S0-AKM-318

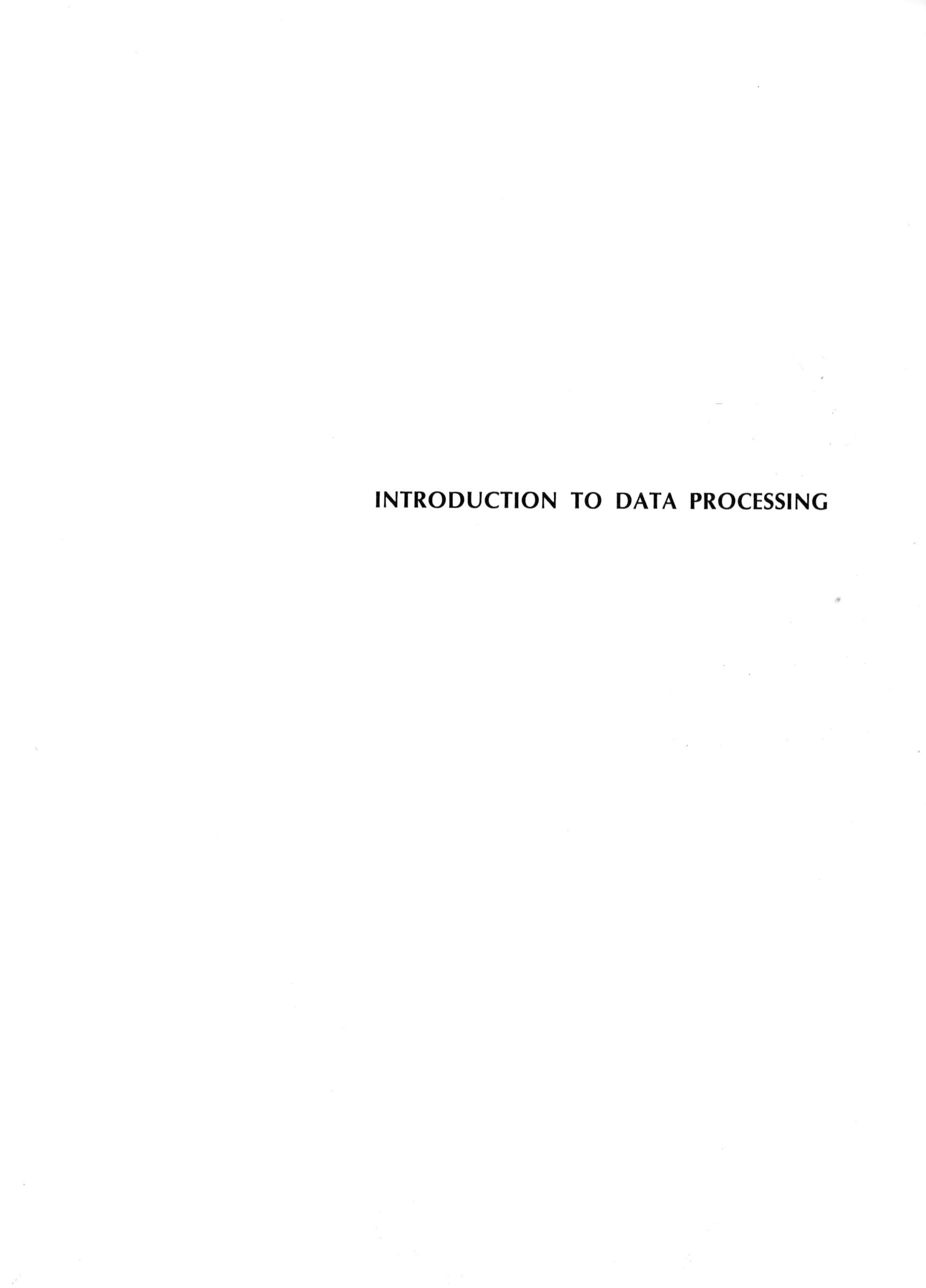

INTRODUCTION TO DATA PROCESSING

WM. C. BROWN COMPANY PUBLISHERS
Dubuque, Iowa

INTRODUCTION TO DATA PROCESSING

CARL FEINGOLD, C.P.A., C.D.P.
West Los Angeles College
Culver City, California

SECOND EDITION

Library of Congress Catalog Card Number: 74–78726

ISBN 0–697–08113–3

Second Printing, 1976

Printed in the United States of America

To Sylvia

Contents

Preface

The field of data processing continues its phenomenal growth with new devices and innovations being announced each day. It is evolving to meet the ever-increasing demands of a technological society and in turn is contributing to even greater technical advancement. Those who work with data processing or have close contact with it must be prepared for a constant learning situation. Regulatory agencies are demanding that those who work with data processing equipment possess some working knowledge of the operations. These agencies are no longer accepting the concept that one does not understand the intricacies of data processing equipment. It is toward this objective that this text was written—to provide a basic understanding of data processing to all concerned with its operations. This book is intended for today's student of data processing who must work from here toward the future. His role is not that of a historian but of a frontiersman in computer technology.

This revised edition preserves the same basic concepts of its predecessor with the addition of new developments in the field. Many chapters have been condensed or expanded from the earlier edition to reflect the current trend in data processing. The purpose of the book is to serve as an introductory text in data processing and as such, presumes no prior knowledge of data processing. It deals with the nature and matter of computer data processing and how these concepts relate to the specific problems of today. The material is presented in simple nontechnical terms with many illustrations. These topics include all areas of data processing which are important for any beginning student of data processing. I have attempted to arrange the subject matter in a logical sequence to provide "in-depth" coverage of the important areas, giving the student an appreciation for the field while furnishng him with a solid background for further courses in data processing.

The introduction presents the importance of data, its source, and the future of data processing itself. Included therein is a case study demonstrating the ways in which computers are being used to solve one of today's most complex problems—traffic congestion.

A brief history of data processing shows the student the natural progression of data processing throughout the ages. Only the important events and devices that have contributed significantly to the present state of data processing are discussed.

Punched-card data processing is discussed briefly in Part II, highlighting the important aspects of unit record processing. Although punched-card data processing does not enjoy the popularity it once had, it still is an integral part of a successful data processing application.

Computer components and arithmetic are important to any student of data processing to provide an insight to the operation of a computer. The hardware and storage features are presented in Part III so that the student can have a complete understanding of the physical operations of a computer. Through simple explanations and illustrations, the student learns the basic calculation functions of the computer and the different number systems employed.

Computer programming is the most important segment of data processing. In Parts IV and V, the student is made aware of the numerous problems encountered in the study, planning, and preparation of computer programs. He is introduced to the various tools, such as flowcharts and decision tables, available to the programmer to make the task of programming easier and more logical. Commonly used programming languages such as RPG, FORTRAN, COBOL, PL/1 and system 360/370 Assembler Language are explained so that the student understands the capabilities and features of each language.

Real time processing and time sharing, the fastest growing segment of the data processing field, are explained in Part VI. New hardware and software features are being introduced daily and the important features of these new techniques and equipment are explained in this section. All components of real time processing such as data communications, conversational and remote batch time sharing, and BASIC programming language are all discussed in this section so that the student has a thorough knowledge of these important features.

Finally Part VII, computer systems and the problems concerned with the management of data processing units are explained. The discussion of the significance of minicomputers, microprogramming, remote job entry terminals, small computers, super computers, and virtual storage are discussed in this section. The problems of operating a data processing unit including staffing and organization are discussed. The current problems in data management including computer security, data security, telecommunications protection, data processing responsibility, and feasibility studies are all discussed in this section.

A detailed explanation of the IBM/System 3 is included in the Appendix. A new glossary includes many of the definitions of the American National Standards Institute.

New features to this edition are:

1. A new chapter on computer systems where the latest innovations in minicomputers, small and large computers as well as virtual storage are discussed.
2. A new chapter on data management highlighting all current problems such as computer security, data security, data processing responsibility, etc.
3. The inclusion of a case study of the Los Angeles Area Freeway Surveillance and Control Project demonstrating the methods whereby computers are being used to solve many of our everyday problems.
4. The latest advance in computer technology such as Fourth Generation Computers, minicomputers, virtual storage, etc.
5. The inclusion of the newest model card-punch machines.
6. The inclusion of the controversial subject "The Growing Threat to Personal Privacy" with many examples to illustrate the significance of this timely topic.

Most chapters have been expanded with new illustrations and explanations. Summaries appear behind each chapter which can serve as an outline of the chapter for review purposes.

This edition will again include a Student Workbook. The objectives and the basic format of the Workbook will remain similar. I have deleted the identification questions from the Workbook and have now included these identification questions in the textbook.

The Instructor's Manual will again include a brief commentary of each chapter. The commentary states the intent of the chapter, useful teaching suggestions and a summary of the important points. The Instructor's Manual also provides answers for each of the discussion questions and the identification questions in the book. The answers for all of the questions in the Student Workbook can be found at the end of the Instructor's Manual.

The book is comprehensive in all aspects of data processing. It is ideally suited as a basic text for introductory data processing or computer science courses for first and second year students in the junior college, university, or technological institution. It may be used as a semester, quarter or a year course depending upon the instructional program of the particular institution. The text will provide the beginning student with all the basic principles of data processing.

BEGINNING DATA PROCESSING COURSE
Business Student
No Emphasis on Programming Languages

Part 1 Introduction and History
Chapter 1 Introduction to Data Processing
2 History of Data Processing

Part 2 Punched-Card Data Processing
Chapter 3 Data Recording Media and Equipment
4 Manipulating, Calculating and Reporting Functions

Part 3 Computer Components and Arithmetic
Chapter 5 Input/Output Devices
6 Processing and Storage Devices
7 Computer Data Representation and Arithmetic

Part 4 Introduction to Programming
Chapter 8 Data Processing Systems and Procedures
9 Preparation for a Computer Program
10 Introduction to Computer Programming

Part 6 Real Time Processing and Time Sharing
Chapter 16 Introduction to Real Time Processing and Time Sharing

Part 7 Computer Systems and Management
Chapter 18 Computer Systems—Mini, Small, and Super Computers, Virtual Storage
19 Management of a Data Processing Installation
20 Data Management

BEGINNING DATA PROCESSING COURSE
Business Programming Student
Emphasis on Programming Languages

Part 1 Introduction and History
Chapter 1 Introduction to Data Processing
2 History of Data Processing

Part 2 Punched-Card Data Processing
Chapter 3 Data Recording Media and Equipment
4 Manipulating, Calculating and Reporting Functions

Part 3 Computer Components and Arithmetic
Chapter 5 Input/Output Devices
6 Processing and Storage Devices
7 Computer Data Representation and Arithmetic

Part 4 Introduction to Programming
Chapter 8 Data Processing Systems and Procedures
9 Preparation for a Computer Program
10 Introduction to Computer Programming

Part 5 Programming Languages
Chapter 11 Report Program Generator
12 FORTRAN
13 COBOL

Part 7 Computer Systems and Management
Chapter 18 Computer Systems—Mini, Small, and Super Computers, Virtual Storage
19 Management of a Data Processing Installation
20 Data Management

BEGINNING DATA PROCESSING COURSE
Business Programming Student
Emphasis on 360/370 Programming

Part 1 Introduction and History
Chapter 1 Introduction to Data Processing
2 History of Data Processing

Part 2 Punched-Card Data Processing
Chapter 3 Data Recording Media and Equipment
4 Manipulating, Calculating and Reporting Functions

Part 3 Computer Components and Arithmetic
Chapter 5 Input/Output Devices
6 Processing and Storage Devices
7 Computer Data Representation and Arithmetic

Part 4 Introduction to Programming
Chapter 8 Data Processing Systems and Procedures
9 Preparation for a Computer Program
10 Introduction to Computer Programming

Part 5 Programming Language
Chapter 15 System 360/370 Assembler Language

Part 7 Computer Systems and Management

Chapter 18 Computer Systems—Mini, Small, and Super Computers, Virtual Storage
19 Management of a Data Processing Installation
20 Data Management

ONE SEMESTER COURSE
Business Student
Emphasis on Terminal Devices

Part 1 Introduction and History
Chapter 1 Introduction to Data Processing
2 History of Data Processing

Part 2 Punched-Card Data Processing
Chapter 3 Data Recording Media and Equipment
4 Manipulating, Calculating and Reporting Functions

Part 3 Computer Components and Arithmetic
Chapter 5 Input/Output Devices
6 Processing and Storage Devices
7 Computer Data Representation and Arithmetic

Part 4 Introduction to Programming
Chapter 8 Data Processing Systems and Procedures
9 Preparation for a Computer Program
10 Introduction to Computer Programming

Part 6 Real Time Processing and Time Sharing
Chapter 16 Introduction to Real Time Processing and Time Sharing
17 Time Sharing Programming—BASIC Programming Language

Part 7 Computer Systems and Management
Chapter 18 Computer Systems—Mini, Small, and Super Computers, Virtual Storage
19 Management of a Data Processing Installation
20 Data Management

FULL YEAR COURSE
Business Student
Emphasis on All Topics

Part 1 Introduction and History
Chapter 1 Introduction to Data Processing
2 History of Data Processing

Part 2 Punched-Card Data Processing

Chapter 3 Data Recording Media and Equipment

4 Manipulating, Calculating and Reporting Functions

Part 3 Computer Components and Arithmetic

Chapter 5 Input/Output Devices

6 Processing and Storage Devices

7 Computer Data Representation and Arithmetic

Part 4 Introduction to Programming

Chapter 8 Data Processing Systems and Procedures

9 Preparation for a Computer Program

10 Introduction to Computer Programming

Part 5 Programming Languages

Chapter 11 Report Program Generator

12 FORTRAN

13 COBOL

14 Programming Language 1

15 System 360/370 Assembler Language

Part 6 Real Time Processing and Time Sharing

Chapter 16 Introduction to Real Time Processing and Time Sharing

17 Time Sharing Programming—BASIC Programming Language

Part 7 Computer Systems and Management

Chapter 18 Computer Systems—Mini, Small, and Super Computers, Virtual Storage

19 Management of a Data Processing Installation

20 Data Management

A SHORT INTENSIFIED COURSE
Executive Type Student

Part 1 Introduction and History

Chapter 1 Introduction to Data Processing

2 History of Data Processing

Part 2 Punched-Card Data Processing

Chapter 3 Data Recording Media and Equipment

4 Manipulating, Calculating and Reporting Functions

Part 3 Computer Components and Arithmetic

Chapter 5 Input/Output Devices

6 Processing and Storage Devices

7 Computer Data Representation and Arithmetic

Part 6 Real Time Processing and Time Sharing
Chapter 16 Introduction to Real Time Processing and Time Sharing

Part 7 Computer Systems and Management
Chapter 18 Computer Systems—Mini, Small, and Super Computers, Virtual Storage
19 Management of a Data Processing Installation
20 Data Management

I wish to thank the Burroughs Corporation, Data 100 Corporation, Data General Corporation, General Electric Corporation, Interdata Corporation, International Business Machines Corporation, National Cash Register Corporation, Pacific Telephone and Telegraph Company, and the Sperry Rand Corporation for graciously granting permission to use the numerous charts, diagrams, illustrations, and photos that make the text more meaningful.

A deep expression of gratitude is due my wife Sylvia for her forbearance during the preparation of the manuscript, her expertise in the typing of the manuscript and her effort, patience, and encouragement without which the text never would have been written.

PART I / INTRODUCTION AND HISTORY

CHAPTER 1
Introduction to Data Processing

The dynamic introduction of the computer in the last quarter century has changed man's information needs entirely. Since the resources of society are limited, man has developed methods of compiling and analyzing large quantities of data with a minimum amount of human intervention. Technological advances in all fields of data processing have been dynamic and extensive as man's thirst for information increases daily. The methods of applying data processing systems to information needs are boundless. With each new application, data processing systems have demonstrated still newer ways in which they can be used to help man increase his productivity and advance civilization a little further. Data processing is not just another new industry or innovation but a giant step forward in man's utilization of science and knowledge as a means of progress.

Computers are perhaps the most useful tools ever invented by mankind. In this, the era of computers, they are used to count our votes, figure our bank accounts, help plan new buildings and bridges, guide our astronauts through space and assist management in its everyday decisions. Recently, a major company was criticized by its shareholders for acknowledged management errors to the effect that it outgrew its cash and management resources. The "new regime" then promised that the company computer would print out daily and weekly reports on orders, cash flow, shipments, accounts receivable, accounts payable and inventories. These reports should clear up this basic problem of the company, which had merely gone about its expansion program without watching its expenses, trying to follow overly optimistic marketing plans.

Our lives are affected each day in some manner by computers. Life as we know it would not be possible without them. Patterns of consumer spending have changed. Credit cards have become a way of life. Almost any of man's needs can be satisfied with a credit card. Payments with cash are rapidly disappearing. Checks are used to make almost all payments. Many companies have initiated plans whereby payroll checks are mailed directly to employee-designated banks.

Daily interest computation on bank savings would be an impossibility without the present methods of processing data. Service industries have greatly increased, providing numerous services to make life more convenient and pleasant. A car is waiting for you as you embark from your plane. To make reservations for some distant hotel or to plan a trip to another part of the world all that is required is to reach for the telephone. Sporting events and other entertainment tickets are now available to us at our favorite stores, conveniently located. No longer is it necessary to make a special trip to the sports complex or theatre or to stand in lines. Every individual is touched by the computer in some manner—some, unhappily, by the Internal Revenue Service.

One of the driving forces behind the development of computers was the need to find faster and more efficient methods of handling paperwork. The clerical operations required to handle the ever-mounting quantities of paper to be processed had increased enormously. Paper handling alone would probably have overwhelmed all of our enormous productive capabilities if clerical mechanization had not kept pace with the technological advances in the field. To see how well this purpose has been fulfilled you need only look at the ways computers serve you in your everyday life.

In this morning's mail there is perhaps a magazine that came days earlier than it used to because it was addressed automatically by the computer. There are probably the usual charge and credit account bills, end products of a valuable service that depends almost entirely on the ability of the computers to collect, process and record vast amounts of credit and billing information.

Another item in the mail may be an insurance premium in which the amount due, the dividend accrued, the date due, and other pertinent information are all calculated and printed by the computer. Also, we may find a bank statement presented in a far more readable and convenient form, computer-generated. Add to this more convenient forms of debiting and crediting, faster processing of checks, more frequent and more complete account reports—all a direct result of the paperwork revolution made possible by special computing systems.

Your paycheck provides a perfect illustration of how a multiplicity of record-keeping requirements can be handled smoothly and accurately by a single data processing system. The stub attached to a paycheck might contain all this information: hours worked, federal and state taxes, hospitalization and insurance deductions, and total wages earned for the year to date. All this in addition to the figure you look at first—the amount on the face of the paycheck.

Computers have gone beyond merely taking over the jobs accomplished by paperwork and doing them faster and better. Computers are doing things for business and industry that could never have been done before.

A company may test the design of a new processing plant by simulating every detail of its operation with a computer. Computer simulation frequently provides more information in a week than an expensive pilot plant could provide in a year of actual operation.

More and more management decisions now are based on information supplied by computers—information about inventories, production schedules, market forecasts and sales analyses (Fig. 1.1). Although management

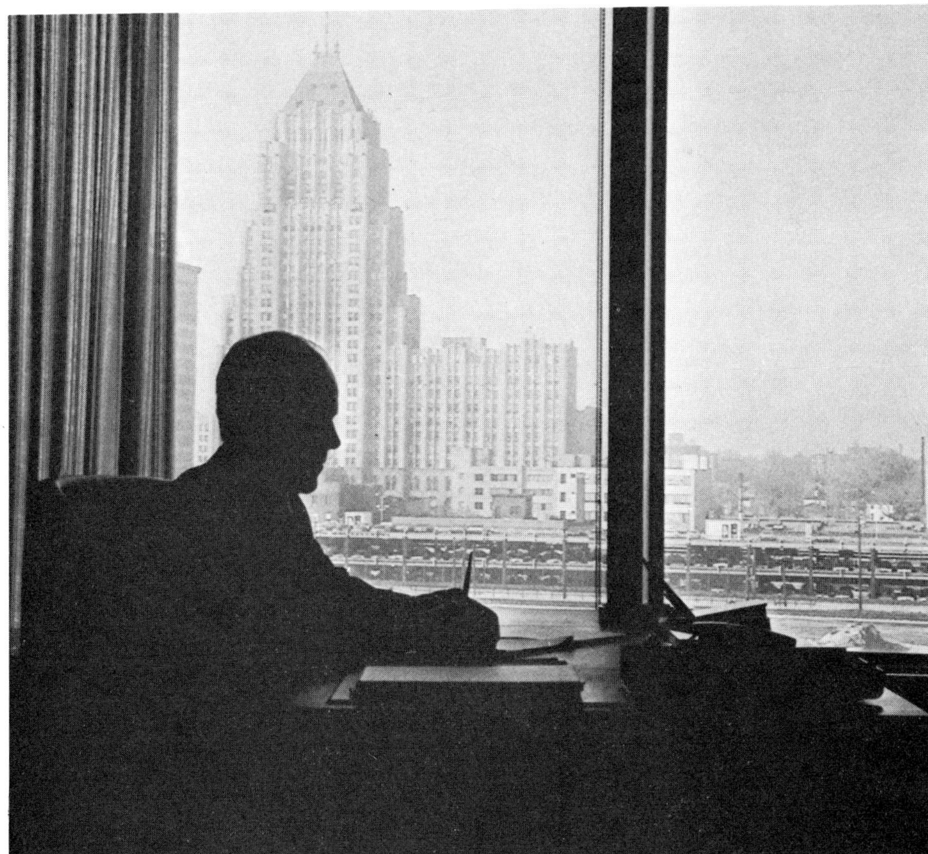

Figure 1–1. Management Decision.

could always get this information, it was not always obtainable in time to take effective action. In some cases today, advanced mathematical techniques, worked out on computers, are used to find answers quickly to complex marketing and production problems that a few years ago would have been solved only with extreme difficulty and a considerable consumption of time.

Computers of the future will go even further toward freeing man from the drudgery of paperwork and repetitive manual tasks. There are many new applications now in the process of development, such as highway traffic control, automatic language translation, automatic processing of maps and pictures. It is obvious that the computer will serve us in many ways that the conventional word "paperwork" could never encompass.

All of the aforementioned activities illustrate ways that data has become a part of life, and indicate the part the computer has played in its development. Great opportunities lie ahead in the data processing field with the addition of the computer. Expanded markets, greater productivity, corporate growth, and increased governmental activity provide the data processor with new challenges each day.

IMPORTANCE OF DATA PROCESSING

Data processing is a planned series of actions and operations upon information, using various forms of data processing equipment, to achieve a desired result. The data processing equipment came into being primarily to satisfy needs for information under increasingly complex conditions. Computer programs and physical equipment are combined into data processing systems to handle business and scientific data at high rates of speed with self-checking accuracy features. The physical data processing equipment consists of various units, such as input and output devices, storage devices, and processing devices to handle information at electronic speed (Fig. 1.2).

Figure 1–2. Data Processing System.

Informational needs have greatly increased as our economy changed from an agricultural to an industrial nation. Data has assumed new importance as there are today more people employed in the handling, processing and distribution of goods and services than in their production. One dollar out of every eight in wages and salaries is paid to white collar workers in the United States. There has been an increase of more than 50 percent in the number of white collar workers in the past ten years as compared to only a 6 percent increase in all employment in manufacturing.

An estimated 26 billion checks circulate annually in the United States. Each check must be handled at least six times before it is finally cancelled and returned (Fig. 1.3). Without the efforts of the computer manufacturers and the American Banking Association, the processing of these checks in a reasonable amount of time would be impossible. Through their efforts, the magnetic character sensing mechanism was developed, making possible the high speed sorting and processing of checks.

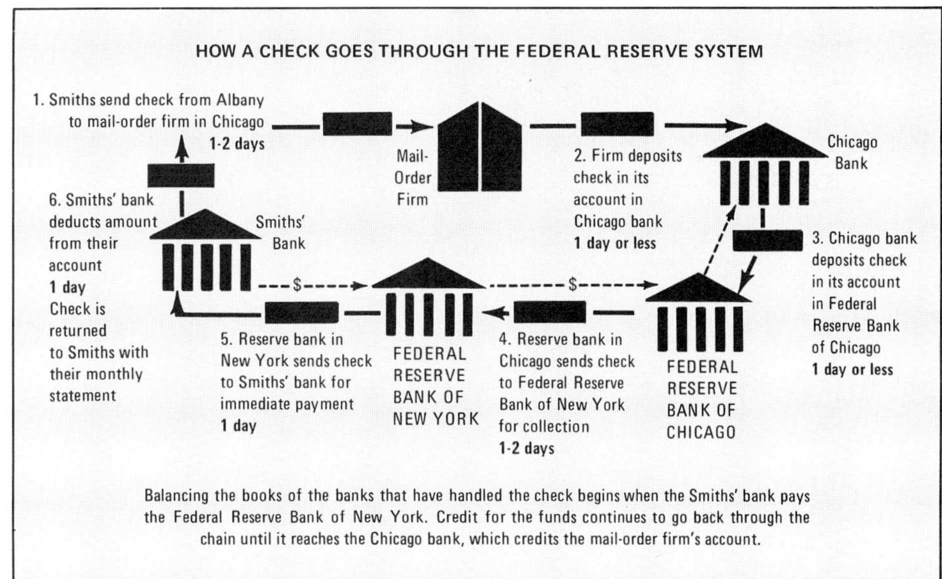
HOW A CHECK GOES THROUGH THE FEDERAL RESERVE SYSTEM
1. Smiths send check from Albany to mail-order firm in Chicago
1-2 days
Mail-Order Firm
2. Firm deposits check in its account in Chicago bank
1 day or less
Chicago Bank
3. Chicago bank deposits check in its account in Federal Reserve Bank of Chicago
1 day or less
FEDERAL RESERVE BANK OF CHICAGO
4. Reserve bank in Chicago sends check to Federal Reserve Bank of New York for collection
1-2 days
FEDERAL RESERVE BANK OF NEW YORK
5. Reserve bank in New York sends check to Smiths' bank for immediate payment
1 day
Smiths' Bank
6. Smiths' bank deducts amount from their account
1 day
Check is returned to Smiths with their monthly statement
$
Balancing the books of the banks that have handled the check begins when the Smiths' bank pays the Federal Reserve Bank of New York. Credit for the funds continues to go back through the chain until it reaches the Chicago bank, which credits the mail-order firm's account.

Figure 1–3. How a Check Goes Through a Federal Reserve System.

Some of the more spectacular examples of the remarkable advances in data processing are *image processing* and *audio response.* The processing of pictures transmitted from the planet Mars was an example of image processing. Rapid microfilm scanning was combined with automatic interpretation of light and dark spots into 0's and 1's for computer storage. These pictures were then displayed on the viewer's screen. The same techniques were used to send pictures to earth from the moon by the various Apollo missions.

The New York Stock Exchange, by means of a recorded voice, can quote the latest stock prices on request. An excellent example of audio response, this is accomplished through the selection and assembly of messages previously stored in the computer.

Computers are used in business for a variety of reasons. When properly applied, they can save time or money (or both) in producing reports for management and government (Fig. 1.4), in preparing checks and earnings statements (Fig. 1.5), in writing invoices to customers (Fig. 1.6), in keeping

PAGE 2 ON HAND STATUS REPORT 12-06-6-

ITEM NO	BIN NO	QTY	CODE	ITEM NO	BIN NO	QTY	CODE	ITEM NO	BIN NO	QTY	CODE	ITEM NO	BIN NO	QTY	CODE
1002000121	229	188	1	1002000122	148	7		1013000134	262	235		1127000179	54	16	
1130002681	468	20		1141029736	29	0	2	1142029746	30	132		1156217368	68	5	
1156321762	19	86		1157316299	336	8		1157332068	561	36		1158260177	1620	261	
1160223466	9067	56		1160223588	10689	29		1160246899	1690	177		1161462133	447	33	
1163281971	887	16		1163281981	893	40		1163281990	78	22		1163282766	79	12	
1164009883	1993	101		1164009944	1110	61		1164009948	1122	70		1164009966	1233	80	
1165002344	10628	17		1165002355	10629	129		1165004141	1988	35		1165012687	474	12	
1168017936	12	48		1173201631	7680	22		1174062812	53	206		1181326819	2216	78	

LOAD REPORT

DATE 9-13-6- PAGE 1

DEPT WK/CTR	BEHIND SCH HRS	1ST PERIOD AVAIL	LOADED	%	2ND PERIOD AVAIL	LOADED	%	3RD PERIOD AVAIL	LOADED	%	4TH PERIOD AVAIL	LOADED	%	FUTURE LOAD
029-001	18.5	40	44.6	111	40	82.1	205	40	66.3	166	80	64.3	80	181.0
049-015		160	64.8	40	160	178.4	111	160	12.4	8	160	2.8	2	
049-020		240	184.3	77	240	200.6	84	240	124.3	52	240	81.5	34	168.0
049-021		40	32.6	81	40	24.2	60	40	17.6	44	40	9.8	25	
049-032	32.6	120	182.4	152	120	105.4	88	120	42.3	35	120	38.7	32	121.2

SALES AND PROFIT, BY SALESMAN, BY CUSTOMER

SALESMAN 5 PAGE 7 12-06-6-

CUSTOMER	CUST NO	THIS PERIOD NET SALES	GROSS PROFIT	CUST % PROFIT	% TOTAL PROFIT	NO INVOICES	TOTAL LINES	AVG $ LINE	YEAR-TO-DATE NET SALES	GROSS PROFIT	CUST % PROFIT	% TOTAL PROFIT	NO INVOICES	TOTAL LINES	AVG $ LINE
ALLIED GROCERY	1006	10000	1500	150	10	15	1900	666	110000	15000	136	9	165	20000	555
LAST YEAR		9000	1080	120	8	14	1400	643	100000	13000	130	9	159	19500	513
PCT INC OR DEC		11.1	38.9	30	2	7.1	35.7	3.6	10.0	15.4	6	0	3.8	2.6	7.2
AL'S SUPER MARKET	1086	8238	1224	149	8	12	1812	545	90268	12872	143	8	131	16120	560
LAST YEAR		7927	1120	141	8	11	1579	512	87197	12242	140	8	126	17063	511
PCT INC OR DEC		3.6	9.3	8	0	9.1	14.8	6.4	3.5	5.1	3	0	4.0	5.5-	9.6
RALPH'S SUPER THRIFT	7263	42681	6492	152	44	16	7919	539	460821	69952	152	43	175	86860	531
LAST YEAR		44800	6787	151	48	16	8517	526	492600	74481	151	51	178	93650	526
PCT INC OR DEC		4.7-	4.3-	1	4-	.0	7.0-	2.5	6.5-	6.1-	1	8-	1.7-	7.3-	1.0
SALESMAN TOTALS THIS YEAR		186534	28017	150	190	190	35395	527	2051874	308602	150	190	2068	385265	533
LAST YEAR		170436	25599	150	180	192	32903	518	1864329	278158	149	190	2116	361304	516
PCT INC OR DEC		8.6	9.4	0	10	1.0-	7.6	1.7	10.1	10.9	1	0	2.3-	6.6	3.3
GRAND TOTALS THIS YEAR		977438	147398	151	1000	997	185824	526	10747621	1627190	151	1000	9425		531
LAST YEAR		950637	142405	150	1000	978	183167	519	9780351	1464119	150	1000	8593		515
PCT INC OR DEC		2.8	3.5	1	0	1.9	1.5	1.3	9.9	11.1	1	0	9.7		3.1

Figure 1–4. Management Reports.

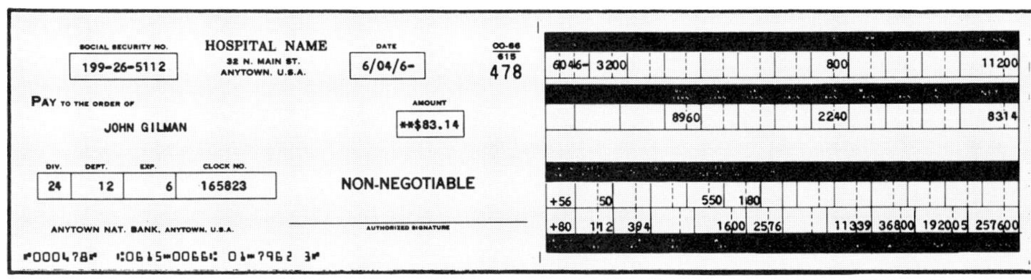

SOCIAL SECURITY NO. 199-26-5112
HOSPITAL NAME
32 N. MAIN ST.
ANYTOWN, U.S.A.
DATE 6/04/6-
00-66 / 615
478
PAY TO THE ORDER OF
JOHN GILMAN
AMOUNT **$83.14
DIV. 24 | DEPT. 12 | EXP. 6 | CLOCK NO. 165823
NON-NEGOTIABLE
ANYTOWN NAT. BANK, ANYTOWN, U.S.A.
AUTHORIZED SIGNATURE
⑈000478⑈ ⑆0615-0066⑆ 01-7962 3⑈

6046-	3200		800	11200
		8960	2240	8314
+56	50	550	180	
+80	112	394	1600	2576
11339	36800	192005	257600	

PAYROLL REGISTER

HOSPITAL NAME

DEPT. NO. 16 — PAY PERIOD END DATE 6/04/6- — DATE 6/07/6- — PAGE 2

CLOCK NO. INITIAL AND LAST NAME	RATE	NO. DEP. MAR. STATUS	MISC. EARNINGS	OTHER 1 EARNINGS OTHER 2 EARNINGS	REG. HOURS REG. EARNINGS	OVERTIME HOURS OVERTIME EARNINGS	DOUBLE HOURS DOUBLE EARNINGS	HOL. HOURS HOL. EARNINGS	VAC. HOURS VAC. EARNINGS	SICK HOURS SICK EARNINGS	ADJ. NET ADJ. GROSS	UNITED FUND ADVANCE	BONDS	ACCTS. REC.	CREDIT UNION	BLUE CROSS	UNION DUES	CITY TAX F.I.C.A. TAX	W/H TAX STATE TAX	GROSS NET
16423 H DENVER	348	4 2			4000 13920	200 1084						150	1000		1500	258		150 658	1377	14964 9871
206471 B DONALDSON	257	2 2			4000 10280							50			1050	200		103 449	1051	10280 7377
164238 A EGGERS	280	1 1			4000 11200	20 84						50	500		1250	180		113 496	1617	11284 7078
200346 W GHORMLEY	325	5 2			3800 12350							100	800			290		124 543	761	12350 9732
92743 C GROVE	275	3 2							4000 11000			100			1000	240		110 488	964	11000 8098
64727 A HARRISON	280	1 1			3200 8960					800 2240		50			550	180		112 394	1600	11200 8314
216432 W HEDLEY	348	7 2			3200 11136							150	350			290		111 490	180	11136 9565
184921 M HOTTINGER	325	2 2			4000 13000	625 3047						100				200		160 706	2020	16047 12861
116488 C JOHNSTON	280	1 1			4000 11200							50			500	180		112 493	1600	11200 8265

MEAL EARNINGS COMMISSION EARNINGS	OTHER 1 EARNINGS OTHER 2 EARNINGS	REG. HOURS REG. EARNINGS	OVERTIME HOURS OVERTIME EARNINGS	DOUBLE HOURS DOUBLE EARNINGS	HOLIDAY HOURS HOLIDAY EARNINGS	VACATION HOURS VACATION EARNINGS	SICK HOURS SICK EARNINGS	ADJ. NET ADJ. GROSS	UNITED FUND ADVANCE	BOND	ACCTS. REC.	CREDIT UNION	BLUE CROSS	UNION DUES	CITY TAX F.I.C.A. TAX	W/H TAX STATE TAX	GROSS NET
		30200 92046	845 4175			4000 11000	800 2240		800	2650		5850	2018		1095 4717	11170	109461 81161

Figure 1–5. Payroll Check and Register.

records of accounts payable to suppliers, and in numerous other ways. In many situations they make it possible to obtain information that would otherwise not be economically justifiable. In some cases, they provide a basis for an improved management control of a business that would not, for time or money reasons, be feasible without computers.

Engineering and scientific computations require the extensive use of computers. Scientific research has itself grown into a multibillion-dollar-a-year undertaking, and the new computer technology has provided most of the impetus for this remarkable growth. Information needs in both of these areas have, obviously, greatly increased, thus giving data, extractable from computers, a vast new importance.

INFORMATIONAL NEEDS

DEMANDS FOR DATA

The demands for data stem basically from two sources; *internal* and *external* demands.

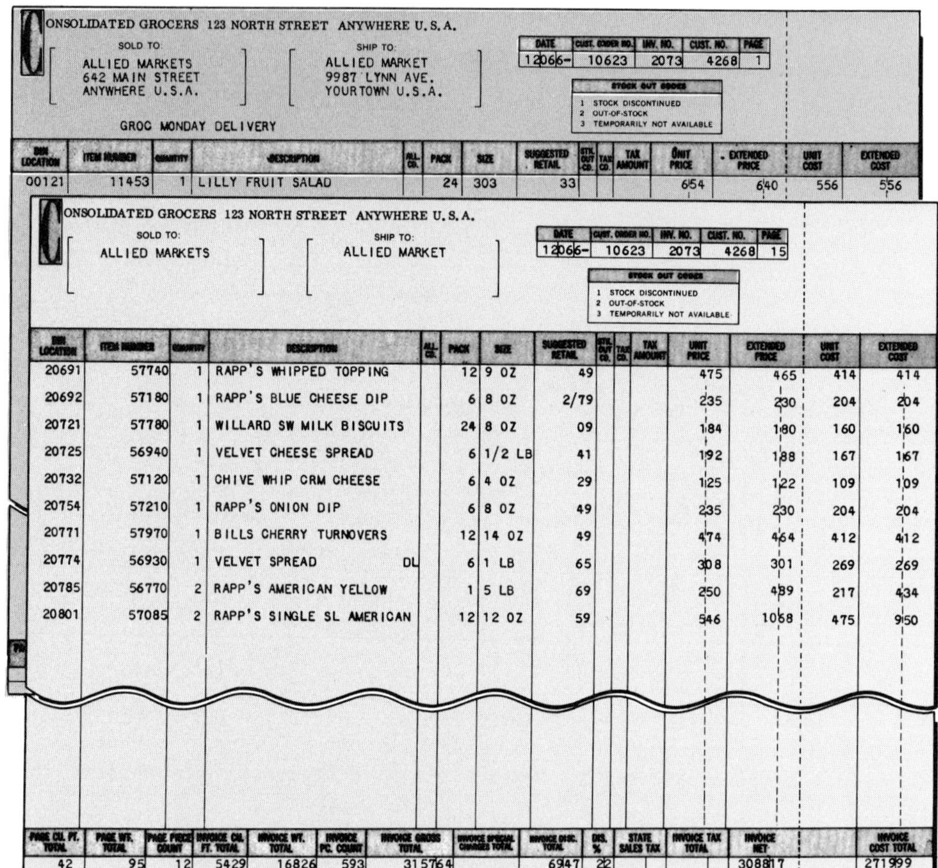

CONSOLIDATED GROCERS 123 NORTH STREET ANYWHERE U. S. A.

SOLD TO: ALLIED MARKETS, 642 MAIN STREET, ANYWHERE U.S.A.

SHIP TO: ALLIED MARKET, 9987 LYNN AVE., YOURTOWN U.S.A.

GROC MONDAY DELIVERY

DATE	CUST. ORDER NO.	INV. NO.	CUST. NO.	PAGE
12066-	10623	2073	4268	1

STOCK OUT CODES
1 STOCK DISCONTINUED
2 OUT-OF-STOCK
3 TEMPORARILY NOT AVAILABLE

BIN LOCATION	ITEM NUMBER	QUANTITY	DESCRIPTION	ALL. CD.	PACK	SIZE	SUGGESTED RETAIL	STK. OUT CD.	TAX CD.	TAX AMOUNT	UNIT PRICE	EXTENDED PRICE	UNIT COST	EXTENDED COST
00121	11453	1	LILLY FRUIT SALAD		24	303	33				654	640	556	556

CONSOLIDATED GROCERS 123 NORTH STREET ANYWHERE U. S. A.

SOLD TO: ALLIED MARKETS

SHIP TO: ALLIED MARKET

DATE	CUST. ORDER NO.	INV. NO.	CUST. NO.	PAGE
12066-	10623	2073	4268	15

STOCK OUT CODES
1 STOCK DISCONTINUED
2 OUT-OF-STOCK
3 TEMPORARILY NOT AVAILABLE

BIN LOCATION	ITEM NUMBER	QUANTITY	DESCRIPTION	ALL. CD.	PACK	SIZE	SUGGESTED RETAIL	STK. OUT CD.	TAX CD.	TAX AMOUNT	UNIT PRICE	EXTENDED PRICE	UNIT COST	EXTENDED COST
20691	57740	1	RAPP'S WHIPPED TOPPING		12	9 OZ	49				475	465	414	414
20692	57180	1	RAPP'S BLUE CHEESE DIP		6	8 OZ	2/79				235	230	204	204
20721	57780	1	WILLARD SW MILK BISCUITS		24	8 OZ	09				184	180	160	160
20725	56940	1	VELVET CHEESE SPREAD		6	1/2 LB	41				192	188	167	167
20732	57120	1	CHIVE WHIP CRM CHEESE		6	4 OZ	29				125	122	109	109
20754	57210	1	RAPP'S ONION DIP		6	8 OZ	49				235	230	204	204
20771	57970	1	BILLS CHERRY TURNOVERS		12	14 OZ	49				474	464	412	412
20774	56930	1	VELVET SPREAD	DL	6	1 LB	65				308	301	269	269
20785	56770	2	RAPP'S AMERICAN YELLOW		1	5 LB	69				250	489	217	434
20801	57085	2	RAPP'S SINGLE SL AMERICAN		12	12 OZ	59				546	1068	475	950

PAGE CU. FT. TOTAL	PAGE WT. TOTAL	PAGE PIECE COUNT	INVOICE CU. FT. TOTAL	INVOICE WT. TOTAL	INVOICE PC. COUNT	INVOICE GROSS TOTAL	INVOICE SPECIAL CHARGES TOTAL	INVOICE DISC. TOTAL	DIS. %	STATE SALES TAX	INVOICE TAX TOTAL	INVOICE NET	INVOICE COST TOTAL
42	95	12	5429	16826	593	315764		6947	22			308817	271999

Figure 1–6. Customer Invoice.

Internal demands are requests from management, which is in need of accurate, classified and summarized data for use in the analysis necessary for the making of decisions on a daily, weekly or cyclical basis. Transactions that occur in the everyday operations of an enterprise provide the necessary historical records. From this group of data, information is extracted and accumulated to provide reports used in business decisions and in facilitating other managerial functions. Unless this information is furnished on a current and accurate basis, the company's competitive position may be weakened. A decision to buy, sell or produce a commodity should be based on information supplied by the data processing system after all significant factors have been evaluated. The computer can present the possible alternative actions, thus providing the user with the information necessary to make an intelligent decision.

External demands for data originate outside the organization. These demands are created by customers, unions, governmental agencies and other parties who have an interest in the operations of the enterprise.

The customer needs a statement or invoice in order to pay his obligations on time and to record the transaction properly in his records. The union has the responsibility of looking after the interests of its members and in order to accomplish this objective, it needs reports relative to the status of the employees. The government with its enormous need for data in the form of tax returns and other reports requires that each report be filed on time and reported accurately.

All of these demands must be integrated into a common purpose which makes an organic whole of the entire organization; all functions must be in a balanced accord. A successful data processing system must combine these demands into an integrated data processing system satisfying the needs of all users without duplicating the effort of processing.

A CASE STUDY

One of the most serious problems in the Los Angeles area is the mounting traffic congestion on the urban freeways. Rush-hour commuting on the Los Angeles Freeway system can be slow and frustrating to many motorists. For some, the trip is delayed due to involvement in an accident, freeway congestion resulting from an accident, or of minor failure of the individual's automobile.

What are the alternatives to the traffic problem? More freeways can be built which will be very costly, or the efficiency of the existing freeways can be increased. It is toward the latter alternative that the efforts of the Los Angeles Area Freeway Surveillance and Control Project are directed.

LOS ANGELES AREA FREEWAY SURVEILLANCE AND CONTROL PROJECT (LAAFSCP)

After three and one-half years of planning, the Los Angeles Area Freeway Surveillance and Control Project emerged with the prime purpose of finding methods to reduce delays in traffic, reduce accidents, relieve motorist frustration, and to provide motorist services. Two computers are used in the system: a mini computer and a medium size computer.

The project is in response to continued and mounting public concern that everything possible be done to maximize the operational effectiveness of the existing highway plant, using advanced electronic technology to the maximum degree. Since these devices and concepts were new as applied to highway operation, it could not be said with certainty that they would produce

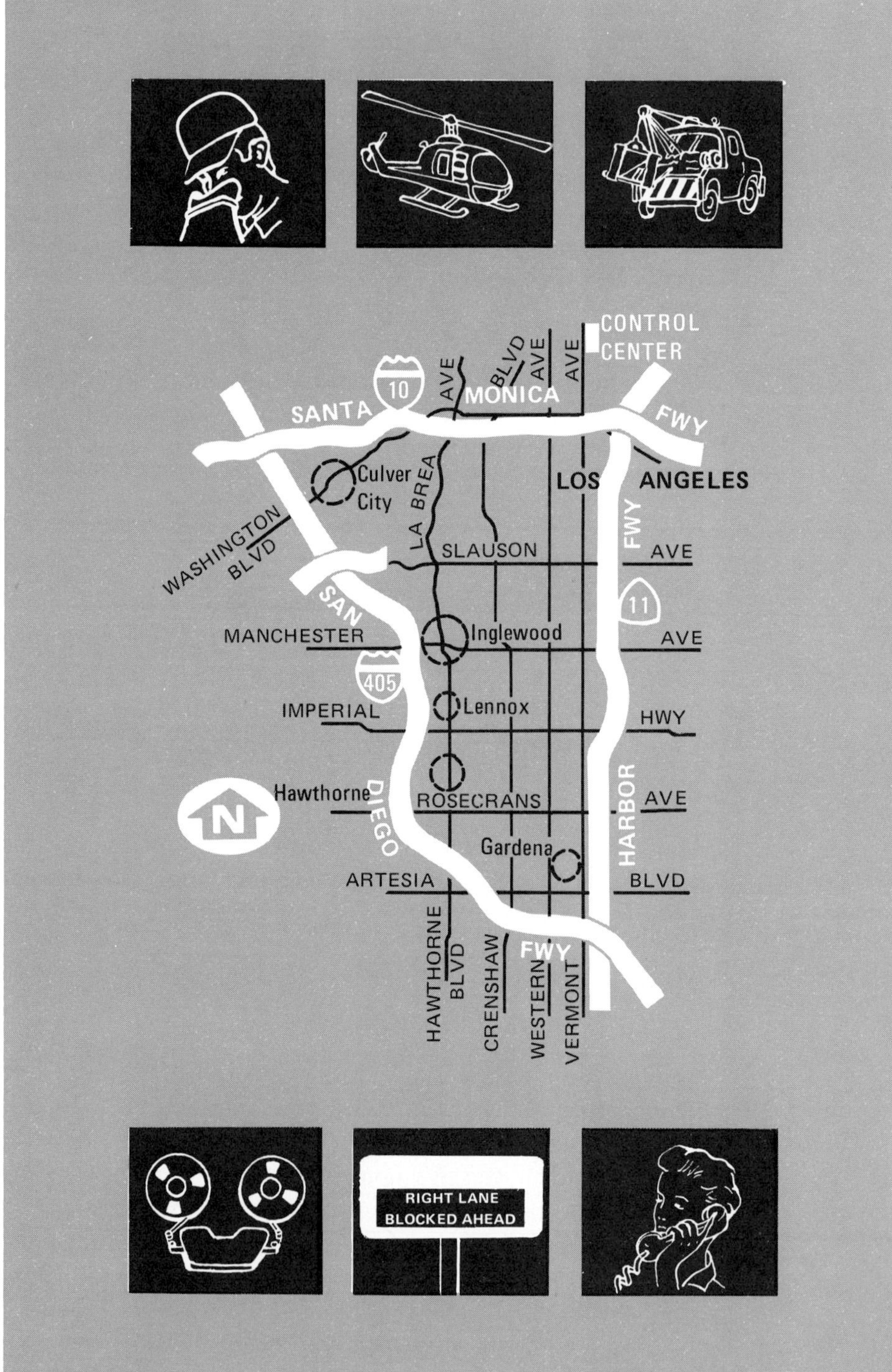

Figure 1–7.
Project Location.

significant changes in traffic flow and safety, nor whether such changes would be worth the capital cost and operating expense.

The project is providing the Department of Public Works and the California Highway Patrol (CHP) an opportunity for coordination of effort in a more specific way than has heretofore been possible. It is providing a test bed for developing techniques of incident management that might be projected to larger networks and in fact to the whole State Highway System. There are real benefits accruing to the motorist; the Department of Public Works and the Highway Patrol are continuing to learn how to improve the service to the motorist.

The project is located in the heart of the Los Angeles urban area on three of the most heavily traveled freeways in the world: the Santa Monica, San Diego and Harbor freeways (Fig. 1.7). Forty-two miles in length, it has within its boundaries fifty-six freeway interchanges. The average daily traffic on these freeways is 175,000 vehicles.

The project contains electronic surveillance and detection, a multidisciplinary team in a control room (Fig. 1.8), communications systems, helicopter borne closed circuit T.V., roving towing trucks, service patrol, commercial radio advisories, changeable message signs, and traffic responsive ramp control.

Every day accidents occur. Within minutes of an accident, the computer in the project control center detects the accident. A blinking red light causes the multidisciplinary team to act. By radio communication, the maintenance man dispatcher sends a tow truck from his roving patrol; the helicopter-borne

Figure 1–8. Control Center Incident Management Team.

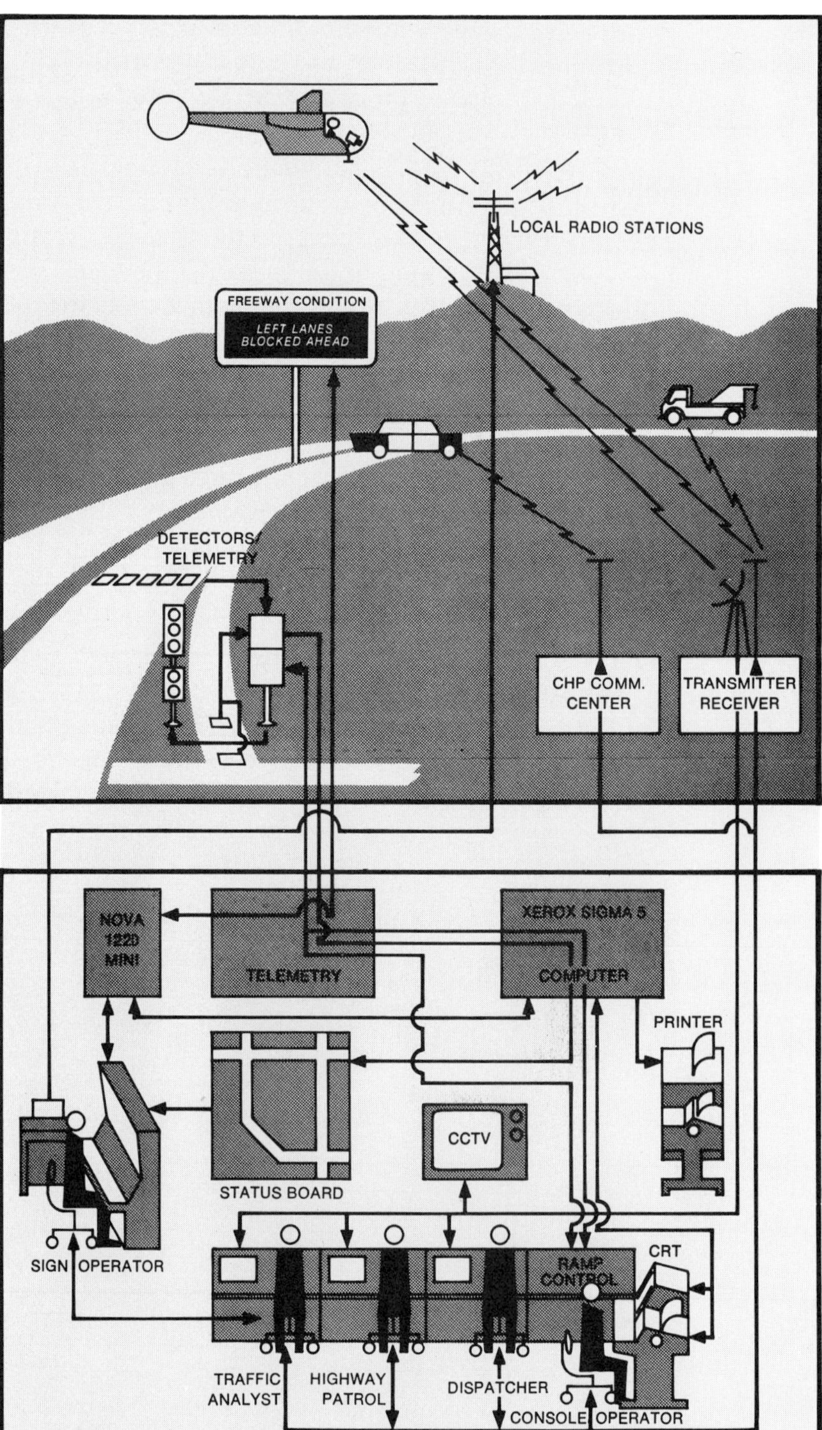

Figure 1–9. Schematic—Los Angeles Area Freeway Surveillance and Control Project.

television also moves to the scene (Fig. 1.9). The CHP control room officer notifies CHP communications. When confirmation of the accident is made (by helicopter or ground units), the traffic analyst relays a message to be teletyped to nine radio stations to notify them of the freeway condition. If the accident is on the Santa Monica freeway, changeable message units controlled by a computer turn on to warn the motorist and provide him with information (Fig. 1.10). If the accident occurred on the San Diego freeway, computer-controlled ramp control signals would automatically change traffic rates on the on-ramps.

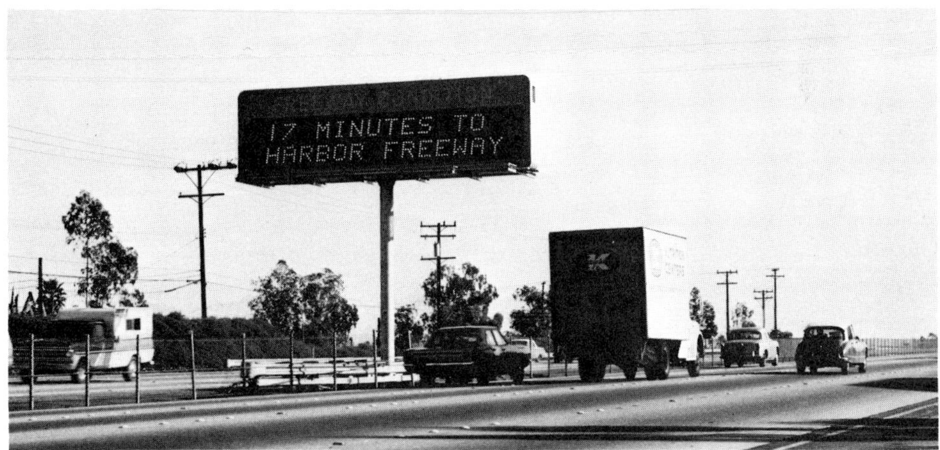

Figure 1–10. Freeway Message.

This description generalizes the operation of the LAAFSCP system. What may appear to be a simple operation is really a complex system of people and electronic hardware.

The aforementioned case study demonstrates one way that computers are being used to solve many of our everyday problems.

SOURCES OF DATA

Data can originate as *internal* or *external data.*

Internal data is the medium on which the data is recorded originally at the time the transaction occurs: a bank check, voucher, sales slip, purchase requisition, etc. The design of these forms can be controlled to make the recording of the data as simple and accurate as possible. The layout of the form should be such that it will provide the data in the sequence in which it will be later transcribed into a data processing media—for example, a punched card. Transcriptions of the data should be kept at a minimum as this will tend to increase the costs of processing and the possibilities for errors.

Internal data can be controlled much more accurately as to the form used, the information to be collected, and the care exercised in the collection of the information. This control is not possible with data originating outside of the organization (external data) as each individual organization prepares forms that will accommodate its own needs.

External data is created outside of the organization, therefore it is designed to satisfy the needs of the supplier. The data may be in the form of a vendor invoice, government tax form, or a utility bill. Transcription of the form to one suitable to the needs of the recipient is usually required. This may necessitate the creation of a new form such as an accounts payable voucher document that contains all the necessary coded information for transcription into a machine processable media.

TYPES OF DATA PROCESSING

Data processing is divided into two main categories: *business data processing* and *scientific data processing*.

In *business data processing*, all necessary activities such as payroll preparation, inventory control, sales analysis and general accounting files are processed, and the required outputs of statements and reports are prepared. *Business data processing is characterized by the processing of many files, used repeatedly, requiring few calculations and many output reports.* For example, a payroll application would require outputs such as updated personnel files, payroll checks, payroll registers, deduction reports and various internal and external reports. All of these reports would be prepared with the same inputs. The reports prepared may be *mandatory* or *operational*.

Mandatory reports are those necessary reports that are required by governmental agencies, stockholders, customers, etc. These reports must be prepared in a fixed format according to the needs of the user. There isn't a great deal of flexibility in the printed output (Fig. 1.11).

Operational reports are the reports that aid management in making the many necessary decisions in everyday operations of a business. In these reports, data processing can provide valuable aids to management. The analysis, ratios, trends and comparisons, heretofore impossible, are now being prepared on a current basis with self-checking accuracy (Fig. 1.12).

Management must make decisions daily relative to the operations of a business. How much to produce, where to sell, budget, pricing are just a few of the problems confronting administrative executives each day. High speed computers provide the analysis and reports stipulating any alternative actions that are available to the decision maker. Computers also provide the necessary paperwork in accordance with these decisions. The *management by exception* technique is used by many companies to reduce the amount of detail that the decision maker is faced with. In this concept, only the exceptional facts are drawn to the attention of those executives. For example, a complete accounts receivable report listing all account balances would not be presented to the credit manager, but only those accounts that are delin-

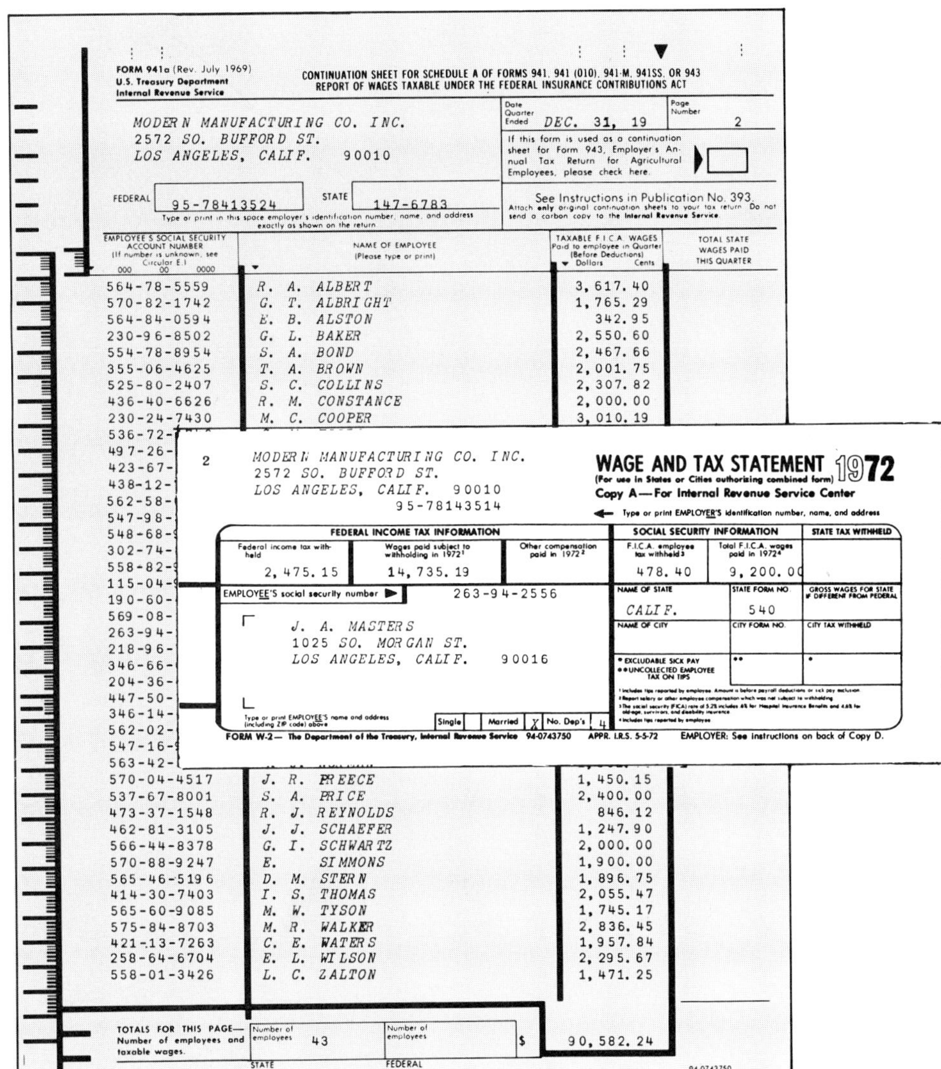

FORM 941a (Rev. July 1969)
U.S. Treasury Department
Internal Revenue Service

CONTINUATION SHEET FOR SCHEDULE A OF FORMS 941, 941 (010), 941-M, 941SS, OR 943
REPORT OF WAGES TAXABLE UNDER THE FEDERAL INSURANCE CONTRIBUTIONS ACT

MODERN MANUFACTURING CO. INC.
2572 SO. BUFFORD ST.
LOS ANGELES, CALIF. 90010

Date Quarter Ended DEC. 31, 19 — Page Number 2

If this form is used as a continuation sheet for Form 943, Employer's Annual Tax Return for Agricultural Employees, please check here.

FEDERAL 95-78413524 — STATE 147-6783

Type or print in this space employer's identification number, name, and address exactly as shown on the return.

See Instructions in Publication No. 393. Attach only original continuation sheets to your tax return. Do not send a carbon copy to the Internal Revenue Service.

EMPLOYEE'S SOCIAL SECURITY ACCOUNT NUMBER (If number is unknown, see Circular E.) 000 00 0000	NAME OF EMPLOYEE (Please type or print)	TAXABLE F.I.C.A. WAGES Paid to employee in Quarter (Before Deductions) Dollars Cents	TOTAL STATE WAGES PAID THIS QUARTER
564-78-5559	R. A. ALBERT	3,617.40	
570-82-1742	G. T. ALBRIGHT	1,765.29	
564-84-0594	E. B. ALSTON	342.95	
230-96-8502	G. L. BAKER	2,550.60	
554-78-8954	S. A. BOND	2,467.66	
355-06-4625	T. A. BROWN	2,001.75	
525-80-2407	S. C. COLLINS	2,307.82	
436-40-6626	R. M. CONSTANCE	2,000.00	
230-24-7430	M. C. COOPER	3,010.19	
536-72-			
497-26-			
423-67-			
438-12-			
562-58-			
547-98-			
548-68-			
302-74-			
558-82-			
115-04-			
190-60-			
569-08-			
263-94-			
218-96-			
346-66-			
204-36-			
447-50-			
346-14-			
562-02-			
547-16-			
563-42-			
570-04-4517	J. R. PREECE	1,450.15	
537-67-8001	S. A. PRICE	2,400.00	
473-37-1548	R. J. REYNOLDS	846.12	
462-81-3105	J. J. SCHAEFER	1,247.90	
566-44-8378	G. I. SCHWARTZ	2,000.00	
570-88-9247	E. SIMMONS	1,900.00	
565-46-5196	D. M. STERN	1,896.75	
414-30-7403	I. S. THOMAS	2,055.47	
565-60-9085	M. W. TYSON	1,745.17	
575-84-8703	M. R. WALKER	2,836.45	
421-13-7263	C. E. WATERS	1,957.84	
258-64-6704	E. L. WILSON	2,295.67	
558-01-3426	L. C. ZALTON	1,471.25	

TOTALS FOR THIS PAGE— Number of employees and taxable wages. — Number of employees 43 (STATE) — Number of employees (FEDERAL) — $ 90,582.24

94-0743750

2

MODERN MANUFACTURING CO. INC.
2572 SO. BUFFORD ST.
LOS ANGELES, CALIF. 90010
95-78143514

WAGE AND TAX STATEMENT 1972
(For use in States or Cities authorizing combined form)
Copy A—For Internal Revenue Service Center

Type or print EMPLOYER'S identification number, name, and address

FEDERAL INCOME TAX INFORMATION			SOCIAL SECURITY INFORMATION		STATE TAX WITHHELD
Federal income tax withheld	Wages paid subject to withholding in 1972[1]	Other compensation paid in 1972[2]	F.I.C.A. employee tax withheld[3]	Total F.I.C.A. wages paid in 1972[4]	
2,475.15	14,735.19		478.40	9,200.00	

EMPLOYEE'S social security number 263-94-2556

NAME OF STATE	STATE FORM NO.	GROSS WAGES FOR STATE IF DIFFERENT FROM FEDERAL
CALIF.	540	
NAME OF CITY	CITY FORM NO.	CITY TAX WITHHELD
* EXCLUDABLE SICK PAY ** UNCOLLECTED EMPLOYEE TAX ON TIPS	**	*

J. A. MASTERS
1025 SO. MORGAN ST.
LOS ANGELES, CALIF. 90016

Type or print EMPLOYEE'S name and address (including ZIP code) above — Single — Married X — No. Dep's 4

[1] Includes tips reported by employee. Amount is before payroll deductions or sick pay exclusion.
[2] Report salary or other employee compensation which was not subject to withholding.
[3] The social security (FICA) rate of 5.2% includes .6% for Hospital Insurance Benefits and 4.6% for old-age, survivors, and disability insurance.
[4] Includes tips reported by employee.

FORM W-2— The Department of the Treasury, Internal Revenue Service 94-0743750 APPR. I.R.S. 5-5-72 EMPLOYER: See instructions on back of Copy D.

Figure 1–11. Mandatory Reports.

quent. Thus, he concentrates only on those accounts that require attention, and is relieved of the tedious task of reviewing all accounts.

The measuring of the actual progress of an organization and the feedback for management control is another important function that data processing equipment is performing for management each day. Reports are prepared periodically that management can compare with predicted results. The feedback can indicate what corrective action, if any, must be taken to achieve management goals.

DATE 9-20-6- QUANTITY DEVIATION REPORT PAGE 1

DEPT WK/CTR	PRODUCTION ORDER NBR	PART NUMBER	OPN SEQ NUMBER	QNTY ORDERED	PREVIOUS OPN QNTY	QNTY COMPL	%	QNTY SCRAP	%	QNTY SHRINKAGE	%
029-001	5200029	5A13982	0200	10000	10000	9000	90	1000	10		
029-001	5200029	5A13982	0300	10000	9000	7000	78			2000	22

SCHOOL NAME U N S C H E D U A B L E S T U D E N T S R E P O R T 9/08/6- PAGE 2

ST.NO.	NAME		COMMENTS
121376	MEADE JOHN D	002 171 192 322 533 724 737 806 808	UNSCHEDUABLE CONFLICT
121564	SMITH JANIS	002 123 313 428 523 723	NO ROOM IN SOME CLASS
121584	SPURSEL DEBORAH	002 121 426 523 635 720 807 809	UNSCHEDUABLE CUTOFF
121616	THOMPSON NANCY	002 133 426 523 635 727 806 808	NO ROOM IN SOME CLASS
121642	TURNER PAUL J	002 171 193 428 533 635 710 807 809	UNSCHEDUABLE CONFLICT
121674	WEAVER ROSALIE W	002 123 533 635 727 806 808 811	NO ROOM IN SOME CLASS
121683	WEAVER WILLIAM R	002 123 533 635 727 735 806 808	NO ROOM IN SOME CLASS
121688	WIEDMAN JOSEPH C	001 113 413 711 726 802 804	UNSCHEDUABLE CONFLICT
121706	YOUNG CLARENCE	001 113 312 413 711 802 804	NO ROOM IN SOME CLASS
121782	ZINDORF ALBERT C	001 123 352 451 496 726 727 806 808	NO ROOM IN SOME CLASS
		TOTAL CONFLICTS 039	

Figure 1–12. Operational Reports.

AGED ACCOUNT BALANCE REPORT

DATE: 05/31/--

	CYCLE: 10	REGULAR	COMBINATION	REVOLVING	CONTRACT	TOTAL
TOTAL OF ACCOUNT BALANCES	CURRENT	$5,560.09	$ 863,891.66	.00	$138,065.07	$1,007,516.82
	30 DAYS		454,096.98	.00	19,591.47	473,688.45
	60 DAYS		268,233.97	.00	8,668.90	276,902.87
	90 DAYS		198,438.51	.00	16,243.91	214,682.42
	120 DAYS		89,439.95	.00	6,724.54	96,164.49
	150 DAYS		54,022.67	.00	4,525.62	58,548.29
	180 DAYS		44,985.18	.00	3,104.90	48,090.08
	OVER 180		.00	.00	.00	.00
	TOTAL	$5,560.09	$1,973,108.92	.00	$196,924.41	$2,175,593.42
	WRITE OFF					.00
TOTAL OF AMOUNT NOW DUE ON ABOVE BALANCE	CURRENT		$ 70,633.12	.00	$ 8,563.01	$ 79,196.13
	30 DAYS		20,438.21	.00	1,956.89	22,395.10
	60 DAYS		11,326.92	.00	1,201.43	12,528.35
	90 DAYS		5,115.63	.00	865.63	5,981.26
	120 DAYS		3,265.88	.00	406.46	3,672.34
	150 DAYS		1,985.25	.00	350.00	2,335.25
	180 DAYS		1,190.01	.00	275.50	1,465.51
	OVER 180		.00	.00	.00	.00
	TOTAL		$ 113,955.02	.00	$ 13,618.92	$ 127,573.94
	REGULAR					5,560.09
	TOTAL					$ 133,134.03

Scientific data processing includes the analysis of the data required and used for engineering and research purposes. It is *mathematically-oriented, usually nonrepetitive in nature or file-oriented, requiring small amounts of input and output data with many calculations.* For example, a mathematical formula is programmed into a computer, a small amount of data is entered into the machine, and one line of output is produced on the printer, although the machine was required to go through many computing cycles.

Space technology would be almost unthinkable without the power of the computer. This is an area of science that requires the combined knowledge of almost all the other sciences—physics, chemistry, thermodynamics, electronics, mathematics, even psychology. Only computers can bring this incredibly large amount of information under control to make it serve rather than impede our efforts.

What can computers do for the scientist?

For almost a century weather scientists have had mathematical formulas for predicting weather changes. Now they are able to work out the astronomical number of calculations the formulas require. They are even working on a mathematical model of the world's weather that may some day enable us to make reasonably accurate weather forecasts a year or more ahead of time.

In medicine, computers are helping researchers test drugs by extrapolating the information gained in limited trials, so that large-scale tests will not only be safer, but will yield far more useful information. Computers are helping doctors make diagnoses by winnowing down the information a doctor has to go through to arrive at a valid conclusion (Fig. 1.13).

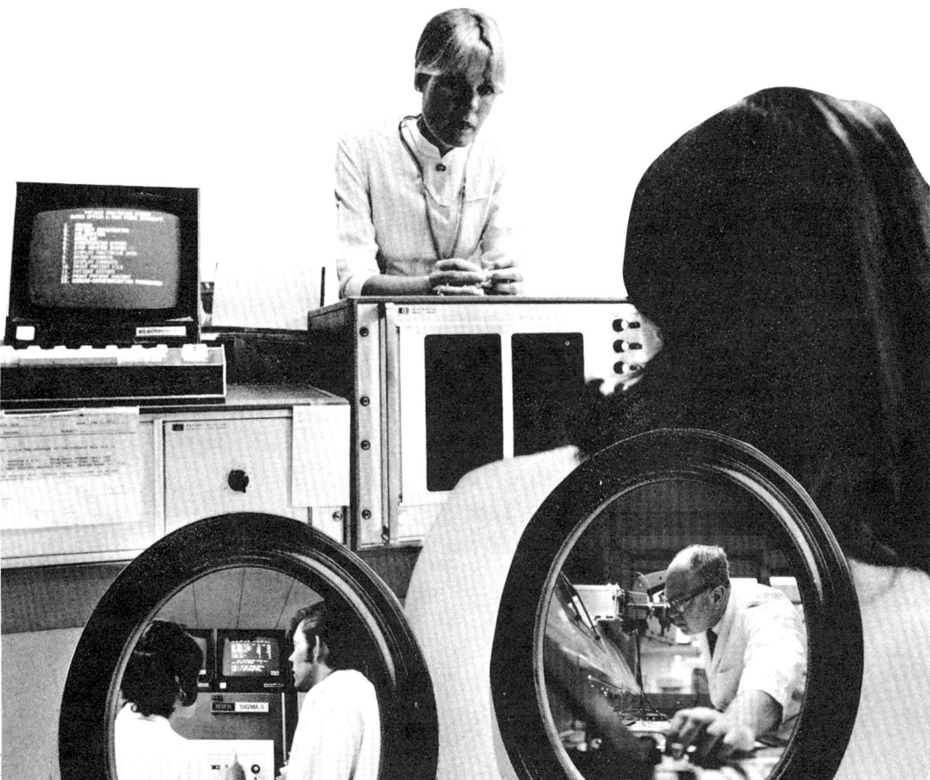

Figure 1–13. Computers in Medicine.

Biochemists are using computers as a sort of mathematical microscope. In delving into the secret of the living cell, they have found a physical limit to the information they can obtain with their instruments. By using computers to comb through and extend the data they have already obtained, they are beginning to construct an accurate picture of the giant molecules that are the building blocks of all living things (Fig. 1.14).

UTAH BIOMEDICAL TEST LABORATORY — 8 JAN 1973, PAGE 3

PRESSURE PROGRAM - 7203
PATIENT CLASS - 0 PROJECT - 2
PATIENT I.D. - 88 UNIT NO. - 32
FROM 1 73 0: 0 TO 365 73 23:59

DATE	TIME	PRES. TYPE	MAX. PRES. MM-HG	MIN. PRES. MM-HG	MEAN PRES. MM-HG	HEART RATE
8 JAN 73	5 :53:21	13	0.	0.	0.	73.
8 JAN 73	6 :9 :21	13	0.	0.	0.	70.
8 JAN 73	6 :25:21	13	0.	0.	0.	95.
8 JAN 73	6 :41:21	13	0.	0.	0.	78.
8 JAN 73	6 :57:21	13	0.	0.	0.	75.
8 JAN 73	7 :13:21	13	0.	0.	0.	61.
8 JAN 73	7 :29:21	13	0.	0.	0.	24.*
8 JAN 73	8 :17:21	13	0.	0.	0.	82.
8 JAN 73	8 :18:4	13	0.	0.	0.	74.
8 JAN 73	8 :33:21	13	0.	0.	0.	89.
8 JAN 73	8 :49:21	13	0.	0.	0.	0.*
8 JAN 73	9 :5 :21	13	0.	0.	0.	81.
8 JAN 73	9 :21:21	13	0.	0.	0.	98.
8 JAN 73	9 :53:21	13	32.	12.	20.*	81.
8 JAN 73	10:25:21	13	23.	-25.	0.	18.*
8 JAN 73	10:57:21	13	31.	-8.	10.	71.

*NOTE-ASTERISK INDICATES AN ALARMED VALUE.

Figure 1–14. Biomedical Reports.

In astronomy, computers, of course, serve as computational workhorses, figuring out the exact positions and orbits of planets, stars and other heavenly bodies. With the growing importance of radio telescopy, computers have been especially valuable in analyzing the patterns of signals received from outer space, separating the meaningful signals from the electronic roar of background "noise" that accompanies them.

The achievements of computers in the fields of space exploration, weather reporting, medical research and other areas of scientific study have been fantastic. The tremendous storage capabilities and rapid processing of data have produced the valuable information necessary for research in the unknown areas of science. Scientific research has moved into the foreground of human activity. In both the pure and applied sciences, computers are being used to multiply man's thinking power—and to multiply the time he can spend thinking!

THE FUTURE

What man foresees in the future for data processing, no one can predict. Obviously, the rate of growth will accelerate with new equipment and devices, and the new methods of data processing being introduced each day. The most rapidly growing industry in the country today is that of the office computing and accounting machines. The computer completely dominates the industry now. Computer output has grown at a staggering rate of nearly 40 percent a year.

Computers will double in number by 1980, it is predicted. Time sharing will continue to spread rapidly. Process computers are expected to increase significantly, and by 1980 nearly ten times as many installations are expected as there were in the mid-1960s when about 1,700 process computers were in use.

Today, computers and computer-directed machines can manufacture steel, turn petroleum into chemicals and chemicals into plastics, sort bank checks, machine engine blocks, route automobile traffic and telephone calls alike, even design and assemble computers that will in turn control machines.

Faster, better communications will be among the important factors in the growth of the economy over the next decade. With fast, flexible data communications, the problems of time and distance which, until now, have limited many computer applications will be eliminated. Prospects for higher quality international communications via satellites will be spectacular and the rapid growth of overseas communications will contribute substantially to the large-scale expansion of international business operations.

One of the significant changes in the future will, hopefully, be the attainment of a maturity level at which it will be recognized that processing data is the purpose of all computing no matter what the source of data, so that the imaginary boundary between "data processor" and "computer scientist" will disappear. Our educational institutions are awakening to the need for more people with better academic training in data processing. In future years, educational institutions at all levels will continue to offer more courses in data processing and computer science. This will hasten the application of the computer to social and environmental problems of man.

If man is to successfully survive and enjoy the benefits of this new era, he must learn the principles and operations of modern data processing systems. He must update himself constantly in the new methods of handling data. Technological developments will limit the employment growth for certain types of clerical workers. To illustrate, the use of computers to produce routine and repetitive work is expected to reduce the number of jobs in such areas as filing, payroll, inventory control and billing. On the other hand, labor-saving innovations will be affected to some extent by growing requirements for clerical personnel to prepare computer inputs. Of the eleven occupations cited by the United States Department of Labor as "expected to grow rapidly during the 1970s", the top three are system analyst, with an anticipated increase from 1968 to 1980 of 183 percent, programmer, 129 percent, and computer operator, 129 percent.

Programming, analysis and computer operating are just a few of the new occupations created with the advent of the computer. No field is immune from the invasion of the computer. More specialized positions are needed in each field of data processing. Information demands are enormous and will continue to increase. Man, who never dreamed of reaching the moon, is now searching for other planets with the aid of the computer.

Governmental agencies have become the largest users of data processing equipment. Increasing pressure from taxpayers for reduced costs of operations, and demands for more detailed and accurate reporting of transactions have caused the conversion of large heretofore manual operations to high speed data processing applications. Many opportunities exist in these fields for all personnel who are properly trained in data processing operations. There exists a serious shortage of trained personnel in many governmental units (as well as in private enterprises) and many units have instituted their own training programs for employees interested in data processing. Most organizations encourage their employees to attend educational institutions to receive training in data processing. These organizations provide promotional opportunities to those employees completing these courses, and pay for their tuition if they receive a satisfactory grade, as well. Many organizations require that the applicant have some basic data processing courses at some institutions and then will train them in the operational and programming techniques on the job.

Accountants, lawyers, business men, administrators, as well as all personnel directly or indirectly connected with data processing equipment, must possess some knowledge pertinent to the operations and functions of the equipment. Recent fraud cases involving the computer has emphasized the need for some knowledge of the operations of the computer in all sectors. Although these individuals need not know the details of programming, they should know the capabilities of the equipment so that they will not expect the impossible of the computer.

Data processing systems are increasingly relied upon for information to assist in the running of an enterprise, aiding in the administrative activities, directing research programs and planning future activities. In a short decade, the computer industry has grown to a stage where it can be called an "industry." It has created almost a quarter of a million new jobs and there is an increasing need for people with the training and vision that computer development requires.

Regardless of the nature of the problem, where there exists a need for a decision based on human judgment, there will also exist a need for a data processing system. As with the tools that preceded it, the computer's beneficial effects are limited only by the imagination and intelligence with which one uses it.

SUMMARY

This chapter was intended to introduce the concepts of data processing, to demonstrate the importance of data processing in our economy, and to explore the vital role played by the computer in this everchanging area.

1. The increasing use of data in our present way of life. The changing of the economy from cash-oriented to credit-based has greatly expanded the use of the computer. New service industries are providing numerous services to make life more convenient and pleasant.
2. Data processing is defined as a planned series of actions and operations upon information using various forms of physical equipment to achieve a desired result. Data processing systems consist of programs and physical equipment. The physical equipment consists of various units such as input and output, storage and processing devices to handle information at electronic speeds.
3. The informational demands both from within and without an organization. The growing need for rapid methods of processing data to satisfy these demands. All demands must be combined into an integrated data processing system to satisfy the needs of all users without duplicating the effort of processing.
4. The case study demonstrated how the computer is being used to solve one of the most complex problems of the day, traffic congestion.
5. The sources of information emphasizing the media upon which they are initially recorded. The problems of controlling the format of the input data. Internal data can be controlled more accurately as to form while the external data is controlled by the individual organizations that create it, thus both types of data are designed to accommodate the needs of the supplier.
6. The types of data processing; business and scientific.

   Business data processing is characterized by the processing of many files, used repeatedly, requiring relatively few calculations and many output reports. The various management reports prepared by the computer help administrators make their everyday decisions and reduce the amount of paperwork.

   Mandatory reports are those necessary reports that are required by governmental agencies, stockholders, customers, etc., that are usually prepared in a fixed format.

   Operational reports are those necessary reports that aid management in their everyday decisions. They help to reduce the cost of operations and so make the organization more competitive.

   Management by exception technique is a concept whereby only the exceptional facts are drawn to the attention of the decision maker relieving him of the tedious task of reviewing the entire report.

Scientific data processing is mathematically oriented, usually nonrepetitive or file oriented, requiring small amounts of input and output with many calculations. The remarkable advances in space technology, weather forecasting, medicine, etc., are just a few of the spectacular achievements made possible by the tremendous calculating speed and storage of the computer.

7. The future of data processing will depend to a large extent upon the ingenuity of its users. Computers are expected to double in number by 1980. Data communications will be an important factor in the growth of data processing during the next decade. Analysts, programmers, and computer operators are expected to grow rapidly in number during the 1970s. More persons will be required to have a knowledge of data processing.

IDENTIFICATION QUESTIONS

Match the following terms with the statements below.

A. Audio Response
B. Business Data Processing
C. Data Processing
D. External Data
E. External Demands
F. Image Processing
G. Internal Data
H. Internal Demands
I. Management By Exception
J. Mandatory Reports
K. Operational Reports
L. Scientific Data Processing

1. The medium in which data is recorded originally at the time the transaction occurs.
2. Reports that aid managment in making the many necessary decisions in everyday operations of a business.
3. Requests from management for information.
4. Rapid microfilming scanning combined with automatic interpretation of light and dark spots into 0's and 1's for computer storage.
5. Characterized by the processing of many files, used repeatedly, requiring few calculations and many output reports.
6. A planned series of actions and operations upon information, using various forms of data processing equipment, to achieve a desired result.
7. Data created outside of an organization.
8. Necessary reports that are required by governmental agencies, stockholders, customers, etc.
9. Response to the human voice through the selection and assembly of messages previously stored in the computer.
10. Characterized by being mathematically-oriented, usually nonrepetitive in nature or file-oriented, requiring small amounts input and output data with many calculations.

11. Requests for data originating outside of the organization.
12. Reduces the amount of detail that a decision maker is faced with.

QUESTIONS FOR REVIEW

1. How does the computer affect our lives?
2. What is data processing and what units constitute a physical data processing system?
3. What are the demands for data and how do they differ?
4. What constitutes a successful data processing system?
5. What are the sources of information and how may the format of each be controlled? Give examples of each form.
6. What are the characteristics of business data processing? Give examples.
7. What are mandatory reports and how do they differ from operational reports?
8. What is "management by exception" and how does it aid the executive in making decisions?
9. What is scientific data processing and how does it differ from business data processing?
10. Why is it important for all personnel directly or indirectly connected with data processing equipment to possess some knowledge of its operations and functions?

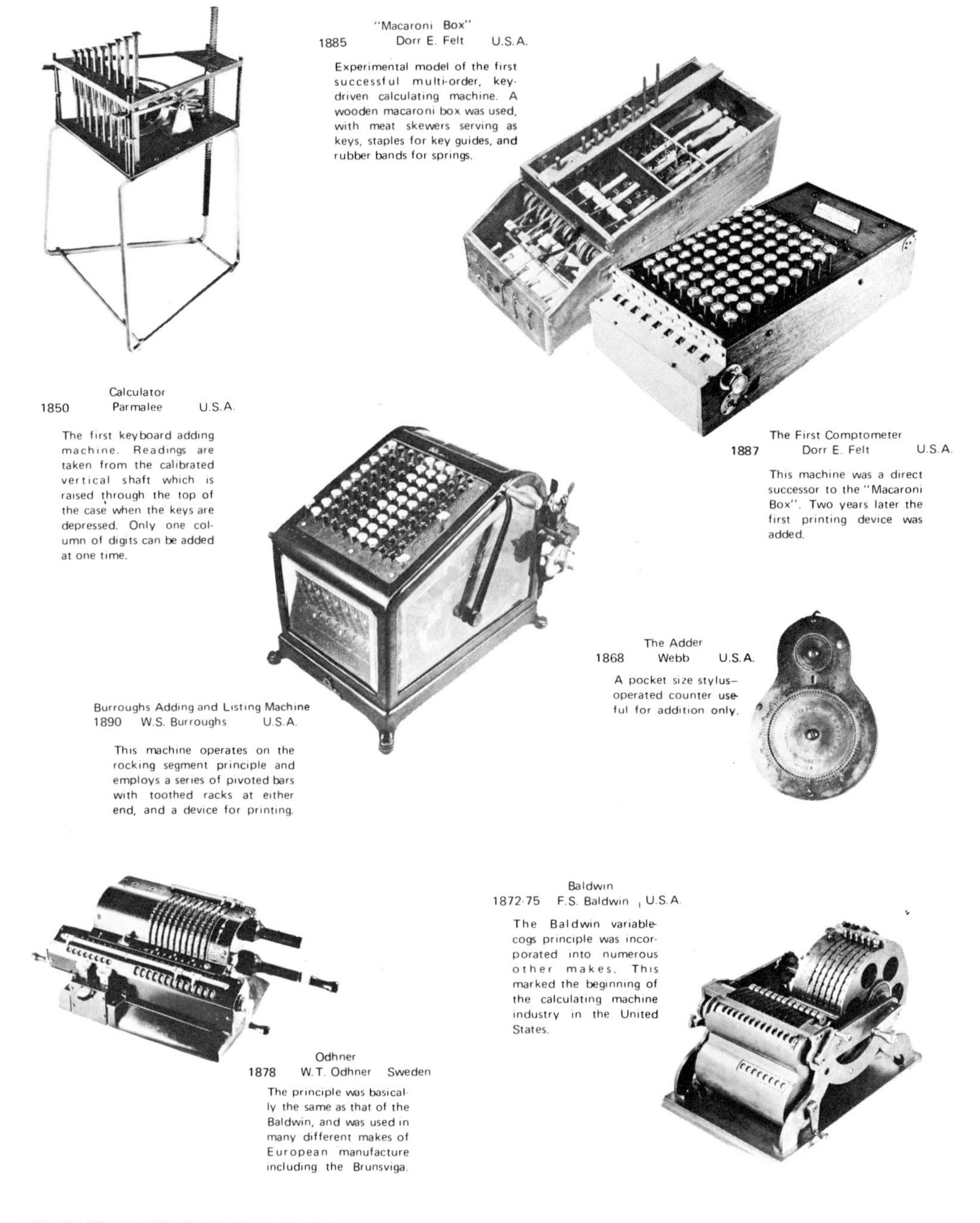

"Macaroni Box"
1885 Dorr E. Felt U.S.A.
Experimental model of the first successful multi-order, key-driven calculating machine. A wooden macaroni box was used, with meat skewers serving as keys, staples for key guides, and rubber bands for springs.
Calculator
1850 Parmalee U.S.A.
The first keyboard adding machine. Readings are taken from the calibrated vertical shaft which is raised through the top of the case when the keys are depressed. Only one column of digits can be added at one time.
The First Comptometer
1887 Dorr E. Felt U.S.A.
This machine was a direct successor to the "Macaroni Box". Two years later the first printing device was added.
The Adder
1868 Webb U.S.A.
A pocket size stylus–operated counter useful for addition only.
Burroughs Adding and Listing Machine
1890 W.S. Burroughs U.S.A.
This machine operates on the rocking segment principle and employs a series of pivoted bars with toothed racks at either end, and a device for printing.
Baldwin
1872-75 F.S. Baldwin U.S.A.
The Baldwin variable-cogs principle was incorporated into numerous other makes. This marked the beginning of the calculating machine industry in the United States.
Odhner
1878 W.T. Odhner Sweden
The principle was basically the same as that of the Baldwin, and was used in many different makes of European manufacture including the Brunsviga.

Figure 2–1. Early Calculating Devices.

CHAPTER 2

History of Data Processing

Although the most dramatic advances in processing information have occurred during the last quarter century, computing can be traced back to the primitive tribes. Ancient calculating involved the manipulation of the fingers to represent various numbers. The first data processing tools were used to facilitate counting. Variations and refinements of counting led to fairly elaborate calculators involving addition, subtraction, multiplication and division (Fig. 2.1). As man continued to work with numbers and the demand for information increased, more complex devices were developed. The computer is the culmination of thousands of years of research to develop a machine capable of processing data at high speeds with self-checking accuracy features (Fig. 2.2).

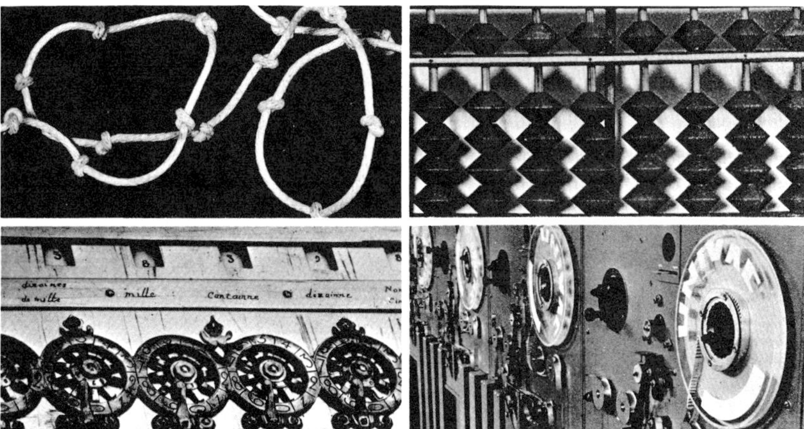

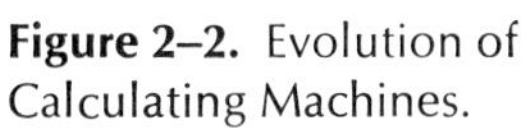

Figure 2–2. Evolution of Calculating Machines.

THE EARLY COMPUTERS

ABACUS (3000 B.C.)

Today's computer is a direct descendent of a device that has been in existence for over four thousand years. The abacus, earliest known calculating device, has been used for so many years it is impossible to ascertain when it was first used (Fig. 2.3). The design of the abacus is so simple that it has remained relatively unchanged from civilization to civilization. Movable beads are strung on a wire frame. These beads are divided into two groups to stipulate the various values of digits. Calculating or counting is performed by the manipulation of these beads. In the simplest form of the abacus the beads or counters are stored at one end of the frame and the computation is performed at the other end by moving the correct number of beads over against the side of the frame.

Figure 2–3. Abacus.

The abacus was the first known device to designate the position of a number to represent a value. Usually in a decimal scale separate wires represent units, tens, hundreds, etc.

Although invented independently by the Greeks and the Chinese, most of the important innovations, such as carrying over to the next position in accumulation, were contributed by the Chinese.

The abacus is still the commonest computer in use in Asia and is used by over one half of the world's population, chiefly in the Far East. Many abacus operators become so adept with the manipulation of the beads that they rival the speed of clerks using modern-day adding machines.

NAPIER'S "BONES" (1617)

John Napier, a Scottish mathematician, is known as the inventor of logarithms. This table of "artificial numbers" provides a convenient method of shortening calculations, particularly in multiplication and division.

Napier's "bones" was a set of rods designed for the purpose of facilitating the numerical operations of multiplication and division. The "bones" or rods were divided into nine squares, each divided diagonally, with the multiples in columns beneath them. The rods were manipulated in such a manner that the answer was found by adding the numbers in horizontally adjacent squares. The purpose of the device was to reduce tedious calculations with large numbers.

Napier's "Bones" were widely employed in Europe for assistance in multiplication, division and the extraction of square and cube roots.

PASCAL (1642)

Blaise Pascal, a well-known French author, philosopher and mathematician, is credited with inventing the first calculating machine (Fig. 2.4). His gear-driven machine was the first machine to perform automatic carry. Each wheel has teeth numbered from 0–9. When a particular wheel was rotated from 9 to 0 in his adding machine, a mechanism moved the wheel next to it

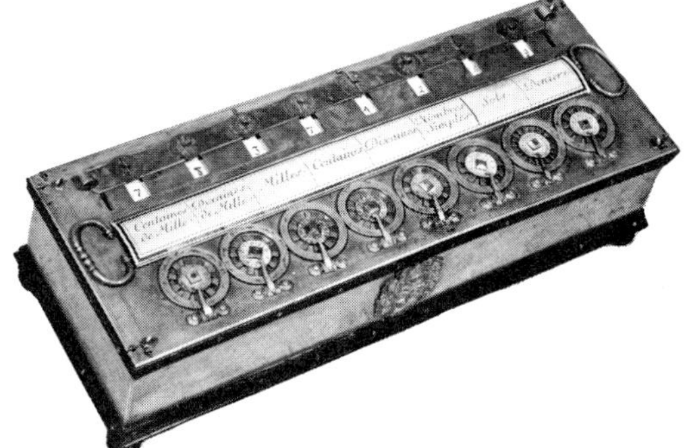

Figure 2–4. Pascal's Machine.

by one digit, thus providing the automatic carry. Addition was executed by stepping the gears a number of intervals equal to the numbers to be added. The basic principles of machine calculation were devised in these machines; automatic carryover to next position, subtraction by turning the various dials in a reverse manner, and the performing of multiplication through repeated additions.

This was the first mechanical calculator, and devices in use today closely resemble the original cylinders and gears of Pascal's machine.

LEIBNITZ (1671)

Gottfried von Leibnitz, a German philosopher, diplomat, and mathematician, utilized Pascal's method to develop a machine that could multiply, divide and extract square roots. These calculations were performed in a series of additions, subtractions and tallies. His "stepped wheel" calculator consisted of a cylindrical drum with nine teeth of increasing length along the surface. When the drum was rotated, it engaged some of the teeth on a sliding gear on the axle, thus rotating them a number of steps. This gear principle is still employed in many of the modern-day calculators.

JACQUARD LOOM (1801)

Joseph Marie Jacquard developed an automatic loom which revolutionized the textile industry; intricate designs were woven from cloth using this loom. A punched card was used and the machine was able to follow the instructions of the punched card. The punched-card principle was later used by Babbage in his "analytical machine" and by Hollerith in his punched-card machines.

BABBAGE (1850)

Charles Babbage, English mathematician and inventor, performed work on desk calculators that revealed to him the feasibility of a machine that would greatly simplify the preparation of mathematical tables. While these simpler machines were still in their early development, he proposed the construction of two such more ambitious machines, the first of which he called a "difference engine" (Fig. 2.5). This machine, designed for the construction and printing of mathematical tables, failed because the necessary parts could not be manufactured precisely.

His second machine, the "analytical engine" was designed for general scientific calculation—stored data that could be manipulated. The data was introduced in a series of levers. The output results were read from an output device and also printed by a typewriter-like method. His "analytical machine"

Figure 2–5. Babbage's "Difference Engine."

worked with punched cards similar to the Jacquard loom. His plans included certain methods of checking the machine for errors.

Although Babbage's basic designs were good, he was never able to complete either of these machines. The English government, which had supported him earlier, withdrew its financial aid and the projects had to be abandoned. One or two "difference engines" were built by others later but they were never used successfully. The "analytical machine" had to wait until the present for the execution of the necessary facilities for reading, storage, recording and control which were beyond the capabilities of those times. Babbage's work is, however, received as an important contribution to the later engineering of the calculating machine.

Despite the failures of most of the early calculating devices, they did make valuable contributions to later developments in data processing equipment.

PUNCHED CARDS

Punched-card history began with Dr. Herman Hollerith, then a statistician employed by the United States Census Bureau, and who, in 1880 was experimenting with a punched-card mechanism. He developed a working model that utilized the "unit record" principle by which data was coded and represented by holes in a card. At that moment in our history, we were experiencing tremendous growth, and the problem of compiling statistics for the Census Bureau was increasing each decade. It had taken seven years to compile the 1880 census statistics and the population had increased by 25 percent in the interim. It became clear that if quicker methods of accumulating data were not found, no census could be completed in the ten years before the next census period.

Although the punched-card system of Dr. Hollerith was crude by today's standards of punched-card data processing, its application caused the 1890 census to be completed in one-fourth the time required for completing the 1880 census. The first card forms used did not resemble the cards as they appear today; they were forty-five columns in length and had round holes instead of the rectangular holes with which we are familiar.

By the year 1900, Dr. Hollerith had developed an automatic sorting machine which could sort at the rate of 300 cards per minute (Fig. 2.6); a card-punch machine, and a semiautomatic tabulating machine (Fig. 2.7).

Realizing the potential of punched-card data processing, Dr. Hollerith organized the Tabulating Machine Company in 1896 to enter the commercial sales market. His first large customers were railroad companies who used the machines to compile freight statistics. In 1924, the Tabulating Machine Company was merged with the Time Recording Company and the Dayton Scale Company to form a new company to be known as the International Business

Figure 2–6. Original Sorting Box.

Figure 2–7. First Census Tabulator.

Machines Corporation. The 80-column IBM card became known as the "Hollerith" card although the form was changed from the original (Fig. 2.8).

Following Dr. Hollerith to the Census Bureau was a little-known statistical engineer, James Powers, who displayed some original ideas for punched cards. In 1908, Mr. Powers patented his card-punch machine. His principle of punching was "simultaneous punching" whereby the operator depresses the keys to cause the punching but the holes in the card are not punched until the operator depresses the release key which punches all the holes in the card at the same time. This has some advantage over the IBM card-punch machine in that it permits the operator to correct a punching error without destroying the card.

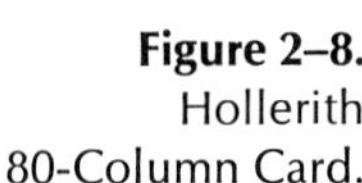

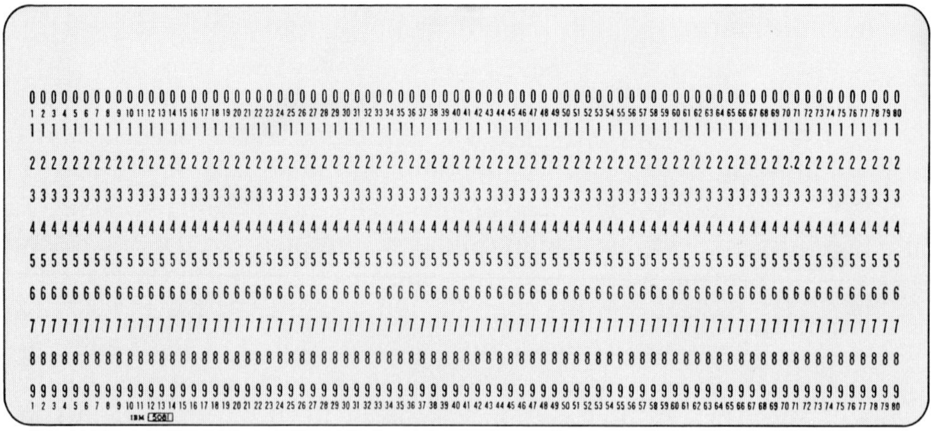

Figure 2–8. Hollerith 80-Column Card.

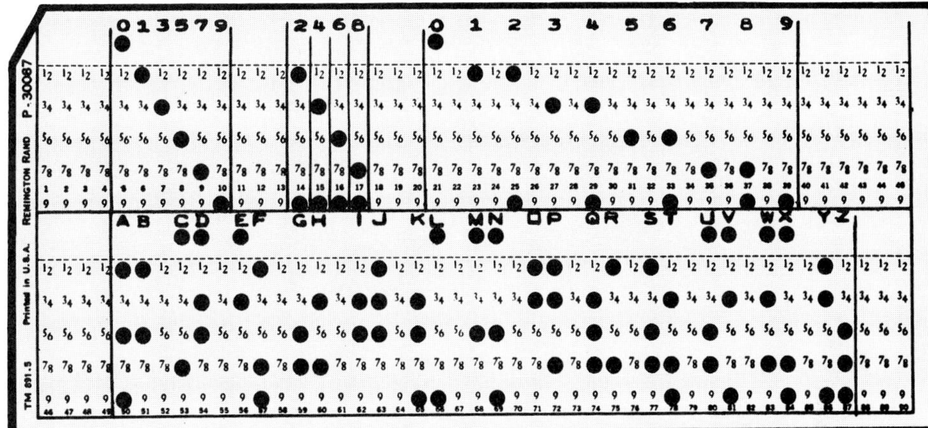

Figure 2–9. Powers 90-Column Card.

Mr. Powers developed a sorting machine, card-punch machines and tabulators which were used in the 1910 census. In 1925, he sold his patent rights to the Remington Rand Corporation who employed his "simultaneous punching" concept as late as 1954. The Remington Rand Corporation merged with the Sperry Gyroscope Company to form the Sperry Rand Corporation which now markets these machines.

Up to the outbreak of World War II, there were just these two companies engaged in the punched-card data processing field in the United States: the IBM Corporation with the 80-column "Hollerith" card, and the Remington Rand Corporation with the "Powers" 90-column card (Fig. 2.9). Little progress was made in the data processing field during the war years.

MODERN COMPUTERS

World War II caused a swift change of pace in data processing needs. Urgent demands in science supplied the early momentum for high speed data processing. New requirements for data were encountered in aircraft design. The atomic bomb created a new dimension in calculating.

MARK I

After five years of effort, the Mark I emerged from the Harvard laboratories, in 1944, under a research grant from the IBM Corporation (Fig. 2.10). This was the world's first automatic computer, in that it had an automatic sequence-controlled calculator operated entirely by mechanical switches. It was an electromechanical machine built by the IBM Corporation and financed by the Navy Department. Punched cards were used for both input and output operations. A typewriter was used as a printing device. The sequencing of instructions was mainly through paper tape input. Limited program branch-

Figure 2–10. Mark I Computer.

ing (the ability to change the sequence of instruction execution), was incorporated into the system later.

The Mark I was a milestone in computer history as it virtually transformed Babbage's "analytical engine" into a reality. It was the first machine to do a long series of arithmetic and logical operations. A series of the machines were built for the Navy Department and they made a vital contribution to the war effort.

ENIAC

The next important machine to appear in the computer field was ENIAC (Electronic Numerical Integrator and Calculator)—in 1946. This machine was originally designed to produce mathematical tables required in the firing of projectiles. In this machine, the switching and controlling functions once trusted to relays were now handled by vacuum tubes. With the replacement of the slow electromechanical relays by electronic tubes, the speed of calculation increased one thousand times.

As the ENIAC was originally designed, each unit had to be set up by making several hundred manual adjustments for the transmission of data from one unit to another. Input and output signals between units provided the sequence for processing. In 1947, a method was designed for converting

ENIAC into a stored program machine. An arrangement was made whereby the sequence of commands was given to the machine in a list of coded instructions necessary to solve a particular problem. A central control system executed these commands in the sequence in which they were written. A limited number of special instructions provided for looping and branching and this became the basis for modern day instruction sets. These *stored program* techniques widened the capabilities of data processing systems and expanded their opportunities for application.

The ENIAC was the first electronic computer and was the first to use stored program (programs stored internally in the machine) techniques. Problems of greater complexity could now be handled by computers. The amount of human effort was greatly reduced due to the centralization of control through the stored program.

The ENIAC is regarded as the prototype of all later computer equipment.

UNIVAC

The first commercial computer, UNIVAC (Universal Automatic Computer), was delivered in 1951 to the Census Bureau and was immediately used in the 1952 biennial census statistics. Several types of input and output, as well as automatic programming, were used by the equipment. UNIVAC was one of the first computers to use magnetic tape for input and output operations.

FIRST GENERATION COMPUTERS

During the years 1954–59, approximately three dozen different engineering groups in the United States and abroad completed the construction of modern and large scale data processing systems. Many assembly lines were producing electronic calculators of varied sizes and speeds, such as the UNIVAC produced by the Sperry Rand Corporation; IBM's 700 series and SAGE computers; Monroe MONOROBOT; CRC102A by the National Cash Register Company; DATATRON by the Electro Data Corp. (now Burroughs Corp.); ELECOM by the Underwood Corporation; IBM's 650; RCA BIZMAC; and DATAMATIC 1000. At this period it seemed that there was a new computer being announced each day by some company. These "first generation" computers were characterized as being rather bulky in size, requiring great amounts of air conditioning to dissipate the heat problem their many vacuum tubes created, and demanding a high rate of maintenance and repair time. However, these computers had many advantages over their earlier electromechanical counterparts—in speed of calculation, in the use of stored and internal programs, in an ability to apply logical decisions to calculated results, and by the introduction of different types of input and output

Figure 2-11. IBM 650 Computer (First-Generation Computer).

media such as magnetic tape, paper tape, etc. These new techniques provided speeds up to fifty to seventy-five times greater than that of cards and brought improvements in input, output and storage capabilities (Figs. 2.11, 2.12).

The computer now had immediate access to instructions given as rapidly as it called for them, inasmuch as the program was stored in a high speed internal memory or storage unit. With this internal storage, the computer could process instructions in the same manner as data. It could modify its own instructions in making simple decisions thus relieving the programmer of vast amounts of costly and repetitive programming. Later computers extended this principle until it became possible for computers to generate a considerable part of their own instructions.

Figure 2–12. IBM 702 Computer (First-Generation Computer).

SECOND GENERATION COMPUTERS

The "second generation" of computers was ushered in during the late 1950s. The significance of this era of computers came into full focus as a result of the replacement of the vacuum tube by the tiny transistor requiring less power and offering greater reliability (Figs. 2.13, 2.14). Thanks to this change, the size of the computers was drastically reduced and the need for large amounts of air conditioning was lessened. High speed card readers and printers were introduced. Access to data and instructions was now thought of in terms of microseconds (millionths of a second). High speed data processing was now a reality. Sophisticated programs and compilers began to appear. The "natural" or mnemonic language was now replacing the machine language in programming. Maintenance costs were reduced by virtue of the reliability of the transistor and the use of new and better components resulting from continuing developments in the electronics and solid state physics field.

Figure 2–13. IBM 1401 Computer (Second-Generation Computer).

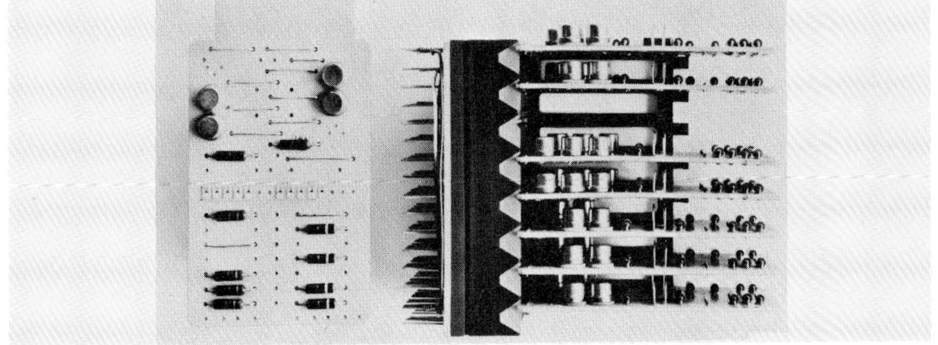

Figure 2–14. Computer Components.

Random (direct) access devices appeared during this period, offering the user random accessing of data in addition to the sequential processing of data. Inline processing was now possible inasmuch as data could be recorded as received instead of having to wait to be batched for subsequent sequential processing. Information could be recorded on or retrieved from the data tracks without regard to the sequential order of the recorded data.

THIRD GENERATION COMPUTERS

In the mid-1960s, the "third generation" of computers appeared. This era is characterized by the advanced miniaturization and the refined components that came with "second generation" computers (Figs. 2.15, 2.16). The nanosecond (one billionth of a second) appeared as a method of measuring access and processing time. Newer and faster methods of input and output were introduced: optical scanning, magnetic ink recognition, data transmission displays, etc. Multiprogramming permitted the simultaneous processing of more than one program at a time. Tremendous storage capabilities permitted immediate access to millions of characters. All operational and functional data can now be stored in a computer and be accessed from any location. Remote terminals located in the same building or across the entire nation can now have access to the data stored in the computer, thus facilitating the

Figure 2–15. IBM 360 Computer (Third-Generation Computer).

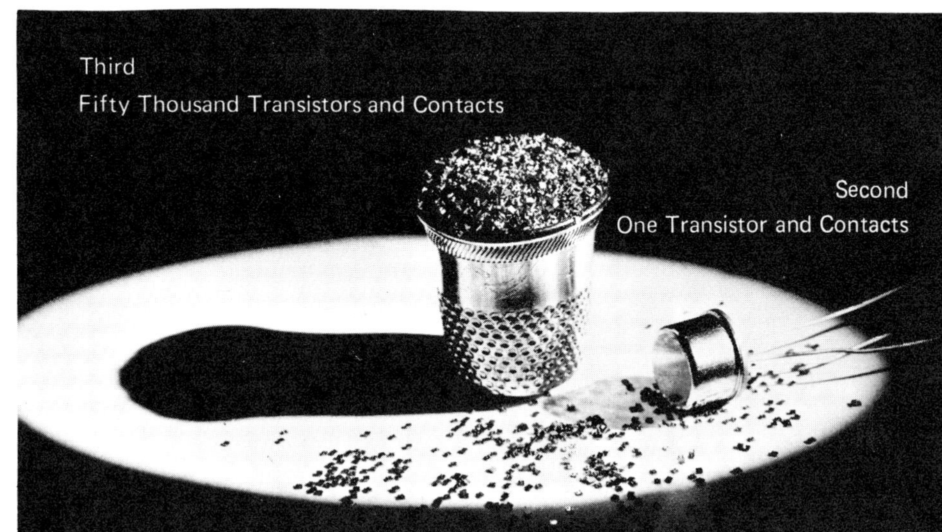

Figure 2–16. Comparison of Second- and Third-Generation Computer Components.

transmission of data over great distances. Inquiries are made through these terminals and the answers can be displayed on a video tube.

FOURTH GENERATION COMPUTERS

The 1970s marked the beginning of a new generation of computers (Fig. 2.17). Although the changes were subtle, there were dramatic announcements in all sectors of the computer field. No previous period saw so many major concepts of data processing undergoing such simultaneous intensive

Figure 2–17. IBM 370 Computer (Fourth-Generation Computer).

study, experimentation and development. The technology of operating systems, multiprogramming, multiprocessing, high-level and user-oriented programming languages, time sharing, data communications, hardware miniaturization and operating speeds were all subject to intensive research in both private and public sectors of the economy.

The IBM System/370 appeared during this period. The system used many of the functions already provided in the third generation System/360 but added this extensive array of enhancements:

- Faster internal performance
- Greater channel capabilities providing more efficient input and output processing of data
- Integrated emulation of other systems
- Added reliability, availability and serviceability
- Enhanced functional capabilities

Of special importance to users of System/360 was the relative ease with which the transition could be made from the System/360 to System/370. Most System/360 input/output equipment, users programs and programming systems can be used on the System/370 without change.

The dramatic announcement of "Virtual Storage" concept increased the main storage capabilities of computers. *Virtual storage is a means of greatly expanding a computer's main storage capacity by allowing a computer to directly access outside storage devices as though they were part of main storage itself.*

The minicomputer made spectacular advances during this period. *A minicomputer may be defined as a small computer system which rents for approximately $3,000 a month, operates under stored program control and includes a master file capability.* It is expected that with new technological advances in the manufacture of minicomputers, a reduction of up to 25 percent in price can be expected during the next five years. These reduced prices plus increased acceptance for small computer operations should produce an average annual sales increase of approximately 22 percent over the same period.

FUTURE COMPUTERS

What is the future for data processing? Automatic programming allows the computer to create its own program from specification sheets or other media written by other than data processing personnel as well as by data processing personnel. This should make programming easier and more manageable in the future. Ultimately scientists hope to develop machines that can read ordinarily printed matter and can respond to the spoken word. Input and output techniques will be improved. Graphic displays will become more popular; and (already available) the user will be permitted to change the output by using a light pen to erase or alter a character. Integrated networks of systems will permit the communication of data from one system to another. Paychecks may entirely disappear as the paymaster can instruct the computer at a bank to credit an employee's account with the net salary earned without the necessity of issuing a document. Physical changes will continue, with the processing unit continuing to decrease in size while the speed and capacity are greatly increased.

Computer hardware will continue its trend toward miniaturization. The era of the complete circuit is just beginning. It is reasonable to assume that within the next ten years we will see a complete computer on a single chip. A "microcomputer" with about eight thousand to sixteen thousand words of storage, an instruction set of sixty-four to ninety-six commands, about sixteen general purpose registers, and input/output bus on a single chip will be a reality within the next two or three years. In ten years, such a chip will probably sell for under fifty dollars. The impact of this type of microcomputer will be felt in all walks of life.

An area of major change will be that of education. The use of machines will permeate the educational process all the way down to the primary grades. Consider the impact of the small computer, similar to the current miniature electronic calculator selling for about fifty dollars. A pocket computer will be as common and as essential as today's pencil and workbook. There will be no need to teach the mechanics of arithmetic—no drills on times tables. Classroom time will be spent teaching the thought processes required to solve problems with the computer as an aid to doing the mechanics of arithmetic and recording, except that the classroom will not be a classroom but a learning laboratory centered around the computer-assisted learning techniques under development today. In the next ten years, all classroom activity will take place in the home or in a community learning center. The campus buildings will become laboratories for research and experimentation.

What will be the impact of the "computer on a chip" on other areas of society? In consumer products, think in terms of an alarm clock with a built-in hundred-year personal calendar; it would be preprogrammed to awaken its owner at an appointed time on each day of the year, excluding weekends and holidays. The same device could be used as an appointment calendar built into a wristwatch. A credit card with an individual's entire credit history stored in an imbedded microcomputer would eliminate the need for credit reports at time of sale; and the same card used to activate the lock on its owner's automobile, home or office, in addition to activating a bank's memory money dispenser, a pay telephone, etc. Think of a computer chip in your electric typewriter, telephone, television set, refrigerator, stove, etc. Toymakers could make truly educational toys. The list of possibilities is endless.

Programming as we know it may cease to exist. Instead, user languages could be developed which would be programmed into language interpreter chips, which may be built into the user's terminal, enabling the terminal to call a central system. Every home could have a built-in communications system, similar to cable television, which would allow the user to have the world's information at his immediate disposal without having to leave his home. If we allow our imagination to work on all potential uses of computers, there will be no end.

From these speculations, we can see the character of the jobs in data processing changing dramatically within the next ten years. The emphasis will be on system analysis, with the definition of "system" expanded to include psychological and sociological aspects of computer use. Preoccupation with jargon, programming problems, and hardware technology must give way to preoccupation with service. Popular acceptance of the computer will depend on our ability to adapt to an environment which emphasizes the importance to the user of service which the computer professional offers.

Computer programs of the future will probably be quite different from those in use today. It will be an interesting future—waiting for each new development and marvelling at each new advance in data processing.

SUMMARY

To obtain a thorough knowledge of data processing, one must study its history and background. Only then will one realize that the computer did not just "happen" along during the last twenty-five years but is the outgrowth of thousands of years of development and research. The object of this chapter has been to trace the most significant events and show how each contributed to the development of the computer.

The history is brief, highlighting only those individuals and equipment that made vital contributions to modern-day processing.

EARLY COMPUTERS

The first important machine in this period was the abacus (3,000 B.C.) which is still in existence today and used by over half of the world's population, chiefly in the Far East. The machine made valuable contributions, including positional notation.

Napier (1617) was the inventor of logarithms. His "bones" facilitated the numeric operations of multiplication and division.

Pascal (1642) invented the first gear-driven calculating machine. Calculating devices in use today closely resemble Pascal's machine.

Leibnitz (1671) improved on Pascal's machine and his gear principle is still used in many modern-day calculators.

Jacquard (1801) developed the punched-card principle used in the textile industry for weaving. His "punched-card" principle was later used by Babbage and Hollerith.

Babbage (1850) constructed large-scale calculating machines. His machines failed because the necessary parts could not be manufactured precisely. Despite failures, his work is received as a valuable contribution to the later engineering of calculating machines.

PUNCHED CARDS

Hollerith (1880) used Jacquard's "punched-card" principle to develop his "unit record" principle by which data was coded and represented by holes in cards. His "punched-card" principle was used successfully by the U.S. Census Bureau in 1890 to compile census statistics in one-fourth of the time required for the 1880 census in spite of a 25 percent increase in population. Hollerith developed an automatic sorting machine, a card-punch machine and semiautomatic tabulating machine. In 1896 he organized the Tabulating Machine Company which was subsequently merged with other companies to form the International Business Machines Corporation in 1924. The 80-column IBM punched card became known as the "Hollerith" card.

Powers (1900) employed "punched-card" principles in developing his sorting machines, card-punch machines and tabulators. His equipment was used in the 1910 census. He later sold his patent rights to the Remington Rand Corporation in 1925. The "Powers" punched card contained 90 columns. In 1966, the 90-column card was discontinued by the Sperry Rand Corporation, successor to the Remington Rand Corporation. Up to the outbreak of World War II, there were just these two companies engaged in punched-card data processing, the IBM Corporation and the Remington Rand Corporation. Little progress was made in data processing field during the war years.

MODERN COMPUTERS

Mark I (1944) was the world's first automatic computer in that it had an automatic sequence controlled calculator operated entirely by mechanical switches. Developed by IBM and the Navy Department, it was the first machine to do a long series of arithmetic and logical operations.

ENIAC (1946) was the first electronic (vacuum tube) computer and was the first to use stored programs (stored internally in the machine). It was the prototype of all later computer equipment.

UNIVAC (1951) was the first commercial computer. It was first used in the 1952 biennial census. Automatic programming, several types of input and output equipment were some of the features of this machine.

First Generation Computers (1954–59) were rather bulky in size, requiring large amounts of air conditioning to dissipate the heat created by the many vacuum tubes. They had a high ratio of maintenance and repair time also. The important advantages over earlier machines were speed of calculation, use of the stored program, the ability to apply logical decisions to calculated results, various types of input and output equipment, magnetic tape, paper tape, ability to modify its own program, etc.

Second Generation Computers (1959–64) replaced the vacuum tubes with the tiny transistor, thus requiring less power and offering greater reliability. The size of the computer was greatly reduced and the need for large amounts of air conditioning was eliminated. High speed card readers and printers were introduced. Sophisticated programs and compilers began to appear. Symbolic programming was replacing machine language programming during this period. Random access devices were introduced. Repair and maintenance time was greatly reduced.

Third Generation Computers (1964–70) were characterized by advanced miniaturization and refinement of computer components. Greater compilers, newer and faster methods of input and output, optical scanners, magnetic ink character readers, data transmission over long distances, displays on video tubes, multiprogramming, tremendous storage capacities, remote terminals with access to central computers—just some of the innovations introduced during this period.

Fourth Generation Computers (1970–) featured many changes in all sectors of the computer field. The technology of operating systems, multiprogramming, multiprocessing, time sharing, data communications, hardware miniaturization, and operating speeds were all subject to intensive research and undergoing changes. The concept of "Virtual Storage" increased the main storage capabilities of computers by allowing a computer to directly access outside storage devices as though they were part of main storage. The minicomputer made spectacular advances during this period. The "mini" is defined as a small computer renting for approximately $3,000 a month and having stored program and master file capabilities.

THE FUTURE

Automatic programming to continue to improve, improvement in input and output devices, greater use of video displays, continued miniaturization of computer hardware, computers that can respond to the spoken word, integrated network of systems to transmit data from one system to another, the possible elimination of the paycheck, are just a few of the new innovations being developed. The appearance of the "microcomputer," a complete circuit on a single chip may affect all aspects of our society. Education, consumer products, programming are just a few areas that will undergo change as a result of the impact of the "microcomputer." Job characters will change with the emphasis being placed on "systems" to include psychological and sociological aspects of using the computer. Computer programs of the future will probably be quite different from those in use today.

IDENTIFICATION QUESTIONS

Match the following terms with the statements that follow.

A. Abacus
B. Babbage
C. Eniac
D. First Generation Computers
E. Fourth Generation Computers
F. Hollerith
G. Jacquard
H. Leibnitz
I. Mark I
J. Napier's 'Bones'
K. Pascal
L. Powers
M. Second Generation Computers
N. Third Generation Computers
O. Univac
P. Virtual Storage

1. First commerical computer.
2. Inventor of first calculating machine.
3. World's first automatic computer.
4. 80 column card.
5. Earliest known calculating device.
6. Bulky in size, requiring large amounts of air conditioning and having a high maintenance rate.
7. Punched card principle used in automatic loom.
8. First electronic computer to use storage program.
9. IBM System/370.
10. 90 column card.
11. Allows computer to directly access outside storage devices.
12. Set of rods for the purpose of facilitating multiplication and division operations.
13. Replaced vacuum tubes with transistors.
14. Invented "stepped wheel" calculator.
15. Advanced miniaturization and refined computer components.
16. Invented large scale calculators.

QUESTIONS FOR REVIEW

1. What were the early data processing devices used for?
2. Who originated the ABACUS and what important contributions did it make to the data processing field?
3. What were the significant developments in the data processing field during the seventeenth century?
4. What important contributions did Babbage make in the field of data processing?
5. Describe the main contributions of Hollerith and Powers to the field of punched card data processing.

6. In the era of modern computers, the following machines made important contributions. What were they? Mark I, ENIAC, UNIVAC.
7. What characterized the "First Generation" computers?
8. What characterized the "Second Generation" computers and how did they differ from the first and third generation computers?
9. What was the significance of the "Fourth Generation" computers?
10. What is "Virtual Storage"? What is its significance?
11. What does the future hold for data processing?

PART II / PUNCHED-CARD DATA PROCESSING

CHAPTER 3

Data Recording Media and Equipment

The punched card has played a major role in the development of rapid data processing. Besides serving as the main input media, punched cards are also used as original documents such as checks, time cards, invoices and many other forms.

Punched-card data processing is the procedure of recording, manipulating and reporting information through the use of holes punched in a card (Fig. 3.1). These holes activate machines to perform certain operations automatically. At the present time, the punched card is the principle source of input and output to both punched card and computer systems.

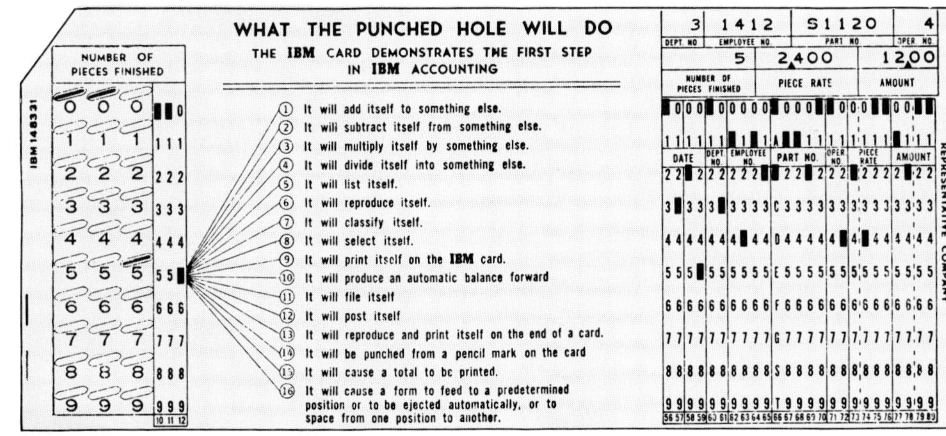

Figure 3–1. What the Punched Hole Will Do.

The computer has greatly increased the uses of the punched card. Familiarity with punched cards is essential to programmers, analysts, clerks, accountants, business people and many other persons who come in contact with these cards. They are a versatile and important tool in data processing. A common use is the preparation of computer programs, in which the instructions for the computer are punched into predefined fields of a card (Fig. 3.2).

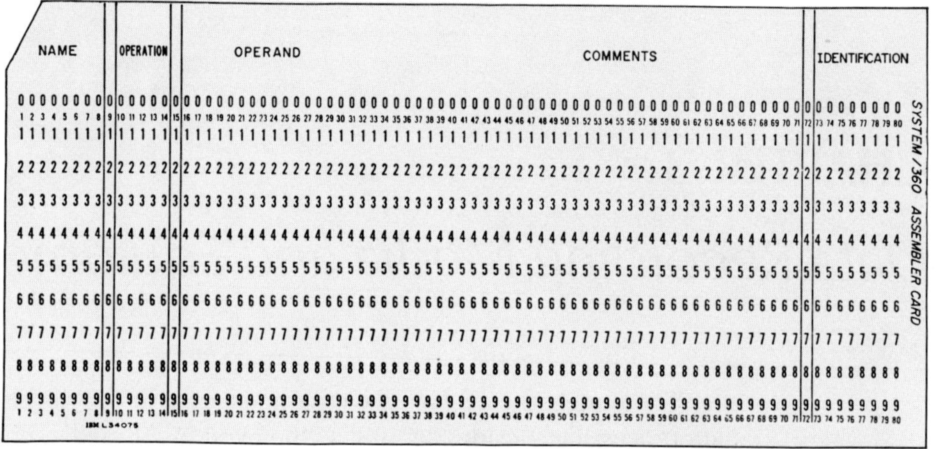

Figure 3–2. Program Card.

There are a variety of uses for punched-card data processing. Primarily, it provides an input media that enters information into a machine. In addition, the card provides an output media for the equipment. The machine language of the card establishes the communication between men and equipment.

Secondly, the machine language capability permits communication between the specialized machines.

Thirdly, the punched card provides the facility for storing information in the form of machine processable files so that this information can be available for use when needed.

UNIT RECORD PRINCIPLE

The principle of punched cards implies that the information concerning a single transaction is usually recorded in one card. This is frequently referred to as the "unit record" principle of data processing. This unit record principle of punched-card data processing permits each card to be processed with other cards or other input media on a single record basis (Fig. 3.3). Because of the unit record principle, each card can be processed by each of the specialized punched-card machines (Fig. 3.4). However, cards must be physically taken from one machine to another for processing.

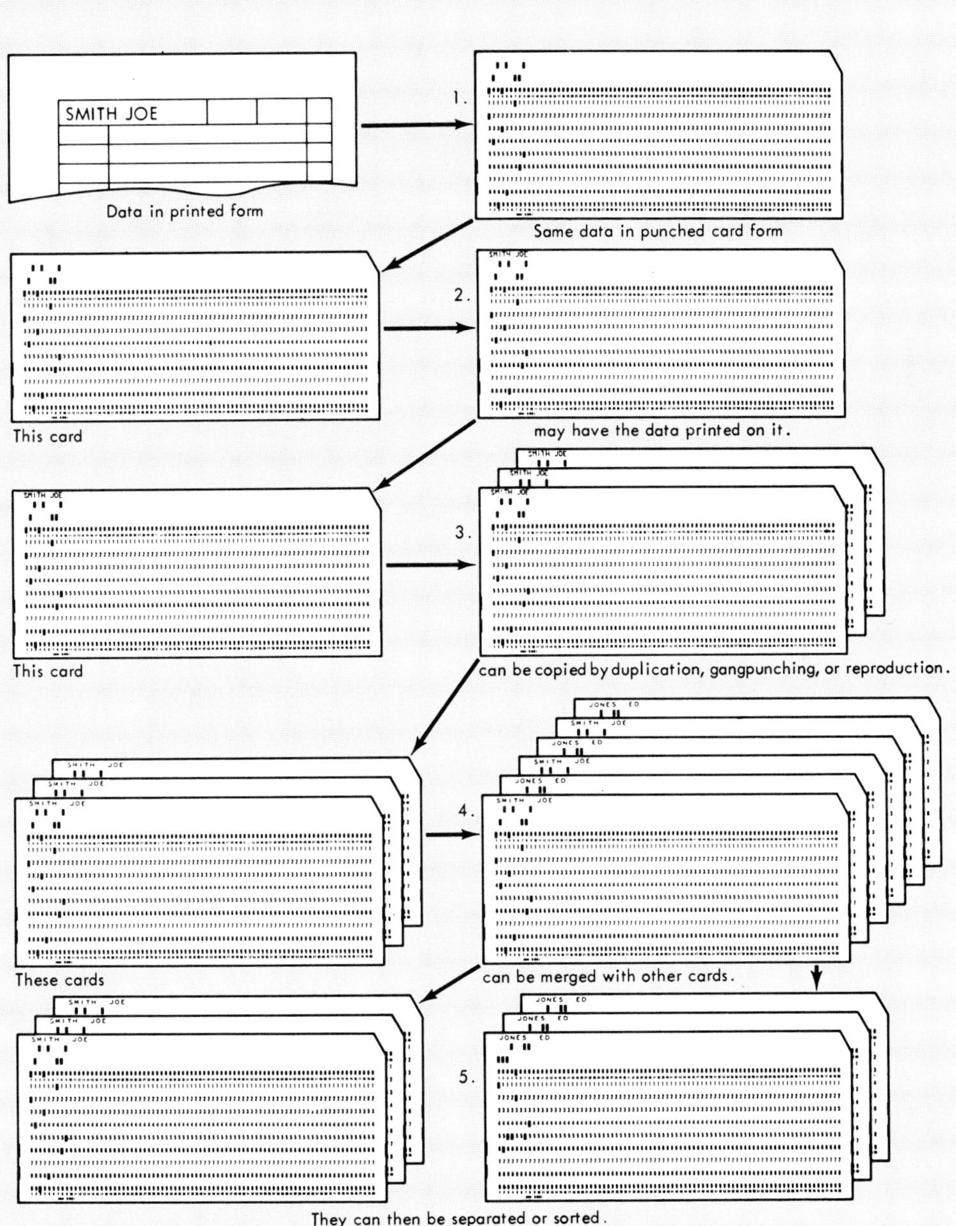

Figure 3–3. Basic Punched-Card Operations.

An operator can select data from printed records and, using a keyboard, can *record* it in cards, in the form of punched holes.

By pressing one key, the operator can cause data that has been recorded in one card to be *duplicated* (punched in the *same* places) in one or more cards that follow it.

If the 26 Printing Card Punch is used, data that is being punched in a card can also be *printed* along the top edge of that card.

24 Card Punch or 26 Printing Card Punch.

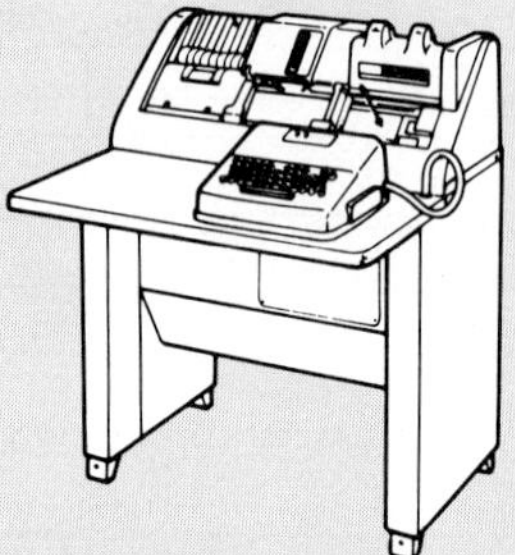

An operator reads (from printed records) the data that has been recorded in the cards and, using a keyboard, *checks the holes* punched in those cards to ensure that the data has been recorded correctly.

56 Card Verifier.

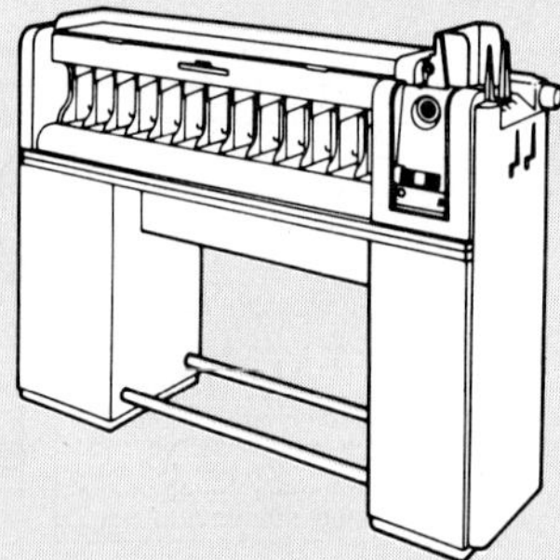

The cards can be sorted (arranged in numerical or alphabetic order) for further machine operations or for filing.

Two files of cards can be *merged* (sorted together) to form one file, in numerical or alphabetic order.

Particular cards can be automatically *separated* from others in a file without disturbing the order of the rest of the cards.

82 or 83 Sorter.

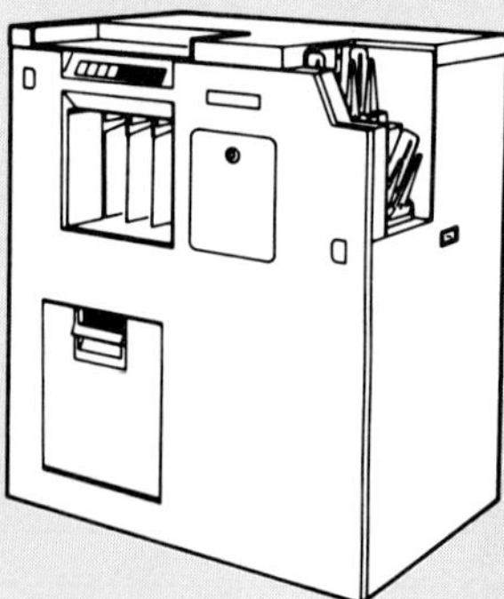

Different types of cards, from two or more files, can be *collated* (combined so that each type of card is followed by another type, in a particular order).

Cards of the same type, arranged in numerical order in separate files, can be *merged* (combined to form one file, still in numerical order).

The Collator can automatically *check the sequence* of the cards, to ensure that they are arranged in numerical order. Particular cards can be separated from others in a file, without changing the order of the rest of the cards.

85 Collator.

Figure 3–4. The Processing of Cards Through Unit Record Equipment.

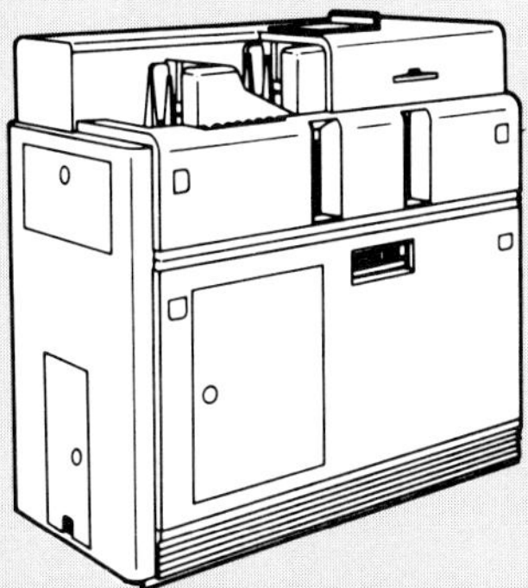

Data recorded in each card, as punched holes, can be *reproduced* (punched in another card) in order to produce a new file of punched cards.

Data that has been recorded (punched) in one card can be *gangpunched* (copied), in the same *or different* columns, in one or more of the cards that follows.

Data recorded *on* each card, by marking in pencil, can be read by the machine (*mark sensing*) and recorded (punched) in that card.

If the 519 is used, some data punched in each card can be *end-printed* (printed across the end of the card). (The drawing shows the 514 Reproducing Punch.)

514 Reproducing Punch or 519 Document-Originating Machine.

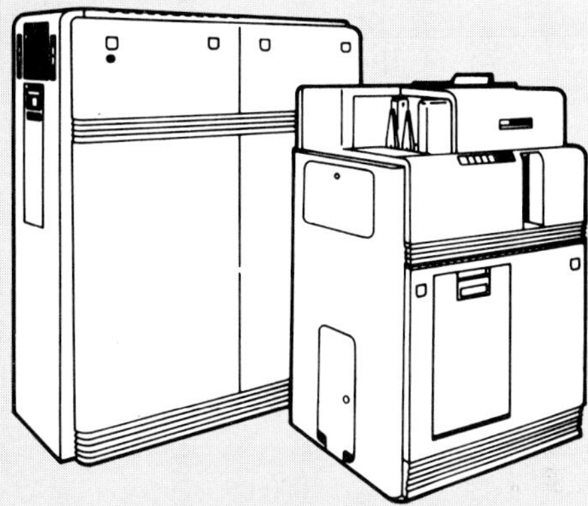

The 521 can read data recorded in the form of punched holes; the 604 can perform *calculations* (adding, subtracting, multiplying, and dividing) with the data, and the 521 can then record (punch) the result in the same card.

Calculations can be performed on data from one or more cards, and results can be recorded (punched) in a following card.

604 Electronic Calculating Punch and 521 Card Read Punch.

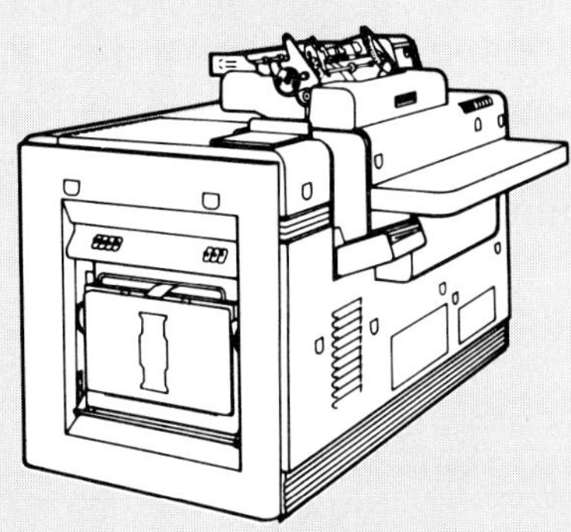

Data recorded in each card, as punched holes, can be listed (printed in a single line) on a report.

Simple calculations (adding and subtracting) can be performed with data recorded in the cards, and the results can be printed on a report.

(The drawing shows the 402 Accounting Machine.)

402 or 407 Accounting Machine.

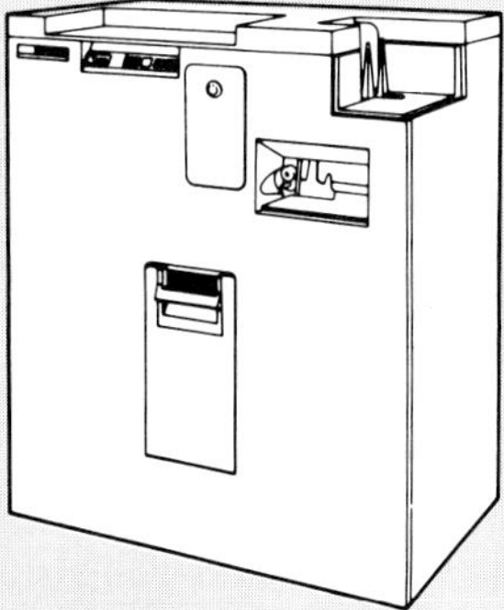

Data recorded in each card, in the form of punched holes, can be *printed* on that card, on either of two lines.

If the 557 Interpreter is used for this operation, the data can be printed on any one of 25 lines.

In another 557 operation, data punched in *one* card can be printed on one or more cards that follow it.

(The drawing shows the 548 Interpreter.)

548 or 557 Interpreter.

Figure 3–4. (Continued).

TYPES OF PUNCHED CARDS

There are two types of cards in use today. The "Hollerith" card is divided into eighty vertical columns with twelve possible punching positions in each column. There are rectangular holes in the cards to represent characters. The "Hollerith" card is used on all IBM equipment (Fig. 3.5).

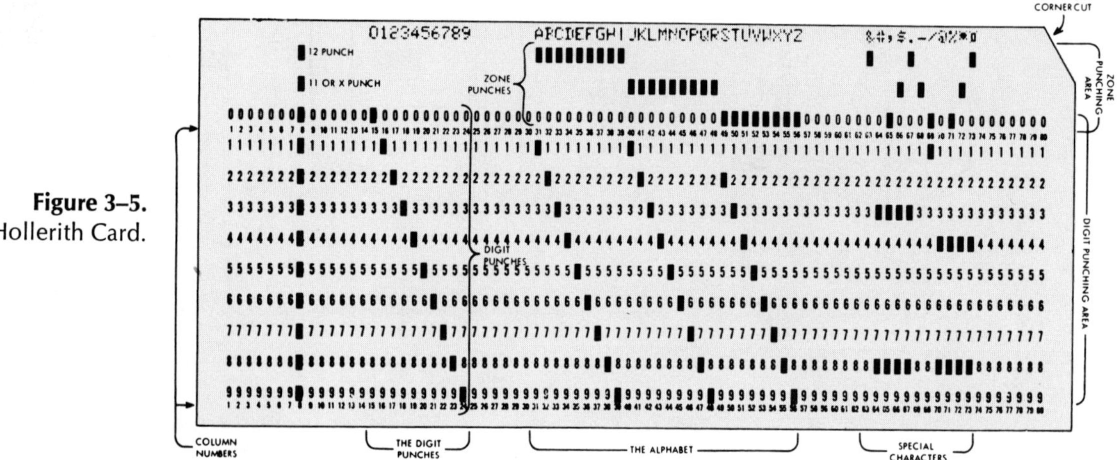

Figure 3–5. Hollerith Card.

The "Powers" card was divided into ninety columns with an upper and lower portion of 45 vertical columns each. Round holes in the card were used to represent characters. This card was manufactured by the UNIVAC Division of the Sperry Rand Corp. In 1966, the Sperry Rand Corp. announced that it was discontinuing its 90-column and related card processing equipment and was adopting the standard 80-column card (Fig. 3.6).

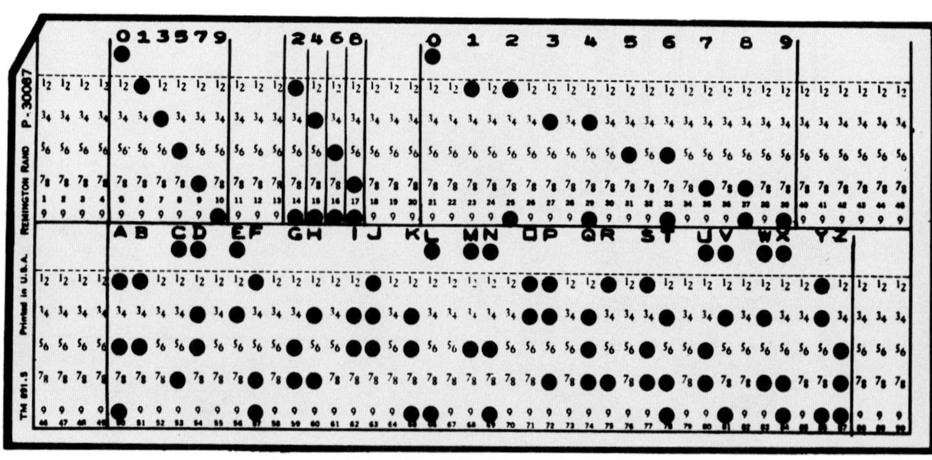

Figure 3–6. Powers 90-Column Card.

The IBM Corporation has announced a 96-column punched card that was designed for use in their System/3 series. The lower section of the card is the punch area, while the upper section of the card is the print area.

The lower section, or punch area is divided into three equal, horizontal sections, called tiers. Each tier contains six vertical groups of six punch positions. There are thirty-two columns of punching positions in each tier (Figs. 3.7, 3.8).

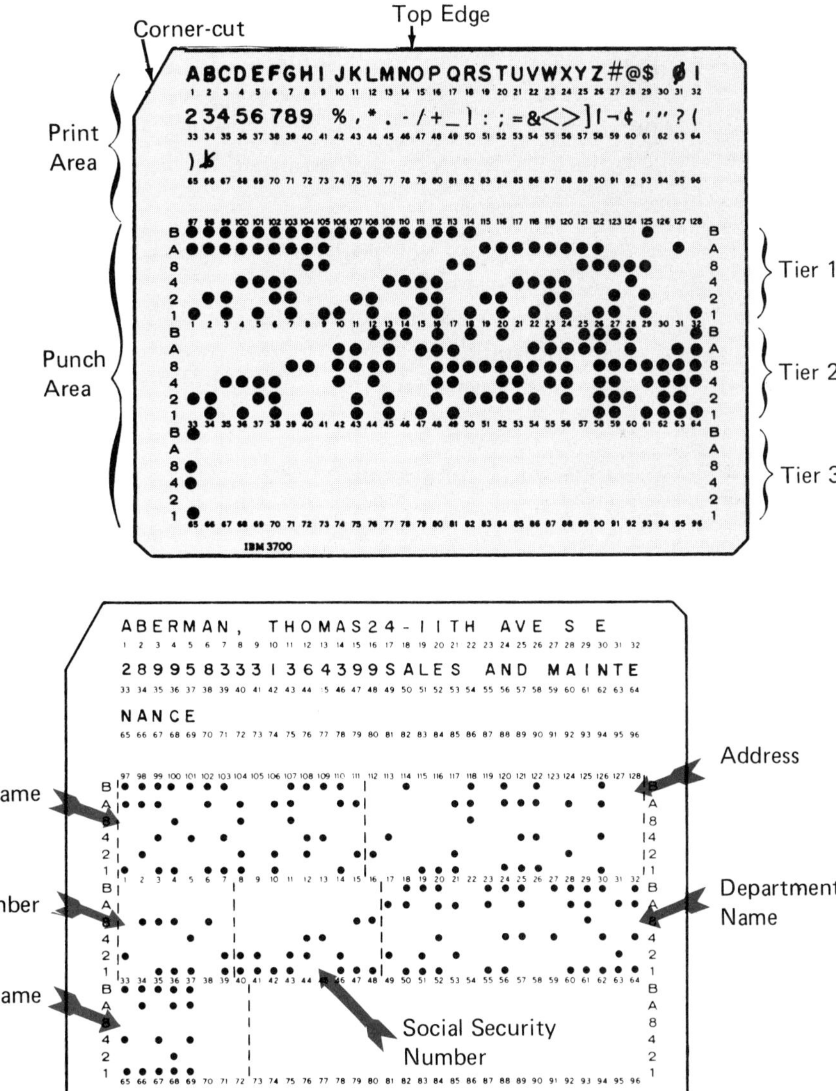

Figure 3–7. System/3 Column Card.

Figure 3–8. System/3 Column Card Fields.

CARD DATA REPRESENTATION

As noted above, the "Hollerith" card is divided into eighty vertical columns with twelve possible punching positions in each column. The top edge of the card is known as the "twelve" edge while the bottom of the card is known as the "nine" edge. Each machine has a designation in the feed mechanism specifying how the card is to enter the machine. For example, "nine edge face down" means the printed side of the card down and the nine edge facing the feeding mechanism of the machine.

The card is divided into two major sections. The upper three rows of the card are known as the "zone" punches and contain holes in the 12, 11, and 0 positions of the card. The numerical section of the card contains the digits 0 through 9. Numeric information is represented by a single punch 0–9. (The 0 punch may be either zone or numeric depending upon its usage.) The zone and numeric punches are combined in the following manner to represent alphabetic characters.

1. A through I are represented by a 12 punch plus the numeric punches 1 through 9.
2. J through R are represented by an 11 punch plus the numeric punches 1 through 9.
3. S through Z are represented by a 0 punch plus the numeric punches 2 through 9.

Special characters may have 1, 2, or 3 punches in a single column.

CARD FIELDS

Data is usually recorded in a card in a group of consecutive columns called fields. A *field* is composed of a group of related characters that are treated as one unit of information. A field may consist of one to eighty characters depending upon the particular need of information to be recorded in it (Fig. 3.9). The left column of a field is known as the *high order* position while the right-hand column is known as *low order* position of a field.

RECORDS

A *record* consists of a field or a series of fields normally grouped together for input and output operations. A card reader reads an entire card, while a card punch would punch an entire card. A record can be reused and become a permanent record; therefore it should contain all the necessary information about a single transaction.

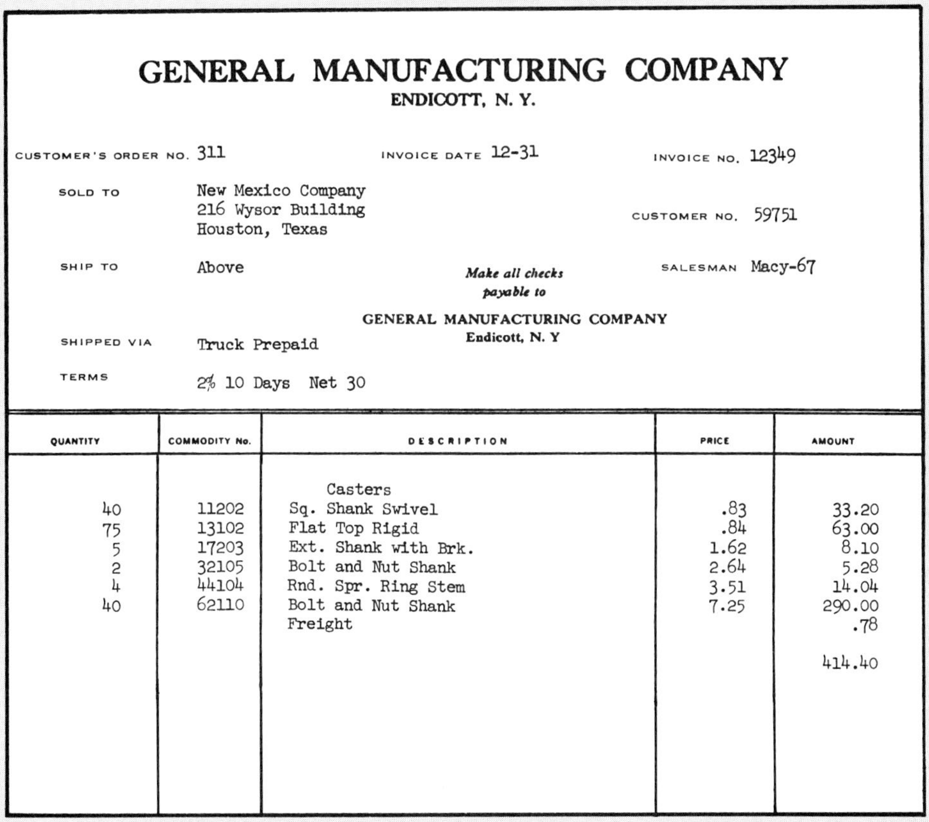

GENERAL MANUFACTURING COMPANY
ENDICOTT, N. Y.

CUSTOMER'S ORDER NO. 311 INVOICE DATE 12-31 INVOICE NO. 12349

SOLD TO New Mexico Company
216 Wysor Building
Houston, Texas

CUSTOMER NO. 59751

SHIP TO Above

Make all checks payable to
GENERAL MANUFACTURING COMPANY
Endicott, N. Y

SALESMAN Macy-67

SHIPPED VIA Truck Prepaid

TERMS 2% 10 Days Net 30

QUANTITY	COMMODITY No.	DESCRIPTION	PRICE	AMOUNT
		Casters		
40	11202	Sq. Shank Swivel	.83	33.20
75	13102	Flat Top Rigid	.84	63.00
5	17203	Ext. Shank with Brk.	1.62	8.10
2	32105	Bolt and Nut Shank	2.64	5.28
4	44104	Rnd. Spr. Ring Stem	3.51	14.04
40	62110	Bolt and Nut Shank	7.25	290.00
		Freight		.78
				414.40

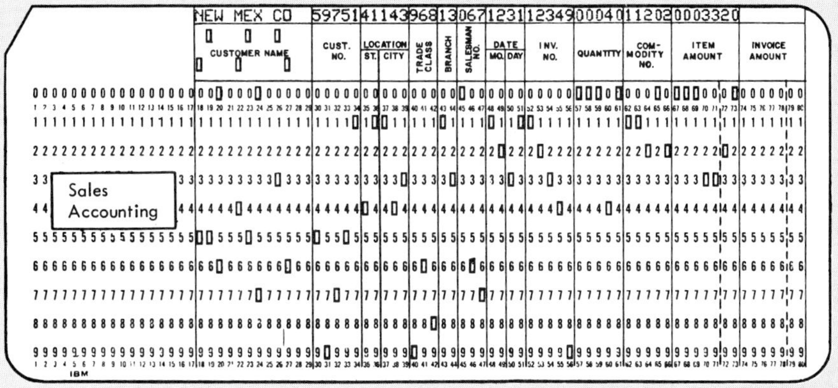

NEW MEX CO 59751411439681306712311234900040112020003320

CUSTOMER NAME | CUST. NO. | LOCATION ST. CITY | TRADE CLASS | BRANCH | SALESMAN NO. | DATE MO. DAY | INV. NO. | QUANTITY | COMMODITY NO. | ITEM AMOUNT | INVOICE AMOUNT

Sales Accounting

IBM

Figure 3–9. Card Fields.

CORNER CUTS

Corner cuts, upper left or upper right, are used to identify a card type and to insure that all cards are facing the same direction. Corner cuts are also used to separate groups of cards; master from detail cards.

COLORS

Cards may be in various colors and with different colored stripes across the front of the card. These colors and stripes are further identification for particular card groups. For example, a yellow card may represent an inventory balance card while the same card format in green may signal a price card.

CARD PUNCH

The initial operation in punched-card data processing is the transcribing of written records into punched cards. This is one of the most expensive operations in data processing as it involves the ratio of one operator to one machine. For many years numerous efforts have been made to reduce the cost of card punching through various methods of converting source documents into a machine language processable format. Porta punches, mark sensing cards, magnetic ink recorders, optical readers and many other devices have been used with a certain degree of success. In spite of all these innovations, the amount of card punching has increased and is continuing to increase, in the face of a critical shortage of trained card-punch operators (Fig. 3.10).

Figure 3–10. IBM 29 Card Punch Machine.

CARD-PUNCH MACHINES—FUNCTIONS AND KEYBOARDS TYPES

The primary function of a card-punch machine is to convert a source document into a punched card. The card punch has numerous other uses, among which are:

1. Replacing cards that have been damaged in processing.
2. Correcting cards that have incorrect punches.
3. Preparing computer program cards.
4. Preparing test cards for the various machines.

There are two types of keyboards available on IBM card-punch machines; the numeric keyboard and the alphanumeric keyboard which combines the numeric and alphabetic punching (Fig. 3.11). The numeric keyboard resembles a ten-key adding machine with the exception that the 1, 2, and 3 keys of the card punch are located in the 7, 8, and 9 positions of the adding machine. The zero key also appears at a different location. These differences present some problems to adding machine-trained operators when they have to use the card punch (Fig. 3.12).

IBM 29 Numeric and Combination Keyboards.

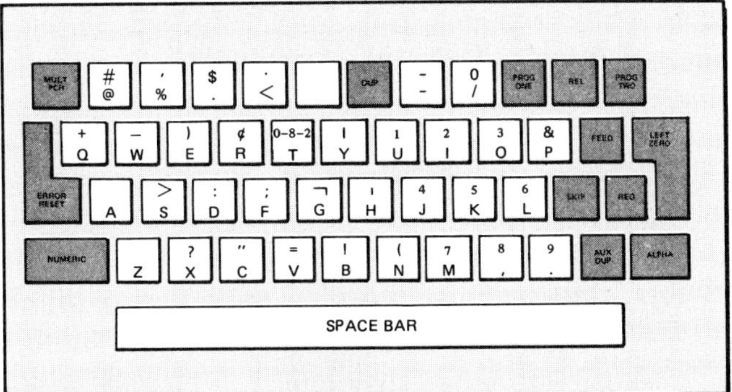

Figure 3–11.

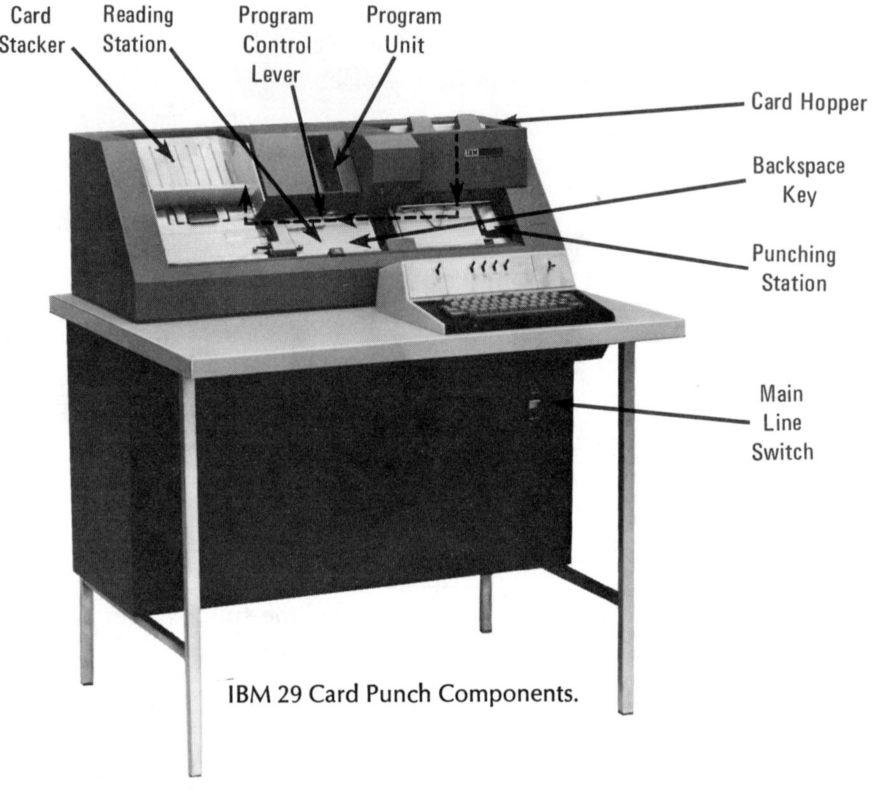

IBM 29 Card Punch Components.

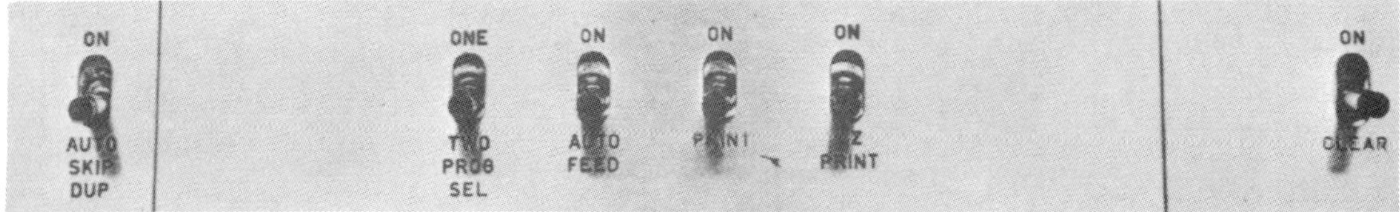

IBM 29 Keyboard Switch Panel.

Figure 3–12.

The alphanumeric keyboard has the same key positions as a standard typewriter with the exception of the numerals and special characters which appear in a different location. The numerals in an alphanumeric keyboard are grouped in a shaded area location of the keyboard, sharing this area with letters. By depressing the numerical shift key located on the lower left of the keyboard, the numerals will be punched into the card for these locations. In the normal mode, an alphabetic character would be punched from this shaded area of letters and numerals.

The most commonly used card-punch machine is the IBM model 29.

IBM MODEL 29 CARD PUNCH

Some of the important features of the model 29 card-punch machine are:

1. A simple means of setting up quickly for automatic control of duplicating operations, automatic insertion of left zeroes, or skipping. Each setup or *program* is made by punching a card and mounting it on a program drum which is inserted in the machine.
2. The card punch can duplicate common information from any preceding card into the following card. This method of duplication avoids much card handling and consequently increases production. The duplicating feature facilitates error correction as the operator need not punch the entire card but can duplicate the card until the error is reached and repunch only the incorrect portion.
3. The keyboard can be moved anywhere on the reading board for the greatest convenience and comfort of the operator.

COMPONENTS OF THE CARD PUNCH

CARD HOPPER

The card hopper feeds cards automatically to the punching station. Approximately 500 cards can be held and fed for continuous punching operations.

PUNCHING STATION

To start an operation, normally two cards are fed into the punch station from the card hopper. While the first card is being punched, the second card remains stationary. When column 80 of the first card passes the punching station, the second card is registered and the next card in the hopper is fed into the punch station. This method of feeding minimizes the time required for feeding and ejecting cards.

READING STATION

As the punched card passes through the read station, the next card is being punched. The two cards move synchronously, column by column, and the information to be duplicated is transferred from one card to the other when required.

CARD STACKER

The card stacker is located on the upper left side of the machine. As the card passes the read station, it feeds automatically into the stacker. The cards are stacked in the original sequence of punching. The capacity of the stacker is the same as that of the hopper, 500 cards.

MAIN-LINE SWITCH

The main-line switch is a toggle switch located at the rear of the stacker. The purpose of the switch is to turn the machine on or off. When the stacker is full, this switch will automatically turn the machine off.

BACKSPACE KEY

The backspace key is located beneath the card bed between the reading and punching stations. As long as the key is held down, the cards at the reading and punching stations will continue to backspace until column one is reached. This key may also be used to unlock the keyboard after it has been locked due to an improper operation.

PROGRAM UNIT

The program unit was designed to allow for fully automatic control of skipping, duplicating, and shifting from numeric to alphabetic and from alphabetic to numeric mode (Fig. 3.13).

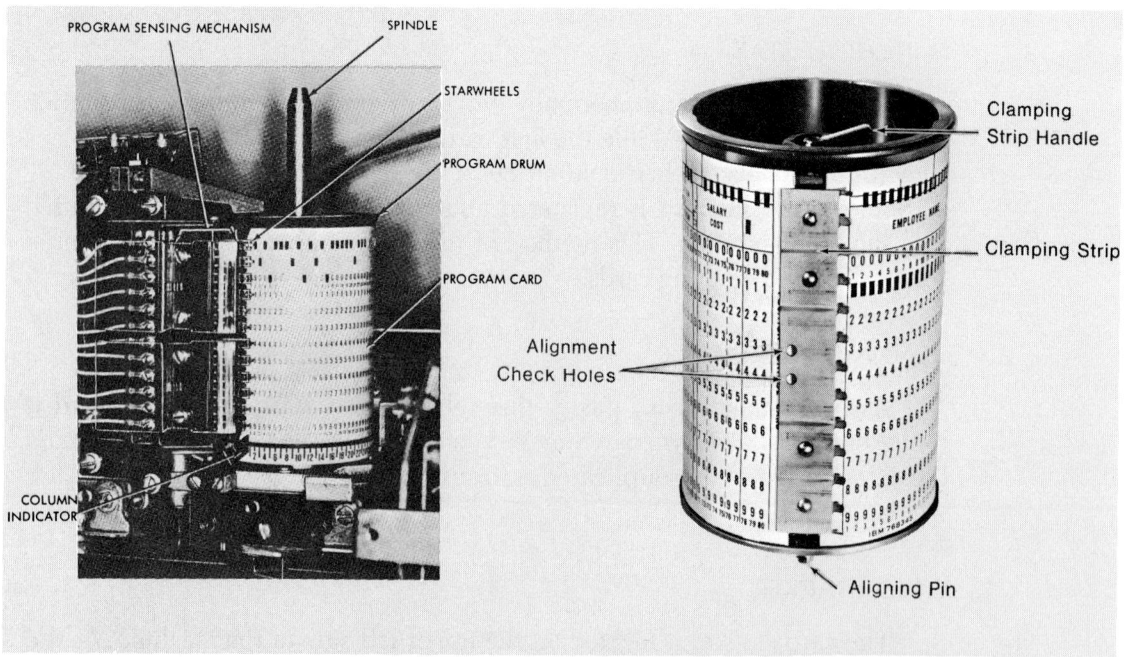

Figure 3–13. Program Unit.

Figure 3–14. Program Drum.

PROGRAM DRUM

Operations designated by a specific code are recorded in a program card. The operator fastens the program card around the drum (Fig. 3.14) and inserts it into the machine where it is read by the sensing mechanism (Fig. 3.15).

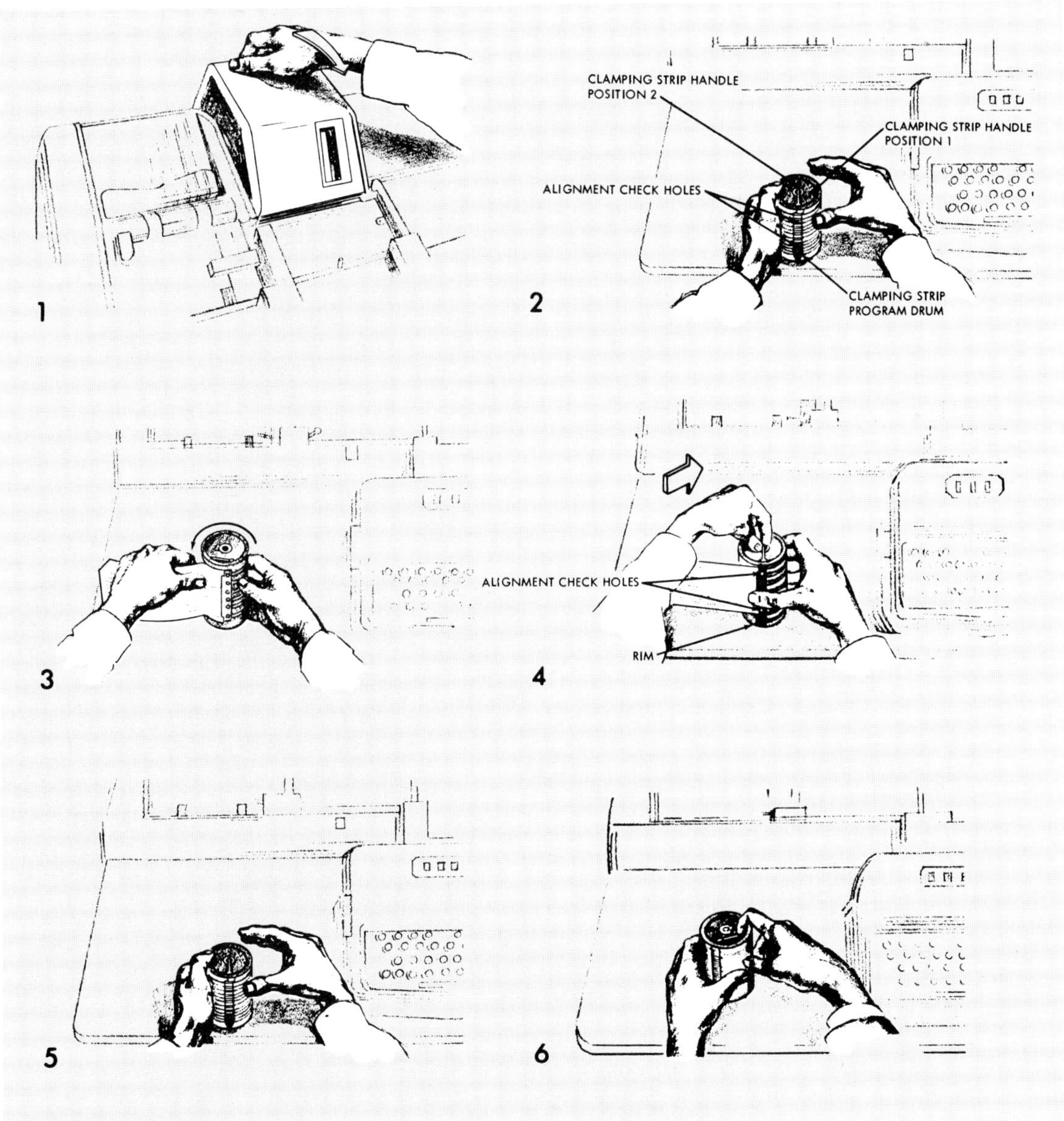

Figure 3–15. Inserting Drum Card.

PROGRAM CONTROL LEVER

The program control lever, located below the program unit (Fig. 3.16), controls the operations of the program card. To disengage the drum, the lever is turned *off*. When the lever is turned *on*, the programming sensing mechanism rests on the drum card activating the operating codes of the program card.

COLUMN INDICATOR

The column indicator is located beneath the program drumholder and indicates the next column to be punched.

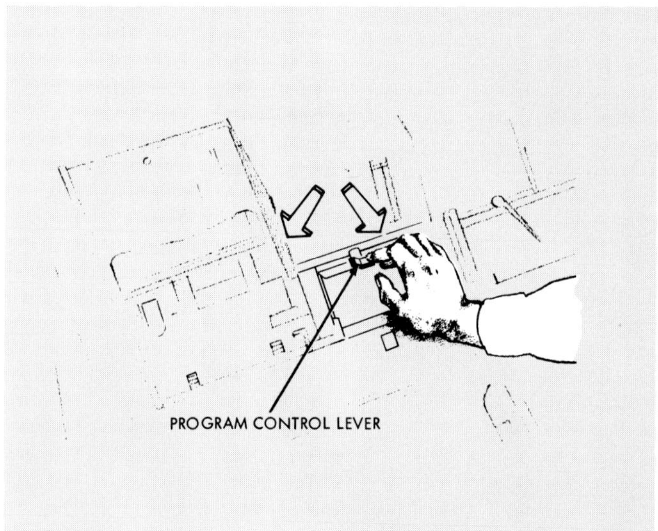

Figure 3–16. Program Control Lever.

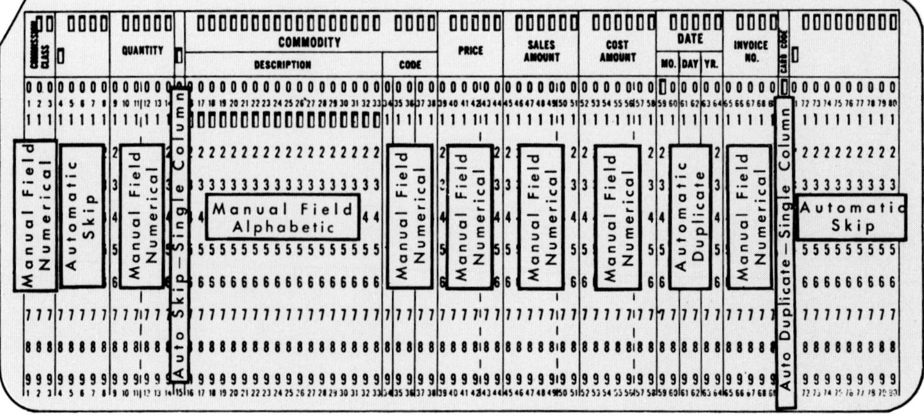

Figure 3–17. Program Card.

PROGRAM CONTROL CARD PUNCHING

A basic part of the program control unit is the program card (Fig. 3.17). The program card controls the automatic skipping, duplicating, and shifting between various modes of operation according to the format of the card to be punched.

PROGRAM CARD CODES

Code	Function to be performed
blank	Initiates beginning of a field to be punched manually with numeric information.
0	Initiates automatic duplication.
1	Initiates beginning of a field to be punched manually with alphabetic information.
11	Initiates automatic skipping.
12	Defines the length of a numeric field.
A	Defines the length of an alphabetic field.

MANUAL PUNCHING

Often it is desirable to insert a card manually, one at a time (Fig. 3.18), to replace a damaged card or to correct a card that has incorrect punches. The following steps should be taken:

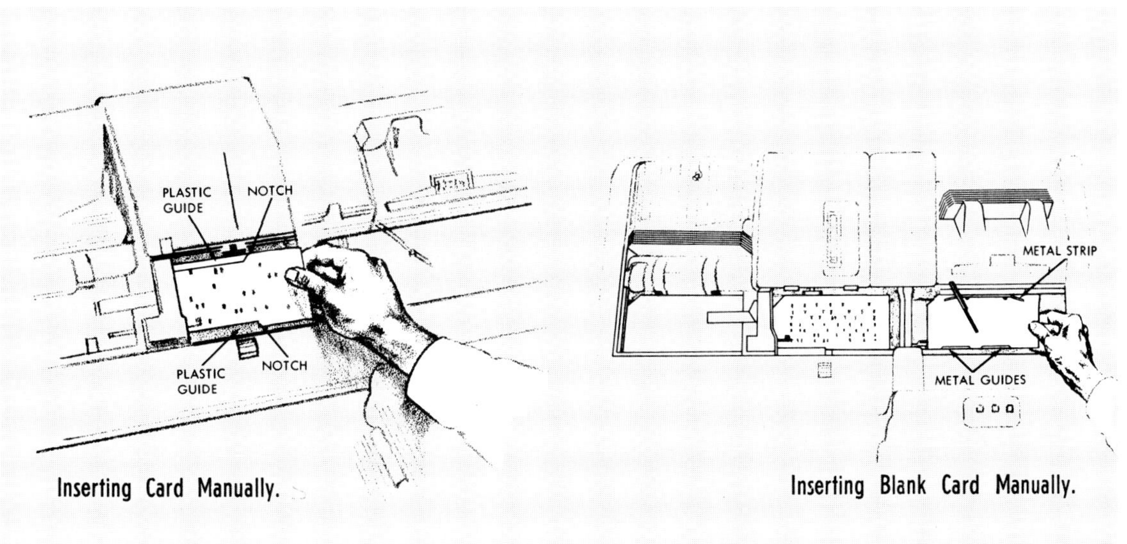

Figure 3–18. Manual Punching.

1. Insert the card to be replaced or corrected in the plastic guides at the read station.
2. Insert a blank card at the punch station.
3. Press the register key. This will align both cards at column one.
4. Depress the duplicating key until the entire card is duplicated.

Where a card is to be corrected, hold the duplicating key down until the desired column is reached, release the key and punch the corrected information, and depress the duplicating key to continue duplication for the remainder of the card.

NOTE

When correcting or replacing cards it is important that the new card and the old card be compared through a sight checking process. Since the reliability of the output depends upon the accuracy of the punched card, the original card after being thoroughly checked should be kept in a "spoiled card" file until the final report is prepared and balanced. Many times in data processing, errors in output are traced to the correction of punched cards that occurred during the processing cycle.

VERIFYING PUNCHED CARDS

As stressed earlier, the reliability of the output depends upon the accuracy of the input data. All possible checks should be taken to assure this. One of the methods of assuring accuracy is the verifier punch.

The verifier closely resembles the card punches in appearance. The differences between the two machines in appearance are that in place of the backspace key on the card-punch machines, the verifier machine has a red light; and instead of punch dies, the verifier has a sensing mechanism consisting of twelve pins.

If an error is signalled, the red light turns on and the machine stops. The verifier operator has two more attempts to check the agreement of the punches before the card is notched above the incorrect column (Fig. 3.19). If the card is correct and properly verified, the card is notched on the right end of the card (Fig. 3.20).

IBM MODEL 129 AND UNIVAC MODEL 1710 CARD PUNCHES

Both of these card punches (Figs. 3.21, 3.22, 3.23) are programmed, data-storage, key-entry, card punching and verifying machines used to punch 80-column cards for data processing operations. Similar in operation to the

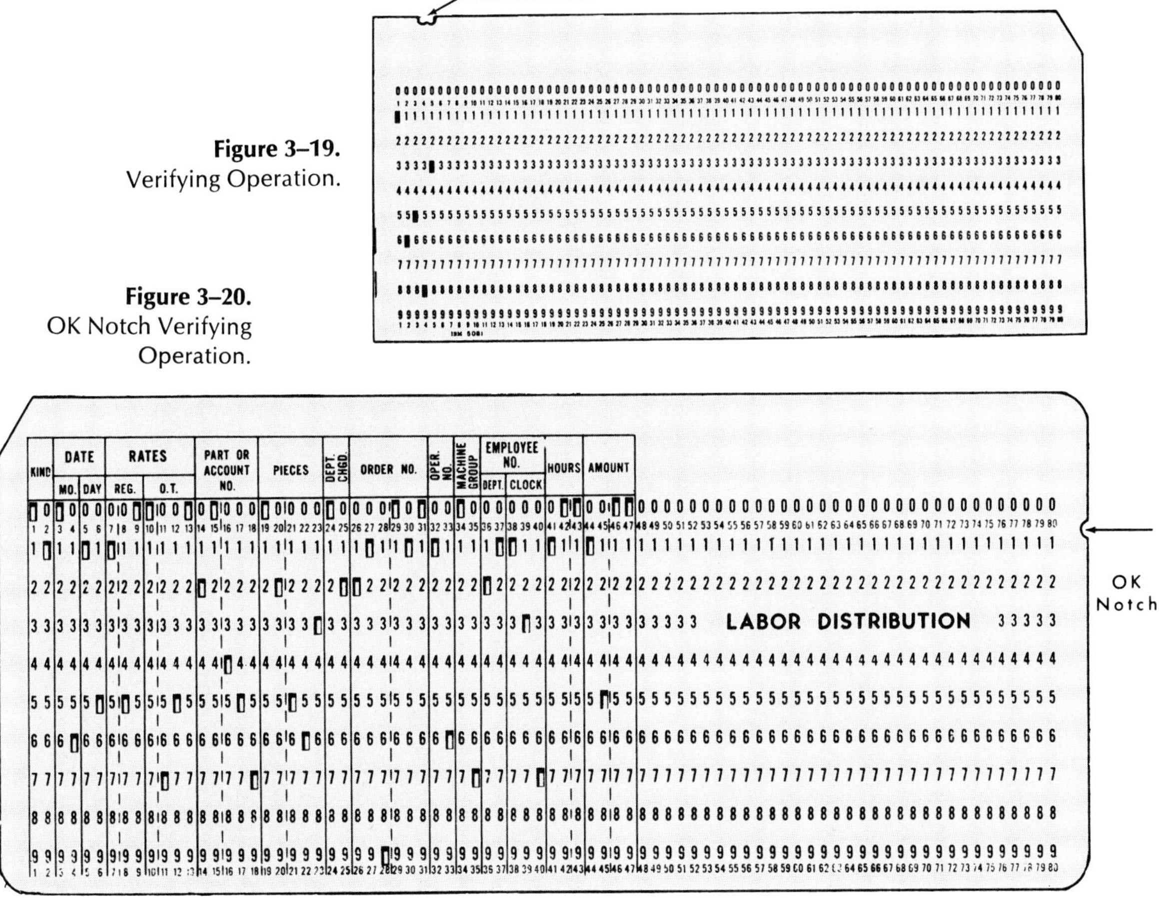

Figure 3–19. Verifying Operation.

Figure 3–20. OK Notch Verifying Operation.

model 29 card punch, these machines offer the following special advantages:

1. *Simultaneous operations*—keyed input data simultaneous with automatic functions. All keypunching is initiated in the normal manner. However, instead of each keystroke causing the card to be punched, data is entered into core storage. When all information for the card is in storage, the punching operation takes place automatically, as information for the next card is being entered.

2. *Instant correction*—sensed keypunching errors corrected before punching.

3. *Verification*—errors detected during verification corrected instantly and corrected card is punched. Error card is segregated.

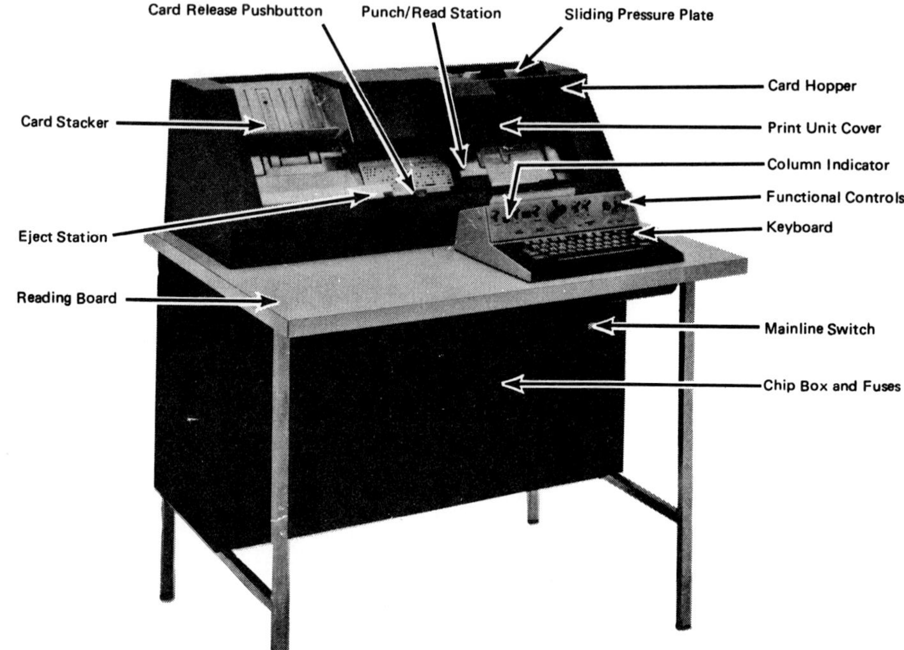
Card Release Pushbutton
Punch/Read Station
Sliding Pressure Plate
Card Hopper
Card Stacker
Print Unit Cover
Column Indicator
Functional Controls
Eject Station
Keyboard
Reading Board
Mainline Switch
Chip Box and Fuses

Figure 3–21. IBM 129 Card Data Recorder.

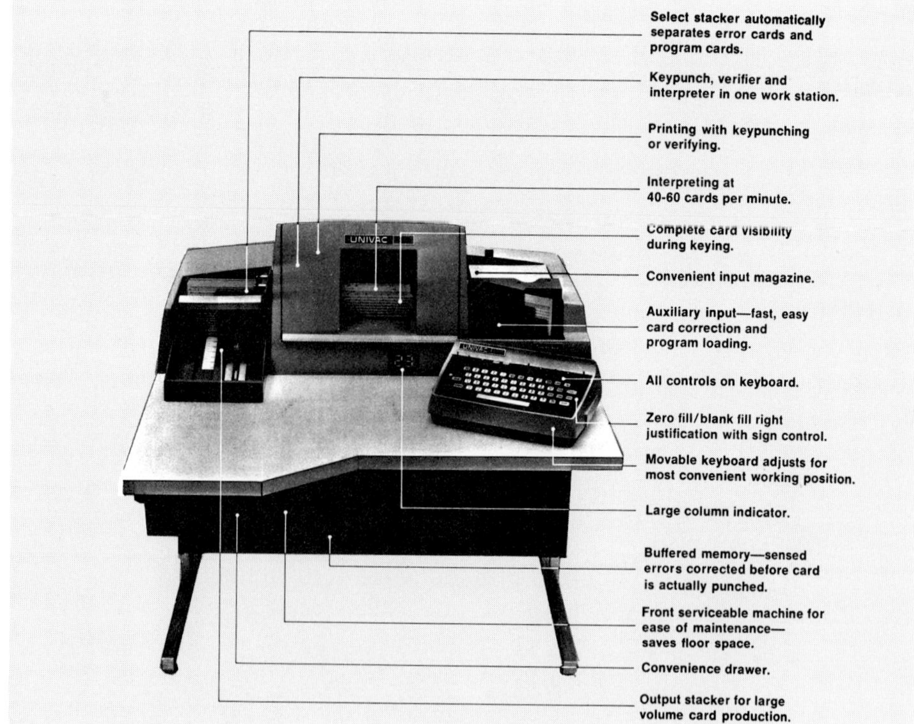
Select stacker automatically separates error cards and program cards.
Keypunch, verifier and interpreter in one work station.
Printing with keypunching or verifying.
Interpreting at 40-60 cards per minute.
Complete card visibility during keying.
Convenient input magazine.
Auxiliary input—fast, easy card correction and program loading.
All controls on keyboard.
Zero fill/blank fill right justification with sign control.
Movable keyboard adjusts for most convenient working position.
Large column indicator.
Buffered memory—sensed errors corrected before card is actually punched.
Front serviceable machine for ease of maintenance—saves floor space.
Convenience drawer.
Output stacker for large volume card production.
UNIVAC

Figure 3–22. UNIVAC 1710 Verifying Interpreting Punch.

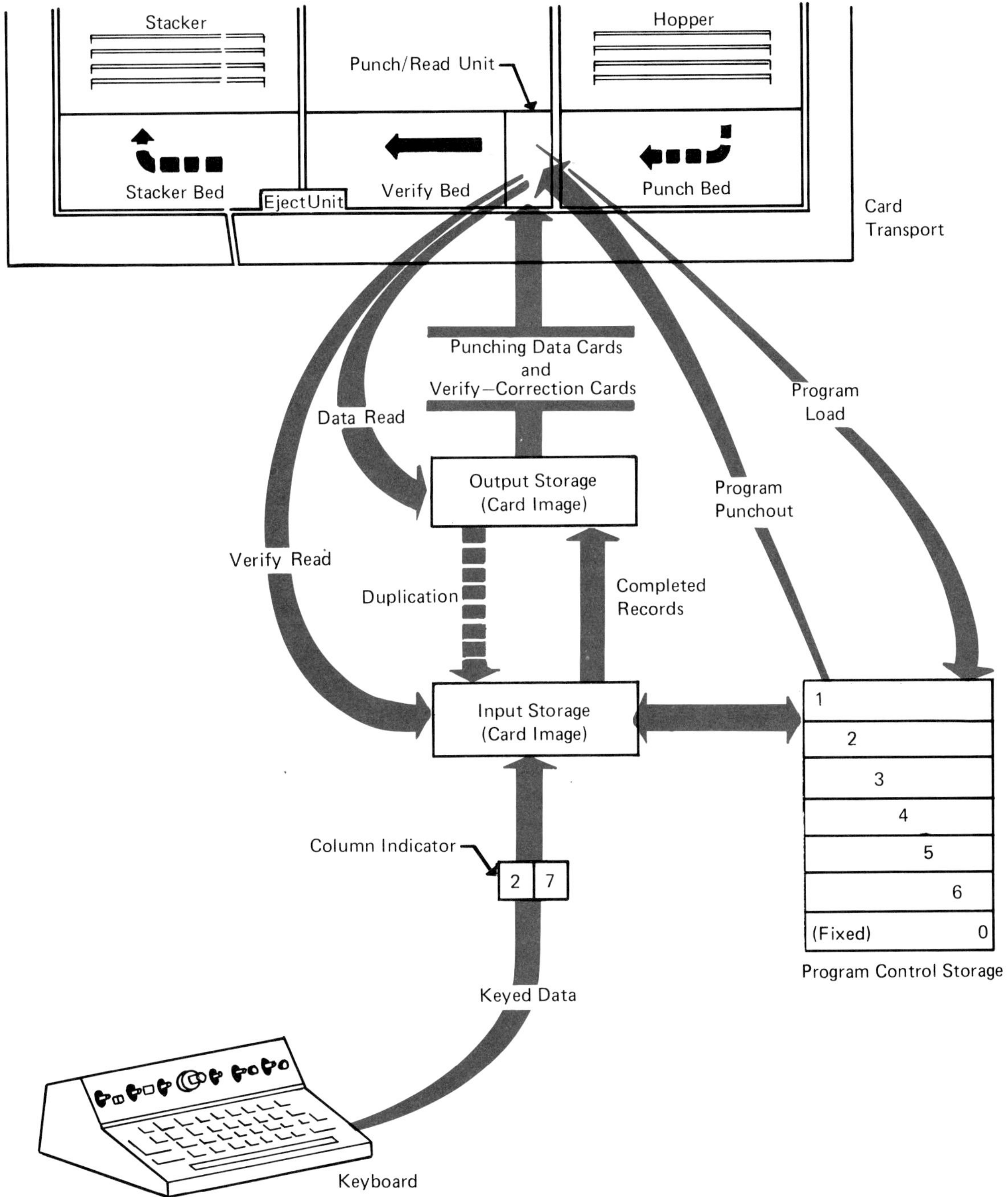

Figure 3–23. IBM 129 Storage and Data Flow.

4. *Instant programming*—programs entered automatically by simply setting switch. IBM Model 129 can store up to nine programs. UNIVAC Model 1710 permits storage for only two programs.

REPRODUCING MACHINES (Figure 3–24)

Optimum efficiency in data processing is the recording of data once, as close to the beginning of the process as possible, and then using this recorded information repeatedly without duplication of the original effort. All or portions of the information thus recorded which might be needed at various

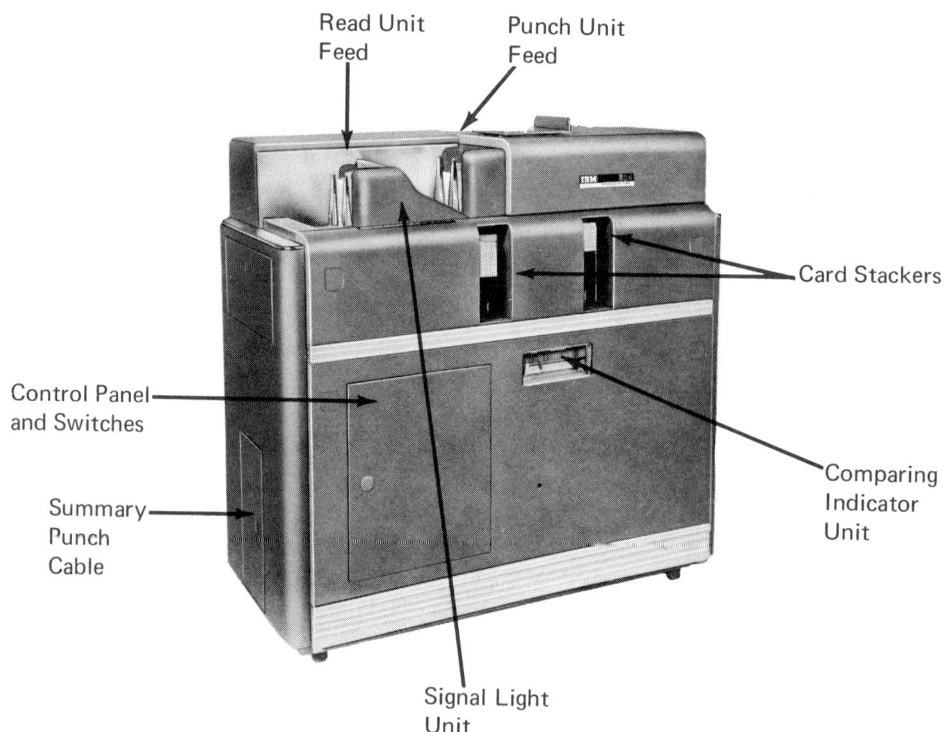

Figure 3–24.
Reproducing Punch.

stages of a program could be reused without requiring duplication of the recording. In some instances, however, partial changes must be made to the original record in order to keep it up to date. Common information such as dates, batch numbers, etc., must be punched in a file of cards.

When the records are maintained in punched card format, the repetitious operations can be performed automatically. Automatic punches were designed to perform these tedious tasks of transferring information from one card to another at relatively high rates of speed with a high degree of duplication accuracy.

AUTOMATIC PUNCH OPERATIONS

The principal operations performed by the automatic punches are reproducing, gangpunching, comparing, summary punching, mark sensing and end printing (available only on the IBM model 519 machine). All of these operations can be performed simultaneously as the card is being processed.

Reproducing—the operation whereby information is transferred from one card to another either in the same field or in different fields (Fig. 3.25).

Gangpunching—the punching of common information from a master card into detail cards, usually in the same field (Fig. 3.26).

Comparing—the process by which the source and the duplicated card can be checked for agreement of punches (Fig. 3.27).

Summary Punching—the process whereby an automatic punch, attached to an accounting machine by a cable, can punch totals into a card at the same time as they are being printed on the accounting machine (Fig. 3.28).

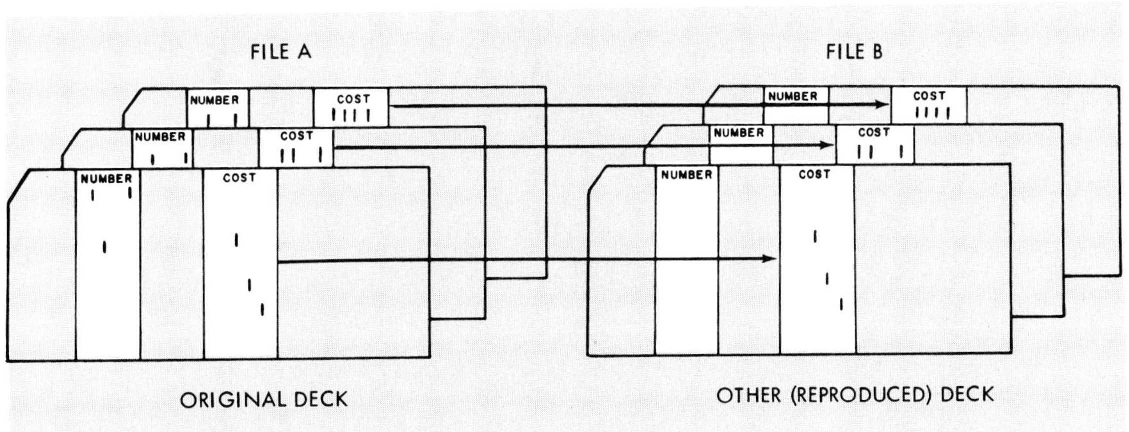

Figure 3–25. Reproducing.

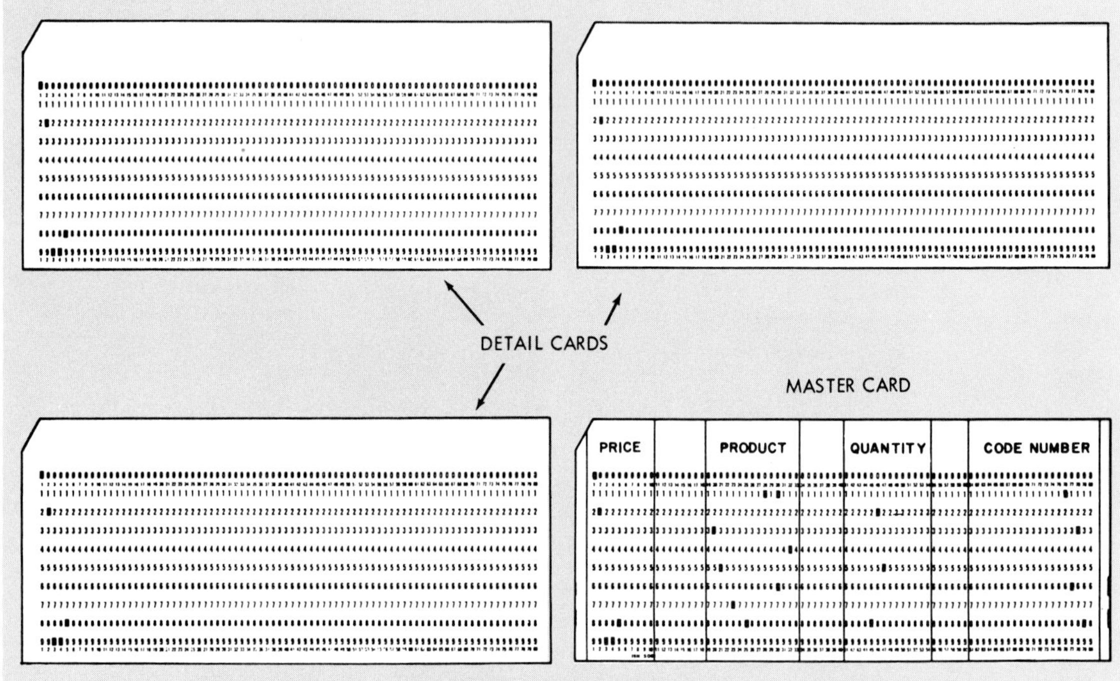

Figure 3–26. Gangpunching.

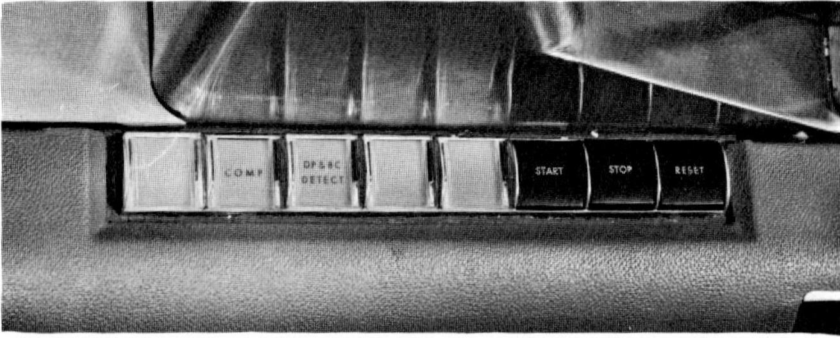

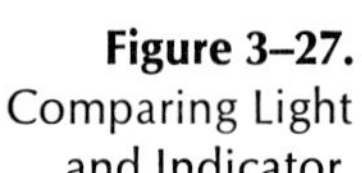

Figure 3–27. Comparing Light and Indicator.

Mark Sensing—the process whereby information is recorded in the form of a pencil mark on a card. This mark can be used to punch holes into the same card automatically. This method of punching eliminates the need for a card-punch operator (Fig. 3.29).

End Printing—a feature available only on the model 519 automatic punch permits the printing of up to eight digits on the face of a card. An additional eight digits may be printed on a second line requiring a subsequent run. The numbers are printed at the end of the card (Fig. 3.30).

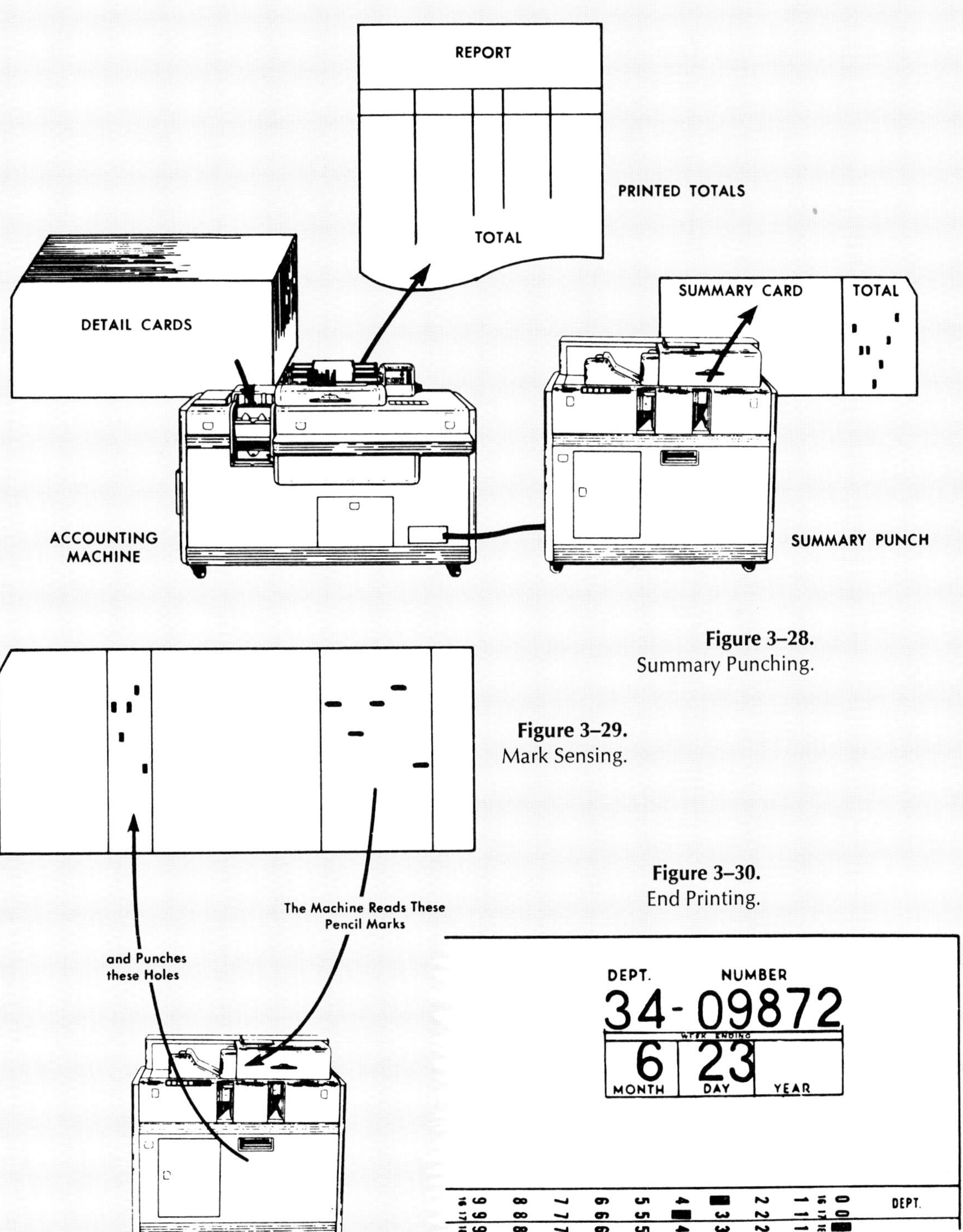

Figure 3–28.
Summary Punching.

Figure 3–29.
Mark Sensing.

Figure 3–30.
End Printing.

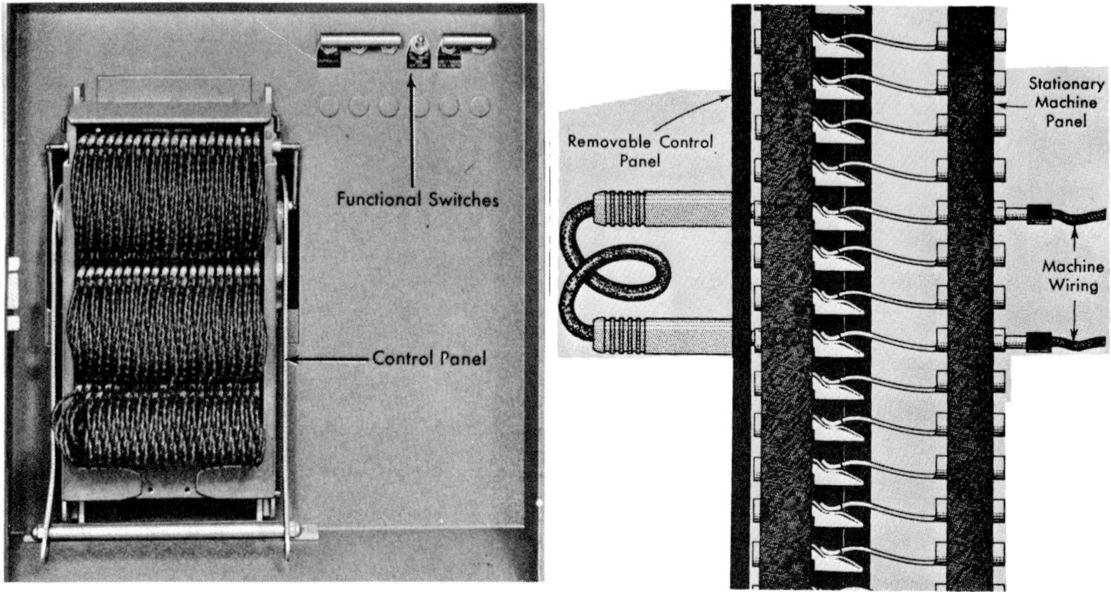

Figure 3–31. Control Panel and Switches.

Figure 3–32. Control Panel Wiring.

CONTROL PANEL

The control panel (Fig. 3.31) provides the flexibility for reproducing, comparing, and gangpunching, regardless of which columns contain the originating information, or into which columns it is to be punched. Automatic operation of the reproducer is achieved by wiring the control panel and the setting of the appropriate switches (Fig. 3.32).

INTERPRETERS

One of the basic concepts of data processing is the conversion of source data into machine language. The machine can sense the holes in the cards and translate them into data that can be processed. However, if the cards are to be used as documents as well as for automatic production of reports, it is desirable that the punched information be translated into a printed form on the card itself. Thus the information in the cards can be read with the same ease as one reads a typewritten document.

Machines designed to print information that has been punched in cards are called interpreters. IBM Models 548 and 557 are the most popular interpreters in use today.

548 Interpreter. Can translate up to sixty columns of punched data into printed characters on the face of the card. To interpret more than sixty columns, the card must be run through the machine twice. Two lines of data

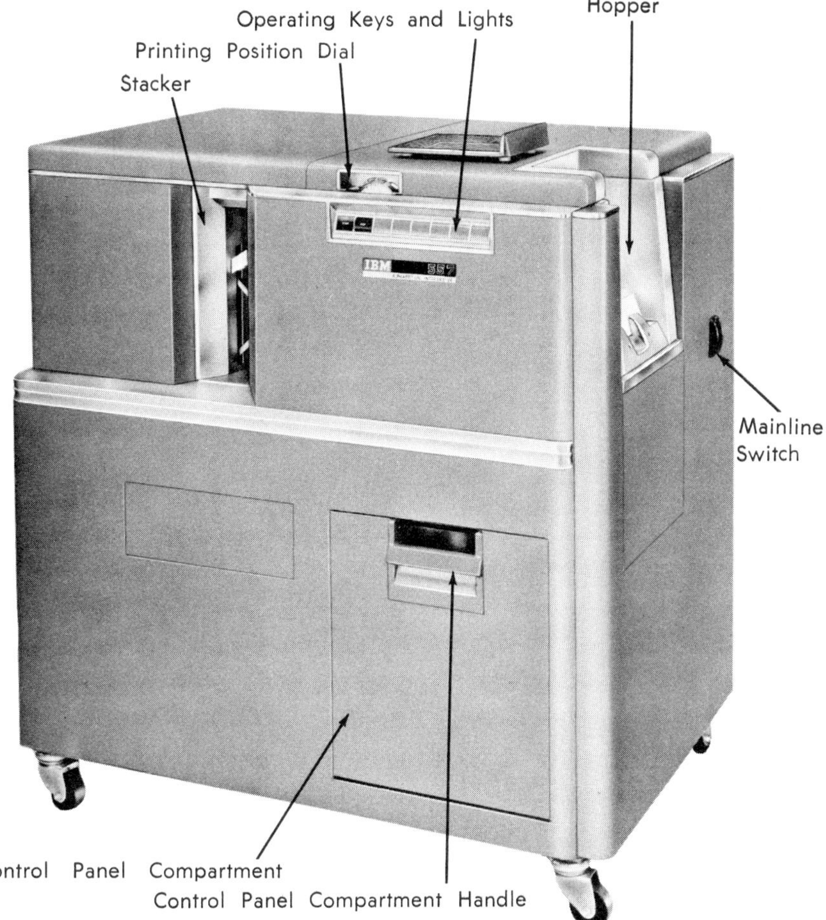

Figure 3–33.
557 Interpreter.

may be printed on a card. The machine operates at a speed of 60 cards per minute (Fig. 3.33).

557 Interpreter. Can print up to sixty columns of punched data in as many as twenty-five lines. Printing is accomplished at the rate of 100 cards per minute and the desired printing is selected manually (Fig. 3.34).

SUMMARY

Punched cards play a major role in a data processing installation. Besides its role as chief input media, the punched card is used for original documents as well as for computer programming. The intent of this chapter is to introduce punched-card data processing concepts and to explain the use of various punched card reading and interpreting machines. In the next chapter, the important functions and uses of other punched-card equipment are discussed.

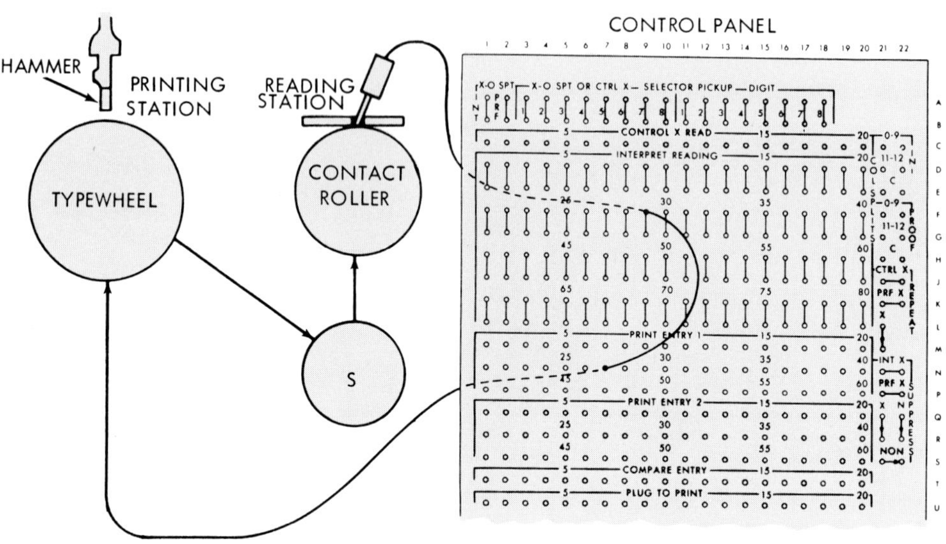

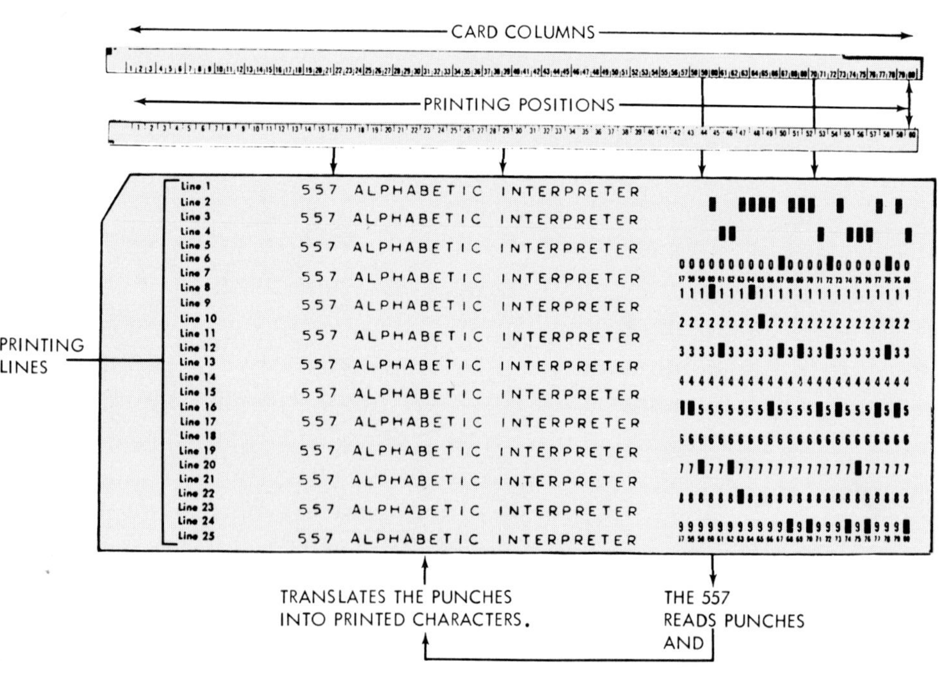

Figure 3–34. 557 Printing.

Although punched-card data processing is not as important as it was twenty-five years ago, it is still a valued part of data processing, and knowledge of the operation and uses of the equipment is essential to all students of data processing.

1. *Punched-card data processing* is defined as the recording, manipulat- and reporting of information through the use of holes punched in the card.
2. *Uses* of punched card as input and output media because of its machine language capabilities. Facilities for storing information in a machine provide processable format for future use.
3. The *"unit record" principle:* information concerning a single transaction is contained in one card, permitting each card to be processed with other cards or input media on a single record basis.
4. *Types of cards:* Hollerith 80-column card, and Powers 90-column card (discontinued). New 96-column card for IBM System/3.
5. *Data representation in cards.* Zone punches (12, 11 and 0) and numeric punches (0–9). Numbers are represented by 0–9 punches. Letters and special characters are represented by combination of zone and numeric punches.

   A–I 12 punch plus 1 through 9 punches.
   J–R 11 punch plus 1 through 9 punches.
   S–Z 0 punch plus 2 through 9 punches.

   Special characters may have 1, 2 or 3 punches in one column.
6. *Field*—related characters that are treated as one unit of information. High-order position of a field (left-hand column) and low order position (right-hand column).
7. *Record*—series of fields (may be one field) grouped together for input and output operations.
8. *Card-Punch Machines.* Functions: Primary function is to convert a source document into a punched card. Other uses as: replacing damaged cards, correcting cards, preparing computer program cards and preparing test cards for data machines.

   Keyboards: Numeric and alphanumeric.
   Components: Include card hopper, punch station, read station, hopper, switches.
   Program Control Unit: Program card, controls by means of coding.
   Verifying. Verifying machine checks reliability of output.
   IBM Model 29 card punch. Most commonly used.
   Other models. IBM model 129 and UNIVAC model 1710 card punches.

9. *Reproducers.* Automatic punches. Functions: reproducing, gangpunching, comparing, mark sensing, summary punching, and end printing, IBM models 514 and 519.

   Control panel provides flexibility for functions and automatic operation of the machine through the setting of the proper switches.

10. *Interpreters.* Function: To translate holes into a printed form on the face of the card itself. IBM models 548 and 557.

IDENTIFICATION QUESTIONS

Match the following terms with the statements that follow.

A. Control Panel
B. End Printing
C. Field
D. Gangpunching
E. Hollerith Card
F. Interpreter
G. Mark Sensing
H. Nine Edge
I. Numerical Punches
J. Powers Card
K. Program Unit
L. Punched Card Data Processing
M. Record
N. Reproducing
O. Summary Punching
P. System/3
Q. Twelve Edge
R. Unit Record Principle
S. Zone Punches

1. A group of related characters treated as one unit of information.
2. 96 column card.
3. Totals punched in card at the same time they are printed.
4. Upper three rows of a card.
5. Information transferred from one card to another either in the same or different fields.
6. Top edge of a card.
7. Information concerning a single transaction usually recorded in one card.
8. Information recorded in the form of pencil marks on a card.
9. Translates punched information into a printed form on a card.
10. 80 column card.
11. Allows for fully automatic control of skipping, duplicating, and shifting of modes of card punching.
12. Bottom edge of a card.
13. Permits printing of eight digits on the face of a card.
14. 0 through 9 punches of a card.
15. Procedure of recording, manipulating, and reporting information through the use of punched holes in cards.
16. 90 column card.
17. Provides for flexibility of operations.
18. Punching of common information from a master card to detail cards.
19. A field or a series of fields grouped together for input and output operations.

QUESTIONS FOR REVIEW

1. What is punched card data processing and why has it played such an important role in the development of data processing?
2. What are the principal uses for punched card data processing?
3. What is the "unit record" principle?
4. What are the different types of punched cards and how do they differ?
5. How is data represented in the "Hollerith" code for alphabetic, numeric and special characters?
6. What is the difference between a field and a record?
7. Differentiate between the high order position and the low order position of a punched card. Give an example.
8. Why is card punching the most expensive operation in data processing?
9. What are the main operations of a card punch machine?
10. What are the two types of keyboards available and how do they differ from the standard typewriter keyboard and adding machine?
11. What are some of the important features of the model 29 card punch?
12. Why is it important to keep the original card after it has been corrected and punched?
13. What is the function of the program unit and program card?
14. In a verifying operation, how many opportunities does the operator have to check the agreement of punches?
15. What additional features does the IBM model 129 and the UNIVAC model 1710 card punches offer?
16. What were automatic punches designed for?
17. What is the main difference between the model 514 and 519 reproducing punch?
18. What are the principal operations performed by the automatic punches and explain the functions of each?
19. What purpose does a control panel serve?
20. What is the principal function of the interpreter?
21. What is the difference between the model 548 and 557 interpreters?

CHAPTER 4

Manipulating, Calculating and Reporting Functions

SORTER

An important part of any data processing system is the sorting and classifying of records. By using punched cards one has the advantage of being able to arrange record cards in sequence very rapidly with the aid of high speed sorters. There are available several model sorters of varying speeds and features. The selection of a particular model depends on the nature and volume of data to be sorted.

The main function of the sorter is to arrange cards in a predetermined sequence. The sorter may also be used to select cards with a specific punch from a group of cards. (Fig. 4.1)

IBM MODEL 82 SORTER—OPERATING PRINCIPLES AND FEATURES

1. The card feed hopper has a capacity of 1,200 cards and is located at the right end of the machine.
2. Cards are placed in the feed hopper face down with the nine edge facing the throat of the machine.
3. The column to be sorted is selected by turning the handle to the desired column. Each turn of the handle moves the reading brush one column. In a sorting operation, one sorts from the low order position (rightmost position of field) to the high order position (leftmost position of field) of a particular field. The sorter can sort only one column at a time (Fig. 4.2).

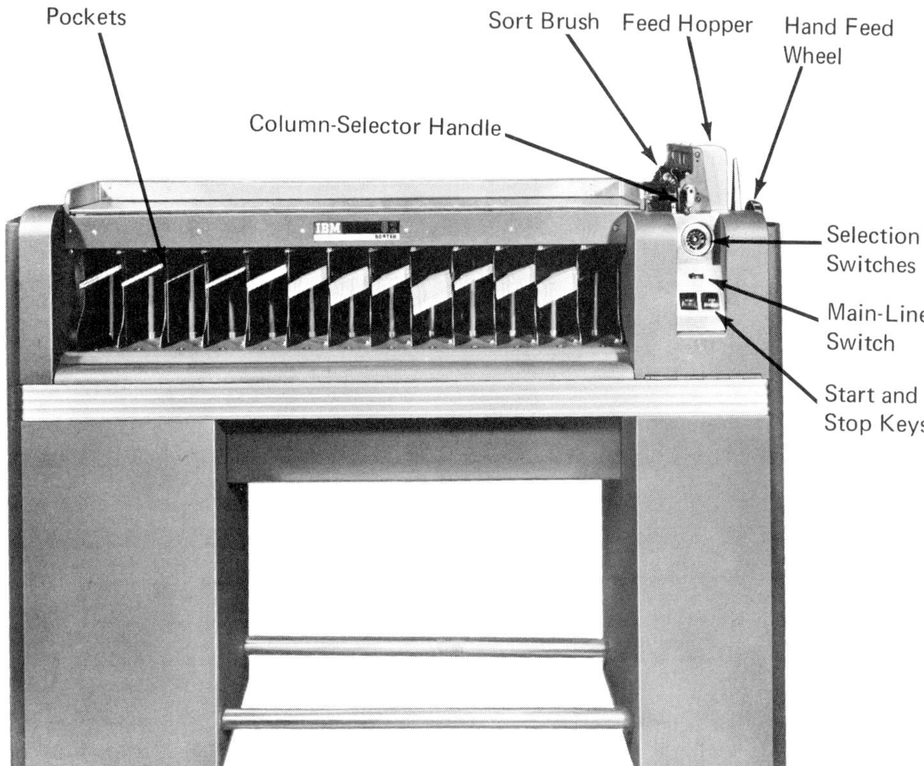

Figure 4–1. 82 Sorter.

4. There are thirteen possible pockets for the cards to fall into; one pocket for each possible punch position plus a reject pocket to hold cards without any punch in that particular column (Fig. 4.3).
5. Sorting is automatic—all cards are fed from the bottom of the deck. Automatic shutoff occurs as soon as the last card is fed or as soon as any pocket is filled.
6. Selection switches make it possible to separate certain types of cards without disturbing the basic sequence of the cards. An alphabetic sorting switch is used in sorting cards alphabetically (Fig. 4.4).

SORTING

NUMERICAL SORTING

To arrange cards in a numerical sequence, each column in a field requires one sort. The first sort should be on the low order position of a field (rightmost column). After the sort is completed, the cards are removed from the pockets right to left: the zero pocket, the one pocket on top of the zero, the two pocket on top of the previous combined group and so forth until all ten

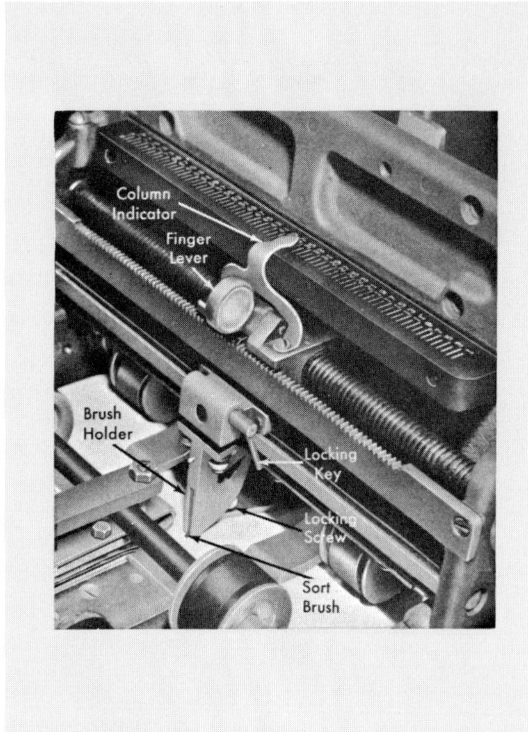

Figure 4–2. Sort Brush and Column Indicator.

Figure 4–4. Selection Switches.

THE SORT BRUSH READS ONE COLUMN AT A TIME

SORT BRUSH

CARD

CHUTE BLADES

A CHUTE OPENS AS SOON AS THE PUNCH IS READ

CARD EDGE

ROLLERS MOVE CARDS THROUGH CHUTES TO THE POCKETS

ROLLER

CHUTE BLADE

9 8 7 6

13 POCKETS

9 8 7 6 5 4 3 2 1 0 11 12 (REJECT)

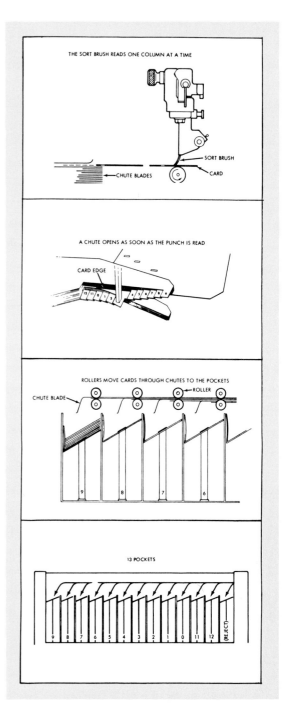

Figure 4–3. Card Feed Path.

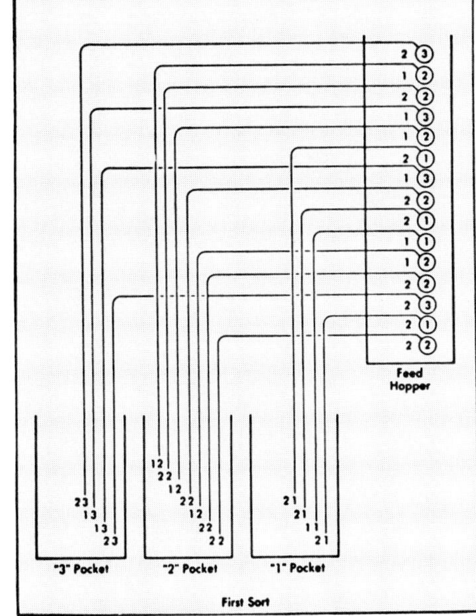

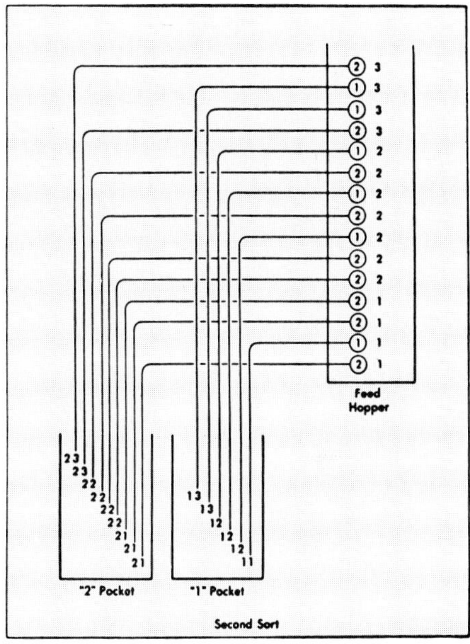

Figure 4–5. Sorting Principle.

pockets are emptied. Cards are now ready for the next column to be sorted. The process is continued until the entire field is sorted, with the last sort being the high order position (leftmost column) (Fig. 4.5).

NOTE

All selection switches must be in the outer position before the sorting operation is started.

In certain sorting operations, it is necessary to sort on more than one field. The sequence of sorting is inverse to the importance of each field. The least important (minor) is sorted first. Next, the more important field (intermediate) and finally the most important field (major) is sorted last (assuming that three fields are to be sorted). Thus to arrange cards in sequence by AREA (major), TERRITORY (intermediate), and CUSTOMER NUMBER (minor), the cards should be sorted to customer number sequence first, then territory, and finally area number, to complete the sort.

ALPHABETIC SORTING

Alphabetic sorting requires two sorts per column, since each letter is represented by two holes, punched in a single column. The letters A–I combine a 12 punch with the numeric digits 1–9; J–R combines an 11 punch with the numeric digits 1–9; and S–Z combines a 0 punch with the numeric digits 2–9.

Each column is sorted on the numerical portion of the letters first. The cards should fall into pockets 1 through 9. The alphabetic switch (red) on an 82 sorter should be pushed towards the center of the dial and cards re-sorted on the same column. This time the cards will fall into pockets, 0, 11, and 12. Alphabetic items may contain blanks, therefore if any cards fall into the reject pocket on the first sort of a particular column, it is not necessary to sort rejected cards a second time on the same column. However, at the completion of the sort, these rejected cards should be placed in front of the file when proceeding to the next column.

VERIFICATION OF SORTING—METHODS

SIGHT CHECKING

When cards are removed from a pocket, they should be checked to see that all of the cards have the same punch in the particular column in question. The cards are joggled and held up to the light. If the cards are properly sorted, the holes form a tunnel through which the light can be seen. If the light is obstructed, this would be an indication that there is at least one missorted card in the group. Such cards must be located, removed and hand-filed in their proper sequence.

To assure accurate sorting, all cards should be sight checked on each column before continuing the sorting operation, particularly on the first column of the sort, to assure that the machine is sorting properly (Fig. 4.6).

NEEDLE CHECKING

Another method of checking the agreement of holes is the use of a sorting needle. The needle has a blunt point and is gently glided (*not forced*) through a group of cards. If the needle comes out through the last card, this

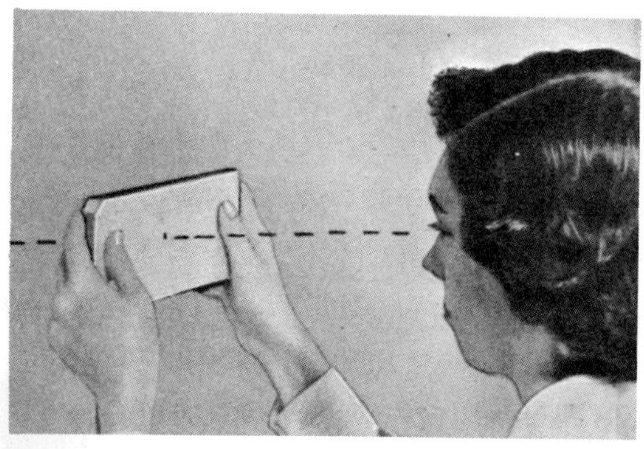

Figure 4–6. Sight Checking.

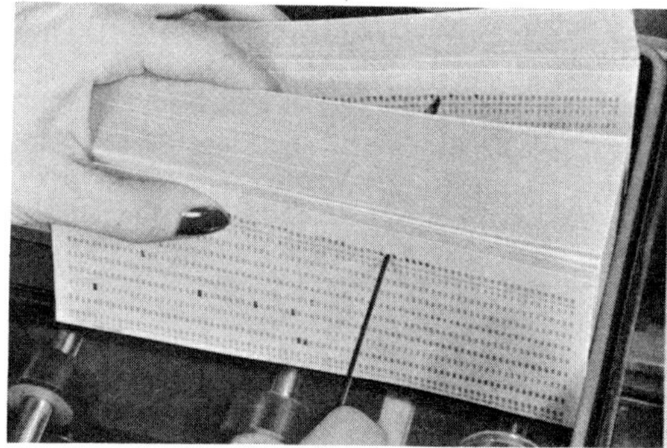

Figure 4–7. Needle Checking.

would be an indication that all the holes are the same. If the needle is obstructed, the point of obstruction locates the missorted card (Fig. 4.7).

TIMING REQUIREMENTS

Due to the large amount of handling time involved in a sorting operation, this time must be considered a factor in estimating the total amount of time required to complete a sorting operation.

In order to calculate the amount of sorting time required, the number of columns to be sorted is multiplied by the number of cards involved in the sort. This product is then divided by the speed of the sorter, thus arriving at the time in minutes. A handling time factor of 25 percent is then added to this figure in order to complete the calculation of total time required for the sorting operation.

The formula for estimating the sorting time for the 82 sorter is

$$\frac{\begin{array}{c}\text{Number of columns}\\\text{to be sorted}\end{array} \times \begin{array}{c}\text{Number of cards}\\\text{to be sorted}\end{array}}{\begin{array}{c}650\\\text{(speed of sorter in units per minute)}\end{array}} \times 125\% = \begin{array}{c}\text{MINUTES}\\\text{SORTING}\\\text{TIME}\end{array}$$

The 25 percent factor is higher than for most machines as the sorter requires more handling due to the stacking, sight checking, needling and joggling of cards (Fig. 4.8). For an inexperienced operator, this 25 percent factor may be low, while for an experienced operator this percentage will be substantially reduced. For example, the length of time required to sort 13,000 cards on columns 14–18 would be as follows:

$$\frac{5 \times 13{,}000}{650} = 100 \times 125\% = 125 \text{ minutes}$$

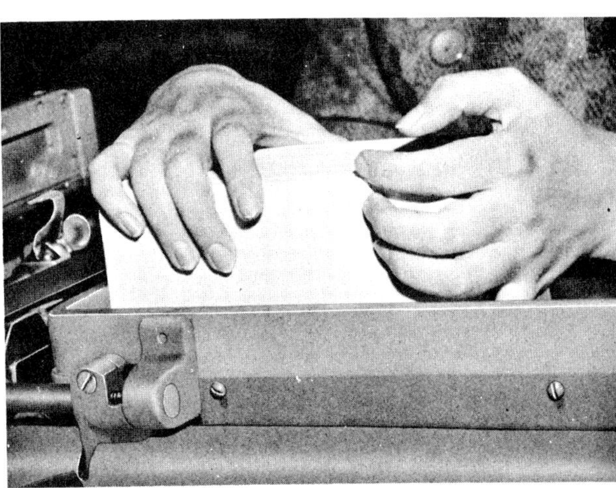

Figure 4–8. Joggling Cards.

COLLATOR

One of the major problems in data processing is the updating and maintenance of files. Records must be kept current and accessible. Filing and extracting cards from a file are a necessary operation in keeping the files up to date.

The principal function of the collator is to compare two or more fields in the same or different cards, and based on this comparison, to separate, segregate or combine the cards. Separation of a file divides one group of cards into two groups. Segregation of a file arranges cards into specific groups. Combining files merges two groups into one. The basic operations that can be performed on the collator are:

1. Checking the sequence of a file of cards (in either ascending or descending sequence). For example, each card in an ascending file should have a control number equal to or greater than the preceding number, 1245, 1247, 1247, 1251, etc. (Fig. 4.9).

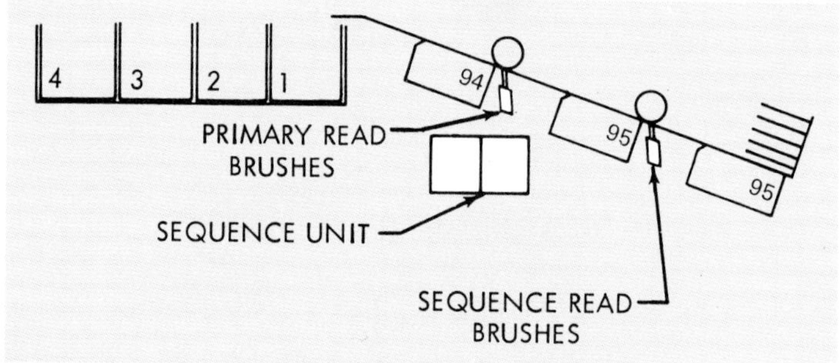

Figure 4–9.
Sequence Checking.

2. Selecting specific cards from a file of cards. For example, it may be necessary to select card(s) from a file without disturbing the sequence of the file. Numbers 10,000 to 19,999 (or any numbers desired) can be extracted from the file in one pocket without altering the sequence of the other group of cards in another pocket of the machine.
3. Merging: combining two files of cards into one file (Fig. 4.10).
4. Match-Merging: merging only matched (equal) cards with the selection of the unmatched cards from both files. For example in a payroll application it may be necessary to merge only the cards of employees who have worked during the current pay period. The master employee name cards would be placed in one card feed while the detail current earning cards could be placed in the other card feed. The merged cards would represent the matched cards (employees that worked the current period), one pocket would contain unmatched master employee cards (employees that did not work), while the other pocket would contain unmatched detail current earning cards (new hires or incorrect employee numbers) (Fig. 4.11).

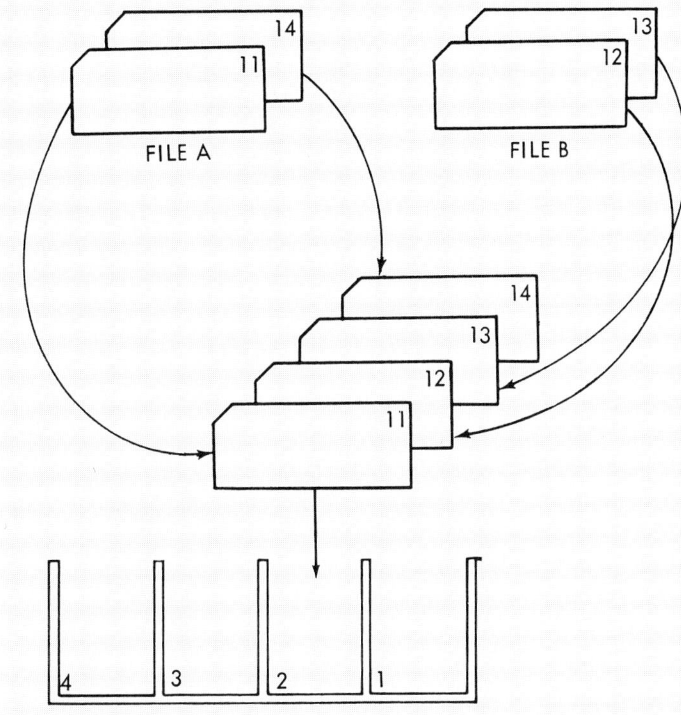

Figure 4–10. Merging Example.

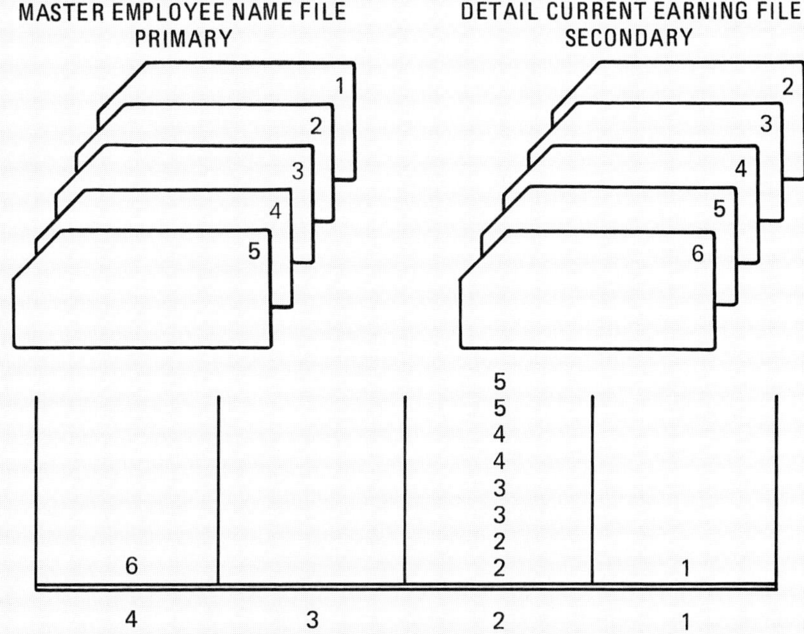

Figure 4–11. Match Merging Example.

Figure 4–12. Match Selecting Example.

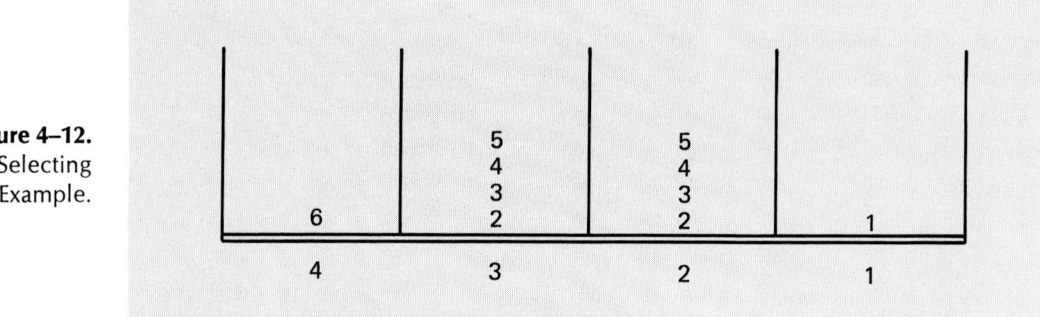

5. Match-Selecting: matching two files with the selection of matched cards (not merged) and the selection of unmatched cards from both files. Using the same example as in the match-merge example, instead of merging the matched master employee name and detail current earning cards, the cards could be selected in adjoining pockets (Fig. 4.12).

The collator is a versatile machine and with it almost every type of filing operation is possible. If a specific filing job is required and the standard operating procedure does not provide for it, the index of the reference manual for the specific collator should be consulted, for in it are numerous illustrations of various operations. One could find the operation desired and substitute the columns of the existing job for the ones given in the manual illustration. Frequent references to the manual can save time in filing operations.

IBM MODEL 85 COLLATOR

The model 85 collator compares and files cards according to the numerical information punched in the card (Fig. 4.13). Cards with numerical, alphabetical or special characters can be processed on the model 87 collator (the alphabetic version of the model 85).

There are two card feeds (primary and secondary) to accommodate two files of cards. Each feed is capable of operating at a speed of 240 cards per minute. The speed of the collator will vary with the type of jobs being processed from a minimum of 240 cards per minute to a maximum of 480 cards per minute. The lower feed unit is called the PRIMARY feed and the upper feed unit is called the SECONDARY feed.

Four pockets are provided for the stacking of the cards. Each pocket can hold up to 1,000 cards and is equipped with a lever that will stop the machine when the pocket is full. The pockets are numbered from right to left (Fig. 4.14) as follows:

1	Selected Primaries	3	Selected Secondaries
2	Merged Cards	4	Selected Secondaries

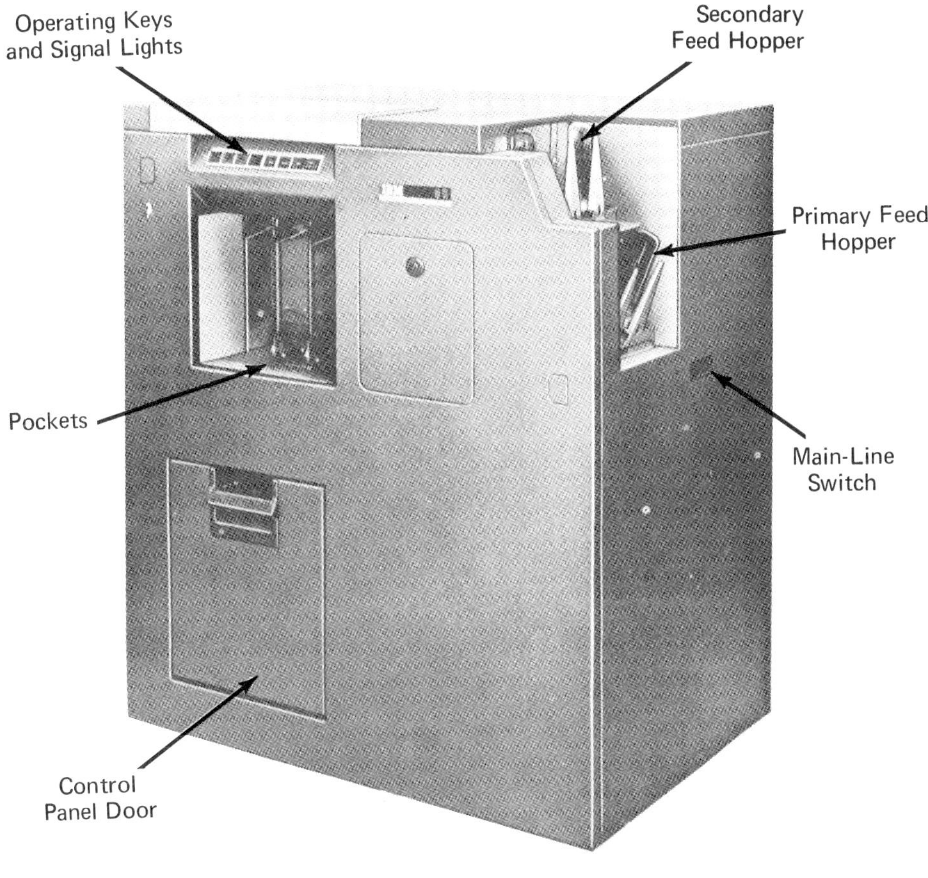

Figure 4–13. 85 Collator.

Primary cards can be stacked only into pocket 1 or 2. If no selection is made, cards from the primary feed will travel into pocket 2. Primary cards pass two sets of brushes on their way to the pocket: sequence and primary brushes.

Cards from the secondary feed pass only one set of brushes—secondary brushes. Secondary cards can be stacked into pockets 2, 3 or 4. Pocket 2 is the normal pocket and unless otherwise directed, all secondary cards will enter pocket 2.

Thus pocket 1 is used for selected primary cards; pocket 2 is the normal pocket for cards from both feeds; pocket 3 and 4 are used for selecting secondary cards.

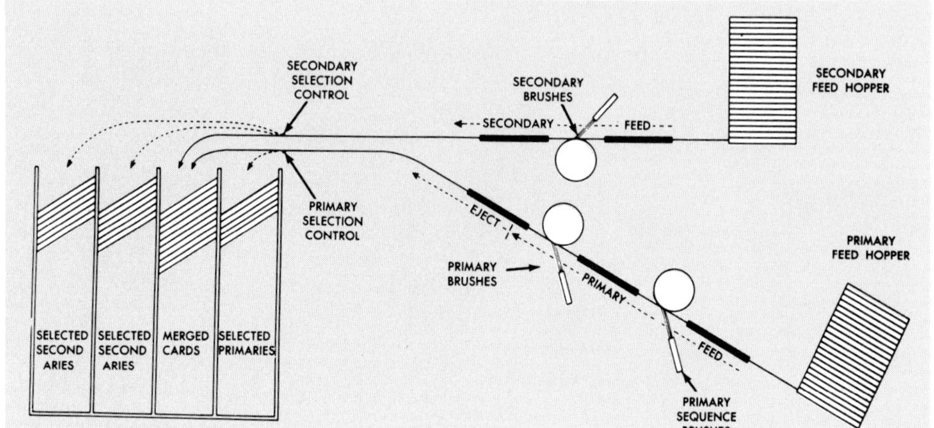

Figure 4–14. 85 Schematic of Card Feeds.

CONTROL PANEL

A double control panel is used for the comparison desired and the determination of the appropriate pockets for the cards (Fig. 4.15).

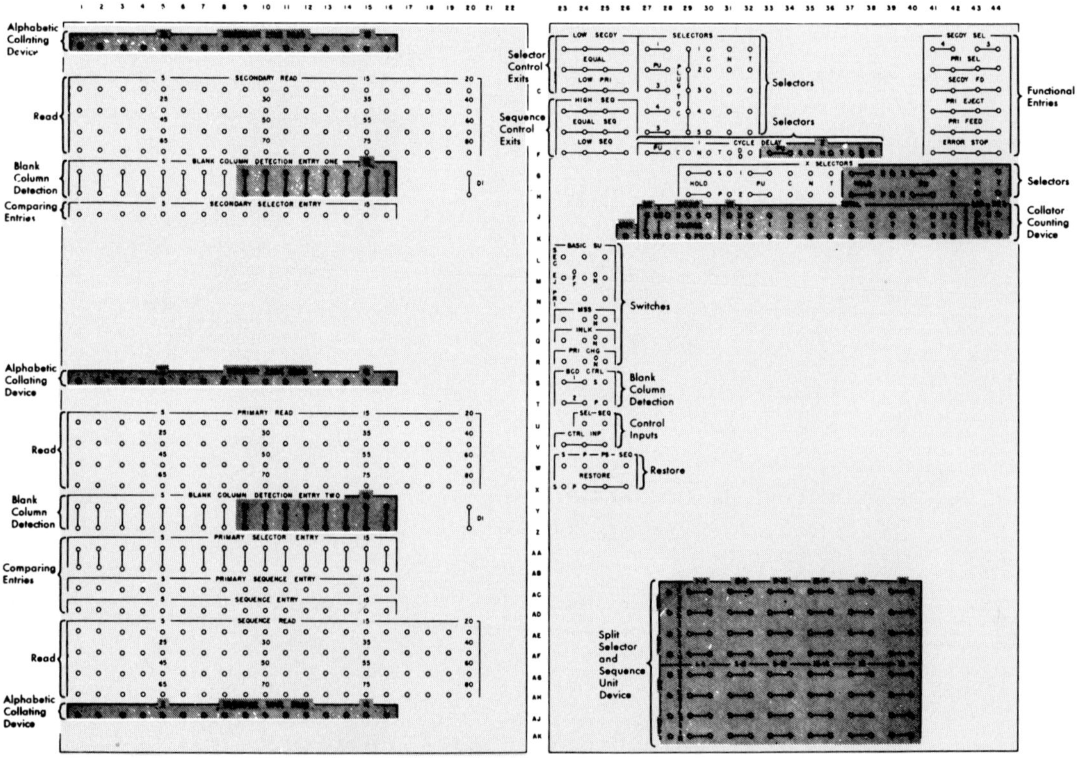

Figure 4–15. 85 Collator Panel.

ADDITIONAL OPERATIONS

Although most of the collator time is spent on the basic operations, there are still many other operations that can be performed on the collator.

1. The selection of certain types of cards from a file, such as the first card of a group; the last card of a group; single cards; cards within a given number group; cards with numbers between two levels, etc.
2. The selection of zero balances in certain fields.
3. The selection of duplicate cards.
4. The selection of cards out of sequence.
5. The detection of blank columns on a card.
6. The insertion of a predetermined number of cards behind or in front of each group.
7. Consecutive number checking.

Numerous other operations can be performed on the collator in addition to those mentioned above. Again, reference to the manual will produce further details.

CARD-PUNCH CALCULATOR

The card-punch calculator is usually not found in a data processing unit that contains a computer since, basically, the computer performs the same functions as a calculator and there would be no justification for using both machines. The important differences between a card-punch calculator and a computer are:

1. The calculator uses an external control panel for programming the machine while the computer uses a program that is stored in the machine.
2. The calculator has a limited storage area compared to the vast storage area of a computer.
3. The computer can process data at a greater rate of speed than the calculator, which is much slower because it is limited by the speed of the punch unit.
4. There is a limit to the number of calculations that can be performed on the calculator. There is no such general limitation in a computer operation.

The most common form of card-punch calculator is the IBM model 604 (Fig. 4.16). The model 604 calculator uses electronic means for performing the basic calculations. All calculations are performed at a constant speed of 100 to 200 cards per minute depending on the model punch used. Up to 60 program steps can be performed at the same time without any increase in processing time.

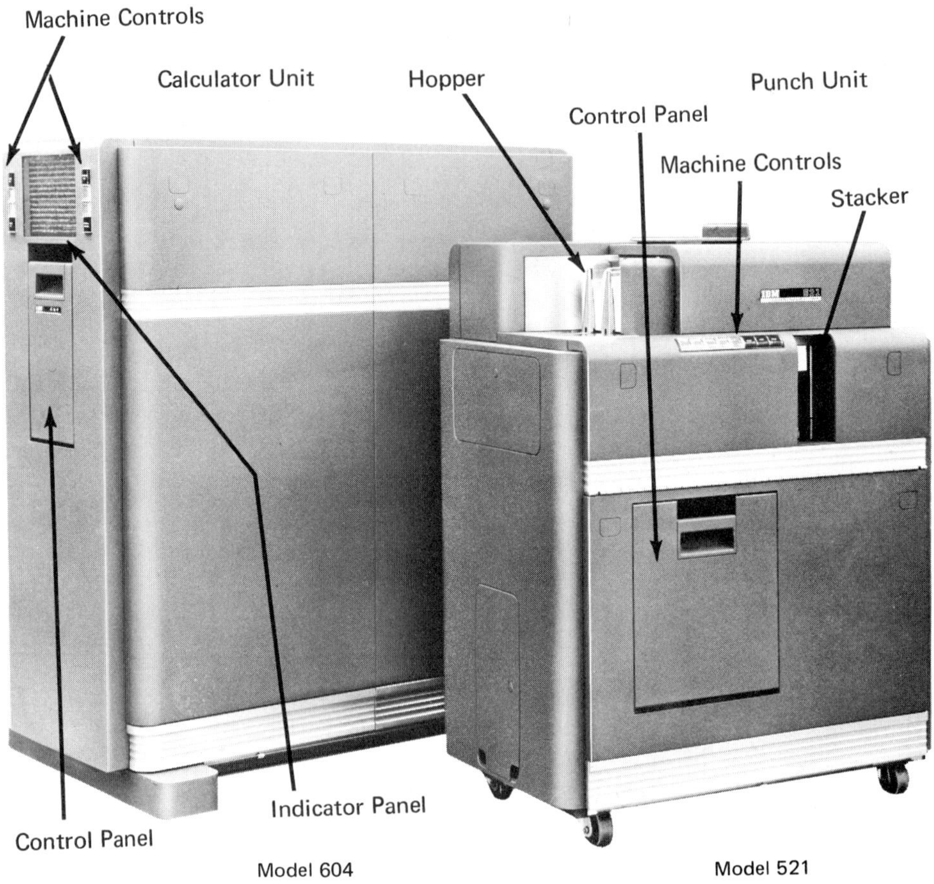

Figure 4–16. 604 Electronic Calculating Punch.

Figure 4–17. 604 Planning Chart Problem.

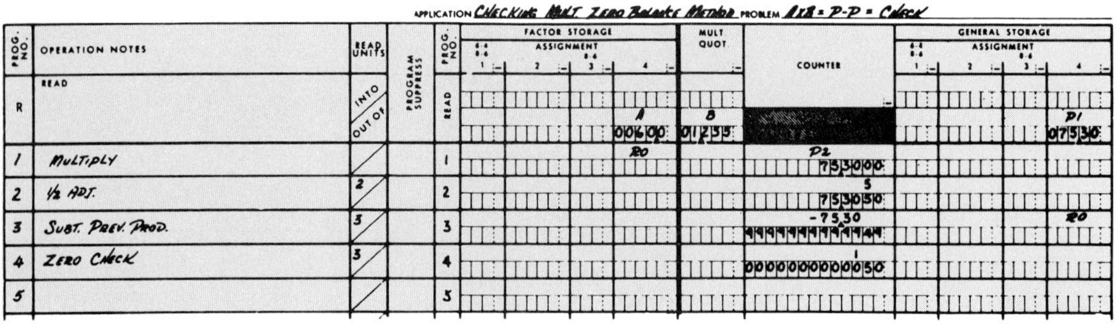

APPLICATION CHECKING MULT. ZERO BALANCE METHOD PROBLEM A×B = P-P = CHECK

PROG. NO.	OPERATION NOTES	READ UNITS (INTO / OUT OF)	PROGRAM SUPPRESS	PROG. NO.	FACTOR STORAGE ASSIGNMENT 1	2	3	4	MULT QUOT	COUNTER	GENERAL STORAGE ASSIGNMENT 1	2	3	4
R	READ			READ				A 00600	B 01235					P1 07530
1	MULTIPLY			1				RO		P2 753000				
2	½ ADJ.	2		2						5 753050				
3	SUBT. PREV. PROD.	3		3						-7530 [illegible]				RO
4	ZERO CHECK	3		4						1 00000000000050				
5				5										

The model 604 was the actual forerunner of the computer, introducing as it did new concepts in data processing. The numerals 8, 4, 2 and 1 were used for the first time to represent the values of data, and the concept of programming a job was initiated (Fig. 4.17).

ACCOUNTING MACHINES

The culmination of all the previous stages involved in data processing—card punching, sorting, collating, reproducing and calculating—is the preparation of the finished product; and one of the most important functions of data processing is the printing of reports. Reports and analyses become the basis of administrative action, and management must be kept constantly informed with current information pertaining to such activities as payroll, sales, inventory, and in many other major areas of concern. The preparation of documents—statements, invoices, checks and reports—is required of every business for efficient operation. The quality and legibility of such forms are of particular importance as they come into the hands of people whose only contact with the business may be through these documents.

The accounting machines perform the function of automatically feeding cards and printing reports. The information read from the card is added, subtracted, selected or compared according to the requirements of individual reports. Information can be read from any of the eighty columns of the card with complete flexibility provided in the arrangement of the printed output. Summary cards may be punched simultaneously with the preparation of the report.

The following are the basic functions of the accounting machine:

1. Summarizing in counters the information punched in cards through addition and subtraction.
2. Printing the summarized information in the forms of totals and subtotals.
3. Punching the summarized information into cards when the accounting machine is connected to the punch by cable.
4. Printing reports (Fig. 4.18).
5. Positioning continuous form paper automatically through carriage tape control.

All the above functions can be performed simultaneously as the card is being read by the machine.

ACCOUNTING MACHINE AND THE COMPUTER PRINTER

Although both the accounting machine and the computer printer perform the same functions of printing, they are entirely different in design and operation.

The printer is connected physically to the computer and receives all of its information from the computer. It is entirely dependent upon the computer for all of its operations.

The accounting machines are entirely independent units complete within themselves with their own accumulators. They are considered "offline" printers while computer printers are considered "online"—so called because of the very nature of the operation of the machines.

The accounting machine prints at the relatively slow speed of 150 lines per minute while the computer printer can list as many as 4,000 lines in a minute. The accuracy and reliability of printing of the two are the same. Both units use tape-controlled carriage for continuous-form spacing and skipping of forms.

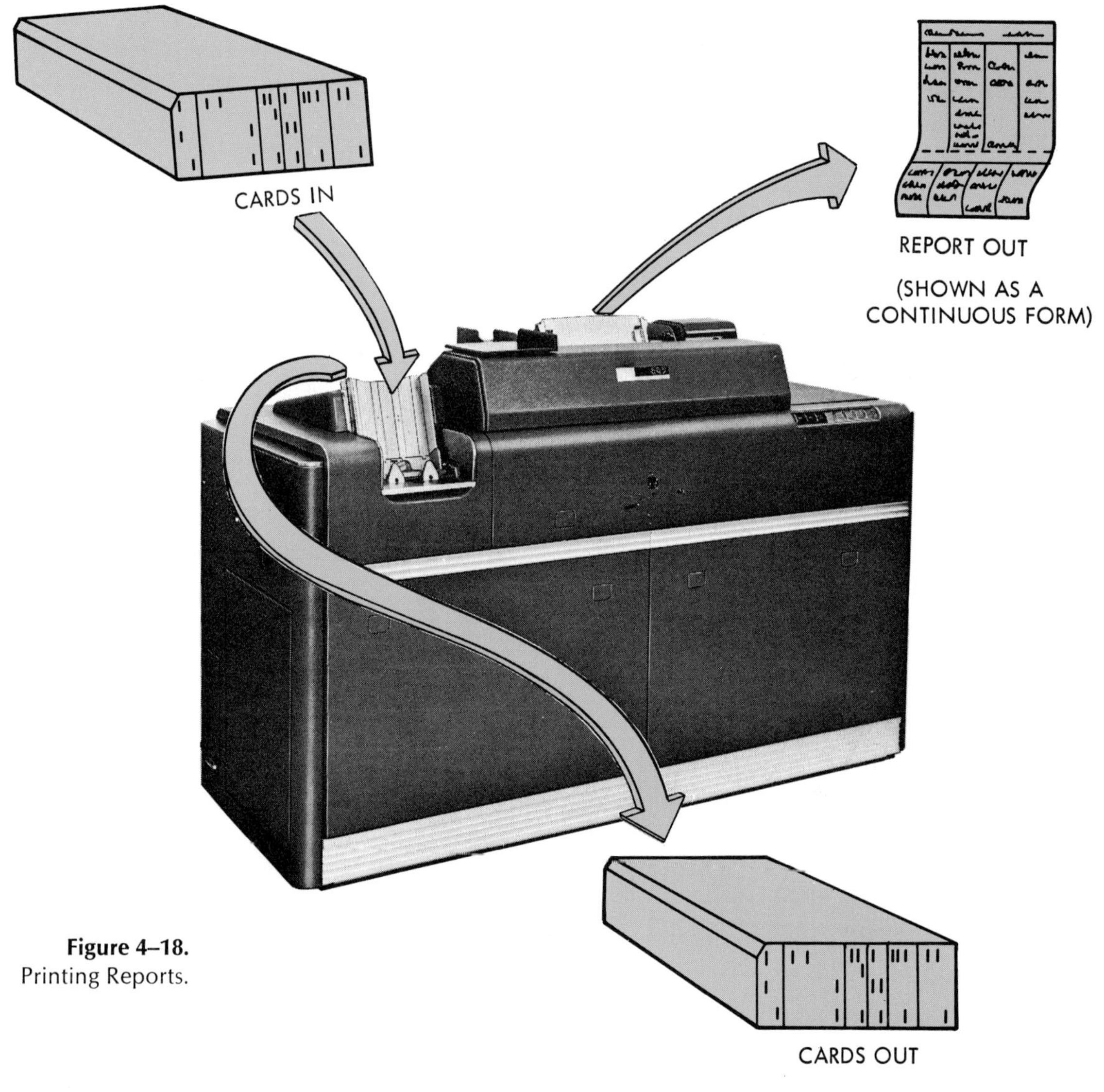

Figure 4–18.
Printing Reports.

IBM 407 ACCOUNTING MACHINE

The 407 accounting machine is the most popular model in use today (Fig. 4.19). The standard 407 has 120 printwheels (Fig. 4.20), each capable of printing the following characters:

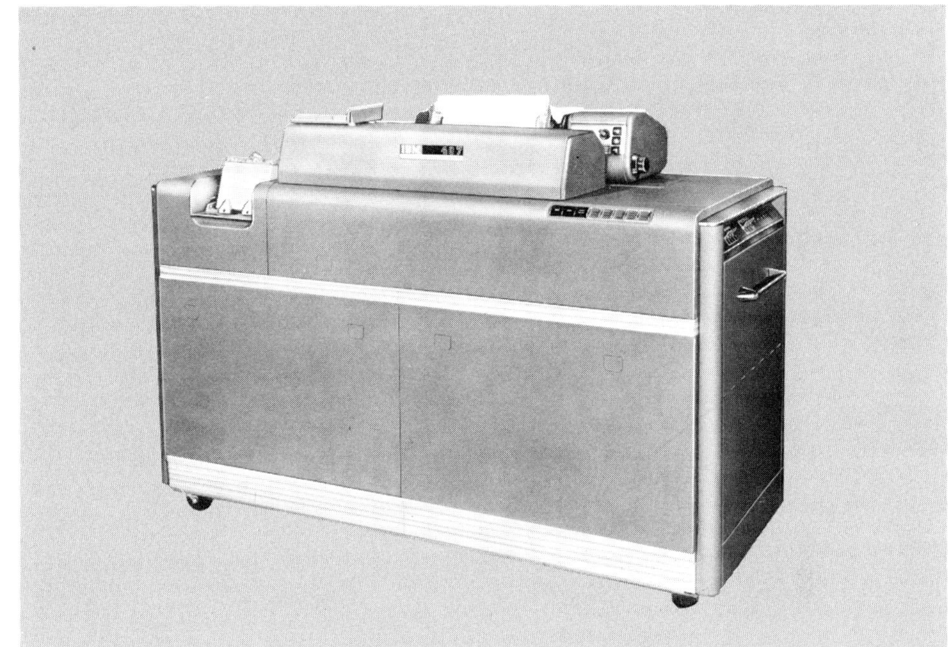

Figure 4–19. 407 Accounting Machine.

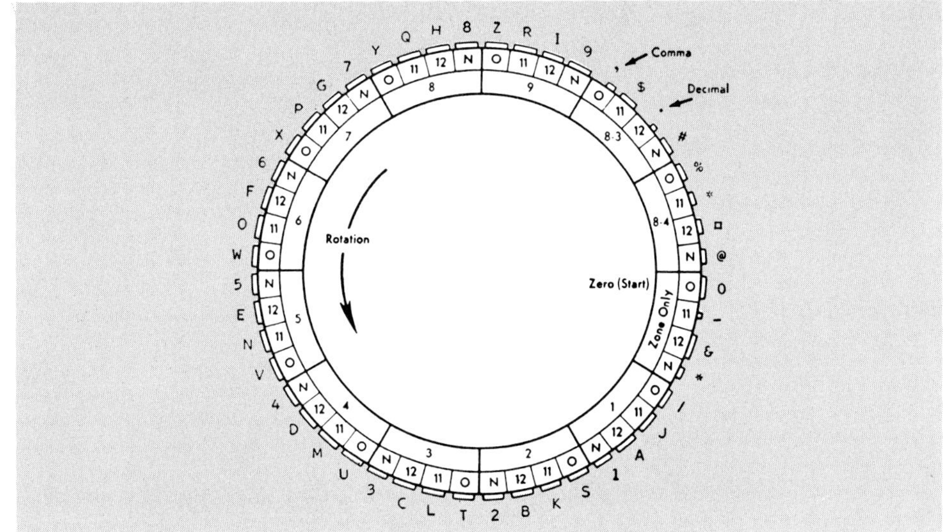

Figure 4–20. 407 Print Wheel.

The twenty-six letters of the alphabet
Ten numerals 0–9
Eleven special characters / $ * % @ & – # □ . ,

The printwheels rotate to the desired character position and then are pressed toward the platen and printed. The accounting machine is capable of both detail printing and tabulating cards at the same rate of speed—150 cards per minute. The machine is also capable of multiple line printing and reading from one card.

ACCOUNTING MACHINE OPERATIONS

Counters. The accumulation of data is performed by a series of counters. These counters are individual adding machine-type accumulators that can be activated individually or coupled together to form larger units.

Programming. Automatic programming steps are possible, as a comparison is made between the two sets of brushes; these tests can be used to generate automatic totals.

Summary Punching. At the same time a report is being prepared, the information can be automatically punched into a summary card. To perform summary punching an automatic punch must be connected to the accounting machine through a summary cable (Fig. 4.21).

Control Panel. This is the control center of the machine. It controls the reading of the information from the card and the printing of the information in the proper place on the form.

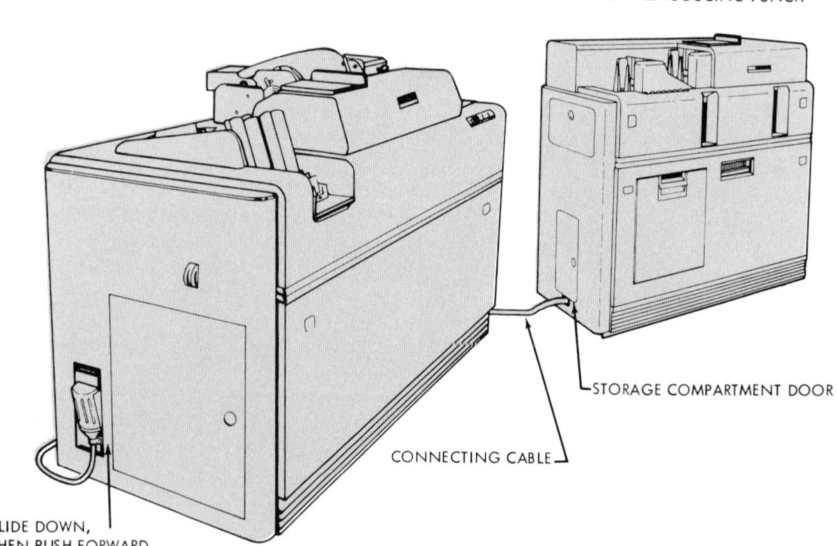

Figure 4–21. Summary Punching.

TAPE-CONTROLLED CARRIAGE

The tape–controlled carriage controls the feeding and spacing of forms. The carriage is standard on all models of accounting machines and printers. A punched hole tape which corresponds to the form controls all the spacing operations. The following are possible with the tape-controlled carriage:

1. Single, double or triple spacing can be varied on the report form by control panel wiring.
2. Overflow skipping from form to form is accomplished by the sensing of a specified punch in the tape which starts the advancing of the form to the first printing line of the following form (Fig. 4.22).
3. Page totals are possible before ejecting the form.
4. Any class of total can be printed on a predetermined line.
5. Channel 12 is the last printing line on the form. When a hole is detected by the carriage in channel 12, the form skips to the next sheet to channel 1 (Fig. 4.23).

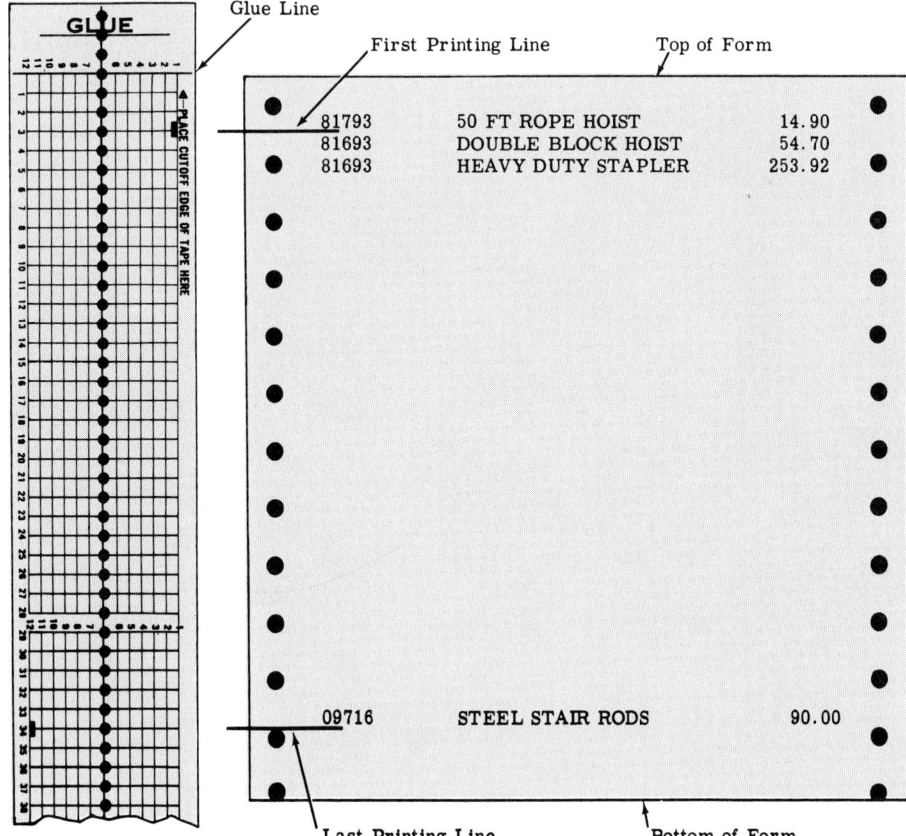

Figure 4–22. Tape Control Carriage.

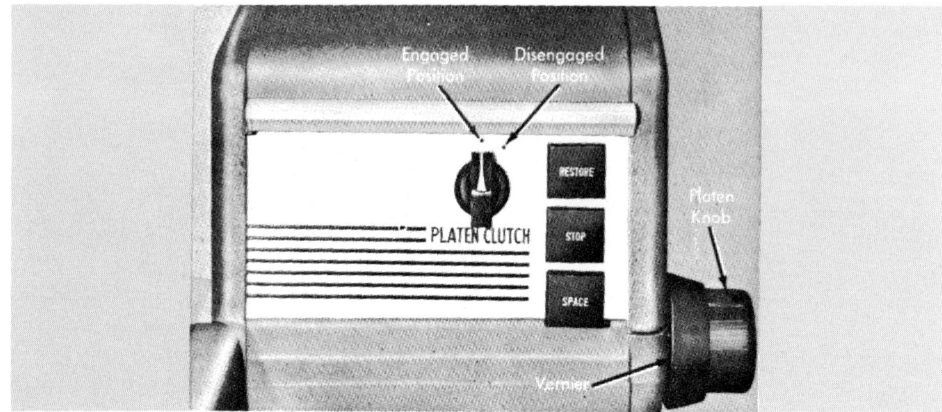

Figure 4–23. Carriage Features.

CARRIAGE TAPE

Channel 1	This channel is always punched for the first printing line of a form. This is known as the "home" position.
Channel 2	This channel is always punched for the first body line of a conventional two part form using heading cards.
Channels 3–11	These channels can be used in any sequence to control form skipping and ejecting to a controlled punch in the carriage tape.
Channel 12	This channel is used as the last printing line of a form. When this channel is sensed by the brushes of the carriage, the form is "overflowed" to channel 1 of the next form (Figs. 4.24, 4.25).

SUMMARY

The ability to manipulate punched cards into a desired sequence or to combine punched cards with other files greatly enhances the uses of punched cards in data processing applications. The calculating and reporting functions are important segments of a data processing operation. An efficient data processing system must possess rapid methods of computations as well as flexible output printers. The intent of the chapter is to demonstrate the uses of punched-card equipment in the manipulating, calculating and reporting operations.

Knowledge of the operation of sorting and collating machines can greatly reduce the processing time of a data processing operation. Valuable computer time can be saved in sorting operations if the cards are presorted before entering a data processing system. Sorters and collators are relatively inexpensive machines and can be extremely helpful in data processing operations.

Since the reliability of the final reports depends upon the accuracy of the computation, it is important that one fully understands the calculating and

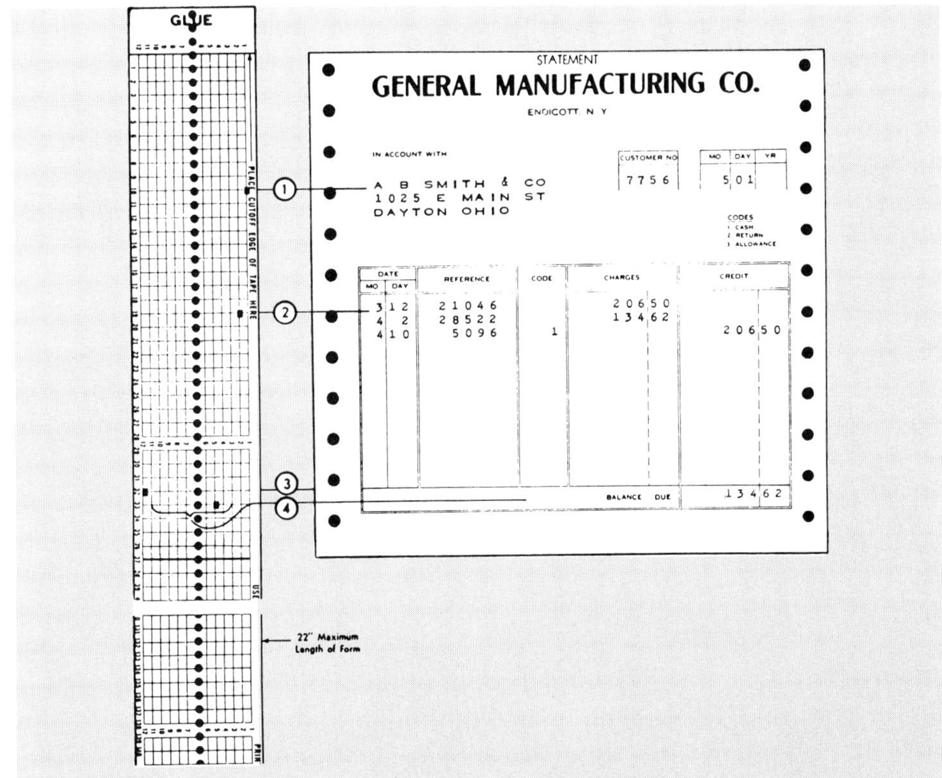

Figure 4–24. Invoice Carriage Control Tape.

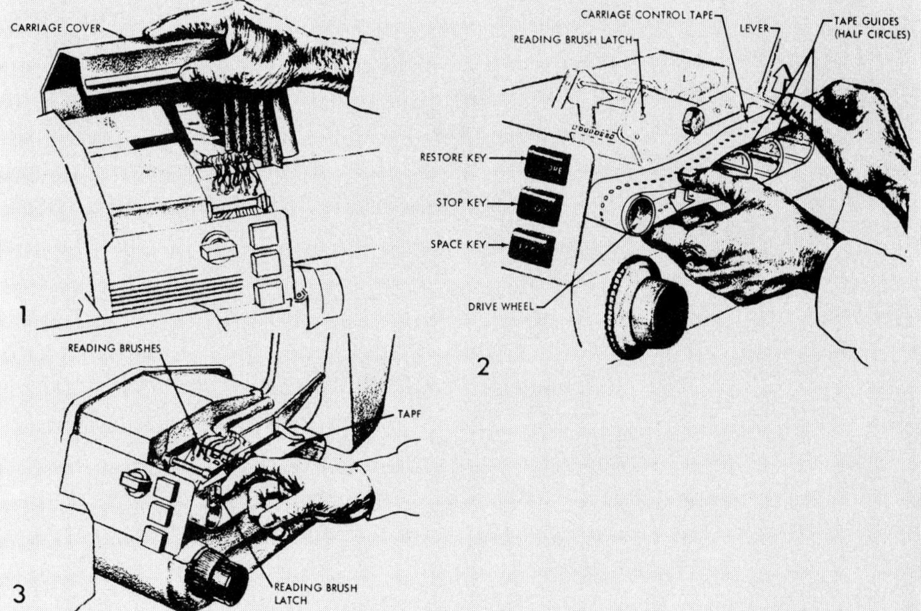

Figure 4–25. Insertion of a Carriage Tape.

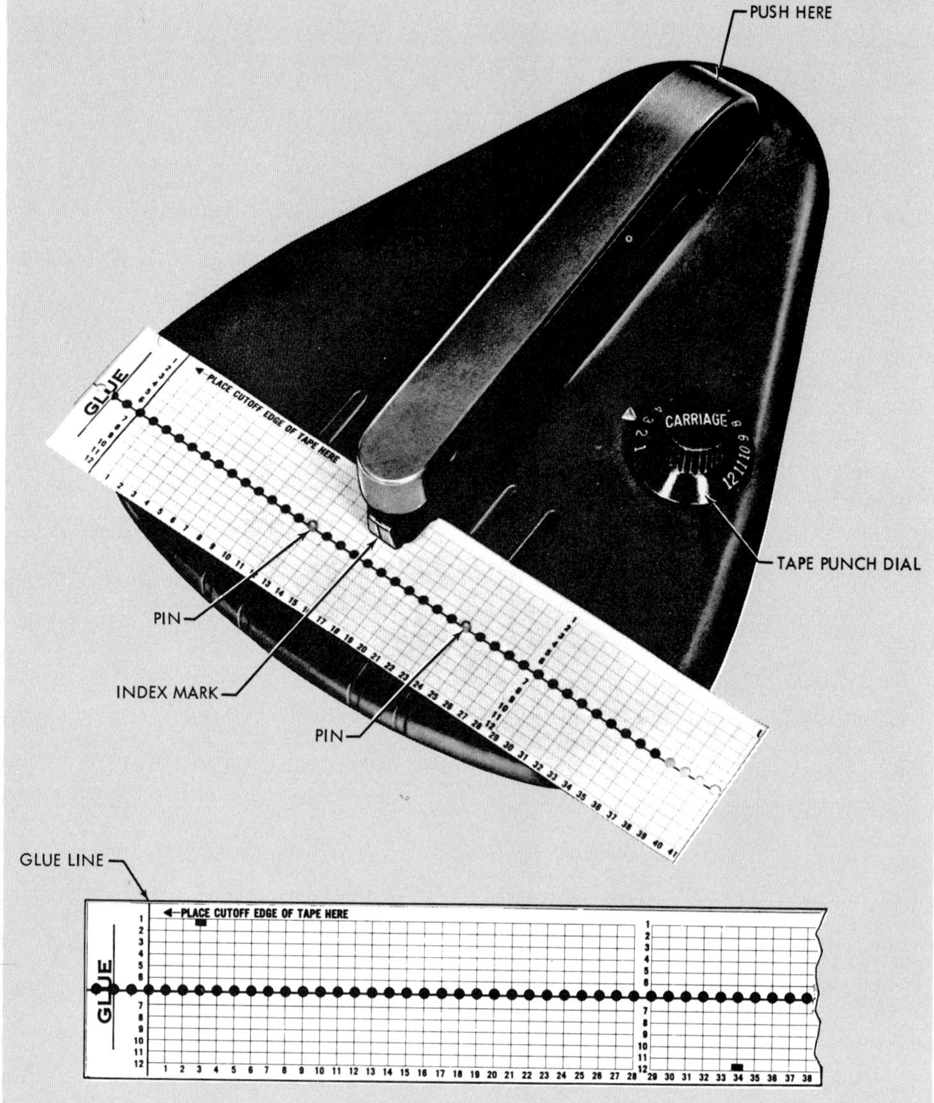

Figure 4–26.
Tape Punch.

reporting operations. Card-punch calculators are usually found only in punched-card installations as the computer performs the same operation. Accounting machines may be found in both types of installations, punched card and computer, as they may be used for "offline" printing operations where the computer is present.

I. *Sorter. Function.* To arrange cards in a predetermined sequence, either numerical or alphabetical. The sorter may also be used to select cards with a specific punch from a group of cards.

A. *Sorting Operations.*
   1. *Numerical Sorting*—sort each column in a field from low order position (rightmost column) to high order position (leftmost column).
   2. *Alphabetical Sorting*—requires two sorts per column, zone and numeric.

B. *Methods of Verifying Sorting Operations.*
   1. *Sight Checking.* Cards are checked to see that all have the same punch in a particular column by holding the cards up to the light.
   2. *Needle Checking.* The agreement of holes is checked by gently gliding a needle through a group of cards.

C. *Timing Requirements.* Formula for estimating sorting time (model 82 sorter).

$$\frac{\text{Number of columns to be sorted} \times \text{Number of cards to be sorted}}{650 \text{ (speed of sorter)}} \times 125\% = \text{MINUTES SORTING TIME}$$

II. *Collator. Function.* To compare two or more fields in the same or different cards and based on the comparison, separate, segregate or combine files of cards.

A. *Collating Operations.*
   1. Checking the sequence of a file of cards (either ascending or descending).
   2. Selecting specific cards from a file of cards.
   3. Merging—combining two files into one.
   4. Match-Merging—merging only matched (equal) cards with selection of unmatched cards from both files.
   5. Match-Selecting—matching of two files with the selection of matched cards (not merged) and the selection of unmatched cards from both files.
   6. Additional Collating Operations—selection of zero balances, selection of duplicate cards, etc.

III. *Calculator. Function.* To perform all necessary arithmetic operations.

A. *Important differences in speed and storage* operations between a calculator and a computer.

B. *Model 604 Calculator* used electronic means for performing calculations and introduces binary concepts (8,4,2,1) for the first time to represent the value of data. The 604 calculator was the forerunner of the computer and introduced the concept of programming a job.

IV. *Accounting Machine. Function.* The printing of reports.

A. *Basic Functions.* Summarizing, printing, punching summarized data, and positioning continuous form paper.

B. *Differences between accounting machine and computer printer.*
   1. Accounting machine not physically connected to computer as is computer printer.
   2. The accounting machine prints at the relative slow speed of 150 lines per minute as compared to the computer printer speed of 4,000 lines per minute. (*Some computer printers are faster now*).

C. *407 Accounting Machine Features.*
   1. *120* printwheels capable of printing 26 letters, 10 numerals and 11 special characters in each of its printwheels.
   2. *Counters*—used to accumulate and store totals.
   3. *Programming*—comparison tests to generate automatic totals.
   4. *Control Panel*—flexibility for reading, accumulating and printing of information.

D. *Tape-Controlled Carriage.* Used in both accounting machine and computer printers.
Function—controls the automatic feeding and spacing of forms.
Carriage Tape is punched in channels as follows:

Channel	1	First printing line of a form.
Channel	2	First printing line of the body of a form using heading cards.
Channels	3–11	May be used in any sequence for automatic control of skipping and spacing.
Channel	12	The last printing line of a form.

IDENTIFICATION QUESTIONS

Match the following terms with the statements that follow.

A. Accounting Machine
B. Alphabetic Sorting
C. Card Punch Calculator
D. Channel 1
E. Channel 12
F. Computer Printer
G. Counters
H. Major
I. Match Merging
J. Match Selecting
K. Merging
L. Minor
M. Needle Checking
O. Numerical Sorting
P. Primary Feed
Q. Programming
R. Secondary Feed
S. Segregation
T. Separation
U. Sight Checking
V. Tape Controlled Carriage

1. Individual adding machines.
2. A blunt point is glided through a group of cards.
3. Combining two files into one.
4. Forerunner of the computer.
5. Lower feed unit of a collator.

6. Merging only equal cards with the selection of unmatched cards from both feeds.
7. Most important field.
8. First printing line of a form.
9. Requires two sorts per column.
10. Online printer.
11. Comparison between two sets of brushes.
12. Dividing one file into two groups.
13. Arrange cards in a numerical sequence.
14. Matching of two fields with selection of unmatched cards from both feeds.
15. Least important field.
16. Last printing line of a form.
17. Holes form a tunnel through which a light can be seen.
18. Separation of cards into various groups.
19. Controls skipping and spacing of forms.
20. Offline printer.
21. Upper feed unit of a collator.

QUESTIONS FOR REVIEW

1. What are the functions of a sorter?
2. Explain the steps in sorting a group of cards in numerical sequence on a model 82 sorter.
3. How does numerical sorting differ from alphabetical sorting?
4. Explain the methods of verifying sorting.
5. Why is handling time such an important factor in sorting?
6. What is the principal function of a collator?
7. What are the four basic operations performed on a collator? Explain.
8. Name the four pockets of the model 85 collator and explain their use.
9. What is the control panel of the collator used for?
10. What are some additional operations in addition to the four basic operations that can be performed on the collator?
11. What are the main differences between a calculator and a computer?
12. What were the new concepts in data processing introduced by the 604 calculator?
13. Explain the basic functions of the accounting machine.
14. What are the major differences between the computer printer and the accounting machine?
15. Explain the basic operations of counters, programming, and summary punching.
16. Explain the functions of the tape controlled carriage and carriage tape?
17. What is channel 1, channel 2, and channel 12 used for?

PART III / COMPUTER COMPONENTS AND ARITHMETIC

CHAPTER 5

Computer Components—Input/Output Devices

Manual data processing has been performed by man since the dawn of recorded history. Since early modern times businesses have relied on pencil and paper to keep records and to figure their profits and losses. The invention of machines to process data helped develop business record-keeping into a system which worked to the profitable advantage of the businessman. The adding machine, the cash register and the calculator are examples of machines which process data by mechanical means. When these mechanical devices are powered by electricity, we had electromechanical data processing. The use of punched-card data processing was the next step in the technological revolution of data processing. Some punched-card systems were quite sophisticated and proved to be adequate for the handling of the data processing needs of many firms. During the punched-card era, data processing machines progressed from the electromechanical, through the electronic (vacuum tube) stage to solid state circuitry (transistors). When the data processing needs of a firm exceeded the capabilities of punched-card equipment, the computer was the ultimate answer (Fig. 5.1).

In 1944, the first computer, the Mark I, appeared in the field of data processing. The Mark I was an experimental computer financed by the Navy Department and built at Harvard University. A new era of data processing was ushered in. These initial machines were first used by mathematicians and scientists to solve complex mathematical problems and to correlate scientific information.

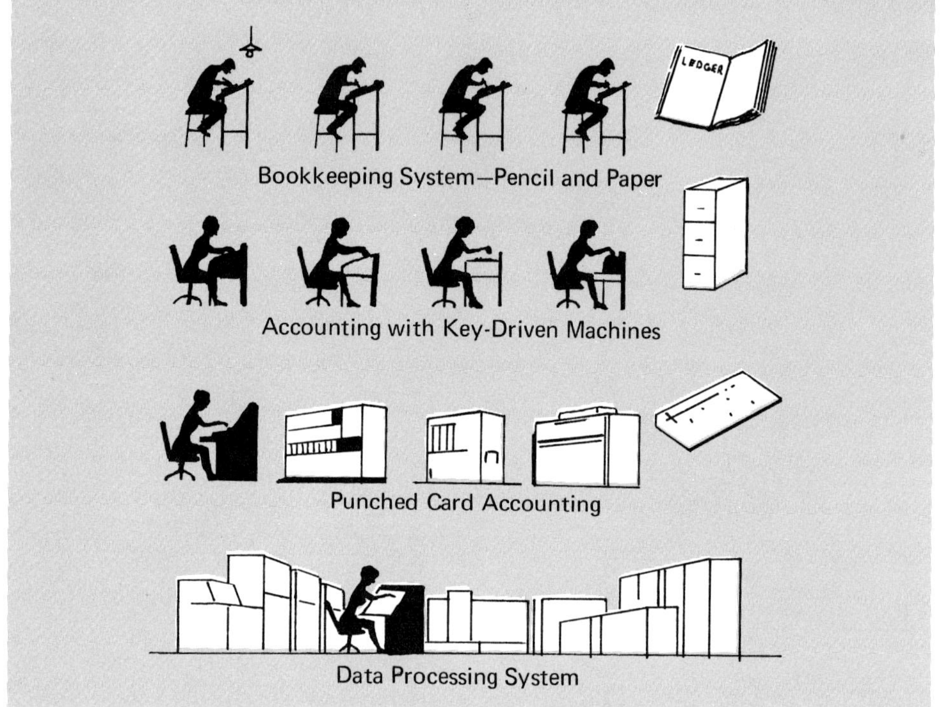

Figure 5–1. Data Processing Systems.

Since 1945, the progress in computer data processing has been phenomenal. With each new application, data processing systems have demonstrated newer methods of handling all of man's informational needs. The undiscovered methods of data processing are endless and no one can predict what developments will occur in the future.

What is this thing called a computer? I don't know how it works. I'm not even sure what it does exactly; I know it's having a tremendous impact on business and science and it seems to have a great deal to do with automation, but how does it relate to me? Can it outthink me? Where will it end—for me—for my children?

These are some thoughts and questions going through many people's minds today relative to the computer. Start a conversation relating to a computer and within a few moments someone will respond with the word "fantastic" or some expression like "it is too complicated for me to understand." To many people, a computer is visualized as a giant electronic monster possessing some sort of mysterious power and wisdom. In reality, nothing could be further from the truth. Computers are not fantastic . . . marvelous . . . awesome. They are the logical development of something that's been going on since man invented his first tool. Their greatest assets are speed and accuracy.

For all the talk about "giant brains," for all the astonishing feats that modern computers do perform, a computer is a remarkably simple machine. Almost every part in a computer has only one job to do; when the time comes for it to act, it must answer either "yes" or "no."

The coming of the computer introduced an entirely new category of data processing equipment. Until that time, the principal method of processing data had been with the use of wired control panel machines. Now, with the addition of the computer, there are two main types of data processing equipment: stored programs (computer) and external control program machines (unit record).

Although punched-card data processing was a major improvement over the preceding manual methods, it did have its serious limitations as compared to computer processing of data. The most important of the limitations are these:

1. *Communication between these specialized machines is limited.* In order to process data through several of the unit record machines, it is necessary to physically transport the cards from one machine to another. This involves the movement of large numbers of cards and also the setting up and insertion of numerous control panels.

The computer can completely process the data with a minimum of human intervention and transportation of cards. The cards are entered in one unit of the system and the desired outputs are produced automatically on one or more units of the system, all under the control of the stored program.

2. *Punched-card systems have a limited logical ability (the ability to make decisions based on conditions arising during the processing).* A complex data processing problem usually had to be solved in sections rather than in one complete continuous process.

A computer does have the logical ability to make comparisons, test the various conditions, and take the appropriate action called for by the result.

3. *Unit record equipment had one primary input record, the punched card, which provides the link between the various components of the system.*

Many different forms of input may be used in computer systems, thus providing more flexibility of processing.

4. *The data processing speed is much greater in computer processing than in punched-card data processing.*

5. *"Exception" routine processing in unit record machines usually requires manual processing.* Exception routines are those out-of-the-ordinary procedures that may arise during the processing of the data, such as invalid code numbers and incorrect format on input data. The computer can handle these conditions through the use of error routines written into the program which permit the continued processing of data while at the same time servicing the exception.

In spite of the above-mentioned limitations, punched-card data processing systems are still in use today, and will most likely be used for many years in the foreseeable future. As companies continue to expand their operations, the need for data processing increases, resulting in larger expenditures for personnel and specialized punched-card machines. At this point, the data processing efficiency declines and a study is usually initiated to consider the possibility of using the computer as a replacement for the punched-card equipment.

Data processing is a series of planned actions and operations upon information to achieve a desired result. All the necessary devices and procedures used in the operation constitute a data processing system. The computer is a major tool used for implementing the solution to data processing problems. In brief, a computer accepts data, processes data and puts out results (Fig. 5.2).

There are many computer systems. They vary in size, complexity, cost, levels of programming systems and applications; but regardless of the nature of the information to be processed, all data processing involves the following basic considerations:

1. The source data entering the system (INPUT). Input relates to the information that goes into a computer. All data—numbers, letters or symbols—must be recorded on punched cards, magnetic tape, punched paper tape or other input media (Fig. 5.3). The computer "reads" the information from these devices. Sometimes information is keyed into the computer directly through the use of a console.

2. The planned processing steps necessary to change the data into the desired result (PROCESSING). The processing operation is carried out in a pre-established system of sequenced instructions that are followed automatically by the computer. The computer without instructions from the man who uses

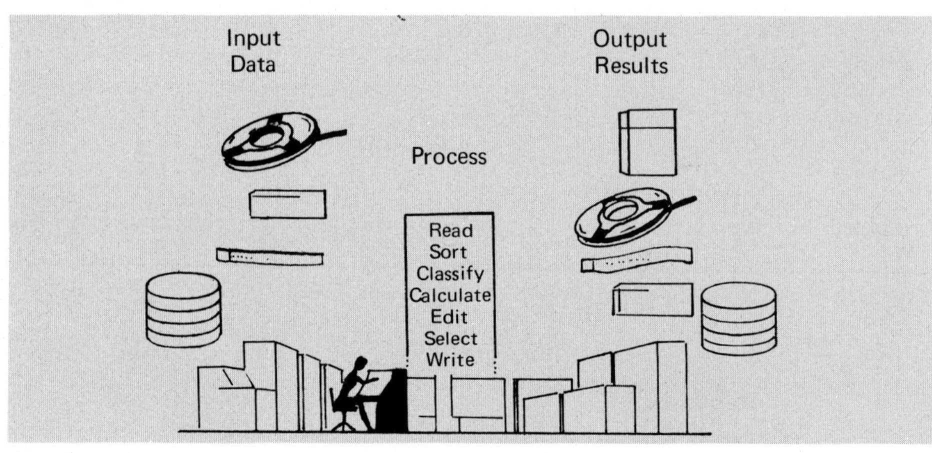

Figure 5–2. Data Processing by Computer.

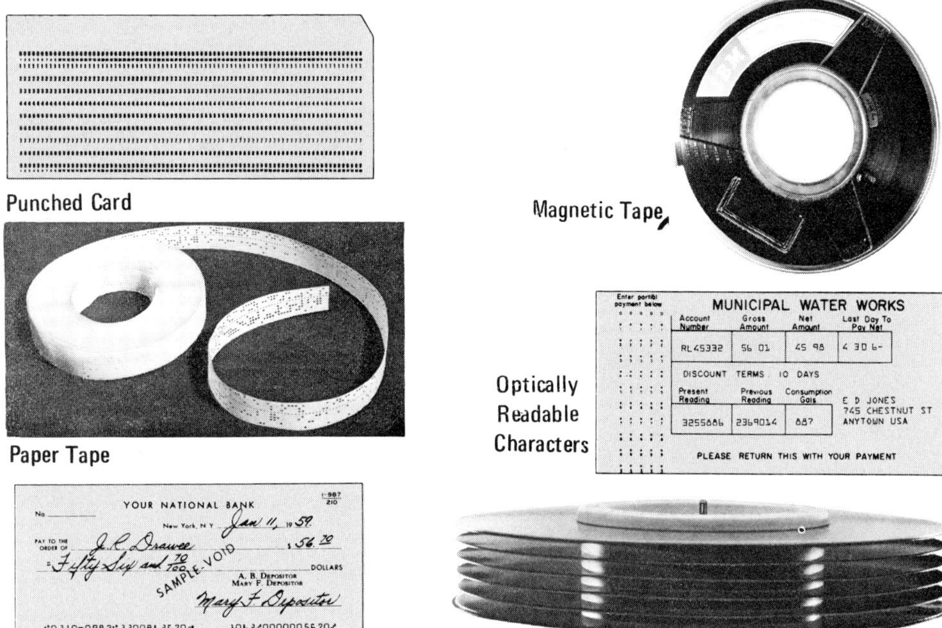

Figure 5–3. Data Recording Media.

its capabilities is worthless. The plan of processing is of human origin and involves calculations, sorting, analysis and other operations necessary to arrive at the desired solution. A series of instructions devised by man and fed into the computer and which accomplishes a particular job needed by man is called a *program*. Assembling the instructions into a logical sequence that the computer will understand is called *programming*. The man who writes the program (programmer) must know how to communicate with the computer; he must understand the computer language.

The Central Processing Unit (CPU) consists of two sections; Control Section and Arithmetic and Logical Section (discussed in greater detail in Chapter 6). The Control Section manipulates the data between core storage and the Arithmetic and Logical section according to the program. The Arithmetic and Logical Section adds, subtracts, multiplies, divides and compares data, and directs the processing unit in making decisions when it comes up against several alternate courses in the middle of a program.

The core storage unit is the computer memory and keeps original information, intermediate results, records, reference tables, and programmed instructions. Each storage location has an "address" so the computer knows where to find the information it wants. The speed of the computer is determined largely by how fast the computer can get this information out of storage and deliver it to another part of the computer.

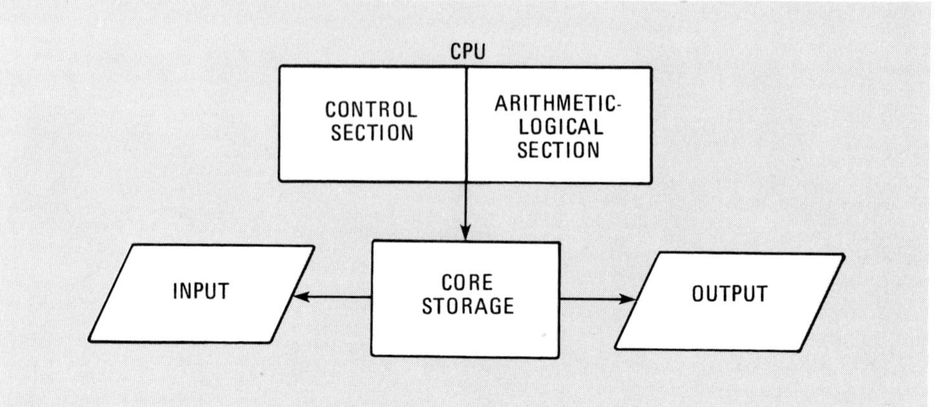

Figure 5–4. Basic Data Processing Pattern.

3. The finished result is the end product of the system (OUTPUT). Output is the end of the line. The computer delivers its processed information in pretty much the same way it was received; on punched cards, paper tape or magnetic tape. In any of these forms, the information is always available for further processing when necessary. Computers can also print out results—often at speeds too fast for the eye to follow (Fig. 5.4).

The basic elements of a computer data processing system consist of its *hardware* and *software* features. *Hardware* is defined as the physical equipment or devices of a system forming a computer and its peripheral equipment. It includes all equipment necessary for the input, processing and output functions of the system. The equipment may be directly connected to the system (online) or it may be used separately, not connected to the system (offline). A card reader would be an example of an online unit and a card punch machine would be considered an offline unit.

Software consists of the totality of programs and routines that are used to extend the capabilities of the computer, such as compilers, assemblers, routines and subroutines. The term may also apply to an application program written for a particular installation. Included are also various utility programs that are written to maintain files and records. COBOL and FORTRAN compilers and Sort/Merge programs are examples of software. Software is perhaps more important than the hardware as it extends the capabilities of the computer. Each year the growing file of software requires increasing numbers of data processing programmers skilled in the writing of software programs for all types of data processing applications.

The major hardware elements of the computer are:

1. *Input Devices*—used to enter data into the data processing system.
2. *Output Devices*—accept data from the system and record it.
3. *Central Processing Unit*—accepts the data for processing and makes results available for output devices.

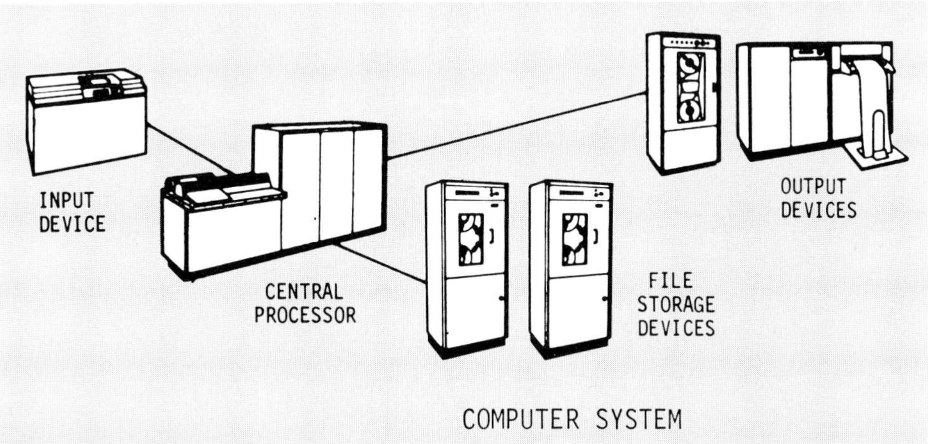

Figure 5–5. Computer System.

4. *Storage Devices*—used for temporary or permanent storage of data (Fig. 5.5).

The presentation of information to a computer system requires that the data be reduced to a set of symbols that can be read, interpreted and processed by various data processing machines. Each medium requires its own specific arrangement of symbols to represent data. The choice of the particular symbols and their meanings is a matter of convention on the part of the system designers. These symbols differ from those most commonly used by man in his daily communication in that the information presented must conform to the design and operation of the data processing equipment. A definite pattern of symbols is interpreted by the machines and provides the link between man and these specialized machines. This *machine language* thus becomes the important communication between people and data processing machines.

Information communicated to computer systems can be in the form of punched cards, paper tape, magnetic tape, magnetic ink characters, optically recognizable characters, microfilm, display screen images, magnetic disks, communication network signals, etc. It seems that each day sees a new information communication medium being announced.

Data processing systems are divided into three types of functional units: input/output devices, central processing unit and storage.

INPUT AND OUTPUT DEVICES

The data processing system requires, as part of its information handling ability, input and output devices that are linked directly to the system. These devices can enter data into and record data from the data processing system. These devices can read or sense coded data and make this information available to the computer. The data for input may be recorded in cards, in paper tape, in magnetic tape, on magnetic disks, as characters on paper documents, as line images created with a light pen.

Output devices record and write information from the computer into cards as punches, as holes in paper tape, or as magnetized spots on magnetic tape. These devices may also print information in the form of reports, generate signals for transmission over telephone lines, produce graphic displays on cathode tubes, and produce microfilm images.

The number and types of input and output devices will depend upon the design of the particular system and the type of computer used. All computer systems have conversion systems that will transcribe information from one medium to another. For example, information initially entered as punched holes in cards can be transcribed automatically to magnetized spots along the length of the magnetic tape.

An input and output device is a unit for putting or getting data out of the storage unit. The device operation is usually initiated by a program instruction that generates a command to a particular input or output device. A control unit acts as intermediary between the command and the input and output device. The control unit decodes the command and synchronizes the device with the data processing system (Fig. 5.6).

The information is read by the input medium as the record moves through the input device. The data is then converted to a computer code and transmitted to the main storage area.

The output involves the transferring of the data from the main storage area to the particular output device. The computer code must be transcribed into the individual output medium.

The input and output devices perform their functions automatically and continue to operate as directed by the program until the entire file is processed. Program instructions select the required device, direct it to read or write, and indicate the storage locations into which the data will be entered or from which the data will be taken (Fig. 5.7).

Data may be also entered directly into storage using a keyboard or switches. In this case, these input and output devices are used for manual entry directly into a computer without any medium for recording the data. The devices used are console keyboards, transmission terminals and graphic display terminals. Terminals may be used at remote locations and the information transmitted over teleprocessing lines (Fig. 5.8). No medium for recording the data is involved. Instead these terminals require some amount of internal storage for holding analyzing signals until the short message is completed or until the terminal is requested to transmit data.

CONTROL UNIT

Because of the many different types of input and output devices that can be attached to a data processing system, a unit is needed to coordinate input

Device
Device
Device
Device
Device
Device
Input Device Control Unit
Input Device Control Unit
Central Processing Unit
Core Storage
Output Device Control Unit
Device
Device
Device
Device

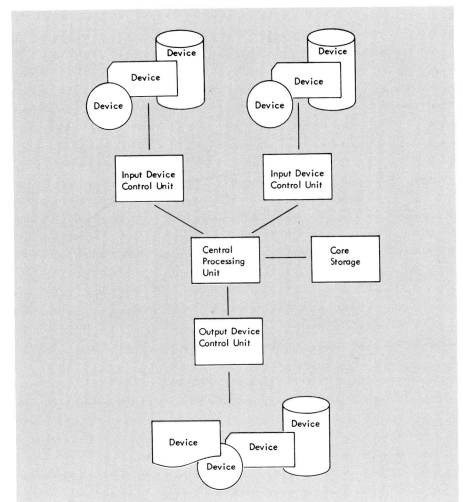

Figure 5–6. Input/Output Units in a Data Processing System.

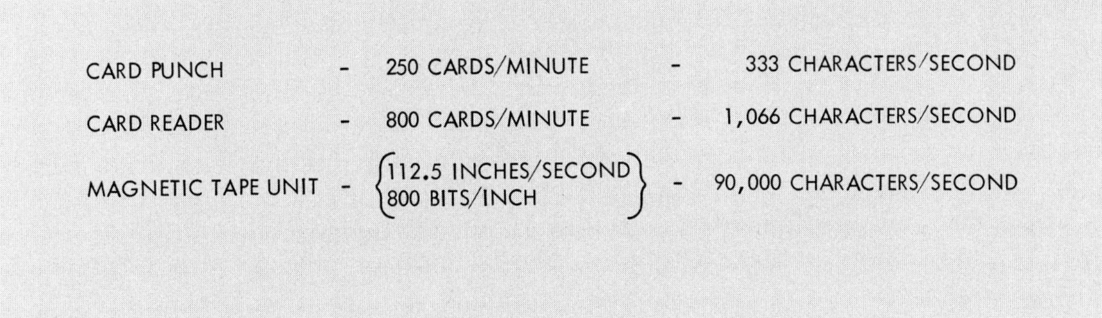

CARD PUNCH	-	250 CARDS/MINUTE	-	333 CHARACTERS/SECOND
CARD READER	-	800 CARDS/MINUTE	-	1,066 CHARACTERS/SECOND
MAGNETIC TAPE UNIT	-	{112.5 INCHES/SECOND 800 BITS/INCH}	-	90,000 CHARACTERS/SECOND

Figure 5–7. Input/Output Processing Speeds.

Figure 5–8.
Terminal Operation.

and output operations with the central processing unit. The control unit performs this function in acting as a traffic policeman, directing information to the various input and output devices as they are read into the system or outputted by the system.

The control unit determines the priority of servicing and signaling device identification when requesting service for the input device.

CHANNEL

A channel is a separate piece of equipment devoted exclusively to managing the input and output control units and devices assigned to it. Once the channel has been activated it carries out its own program, independent of the central processing unit. This permits the overlapping of input and output operations and computer processing. Sometimes this is performed in an interweaving pattern working with several input/output control units at one time and maintaining the proper destinations for storage allocation (input) or the control unit and device (output) (Fig. 5.9).

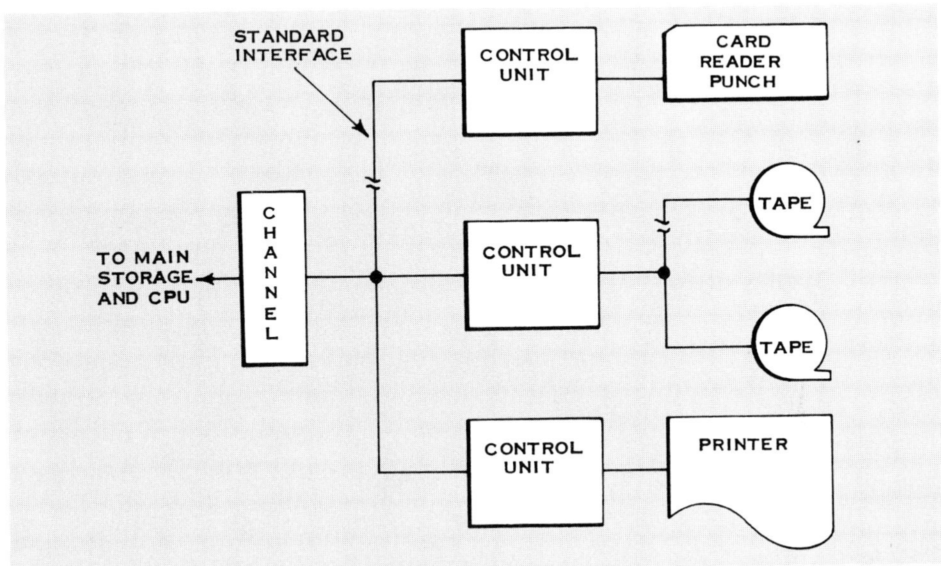

Figure 5–9. Channel Organization.

The channel operates in the same manner as the central processing unit to the extent that it is free to step through its commands (starting and terminating input/output operations). The channel serves as an intermediary input/output device, constantly switching the various input/output operations to make the most efficient use of the time not only by overlapping operations of input and output units, but by doing so without tying up the central processing unit.

The channel thus performs the important function of permitting the simultaneous operation processing of input/output devices with the computer processing of data (Fig. 5.10).

BUFFERS

The efficiency of any data processing system can be increased to that degree to which input, output and internal data handling operations can be overlapped and allowed to occur simultaneously (Fig. 5.11). The usefulness of a computer is directly related to the speed at which it can complete a given procedure. To accomplish this, the Central Processing Unit must be used to its full capacity. The speed of input/output units should be so arranged that the CPU (Central Processing Unit) is always kept busy.

Input is divided into specific units or logical combinations of data that enter storage under the control of the program. A number of output results

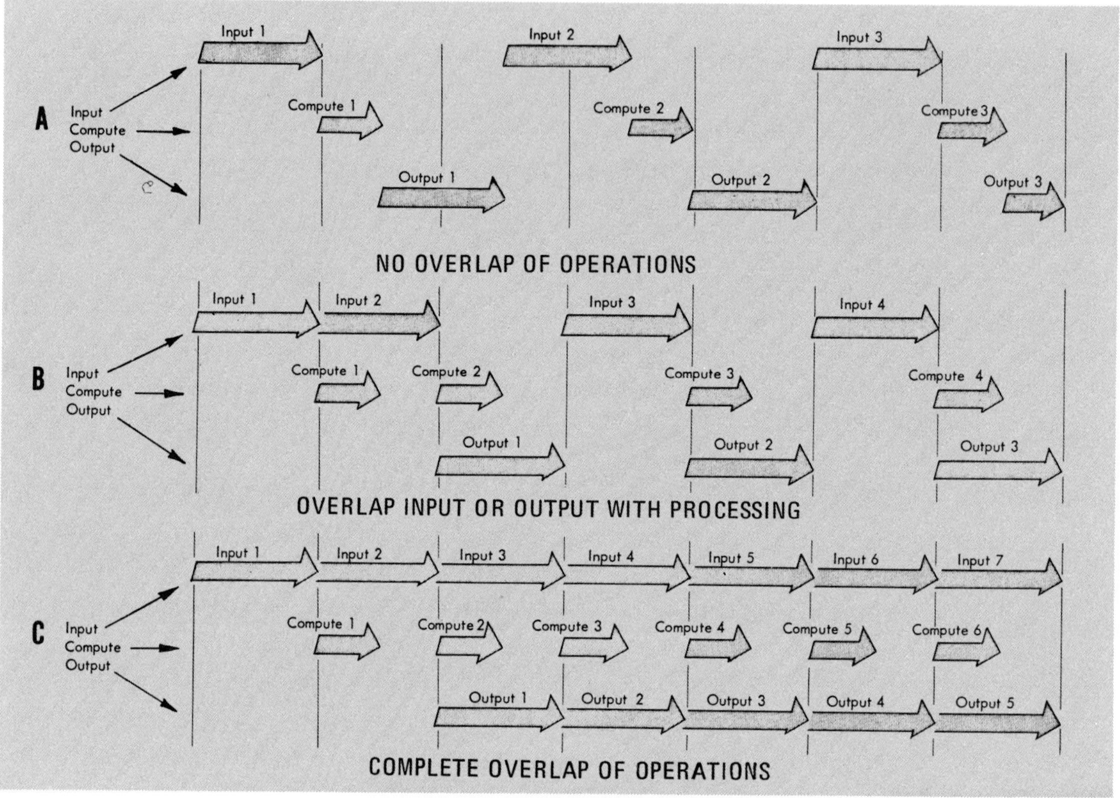

Figure 5–10. Channel Processing.

can be developed from a single input or conversely several input units can be combined to form one output unit. Inefficiency can result if processing is suspended during the reading and writing operations.

To synchronize the processing of input/output operations and to provide an overlap of operations, a buffering system is used. Data is entered first into an external unit known as a buffer. When information is requested by the program, it is transferred to main storage in a fraction of the time necessary to read the information from the unit directly. Likewise output information is assembled in the buffer unit while the Central Processing Unit is computing or manipulating the data. Processed data can be placed in these buffers at high speed. The output device proceeds to write the data while the CPU is free to continue its processing.

Large computer systems have many buffers and buffering techniques to overlap the processing operations with the many input/output devices attached to the system.

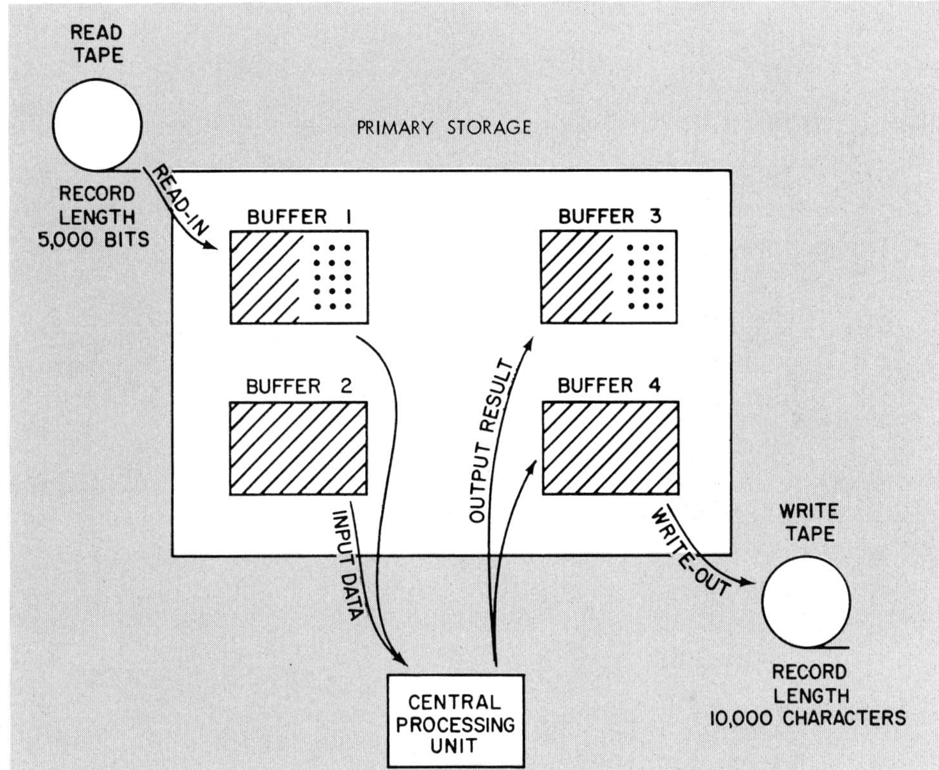

Figure 5–11. Buffer Operation.

CARD READING AND PUNCHING DEVICES

The punched card is the most common medium for communication with the data processing machines. Data is recorded in a pattern of small rectangular holes punched in specified locations to represent numerals, alphabetic characters and special characters. The special characters may be $. % # or other symbols commonly used in data processing applications (Fig. 5.12). A card reader (input) interprets the pattern of holes in the card and automatically converts the data into electronic impulses, thereby entering the information into the machine. The information can also be punched into a card (output) through the use of an automatic card punch. Thus the card can be used as original data and as a common medium of exchange of information between the machines.

ADVANTAGES OF PUNCHED CARDS

The use of punched cards provides the following advantages:

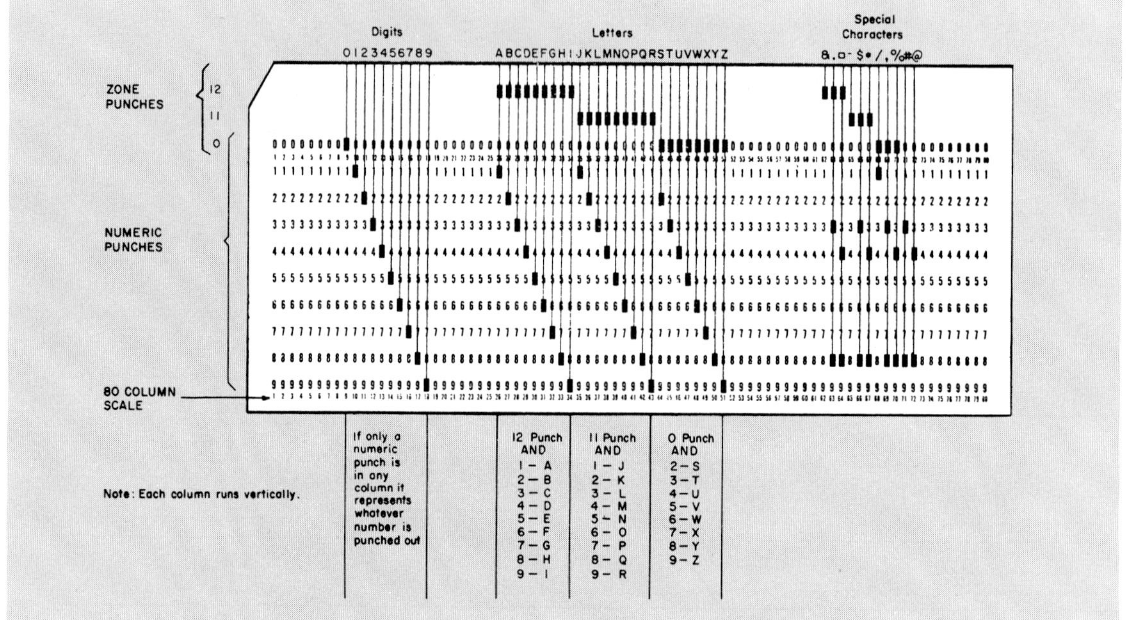

Figure 5–12. Hollerith Coded Punched Card.

1. The standardized card format used can be combined with other media in efficient data processing operations.
2. The cards may be stored in an external file for future processing or for visual reference.
3. The cards may be processed through unit record as well as other data processing equipment.
4. The necessary information concerning a single transaction is usually recorded in a single card.
5. The punched card can be used as an original document—checks, time cards, invoices, etc.
6. The punched card can serve as a communication between the computer and the user programs in the form of job control cards and also as test media for the various computer programs.

DISADVANTAGES OF PUNCHED CARDS

Some of the important disadvantages of punched-card processing are:

1. The limitation of eighty columns for information.
2. The relatively slow input and output access time to computer systems.
3. Cards may not be bent, mutilated or damaged in any manner.

4. Large storage areas are required to store cards. Card file cabinets, racks, trays, can represent a sizable investment in equipment.
5. Because of the bulkiness of cards, transporting them from one location to another can be a problem.
6. Standardized card fields limit the flexibility of operations.

CARD READERS

Card reading devices introduce punched-card records into a data processing system (Fig. 5.13). The cards move past a reading unit that converts the data into a machine-processable electronic format. Two types of reading units are available: reading brushes and photoelectric cells (Fig. 5.14).

Figure 5–13. Card Read Punch.

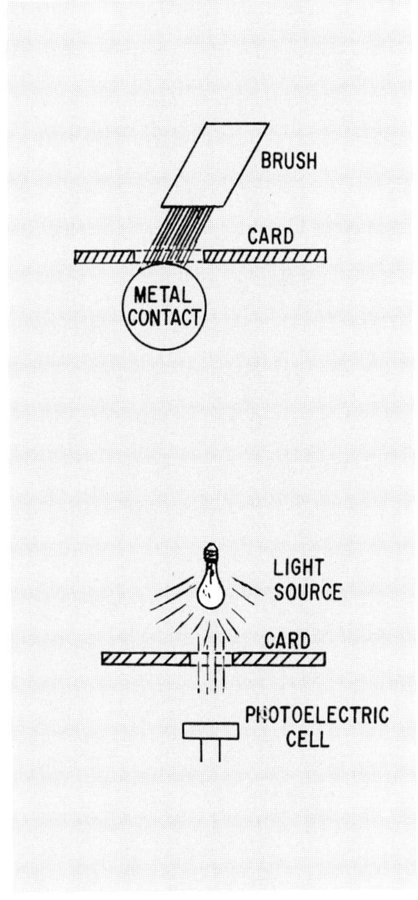

Figure 5–14.
Card Reading Methods.

In the brush type reader, the cards are mechanically moved from the card hopper past the reading brushes that electrically sense the presence or absence of holes in each column of the punched card. The card then proceeds to a card stacker in the same sequence. The electronic sensing converts the information in the card into electrical impulses that can be detected by the card reader circuitry and later stored as data (Fig. 5.15). Some readers have two sets of reading brushes. As a check on the reading, the card can be read twice with the second reading checking the validity of the first reading.

The photoelectric type of card reader acts in the same manner as the brush type; the basic difference is in the method of sensing the holes. As the punched card is read, photoelectric cells are activated by the presence of light as the light source passes over the punched card. There is one cell for each column of the card.

The speed of card reading devices will vary from 12 cards to 1,000 cards per minute depending on the particular type of card reader.

CARD PUNCHES

The output from a data processing system can be punched into a card by a card-punching device. This is the slowest manner of getting information out of a computer except for typewriter output, but is often used when the information is to be stored in cards for subsequent processing. Blank cards are automatically fed into the punch unit one at a time from the card hopper. A punching mechanism punches data into the card as it receives the information

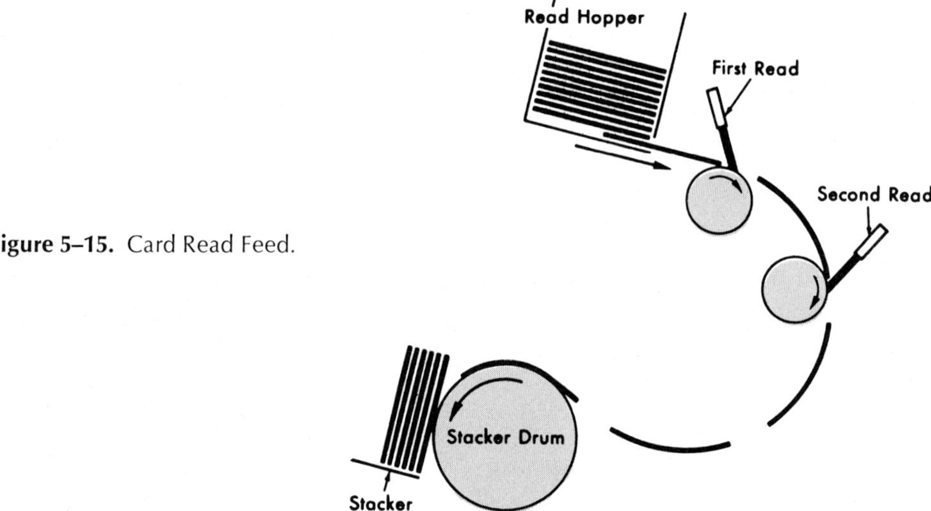

Figure 5–15. Card Read Feed.

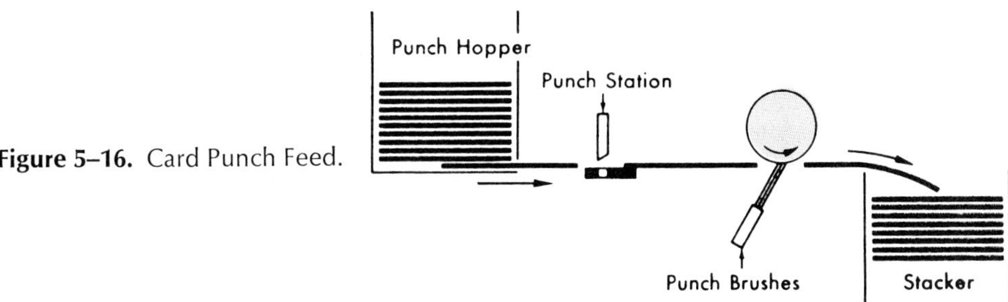

Figure 5–16. Card Punch Feed.

from storage of the computer. After the card is punched, it is moved to a checking station where the data is read and checked against the information that was received at the punching station (Fig. 5.16).

The speed of the card punch varies from 12 to 500 cards per minute depending upon the type of card-punch machine used.

MAGNETIC TAPE DEVICES

Magnetic tape is the basic ingredient for the fastest method of entry of data into a computer system. It is the principal input/output recording media. Its primary uses are for storing intermediate results of calculations and for compact storage of large files of data. In addition to its high speed entry, magnetic tape offers efficient, extremely fast recording of processed data. Up to 640,000 numerical characters per second can be read from or written onto a tape.

The magnetic tape operates in the same manner as a home tape recorder. A read/write head accomplishes the actual reading and writing of the information on the tape. The symbols are recorded as a series of magnetized areas called bits arranged in a specific pattern along the length of the tape (Fig. 5.17). The recordings can be retained indefinitely and reused many times

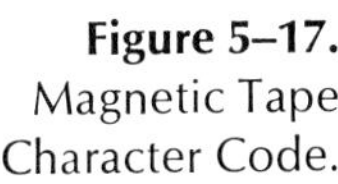

Figure 5–17. Magnetic Tape Character Code.

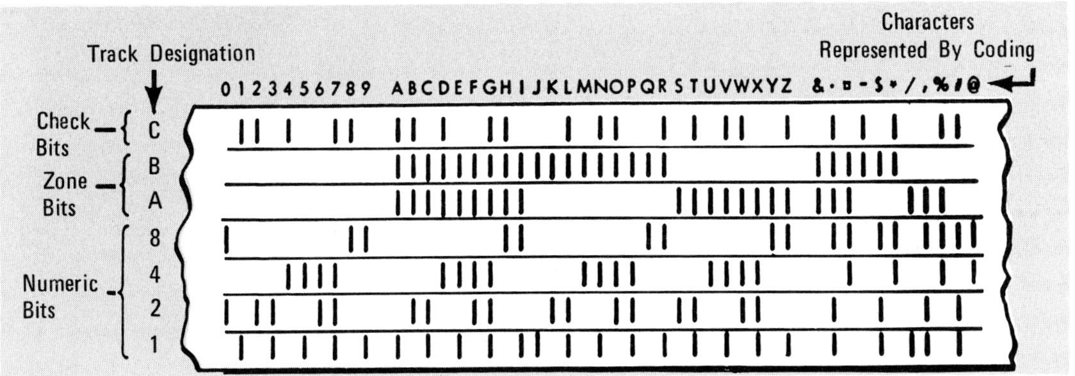

with continued high reliability. The information on the tape is automatically erased by a new recording superimposed in the area. This is known as "destructive read in."

The tape, ½-inch wide, is supplied in lengths up to 2,400 feet per reel (Fig. 5.18). It can be easily handled and stored. Simplified automatic threading and high speed rewind decreases the processing time of magnetic tape. One inch of tape can store the contents of many cards (Fig. 5.19).

The tape is recorded in character densities of up to 1,600 characters per inch. The spacing between the vertical rows is automatically generated during the write operation (Fig. 5.20). Records are recorded in blocks separated by a space called the interblock gap (formerly referred to as the interword gap).

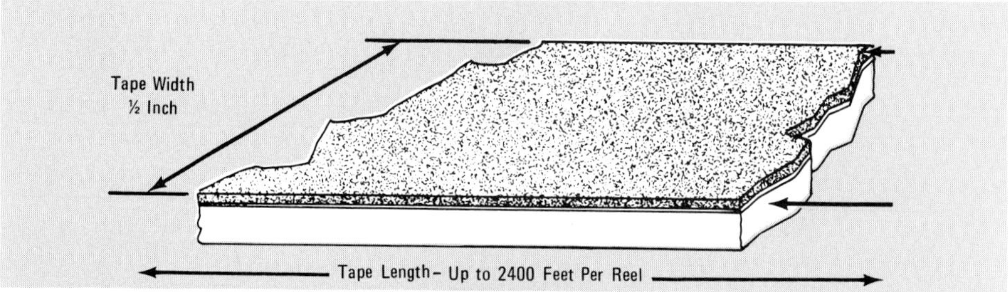

Figure 5–18. Magnetic Tape Composition.

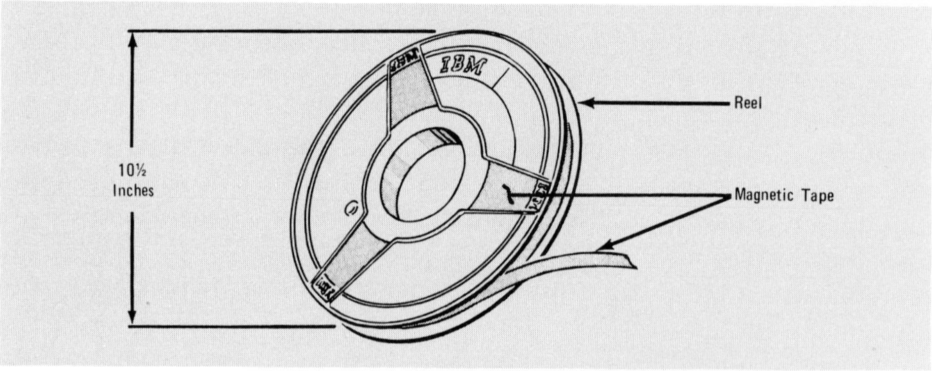

Tape Width ½ Inch

Tape Length– Up to 2400 Feet Per Reel

Figure 5–19. Reel of Magnetic Tape.

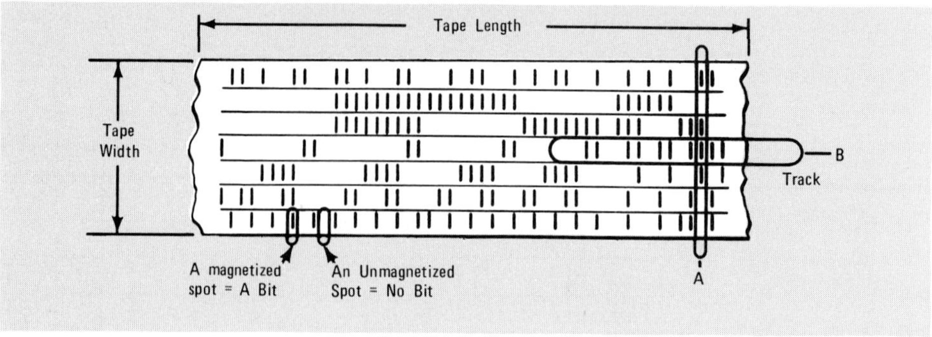

10½ Inches

Reel

Magnetic Tape

Figure 5–20. Data Coded on a Section of Magnetic Tape.

Tape Length

Tape Width

Track

B

A

A magnetized spot = A Bit

An Unmagnetized Spot = No Bit

ADVANTAGES OF MAGNETIC TAPE

1. High speed input and output recording media.
2. Records not limited in size; can be as long or as short as needed.
3. Intermediate results can be stored on tape for subsequent processing.
4. Compact storage for large files of information.
5. High reliability of reading and recording due to many self-checking accuracy features.
6. Compact size assures ease of transport.
7. Many tape units can be used simultaneously with computer.
8. Errors can be corrected merely by writing corrected information over areas containing errors.
9. Available in different densities and lengths to serve individual processing needs.
10. Relative low cost of information storage.

DISADVANTAGES OF MAGNETIC TAPE

1. Sequential reading makes it necessary for each record to be examined in order to locate the desired record. This type of processing can be wasteful as the tape will have frequent stops, starts and rewinds.
2. Magnetic tape is affected by physical elements such as dust, humidity, heat, etc., which can affect the recording of the magnetized data on the tape.
3. Information can be lost if the tape is broken, despite the splicing done. The greater the density of the tape, the more information that can be destroyed.
4. A tape that is wound too tightly may cause a "bleed-through" on another part of the tape. Some of the information of one section could thus be printed on another portion of the tape within the reel. Frequent rewinding of the tape could prevent some of the "bleeding" problems.

High speed data processing demands high speed input and output devices so that the system operations are not slowed by waiting for data or by an inability to get processed data out of a computer. Magnetic tape units, with their dual capacity of input/output and storage, have provided the increased speed necessary to transmit the data to and from the computer and at the same time have provided increased storage capacity for data.

All magnetic tape units are basically the same but design improvements have increased the tape applications and provided easier operating methods. The tape unit moves past a recording head in a continuous movement at a constant rate of speed. During the reading and writing operations, the tape is constantly in motion. A full tape reel holding 2,400 feet of half-inch wide tape weighs about four pounds, and contains the equivalent of information contained in approximately 400,000 fully punched cards.

Before tape units can read or write, they must be prepared for operation (Fig. 5-21). Two tape reels are mounted on the unit and the tape is threaded through the tape transport mechanism. The head assembly can be separated for ease of threading and it is then closed to make contact with the read/write heads for the reading and writing of the tape.

During the operation, the tape moves from the file reel through the left vacuum column across the read/write head, through the right vacuum column to the machine reel. The purpose of the loop in each vacuum column is to act as a buffer to prevent high speed stops and starts from snapping the tape (Fig. 5.22). Some tape units are vertical vacuum columns while others use horizontal columns. Vacuum activated switches in the column control clutches permit two reels of tape to rotate independently. The file reel feeds the tape when the loop reaches the minimum reserve length in the left vacuum column and the machine reel winds the tape when the loop reaches a point near the bottom of the right vacuum column.

Tape may be rewound or backspaced to the beginning of the reel. Rewind speeds are as high as 500 inches per second. The loading of the tape reel cartridge is accomplished automatically after the cartridge is placed on the drive by the operator. The time-consuming manual threading involved in the original loading of the tape has been eliminated.

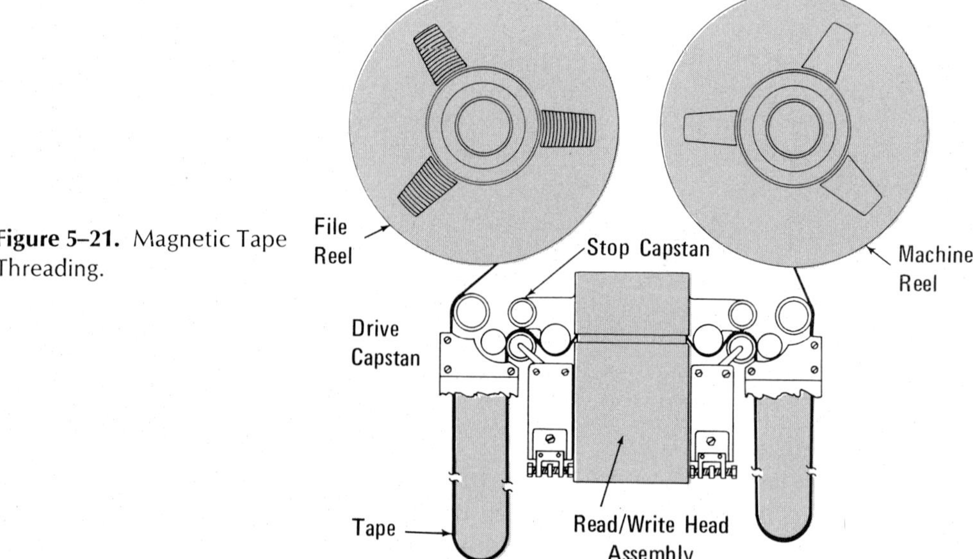

Figure 5–21. Magnetic Tape Threading.

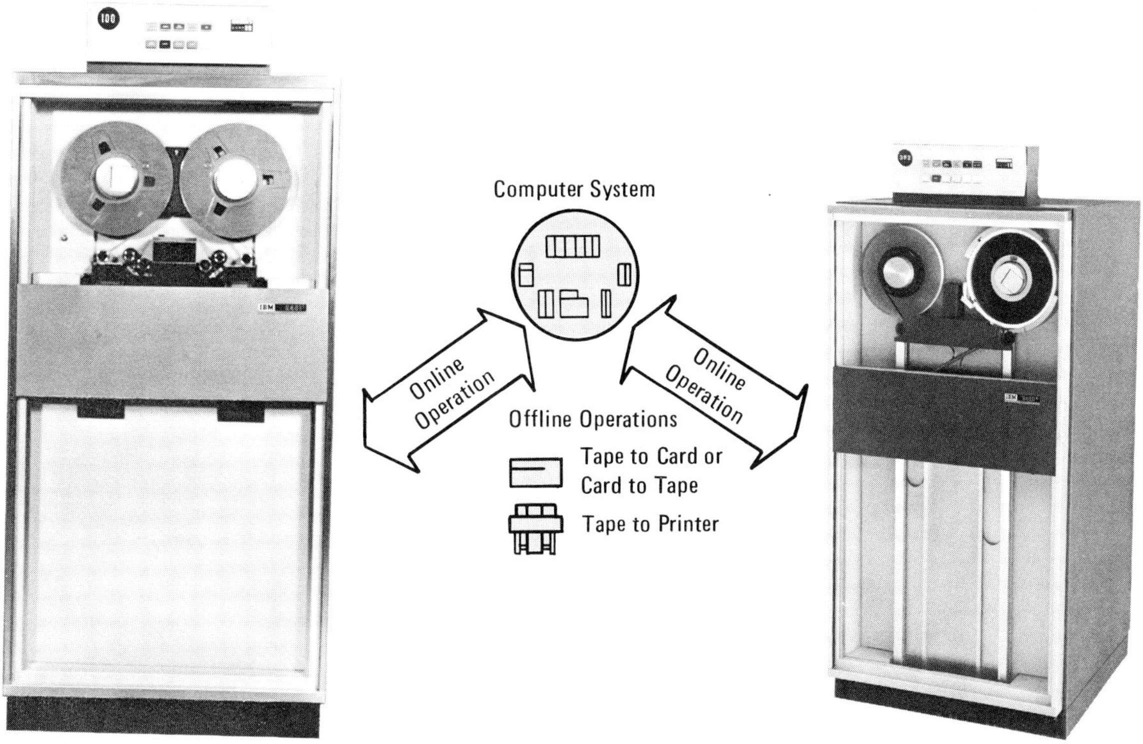

Figure 5–22. Magnetic Tape Operation.

READING/WRITING ON MAGNETIC TAPE

The magnetic tape unit reads or writes the data as the tape moves past the read/write head (Fig. 5.23). The writing on magnetic tape is destructive in that the new information erases the old (destructible) information on the tape. A tape may be read repeatedly with the information on the tape remaining unaltered (Figs. 5.24, 5.25). Reading therefore is nondestructive.

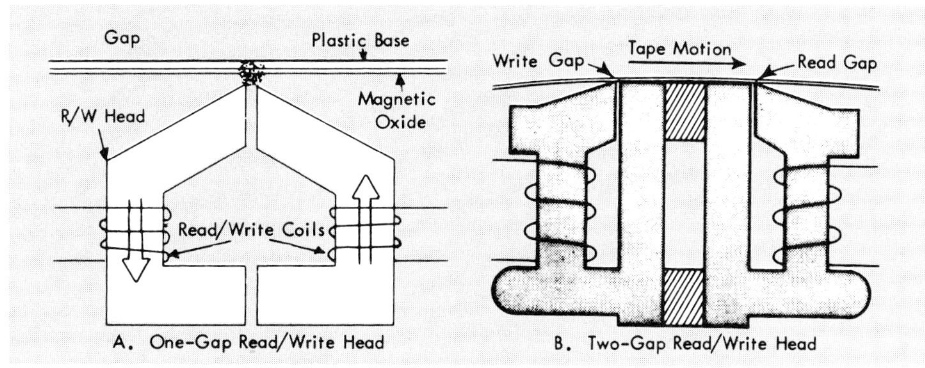

Figure 5–23. Magnetic Tape Read/Write Heads.

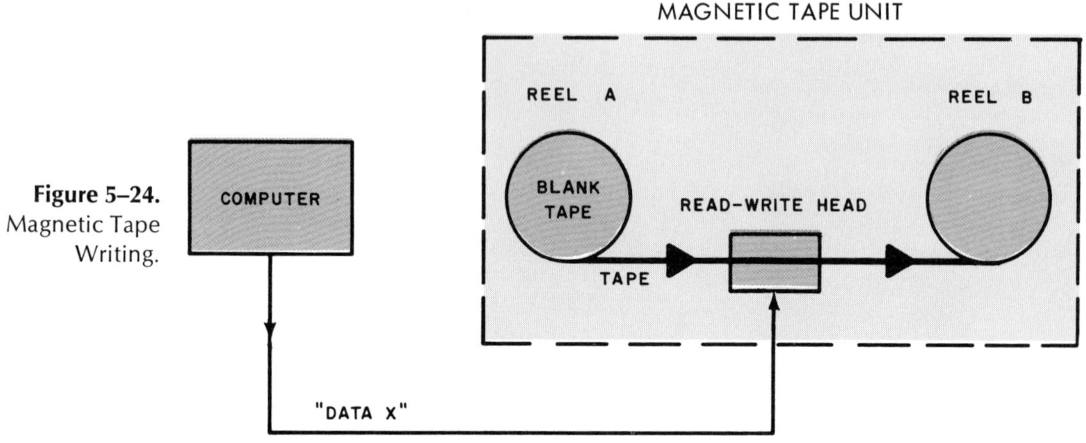

Figure 5–24. Magnetic Tape Writing.

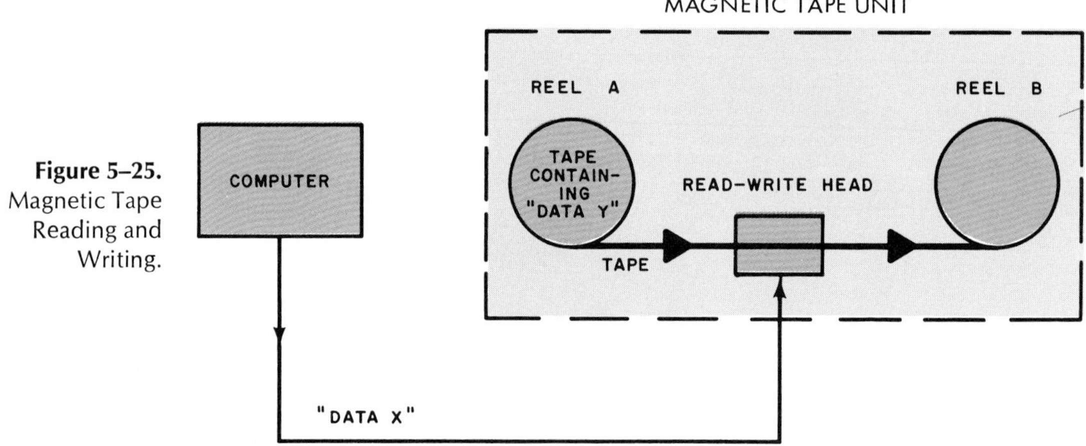

Figure 5–25. Magnetic Tape Reading and Writing.

Information is written in tape by magnetizing areas in parallel tracks along the length of the tape (Fig. 5.26). Data recorded in tape must be checked for accuracy so that any information errors are not transmitted through the system. The data is checked to insure that only valid characters are recorded and also to verify that the recorded bits are of effective magnetic strength. A *parity check* is made as the information is read from a magnetic tape. A character code check (vertical) is made on each column of information to ensure that an even number of bits is detected for each character read. If an odd number of bits is detected for any character, an error is indicated unless the computer operates in odd parity; then the reverse would be true (Fig. 5-27).

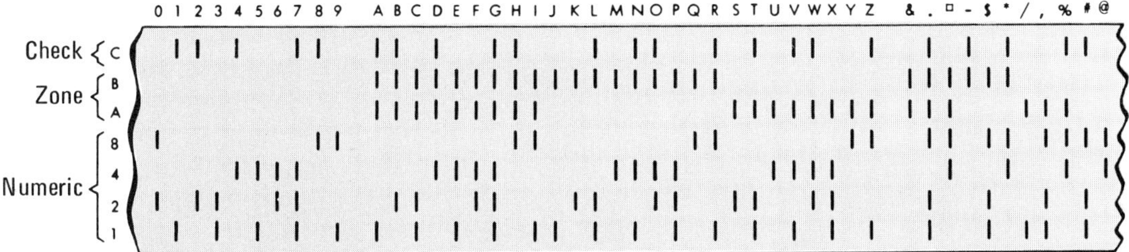

Figure 5–26. Magnetic Tape Characters.

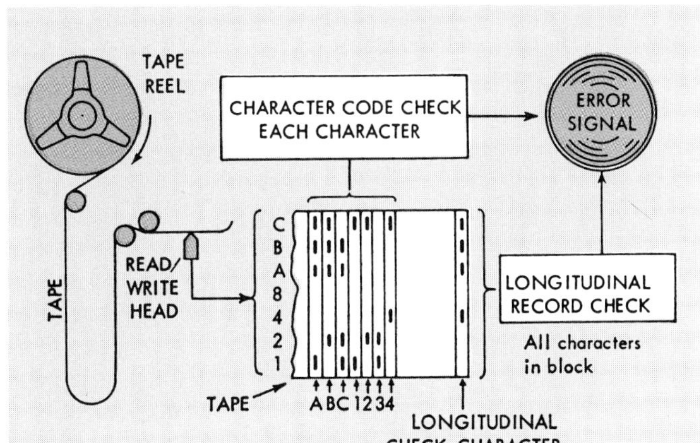

Figure 5–27. Seven-Track Validity Checking.

MAGNETIC TAPE RECORDS

Records on tape are not restricted to any fixed record size of characters, words or blocks. They may be of any size within the limits of the particular computer.

Blocks of records (which may be a single record or several records) are separated on the tape by an interblock gap, a length of blank tape averaging about .6 in. to .75 in. This gap is automatically produced at the end of each block of records during the writing of a tape. During the reading, the block begins with the first character sensed after the gap and continues the reading without interruption until the next gap is reached. The interblock gap provides the necessary time for starting and stopping the tape between blocks of records. The end of a file of records is indicated by a tapemark, which is written and read by most computers (Fig. 5.28).

The major performing consideration among tape units is the speed at which the tape is moved across the read/write head and the recording density of the data on the tape.

The total time required to read a record must include time to space over the gap. Access time for tape units is based on the tape speed plus the length

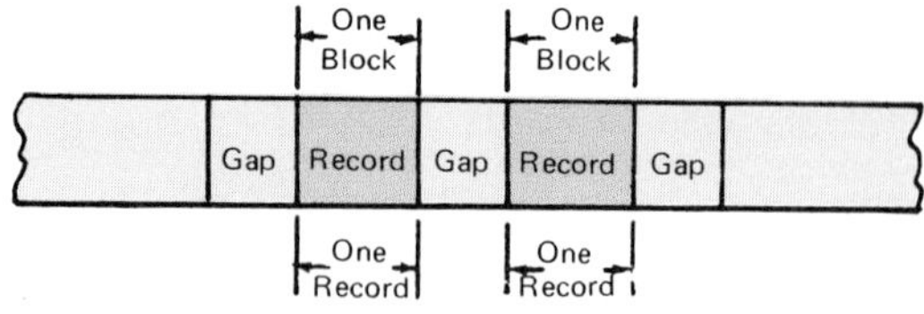

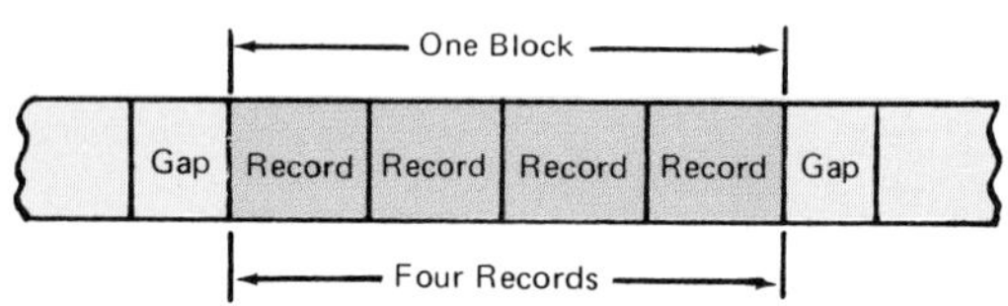

On magnetic tape, a single unit or block of information is marked by an interblock gap before and after the data. A record block may contain one record or several.

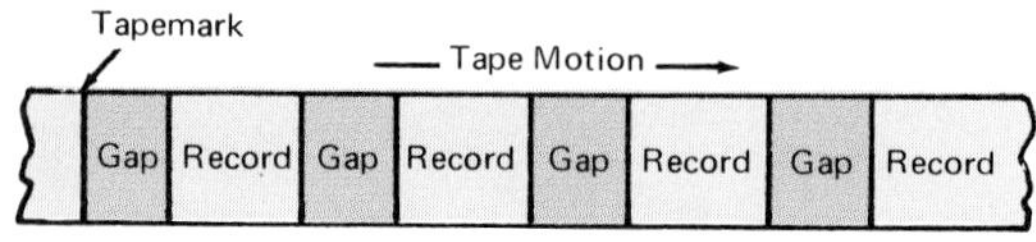

The interblock gap followed by a unique character record is used to mark the end of a file of information. The unique character, a tapemark, is generated in response to an instruction and is written on the tape following the last record of the file.

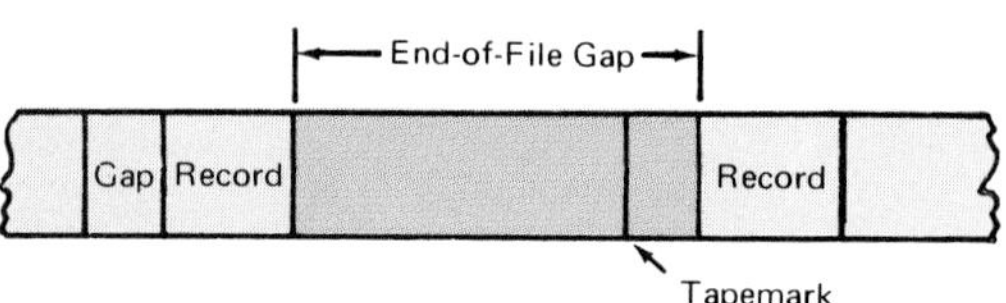

Figure 5–28. Magnetic Tape Records.

of the interblock gap. Access time is an important factor in determining the actual or effective character rate of a tape unit.

Blank space must be provided at the beginning and ending of a reel to allow threading through the feed mechanism. A reflective strip called a marker is usually placed at the beginning and ending of the tape to enable the photoelectric cells in the tape unit to sense the loadpoint (where the reading or writing is to begin), see Figure 5.29, or the end-of-reel marker where the writing is to stop. The tape unit does not recognize the end-of-reel marker when reading the tape; a tapemark written on the tape signals an end-of-reel condition.

Figure 5–29. Loadpoint Marker.

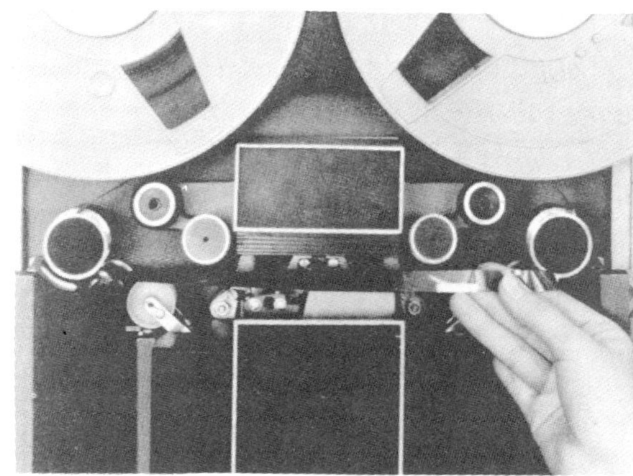

Figure 5–30. File Protection Devices.

On noncartridge tape, the file protection device is a plastic ring that fits into a round groove molded in the tape reel. When the ring is in place, either reading or writing can occur. When the ring is removed, writing is suppressed and only reading can take place; thus, the file is protected from accidental erasure.

Because of the destructive read-in feature of the write operation, it is wise to use a file protection device ring to prevent the accidental erasure of information that is to be saved for future reference. This device is a plastic ring that fits into a round groove molded in the tape reel. When the ring is in place, either reading or writing can occur. When the ring is removed, writing is suppressed and only reading can take place; thus the file is protected from accidental erasure (Fig. 5.30).

PAPER TAPE DEVICES

Paper tape serves the same purpose as punched cards. It is a continuous recording medium compared to the eighty-character limit of punched cards. The tape can be used to record data in records of any length limited only by the storage media into which the data is to be placed or from which the data is received. The data is recorded as a special arrangement of punched holes along the length of the tape.

A paper tape reader interprets the data (input) and a paper tape punch (output) punches holes in the paper tape. The data is recorded (punched) and read as holes in channels along the length of the tape. The tape is classified according to the number of channels. One column, similar to punched cards, is used to represent characters either alphabetic, numeric or special. The eight-channel tape is the most commonly used. The lower four channels (excluding feed holes) are labeled 8, 4, 2, 1 and are used to represent numeric values of characters. The sum of the values indicates the number value; for example, a combination of 1 and 4 is used to represent a numeric five.

The X and O channels are similar to zone punches of punched cards.

These punches combined with the numeric values are used to form alphabetic and special characters. A check hole must be present for any channel whose basic code consists of an even number of holes. This technique is used to check that each character is recorded correctly in the tape with an odd number of holes (Fig. 5.31).

ADVANTAGES OF PAPER TAPE

1. Paper tape can be used to transport data long distances over telephone or telegraph wires to produce a duplicate tape at the other end.
2. Punched cards can be converted to punched tape at the other end of

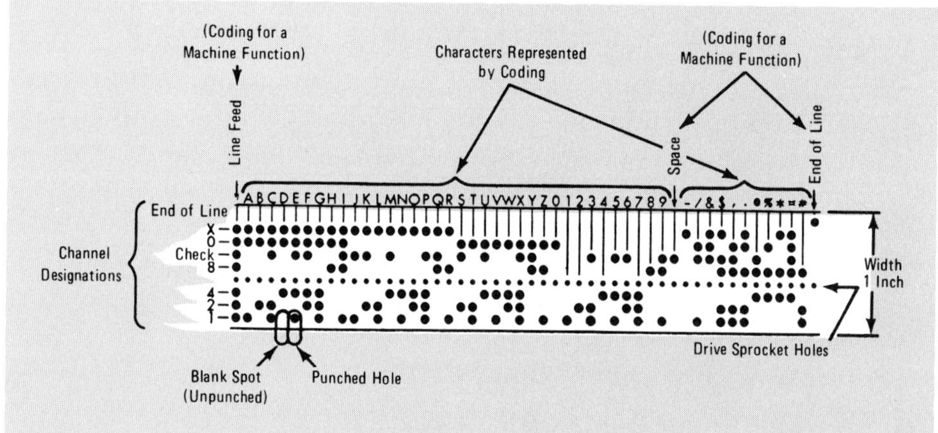

Figure 5–31. Paper Tape Coding.

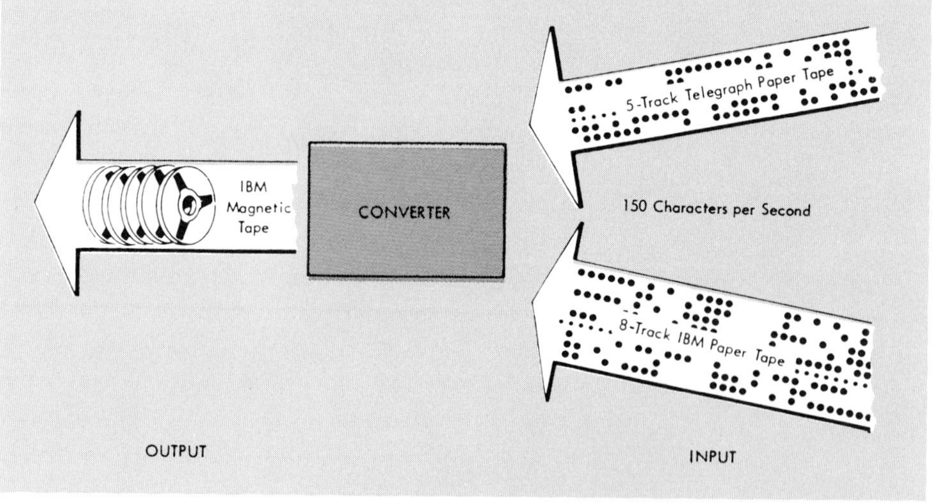

Figure 5–32. Data Conversion—Paper Tape to Magnetic Tape.

the wire and later reconverted to punched cards on magnetic tape for processing (Fig. 5.32).
3. Paper tape, neither as heavy nor as bulky as punched cards, is easy to transport and mail.
4. Paper tape is cheaper to produce (twenty-five cents per 100 feet).
5. Paper tape can be produced as a by-product of another operation; for example, a summary of cash register receipts can be punched in a paper tape and submitted to the data processing unit for processing.
6. The paper tape is not limited in record size as are punched cards.
7. The paper tape can be read into and out of a computer at a greater rate of speed than punched cards.

DISADVANTAGES OF PAPER TAPE

1. As compared to other input media (magnetic tape), paper tape is rather slow.
2. Paper tape is not as durable as punched cards.
3. The data in paper tape must be converted to another form before the information can be manipulated.
4. The data in paper tape cannot be altered without punching another tape.

Originally developed for transmitting telegraphic messages over wire, paper tape is now extensively used for data processing communications as well. For long distance transmission, the machines convert the information punched in cards and keyboard strokes to paper tape, then send the information over telephone or telegraph wires to produce a duplicate paper tape at the other end. The information is then reconverted and punched into cards for further processing.

Paper tape may also be punched as a by-product of a cash register. As the register is recording the cash receipts, the information is being summarized and is being punched into a paper tape that is mailed to a central data processing center for further processing. A flexowriter typewriter can also be used to punch a tape at the same time that the information is being typed on a "hard copy." Later this tape can be transmitted to the computer center for entry into the data processing system. Many additional uses for paper tape are being developed constantly.

The data punched in the paper tape is read or interpreted by a paper tape reader and recorded by a paper tape punch.

PAPER TAPE READER

The paper tape reader reads the punched holes in five-, six-, seven-, or eight-channel tapes at a rate of up to 1,000 characters per second. As the tape is moved or fed past a reading unit, the absence or presence of holes in the tape is sensed and converted to electronic impulses acceptable to the computer. Built-in self-checking devices such as the parity check are part of the checking features. The speed of reading varies from 150 to 1,000 characters per second depending on the type of reader and length of records (Fig. 5.33).

For faster tape input to the data processing system, the data may be converted to magnetic tape in an offline device at a speed of 150 paper tape characters per second. The recorded tape may be then placed on a magnetic tape unit and read into the system at high rate magnetic tape input speeds.

Figure 5–33. IBM 2671 Paper Tape Reader and 2822 Tape Reader Control.

PAPER TAPE PUNCH

As the data is received from main storage, it is converted to tape code and is punched into a blank tape as the tape moves past the punching mechanism. Self-checking circuitry is built in. The tape is punched at a density of 10 characters per inch at rates of 15 and 150 characters per second depending upon model punch (Fig. 5.34).

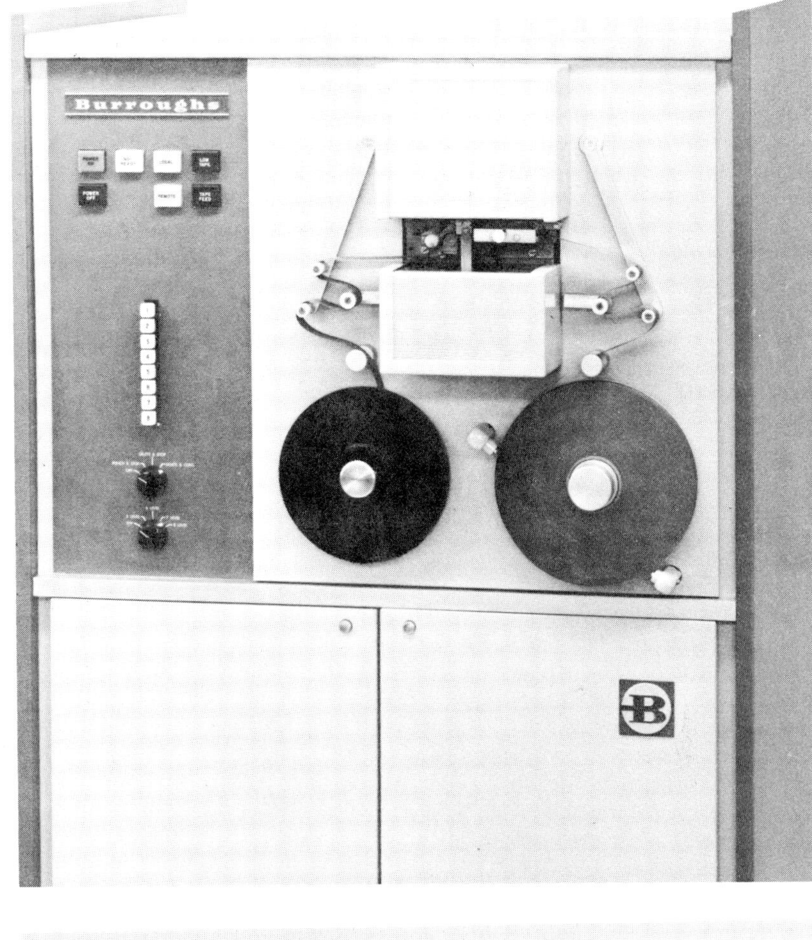

Figure 5–34.
Paper Tape Punch.

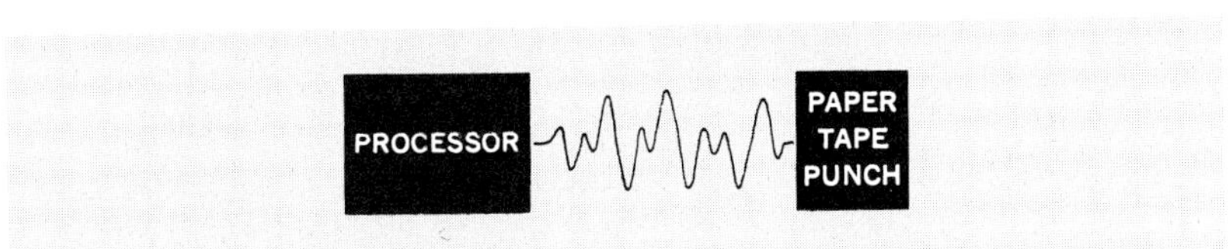

MAGNETIC INK CHARACTER RECOGNITION DEVICES

Machine-recognizable characters are printed on a paper document by a machine. The paper document may be of random size. This created language is readable by both man and machine. The shape of the characters permits the easy visualization by man and the special magnetic ink permits the same interpretation by the machine (Fig. 5.35). This information can be entered

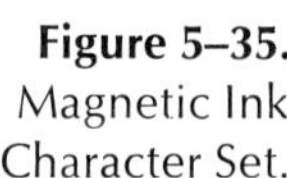

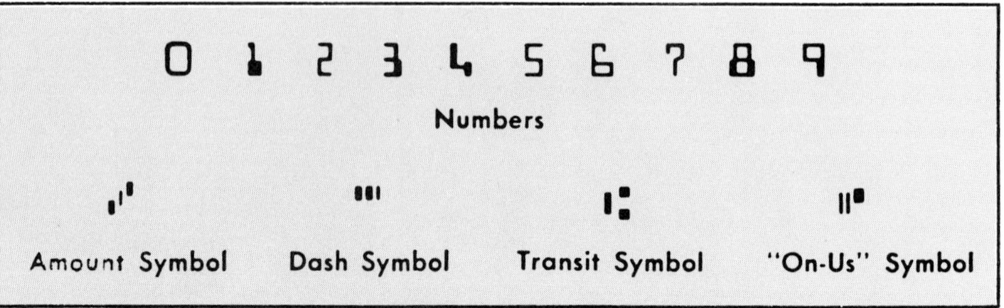

Figure 5–35. Magnetic Ink Character Set.

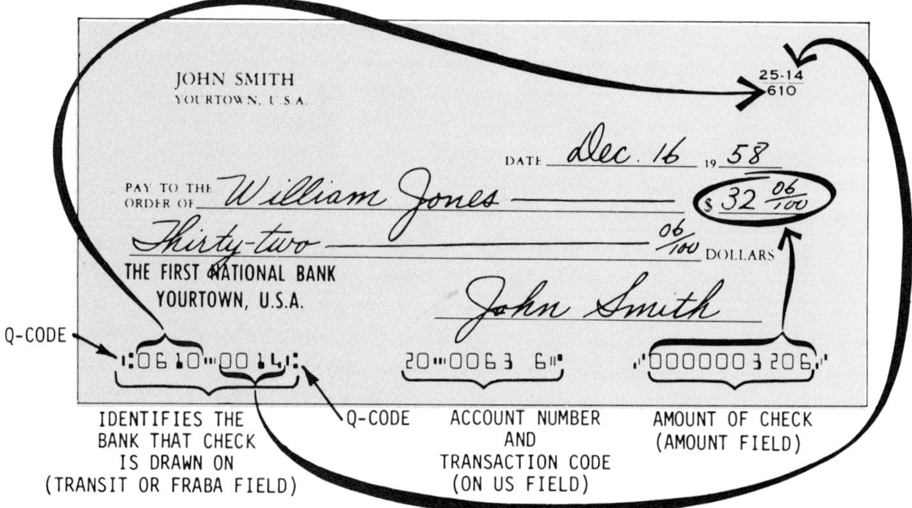

Figure 5–36. Sample Check with MICR Encoding.

directly into a data processing system without any further transcribing. These readers are used extensively in banking operations and are directly responsible for the wide use of checks in the consumer world (Fig. 5.36). These machines have the capability of reading card and paper documents at a relatively high rate of speed. In addition, these documents can be sorted in offline operations. There are many built-in validity checking devices to assure the accuracy of the readings.

These time-saving methods of recording and processing large volumes of data have greatly reduced the costs of checking operations for banks, thereby vastly increasing the use of checks in all phases of business operations.

ADVANTAGES OF MAGNETIC INK CHARACTER READERS

1. Have the ability to read paper documents directly and enter the information into a data processing system.

2. Timesaving in processing large quantities of paper documents.
3. Are able to sort documents at a high rate of speed.
4. Characters readable by both man and machine.

DISADVANTAGES OF MAGNETIC INK CHARACTER READERS

1. Magnetic ink must be inscribed properly, otherwise data will be read incorrectly.
2. Torn or otherwise mutilated paper documents cannot be read by the reader. The documents must be manually entered into the system.
3. Information read cannot be transferred over communication lines.

MAGNETIC INK CHARACTER READERS

These machines read card and paper documents inscribed with magnetic ink characters. The shape of this character permits easy recognition, visualization and interpretation. The special magnetic ink is read by the reader and interpreted for the system.

As the document is being read, the reader examines the shape of each magnetic ink character passing under the read head, and ten data channels send signals to an electronic storage device called the character matrix (Fig. 5.37). After the entire character area has passed under the read head and all segments have been read, a pattern of the character shape in the character matrix is made as a configuration of 0 bits and 1 bits. To verify the accuracy of the processed data, the reader automatically checks each character as it is being read. When the reader determines that the character read is valid, it stores the character in the computer. If the machine determines that the pattern is invalid, an error signal is indicated.

Another important feature of magnetic ink character readers is their ability to sort magnetically inscribed documents in offline operations. As many as 1,200 documents can be sorted in one minute.

OPTICAL CHARACTER RECOGNITION DEVICES

Another method of representing data in paper documents for input to a data processing system is to use optically readable characters (Fig. 5.38). Optical character readers can read upper case letters, numbers, and certain special characters from printed paper documents and enter the data into a computer system. Printed reports produced on computer printers can also be read by the optical character reader. Printed paper tape from cash registers and adding machine tapes can also be read by these readers. This eliminates the necessity of transcribing the source document into cards or tape and the

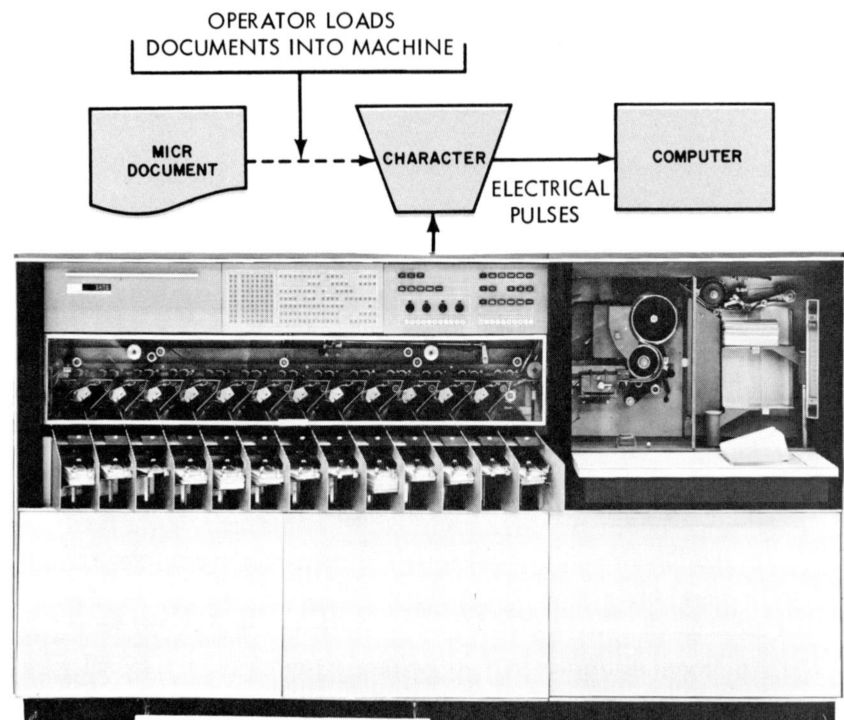

Figure 5–37. Magnetic Document Sorter and Reader.

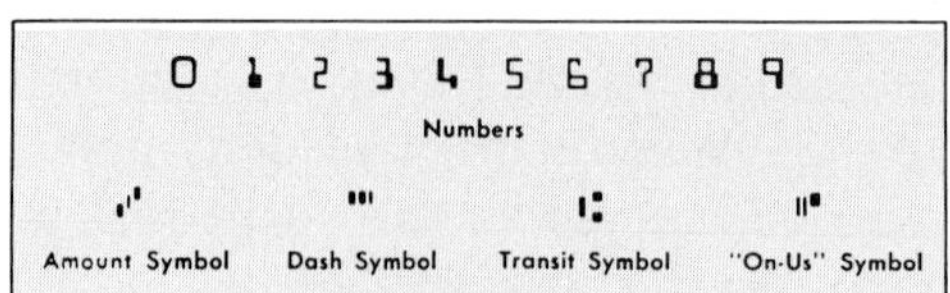

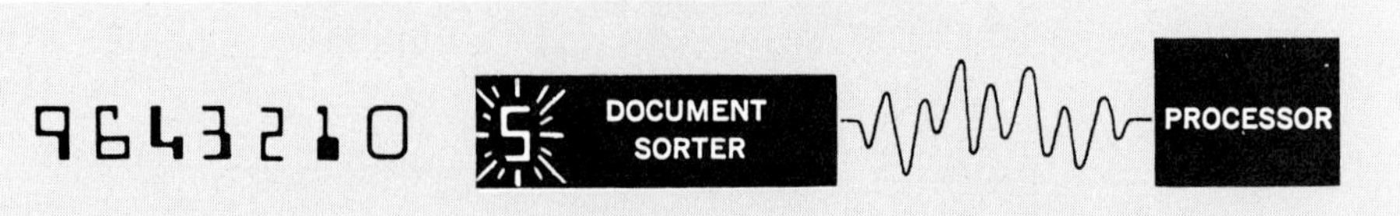

time between the receipt of the source documents and their entry into the data processing system is greatly reduced.

In addition, mark sensed information (the recording of ordinary pen and pencil markings in specified locations in the source document) can be read by the optical character reader.

Common uses of the optical character reader are insurance premium notices, charge sales invoices, utility bills, etc. Partial payments can be

ABCDEFGHIJKLMNOPQRSTU
VWXYZ , . $ / * - 1234567890

Figure 5–38. OCR Character Set.

processed directly to a customer's bill and immediate processing of the payment can be made. The Social Security Board is one of the largest users of optical character readers, employing them for reading its quarterly payroll reports as submitted by employers.

ADVANTAGES OF OPTICAL CHARACTER READERS

1. The greatest advantage lies in the reading directly of the paper document into the system thus reducing the processing time between the receipt of the document and processing into the system.
2. Ordinary hand written, typed, computer printed and other source documents can be read into the system.
3. Mark sensed information can be read by the reader.

DISADVANTAGE OF OPTICAL CHARACTER READERS

The one big disadvantage still rests on the degree of reliability (or unreliability) of the reading of these printed symbols. Although the readers are being improved each day, there still are quite a few printed characters that cannot be read for various reasons and must be processed manually.

OPTICAL CHARACTER READER

A rotating drum in the reader transports the documents from a hopper past an optical scanner. The scanner consists of a powerful light that distinguishes between black and white patterns of reflected light. These light patterns are read as a number of small dots and are converted into electrical impulses to develop a character. When the optically-read character matches a character pattern in the character recognition circuitry, the character is recorded and entered into the data processing system. The read and recognition operation is automatic and takes place at electronic speeds (Fig. 5.39).

Mark sensing operations can be combined with optical character reading. Mark sensing is the reading of ordinary pen and pencil markings representing specific information, in a specified location on the source document.

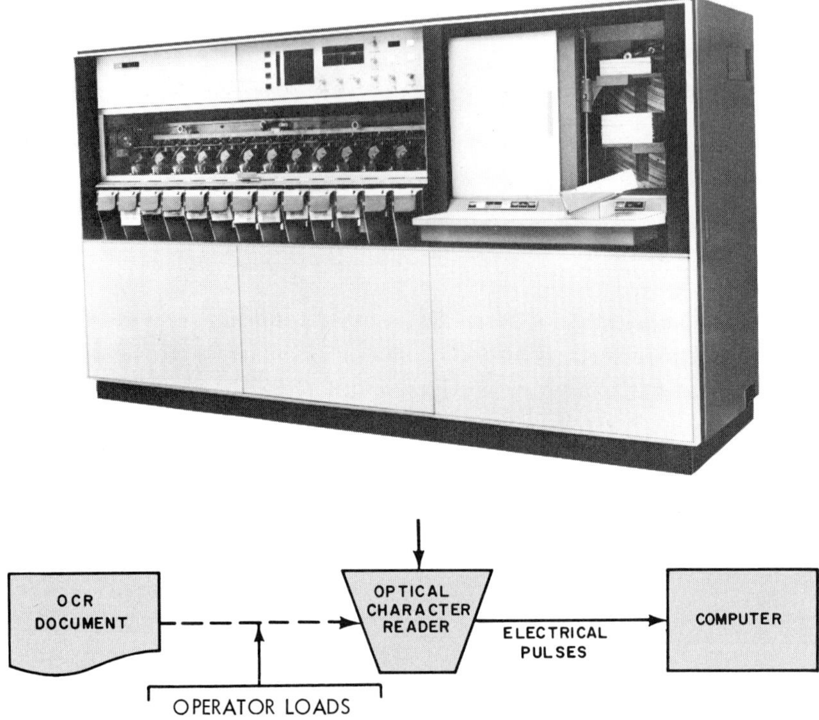

Figure 5–39.
Optical Character

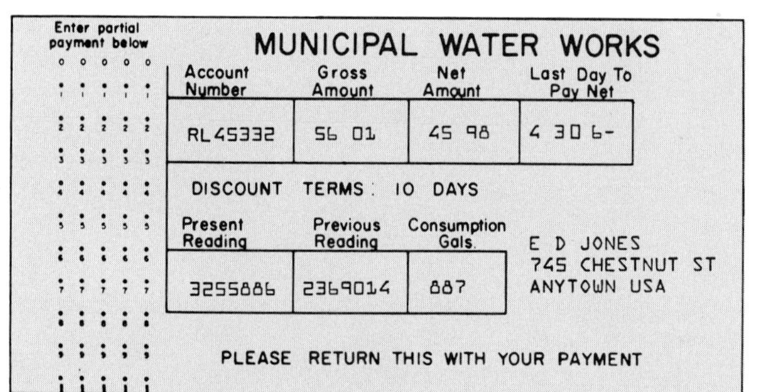

Enter partial payment below

MUNICIPAL WATER WORKS

Account Number	Gross Amount	Net Amount	Last Day To Pay Net
RL45332	56 01	45 98	4 30 6-

DISCOUNT TERMS : 10 DAYS

Present Reading	Previous Reading	Consumption Gals.
3255886	2369014	887

E D JONES
745 CHESTNUT ST
ANYTOWN USA

PLEASE RETURN THIS WITH YOUR PAYMENT

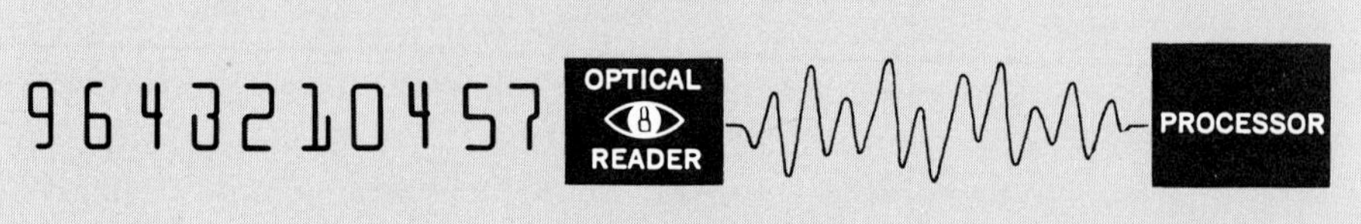

VISUAL DISPLAY UNITS

Visual display units permit the user of a data processing system to see, on a cathode tube, reports that would take many times longer to produce on any other output device (Fig. 5.40). The display units present tables, charts, graphs and various other configurations of alphameric letters and figures on a cathode tube screen. An operator console is used in conjunction with the display unit. Included among the possible applications are:

1. An inquiry for vital information from a computer. This can be made by an executive at a terminal located near his office. The information can be displayed on the unit and the necessary decision can be made.
2. An inquiry received by telephone for information about the status of a client's account. The account can be retrieved and presented on the display unit. The record can be updated immediately using the entry keyboard, and the corrected record placed in storage.
3. Inquiries for payroll information relative to an employee's record.
4. Inventory information inquiries relative to the status of stock items.

These are just a few of the many possible uses for visual display devices in a business organization.

Terminals are commonly used to produce a visual display of the records in storage. An operator initiates the request for information and the data is transferred to and from the computer at the rate of 2,560 characters per second. The displayed information can be retained as long as needed. Remote

Figure 5–40. Visual Display Operation.

terminals can be used to transfer data over telephone lines at a speed of 120 or 240 characters per second.

The display station has a four-by-nine-inch receiving area. As many as six to twelve rows of 40 or 80 characters can be displayed depending upon the model used. Thirty-six alphameric plus 25 special characters are displayed on a matrix with an appearance similar to a printer.

All input to be displayed is through an alphameric or numeric keyboard. The keyed information is displayed immediately on the tube for a visual accuracy check. The operator can correct, erase, backspace, reenter or clear an entire input message before the information is released to the computer.

Output information is written on the tube face under operator or program control. The information can be written in a cleared display unit or added to an existing display on the tube face. The display may also be directed to an output printer.

The most important advantage of visual display devices is the reduction of the time gap between the actual occurrence of the transaction and its subsequent entry into the data processing system. Real time processing has become an actuality in that it is possible to process the actual transaction almost the moment it occurs. Remote terminals can communicate directly with the data processing system. These terminals can be strategically located throughout an organization with inquiries possible from any station in the building or throughout the United States. The distance gap between the location of the transaction and the computer has been bridged.

The chief disadvantage in the extensive use of display units is the cost factor. Data transmission of large quantities of data over the telephone and by other communication devices is still rather expensive. However the costs of terminals and transmissions are gradually being reduced and this method of input/output to a data processing unit is growing in popularity each day.

PRINTERS

The printers provide the permanent visual record (hard copy) from a data processing system. As an output device, the printer receives data from the computer and prints the reports (Fig. 5.41). A paper transport automatically spaces the form as the report is being prepared. The principal printing devices are print-wheel printers, wire-matrix printers, chain printers, incremental bar printers and the typewriter.

The print-wheel printer is equipped with 120 rotary wheels each capable of printing 47 characters of a type including numerals, alphabetic symbols and special characters (Fig. 5.42). All 120 printwheels are correctly positioned to represent the data to be printed. A complete line of 120 characters is printed each time at a speed of 150 lines per minute.

Figure 5–41. IBM 1403 Printer and Printed Report.

ACCOUNT NUMBER	BALANCE DUE	DATE OF LAST PAYMENT	
8332	$ 308.65	6/09/62	*
9818	$ .02	12/08/62	*
10003	$1,803.17	6/14/63	
10015	$ .89	10/13/62	*
11007	$1,000.56	6/01/63	
20005	$ 756.79	5/18/63	

A wire-matrix printer prints each character in a pattern formed by ends of small wires arranged in a five-by-seven rectangle. The wires are extended to form patterns that are arranged in 47 different characters including all letters of the alphabet, the ten numeric digits and eleven special characters used for punctuation and report writing (Fig. 5.43). These wires are pressed against a ribbon causing the character to be printed. 120 characters are printed on a line at speeds of 500 to 1,000 lines per minute depending upon device used.

The chain printer is an electromechanical line printer employing engraved type. All characters are assembled in a chain and as the chain moves horizontally, each character is printed as it is positioned opposite a magnetically activated hammer that presses the paper against one piece of type in the moving chain (Fig. 5.44). Up to 132 characters may be printed in one

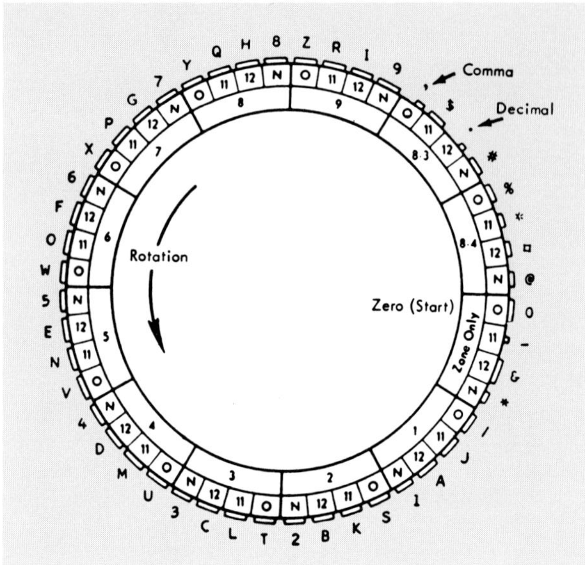

Figure 5–42. Print Wheel.

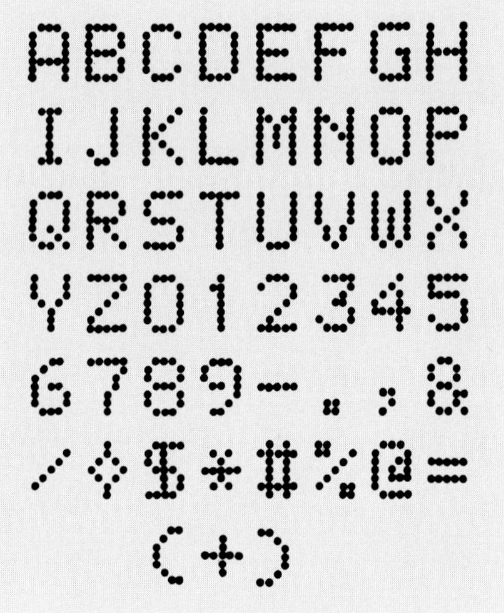

Figure 5–43. Wire Matrix Dot Pattern.

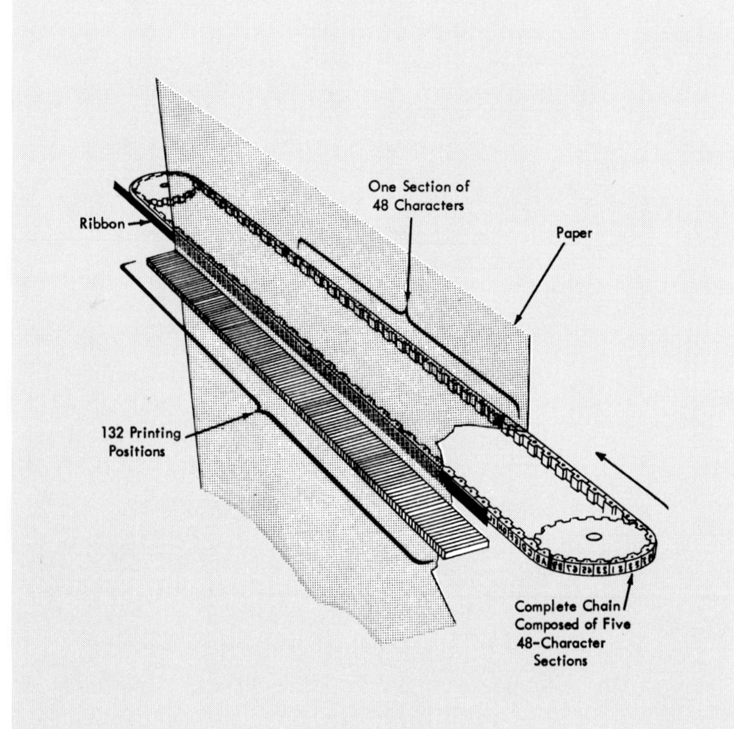

Figure 5–44. Print Chain.

Figure 5–45. IBM 1052 Printer Keyboard.

line at speeds up to 1,285 lines per minute. The print chain can easily be changed to provide a variety of print fonts.

The incremental bar printer has a bar which contains print characters and travels back and forth in a horizontal plane. To print a character, a magnet releases a spring-loaded hammer at the proper time so that the desired character can be printed. Up to 240 characters can be printed in a minute.

The typewriter used as an output device is similar to one that is used manually except that the printing occurs automatically under the control of the stored programs (Fig. 5.45). Up to 600 characters per minute can be printed with automatic spacing and carriage return.

Other printers available using any of the above printing mechanisms can achieve speeds as high as 2,000 to 4,000 lines per minute.

CONSOLES

The console of a data processing system is used by the operator to control the system and monitor its operations. Keys, switches, audible tone signals and display lights are some of the manual controls available to the operator for manipulation and checking of the program (Fig. 5.46).

Although the console of a data processing system is not ordinarily used as a data recording medium (except in small computer systems), small quantities of information can be entered at a relatively slow speed to keep a system operational. In many data processing systems that are used for engineering

Figure 5–46.
IBM 370 Console.

applications, console typewriters are used to insert data needed to complete the computations.

If the system is bottled up by an error condition, or a condition requiring the entry of data into the system such as code or reference numbers, etc., the console operator can cause the operation of the system to be resumed by typing the correct information on the console (Fig. 5.47).

Communication network signals, microfilm, and audio tones, are just a few of the methods used to communicate with the computer. By virtue of the moon exploration, it is conceivable that in the future, data will be entered into and extracted from computers on the moon via the various satellites. The list of data recording media grows larger each year.

TYPEWRITER CONSOLES

Typewriter consoles can be attached to a data processing system for communication between operator and system, such as operator-to-program or program-to-operator communication for program checking, program correction and job logging.

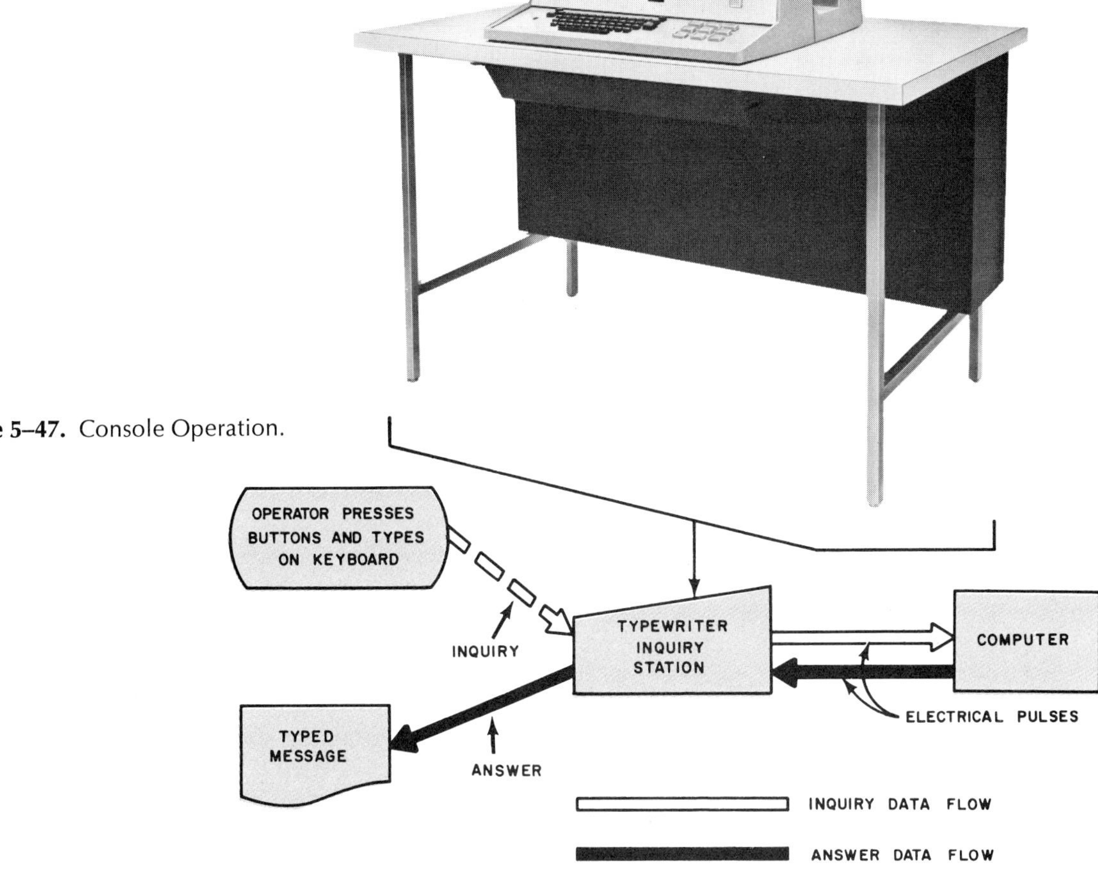

e 5–47. Console Operation.

The keyboard and the printing are electrically or mechanically independent of each other. The keyboard can be used for system input and the printer will accept computer output. The printer prints at a rate of 14.8 characters per second and has a replaceable printing head and typewriter-style keyboard.

TERMINALS

Terminals are used in telecommunications within a data processing system. Terminal units at the sending location accept data from cards, magnetic tape or data entered manually into a system through a keyboard, and partially conditions this data for transmission over telephone, telegraph, radio and microwave circuits (Fig. 5.48). At the receiving station, the data is punched into cards, written on a magnetic tape, printed as a report or entered directly into a data processing system. Several automatic checking features insure validity of all transmitted data.

Figure 5–48. IBM 3780 Data Communications Terminal.

SUMMARY

The study of computer components is important in providing insight to the operation of the computer. In this and the succeeding chapter, the hardware and storage devices are explained so that one can have a complete understanding of the physical operation of a computer. The intent of this chapter is to describe the physical characteristics of the input and output devices as well as to serve as an introduction to computer processing. The advantages and disadvantages of each input and output type are so listed that the user can become familiar with the media used to record data and be able to evaluate each in order to determine the one best suited for a particular application.

The operations of input and output devices is essential to the understanding of data processing procedures. The input and output devices are one of the most important segments of computer processing. An efficient data processing installation must have a balanced input and output system. Because of the variety of input and output devices, it is important that one understands the operations, features and capabilities of each type of device.

I. *Introduction to Computer Processing*
   A. *Limitations of punched-card processing*—no communication between these specialized machines, limited logical ability, one primary input, speed limitation, "exception routine" processing difficulties.
   B. *Basic considerations in data processing.*
      1. *Input*—source data entering system.
      2. *Processing*—the planned steps necessary to change the data into the desired result.
      3. *Output*—the finished result, the end product of the system.
   C. *Basic elements of a computer data processing system.*
      1. *Hardware*—the physical devices of a data processing system; input and output devices, central processing unit, storage.
      2. *Software*—the totality of programs and routines that are used to extend the capabilities of the computer, such as compilers, routines and subroutines.
   D. *Hardware elements of a computer.*
      1. *Input devices*—used to enter data into a data processing system.
      2. *Output devices*—accept data from the system and record it.
      3. *Central processing unit*—accepts data for processing and makes results available for output devices.
      4. *Storage devices*—used for temporary and permanent storage of data.

II. *Input and Output Devices.*
   A. *Functions*—units for getting and putting data into and out of a storage unit of a computer.
   B. *Control unit*—coordinates input and output units with the central processing unit.
   C. *Channel*—manages input and output control units and devices.
   D. *Buffer*—external device used to store data prior to entry into storage or prior to output. Overlapping of operations between input and output devices and processing functions.
   E. *Card reading and punching devices.*

1. Most commonly used data processing media.
2. Data recorded in a pattern of small rectangular holes in specified locations to represent all characters.
3. *Advantages*—standardized card format, storage capability, unit record principle, can be used as original documents, etc.
4. *Disadvantages*—limitation of 80 columns, slow input and output, bulky, etc.
5. *Card readers*—introduce punched-card records into a data processing system.
6. *Card punches*—punches information into cards.

F. *Magnetic Tape Devices.*
   1. Fastest method of entry into a computer.
   2. Data recorded as a series of magnetized areas along the tape.
   3. *Advantages*—high speed input and output media, records not limited in size, compact size, errors can be corrected in same area of tape, high reliability of reading and recording, etc.
   4. *Disadvantages*—sequential reading (each record must be examined), affected by physical elements, information lost if tape is broken, etc.
   5. *Parity check*—used to insure correct number of bits in each character.
   6. *Interrecord gap*—separates blocks of records.
   7. *File protection device ring*—prevents accidental erasure of data on tape.

G. *Paper Tape Devices.*
   1. Continuous recording medium
   2. Data recorded as special arrangement of punched holes in tape.
   3. *Advantages*—electronic transportation over long distances, not heavy or bulky, may be by-product of another operation, records not limited in size, etc.
   4. *Disadvantages*—slow input and output as compared to other media, not durable, must be converted to another form before processing, cannot be altered without repunching a new tape, etc.
   5. *Paper tape reader*—reads the punched holes in tape.
   6. *Paper tape punch*—punches holes into blank tape as data is received from main storage.

H. *Magnetic Ink Character Recognition Devices.*
   1. Readable by both man and machine.
   2. Data printed on paper documents by machine.
   3. Used extensively in banking operations.

4. *Advantages*—paper document can be read directly into system, timesaving in sorting and processing of paper documents, etc.
5. *Disadvantages*—data is read incorrectly if not properly inscribed, torn or multilated documents must be manually processed, cannot be transmitted over communication lines.
6. *Magnetic Ink Character readers*—read card and paper documents inscribed with magnetic ink characters.

I. *Optical Character Recognition Devices.*
   1. Can be read by both man and machine.
   2. Printed by typewriters, printing devices, computer printers or even handwritten.
   3. Used for insurance premium notices, sales invoices, utility bills, etc.
   4. *Advantages*—paper documents can be read directly into system without transcriptions; includes handwritten, typed or printed documents.
   5. *Disadvantage*—reliability of reading of printed systems, etc.
   6. *Optical Character Reader* can read some hand-printed or machine-printed numeric digits and certain alphabetic characters from paper or card documents.

J. *Visual Display units.*
   1. Data displayed on cathode tube.
   2. Used in conjunction with terminals at remote distances from the computer.
   3. *Advantage*—reduction of time gap between actual occurrence and entry into the system.
   4. *Disadvantage*—cost is high for transmission of data.

K. *Printers.*
   Provide the permanent visual record (hard copy) from a data processing system. Available in a variety of types and speeds.

L. *Consoles.*
   Used to enter small amounts of data into a system. Used by the operator to control the system and monitor its operations.

M. *Terminals.*
   Used in telecommunications within a data processing system. Terminal units at the sending location accept data from cards, magnetic tape or data entered manually into a system through a keyboard; partially conditions this data for transmission over telephone, telegraph, radio and microwave circuits.

IDENTIFICATION QUESTIONS

Match the following terms with the statements that follow.

A. Arithmetic and Logical Section
B. Bits
C. Buffer
D. Card Punch
E. Card Reader
F. Central Processing Unit
G. Channel
H. Console
I. Control Section
J. Control Unit
K. Data Processing System
L. Destructive Read In
M. Electromechanical
N. Electronic
O. Exception Routines
P. File Protection Ring
Q. Hardware
R. Input
S. Interblock Gap
T. Machine Language
U. Mag. Ink Character Reader
V. Magnetic Tape
W. Offline
X. Online
Y. Optical Character Reader
Z. Output
AA. Paper Tape Punch
BB. Paper Tape Reader
CC. Parity Check
DD. Printers
EE. Processing
FF. Program
GG. Software
HH. Solid State
II. Tapemark
JJ. Terminal
KK. Visual Display Unit

1. Punches output from a data processing system into cards.
2. Provides permanent visual record from a data processing system.
3. Directly connected to the data processing system.
4. Transistors.
5. A definite pattern of symbols interpreted by a machine.
6. A space that separates records recorded in blocks.
7. Transmits data over communication lines.
8. Accepts data for processing and makes results available for output.
9. A series of instructions in a logical sequence which accomplishes a particular job.
10. Synchronizes the processing of input and output operations with the processing of the data.
11. Reads cards and paper documents inscribed with magnetic ink.
12. The finished result.
13. Mechanical devices that are powered by electricity.
14. Prevents accidental erasure of data.
15. Coordinates input and output operations with the central processing unit.
16. Indicates end of file for tape records.
17. Not directly connected to the system.
18. Symbols recorded as a series of magnetized areas along the length of a tape.
19. All necessary devices and procedures used in a data processing operation.
20. Source data entering a system.
21. Reads upper case letters, numerals, and special characters into a computer system.
22. A separate piece of equipment devoted exclusively to managing input and output control units and devices assigned to it.
23. Insures that only valid characters are recorded in a data processing system.

24. Each new recording erases previous data.
25. Reads punched holes in tape.
26. Out-of-the-ordinary routines that may arise during the processing of data.
27. Punches coded data into tape.
28. Planned processing steps necessary to change data into the desired result.
29. Totality of programs and routines that are used to extend the capabilities of the computer.
30. Vacuum tubes.
31. Controls the system and monitors its operations.
32. Fastest method of entering data into a data processing system.
33. Performs all functions of arithmetic and directs the processing unit in making decisions.
34. Permits user of a data processing system to see data displayed on a cathode tube.
35. Physical equipment and devices of a system forming a computer and its peripheral devices.
36. Manipulates data between core storage and the arithmetic and logical section.
37. Introduces punched cards into a data processing system.

QUESTIONS FOR REVIEW

1. What new category of data processing equipment was introduced by the computer?
2. What are the important limitations of punched card data processing equipment as compared to computer data processing?
3. A computer accepts data, processes data, and puts out results. List the basic considerations in computer data processing.
4. Differentiate between "hardware" and "software" features of a computer system.
5. What is the difference between "online" and "offline" equipment? Give examples of each type.
6. What are the major hardware elements used in a computer? Explain the function of each element.
7. What is the primary function of the input/output devices?
8. What function does a control unit perform in an input/output device?
9. Explain the main function of a channel.
10. What part does the buffering system play in the processing of input/output operations?
11. Differentiate between the two types of reading units in card reading devices.
12. What are the main advantages and disadvantages of punched cards?
13. Explain the operation of a magnetic tape device.
14. How is data recorded on magnetic tape?
15. What are the important advantages and disadvantages of magnetic tape?
16. Explain the purpose of a parity check.
17. How are tapes recorded? What is the purpose of the interrecord gap?

18. What are the main uses of paper tape?
19. What are the important advantages and disadvantages of paper tape?
20. Explain the uses of two major character recognition devices. Give examples.
21. What is the importance of magnetic ink character readers in the banking field?
22. What is a visual display unit used for?
23. What is the importance of visual display units? List some possible applications.
24. What is the important advantage of a visual display unit? What is a serious disadvantage?
25. What is the primary function of a console?
26. How can a console aid in the operation of a data processing unit?
27. What are terminals and when are they used?

CHAPTER 6

Computer Components—Processing and Storage Devices

CENTRAL PROCESSING UNIT (CPU)

The central processing unit is the heart of the entire data processing system. It supervises and controls the data processing components, performs the actual arithmetic, and makes the logical decisions. Processing includes the data movement, the computations, and the logical decisions necessary to edit the data into meaningful information in the desired format of the output.

The central processing unit (CPU) is not limited by speeds of peripheral units. Being the unit that performs all the internal processing, it is permitted to do most of its arithmetic and logical functions while the other units in the system are performing their assigned tasks.

The central processing unit is divided into two sections: the Arithmetic and Logical section and the Control section plus Main Storage (Fig. 6-1).

ARITHMETIC AND LOGICAL SECTION

The arithmetic and logical section contains the circuitry which makes the necessary arithmetic computations and logical decisions called for by the computer commands (Fig. 6.2). A computer can execute thousands of arithmetic operations per second compared to the several problems per minute performed by an experienced desk-calculator operator. The arithmetic portion performs operations such as addition, subtraction, multiplication,

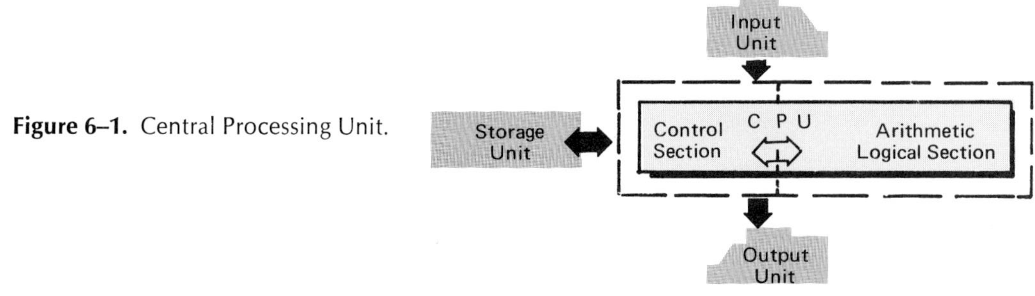

Figure 6–1. Central Processing Unit.

Figure 6–2. Control, Arithmetic and Logical Sections.

division, shifting, moving and storing under control of the stored program. The logical portion of the section is capable of decision making to test various conditions encountered during the processing and to alter the sequence of the instruction execution. Logical decisions determine the relationship between two items, such as equal to, less than or greater than. Once the relationship is established, the computer follows the instructions programmed for that condition.

Certain logical decisions, such as a compare instruction, can be made and acted upon as the situation requires. Based on whether or not a stated condition exists, the processing unit can be directed to go to one series of instructions or another. For example, in an inventory application, when a disbursement quantity is subtracted from the stock balance, a negative balance may occur. Noting this condition, the processing unit can be directed to another series of instructions that will call the attention of the user of the report to this condition in the form of a printed output.

CONTROL SECTION

The control section acts as a traffic manager directing and coordinating all operations called for by the instructions of the computer system. This involves control of input/output devices, entry and removal of information from storage, routing of information between storage and the arithmetic and logical section. The control section automatically integrates the operation of the entire computer system.

The control aspect of the processing unit comes from the individual commands contained in the program. These commands are instructions to the various devices to perform a function as specified. Each time a card is read or punched, or a line is printed on the output printer, or two amounts are added together, it is because an instruction in the processing unit caused it to happen. An instruction tells the computer what operation is to be done (add, subtract, multiply, move, read a card) and where the data is that will be affected by this operation.

This section directs the system according to the procedure and instructions received from its human operators and programmers.

OPERATIONAL UNITS

REGISTERS

A register is a device capable of storing information temporarily, receiving information from other areas, and transferring information as directed by the control section.

Registers are named according to the function they perform (Fig. 6.3). For example, an accumulator accumulates results, a storage register contains information that is taken from or being sent to storage, an address register contains the address of a storage location or device, and an instruction register contains the instruction being executed. The IBM System/360/370 has sixteen general purpose registers that can be used as index registers, relocation registers, accumulators for fixed point arithmetic and logical operations.

Registers differ in size, capacity and use. A register may be used to test an overflow condition that may result from an arithmetic operation. Registers may also be used to shift results right or left. In other instances, registers can contain data which may be analyzed by other associated units. For example,

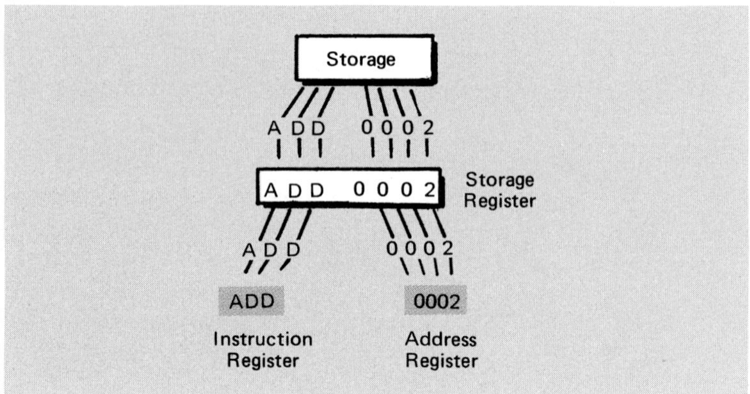

Figure 6–3. Register Nomenclature and Function.

an instruction placed in a register can be analyzed by associated circuits to determine the operation to be performed, the location of the data involved in the operation and where the result is to be placed. Data may also be checked for validity within the specific register.

The more important registers have small lights associated with them which may be displayed on a console. These lights are located on the machine console and are used to display the register contents and various program conditions.

COUNTER

A counter is closely related to a register and performs the same functions. It can function as an accumulator in that its contents may be increased or decreased. Counter functions will vary depending upon the computer. Usually their contents may be displayed upon the console.

ADDER

The adder performs arithmetic functions to the extent that it accumulates the value of two data items and sends the results to an accumulator or register. Automatic carries to the next higher order position are performed on the data. When a command is given, the addition, subtraction, multiplication or division will be performed in the adder, and then the answer will be stored in a counter or register (Fig. 6.4).

MACHINE CYCLES

In computer usage, time is stated in terms of milliseconds, microseconds, and nanoseconds. How short is a period of time? The blink of an eye takes one tenth of a second or 100 milliseconds. The following are some abbreviations for time intervals.

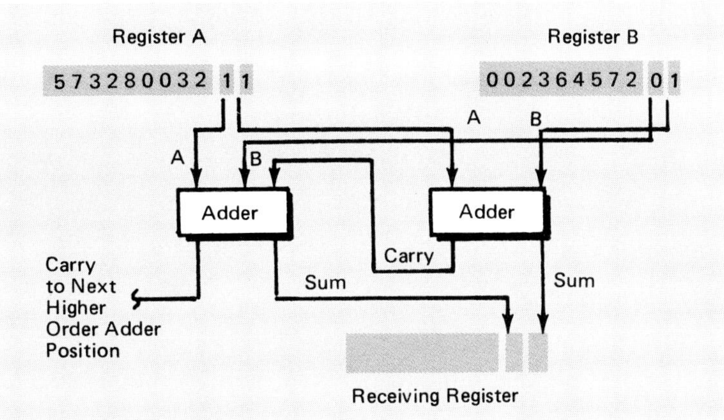

Figure 6–4. Adders in a Computer System.

.1 = 1/10 second = 100 milliseconds
.001 = 1/1,000 second = 1 millisecond (MS)
.000001 = 1/1,000,000 second = 1 microsecond (m sec)
.000000001 = 1/1,000,000,000 second = 1 nanosecond (NS)

During a machine cycle, the computer can perform a specific machine operation. The number of operations required to execute a single instruction will depend on the instruction. Many machine operations are combined to execute each program instruction.

INSTRUCTIONS

There are at least two parts to each instruction: an operation and operand. The *operation* denotes the function that the machine is to perform such as add, subtract, multiply, write, move, or read. The *operand* can be the address of the data or an instruction in main storage, or the address of a program in secondary storage, or the address of an input/output device.

During an instruction cycle, an instruction is selected from storage and analyzed by the central processing unit. The operation portion of the instruction indicates the operation to be performed. This is coded information that has a particular meaning to the computer. For example, in an IBM System/360/370 computer, the letter A is interpreted as "Add" and the letter C as "Compare." Each computer has its own unique coding techniques.

The operand further defines or augments the function of the operation. For example, to perform an arithmetic operation, the storage location of one or both of the factors involved would be indicated. For reading or writing operations, the area of storage needed for the input and output is indicated or fixed by machine design.

In most data processing units, no particular area of storage is reserved for instructions. They are usually grouped together in ascending sequential locations according to the sequence in which the instructions are to be executed normally. Unless altered by a branch–type instruction (the changing of the sequence of instruction execution due to a condition detected during the processing), the process is as follows:

1. The computer locates the first instruction either in a predetermined location of storage assigned for this purpose or by the manual resetting of the switches on the console.
2. After each instruction is executed, the next sequential instruction is fetched unless the program directs it to another location.
3. The process continues automatically, instruction by instruction, until the program is complete or the computer is instructed to stop.

To receive, interpret and execute the various instructions, the central processing unit must operate in a prescribed sequence.

INSTRUCTION CYCLE

The following operations occur during the instruction cycle (Fig. 6.5):

1. The instruction is brought to the CPU from main storage.
2. The operation code is decoded.
3. The operand is placed in an address register, indicating the location of the factors involved in the operation.
4. The location of the next instruction to be executed is indicated.

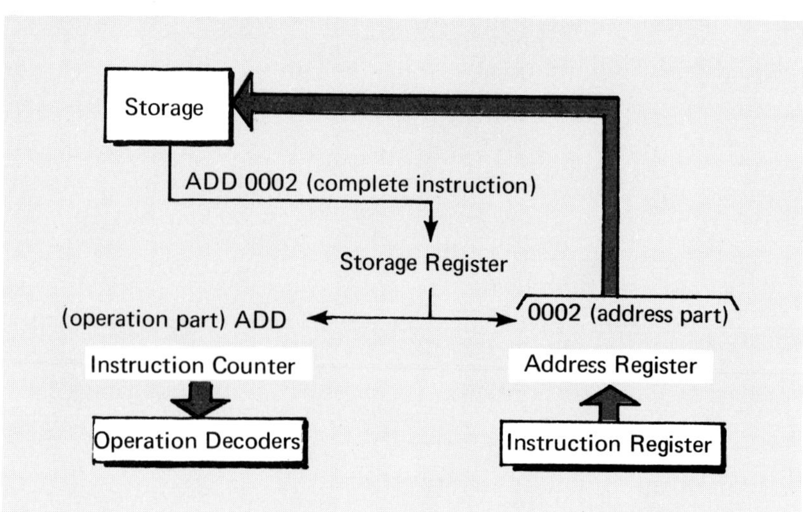

Figure 6–5. Instruction Cycle.

EXECUTION CYCLE

The execution cycle follows the instruction cycle (Fig. 6.6). The number of execution cycles to be performed will depend on the instruction to be executed.

The address register may contain information other than the location of the data. The address of the input/output device or a control function to be performed can be indicated. The operating portion of the instruction informs the computer how to interpret the information (Fig. 6.7).

STORAGE

All data entering a computer to be processed must be placed in storage first. Storage can be compared to a giant electronic file cabinet, completely indexed and available for instant accessing. Information is entered into storage by an input device and is then available for internal processing. Storage is so arranged that each position has a specific location called an *address*, just as your house has its own street address. This unique address enables the programmer to have access to data stored in storage as well as to place new data into storage. For example, consider a group of numbered mailboxes in a post office (Fig. 6.8). Each of these boxes is identified and located by its unique number. In the same manner storage is divided into locations, each with its assigned address. Each location holds a special character of information. However, unlike the mailbox, a computer storage location holds only one piece of information at a time; the placing of another piece of information into this same location automatically erases its previous contents.

Data may be rearranged by sorting and collating different types of information received from the various input units. Data may also be taken from

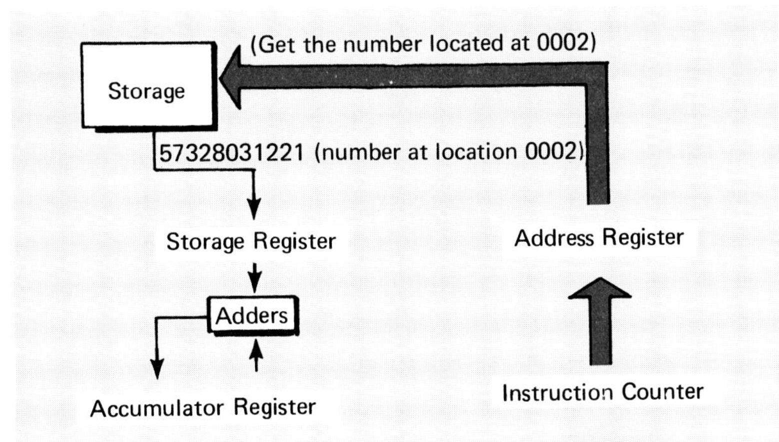

Figure 6–6. Execution Cycle.

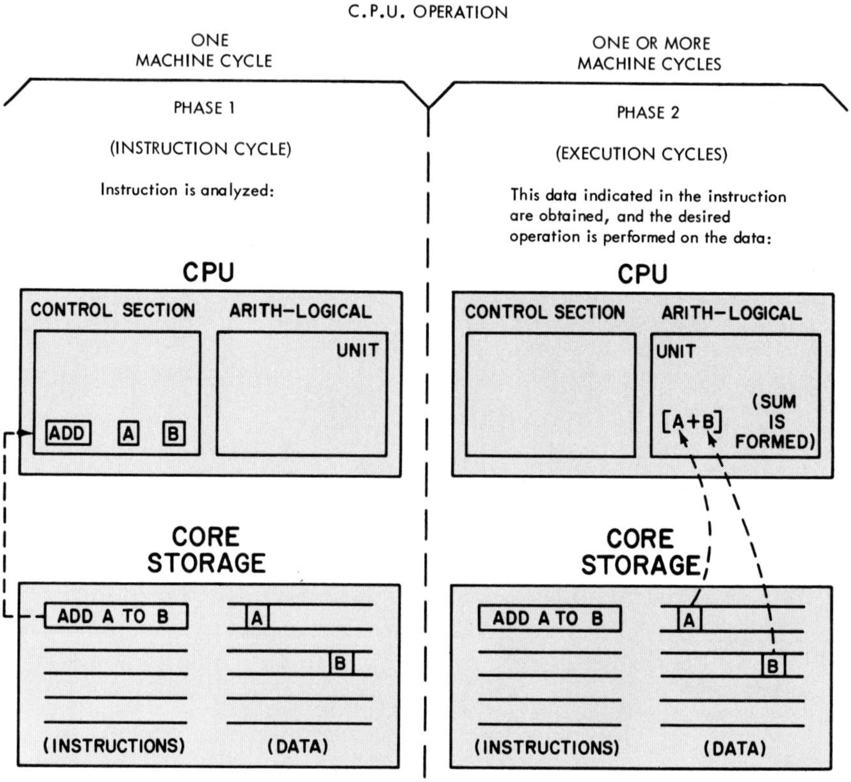

C.P.U. OPERATION

ONE MACHINE CYCLE

PHASE 1

(INSTRUCTION CYCLE)

Instruction is analyzed:

CPU

CONTROL SECTION

ADD A B

ARITH–LOGICAL UNIT

CORE STORAGE

ADD A TO B

A

B

(INSTRUCTIONS) (DATA)

ONE OR MORE MACHINE CYCLES

PHASE 2

(EXECUTION CYCLES)

This data indicated in the instruction are obtained, and the desired operation is performed on the data:

CPU

CONTROL SECTION

ARITH–LOGICAL UNIT

[A+B] (SUM IS FORMED)

CORE STORAGE

ADD A TO B

A

B

(INSTRUCTIONS) (DATA)

Figure 6–7. Schematic-Instruction and Execution Cycle.

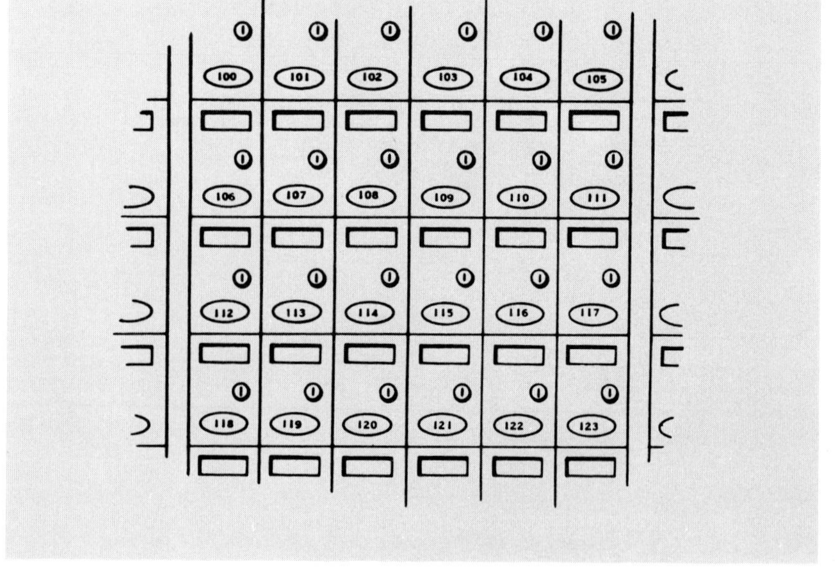

Figure 6–8. Post Office Mail Boxes.

storage, processed and the result placed back in storage. The size and capacity of storage determines the amount of information that can be held within a system at one time. The larger the capacity, the more powerful and expensive the computer. A computer containing 256,000 storage locations is commonly referred to as 256K System. (K stands for 1,000. 256K = 256 × 1000, or 256,000.) In some computers, the storage capacity is measured in millions of characters while other systems have smaller storage facilities. The capacity and design of the storage unit has an effect upon the method of processing data through the computer. Storage may be classified as main or auxiliary storage (Fig. 6.9).

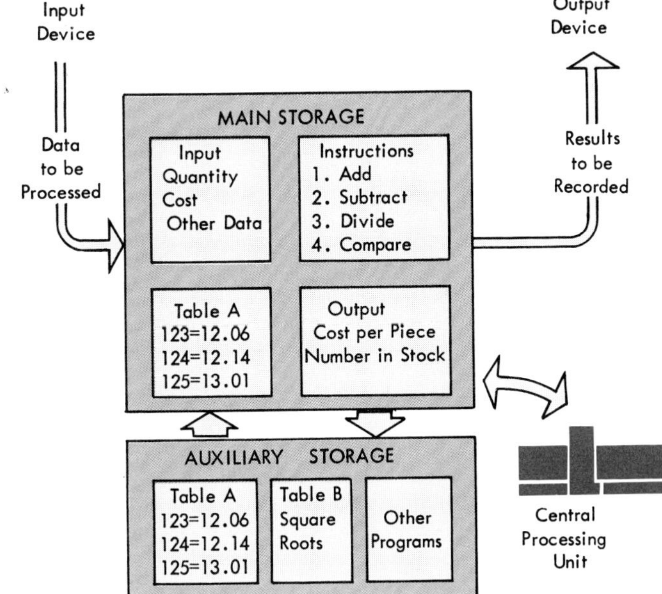

Figure 6–9. Schematic Main and Auxiliary Storage.

MAIN STORAGE

Main storage is usually referred to as core storage. *All data to be processed must pass through main storage.* Main storage accepts the data from the input unit, holds processed data, and can furnish data to an output unit. Since all data passes through main storage, the unit must therefore have capacity to retain a usable amount of data and all necessary instructions for processing.

If additional storage is required, the capacity of main storage is augmented by auxiliary storage units, however all information to and from auxiliary storage must be routed through main storage.

AUXILIARY STORAGE

There are two types of auxiliary storage.

Random (Direct) Access Units

Drum, disk and data cell devices can process data randomly. That is, records can be accessed without reading from the beginning of a file to find them.

Sequential Access Units

The magnetic tape unit is the chief type of sequential access unit. This type of processing indicates that the tape reels must be read from the beginning of tape to find the desired record.

STORAGE PROCESSING

All data in storage is so arranged that it can be accessed by its individual address. Each location holds a specific unit of data, be it a character, a digit, a word or an entire record, depending upon the particular computer. To insert or remove data at a location, the address must be known either to the programmer or to a control program.

When information is placed in a location, it replaces the previous contents of that location. Once stored, the same data may be used repeatedly. The original contents remain unaltered when information is moved from one location to another.

Access time is the time required to locate and transfer information to and from storage. Access time is measured in billionths of a second. To fully appreciate such a minute interval of time, one imagines a spaceship traveling at 100,000 miles per hour. In one microsecond (millionth of a second) the spaceship would have traveled about 1¾ inches while in a nanosecond (billionth of a second) it would travel one thousandth of 1¾ inches.

In all data processing systems, the access time has a direct bearing on the efficiency of the entire system.

CORE STORAGE

A magnetic core is a doughnut-shaped ferromagnetic-coated material, vertically aligned. The tiny ring measures a few hundredths of an inch in diameter. Aside from its compact size, the core is easily magnetized in a few millionths of a second and unless changed retains its magnetism indefinitely.

Cores are placed on a wire in a series similar to a string of beads (Fig. 6.10). An electric current is sent through, magnetizing the individual cores. The direction of the current determines the polarity of the magnetic state of the core. By reversing the current, the magnetic state of the core can be

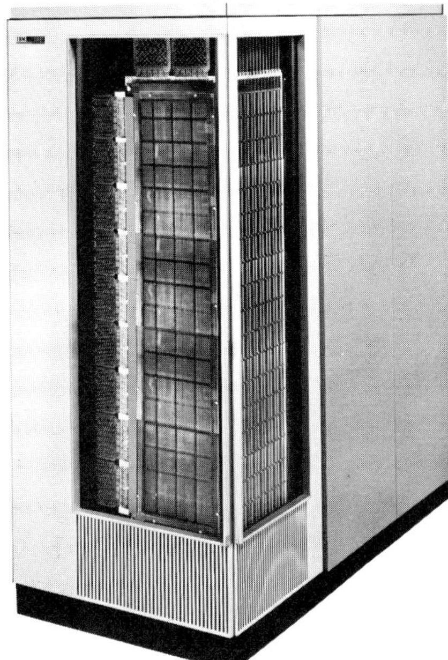

Figure 6–10. IBM 2361 Core Storage. One Core Plane from a Magnetic Core Storage.

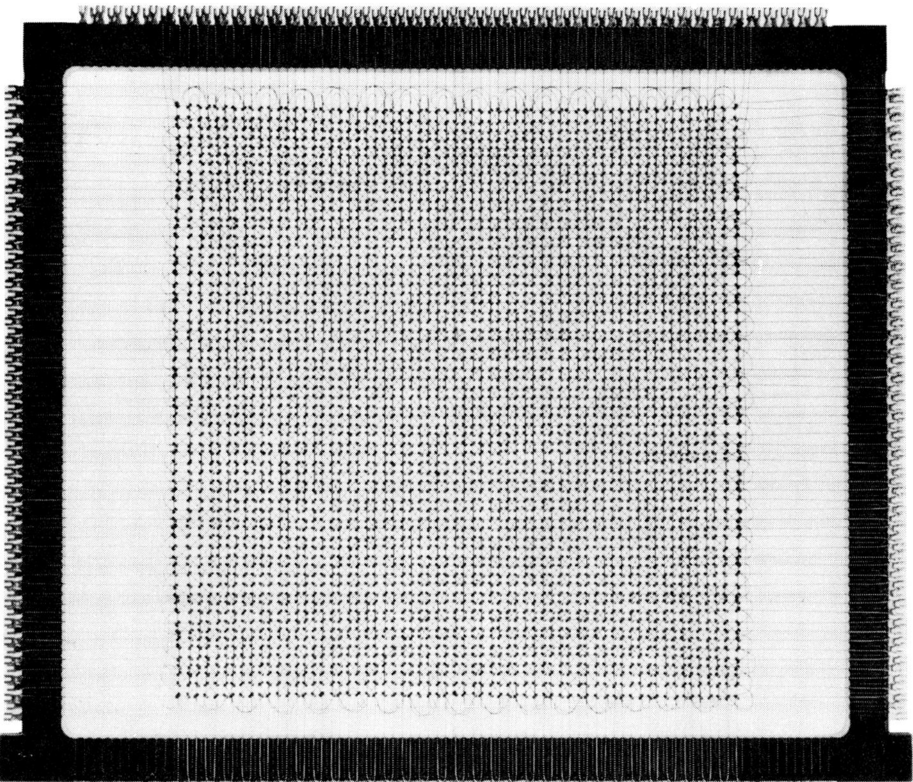

reversed (Fig. 6.11). In a binary system of information, only one of two conditions need be tested. Core storage lends itself perfectly to binary in that each position will have a reading of 1 or 0 depending upon the state of the magnetism (Fig. 6.12). Any single core can be selected for reading without affecting the others. Any combination of 1's (ones) or 0's (zeros) representing a character can be written magnetically or read back when needed (Fig. 6.13).

To select certain cores to be magnetized, two wires are run through each core at right angles to each other. When half the current needed to magnetize

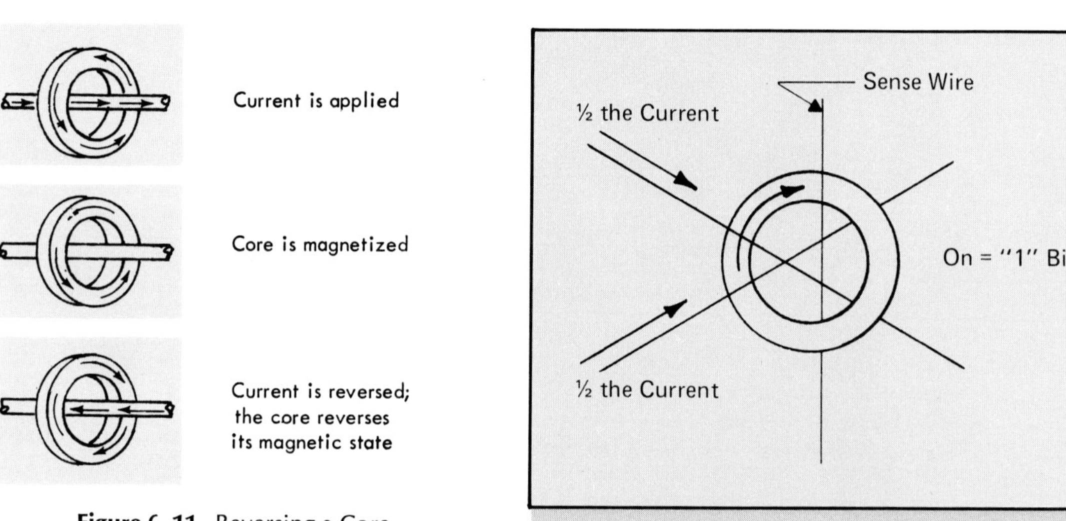

Figure 6–11. Reversing a Core.

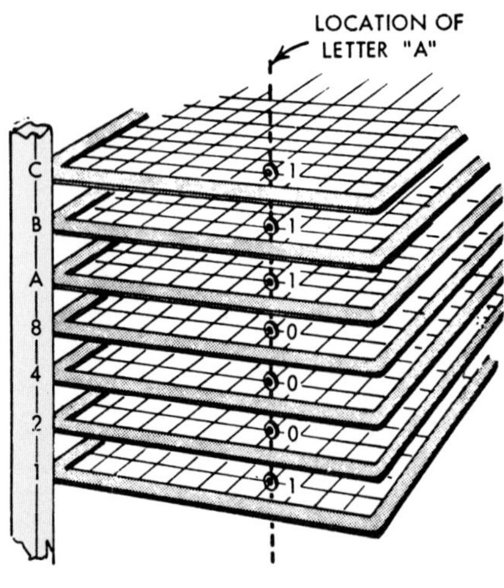

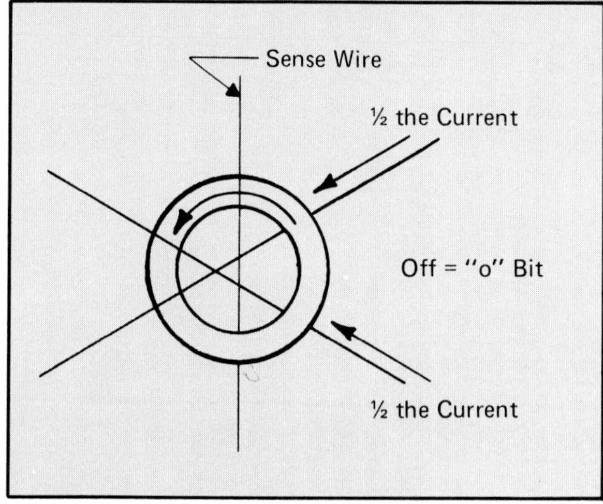

Figure 6–13. Magnetic Core Location.

Figure 6–12. Schematic Magnetic Core.

is sent through each wire, only the core at the intersection is magnetized. No other core in the string is affected. Employing these principles, any single core in a screen may be selected for storage or reading without affecting any other (Fig. 6.14).

If the magnetic state of the core is reversed, the abrupt change induces current in a third wire. This signal is sent by the sense wire and can be used to determine whether the core contained a 1 or *on* status. Since only one core at any one time in any plane is tested for its magnetic state, only one sense wire is needed for an entire plane.

The core storage is the "workhorse" of a computer system. All processing takes place in magnetic core. Core storage is the most expensive storage device in terms of cost per storage location but it provides the fastest access time and thus may be the least expensive per machine calculation.

MAGNETIC DRUM

Drum storage devices (Fig. 6.15) are usually used in larger computer systems. A drum is vertically mounted in a shaft and the data is recorded on its outer surface. Data is recorded around the drum in a series of tracks. The drum has a fixed read/write head for each track. Data is transferred to and

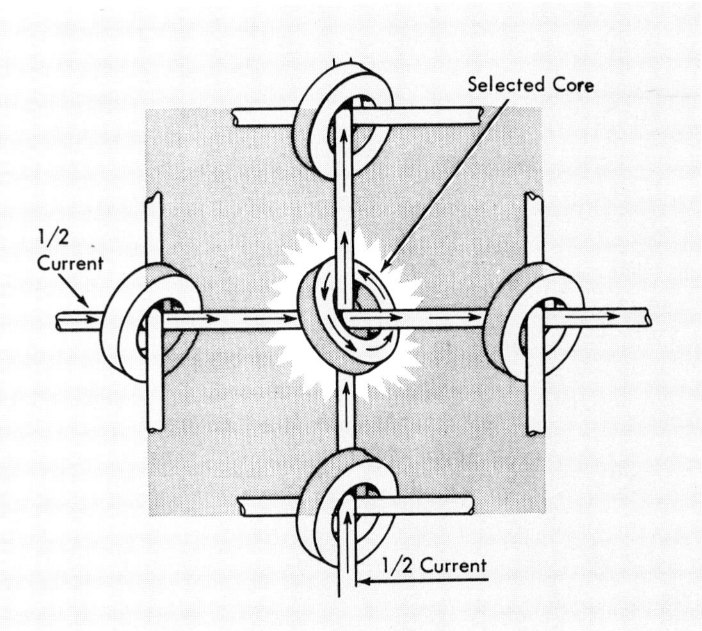

Figure 6–14. Selecting a Core.

Figure 6–15. IBM 2303 Drum Storage.

from the drum as the single recording surface rotates past the fixed head. A drum storage device has a maximum capacity of over 4 million characters.

A *magnetic drum* is a constant-speed rotating cylinder with an outer surface coated with magnetic material. The chief function of the drum is to serve as a low capacity, intermediate access (storing results temporarily for future processing) storage device (Fig. 6.16). The primary uses of a magnetic drum are: as a storage for data that are repetitively referenced during processing (tables, rates, codes); or as a supplementary storage for core storage. Another important use today is to serve as a random access device to provide program storage, program modification of data, and as a temporary storage for high activity random access operations involving limited amounts of data.

The outer surface of the cylinder can be magnetized and read repeatedly as the drum rotates at a constant speed (Fig. 6.17). Each time new data is read into the area, the old data is automatically erased. The data is read or written by a read/write head that is suspended at a slight distance from the drum. The read/write head consists of fine wires wound around tiny cores. By sending current to the write coils in the read/write head, the surface of

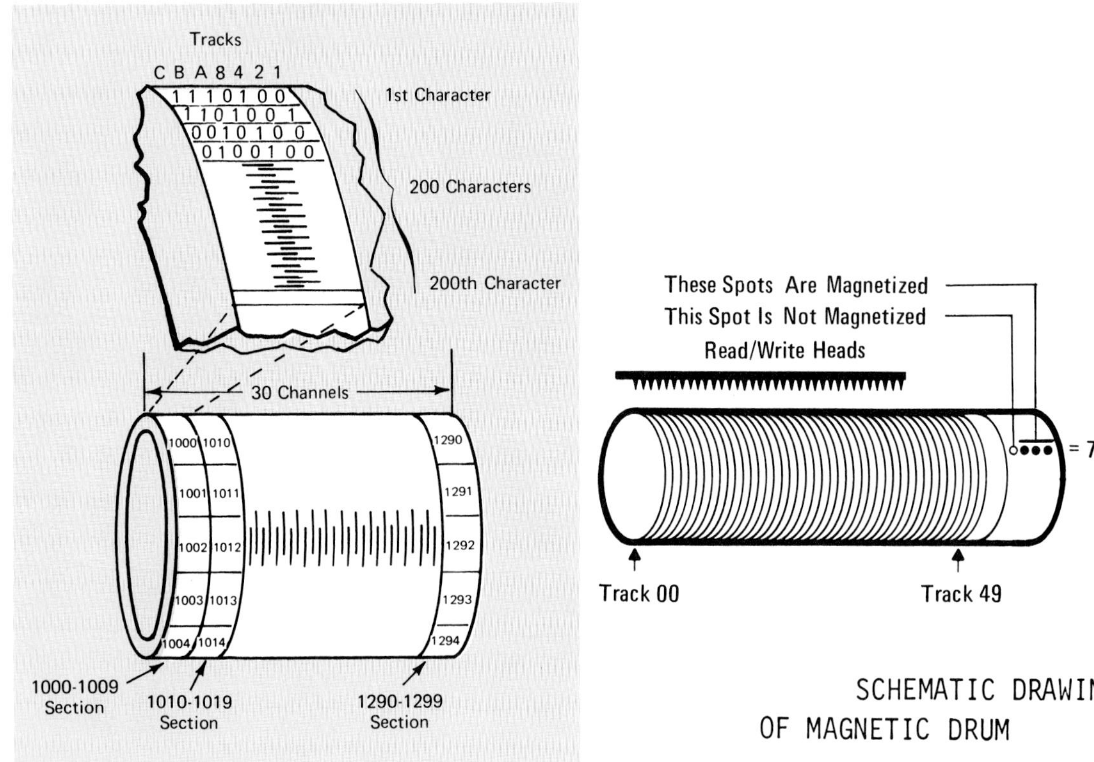

Figure 6–16. Magnetic Drum Storage.

Figure 6–17. Schematic Drawing of Magnetic Drum.

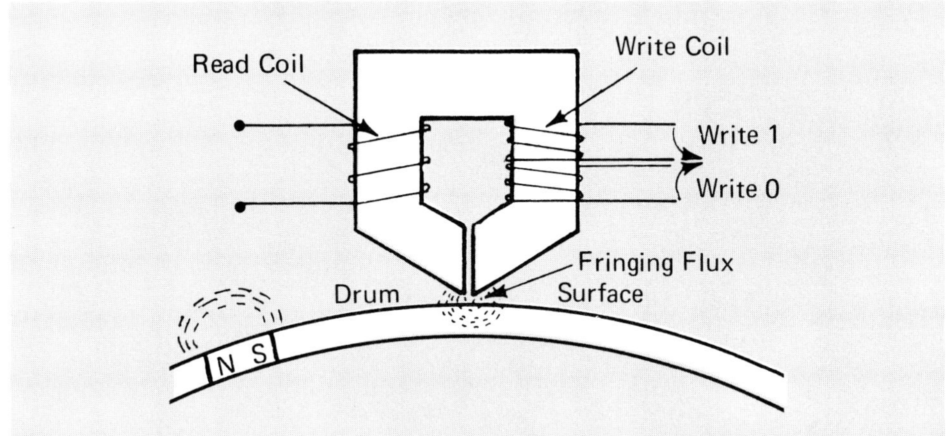

Figure 6–18. Drum Recording.

the magnetic drum is magnetized. The read coils read magnetized spots as they pass by the head (Fig. 6.18). There are a specific number of storage locations addressable by the computer on each drum. The capacity of each storage location depends upon the design of the drum and the particular type of data representation used.

Drum storage offers the advantage of lower direct cost to offset the faster speed of the core storage units.

MAGNETIC DISK

Disk storage is the most popular type of auxiliary storage in use today. Magnetic disk, like drum storage, provides data processing systems with the ability to read or retrieve records sequentially or randomly (direct access). The *magnetic disk* is a thin disk of metal coated on both sides with magnetic recording material.

Data is stored as magnetic spots on concentric tracks on each surface of the disk. These tracks are accessible for reading by positioning the read/write heads between the spinning disks.

Independent portable disks can be used with interchangeable disk packs. Each disk pack has a capacity of over 7 million characters. Six disk packs are mounted as a single unit which can be readily removed from the disk drive and stored in a library of disk packs. Read/write heads are mounted on an access arm arranged like teeth on a comb that moves horizontally between the disks. Two read/write heads are mounted on each arm with one head serving the bottom surface of the top disk and the other head servicing the top surface of the lower disk. Thus it is possible to read or write on either side of the disk (Fig. 6.19).

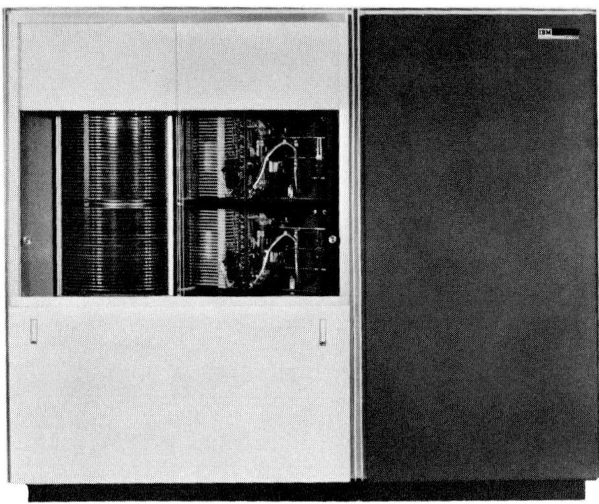

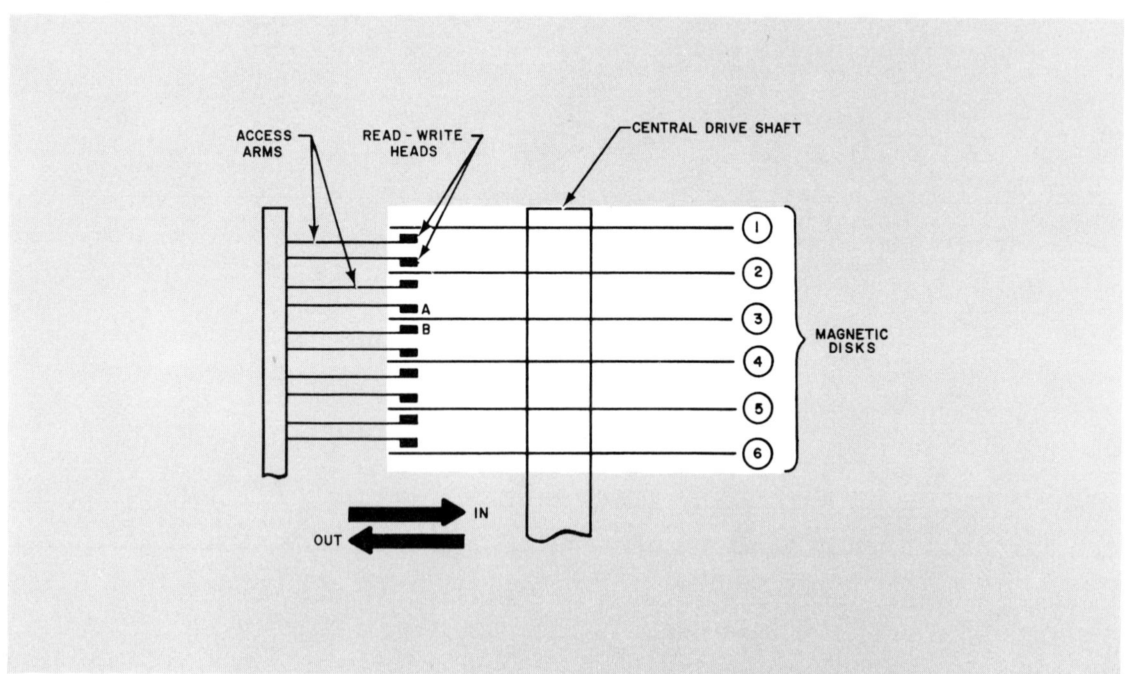

Figure 6–19. Magnetic Disk Schematic Drawing.

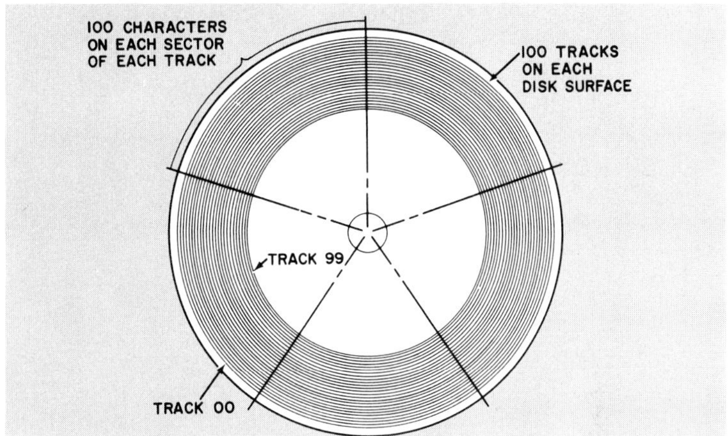

Figure 6–20. Magnetic Disk Layout.

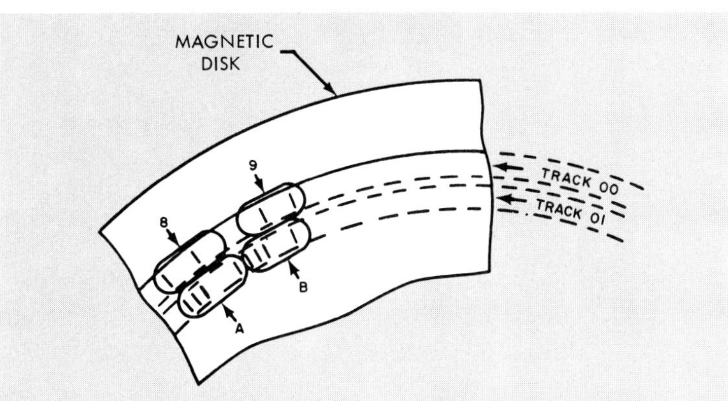

Figure 6–21. Magnetic Disk Recording.

Each disk surface contains 100 tracks which are divided into 20 sectors. The capacity of each sector may be as many as 100 characters (Figs. 6.20, 6.21). With proper file organization, a minimum of access time is required for retrieval of a disk record. The concept of removable disk packs means that only those disk records needed for a particular application need be in use. Data records for other applications can be removed and stored.

The types of disk storage devices presently available are: (1) devices with removable disk packs, (2) devices with nonremovable disk packs, and (3) direct access storage facility.

REMOVABLE DISK PACKS

Each drive consists of six disks mounted on a vertical shaft that may be removed from the drive and enclosed in a protective cover. The disks are fourteen inches in diameter and contain ten recording surfaces. A disk pack has a maximum capacity of over 7 million characters (Fig. 6.22).

Figure 6–22. Removable Disk.

NONREMOVABLE DISC PACKS

These disk units are available in two models. One model contains one module while the other has two modules, one mounted above the other. Each module consists of twenty-five disks, similar to the removable disks, except that they are twenty inches in diameter. There are forty-six surfaces on these disks available for recording data. Each module has a maximum capacity of over 113 million characters with the two-module type having a capacity of over 226 million characters (Fig. 6.23).

DIRECT ACCESS STORAGE FACILITY

This unit consists of five or nine drives depending upon the particular model (Fig. 6.24). All five, or any of eight of the nine (one drive is used as a backup if one of the other drives requires service), can be online at the same time. The devices use removable disk packs. The disk packs are larger than the six disk packs of the removable disk pack drives. Each pack consists of eleven disks with twenty recording surfaces. The five drives have a capacity of over 146 million characters. The direct access storage facility has a capacity of over 233 million characters.

The recording of each of the different types of disk storage devices operates in the same manner. The recording surface is divided into *tracks*. A *track* is defined as the circumference of the recording surface.

The access mechanism transfers data to and from the device. Each access

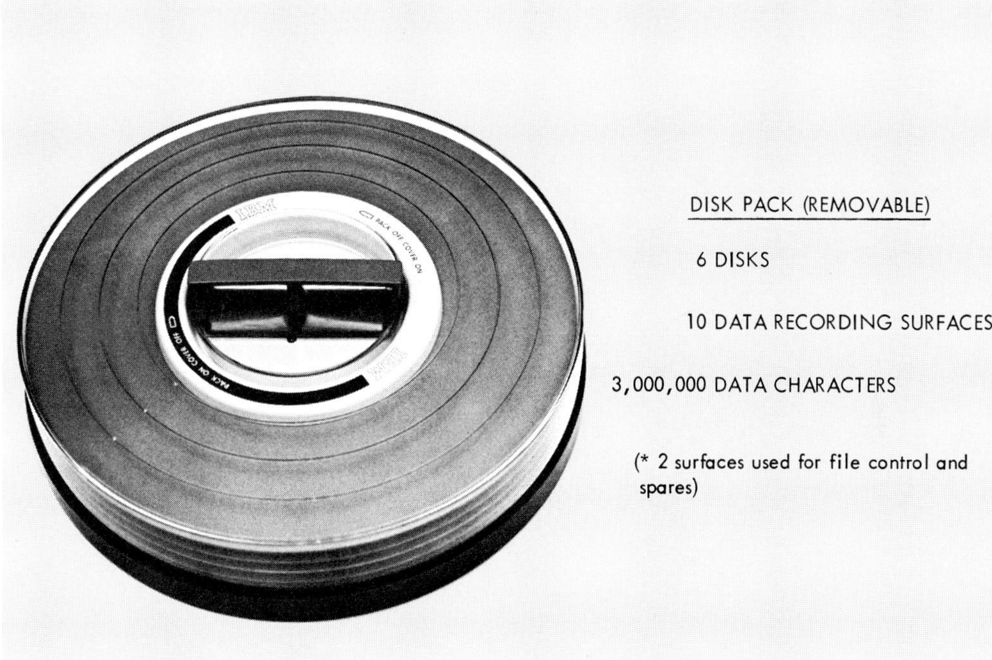

Figure 6–23. ›sk Packs and Modules.

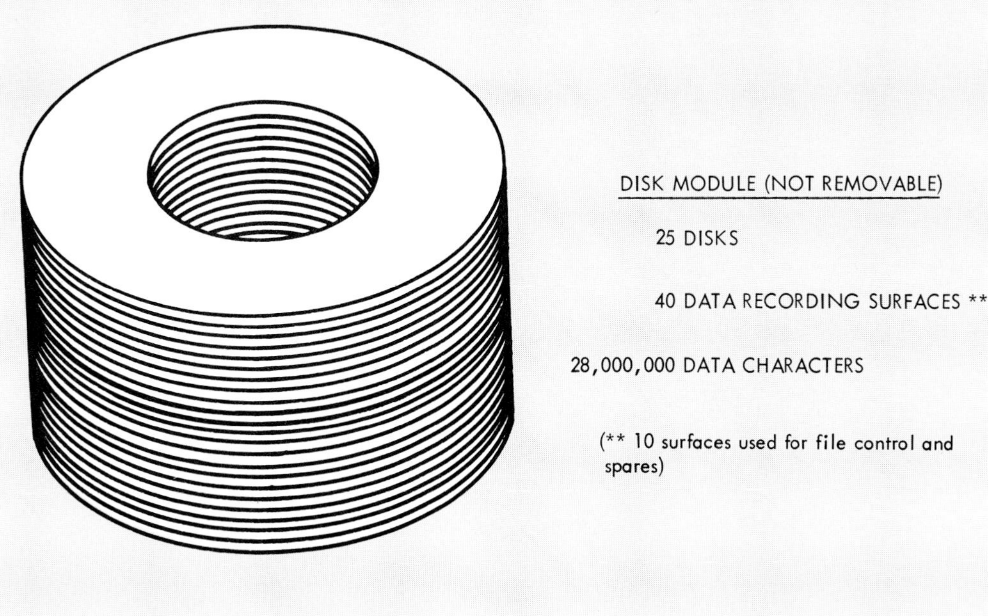

Figure 6–24. IBM 2314 Direct Access Storage Fàcilities.

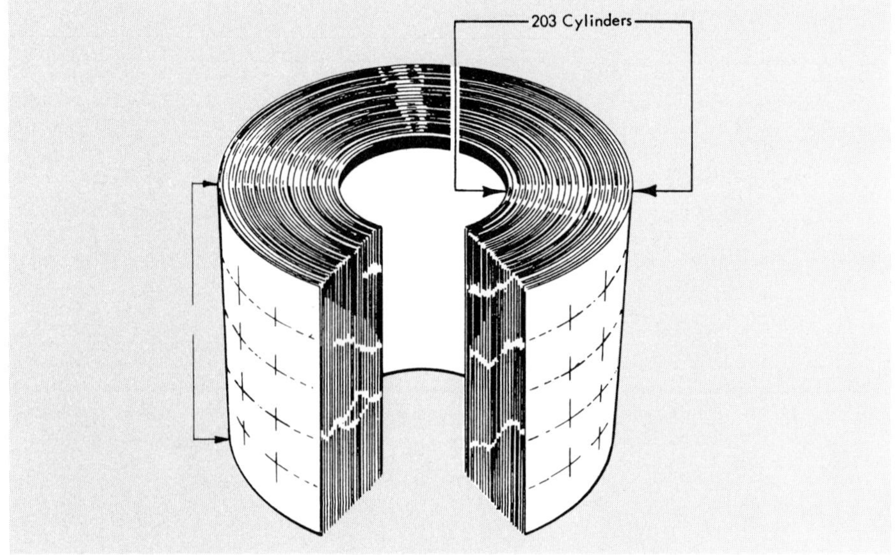

Figure 6–25. IBM 2311 Cylinders.

mechanism consists of a number of read/write heads arranged in a comb-type assembly that can be moved horizontally across the tracks. Only one head can be transferring data (either reading or writing) at any one time.

Each pack is divided into *cylinders* (Fig. 6.24). A *cylinder* of data is that amount of information that is accessible with one position of the access mechanism. Since the movement of the access mechanism requires a significant portion of the time needed to access and transfer data, the storing of a large amount of data in a single cylinder can save time in the processing by minimizing the amount of the access mechanism.

Disks provide the data processing systems with the ability to read and retrieve records randomly or sequentially. They permit the immediate access to specific areas of information without the need to examine each record as in magnetic tape operations.

Most disk storage devices are slower than drum storage but offer the advantage of capacities of millions of characters.

DATA CELLS

The data cell drive (Fig. 6.25) economically extends the online random access storage capabilities to a volume of data beyond that of other storage devices. A data cell device consists of ten cells. Each cell is divided into twenty subcells. Each subcell contains ten strips which are the recording medium for the device. Each strip is 2¼ inches wide, 13 inches long, and about three times as thick as magnetic tape. The strips are held in place at the bottom of the cell and by the adjacent strips.

The strips are processed by being wrapped around a drum. The data is recorded on concentric tracks, not a spiral track as on a phonograph record. The strips are selected for processing. As the drum continues to rotate, the strip is withdrawn from the subcell and wrapped around the drum. As the rotation continues, the strip moves past a bar of twenty read/write heads. There is no actual physical contact between the head and the strip since there is an air cushion between them. The strip remains attached to the drum until another strip is selected

The maximum capacity of a data cell drive is 400 million characters.

OTHER OPERATIONS

Other operations are performed to free the computer from the slow processing and conversion operations. Input/output and data conversion operations are relatively slow operations compared to the high speed of the CPU, so many offline operations are performed to convert data to faster input media. For example, magnetic tape is the fastest input/output medium, while

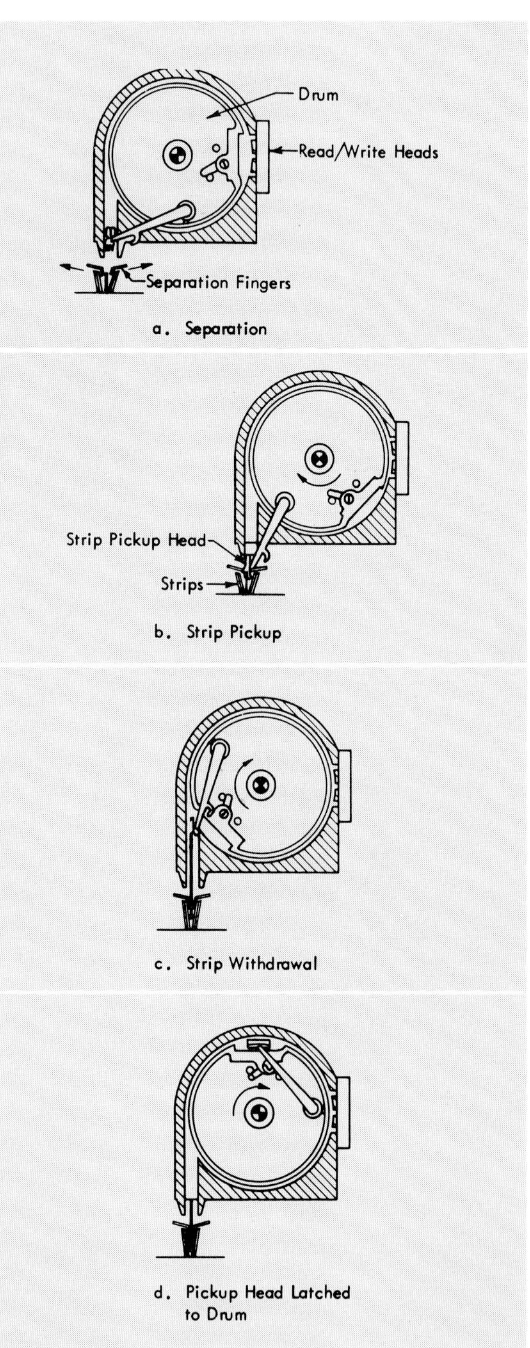

Figure 6–26. IBM 2321 Drive, Cell, Subcell Operation.

punched cards are the slowest. The punched cards can be converted to magnetic tape in an offline operation and the data entered into the system at the high speed rate of magnetic tape. Similarly, the output can be in the form of magnetic tape and later converted to punched cards in offline operations.

These auxiliary operations have progressed to a point where it is not unusual to find a small data processing unit performing these offline operations in a large data processing system. The big advantage is of course to free the computer from these routine tasks and to allow it more time for data manipulating and computing.

DIRECT ACCESS

"Inline" processing denotes the ability of the data processing system to process the data as soon as it becomes available. This implies that the input data does not have to be sorted in any manner, manipulated, or edited, before it is entered into the system, whether the input consists of transactions of a single application or of many applications.

Direct access mass storage devices have made inline processing feasible for many applications. While sorting transactions are still advantageous before certain processing runs, in most instances the necessity for presorting has been eliminated. The ability to process data inline provides solutions to problems which heretofore were thought impractical. A typical application of inline processing is inventory control where direct access processing is now being used extensively. For example, a large school district established a central warehouse for distributing supplies to its many schools. The records for the 20,000 items of inventory are maintained using a nine-digit stock number for identification purposes. Minimum balances which allow the storekeeper ample time to reorder each item are established for all items of inventory. The storekeeper wishes to be notified immediately when this minimum balance has been reached to avoid an out-of-stock condition. Under the previous system, all transactions were batched and processed together. All transactions affecting inventory were accumulated and sorted into stock number sequence and processed against the master file. This type of processing would result in a delay of days from the time the transaction occurred until it was processed. Sufficient time was not provided for the necessary reordering procedures. The problem was solved with the installation of direct access devices whereby the transactions were processed inline, as they occurred, and the required notifications of stock status would be provided almost immediately to the storekeeper.

Direct access storage enables the user to maintain current records of diversified applications and to process nonsequential and intermixed data for multiple application areas.

DIRECT ACCESS PROCESSING—APPLICATIONS

INQUIRIES

Prior to the development of direct access devices, the ability to request information directly from a storage device was limited. It involved the preparation of a complex time-consuming interruption procedure that did not always provide current information. The ability of direct access storage systems to process input data of various types inline for multiple applications and in addition to immediately update all the affected records makes it possible to interrogate the system and receive current information directly in readable form. There is no longer a need to disrupt the normal processing of the data, nor is there a delay between the request for information and the response. For example, a bank teller may need information immediately as to the status of a depositor's account. All that need be done is for the teller to insert the depositor's account number in an input device and the information will be displayed in readable format.

This ability to request information directly from the computer and receive an immediate response may in itself be a justification for the use of direct access storage devices.

MODIFICATION OF RECORDS

In most data processing applications, there is an interrelationship between records. Various applications may require the same input records, or, for processing, require reference to the same master file records used in other applications. Modification of existing records to change the sequence of file referencing and/or to accommodate additional references is more easily accomplished with direct access storage systems. For example, if the company manufactured a new product and several procedures had to be altered, all necessary activities could be changed at the same time. Direct access units, containing the records of production control, inventory maintenance and budgeting could be changed with a minimum of effort to accommodate the new product.

Another example is a payroll activity where a change is required for rate, number of exemptions, etc. The payroll change could be entered into the system once and the necessary records of personnel and payroll updated at the same time.

This provides solutions to data processing problems where multiple interdependent activities and multiple references to interrelated records are required.

LOW ACTIVITY DATA PROCESSING

Many applications involve a limited number of input transactions with a large master file of records. Although a small portion of the master file is referenced by the input data for a particular run, the entire master file, which is maintained in sequence, must be searched. For example, in an inventory application of 20,000 items where only 2,000 items may be active each day, the 2,000 items must be collected and sorted in a predetermined sequence and processed against the file.

Direct access devices permit the retrieval of a single record without the extensive searching of an entire file.

ONLINE PROCESSING

Online processing permits the operation of input and output devices under the control of the central processing unit at the same time the processing function is being performed. The online devices are physically connected to the CPU; a printer, for example. A data communication unit such as a teletypewriter is considered "online" even though it is not "physically" connected to the central processing unit, because a communication device provides the linkage between the two. In the previously mentioned example of inventory control, an inquiry as to the status of a particular item of stock can be made from any location. With a direct access storage system, the inventory items are kept current all the time and the information is available to all users. Without these "online" activities of teleprocessing, the ability to change records or to inquire regarding information relative to these records would be difficult.

DIRECT ACCESS STORAGE DEVICES

The term *direct access* implies access at random by multiple users of data (files, programs, subroutines, programming aids) involving mass storage devices. These storage devices differ in physical appearance, capability and speed but functionally they are similar in terms of data recording, checking and programming. The direct access devices used for mass memory storage are drums, disks and data cells.

DATA ORGANIZATION

Information is recorded on all devices in a format which is prescribed by the control unit and which is identical for each device. Each track contains certain nondata information such as the address of the track, the address of each record, the length of each record and a gap between areas, as well as data information (Figs. 6.27, 6.28).

Index Point
Track Descriptor Record (R0)
Data Record (R1)
Data Record (Rn)
G HA G Count Area G Data Area G A G Count Area G Data Area G G A G Count Area G Data Area
A. Count-data format

Index Point
Gap
Home Address
Track Descriptor Record (R0)
Data Record (R1)
Data Record (Rn)
G HA G Count Area G Data Area G A G Count Area G Key Area G Data Area G G A G Count Area G Key Area G Data Area
F C H CC
Cyclic Check
Head Number
Cylinder Number
Flag
F C H R KL DL CC
Cyclic Check
Data Length
Key Length
Record Number
Head Number
Cylinder Number
Identifier
Flag
Address Marker
B. Count-key-data format

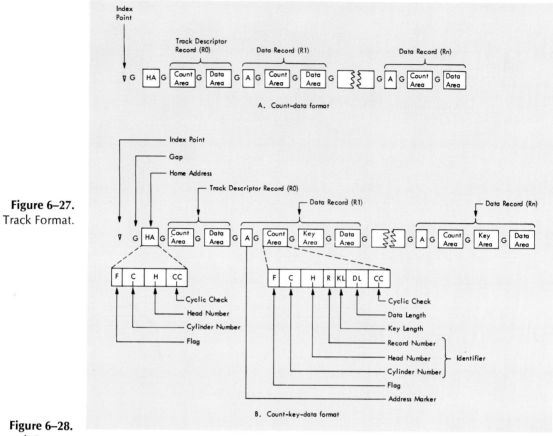

Figure 6–27.
Track Format.

Figure 6–28.
Record Format.

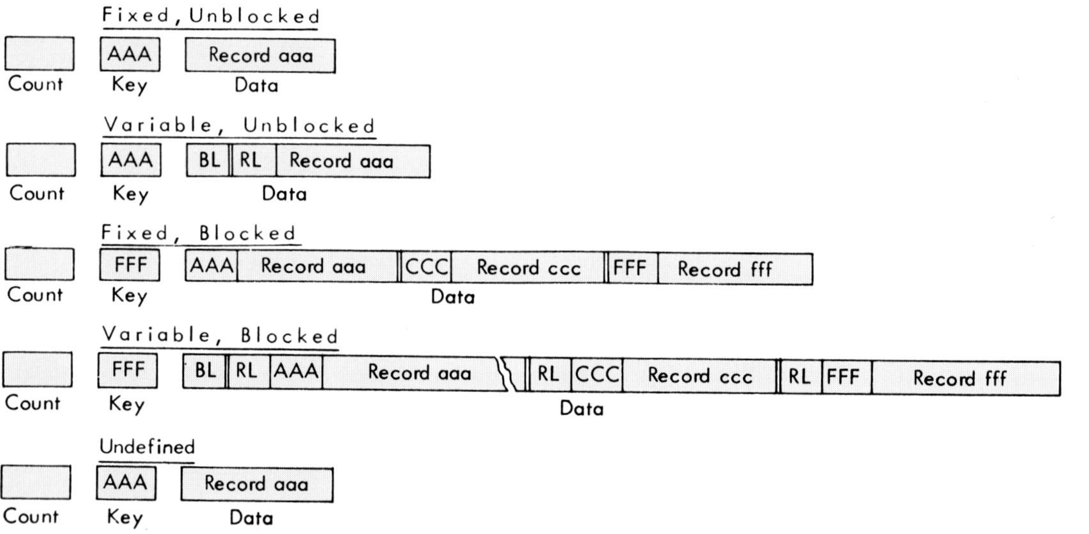

FIXED UNBLOCKED RECORDS

All records in the file are of the same length. Each data area contains one logical record. If keys are used, they are usually not repeated in each of the data areas.

VARIABLE UNBLOCKED RECORDS

The logical records contained in a file are of various lengths. Individual data areas contain one logical record. Special fields are added to define the block and record lengths. A block length (BL) indicates the number of characters in each block and a record length field (RL), indicates the number of characters in each logical record.

BLOCKED RECORDS

The primary reason for blocking is to pack more information in a storage area. This method uses direct access storage more efficiently as it is only necessary to have address marker, count areas, key areas and interrecord gaps for each block of records rather than for each logical record.

If the records are to be processed consecutively, there is an advantage in blocking records as there is only one rotational delay before the reading or writing of a block of records. However, if records are not processed consecutively, blocking may be a disadvantage since it takes longer to transfer an entire block than a single record.

FIXED BLOCKED RECORDS

All the records in the file are of the same length and each data area contains more than one logical record. All blocks are of the same length except possibly the last block, which may be shorter. The key appears in each logical record in the same location and is used for identification purposes during processing. The *key area* usually contains the key of the highest logical record in the block.

VARIABLE BLOCKED RECORDS

The logical records in these files are of varying lengths. Each data area contains a block of logical records. A block length field and record length field are used to indicate the sizes of blocks and records.

UNDEFINED RECORDS

This particular format is used to permit the handling of records that do not fit any of the aforementioned formats. One record per block is used. An example would be a variable length record without a block length or record length field.

In order to retrieve records efficiently for data processing operations, the records within the file must be properly organized. There are several important considerations in selecting an efficient method for file organization.

FILE ORGANIZATIONS—CONSIDERATIONS

VOLATILITY

The time it takes to add or delete records from a file must be considered. A *static file* is one that has a low percentage of additions and deletions while a *volatile file* is active at all times, requiring many additions and deletions. The file must be organized so that these additions and deletions are handled with ease. Some methods of organization are more suited to these types of transactions than others.

ACTIVITY

The percentage of activity is an important factor in considering file organization. If a small percentage of the records stored in a file are active at any one time, the file should be so organized that these active records can be quickly located without the necessity for searching the entire file. The records that are processed frequently should be so located that they are retrieved quickly.

SIZE

A file should be so planned as to anticipate growth over a period of time. In the process of this planning the possibility that the growth may exceed the present size of storage facilities should also be considered.

A file that is so large that it is not available to the system at one time (online) must be organized and processed in certain ways. On the other hand, a file may be so small that its organization will make little difference in processing time no matter how it is organized.

PROCESSING TECHNIQUES

SEQUENTIAL PROCESSING

In sequential processing, input transactions are grouped together and sorted into a predetermined sequence and processed against the master file. When information is recorded in magnetic tape or punched cards, the most efficient method of processing is sequential. Direct access storage devices are also efficient sequential processors, especially when the percentage of activity against the master file is high.

RANDOM PROCESSING

The processing of detail transactions against a master file, regardless of the sequence of the input documents, is called random processing. With direct access devices, it can be very efficient, especially if the files are organized in such a manner that each record can be located quickly. It is possible to process input transactions against more than one file in a single run. This saves time in both setup and sorting, and minimizes the control problems, since the transactions are handled less frequently. It is feasible to handle transactions without the necessity of accumulating them. The transactions may be processed inline as soon as they are available. Inquiries to master files need not be scheduled. This is particularly significant in teleprocessing systems where many inquiries can be made regarding the status of records within a file.

The use of direct access storage devices makes it possible to select the processing techniques that will suit the application best. Thus some applications may be processed sequentially while those in which the time required to sort or the delay associated with batching processes is a material factor, can be processed randomly. Real savings in overall processing time for a job can be made by combining runs in which the same input data affects several files, the detail items can be processed sequentially against a primary file and randomly against the secondary file, all in one run. This is the basis of inline processing.

DATA FILE ORGANIZATIONS

This term refers to the physical arrangement of data records within a file. To give the programmer maximum flexibility and efficiency in reading and writing data sets from direct access devices, the following methods of data file organizations are used: Sequential, Indexed Sequential, Direct (Random), and Partitioned.

SEQUENTIAL ORGANIZATION

In a sequential file, records are organized solely on the basis of their successive physical locations in the file (Fig. 6.29). The records are written one

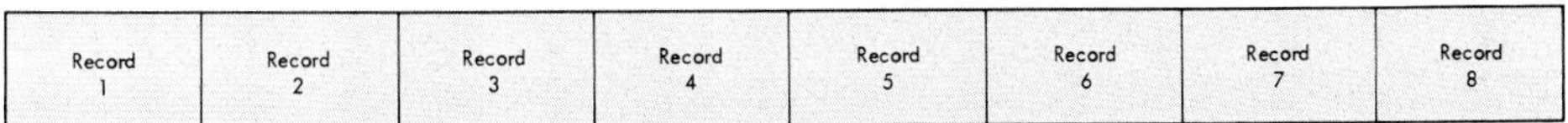

Figure 6–29. A Sequentially Organized Data Set.

after the other—track by track, cylinder by cylinder—at successively higher locations. The records are usually, but not necessarily in sequence according to their keys (control numbers). The records are usually read or updated in the same sequence as that in which they appear. For example, record 6 will be read only after the first five records have been read.

Random processing of a sequential file is very inefficient. Individual records cannot be located rapidly. Records cannot be inserted or deleted unless the entire file is rewritten. This method of organization is generally used where most of the records of a file are processed each time the file is used.

Sequential organization of a file is used in direct access storage devices primarily for tables, and intermediate storage rather than master files. Its use is recommended for master files only if there is a high percentage of activity of a file each time the file is processed, or if virtually all processing of the file is sequential.

INDEXED SEQUENTIAL ORGANIZATION

An indexed sequential organization file is a sequential file with indexes that permit the rapid access to individual records as well as rapid sequential processing (Fig. 6.30). The indexes are created and written by the system as the file is created or reorganized. A key precedes each block of data. An index

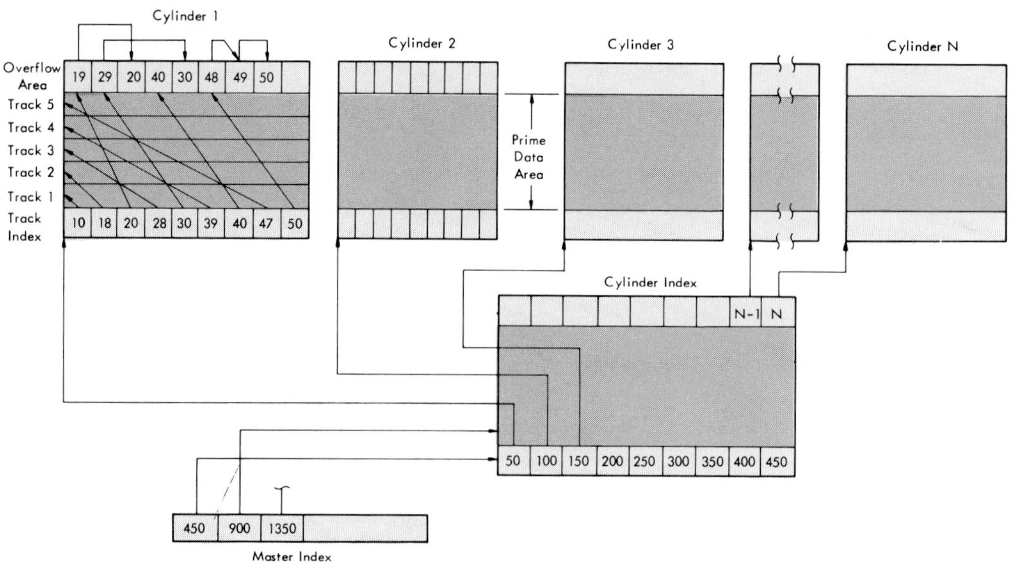

Figure 6–30. Index Structure for an Indexed Sequential Data Set.

sequential file is similar to a sequential file; however, by referring to the indexes maintained within the file, it is possible to quickly locate individual records for random processing. Moreover a separate area can be set aside for additions which makes it unnecessary to rewrite the entire file, a process that would be required for sequential processing (Fig. 6.31). Although the records are not maintained in key sequence, the indexes are referred to in order to retrieve the added records in key sequences, thus making rapid sequential processing possible.

The programming system has control over the location of the individual record in this method of organization. The user need do very little input and output programming; the programming system does most of it inasmuch as the characteristics of the file are known.

Indexed sequential organization gives the programmer greater flexibility in the operations he can perform on the data file. He has the ability to read or write records in a manner similar to that for sequential organization. He can also read or write individual records whose keys may be in any order, and add logical records with new keys. The system locates the proper position in

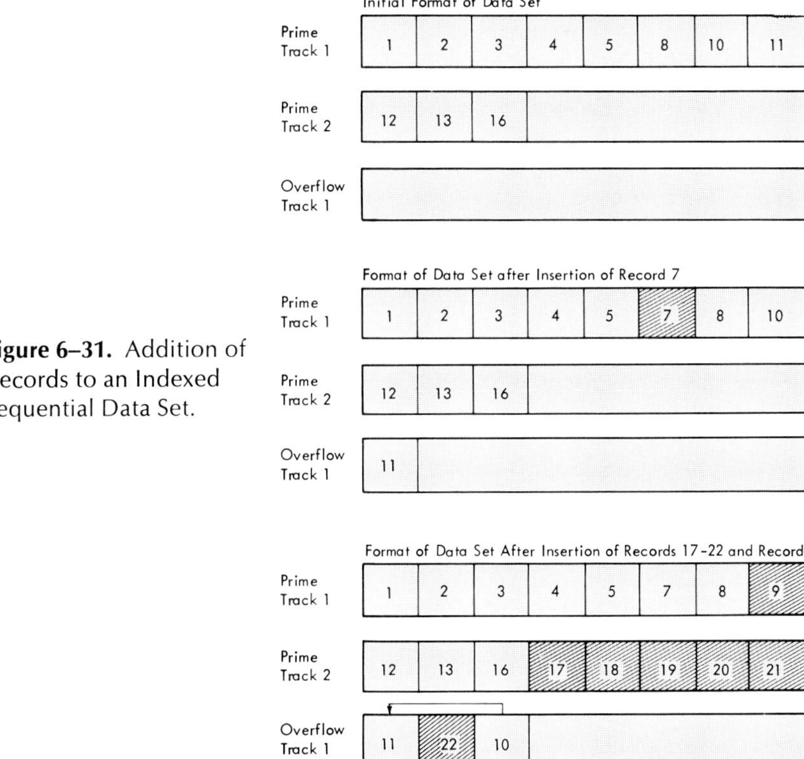

Figure 6–31. Addition of Records to an Indexed Sequential Data Set.

the data file for the new record and makes all the necessary adjustments to the indexes.

DIRECT (RANDOM) ORGANIZATION

A file organized in a direct (random) manner is characterized by some predictable relationship between the key of a record and the address of that record in a direct access storage device. The relationship is established by the user and permits the rapid access to any record of the file if the file is carefully organized. The records will probably be distributed nonsequentially throughout the file. If so, processing the records in key sequence requires a preliminary sort or the use of a finder file.

When a request to store or retrieve a record is made, an address relative to the beginning of the file or an actual address (i.e., device, cylinder, track, record position) must be furnished. This address can be specified as being the address of the desired record or as a starting point within the file where the search for the record begins. When a record search is specified, the programmer must also furnish the key (e.g., part number, customer number) that is associated with the desired record. With direct addressing, every possible key in the file converts to a unique address, thus making it possible to locate any record in the file with one search and one read (Fig. 6.32).

The user has complete freedom in deciding where records are to be located in a direct organized file. When creating or making additions to the file, the user may specify the location for a record key by supplying the track address and identifier or just simply the track address and let the system find a

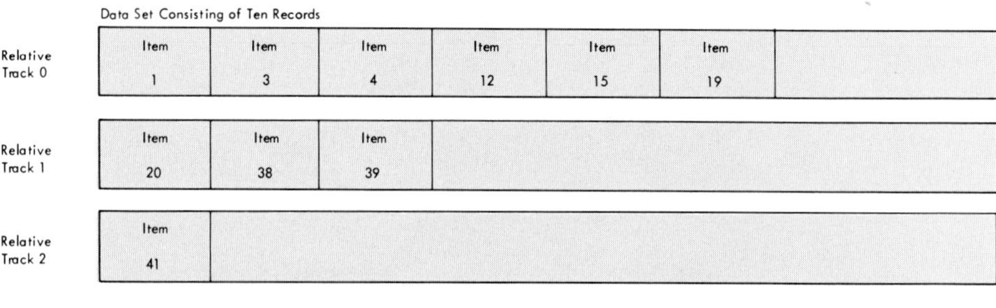

Figure 6–32. Addition of Records to a Direct Data Set.

location for the record. The record is written in the first available location on the track specified. If the specified track is full, the system continues to search successive tracks until a location is found.

Direct organization is generally used for files whose characteristics do not permit the use of sequential or indexed sequential organizations, or for files where the time required to locate individual records must be kept at a minimum. This method has considerable flexibility but has a serious disadvantage in that the programming system provides the routines to read a file of this type. The user is largely responsible for the logic and programming requirements to locate records since he establishes the relationship between the key of the record and the address in the direct access storage device.

PARTITIONED ORGANIZATION

A partitioned file is one that is divided into sequentially organized members made up of one or more records. Each member has a unique name (Fig. 6.33). The file also includes a directory containing the names and beginning address of each member. Enough storage space is required to hold the sequentially organized members and the directory. As new members are added, the system allocates additional areas of assigned storage, if the assigned areas are filled. If the directory is filled, no new members may be added without reorganizing the file.

Members may be added or deleted as required. The records within the members are organized sequentially and are retrieved or stored successively according to their physical sequence.

Partitioned organization is used mainly for the storage of sequential data, such as programs, subroutines, compilers and tables. The main advantage of

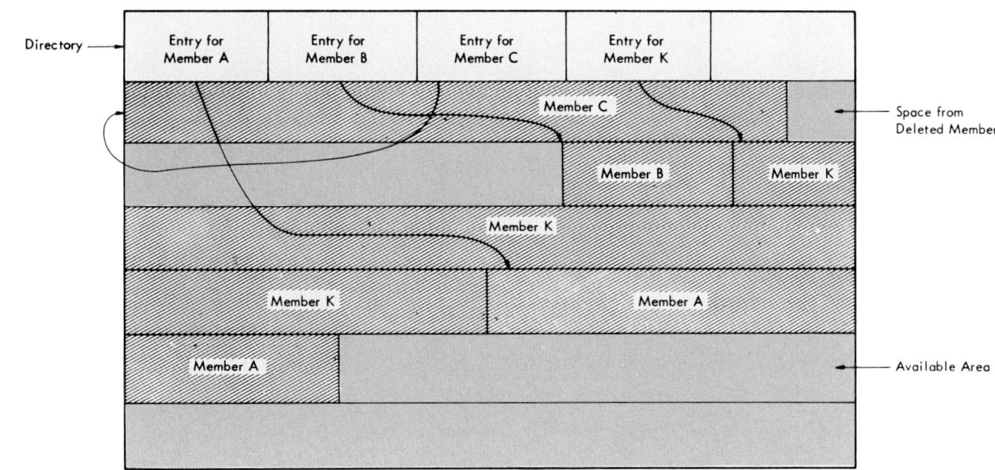

Figure 6–33. Partitioned Data Set.

a partitioned file is that it makes it possible for the programmer to retrieve specific members. For example, a library of subroutines might be a partitioned file whose members are subroutines. Within each subroutine, the records are sequentially organized.

SUMMARY

The effectiveness of a data processing system is measured by its ability to process data as soon as it becomes available. In order to accomplish this all-important objective, the data processing system must have the capacity to store large amounts of data. Direct access storage devices have made real time processing a reality. The ability to process data as soon as it becomes available implies that the input does not have to be sorted or manipulated in any manner before it is introduced into the system. Direct access mass storage devices have made inline processing feasible for many applications by virtue of the fact that it enables the user to maintain current records of diversified applications, and to process nonsequential and intermixed records of multiple application areas. The intent of this chapter is to describe the various components of a central processing unit, the physical characteristics of storage devices available to the users of the equipment and direct access processing concepts together with the operation of the direct access devices.

The methods of processing data and the function of each of the units involved is essential to a clear understanding of the data processing function. One should be aware that the computer processing unit is composed of a series of devices that act together in processing the data to produce the desired output, and that each of these individual units has a particular function to perform. Further it is important to know the different methods of storing data and the operation of direct access units. How data is organized has a direct effect on the retrieval time. Certain data organizations are best suited for certain data processing applications and will reduce actual processing time for those applications.

The potential processing capabilities of any computer system is determined by its storage capacity. Computer storage is an important factor in determining the number of operations and the extent of processing to be performed by the computer. Direct access storage devices are used more extensively in data processing applications each day. Large storage capacities have reduced the price of storage and have made possible heretofore impractical applications. One should possess knowledge of all types of storage available and how each operates within a data processing system.

I. *Central Processing Unit* (*CPU*).
   A. *Function*—supervises and controls data processing components.
   B. *Arithmetic and Logical Section*—performs the necessary arithmetic and logical operations.

C. *Control Section*—automatically integrates operations of the entire system.

II. *Operational Units.*

A. *Registers*—capable of storing information temporarily. Classified according to function performed.

B. *Counter*—acts as an accumulator.

C. *Adder*—performs the actual accumulating process.

D. *Machine cycles*—the time to perform a specific operation. Time intervals, milliseconds, microseconds, nanoseconds.

III. *Instructions.*

A. *Function*—a command to the system to perform an operation.

B. *Parts of an instruction.*

1. *Operation*—the function the machine is to perform: add, move, shift, etc.
2. *Operand*—the address of the data in storage, or a program in storage, or an input/output device.

C. *Processing.*

1. *Function*—sequential execution of instructions except for branch-type instructions.
2. *Instruction cycle*—instruction brought from main storage and decoded.
3. *Execution cycle*—the actual processing of the data.

IV. *Storage.*

A. *Function*—receives information from input/output devices and makes information available for processing. Information stored in addressable locations.

B. *Main Storage (core)*—all data to be processed must pass through main storage.

C. *Auxiliary storage*—additional storage to augment main storage. All data must be transferred to main storage for processing.

1. *Random (direct) access units*—records may be accessed randomly.
2. *Sequential access units*—each record must be examined before desired record is reached.

D. *Storage processing.*

1. *Access time*—the time required to locate and transfer data to and from storage.
2. *Core storage*—all processing takes place here; doughnut-shaped ferro-magnetic-coated material, vertically aligned.
3. *Drum storage*—serves as intermediate storage; constant-speed rotating cylinder with an outer surface coated with magnetic material. Usually valuable in large data processing systems. Capacity of over 4 million characters.

4. *Disk storage*—used to retrieve records randomly and sequentially; large capacity storage device; thin metal disk coated on both sides with magnetic recording material.
   a) *Removable disk packs*—six-disk packs with capacities over seven million characters, mounted on a vertical shaft that can be removed from the device.
   b) *Nonremovable disk packs*—available with twenty-five disks with a capacity of 113 million characters.
   c) *Direct access storage facility*—consists of five or nine devices depending upon the particular model. Removable disk packs with a total capacity ranging from 146 million characters (five devices) to 233 million characters (nine devices).
5. *Data cells*—used to retrieve records randomly and sequentially: large capacity storage device; storage medium is a strip of magnetic film 2¼ inches wide by 13 inches long; extends the only random access capabilities to a volume of data beyond that of other storage devices. A maximum capacity of over 400 million characters.

Other operations—input/output conversion, offline operations.

V. *Direct Access Processing Applications.*
   A. *Inquiries*—information can be requested directly from the computer and an immediate response received.
   B. *Modification of records*—makes possible the changing of many interrelated records in a data processing system at the same time.
   C. *Low activity data processing*—it becomes possible to retrieve a single record without the extensive searching of an entire file where there is a limited number of transactions with a large master file of records.
   D. *Online processing*—input and output operations can be performed at the same time the processing function is performed.

VI. *Data Organization.*
   A. *Record formats.*
      1. *Fixed unblocked records*—all records in file are of the same length and each data area contains one logical record.
      2. *Variable unblocked records*—all records in file are of various lengths and each data area contains one logical record.
      3. *Fixed blocked records*—all records in file are of the same length, and each data area contains more than one logical record.
      4. *Variable blocked records*—all records in file are of various lengths and each data area contains more than one logical record.
      5. *Undefined*—all records in file do not fit any of the aforementioned formats and there is one logical record per block.

B. *Data file organization considerations.*
   1. *Volatility*—the time it takes to add or delete records from a file.
   2. *Activity*—the percentage of activity of each of the logical records in the file.
   3. *Size*—should be planned to anticipate growth over a period of time.

C. *Processing techniques.*
   1. *Sequential processing*—input records are grouped together, sorted in a predetermined sequence and processed against the master file.
   2. *Random processing*—detail transactions are not sorted, and processed against file regardless of sequence.

D. *Data file organization.*
   1. *Sequential file organization*—all records are organized solely on their successive physical locations in a file.
   2. *Indexed sequential file organization*—a sequential organized file with indexes that permit rapid access to individual records as well as sequential processing. The indexes are created by the system as the file is being organized.
   3. *Direct (random) file organization*—there is some predictable relationship between the key of the records and the address of the record in the file.
   4. *Partitioned organization file*—is divided into sequentially organized members made up of one or more records with each member having a unique name.

IDENTIFICATION QUESTIONS

Match the following terms with the statements that follow.

A. Access Time
B. Adder
C. Address
D. Blocked Records
E. Counter
F. Data Cells
G. Data File Organization
H. Direct Access
I. Direct (Random) Organization
J. Execution Cycle
K. Fixed Records
L. Indexed Sequential Organization
M. Inline Processing
N. Instruction Cycle
O. Magnetic Core
P. Magnetic Disk
Q. Magnetic Drum
R. Main Storage
S. Microsecond
T. Millisecond
U. Nanosecond
V. Online Processing
W. Operand
X. Operation
Y. Partitioned Organization
Z. Random Access Units
AA. Random Processing
BB. Register
CC. Sequential Access Unit
DD. Sequential Organization
EE. Sequential Processing
FF. Static File
GG. Storage
HH. Variable Records
II. Volatile File

1. Thin metal disk coated on both sides with magnetic material.
2. Denotes the function that the machine is to perform.
3. Characterized by some predictable relationship between the record and its location in main storage.
4. All data must pass through this unit.
5. Acts as an accumulator.
6. Records grouped together.
7. Physical arrangement of data records within a file.
8. The time required to locate and transfer data to and from storage.
9. Low percentage of additions and deletions.
10. Accumulates values of two data items and sends results to accumulator.
11. Giant electronic cabinet, completely indexed and available for instant access.
12. Metallic recording medium strip.
13. Records are arranged solely on the basis of their physical location in a file.
14. One thousandth of a second.
15. Access at random by multiple users of data involving mass storage devices.
16. Active at all times
17. A device capable of storing information temporarily and receiving and transferring information as directed by the Control Section.
18. A sequential file with indexes that permit rapid access to individual items.
19. Doughnut shaped ferromagnetic-coated material vertically aligned.
20. One billionth of a second.
21. The processing of detail transactions against a master file regardless of sequence.
22. The address of data, instructions, program, or input or output devices.
23. A constant speed rotating cylinder with an outer surface coated with magnetic material.
24. Operation of input and output devices at the same time that processing takes place.
25. A file that is divided into sequentially organized members made of one or more records.
26. One millionth of a second.
27. All records in the file are of the same length.
28. Devices that can process data randomly.
29. The ability to process data as soon as it becomes available.
30. All records in the file are of various lengths.
31. Input transactions are grouped together, sorted in a predetermined sequence and processed against the file.
32. Instructions brought from main storage and decoded.
33. A specific location in storage.
34. Data must be read from the beginning of the file to find the desired record.
35. The actual performance of an instruction.

QUESTIONS FOR REVIEW

1. What is the chief function of the central processing unit?
2. What two sections compose the central processing unit and what is the main function of each section?
3. How is a register used in data processing?
4. What is a machine cycle?
5. What are the two parts of each instruction?
6. What steps are involved in an instruction process?
7. What is storage?
8. What is main storage? Auxiliary storage?
9. What is meant by access time?
10. Describe the different types of storage available and enumerate the important aspects of each type.
11. Describe an offline operation that can speed up the processing of data.
12. What is inline processing?
13. What is the basic purpose of direct access storage devices in inline processing?
14. Describe some of the principal uses for direct access processing.
15. What are direct access storage devices?
16. What is a format?
17. Describe briefly the five record formats available.
18. What are the reasons for blocking records?
19. List the important considerations in selecting an efficient method for file organization.
20. What is the important difference between sequential processing and random processing?
21. What is data file organization?
22. Describe sequential organization and state why it is inefficient in random processing.
23. Describe an indexed sequential file organization and list its main advantages.
24. What is a direct organization file? What is its main use?
25. What is a partitioned organization file and what is its principal use?

CHAPTER 7

Computer Data Representation and Arithmetic

Numeric symbols or numbers were invented to facilitate counting. Over the years, numerous symbols were used to represent and communicate information. Early number systems frequently employed cumbersome symbols and inconvenient rules which hindered the advance of systematic mathematical solutions. These early computers were designed to manipulate the data in decimal and alphabetic formats (Fig. 7.1). The use of these early symbolic codes in a modern computer would make the solution of the complex mathematical problems of today extremely complicated—if even possible. As a result, simpler and faster methods of representing data had to be found.

Most computers today employ the simplest form of arithmetic, a two digit code. Known as the binary system, it uses a combination of ones and zeroes in

As you know, the decimal system is based on ten digits, "0" through "9."

1	,	2	6	4
THOUSANDS		HUNDREDS	TENS	UNITS

Figure 7–1. Decimal Counting System.

This is just one other way of representing one thousand two hundred and sixty four units . . . each carrying a value of one (1).

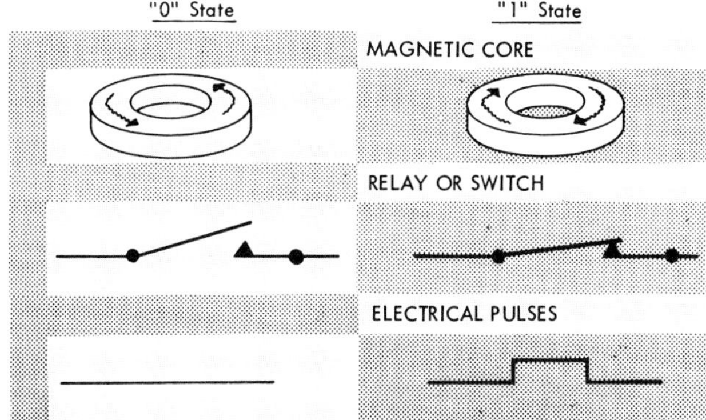

Figure 7–2. Binary Components.

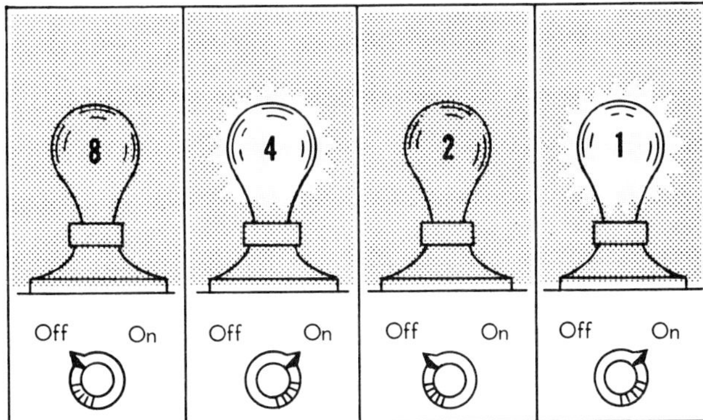

Figure 7–3. Representing Data with Binary Components.

various configurations, by which a computer can represent all numerals, letters and special characters. The binary form indicates the presence of only two conditions, the presence of a bit (on) or the absence of a bit (off) (Fig. 7.2). This principle can be compared to an electric light bulb which functions in the binary mode; either it is in the on or the off position. The position of a particular bit establishes its value (Fig. 7.3). The bit values start at the right with one value and then proceed upward by 2, 4, 8, 16, etc. Thus the decimal values 0 through 15 can be expressed with these four bits, 8, 4, 2, and 1 (Fig. 7.4). It is the binary method of data representation and computation that permits the computer to process data at fantastic speed, as it is necessary for the machine to test for only one of two possible conditions.

Light bulbs, of course, are not used in computers, but the same principles are used in the various computer components. Vacuum tubes and transistors are either conducting or nonconducting; a magnetized device is magnetized with either one or two polarities; a position in a card is either punched or left blank (Fig. 7.5).

The data is encoded in binary form by the presence or absence of an

DECIMAL NUMBER	BINARY NUMBER
0	0 0 0 0 0
1	0 0 0 0 1
2	0 0 0 1 0
3	0 0 0 1 1
4	0 0 1 0 0
5	0 0 1 0 1
6	0 0 1 1 0
7	0 0 1 1 1
8	0 1 0 0 0
9	0 1 0 0 1
10	0 1 0 1 0
11	0 1 0 1 1
12	0 1 1 0 0
13	0 1 1 0 1
14	0 1 1 1 0
15	0 1 1 1 1
16	1 0 0 0 0
BIT VALUES →	16 8 4 2 1

Figure 7–4. Binary and Decimal Numbers.

Figure 7–5. Binary Representation.

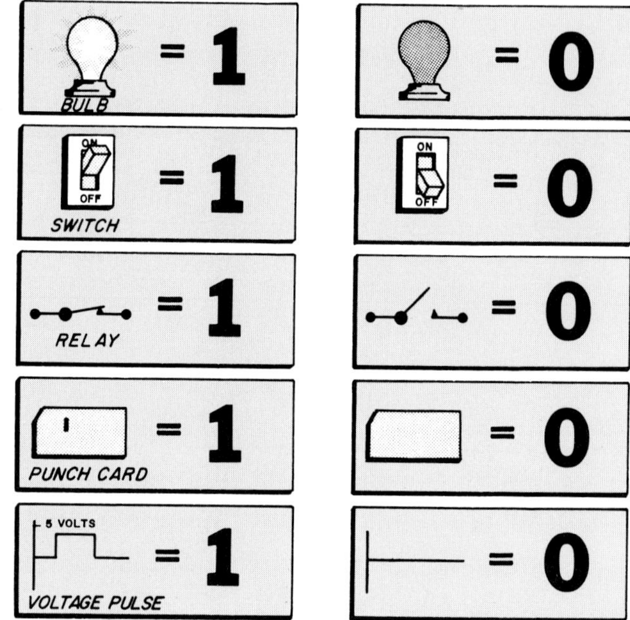

Binary Representation

electrical impulse or by the direction of magnetization. Tiny magnetic cores are used to store individual binary bits and the direction of polarity indicates a 1 (one) or 0 (zero) bit.

There are various binary coding systems used by different computers. In the computer, the code relates to a fixed number of binary indicators. By the proper arrangement of these indicators, it is possible to represent numeric, alphabetic and special characters.

COMPUTER NUMBER SYSTEMS

The Arabs invented the numerical symbols and system of positional notation on which our present decimal and other number systems are based. Each numeric symbol has a fixed value one higher than that of the symbol immediately preceding it in the progression from the smallest to the largest number; 0, 1, 2, 3, 4, 5, 6, 7, 8, 9. When several positions are used, the value is dependent upon the relative position of the digits as well as the digit values themselves. In any system of numbers, the digit position on the extreme right has the smallest value and is known as the low order position (least significant digit). The increase in value of each digit position depends upon the *base* or *radix* of the number system. Each numbering system is identifiable by its base or radix which indicates the number of digits used in the system. The decimal system with a base of 10, uses the different digits 0–9. *The highest number to be represented by a single digit is one less than the base.*

Characteristic of all numbering systems is the positional numbering system. Thus in the decimal numbering system, each digital position is assigned a value equal to a power of 10. These positions of the decimal system are commonly called units, tens, hundreds, thousands, etc. The following table contains some values of powers of 10.

$10^0 = 1$	$10^4 = 10{,}000$
$10^1 = 10$	$10^5 = 100{,}000$
$10^2 = 100$	$10^6 = 1{,}000{,}000$
$10^3 = 1{,}000$	$10^7 = 10{,}000{,}000$

The values positioned to the left of the least significant digit increases by powers of 10. For example, the decimal number 8,952 actually implies

8 THOUSANDS + 9 HUNDREDS + 5 TENS + 2 UNITS or = 8,952
8,000 + 900 + 50 + 2

These positional values can be expressed more simply using the powers of 10 for each position. Positional notation is not possible without the zero. Its presence within a number means that the power of the base is not used by that digit position.

Thousands	*Hundreds*	*Tens*	*Units*
10^3 or 1,000	10^2 or 100	10^1 or 10	10^0 or 1
8	9	5	2
4	0	0	8

The decimal number in each digital position is multiplied by its respective digital position value. The products added together form the total.

The first number

$$
\begin{array}{rcrcr}
8 & \times & 1{,}000 & = & 8{,}000 \\
9 & \times & 100 & = & 900 \\
5 & \times & 10 & = & 50 \\
2 & \times & 1 & = & 2 \\
\hline
 & & & & 8{,}952
\end{array}
$$

The second number

4	×	1,000	=	4,000
8	×	1	=	8
				4,008

In the decimal number 8,952, the rightmost digit (2) has the smallest value and is considered the least significant digit while the leftmost digit (8) has the highest value and is considered the most significant digit.

An important rule to be remembered which is applicable to any positional numbering system; any base (or radix) to the zero power equals (1). $2^0 = 1$, $8^0 = 1$, $10^0 = 1$, $16^0 = 1$.

BINARY NUMBER SYSTEM

The number system we're all familiar with jumps one place when it gets to 10 (after 9, you start with one again and add 0; 9 becomes 10, 99 becomes 100). The two digit, or binary system of numbers does the same thing—but does it every two digits. Thus one is 1, two is 10, three is 11, four is 100, five is 101, and so on.

The complexity of electronic circuitry needed for utilizing the decimal number has resulted in a simpler two-digit system for computer use. The binary (base 2) uses only two distinct symbols—0 and 1—which signifies "no bits," and the presence of a bit, respectively. (Binary digits are called *bits,* a word that is a contraction of the words *BI*nary digi*T*.) In contrast to the decimal system, the place values of binary digits to the left of the least significant digit increase by powers of two compared to the decimal increments of ten. For example, the decimal number 435 is merely the sum of 4 × 100 plus 3 × 10 plus 5 × 1 or 435. In the binary system, we multiply by 2 as we go left. Thus the binary number 111 is really 1 × 4 plus 1 × 2 plus 1 × 1 or 7.

The binary system lends itself to computer circuitry, as only one of the two conditions need be tested to determine the value of the bit position. In the binary system, each digital position is assigned an ascending power of 2 beginning with the right digital position and progressing to the left (Fig. 7.6). The following table contains some of the decimal values of the powers of two (Fig. 7.7).

$2^0 = 1$	$2^4 = 16$	$2^8 = 256$
$2^1 = 2$	$2^5 = 32$	$2^9 = 512$
$2^2 = 4$	$2^6 = 64$	$2^{10} = 1024$
$2^3 = 8$	$2^7 = 128$	$2^{11} = 2048$

To represent a quantity, each bit (either 0 or 1) is multiplied by its respective bit (digital) position. The products are then added together giving the decimal equivalent of the binary number. Since the multiplier is either 1

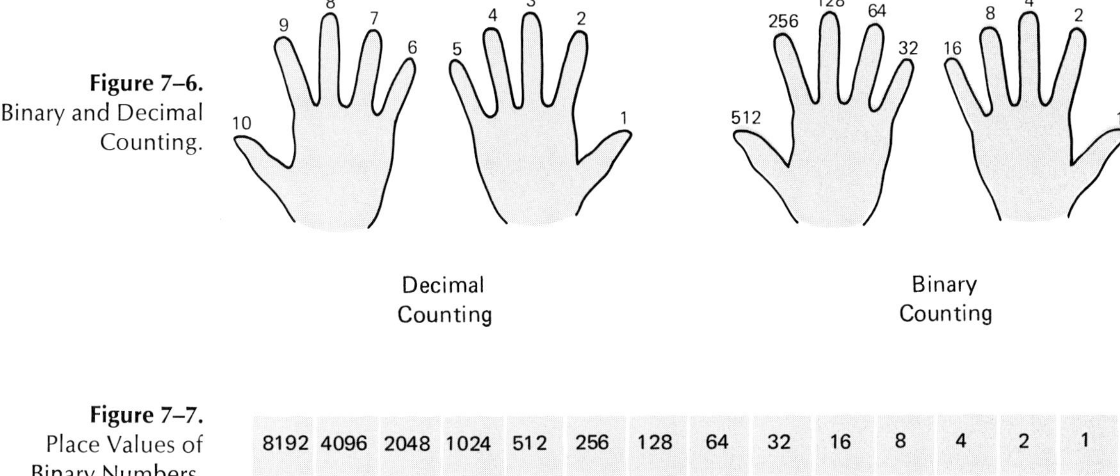

Figure 7–6. Binary and Decimal Counting.

Figure 7–7. Place Values of Binary Numbers.

8192	4096	2048	1024	512	256	128	64	32	16	8	4	2	1

or 0, it is only necessary to add the value of the binary digital positions where the 1s appear. For example, the binary number 101101 signifies

Decimal Value	32	16	8	4	2	1	
Power	2^5	2^4	2^3	2^2	2^1	2^0	
Binary Number	1	0	1	1	0	1	
	$32 + 8 + 4 + 1 = 45$						*decimal equivalent number*

To avoid confusion when several different numbering systems are used, it is customary to enclose each number in parentheses and to write the base as a subscript. For example, the numbers in the previous example would be expressed as

$$(101101)_2 = (45)_{10}$$

BINARY TO DECIMAL CONVERSION

Two methods may be used to convert binary numbers to their decimal equivalent; the expansion method and the double-dabble method.

EXPANSION METHOD OF CONVERTING BINARY NUMBERS TO DECIMAL

Binary numbers may be easily converted to decimal numbers by direct expansion in powers of two. The literal method of expansion of the numbers of its base readily yield the *decimal* equivalent of the number provided all arithmetic is carried out in the decimal system. Each position has its own assigned value. Simply write down the power of two of the binary number in column format beginning with the least significant digit. The values are then added together to obtain the decimal equivalent.

For example, convert 111011 to a decimal number.

	32	16	8	4	2	1	
	1	1	1	0	1	1	
Add values	32	16	8		2	1	= 59

DOUBLE-DABBLE METHOD OF CONVERTING BINARY NUMBERS TO DECIMAL

The double-dabble method (double and add) is a short–cut method of performing the binary to decimal conversion. The procedure is as follows:

1. Double the highest-order (leftmost) binary digit and add it to the digit at its right.
2. Double the sum and add 1 or 0 depending upon whether the next digit to the right is 1 or 0.
3. Repeat the process until the sum contains the lowest order digit at the right.

Using the previous example, convert 111011 to a decimal number using a double-dabble system.

Binary Digits 1 1 1 0 1 1

Decimal Numbers

$2 + 1 = 3 \times 2 + 1 = 7 \times 2 + 0 = 14 \times 2 + 1 = 29 \times 2 + 1 = 59$

(each "× 2" step labelled double; each "+" step labelled add)

This double-dabble technique has a decided advantage over the expansion method in large binary numbers. The technique can be applied quickly with simple practice by properly remembering to double each time if the next digit is 0 and to double and add 1 if the next digit is 1. In most cases, the partial sums can be retained mentally without the necessity for writing them down.

DECIMAL TO BINARY CONVERSION

The most often used method of decimal to binary conversion is the *remainder* method. The decimal is divided by two and that quotient and all succeeding quotients are in turn divided by two. The division is repeated until a quotient of 0 is obtained. The equivalent binary number is composed of the remainders, the first remainder being the rightmost or least significant digit, while the final remainder is the leftmost, most significant digit.

For example, convert decimal number 27 to a binary number.

Divide the decimal number by the base.

```
                  13 quotient
Binary base   2 ) 27
                  26
                  --
                   1 remainder
```

The conversion is not complete. *The binary base is now divided into the quotient of the previous division. The remainder from the previous division is retained.*

```
                   6
Binary base   2 ) 13 quotient from previous division
                  12
                  --
                   1 remainder
```

The process is repeated until the quotient of a division is zero. The remaining divisions for the problem are shown below.

```
              3
          2 ) 6
              6
              -
              0 remainder

              1
          2 ) 3
              2
              -
              1 remainder

              0 (quotient = 0; division portion of conversion now
                complete).
          2 ) 1
              0
              -
              1 remainder
```

All the divisions are now complete and the remainders are either 0 or 1. These remainders become the bits of the binary number. In order to determine the positional notation of each bit, the order of the divisions must be carefully noted. The first division yields the remainder that becomes the least significant or rightmost bit while the last division performed yields the remainder that is the most significant or leftmost bit of the binary number as illustrated in the following diagram:

13	6	3	1	0
$2\overline{)27}$	$2\overline{)13}$	$2\overline{)6}$	$2\overline{)3}$	$2\overline{)1}$
26	12	6	2	0
1 rem.	1 rem.	0 rem.	1 rem.	1 rem.

1 1 0 1 1

Multiply each bit position by the decimal value of its bit position and add the products together to verify the accuracy of the conversion.

Decimal Value	16	8	4	2	1
Binary Number	1	1	0	1	1

$16 + 8 + 2 + 1 = 27$

Another Example

Convert the decimal number 51 to a binary number.

25	12	6	3	1	0
$2\overline{)51}$	$2\overline{)25}$	$2\overline{)12}$	$2\overline{)6}$	$2\overline{)3}$	$2\overline{)1}$
50	24	12	6	2	0
1 rem.	1 rem.	0 rem.	0 rem.	1 rem.	1 rem.

1 1 0 0 1 1

CHECK

Decimal Value	32	16	8	4	2	1
Binary Number	1	1	0	0	1	1

$32 + 16 + 2 + 1 = 51$

This division method can convert any decimal number to binary. It can also be used to convert decimal numbers to other numbering systems by substituting the base of those numbering systems as the divisor.

BINARY ADDITION

Binary arithmetic follows the same general rules as decimal arithmetic with one exception: a base of two is used instead of base 10 tables. Addition is essentially a shortcut to counting. Whenever the sum of two digits exceeds the available number symbols of the system (limit of any digit position), a one is carried to the next high order digit position. Thus in the decimal system, $4 + 3 = 7$, while $9 + 1 = 0$ with a carry of 1 (that is, 10).

In binary addition only two symbols, 0 and 1, are used. Hence adding 1 to 1 in binary arithmetic exceeds the limit of counting and the result is 0 with a one carried to the next high order digit position. The rules for binary addition are

BINARY		ADDITION
0 + 0	=	0
0 + 1	=	1
1 + 0	=	1
1 + 1	=	0 with a carry of 1.

EXAMPLES OF BINARY ADDITION

In the following examples, we will perform the addition calculations just as they would be performed in decimal arithmetic starting with the rightmost bit position and proceeding to the leftmost bit position generating any necessary carries.

Example 1

BINARY	DECIMAL
1 0 1 0	10
+ 0 1 0 1	+ 5
1 1 1 1	15

Bit Position	Computation	Result	Carries
1	0 + 1	1	0
2	1 + 0	1	0
3	0 + 1	1	0
4	1 + 0	1	0

Example 2

	BINARY	DECIMAL
Carries	1 1 1	1
	1 0 1 1	11
	+ 1 0 0 1	+ 9
	1 0 1 0 0	20

Bit Position		Computation	Result	Carries
1		1 + 1	0	1
2	Carry (1)	+ 1 + 0	0	1
3	Carry (1)	+ 0 + 0	1	0
4		1 + 1	0	1
5	Carry (1)		1	0

Example 3

	BINARY	DECIMAL
Carries 1	1 1	1
	1 1 1 0 0 1	57
	+ 1 0 0 0 1 1	+35
	1 0 1 1 1 0 0	92

Bit Position		Computation	Result	Carries
1		1 + 1	0	1
2	Carry (1) +	0 + 1	0	1
3	Carry (1) +	0 + 0	1	0
4		1 + 0	1	0
5		1 + 0	1	0
6		1 + 1	0	1
7	Carry (1)		1	0

When adding several binary numbers, more than one carry may be developed to a single column. Decimal-binary tables are very helpful when adding a list of binary numbers. Below is a partial decimal-binary table.

DECIMAL	BINARY	DECIMAL	BINARY
0	0	5	101
1	1	6	110
2	10	7	111
3	11	8	1000
4	100	9	1001

Example 4

	BINARY	DECIMAL
Carries 1	1 1	2
	1 0 1 1	11
	1 1 0 1	13
	1 0 0 1	9
	0 0 0 1	1
	+ 1 0 0 1	9
	1 0 1 0 1 1	43

Bit Position			Computation	Result	Carries
1			$1+1+1+1+1$	1	1 carry to 3 bit position
2			$1+0+0+0+0$	1	0
3	Carry (1)	+	$0+1+0+0+0$	0	1
4	Carry (1)	+	$1+1+1+0+1$	1	1 carry to 6 bit position
5				0	
6	Carry (1)			1	

In the above problem, the first bit position addition equalled 5. By referencing the decimal-binary table, we find the binary number for 5 as 101. We only carry the 1 to the 3 bit position as zeros are not carried. The same procedure is followed when adding the 4 bit position.

To verify the accuracy of binary addition, binary numbers should be converted to decimal and the results checked.

BINARY SUBTRACTION

In checking out programs, it is necessary to be familiar with the conventional direct method of subtraction, "borrowing" when necessary. One of the first things taught in elementary school was that subtraction is the reverse of addition. We also learned that when a digit being subtracted is larger than the digit from which it is being subtracted, you must "borrow" a quantity from one of the next higher positions.

The rules for direct binary subtraction are as follows:

$0-0=0$
$1-0=1$
$1-1=0$
$0-1=1$ with a borrow of "1" from a next high order position.

By incorporating the borrow concept, the last rule is interpreted as $10-1=1$ or the decimal equivalent of $2-1=1$.

EXAMPLES OF BINARY SUBTRACTION

In the following examples, we will perform the subtraction calculations just as they would be performed in decimal arithmetic starting with the rightmost bit position and proceeding to the leftmost bit position employing any necessary borrowing procedures.

Example 1

Decimal problem

$$
\begin{array}{r}
1,000 \\
-\quad\quad 1 \\
\hline
999
\end{array}
\quad \text{or} \quad
\begin{array}{lrrrr}
\text{Borrow} & 0 & 9 & 9 & 10 \\
 & \not{1} & \not{0} & \not{0} & \not{0} \\
 & - & & & 1 \\
\hline
 & & 9 & 9 & 9
\end{array}
$$

In the decimal problem above, it was necessary to borrow "1" in the thousands position. While we have learned to mentally short-cut this process, we could have written the quantity (after borrowing) as zero 1000s, nine 100s, and nine 10s and ten 1s. Then when we perform the subtraction we would obtain the answer 999.

Binary problem

$$
\begin{array}{lrrrr}
 & \multicolumn{4}{c}{\text{BINARY}} \\
\text{Borrows} & & 0 & 1 & 10 \\
 & 0 & \not{1} & \not{0} & \not{0} \\
 & -0 & 0 & 0 & 1 \\
\hline
 & 0 & 0 & 1 & 1
\end{array}
\qquad\qquad
\begin{array}{r}
\text{DECIMAL} \\
\\
4 \\
-1 \\
\hline
3
\end{array}
$$

Subtraction in binary arithmetic follows the same rules of "take-away and borrow" used in decimal arithmetic. In the above example of binary subtraction, we could not subtract "1" from "0" in the first bit position, so we moved to the left searching for something to borrow from. The first quantity we could borrow was the "1" in the third bit position. Since we were borrowing the quantity "4" we distributed the quantity over the remaining low-order positions. To do this we changed the third bit position from "1" to "0" to reflect the borrow, changed the second bit position from "0" to "1" and changed the first bit position from "0" to "10" (2). If you add the distribution across, you will find that the binary number still represents the quantity "4." Now, however, we have a condition where we can perform the subtraction.

We will use the same technique of "borrowing" in each of the following examples.

Example 2

$$
\begin{array}{lrrrr}
 & \multicolumn{4}{c}{\text{BINARY}} \\
\text{Borrows} & 0 & 1 & 1 & 10 \\
 & \not{1} & \not{0} & \not{0} & \not{0} \\
 & -0 & 0 & 0 & 1 \\
\hline
 & 0 & 1 & 1 & 1
\end{array}
\qquad\qquad
\begin{array}{r}
\text{DECIMAL} \\
\\
8 \\
-1 \\
\hline
7
\end{array}
$$

In the above problem, it was necessary to borrow from the fourth bit position and distribute the remaining quantity amongst the remaining low-order positions.

Example 3

	Binary							Decimal
Borrows			0	10				
				Ø	10			
	1	0	1̸	1̸	Ø	1	1	91
	−1	0	0	1	1	1	1	−79
	0	0	0	1	1	0	0	12

In the above problem, it was necessary to borrow as follows:

To Bit Position	From Bit Position
3	4
4	5 (because bit position was "0" from the previous borrowing)

Example 4

	Binary						Decimal
Borrows	0	10					
		Ø	1	10			
	1̸	1̸	Ø	Ø	1	1	51
	−0	1	1	1	0	1	−29
	0	1	0	1	1	0	22

In the above example, it was necessary to borrow as follows:

To Bit Position	From Bit Position
3	5
5	6 (because bit position was "0" from the previous borrowing)

With the numerous borrowings required to carry out subtractions, which may become confusing at times, it is advisable to write down the numerals once again after all the borrowings have been completed.

BINARY MULTIPLICATION

There are simple rules for binary multiplication:

Binary Multiplication

$$0 \times 0 = 0$$
$$0 \times 1 = 0$$
$$1 \times 0 = 0$$
$$1 \times 1 = 1$$

Actually it is not necessary to remember the rules. Simply *copy the multiplicand* (top number of the problem) whenever the multiplier digit (on the bottom) is 1 and shift an extra place to the left for each digit that is zero. For example,

```
BINARY     DECIMAL     BINARY     DECIMAL
  011         3           111         7
 ×011        ×3          ×110        ×6
   11                    1110
  11                    111
 1001         9        101010        42
```

BINARY DIVISION

Binary division is performed in a series of subtractions. For example, to verify the result of the second multiplication example:

PROBLEM

```
BINARY      DECIMAL
   111          7
  ×110         ×6
101010         42
```

CHECK

```
                 110      (6)
(7)   111  )101010       (42)
            111
             111
             111
```

OCTAL NUMBER SYSTEM

Binary numbers are rather bulky and become unwieldy and extremely difficult to communicate other than in a computer. A binary number requires several times as many positions for display as does the equivalent decimal number. A long string of ones and zeroes can be extremely difficult to transmit from one individual to another. Since the internal circuitry of the computer understands only binary 1s (ones) and 0s (zeroes), some shorthand method becomes necessary. The octal number system is a shorthand method of displaying binary numbers. Because of their simple relationship to binary, octal numbers can be converted from one system to another by inspection. The base or radix of the octal system is eight, which means that the largest possible single digit is 7 (0, 1, 2, 3, 4, 5, 6, 7). There are no 8s or 9s in an octal

BINARY	OCTAL	DECIMAL
000	0	0
001	1	1
010	2	2
011	3	3
100	4	4
101	5	5
110	6	6
111	7	7

At this point, a carry to the next-higher position of the number is necessary, since all eight symbols have been used.

BINARY	OCTAL	DECIMAL
001 000	10	8
001 001	11	9
001 010	12	10
001 011	13	11
001 100	14	12
•	•	•
•	•	•

Figure 7–8. Binary-Octal-Decimal Conversion.

Figure 7–9. Octal Bit Equivalents.

OCTAL NUMBER	BIT EQUIVALENTS
0	0 0 0
1	0 0 1
2	0 1 0
3	0 1 1
4	1 0 0
5	1 0 1
6	1 1 0
7	1 1 1
BIT VALUES →	4 2 1

number system. The conversion from binary to octal is rather simple since one octal position is equivalent to three binary positions (Fig. 7.8).

Any binary number can be converted to octal by grouping the bits in 3s, starting at the rightmost bit and then reconverting each group into its octal equivalent (Fig. 7.9). For example, to convert the following binary number to octal; 1 1 0 0 1 0 1 0

$$\frac{011}{3}\ \frac{001}{1}\ \frac{010}{2} = 312 \text{ octal equivalent}$$

Necessary zeroes are added to left if less than 3. Convert the following number to binary 431.

$$\frac{4}{1\,0\,0}\quad \frac{3}{0\,1\,1}\ \frac{1}{0\,0\,1} = 1\,0\,0\,0\,1\,1\,0\,0\,1 \text{ binary equivalent}$$

OCTAL TO DECIMAL CONVERSION

By remembering what a number represents in octal (or binary), the number can be easily converted to decimal using the following table.

Octal Values

$8^0 = 1$	$8^4 = 4{,}096$
$8^1 = 8$	$8^5 = 32{,}768$
$8^2 = 64$	$8^6 = 262{,}144$
$8^3 = 512$	

To represent a quantity, each octal digit is multiplied by its digital position value (power of 8) and the products are added together. The total, then, is the decimal equivalent of the octal value. For example, the value of an octal number 765 is determined below.

Decimal Value	64	8	1
Power	8^2	8^1	8^0
Octal Number	7	6	5

Digit		Digit Position Value	Value
5	×	1	5
6	×	8	48
7	×	64	448
			501 Decimal value of octal number 765

Example: Convert the binary number 1 0 0 1 1 1 to its octal equivalent and prove your answers in decimal.

Binary number	1 0 0	1 1 1
Octal number	4	7

$$(100111)_2 = (47)_8$$

CHECK

BINARY

32	16	8	4	2	1
1	0	0	1	1	1

1
2
4
32
39

$$(100111)_2 = (39)_{10}$$

OCTAL

8	1
4	7

7
32 (4 × 8)
39

$$(47)_8 = (39)_{10}$$

Another method by which to convert an octal number to its decimal equivalent (similar to the Double-Dabble method of converting binary numbers to decimal), continuously multiply by eight and add the next octal digit. For example, to convert the octal number 312 to its decimal equivalent:

3 1 2 octal equivalent number

```
   3
 × 8
 ---
  24
+  1
 ---
  25
×  8
 ---
 200
+  2
 ---
 202        decimal equivalent
```

DECIMAL TO OCTAL CONVERSION

Conversion from a decimal to its octal equivalent can be accomplished by using the division discussed earlier in the binary system. The divisor must be the base of the numbering system; in this case it is 8. To convert a decimal number to octal, divide the number continuously by 8 until the quotient is zero and develop the actual number from the remainders of each division.

For example, convert the decimal number 202 to its octal equivalent.

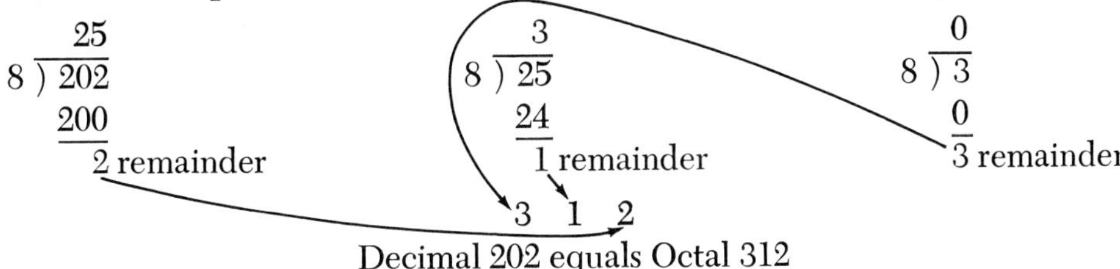

Decimal 202 equals Octal 312

All actual arithmetic operations in octal are performed in a manner similar to binary except that the base is 8 instead of 2. The last remainder is the most important with the first remainder being the least important.

OCTAL ADDITION

	OCTAL	DECIMAL
Carries	1 1	1
	2 3 6	158
	7 7	+ 63
	3 3 5	221

The addition is performed as follows:

Digit Position	Computation	Result	Carry
1	$6 + 7 = 13$	5	1

The base 8 is subtracted from sum (13) leaving a remainder of 5 and a carry of 1.

2	Carry (1) + 3 + 7 = 11 The base 8 is subtracted from the sum (11) leaving a remainder of 3 and a carry of 1.	3	1
3	Carry (1) + 2	3	0

CHECK

To check sum convert octal number 335 to its decimal equivalent.

64	8	1		
3	3	5	5 × 1	5
			3 × 8	24
			3 × 64	192
				221 Decimal equivalent

OCTAL SUBTRACTION

	OCTAL	DECIMAL
Borrows	4 12	
	7 5 4	492
	−3 4 5	−229
	4 0 7	263

A borrow of the base 8 was made from the second digit position (5 − 1 = 4) and added to the value appearing in the first position (4 + 8 = 12). Now the subtraction can be performed. Rules are the same as for decimal and binary arithmetic with one exception; the base is now 8.

CHECK Convert octal number 407 to its decimal equivalent.

64	8	1		
4	0	7	7 × 1	7
			0 × 8	0
			4 × 64	256
				263 decimal equivalent

OCTAL MULTIPLICATION

	OCTAL	DECIMAL
	2 7	23
	× 3 2	× 26
		598
First partial product	56	
Second partial product	105	
Product	1126	

The first steps involved in the multiplication problem above are as follows:

First partial product

```
Carries   1
          2 7
        × 2
        -----
          5 6
```

1. 2 × 7 = 14. Subtract base 8 leaving a remainder of 6 with a carry of 1.
2. 2 × 2 + Carry (1) = 5.

Second partial product

```
Carries    2
           2 7
        ×    3
        ------
         1 0 5
```

1. 3 × 7 = 21. Subtract base 8 leaving a remainder of 5 with a carry of 2 (two multiples of 8).
2. 3 × 2 + Carry (2) = 8. Subtract base 8 leaving a remainder of 0 and a carry of 1.
3. Carry (1).

Add partial products together

```
        Carry             1
First partial product      56
Second partial product   105  ← Indented—each subsequent partial product
                         ----
                         1126   will be indented one additional position.
```

1. 6 +	=	6
2. 5 + 5	=	10. Subtract base 8 leaving remainder of 2
3. Carry (1) + 0	+	1. with a carry of 1.
4. 1		1.

CHECK

512	64	8	1
1	1	2	6

```
6 ×   1     6
2 ×   8    16
1 ×  64    64
1 × 512   512
          ---
          598 decimal equivalent
```

OCTAL DIVISION

To check octal multiplication, use octal division.

```
                      2 7
                  8
Borrows       0   ø  10
         32 / ɫ   ɫ   ź 6
                  6   4
                  2   6 6
                  2   6 6
```

The division was performed as follows.

1. $32 \times 2 = 64$.
2. $112 - 64 = 26$.
3. Bring down 6 to form 266.
4. $32 \times 27 = 266$.

HEXADECIMAL NUMBER SYSTEM

The hexadecimal number system, like the octal number system, is simply a shorthand method of expressing the binary bit patterns within a computer. Each hexademical digit stands for *four* binary bits. Hexadecimal means 16 and the system requires 16 symbols to represent the possible values. It does not count to 16 but uses the 10 decimal digits (0 — 9) plus the letters, A, B, C, D, E, F, to represent these values. The entire list of hexadecimal symbols consists of 0,1,2,3,4,5,6,7,8,9,A, B, C, D, E, F (Fig. 7.10).

Figure 7–10. Decimal, Hexadecimal, and Binary Notation.

Decimal	*Hexadecimal*	*Binary*	*Decimal*	*Hexadecimal*	*Binary*
0	0	0000	16	10	10000
1	1	0001	17	11	10001
2	2	0010	18	12	10010
3	3	0011	19	13	10011
4	4	0100	20	14	10100
5	5	0101	21	15	10101
6	6	0110	22	16	10110
7	7	0111	23	17	10111
8	8	1000	24	18	11000
9	9	1001	25	19	11001
10	A	1010	26	1A	11010
11	B	1011	27	1B	11011
12	C	1100	28	1C	11100
13	D	1101	29	1D	11101
14	E	1110	30	1E	11110
15	F	1111	31	1F	11111

Figure 7–11. Hexadecimal Bit Equivalents.

DECIMAL VALUE	HEXADECIMAL NOTATION	GROUP OF FOUR BITS
0	0	0 0 0 0
1	1	0 0 0 1
2	2	0 0 1 0
3	3	0 0 1 1
4	4	0 1 0 0
5	5	0 1 0 1
6	6	0 1 1 0
7	7	0 1 1 1
8	8	1 0 0 0
9	9	1 0 0 1
10	A	1 0 1 0
11	B	1 0 1 1
12	C	1 1 0 0
13	D	1 1 0 1
14	E	1 1 1 0
15	F	1 1 1 1
	BIT VALUES →	8 4 2 1

To convert a binary number to a hexadecimal equivalent, it is only necessary to divide the number into groups of four binary digits starting from the right and replacing each group of four by the hexadecimal equivalent (Fig. 7.11).

For example, to convert the following binary number to its hexadecimal equivalent:

$$(1\,1\,1\,1\,1\,0\,0\,1\,1\,0\,1\,1\,0\,1\,0\,0\,1\,1)_2 = \frac{0011/\,1110/\,0110/\,1101/\,0011}{(\ \ 3\ \ \ \ E\ \ \ \ \ 6\ \ \ \ D\ \ \ \ 3)_{16}}$$

$$3E6D3 = \text{hexadecimal equivalent.}$$

Note: If left–hand group is incomplete (less than four bits) fill in excess positions at left with zeros.

Similarly, to convert hexadecimal numbers into binary, substitute the corresponding group of four binary digits for each hexadecimal number.

For example, convert the following hexadecimal number to its binary equivalent.

$$(6C4F2E7B8)_{16}$$

6	C	4	F	2	E	7	B	8
0110	1100	0100	1111	0010	1110	0111	1011	1000

$$(11011000100111100101110011110111000)_2$$
$$= \text{equivalent binary number}$$

HEXADECIMAL TO DECIMAL INTEGER CONVERSION

Although division can be used for conversion of hexadecimal integers into decimal, the following three methods will be found to give results more rapidly. The *direct method* consists of expanding hexadecimal numbers into powers of 16, using the decimal for the calculations (Fig. 7.12). The rules for this method are:

Multiply the decimal equivalent of each hexadecimal digit by the place value of the digit expressed in decimal (that is by the power of 16).

	Hexadecimal Values		
16^0	1	16^3	4,096
16^1	16	16^4	65,536
16^2	256	16^5	1,048,576

	0	1	2	3	4	5	6	7	8	9	A	B	C	D	E	F
0000	0000	0001	0002	0003	0004	0005	0006	0007	0008	0009	0010	0011	0012	0013	0014	0015
0010	0016	0017	0018	0019	0020	0021	0022	0023	0024	0025	0026	0027	0028	0029	0030	0031
0020	0032	0033	0034	0035	0036	0037	0038	0039	0040	0041	0042	0043	0044	0045	0046	0047
0030	0048	0049	0050	0051	0052	0053	0054	0055	0056	0057	0058	0059	0060	0061	0062	0063
0040	0064	0065	0066	0067	0068	0069	0070	0071	0072	0073	0074	0075	0076	0077	0078	0079
0050	0080	0081	0082	0083	0084	0085	0086	0087	0088	0089	0090	0091	0092	0093	0094	0095
0060	0096	0097	0098	0099	0100	0101	0102	0103	0104	0105	0106	0107	0108	0109	0110	0111
0070	0112	0113	0114	0115	0116	0117	0118	0119	0120	0121	0122	0123	0124	0125	0126	0127
0080	0128	0129	0130	0131	0132	0133	0134	0135	0136	0137	0138	0139	0140	0141	0142	0143
0090	0144	0145	0146	0147	0148	0149	0150	0151	0152	0153	0154	0155	0156	0157	0158	0159
00A0	0160	0161	0162	0163	0164	0165	0166	0167	0168	0169	0170	0171	0172	0173	0174	0175
00B0	0176	0177	0178	0179	0180	0181	0182	0183	0184	0185	0186	0187	0188	0189	0190	0191
00C0	0192	0193	0194	0195	0196	0197	0198	0199	0200	0201	0202	0203	0204	0205	0206	0207
00D0	0208	0209	0210	0211	0212	0213	0214	0215	0216	0217	0218	0219	0220	0221	0222	0223
00E0	0224	0225	0226	0227	0228	0229	0230	0231	0232	0233	0234	0235	0236	0237	0238	0239
00F0	0240	0241	0242	0243	0244	0245	0246	0247	0248	0249	0250	0251	0252	0253	0254	0255

Figure 7–12. Hexadecimal-Decimal Integer Conversion Table—Small Numbers.

For example, the value of hexadecimal number 6AE is determined below.

Decimal Value	256	16	1
Power	16^2	16^1	16^0
Hexadecimal Number	6	A	E

Digit		Digit Position Value	Value
14 (E)	×	1	14
10 (A)	×	16	160
6	×	256	1,536 Decimal value of
			1,710 hexadecimal number 6AE

The above method requires memorization of the powers of 16 and becomes unwieldy for large size hexadecimal numbers. Another technique which is a *combination of multiplication and* addition is frequently easier than the direct expansion method. (Similar to Double-Dabble method used in binary). The following rules are used in this method.

1. Multiply the decimal equivalent of the high order (leftmost) hexadecimal digit by 16.
2. Add to the product, the decimal equivalent of the next lower hexadecimal digit to the right and multiply sum by 16.
3. Continue the process until the last (rightmost) hexadecimal is added to the product.
4. The last sum is the decimal equivalent. *Do not multiply it by 16.*

For example, use the previous example $(6AE)_{16}$ to convert to decimal.

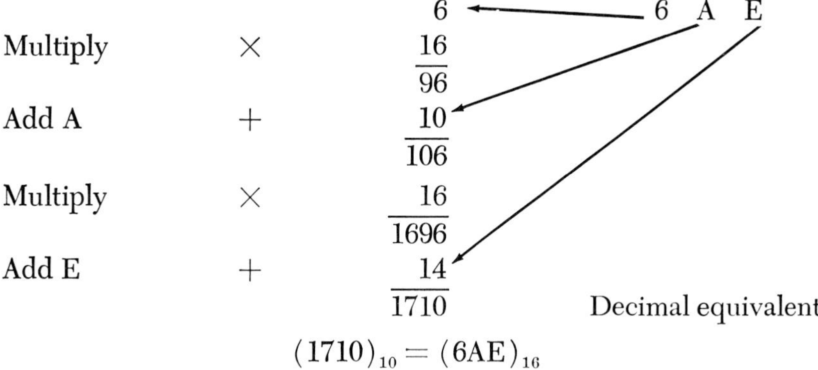

6
6 A E
Multiply
×
16
96
Add A
+
10
106
Multiply
×
16
1696
Add E
+
14
1710
Decimal equivalent

$$(1710)_{10} = (6AE)_{16}$$

The conversion of large hexadecimal numbers by either the direct expansion or the multiplication and addition method is quite tedious and difficult. Reference conversion tables should be used whenever available for conversion from hexadecimal to decimal or from decimal to hexadecimal.

For example, to convert the hexadecimal number of the previous example to its decimal equivalent:

$(6AE)_{16}$	E in hexadecimal position 1 equals	14
	A in hexadecimal position 2 equals (10×16)	160
	6 in hexadecimal position 3 equals (6×256)	1536
$(6AE)_{16}$	$= \quad (1710)_{10}$	1710

DECIMAL TO HEXADECIMAL CONVERSION

Two methods may be used to convert a decimal number into its hexadecimal equivalent. The first, division method, is similar to the ones discussed earlier in the binary and octal systems. The divisor must be the base of the numbering system, which is 16 in this case. The division method is as follows:

1. Divide the decimal number repeatedly by 16 until a zero quotient is obtained.
2. Convert remainders of 10–15 into hexadecimal symbols A–F.
3. The first remainder is the least significant hexadecimal digit, with the last remainder the most significant.
   For example, convert the decimal number 1710 to its hexadecimal equivalent:

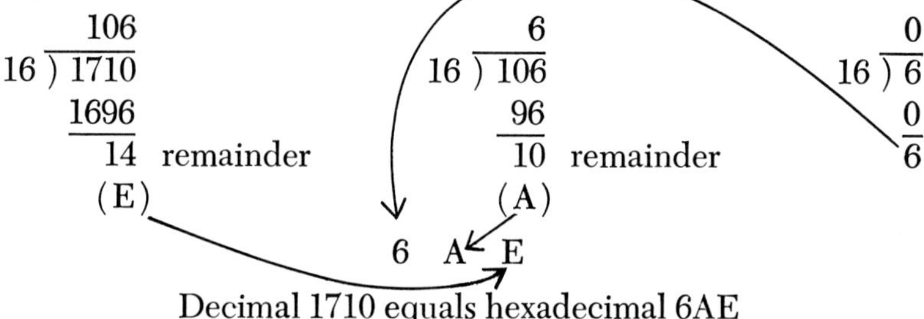

Decimal 1710 equals hexadecimal 6AE

Another method for converting numbers into hexadecimal digits is using the hexadecimal-decimal integer conversion tables whenever available. The following method is used (Figs. 7.13, 7.14).

1. Look up the next smaller number in the table. Note the hexadecimal equivalent position.
2. Subtract the decimal value of the hexadecimal digit in the table from the hexadecimal number.
3. Look up the remainder in the table and repeat the process until all hexadecimal digits are converted.

Figure 7–13. Hexadecimal-Decimal Integer Conversion Table—Small and Large Numbers.

HEX	DEC	HEX	DEC	HEX		HEX	DEC	HEX	DEC	HEX	DEC	HEX	DEC	HEX	DEC
0	0	0	0	0	0	0	0	0	0	0	0	0	0	0	0
1	268,435,456	1	16,777,216	1	1,048,576	1	65,536	1	4,096	1	256	1	16	1	1
2	536,870,912	2	33,554,432	2	2,097,152	2	131,072	2	8,192	2	512	2	32	2	2
3	805,306,368	3	50,331,648	3	3,145,728	3	196,608	3	12,288	3	768	3	48	3	3
4	1,073,741,824	4	67,108,864	4	4,194,304	4	262,144	4	16,384	4	1,024	4	64	4	4
5	1,342,177,280	5	83,886,080	5	5,242,880	5	327,680	5	20,480	5	1,280	5	80	5	5
6	1,610,612,736	6	100,663,296	6	6,291,456	6	393,216	6	24,576	6	1,536	6	96	6	6
7	1,879,048,192	7	117,440,512	7	7,340,032	7	458,752	7	28,672	7	1,792	7	112	7	7
8	2,147,483,648	8	134,217,728	8	8,388,608	8	524,288	8	32,768	8	2,048	8	128	8	8
9	2,415,919,104	9	150,994,944	9	9,437,184	9	589,824	9	36,864	9	2,304	9	144	9	9
A	2,684,354,560	A	167,772,160	A	10,485,760	A	655,360	A	40,960	A	2,560	A	160	A	10
B	2,952,790,016	B	184,549,376	B	11,534,336	B	720,896	B	45,056	B	2,816	B	176	B	11
C	3,221,225,472	C	201,326,592	C	12,582,912	C	786,432	C	49,152	C	3,072	C	192	C	12
D	3,489,660,928	D	218,103,808	D	13,631,488	D	851,968	D	53,248	D	3,328	D	208	D	13
E	3,758,096,384	E	234,881,024	E	14,680,064	E	917,504	E	57,344	E	3,584	E	224	E	14
F	4,026,531,840	F	251,658,240	F	15,728,640	F	983,040	F	61,440	F	3,840	F	240	F	15
Hexadecimal Positions	8		7		6		5		4		3		2		1

For example, using the previous example $(1710)_{10}$, convert to a hexadecimal number.

Find the hexadecimal equivalent of 1710 on the conversion chart:

	1710
6 in hexadecimal position 3 equals	−1536
	174
A in hexadecimal 2 equals	− 160
	14
E in hexadecimal position 1 equals	− 14

Therefore $(1710)_{10} = (6AE)_{16}$

HEXADECIMAL ADDITION

Addition in hexadecimal follows the same rules as those in decimal, binary and octal addition. Working with alphameric characters (numbers and letters), will appear strange at first since the results long familiar under the decimal system have a different value in hexadecimal arithmetic. For instance $5 + 4 = 9$ in both decimal and hexadecimal arithmetic while $8 + 6 = E$ (not 14) in hexadecimal. Whenever the sum of two hexadecimal digits exceeds F (15), the highest single digit value in the system, a carry of one is developed and is added to the next high order value hexadecimal position. Thus $8 + 8 = 10$ (0 with a 1 carry), $9 + 9 = 12$ (2 with a carry of 1), and $D + 8 = 15$ (5 with a carry of 1), etc.

Figure 7–14. Hexadecimal-Decimal Fraction Conversion Table.

HEX	0123 DEC	HEX	4 5 6 7 DECIMAL	HEX	0 1 2 3 DECIMAL	HEX	4 5 6 7 DECIMAL EQUIVALENT
.0	.0000	.00	.0000 0000	.000	.0000 0000 0000	.0000	.0000 0000 0000 0000
.1	.0625	.01	.0039 0625	.001	.0002 4414 0625	.0001	.0000 1525 8789 0625
.2	.1250	.02	.0078 1250	.002	.0004 8828 1250	.0002	.0000 3051 7578 1250
.3	.1875	.03	.0117 1875	.003	.0007 3242 1875	.0003	.0000 4577 6367 1875
.4	.2500	.04	.0156 2500	.004	.0009 7656 2500	.0004	.0000 6103 5156 2500
.5	.3125	.05	.0195 3125	.005	.0012 2070 3125	.0005	.0000 7629 3945 3125
.6	.3750	.06	.0234 3750	.006	.0014 6484 3750	.0006	.0000 9155 2734 3750
.7	.4375	.07	.0273 4375	.007	.0017 0898 4375	.0007	.0001 0681 1523 4375
.8	.5000	.08	.0312 5000	.008	.0019 5312 5000	.0008	.0001 2207 0312 5000
.9	.5625	.09	.0351 5625	.009	.0021 9726 5625	.0009	.0001 3732 9101 5625
.A	.6250	.0A	.0390 6250	.00A	.0024 4140 6250	.000A	.0001 5258 7890 6250
.B	.6875	.0B	.0429 6875	.00B	.0026 8554 6875	.000B	.0001 6784 6679 6875
.C	.7500	.0C	.0468 7500	.00C	.0029 2968 7500	.000C	.0001 8310 5468 7500
.D	.8125	.0D	.0507 8125	.00D	.0031 7382 8125	.000D	.0001 9836 4257 8125
.E	.8750	.0E	.0546 8750	.00E	.0034 1796 8750	.000E	.0002 1362 3046 8750
.F	.9375	.0F	.0585 9375	.00F	.0036 6210 9375	.000F	.0002 2888 1835 9375
Hexadecimal Positions	1		2		3		4

Example 1 (Having a table of the values of decimal and hexadecimal numbers above 9 handy, will greatly simplify hexadecimal calculations. Digits up to 9 are the same in both systems.)

DECIMAL	HEXADECIMAL
10	A
11	B
12	C
13	D
14	E
15	F

	HEXADECIMAL	DECIMAL
Carries	1 1	
	6 A E	1710
	+ 1 F A	−506
	8 A 8	2216

Digit Position	Computation	Result	Carry
1	14(E) + 10(A) = 24	8	1
	The base of 16 is subtracted from the sum (24) leaving a remainder of 8 and a carry of 1.		
2	Carry (1) + 10(A) + 15(F) = 26	A	1
	The base of 16 is subtracted from the sum (26) leaving a remainder of A(10) and a carry of 1.		
3	Carry (1) + 6 + 1 = 8	8	0

CHECK: Convert hexadecimal number 8A8 to its decimal equivalent.

256	16	1
8	A	8

8	× 1	8
10(A)	× 16	160
8	× 256	2,048
		2,216 Decimal equivalent

Example 2

						DECIMAL
	HEXADECIMAL					
Carries	1	1		1		
		8	F	9	7	36759
	+	D	4	4	C	+54348
	1	6	3	E	3	91107

Digit Position	Computation	Result	Carry
1	7 + 12(C) = 19	3	1
	The base of 16 is subtracted from the sum (19) leaving a remainder of 3 and a carry of 1.		
2	Carry (1) + 9 + 4 = 14 (E)	E	0
3	15(F) + 4 = 19	3	1
	The base 16 is subtracted from the sum (19) leaving a remainder of 3 and a carry of 1.		
4	Carry (1) + 8 + 13(D) = 22	6	1
	The base 16 is subtracted from the sum (22) leaving a remainder of 6 and a carry of 1.		
5	Carry (1)	1	0

CHECK: Convert hexadecimal number 163E3 to its decimal equivalent.

65536	4096	256	16	1
1	6	3	E	3

3	× 1	3
14(E)	× 16	224
3	× 256	768
6	× 4096	24576
1	× 65536	65536
		91107 Decimal equivalent

Hexadecimal addition can be greatly simplified when hexadecimal-addi-

	1	2	3	4	5	6	7	8	9	A	B	C	D	E	F	
1	02	03	04	05	06	07	08	09	0A	0B	0C	0D	0E	0F	10	1
2	03	04	05	06	07	08	09	0A	0B	0C	0D	0E	0F	10	11	2
3	04	05	06	07	08	09	0A	0B	0C	0D	0E	0F	10	11	12	3
4	05	06	07	08	09	0A	0B	0C	0D	0E	0F	10	11	12	13	4
5	06	07	08	09	0A	0B	0C	0D	0E	0F	10	11	12	13	14	5
6	07	08	09	0A	0B	0C	0D	0E	0F	10	11	12	13	14	15	6
7	08	09	0A	0B	0C	0D	0E	0F	10	11	12	13	14	15	16	7
8	09	0A	0B	0C	0D	0E	0F	10	11	12	13	14	15	16	17	8
9	0A	0B	0C	0D	0E	0F	10	11	12	13	14	15	16	17	18	9
A	0B	0C	0D	0E	0F	10	11	12	13	14	15	16	17	18	19	A
B	0C	0D	0E	0F	10	11	12	13	14	15	16	17	18	19	1A	B
C	0D	0E	0F	10	11	12	13	14	15	16	17	18	19	1A	1B	C
D	0E	0F	10	11	12	13	14	15	16	17	18	19	1A	1B	1C	D
E	0F	10	11	12	13	14	15	16	17	18	19	1A	1B	1C	1D	E
F	10	11	12	13	14	15	16	17	18	19	1A	1B	1C	1D	1E	F
	1	2	3	4	5	6	7	8	9	A	B	C	D	E	F	

Figure 7–15. Hexadecimal-Addition Table.

tion tables are available (Fig. 7.15). To perform hexadecimal addition, the hexadecimal addition tables can be used. The use of the table is simple.

1. Locate the two hexadecimal digits involved in the addition in the respective row and column of the table (it doesn't matter which digit is selected from a column or row).
2. Find the intersection of the two digits by row and column. This is the sum of the two hexadecimal digits.

In the first example, where we are adding the hexadecimal numbers 6 A E to 1 F A, the values of the first digits E and A could be located on the hexadecimal addition table as having the sum of 18. This would indicate a digit of 8 with a carry of 1. The second digit would be the sum of 1 + A + F equals the sum of 1A. A would be the digit with a carry of 1 to the next higher-order value. The third digit would be 1 + 6 + 1 = 8.

The use of the table greatly simplifies the addition of hexadecimal numbers. When a large number of hexadecimal amounts are to be added in a column, it is advisable to convert them to their decimal equivalent and perform the addition in decimal for checking purposes.

Whenever feasible, the decimal conversion addition should be used to verify the results of a hexadecimal addition.

HEXADECIMAL SUBTRACTION

Hexadecimal subtraction follows the same rules as decimal, binary and octal subtraction with the proviso that a carry or borrow of 1 in hexadecimal represents 16. For example,

		Hexadecimal			Decimal
(Borrows)		19			
	7	~~9~~	18		
	~~8~~	~~A~~	~~8~~		2216
	−1	F	A		− 506
	6	A	E		1710

						Decimal
(Borrows)	0	15	13	D	13	
	~~1~~	~~0~~	~~3~~	~~E~~	~~3~~	91107
	−	D	4	4	C	−54348
		8	F	9	7	36759

In example 1, starting with the lowest-order digit at the right, A cannot be subtracted from 8 since it exceeds 8. Hence hexadecimal 10 is borrowed from the next high-order digit at left reducing the digit to 9 (A − 1) and increasing the minuend digit to 18. Using the addition table under the A column (subtrahend), the minuend digits 18 appear in the E row, therefore 18 − A = E. Proceeding to the next-higher-order digit position, F cannot be subtracted from 9, hence a 1 is borrowed from the 8 at the left reducing it to 7 and increasing the minuend to 19. In the table going down in the F column (subtrahend), the A is put down. Finally the difference between the 7 and 1 is 6. The 6 is put down to complete the result.

HEXADECIMAL MULTIPLICATION

The rules of hexadecimal multiplication are the same as those for decimal, binary and octal. The process is fairly complicated and a table is necessary to determine the product of multiplying two decimal digits (Fig. 7.16). For example,

Hexadecimal						Decimal
9	D	7				2519
×	5	A				× 90
						226710
	4	6		(A × 7)	Partial Products	
8	2			(A × D)	First Decimal Digit	

1	2	3	4	5	6	7	8	9	A	B	C	D	E	F
2	04	06	08	0A	0C	0E	10	12	14	16	18	1A	1C	1E
3	06	09	0C	0F	12	15	18	1B	1E	21	24	27	2A	2D
4	08	0C	10	14	18	1C	20	24	28	2C	30	34	38	3C
5	0A	0F	14	19	1E	23	28	2D	32	37	3C	41	46	4B
6	0C	12	18	1E	24	2A	30	36	3C	42	48	4E	54	5A
7	0E	15	1C	23	2A	31	38	3F	46	4D	54	5B	62	69
8	10	18	20	28	30	38	40	48	50	58	60	68	70	78
9	12	1B	24	2D	36	3F	48	51	5A	63	6C	75	7E	87
A	14	1E	28	32	3C	46	50	5A	64	6E	78	82	8C	96
B	16	21	2C	37	42	4D	58	63	6E	79	84	8F	9A	A5
C	18	24	30	3C	48	54	60	6C	78	84	90	9C	A8	B4
D	1A	27	34	41	4E	5B	68	75	82	8F	9C	A9	B6	C3
E	1C	2A	38	46	54	62	70	7E	8C	9A	A8	B6	C4	D2
F	1E	2D	3C	4B	5A	69	78	87	96	A5	B4	C3	D2	E1

Figure 7–16. Hexadecimal-Multiplication Table.

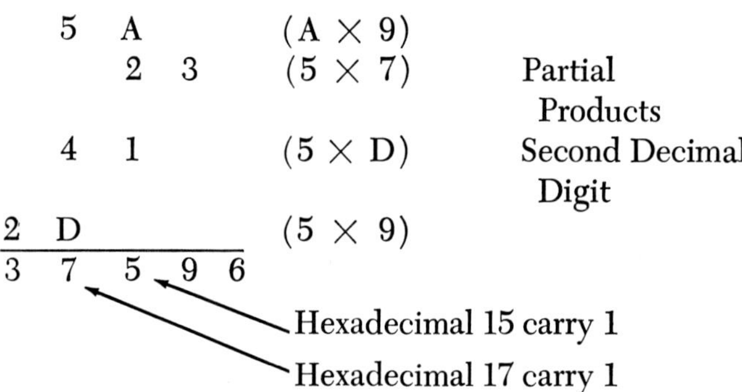

5 A (A × 9)
2 3 (5 × 7)
Partial Products
4 1 (5 × D)
Second Decimal Digit
2 D (5 × 9)
3 7 5 9 6
Hexadecimal 15 carry 1
Hexadecimal 17 carry 1

Note that each of the partial products of a multiplication digit are shifted one place to the left with respect to the previous product. Care must be taken to shift the first partial product of the *second* multiplier digit (23) above only one place with respect to the first partial product of the first multiplier digit (46) above, as in decimal multiplication. In adding up the partial products use is made of the hexadecimal addition tables and any resulting carries are applied to the next-higher-order digit positions.

HEXADECIMAL DIVISION

The rules for hexadecimal division are the same as those for decimal, binary and octal. For example, to verify the previous multiplication problem:

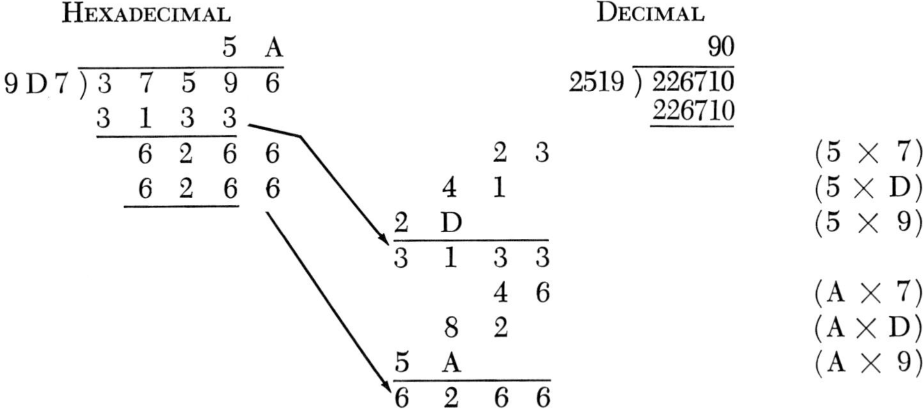

All multiplication and addition in hexadecimal is performed using the hexadecimal multiplication and addition tables.

All answers should be verified by conversion to decimal and checking the decimal results against hexadecimal results.

COMPUTER CODES

The method used to represent (symbolize) data in a data processing system is known as a code or system. In the computer, the code relates to a fixed number of symbols (binary numbers). For example, a code used to represent numeric and alphabetic characters may use eight positions of binary numbers. By the proper arrangement of these binary numbers (0 bit and 1 bit), all characters can be represented by a different combination of bits. Parity checking is used to check the computer code to assure that no bits are lost in the transmission of the data throughout the system.

Two of the computer codes in use are the 8 bit hexadecimal number system, and the 7 bit binary coded decimal system.

8 BIT HEXADECIMAL NUMBER SYSTEM

The hexadecimal number system requires the use of sixteen different symbols to represent the sixteen values. Since the decimal system only provides ten numerals (0–9), the letters A, B, C, D, E, F were added (Fig. 7.17). By using eight bit positions, 256 different characters can be coded. These codes permit the coding of upper case and lower case alphabetic letters, which allows a much wider range of special characters and many control characters that are meaningful to certain input/output devices (Fig. 7.18).

All operations are performed in binary arithmetic, which indicates the presence of a power of two up to the size of the designated field. However the communication with the system is through the hexadecimal number system.

DECIMAL SYSTEM	HEXADECIMAL SYSTEM	BINARY SYSTEM 8 4 2 1 Bit values
0	0	0 0 0 0
1	1	0 0 0 1
2	2	0 0 1 0
3	3	0 0 1 1
4	4	0 1 0 0
5	5	0 1 0 1
6	6	0 1 1 0
7	7	0 1 1 1
8	8	1 0 0 0
9	9	1 0 0 1
10	A	1 0 1 0
11	B	1 0 1 1
12	C	1 1 0 0
13	D	1 1 0 1
14	E	1 1 1 0
15	F	1 1 1 1

Figure 7–17. Relationship Among Decimal, Hexadecimal, and Binary.

The IBM system 360/370, principal user of 8 bit (byte) computer code, uses each byte as though it were two hexadecimal number systems. For example,

Decimal	248	
Binary	1111	1000
Hexadecimal	F	8

The output representation in hexadecimal is just the division of the binary numbers into groups of four binary digits starting from right to left. The hexadecimal number system employs four zone bits plus four numeric bits to represent each character. The hexadecimal number system is simply a shorthand notation used to express the binary bit patterns within a computer such as the IBM system 360/370.

7 BIT—A STANDARD BINARY CODED DECIMAL SYSTEM

In this particular number system, seven bits are used to represent all characters. In this method of coding, all characters are coded using one check bit, two zone position bits and four numeric position bits (Fig. 7.19).

The four numeric bit positions, 8, 4, 2, 1, represent a binary coded decimal, and form the digits 0–9. The zone bits B and A are not used, and are coded with zeros when only numeric digits are represented.

Combinations of zone and numeric bits are used to represent alphabetic and special characters (Fig. 7.20). Four possible bit combinations, 10, 01, 11, and 00 provide the needed zone configuration.

The check bit is used as a check code. An even parity code indicates that the total number of bits used represent an even total. A check bit is added if

EBCDIC	Bit Configuration
NUL	0000 0000
SOH	0000 0001
STX	0000 0010
ETX	0000 0011
PF	0000 0100
HT	0000 0101
LC	0000 0110
DEL	0000 0111
	0000 1000
RLF	0000 1001
SMM	0000 1010
VT	0000 1011
FF	0000 1100
CR	0000 1101
SO	0000 1110
SI	0000 1111
DLE	0001 0000
DC1	0001 0001
DC2	0001 0010
TM	0001 0011
RES	0001 0100
NL	0001 0101
BS	0001 0110
IL	0001 0111
CAN	0001 1000
EM	0001 1001
CC	0001 1010
CU1	0001 1011
IFS	0001 1100
IGS	0001 1101
IRS	0001 1110
IUS	0001 1111
DS	0010 0000
SOS	0010 0001
FS	0010 0010
	0010 0011
BYP	0010 0100
LF	0010 0101
ETB	0010 0110
ESC	0010 0111
	0010 1000
	0010 1001
SM	0010 1010
CU2	0010 1011
	0010 1100
ENQ	0010 1101
ACK	0010 1110
BEL	0010 1111
	0011 0000
	0011 0001
SYN	0011 0010
	0011 0011
PN	0011 0100
RS	0011 0101
UC	0011 0110
EOT	0011 0111
	0011 1000
	0011 1001
	0011 1010
CU3	0011 1011
DC4	0011 1100
NAK	0011 1101
	0011 1110
SUB	0011 1111
SP	0100 0000
	0100 0001
	0100 0010
	0100 0011
	0100 0100

EBCDIC	Bit Configuration
	0100 0101
	0100 0110
	0100 0111
	0100 1000
	0100 1001
¢ [	0100 1010
.	0100 1011
<	0100 1100
(	0100 1101
+	0100 1110
|	0100 1111
&	0101 0000
	0101 0001
	0101 0010
	0101 0011
	0101 0100
	0101 0101
	0101 0110
	0101 0111
	0101 1000
	0101 1001
!]	0101 1010
$	0101 1011
*	0101 1100
)	0101 1101
;	0101 1110
¬	0101 1111
–	0110 0000
/	0110 0001
	0110 0010
	0110 0011
	0110 0100
	0110 0101
	0110 0110
	0110 0111
	0110 1000
	0110 1001
7/12	0110 1010
,	0110 1011
%	0110 1100
_	0110 1101
>	0110 1110
?	0110 1111
	0111 0000
	0111 0001
	0111 0010
	0111 0011
	0111 0100
	0111 0101
	0111 0110
	0111 0111
	0111 1000
6/0	0111 1001
:	0111 1010
#	0111 1011
@	0111 1100
'	0111 1101
=	0111 1110
"	0111 1111
	1000 0000
a	1000 0001
b	1000 0010
c	1000 0011
d	1000 0100
e	1000 0101
f	1000 0110
g	1000 0111
h	1000 1000
i	1000 1001

EBCDIC	Bit Configuration
	1000 1010
	1000 1011
	1000 1100
	1000 1101
	1000 1110
	1000 1111
	1001 0000
j	1001 0001
k	1001 0010
l	1001 0011
m	1001 0100
n	1001 0101
o	1001 0110
p	1001 0111
q	1001 1000
r	1001 1001
	1001 1010
	1001 1011
	1001 1100
	1001 1101
	1001 1110
	1001 1111
	1010 0000
—	1010 0001
s	1010 0010
t	1010 0011
u	1010 0100
v	1010 0101
w	1010 0110
x	1010 0111
y	1010 1000
z	1010 1001
	1010 1010
	1010 1011
	1010 1100
	1010 1101
	1010 1110
	1010 1111
	1011 0000
	1011 0001
	1011 0010
	1011 0011
	1011 0100
	1011 0101
	1011 0110
	1011 0111
	1011 1000
	1011 1001
	1011 1010
	1011 1011
	1011 1100
	1011 1101
	1011 1110
	1011 1111
PZ 7/11	1100 0000
A	1100 0001
B	1100 0010
C	1100 0011
D	1100 0100
E	1100 0101
F	1100 0110
G	1100 0111
H	1100 1000
I	1100 1001
	1100 1010
	1100 1011
ʃ	1100 1100
	1100 1101
⑂	1100 1110

EBCDIC	Bit Configuration	ASCII-8
	1100 1111	
<	1101 0000	
J	1101 0001	
K	1101 0010	
L	1101 0011	
M	1101 0100	
N	1101 0101	
O	1101 0110	
P	1101 0111	
Q	1101 1000	
R	1101 1001	
	1101 1010	
	1101 1011	
	1101 1100	
	1101 1101	
	1101 1110	
	1101 1111	
‡	1110 0000	
	1110 0001	a
S	1110 0010	b
T	1110 0011	c
U	1110 0100	d
V	1110 0101	e
W	1110 0110	f
X	1110 0111	g
Y	1110 1000	h
Z	1110 1001	i
	1110 1010	j
	1110 1011	k
	1110 1100	l
	1110 1101	m
	1110 1110	n
	1110 1111	o
	1111 0000	p
1	1111 0001	q
2	1111 0010	r
3	1111 0011	s
4	1111 0100	t
5	1111 0101	u
6	1111 0110	v
7	1111 0111	w
8	1111 1000	x
9	1111 1001	y
	1111 1010	z
	1111 1011	
	1111 1100	
	1111 1101	
	1111 1110	ESC
	1111 1111	DEL

Figure 7–18. 8 Bit Hexadecimal Number Code.

the total number is odd. In an odd parity check, a check bit is added to an even number of bits.

The standard Binary Coded Decimal System provides compatibility among the computer systems. Sixty-four different configurations are possible (Fig. 7.21).

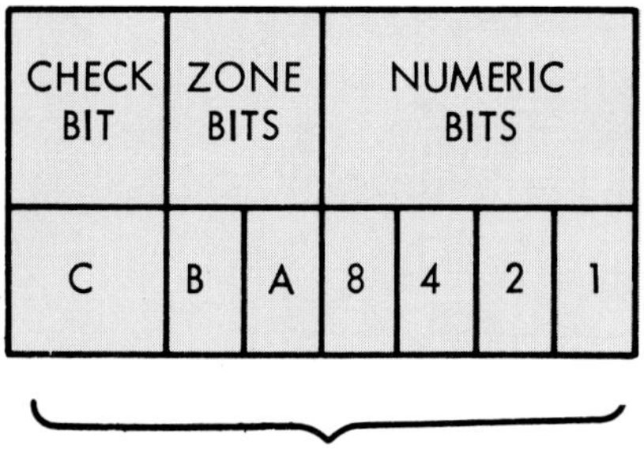

CHECK BIT	ZONE BITS		NUMERIC BITS			
C	B	A	8	4	2	1

Figure 7–19. 7 Bit Alphameric Character.

Decimal Digits	2	6	5	4	9	8
Binary Value	0 0 1 0	0 1 1 0	0 1 0 1	0 1 0 0	1 0 0 1	1 0 0 0
Place Value	8 4 2 1	8 4 2 1	8 4 2 1	8 4 2 1	8 4 2 1	8 4 2 1

Figure 7–20. Binary Coded Decimal Representation of Decimal Numbers.

COLLATING SEQUENCE (Low → High)

CHARACTER Report	CHARACTER Program	CARD CODE	BCD CODE (Core Storage)						
			C	B	A	8	4	2	1
b (Low)		No Punches	C						
.		12-3-8		B	A	8		2	1
□	)	12-4-8	C	B	A	8	4		
[		12-5-8		B	A	8	4		1
<		12-6-8		B	A	8	4	2	
≢		12-7-8	C	B	A	8	4	2	1
&	+	12	C	B	A				
$		11-3-8	C	B		8		2	1
*		11-4-8		B		8	4		
]		11-5-8	C	B		8	4		1
;		11-6-8	C	B		8	4	2	
Δ		11-7-8		B		8	4	2	1
—		11		B					
/		0-1	C		A				1
,		0-3-8	C		A	8		2	1
%	(	0-4-8			A	8	4		
⌒		0-5-8	C		A	8	4		1
\		0-6-8	C		A	8	4	2	
⧻		0-7-8			A	8	4	2	1
ƀ		2-8			A				
#	=	3-8				8		2	1
@	'	4-8	C			8	4		
:		5-8				8	4		1
>		6-8				8	4	2	
√		7-8	C			8	4	2	1
?		12-0	C	B	A	8		2	
A		12-1		B	A				1
B		12-2		B	A			2	
C		12-3	C	B	A			2	1
D		12-4		B	A		4		
E		12-5	C	B	A		4		1
F		12-6	C	B	A		4	2	
G		12-7		B	A		4	2	1
H		12-8		B	A	8			
I		12-9	C	B	A	8			1
!		11-0		B		8		2	
J		11-1	C	B					1
K		11-2	C	B				2	
L		11-3		B				2	1
M		11-4	C	B			4		
N		11-5		B			4		1
O		11-6		B			4	2	
P		11-7	C	B			4	2	1
Q		11-8	C	B		8			
R		11-9		B		8			1
‡		0-2-8			A	8		2	
S		0-2	C		A			2	
T		0-3			A			2	1
U		0-4	C		A		4		
V		0-5			A		4		1
W		0-6			A		4	2	
X		0-7	C		A		4	2	1
Y		0-8	C		A	8			
Z		0-9			A	8			1
Ø		0	C			8		2	
1		1							1
2		2						2	
3		3	C					2	1
4		4					4		
5		5	C				4		1
6		6	C				4	2	
7		7					4	2	1
8		8				8			
9 (High)		9	C			8			1

NOTE: Tape may use even parity.

Figure 7–21. 7 Bit Alphameric Code.

SUMMARY

In the study of computer processing, one should understand the meaning and operation of various number systems used in data processing. Most of us are familiar with the decimal number system. It is the intent of this chapter to present the operations of various computer number systems and the coding systems used in computers.

Knowledge of binary numbers and its related number systems is mandatory to the understanding of computer operations regardless of the depth into which one will ultimately go in data processing. Binary arithmetic is basic for octal and hexadecimal number systems. A thorough knowledge of the operations of octal and hexadecimal number systems is important as they are used extensively in data processing operations.

One should be able to convert numbers from one system to the symbols of any other system.

I. *Computer Number Systems.* The value of each digit position is dependent upon the relative position of the digits as well as the digit value itself.

Definitions:

Least significant digit (extreme right)—low order position with smallest value.

Most significant digit (extreme left)—high order position with largest value.

Base (radix)—indicates the number of digits used in the number system. The increases in value of each digit depends upon the *base* of the number system. The highest number that can be represented by a single digit is *one less* than its base.

A. *Binary number system*—two possible numbers (0, 1).

1. *Operation*—simple two digit system for computer use. Symbol "0" represents "no bits" and symbol "1" signifies the presence of a bit. Bit is a contraction of *BI*nary Digi*T*.
2. *Binary to decimal conversion*—convert binary numbers to decimal equivalents.
   a) *Expansion method*—using direct expansions in powers of two, write down the power of the binary number in columnar format beginning with the least significant digit and proceeding to the most significant digit. The values are then added together to obtain the decimal equivalent number.
   b) *Double-dabble method*—double the high order (leftmost) binary digit and add to it the digit at right. Double the sum obtained and add the next digit at right. Repeat process until the sum contains the lowest digit at right.
3. *Decimal to binary conversion*—convert decimal numbers to binary

equivalents. *Remainder method*—The decimal is divided by two and that quotient and all succeeding quotients are in turn divided by two until quotient is zero. The equivalent binary number is composed of the remainders of each division in reverse sequence of division. Last division remainder produces the most significant digit and the first division remainder produces the least significant digit.

4. *Binary, addition, subtraction, multiplication and division.* Binary arithmetic follows the same general rules as decimal with the exception that a base of two is substituted for ten.

B. *Octal number system*—eight possible numbers (0,1,2,3,4,5,6,7).

1. *Operation*—The octal number system is a shorthand method of displaying binary numbers. Each octal digit is assigned ascending powers of 8 beginning with the rightmost digital position and proceeding to the leftmost digital position.
2. *Binary to octal conversion*—each octal position is equivalent to *three* binary digits. Any binary number can be converted to octal by grouping the bits in 3s starting at the rightmost bit and reconverting each group into its octal equivalent.
3. *Octal to decimal conversion*—convert octal numbers to decimal equivalent. Each octal digit is multiplied by its digital position value (power of 8) and the products are added together to produce the decimal number.
4. *Decimal to octal conversion*—convert decimal number to its octal equivalent. The *remainder method* discussed in decimal to binary conversion is used substituting a divisor of 8 instead of two, the remainders from the division producing the octal number equivalent.
5. *Octal addition, subtraction, multiplication and division.* Octal arithmetic follows the same general rules as decimal except that a base of eight is used instead of ten.

C. *Hexadecimal number system*—sixteen possible numbers (0,1,2,3,4,5, 6,7,8,9,A,B,C,D,E,F).

1. *Operation*—The hexadecimal number system is shorthand method of displaying binary numbers. Each hexadecimal digit is assigned ascending powers of 16 beginning with the rightmost digital position and proceeding to the leftmost digital position.
2. *Binary to hexadecimal conversion*—convert binary numbers to hexadecimal equivalent. Each hexadecimal position is equivalent to *four* binary positions. Any binary number can be converted to hexadecimal by grouping the bits into groups of 4 starting at the

rightmost bit and reconverting each group into its hexadecimal equivalent.

3. *Hexadecimal to decimal conversion*—convert hexadecimal number to decimal equivalent. Each hexadecimal digit is multiplied by its digital position value (power of 16) and the products are added together to produce the decimal number.
4. *Decimal to hexadecimal conversion*—convert decimal number to its hexadecimal equivalent.
   a) *Remainder method* is similar to the one discussed in binary conversion except that a divisor of 16 is used instead of two. The remainder from each division produces the hexadecimal equivalent number.
   b) *Hexadecimal—decimal integer conversion table.* Look up in the table the next smaller number. Note the hexadecimal equivalent position. Subtract the decimal value of the hexadecimal digit in the table from the hexadecimal number. Look up the remainder in the table and repeat the process until all hexadecimal digits are converted.
5. *Hexadecimal addition, subtraction, multiplication and division.* Hexadecimal arithmetic follows the same general rules as decimal except that a base of 16 is used instead of ten.

II. *Computer Codes.* Used to symbolize data in a data processing system. The code relates to the fixed number of symbols (binary numbers).

A. *8 Bit Hexadecimal Number System.* Eight bits are used to represent all characters: four zone bits and four numeric bits. Used principally in the IBM System 360/370 computers.

B. *7 Bit Standard Binary Coded Decimal System.* Seven bits are used to represent all characters; one check bit, two zone bits and four numeric positions. The check bit is used as a parity check to insure the correct number of bits for each character.

IDENTIFICATION QUESTIONS

Match the following terms with the statements that follow.

A. 7 Bit Standard Binary Coded Decimal System
B. 8 Bit Hexadecimal Number System
C. Base (Radix)
D. Binary Number System
E. Bit
F. Double-Dabble Method
G. Hexadecimal Number System
H. Least Significant Digit
I. Most Significant Digit
J. Octal Number System
K. Remainder Method

1. Contraction of the words binary and digit.
2. The digit position at the extreme left with the highest value.

3. A code consisting of one check bit, two zone bits, and four numeric bits to represent sixty-four characters.
4. A number system consisting of two digits.
5. Double and add method of converting binary numbers to their decimal equivalent.
6. A number system consisting of eight digits where each digit represents three binary digits.
7. A method whereby each number is divided by its base and each succeeding quotient is divided by the base until a quotient of zero is reached. The equivalent number composed of the remainders in reverse sequence.
8. The digit position at the extreme right with the lowest value.
9. The number of digits in a system.
10. A number system consisting of sixteen digits where each digit represents four binary digits.
11. The use of sixteen different numbers consisting of four zone bits and four numeric bits to represent characters.

QUESTIONS FOR REVIEW

1. Why is the binary form of arithmetic used in most computers today?
2. Describe the basic principles of a number system.
3. Explain the binary number system.
4. What are the two methods most commonly used to convert binary numbers into their decimal equivalents?
5. What is the remainder method?
6. What are the main advantages of using an octal number system?
7. How do you convert a decimal number to its octal equivalent?
8. Describe the hexadecimal number system and its importance in computer arithmetic.
9. Describe the direct method of converting hexadecimal numbers to their decimal equivalents.
10. What is the importance of conversion tables?
11. Describe the division method of converting a decimal number to its hexadecimal equivalent.
12. What is a computer code?
13. Describe the eight bit hexadecimal number system code.
14. Describe the seven bit standard binary coded decimal code.

PART IV / INTRODUCTION TO PROGRAMMING

CHAPTER 8

Data Processing Systems and Procedures

Industry is becoming aware of its paperwork burden: the size of its clerical force, the amount and kinds of records that it must keep of its products, purchases and other transactions, the reports that it must make periodically on its operations. Companies are attempting to expand their use of computers as an aid in their battle to reduce both their data processing costs and the time lag between source document information availability and the distribution of the ultimate report on that specific.

Management is conscious today of the enormous number of problems involved in making data processing an effective management decision-making tool. Growing awareness of these problems on the part of management defines on the one hand the realistic limits of what should be expected of a computer and on the other hand how to expand its capabilities. A constant challenge to management lies in extracting more and more from this potent management tool.

The computer today is in a period of transition from initial acceptance to massive exploitation by business. The computer must be applied to the increasing number of variables and the accelerating rate of changes with which every business has to deal. It is difficult to find a company today that does not lease or own a computer.

The transition in data processing today is from the single self-contained computer to complex electronic systems in which the computer plays only a part. Data processing has changed from accounting and record-keeping to a far broader range of management information systems that are necessary for effective decision making. Also there has been a great increase in the breadth of expectations held by management for data processing. Initially most computers were installed on the strength of anticipated cost reductions in clerical activities. Now the shift is toward the infinitely broader concept of profit improvement.

SYSTEMS ANALYSIS

A good data processing system is designed to solve a particular problem and, if well done, it in itself will never become a problem. *A system reflects a cohesive collection of items or a representation of connected parts that are related by a "network of relationships." It includes the required information that makes possible the exercise of effective controls* (Fig. 8.1).

When it is decided to use the data processing system to solve a problem, it is seldom clear what results are expected. Many data processing applications have proved a disappointment due to an inadequate system study.

The best results in a data processing system design are achieved if a fully defined sequence of steps is followed. The system analyst is familiar with these steps from training and experience. He believes in them and will try to follow them. To anticipate the thoughts of the system analyst and understand what he is trying to accomplish, top management should be familiar with these phases of system design and the operations peculiar to each phase. This familiarity on the part of management will ultimately prove helpful to the system analyst in the preparation of the best system possible. Therefore the analyst must be given a free hand to cut across departmental lines to learn all aspects of the problem so that he can make worthwhile recommendations (Figs. 8.2, 8.3, 8.4, 8.5).

The initial step in a system analysis study is the survey. *A survey, in this case, determines whether or not a proposed computer system is feasible; whether or not it will give improved operation at a lower cost.* Initially, someone gets the idea that there may be benefits to be reaped by computerizing some data processing operation. A survey of the area is made to determine the feasibility of such a step. If the computerization is feasible as defined, responsibility for the construction of the new data processing operation is detailed. The creation of an information processing system for an application can be divided into three phases: problem definition, analysis and design, and procedure programs and conversion.

PROBLEM DEFINITION

The key to a good information system involves a total understanding of the entire problem. *Proper problem definition will help insure the achievement of the objectives—the creation of an efficient and effective data processing system to solve the specific problem.*

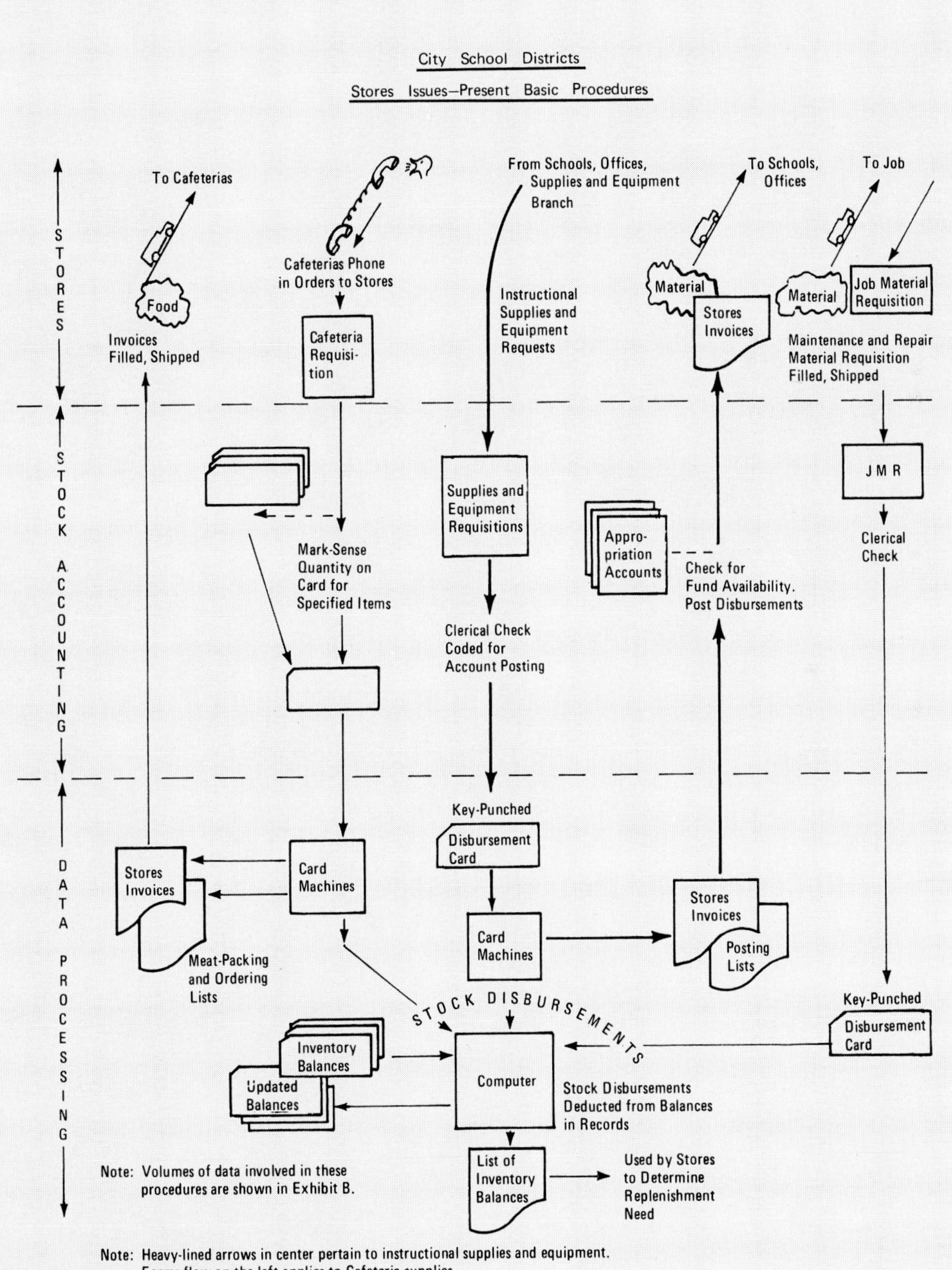

Figure 8–1. Procedural Flowchart.

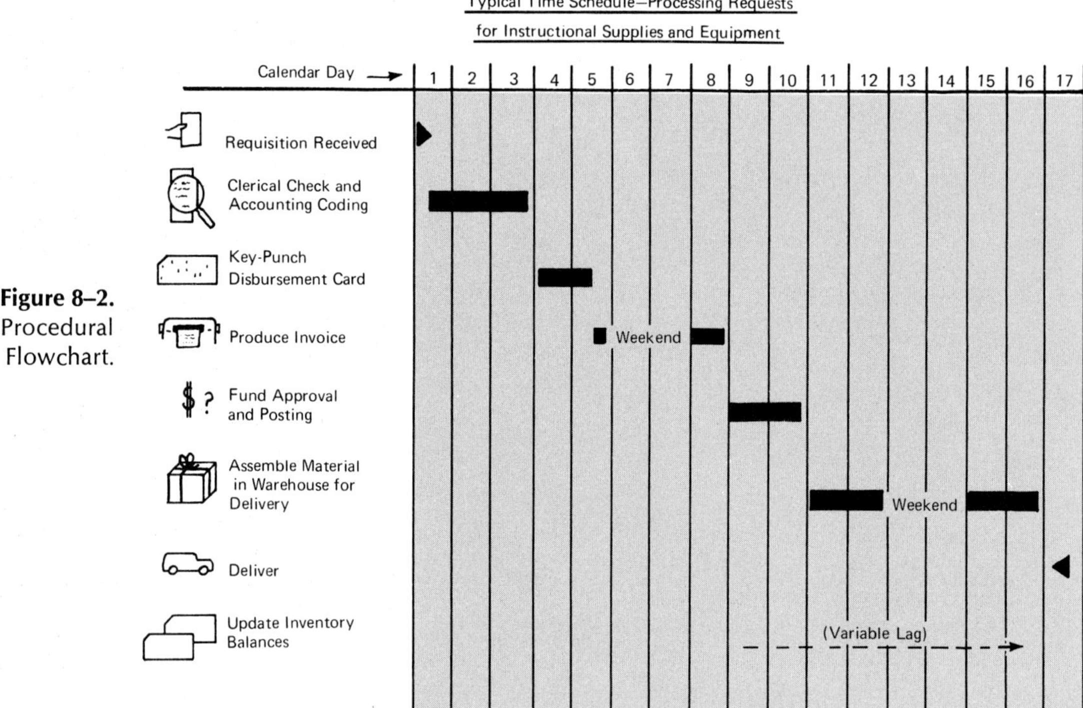

Figure 8–2. Procedural Flowchart.

1. A complete record of the present operations should be obtained for analysis.
2. Key personnel should be interviewed to determine the flow of data.
3. Sample source documents should be collected for analysis.

Upon completion of the analysis, a flowchart of the existing procedures in a sequence of operations should be prepared (Fig. 8.6).

ANALYSIS AND DESIGN

System analysis consists of two phases: defining area objectives and reviewing existing procedures. In defining area objectives, the scope of the area to be covered is analyzed, the overall objectives are determined, and the functions required to meet these objectives are evaluated. Also, an appraisal is made of how this area relates to other data processing operations and to the company as a whole.

In reviewing existing procedures, a study is made of the operation with emphasis on exceptional as well as routine characteristics. All basic docu-

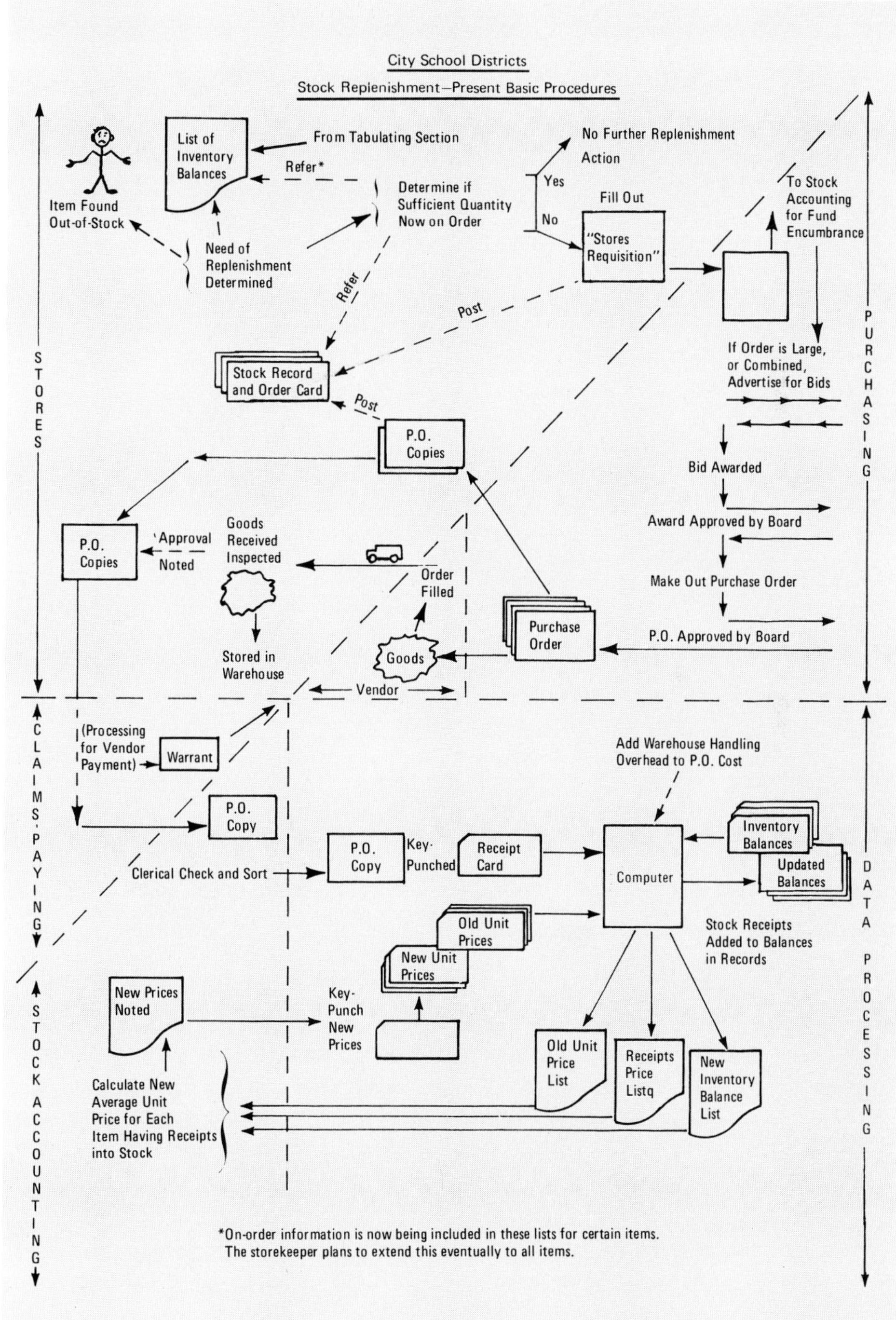

Figure 8–3. Procedural Flowchart. Flowchart

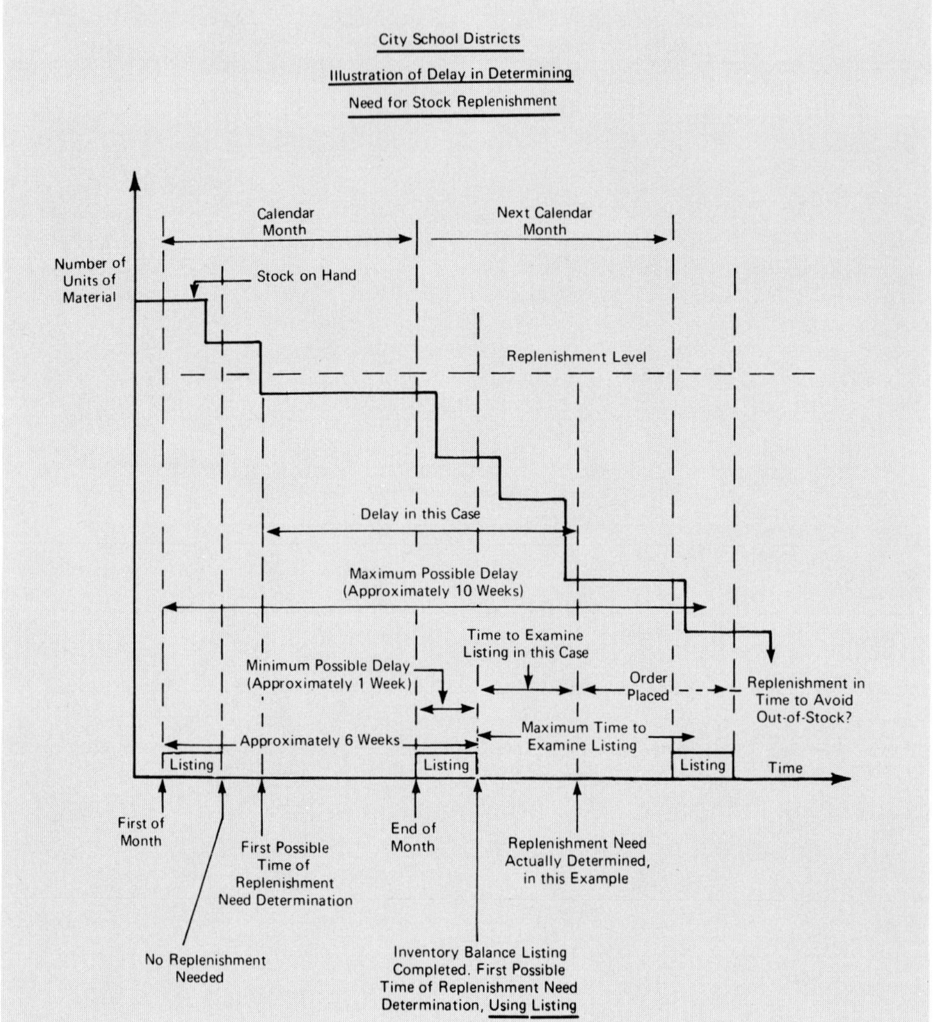

Figure 8–4. Procedural Flowchart.

ments are reviewed as to origin, distribution, material and format, master record reference, etc. All outputs are studied to reveal distribution, content and format of finished reports, vouchers, checks, etc. Another phase of this study determines operating restrictions which must be adhered to in the new system.

The *System Design* step begins with a study of the documentation prepared during system analysis. This study is made for the purpose of determining the relationships between all parts of the system. Next, a layout is prepared depicting the major relationships in the proposed system and giving

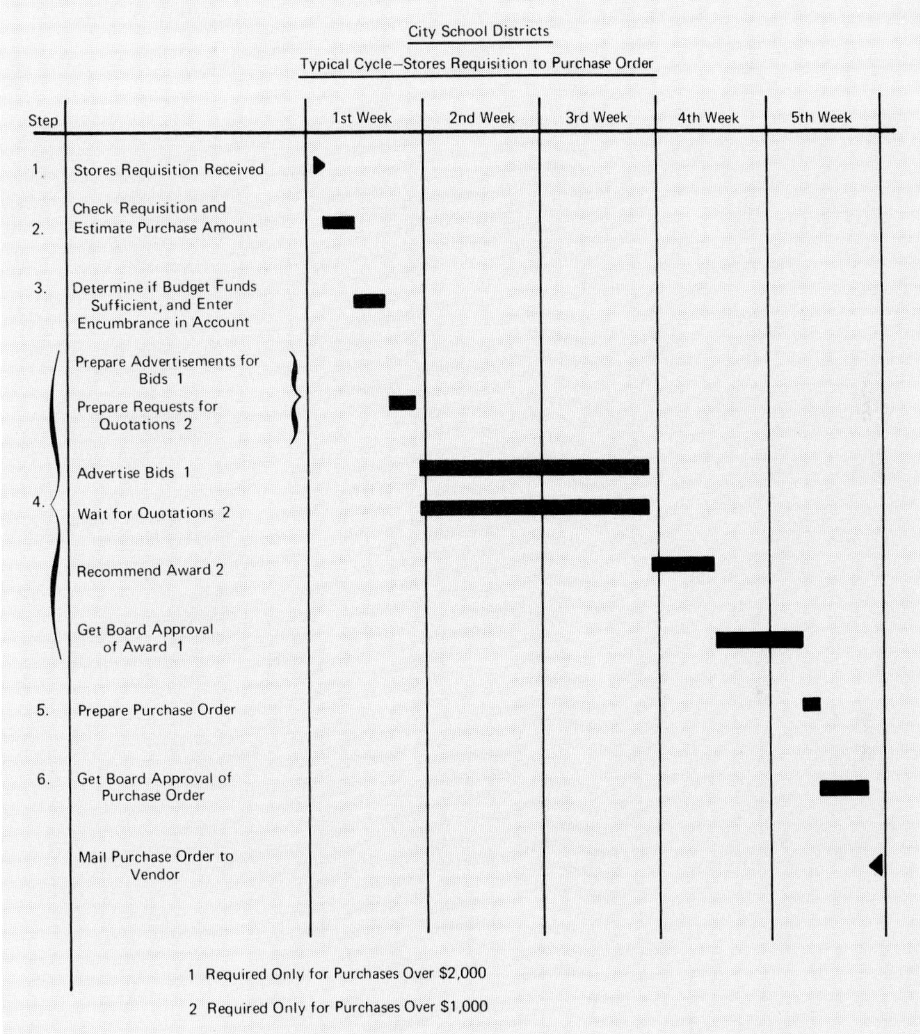

Figure 8–5. Procedural Flowchart.

consideration to what reference records must be created. Following this, an analysis of the report to be generated is made with emphasis on the fulfillment of legal and management control requirements. The source and reference data required to produce the desired reports are then defined.

The important points to be remembered are:

1. The main objective is to design a system that will meet all the established requirements.
2. The method is one of basic problem definition concerning the organization of the data files, and the required reports.

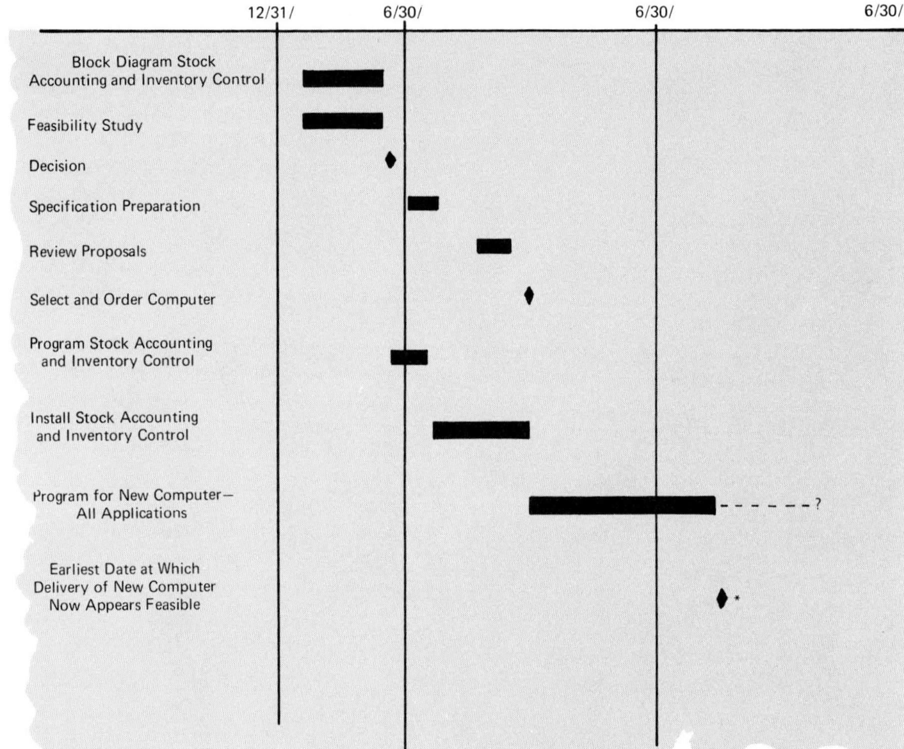

Figure 8–6. Procedural Flowchart.

3. Key documents must be examined in terms of content, frequency and purpose.
4. Key personnel must review the proposed procedures to insure an understanding of the methods and end products. At this stage, output specifications must become firm and complete.
5. The analysis and preliminary design are completed when the present revisions are acceptable and the final flowcharts and documents prove satisfactory to all personnel concerned (Figs. 8.7, 8.8).

PROCEDURES, PROGRAMS AND CONVERSION

During this phase, the procedures are converted to flowcharts and the programming function begins. During *programming*, the run descriptions are

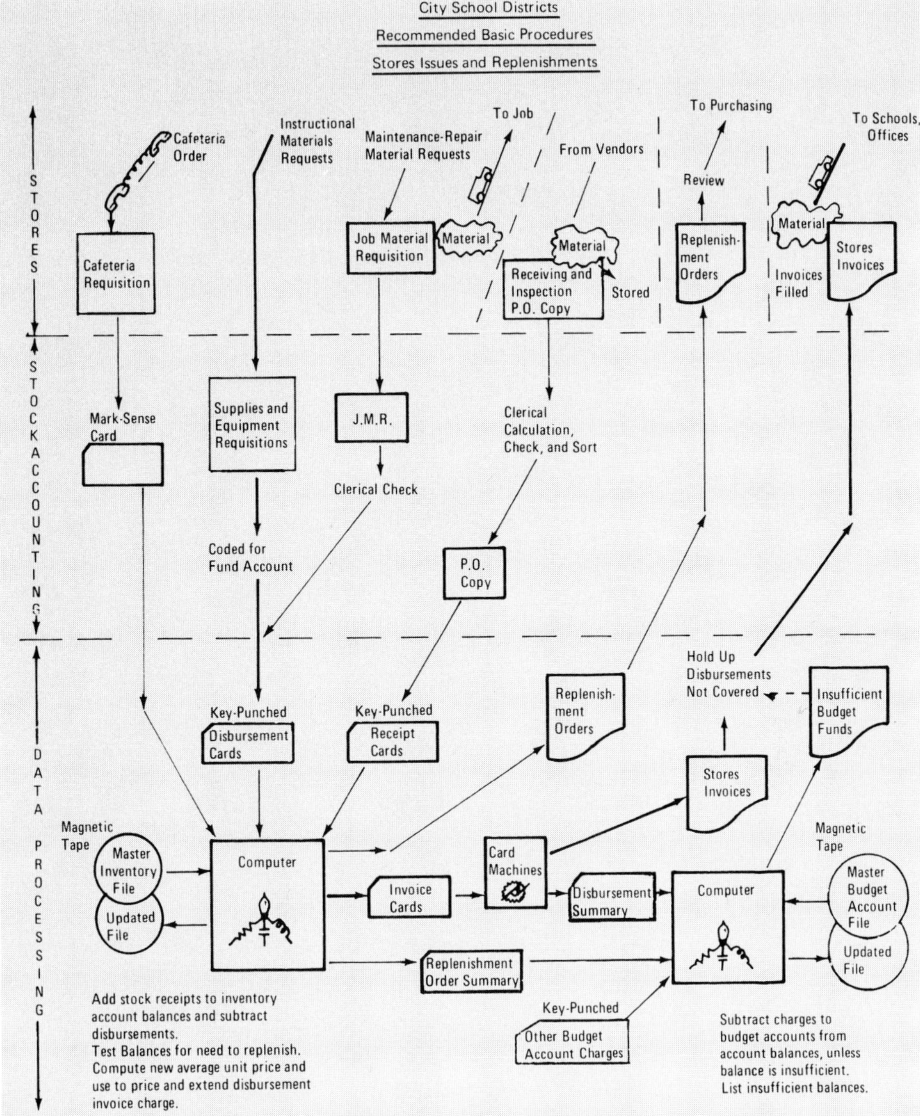

Figure 8–7. Procedural Flowchart.

parceled out to programmers. The programmer's first step is to analyze the run description and prepare a flowchart which pictures in detail how this run is to be executed on the computer. The flowchart is used for coding the run in computer language. After the coding has been completed, the run is tested for accuracy by processing specific transaction material on the computer (this is the "debugging" process). On completion of the testing, a run book and computer center procedures are prepared.

CITY SCHOOL DISTRICTS

Approximate Present Costs Displaceable by Computer System

	Number of People	Monthly Cost
Clerical:		
Equivalent clerical time of clerks in stores branch to determine replenishment needs	6	$ 3,000
Equivalent clerical time spent in calculating new moving average unit inventory prices	1/2	250
Equivalent clerical time spent checking budget fund coverage and posting to budget accounts	5	2,500
Equivalent clerical time spent in checking incoming stores materials requests	1	500
	12 1/2	6,250
Tabulating Section:		
1/2 of approximate monthly average costs	$9,640	
Estimated 1/2 of present stock accounting work		4,820
		$11,070
Estimated Recurring Computer Costs:		
100 hours per month, at $38.00 (second shift hourly rental rate)		$ 3,800
Estimated Net Displaceable Costs, Per Month*		$ 7,270

*In an organization as large as the School Districts, many vacancies occur through voluntary terminations and through the opening of additional positions caused by natural expansion. This situation should easily enable the Districts to find desirable positions for employees who are displaced by the installation of electronic equipment.

Figure 8–8. Feasibility Report Analysis Sheet.

Filemaking constitutes a major part of the work in the initial application of a computer system. It involves construction of the records used for reference to obtain information or to accumulate data. For example, in a payroll system, a file is maintained on a disk of each employee's record, including such data as earnings, deductions, accumulated data for the year, etc.

Defining the files required and their format is an important phase of the job. In addition, arrangements must be made to enable the clerical organization to gather the necessary data and establish the file. The data is then converted to disk and an audit of the file is made. Finally, after establishing the file, but before going into production, the file is updated.

The installation of a new computer system will involve changes in clerical routings and thus will require documentation of these manual procedures. After documentation has been completed, training must be provided for all personnel involved in the new system. Following the completion of the training phase, the new system is tried with test data before it is installed on a production basis.

Testing and installation of the computer system, is the last step, one that involves testing the system prior to installation and making the necessary changes to produce the required data. The system is then turned over to operations personnel.

The important features to be remembered are these:

1. The objective is to write detailed procedures for the overall system.
2. The method is to analyze the flowcharts, documentation and narrative from the analysis and design phase. These will show the final system that was agreed upon by all.
3. The technique of system design should include
   a. A detailed outline of the new system.
   b. Samples of source documents together with scaled images of reports.
   c. Detailed procedures.
4. The entire system should be submitted to management for approval.
5. Upon written authorization, the installation of the new system should begin.
6. The system should be released to operating personnel.
7. A follow–up should be made after the release of the new system to operating personnel to confirm results and the adequacy of the procedures. Any evidence of "back sliding" to the old system should be stoped. A ninety-day follow–up is also a long enough trial period to make a realistic cost analysis of the system.

Before the installation of a computer is undertaken, management must be convinced of the practicability as well as the cost justification of the application (Fig. 8.9).

SYSTEMS AND PROCEDURES APPROACH

1. The objective of systems and procedures is to reduce everyday activities to simple routines, thereby minimizing the task of decision making, and relieving the employees of many details of execution.
2. The system will be a network of procedures which are integrated and designed to carry out a major activity.
3. The size and number of work specialities make it difficult and time–consuming for managers to inspect each operation personally. The manager should secure pertinent information regarding operations via the system and procedure methods.
4. The use of systems expedites comprehension, forces the identification of activities, and prescribes the sequence of operations to achieve the stated goal. The *system problem* is to design a system that will bring together all forces to accomplish an effective pattern.

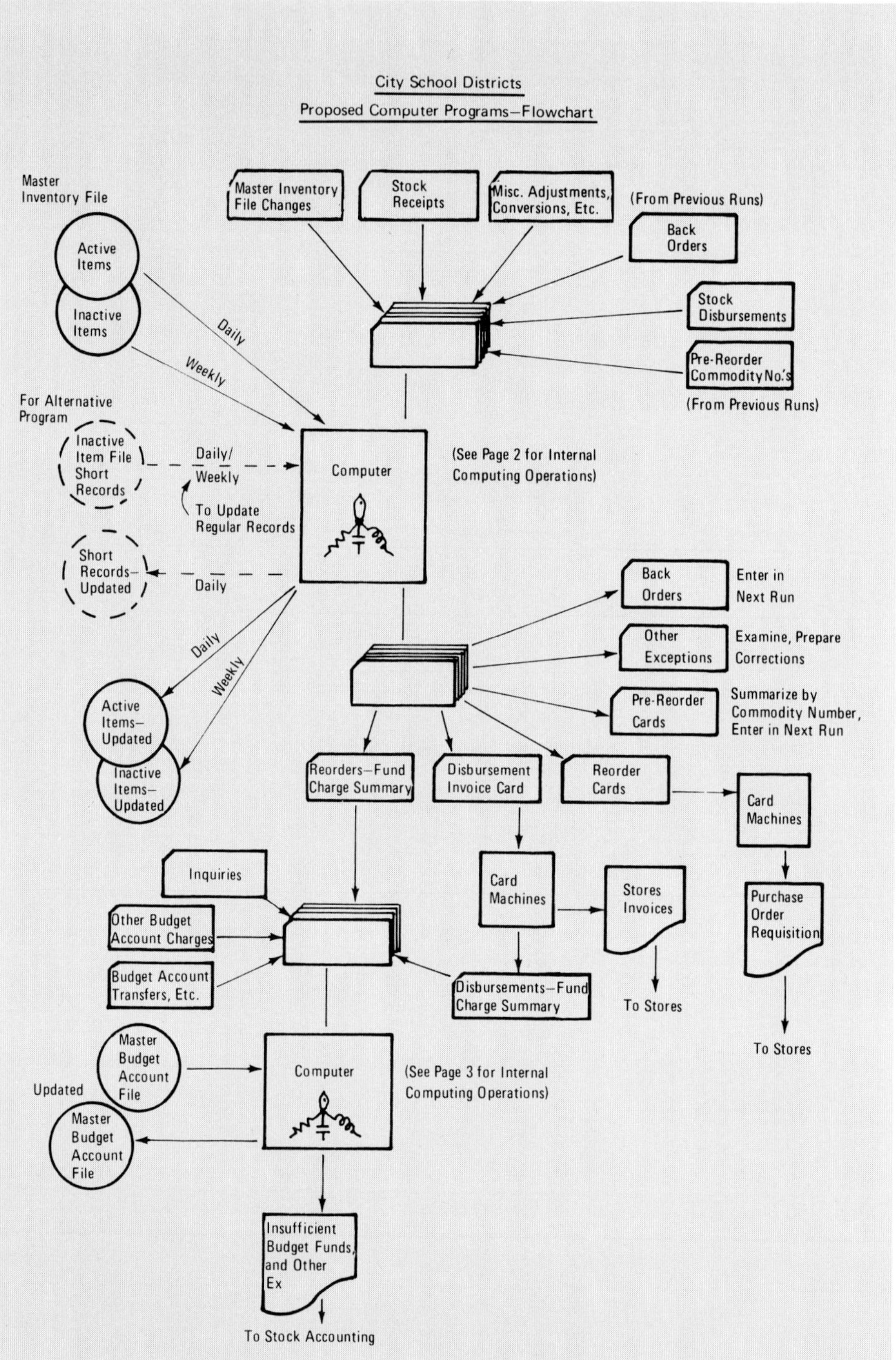

Figure 8–9. System Flowchart Example.

SYSTEMS ELEMENTS

Objectives. The basic goals of the organization.

Decisions. Selections that must be made between alternative actions.

Policies. Written guidelines of management for guiding administrative action.

Procedures. Activities to carry out the management policies. A series of related steps to carry out an activity.

System. A network of procedures that is large in scope.

Subsystem. Subordinate to the system that is an integral part of the larger system usually consisting of two or more procedures.

Integrated Information System. A network of related subsystems developed according to an integrated scheme. A single transcription of the source data will be used and combined with all interrelated activities without the necessity of recopying the original data.

System Flowchart. An overall visual of the system showing the flow of information from the input to the output media.

Program Flowchart. The breakdown, step–by–step, in sequence, of each procedure of the operation to be performed.

Block Diagram. A further breakdown of the program flowchart. Both the program flowchart and the block diagram are used in the coding of the program.

SYSTEM DESIGN CONCEPTS

1. A good system should permit reasonably rapid changes to be made as the necessity arises, without completely disrupting the entire operation.
2. Data should be captured in machine-acceptable format as close to the source as is economically possible: e.g. punched cards, paper tape, magnetic tape, etc. This prevents repetitive copying.
3. Adequate controls should be maintained over all parts of the system. Costs should be ascertained at the different degrees of control to assure the most economical cost consistent with adequate controls. There is a tendency to "over control" a system. Too many checkpoints intend to increase costs without compensatory benefits.
4. There should be a straight line flow of the operating procedures. Backtracking should be avoided.
5. Exception procedures should be eliminated if possible, or at least minimized.
6. Authority should be defined so that decisions can be made as close to point of operation as possible.
7. The system must be sold to all levels of management to gain acceptance.

ADVANTAGES OF SYSTEMS AND PROCEDURES

The important advantages of an effective system procedures program are:

1. It supplies an overall look at the enterprise. The overall objectives are defined.
2. It increases the appreciation of the total problem. The limited departmentalized and outmoded notions are cut through by the system.
3. The input and output ingredients are identified. Source documents are standardized and output formats are formalized.
4. The system brings order and a desirable mode of operations to office work. The work patterns are reduced to simple routines.
5. It provides uniformity of action and formalized work. Procedures and other types of manuals guarantee uniform operating procedures.
6. The emphasis is on accurate and reliable controls. With an effective system, management has tighter control of the operations.
7. Problems that arise are more readily identified and isolated.
8. Uniform management policies are encouraged through a standardized system of operation.
9. It facilitates automatic data processing. The installation of a data processing system is simplified if there is an effective system in operation.
10. Personnel training is simplified. New personnel are more easily trained as the duties of each job are properly defined.
11. Service to the operating departments is improved with a more effective system reducing the amount of confusion.
12. Savings in operating costs usually accrue as the result of the elimination of duplicated activities and simplified methods of operation.

SELLING THE SYSTEM

"The job of the systems man is 10 percent technique and 90 percent salesmanship," because there is often a wide divergence between the objectives of the individual employee, the functional area, and the business enterprise as a whole.

Even if this situation does not exist in fact, it is imagined by many employees. Hence, an *extraordinary* sales effort is required on the part of the systems man. The selling starts with the receipt of the assignment and does not end until full implementation of the new system has been accomplished.

Selling should not be limited to top management. If the system is not sold to all personnel involved, it is destined to fail. It will be sabotaged in a myriad of subtle ways by the operations personnel, who can make the most unlikely system operable or the best system fail.

The success of the system depends on the acceptance by operating personnel. All people need to "belong" and all want status; the systems person must be sure to fulfill these needs. If properly approached, most operating personnel will be anxious to join a systems staff effort. The operating staff must gain confidence in the new system to remove all the mystery.

People fear what they don't understand. The rank and file basically fear for their security when confronted with system change and improvement. Operations personnel should be assigned to the systems staff for the duration of the project to orient them in the techniques that are applicable to each domain.

The proposed new system should be presented formally after the preliminary work of selling has been accomplished. The purpose of the presentation:

1. To gain management commitment.
2. To gain political support for a proposed system; approval is not sought in this presentation.
3. To orient indirectly-concerned members of management about the direction and goals of the new system.

The presentation should include the history of the system study, who requested the study, participants and the development status. It is not necessary to depict the existing system in terms of computer logic, matching flow or multiple card formats; it is only necessary to simply provide a basic understanding of the existing system.

Several organizations will benefit from the new system and these benefits, both corporate and by individual department, should be pointed out. All points should be covered in the presentation, inviting questions and comments from all personnel. All questions should be answered honestly.

The presentation should end with a summary of decisions made and the future correspondence necessary to confirm decisions. A successful presentation can be made only if the listener fully understands the value of the system to him and his organization.

SUMMARY

A good data processing system is designed to solve a particular problem, and if well done it will never become a problem. A data processing application doesn't just happen. It is the culmination of the work of many people who contribute their knowledge toward the conversion of manual procedures to a computer application. Systems and procedures are an important part of the data processing area. Before the programming phase can begin, a thorough system analysis must be completed. The intent of this chapter is to present the numerous procedures and problems involved in a systems study. One should be aware of the complexity of system analysis, conversion problems and many of the terms used in a system study.

The eventual success of the entire data processing effort is dependent upon a good systems study. Many persons have the impression that programming is the most important phase of computer processing. It should be pointed out that the programming effort is begun only after the entire problem has been properly defined—the flowcharts, analysis sheets and other documents prepared that have resulted from the systems study. The entire study is centered around management objectives and what management expects from data processing.

I. *Systems Analysis.*
  A. *System-Definition*—a cohesive collection of items or a representation of connected parts that are related through a "network of relationships."
  B. *Survey-Definition*—the determination of whether or not a proposed system is feasible; whether or not it will give improved operation at a lower cost.
  C. *Problem-Definition*—will insure the setting up of objectives for creating an efficient and effective data processing system to solve a particular problem.
  D. *Analysis and Design.*
    1. *System analysis*—defining area objectives and reviewing existing procedures.
    2. *System design*—determining the relationship between all parts of a system and designing the system with emphasis on the fulfillment of legal and management control requirements.
  E. *Procedures, Programs and Conversion*—procedures are converted to flowcharts and the programming function begins.
    1. *Filemaking*—construction of records to be used for reference to obtain information or to accumulate data.
    2. *Installation of a new system*—changes in personnel, training new personnel, documentation, testing the new system, etc.
    3. *Follow-up*—to confirm results of system installation and the adequacy of the procedures.

II. *Systems and Procedures Approach.*
  A. *Systems elements.*
    1. *Objectives*—basic goals of management.
    2. *Decisions*—selection between alternatives.
    3. *Policies*—guidelines for administrative action.
    4. *System*—network of procedures that is large in scope.
    5. *Subsystem*—a segment of a large system.

6. *Integrated Information System*—network of related systems developed according to an integrated scheme.
7. *System flowchart*—overall view of the system.
8. *Program flowchart*—procedure sequence of the operations to be performed.
9. *Block diagram*—a further breakdown of the program flowchart.

B. *Advantages of systems and procedures*—overall look at an enterprise, identification of input and output ingredients, appreciation of total problem, control, savings, etc.

C. *Selling the system.*

1. Must be sold to all persons concerned.
2. Success depends upon acceptance by all operating personnel.
3. Gain management commitment.
4. Orient indirectly concerned members of management about direction and goals of new system.
5. Summary benefits of new system.

IDENTIFICATION QUESTIONS

Match the following terms with the statements that follow.

A. Block Diagram
B. Decisions
C. Filemaking
D. Integrated Information System
E. Objectives
F. Policies
G. Procedures
H. Program Flowchart
I. Subsystem
J. Survey
K. System
L. System Flowchart

1. Written guidelines of management for guiding administrative action.
2. To determine whether or not a proposed system is feasible.
3. A network of procedures that is large in scope.
4. The breakdown step-by-step in sequence of each procedure to be performed.
5. The selections that must be made between alternatives.
6. The construction of the records used for reference to obtain information or to accumulate data.
7. A network of related subsystems developed according to an integrated scheme.
8. An integral part of a larger system consisting of two or more procedures.
9. The basic goals of an organization.
10. A further breakdown of a program flowchart.
11. The necessary activities to carry out the management policies.
12. An overall visual of the system showing the flow of information from input to output.

QUESTIONS FOR REVIEW

1. Why is management involved with data processing problems?
2. What important changes have been made in data processing?
3. What requirements are necessary to correctly define the problem?
4. What is the purpose of system analysis?
5. What are the objectives of the analysis and design phase of the study?
6. What are the important aspects of the procedures, programs, and conversion phase of the study?
7. Describe the important points in the systems and procedures approach.
8. What are the important system design concepts?
9. List the important advantages of systems and procedures.
10. Why is it important that the system be sold to all personnel involved? What are the important points to be reiterated in the selling of the system?

CHAPTER 9

Preparation for a Computer Program

A computer really is a simple machine, made up of simple components that operate on simple physical principles. What makes a computer complicated, what gives it its wonderful capabilities, is the ingenious logic with which its parts are organized. And that logic—that organization—is something its human designers are responsible for.

INTRODUCTION TO COMPUTER PROGRAMMING

Running an automatic machine is such an easy job that it is easy to overlook the many hours that have to be spent in designing, testing, and adjusting all of the automatic features until the operation becomes effortless. The same meticulous care and preparation is necessary before the computer can function automatically. It must be instructed in how to perform every task. This job of writing detailed instructions for the computer and making them work correctly is called *programming*.

The initial assignment consists of a precise problem statement which has been developed by a system analyst. It should contain a job description, special processing information, a description of the kind of data desired and the layout specifications for input and output of that data. The information contained in the problem statement will be further translated into the necessary tools that enable the programmer to both solve and program the problem (Fig. 9.1). In the absence of such information, the programmer must develop such specifications as are necessary for solving the problem.

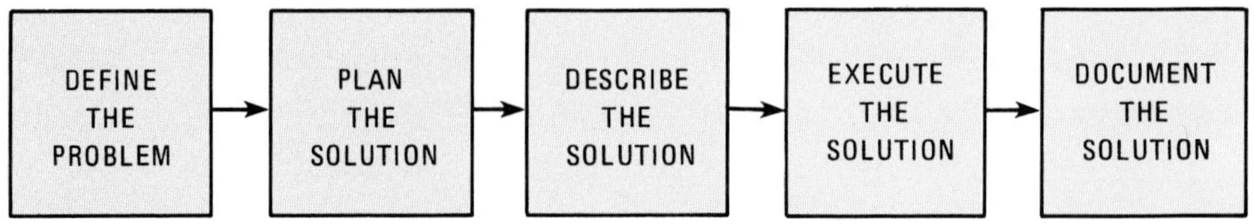

Figure 9–1. Problem Solving.

In order to process data with a computer, the machine must be provided with a set of instructions (program). *The instruction is a command to the machine, expressed in a coded combination of characters, to carry out some operation.* With the preliminary data processing tasks of analysis and definition of the problem accomplished, the job of coding is put together in a set of elementary instructions to carry out the prescribed task. When these instructions are loaded into the predetermined storage area of the computer, the data is entered and the instructions are ready to be executed by the machine and the desired data processing project is accomplished. The ability of the machine to store its own program internally allows the computer to alter its own instructions at electronic speeds to conditions encountered during the processing of the data. This ability to manipulate instructions during processing provides the almost unlimited flexibility and the so-called logical capability of the stored program system.

INSTRUCTIONS

After a programmer has developed the necessary tools, he must next develop a program (Fig. 9.2). *A program is a series of instructions which, when properly translated, will direct the computer in how it will receive data, process it, and output it* (Fig. 9.3).

The repertory of instructions allows the programmer to specify all operations quickly and easily. *An instruction is a coded statement used to write a program which, when combined with other instructions, is used by the computer to solve a specific problem* (Fig. 9.4). A computer instruction is an order to carry out some elementary operation. Each instruction has a standard format and may range in complexity from a simple element operation code to an operation code with many elements. All instructions have an *operation code which uniquely identifies the operation to be performed.* Some instructions may include variant characters which are used to further define an operation or to specify a piece of data to be used in the operation (Fig. 9.5).

Some instructions call for information to be read into internal storage from an input device such as a card reader, or to be written out on an output device such as a printer. Other instructions perform arithmetic operations. Still other instructions move and rearrange data within a computer and make various decisions based on data or results of processing. Some instructions can

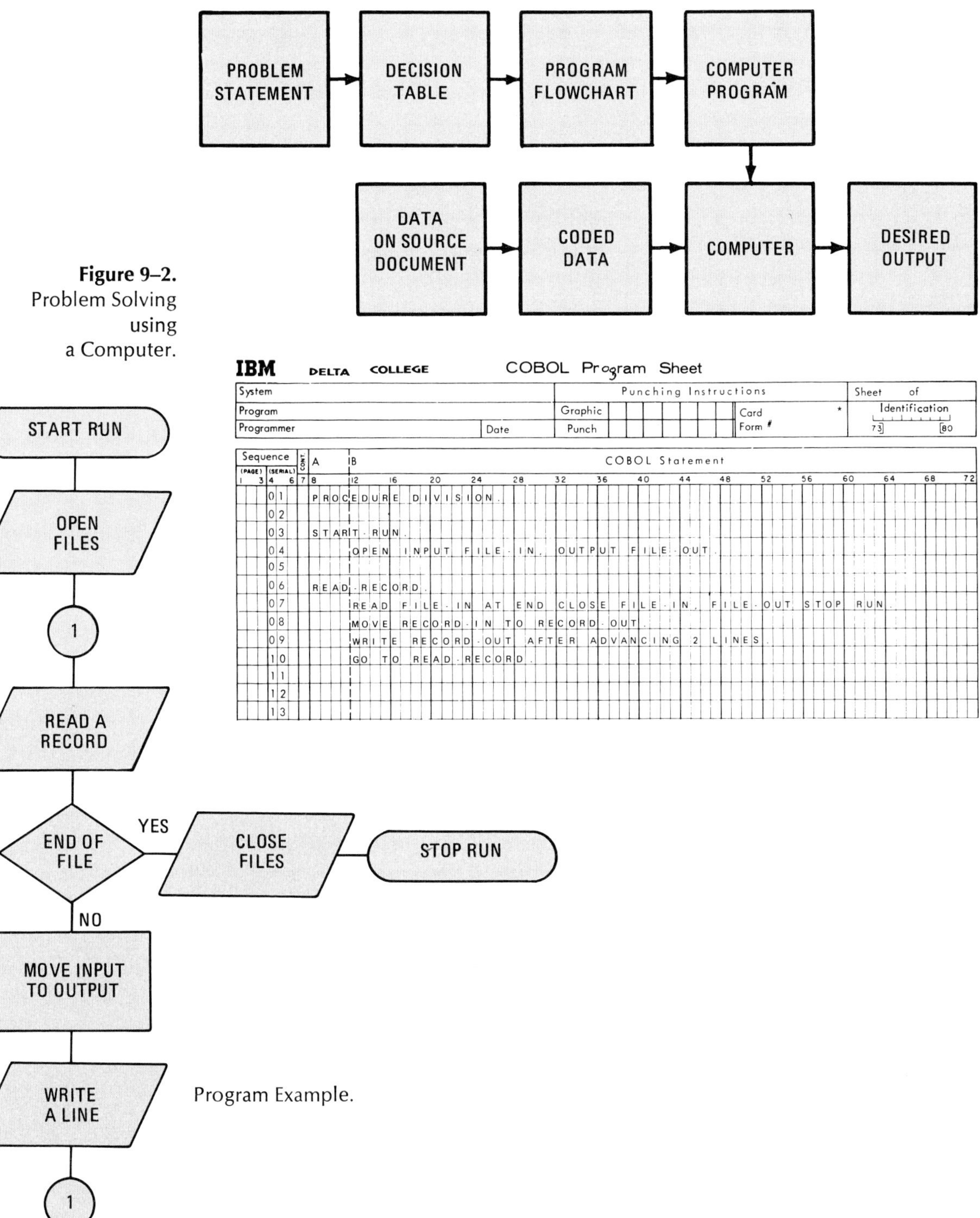

Figure 9–2. Problem Solving using a Computer.

IBM DELTA COLLEGE COBOL Program Sheet

System	Punching Instructions	Sheet of
Program	Graphic	Card Form #	Identification 73 80
Programmer / Date	Punch	

```
Sequence  A   B                                   COBOL Statement
(PAGE)(SERIAL)
01        PROCEDURE DIVISION.
02
03        START-RUN.
04            OPEN INPUT FILE-IN, OUTPUT FILE-OUT.
05
06        READ-RECORD.
07            READ FILE-IN AT END CLOSE FILE-IN, FILE-OUT STOP RUN.
08            MOVE RECORD-IN TO RECORD-OUT.
09            WRITE RECORD-OUT AFTER ADVANCING 2 LINES.
10            GO TO READ-RECORD.
11
12
13
```

Program Example.

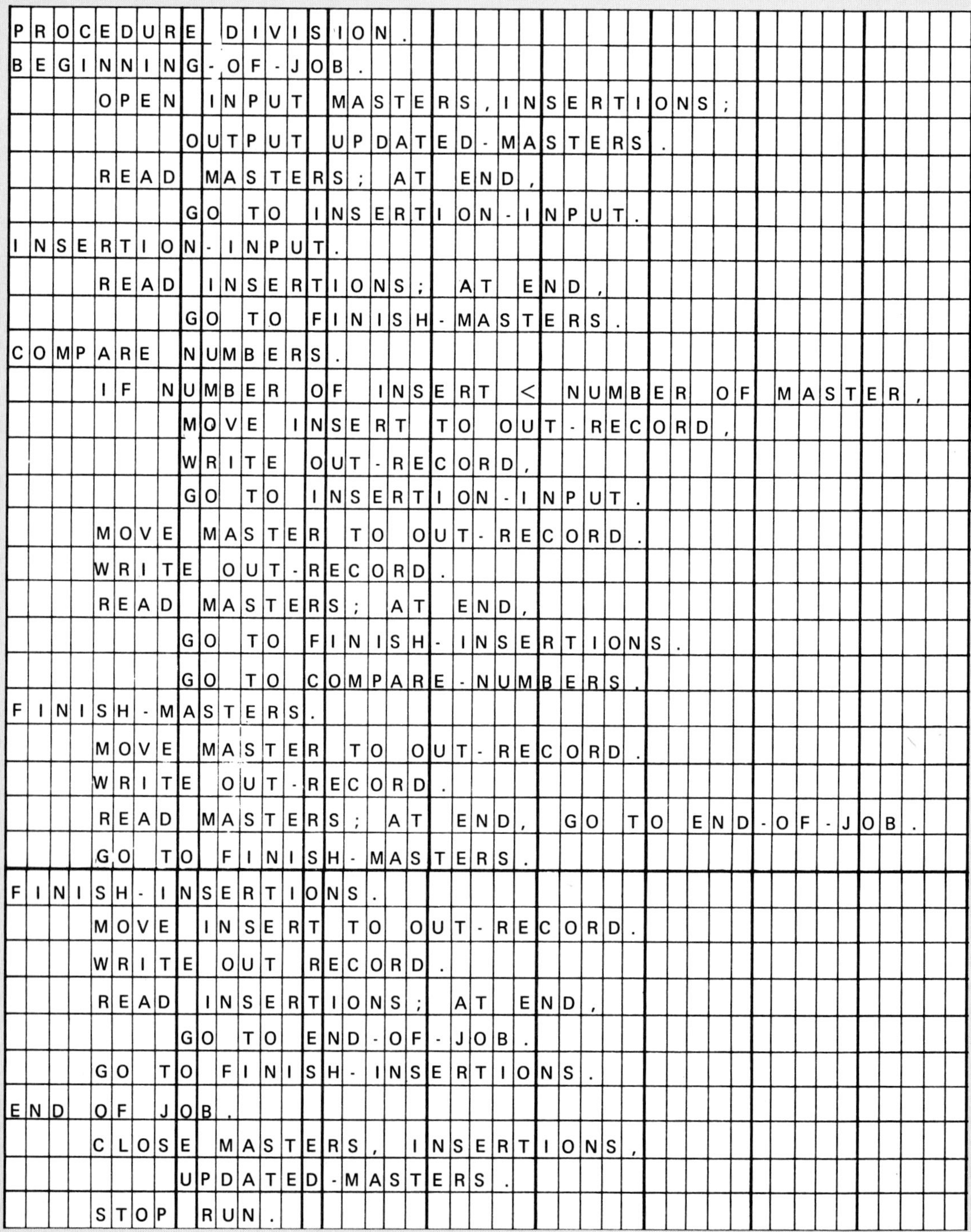

```
PROCEDURE DIVISION.
BEGINNING-OF-JOB.
    OPEN INPUT MASTERS, INSERTIONS;
        OUTPUT UPDATED-MASTERS.
    READ MASTERS; AT END,
        GO TO INSERTION-INPUT.
INSERTION-INPUT.
    READ INSERTIONS; AT END,
        GO TO FINISH-MASTERS.
COMPARE NUMBERS.
    IF NUMBER OF INSERT < NUMBER OF MASTER,
        MOVE INSERT TO OUT-RECORD,
        WRITE OUT-RECORD,
        GO TO INSERTION-INPUT.
    MOVE MASTER TO OUT-RECORD.
    WRITE OUT-RECORD.
    READ MASTERS; AT END,
        GO TO FINISH-INSERTIONS.
        GO TO COMPARE-NUMBERS.
FINISH-MASTERS.
    MOVE MASTER TO OUT-RECORD.
    WRITE OUT-RECORD.
    READ MASTERS; AT END, GO TO END-OF-JOB.
    GO TO FINISH-MASTERS.
FINISH-INSERTIONS.
    MOVE INSERT TO OUT-RECORD.
    WRITE OUT RECORD.
    READ INSERTIONS; AT END,
        GO TO END-OF-JOB.
    GO TO FINISH-INSERTIONS.
END OF JOB.
    CLOSE MASTERS, INSERTIONS,
        UPDATED-MASTERS.
    STOP RUN.
```

Figure 9–3. Computer Program.

```
NEXTREC  GET    TPDATA,TRANAREA
         CLI    TRANCODE,2                     Determine if replacement or other
*                                              transaction
         BL     REPLACE                        Branch if replacement
         READ   DECBRW,KU,,'S','S',MF=E        Read record for update
         CHECK  DECBRW,DSORG=IS                Check exceptional conditions
         CLI    TRANCODE,2                     Determine if change or append
         BH     CHANGE                         Branch if change
         ...
```

Figure 9–4. Instructions.

Operation	Operand
Select	Tape Unit 200
Read	One Record into Storage Positions 1000–1050
Clear & Add	Quantity in Storage Location 1004 in Accumulator
Subtract	Quantity in Storage Location 1005 from Contents of Accumulator
Store	Result in Storage Location 1051
Branch	To Instruction in Storage Location 5004

Figure 9–5. Instruction Format.

specify the location of the next instruction, and in this way may be used to alter the sequence in which any instruction or block of instructions are executed.

An important thing to realize is that the program of instructions must be prepared before the processing can be done, and the program must be in storage before it is executed. Since it is frequently necessary to repeat the execution of groups of instructions or to skip around in the program, we must have some way to identify an instruction by where it is located in storage.

The instructions must be storable in the same location that is used for storing data. The instructions must be set up to handle data of a general type. If a condition occurs in a program that was not anticipated, the program will do what the instructions say to do even though the result may be meaningless. The fundamental thing to remember is that by the time the instructions are executed by the machine, the human factor is no longer part of the picture.

The instruction address is not part of the instruction; it merely tells where the instruction is located in storage (or, rather where it will be located after the program is put into storage).

The only distinction between instructions and data lies in the time they are brought into the central processing unit. A program may be stored in any location that does not conflict with the storage of data. Since the program is stored in the same manner as data there must be no overlapping. If the information is brought in during an instruction cycle, it is interpreted as an instruction; at any other time, it is interpreted as data. The computer can operate upon its own instructions if the instructions are supplied as data. A storage location can store one character of an instruction or one character of data.

METHODS OF PROCESSING DATA

The two methods of processing data through a computer are sequential (batch) processing and direct access (inline) processing. The type of method used depends upon the application requirements.

SEQUENTIAL (BATCH) PROCESSING

In sequential processing, data is recorded in files outside of the computer, on magnetic tape, for example, and is arranged in a predetermined sequence. Each record has to be examined for possible processing. Before the transaction record can be applied against the main or master file it must be arranged in the same sequence as the master file; it is feasible, therefore, to accumulate these records in convenient groups or batches for subsequent processing.

Sequential processing is feasible in operations that have a high rate of activity—payroll, for instance, where a large percentage of the records are active each time the payroll is processed. Transactions are batched for processing at one time (Fig. 9.6).

One of the principal objections to sequential processing is the fact that each record has to be examined and processing cannot occur as the transaction appears. For economical operations, data is accumulated in batches for subsequent processing at one time. It does, however, have the advantage of rather fast processing time for read and process when compared to random processing.

RANDOM PROCESSING (INLINE)

In random processing, the data is usually stored in large capacity storage units, such as magnetic disks, and is fed into the computer as the need for processing occurs. All records need not be examined, only those that need updating. Transactions are not batched and there is no need for sorting as in sequential processing. A low-activity operation such as inventory updating where a small percentage of the records are active at any one time is a typical example of a random access application (Fig. 9.7).

Random access does have the advantage of processing the transaction as the activity occurs without having to wait to batch the items.

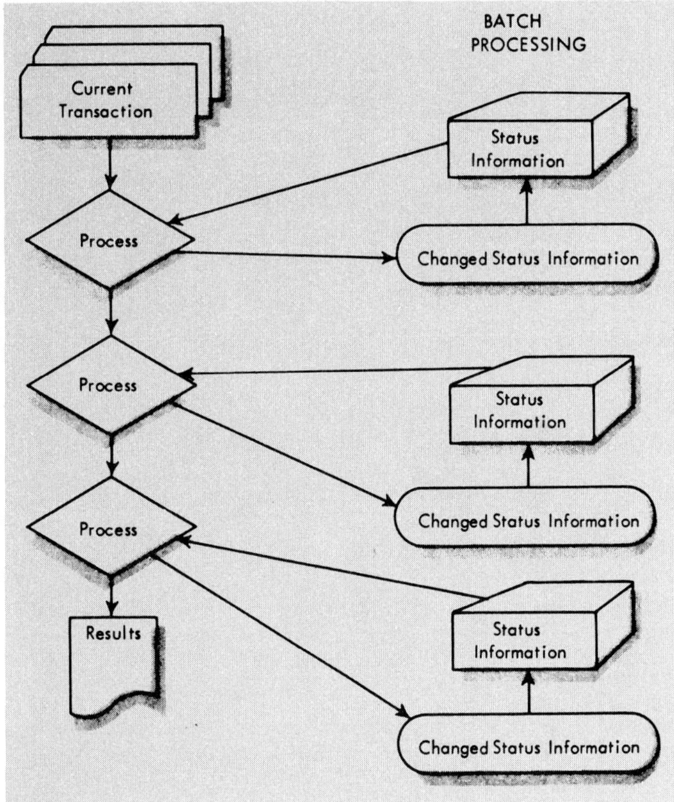

Figure 9–6.
Sequential Batch
Processing.

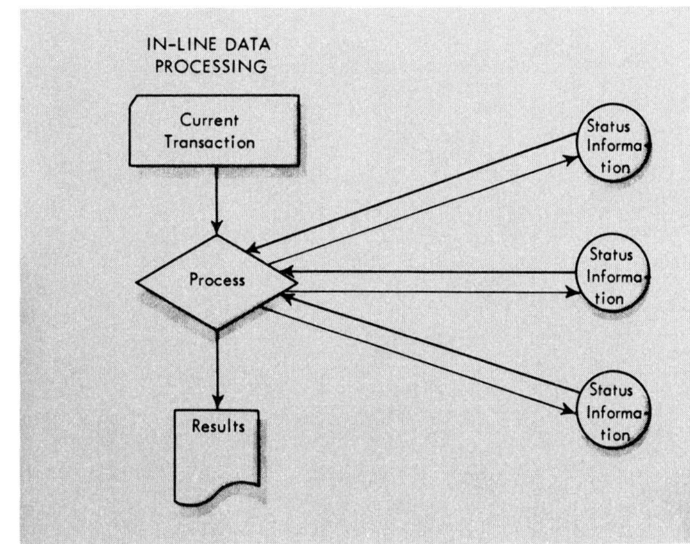

Figure 9–7.
Random (In Line)
Processing.

DECISION TABLES

In order to establish an exact picture of the problem statement and possible actions resulting from its conditions, the programmer may set up a decision table. The decision table is very useful in reducing the problem statement to a table of condition/action statements. In addition, it will clarify the relationships between the various operations to be performed and the decisions which must be made, and which are expressed as condition/action statements in the table (Fig. 9.8).

A decision table is a tool of convenience for the programmer and should be used as a supplement to the program flowchart. The complexity of the problem determines the extent to which the table is necessary. There are many times when the problem statement is so concise that the construction of a decision table would be time-consuming and of little value. However, when the problem statement requires close discriminations involving many complex logic decisions, the decision table provides a form for recording them

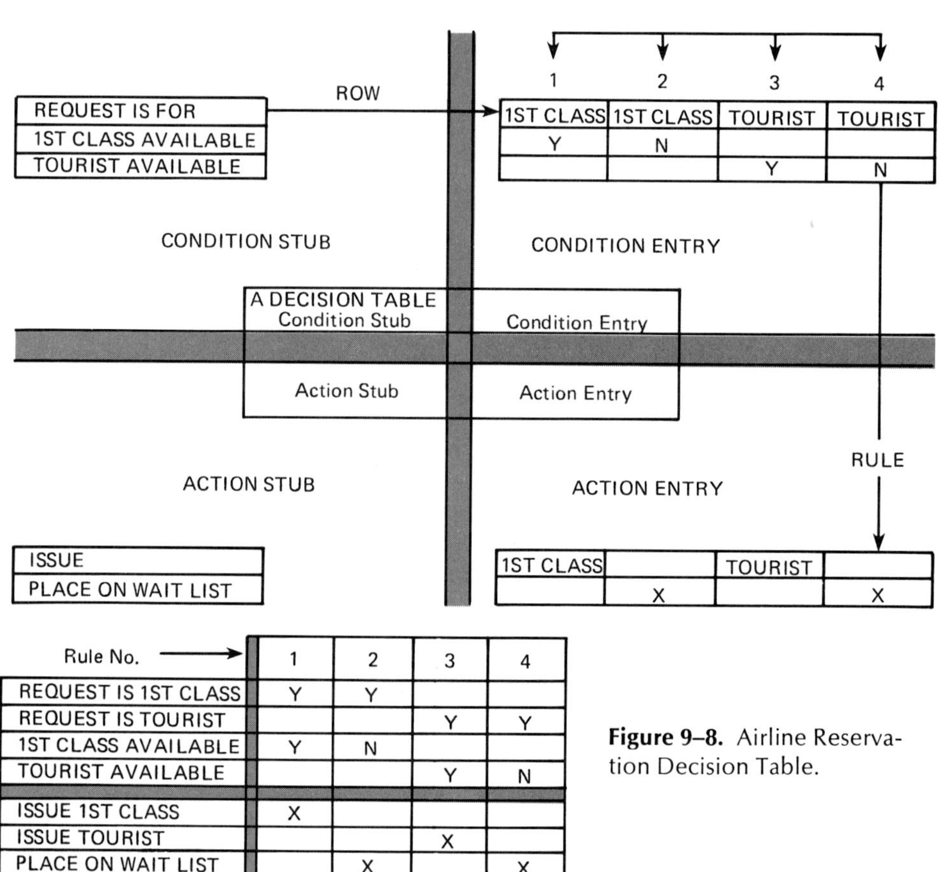

Rule No.	1	2	3	4
REQUEST IS 1ST CLASS	Y	Y		
REQUEST IS TOURIST			Y	Y
1ST CLASS AVAILABLE	Y	N		
TOURIST AVAILABLE			Y	N
ISSUE 1ST CLASS	X			
ISSUE TOURIST			X	
PLACE ON WAIT LIST		X		X

Figure 9–8. Airline Reservation Decision Table.

PROBLEM STATEMENT:

If customer's credit is OK, and quantity ordered is equal to or less than order limit, and quantity ordered is equal to or less than quantity on hand, ship item. If customer's credit is not OK, or quantity ordered is greater than order limit, reject order. If quantity ordered is greater than quantity on hand, back order.

DECISION TABLE -

Customer's credit is OK	Y	N		
Quantity ordered is less than or equal to order limit	Y		N	
Quantity ordered is less than or equal to quantity on hand	Y			N
Ship item	X			
Reject order		X	X	
Back order				X

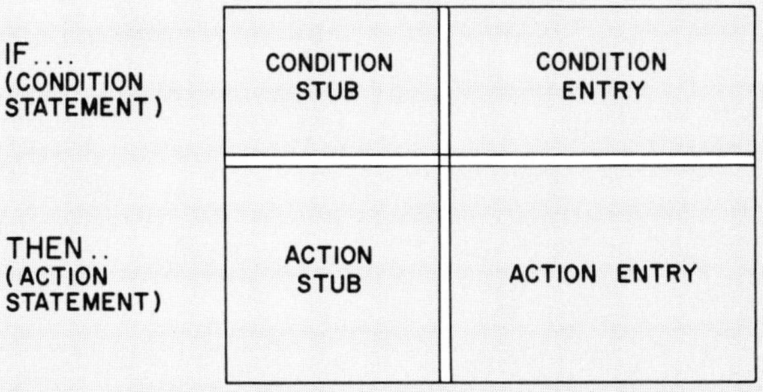

IF.... (CONDITION STATEMENT)	CONDITION STUB	CONDITION ENTRY
THEN.. (ACTION STATEMENT)	ACTION STUB	ACTION ENTRY

Figure 9–9. Decision Table—Example.

(Fig. 9.9). A programmer should have a working knowledge of the elements of a decision table.

Decision tables are divided into four sections. Each section is marked off by a set of double vertical and horizontal lines.

1. The first section contains the *conditions* listed in the problem statement.
2. A second section contains the *actions* listed in the problem statement.
3. A third section contains a pattern of *yes* (Y) and *no* (N) answers to the *conditions*.
4. The fourth section indicates by an "X" what action should be taken based on the answers found in the third section. Each "X" indicates that a *decision* should be made to take the *action* listed in the same row in the second section (Fig. 9.10).

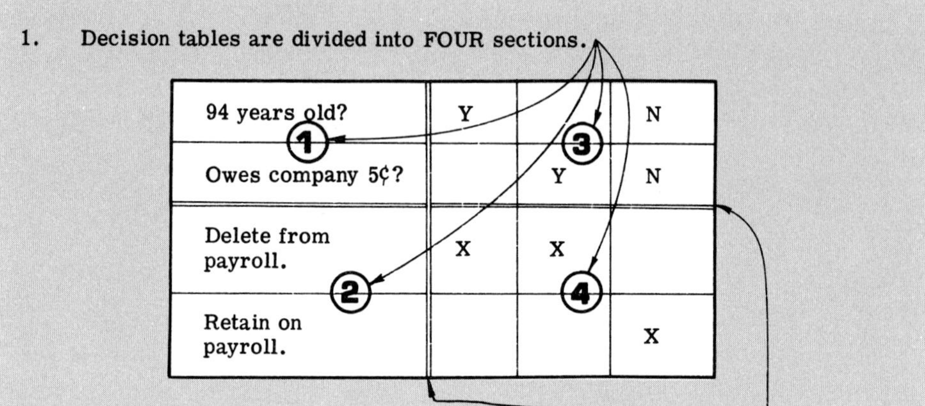
1. Decision tables are divided into FOUR sections.
1
2
3
4

94 years old?	Y		N
Owes company 5¢?		Y	N
Delete from payroll.	X	X	
Retain on payroll.			X

Figure 9–10. Decision Table Sections.

2. Each section is marked off with a set of double vertical and horizontal lines.
3. The section labeled (1) contains the conditions listed in the problem statement.
4. The section labeled (2) contains the actions listed in the problem statement.
5. The section labeled (3) contains a pattern of yes (Y) and no (N) answers to the conditions.
6. The section labeled (4) indicates by an "X" what action should be taken based on the answers found in section (3). Each X indicates that a decision should be made to take the action listed on the same row in section (2).

Every possible combination of "yes" and "no" answers does not have to be shown. A decision table will only contain the basic pattern of answers necessary to determine which action is to be taken.

A decision table shows the major aspects of a problem; the major decisions and processing routines that must be established so that the data can be processed. As such, the decision table is oriented toward the problem.

Before a computer program can be written, the processing steps to be taken by the computer must be described in greater detail. This can be done by a succession of decision tables each showing more of the detail of a particular routine. To plan a computer program, the *program flowchart* is constructed like a decision table. The program flowchart is a means of representing visually a logical sequence of procedure steps which a computer must take in processing data. As such, the program flowchart is oriented toward the computer.

Figure 9–11. Flowcharting.

FLOWCHARTS

The increased use of data processing has focused attention upon the need for the logical representation of data flows. Once the problem has been defined and the objectives established, the next step is the orderly presentation of procedures so that the objectives can be realized sequentially (Fig. 9.11). Any successful program depends upon well-defined steps prior to the actual program. The steps involve the processes to be performed and the sequence of these processes. The processes must be precisely stated before any programming can begin.

The programmer must know all the different operations to be performed. A complete analysis of the procedures, both existing and proposed, must be made to ascertain the ultimate goals to be accomplished. Many times, data processing applications fail or fall short of expectations due to inadequate planning or analysis.

The analysis is normally accomplished by developing flowcharts. *The flowchart is a graphic representation of the flow of information through a system in the course of which the information is converted from the source document to the final reports.* Because most data processing applications involve a large number of alternatives, variations, decisions, exceptions, etc., it would be impractical to attempt to state these possibilities verbally. The value of a flowchart is that it can show graphically, at a glance, the organized procedures

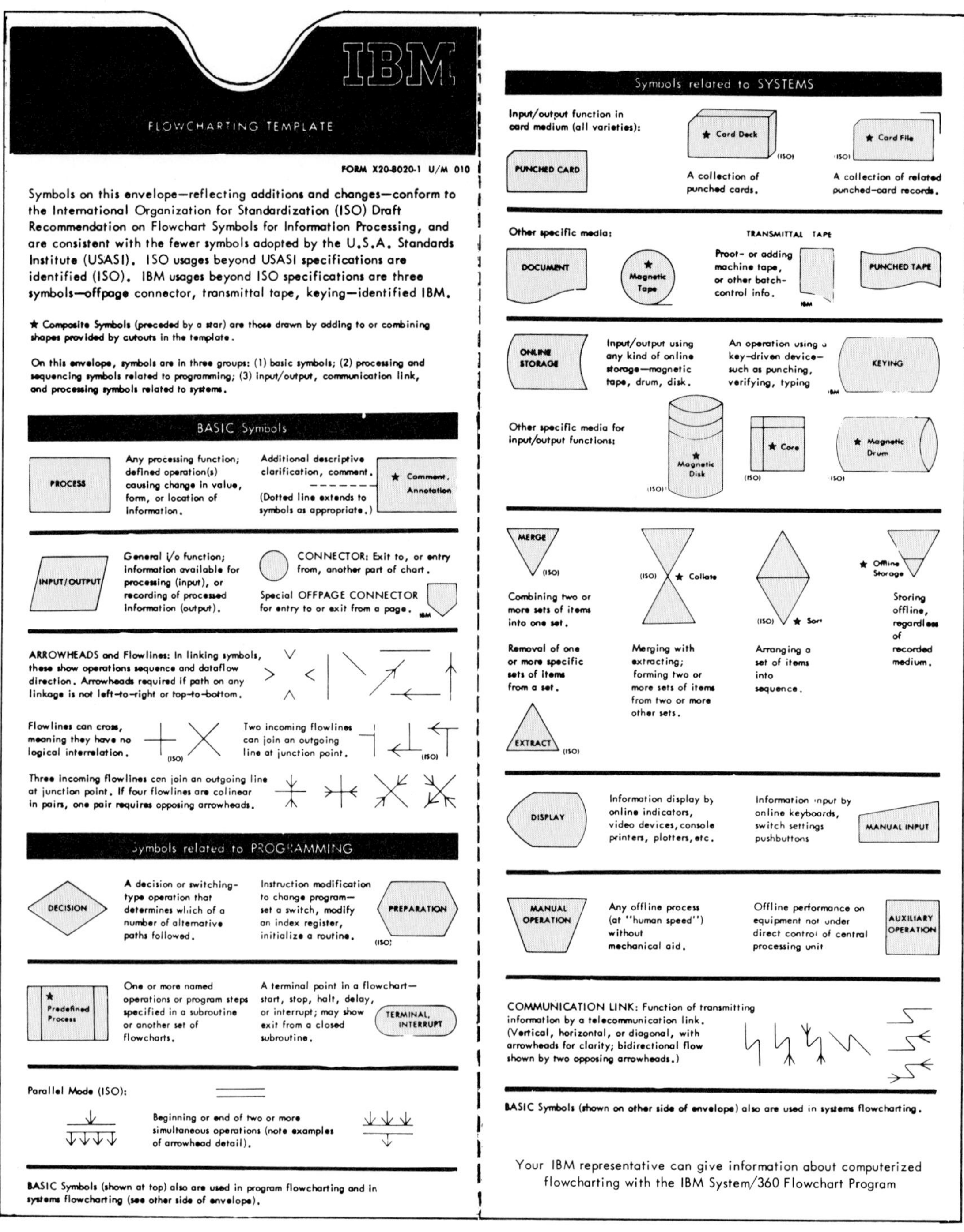

IBM

FLOWCHARTING TEMPLATE

FORM X20-8020-1 U/M 010

Symbols on this envelope—reflecting additions and changes—conform to the International Organization for Standardization (ISO) Draft Recommendation on Flowchart Symbols for Information Processing, and are consistent with the fewer symbols adopted by the U.S.A. Standards Institute (USASI). ISO usages beyond USASI specifications are identified (ISO). IBM usages beyond ISO specifications are three symbols—offpage connector, transmittal tape, keying—identified IBM.

★ Composite Symbols (preceded by a star) are those drawn by adding to or combining shapes provided by cutouts in the template.

On this envelope, symbols are in three groups: (1) basic symbols; (2) processing and sequencing symbols related to programming; (3) input/output, communication link, and processing symbols related to systems.

BASIC Symbols

PROCESS — Any processing function; defined operation(s) causing change in value, form, or location of information.

★ Comment, Annotation — Additional descriptive clarification, comment. (Dotted line extends to symbols as appropriate.)

INPUT/OUTPUT — General I/O function; information available for processing (input), or recording of processed information (output).

CONNECTOR: Exit to, or entry from, another part of chart.

Special OFFPAGE CONNECTOR for entry to or exit from a page. IBM

ARROWHEADS and Flowlines: In linking symbols, these show operations sequence and dataflow direction. Arrowheads required if path on any linkage is not left-to-right or top-to-bottom.

Flowlines can cross, meaning they have no logical interrelation. (ISO)

Two incoming flowlines can join an outgoing line at junction point. (ISO)

Three incoming flowlines can join an outgoing line at junction point. If four flowlines are colinear in pairs, one pair requires opposing arrowheads.

Symbols related to PROGRAMMING

DECISION — A decision or switching-type operation that determines which of a number of alternative paths followed.

PREPARATION — Instruction modification to change program—set a switch, modify an index register, initialize a routine. (ISO)

★ Predefined Process — One or more named operations or program steps specified in a subroutine or another set of flowcharts.

TERMINAL, INTERRUPT — A terminal point in a flowchart—start, stop, halt, delay, or interrupt; may show exit from a closed subroutine.

Parallel Mode (ISO): Beginning or end of two or more simultaneous operations (note examples of arrowhead detail).

BASIC Symbols (shown at top) also are used in program flowcharting and in systems flowcharting (see other side of envelope).

Symbols related to SYSTEMS

Input/output function in card medium (all varieties): PUNCHED CARD

★ Card Deck (ISO) — A collection of punched cards.

★ Card File (ISO) — A collection of related punched-card records.

Other specific media: DOCUMENT; ★ Magnetic Tape; TRANSMITTAL TAPE — Proof- or adding machine tape, or other batch-control info. IBM; PUNCHED TAPE

ONLINE STORAGE — Input/output using any kind of online storage—magnetic tape, drum, disk.

KEYING — An operation using a key-driven device—such as punching, verifying, typing. IBM

Other specific media for input/output functions: ★ Magnetic Disk (ISO); ★ Core (ISO); ★ Magnetic Drum (ISO)

MERGE (ISO) — Combining two or more sets of items into one set.

EXTRACT (ISO) — Removal of one or more specific sets of items from a set.

(ISO) ★ Collate — Merging with extracting; forming two or more sets of items from two or more other sets.

(ISO) ★ Sort — Arranging a set of items into sequence.

★ Offline Storage — Storing offline, regardless of recorded medium.

DISPLAY — Information display by online indicators, video devices, console printers, plotters, etc.

MANUAL INPUT — Information input by online keyboards, switch settings pushbuttons

MANUAL OPERATION — Any offline process (at "human speed") without mechanical aid.

AUXILIARY OPERATION — Offline performance on equipment not under direct control of central processing unit

COMMUNICATION LINK: Function of transmitting information by a telecommunication link. (Vertical, horizontal, or diagonal, with arrowheads for clarity; bidirectional flow shown by two opposing arrowheads.)

BASIC Symbols (shown on other side of envelope) also are used in systems flowcharting.

Your IBM representative can give information about computerized flowcharting with the IBM System/360 Flowchart Program

Figure 9–12. Flowchart Template Symbols.

and data flows so that their apparent interrelationships are readily understood by the reader. Such relationships would be difficult to abstract from a detailed narrative text. Meaningful symbols are used in place of narrative statements. The flowchart is the "roadmap" by which the data travels through the entire system.

Flowcharting systematizes the thinking of the systems analyst and clarifies intricate procedures for the programmer. When properly prepared by a systems analyst or programmer, a flowchart opens the way to communication among the individuals who work on or are affected by the data processing system. For this reason, standardization of flowcharts are a necessity. Often the coding and flowcharting functions are done by different programmers or the entire program writing assignment is transferred from one programmer to another. If flowcharts have been properly prepared, communication will be accurate and smooth. The drawing of the flowchart is often more difficult than the translation of the flowchart into computer instructions.

While flowcharts are widely used in the field of data processing, they have occasionally been misinterpreted, due primarily to the lack of uniformity in the meanings assigned to and the use of the symbols. As a result, a uniform set of flowcharting symbols was prepared by a subcommittee of the United States of America Standards Institute (Figs. 9.12, 9.13).

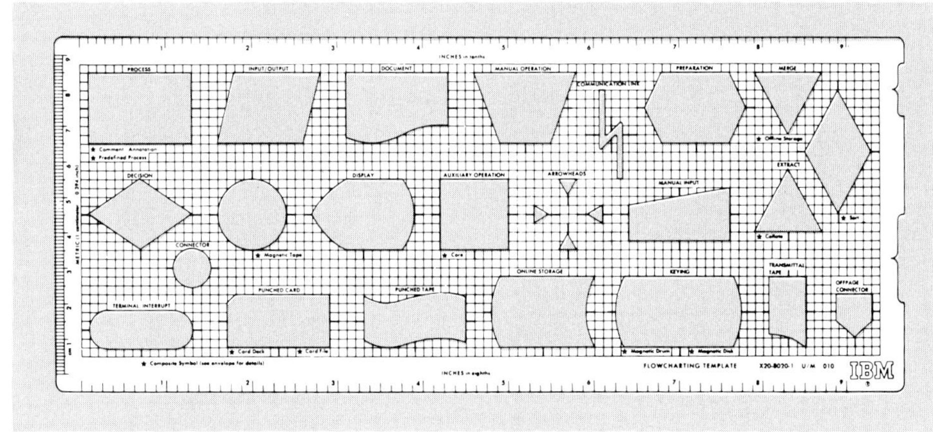

Figure 9–13. Flowchart Template.

There are two types of flowcharts widely used in data processing operations: a system flowchart and a program flowchart.

SYSTEM FLOWCHARTS

Before the system of programs is flowcharted, a systems analyst researches the problem, analyzes and summarizes existing methods of doing the job and proposes a computer solution. The systems analyst determines the input and output requirements, surveys the existing computer system and determines the necessary programs and hardware to perform the overall job. He usually prepares the system flowcharts.

The system flowchart is a diagram that illustrates the flow of data into, through, and out of a system of programs. This flowchart establishes relationships between system inputs and outputs by means of intermediate files, and establishes relationships concerning individual programs that compose the system.

A system flowchart is normally used to illustrate the overall objectives for the benefit of data processing as well as nondata processing personnel. The flowchart provides a picture indicating what is to be accomplished. Emphasis is on the documents and the work stations they must pass through. The flowchart also provides an application where source media is converted to a final report or stored in files. A brief mention is made of the actual operations to be performed.

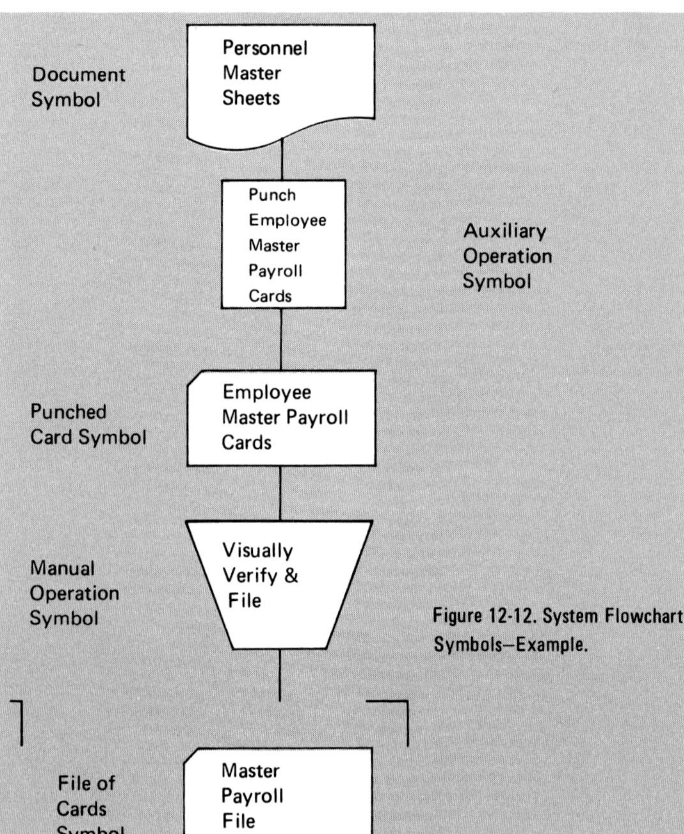

Figure 9–14. System Flowchart Symbols—Example.

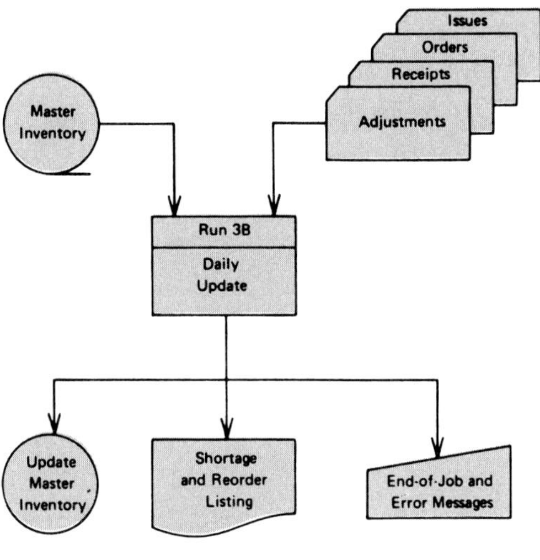

Figure 9–15. System Flowchart.

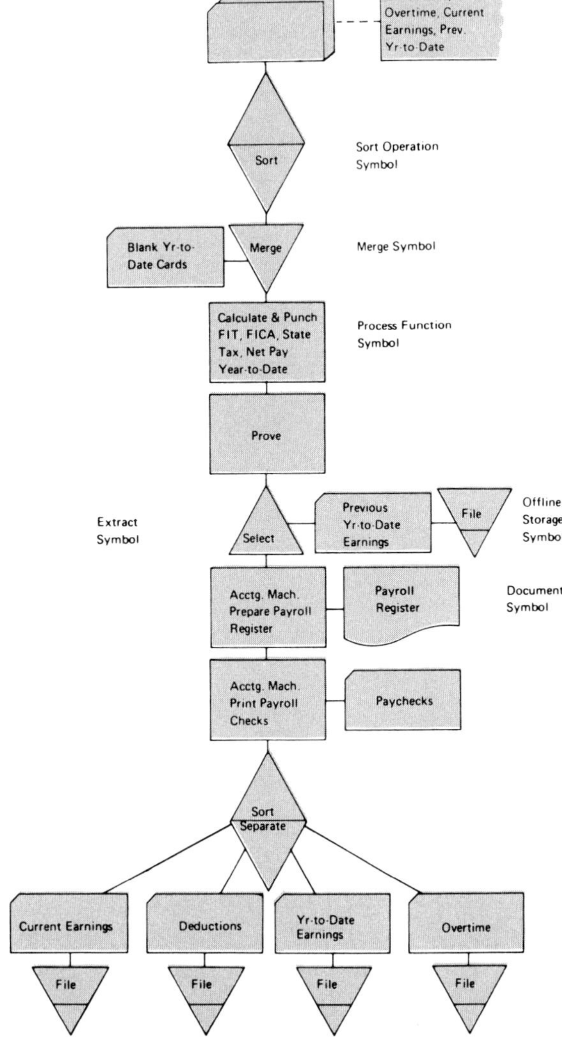

Figure 9–16. System Flowchart Punched Card Symbols.

Many symbols depicting documents and operations are used throughout the system flowchart. The symbols are designed so that they are meaningful without too much further comment or text. Card symbols are used to indicate when the input or output may be a card. Document symbols are used to represent the prepared reports. The system flowchart is usually prepared on one sheet of paper for facilitating the presentation of the overall picture of the system to administrative personnel and executives (Fig. 9.14).

A system flowchart indicates the job to be done without detailing the steps involved (Figs. 9.15, 9.16).

There follows a brief description of some of the most frequently used system flowchart symbols.

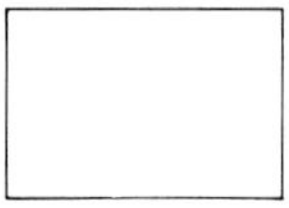

This symbol represents any processing function. It also stands for a computer program on both the system and program flowcharts.

The tab card symbol represents an input or an output function in which the medium is a punched card.

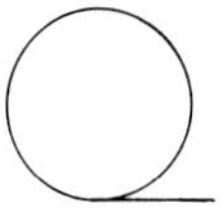

The magnetic tape symbol represents an input, output or filing function in which the medium is magnetic tape.

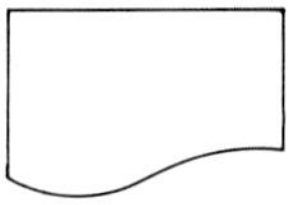

This symbol represents an input or output function in which the medium is a document. A document can be anything from a check to a printed report.

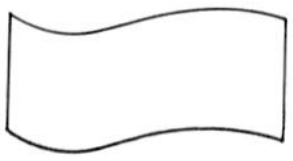

The punched–tape symbol represents an input or output function in which the medium is punched paper tape.

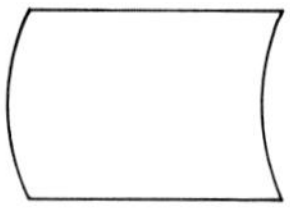

This symbol represents an input or output function utilizing auxiliary mass storage of information that can be accessed online. An example of this might be a banking situation where a savings account master file is held on a magnetic disk.

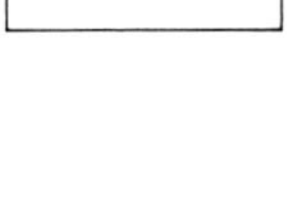

The display output symbol represents an output function in which the information is displayed visually at the time of processing. This is done by means of online indicators such as a visual display device.

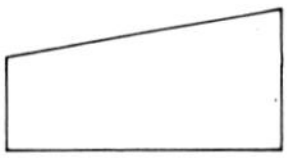

The manual input symbol represents an input or output function in which the information is entered manually at the time of processing by means of an online keyboard. A teletype would be an example.

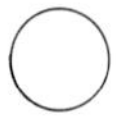

The connector symbol represents an interruption or a continuation after an interruption in a line of flow. This symbol on a system or program flowchart designates programs which are sources and destinations of files.

The communication link represents an input or an output function in which information is transmitted from one location to another. An example of this would be a branch banking situation where a computer in the home office is accessed from a branch office in the suburbs via telephone lines. The arrowheads are optional and denote the direction of the data flow.

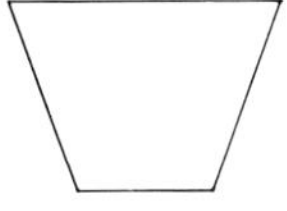

The manual operation symbol represents any offline process geared to the speed of a human being, such as cards being punched by a keypunch operator. This should not be confused with the manual input symbol. The manual input symbol is used for an online operation; the manual operation symbol is used for an offline operation.

The auxiliary operation symbol represents an offline operation that is not geared to the speed of a human being. An example of this is a card sort operation or a report prepared on a tab system that is not under direct control of the central processing unit.

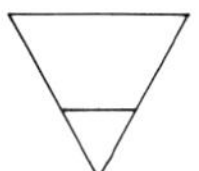

The offline storage symbol represents any offline storage of information regardless of the medium on which the information is recorded.

Example
A bank keeps customers' checking account records in disk files. Information about the day's checks and deposits is recorded on punched cards. The system flowchart for the daily updating run is shown below (Fig. 9.17).

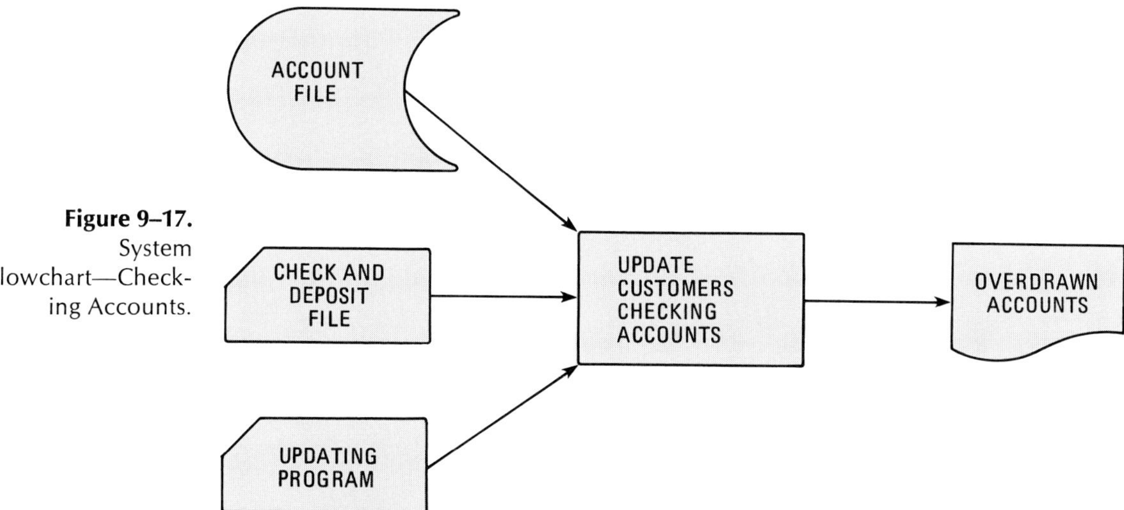

Figure 9–17. System Flowchart—Checking Accounts.

PROGRAM FLOWCHART

A program flowchart is a graphic representation of the procedures by which data is to be processed (Fig. 9.18). The chart provides a picture of the problem solution, the program solution, the program logic used for coding, and the processing sequences. Specifically, it is a diagram of the operations and decisions to be made and the sequence in which they are to be performed by the machine. The major functions and sequences are shown and if any detail is required, a *block diagram* is prepared (Fig. 9.19).

The program flowchart shows the relationship of one part of the program to another. The flowchart can be used to experiment or verify the accuracy of different approaches to coding the application. Where large segments of the program are indicated, a single processing symbol may be used and the detail for the segment shown in a separate block diagram which would be used for the machine coding. Once the flowchart has been proven sound and the procedures developed, it may be used for coding the program.

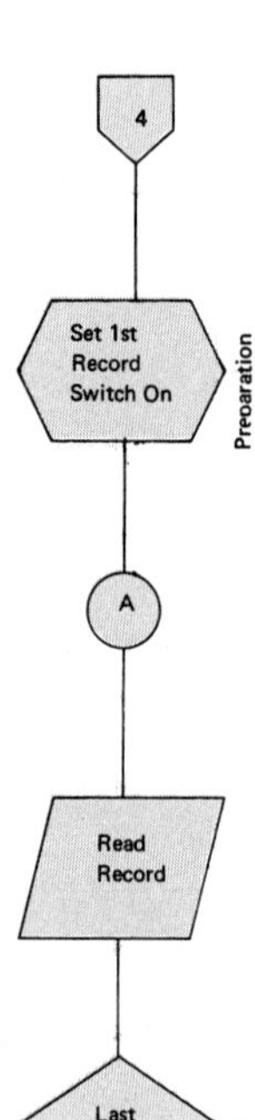

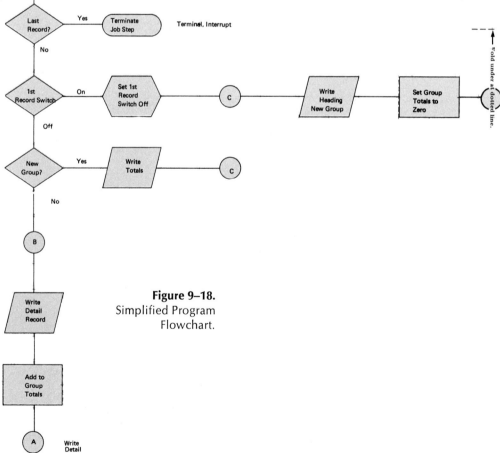

Figure 9–18. Simplified Program Flowchart.

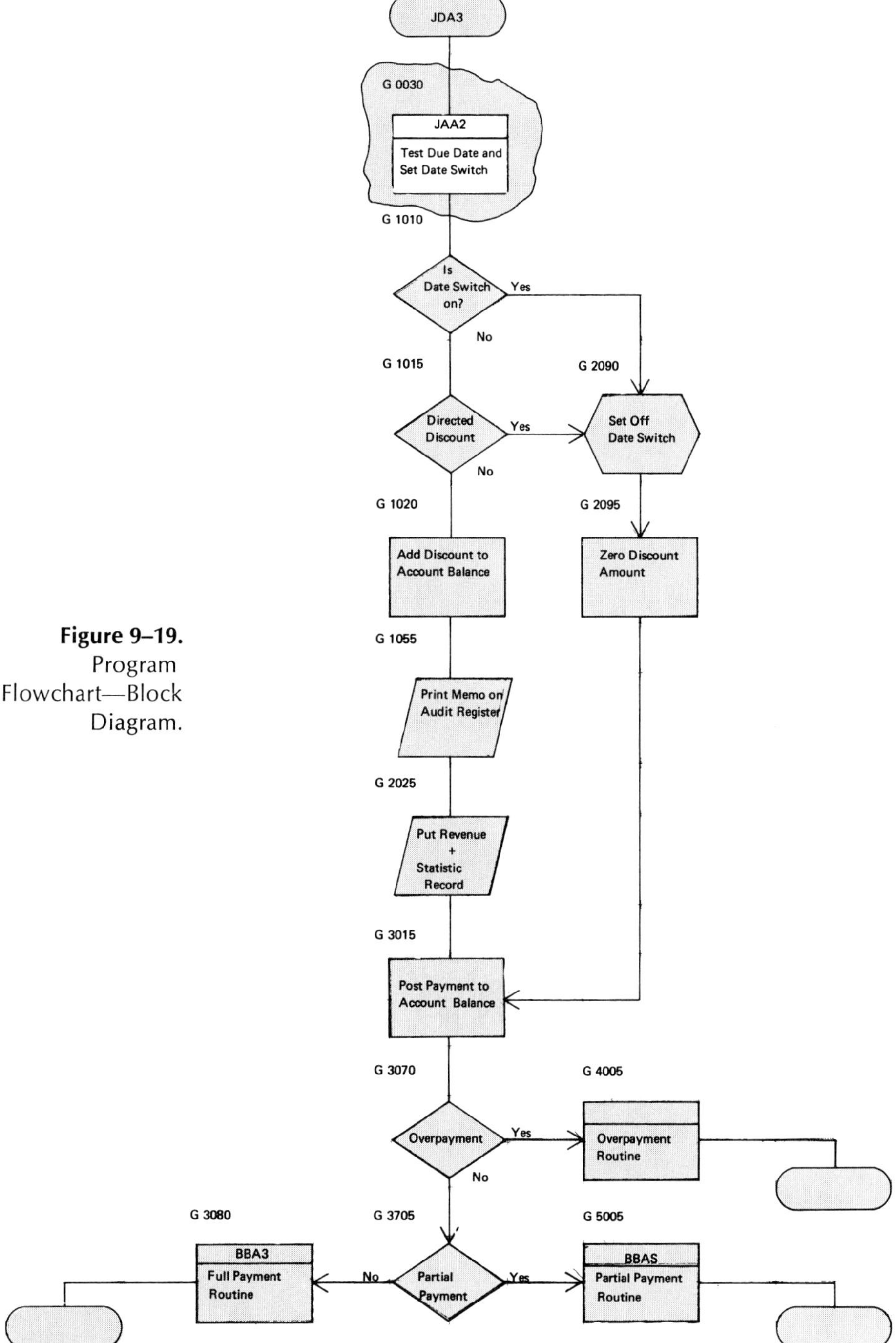

Figure 9–19. Program Flowchart—Block Diagram.

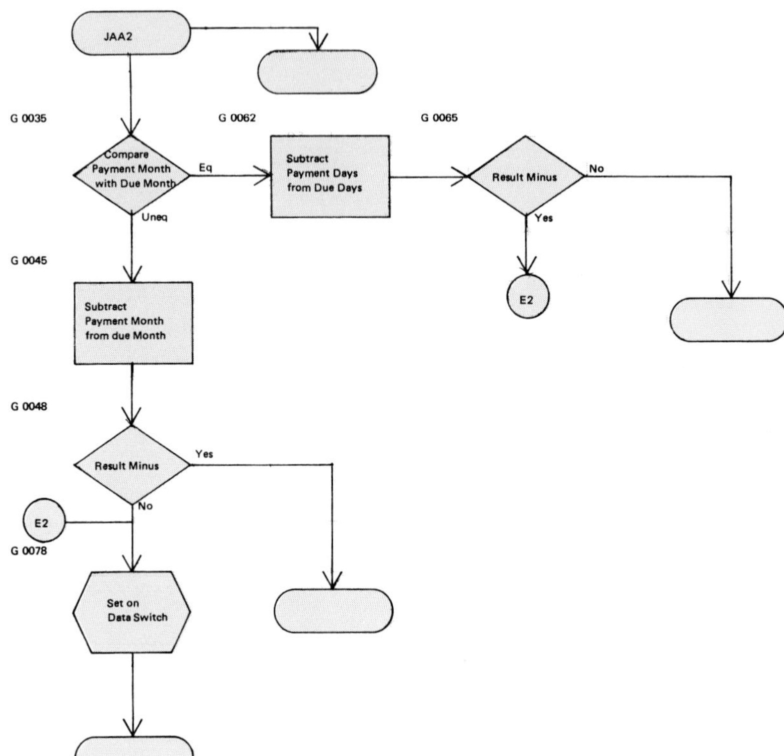

Figure 9–19. (continued)

A program flowchart (Figs. 9.20, 9.21, 9.22) should provide:

1. A pictorial diagram of the problem solution to act as a map of the program.
2. A symbolic representation of the program logic used for coding, desk checking and debugging while testing all aspects of the program.
3. Verification that all possible conditions have been considered and have been taken care of (Figs. 9.23, 9.24).
4. Documentation of the program, necessary to give an unquestionable historical reference record.
5. Aid in the development of programming and coding.

These are the important features and phases of program flowcharting:

1. It provides the programmer with a means of visualizing the entire program during its development. The sequence, the arithmetic and logical operations, the inputs and outputs of the system and the relationship of one part of the program to another—all are indicated.
2. The system flowchart provides the various inputs and outputs, the general objective of the program and the general nature of the opera-

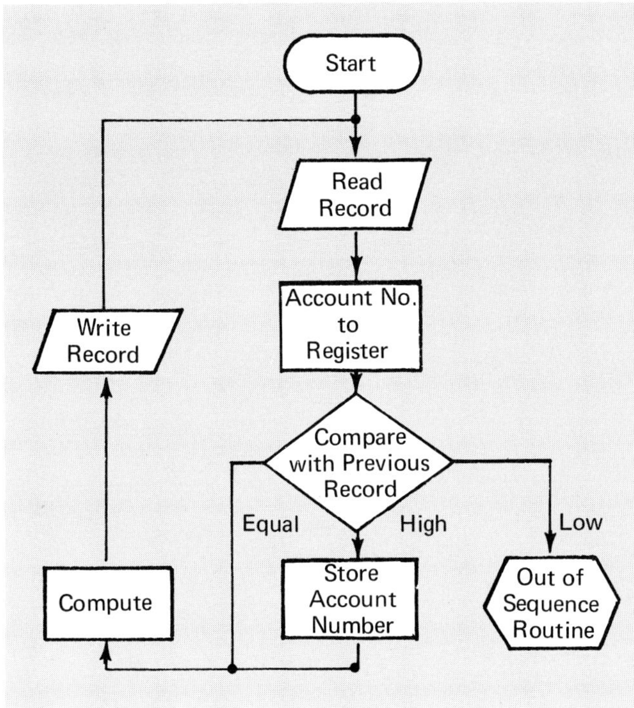

Figure 9–20. Program Flowchart—Sequence Checking.

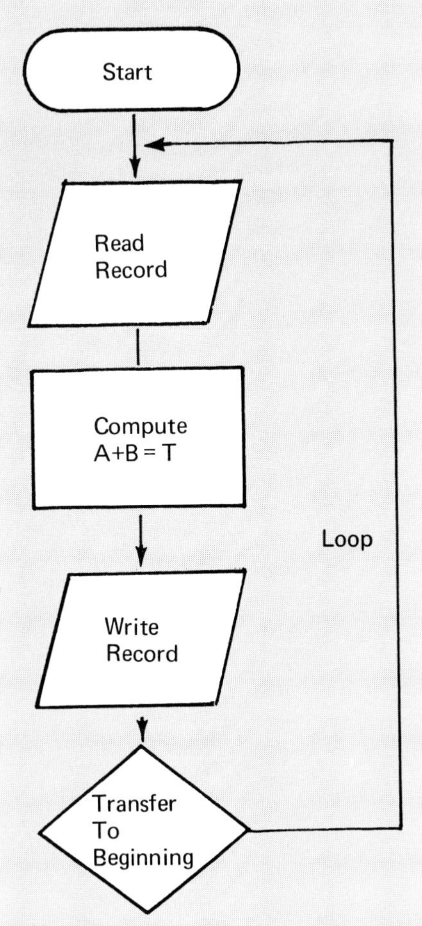

Figure 9–21. Program Flowchart—Loop.

tion. A program flowchart, however, will be prepared for each run and will serve as a means of experimenting with the program specifically, in order to achieve the most efficient program.

3. Starting with the symbol representing the major functions, the programmer must develop the overall logic by depicting blocks for input and output, identification, decisions, etc.
4. After the overall logic has been developed by the programmer, he will extract the larger segments of the program and break them down into smaller detailed block diagrams.
5. After the flowchart has been proven sound, the coding for the program will commence.
6. Upon completion of the coding, the program will be documented for

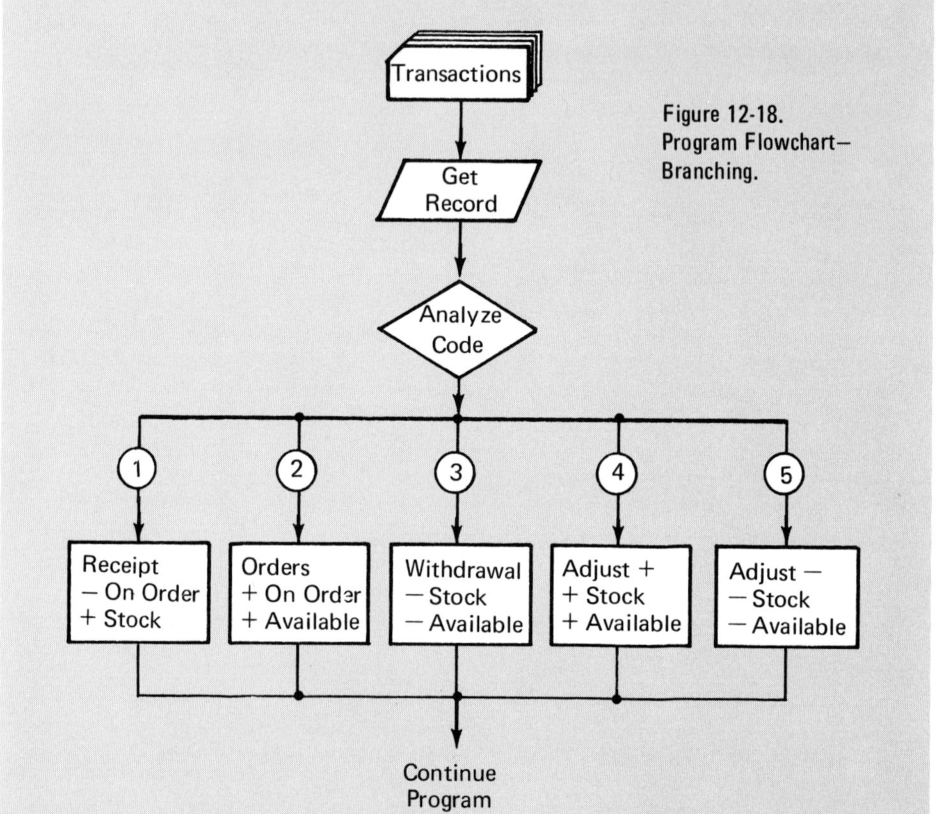

Figure 9–22. Program Flowchart—Branching.

further modification which will always occur after the testing, installation and operational stages.

7. Final documentation should encompass the overall main logic, the system flowcharts, the program flowcharts—right down to the detailed block diagrams. The general system flowcharts help in the understanding of the more detailed program flowcharts.

The use of standard techniques for the preparation of flowcharts for data processing systems will greatly enhance the effectiveness of the programmer's conversion of the problem into a meaningful program. It will reduce the time necessary to program the application and if properly done, will provide a proper communication between the analyst and the many groups with whom he must deal.

Flowcharts are used extensively in the field and are the fundamental basis for all operations in data processing. A clear understanding of flowcharting

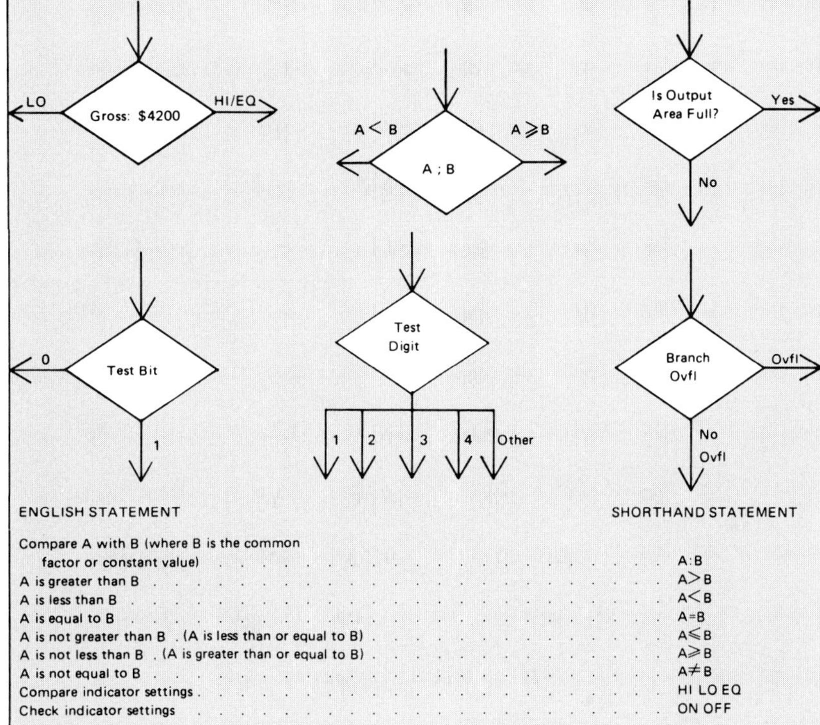

ENGLISH STATEMENT	SHORTHAND STATEMENT
Compare A with B (where B is the common factor or constant value)	A:B
A is greater than B	A>B
A is less than B	A<B
A is equal to B	A=B
A is not greater than B . (A is less than or equal to B)	A≤B
A is not less than B . (A is greater than or equal to B)	A≥B
A is not equal to B	A≠B
Compare indicator settings	HI LO EQ
Check indicator settings	ON OFF

Figure 9–23. Examples of Decision Techniques.

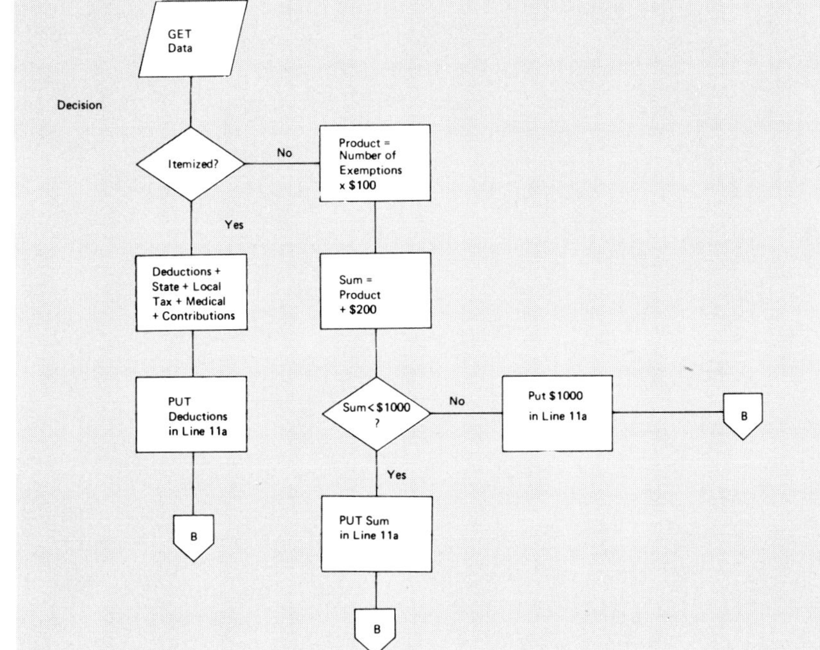

Figure 9–24. Program Flowchart—Logical Decision Example.

techniques is a must for everyone who becomes involved with data processing at any level.

The program flowchart shows, in graphic form, the logical sequence of steps to be taken during the production run. Before you can begin to prepare flowcharts, you need practice in thinking about problem solutions as logical sequences of steps.

Suppose that you were to add two numbers in your head and write down the answer. You want to continue the process until all numbers on the sheet had been added. If you analyzed this mental process in detail, you would find that it went about like this:

1. Start (thinking)
2. Read the first number
3. Store the number in your memory
4. Read the second number
5. Store the second number
6. Add the second number to the first number
7. Write out the total
8. Are there any more pairs of numbers to be added? (if yes, go back to step 2, if no, continue to step 9).
9. Stop (thinking)

Let us apply the same logic to the following problem and prepare a program flowchart for the problem solution.

The input file is made up of punched–card records, each of which contains two number fields, one called *A*, the other *B*. The pairs of numbers in each record are to be added.

The program flowchart on page 277 represents the steps in a very simple program.

The following is a brief description of some of the most often used program flowchart symbols.

The processing symbol represents a processing function; for example, the process of executing a defined operation or group of operations resulting in a change in value, form, or location of information.

The predefined process symbol is drawn by adding two vertical lines within the processing symbol. This symbol represents a named process consisting of one or more operations or program steps, such as a subroutine, that is flowcharted elsewhere in the same flowchart.

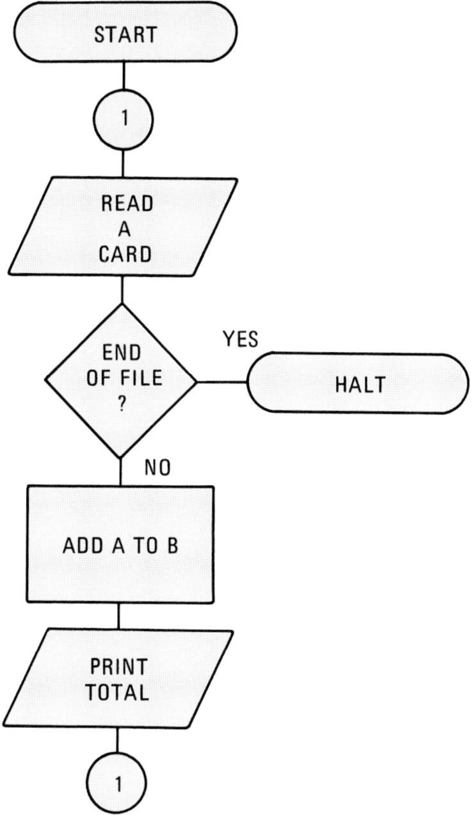

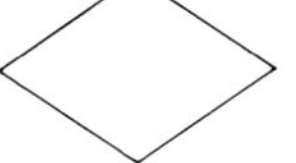

The decision symbol represents a decision operation that determines which of a number of alternate paths is to be followed.

The input-output symbol represents input/output functions; that is, the making available of data for processing (input) or the recording of processed information (output). There are no punched-card, punched-tape, etc., symbols for program flowcharts; instead, the input/output symbol is used.

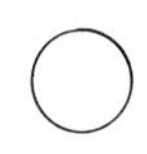

The connector symbol represents an interruption or a continuation after an interruption in a line of flow. A set of two connectors represents a continued flow direction when the flowline is broken for a reason such as physical limitation of the flowchart page.

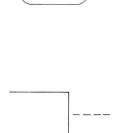

This symbol represents a terminal point of a program. The appearance of this symbol indicates that there is no further continuation of the logical path within the program. The terminal symbol appears, usually, at the beginning of the program indicating the start of the program.

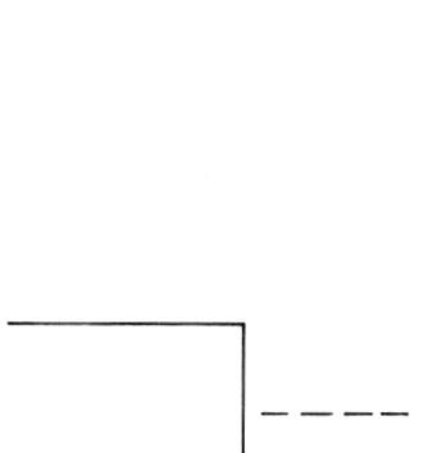

The annotation symbol encloses the addition of descriptive explanatory notes or cross references to the flowline. These notes provide information necessary for the programmer's use at a particular point in preparing a program. The annotation is drawn by using the processing symbol with the left-hand (or right-hand) end open. The symbol is then connected to the flowline by a broken line at a point where the annotation is meaningful. (See Figs. 9.25, 9.26.)

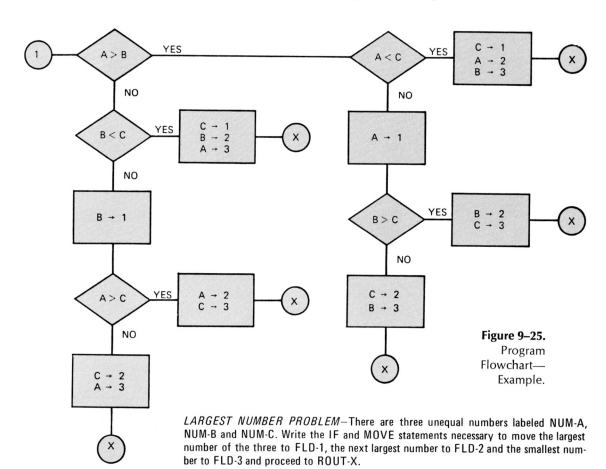

Figure 9–25. Program Flowchart—Example.

LARGEST NUMBER PROBLEM—There are three unequal numbers labeled NUM-A, NUM-B and NUM-C. Write the IF and MOVE statements necessary to move the largest number of the three to FLD-1, the next largest number to FLD-2 and the smallest number to FLD-3 and proceed to ROUT-X.

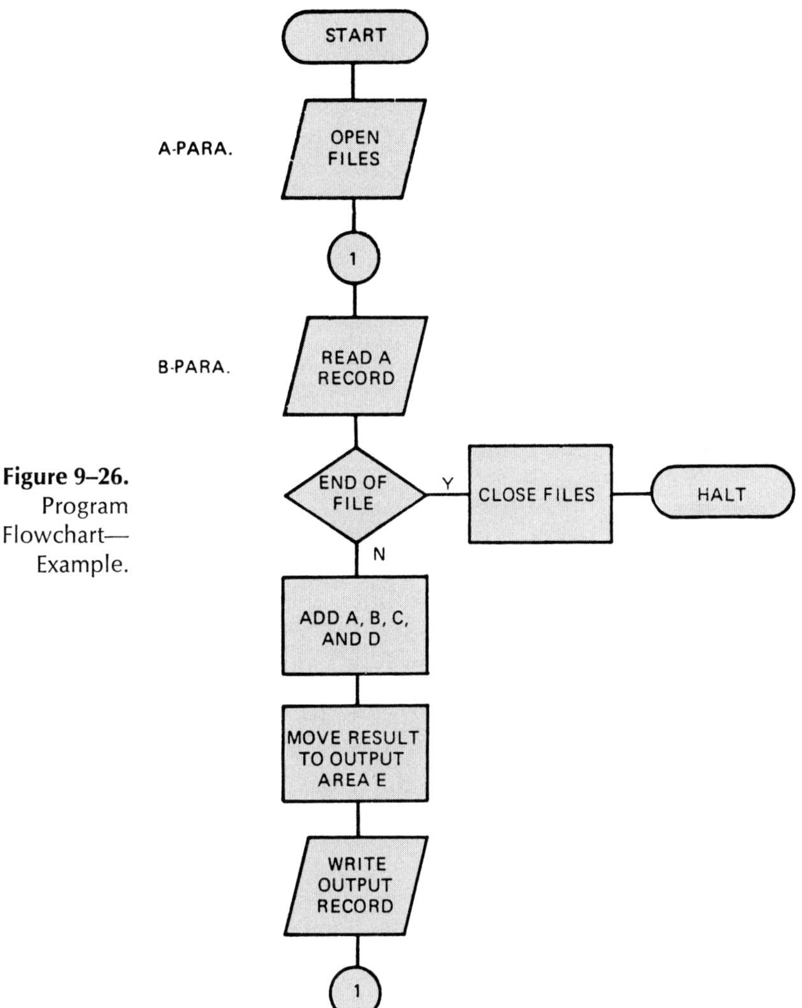

Figure 9–26. Program Flowchart—Example.

PROGRAMMING

The success of a computer program depends upon the ability of the programmer to (1) Analyze the problem, (2) Prepare a program to solve the particular problem (Fig. 9.27), (3) Operate the program (Fig. 9.28).

ANALYSIS

A problem must be thoroughly analyzed before any attempt is made at a solution. This requires that boundary conditions be established so that the solution does not exceed the objectives of management nor become too narrow to encompass all the necessary procedures. Output needs should be

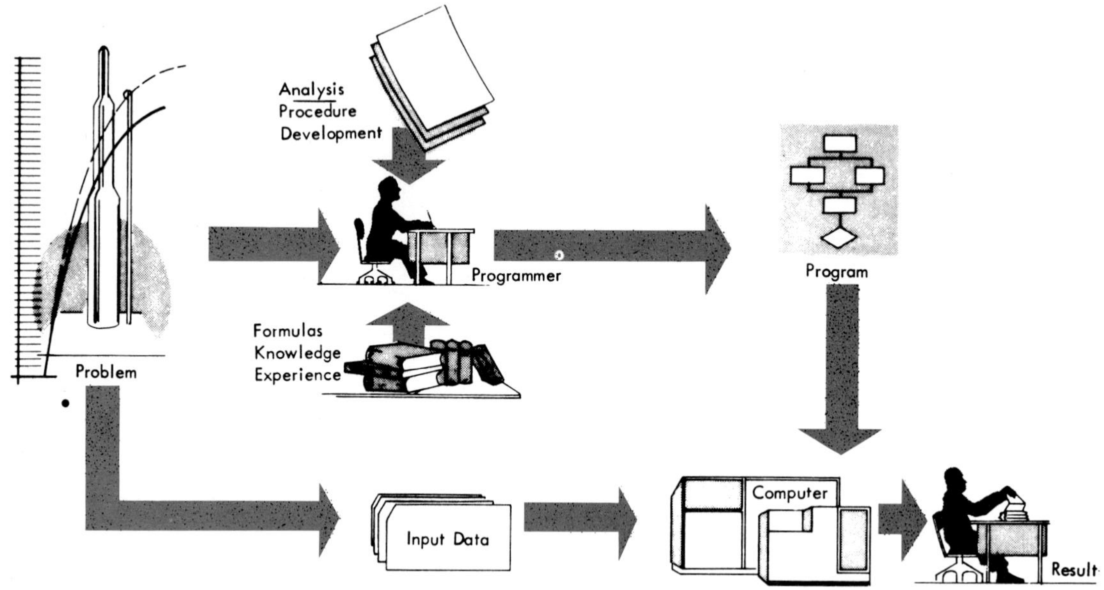

Figure 9–27. Direct Conversion of Problem to Computer Program.

Figure 9–28. Steps in Problem Solving.

STEP	GENERAL TERMS	PROGRAMMING TERMS
1	Defining the problem	Preparing job specifications
2	Planning the problem solution	Flowcharting (the program)
3	Describing the problem solution	Coding (the program)
4	Executing the problem solution	Program 'Translation' Program Testing Production Run
5	Documenting the problem solution	Documentation

clearly stated and the necessary input to produce the desired results should be carefully studied. If necessary, the source documents (input) should be revised so that they can be more readily converted into machine language for data processing operations. The relationship between the inputs and outputs must be clearly shown. The flowcharts will show the orderly logical steps necessary to arrive at the computer solution to the problem.

PREPARATION

After a careful analysis of the problem and flowcharting, the computer program should be written. Instructions are coded in the particular computer language using the program flowchart as a guide. The sequence of instructions will determine the computer program.

OPERATION

The next step is usually the placing of the program and data into the storage unit of the computer. The program must be prepared on punched cards or other media for entry into the machine. The data must also be made available to the computer through some input unit. The program must be thoroughly checked with the test data and all necessary "debugging" accomplished before the program is ready for operation upon actual data.

The following items should be checked to insure that the proper analysis and coding was made and that the computer will operate properly.

1. **Precise statement of the problem.** The statement must be exact, specifying what the program is to accomplish. "To Compute Social Security Tax, Multiply A by B to Arrive at C, Etc."
2. **List of inputs.** All sample copies of inputs to be used together with the size of the fields, the type (alphabetic or numeric), control fields, etc., should be included.
3. **Outputs desired.** Samples of all outputs should be included with all headings indicated. The number of copies desired, type and size of paper to be used, tape density (if used)—these are some of the items of information to be included in this section.
4. **Flowcharts.** Include all necessary system flowcharts, program flowcharts and block diagrams.
5. **Decision tables.** These tables will show relationships of conditions and actions pertaining to a particular problem.
6. **Program.** A printed copy of the computer program with all necessary comments.
7. **Test data.** Sample data to be used to test programs.
8. **Job control cards.** All job control cards necessary to load the program and the data into the computer.
9. **Test results.** Output listings and/or cards used to test the accuracy of the program.

PLANNING A PROGRAM

A computer program is the outcome of a programmer's applied knowledge of the problem and the operation of a particular computer. Problem definition, analysis, documentation and flowcharting are just the initial steps in the preparation of a program. The following must be considered even in the simplest of programs (Fig. 9.29).

1. The allocation of storage locations for the storing of data, instructions, work areas, constants, etc.
2. The necessary input procedures to convert the source data into machine-processable media.
3. The various reference tables and files that are essential to the program.
4. The checking of the accuracy of the data and the calculations.
5. The ability to restart the system in case of unscheduled interruptions, machine failures or error conditions.
6. The necessary housekeeping procedures to clear storage areas, register, and indicators prior to the execution of the program.
7. A thorough knowledge of the arithmetic and logical procedures to be used in the program.
8. The output formats of cards, printed reports, displayed reports, magnetic tapes, etc.
9. The subroutines available from other procedures to be used in the program.

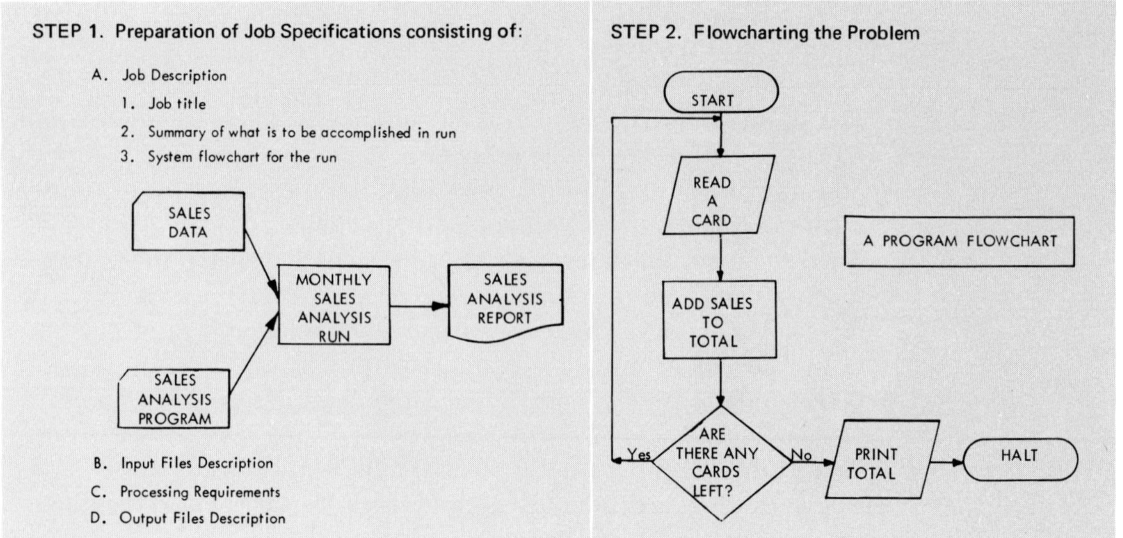

Figure 9–29. Documentation of a Program.

STEP 3.

FORTRAN Coding Form

PROGRAM: SAMPLE PROGRAM — PAGE 1 OF 3

```
      REAL X(100),Y(100),W(21),Z(11),A(11),B(11,12)
    1 FORMAT (I2,I3/(4F14.7))
    2 FORMAT (5E15.6)
      READ (5,1) M,N,(X(I),Y(I),I=1,N)
      LW = 2*M+1
      LB = M+2
      LZ = M+1
      DO 5  J=2,LW
    5 W(J) = 0.0
      W(1) = N
      DO 6  J=1,LZ
    6 Z(J) = 0.0
      DO 16  I=1,N
      P = 1.0
      Z(1) = Z(1)+Y(I)
      DO 13  J=2,LZ
      P = X(I)*P
      W(J) = W(J)+P
   13 Z(J) = Z(J)+Y(I)*P
      DO 16  J=LB,LW
      P = X(I)*P
```

PROGRAMMING FORM

STEP 4. Program 'Translation'; Program Testing; and Production Run

A. Program Translation

B. Program Testing

C. Production Run: execution of translated program on actual input data to produce final results.

NOTE: The systems flowchart, prepared as part of the Job Specifications, diagrams the production run.

STEP 5. Documentation

Preparation of a permanent job file containing all documents produced in previous steps.

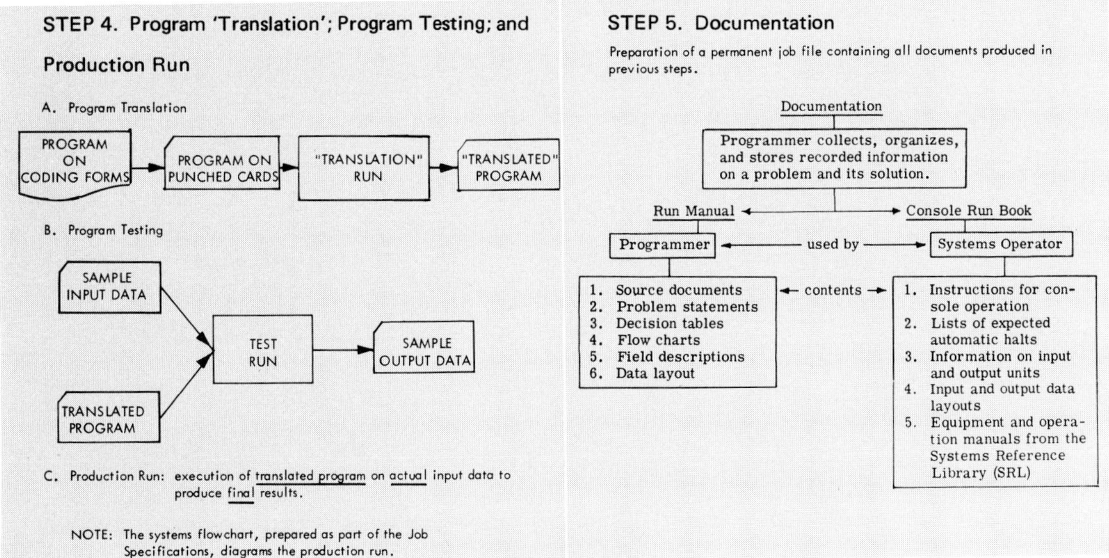

Figure 9–29. (continued)

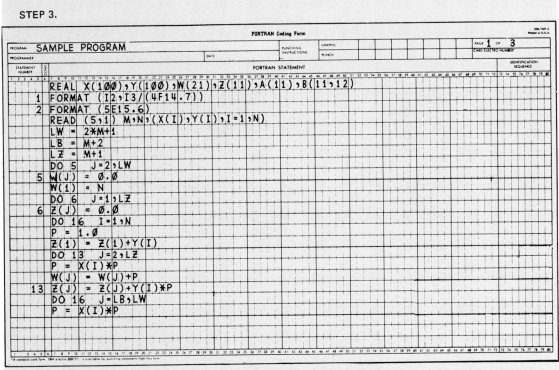

INPUT

All data entering a computer system must be read by an input device and stored at a preassigned location so that the information is available to the programmer (Fig. 9.30). The storage should be located in a logical manner so that the instructions can have access to these files as the data is being manipulated. It is necessary to know at all times where to find the information in the successive stages of processing. The instruction of the program can later specify the location where these records may be found. The input device is selected by the programmer before the actual reading begins. The reference is made to the particular device number known to the programmer. These device numbers are assigned by the system programmer to be used in all programs. The programmer determines the sequence of read instructions in which the files are to be read. The storage need is determined by the length and type of records and the construction of the files.

The read instruction causes the actual transfer of data to the particular area of storage assigned for input records. A number of areas may be assigned to handle several related records. These records are now available to the programmer for processing (Fig. 9.31).

In most data processing installations, certain areas of storage are assigned for individual programs and the programmer must confine himself to these storage boundaries. These restraints prevent the programmer from wandering into different areas reserved for other programs. This also eliminates the possibility of essential information being erased by the erroneous imposition of another program (Fig. 9.32).

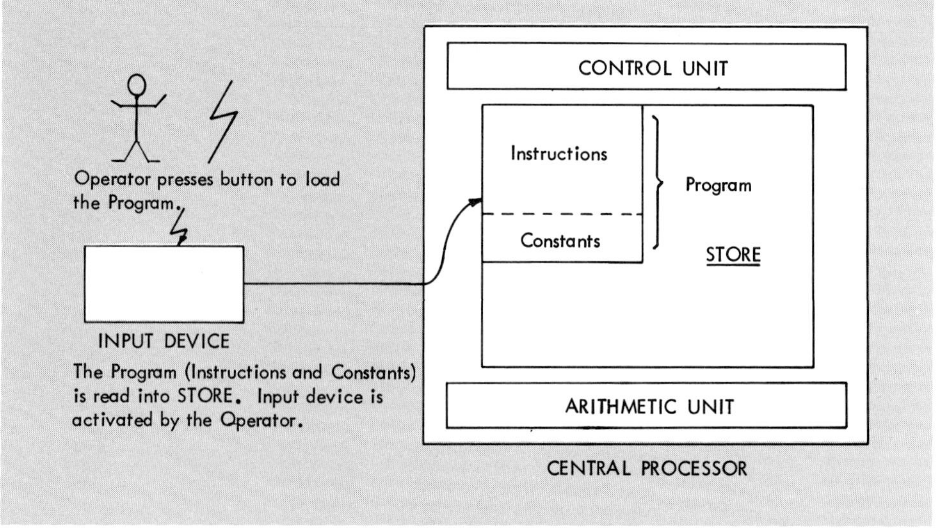
Operator presses button to load the Program.
INPUT DEVICE
The Program (Instructions and Constants) is read into STORE. Input device is activated by the Operator.
CONTROL UNIT
Instructions
Constants
Program
STORE
ARITHMETIC UNIT
CENTRAL PROCESSOR

Figure 9–30. Loading the Program.

Figure 9–31. Processng the Data.

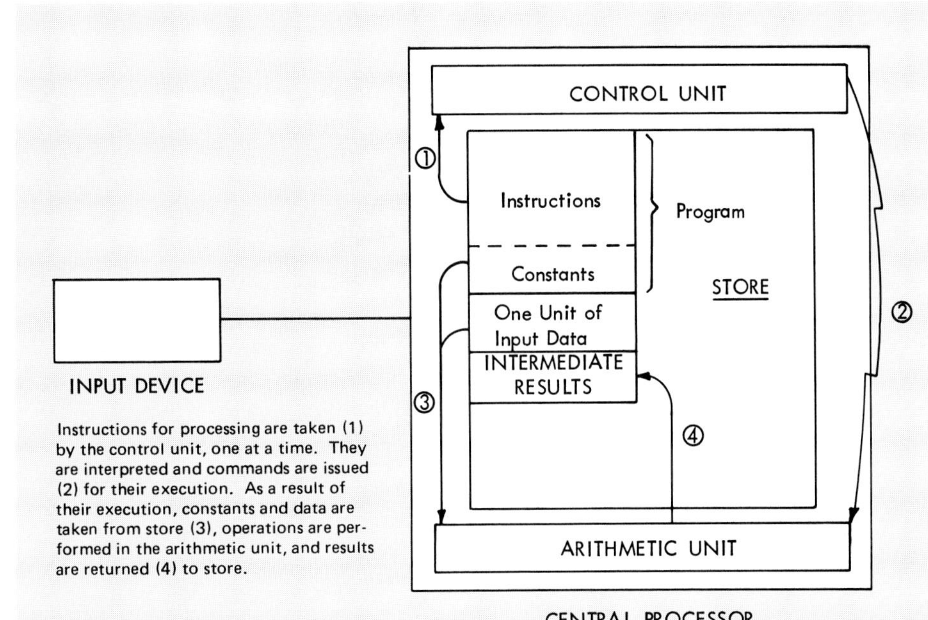

Instructions for processing are taken (1) by the control unit, one at a time. They are interpreted and commands are issued (2) for their execution. As a result of their execution, constants and data are taken from store (3), operations are performed in the arithmetic unit, and results are returned (4) to store.

Figure 9–32. Assembling and Writing Output.

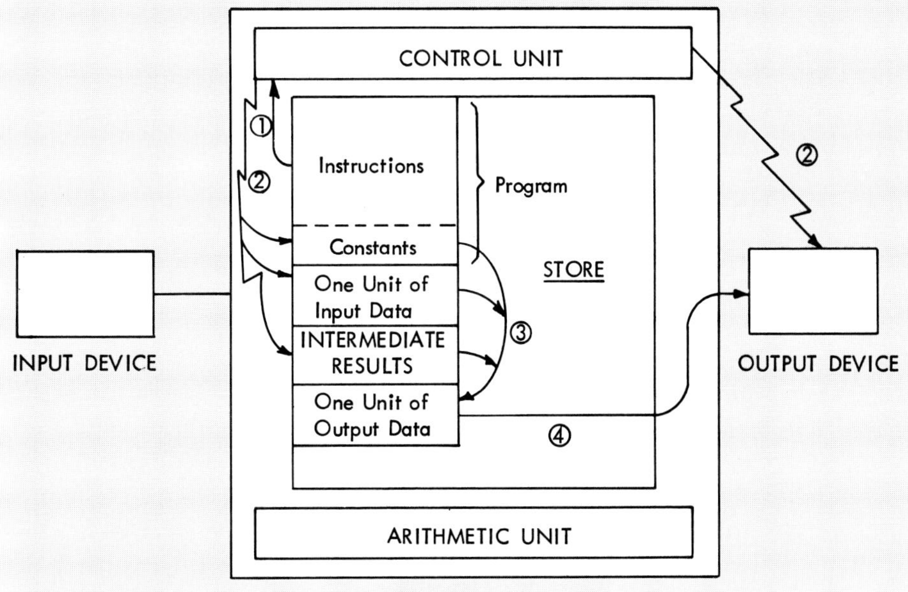

Instructions for this step are taken (1) by the control unit for interpretation. Commands (2) are issued to store, resulting in the assembly of a unit of output data (3), and to the output device (2), resulting in the writing (4) of a unit of output data.

ARITHMETIC

Once the data has been read into the system by an input device, calculation can begin. Calculation in computer systems is carried out at much higher rates of speed than the reading of input or the writing of output. The input and output devices are mechanical and as such operate at a relatively slow speed while the calculating operations are performed at electronic speeds. Programs are so written as to overlap the operations of input and output with the processing function to increase the efficiency of the system. In most business operations, calculations are rather simple and the overall speed of the system is governed by the input and output units. In scientific operations, the calculations are more involved and complex and high calculating speeds are essential. A successful system will have a balance between input and output devices and processing operation.

Each computer has the capacity for performing addition, subtraction, multiplication and division as built-in operations or under the control of the program. In the simplest calculation, at least two factors are involved in all arithmetic operations, such as a dividend and divisor, or multiplier and multiplicand. All these factors must be available in storage and accessible to the arithmetic unit of the machine so that the results can be calculated. The address portion of the instruction will specify the storage location of each of the factors involved in the calculation. The operation code of the instruction specifies the particular arithmetic operation to be performed on these factors. Any practical number of calculations can take place on many factors in a single series of instructions.

Arithmetic factors may be computed on a storage-to-storage basis where the calculation is performed in storage with the results being placed in storage or the calculation can be performed in a register with one factor in a register and the other factor in storage or another register. The final result appears in a register and may be later moved to a storage location. The method of calculation employed will depend upon the program and the computer involved.

All calculations take into account the algebraic values of the factors; that is, the individual signs of the numbers. The computer follows the rules of algebra in all basic arithmetic calculations. The programmer must assign an area large enough to contain the result of the calculation. If the storage area assigned for the result is too small to contain the entire answer, truncation of the result will occur and the answer will be unpredictable. Other operations of shifting and rounding results are also provided to shorten or lengthen or otherwise adjust the result. With these capabilities, decimal values may be handled by the computer and directions for placing the decimal point may be given to the system.

The design of a particular system must achieve a realistic balance between the calculating ability and the record handling ability.

LOGIC

The logic of the computer is determined by its ability to make comparisons, test the various conditions, and take the appropriate action called for by the result. The sequence of the computer instructions may be altered by the condition tested. The comparison of an identifying field in one record with that of another enables the computer to make these tests. The results of the comparison are registered as *low,* where the test number in one record is lower than the corresponding number of the other record; or *high* where the test number exceeds the other; or *equal* where both numbers are equal to each other. Each condition tested can be used to set an indicator which may be interrogated later in the program.

Both fields of a record are placed in predetermined locations in storage and a *compare*-type instruction compares the first record with the second, and sets the appropriate indicator based on the resulting condition. A *branch*-type instruction specifies the location of the next instruction to be executed if a certain condition exists. This permits the program to handle alternative actions due to exceptions in the procedure without the necessity of writing a complete program for each different record in a file. A program may be so arranged that the machine can recognize one or more types of records in a single file and process each according to its individual requirements. This method of computation can be revised according to the particular type of record in a storage unit. For example, in an inventory application containing many different records such as receipts, disbursements, back orders and adjustments, each different type of record could be identified by a particular code. The program could be written to test for each of these codes and, based on the type, the program will branch to the appropriate procedure which will process the particular record.

The sequence checking of files is another application of the logical ability of the computer. If a file is in ascending sequence, each incoming record should be equal to or higher than the previous record otherwise the record is out of sequence. Duplicate records can also be selected if the second record is equal to the first. The same principle can be used to sort records into a predetermined sequence by testing the code number of each succeeding record. For example, in a payroll application it is known that each employee should have a single master record. If by error the old record was not removed when a change was made, duplicate records result. The computer through its logic ability could be so programmed to test for this condition by comparing each record with the preceding record. If an equal condition is detected, the program could branch to an error routine.

Another possible application is *conditional transfer,* where the program is repeated if some predetermined condition has occurred. The conditional transfer may be used to execute a special purpose subroutine out of the normal portion of the program. This routine will be executed only if the predetermined condition exists. For example, when computing the social security taxes in a payroll procedure, it is necessary to test the accumulated earnings of each employee to see if they have reached the maximum for social security taxes. If this limit has been reached, the program would branch to a subroutine that bypasses the calculations for social security taxes and continues with the payroll procedure.

A logical operation may be used to vary the program by changing the operation part or the address of the instruction. The operation portion of an instruction can be altered as a result of a previous comparison or test of indicators. A *switch*-type instruction can be inserted in the program at a predetermined location. This switch will be turned on as a result of a certain condition and the operation code of the next instruction changed. If the test condition does not exist, the switch will be skipped and the next instruction executed in the normal manner. For example, in an inventory updating application, it is known that each record is in ascending sequence, otherwise the processing should be terminated. Each succeeding record is compared with the previous one and a switch is set if an out-of-sequence condition is detected. The switch will cause the program to be aborted.

The address part of an instruction may be treated as data which can be modified by arithmetic. An index register can add or subtract variable quantities contained in one or more special purpose registers to the address portion of an instruction. This index feature permits repetitious calculations and other operations to be performed using the same program, thus reducing the sequential number of instructions. For example, in an inventory application it is necessary to total all the on-hand values of each item. There are 20,000 items of inventory, each with a stock number separated by 10 digits. Twenty thousand or more program steps could be written to add these amounts from each inventory record or an index register could be initialized with a value of 10 and this could be added to the address in each instruction (modify the address) thus reducing the program to a few instructions. The program could be *looped* (repeated processing) until all of the 20,000 items have been accumulated.

The logical ability greatly expands the use of the computer. It permits the computer to alter its program to accommodate changed conditions without the intervention of the programmer. This ability increases the potential use applications of computer operations.

SUMMARY

The ability to solve computer problems logically hinges on the proper preparation of flowcharts, decision tables and other tools available to the programmer. A majority of the persons entering the data processing field will spend a considerable amount of time programming. The progress of potential programmers will depend on their ability to solve problems logically. To accomplish this objective, one must learn how to prepare for the programming effort. The intent of this chapter is to introduce the programming phase of data processing. The construction of flowcharts is important in solving complex problems. The use of decision tables is becoming increasingly more popular with programmers.

It is equally important that one learns the other facets of programming, such as, instructions, methods of processing data, planning the programming and the program itself. The computer program will be the result of the programmer's knowledge as applied to the problem, and to the operation of the specific computer. The success of the computer program will depend upon the ability of the programmer to analyze the problem properly, prepare the program to solve the particular problem and the program's operation.

I. *Introduction to computer programming.*
   A. *Instruction*—a coded statement used to write a program; when combined with other instructions is used by the computer to solve a specific problem.
      1. *Operation code*—uniquely identifies the operation to be performed.
      2. *Instruction address*—the address of the instruction in storage.
      3. *Program*—series of instructions that tell the computer how to receive, process and return the data.
   B. *Methods of processing data.*
      1. *Sequential (batch) processing*—data is arranged in predetermined sequence and each record must be examined prior to processing.
      2. *Random (inline) processing*—transactions are not batched. All records need not be examined, only those requiring updating.
   C. *Decision tables*—reduces the problem statement to a table or to a condition and action statement.
   D. *Flowcharts*—a graphic representation of the flow of information through a system in which the information is converted from the source document to the final report.
      1. *System flowchart*—illustrates the overall flow of data through a system.
      2. *Program flowchart*—graphic representation of the procedures by which data is processed. Used to write the program.

II. *Programming.*
   A. *Analysis*—hardware, output needs, source document analysis, etc.
   B. *Preparation*—writing computer programs using program flowcharts as a guide.
   C. *Operation*—placing programs and data into storage of the computer, debugging operations.
   D. *Planning a program*—allocation of storage, input and output procedures, arithmetic and logical procedures to be used in programming, output format, subroutines.
   E. *Input*—data read by input device and stored at preassigned location in storage.
   F. *Arithmetic*—calculation functions at high speeds whether data is in register or in storage.
   G. *Logic*—the ability of the computer to make comparisons, test various conditions, and then take the appropriate action called for by the results.

IDENTIFICATION QUESTIONS

Match the following terms with the statements that follow.

A. Block Diagram	E. Instructions	I. Program Flowchart
B. Conditional Transfer	F. Looped	J. Programming
C. Decision Table	G. Operation Code	K. Random Processing
D. Flowchart	H. Program	L. Sequential Processing
		M. System Flowchart

1. A command to the machine, expressed in a coded combination of characters, to carry out some operation.
2. Reduces the problem to a table of condition/action statements.
3. A diagram that illustrates the flow of data into, through, and out of a system of programs.
4. The writing of detailed instructions for the computer and making them work correctly.
5. A code that uniquely identifies the operation to be performed.
6. The major functions and sequences are shown in detail.
7. A series of instructions which will direct the computer on how to read, process, and output the data.
8. All records need not be examined, only those requiring updating.
9. A graphic representation of the flow of data through a data processing system.
10. The program is repeated if some predetermined condition has occurred.
11. Each record has to be examined for possible processing.
12. Repeated processing.
13. A graphic representation of the procedures by which data is processed.

QUESTIONS FOR REVIEW

1. How is data processed within a computer?
2. What is an instruction and what is its chief function?
3. What is the difference between instructions and data in storage?
4. What is the difference between sequential and random processing?
5. What are the important advantages and disadvantages of sequential and random processing? Give examples of each.
6. How are the decision tables used in defining data processing problems?
7. What is the importance of flowcharting in data processing?
8. Explain the use of the two main types of flowcharts used in data processing and their purpose.
9. List the important points in program flowcharting.
10. Describe the steps in programming.
11. List the necessary steps to insure that a proper analysis and coding was made.
12. What are the important considerations in planning a program?
13. Why is it important to arrange input data properly in computer storage?
14. Describe the operation of the arithmetic unit in a computer.
15. Describe the logic operation of the computer.

CHAPTER 10

Introduction to Computer Programming

The capabilities of computers are expanding at a fantastic rate and the technology of ultilization and control is advancing at an equal pace. The improvements in programming techniques are as vitally important as the design of the data processing system itself. To a large extent, the future of computers is dependent not only on increases in speed, logical ability, and storage capacity, but on the efficient use of these facilities as they become available.

A computer program is much more than a set of detailed instructions. It is the outcome of the programmer's applied knowledge of the problem and the operation of the computer system. The programmer receives a problem statement that contains a job description, a description of the different types of data involved, and layout specifications for input and output of the data. After a complete analysis of the problem statement, the completed problem statement must be translated into the appropriate tools available to the programmer—the flowcharts and decision tables. The flowcharts and any necessary decision tables must be translated into a program, a series of instructions, which will instruct the computer how the data will be received, how to process the data and what outputs to develop (Fig. 10.1).

The problem is first analyzed in terms of operations that the computer can perform. The program is then written by the programmer who supplies the necessary tables, formulas, codes or other reference material specified by the application. The problem thus becomes the input data, and the computer with its calculating and manipulating functions produces the desired output.

Before the physical components of an electronic data processing system can solve any problem, the programmer must be able to communicate the

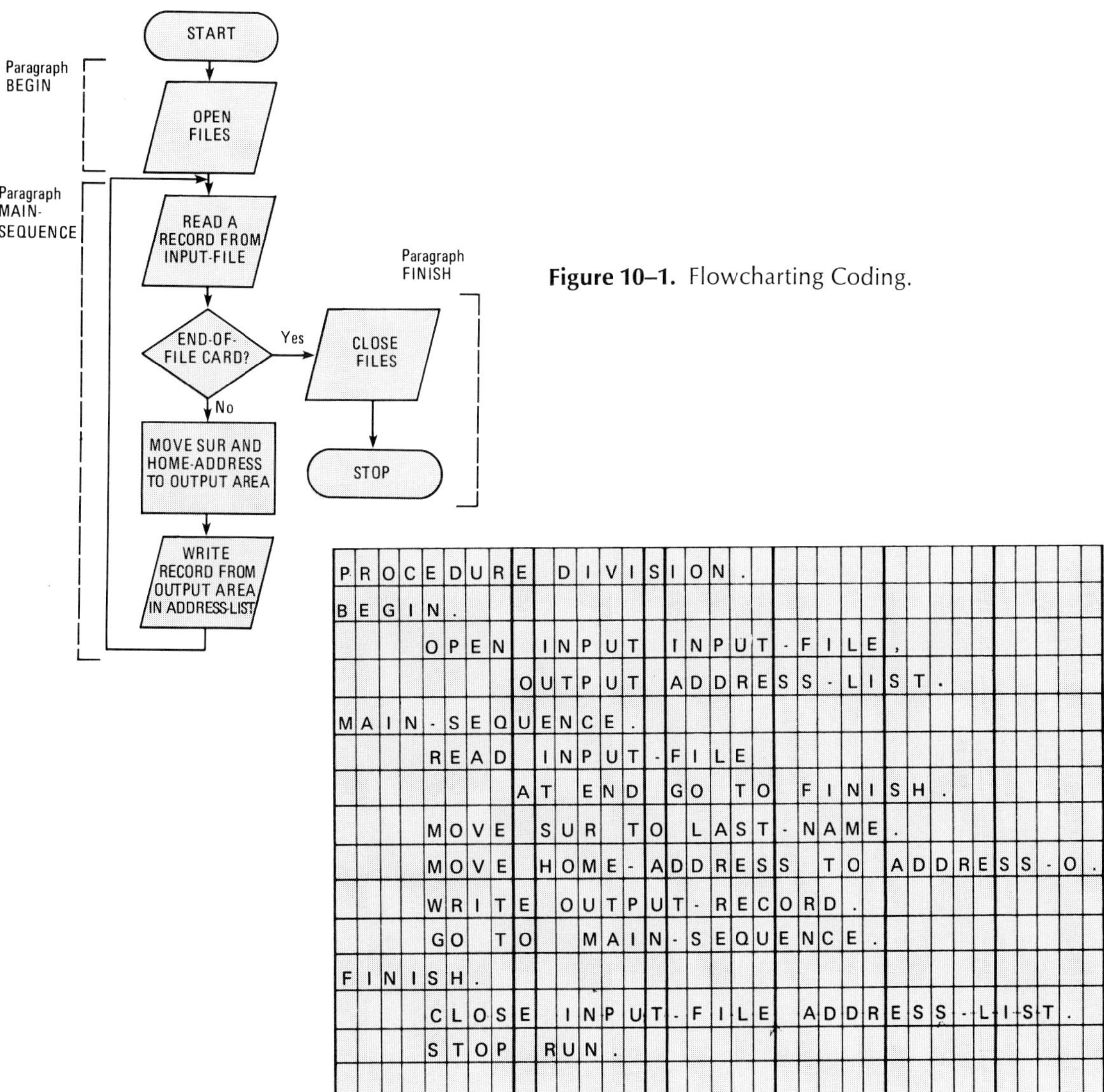


```
PROCEDURE DIVISION.
BEGIN.
      OPEN INPUT INPUT-FILE,
           OUTPUT ADDRESS-LIST.
MAIN-SEQUENCE.
      READ INPUT-FILE
           AT END GO TO FINISH.
      MOVE SUR TO LAST-NAME.
      MOVE HOME-ADDRESS TO ADDRESS-O.
      WRITE OUTPUT-RECORD.
      GO TO MAIN-SEQUENCE.
FINISH.
      CLOSE INPUT-FILE ADDRESS-LIST.
      STOP RUN.
```

Figure 10–1. Flowcharting Coding.

instructions that he has evolved in a decision table and/or flowchart to the hardware. Both the data and the instructions are stored in the computer in configurations of 1-bits and 0-bits. The characters these bits represent make up the language of the computer called *machine language*. Though programmers can, and sometimes do, communicate with the computer in machine language, the process of writing computer instructions in binary representation is a cumbersome and time-consuming task.

Computer programs may be expressed in either machine language—a language directly interpreted by the machine—or a symbolic language which

Figure 10–2. Machine and Symbolic Codes.

Machine	Symbolic
01011000000100000000000110000000	L REG1,384
01011010000100000000000110001000	A REG1, 392

is more meaningful to the programmer. The symbolic language must be later translated into machine language before the program can be executed by the computer (Fig. 10.2).

MACHINE LANGUAGE

Machine language is the common language of the particular computer and hence does not require further modification before execution by the computer. After the proper definition of the problem, the programmer proceeds to code the operation using codes that the computer can interpret. A thorough knowledge of the machine operation codes and instruction formats for the particular computer is required before a successful program can be written. It is the responsibility of the programmer to assign actual storage locations for the input data, work areas, constant data, output areas, reference tables, etc. A record of these locations must be kept so that they may be used in the program. The program is written in machine language using the various tables, formulas, codes and other reference material necessary to the program for the specific data processing application.

Some of the problems in using programs written in actual machine language are the following:

1. In writing programs with actual addresses, many difficulties arise in assigning data to storage locations. The programmer has the sole responsibility for the assignment of all storage areas.
2. When several people must work with the same program, problems arise, inasmuch as the full burden of the logic and program organization rests entirely with the original programmer.
3. The programmer must fully understand the details of the computer. Registers and indicator functions must be programmed in their entirety by the programmer.
4. Instructions must be written in the exact sequence in which they are to be executed by the computer. Programs written in machine language are difficult to correct or modify. "Patching," inserting of instructions into a program, is impractical in machine language programming. If one or more instructions have been omitted in error, all succeeding locations must be relocated to make room for these additional instructions.
5. It is difficult to write a cross-reference within a program. If subroutines or other tested programs outside of the program are to be used,

they must be linked to the program by additional individually handwritten instructions.

6. All instructions must be coded in machine language which may be impractical for some computers.

SYMBOLIC LANGUAGE

The development of larger and more versatile data processing systems has resulted in a greater number of and more complex machine language instructions. Therefore, not only does machine language coding now require memorization of a great many codes, but to compound the situation, the length and intricate design of programs written in machine language make them prone to logical and clerical errors. The problem of correcting errors in an actual machine language program is intensified because of the difficulty in tracing the steps of machine language programs to include corrections and relocate the problem in storage.

Many of the difficulties and inconveniences of machine language coding can be eliminated or simplified by the more advanced systems of program writing (Fig. 10.3). Programs can be made compatible by the computer thus eliminating the need for direct machine coding. A computer can be programmed to recognize instructions written in a symbolic language and to translate these statements into the machine language of that particular com-

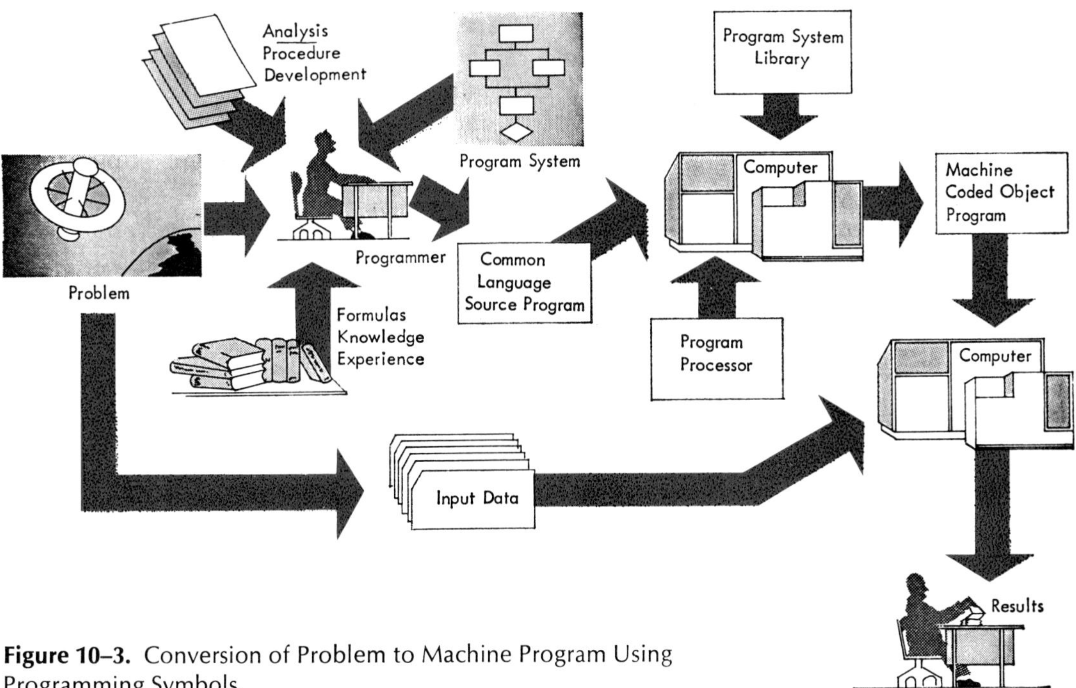

Figure 10–3. Conversion of Problem to Machine Program Using Programming Symbols.

Machine language Symbolic language

```
  LOC  OBJECT CODE    ADDR1 ADDR2 STMT   SOURCE STATEMENT

                                     1          PRINT NOGEN
000000                               2 ACCTNO   START 0
000000 05B0                          3 BEGIN    BALR  11,0
000002                               4          USING *,11
000002 4130 0001            00001    5          LA    3,1           REG 3 WILL HAVE SIGN REVERSED IN LOOP
000006 4140 0009            00009    6          LA    4,9           COUNTER FOR 9 DIGITS IN NUMBER
00000A D201 B064 B066 00066 00068    7          MVC   SUM,ZERO      SUM OF DIGITS KEPT IN SUM
000010 1B55                          8          SR    5,5           CLEAR REG 5
000012 4354 B059            0005B    9 LOOP     IC    5,ACCT-1(4)   PICK UP 1 DIGIT OF INDEXED NUMBER
000016 8950 0004            00004   10          SLL   5,4           SHIFT LEFT 4 BITS
00001A 5650 B06A            0006C   11          O     5,PLUS        ATTACH A PACKED PLUS SIGN
00001E 4250 B068            0006A   12          STC   5,DIGIT       STORE IN TEMPORARY LOCATION
000022 FA10 B064 B068 00066 0006A   13          AP    SUM,DIGIT     ADD TO SUM OF DIGITS
000028 1333                         14          LCR   3,3           REVERSE SIGN OF REG 3
00002A 4720 B038            0003A   15          BC    2,EVEN        SKIP NEXT 2 INSTR ON PLUS ODD TIMES THRU
00002E FA10 B064 B068 00066 0006A   16          AP    SUM,DIGIT     IF NOT SKIPPED ADD DIGIT TO SUM
000034 FA10 B064 B068 00066 0006a   17          AP    SUM,DIGIT     SAME. HAS EFFECT OF MULTIPLYING BY 3
00003A 4640 B010            00012   18 EVEN     BCT   4,LOOP        BRANCH BACK IF NOT ALL DIGITS PROCESSED
00003E 4350 B063            00065   19          IC    5,ACCT+9      PUT CHECK DIGIT IN REG 5
000042 8950 0004            00004   20          SLL   5,4           SHIFT LEFT 4 BITS
000046 5650 B06A            0006C   21          O     5,PLUS        ATTACH SIGN TO PUT IN SAME FORMAT AS SUM
00004A 4250 B064            00066   22          STC   5,SUM         PUT ONE BYTE IN LEFT BYTE OF SUM
00004E D500 B064 B065 00066 00067   23          CLC   SUM(1),SUM+1  IS THIS BYTE SAME AS CHECK DIGIT
000054 4770 B058            0005A   24          BNE   ERROR         BRANCH TO ERROR ROUTINE IF NOT EQUAL
                                    25 OUT      EOJ                 PROGRAM WOULD NORMALLY CONTINUE HERE
                                    28 ERROR    EOJ
00005C                              31 ACCT     DS    CL9
000065                              32 CHECK    DS    CL1
000066                              33 SUM      DS    CL2
000068 000C                         34 ZERO     DC    PL2'0'
00006A                              35 DIGIT    DS    CL1
00006C                              36          DS    0F
00006C 0000000C                     37 PLUS     DC    XL4'0C'
000000                              38          END   BEGIN
```

Figure 10–4. Machine and Symbolic Coding.

puter (Fig. 10.4). A number of programming languages have been developed that are easier to use and understand than machine language.

Symbolic programming, the use of mnemonic characters to write a program, has been developed to facilitate computer programming. When the mnemonic instructions are used, data may be referred to in terms which are logical to the nondata processing personnel as well as to the experienced programmer. One of the important advantages of symbolic programming is that the checking of each program may be performed by a person other than the programmer. The program written in the symbolic language is known as the *source program.*

The use of symbolic names (labels) makes a program independent of actual machine locations. Programs and routines written in symbolic language can be relocated and combined as desired. Routines within a program can be written independently without any loss of efficiency in the final program.

Symbolic instructions may be added or deleted without the necessity of reassigning storage addresses. The instructions can be inserted into the exact point in the program where they are needed.

The source program requires translation into an actual machine language program (object program) before the computer can execute it. To bridge the gap between the source program and the machine language, a special type of conversion program must tell the computer how to change the operations from the symbolic language (source program) to actual machine instructions (object program). Any programming language must have a rigid structure so that a conversion program can be written from it to accomplish the language translation. Several types of conversion programs, especially written by the programmer or supplied by the computer manufacturer in its software package, are able to convert a symbolic language program to a machine language program. The choice of program depends on the hardware and the purpose of the program.

Initially these translations were performed on a one-for-one basis, that is, each instruction was translated into a single machine language instruction. The processor program was called an *assembler*. An assembly program (or an assembler) converts a program written in symbolic form into a machine language program (Figs. 10.5, 10.6). An assembler translates item for item,

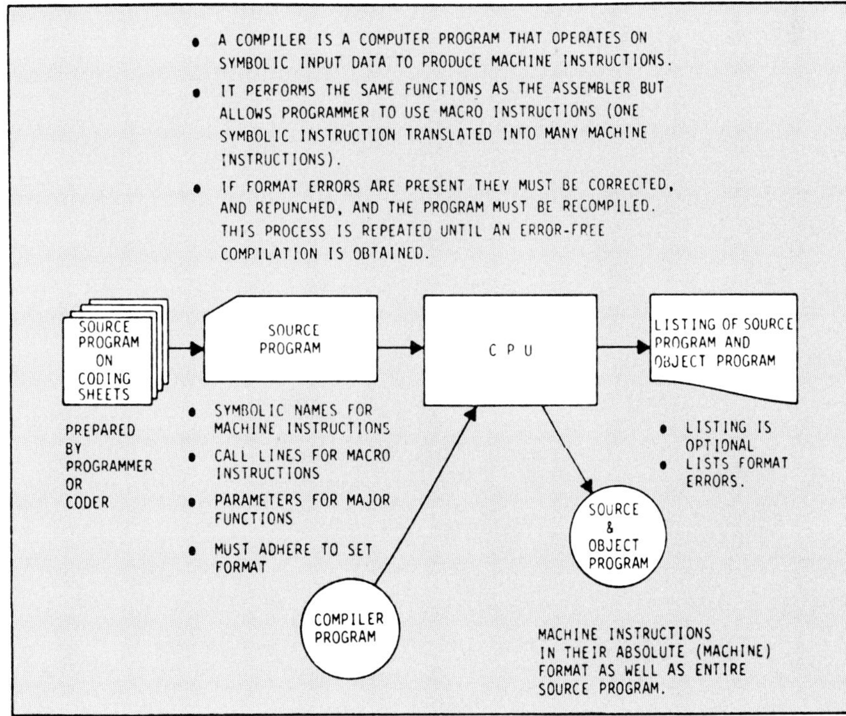

Figure 10–5. Assembly Process.

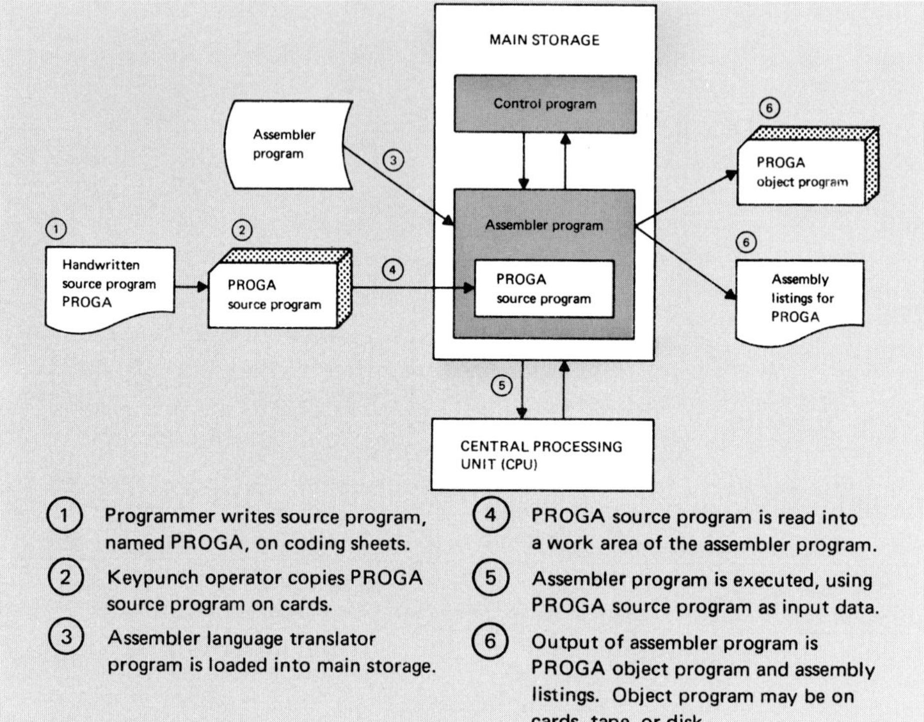

Figure 10–6. Assembly of a Problem Program.

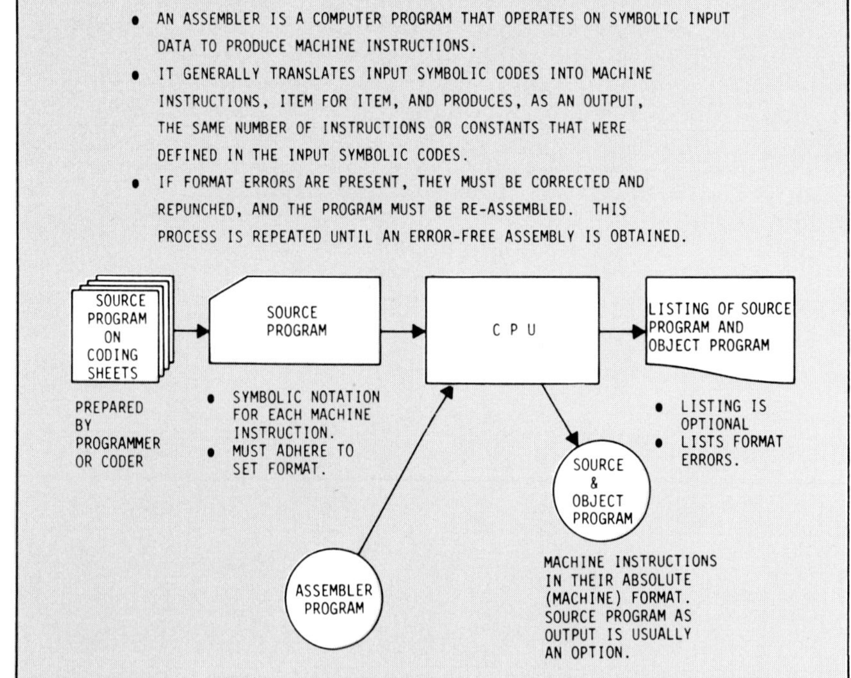

Figure 10–7. Compilation Process.

i.e., it produces an object program with the same number of instructions and constants as the source program. All symbolic entries are analyzed by the assembler and the conversion is made to actual machine operating data and instructions establishing specified relationships between them.

A compiling program (called a *compiler*) converts a symbolic program into a machine language program (Figs. 10.7, 10.8). A compiler differs from an assembler in that the compiler may generate a series of machine language instructions from one instruction written in the compiler program language. When using the compiler language, the programmer gives just one symbolic language instruction; the compiler program generates the many absolute or machine language instructions that are needed to perform the task. Most compiler languages allow many different macro instructions. (A macro instruction is equivalent to a specified sequence of machine instructions.) Some compiler languages allow the user to write his own macros and add them to the compiler group of macros.

Because of the macro capability, the compiler language is more powerful than the assembler language (Fig. 10.9). The compiler performs the same functions as the assembler plus the use of macros. This development greatly increases the power of symbolic languages. The art of programming has so

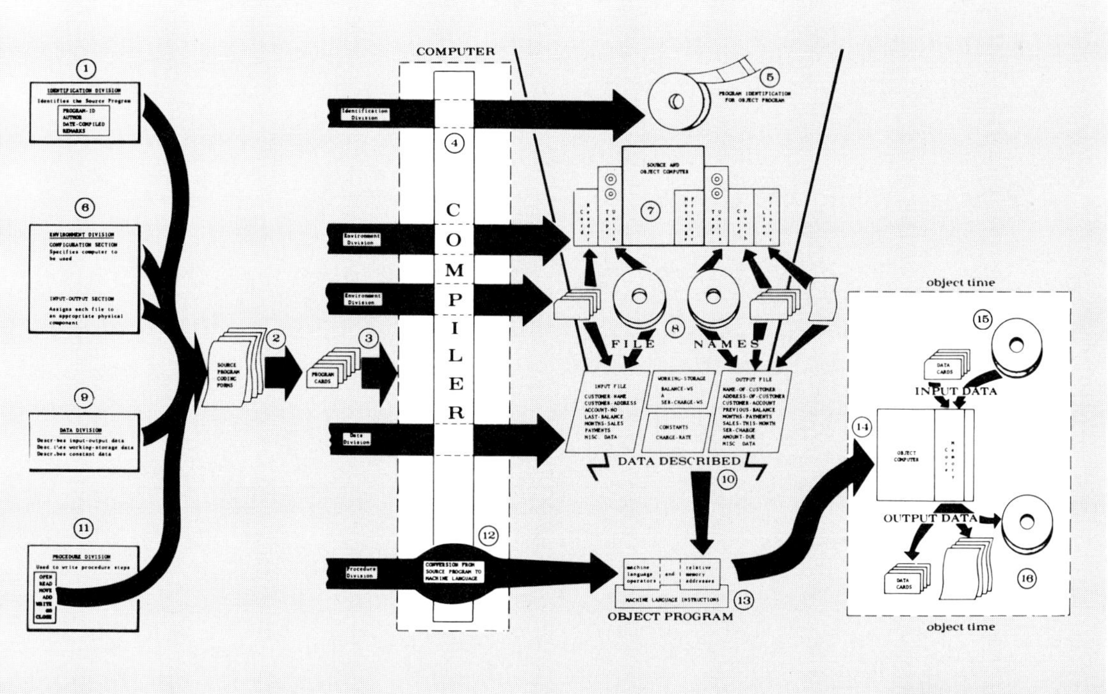

Figure 10–8. Compilation of a Source Program.

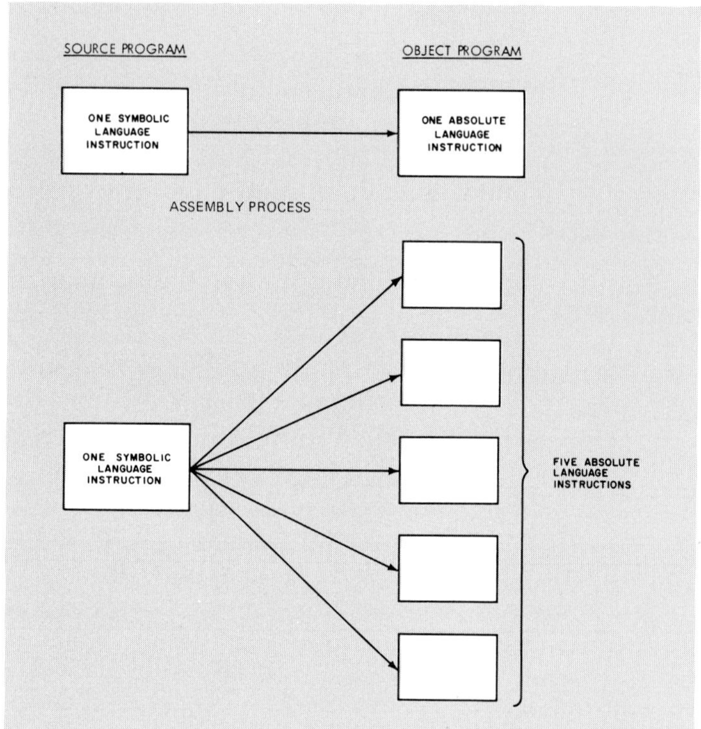

Figure 10–9. Compiling Processes.

advanced that it is possible to write instructions in a near-English format or mathematical format and have the compiler understand these statements and convert them into machine language instructions.

As an additional feature, compiled programs also indicate various types of errors such as coding, or out-of-sequence cards. Symbolic programming saves time and simplifies coding because the actual machine addresses of the data and instructions are assigned automatically by the processor. The programmer need not concern himself with detail. He can, however, refer to these addresses symbolically.

Once there is an agreement on label terminology, subroutines (short programs or routines common to a number of programs) may easily be incorporated into any program and a major program may be written in independent parts without any loss of efficiency in the final program. Corrections and modifications of program instructions will not require reassignment of addresses by the programmer. Finally, the automatic assignment of addresses makes programs and subroutines readily relocatable; they can be placed in varying machine locations as desired.

In summary, the significant advantages of symbolic programming are as follows:

1. *Simplifies program writing and organization.* It is easier to write and refer to an instruction using the symbolic names than to look up the actual machine address.
2. *Provides continuity for group programming efforts.* Once the label terminology has been agreed upon, program routines can be written efficiently and independently, and can be combined for compilation because addresses are automatically assigned by the processor.
3. *Simplifies program adjustment.* If programs require partial revision, only the affected routines need to be rewritten.
4. *Detects coding errors.* Illegal operation codes, invalid addressing, sequence errors, etc. are detected by the compiler and listed before the program is compiled.
5. *Facilitates program testing.* Explanatory comments may be listed next to the program instructions.

Symbolic programming permits the programmer to code in a symbolic language that is more meaningful and easier to handle than numerical machine language. The difficulties of coding in machine language, a tedious and time–consuming task, are thus eliminated. The compiler automatically assigns and keeps a record of storage locations, and checks for coding errors. By relieving the programmer of these burdensome tasks, symbolic programming reduces the amount of programming time and effort required.

OPERATION OF COMPILERS

A compiler is a processor program supplied by the computer manufacturer that translates the program created by the programmer (source program) into a machine language program (object program) for the particular computer. The compiler is loaded into the storage area of the computer. A source program is written by the programmer on a coding form that will be used as a guide for the punching of the program into cards. These cards will be entered into the machine and will be subsequently translated into an object program with the help of the computer. After the entire program has been written in the symbolic language, the source program is entered into the computer with the use of job control cards. The computer translates the symbols into the operation codes and absolute addresses in machine language coding according to the sequence and logic set up by the programmer. The object program may then be run to produce the problem results (Fig. 10.10).

It is worth emphasizing that the compiler itself is a program, not a machine. It translates the source program into the object program—it does not cause the object program to be executed. In some systems, the object program may be executed, while in other systems the object program is not in an

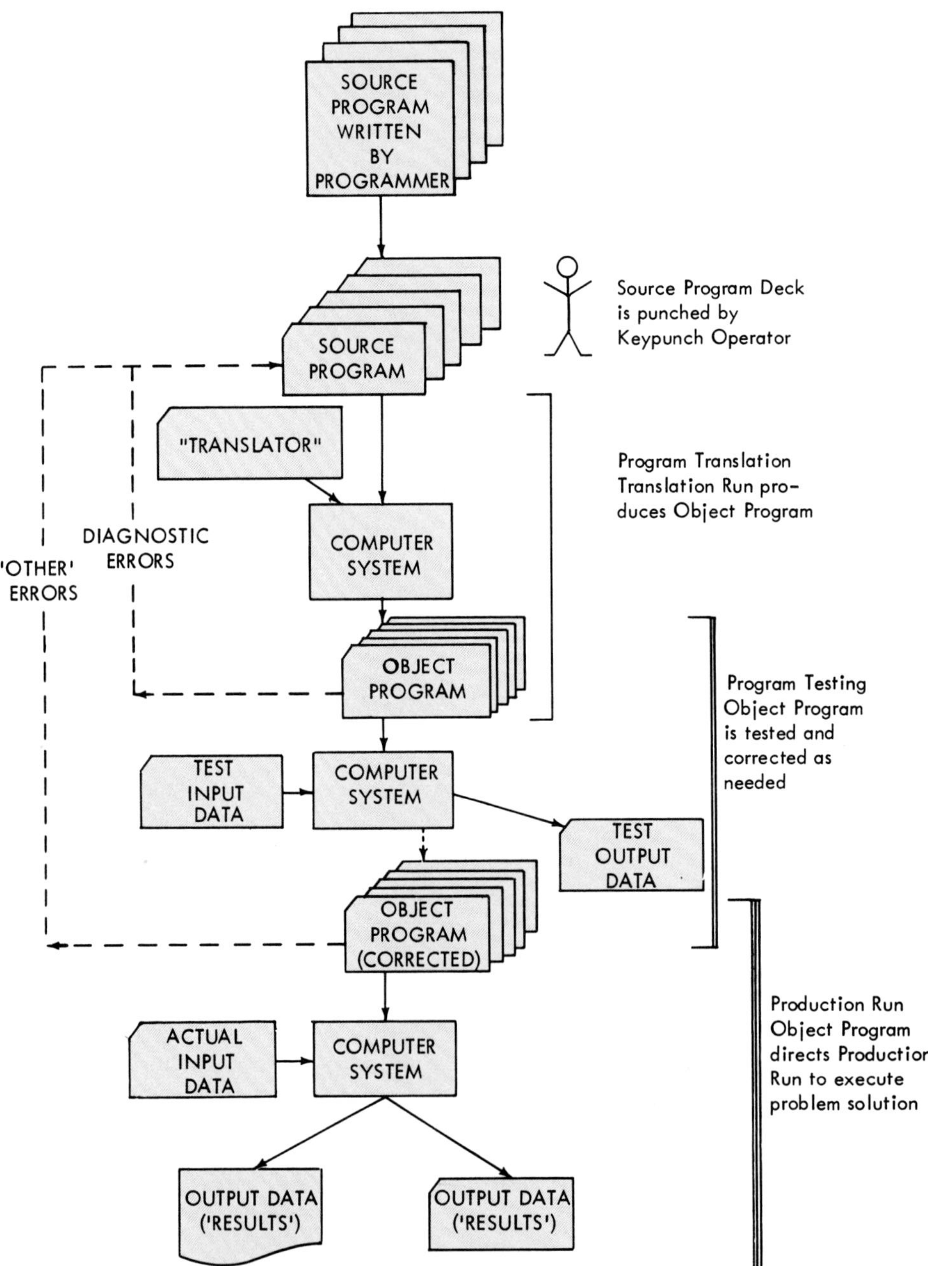

Figure 10–10. Execution: Program Translation and Testing and Production Run.

executable format but must be processed by another program called the *linkage editor* which produces the executable program.

Some examples of compilers (language processors) are COBOL and FORTRAN. These programming languages are written either in English-like statements or with mathematical formulas. Each of the individual statements is translated into one or more object program instructions.

LANGUAGE TRANSLATION

The output of a language processor is used to instruct the computer to solve a particular problem. The processor is itself a program with rules for grammar and execution. Its main function is the translation of the symbolic program of the programmer into the machine language of the particular computer.

The source program is written by the programmer after a thorough analysis of the problem. The method and logic of the solution is stated by the programmer in the language of the processor system. The language processor will then convert the source program into the corresponding object program that is understood by the computer. Other information such as subroutines, reference tables, constant factors, may be required within the computer to support the object program. This data must be inserted into the computer before the execution of the program can begin.

The processing involves the translation of the source statements into machine language, the assignment of storage locations to instructions and other elements of the program, and the performance of the auxiliary compilatory function designated by the programmer. The output of the compilation is the object program, a machine language translation of the source program. The compiler furnishes a printed listing of the source statements and object program statements, and additional information such as error indications useful to the programmer in analyzing his program.

After the object program has been executed, the output may be recorded on magnetic tape or disk, or in punched cards for later processing on offline equipment. The output results may be printed in the form of a report directly from the computer at the same time as the processing of the data.

Once an object program has been compiled, it can be used over and over again each time the particular job is run. Data processing applications which are of the production type, such as payroll, inventory control, sales analysis, may use a previously prepared object program each time it is needed merely by requesting it from storage.

MACHINE-ORIENTED PROGRAMMING LANGUAGE

In a machine-oriented programming language, the symbolic program is written by the programmer for a particular computer. The language was so designed by the computer manufacturer as to allow the programmer to take full advantage of the features and capabilities of the computer. For this reason, the most efficient program next to machine language that can be prepared for an individual computer is usually written using a machine-oriented language. The machine-oriented language differs from a problem-oriented or procedure-oriented language in that the former is meant to be processed on a particular computer while a problem-oriented or procedure-oriented language is written to solve a problem and may be processed on many different types of computers.

The programmer uses names and symbolic codes to designate the operations that the computer is to perform, or the storage locations of the data to be used in the data processing operation. The assembler processor then proceeds to translate the instruction into machine language instructions with actual machine storage locations.

An example of machine-oriented language is the IBM System/360/370 Assembler language. Coding sheets are used to write each instruction the machine is to perform (Fig. 10.11). Each line of the coding sheet is punched into a card. The form corresponds to the eighty columns of a punched card. Instructions for punching and program identification are provided for on the form.

IBM — IBM System/360 Assembler Coding Form

PROGRAM: AJAX PAYROLL REPORT — PAGE 4 OF 8

```
A3Ø      ZAP   CURFICA,=P'Ø'
         CP    YTDFICA,=P'29Ø4Ø'       COMPUTE
         BC    1Ø,B
         ZAP   CURFICA,GROSS           NEW
         MP    CURFICA,=P'44ØØ'
         AP    CURFICA,=P'5ØØØØ'       FICA
         MVO   CURFICA,CURFICA(4)
         ZAP   UNPDFICA,=P'29Ø4Ø'      DEDUCTION
         SP    UNPDFICA,YTDFICA
         CP    CURFICA,UNPDFICA        AND
         BC    12,A5Ø
         ZAP   CURFICA,UNPDFICA        YTD FICA
A5Ø      AP    YTDFICA,CURFICA
*
B        ZAP   NETPAY,GROSS            COMPUTE
         SP    NETPAY,CURFICA          NET
         SP    NETPAY,CURWH(5)         PAY
*
```

Figure 10–11. Machine-Oriented Programming Language.

The coding form permits a maximum of four fields in each line. These fields are called name, operation, operand and comment. The *name,* which is created by the programmer, provides a reference identification (label) in case other parts of a program need to refer to it. A symbol entered in the same field may be used in the operand field to address the beginning of an instruction or data field generated by the named statement line. Names are not required for every line. They are commonly used to identify data elements and instructions to which branches are made. Names may also be used for the identification of an instruction to which a branch is not made.

An *operation* is a mnemonic operation code specifying the machine operation or assembler function desired. An operation is required for every statement line except a line that is used only for comments or is a continuation line. A comment is indicated by an asterisk (*) in the first column, followed by the statement.

The content and the format of the entries in the *operand* field are governed by the requirements of the entry in the operation field. Operand entries indicate the storage location of the data to be processed. In addition, they specify the storage area lengths, types of data, etc. Depending upon the nature of the instruction, several operands may be used. The actual operand may be extended to the next line and be so indicated in the continuation column.

The *comments* entries may begin following the operand field as long as there is at least one space following the operand field entry. Comments are descriptive entries regarding the program. They usually provide the reader with the purpose of each instruction. A complete line may be used for comments by placing an asterisk in the first column. Comments appear on the listing solely for the convenience and information of the programmer.

The assembly program offers, also for the convenience of the programmer, extended mnemonic codes—symbolic codes that assemble a machine operation code with a portion of an instruction. Used in branching instructions, they permit the programmer to specify the branch and reason for branching. For example, the instruction BO (Branch on Overflow) combines the reason and branch into one instruction.

There are many more features in the IBM System/360/370 Assembler programming which will be discussed in greater detail later in the text.

Despite the many advantages in using machine-oriented programming languages (such as program efficiency), there are some serious disadvantages.

1. The great number of instructions and variations of instructions in a machine-oriented language make it difficult for the average programmer to write a program and debug it in a short period of time.
2. Any extensive revision or modification of a program can cause major

changes in the program, at which point the possibility of reprogramming the entire problem exists. Most machine-oriented language instructions are compatible only within the same system for a particular computer. They are not compatible upwards as most computer manufacturers claim. A large system of the same computer family usually requires reprogramming when upgraded from a small system.

3. Programmers have difficulty in learning the program because of the detail involved in each instruction format.

For these and other reasons machine-oriented language programs are written mainly for system and supervisory programs. Problem-oriented and procedure-oriented programming languages have become very popular for the writing of application programs.

PROBLEM-ORIENTED AND PROCEDURE-ORIENTED PROGRAMMING LANGUAGES

The use of problem- and procedure-oriented programming languages in data processing applications is increasing daily. Both of these programming languages are tailored to the solution of a particular problem rather than to a particular machine. *A problem-oriented programming language describes the problem to the computer and the compiler generates the necessary procedures for the solution of the problem while the procedure-oriented programming language describes the procedures to the computer* (Fig. 10.12).

A program written in this type of language can be compiled and executed

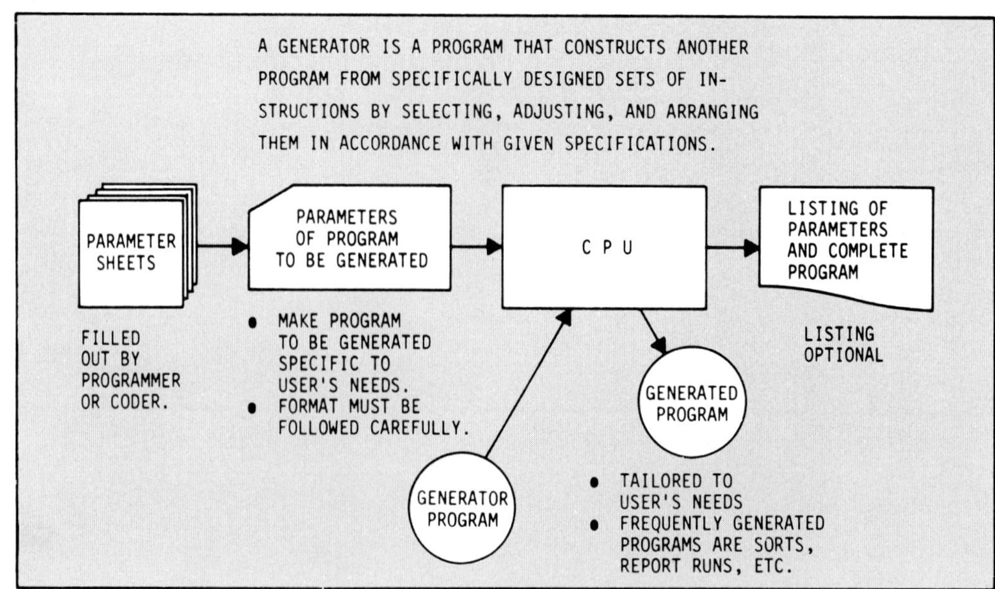

Figure 10–12. Generating a Program.

on many different computers with only minor changes in the program for each computer. These programs are written in a more flexible form than the machine-oriented language. English-like statements and mathematical expressions are used in the writing of these programs. The fact is that the programs written bear little resemblance to the machine language instruction, and the programmer need not be concerned with the method of translation.

One of the important advantages of these programming languages is that learning time is greatly reduced, especially for new programmers because they are writing in a form that is familiar to them. Nondata processing personnel as well as experienced programmers can read these languages. Debugging time is reduced because of the ease of reading and writing them.

These languages are easier to change and modify without any drastic reprogramming. Programs can be changed by personnel other than the original programmer. Many instructions in machine language can be created from a single problem- or procedure-oriented language instruction. The program can be compiled and executed on a variety of computers with minor revisions for each different type of computer. Prewritten subroutines may be included at compilation time with less effort than that required for a machine-oriented programming language.

The Report Program Generator (RPG) language is a problem-oriented language. RPG is a symbolic language which is designed specifically to ease the programmer's task in writing programs that produce reports. It is a very simple way of adapting an application to a computer. The file definition and input/output control considerations normally required of the programmer by other programming languages are reduced to filling out of simplified control forms. The File Description form details the file names for the program and the type of device which will handle each; the Input Specification form tells the machine what kind of information it is to receive; and the Output-Format Specification describes how the desired output should appear. The calculations form is the heart of the logic of the program and describes the operations to be performed on the data (Fig. 10.13).

RPG language simplifies the programmer's job by eliminating the task of developing processing steps. Cards are punched from the specification sheets and read into the computer, which, when used with the RPG compiler, will generate the desired report.

COBOL (*CO*mmon *B*usiness *O*riented *L*anguage) is an example of a procedure-oriented language that is used primarily in business applications (Fig. 10.14). The language was developed to meet the need for a programming language to solve business problems that could be processed on various computers with minimal modification of the original program. The program is written in readable English-like statements that are translated by the compiler into machine language instructions.

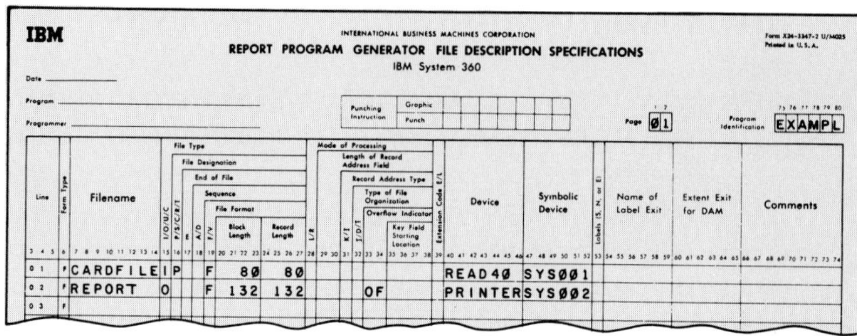

IBM — INTERNATIONAL BUSINESS MACHINES CORPORATION
REPORT PROGRAM GENERATOR FILE DESCRIPTION SPECIFICATIONS
IBM System 360

Page Ø1 — Program Identification EXAMPL

Line	Form Type	Filename	File Type	File Designation	File Format	Block Length	Record Length	Overflow Indicator	Device	Symbolic Device
01	F	CARDFILE	I	P	F	8Ø	8Ø		READ4Ø	SYSØØ1
02	F	REPORT	O		F	132	132	OF	PRINTER	SYSØØ2
03	F									

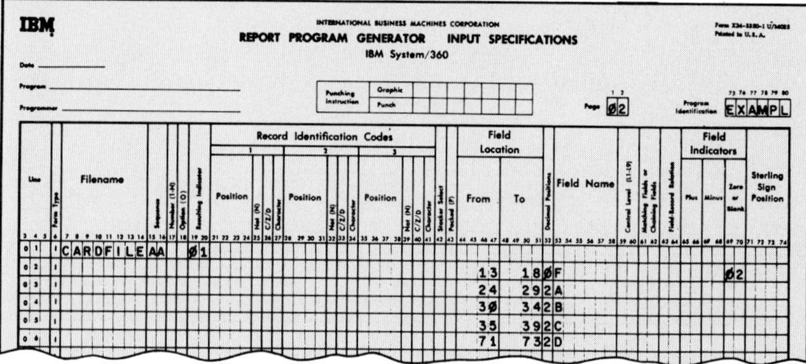

IBM — INTERNATIONAL BUSINESS MACHINES CORPORATION
REPORT PROGRAM GENERATOR INPUT SPECIFICATIONS
IBM System/360

Page Ø2 — Program Identification EXAMPL

Line	Form Type	Filename	Sequence	Resulting Indicator	Field Location From	Field Location To	Decimal Positions	Field Name	Field Indicators Zero or Blank
01	I	CARDFILE	AA	Ø1					
02	I				13	18	Ø	F	Ø2
03	I				24	29	2	A	
04	I				3Ø	34	2	B	
05	I				35	39	2	C	
06	I				71	73	2	D	

Figure 10–13. RPG Forms.

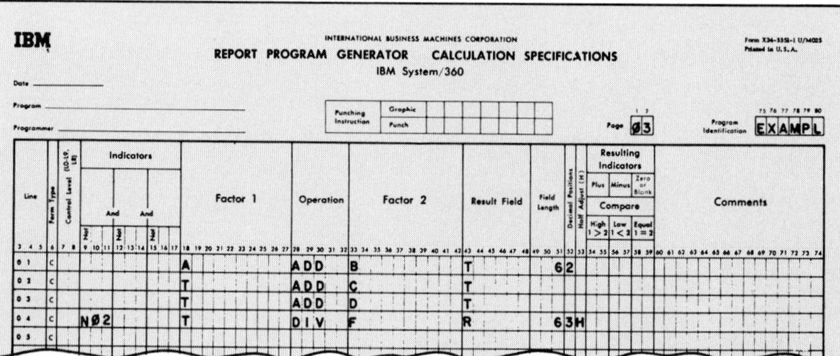

IBM — INTERNATIONAL BUSINESS MACHINES CORPORATION
REPORT PROGRAM GENERATOR CALCULATION SPECIFICATIONS
IBM System/360

Page Ø3 — Program Identification EXAMPL

Line	Form Type	Indicators	Factor 1	Operation	Factor 2	Result Field	Field Length	Decimal Positions	Half Adjust (H)
01	C		A	ADD	B	T	6	2	
02	C		T	ADD	C	T			
03	C		T	ADD	D	T			
04	C	NØ2	T	DIV	F	R	6	3	H
05	C								

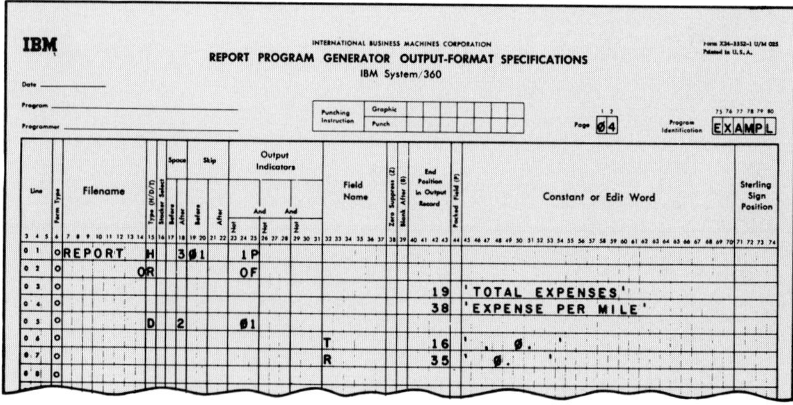

IBM — INTERNATIONAL BUSINESS MACHINES CORPORATION
REPORT PROGRAM GENERATOR OUTPUT-FORMAT SPECIFICATIONS
IBM System/360

Page Ø4 — Program Identification EXAMPL

Line	Form Type	Filename	Type (H/D/T)	Space Before	Skip Before	Output Indicators	Field Name	End Position in Output Record	Constant or Edit Word
01	O	REPORT	H	3	Ø1	1P			
02	O		OR			OF			
03	O							19	'TOTAL EXPENSES'
04	O							38	'EXPENSE PER MILE'
05	O		D	2		Ø1			
06	O						T	16	' , Ø. '
07	O						R	35	' Ø. '
08	O								

IBM COBOL PROGRAM SHEET

```
PROCEDURE DIVISION.

START-RUN.
    OPEN INPUT MASTER-FILE; OUTPUT CREDIT-LETTERS.

READ-MASTER.
    MOVE SPACES TO OUTPUT-LINE
    READ MASTER-FILE;
        AT END, CLOSE MASTER-FILE, CREDIT-LETTERS; STOP RUN.
    MOVE CUSTOMER-NAME TO DATA-AREA.
    WRITE OUTPUT-LINE AFTER ADVANCING 0.
    MOVE STREET-ADDRESS TO DATA-AREA.
    WRITE OUTPUT-LINE AFTER ADVANCING 1.
    MOVE CITY TO DATA-AREA.
    WRITE OUTPUT-LINE AFTER ADVANCING 1.
    GO TO READ-MASTER.
```

Figure 10–14. COBOL Program Sheet.

The COBOL compiler writes the instructions for the object program. Therefore, the programmer does not make as many clerical errors as he would make if he were writing in the assembler language. In a COBOL program, the programmer's errors would be in logic or in the use of the COBOL format. (Refer to the section on Checking the Program further on in this chapter.) Thus, there are fewer places that the programmer must check for errors. The COBOL programming language has two advantages: it makes testing COBOL programs easy, and it assures clear program documentation. These COBOL statements, which can be easily read and understood by people, provide excellent documentation of the program being defined and solved by the COBOL program.

An instruction such as ADD GROSS TO Y-T-D-GROSS can be translated by the compiler into the appropriate number of machine language instructions to accomplish the necessary operation. COBOL is widely used in all types of data processing operations for processing business data processing problems.

Another popular procedure-oriented language that is used extensively is FORTRAN (*FOR*mula *TRAN*slator). The FORTRAN language is similar to COBOL in concept. Whereas COBOL uses English-like statements, FORTRAN, a scientific-oriented language, uses mathematical formulas to state the problem (Fig. 10.15). The COBOL instruction ADD GROSS TO Y-T-D-

IBM FORTRAN CODING FORM

Form X28-7327-4 Printed in U.S.A.

Program SAMPLE PROGRAM 1		Punching Instructions: Graphic / Punch	Card Form #	Page 1 of 1
Programmer	Date			Identification 73–80

C FOR COMMENT — STATEMENT NUMBER (1–5) — Cont. (6) — FORTRAN STATEMENT (7–72)

```
C PRIME NUMBER GENERATOR
      WRITE (3,1)
    1 FORMAT ('1FOLLOWING IS A LIST OF PRIME NUMBERS FROM 2 TO 1ØØØ'/
     *19X,'2'/19X,'3')
      DO 4 I=5,1ØØØ,2
      K=SQRT(FLOAT(I))
      DO 2 J=3,K,2
      IF (MOD(I,J)) 2,4,2
    2 CONTINUE
      WRITE (3,3) I
    3 FORMAT (I2Ø)
    4 CONTINUE
      WRITE (3,5)
    5 FORMAT (' THIS IS THE END OF THE PROGRAM')
      STOP
      END
```

Figure 10–15. FORTRAN Coding Form.

GROSS would have to be rewritten in a mathematical expression and abbreviated as follows to accommodate the FORTRAN compiler;

YTDGR = YTDGR + GROSS

The FORTRAN language is characterized by mathematical statements that indicate actions to be taken. These FORTRAN statements are input to the FORTRAN compiler program. The program generates machine language instructions which perform the actions indicated in the original FORTRAN statements.

FORTRAN permits the programmer to use familiar arithmetic conventions to formulate a program. The symbols + — * / ** denote addition, subtraction, multiplication, division and exponentiation. FORTRAN gives the mathematician or scientist a language he can use to communicate with the computer, leaving him to concentrate on a problem rather than on the computer's machine language.

RPG, COBOL and FORTRAN as well as other widely used programming languages will be discussed in greater detail later in the text.

It is important to recognize the role that procedure and problem-oriented languages are playing in modern day data processing. More and more application programs are being written in these languages. With the continued improvements in software, compilers are becoming more powerful, permitting the programmer to write more complex programs with a minimum number of instructions. With the built-in facility for program testing, capabilities of parallel program execution, self-monitoring systems and procedure- and problem-oriented languages, the programming task has been simplified to the point where the definition of the problem and the subsequent analysis and solution are the most important aspects of computer programming, with the actual program coding being reduced to the writing of a series of statements in a language familiar to the programmer.

OTHER PROGRAMMING ELEMENTS

MACRO INSTRUCTIONS

A macro instruction is a symbolic statement that combines several operations into one. It provides a convenient way to generate a desired sequence of source program instructions many times in one or more source programs. The macro definition is written only once in a single statement. A macro instruction is written each time a programmer wants to generate the desired sequence of statements. This facility greatly simplifies the coding of programs, reduces chances of programming errors and insures that standard sequences of source program statements are used to accomplish desired functions.

Most of the macro instructions are supplied by the computer manufacturer but any programmer may develop his own to satisfy his own particular needs. The macro instruction statement is a source program statement that can produce a variable number of machine instructions for each occurrence of the same macro instruction. These generated statements are processed in the same manner as any other source statement.

The operations to be performed by the macro statement must be defined and written prior to the compilation operation. Before a macro statement can be compiled, the macro definition must be made available to the compiler. The macro definition consists of a series of statements that provide the compiler with (1) the mnemonic operation code and the format of the macro instruction, and (2) the sequence of statements the compiler generates when the macro instruction appears in the source program (Fig. 10.16).

The same macro definition may be made available to more than one source program by placing the macro definition in the macro library. The macro library is a collection of macro definitions available for use by all programmers in an installation. Once a macro definition has been placed in the macro library, it may be used by writing the corresponding macro instruction in a source program.

The macro, when defined, written and tested is placed along with previously prepared macros in a macro library. Then during the compilation process when a macro statement is encountered, the coding in the macro library is substituted in the source program for the macro written by the programmer.

Figure 10–16. Macro Instruction—Example.

	Name	Operation	Operand
Header		MACRO	
Prototype	&NAME	MOVE	&TY, &P, &TO, &FROM
Model	&NAME	ST&TY	2, SAVEAREA
Model		L&TY	2, &P&FROM
Model		ST&TY	2, &P&TO
Model		L&TY	2, SAVEAREA
Trailer		MEND	
Macro	HERE	MOVE	D, FIELD, A, B
Generated	HERE	STD	2, SAVEAREA
Generated		LD	2, FIELDB
Generated		STD	2, FIELDA
Generated		LD	2, SAVEAREA

For example, assume in a particular installation a standard routine exists that must be included in many programs. Instead of each programmer writing the routine as part of his own program, one programmer could write it as a macro and all other programs could call it in the form of a macro statement whenever needed. Thus the macro is similar to compiler statements in that many instructions are generated from one source statement.

Machine oriented languages have their own macro instructions supplied by the computer manufacturer and included in the compiler. However, many programmers like to develop their own macros to increase the effectiveness of the machine-oriented programming language and enlarge the functions of the compiler. Problem- and procedure-oriented languages also have their own macros which are supplied with the compiler, and which reduce the number of source program instructions.

SUBROUTINES

A subroutine is a subprogram consisting of a set of instructions that performs some subordinate function within the program. There are two means by which the subroutine may be included in a program. The best method is to insert the subroutine directly into the main program at the point at which it is needed. A subroutine used in this manner is known as an *open* subroutine (Fig. 10.17). However, if the program requires the execution of the subroutine several times during the operation of the main program, the use of an open subroutine is not practical because of the storage limitations and the apparent

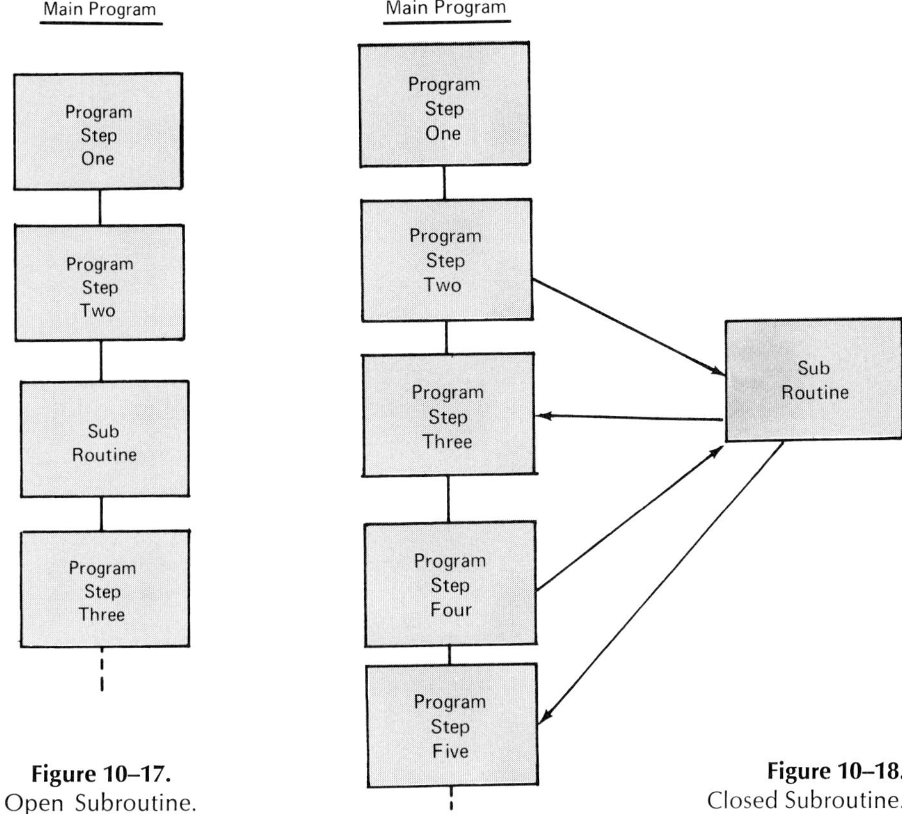

Figure 10–17.
Open Subroutine.

Figure 10–18.
Closed Subroutine.

waste of time and storage that would result from repeating the same set of instructions many times over.

A *closed* subroutine is included in a program only once but is referred to whenever the desired function is needed (Fig. 10.18). This avoids the repetition of instructions. The closed subroutine presents the problem of returning to the main program at the proper place.

Subroutines ease the task of the programmer by reducing the number of instructions to be written, and by enabling him to include pretested routines in his program. These subroutines can be written as a separate job by a programmer not acquainted with the main program. Routines that are reused in a large variety of programs can be kept in a library where they can be made available to all users.

CHECKING THE PROGRAM

After the successful coding and compilation of the source program has been completed, the next phase in the program checkout procedure is to check the resultant machine language program with the data (Fig. 10.19). *Program testing or debugging is the determination that the program will ac-*

```
  LOC   OBJECT CODE      ADDR1 ADDR2  STMT    SOURCE STATEMENT

000100                                  1 PROGC      START 256
000100 05B0                             2 BEGIN      BALR  11,0
000102                                  3            USING *,11
000102 5820 B01E            0012^       4            L     2,DATA
000106 5A20 B026            00126       5            A     2,CON
                                        6            SLS   2,1
           *** ERROR ***
00010A 0000 0000            00000       7            S     2,DATA4
           *** ERROR ***
00010E 5020 B02A            0012C       8            ST    2,RESULT
000112 0000 0000            00000       9            L     6BIN1
           *** ERROR ***
000116 5A60 B02E            00130      10            A     6,BIN2
00011A 0000 0000            00000      11            CVD   6,BIN1
           *** ERROR ***
                                       12            EOJ
                                       13+* 360N-CL-453 EOJ        CHANGE LEVEL 3-0
00011E 0A0E                            14+           SVC   14
000120 00000019                        15 DATA       DC    F'25'
000124 4CB016EA                        16            DC    F'9876543210'
           *** ERROR ***
000128 0000000A                        17 CON        DC    F'10'
00012C                                 18 RESULT     DS
           *** ERROR ***
00012C 0000 0000            00000      19 IN1        C     '12'
           *** ERROR ***
000130 0000004F                        20 BIN2       DC    F'78'
000138                                 21 DEC        DS    D
000140 00000019                        22 DATA       DC    F'25'
           *** ERROR ***
000100                                 23            END   BEGIN
```

```
                           DIAGNOSTICS

STMT   ERROR CODE   MESSAGE

   6   IJQ088       UNDEFINED OPERATION CODE
   7   IJQ024       UNDEFINED SYMBOL
   9   IJQ039       INVALID DELIMITER
   9   IJQ039       INVALID DELIMITER
  11   IJQ024       UNDEFINED SYMBOL
  16   IJQ017       DATA ITEM TOO LARGE
  18   IJQ031       UNKNOWN TYPE
  18   IJQ009       MISSING OPERAND
  19   IJQ039       INVALID DELIMITER
  19   IJQ018       INVALID SYMBOL
  22   IJQ023       PREVIOUSLY DEFINED NAME

  8 STATEMENTS FLAGGED IN THIS ASSEMBLY
```

Figure 10–19. Assembly Listing with Errors.

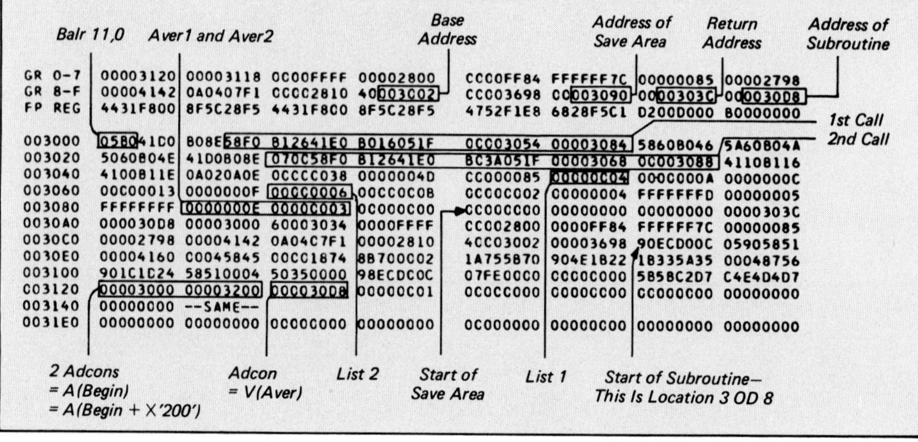


```
GR 0-7   00003120 00003118 0C00FFFF 00002800   CCC0FF84 FFFFFF7C 00000085 00002798
GR 8-F   00004142 0A0407F1 CCCC2810 40003C02   CC003698 CC003090 0000303C 000030D8
FP REG   4431F800 8F5C28F5 4431F8C0 8F5C28F5   4752F1E8 6828F5C1 D200D000 B0000000

003000   05B041C0 B08E58F0 B12641E0 B016051F   0CC03054 00003084 5860B046 5A60B04A
003020   5060B04E 41D0B08E 070C58F0 B12641E0   BC3A051F 00003068 0C003088 41108116
003040   4100B11E 0A020A0E 0CCCC038 0000004D   CC000085 00000C04 000C000A 0000000C
003060   00C00013 0000000F 00CC0006 00CC0C0B   CCC0C002 C0000004 FFFFFFFD 00000005
003080   FFFFFFFF 0000000E 00000003 0C000C00   CC00C000 00000000 00000000 0000303C
0030A0   000030D8 00003000 60003034 0000FFFF   CC002800 0000FF84 FFFFFF7C 00000085
0030C0   00002798 00004142 0A04C7F1 00002810   4CC03002 00003698 90ECD00C 05905851
0030E0   00004160 C0045845 00CC1874 8B700002   1A755870 904E1B22 1B335A35 00048756
003100   901C1C24 58510004 50350000 98ECDC0C   07FE00C0 CCC0C000 5B5BC2D7 C4E4D4D7
003120   00003000 00003200 000030D8 00000C01   0C0CC000 C000CC00 CC0000C0 00000000
003140   00000000 --SAME--
0031E0   00000000 00000000 0C000000 00000000   0C000000 00000C00 00000000 00000000
```

Figure 10–20. Dump of Storage.

complish the desired results. Few programs are written that work correctly the first time they are tried with actual data. Usually several runs are necessary before all mistakes are found and corrected. The most frequent cause of errors in the source program is that the problem has been improperly or incompletely stated. Most of the obvious errors, such as unnamed storage areas called for by the program, card-punching errors, or arithmetic format errors, will be detected by the compiler. Computers rarely make mistakes, although at times during the debugging stage, it appears that some errors have been made by the computer. Built-in detection circuits will normally reflect the type of mistake the computer has made by turning on an indicator and stopping the computer. The matter of detecting and classifying programmer errors is more complex and difficult.

The two major types of errors that cause difficulty in programs are the logical errors and the clerical errors. *Logical errors result from poor analysis.* For example, the failure to anticipate the possibility of an employee having a negative amount of pay due to excessive payroll deductions. The omission of a test for this possible condition could result in a paycheck being written for this negative amount. Errors of this type can result from a lack of understanding by the programmer of all the possibilities of this data processing application. A more comprehensive analysis of the problem can eliminate many errors like these.

The clerical error usually occurs during the coding stage. A programmer, in error, may assign two different symbolic names for the same parameter or he may use the wrong operation code symbol, or omit one or more instructions.

As the size and complexity of programs increase, the debugging phase will consume more and more time. Many techniques exist to aid the programmer in this checkout stage. The use of a particular technique will depend on the programmer's estimate of the extent and nature of the errors. Techniques that involve the testing of the program by the use of switches on the operator's console of the computer are very wasteful of valuable computer time and should be prohibited.

A successful technique of debugging is the printing out of storage contents relating to the particular problem. The contents of storage, registers and indicators are presented in printed form. This printout (dump) routine will locate many errors on the listing which the programmer may correct at this time (Fig. 10.20).

If the visually checked procedures do not reveal all the errors of a particular program, a tracing routine may be used. This method involves a routine program that executes a number of instructions for each program being traced. The printout received while tracing normally involves the location of the instruction being executed, and the contents of the registers after execution of the instruction. This technique involves a great amount of computer time and should be used only after all other techniques have failed to locate the error.

The tracing technique can be modified so as to print only the contents of selected storage locations when the program reaches the specified point in the program.

When all bugs have been eliminated from the source program, it should be run with test data. The test data should include all possible conditions, particularly exception routines. The data should force the program through most of the exception routines. The test data should be checked with predetermined results to assure that the program is free from error.

Debugging will find most of the errors in a program and reduce the possibility of others but it will not eliminate the possibility that some errors still exist that may be detected with actual data. The time consumed by the necessary debugging processes can be reduced if certain rules are followed.

1. Be aware of all debugging techniques available and do not hesitate to use them. Do not be satisfied with concentrating on one basic technique.
2. A successful debugging does not assure that the program will run to completion with the actual data. The actual data may be too large for the storage area assigned, too slow for the processing procedure, or not in the planned format.
3. Ascertain that the program does all that is expected of it.
4. Document each program thoroughly wherever possible to enable the reader to understand what each program step is to accomplish.
5. Leave room in the program for the possible insertion of testing or printing routines that may be used to test the program.
6. Check all source cards with documentation before compilation and test runs.

After all the expense and complexity of the debugging process it is still impossible to determine that a complex program is completely error-free. This frustrating phase of programming may be lessened if the six rules above are followed. Debugging procedures are relatively ineffective with synthetic data as the program is not aware of all errors. In a complex program, it is difficult, if not virtually impossible, to write branches to test all possible clerical errors.

SUMMARY

The future of computers is dependent not only on increases in speed of processing, logical ability, and storage capacities but on the constant improvement in programming techniques as well. After a complete analysis of the problem, the completed problem statement must then be translated into the appropriate tools available to the programmer: the flowcharts and decision tables. The flowchart and necessary decision tables are then translated into a program, a series of instructions. The intent of this chapter is to furnish the transition between the expression of the problem in flowchart form and the technical methods for the processing of the data in the form of a complete program. One must learn to understand computer programming languages in order to be able to communicate with the computer.

One must learn the meanings of machine language, symbolic language, compilers, macro instructions, subroutines, machine-, problem-, and procedure-oriented programming languages.

I. *Machine Language.*
   A. *Definition*—a common language of a particular computer that does not require further modification before execution by computer.
   B. *Problems in using machine language*—programs must be written with actual addresses; the logic and program organization is the responsibility of the original programmer; must know the details of the computer, requires memorization of many codes.

II. *Symbolic language.*
   A. *Definition*—uses mnemonic characters to write programs (source program) that must be later translated (compiler or assembler) into the machine language (object program) of a particular computer.
   B. *Advantages*—simplifies program writing and organization, simplifies program adjustments, facilitates program testing, eliminates the need for direct machine coding.
   C. *Assembler*—a processor program supplied by the computer manufacturer, that translates a program written in symbolic form into a machine language on a one-for-one basis, that is, one symbolic instruction for one machine language instruction.
   D. *Compiler*—is a processor program supplied by the computer manufacturer that translates the source program into an object program. A compiler differs from an assembler in that the compiler may generate a series of machine language instructions for one instruction written in the compiler programming language.
   E. *Machine-oriented programming language*—a symbolic programming language written by a programmer for a particular computer; allows the programmer to take full advantage of the features and capabilities of the particular computer. Example of a machine-oriented programming language is the IBM System/360/370 Assembler language.

      Coding form provides the following:

      1. *Name*—any necessary labels.

2. *Operation code*—specifies the operation the machine is to perform.
3. *Operand*—the storage location address of the data to be processed.
4. *Comments*—the descriptive entries regarding the program.

Disadvantages of machine-oriented programming language—a large variety of instructions makes it difficult for the average programmer to write, debug and use the program.

F. *Problem-oriented and procedure-oriented programming languages*—symbolic languages tailored to the solution of the problem rather than to the particular machine.
   1. *Problem-oriented programming language*—describe the problem to the computer and the computer generates the necessary procedures for the solution of the problem. Example: Report Program Generator (RPG).
   2. *Procedure-oriented programming language*—describes the procedures to the computer and the compiler translates the source program into the necessary machine language instructions to solve the program. Examples: COmmon Business Oriented Language (COBOL), and FORmula TRANslator (FORTRAN).
   3. *Advantages of problem-oriented and procedure-oriented programming languages*—easy to write because one is writing in a form familiar to him; debugging time is reduced because of the use of macros; easy to modify and change; may be run on a variety of computers.

III. *Other programming elements.*
   A. *Macro instructions*—a symbolic statement that combines several operations into one.
      1. Most macros supplied by computer manufacturers.
      2. Available to other programs.
      3. Simplifies coding and reduces processing errors.
   B. *Subroutines*—a subprogram consisting of a set of instructions, that performs some subordinate functions within a program.
      1. *Open subroutine*—inserted directly into the main program where needed.
      2. *Closed subroutines*—included in main program only once but referred to whenever needed.
   C. *Checking programs*—debugging the program.
      1. *Logical errors*—result from poor analysis of problem.
      2. *Clerical errors*—result from poor coding of program.
      3. *Storage dumps*—printing the contents of storage, registers and indicators.

IDENTIFICATION QUESTIONS

Match the following terms with the statements that follow.

A. Assembler
B. Cobol
C. Compiler
D. Clerical Errors
E. Debugging
F. Fortran
G. Linkage Editor
H. Logical Errors
I. Machine Language
J. Machine-Oriented Programming Language
K. Macro
L. Object Program
M. Problem-Oriented Programming Language
N. Procedure-Oriented Programming Language
O. RPG
P. Source Program
Q. Subroutines
R. Symbolic Language

1. A processor program that translates a source program into a machine language program generating many machine language instructions for each symbolic instruction.
2. A symbolic language that describes the problem to the computer and the compiler generates the necessary procedures.
3. Report Program Generator—a problem-oriented programming language.
4. The common language of the particular computer.
5. It produces the executable program.
6. Formula Translator—a procedure-oriented programming language.
7. A program written in machine language.
8. An instruction that is equivalent to a specific sequence of machine instructions.
9. A symbolic language that describes procedures to the computer.
10. The use of mnemonic characters to write a program.
11. A processor program that translates a source program into a machine language program on a one-for-one basis.
12. A symbolic programming language written for a particular computer.
13. The determination that the program will accomplish the desired result.
14. Errors that result from poor coding.
15. A program written in a symbolic language.
16. Errors that result from poor analysis.
17. Common Business Oriented Language—a procedure-oriented programming language.
18. Short routines or programs common to a number of programs.

QUESTIONS FOR REVIEW

1. What does the future of computers depend on?
2. List the steps involved in programming.
3. How is the program written by the programmer?
4. What is the difference between a machine language and a symbolic language programs?
5. What problems arise in using a program written in actual machine language?

6. How does the symbolic programming overcome some of the disadvantages of machine language coding?
7. What are the important advantages of symbolic programming?
8. What is a compiler? What is its main function? Give examples.
9. What is a machine-oriented programming language? Give an example.
10. Explain the function of the four fields of the IBM System/360/370 coding form. Name, Operation, Operand, Comments.
11. What are the serious disadvantages in using machine-oriented programming languages?
12. Describe problem- and procedure-oriented programming languages and tell how they differ from a machine-oriented programming language. Give examples of problem- and procedure-oriented programming languages.
13. What is a macro instruction and how is it used in writing programs?
14. What is a subroutine? What is the difference between an open and closed subroutine?
15. What are the two main types of programming errors? Give examples of each.
16. What is a dump routine? How can it help programmers to debug their program?
17. What are some rules for successful programming?

PART V / PROGRAMMING LANGUAGES

CHAPTER 11

Report Program Generator

Report Program Generator (RPG) is a problem-oriented language designed to solve a particular problem. A problem-oriented language describes the problem without detailing the procedures involved.

The Report Program Generator (RPG) source language was designed to provide the programmer with an easy and efficient method of generating programs. It is a simple way of adapting an application to a computer (Fig. 11.1). The file definitions and the input/output control considerations re-

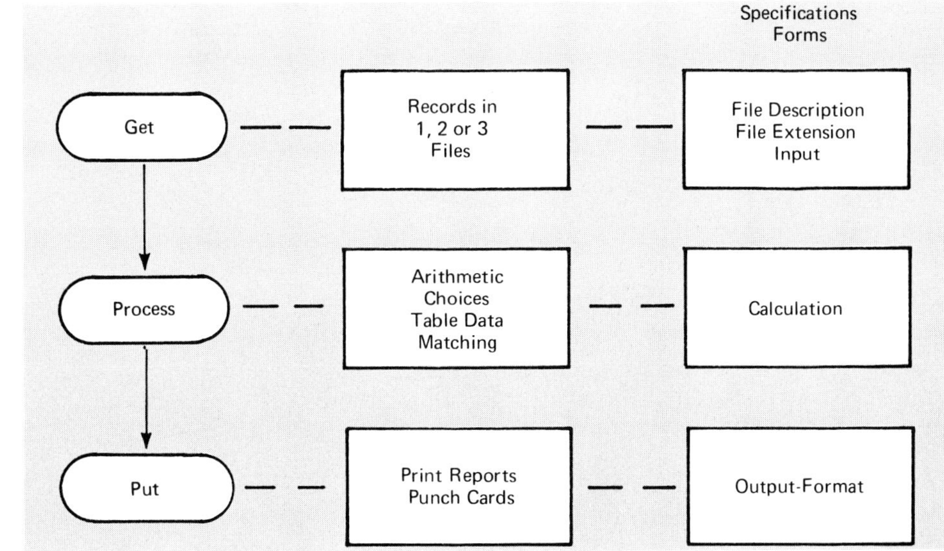

Figure 11–1. RPG Specification Form Usage.

quired normally of other programming languages are reduced to the filling out of simplified forms. Output reports are described on specification sheets to the compiler. Specification sheets are also written for the input source document formats. The calculation form, which is the heart of the logic of the program, will perform the necessary calculations of the two addresses and store the result in the third. All operands are described on forms. All that need be specified for the calculation forms are

1. The sequence in which the calculations are to be performed,
2. The types of calculations to be performed on the data, and
3. Any tests to be made on the results.
   (See Fig. 11.2).

It is easier to describe jobs to a computer than to write a program for doing them (Fig. 11.3).

Many different reports may be prepared from the same input specifications. The specification sheets with their self-explanatory headings make it possible for the nonprogrammer to write programs.

The RPG language is upwards compatible on all models of computers. It can support the minimum configuration of a system as well as the largest full operating system.

SPECIFICATION SHEETS—FUNCTIONS

The specification sheets will generate machine-language program instructions together with automatically assigned storage areas for data input and output, work areas and constants (Fig. 11.4). The created machine language will be combined with the input data files to produce finished output reports and files.

PRINCIPLES OF RPG PROGRAMMING

In planning a job using RPG, there are four points to be considered.

1. Find out what is wanted.
2. Find out about the records used to produce what is wanted.
3. Note the kinds of operations to be done in order to get what is wanted from the records used.
4. Note any additional requirements of job.

Before any attempt is made to fill out the specification forms, a thorough analysis must be made of the procedures to determine the descriptions of the source data and its formats, how the data is to be processed to develop the finished report, and all other information relative to the processing of the data. System and program flowcharts should be drawn to show the flow of data through the system.

The preparation of a report by means of RPG consists of the following steps (Fig. 11.5):

Figure 11–2. RPG Specification Forms.

IBM — INTERNATIONAL BUSINESS MACHINES CORPORATION

REPORT PROGRAM GENERATOR FILE DESCRIPTION SPECIFICATIONS

IBM System 360

Form X24-3347-2 U/M025 Printed in U.S.A.

Date ______ Program ______ Programmer ______

Punching Instruction: Graphic / Punch — Page: Ø1 — Program Identification: EXAMPL

Line	Form Type	Filename	File Type	File Designation	End of File	Sequence	File Format	Block Length	Record Length	Overflow Indicator	Device	Symbolic Device
01	F	CARDFILE	I	P			F	8Ø	8Ø		READ4Ø	SYSØØ1
02	F	REPORT	O				F	132	132	OF	PRINTER	SYSØØ2
03	F											

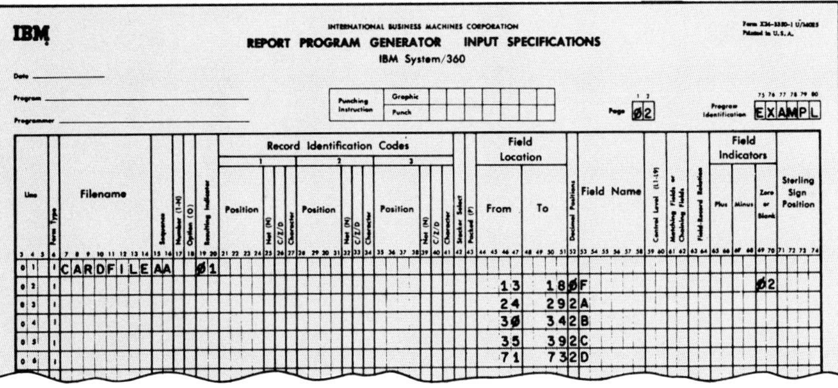

IBM — INTERNATIONAL BUSINESS MACHINES CORPORATION

REPORT PROGRAM GENERATOR INPUT SPECIFICATIONS

IBM System/360

Form X24-3350-1 U/M025 Printed in U.S.A.

Date ______ Program ______ Programmer ______

Punching Instruction: Graphic / Punch — Page: Ø2 — Program Identification: EXAMPL

Line	Form Type	Filename	Sequence	Resulting Indicator	Field Location From	Field Location To	Decimal Positions	Field Name	Field Indicators Plus	Field Indicators Minus	Field Indicators Zero or Blank
01	I	CARDFILE	AA	Ø1							
02	I				13	18	Ø	F			Ø2
03	I				24	29	2	A			
04	I				3Ø	34	2	B			
05	I				35	39	2	C			
06	I				71	73	2	D			

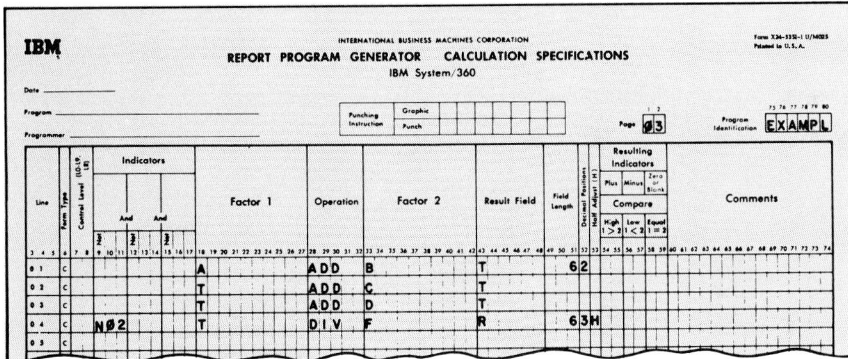

IBM — INTERNATIONAL BUSINESS MACHINES CORPORATION

REPORT PROGRAM GENERATOR CALCULATION SPECIFICATIONS

IBM System/360

Form X24-3351-1 U/M025 Printed in U.S.A.

Date ______ Program ______ Programmer ______

Punching Instruction: Graphic / Punch — Page: Ø3 — Program Identification: EXAMPL

Line	Form Type	Indicators	Factor 1	Operation	Factor 2	Result Field	Field Length	Decimal Positions	Half Adjust (H)
01	C		A	ADD	B	T	6	2	
02	C		T	ADD	C	T			
03	C		T	ADD	D	T			
04	C	NØ2	T	DIV	F	R	6	3	H
05	C								

IBM — INTERNATIONAL BUSINESS MACHINES CORPORATION

REPORT PROGRAM GENERATOR OUTPUT-FORMAT SPECIFICATIONS

IBM System/360

Form X24-3352-1 U/M 025 Printed in U.S.A.

Date ______ Program ______ Programmer ______

Punching Instruction: Graphic / Punch — Page: Ø4 — Program Identification: EXAMPL

Line	Form Type	Filename	Type (H/D/T)	Space After	Skip Before	Output Indicators	Field Name	End Position in Output Record	Constant or Edit Word
01	O	REPORT	H	3	Ø1	1P			
02	O	OR				OF			
03	O							19	'TOTAL EXPENSES'
04	O							38	'EXPENSE PER MILE'
05	O		D	2		Ø1			
06	O						T	16	' , Ø. '
07	O						R	35	' Ø. '
08	O								

STOCK INVENTORY REPORT

7/01/65

MATERIAL NO.	STOCK NO.	DESCRIPTION	UNIT COST	QUANTITY ON HAND	ON HAND COST	
25	96543	CARBORUNDUM WHEELS	10.25	4,646	47,622	
	THE TOTAL ON HAND COST IN DOLLARS FOR MATERIAL NUMBER 25 IS $				47,622	**
111	00986	STAINLESS SET SCREWS NSP	.42	5,986	2,514	
111	01598	STAINLESS RODS	8.59	934	8,023	
111	09346	HI GRADE CARBON	4.82	52	251	
111	11632	CARBON STEEL	5.96	1,598	9,524	
111	11723	STAINLESS PINS	9.17	52	477	
111	11725	STAINLESS TUBING	1.15	915	1,052	
111	11899	STAINLESS FITTINGS	15.67	1,792	28,081	
111	55292	STEEL SHANK 4X9X1	.14	4,138	579	
111	62549	HEX STOCK TITANIUM	100.48	89	8,943	
111	65342	TITANIUM BARS	95.89	85	8,151	
111	72359	STEEL PLATE	11.86	98	1,162	
111	81192	FLAT ROLLED STEEL SHEETS	15.92	1,139	18,133	
111	81536	STEEL FLANGE	4.80	1,985	9,528	
	THE TOTAL ON HAND COST IN DOLLARS FOR MATERIAL NUMBER 111 IS $				96,417	**
123	45678	ALLIGATOR PUMPS	965.43	9,999	9,653,335	
	THE TOTAL ON HAND COST IN DOLLARS FOR MATERIAL NUMBER 123 IS $				9,653,335	**

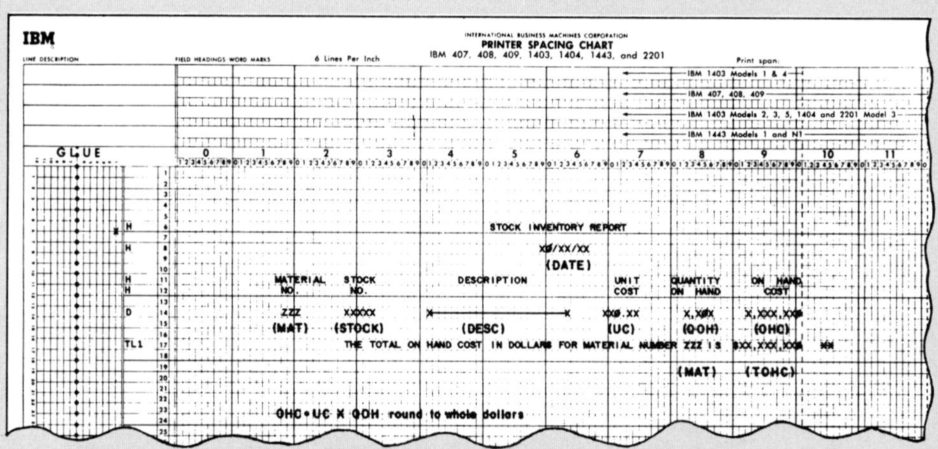

A detail printed report titled, STOCK INVENTORY REPORT, is to be produced from a file of card records arranged in ascending numerical order (by the material number field). For each record, the Unit Cost and Quantity On Hand shall be multiplied to calculate the On Hand Cost. This cost shall be rounded to the nearest whole dollar. A total On Hand Cost is to be calculated for each group of records. A date card precedes the file of cards. The report will have 6 columns of information: Material Number, Stock Number, Description, Unit Cost, Quantity On Hand, and On Hand Cost. A column heading is to be printed over each of these columns. Detail lines shall be double spaced, while total lines shall be 3 spaces ahead of the next group. The input card records are described below.

Stock Card Record

Columns	Decimals	Field
7-9	0	Material Number
12-16	0	Stock Number
19-23	2	Unit Cost
26-49		Item Description
70-73	0	Quantity on Hand
79		Code; Letter M

Date Card Record

Columns	Decimals	Field
1-6	0	Date
79		Code; Letter D

Figure 11–3. RPG Job Layout.

REPORT PROGRAM GENERATOR SPECIFICATIONS FORMS	
FORM	**USE**
1. File Description	A. Describes each file as either input, output, or combined.
2. Input	A. Identifies each record type that is in each input or combined file. B. Locates the data to be used from each record.
3. Calculation	A. Specifies the operations to be performed with the located data.
4. Output-Format	A. Specifies the arrangement of output data in printed lines or punched cards.

Figure 11–4. RPG Specification Form Functions.

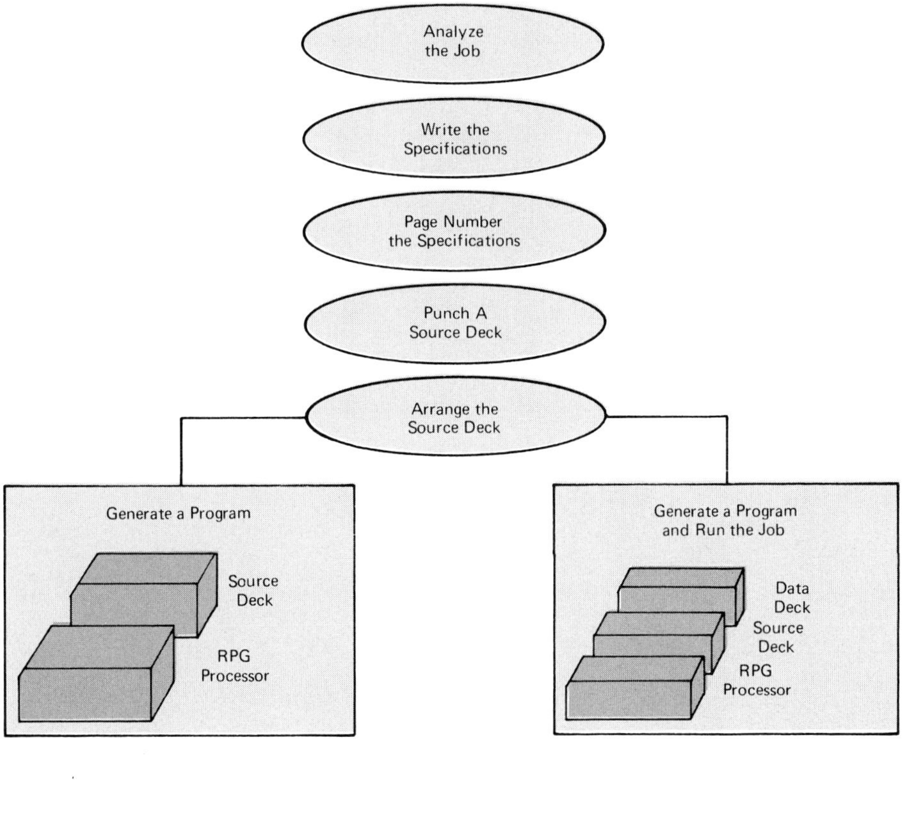

Figure 11–5. RPG Job Steps.

1. The programmer must evaluate the program through the preparation of flowcharts, analysis sheets, input and output requirements and processing requirements. For example, he determines what fields in the input records are to be used, what calculations are to take place, where the data is to be located in the output record and how many and what kinds of totals must be accumulated.
2. After the programmer has evaluated the requirements of the report, he must carefully define the output requirements by preparing a Printer Spacing Chart.
3. The programmer must provide the information to the RPG compiler in the form of specification sheets.
   a. He describes all files used by the object program (input files, output files, table files, etc.) by making entries on the File Description Specification sheets.
   b. If the programmer uses record address files, tables or arrays in his object program, he furnishes information about them through entries on the Extension Specification sheets.
   c. He describes his input (record layout fields used, etc.). This is done by making entries on the Input Specifications sheets.
   d. He states what processing is to be done (add, subtract, multiply, divide, etc.) by means of entries on a Calculation Specifications sheet.
   e. He defines the layout of the report (print positions, carriage control, etc.). This is accomplished by making entries on the Output-Format Specification sheets.
4. After the specifications have been written on the appropriate forms, the data on the forms is recorded in punched cards. Each line on the form is punched in one card.
5. These punched cards (called a source deck) are preceded by the RPG job control cards. The source deck and the control cards are placed in the card reader device and processed by the RPG compiler. At the end of the processing run (referred to as the compilation run), the object program is produced and stored in the computer. The program contains all the machine instructions required to prepare the desired report.
6. The programmer may now have the object program punched into cards for storage or he may proceed directly to processing the object program.
7. The input files are read in for the preparation of the desired output reports and files.

PRINTER SPACING CHART

Prior to the writing of the specification sheets, the programmer should create a work sheet for the printer to be used as a form for coding the particular operations (Fig. 11.6).

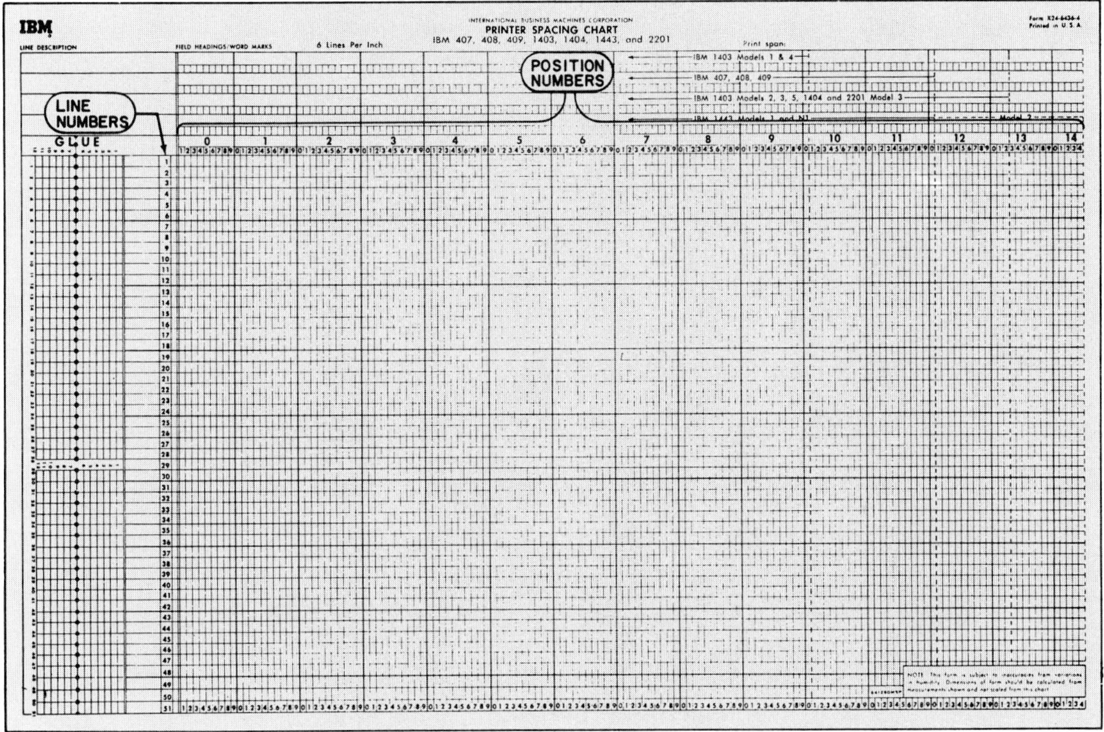

Figure 11–6. Printer Spacing Chart.

The Printer Spacing Chart will provide the programmer with the following information.

1. The format of the desired headings.
2. The number of printing positions necessary for output including editing symbols such as commas, periods, dollar signs, etc.
3. The number of characters in each field and whether they are alphabetic, numeric, or alphanumeric characters.
4. The total lines and different levels of totals desired.
5. Any special skipping or vertical spacing.
6. Any zero suppression desired.
7. Any constant data needed.

Each field that is used must be given a name so that it can be referred to in the program. This is usually done at the same time the spacing chart is prepared, since the names should be close to the fields for easy identification. The names are assigned by the programmer and should be similar to the actual field names for referral (Fig. 11.7).

SPECIFICATION FORMS

After the problem has been evaluated as to the requirements of the desired report, the programmer must make the information available to the RPG processor program. This is accomplished through the preparation of the following specification sheets (Fig. 11.8).

COMMON ENTRIES

The following entries on a RPG coding sheet are common to all specification forms.

1. Columns 1–2	PAGE
2. Columns 3–5	LINE
3. Column 6	FORM TYPE
4. Column 7	COMMENTS
5. Columns 75–80	PROGRAM IDENTIFICATION

PAGE—Columns 1–2

Columns 1–2 in the upper right corner of each sheet are used to number the specification sheets for each job. More than one type of sheet may be used if needed, but all specification sheets of the same type must be kept together. When all the specification sheets are filled out, they are arranged in the following order:

1. *Control Card and File Description.* The control card is required for every program. The control card may provide special information about the program. An *H* must be entered in column 6 of the control card even if all the other control card columns are left blank.
2. *Extension and Line Counter.*
3. *Input.*
4. *Calculation.*
5. *Output-Format.*

The sheets should be numbered in ascending order.

LINE—Columns 3–5

Columns 3–5 are used to number the lines on each page. Columns 3–4 are preprinted on each sheet, so in most cases line numbering is already done. A zero may be added to column 5.

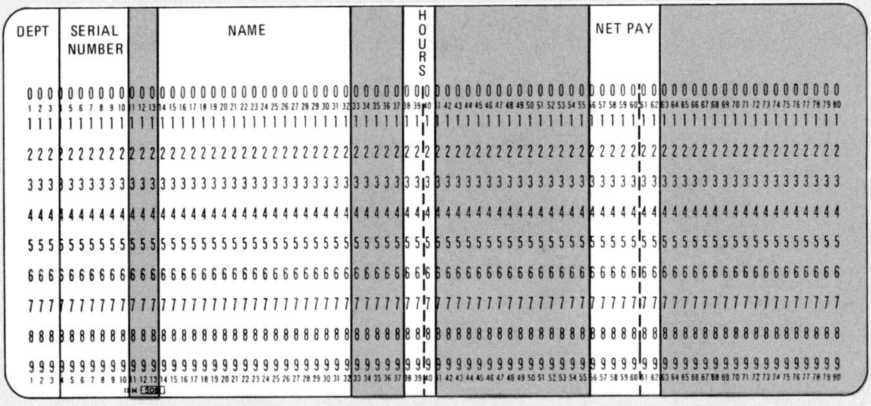

DEPT.	SERIAL NUMBER	N A M E		HOURS WORKED		NET PAY
1	1234560	SMITH	JW	40.1		285.15
1	1892750	JONES	RA	39.6		152.16
1	8929016	MAUS	JB	62.5		182.55
					$	619.86
2	0238648	GOLDMAN	H	31.7		100.25
2	0333367	WOLFE	DJ	9.5		26.60
					$	126.85

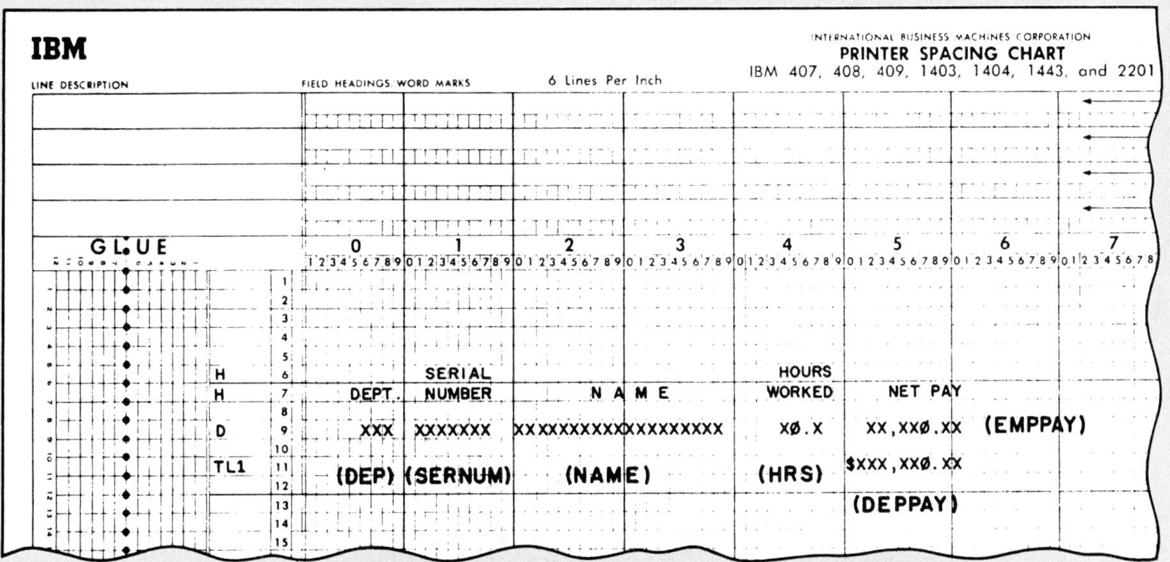

Figure 11–7. Printer Spacing Chart—RPG Layout.

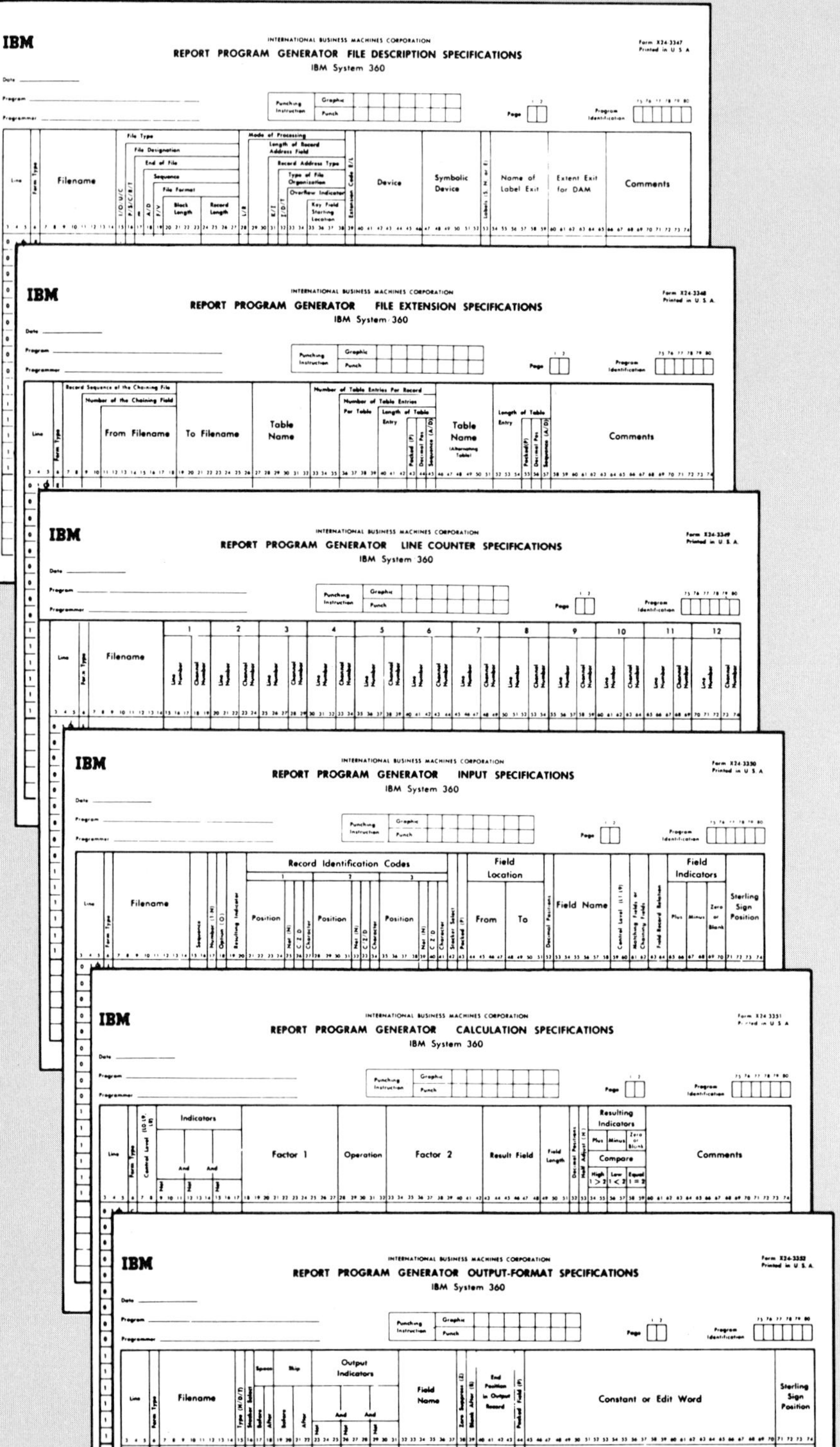

IBM

INTERNATIONAL BUSINESS MACHINES CORPORATION

REPORT PROGRAM GENERATOR FILE DESCRIPTION SPECIFICATIONS

IBM System 360

Form X24-3347
Printed in U.S.A.

Date
Program
Programmer

Punching Instruction: Graphic / Punch

Page

Program Identification

Line | Form Type | Filename | File Type | File Designation | End of File | Sequence | File Format | Block Length | Record Length | Mode of Processing | Length of Record Address Field | Record Address Type | Type of File Organization | Overflow Indicator | Key Field Starting Location | Extension Code E/L | Device | Symbolic Device | Labels | Name of Label Exit | Extent Exit for DAM | Comments

IBM

INTERNATIONAL BUSINESS MACHINES CORPORATION

REPORT PROGRAM GENERATOR FILE EXTENSION SPECIFICATIONS

IBM System 360

Form X24-3348
Printed in U.S.A.

Date
Program
Programmer

Punching Instruction: Graphic / Punch

Page

Program Identification

Line | Form Type | Record Sequence of the Chaining File | Number of the Chaining Field | From Filename | To Filename | Table Name | Number of Table Entries Per Record | Number of Table Entries Per Table | Length of Table Entry | Packed (P) | Decimal Pos | Sequence (A/D) | Table Name (Alternating Table) | Length of Table Entry | Packed (P) | Decimal Pos | Sequence (A/D) | Comments

IBM

INTERNATIONAL BUSINESS MACHINES CORPORATION

REPORT PROGRAM GENERATOR LINE COUNTER SPECIFICATIONS

IBM System 360

Form X24-3349
Printed in U.S.A.

Date
Program
Programmer

Punching Instruction: Graphic / Punch

Page

Program Identification

Line | Form Type | Filename | 1 | 2 | 3 | 4 | 5 | 6 | 7 | 8 | 9 | 10 | 11 | 12 (each: Line Number, Channel Number)

IBM

INTERNATIONAL BUSINESS MACHINES CORPORATION

REPORT PROGRAM GENERATOR INPUT SPECIFICATIONS

IBM System 360

Form X24-3350
Printed in U.S.A.

Date
Program
Programmer

Punching Instruction: Graphic / Punch

Page

Program Identification

Line | Form Type | Filename | Sequence | Number (1-N) | Option (O) | Resulting Indicator | Record Identification Codes (1, 2, 3: Position, Not (N), C/Z/D, Character) | Stacker Select | Packed (P) | Field Location: From, To | Decimal Positions | Field Name | Control Level (L1-L9) | Matching Fields or Chaining Fields | Field Record Relation | Field Indicators: Plus, Minus, Zero or Blank | Sterling Sign Position

IBM

INTERNATIONAL BUSINESS MACHINES CORPORATION

REPORT PROGRAM GENERATOR CALCULATION SPECIFICATIONS

IBM System 360

Form X24-3351
Printed in U.S.A.

Date
Program
Programmer

Punching Instruction: Graphic / Punch

Page

Program Identification

Line | Form Type | Control Level (L0-L9, LR) | Indicators: Not, And, Not, And, Not | Factor 1 | Operation | Factor 2 | Result Field | Field Length | Decimal Positions | Half Adjust (H) | Resulting Indicators: Plus, Minus, Zero or Blank; Compare: High 1 > 2, Low 1 < 2, Equal 1 = 2 | Comments

IBM

INTERNATIONAL BUSINESS MACHINES CORPORATION

REPORT PROGRAM GENERATOR OUTPUT-FORMAT SPECIFICATIONS

IBM System 360

Form X24-3352
Printed in U.S.A.

Date
Program
Programmer

Punching Instruction: Graphic / Punch

Page

Program Identification

Line | Form Type | Filename | Type (H/D/T) | Stacker Select | Space: Before, After | Skip: Before, After | Output Indicators: Not, And, Not, And, Not | Field Name | Zero Suppress (Z) | Blank After (B) | End Position in Output Record | Packed Field (P) | Constant or Edit Word | Sterling Sign Position

Figure 11–8. RPG Specification Forms.

FORM TYPE—Column 6

Column 6 contains a preprinted letter on all sheets. The letter identifies the type of specifications for each line of coding. The control card containing *H* in column 6 must always be the first card in the RPG source program deck.

Entry	*Explanation*
H	Header card (control card specification)
F	File description specifications
E	Extension specifications
L	Line counter specifications
I	Input specifications
C	Calculation specifications
O	Output-format specifications

COMMENTS—Column 7

Comments are often written to help you understand or remember what you are doing in a certain section of coding. RPG allows you to use an entire line for these comments. The comment line is identified by placing an asterisk in column 7. Any characters in the character set may be used in a comment line. A card is punched from this line and the comments appear in the source program listing.

Comments are *not* instructions to the RPG program. They serve only as a means of documenting your program.

PROGRAM IDENTIFICATION—Columns 75–80

Columns 75–80 may contain any characters. These columns are used to identify the program. These entries are ignored by the compiler but will appear in the source program listing.

FILE DESCRIPTION SPECIFICATIONS

These forms are used to describe all files to be used by the object program (Fig. 11.9). Each line of the form describes one file. The forms will also be used to identify input and output devices associated with the files.

FILE EXTENSION AND LINE COUNTER SPECIFICATIONS (Figs. 11.10, 11.11)

These forms contain two types of specifications:

1. Extension specifications provide information about tables, arrays, and record address files.
2. Line counter specifications provide information about the number of lines to be printed on the forms that are used.

RPG CONTROL FILE DESCRIPTION SPECIFICATIONS

Date ______ Program ______ Programmer ______

Punching Instruction: Graphic / Punch — Page (1 2) — Program Identification (75 76 77 78 79 80)

File Description Specifications

Line (3-5)	Form Type (6)	Filename (7-14)	File Type I/O/U/C/D (15)	File Designation P/S/C/R/T/D (16)	End of File E (17)	Sequence A/D (18)	File Format F/V (19)	Block Length (20-23)	Record Length (24-27)	L/R (28)	Length of Key Field or of Record Address Field (29-30)	Record Address Type A/K/I (31)	Type of File Organization or Additional Area I/D/T or 1-9 (32)	Overflow Indicator (33-34)	Key Field Starting Location (35-38)	Extension Code E/L (39)	Device (40-46)	Symbolic Device (47-52)	Labels (S, N, or E) (53)	Name of Label Exit (54-59)	Extent Exit for DAM / Core Index (60-65)	A/U (66)	File Addition/Unordered (67)	Number of Tracks for Cylinder Overflow (68-69)	N/U (70)	Number of Extents (71-72)	Tape Rewind (73)	File Condition U1-U8 (74)
0 2	F	NAMECARD	I	P			F	80									READ40	SYSIPT										
0 3	F	LISTING	O				F	132						OF			PRINTER	SYSOPT										
0 4	F																											
0 5	F																											
0 6	F																											
0 7	F																											
	F																											
	F																											

Figure 11–9. RPG File Description Form—Example.

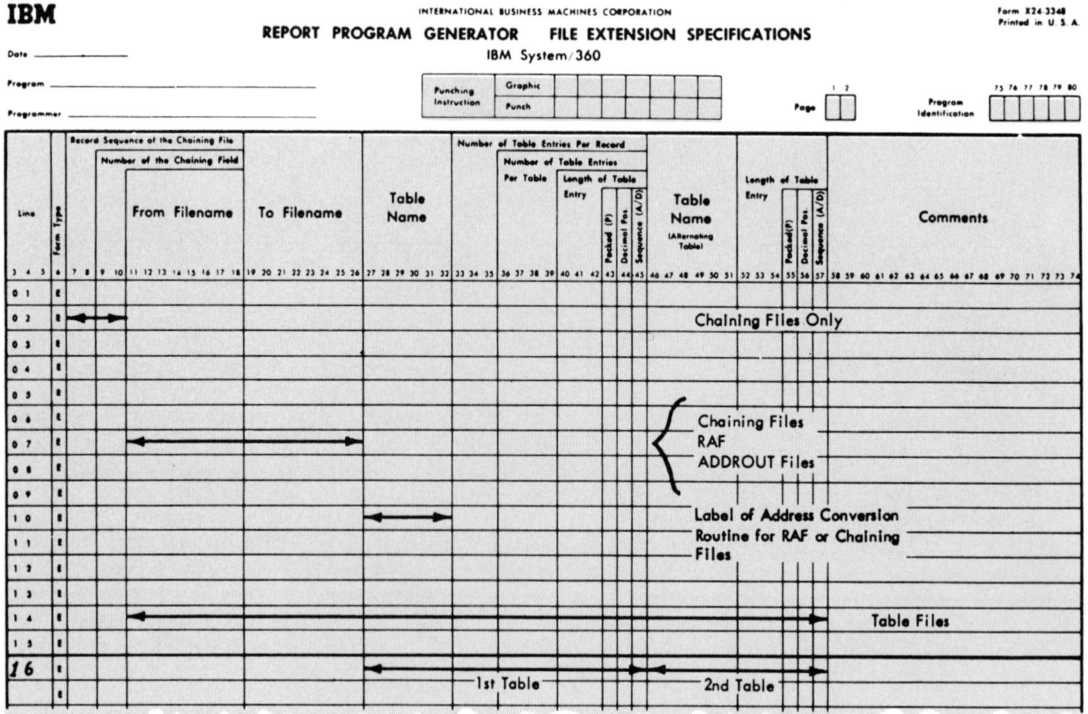
IBM

INTERNATIONAL BUSINESS MACHINES CORPORATION

REPORT PROGRAM GENERATOR FILE EXTENSION SPECIFICATIONS

IBM System/360

Form X24-3348
Printed in U. S. A.

Date ______ Program ______ Programmer ______

Punching Instruction: Graphic / Punch — Page (1 2) — Program Identification (75 76 77 78 79 80)

Line (3-5)	Form Type (6)	Record Sequence of the Chaining File (7-8)	Number of the Chaining Field (9-10)	From Filename (11-18)	To Filename (19-26)	Table Name (27-32)	Number of Table Entries Per Record (33-35)	Number of Table Entries Per Table (36-39)	Length of Table Entry (40-42)	Packed (P) (43)	Decimal Pos. (44)	Sequence (A/D) (45)	Table Name (Alternating Table) (46-51)	Length of Table Entry (52-54)	Packed (P) (55)	Decimal Pos. (56)	Sequence (A/D) (57)	Comments (58-74)
0 1	E																	
0 2	E	←→											Chaining Files Only					
0 3	E																	
0 4	E																	
0 5	E																	
0 6	E																	
0 7	E			←→	←→								Chaining Files / RAF / ADDROUT Files					
0 8	E																	
0 9	E																	
1 0	E					←→							Label of Address Conversion Routine for RAF or Chaining Files					
1 1	E																	
1 2	E																	
1 3	E																	
1 4	E			←→	←→	←→	←→	←→	←→	←→	←→	←→	←→	←→	←→	←→	←→	Table Files
1 5	E																	
16	E					←→ 1st Table	←→	←→	←→	←→	←→	←→	←→ 2nd Table	←→	←→	←→	←→	
	E																	

Figure 11–10. RPG File Extension Form.

ELECTRICAL SHEET STEEL STANDARD GAUGE

Gauge #	Thickness	Gauge #	Thickness
11	0.1250	17	0.0560
12	0.1090	18	0.0500
13	0.0940	19	0.0435
14	0.0780	20	0.0375
15	0.0700	21	0.0340
16	0.0625	22	0.0310

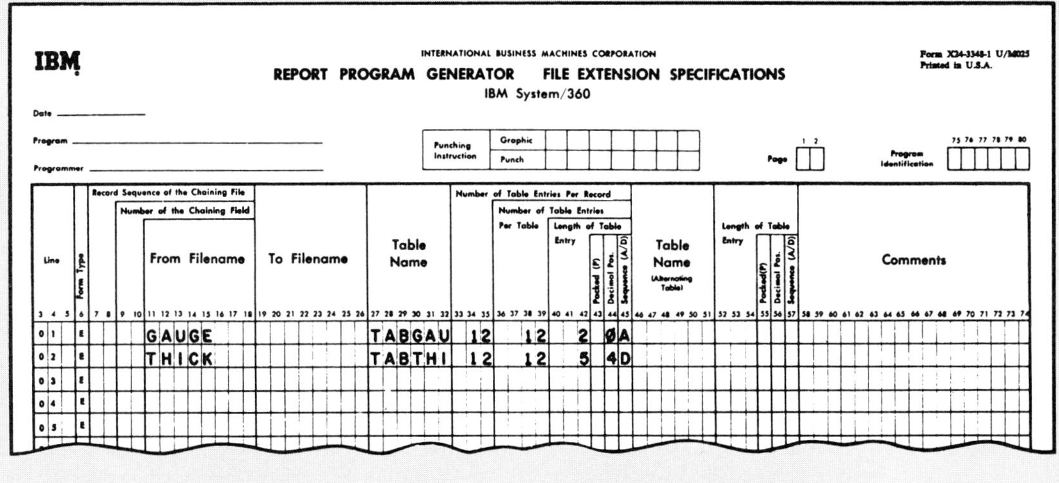

IBM INTERNATIONAL BUSINESS MACHINES CORPORATION

REPORT PROGRAM GENERATOR FILE EXTENSION SPECIFICATIONS

IBM System/360

Form X24-3348-1 U/M025
Printed in U.S.A.

Date
Program
Programmer

Punching Instruction: Graphic / Punch

Page 1 2 — Program Identification 75 76 77 78 79 80

Line (3–5)	Form Type (6)	Record Sequence of the Chaining File (7–8)	Number of the Chaining Field (9–10)	From Filename (11–18)	To Filename (19–26)	Table Name (27–32)	Number of Table Entries Per Record (33–35)	Number of Table Entries Per Table (36–39)	Length of Table Entry (40–42)	Packed (P) (43)	Decimal Pos. (44)	Sequence (A/D) (45)	Table Name (Alternating Table) (46–51)	Length of Table Entry (52–54)	Packed(P) (55)	Decimal Pos. (56)	Sequence (A/D) (57)	Comments (58–74)
01	E			GAUGE		TABGAU	12	12	2		Ø	A						
02	E			THICK		TABTHI	12	12	5		4	D						
03	E																	
04	E																	
05	E																	

Figure 11–11. RPG File Extension Form—Example.

INPUT SPECIFICATIONS (Figs. 11.12, 11.13)

These forms are used to describe the input files, such as record layouts and fields within the record. The records within each input or combined file are described. The relationship of one record to another record is also specified in these forms. The first half of the form is used for record identification while the remaining columns are used to describe each field within a record. One line is used for each record and a separate line is used for each field. The specific input units used need not be identified on these forms inasmuch as they have been specified in the file description sheets.

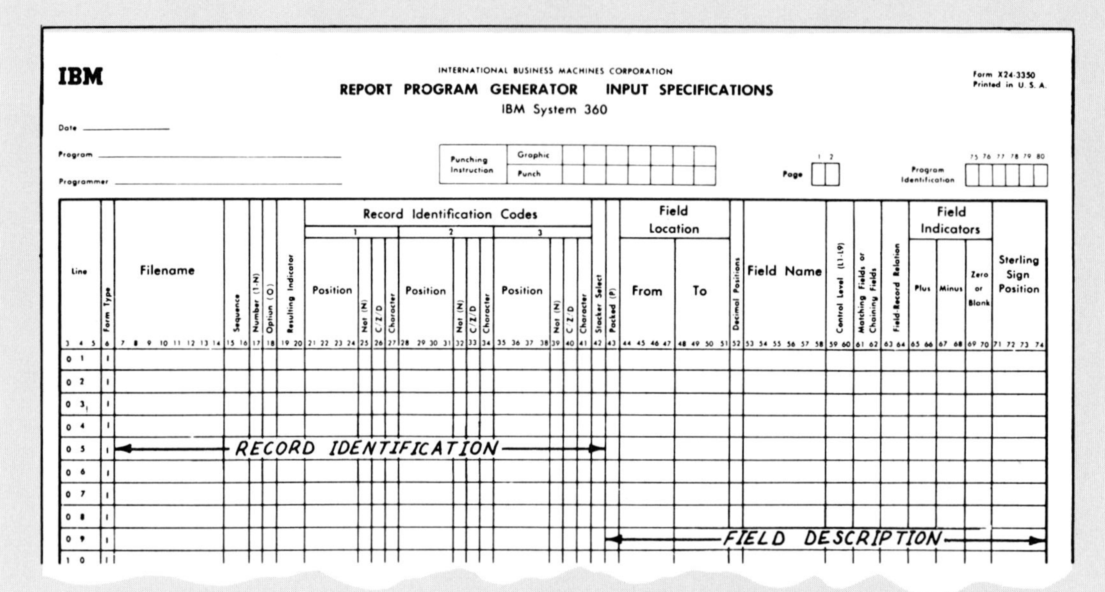

IBM

INTERNATIONAL BUSINESS MACHINES CORPORATION

REPORT PROGRAM GENERATOR INPUT SPECIFICATIONS

IBM System 360

Form X24-3350
Printed in U.S.A.

Date ______
Program ______
Programmer ______

Punching Instruction: Graphic / Punch

Page 1 2

Program Identification 75 76 77 78 79 80

Line	Form Type	Filename	Sequence	Number (1-N)	Option (O)	Resulting Indicator	Record Identification Codes 1: Position	Not (N)	C/Z/D	Character	2: Position	Not (N)	C/Z/D	Character	3: Position	Not (N)	C/Z/D	Character	Stacker Select	Packed (P)	Field Location: From	To	Decimal Positions	Field Name	Control Level (L1-L9)	Matching Fields or Chaining Fields	Field-Record Relation	Field Indicators: Plus	Minus	Zero or Blank	Sterling Sign Position
3 4 5	6	7 8 9 10 11 12 13 14	15 16	17	18	19 20	21 22 23 24	25	26	27	28 29 30 31	32	33	34	35 36 37 38	39	40	41	42	43	44 45 46 47	48 49 50 51	52	53 54 55 56 57 58	59 60	61 62	63 64	65 66	67 68	69 70	71 72 73 74
0 1	I																														
0 2	I																														
0 3	I																														
0 4	I																														
0 5	I	← RECORD IDENTIFICATION →																													
0 6	I																														
0 7	I																														
0 8	I																														
0 9	I																					← FIELD DESCRIPTION →									
1 0	I																														

Figure 11–12. RPG Input Specification Forms.

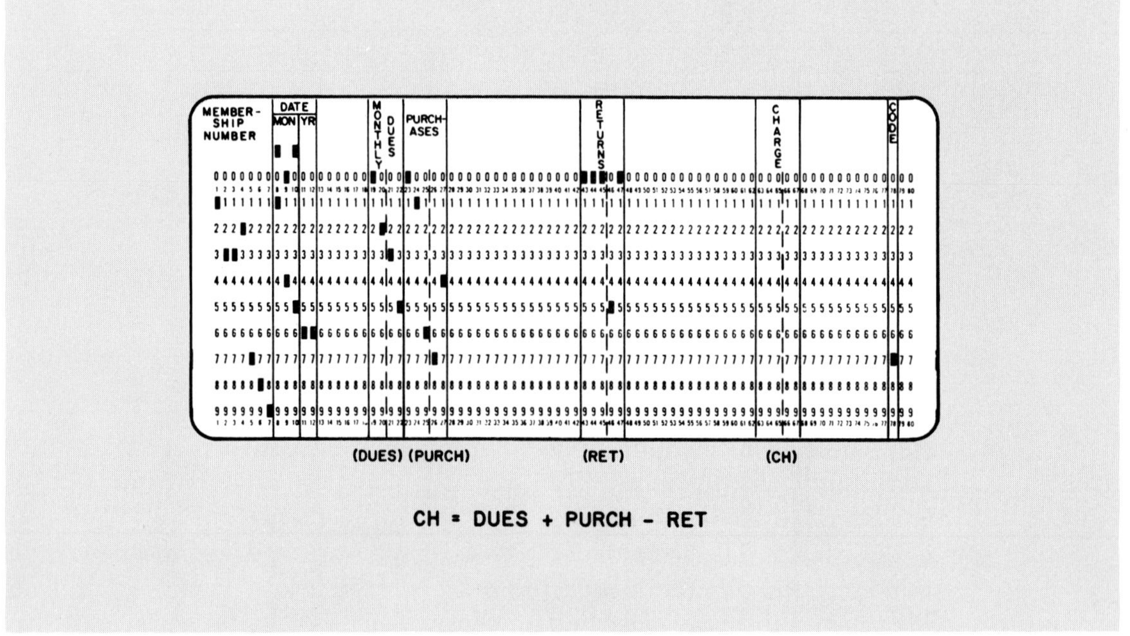

Figure 11–13. RPG Input Specification Form—Example.

CALCULATION SPECIFICATIONS (Figs. 11.14, 11.15)

These forms are used to specify all the operations to be performed on the data. The nature of the processing such as add, subtract, multiply, divide, are

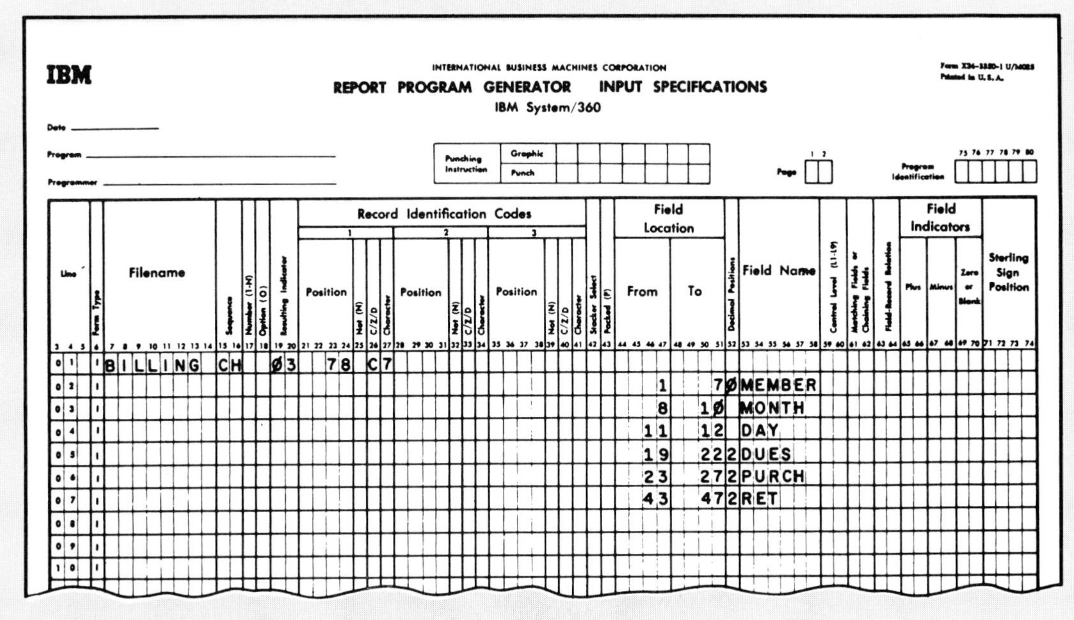

IBM

INTERNATIONAL BUSINESS MACHINES CORPORATION

REPORT PROGRAM GENERATOR INPUT SPECIFICATIONS

IBM System/360

Date ______ Program ______ Programmer ______

Punching Instruction: Graphic / Punch — Page — Program Identification

Line	Form Type	Filename	Sequence	Number (1-N)	Option (O)	Resulting Indicator	Record Identification Codes 1: Position	Not (N)	C/Z/D	Character	Field Location: From	To	Decimal Positions	Field Name
01	I	BILLING	CH			Ø3	78		C	7				
02	I										1	7	Ø	MEMBER
03	I										8	1Ø		MONTH
04	I										11	12		DAY
05	I										19	22	2	DUES
06	I										23	27	2	PURCH
07	I										43	47	2	RET
08	I													
09	I													
10	I													

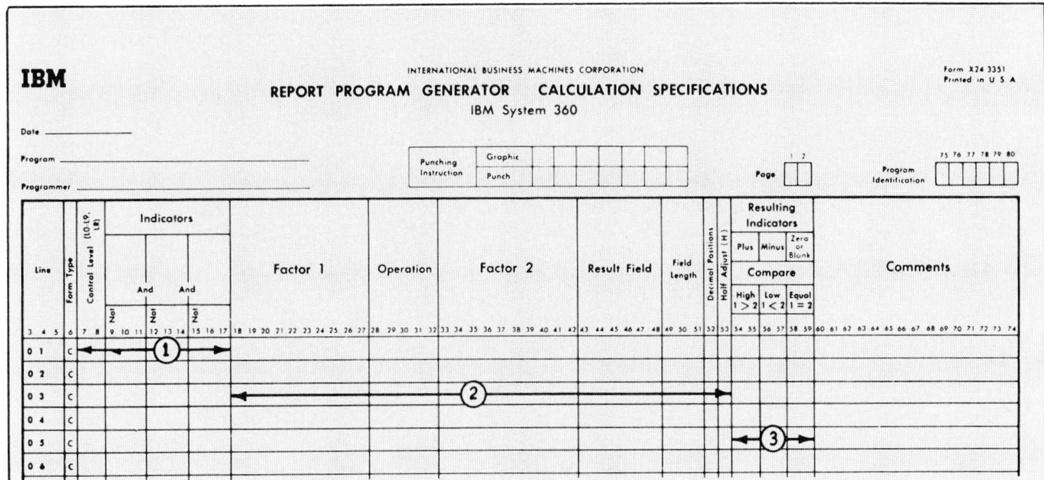

IBM

INTERNATIONAL BUSINESS MACHINES CORPORATION

REPORT PROGRAM GENERATOR CALCULATION SPECIFICATIONS

IBM System 360

Form X24 3351 Printed in U.S.A.

Date ______ Program ______ Programmer ______

Punching Instruction: Graphic / Punch — Page — Program Identification

Line	Form Type	Control Level (L0-L9, LR)	Indicators (Not, And Not, And Not)	Factor 1	Operation	Factor 2	Result Field	Field Length	Decimal Positions	Half Adjust (H)	Resulting Indicators: Plus / Minus / Zero or Blank — Compare: High 1 > 2 / Low 1 < 2 / Equal 1 = 2	Comments
01	C	← (1) →										
02	C											
03	C			← (2) →								
04	C											
05	C										← (3) →	
06	C											

Figure 11–14. RPG Calculation Form.

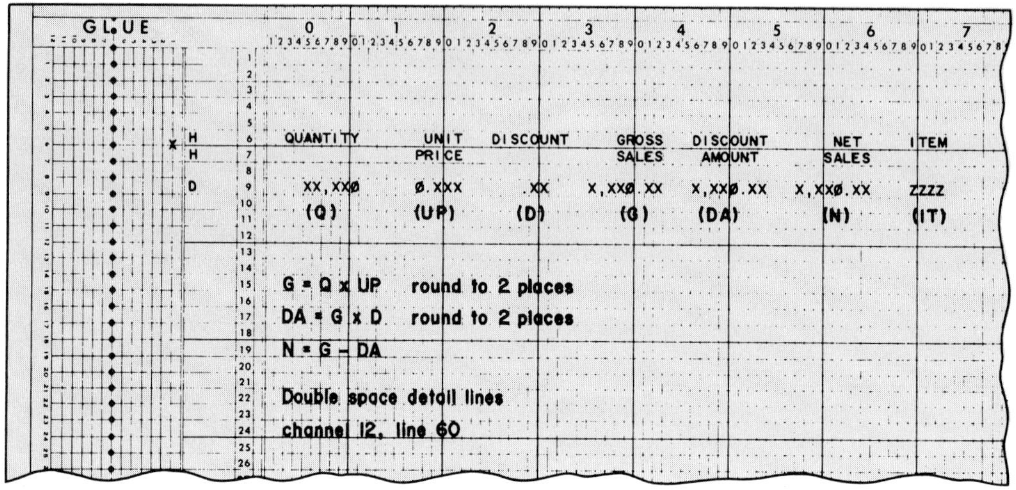

Problem Statement:

Compute the value for Gross Sales (G) and Discount Amount (DA), rounding each to the nearest cent. Next, compute the value of Net Sales (N). The formulas for these calculations are shown on the spacing chart. Each input record has these fields:

Quantity	5 positions	no decimals
Unit Price	4 positions	3 decimals
Discount	2 positions	2 decimals

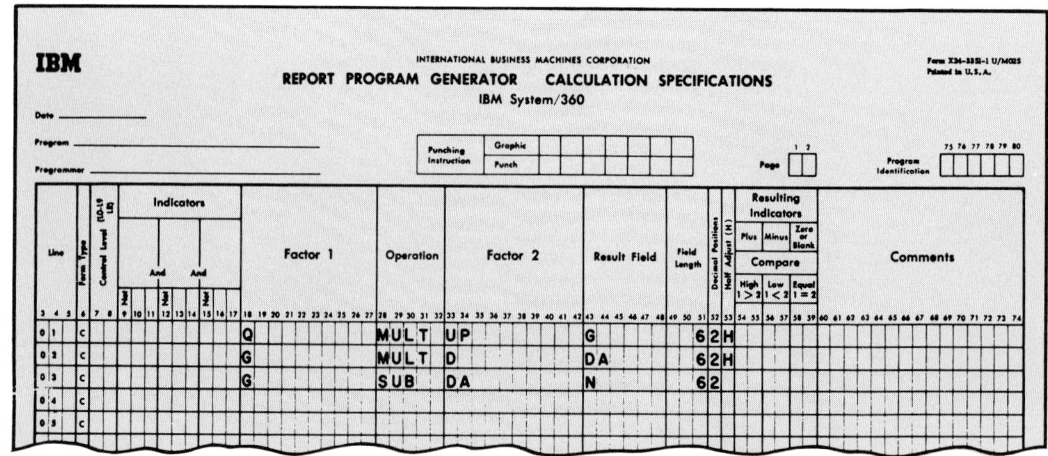

IBM INTERNATIONAL BUSINESS MACHINES CORPORATION

REPORT PROGRAM GENERATOR CALCULATION SPECIFICATIONS

IBM System/360

Line	Form Type	Control Level	Indicators	Factor 1	Operation	Factor 2	Result Field	Field Length	Decimal Positions	Half Adjust (H)	Resulting Indicators	Comments
01	C			Q	MULT	UP	G	6	2	H		
02	C			G	MULT	D	DA	6	2	H		
03	C			G	SUB	DA	N	6	2			
04	C											
05	C											

Figure 11–15. RPG Calculation Form—Example.

described in these forms. Each operation is specified on a separate line of the form in the sequence in which it is to be processed. All detail calculations are performed before the total calculations.

OUTPUT-FORMAT SPECIFICATIONS (Figs. 11.16, 11.17)

These forms describe how the finished report is to look. The types of output files to be produced as well as the location of the data in output records and reports are also described. The specification of these forms will identify the output records of which the files are comprised. The selection of the appropriate stacker for the cards, the spacing in the printed reports and under what conditions the report is to be produced will also be described in these sheets.

All field descriptions will be written in entries immediately following the file in which they appear. These specifications will tell when and where the fields are to be placed in the output record. The specific output device need not be specified in these forms as the file description forms indicate the device to be used for each file. All that is required for identification with the file is the writing of the record on the output form.

Edit words are used to punctuate numeric fields with the necessary commas, dollar signs, periods, and signs to make the output data more readable (Figs. 11.18, 11.19, 11.20).

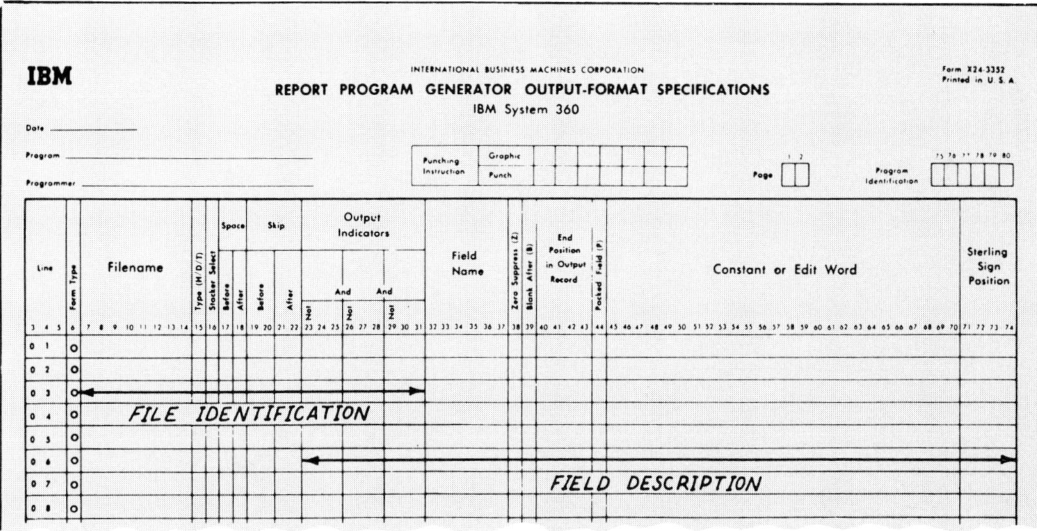
IBM

INTERNATIONAL BUSINESS MACHINES CORPORATION

REPORT PROGRAM GENERATOR OUTPUT-FORMAT SPECIFICATIONS

IBM System 360

Form X24-3352
Printed in U. S. A.

Date ______

Program ______

Programmer ______

Punching Instruction: Graphic / Punch

Page (1 2)

Program Identification (75 76 77 78 79 80)

Line (3–5)	Form Type (6)	Filename (7–14)	Type (H/D/T) (15)	Stacker Select (16)	Space Before (17)	Space After (18)	Skip Before (19–20)	Skip After (21–22)	Output Indicators Not (23–25)	And Not (26–28)	And Not (29–31)	Field Name (32–37)	Zero Suppress (Z) (38)	Blank After (B) (39)	End Position in Output Record (40–43)	Packed Field (P) (44)	Constant or Edit Word (45–70)	Sterling Sign Position (71–74)
0 1	O																	
0 2	O																	
0 3	O	←									→							
0 4	O	FILE IDENTIFICATION																
0 5	O																	
0 6	O								←									→
0 7	O														FIELD DESCRIPTION			
0 8	O																	

Figure 11–16. RPG Output Specification Form.

GLUE

Line		
3–4		GROSS/NET SALES REPORT
7–8		OFFICE | GROSS SALES | NET SALES
10	D	XXX | $XX,XXØ.XX | $XX,XXØ.XX
11–12		(OFFICE) | (GROSS) | (NET)
14	TLR	TOTALS | $X,XXX,XXØ.XX | $X,XXX,XXØ.XX
15–16		| (TGROSS) | (TNET)

Single space detail lines
channel 12, line 48

GROSS/NET SALES REPORT

OFFICE	GROSS SALES	NET SALES
008	$14,000.00	$ 3,500.00
017	$ 6,500.00	$ 1,500.00
023	$10,570.00	$ 2,480.65
024	$ 1,256.00	$ 840.60
030	$12,000.00	$ 8,009.75
031	$ 7,840.00	$ 4,400.00
032	$11,248.00	$10,000.00
247	$22,350.00	$ 4,100.00
TOTALS	$1,053,420.00	$ 911,580.65

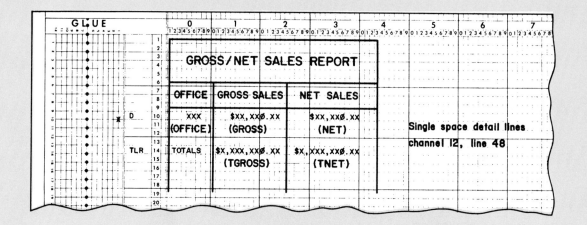

IBM — INTERNATIONAL BUSINESS MACHINES CORPORATION
REPORT PROGRAM GENERATOR OUTPUT-FORMAT SPECIFICATIONS
IBM System/360

Form X24-3352-1 U/M 085
Printed in U.S.A.

Line	Form Type	Filename	Type (H/D/T)	Stacker Select	Space Before	Space After	Skip Before	Skip After	Output Indicators	Field Name	Zero Suppress (Z)	Blank After (B)	End Position in Output Record	Packed Field (P)	Constant or Edit Word	Sterling Sign Position
01	O	GROSSNET	D			1			Ø1							
02	O									OFFICE			7			
03	O									GROSS			23		'$, Ø. '	
04	O									NET			39		'$, Ø. '	
05	O		T		3				LR							
06	O												7		'TOTALS'	
07	O									TGROSS			23		'$, , Ø. '	
08	O									TNET			39		'$, , Ø. '	
09	O															

Figure 11–17. RPG Output Specification Form—Example.

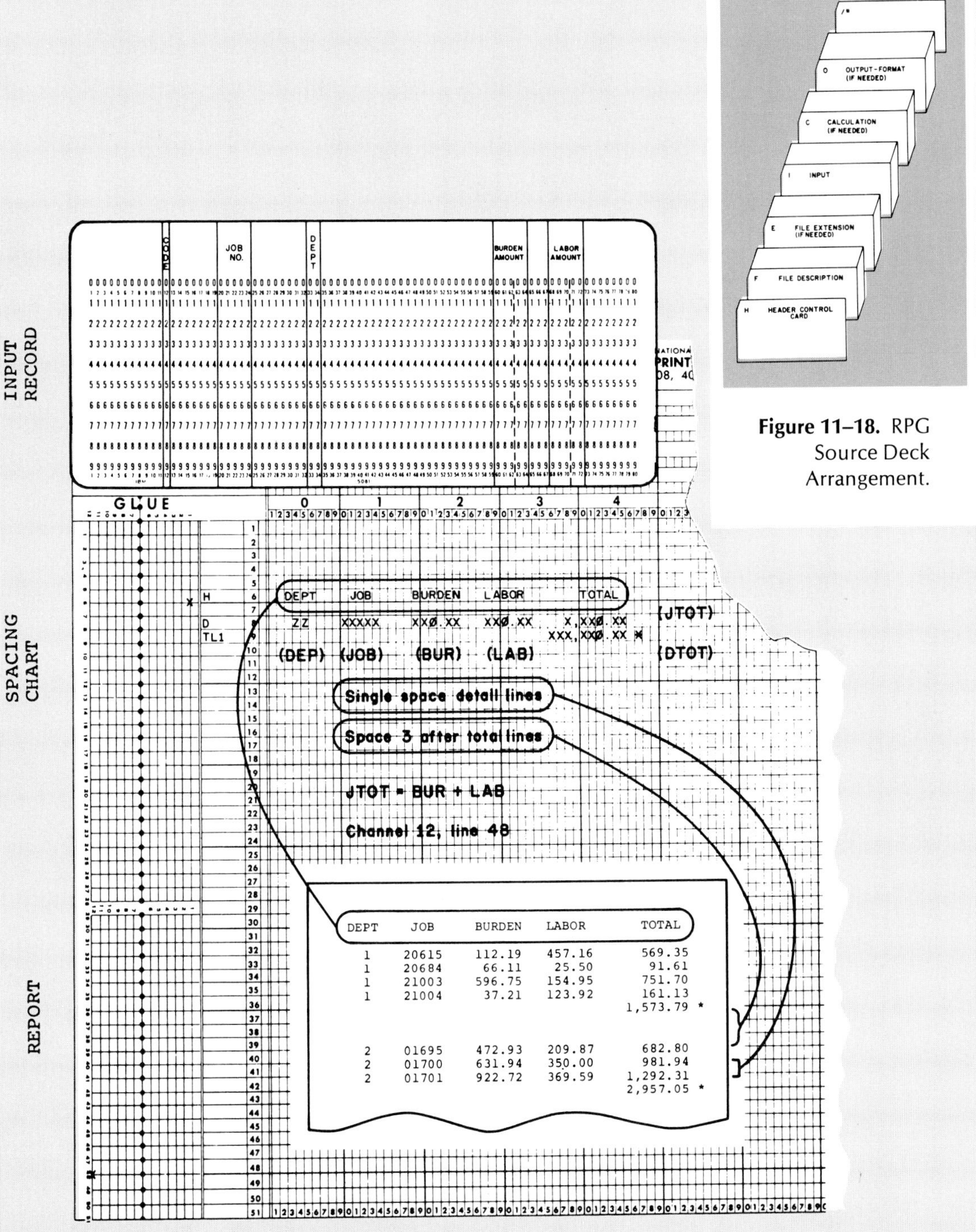

Figure 11–18. RPG Source Deck Arrangement.

Figure 11–19. RPG Programming Example.

SPECIFICATIONS FORMS

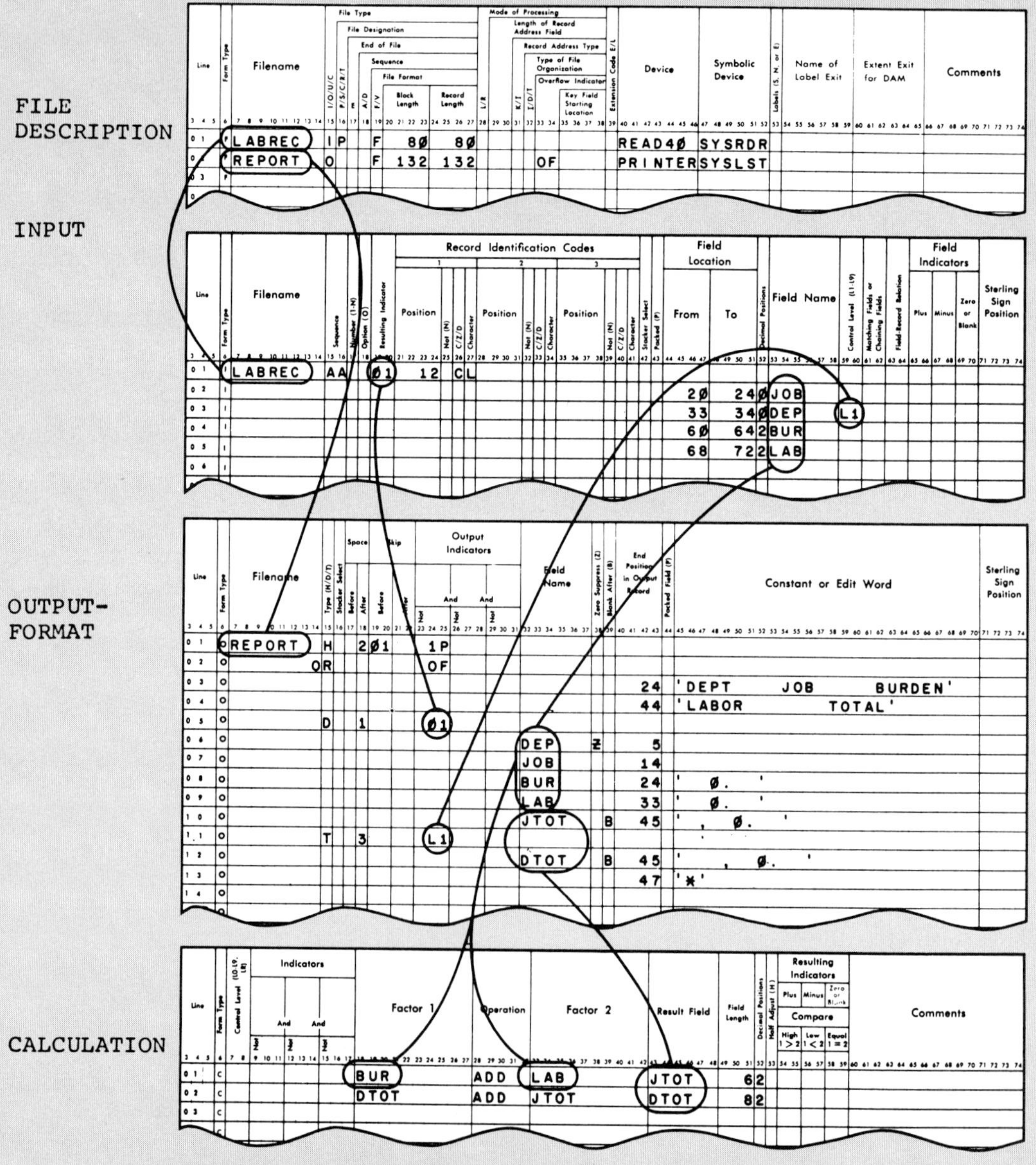

Figure 11–20. RPG Programming Example.

SUMMARY

Report Program Generator is a problem-oriented programming language designed to solve a particular problem. A problem-oriented programming language describes the problem to the computer without detailing the procedures involved. It is the intent of the chapter to describe the features of the most widely used problem-oriented programming language, Report Program Generator (RPG).

I. *Report Program Generator (RPG).*
   A. *Purpose*—to provide the programmer with an easy and efficient method of generating a computer program.
   B. *Specification sheets*—generate machine language program instructions together with assigned storage areas for data input and output, work areas, and constants.
   C. *Principles of RPG programming.*
      1. *Problem defined*—flowcharts prepared.
      2. *Printer spacing chart*—outputs defined. A work sheet for the printer to be used as a form for coding specification sheets.
      3. *Specification sheets prepared.*
         a) *File Description*—describes each file to be used by the program.
         b) *Input*—describes input records, including record layouts and file fields within records.
         c) *Calculation*—specifies all operations to be performed on the data.
         d) *Output-Format*—describes how the finished report is to look.
      4. Cards are punched from specification sheets.
      5. Punched cards together with necessary Job Control Cards are entered into the machine for compilation.
      6. If compilation is successful, input cards are read in from preparation of the desired output.

IDENTIFICATION QUESTIONS

Match the following terms with the statements that follow.

A. Calculation Specifications
B. Comments
C. Edit Words
D. File Description Specifications
E. File Extension and Line Counter
F. Input Specifications
G. Output-Format Specifications
H. Printer Spacing Chart
I. Problem-Oriented Programming Language
J. Specification Sheets

1. A means of documenting a program.
2. These forms provide information about tables, arrays, etc., and also specify the number of lines to be printed.
3. A programming language that describes the problem to the computer without detailing the procedures involved.
4. These forms specify all operations to be performed on the data.

5. These entries are used to punctuate fields to make the output more readable.
6. These forms automatically generate machine language instructions together with automatically assigned storage areas.
7. These forms describe fields and record layouts on input files.
8. These forms define the output format and serve as a coding form for the particular operation.
9. These forms are used to describe the finished report.
10. These forms are used to describe all files to be used by the object program.

QUESTIONS FOR REVIEW

1. What are the main reasons for using RPG?
2. What are the main functions of RPG?
3. What steps are necessary to prepare a RPG program?
4. What information must appear on a Printer Spacing Chart?
5. What are the principal types of specification forms used in RPG and what are the principal purposes of each?
6. What are the main functions of each type of RPG specification form?

CHAPTER 12
FORTRAN

The FORTRAN (FORmula TRANslation) language is a procedure-oriented programming language designed primarily for writing programs to solve scientific and engineering problems involving mathematical computations. FORTRAN is a compromise between the language of the computer and the language of the engineer and scientist. To satisfy the computer, symbols are used that the computer can understand. This requires that the rules for their use be followed closely. To satisfy the engineer and scientist, as many of the detailed computer control operations as possible are eliminated from writing of the programs, and a problem statement format close to that of the mathematical notation is used.

The FORTRAN language is especially useful in writing programs for applications that involve mathematical computations and other manipulation of numeric data, and with the increased use of mathematics in business, more and more FORTRAN programs are being written for commercial applications.

Source programs are written in the FORTRAN language. They consist of a set of statements constructed from the language elements described herein. In the compilation process, the source statements are translated into machine language (object program). In addition, when the FORTRAN compiler detects errors in the source program, it produces appropriate diagnostic messages (Fig. 12.1).

ELEMENTS OF FORTRAN

STATEMENTS

Source programs consist of a set of statements from which the compiler generates machine instructions, constants and storage areas. The FORTRAN

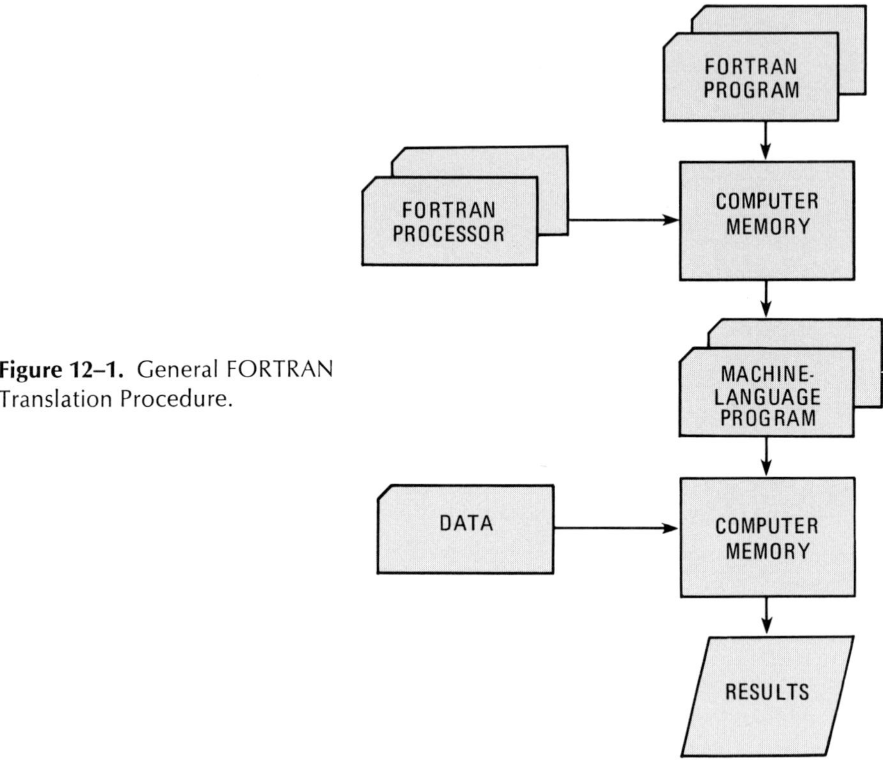

Figure 12–1. General FORTRAN Translation Procedure.

language is composed of statements (individual commands) of a program consisting of operation symbols (+, −, *, /, **) and expressions ($A + B - C$).

Statements are the sentences of FORTRAN and they may

1. Define the arithmetic steps which are to be accomplished by the computer,
2. Provide information for control of the computer during the execution of the program,
3. Describe the input and output operations which are necessary to bring in data and punch or write the results,
4. Specify certain additional facts such as the size of the input data that is read by the program.

FORTRAN statements consist of certain keywords that are used in conjunction with certain basic elements of the language: constants and variables. They may be divided into categories according to their function (Fig. 12.2).

a. **Arithmetic Statements** specify the mathematical calculations to be performed.

TYPE	PURPOSE	EXAMPLES
Arithmetic	Specifies a numerical computation	A = C + D − G
Control	Governs the flow of control in the program	GO TO 20 GO TO (25, 31, 9), ITEM IF (X) 6, 8, 12 DO 6 I = 1, 10 CONTINUE PAUSE STOP END
Input or Output	Provides the means of getting information into or out of the computer	READ (5, 6) A, B, C WRITE (6, 76) N, A, B
Specification	Describes the arrangement of data on input or printed line, and also supplies information to the processor	DIMENSION B(25, 50), TABLE (5, 8, 4) INTEGER DEV, SMALL REAL ITA, JOB COMMON A, B, C, R (100) FORMAT (I3, F6.2/I5, F6.2) EQUIVALENCE (B, D(1))
Subprogram	Enables the programmer to define and use subprograms	CALL MATMPY (X, 5, 40, Y, 7, 2) FUNCTION DAV (D, E, F) SUBROUTINE COPY (A, B, N) RETURN

Figure 12–2. Types of FORTRAN Statements.

b. **Control Statements** determine the sequence in which the statements will follow. These statements enable the user to govern the flow and terminate the execution of the program.
c. **Input/Output Statements** read data into the computer for printing or punching the results of the program. In addition to controlling the input and output devices, these statements enable the user to transfer data between internal storage and an input/output media.
d. **Specification Statements** tell the FORTRAN program the amount and kind of input and output data it will process. In addition, these statements specify the amount of storage to be used by variables and the placement of alphabetic and numerical information on the printed page.

CHARACTER SET

The FORTRAN character set is composed of the following characters:

1. Twenty-six letters to the alphabet, A–Z.
2. Ten numerical digits, 0–9.

3. Punctuation characters

period	.	apostrophe	'
comma	,	dollar sign	$
left parenthesis	(	space (indicated	
right parenthesis	)	by a small b)	b

4. Six algebraic symbols

add	+	divide	/
subtract	—	exponentiation	**
multiply	*	equal	=

FORTRAN CODING FORMS

A FORTRAN coding form is available for use as a guide when preparing a source program. Besides providing a written record of the program, the form facilitates the subsequent transfer of the source statements to cards.

The statements of a FORTRAN source program can be written on a standard FORTRAN coding form (Fig. 12.3). Each line of the form represents one 80-column card, and the FORTRAN statements are written one to a line on these forms. If a statement is too long to be completed on one line of the form, it may be continued on as many as 19 successive lines by placing

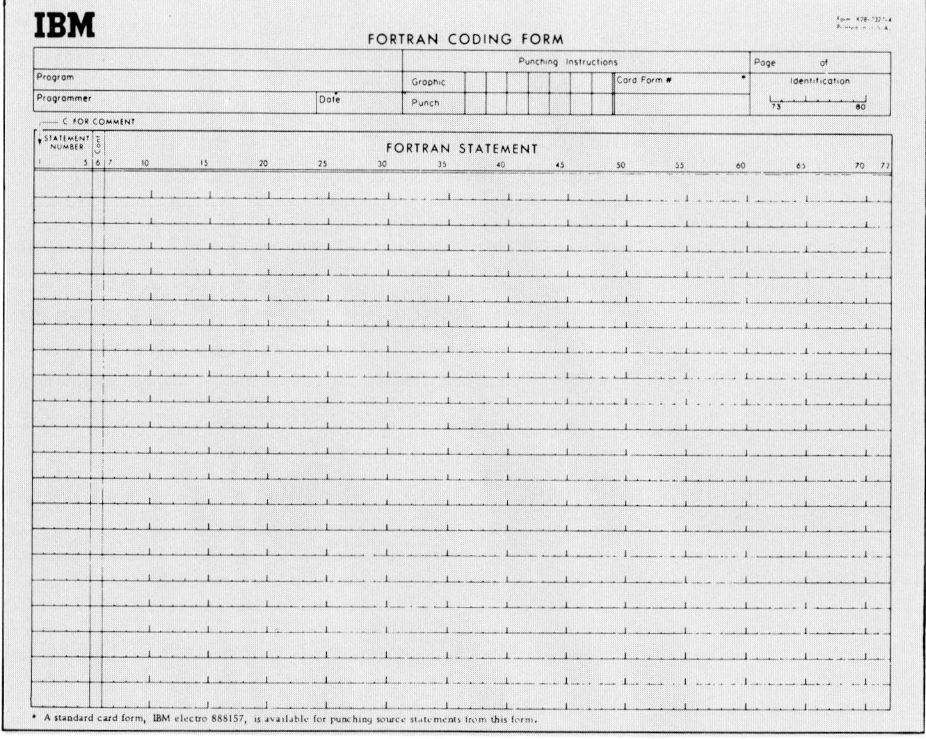
IBM

FORTRAN CODING FORM

Program | Programmer | Date

Punching Instructions: Graphic | Punch | Card Form *

Page of | Identification 73 80

C FOR COMMENT

STATEMENT NUMBER 1 5 | CONT. 6 | FORTRAN STATEMENT 7 10 15 20 25 30 35 40 45 50 55 60 65 70 72

* A standard card form, IBM electro 888157, is available for punching source statements from this form.

Figure 12–3. FORTRAN Coding Sheets.

a continuation indicator in column 6 (any character other than blank or zero). The first card of a statement must always be blank (or contain a zero) in column 6.

Blanks may be inserted anywhere in FORTRAN statements (except literals) to improve the readability of the statement.

The different fields of a FORTRAN coding form are (Fig. 12.4):

1. *Column 1*   *Comment.* A *C* in the first column indicates that a comment is written in that statement. Comments are used as notes and help to clarify some of the statements and improve the readability of the statement. Comments may be written from column 2 through 72 of the form (Fig. 12.5). The comments will be listed with the program; however, they are not processed by the FORTRAN compiler and no part of the comment is translated into machine language. A comment may appear between FORTRAN statements but must not precede a continuation card.

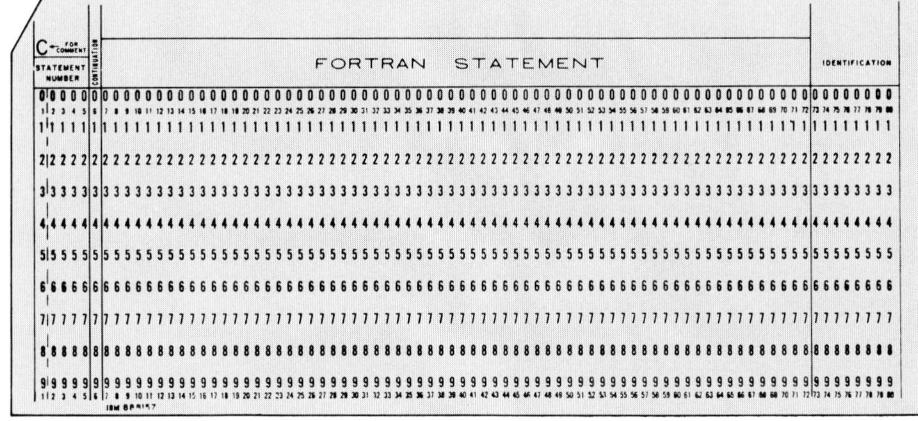

Figure 12–4.
FORTRAN Card.

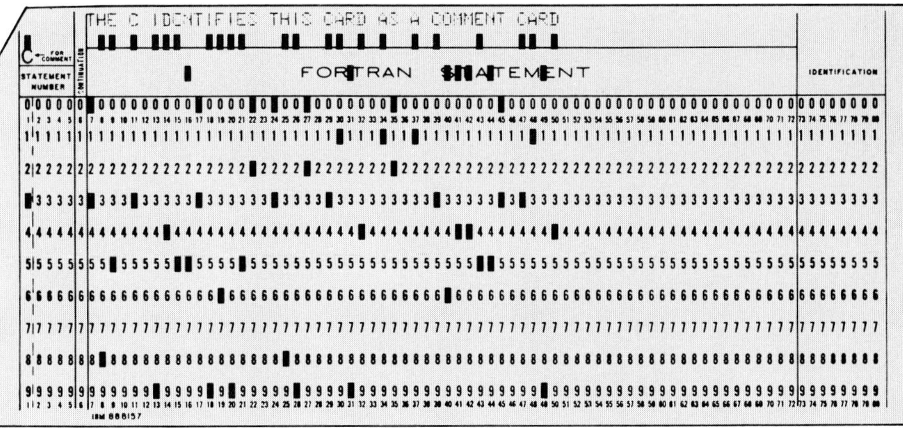

Figure 12–5.
Comment Card.

2. *Columns 1–5* *Statement Number.* These columns are used to write the statement number. A statement number may consist of one to five decimal digits. Blanks or zeros that may precede the statement number are ignored by the compiler. These numbers may be assigned in any order; the value of the statement number does not affect the sequence in which the statements are executed in a FORTRAN program. These numbers will be used as labels to be referred to by other statements in program.

3. *Column 6* *Continuation Indicator.* A nonblank or nonzero character in this field indicates the continuation of a statement from the previous line.

4. *Columns 7–72* *FORTRAN Statement.* Starting in column 7, FORTRAN statements are written up to column 72. One statement per card is punched into a card with the possible exception of a continuation as indicated above.

5. *Columns 72–80* *Identification.* These columns are not significant to the FORTRAN compiler and are used for program identification, sequencing or any other purpose.

Mathematical problems usually contain some data that does not change throughout the entire problem and still other data that may change many times during calculation. These two kinds of data are referred to as "constants" and "variables" respectively. Both constants and variables can be used in FORTRAN programs if they are so written that the processor can distinguish one from the other.

CONSTANTS

A constant is a fixed, unvarying quantity which is used without change from one execution of the program to the next. It appears in its actual numeric form in the source statement. For example, to calculate employee social security tax, the FORTRAN formula would be:

SSTAX = GROSS * .0585

.0585, the current social security tax rate, will remain unchanged for the execution of the program for each employee.

Numerical constants may be *integer* or *real.*

An *integer constant* is a whole number without a decimal point. It may be positive, negative, or zero. It may contain a sign. If unsigned, it is assumed to be positive. The constant may not contain embedded commas. For example:

Valid Integer Constants
0
152
−7452438
+64217

Invalid Integer Constants	
452.	Contains a decimal point.
5,396	Contains a comma.

A *real constant* is a string of decimal digits with a decimal point. The constant may be positive, negative, or zero. If unsigned, it is assumed to be positive. For example:

Valid Real Constants
+456.78
—0.

Invalid Real Constants	
456,678.91	Contains a comma.
589	Contains no decimal point.

Another type of constant is a *literal constant.* A *literal constant* is a string of alphameric and/or special characters which may be enclosed in apostrophes or the string can be preceded by *w*H where *w* is the number of characters in the string. For example, if it is necessary to print a heading at the top of a report, one might write the FORTRAN instruction in either of the following ways:

```
   WRITE (3,3)
3  FORMAT ('SALES ANALYSIS REPORT')
```

or

```
   WRITE (3,3)
3  FORMAT (21HSALES ANALYSIS REPORT)
```

In both cases, when the WRITE statement is executed, the literal constant SALES ANALYSIS REPORT will be printed.

VARIABLES

When a quantity in a FORTRAN problem varies for different executions of a program, it is known as a variable quantity. Variable names are symbols used to distinguish one variable from another. When reading the descriptions of variables, it is important to distinguish between the *value* of a variable and the *name* of a variable. For example, VOLT could be the variable name assigned to a series of values used in a calculation of current in a circuit.

The use of meaningful variable names can serve as an aid in documenting a program so that someone other than the programmer may look at the program and understand its function. It will be easier to follow the flow if meaningful symbols are used whenever possible. For example to compute the distance a car traveled in a certain amount of time at a given rate of speed, you could use the following statement $X = Y * Z$. However, it could be more meaningful to someone reading this statement if the programmer had written DIST = RATE * TIME.

A variable name is a symbolic name that may consist of one to six alphameric characters (Alphabet A–Z, numeric 0–9, and $). The first character must be a letter or $. For example:

Valid Variable Names
C4578
UNIT
$VAR

Invalid Variable Names	
B789456	Contains more than six characters.
5NUMB	First character is not alphabetic.
BJ.7	Contains a special character.

An *integer* variable name begins with the letters I through N. For example:

Data	Variable Name	
3467	JOB	
2145.76	NUMBER	Invalid variable name as data is in real mode
−2467	INCR	

A variable name corresponds to the type of data the variable represents. A *real* variable name begins with the letters A through H and/or O through Z. The data must be in the real mode as explained in real constants.

Data	Variable Name	
1234	UNIT	Invalid variable name as data is in integer mode
1234.56	AMOUNT	
−64.78	RATE	

EXPRESSIONS

Expressions in their simplest form consist of a single constant or variable. They may also designate a computation between two or more constants and/or variables. Expressions may appear in arithmetic statements and in certain control statements (Fig. 12.6).

An expression in FORTRAN consists of a series of constants, variables, and their functions, separated by parentheses, commas, and/or operation symbols so as to form a mathematical expression.

ARITHMETIC STATEMENTS

The numerical computations that are to be performed in an object program are defined by arithmetic statements that closely resemble conventional arithmetic formulas. The simplest arithmetic expression consists of a single constant and/or a variable. The variable to be computed is followed by an equal (=) sign, followed by an arithmetic expression. For example, the

Figure 12–6. Examples of FORTRAN Expressions and Their Mathematical Meaning.

FORTRAN EXPRESSION	MEANING
(C – D)/E	$\frac{C-D}{E}$
C –D/E	$C-\frac{D}{E}$
E/(C – D)	$\frac{E}{C-D}$
A/B *D	$\frac{A}{B} \times D$
A/(B*D)	$\frac{A}{B \times D}$
A/B/D	$\frac{A}{B} \div D$
A + C*B**D	$A + C \times B^D$

arithmetic statement $Z = A - JOE$ means to replace the value of the variable on the left side of the equal sign with value of the expression on the right side of the equal sign. The meaning of the equal (=) sign is important in writing FORTRAN programs. The equal sign means "to be replaced by" rather than "is equivalent to" (Fig. 12.7).

```
      READ (5,10) A,B,C,D
10    FORMAT (4F.5.2)
      G =A +B
      H =C +D
      WRITE (6,11) G,H
11    FORMAT (F8.2,2X,F7.3)
      STOP
      END
```

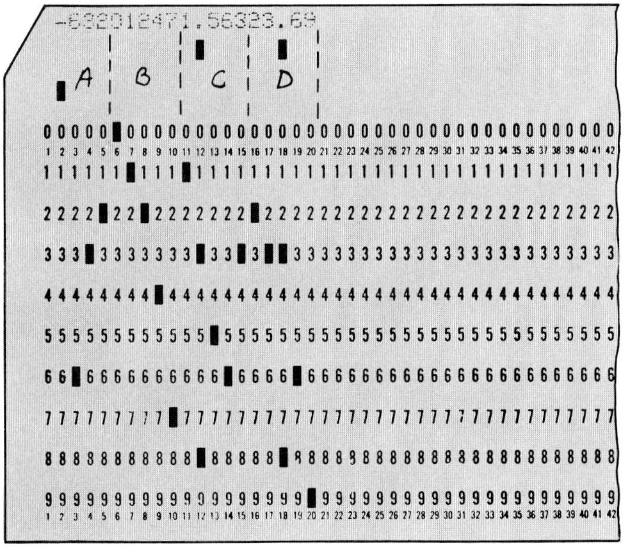

Figure 12–7. Example—FORTRAN Problem—Arithmetic Operation.

Five basic arithmetic operations may be performed in FORTRAN: addition, subtraction, multiplication, division, exponentiation. The arithmetic operators used in FORTRAN are as follows:

ARITHMETIC OPERATOR	FUNCTION
+	Addition
−	Subtraction
*	Multiplication
/	Division
**	Exponentiation

Examples of Arithmetic Statements

Statement	Description
AMT = UNITS * RATE Variable Arithmetic Expression	The product of UNITS and RATE replaces the value of the variable AMT.
Arithmetic Statement	
SSTAX = EARN * .0585	The product replaces the value of SSTAX.
SUM = PRINC	The value of SUM is replaced by the current value of PRINC.

Order of Computations

Computations are performed from left to right according to the hierarchy of operations as follows:

1. Parenthetical expressions from innermost to outermost pairs.
2. Exponentiation.
3. Multiplication and division from left to right.
4. Addition and subtraction from left to right.

Consider the following examples:

Example 1. The mathematical statement $E = \frac{AB}{CD}$ can be correctly written in FORTRAN as

E = A * B / (C * D)

and will be effectively evaluated in the following order:

1. (C * D)	Call the result X	A * B / X
2. A * B	Call the result Y	Y / X
3. Y / X	Final operation.	

Example 2. The arithmetic statement D = B + ((A + B) * C) + A ** 2 will be effectively evaluated in the following order:

1. (A + B)	Call the result X	B + (X * C) + A ** 2
2. (X * C)	Call the result Y	B + Y + A ** 2
3. A ** 2	Call the result Z	B + Y + Z
4. B + Y	Call the result W	W + Z
5. W + Z	Final operation.	

CONTROL STATEMENTS

Normally FORTRAN statements in a program are executed sequentially as they are written on a coding sheet *unless a different sequence is specified.*

Control statements provide flexibility to program development. If statements could only be followed sequentially in a fixed pattern, a program would have to follow a single path of operation without any possibility of dealing with predefined exceptions to the procedure, and without any ability to choose alternatives based upon conditions encountered during the processing of the program.

Some of the statements that are commonly used to alter and control the normal execution of statements in a program are GO TO and IF statements.

GO TO STATEMENTS

GO TO statements permit the transfer of control to an executable statement specified by the number in the GO TO statement. Control may be transferred unconditionally or conditionally. The GO TO statements are:

1. Unconditional GO TO statement.
2. Computed GO TO statement.

Unconditional GO TO statement.

The unconditional GO TO statement causes transfer of control to the statement number specified every time the GO TO statement is executed.

In the following example, every time statement 50 is executed, control is transferred to statement 25.

```
50 GO TO 25
10 A = B + 6
      .
      .
25 C = E ** 2
```

Computed GO TO statement

The computed GO TO statement causes transfer of control to the statement number specified depending upon the current value of the item in the statement. For example:

```
GO TO (35,25,17), ITEM
        .
        .
17 AMT = UNITS * .15
        .
        .
35 AMT = UNITS * .10
        .
        .
25 AMT = UNITS * .05
```

If the value of integer variable ITEM is 1, statement 35 will be executed next. If the value of ITEM is 2, statement 25 is executed, and if the value of ITEM is 3, statement 17 is executed. If any other value is present in ITEM the next statement after GO TO is executed.

IF STATEMENTS

The IF statement is used to test variables and cause control to be transferred to the statement related to the value of the variable tested. There are two types of IF statements. They are (1) Arithmetic IF statements, and (2) Logical IF statements.

Arithmetic IF Statement

The arithmetic IF statement causes control to be transferred to a particular statement number when the value of the arithmetic expression is negative, zero, or positive. Consider the following examples:

Example 1.

```
IF (YTDEAR – 13200.00) 10,20,20
        .
        .
10 SSTAX = EARN * .0585
        .
        .
20 SSTAX = 0
        .
        .
```

In the above example, if the year-to-date earnings are equal to or greater than 13200, control is transferred to statement 20 where no social security tax is calculated. If the earnings are less than 13200, control is transferred to statement 10 where the appropriate social security taxes are calculated.

Example 2.

```
IF (A—B)10,20,30
  .
  .
10 C = E + F
  .
  .
20 G = H * * 2
  .
  .
30 D = (F * B)/D − 1
```

In the above example, if the value of the expression A − B is negative, the statement 10 is executed next. If the value of the expression is zero, the statement 20 is executed next. If the value of the expression is positive, the statement 30 is executed next.

Logical IF Statement

The logical IF statement is used to evaluate a logical expression and to execute or skip the statement depending on whether the value of the expression is .TRUE. or .FALSE.

RELATIONAL OPERATORS

The six relational operators, each of which must be preceded and followed by a period are as follows:

Relational Operators	Meaning
.GT.	Greater than ($>$)
.GE.	Greater than or equal to ($\geq$)
.LT.	Less than ($<$)
.LE.	Less than or equal to ($\leq$)
.EQ.	Equal to ($=$)
.NE.	Not equal to ($\neq$)

The relational operators express an arithmetic condition which can be true or false. For example:

```
IF(A.LE.O.O) GO TO 25
 C = D − E
IF (A.EQ.B) ANSWER = 2.0 * A/C
 F = G/H
  .
  .
25 W = X ** 2
```

In the first statement, if the value of the expression is .TRUE. (A is less than or equal to 0.0), the statement GO TO 25 is executed next and control is passed to the statement 25. If the statement is .FALSE. (A is greater than 0.0), the statement GO TO 25 is ignored and the next statement is executed.

In the third statement, if the value of the expression is .TRUE. (A is equal to B), the value of ANSWER is replaced by the value of the expression (2.0*A/C) and then the fourth statement is executed. If the value of the expression is .FALSE. (A is not equal to B), the value of ANSWER remains unchanged and the fourth statement is executed next.

LOGICAL OPERATORS

The three logical operators, each of which must be preceded and followed by a period, are as follows; (where A and B represent logical constants or variables or expressions containing relational operators).

Two logical operators may appear in sequence only if the second one is the logical operator.

Logical Operator	Use	Meaning
.NOT.	.NOT.A	If A is .TRUE., then NOT.A has the value .FALSE.; if A is .FALSE., then A. or.B. has the value .TRUE.;
.AND.	A.AND.B	If A and B are both .TRUE., then A.AND.B has the value .TRUE.; if either A or B or both are .FALSE.; then A.AND.B has the value .FALSE.
.OR.	A.OR.B	If either A or B or both are .TRUE., then A. or .B has the value .TRUE.; If neither A nor B is TRUE then A. or.B has the value. FALSE.

For example:

Assume that P and Q are logical variables.

```
      .
      .
IF (P.OR..NOT.Q) A = B
C = B ** 2
```

In the first statement if the value of the expression is .TRUE., the value of A is replaced by the value of B and the second statement is executed. If the value of the expression is .FALSE., the statement A = B is skipped and the second statement is executed.

INPUT/ OUTPUT STATEMENTS

The input/output statements enable the user to transfer data belonging to a named collection of data, between input/output devices (such as card readers, disk units, and magnetic tape units) and internal storage (Fig. 12.8). The named collection of data is called a *data set* and is a continuous string of data that may be divided into FORTRAN records.

```
      READ (5,8) DEDUCT,HOURS,YRDATE,WEARN
 8    FORMAT (F2.0,F4.1,F7.2,F6.2)
      WRITE (6,9) DEDUCT,HOURS
      WRITE (6,10) YRDATE,WEARN
 9    FORMAT (F4.0,F6.1)
10    FORMAT (F9.2,F8.2)
      STOP
      END
```

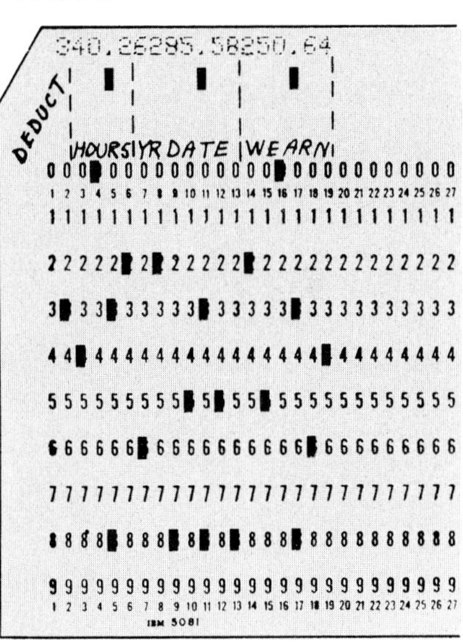

Figure 12–8. Example—FORTRAN Problem—Input/Output Operation.

Input and output statements in FORTRAN are primarily concerned with the transfer of data between storage locations in a FORTRAN program and records which are external to the program. On input, data is taken from a record and placed into storage locations that are not necessarily contiguous. On output, data is gathered from diverse storage locations and placed into a record. An input/output list containing variable names is used to specify which storage locations are used.

Input statements are used to read data into storage and output statements are used to print, punch or otherwise output the results. There are three principal types of FORTRAN statements that are used for input/output operations; READ, WRITE, and FORMAT (which is actually a specification statement and discussed in greater detail in the Specification Statements section that follows shortly.)

The general format of the READ statement is

READ (A, B) list

A—symbolic number of an input device.

B—statement number of the FORMAT statement describing the records being read.

list—input/output list of variable names, separated by commas.

The input and output statements, each with its corresponding FORMAT statement specifies the number and sequence of the data input and output fields, the length of the data fields and what mode they are in. For example:

```
READ (1,4)K,M,A
4 FORMAT (I5, I4, F7.3)
```

The READ statement causes data to be read from the card reader (1) at object time and causes the quantities to become the values of the variables named in the list (K, M, A).

According to the FORMAT statement (4), the first variable in the card, K, has been assigned the format I5 which tells the processor that the first field in the card contains five columns and also that the number is in the fixed point mode.

The next variable M has been assigned the format of I4, which tells the processor that the next field is in the fixed point mode and consists of 4 columns.

The floating point variable A is read next according to F7.3. This format tells the processor that the value is to be a floating point number and that the field contains seven digits and there will be three digits to the right of the decimal point.

The general format of the WRITE statement is WRITE (A,B,) list

A—symbolic number of the output device.

B—statement number of the FORMAT statement describing the records being written.

list—optional, and is the input/output list of variable names, separated by commas.

For example:

```
WRITE (3,15) A,B,J
15 FORMAT (F8.2,F8.3,I5)
```

This WRITE statement causes the printer (3) to print the information as follows:

1. The value of A as eight digits with two decimal positions.
2. The value of B as eight digits with three decimal positions.
3. The value of J as five digits with no decimal positions.

The WRITE statement may also be used without the list option. For example, to print the heading JOB ORDER LIST with three blank spaces on the left, the following FORTRAN statement may be written.

```
WRITE (3,10)
10 FORMAT (3X,'JOB ORDER LIST')
```

SPECIFICATION STATEMENTS

The specification statements provide the compiler with information about the nature of the data uses in the source program. In addition, they supply the information required to allocate locations in storage for this data. Specifications statements may appear anywhere in the program but must precede any statement which refers to them.

The FORMAT statement type tells the FORTRAN processor the length of each input and output data field and whether the field is (or will be) in fixed point or floating point mode. The DIMENSION statement provides the processor with information necessary to allocate storage in the object program for arrays of quantities.

A DIMENSION or FORMAT statement is a nonexecutable statement inasmuch as neither one creates instructions in the object program but merely supplies information to the processor.

The following are some of the principal forms of FORTRAN FORMAT statements.

I FORMAT CODE

The I FORMAT code is used in transmitting integer data. For example:

```
READ (1,4) J
4 FORMAT (I5)
```

In the above statements, for the variable J, an integer of five digits will be read.

F FORMAT CODE

The F FORMAT code is used in transmitting floating point (real) data. For example:

```
READ (1,4) A
4 FORMAT (F5.3)
```

In the above statements, for the variable A, a floating point number of 5 digits with three decimal positions will be read.

H FORMAT CODE

If the H FORMAT code is used, the literal data following the H is printed according to the number specified before the H. For example, in the statements

```
WRITE (3,25)
25 FORMAT (20H    THIS IS MY REPORT)
```

twenty characters will be printed including the three blanks preceding the word THIS.

T FORMAT CODE

The T FORMAT code specifies the position in the FORTRAN record where the transfer of data is to begin. For example, in the statements

```
WRITE (3,25)
25 FORMAT (T4, 'THIS IS MY REPORT')
```

the heading THIS IS MY REPORT will print starting in the third printing position as the first print position is reserved for carriage control.

X FORMAT CODE

The X FORMAT code specifies a field of characters to be skipped on input or filled with blanks on output. For example, the following statements

```
READ (1,5)   I,J,K,L,M
5 FORMAT (I10, 10X, 4I10)
```

cause the first ten characters of the input record to be read into variable I, the next ten characters are to be skipped without transmission and the next four fields (the 4 before I indicates the number of repetitions of the field in the same form) to be read into variables, J,K,L, and M.

DIMENSION

The DIMENSION statement is used to set aside arrays of data into storage locations. For example, in the statement,

```
DIMENSION JOBS (12)
```

the compiler will set aside four contiguous storage locations for the variable JOBS (Figs. 12.9, 12.10, 12.11).

SUMMARY

FORTRAN (*FOR*mula *TRAN*slator) is a procedure-oriented programming language designed primarily for writing programs to solve scientific and engineering problems involving mathematical computations. With the increased use of mathematics in business, more and more FORTRAN programs are being written for commercial applications that involve mathematical computations or other manipulations of numeric data. It is the intent of this chapter to describe the features of the most widely used scientific programming language FORTRAN.

A. *Purpose*—primarily designed to solve scientific and engineering problems involving mathematical computations. With the increased use of mathematics in business it is used more and more in solving business problems.
B. *Operation*—uses English-like statements plus operators in a formula type method of instructions.

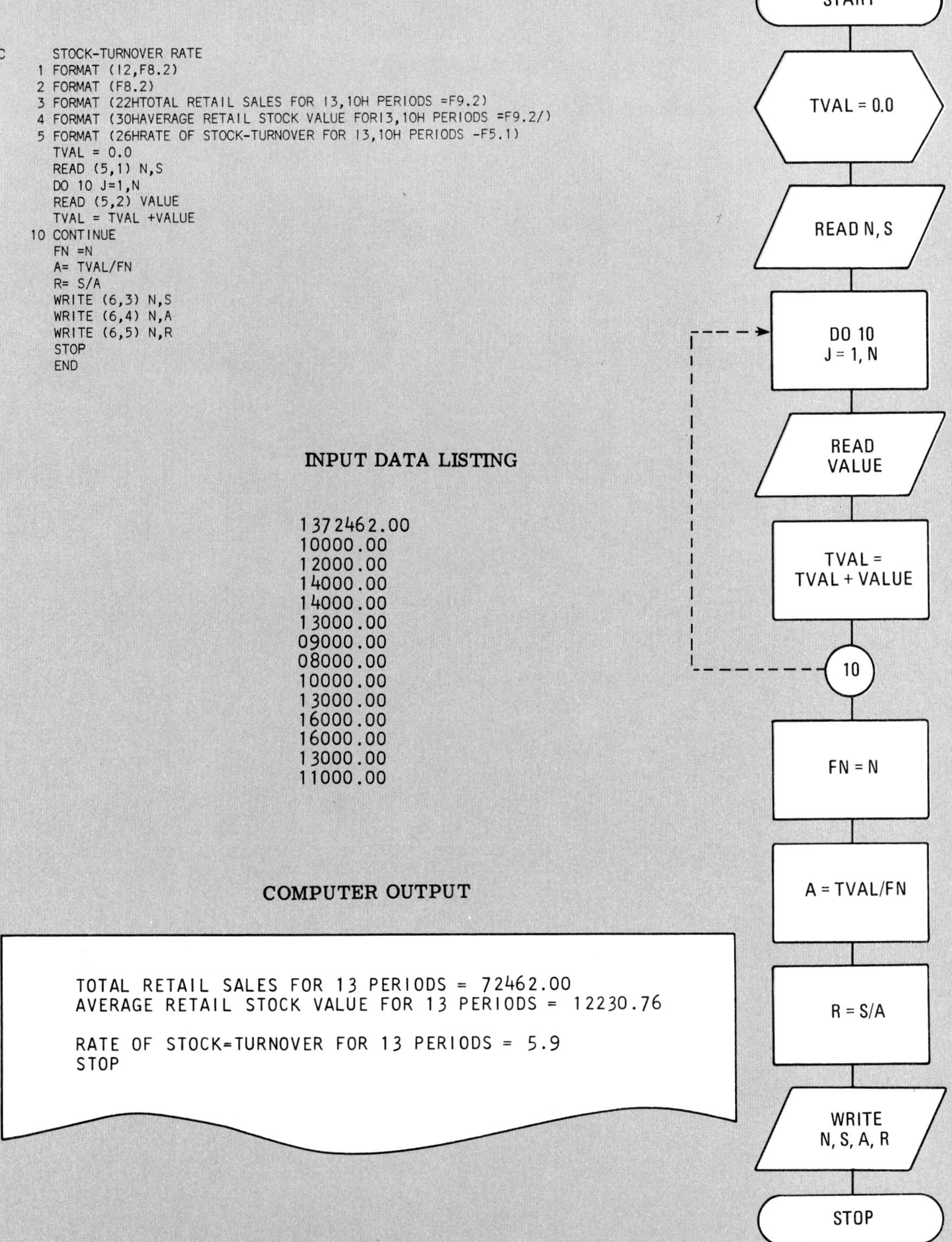

C STOCK-TURNOVER RATE
1 FORMAT (I2,F8.2)
2 FORMAT (F8.2)
3 FORMAT (22HTOTAL RETAIL SALES FOR I3,10H PERIODS =F9.2)
4 FORMAT (30HAVERAGE RETAIL STOCK VALUE FORI3,10H PERIODS =F9.2/)
5 FORMAT (26HRATE OF STOCK-TURNOVER FOR I3,10H PERIODS -F5.1)
TVAL = 0.0
READ (5,1) N,S
DO 10 J=1,N
READ (5,2) VALUE
TVAL = TVAL +VALUE
10 CONTINUE
FN =N
A= TVAL/FN
R= S/A
WRITE (6,3) N,S
WRITE (6,4) N,A
WRITE (6,5) N,R
STOP
END
START
TVAL = 0.0
READ N, S
DO 10
J = 1, N
READ
VALUE
TVAL =
TVAL + VALUE
10
FN = N
A = TVAL/FN
R = S/A
WRITE
N, S, A, R
STOP
INPUT DATA LISTING
1372462.00
10000.00
12000.00
14000.00
14000.00
13000.00
09000.00
08000.00
10000.00
13000.00
16000.00
16000.00
13000.00
11000.00
COMPUTER OUTPUT
TOTAL RETAIL SALES FOR 13 PERIODS = 72462.00
AVERAGE RETAIL STOCK VALUE FOR 13 PERIODS = 12230.76
RATE OF STOCK=TURNOVER FOR 13 PERIODS = 5.9
STOP

Figure 12–9. Example—FORTRAN Problem—Stock Turnover Rate.

START

READ RMORT, RSAV, COUT, CHAND, CHECK

RTOT = FUND + RMORT + RSAV
OTOT = CHAND + CHECK + COUT

RECON = OTOT – RTOT

CHAND = FUND?

Less: REIMB = FUND – CHAND; DEPOS = CHECK

= or Greater: REIMB = 0.0; DEPOS = CHECK + (CHAND – FUND)

WRITE RECON CHAND, CHECK, REIMB, DEPOS

STOP

C DAILY CASH REPORT

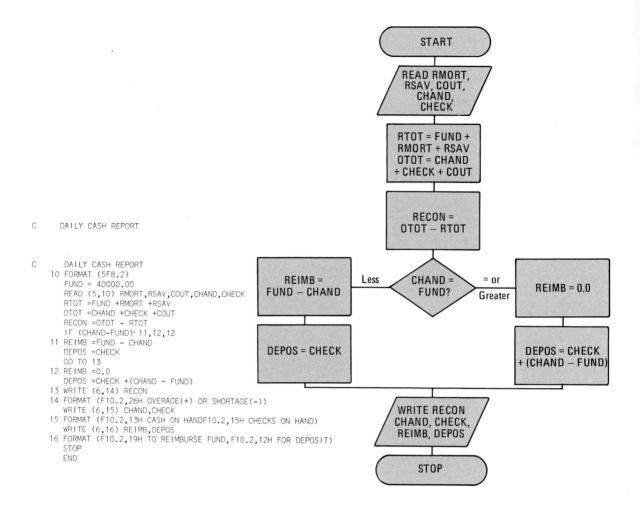

```
C      DAILY CASH REPORT
   10 FORMAT (5F8.2)
      FUND = 40000.00
      READ (5,10) RMORT,RSAV,COUT,CHAND,CHECK
      RTOT =FUND +RMORT +RSAV
      OTOT =CHAND +CHECK +COUT
      RECON =OTOT - RTOT
      IF (CHAND-FUND) 11,12,12
   11 REIMB =FUND - CHAND
      DEPOS =CHECK
      GO TO 13
   12 REIMB =0.0
      DEPOS =CHECK +(CHAND - FUND)
   13 WRITE (6,14) RECON
   14 FORMAT (F10.2,26H OVERAGE(+) OR SHORTAGE(-))
      WRITE (6,15) CHAND,CHECK
   15 FORMAT (F10.2,13H CASH ON HANDF10.2,15H CHECKS ON HAND)
      WRITE (6,16) REIMB,DEPOS
   16 FORMAT (F10.2,19H TO REIMBURSE FUND,F10.2,12H FOR DEPOSIT)
      STOP
      END
```

INPUT DATA LISTING

15000.0008050.0005000.0035000.0023000.00

COMPUTER OUTPUT

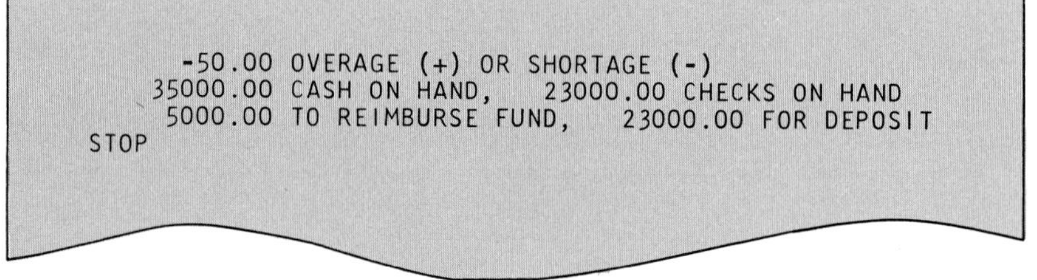

```
   -50.00 OVERAGE (+) OR SHORTAGE (-)
 35000.00 CASH ON HAND,    23000.00 CHECKS ON HAND
  5000.00 TO REIMBURSE FUND,    23000.00 FOR DEPOSIT
STOP
```

Figure 12–10. Example—FORTRAN Problem—Daily Cash Report.

```
C                   ----COMPOUND INTEREST WITH
C     VARYING INITIAL PERIODS AND PERIOD INCREMENTS
      DIMENSION A(25,8),RATE(8)
      READ (5,100) NI,NL,NINC,CON,RINC,NRATE,P
      DO 50 KRATE=1,NRATE
      ZRATE=KRATE
      RATE(KRATE) =CON +ZRATE*RINC
      DO 50 N =NI,NL,NINC
      J =(N-NI)/NINC +1
      A(J,KRATE) =P*(1. +RATE(KRATE))**N
   50 CONTINUE
      WRITE (6,200) P
      WRITE (6,201)
      WRITE (6,202) (RATE(KRATE),KRATE=1,NRATE)
      DO 75 N=NI,NL,NINC
      J =(N-NI)/NINC +1
   75 WRITE (6,203) N, (A(J,KRATE),KRATE=1,NRATE)
      STOP
  100 FORMAT (3I2,2F4.2,I2,F8.2)
  200 FORMAT (13X,34HCOMPOUND INTEREST TABLE PAYMENT -F8.2/)
  201 FORMAT (25X,13HINTEREST RATE)
  202 FORMAT (6HPERIOD,8X,8(F4.2,5X)/)
  203 FORMAT (2X,I2,6X,8F9.2)
      END
```

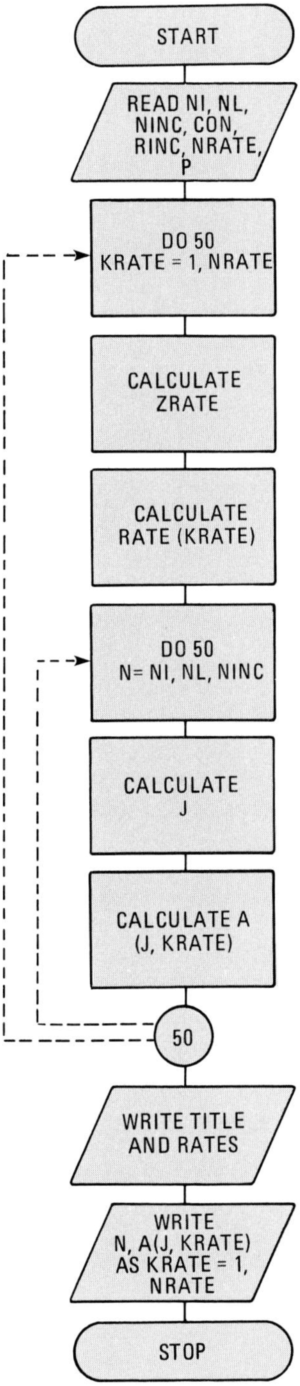

INPUT DATA LISTING

```
1050050.000.010600100.00
```

COMPUTER OUTPUT

```
              COMPOUND INTEREST TABLE   PAYMENT =   100.00

                          INTEREST RATE
PERIOD        .01      .02      .03      .04      .05      .06
  10       110.46   121.89   134.39   148.02   162.88   179.08
  15       116.09   134.58   155.79   180.09   207.89   239.65
  20       122.01   148.59   180.61   219.11   265.32   320.71
  25       128.24   164.06   209.37   266.58   338.63   429.18
  30       134.78   181.13   242.72   324.33   432.19   574.34
  35       141.66   199.98   281.38   394.60   551.60   768.60
  40       148.88   220.80   326.20   480.10   703.99  1028.57
  45       156.48   243.78   378.15   584.11   898.50  1376.46
  50       164.46   269.15   438.39   710.66  1146.73  1842.01
STOP
```

Figure 12–11. Example—FORTRAN Problem—Compound Interest.

C. *Elements of FORTRAN.*
   1. *Statements*—sentences of FORTRAN consisting of keywords that are used in conjunction with certain basic elements of the language that define the operations to be performed. Types of statements are:
      Arithmetic—specify mathematical calculations to be performed on the data.
      Control—determine the sequence in which the statements will follow.
      Input and output—read data into the computer for printing or punching of results.
      Specification—specifies type of input/output data to be processed and the amount of storage to be used by variables and constants.
   2. *Character set*—consists of following: 26 letters of the alphabet, 10 numerical digits, 7 punctuation characters and 6 algebraic symbols.

D. *Coding forms*—used as a guide when preparing a source program. Each line of the form represents one 80 column card. Statements that cannot be completed on one line may be continued on as many as 19 successive lines by placing a continuation indicator in column 6 (any nonblank or nonzero character).
   1. *Column 1—Comment.* A C in the first column indicates that a comment is to be written. Comments are notes that help clarify some of the meanings of statements and improve the readability.
   2. *Columns 1–5—Statement number.* May consist of 1 to 5 decimal digits. Used as labels to be referred to by other statements. Does not affect the sequence in which the statements are to be executed.
   3. *Column 6—Continuation indicator.* A nonblank or nonzero character that indicates the continuation of a statement from the previous line.
   4. *Columns 7–72—FORTRAN statement.* Statement is written starting column 7 and may be continued up to column 72. If additional columns are needed, the statement is continued as indicated above.
   5. *Columns 73–80—Identification.* These columns are not significant to the program and may be used for identification purposes or sequence control of cards.

E. *Constants.* A fixed unvarying quantity value that is used without change from one execution of the program to another.
   1. *Integer constant*—a whole number without a decimal point.
   2. *Real constant*—a string of decimal digits with a decimal point.
   3. *Literal constant*—a string of alphameric and/or special characters enclosed in apostrophes used to denote headings or messages.

F. *Variables*—a quantity that may change many times during the execution of a program. Variable names consist of 1 to 6 alphameric characters assigned to the type of data that the variable represents.

1. *Real variable name*—begins with the letters A through H and/or O through Z. The data must be in a real mode.
2. *Integer variable name*—begins with the letters I through N. The data must be in integer mode.

G. *Expressions.* A series of constants and/or variables separated by operators so as to form a mathematical expression.

H. *Arithmetic statements.* These statements closely resemble conventional arithmetic formulas that stipulate calculation operations to be performed. The equal sign means "to be replaced by" rather than "is equivalent to." The basic arithmetic operators used in FORTRAN are addition, subtraction, multiplication, division and exponentiation.

I. *Control statements.* These statements control sequence of program instruction execution. The types of control statements are:

1. *GO TO*—permits the transfer of control to an executable statement specified by the number in the GO TO statement. This statement may be unconditional or conditional.
   Unconditional—causes transfer of control to the statement number specified every time the GO TO statement is executed.
   Conditional (Computed GO TO)—causes transfer of control to the statement number specified depending on the current value of the item in the statement.
2. *IF*—tests variables and causes control to be transferred to the statement number related to the value of the variable tested. There are two types of IF statements.
   Arithmetic IF—causes control to be transferred to a particular statement when the value of an arithmetic statement is negative, zero or positive.
   Logical IF—is used to evaluate a logical expression and to execute or skip a statement depending on the value of the expression (true or false).

J. *Relational operators*—must be preceded and followed by a period.

1. .GT. Greater than.
2. .GE. Greater than or equal to.
3. .LT. Less than.
4. .LE. Less than or equal to.
5. .EQ. Equal to.
6. .NE. Not equal to.

K. *Logical operators*—must be preceded and followed by a period.

1. .NOT. Negate a statement.
2. .AND. Combine two or more statements.
3. .OR. Either statement.

L. *Input and output statements.* These statements are used to read in data and output results.
   1. *READ statement*—causes data to be read into the computer.
   2. *WRITE statement*—causes data to become output from the computer.

M. *Specification statements (FORMAT)*—provides information to the computer regarding the nature of the data. May also be used to allocate storage for data.
   1. *I FORMAT code*—used in transmitting integer data.
   2. *F FORMAT code*—used in transmitting floating point (real) data.
   3. *H FORMAT* code—used in transmitting literal data.
   4. *T FORMAT* code—position the FORTRAN record where the transfer of data is to begin.
   5. *X FORMAT code*—specifies a field of characters to be skipped on input or filled with blanks on output.
   6. *DIMENSION statement*—is used to set aside arrays of data into storage locations.

IDENTIFICATION QUESTIONS

Match the following terms with the statements that follow.

A. Arithmetic Statements
B. Constant
C. Control Statements
D. Dimension Statement
E. Expression
F. Format Statement
G. Go To Statement
H. If Statement
I. Input/Output Statements
J. Integer Constant
K. Integer Variable Name
L. Literal Constant
M. Logical Operator
N. Read Statement
O. Real Constant
P. Real Variable Name
Q. Relational Operators
R. Specification Statements
S. Statements
T. Variable
U. Write Statement

1. A quantity that varies in value for different executions of the program.
2. Statements that determine the sequence in which the statements will follow.
3. A fixed unvarying quantity that is used without change from one execution of the program to another.
4. A constant string of alphameric characters enclosed in apostrophes.
5. A variable name that begins with the letters I through N.
6. A statement that consists of constants and variables, etc., so as to form a mathematical expression.
7. These operators are used in compare operations.
8. These statements specify to the processor the length and mode of input and output data.
9. The individual commands of the program.
10. Statements that read data into the computer and put out results.
11. A whole number constant without a decimal point.

12. A variable name that begins with the letters A through H and/or O through Z.
13. This operator is used to determine whether the expression is true or false.
14. This statement causes data to be transferred from internal storage to output.
15. Statements that specify the mathematical calculations to be performed.
16. A constant string of decimal digits with a decimal point.
17. This statement permits transfers of control conditionally or unconditionally to another statement.
18. This statement provides the processor with information to allocate storage for arrays.
19. A statement that specifies the kind of input and output data.
20. This statement causes data to be transferred from the record to internal storage.
21. This statement permits transfer of control if certain conditions are satisfied.

QUESTIONS FOR REVIEW

1. What is the importance of FORTRAN as a programming language?
2. Describe the different types of FORTRAN statements with their main functions.
3. What is the FORTRAN character set composed of?
4. What is the main purpose of a FORTRAN coding form?
5. What are the different fields of a FORTRAN coding form used for?
6. Briefly explain the following FORTRAN terms. Give examples of each: Constant, Variable, Expression.
7. Explain how mathematical calculations are performed in FORTRAN. Give an example.
8. What is the purpose of control statements?
9. Differentiate between the GO TO and IF statements. Give examples of each.
10. What function do relational and logical operators perform?
11. What is the main function of input/output statements?
12. What are the primary functions of the READ and WRITE statements? Give examples.
13. Differentiate between the FORMAT and DIMENSION statements.

CHAPTER 13
COBOL

COBOL is defined as a *CO*mmon *B*usiness *O*riented *L*anguage. As such it is the result of the efforts of computer users, both in industry and government, to establish a standard language for programming business data processing applications. The COBOL language bears little resemblance to machine language and the problem programmer has little direct concern with the method by which the COBOL language program is translated into machine language.

COBOL is a high-level language that is procedure-oriented and relatively machine independent. Designed with the programmer in mind, COBOL frees him from the many machine-oriented instructions of other languages and allows him to concentrate on the logical aspect of a program. The program is written in an English-like syntax that looks and reads like ordinary business English (Fig. 13.1). Organization of the language is simple in comparison to machine-oriented languages; as such it is much easier to teach to new programmers, thus reducing training time (Fig. 13.2).

```
SUBTRACT DEDUCTIONS FROM GROSS GIVING NET-AMOUNT.

MULTIPLY UNITS BY LIST-PRICE GIVING BILLING-AMT.

IF ON-HAND IS LESS THAN MINIMUM-BALANCE GO TO
REORDER-ROUTINE.
```

Figure 13–1. Typical COBOL Statements.

COMPATIBILITY—COBOL makes it possible for the first time to use the same program on different computers with a minimum of change. Reprogramming can be reduced to making minor modifications in the COBOL source program, and re-compiling for the new computer.

STANDARDIZATION—The standardization of a computer programming language overcomes the communication barrier which exists among programming language systems which are oriented to a single computer or a single family of computers.

COMMUNICATION—Easier communication between decision-making management, the systems analyst, the programmer, the coding technician, and the operator is established.

AUTOMATIC UNIFORM DOCUMENTATION—Easily understandable English documentation, provided automatically by the compiler, facilitates program analysis and thus simplifies any future modifications in the program.

COMPLETELY DEBUGGED PROGRAMS—Programs produced by the COBOL compiler are free from clerical errors.

CORRECTIONS AT ENGLISH LEVEL—Corrections and modifications in program logic may be made at the English level.

EASE OF TRAINING—New programming personnel can be trained to write productive programs with COBOL in substantially less time than it takes to train them in machine coding.

FASTER AND MORE ACCURATE PROGRAMMING—The English language notation expressed by the user and the computer-acceptable language produced by the COBOL computer ensure greater programming accuracy and a reduction in programming time.

REDUCTION IN PROGRAMMING COSTS—The ability to program a problem faster reduces the cost of programming. Also, reprogramming costs are greatly reduced since a program run on one system may be easily modified to run on another without being entirely recoded.

Figure 13–2. Benefits Derived from Using COBOL.

ADVANTAGES

There are many advantages in using COBOL as a programming language.

1. Principal advantage of the COBOL system is found in the area of establishment of communication. The ability to use English-like statements solves language difficulties that have often existed between the advanced programmer and decision-making management.
2. The program is written in the English language, thus removing the programmer from the individual symbolic machine or language in-

structions required in the program. Although a knowledge of the individual instructions (symbolic and machine) are not required in COBOL programming, it is very useful to the writing of an efficient program if the programmer possesses some knowledge of the hardware and coding of the particular computer.

3. Pretested modules of input and output are included in the COBOL processor which relieve the programmer of the tedious task of writing input and output specifications and testing them.
4. The programmer is writing in a language that is familiar to him, which reduces the documentation required since the chance for clerical error is diminished. Generally, the quality and the quantity of documentation provided by the COBOL compiler is far superior to that of other language processors. The printed output resulting from the compilation provides an added improvement in the communication problems of man to man and man to machine.
5. While COBOL is not completely machine-independent, a program written for one type of machine can be easily converted for use on another with minimum modification. The standardization of a COBOL program provides this benefit.
6. Because of the separate divisions in COBOL, a large program can be broken down into various segments, and each programmer may write one division. The format definition can be made available to all programmers engaged in the problem.
7. Nonprogrammers and managers can read the COBOL program in English, which provides them with the opportunity of judging the logic of the program.
8. During the compilation phase, the COBOL language processor generates a list of diagnostics. *A diagnostic is a statement provided by the compiler indicating all errors in a source program, excluding errors in logic.* Because diagnostics affect the measurement of compiling efficiency, these as well as compiling speed become important conditions for measuring the superior attributes of COBOL. This advantage derived from the attributes of COBOL can materially reduce the "debugging" time.

DISADVANTAGES

Most of the disadvantages of using COBOL arise with the failure of personnel to fully understand the language and its use, such as:

1. The expectation that a single COBOL program will provide a permanent solution without ever reprogramming.
2. Assuming that the programmer need be taught only the COBOL language without any knowledge of the hardware or the operation of the computer.

3. COBOL will not generate a sophisticated program similar to one written in the actual language of the particular computer.
4. COBOL processors will operate only with a computer having a certain storage capacity. The newer COBOL compilers have drastically reduced the storage requirements. With the introduction of larger and larger storage units, this problem has been greatly reduced.

COMPONENTS OF COBOL

COBOL is similar to the English language in the use of words, sentences, and paragraphs. The programmer can use English words and conventional arithmetic symbols to direct and control the operations of a computer.

```
ADD QUANTITY TO ON-HAND.
MULTIPLY GROSS-EARN BY SS-RATE GIVING SS-TAX.
IF Y-T-D-EARN IS LESS THAN SS-LIMIT, GO TO SS-PROC.
```

Each of the above sentences is understandable by the computer, but all must be first translated into the particular machine language of the computer before the program can be executed. During the compilation stage, a special system program known as a compiler is first entered into the computer.

The COBOL system consists of two basic elements; the *source program,* which is a set of rules and/or instructions that carry out the logic of the particular data processing application; and the *compiler,* the intermediate routine that converts the English-like statements of COBOL into computer-acceptable instructions. Since the COBOL language is directed primarily at those unfamiliar with machine coding, terms common to business applications rather than to computing systems are used in the language.

In order to write a COBOL program, the programmer should familiarize himself with the basic components of COBOL programming. There are many terms, rules, entry formats, and program structures to be learned before any attempt at COBOL programming is made.

Some of the terms used in COBOL are explained below.

Source Program. The problem-solving program written in the COBOL language which will be later compiled and translated into the machine language of the particular computer.

Object Program. The machine language that resulted from the compilation of the COBOL source program which will be used to process the data.

Compiler. A program supplied by a computer manufacturer that will translate a COBOL source program into the machine-language object program.

Source Computer. The computer that is used to compile the source program. Usually the same computer is used for the object computer.

Object Computer. The computer upon which the machine-language program will be processed.

Figure 13–3. COBOL Character Set.

CHARACTER SET

Digits 0 through 9
Letters A through Z
Special characters:
- Blank or space
- + Plus sign
- − Minus sign or hyphen
- * Check protection symbol, asterisk
- / Slash
- = Equal sign
- > Inequality sign (greater than)
- < Inequality sign (less than)
- $ Dollar sign
- , Comma
- . Period or decimal point
- ' Quotation mark
- (Left parenthesis
-) Right parenthesis
- ; Semicolon

The following characters are used for words:
- 0 through 9
- A through Z
- - (hyphen)

The following characters are used for punctuation:
- ' Quotation mark
- (Left parenthesis
-) Right parenthesis
- , Comma
- . Period
- ; Semicolon

The following characters are used in arithmetic expressions:
- + Addition
- − Subtraction
- * Multiplication
- / Division
- ** Exponentiation

The following characters are used in relation tests:
- > Greater than
- < Less than
- = Equal to

Character Set. The complete set of COBOL characters consists of fifty-one characters. These are the characters (alphabetic, numeric, and special characters or symbols) the computer manufacturer has included in the COBOL programming package (Fig. 13.3).

Names. Names are a means of establishing words to identify certain data within the program. A symbolic name is attached to an item that is being used in the program. All reference to the item will be through this name although the value may change many times throughout the execution of the program. The name must be unique or identified with a file in which it is found.

TYPES OF NAMES

Data-names are words assigned by the programmer to identify data items in the COBOL program. All items used in the Data Division must be identified by a unique or qualified name (Fig. 13.4).

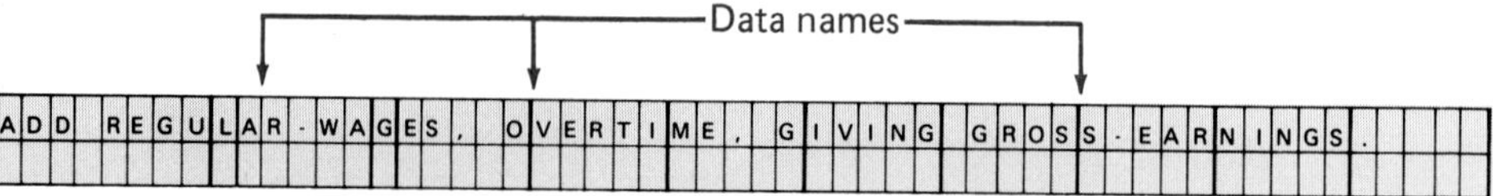

Figure 13–4. Example—Data Names.

Procedure-names are symbolic names attached to the various segments of the Procedure Division (Fig. 13.5) and used for reference by the program in a decision-making operation. The basic concept of computer programming is the ability of the program to leave the sequential order to another part of the program for further processing.

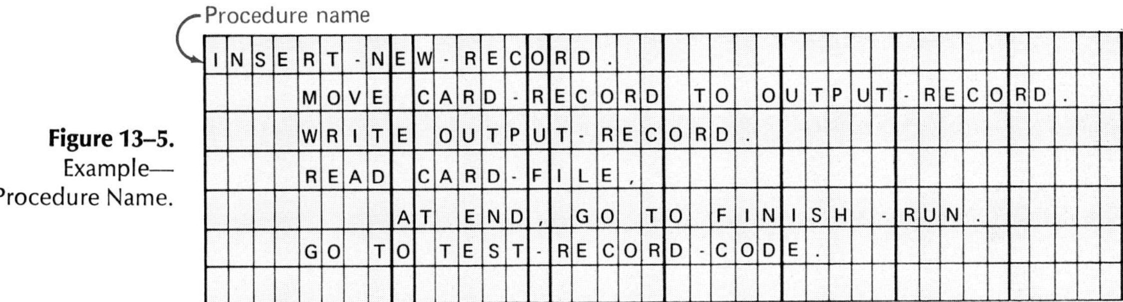

Figure 13–5. Example—Procedure Name.

Condition-names are assigned to an item that may have various values. The data item itself is called a condition variable and may assume a specific value, a set of values, or a range of values (Fig. 13.6). Condition-names are often used in the Procedure Division to specify certain conditions for branching to another part of the program.

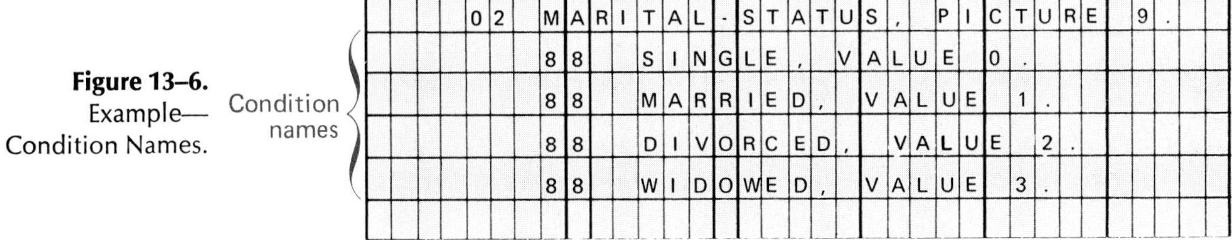

Figure 13–6. Example—Condition Names.

Special-names are the mnemonic names that are assigned to various components of the Environment Division. The term special-names refers to the mnemonic name that is associated with a function-name. Function-names are fixed for each different type of computer (Fig. 13.7).

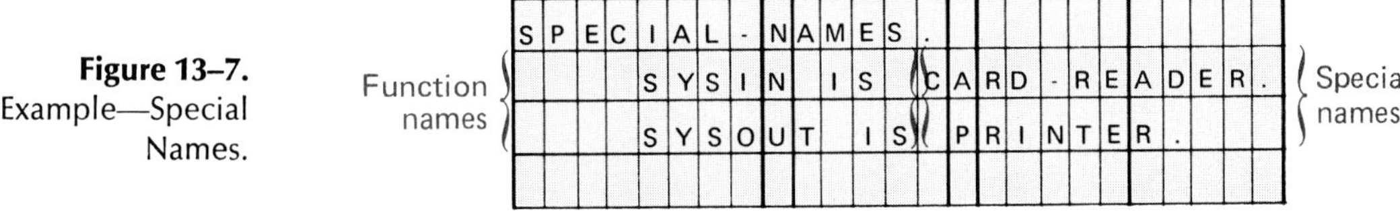

Figure 13–7. Example—Special Names.

Rules for the Assignment of Names

1. Names may range from one to thirty characters in length.
2. No spaces (blanks) may appear within a name.
3. Names may be formed from the alphabet, numerals, and the hyphen. No special characters may appear in a name except the hyphen.
4. Although a hyphen may appear in a name, no name may begin or end with a hyphen.
5. The procedure-name may consist entirely of numerals, but all other names must have at least one alphabetic character.
6. Names which are identical must be qualified with a higher level name.

WORDS

A COBOL word consists of one or more COBOL characters chosen from the character set. A word is followed by a space or by a period, right parenthesis, comma, or semicolon (Fig. 13.8).

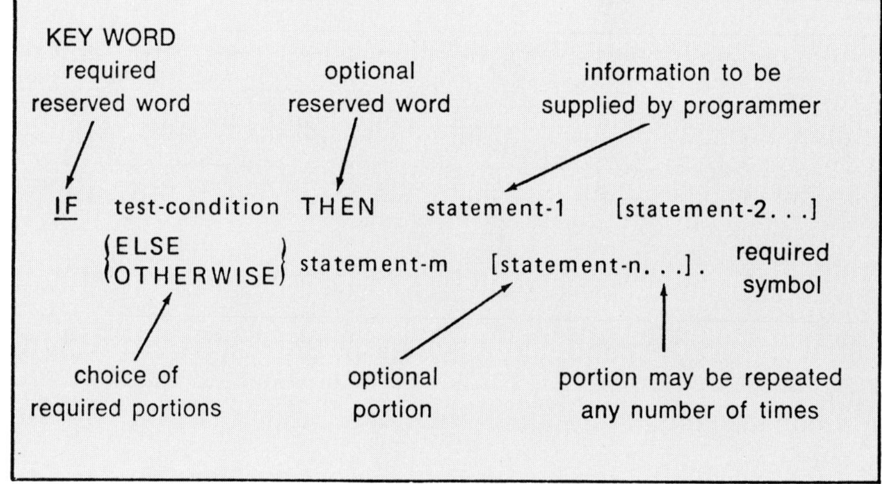

Figure 13–8. COBOL Words.

Reserved Words have preassigned meanings and must not be altered, mispelled, or changed in any manner from the specific purpose of the word (Fig. 13.9). Each of these COBOL reserved words has a special meaning to the compiler; hence, it should not be used out of context. A list of reserved

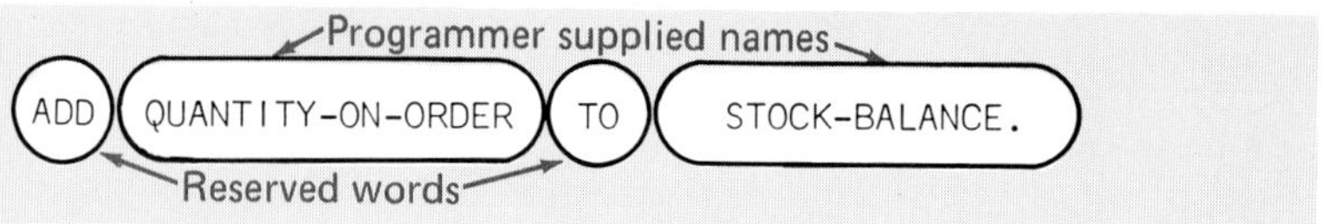

Figure 13–9. Example—Reserved Words and Programmer Supplied Names.

words is available for all computers and must be checked before attempting to program, since there are slight differences in the lists among the different computers.

CONSTANTS

A constant is an actual value of data that remains unchanged during the execution of the program. The value for the constant is supplied by the programmer at the time the program is loaded into storage.

There are two types of constants used in COBOL programming—literals and figurative constants.

Literals are composed of a string of characters where the value is determined by the set of characters of which the literal is a part.

There are two types of literals—numeric and nonnumeric (Fig. 13.10).

Numeric literal

```
   MULTIPLY SALES BY .0525 GIVING BONUS.
```

Nonnumeric literal

```
77 MESSAGE-4 PICTURE A(12)
       VALUE 'OUT OF STOCK'.
```

Figure 13–10. Example—Numeric and Nonnumeric Literals.

A *numeric literal* is a string of characters chosen from the digits 0–9, the plus or minus sign, and the decimal point. The value of the literal is implicit in the character itself. Thus, 842 is both the literal and the value itself. The primary use of numeric literals is in arithmetic computations.

A *nonnumeric literal* is composed of a string of any character in the COBOL character set except the quotation marks, enclosed in quotation marks. Nonnumeric literals are used mainly for displaying messages and printing headings for reports.

Figurative constants are reserved words that have a predefined value recognized by the COBOL compiler (Fig. 13.11). These words are frequently used in programming so that the programmer is relieved of the responsibility of assigning names for commonly used constants. The use of the figurative constant ZEROS in the statement MOVE ZEROS TO WORK, will fill the entire area WORK with zeros. Similarly, the use of the figurative constant SPACES in the statement MOVE SPACES TO OUT will blank out the entire area OUT.

HIGH-VALUE(S)	are assigned the highest value in the computer collating sequence
LOW-VALUE(S)	are assigned the lowest value in the computer collating sequence
ZERO ZEROS ZEROES	are assigned the value 0
SPACE SPACES	are assigned to one or more spaces (blanks)
QUOTE QUOTES	are assigned to one or more quotation mark characters (apostrophes)

ALL "any literal" will represent a continuous sequence of "any literal."

The singular and plural forms of figurative constants are interchangeable.

Figure 13–11. Figurative Constants.

Operators. Operators are used in the COBOL language to specify some sort of action or relationship between two items in a program. Symbols are special characters that have a specific meaning to the compiler. The type of operators and their symbolic forms are as follows;

Arithmetic Expression Operators are used in the COMPUTE statement and in relational conditions (Fig. 13.12). The characters used in arithmetic expressions are as follows:

Meaning	Symbol	Name
ADDITION	+	Plus
SUBTRACTION	—	Minus
MULTIPLICATION	*	Asterisk (times)
DIVISION	/	Slash (divided by)
EXPONENTIATION	**	Double Asterisk (raise to the power of)
EQUAL	=	Make equivalent to
PARENTHESIS	( )	To control sequence of calculations

Relational Expression Operators. The logical flow of a program frequently depends on the ability to make comparisons of the current value of a data-name and/or to compare this value with another or predetermined value. The expression can be reduced to a true or false statement. If the statement is

Figure 13–12. Example—Arithmetic Expression Operators.

```
COMPUTE CAPACITY = (UTILITY * SPAN)/
   (RANGE + CONSUMPTION * EFFICIENCY).
```

true, the remainder of the statement is executed. If the statement is false, the program is directed to the next sentence unless an alternative action is specified (Fig. 13.13). The following are the symbols used in relational expressions together with their meanings.

Meaning	Symbol	Name
EQUAL	=	"IS EQUAL TO"
GREATER THAN	>	"IS GREATER THAN"
LESS THAN	<	"IS LESS THAN"
PARENTHESIS	( )	To control the sequence of statements to be evaluated.

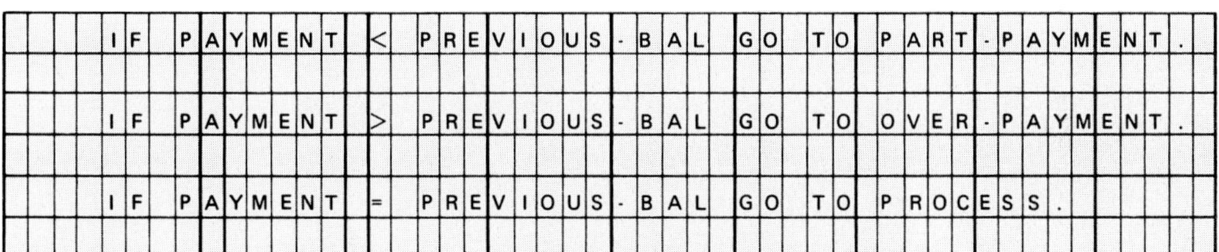

```
IF PAYMENT < PREVIOUS-BAL GO TO PART-PAYMENT.
IF PAYMENT > PREVIOUS-BAL GO TO OVER-PAYMENT.
IF PAYMENT = PREVIOUS-BAL GO TO PROCESS.
```

Figure 13–13. Example—Relational Operators.

Logical Expression Operators are used to combine simple statements in the same expression for the purpose of testing the condition of the expression (Fig. 13.14). The following are the operators used in logical operations together with their meanings.

Operator	Meaning
AND	Used to evaluate both statements.
OR	Used to evaluate either or both statements.
NOT	Used to negate a positive condition.
( )	Used to control the sequence of enclosed statements.

```
IF A > B OR A = C AND D IS POSITIVE, GO TO PROC-1.
```

Figure 13–14. Example—Logical Operators.

READ BILL-FILE; AT END, GO TO FINISH.

Figure 13–15. Example—Punctuation Symbols.

Punctuation Symbols are important to the successful execution of a COBOL program (Fig. 13.15). Unless the correct usage of symbols is employed, many diagnostic errors can be generated during the compilation phase. The following are the symbols and their meanings as used to punctuate entries.

Name	Symbol	Meaning
PERIOD	.	Used to terminate entries.
COMMA	,	Used to separate operands, clauses in a series of entries.
SEMICOLON	;	Used to separate clauses and statements.
QUOTATION MARK	'	Used to enclose nonnumeric literals.
PARENTHESES	( )	Used to enclose subscripts.

STATEMENTS

A statement is a syntactically valid combination of words and symbols written in the Procedure Division and used to express a thought in COBOL. The statement combines COBOL reserved words with programmer-defined operands.

A COBOL statement may be either a simple or compound expression. A *simple* statement would specify one action, while a *compound* statement, usually joined by a logical operator, would specify more than one form of action.

The statement may be either imperative or conditional. An *imperative* statement directs the program to perform a particular operation under *all* conditions (Fig. 13.16), while a *conditional* statement specifies that the operation be performed only if the condition is satisfied (true) or not (false) Fig. 13.17).

Figure 13–16. Example—Simple Imperative Statement.

```
GO TO READ-RECORD.
```

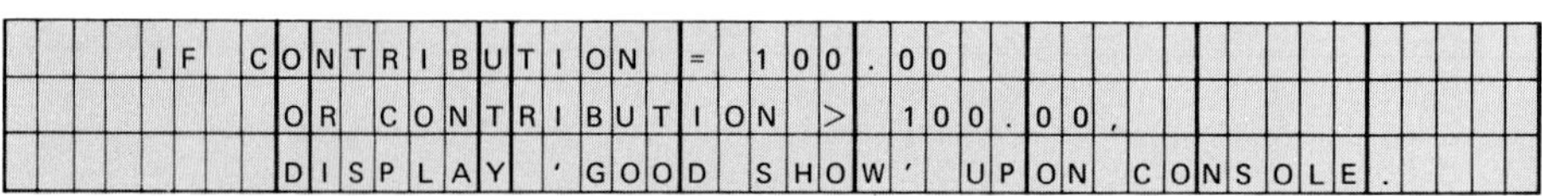

IF CONTRIBUTION = 100.00
OR CONTRIBUTION > 100.00,
DISPLAY 'GOOD SHOW' UPON CONSOLE.

Figure 13–17. Example—Compound Conditional Statement.

WRITING COBOL PROGRAMS

COBOL Program Sheet Format. The source program is written by the programmer on a COBOL Program Sheet Coding Form. The program sheet provides the programmer with a standard method of writing COBOL source programs. Despite the necessary restrictions, the program is written in rather free form. However, there are precise rules for using this form. Unless these rules are followed, especially with respect to spacing, many diagnostic errors will be generated unnecessarily (Figs. 13.18, 13.19).

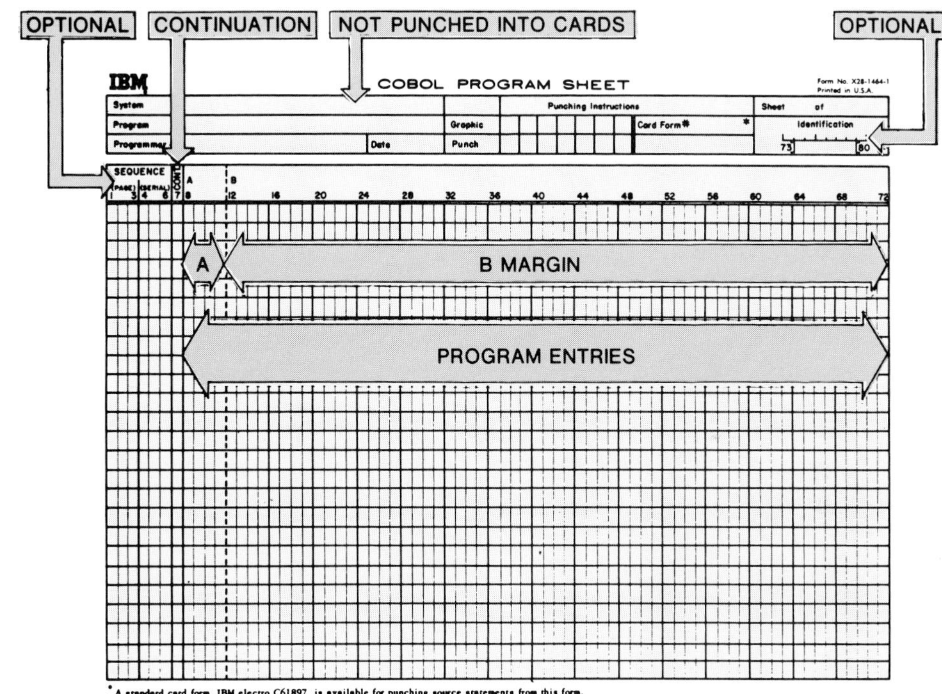

Figure 13–18. COBOL Program Sheet Rules.

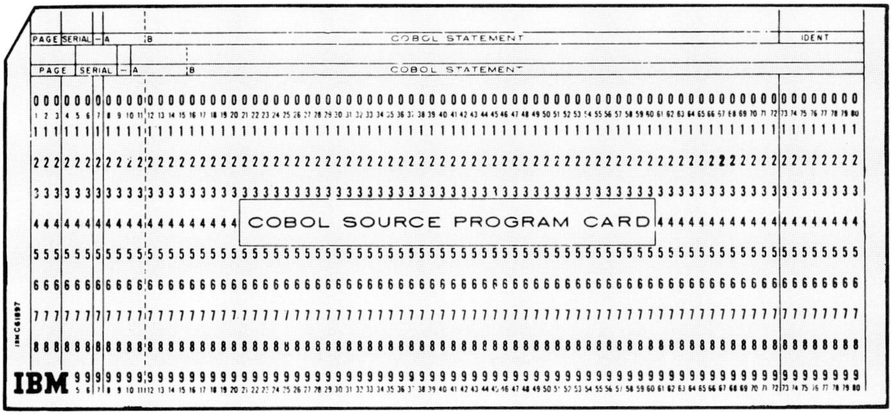

PAGE SERIAL – A B COBOL STATEMENT IDENT

COBOL SOURCE PROGRAM CARD

IBM

Figure 13–19. COBOL Program Card.

Sequence Numbers (1–6). The sequence numbers are written in columns 1 through 6 of the form. The sequence number consisting of six digits is used to identify numerically each card to the COBOL compiler. The use of these sequence numbers has no effect on the object program. It is a good practice to use these sequence numbers since they will provide a control on the sequence of the cards if the cards are scattered or if an insertion is to be made in the program. If sequence numbers are used they must be in ascending order as the compiler will check the sequence and indicate any sequence errors. No sequence check is made if the columns are left blank.

Continuation Indicator (7). A coded statement may not extend beyond column 72 of the coding form. To continue a statement on a succeeding line, it is not necessary to use all the spaces up to column 72 on the first line. Any excess spaces are disregarded by the compiler. If a statement must be continued on a succeeding line (split words or literals), the continuing word must begin at the B margin (column 12 or any column to the right of column 12), and a hyphen placed in column 7 (Fig. 13.20).

Sequence (PAGE) 1–3	Sequence (SERIAL) 4–6	CONT. 7	A 8	B 12 … 72
	01			
	02			02 TITLE, PICTURE A(38), VALUE 'LISTING OF DATA RECORDS IN F
	03	-		'ILE NUMBER'.

Figure 13–20. Continuation Nonnumeric Literal.

Program Statements (8–72). These columns are used to write source program entries. These columns are grouped as to margins. *A* margin begins at column 8 and continues through column 11. Any information between these two columns is considered to be written at the *A* margin. The *B* margin begins at column 12 and continues through column 72. Any information written between these two columns is considered to be written at the *B* margin. There are important rules for entries that are to begin at the *A* or *B* margins.

Identification Code (73–80). These columns are used for the names of the program for identification purpose. The code has no effect on the object deck or compilation, and may be left blank.

PROGRAM STRUCTURE

COBOL programs are arranged in a series of entries that comprise divisions, sections, and paragraphs. A division is composed of a series of sections, while a section is made up of paragraphs. Paragraphs are composed of a series of sentences containing statements (Figs. 13.21, 13.22).

Divisions. Four divisions are required in every COBOL program. They are Identification, Environment, Data, and Procedure. These divisions must always be written in the aforementioned sequence. A fixed name header

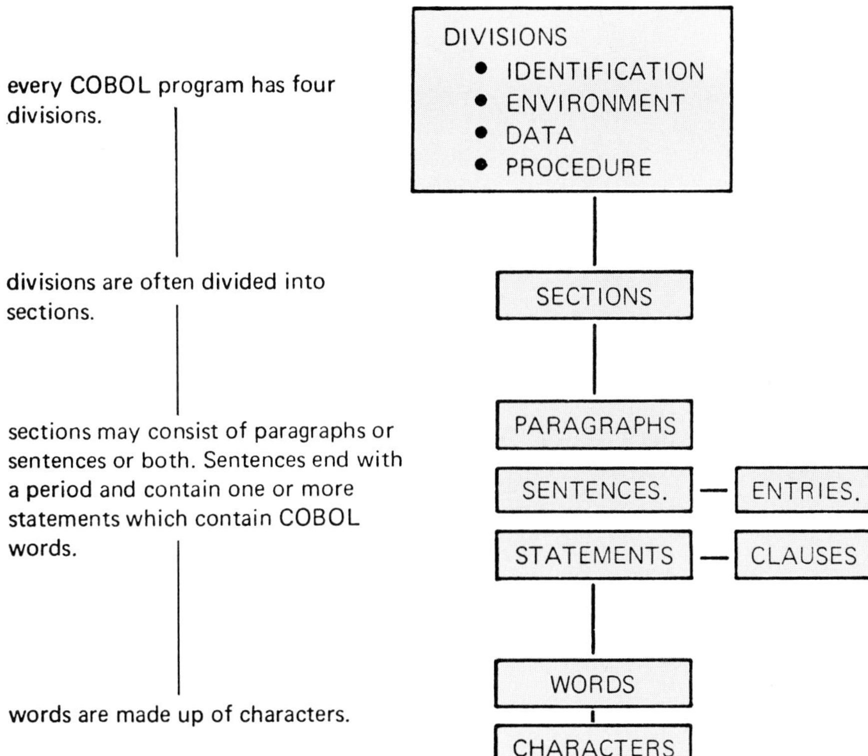
COBOL PROGRAM STRUCTURE
every COBOL program has four divisions.
DIVISIONS
• IDENTIFICATION
• ENVIRONMENT
• DATA
• PROCEDURE
divisions are often divided into sections.
SECTIONS
sections may consist of paragraphs or sentences or both. Sentences end with a period and contain one or more statements which contain COBOL words.
PARAGRAPHS
SENTENCES. — ENTRIES.
STATEMENTS — CLAUSES
words are made up of characters.
WORDS
CHARACTERS

Figure 13–21. COBOL Program Structure—Schematic.

consists of the division name followed by a space and the word DIVISION, and a period on a line by itself.

Sections. The next group in the hierarchy is sections. All divisions do not necessarily contain sections. The Environment and Data Division always contain sections with fixed names. Sections are never found in the Identification Division, while the Procedure Division sections are optional and are created by the programmer if needed.

The beginning of each section is preceded by the name of the section followed by a space, the word SECTION, and a period on a line by itself.

Paragraphs. All divisions except the Data Division contain paragraphs. In the Identification and Environment Divisions, the paragraphs have fixed names. The paragraph names in the Procedure Division are supplied by the programmer.

Each paragraph is identified by a paragraph name followed by a period and space. Paragraph headers *do not* contain the word PARAGRAPH. The paragraph header need not appear on a line by itself; however, it must be the first entry, and can be followed on the same line by a series of entries.

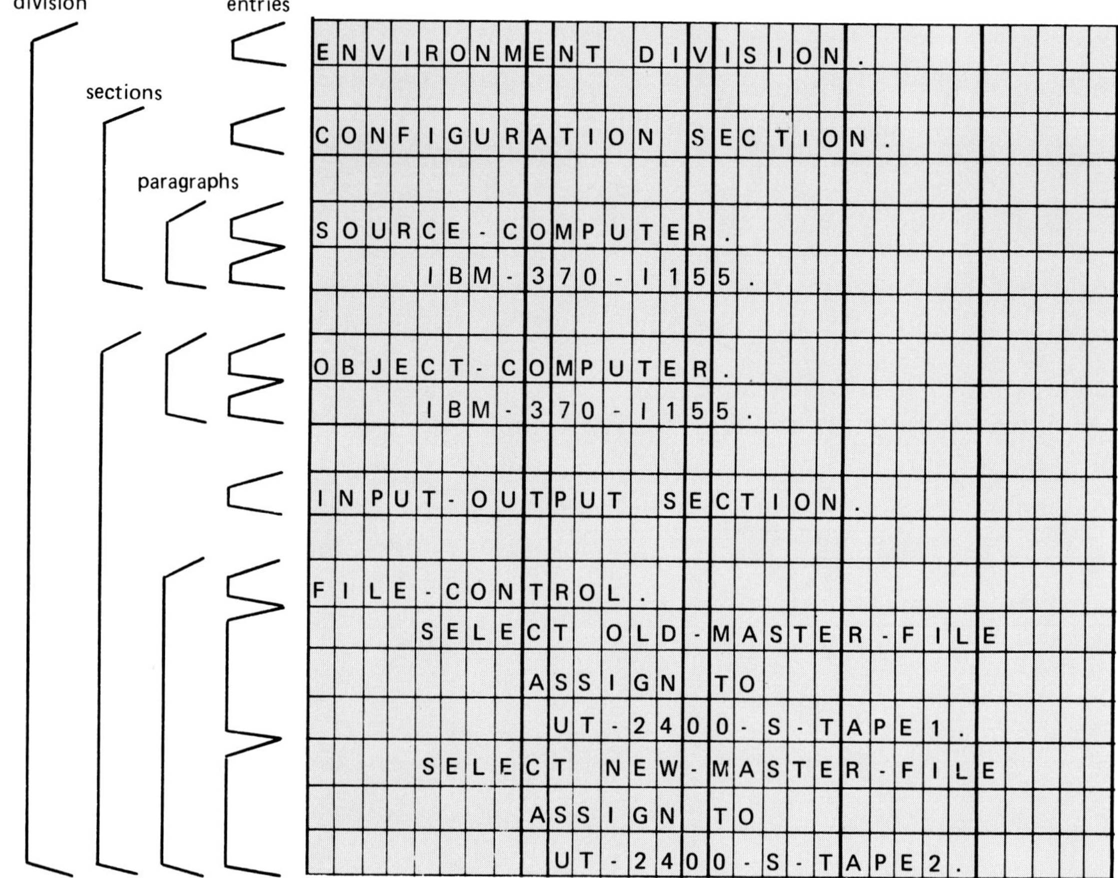

Figure 13–22. Example—COBOL Program Structure.

A paragraph header entry consists of either a reserved word or a data-name and a period.

Entries (sentences) consist of a series of statements terminated by a period and a space. These statements must follow precise format rules as to sequence.

DIVISIONS OF COBOL

Every COBOL source program is divided into four divisions (Fig. 13.23). Each division must be placed in its proper sequence, beginning with a division header, and all the format rules for the particular division must be abided by. The four divisions listed in sequence with their main functions are:

Identification Division — Identifies the program to the computer.

Environment Division — Describes the computer to be used and the hardware features to be used in the program.

Figure 13–23. The Four Divisions of a COBOL Program.

IDENTIFICATION DIVISION. Provides all of the necessary documentation for the program such as:

the program name and number,
the programmer's name,
the system or application to which the program belongs,
the security restrictions on the use of the program,
a brief description of the processing performed and the output produced,
the dates on which the program was written and compiled.

ENVIRONMENT DIVISION.

CONFIGURATION SECTION.
SOURCE-COMPUTER. What computer will be used for compilation?
OBJECT-COMPUTER. What computer will be used for running the compiled object program?
SPECIAL-NAMES. What names have you assigned to the sense (alteration) switches and the channels of the paper tape loop on the printer?
INPUT-OUTPUT SECTION.
FILE-CONTROL. What name and hardware device have you assigned to each file used by the object program?

DATA DIVISION.

FILE SECTION. For each file named in the FILE-CONTROL paragraph above:
the file name,
the record name,
the layout of the record—the name, location, size, and format of each field.
WORKING-STORAGE SECTION. The size, format, and content of every counter, storage area, or constant value used by the program.

PROCEDURE DIVISION. The individual processing steps, written as COBOL-language statements. This division is divided into programmer-created paragraphs, each containing all of the procedure statements which constitute one particular routine.

Data Division	Defines the characteristics of the data to be used, including the files, record layouts, and storage areas.
Procedure Division	Consists of a series of statements directing the processing of the data according to the program logic as expressed in the detailed program flowchart.

IDENTIFICATION DIVISION

The Identification Division contains the necessary information to identify the program that is written and compiled. A unique data-name is assigned to the source program (Fig. 13.24).

The Identification Division must appear first at compile time. The intended use of the division is to supply information to the reader. Usually it contains information as to when the program was written, by whom, and any security information relative to the program. The REMARKS paragraph usually contains the purpose of the program, a brief description of the processing to be performed, and the outputs produced. This information will serve as documentation for the program (Fig. 13.25).

ENVIRONMENT DIVISION

Although COBOL is to a large degree machine-independent, there are some aspects of programming that depend upon the particular computer to be used and the associated input and output devices. The Environment Division is the one division that is machine-dependent since it contains the necessary information about the equipment that will be used to compile and exe-

```
IDENTIFICATION DIVISION.
PROGRAM-ID. program-name.
[AUTHOR. [comment-entry]...]
[INSTALLATION. [comment-entry]...]
[DATE-WRITTEN. [comment-entry]...]
[DATE-COMPILED. [comment-entry]...]
[SECURITY. [comment-entry]...]
[REMARKS. [comment-entry]...]
```

Figure 13–24. Identification Division Format.

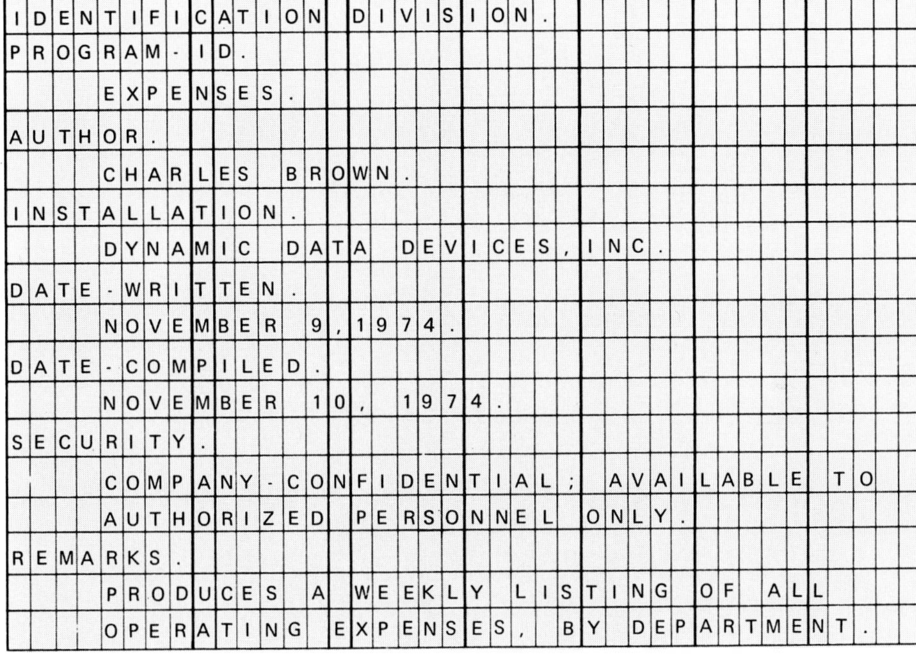

```
IDENTIFICATION DIVISION.
PROGRAM-ID.
    EXPENSES.
AUTHOR.
    CHARLES BROWN.
INSTALLATION.
    DYNAMIC DATA DEVICES, INC.
DATE-WRITTEN.
    NOVEMBER 9, 1974.
DATE-COMPILED.
    NOVEMBER 10, 1974.
SECURITY.
    COMPANY-CONFIDENTIAL; AVAILABLE TO
    AUTHORIZED PERSONNEL ONLY.
REMARKS.
    PRODUCES A WEEKLY LISTING OF ALL
    OPERATING EXPENSES, BY DEPARTMENT.
```

Figure 13–25. Example—Identification Division.

cute the source program. To exchange a COBOL program from one computer to another, the Environment Division would have to be modified or even replaced to make the source program compatible to the new computer.

The Environment Division describes the hardware features of the source as well as the object computer. Each data file to be used in the program must be assigned to an input or output device. If special input or output techniques are to be used in the program, they have to be specified in this division. Any special-names assigned to hardware devices must be stipulated here (Figs. 13.26, 13.27).

```
ENVIRONMENT DIVISION.
CONFIGURATION SECTION.
SOURCE-COMPUTER paragraph
OBJECT-COMPUTER paragraph
[SPECIAL-NAMES paragraph]
[INPUT-OUTPUT SECTION.
FILE-CONTROL paragraph
[I-O-CONTROL paragraph]]
```

Figure 13–26. Environment Division Format.

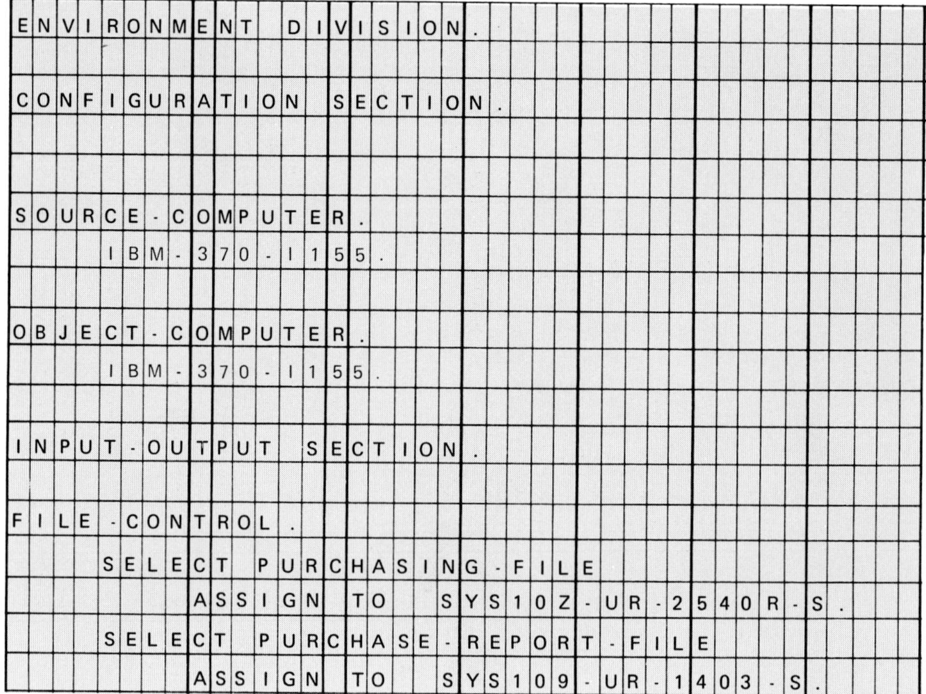

```
ENVIRONMENT DIVISION.

CONFIGURATION SECTION.


SOURCE-COMPUTER.
        IBM-370-I155.

OBJECT-COMPUTER.
        IBM-370-I155.

INPUT-OUTPUT SECTION.

FILE-CONTROL.
        SELECT PURCHASING-FILE
            ASSIGN TO SYS10Z-UR-2540R-S.
        SELECT PURCHASE-REPORT-FILE
            ASSIGN TO SYS109-UR-1403-S.
```

Figure 13–27. Example—Environment Division.

DATA DIVISION

The Data Division describes the formats and the detailed characteristics of the input and output data to be processed by the object program. The programmer attaches unique names to the files, the records within the files, and the items within the records (Fig. 13.28). All files that are named in the Environment Division must be described therein.

Figure 13–28. Data Division Format.

```
DATA DIVISION.
FILE SECTION.
{file description entry
{record description entry}...}...
WORKING-STORAGE SECTION.
[data item description entry]...
[record description entry]...
```

In addition to the file and record descriptions of data, work areas, and constants to be used in the program must be described in the Working-Storage Section of the division (Fig. 13.29).

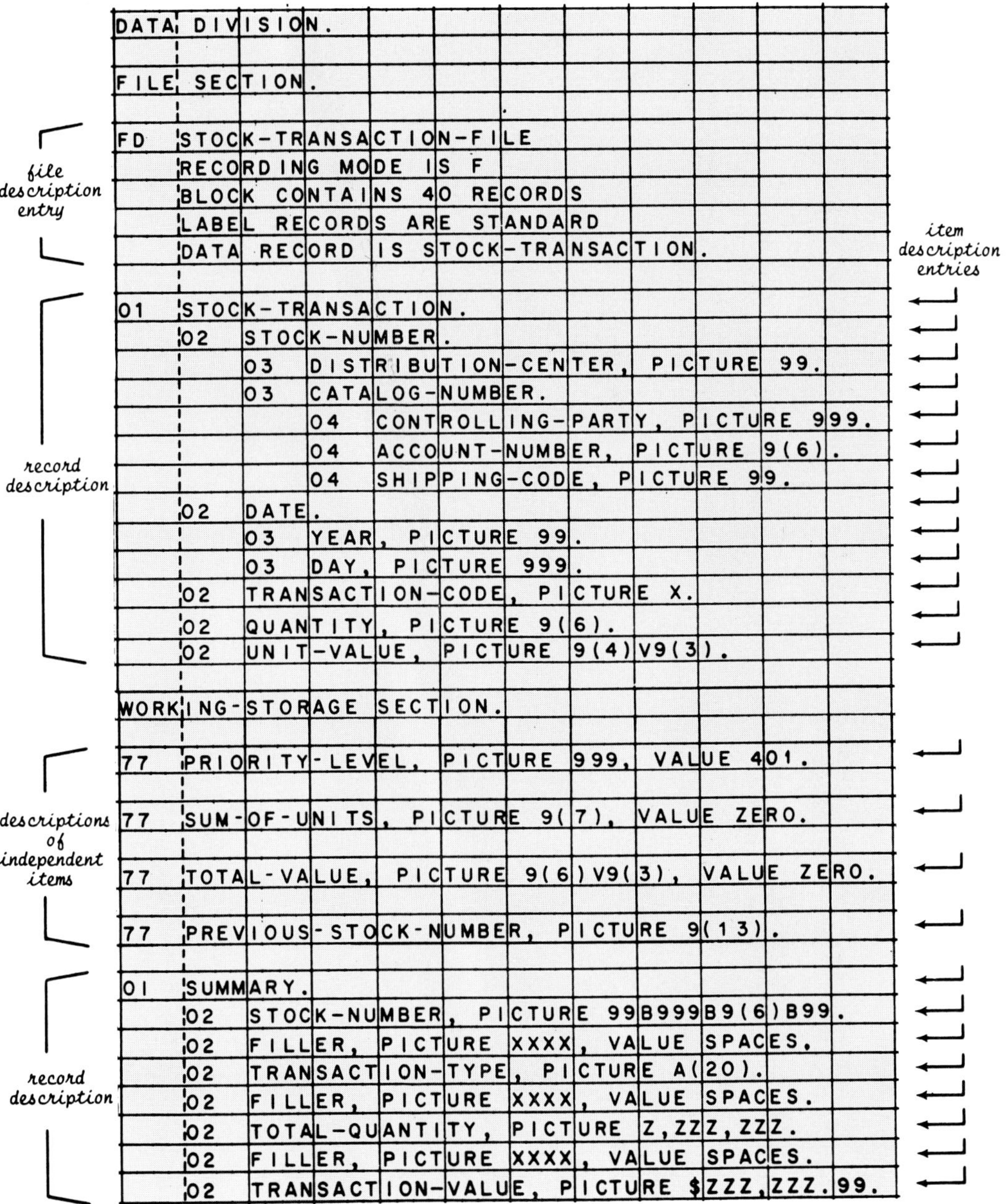

```
DATA DIVISION.

FILE SECTION.

FD  STOCK-TRANSACTION-FILE
    RECORDING MODE IS F
    BLOCK CONTAINS 40 RECORDS
    LABEL RECORDS ARE STANDARD
    DATA RECORD IS STOCK-TRANSACTION.

01  STOCK-TRANSACTION.
    02  STOCK-NUMBER.
        03  DISTRIBUTION-CENTER, PICTURE 99.
        03  CATALOG-NUMBER.
            04  CONTROLLING-PARTY, PICTURE 999.
            04  ACCOUNT-NUMBER, PICTURE 9(6).
            04  SHIPPING-CODE, PICTURE 99.
    02  DATE.
        03  YEAR, PICTURE 99.
        03  DAY, PICTURE 999.
    02  TRANSACTION-CODE, PICTURE X.
    02  QUANTITY, PICTURE 9(6).
    02  UNIT-VALUE, PICTURE 9(4)V9(3).

WORKING-STORAGE SECTION.

77  PRIORITY-LEVEL, PICTURE 999, VALUE 401.

77  SUM-OF-UNITS, PICTURE 9(7), VALUE ZERO.

77  TOTAL-VALUE, PICTURE 9(6)V9(3), VALUE ZERO.

77  PREVIOUS-STOCK-NUMBER, PICTURE 9(13).

01  SUMMARY.
    02  STOCK-NUMBER, PICTURE 99B999B9(6)B99.
    02  FILLER, PICTURE XXXX, VALUE SPACES.
    02  TRANSACTION-TYPE, PICTURE A(20).
    02  FILLER, PICTURE XXXX, VALUE SPACES.
    02  TOTAL-QUANTITY, PICTURE Z,ZZZ,ZZZ.
    02  FILLER, PICTURE XXXX, VALUE SPACES.
    02  TRANSACTION-VALUE, PICTURE $ZZZ,ZZZ.99.
```


Figure 13–29. Example—Data Division Entries.

Entries in this division will describe how the items are grouped and organized into records to be used in the processing. Information, such as the type of data and usage of the data, will be found in the division (Fig. 13.30).

The Environment Division describes the computer upon which the source program will be compiled and the computer that will be used to execute the object program; the Data Division describes the characteristics of the data; and the Procedure Division will describe the logical steps necessary to process the data.

```
01  ACCOUNTS-RECEIVABLE-RECORD.
    02  CUSTOMER.
        03  NUMBER          PICTURE X(6).
        03  NAME            PICTURE X(30).
    02  SALESMAN.
        03  BRANCH-OFFICE   PICTURE 999.
        03  SERIAL-NUMBER   PICTURE 9(5).
    02  INVOICE.
        03  NUMBER          PICTURE 9(5).
        03  DATE.
            04  MONTH       PICTURE 99.
            04  DAY         PICTURE 99.
            04  YEAR        PICTURE 99.
        03  AMOUNT          PICTURE 9(4)V99.
    02  PAYMENT.
        03  DATE.
            04  MONTH       PICTURE 99.
            04  DAY         PICTURE 99.
            04  YEAR        PICTURE 99.
        03  DISCOUNT        PICTURE 9(4)V99.
        03  NET-AMOUNT      PICTURE 9(4)V99.
    02  RECORD-CODE         PICTURE X.
```


Figure 13–30. Example—Record Description Entries, Levels.

PROCEDURE DIVISION

The Procedure Division specifies the actions expected of the object program to process the data to achieve the desired outputs. The division indicates the sequential order of the processing steps and also any alternate paths of actions where necessitated by decisions encountered during the processing (Fig. 13.31).

This division is usually written from the program flowchart. The names of the data described in the Data Division are used to write sentences, employing program verbs to direct the computer to perform some action. The main types of action that may be specified are input and output, arithmetic, data transmission, and sequence control. All sentences are imperative even though they may be preceded by IF, since they direct the computer to perform some action (Fig. 13.32).

Examples of Program Verbs

Input and Output	OPEN, READ, WRITE, CLOSE, ACCEPT, DISPLAY
Arithmetic	ADD, SUBTRACT, MULTIPLY, DIVIDE, COMPUTE
Data Transmission	MOVE, EXAMINE
Sequence Control	GO TO, PERFORM, ALTER, STOP

OPERATION OF A COBOL PROGRAM

An example of a COBOL entry will best illustrate the basic principles of operation of a procedure-oriented COBOL program.

Assume that the programmer wished to move data from one area in storage to another.

MOVE INVENTORY-MASTER TO OUTPUT-REPORT.

Before the above statement can be executed, the data names INVENTORY-MASTER and OUTPUT-REPORT must have been described in the Data Division. Such information about the data as the maximum size and how the data is expressed (alphabetic, numeric, alphanumeric) are stated in the Data Division and are necessary to the successful execution of the instruction.

Figure 13–31. Procedure Division Format.

```
PROCEDURE DIVISION
procedure-name .
   sentence . . .
[procedure-name .
   sentence . . .] . . .
```

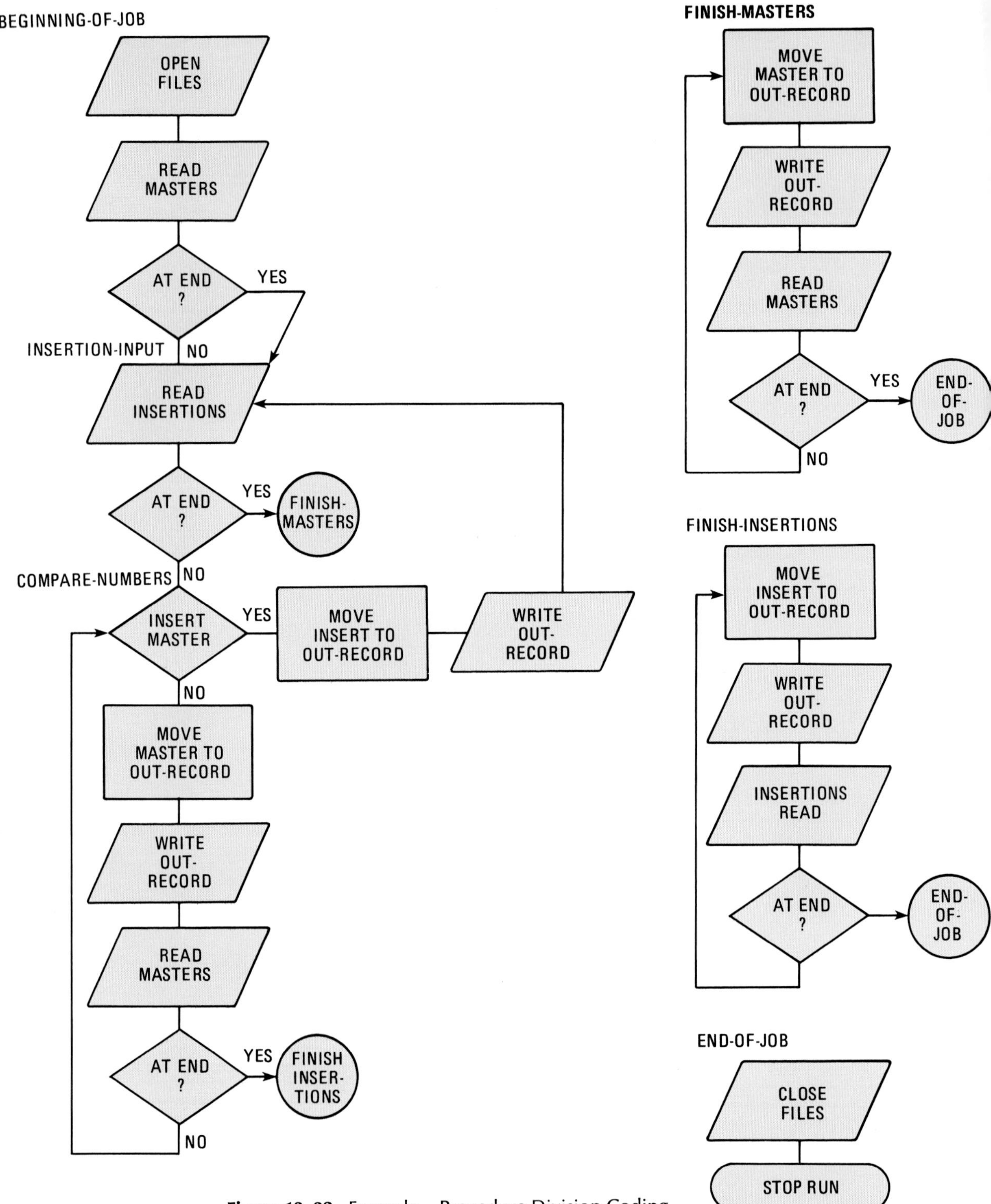

Figure 13–32. Example—Procedure Division Coding.

```
PROCEDURE DIVISION.
BEGINNING-OF-JOB.
    OPEN INPUT MASTERS, INSERTIONS;
        OUTPUT UPDATED-MASTERS.
    READ MASTERS; AT END,
        GO TO INSERTION-INPUT.
INSERTION-INPUT.
    READ INSERTIONS; AT END,
        GO TO FINISH-MASTERS.
COMPARE NUMBERS.
    IF NUMBER OF INSERT < NUMBER OF MASTER,
        MOVE INSERT TO OUT-RECORD,
        WRITE OUT-RECORD,
        GO TO INSERTION-INPUT.
    MOVE MASTER TO OUT-RECORD.
    WRITE OUT-RECORD.
    READ MASTERS; AT END,
        GO TO FINISH-INSERTIONS.
        GO TO COMPARE-NUMBERS.
FINISH-MASTERS.
    MOVE MASTER TO OUT-RECORD.
    WRITE OUT-RECORD.
    READ MASTERS; AT END, GO TO END-OF-JOB.
    GO TO FINISH-MASTERS.
FINISH-INSERTIONS.
    MOVE INSERT TO OUT-RECORD.
    WRITE OUT RECORD.
    READ INSERTIONS; AT END,
        GO TO END-OF-JOB.
    GO TO FINISH-INSERTIONS.
END OF JOB.
    CLOSE MASTERS, INSERTIONS,
        UPDATED-MASTERS.
    STOP RUN.
```

-32.
ued).

When the translator encounters this statement, it has access to certain information that will aid in the translation. The exact procedure of translation will vary with the different types of computers used. In any case, the problem programmer is not concerned with the details of translation into machine language.

The translator examines first, the word MOVE. A special list of reserved words are part of the translator program. The necessary machine-language instructions are inserted in the object program to accomplish the movement of the data.

The next word in the statement is INVENTORY-MASTER. From the format of the verb MOVE, the translator ascertains that this is a data name supplied by the programmer and should be described in the Data Division. Information as to how and where the data is stored in the computer is obtained from this division and the translator will then proceed to insert in the object program the necessary machine-language instructions needed to locate and obtain the data.

When the word TO is encountered, the translator again consults the special word list for the interpretation of the word. In this instance, the TO directs the information to be moved to another location.

The OUTPUT-REPORT word is then examined by the translator by referral to the description of the item in the Data Division. Certain information about the data word is obtained and this will be used by the translator in accomplishing the move.

For example, if the item (INVENTORY-MASTER) is shorter in length than the receiving area (OUTPUT-REPORT), certain functions have to be performed. If numeric data is involved in the move, the source data is aligned to the decimal point in the receiving area. Excess positions at either end of the receiving field are filled with zeros. In addition, if the receiving area specifies editing, zero suppression, insertion of dollar signs, etc., all will take place in the receiving area at the time of the move.

On the other hand, if alphabetic or alphanumeric information is included in the move, the source data is placed in the receiving field beginning at the left-most position and continuing until all the source data is transferred. All excess positions at the right of the receiving field are filled with spaces.

As in English statements, a period (.) at the end of the statement terminates the sentence. The effect of the period in the COBOL translator is quite simple as it tells the translator that it has received the last word to which the MOVE statement applies.

The previously described steps are performed by the compiler in the translation of a source program into an object program. Procedures may not always be performed in the same sequence because machines vary and each translator is adapted to a certain machine. However, regardless of the machine, the same COBOL-language sentence produces the necessary machine-language instructions to move the data INVENTORY-MASTER to a location called OUTPUT-REPORT (Figs. 13.33, 13.34).

ACCOUNTS RECEIVABLE PROBLEM

CALCULATIONS TO BE PERFORMED

1. Calculate Accounts Receivable = Amount Paid + Discount Allowed.
2. Final Totals for Accounts Receivable, Discount Allowed and Amount Paid.

OUTPUT

Print a report as follows:

ACCOUNTS RECEIVABLE REGISTER

CUST. NO. CUST. NAME INV. NO. ACCTS. REC. DISCT. ALLOW. AMT. PAID

TOTALS

ACCOUNTS RECEIVABLE PROBLEM

START

INIT. OPEN FILES

PRT HDG. PRINT HEADINGS

1

AGAIN. READ A RECORD

END OF FILE — FINISH

ADD DISCT IN, AMT-PD-IN, GIVING ACCT-REC WS

ADD ACCT-REC-WS TO ACCT-REC T WS

ADD DISCT-IN TO DISCT T WS

ADD AMT PD IN TO AMT PD T WS

2

2

MOVE CUST-NAME-IN TO CUST-NAME-O

MOVE CUST-NO-IN TO CUST-NO-O

MOVE INV-NO-IN TO INV-NO-O

MOVE ACCT-REC-WS TO ACCT-REC-O

MOVE DISCT-IN TO DISCT-O

MOVE AMT-PD-IN TO AMT-PD-O

WRITE DETAIL-LINE

1

FINISH. MOVE ACCT-REC-T WS TO ACCT-REC-T-O

MOVE DISCT-T-WS TO DISCT-T-O

MOVE AMT-PD-T WS TO AMT-PD-T-O

WRITE TOTAL-LINE

CLOSE FILES

STOP

Figure 13–33. Example—COBOL Program.

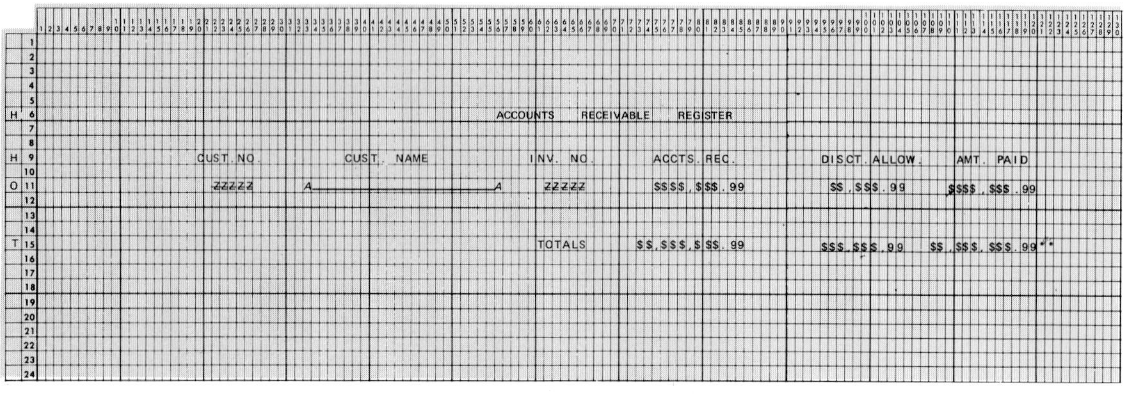


```
                              IBM DOS AMERICAN NATIONAL STANDARD COBOL         CBF CL3-5         10/27/72

001010 IDENTIFICATION DIVISION.                                         ACCTSREC
001020 PROGRAM-ID. ACCTS-REC.                                           ACCTSREC
001030 AUTHOR. C FEINGOLD.                                              ACCTSREC
001040 DATE-WRITTEN. JUNE 14 1972.                                      ACCTSREC
001045 DATE-COMPILED. 10/27/72                                          ACCTSREC
001050 INSTALLATION. WEST LOS ANGELES COLLEGE.                          ACCTSREC
001060 REMARKS. THIS PROGRAM PREPARES AN ACCOUNTS RECEIVABLE            ACCTSREC
001070     REGISTER.                                                    ACCTSREC
002010 ENVIRONMENT DIVISION.                                            ACCTSREC
002020 CONFIGURATION SECTION.                                           ACCTSREC
002030 SOURCE-COMPUTER. IBM-360-H50.                                    ACCTSREC
002040 OBJECT-COMPUTER. IBM-360-H50.                                    ACCTSREC
002045 SPECIAL-NAMES. CO1 IS SKIP-TO-ONE.                               ACCTSREC
002050 INPUT-OUTPUT SECTION.                                            ACCTSREC
002060 FILE-CONTROL.                                                    ACCTSREC
002070     SELECT FILE-IN ASSIGN TO SYS009-UR-2540R-S.                  ACCTSREC
002080     SELECT FILE-OUT ASSIGN TO SYS005-UR-1403-S                   ACCTSREC
002085     RESERVE NO ALTERNATE AREA.                                   ACCTSREC
003010 DATA DIVISION.                                                   ACCTSREC
003020 FILE SECTION.                                                    ACCTSREC
003030 FD  FILE-IN                                                      ACCTSREC
003040     RECORDING MODE F                                             ACCTSREC
003050     LABEL RECORDS OMITTED                                        ACCTSREC
003060     DATA RECORD IS CARD-IN.                                      ACCTSREC
003070 01  CARD-IN.                                                     ACCTSREC
003080     02 ENTRY-DATE-IN          PICTURE 9(5).                      ACCTSREC
003090     02 ENTRY-IN               PICTURE 99.                        ACCTSREC
003100     02 CUST-NAME-IN           PICTURE X(22).                     ACCTSREC
003110     02 INV-DATE-IN            PICTURE 9(4).                      ACCTSREC
003120     02 INV-NO-IN              PICTURE 9(5).                      ACCTSREC
003130     02 CUST-NO-IN             PICTURE 9(5).                      ACCTSREC
003140     02 LOC-IN                 PICTURE 9(5).                      ACCTSREC
003150     02 FILLER                 PICTURE X(14).                     ACCTSREC
003160     02 DISCT-IN               PICTURE 9(3)V99.                   ACCTSREC
003170     02 AMT-PD-IN              PICTURE 9(4)V99.                   ACCTSREC
003180     02 FILLER                 PICTURE X(7).                      ACCTSREC
004010 FD  FILE-OUT                                                     ACCTSREC
004020     RECORDING MODE F                                             ACCTSREC
004030     LABEL RECORDS OMITTED                                        ACCTSREC

       2

004040     DATA RECORD IS PRINTOUT.                                     ACCTSREC
004050 01  PRINTOUT          PICTURE X(133)                             ACCTSREC
004060 WORKING-STORAGE SECTION.                                         ACCTSREC
```

Figure 13–33. (Continued).

```
004070 77  ACCT-REC-WS      PICTURE 9(6)V99.                          ACCTSREC
004080 77  ACCT-REC-T-WS    PICTURE 9(7)V99   VALUE ZEROS.            ACCTSREC
004090 77  DISCT-T-WS       PICTURE 9(5)V99   VALUE ZEROS.            ACCTSREC
004095 77  AMT-PO-T-WS      PICTURE 9(7)V99   VALUE ZEROS.            ACCTSREC
004100 01  HDG-1.                                                     ACCTSREC
004110     02 FILLER        PICTURE X(56) VALUE SPACES.               ACCTSREC
004120     02 FILLER        PICTURE X(30)                             ACCTSREC
004130         VALUE 'ACCOUNTS RECEIVABLE REGISTER'.                  ACCTSREC
005010 01  HDG-2.                                                     ACCTSREC
005020     02 FILLER        PICTURE X(20) VALUE SPACES.               ACCTSREC
005030     02 FILLER        PICTURE X(9)  VALUE 'CUST. NO.'.          ACCTSREC
005040     02 FILLER        PICTURE X(10) VALUE SPACES.               ACCTSREC
005050     02 FILLER        PICTURE X(10) VALUE 'CUST. NAME'.         ACCTSREC
005060     02 FILLER        PICTURE X(11) VALUE SPACES.               ACCTSREC
005070     02 FILLER        PICTURE X(8)  VALUE 'INV. NO.'.           ACCTSREC
005080     02 FILLER        PICTURE X(7)  VALUE SPACES.               ACCTSREC
005090     02 FILLER        PICTURE X(11) VALUE 'ACCTS. REC.'.        ACCTSREC
005100     02 FILLER        PICTURE X(8)  VALUE SPACES.               ACCTSREC
005110     02 FILLER        PICTURE X(13) VALUE 'DISCT. ALLOW.'.      ACCTSREC
005120     02 FILLER        PICTURE X(5)  VALUE SAPCES.               ACCTSREC
005130     02 FILLER        PICTURE X(9)  VALUE 'AMT. PAID'.          ACCTSREC
005140 01  DETAIL-LINE.                                               ACCTSREC
005150     02 FILLER        PICTURE X(22) VALUE SPACES.               ACCTSREC
005160     02 CUST-NO-O     PICTURE 2(5).                             ACCTSREC
005170     02 FILLER        PICTURE X(7)   VALUE SPACES.              ACCTSREC
005180     02 CUST-NAME-O   PICTURE X(22).                            ACCTSREC
005190     02 FILLER        PICTURE X(6)   VALUE SPACES.              ACCTSREC
005200     02 INV-NO-O      PICTURE 2(5).                             ACCTSREC
005210     02 FILLER        PICTURE X(8)  VALUE SPACES.               ACCTSREC
005220     02 ACCT-REC-O    PICTURE $$$$,$$$.99.                      ACCTSREC
005230     02 FILLER        PICTURE X(10) VALUE SPACES.               ACCTSREC
005240     02 DISCT-O       PICTURE $$,$$$.99.                        ACCTSREC
005250     02 FILLER        PICTURE X(6)  VALUE SPACES.               ACCTSREC
006010     02 AMT-PD-O      PICTURE $$$$,$$$.99.                      ACCTSREC
006020 01  TOTAL-LINE.                                                ACCTSREC
006030     02 FILLER        PICTURE X(61) VALUE SPACES.               ACCTSREC

   3

006040     02 FILLER        PICTURE X(6)  VALUE 'TOTALS'.             ACCTSREC
006050     02 FILLER        PICTURE X(6)  VALUE SPACES.               ACCTSREC
006060     02 ACCT-REC-T-O  PICTURE $$,$$$,$$$.99.                    ACCTSREC
006070     02 FILLER        PICTURE X(9)  VALUE SPACES.               ACCTSREC
006080     02 DISCT-T-O     PICTURE $$$,$$$.99.                       ACCTSREC
006090     02 FILLER        PICTURE X(4)  VALUE SPACES.               ACCTSREC
006100     02 AMT-PD-T-O    PICTURE $$,$$$,$$$.99.                    ACCTSREC
006110     02 FILLER        PICTURE X(3)  VALUE ' **'.                ACCTSREC
007010 PROCEDURE DIVISION.                                            ACCTSREC
007020 INIT. OPEN INPUT FILE-IN, OUTPUT FILE-OUT.                     ACCTSREC
007030 PRT-HDG. WRITE PRINTOUT FROM HDG-1 AFTER ADVANCING SKIP-TO-ONE ACCTSREC
007040     LINES                                                      ACCTSREC
007050     WRITE PRINTOUT FROM HDG-2 AFTER ADVANCING 3 LINES.         ACCTSREC
007060     MOVE SPACES TO PRINTOUT.                                   ACCTSREC
007070     WRITE PRINTOUT AFTER ADVANCING 1 LINES.                    ACCTSREC
007080 AGAIN. READ FILE-IN AT END GO TO FINISH.                       ACCTSREC
007090     ADD DISCT-IN, AMT-PD-IN GIVING ACCT-REC-WS.                ACCTSREC
007100     ADD ACCT-REC-WS TO ACCT-REC-T-WS.                          ACCTSREC
007110     ADD DISCT-IN TO DISCT-T-WS.                                ACCTSREC
007120     ADD AMT-PD-IN TO AMT-PD-T-WS.                              ACCTSREC
007130     MOVE CUST-NAME-IN TO CUST-NAME-O.                          ACCTSREC
007140     MOVE CUST-NO-IN TO CUST-NO-O.                              ACCTSREC
007150     MOVE INV-NO-IN TO INV-NO-O.                                ACCTSREC
007160     MOVE ACCT-REC-WS TO ACCT-REC-O.                            ACCTSREC
007170     MOVE DISCT-IN TO DISCT-O.                                  ACCTSREC
007180     MOVE AMT-PD-IN TO AMT-PD-O.                                ACCTSREC
007190     WRITE PRINTOUT FROM DETAIL-LINE AFTER ADVANCING 1 LINES.   ACCTSREC
007200     GO TO AGAIN.                                               ACCTSREC
007210 FINISH. MOVE ACCT-REC-T-WS TO ACCT-REC-T-O.                    ACCTSREC
007220     MOVE DISCT-T-WS TO DISCT-T-O                               ACCTSREC
007230     MOVE AMT-PD-T-WS TO AMT-PD-T-O.                            ACCTSREC
007240     WRITE PRINTOUT FROM TOTAL-LINE AFTER ADVANCING 4 LINES.    ACCTSREC
007250     CLOSE FILE-IN FILE-OUT.                                    ACCTSREC
007260     STOP RUN.                                                  ACCTSREC
```

Figure 13–33. (Continued).

ACCOUNTS RECEIVABLE REGISTER

CUST. NO.	CUST. NAME	INV. NO.	ACCTS. REC.	DISCT. ALLOW.	AMT. PAID
67451	ACME MFG CO	345	$697.17	$13.67	$683.50
67452	AMERICAN STEEL CO	347	$1,398.93	$27.43	$1,371.50
67453	TAIYO CO LTD	447	$1,211.25	$23.75	$1,187.50
67454	ALLIS CHALMERS CO	451	$2,307.75	$45.25	$2,262.50
67455	XEROX CORP	435	$163.71	$3.21	$160.50
67456	GLOBE FORM CO	435	$229.50	$4.50	$225.00
67457	WATSON MFG CO	428	$113.73	$2.23	$111.50
67458	CALCOMP CORP	429	$165.75	$3.25	$162.50
67459	SHOP--RITE MARKETS	433	$168.30	$3.30	$165.00
67460	MICROSEAL CORP	440	$5.61	$.11	$5.50
67461	MITSURISHI LTD	420	$2,305.20	$45.20	$2,260.00
67462	MARK KLEIN & SONS	431	$1,393.32	$27.32	$1,366.00
67463	HONEYWELL CORP	432	$11.73	$.23	$11.50
67464	SPERRY RAND CORP	449	$2,345.49	$45.99	$2,299.50
67465	WESTINGHOUSE CORP	460	$3,047.25	$59.75	$2,987.50
67466	GARETT CORP	399	$184.62	$3.62	$181.00
67467	NANCY DOLL TOY CO	400	$22.95	$.45	$22.50
67468	RAMONAS FINE FOODS	430	$3,557.25	$69.75	$3,487.50
67469	FL CHOLOS	436	$1,795.71	$35.21	$1,760.50
67470	DATAMATION INC	437	$2,247.00	$374.50	$1,872.50
67471	MICROFICHE CORP	441	$2,555.10	$50.10	$2,505.00
67472	REALIST INC	389	$2,872.32	$56.32	$2,816.00
67473	EASTMAN KODAK CO	401	$2,311.32	$45.32	$2,266.00
67474	UNIVAC INC	410	$3,348.15	$65.65	$3,282.50
67475	AVCO CO	411	$5,015.85	$98.35	$4,917.50
67476	TRW SYSTEMS GROUP	412	$2,311.32	$45.32	$2,266.00
67477	BELL HELICOPTER CO	413	$2,878.95	$56.45	$2,822.50
67478	BOEING AEROSPACE CORP	414	$2,328.15	$45.65	$2,282.50
		TOTALS	$46,993.38	$1,251.88	$45,741.50**

Figure 13–33. (Continued).

PAYROLL REGISTER PROBLEM

INPUT

Field	Card Columns	
Department	14-16	
Serial	17-21	
Gross Earnings	57-61	XXX.XX
Insurance	62-65	XX.XX
Withholding Tax	69-72	XX.XX
State UCI Tax	73-75	X.XX
Miscellaneous Deductions	76-79	XX.XX
Code (Letter E)	80	

Figure 13–34. Example—COBOL Program.

CALCULATIONS TO BE PERFORMED

1. FICA TAX = Gross Earnings x .052 (Founded to 2 decimal places).
2. NET EARNINGS = Gross Earnings − Insurance − FICA Tax − Withholding Tax − State UCI − Miscellaneous Deductions.
3. Department Earnings value is the sum of the Net Earnings for each employee.
4. The Total Net Earnings is the sum of the Net Earnings for each department.

OUTPUT

Print a report as follows:

WEEKLY PAYROLL REGISTER

Employee No. Dept.	Serial	Gross Earnings	Insurance	FICA Tax	Withhold-ing Tax	State UCI	Misc. Ded.	Net Amount

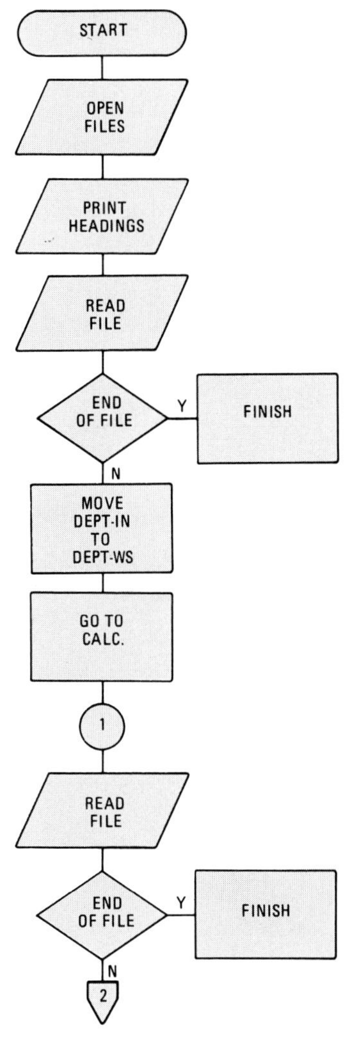

2
DEPT-IN < DEPT-WS
Y
SEQ-ERROR
N
DEPT-IN > DEPT-WS
Y
DEPT-PROC.
N
CALC.
MULTIPLY GROSS-IN BY .052 GIVING FICA-WS ROUNDED
ADD FICA-WS INS-IN, WITH-IN, UCI-IN, MISC-IN GIVING TOT-DED-WS
SUBTRACT TOT-DED-WS FROM GROSS-IN GIVING NET-WS
ADD NET-WS TO DEPT-TOT-WS
MOVE GROSS-IN TO GROSS-O
MOVE FICA-WS TO FICA-O
MOVE INS-IN TO INS-O
MOVE WITH-IN TO WITH-O
3

Figure 13–34. (Continued).

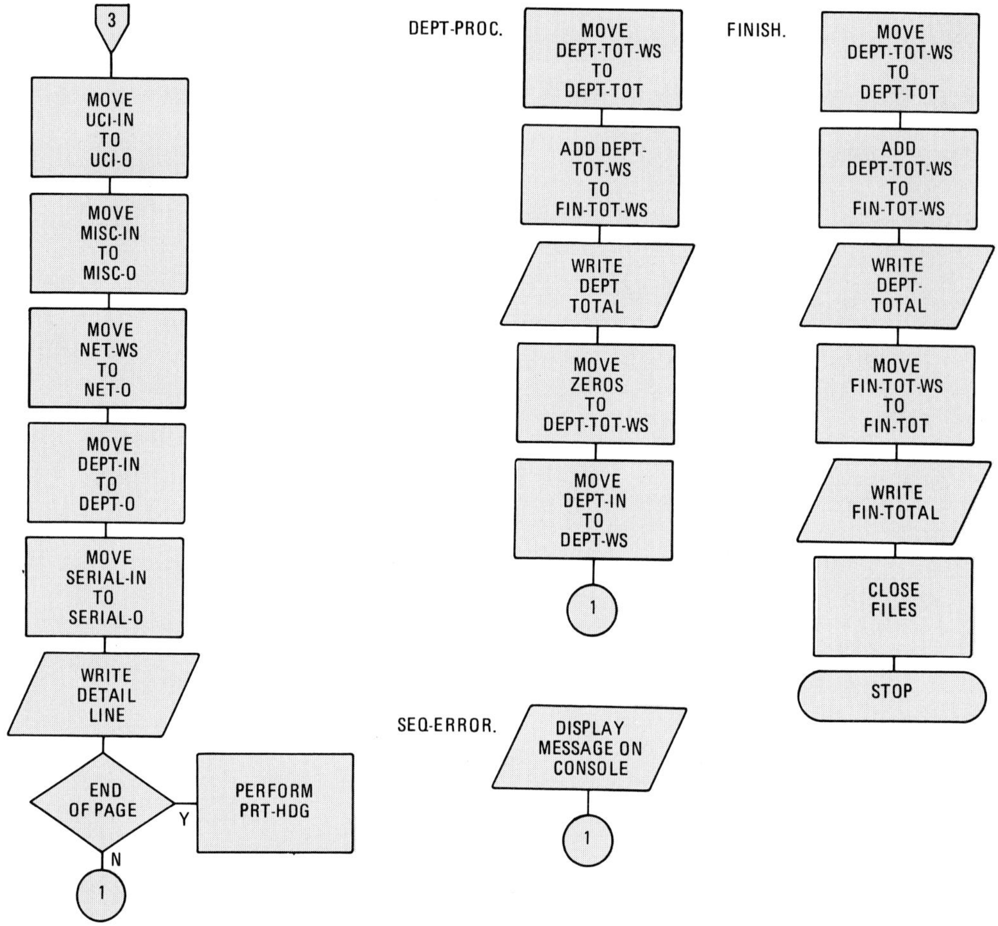

3

MOVE UCI-IN TO UCI-O

MOVE MISC-IN TO MISC-O

MOVE NET-WS TO NET-O

MOVE DEPT-IN TO DEPT-O

MOVE SERIAL-IN TO SERIAL-O

WRITE DETAIL LINE

END OF PAGE

Y

PERFORM PRT-HDG

N

1

DEPT-PROC.

MOVE DEPT-TOT-WS TO DEPT-TOT

ADD DEPT-TOT-WS TO FIN-TOT-WS

WRITE DEPT TOTAL

MOVE ZEROS TO DEPT-TOT-WS

MOVE DEPT-IN TO DEPT-WS

1

SEQ-ERROR.

DISPLAY MESSAGE ON CONSOLE

1

FINISH.

MOVE DEPT-TOT-WS TO DEPT-TOT

ADD DEPT-TOT-WS TO FIN-TOT-WS

WRITE DEPT-TOTAL

MOVE FIN-TOT-WS TO FIN-TOT

WRITE FIN-TOTAL

CLOSE FILES

STOP

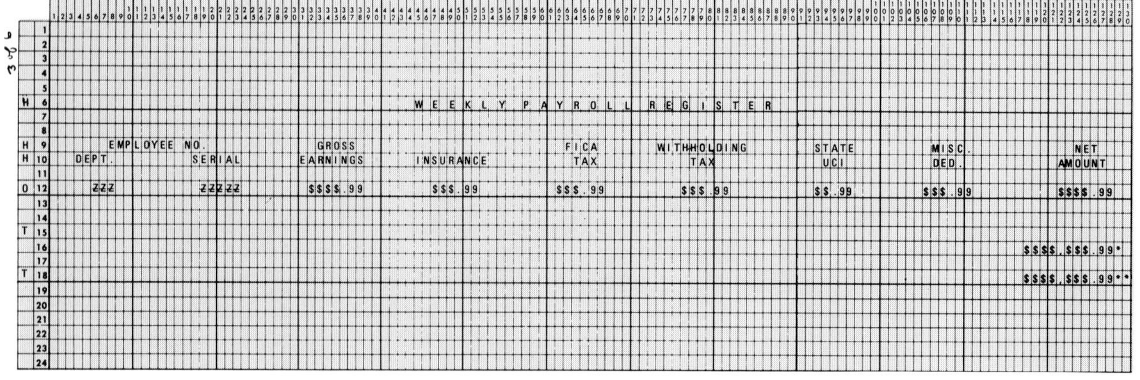

Figure 13–34.
(Continued).

```
1                                   IBM DOS AMERICAN NATIONAL STANDARD COBOL        CBF CL3-5          10/27/72

001010 IDENTIFICATION DIVISION.                                          PAYREGIS
001020 PROGRAM-ID. PAYROLL-REGISTER.                                     PAYREGIS
001030 AUTHOR. C FEINGOLD.                                               PAYREGIS
001040 DATE-WRITTEN. JUNE 14 1972.                                       PAYREGIS
001045 DATE-COMPILED. 10/27/72                                           PAYREGIS
001050 REMARKS. THIS IS A WEEKLY PAYROLL REGISTER.                       PAYREGIS
001060 ENVIRONMENT DIVISION.                                             PAYREGIS
001070 CONFIGURATION SECTION.                                            PAYREGIS
001080 SOURCE-COMPUTER. IBM-360-H50.                                     PAYREGIS
001090 OBJECT-COMPUTER. IBM-360-H50.                                     PAYREGIS
001100 INPUT-OUTPUT SECTION.                                             PAYREGIS
001110 FILE-CONTROL.                                                     PAYREGIS
001120     SELECT FILE-IN ASSIGN TO SYS009-UR-25408-S.                   PAYREGIS
001130     SELECT FILE-OUT ASSIGN TO SYS005-UR-1403-S                    PAYREGIS
001131          RESERVE NO ALTERNATE AREA.                               PAYREGIS
002010 DATA DIVISION.                                                    PAYREGIS
002020 FILE SECTION.                                                     PAYREGIS
002030 FD  FILE-IN                                                       PAYREGIS
002040     RECORDING MODE F                                              PAYREGIS
002050     LABEL RECORDS OMITTED                                         PAYREGIS
002060     DATA RECORD IS CARD-IN.                                       PAYREGIS
002070 01  CARD-IN.                                                      PAYREGIS
002080     02 FILLER         PICTURE X(13).                              PAYREGIS
002090     02 DEPT-IN        PICTURE 999.                                PAYREGIS
002100     02 SERIAL-IN      PICTURE 9(5).                               PAYREGIS
002110     02 FILLER         PICTURE X(35).                              PAYREGIS
002120     02 GROSS-IN       PICTURE 9(31)V99.                           PAYREGIS
002130     02 INS-IN         PICTURE 99V99.                              PAYREGIS
002140     02 FILLER         PICTURE X(3).                               PAYREGIS
002150     02 WITH-IN        PICTURE 99V99.                              PAYREGIS
002160     02 UCI-IN         PICTURE 9V99.                               PAYREGIS
002170     02 MISC-IN        PICTURE 99V99.                              PAYREGIS
002180     02 KODE-IN        PICTURE X.                                  PAYREGIS
003010 FD  FILE-OUT                                                      PAYREGIS
003020     RECORDING MODE F                                              PAYREGIS
003030     LABEL RECORDS OMITTED                                         PAYREGIS
003040     DATA RECORD IS PRINTOUT.                                      PAYREGIS
003050 01  PRINTOUT          PICTURE X(133).                             PAYREGIS
003060 WORKING-STORAGE SECTION.                                          PAYREGIS
```

Figure 13–34.
(Continued).

```
2

003070 77  DEPT-WS           PICTURE 999 VALUE ZEROS.                    PAYREGIS
003080 77  FICA-WS           PICTURE 99V99 VALUE ZEROS.                  PAYREGIS
003088 77  TOT-DED-WS        PICTURE 999V99 VALUE ZEROS.                 PAYREGIS
003090 77  NFT-WS            PICTURE 999V99 VALUE ZEROS.                 PAYREGIS
003100 77  DEPT-TOT-WS       PICTURE 9(4)V99 VALUE ZEROS.                PAYREGIS
003110 77  FIN-TOT-WS        PICTURE 9(6)V99 VALUE ZEROS.                PAYREGIS
003130 01  HDG-1.                                                        PAYREGIS
003140     02 FILLER         PICTURE X(45) VALUE SPACES.                 PAYREGIS
003150     02 FILLER         PICTURE X(43) VALUE 'W E E K L Y  P A Y R O LPAYREGIS
003160-    ' L  R E G I S T E R'.                                        PAYREGIS
003170 01  HDG-2.                                                        PAYREGIS
003180     02 FILLER         PICTURE X(8) VALUE SPACES.                  PAYREGIS
003190     02 FILLER         PICTURE X(119) VALUE 'EMPLOYEE NO.          PAYREGIS
003200-    '  GROSS                        FICA        WITHHOLDING       PAYREGIS
003210-    '  STATE            MISC.              NFT'.                  PAYREGIS
004010 01  HDG-3.                                                        PAYREGIS
004020     02 FILLER         PICTURE X(4) VALUE SPACES.                  PAYREGIS
004030     02 FILLER         PICTURE X(60) VALUE 'DEPT.         SERIAL   PAYREGIS
004040-    '   EARNINGS        INSURANCE               '.                PAYREGIS
004050     02 FILLER         PICTURE X(64) VALUE 'TAX           TAX      PAYREGIS
004055-    '     UCI              DED.               AMOUNT'.            PAYREGIS
004060 01  DETAIL-LINE.                                                  PAYREGIS
004070     02 FILLER         PICTURE X(6) VALUE SPACES.                  PAYREGIS
004080     02 DEPT-O         PICTURE 777.                                PAYREGIS
004090     02 FILLER         PICTURE X(10) VALUE SPACES.                 PAYREGIS
004100     02 SERIAL-O       PICTURE 2(5).                               PAYREGIS
004110     02 FILLER         PICTURE X(8) VALUE SPACES.                  PAYREGIS
004120     02 GROSS-O        PICTURE $$$$.99.                            PAYREGIS
004130     02 FILLER         PICTURE X(8) VALUE SPACES.                  PAYREGIS
004140     02 INS-O          PICTURE $$$.99.                             PAYREGIS
004150     02 FILLER         PICTURE X(9) VALUE SPACES.                  PAYREGIS
004160     02 FICA-O         PICTURE $$$.99.                             PAYREGIS
004170     02 FILLER         PICTURE X(9) VALUE SPACES.                  PAYREGIS
```

```
004180       02 WITH-O          PICTURE $$$.99.                                   PAYREGIS
004190       02 FILLER          PICTURE X(9) VALUE SPACES.                        PAYREGIS
004200       02 UCI-O           PICTURE $$.99.                                    PAYREGIS
005010       02 FILLER          PICTURE X(9) VALUE SPACES.                        PAYREGIS
005020       02 MISC-O          PICTURE $$$.99.                                   PAYREGIS
005030       02 FILLER          PICTURE X(10) VALUE SPACES.                       PAYREGIS
```

3

```
005040       02 NET-O           PICTURE $$$$.99.                                  PAYREGIS
005050 01    DEPT-TOTAL.                                                          PAYREGIS
005060       02 FILLER          PICTURE X(118) VALUE SPACES.                      PAYREGIS
005070       02 DEPT-TOT        PICTURE $$$$.$$$.99.                              PAYREGIS
005080       02 FILLER          PICTURE X VALUE '*'.                              PAYREGIS
005090 01    FIN-TOTAL.                                                           PAYREGIS
005100       02 FILLER          PICTURE X(118) VALUE SPACES.                      PAYREGIS
005110       02 FIN-TOT         PICTURE $$$$.$$$.99.                              PAYREGIS
005120       02 FILLER          PICTURE XX VALUE '**'.                            PAYREGIS
006010 PROCEDURE DIVISION.                                                        PAYREGIS
006020 INIT. OPEN INPUT FILE-IN OUTPUT FILE-OUT.                                  PAYREGIS
006030 PRT-HOG. WRITE PRINTOUT FROM HDG-1 AFTER POSITIONING 0 LINES.              PAYREGIS
006040          WRITE PRINTOUT FROM HDG-2 AFTER POSITIONING 3 LINES.              PAYREGIS
006050          WRITE PRINTOUT FROM HDG-3 AFTER POSITIONING 1 LINES.              PAYREGIS
006051 BEGIN. READ FILE-IN AT END GO TO FINISH.                                   PAYREGIS
006052     MOVE DEPT-IN TO DEPT-WS.                                               PAYREGIS
006053     GO TO CALC.                                                            PAYREGIS
006060 AGAIN. READ FILE-IN AT END GO TO FINISH.                                   PAYREGIS
006070     IF DEPT-IN < DEPT-WS GO TO SEQ-ERROR.                                  PAYREGIS
006080     IF DEPT-IN > DEPT-WS GO TO DEPT-PROC.                                  PAYREGIS
006090 CALC. MULTIPLY GROSS-IN BY .052 GIVING FICA-WS ROUNDED.                    PAYREGIS
006100     ADD FICA-WS, INS-IN. WITH-IN, UCI-IN, MISC-IN.                         PAYREGIS
006105     GIVING TOT-DED-WS.                                                     PAYREGIS
006110     SUBTRACT TOT-DED-WS FROM GROSS-IN GIVING NET-WS.                       PAYREGIS
006120     ADD NET-WS TO DEPT-TOT-WS.                                             PAYREGIS
006130     MOVE GROSS-IN TO GROSS-O.                                              PAYREGIS
006140     MOVE FICA-WS TO FICA-O.                                                PAYREGIS
006150     MOVE INS-IN TO INS-O.                                                  PAYREGIS
006160     MOVE WITH-IN TO WITH-O.                                                PAYREGIS
006170     MOVE UCI-IN TO UCI-O.                                                  PAYREGIS
006180     MOVE MISC-IN TO MISC-O.                                                PAYREGIS
006190     MOVE NET-WS TO NET-O.                                                  PAYREGIS
006200     MOVE DEPT-IN TO DEPT-O.                                                PAYREGIS
006210     MOVE SERIAL-IN TO SERIAL-O.                                            PAYREGIS
006230     WRITE PRINTOUT FROM DETAIL-LINE AFTER POSITIONING 2 LINES              PAYREGIS
006235     AT END-OF-PAGE PERFORM PRT-HDG.                                        PAYREGIS
006240     GO TO AGAIN.                                                           PAYREGIS
007010 DEPT-PROC.  MOVE DEPT-TOT-WS TO DEPT-TOT                                   PAYREGIS
007015     ADD DEPT-TOT-WS TO FIN-TOT-WS.                                         PAYREGIS
```

4

```
007020     WRITE PRINTOUT FROM DEPT-TOTAL AFTER POSITIONING 3 LINES.              PAYREGIS
007030     MOVE ZEROS TO DEPT-TOT-WS.                                             PAYREGIS
007035     MOVE DEPT-IN TO DEPT-WS.                                               PAYREGIS
007040     GO TO CALC.                                                            PAYREGIS
007050 SFQ-ERROR. DISPLAY 'EMPLOYEE NUMBER ' DEPT-IN SERIAL-IN'IS OUT OPAYREGIS
007060-    'F SEQUENCE' UPON CONSOLE.                                             PAYREGIS
007070     GO TO AGAIN.                                                           PAYREGIS
007071 FINISH.  MOVE DEPT-TOT-WS TO FIN-TOT-WS.                                   PAYREGIS
007072     ADD DEPT-TOT-WS TO FIN-TOT-WS.                                         PAYREGIS
007073     WRITE PRINTOUT FROM DEPT-TOTAL AFTER POSITIONING 3 LINES               PAYREGIS
007074     MOVE FIN-TOT-WS TO FIN-TOT.                                            PAYREGIS
007090     WRITE PRINTOUT FROM FIN-TOTAL AFTER POSITIONING 3 LINES.               PAYREGIS
007100     CLOSE FILE-IN FILE-OUT. STOP RUN.                                      PAYREGIS
```

Figure 13–34.
(Continued).

WEEKLY PAYROLL REGISTER

EMPLOYEE NO. DEPT.	SERIAL	GROSS EARNINGS	INSURANCE	FICA TAX	WITHHOLDING TAX	STATE UCI	MISC. DED.	NET AMOUNT
9	1217	$84.17	$.00	$4.38	$8.90	$.84	$.00	$70.05
9	1218	$100.65	$1.00	$5.23	$16.02	$1.19	$1.75	$75.46
9	1219	$116.40	$3.00	$6.05	$12.57	$1.34	$.00	$93.44
								$238.95*
10	374	$156.80	$2.00	$8.15	$18.90	$1.85	$2.00	$123.90
10	375	$186.57	$2.00	$9.70	$22.46	$2.02	$.00	$150.39
10	940	$67.20	$.00	$3.49	$4.80	$.60	$.75	$57.56
10	992	$75.38	$1.25	$3.92	$9.75	$.78	$.00	$59.68
								$391.53*
19	1217	$84.17	$.00	$4.38	$8.90	$.84	$.00	$70.05
19	1218	$100.65	$1.00	$5.23	$16.02	$1.19	$1.75	$75.46
19	1219	$116.40	$3.00	$6.05	$12.57	$1.34	$.00	$93.44
								$238.95*
20	374	$156.80	$2.00	$8.15	$18.90	$1.85	$2.00	$123.90
20	375	$186.57	$2.00	$9.70	$22.46	$2.02	$.00	$150.39
20	940	$67.20	$.00	$3.49	$4.80	$.60	$.75	$57.56
20	992	$75.38	$1.25	$3.92	$9.75	$.78	$.00	$59.68

WEEKLY PAYROLL REGISTER

EMPLOYEE NO. DEPT.	SERIAL	GROSS EARNINGS	INSURANCE	FICA TAX	WITHHOLDING TAX	STATE UCI	MISC. DED.	NET AMOUNT
								$391.53*
29	1217	$84.17	$.00	$4.38	$8.90	$.84	$.00	$70.05
29	1218	$100.65	$1.00	$5.23	$16.02	$1.19	$1.75	$75.46
29	1219	$116.40	$3.00	$6.05	$12.57	$1.34	$.00	$93.44
								$238.95*
30	374	$156.80	$2.00	$8.15	$18.90	$1.85	$2.00	$123.90
30	375	$186.57	$2.00	$9.70	$22.46	$2.02	$.00	$150.39
30	940	$67.70	$.00	$3.49	$4.80	$.60	$.75	$57.56
30	992	$75.38	$1.25	$3.92	$9.75	$.78	$.00	$59.68
								$391.53*
39	1217	$84.17	$.00	$4.38	$8.90	$.84	$.00	$70.05
39	1218	$100.65	$1.00	$5.23	$16.02	$1.19	$1.75	$75.46
39	1219	$116.40	$3.00	$6.05	$12.57	$1.34	$.00	$93.44
								$238.95*
								$2,130.39**

Figure 13–34.
(Continued).

SUMMARY

COBOL (*CO*mmon *B*usiness *O*riented *L*anguage) is a procedure-oriented programming language designed as a standard language for programming business data processing applications. COBOL is the most popular programming language used in business. The program is written in an English-like syntax using words, sentences and paragraphs that look and read like ordinary business English. It is the intent of this chapter to describe the features of the most widely used business programming language, COBOL.

A. *Purpose*—to establish a standard language for programming business data processing applications.
B. *Advantages.*
   1. English-like statements solve language difficulties between programmers and management.
   2. English-like statements remove the programmer from individual machine or symbolic instructions.
   3. Pretested modules of input and output relieve the programmer of the tedious task of writing input and output operations.
   4. Documentation requirements are less because the programmer is writing in a language that is familiar to him.
   5. COBOL programs written for one computer can be easily adapted for use on another computer.
   6. Separate divisions of a COBOL program permit a large program to be broken down into segments.
   7. Nonprogrammers can read English-like programs.
   8. Debugging time is reduced because of the simplicity of the diagnostics.
C. *Disadvantages.*
   1. Expectation that a single COBOL program will provide a permanent solution to a problem.
   2. Programmers must possess some knowledge of the hardware and operation of the computer.
   3. Will not generate as sophisticated program as one actually written in the actual language of the computer.
   4. COBOL processors operate only with computers having certain storage capacities.
D. *Components.* Similar to the English language in the use of words, sentences and paragraphs.
   1. *Source program*—problem-solving COBOL program which will be later compiled and translated into the machine language of the particular computer.
   2. *Object program*—the machine-language program resulting from the compilation of the source program.

3. *Compiler*—a program supplied by the computer manufacturer that translates the COBOL source program into the machine-language object program.
4. *Source-Computer*—The computer used to compile the COBOL source program.
5. *Object-Computer*—The computer that will be used to process the machine language program. Usually the same computer as the Source-Computer.
6. *Character set*—Fifty-one characters composed of alphabetic, numeric and special characters.
7. *Names*—a means of establishing words to identify certain data within a program.
   a) *Data-names*—assigned names to identify data items in a program.
   b) *Procedure-names*—symbolic names attached to various segments of the Procedure Division for reference.
   c) *Condition-names*—assigned names to items that may have various values.
   d) *Special-names*—mnemonic names to various components of the Environment Division.
8. *Rules for assignment of names.*
   a) Names may range from one to thirty characters in length.
   b) No spaces may appear within a name.
   c) Names may be formed from the alphabet, numerals, and the hyphen. No other special characters may appear in a name. If the hyphen is used, it may not be the first or last character of the name.
   d) Procedure-names may be all numerals but all other names must contain at least one alphabetic character.
   e) If names are identical, they must be qualified.
9. *Reserved words*—have preassigned meanings and must not be altered, misspelled or changed in any manner from the specific purpose of the word.
10. *Constants*—actual values of data that remains unchanged during the execution of the program.
    a) *Literals*—a string of characters whose value is determined by a set of characters of which the literal is a part.
       Numeric literal—a string of characters chosen from the digits 0–9, the plus or minus sign, and the decimal point. Primarily used for arithmetic computations.
       Nonnumeric literal—a string of any character in the COBOL character set, enclosed in quotation marks. Primarily used for displaying messages and printing report headings.

   b) *Figurative constants*—reserved words that have predefined value recognized by the COBOL compiler.

11. *Operators*—specify some sort of action or relationship between two items in a program.
    a) *Arithmetic expression*—addition (+), subtraction (−), multiplication (*), division (/), exponentiation (**), equal (=), greater than (>), less than (<), parenthesis (()).
    b) *Logical expression*—evaluate both statements (AND), evaluate either or both statement (OR), negate a positive condition (NOT), control sequence (()).
    c) *Punctuating symbols*—terminate entries (.), separate operands, clauses and statements in a series of entries (,), separate clauses and statements (;), enclose nonnumeric literals (').
12. *Statements*—a syntactically valid combination of words and symbols written in the Procedure Division used to express a thought in COBOL.

E. *Coding forms*—provides programs with a standard method of writing COBOL source programs.
   1. *Columns 1–6 Sequence Number*—Six digits used to identify numerically each card to the COBOL compiler.
   2. *Column 7 Continuation Indicator*—a hyphen in this column will cause the continuation of the statement from the previous line.
   3. *Columns 8–72 Program Statement*—used to write source program entries. These columns grouped as to margins. *A* margin begins with column 8 and continues through column 11. *B* margin begins at column 12 and continues through column 72.
   4. *Columns 73–80 Identification Code*—used for names of programs for identification purposes.

F. *Program structure*—COBOL programs are arranged in a series of entries that comprise divisions, sections, and paragraphs.
   1. *Divisions*—composed of a series of sections. Four divisions are required in every COBOL program in the following sequence; Identification, Environment, Data and Procedure. Each division must appear on a line by itself and contain the word "division."
   2. *Sections*—composed of a series of paragraphs. All divisions need not contain sections. Each section must appear on a line by itself and contain the word "section."
   3. *Paragraphs*—composed of a series of sentences containing statements. All divisions except the Data Division contain paragraphs. Paragraphs need not appear on a line by themselves.
   4. *Entries* (*sentences*)—consist of a series of statements terminated by a period.

G. *Divisions.*
   1. *Identification Division*—appears first at compile time and contains the necessary information to identify the program that is written and compiled.
   2. *Environment Division*—is a machine-dependent division that describes the computer to be used and the hardware features to be used in the program.
   3. *Data Division*—defines the characteristics of the data to be processed, including files, record layouts, and storage areas.
   4. *Procedure Division*—consists of a series of statements directing the processing of the data according to the program logic as expressed in the detailed program flowchart.

IDENTIFICATION QUESTIONS

Match the following terms with the statements that follow.

A. Compiler
B. Constant
C. Data Division
D. Diagnostic
E. Division
F. Entries
G. Environment Division
H. Figurative Constants
I. Identification Division
J. Literal
K. Names
L. Object Computer
M. Object Program
N. Operators
O. Paragraph
P. Procedure Division
Q. Reserved Words
R. Section
S. Source Computer
T. Source Program
U. Statement
V. Word

1. Composed of a series of sentences.
2. Consists of one or more COBOL characters chosen from the character set.
3. The computer used to compile the source program.
4. The machine language that will be used to process the data.
5. The actual value of data that remains unchanged during the execution of the program.
6. Words that specify some sort of action or relationship between two items in the program.
7. Composed of a series of paragraphs.
8. Describes the computer to be used and the hardware features to be used in the program.
9. A set of statements that direct the computer to perform the necessary processing.
10. A statement provided by the compiler indicating all errors in a source program excluding logic errors.
11. A program supplied by the computer manufacturer that is used to translate a source program.
12. The computer upon which the object program will be processed.
13. A string of characters where the value is determined by the set of characters in which the literal is a part.

14. A syntactically valid combination of words and symbols used to express a thought.
15. Composed of a series of statements.
16. A problem-solving program which will later be compiled into the machine language of a particular computer.
17. A means of establishing words to identify certain data within a program.
18. Words that have a predefined value recognized by the compiler.
19. Composed of a series of sections.
20. Identifies program to the computer.
21. Defines the characteristics of the data to be processed.
22. Words that have preassigned meaning that cannot be altered in any manner.

QUESTIONS FOR REVIEW

1. What is COBOL and what is its main purpose?
2. What are the important advantages of COBOL as a programming language?
3. COBOL has some serious disadvantages. What are they?
4. What is the difference between the source computer and the object computer in a COBOL program?
5. What is the significance of the following COBOL terms: Name, Reserved Word, Figurative Constant, Operator, Statement, Literals.
6. Describe the program structure of a COBOL program.
7. What are the divisions of COBOL and what are their main purpose?

CHAPTER 14

Programming Language 1 (PL/1)

The increase in the use of computer systems during the past decade has led to the development of programming languages of increasing versatility and utility. In the past, throughout the data processing field, certain computers were identified with a particular field of activity, either scientific or business. Programming languages were also specialized in the same manner. FORTRAN programming language was developed for scientific programming applications while COBOL programming language is primarily used for commercial applications.

New computing systems have recently become available, systems which are able to handle problems from both scientific and business fields with equal facility and which also possess increased data-handling capabilities. Existing higher-level programming languages do not come up to the capability levels of such new systems.

Until the recent interest in linear programming and management decision making, business applications could generally be characterized by simple arithmetic operations on great masses of data. By contrast, the scientific applications usually involved comparatively small amounts of data but rather lengthy and intricate computations. In business applications, programs are used repetitively for periods of time measured in months or years, so that the time to write and compile a program forms a comparatively insignificant percentage of the total, and the efficiency of the object program is of prime importance. By contrast, machine running time is less significant than the time required to define, write, compile, and test a program for most scientific applications.

With the development of more and more decision-making, forecasting and teleprocessing uses for computers, the business programmer requires frequent changes in his program and wider scope of computation becomes necessary. The scientific programmer on the other hand is faced with the task of handling problems with ever-greater masses of data, with a wide variety of input and output requirements. The differences between scientific and business programming is becoming less and less distinct. PL/1 is a broad base language that may be used for both scientific and business applications.

In a procedure-oriented language, the notation reflects the type of problem being solved rather than the computer on which the program is to be processed. In COBOL, the notations used resemble English statements and in FORTRAN programs, the notation resembles mathematical formulas. The PL/1 notations combine the features of both COBOL and FORTRAN notations (Fig. 14.1).

```
NEW_RECORD:   GET FILE (INPUT) LIST (PAY_#, PAYMENT);
MASTER_FILE:  GET FILE (MASTER) LIST ( LOAN_#, PRINCIPAL, RATE);
              INTEREST = PRINCIPAL * RATE/12;
              IF LOAN_# ¬ = PAY_#
                 THEN DO;
                    PRINCIPAL = PRINCIPAL + INTEREST;
                    PUT FILE (NEW_MASTER) LIST (LOAN_#, PRINCIPAL, RATE);
                    GO TO MASTER_FILE;
                    END;
                 ELSE IF PAYMENT <= PRINCIPAL + INTEREST
                    THEN BALANCE = PRINCIPAL + INTEREST - PAYMENT;
                    ELSE DO;
                       BALANCE = 0;
                       REFUND = PAYMENT - PRINCIPAL + INTEREST;
                       PUT FILE (OUTPUT) LIST (LOAN_#, 'REFUND:', REFUND);
                       END;
              PUT FILE (OUTPUT) LIST (LOAN_#, PRINCIPAL, INTEREST, PAYMENT, BALANCE);
              IF BALANCE = 0
                 THEN GO TO NEW_RECORD;
                 ELSE PUT FILE (NEW_MASTER) LIST (LOAN_#, BALANCE, RATE);
              GO TO NEW_RECORD;
```

Figure 14–1. Sample—PL/1 Entries.

Just as restrictions exist in the notation of English and mathematics, there also exist restrictions in the notation of procedure-oriented languages. Only a specified set of numbers, letters, and special characters may be used in the writing of programs. Special rules must be followed for the use of punctuation and blanks.

BASIC ELEMENTS

PL/1 FORMAT

In most programming languages, the length of an individual instruction or statement depends upon the limits of a single punched card. If the statement exceeds these limits, a notation must be made in the form of a punch in a particular column to indicate that the statement is continued in the following card.

PL/1 does not place any artificial limitation on input data. There are no fixed length formats for input although several card columns may be reserved by the compiler. Within the available card area, PL/1 can be written in rather free form; the computer recognizes a continuous stream of input. Just as a period indicates the end of an English statement, a semicolon is used to indicate the end of a PL/1 statement. The next statement may begin immediately in the next available location whether a card column, a tape character, a typewriter space, or any number of blanks intervene.

Thus PL/1 allows the programmer to write his program in a free format, eliminating the need for coding on special forms or for punching items in particular columns of a card.

Depending on the particular machine configuration or the particular compiler being used, conventions can be established so that a program can be prepared for a computer through the medium of punched cards. If this be the case, certain predetermined fields in the records could be used for the program.

For example, card columns 2 through 72 could be used for the source text and columns 73 through 80 could be used as a sequence number field.

CHARACTER SET

The PL/1 character set comprises sixty characters. These characters are English language alphabetic characters, decimal digits, and special characters.

There are twenty-nine characters known as alphabetic characters. The alphabetic characters are letters A through Z, the currency symbol ($), the commercial "at" sign @ and the number sign (#).

There are ten digits, 0–9.

There are twenty-one special characters as follows:

NAME	CHARACTER
Blank	—
Equal or assignment symbol	=
Plus sign	+
Minus sign	—
Asterisk or multiply symbol	*
Slash or divide symbol	/

Left parenthesis	(
Right parenthesis	)
Comma	,
Point or period	.
Single quote mark or apostrophe	'
Percent symbol	%
Semicolon	;
Colon	:
"Not" symbol	¬
"And" symbol	&
"Or" symbol	|
"Greater Than" symbol	>
"Less Than" symbol	<
Break character	_
Question mark	?

Special characters may be combined to create other symbols; for example, $<=$ means "less than or equal to," ¬= means "not equal to." The combination ** denotes exponentiation (X**2 means X^2). Blanks are not permitted in such character combinations.

A PL/1 program consists of words, delimiters, expressions, comments, and statements.

WORDS

Words belong to one of two categories; identifiers or constants. Adjacent words can be separated by one or more delimiters and/or blanks. For example, CALLA is considered to be one identifier; CALL A is considered to be two identifiers; AB + BC is considered to be two identifiers separated by the delimiter +, and is equivalent to AB + BC where + is surrounded by blanks.

IDENTIFIERS

An identifier can be a word created by the user to identify a file or a data item in any or all parts of his program; or it can be a *keyword* which when used in the proper context has a specific meaning to the compiler. Examples of keywords are READ, WRITE, GO TO, etc. (Fig. 14.2).

A	BINARY
LOOP	WRITE
SALESNUMBER	FILE2
XR25	#1200
DECIMAL	PAY_NUMBER

The last of these examples (PAY_NUMBER) illustrates the use of the break character to improve the readability of an identifier, since blanks are not permitted.

Figure 14–2. Examples of Identifiers.

CONSTANTS

An identifier is a variable symbolic name having a value that may change during the execution of the program. The value of a variable at any specific time is the data item to which it refers at that time.

A constant which is not given a symbolic name is an unchanging data item. For example, AREA—RADIUS **2*3.141593. AREA and RADIUS are variables while 2 and 3.141593 are constants.

The characteristics of a constant are inherent in its representation of the constant. The constant does more than state a value: it demonstrates the various characteristics of the data item. For example in a PL/1 program, the constant 98.6 is a data item that represents a numeric value. This constant specifies that the data item is a decimal data item with two digits to the left of the decimal point and one digit to the right of the decimal point.

DELIMITERS

There are two classes of delimiters in PL/1. They are separators and operators.

The separators, with their use and the graphics by which they are represented, are shown below.

Name of Separator	Graphic	Use
Comma	,	Separates elements of a list.
Semicolon	;	Terminates statements.
Colon	:	Follows statement labels and condition prefixes.
Period	.	Separates name qualifiers.
Parenthesis	( )	Used in expressions and for enclosing lists and specifying information associated with certain key words.

Operators are divided into four classes: arithmetic operators, comparison operators, logical operators, and concatenation operator.

The *arithmetic operators* are

Operator	Use
+	denoting addition or positive quantity
—	denoting subtraction or negative quantity
*	denoting multiplication
/	denoting division
**	denoting exponentiation

The *comparison operators* are

OPERATOR	USE
>	denoting greater than
¬>	denoting not greater than
>=	denoting greater than or equal to
=	denoting equal to
¬=	denoting not equal to
<=	denoting less than or equal to
<	denoting less than
¬<	denoting not less than

The *logical operators* are

¬	denoting not
&	denoting and
|	denoting or

The *concatenation operator* is

||	denoting linkage

EXPRESSIONS

Any identifier, other than language keywords, written in PL/1 program is called an *expression. An expression may be a single constant or a name, or it may be a combination of them, including operators or other delimiters.*

An arithmetic expression combines arithmetic data identifiers and arithmetic operators. A number of arithmetic operations may be included in a single expression. For example A + B – C * D ** C.

Although the expression may contain more than one data item, it represents a single value obtained after the expression is evaluated.

COMMENTS

Programmers frequently insert comments into their programs to clarify the action that occurs at a given point. Comments are permitted wherever blanks are allowed in the program.

```
/* COMMON */
```

The character pair, /* indicates the beginning of a comment. The same characters reversed */ indicate the end of the comment.

```
/* THIS WHOLE SENTENCE COULD BE INSERTED
            AS A COMMENT */
```

Comments can consist of one or more of the characters permitted for a particular machine configuration.

STATEMENTS

Words, delimiters, expressions, blanks and comments are used to form statements. *Statements are the basic program element used to construct a PL/1 program.* They are used for the description of the data, for the actual processing of the data and for the control of the execution sequence of other statements. A semicolon terminates a statement.

DECLARE STATEMENT

The DECLARE statement is used to describe named data as it is represented within the internal storage of a computer (Fig. 14.3). These properties

Figure 14–3. Example—DECLARE Statement.

```
DECLARE SALARY DECIMAL FIXED (7, 2),
  ESTIMATE FLOAT DECIMAL (10),
  COUNTER FIXED (5) BINARY,
  MEAN BINARY (10) FLOAT;
```

that characterize a data item are called *attributes.* The attributes of a named data item are in a DECLARE statement. For example, DECLARE wages DECIMAL FIXED (5,2); wages is the data name.

DECIMAL attribute specifies that the data item in the DECLARE statement is decimal type data.

FIXED attribute specifies that the data item is represented in fixed point format.

The precision attribute specifies the maximum number of digits and also the location of the assumed decimal point. In the above example, the precision attribute (5,2) declared for wages specifies that no data item assigned to *wages* should contain more than five digits and that each data item is assumed to have a decimal point immediately preceding the last two digits.

GO TO STATEMENT

The GO TO statement transfers control to a specified statement. There are two forms of the GO TO statement: 1) GO TO label constant; and 2) GO TO label name.

In the first form, control is sent to the statement that has the label constant as its label. For example; GO TO LOOP—3. In the second form the GO TO statement has the effect of a multi-way switch; control is transferred to the statement identified by the current value of the label name. Because the label name may have different values at each execution of the GO TO statement, control may not always pass to the same statement. The label name may also be the name of an array of labels. The following example illustrates the use of a GO TO statement that is in effect a multi-way switch.

```
        Switch:  PROCEDURE
                     .
                     .
                     .
                 DECLARE L LABEL (L1,L2)
                 INITIAL (L2);
                 GO TO Meet;
L1               X = Y - 1;
                 L = L2;
                 GO TO Meet;
L2               Y = X - 1;
                 L = L1,
Meet             CALL Fudge (X,Y,Z);
                 IF Z = Limit THEN GO TO L;
                     .
                     .
END              Switch;
```

When the value of L is L2, the GO TO statement sends control to the CALL statement. When L1 is the value of L, control is sent to the first assignment statement.

The value of label name is changed to L1 by executing the assignment L = L1.

IF STATEMENT

It is often desirable to execute a statement or a series of statements only under certain circumstances (Fig. 14.4). In such a situation, it might be convenient to evaluate an expression and, on the basis of this evaluation, select or reject the statement or statements to be executed. PL/1 provides the IF statement for this purpose. It also provides eight comparison operators that are used to construct comparison expressions that may be either true or false. *These expressions are used in the IF statement to determine whether or not the statement or statements are to be executed.*

Comparison Expressions

		=	(equal to)
>	(greater than)	¬=	(not equal to)
¬>	(not greater than)	<	(less than)
>=	(greater than or equal to)	¬<=	(not less than or equal to)

```
IF SALES > 1000
   THEN BEGIN;
         DECLARE GROSS FIXED (7, 2),
         NET FIXED (6, 2);
         GET FILE (DETAIL) EDIT (GROSS,
         NET) (F(7, 2), F(6, 2));
         CALL ANALYSIS (GROSS, NET);
         PUT FILE (REPORT) LIST
         (PROFIT);
       END;
   ELSE DO;
         CALL TAX (SALES);
         GO TO ADJUSTMENT;
       END;
```

When the numeric value of SALES is greater than 1000 the begin block after the THEN is executed and the DO group after the ELSE is skipped; otherwise the DO group is executed and the begin block is skipped.

Figure 14–4. Example—IF Statement.

These operators are used with data names and constants to form comparison expressions. For example, the expression:

COUNT > 10

is a comparison expression in which the numeric value of COUNT is compared to the constant 10. If the value of COUNT is greater than 10 the expression is true; otherwise it is false.

An IF statement can assume one of 2 forms:

IF comparison expression THEN unit
IF comparison expression THEN unit 1 ELSE unit 2

Each unit is either a single statement, a begin block, or a group. *A group consists of a sequence of statements and/or blocks preceded by a DO statement and terminated by an END statement.* An example of a group is the following sequence of statements:

```
DO; GET LIST (Gross, Net);
CALL Profit; END;
```

This group may appear in an IF statement as follows:

```
IF Sales = 22500 THEN DO; GET LIST (Gross, Net); CALL profit; END;
```

In this example, if the numerical value of Sales is equal to constant 22500, the group of statements following the keyword THEN is executed; otherwise the group is skipped and control passes to the statement after the END statement of the group.

When the unit is a single statement, the DO and END statements need not be specified unless iteration by means of the DO statement is desired. The following is an example of a single statement "unit."

IF Profit $<$ 0 THEN GO TO Loss;

When the numeric value of profit is less than zero, control is sent to the statement labeled Loss; otherwise, the statement following GO TO Loss; is executed.

DO STATEMENT

The DO statement is used to define and specify control for a group of statements to be used as a loop, that is, a series of statements to be executed and re-executed one or more times before control moves on to the next statement after the group (Fig. 14.5). Every DO statement must have an associated END statement to define the end of the group.

The DO statement, used together with an END statement, provides a means of grouping a set of statements. It also provides for the repeated execution of a sequence of statements and permits modification and testing of data items to control the repetition. Being able to repeat the execution of a set of statements a specified number of times generally results in a smaller and more efficient program. A DO statement can be specified in several ways.

Consider the following example:

```
DO COUNTER = 1 TO 10
statement—1
statement—2
statement—3
END;
statement—4
```

The DO and END statements specify that statements 1, 2 and 3, whatever they may be, are a DO group. The DO statement rather specifies that these statements are to be executed, as a group, ten times before control is transferred to statement 4. The variable COUNTER is used to control the

```
LOOP:   DO I = 1 TO 100;
        IF NAME = NAME__LIST (I)
           THEN GO TO FIND;
        END LOOP;
FIND:   NUMBER = NUMBER_LIST (I)
```

During execution of the DO loop, NAME is compared with each of the elements in NAME_LIST, beginning with the first. As I is incremented, NAME_LIST (I) refers to successive elements in the array. When a match is found between NAME and an element of NAME_LIST, the telephone number for that name is secured from the corresponding position in the array NUMBER_LIST and is assigned to NUMBER.

Figure 14–5. Example—DO Statement.

number of times the group is executed. When the DO statement is executed for the first time, COUNTER is assigned the value 1. Statements 1, 2 and 3 are then executed. When the END statement is reached, COUNTER is incremented by one, and the control is transferred back to the beginning of the group where COUNTER is tested to see that it is no larger than 10. This looping continues until the value of COUNTER exceeds 10, when control passes on to statement 4.

Another form of the DO statement:

```
DO WHILE (comparison expression);
statement 1
      .
      .
      .
statement n
END;
```

This use of the DO statement causes the indicated sequence of statements to be executed repeatedly as long as the value of the comparison expression remains true.

INPUT AND OUTPUT

The basic function of input and output is data transmission—getting the data to be processed and returning the results of the processing. Before a computer can process data that is recorded on external media, the data must be reproduced within the computer. This reproduction process is called input. Likewise, when processing has been completed, the processed data is made available by reproducing it on an external media (output).

INPUT/OUTPUT ATTRIBUTES

One of these attributes (INPUT, OUTPUT or UPDATE) may be specified to describe the type of data transmission that is permitted for a file. The INPUT attribute is used for files that are only to be read. The OUTPUT attribute is used for files that are to be created; output files may only be written on. The UPDATE attribute is used for existing files that are to be read, or have new records added, or existing records altered or deleted. For example in the following statement,

```
DECLARE DETAIL FILE INPUT,
        REPORT FILE OUTPUT,
        MASTER FILE UPDATE;
```

DETAIL is the name of an input file; REPORT is the name of an output file; MASTER is the name of a file that is used both for input and output.

GET AND PUT

Using one of the simplest forms of input and output, a programmer need only write the nature of the operation GET or PUT and a list of data names where the data is stored or where the data to be written can be found. *The GET statement is used to transmit data from external to internal storage and the PUT statement to transmit data from internal to external storage.*

The following information is required for each GET or PUT statement:

1. The name of the file from which data is to be obtained or to which data is to be assigned.
2. A list of data names representing storage areas to which data items are to be assigned during input, or from which data items are to be obtained during output. Such a list is known as a data list.
3. The format of each data item.

Under certain circumstances, all of this required information can be implied; in other cases, only a portion of it need be stated explicitly.

The full range of I/O operations allows a programmer to edit data and insert symbols such as dollar signs and decimal point and to control the format and layout of the printed page.

PL/1 deals with data sets in two different kinds of data transmission; stream-oriented and record-oriented. With *stream-oriented transmission, the data set is considered to be a continuous stream of data items in character form, to be assigned from the stream to variables (data names) and from variables to streams. In a record-oriented transmission, the data set is considered to consist of a collection of physically separated records, each of which consists of one or more data items in any form.* Each record is transmitted as an entity to or from a variable or directly to or from an addressable buffer.

The basic input and output statements in a stream-oriented transmission are GET and PUT. They get the next data item from the stream or put the specified items into the stream.

The data list in a list-directed GET statement is a list of variables (representing internal storage areas) to which data items in the data stream are to be assigned. The variables in a data list are separated by commas. An example of a list-directed GET statement follows:

```
GET FILE (MASTER) LIST
(LOAN_#, PRINCIPAL, RATE);
```

The GET statement in the above example causes three data items from MASTER file to be assigned to the variables of the data list in the sequence in which they are listed; that is, the first data item is assigned to LOAN_#, the second to PRINCIPAL, and the third to RATE. Assignment stops at this point because the data list has been exhausted.

The data list in a list-directed PUT statement differs from that of a GET statement only in that a data item may be represented by an expression other than its name, for example, an arithmetic expression whose value is the item to be written. Once evaluated, the value represented by an expression is transmitted in the same way that the value represented by a variable is transmitted. Items in the data list (including expressions, if any) are separated by commas. An example of a list-directed PUT statement follows:

```
PUT FILE (OUT)
LIST (NAME, 6.3*RATE,NUMBER—10);
```

The PUT statement in the above example causes three data items to be written in the file named OUT. The sequence in which the data items are written follows the sequence of the items in the data list; the first data item is the value represented by the variable NAME, the second is the value resulting from the evaluation of the expression 6.3*RATE, the third is the value resulting from the evaluation of the expression NUMBER—10. Writing stops at this point.

The internal and external representation of a data item in list-directed transmission is determined by the attributes declared for it by the programmer. To better understand how this applies to list-directed GET and PUT statements, assume that the standard input file contains the following data:

```
'NEW YORK', 'JANUARY', —6.5, 72.6
```

Assume, further, that the following two statements appear in the program.

```
DECLARE CITY CHARACTER (12), MONTH
CHARACTER (9), MINTEN FIXED DECIMAL (4,2),
MAXTEM FIXED DECIMAL (5,2);
GET LIST (CITY, MONTH, MINTEM, MAXTEM);
```

The GET statement would cause the data items to be assigned as follows:

1. CITY is assigned the character string NEW YORK, left adjusted and padded on the right with four blanks.
2. MONTH is assigned the character string JANUARY, left adjusted and padded on the right with two blanks.
3. MINTEM is assigned the value —06.50.
4. MAXTEM is assigned the value —72.60.

The character strings are padded on the right with blanks to conform with the declared length of the strings; quotation marks are not maintained internally. The decimal fixed-point numbers are aligned on the assumed decimal point, to conform with declared precision. Consider the result of the following PUT statement:

```
PUT, LIST (CITY, MONTH, MAXTEM,MINTEM, 'RANGE',
           MAXTEM-MINTEM);
```

The record would be printed as

```
NEW YORK JANUARY 72.6 –6.5 RANGE: 79.1
```

Note that if a character string is printed, the single quotation marks are not written, whether the string is specified as the value of a variable (CITY and MONTH) or is specified as a character constant ('RANGE:'). If a character string is written in a file that does not have the PRINT attribute, the enclosing quotation marks are supplied if necessary and are written.

In record-oriented transmission, the comparable statements are READ and WRITE, read the next record directly from the data set or within the specified record directly into the data set. Consider the following example:

```
DECLARE 1 PAYROLL,
          2 NAME,
             3 LAST CHARACTER (12),
             3 FIRST CHARACTER (8),
             3 MIDDLE CHARACTER (1),
          2 PAY_NO CHARACTER (5),
          2 RATE,
             (3 REGULAR,
              3 OVERTIME)
                FIXED DECIMAL (3,2);
READ FILE(INFILE) INTO (PAYROLL)
```

The READ statement causes the record to be read directly into the structure PAYROLL. There is no conversion of data types to conform to the attributes declared for the names. The data in the record must exactly match the declaration of PAYROLL; that is, the first twelve characters (including any blanks necessary to extend the string to its declared length) must represent the last name, the next eight characters the first name, etc. And the portion of the records that will be assigned to RATE must be the valid internal representation of fixed-point decimal numbers. Since there is no conversion, the data in the record could not be written in character form. A record of this sort must have been written by a previously executed program.

The following statements might also be part of the same program:

```
DECLARE 1 PAY_RECORD,
          2 NAME,
             3 LAST CHARACTER (12),
             3 FIRST CHARACTER (8),
             3 MIDDLE CHARACTER (1),
```

```
                         2 HOURS,
                           (3 REGULAR,
                            3 OVERTIME)
                              FIXED DECIMAL (2),
                         2 PAY,
                           (3 REGULAR,
                            3 OVERTIME)
                                FIXED DECIMAL (5,2);
         GET FILE (TIME_CARD) LIST (PAY_RECORD, NAME,
             PAY_RECORD.HOURS);
TEST:  IF PAYROLL.NAME = PAY_RECORD.NAME
       THEN DO
             PAY = HOURS*RATE
             WRITE FILE (WAGES) FROM
               (PAY_RECORD);
             END;
        ELSE DO;
             READ FILE (INFILE) INTO (PAYROLL);
             GO TO TEST;
             END;
```

As shown in the example, both record-oriented and stream-oriented statements may appear in the same procedure. Assume that the file TIME CARD, specified in the GET statement, represents a data set of punched cards being read from a card reader. Each card has the employee's name and the hours worked. The GET statement would cause the data, punched in character form, to be converted to fixed decimal notation for the data assigned to HOURS. The WRITE statement, however, would write the record from PAY_RECORD into the file WAGES exactly as the data appears in internal storage, presumbaly for some other program, since the data in internal format could not be printed directly.

PROCEDURES

In PL/1, a program may consist of a single procedure or of several procedures. During the execution of a program, control can go from one procedure to another and can return to a previously executed or partly executed procedure.

A procedure is headed by a PROCEDURE statement and ended with an END statement as follows:

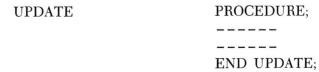

```
UPDATE          PROCEDURE;
                ------
                ------
                END UPDATE;
```

Each procedure must have a name; that is, each procedure statement must be labeled. A procedure name provides an entry through which control can be transferred to a procedure (Fig. 14.6).

The division of a program into several procedures is a feature of PL/1 that provides a special convenience to programmers. The procedures can be separately executed as a single program. A long program can be divided into logical blocks; separate procedures can be written for special purposes (Fig. 14.7).

Control does not pass automatically from one procedure to the next. Each procedure, except the first must be involved, or called separately from some other procedure. This usually occurs with the execution of a CALL statement: for example CALL UPDATE.

Execution of this statement in another procedure would transfer control to the entry point of the procedure called UPDATE.

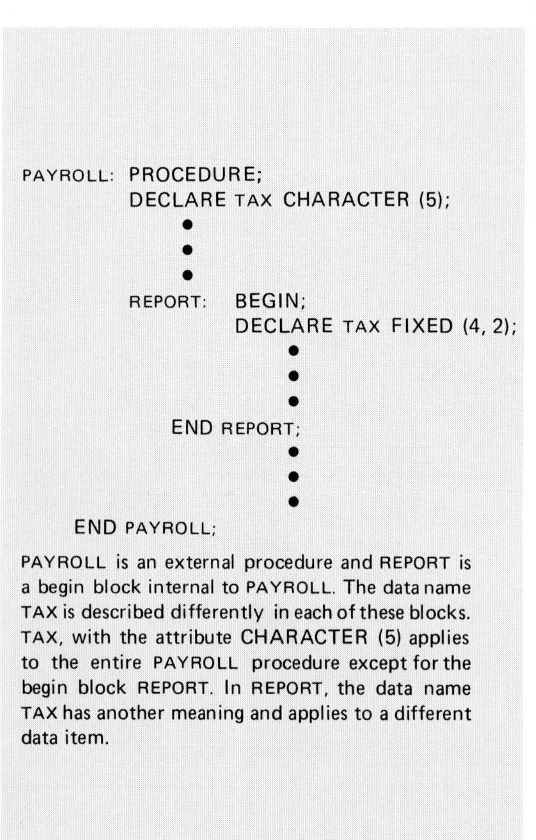

```
PAYROLL: PROCEDURE;
         DECLARE TAX CHARACTER (5);
            •
            •
            •
         REPORT:   BEGIN;
                   DECLARE TAX FIXED (4, 2);
                      •
                      •
                      •
             END REPORT;
                      •
                      •
                      •
     END PAYROLL;
```

PAYROLL is an external procedure and REPORT is a begin block internal to PAYROLL. The data name TAX is described differently in each of these blocks. TAX, with the attribute CHARACTER (5) applies to the entire PAYROLL procedure except for the begin block REPORT. In REPORT, the data name TAX has another meaning and applies to a different data item.

Figure 14–6. Example—PROCEDURE Statement.

```
PROC_1:  PROCEDURE;
         statement–1
         statement–2
         CALL PROC_A;
         PROC_A:  PROCEDURE;
                  statement–1a
                  statement–2a
                  CALL PROC_B;
                  PROC_B:  PROCEDURE;
                           statement–1b
                           statement–2b
                           statement–3b
                           END;
                  statement–4a
                  statement–5a
                  statement–6a
                  END;
         statement–4
         statement–5
         CALL PROC_C;
         PROC_C:  PROCEDURE;
                  statement–1c
                  statement–2c
                  statement–3c
                  END;
         statement–7
         statement–8
         statement–9
END_1:   END;
```

PROC_A, PROC_B, and PROC_C are all contained in PROC_1. PROC_B also is contained in PROC_A. PROC_1 can invoke either PROC_A or PROC_C; either PROC_A or PROC_C might invoke one another; but only PROC_A can invoke PROC_B.

Figure 14–7. Example—PROCEDURE Statement.

COMPARISON: COBOL AND PL/1

COBOL and PL/1 programming languages are similar in many respects, yet there are important differences in the structure and use of each. Some of the important similarities are noted below.

LANGUAGE NOTATION

SIMILARITIES—BOTH LANGUAGES USE

1. Programmer-defined words consisting of alphabetical characters and numerical digits.
2. Expressions consisting of sequences of names, constants, and separators.
3. Keywords that identify language elements.
4. Punctuation characters that separate elements.
5. Statements that have English-like appearance.

DIFFERENCES

1. In both PL/1 and COBOL, keywords have preassigned meanings but in PL/1 keywords are not reserved for special purposes and may appear wherever a programmer-defined word is permitted. In PL/1, different meanings for the same word are determined from the context. In COBOL, keywords are reserved and may be used only for their intended purpose.
2. COBOL requires a programming form. PL/1 does not. In PL/1 punctuation characters determine the significance of the groupings of language elements.
3. In COBOL, arithmetic operators must be surrounded by blanks. In PL/1 blanks are only required between successive words.
4. COBOL restricts comments to the PROCEDURE division in the form of a NOTE statement. PL/1 allows comments to appear through the program wherever blanks may appear.
5. COBOL uses a fifty-one-character set. PL/1 uses a sixty-character set.
6. In PL/1 all statements are terminated with a semicolon. In COBOL, all sentences are terminated with a period.

DATA DESCRIPTION

SIMILARITIES—IN BOTH LANGUAGES

1. Programmer-defined words are used to name data items,
2. Keywords are used to specify the characteristics of named data items.
3. Data items may be collected into aggregates.

4. Constants may be specified for each data type.
5. Data names may be assigned initial values.
6. A picture specification may serve as an alternative method for describing data.

DIFFERENCES

1. COBOL describes data in the Data Division in separate sections for different types of data. PL/1 uses a DECLARE statement and does not require a separation of the various data types in the DECLARE statement.
2. All programmer-supplied words used in a COBOL program must be defined in the Data Division. PL/1 allows programmer-supplied words to be used in the program without being described in the DECLARE statement. The meaning is determined from the context.
3. In COBOL, the description of data in external storage media is specified in the Data Division. In PL/1, the input and output statements specify the description of externally stored data.
4. COBOL has figurative constants (symbols that are represented by their names). PL/1 does not use them.

INPUT AND OUTPUT

SIMILARITIES

Both languages employ similar methods of transmitting data between internal and external areas to the extent that input/output statements process files and identification records (label records) in files may be processed both in input and on output.

DIFFERENCES

1. COBOL data transmission implies that files are composed of logical records. One or more data items form a logical record. The data is transmitted at the rate of one logical record at a time. PL/1 provides two types of data transmissions; record-oriented and stream-oriented transmissions. Record-oriented transmission operates like COBOL in that it deals with logical records. Stream-oriented handles individual data items. A file is thought of as one continuous stream of data items rather than a collection of logical records.
2. PL/1 provides control format specifications that regulate printing and spacing operations. COBOL does not provide these.

3. COBOL permits a file name to be used as a name qualifier. PL/1 does not.
4. In PL/1, the characteristics of a file are specified in the DECLARE statement or in an OPEN statement. In COBOL, file characteristics are specified in the file description entry in the Data Division.

In PL/1, as in FORTRAN, addition (as other arithmetic operations) can be specified by the standard operators +, —, /, *, **. For example INCOME = DIVIDENDS + INCOME; PL/1 differs from FORTRAN only in the use of the semicolon (;) which ends a statement, and in that this statement can be written in free form as found convenient by the program.

Addition can also be indicated by a statement which looks like a COBOL statement, such as SUM = ADD (DIVIDENDS, INCOME 8,2). This will put the results of adding DIVIDENDS to INCOME into an address called SUM which has an eight position field, including two positions to the right of the decimal point.

PL/1 is a multipurpose programming language that can be used for both commercial and scientific programs to handle all of the programming work and provide the widest range of control over the computer. The language provides many options in statements and in descriptions of data and files. *Wherever there are alternatives, the compiler makes an assumption if no choice is stated by the programmer. In each case, the assumption, called a default, is the alternative that would be required in a majority of cases.* The default concept is an important part of the simplicity of PL/1. In many cases, the beginning programmer need not know what alternatives exist (Figs. 14.8, 14.9, 14.10, 14.11, 14.12, 14.13).

SUMMARY

PL/1 is a procedure-oriented programming language that may be used for both scientific and business applications. In the past, programming languages were identified with a particular field of activity, either scientific or business. FORTRAN programming was developed for scientific programming applications while COBOL programming language is primarily used for commercial applications. In COBOL the notation used resembles English statements, and in FORTRAN programs the notation resembles mathematical formulas. The distinction between a scientific and business program is becoming less distinct. PL/1 notations combine the features of both COBOL and FORTRAN notations. It is the intent of this chapter to describe the features of PL/1 programming language.

I. *PL/1 (Programming Language 1).*
   A. *Purpose*—a broad base programming language useful for scientific and business applications.

```
UPDATE:      PROCEDURE;
             DECLARE PAY_# DECIMAL FIXED (7),
                  LOAN_# DECIMAL FIXED (7),
                  PRINCIPAL DECIMAL FIXED (8,2),
                  BALANCE DECIMAL FIXED (8,2),
                  PAYMENT DECIMAL FIXED (6,2),
                  REFUND DECIMAL FIXED (6,2),
                  INTEREST DECIMAL FIXED (5,2),
                  RATE DECIMAL FIXED (3,3),
                  MASTER FILE INPUT,
                  NEW_MASTER FILE OUTPUT,
                  INPUT FILE INPUT,
                  OUTPUT FILE OUTPUT;
             ON ENDFILE (INPUT) GO TO MASTER FILE;
NEW_RECORD:  GET FILE (INPUT) LIST (PAY_#,PAYMENT);
MASTER_FILE: GET FILE (MASTER) LIST (LOAN_#,PRINCIPAL, RATE);
             INTEREST=PRINCIPAL * RATE/12;
             IF LOAN_# ¬=PAY_#
               THEN DO;
                  PRINCIPAL=PRINCIPAL+INTEREST;
                  PUT FILE (NEW_MASTER) LIST (LOAN_#,PRINCIPAL,RATE);
                  GO TO MASTER_FILE;
                  END;
               ELSE IF PAYMENT<=PRINCIPAL+INTEREST
                  THEN BALANCE=PRINCIPAL+INTEREST-PAYMENT:
                  ELSE DO;
                      BALANCE=0;
                      REFUND=PAYMENT-PRINCIPAL+INTEREST;
                      PUT FILE (OUTPUT) LIST (LOAN_#, 'REFUND: ', REFUND);
                      END;
             PUT FILE (OUTPUT) LIST (LOAN_#,PRINCIPAL, INTEREST,PAYMENT,BALANCE);
             IF BALANCE=0
               THEN GO TO NEW_RECORD;
               ELSE PUT FILE (NEW_MASTER) LIST (LOAN_#,BALANCE,RATE);
             GO TO NEW_RECORD;
             END UPDATE;
```

From INPUT		From MASTER		
Assigned to PAY_#	Assigned to PAYMENT	Assigned to LOAN_#	Assigned to PRINCIPAL	Assigned to RATE
8212345	50.00	8212345	600.00	.050
8212347	40.00	8212346	1200.00	.055
8212348	60.30	8212347	24.00	.050
8212349	1000.00	8212348	60.00	.060
		8212349	24000.00	.055
		8212350	880.00	.060
		8212351	72.00	.050

Written in OUTPUT				
Written from LOAN_#	Written from PRINCIPAL	Written from INTEREST	Written from PAYMENT	Written from BALANCE
8212345	600.00	2.50	50.00	552.50
8212347	REFUND: 15.90			
8212347	24.00	.10	40.00	0
8212348	60.00	.30	60.30	0
8212349	24000.00	110.00	1000.00	23110.00

Written in NEW_MASTER		
Written from LOAN_#	Written from PRINCIPAL	Written from RATE
8212345	552.50	.050
8212346	1205.50	.055
8212349	23110.00	.055
8212350	884.40	.060
8212351	72.30	.050

Figure 14–8. PL/1 Program Example.

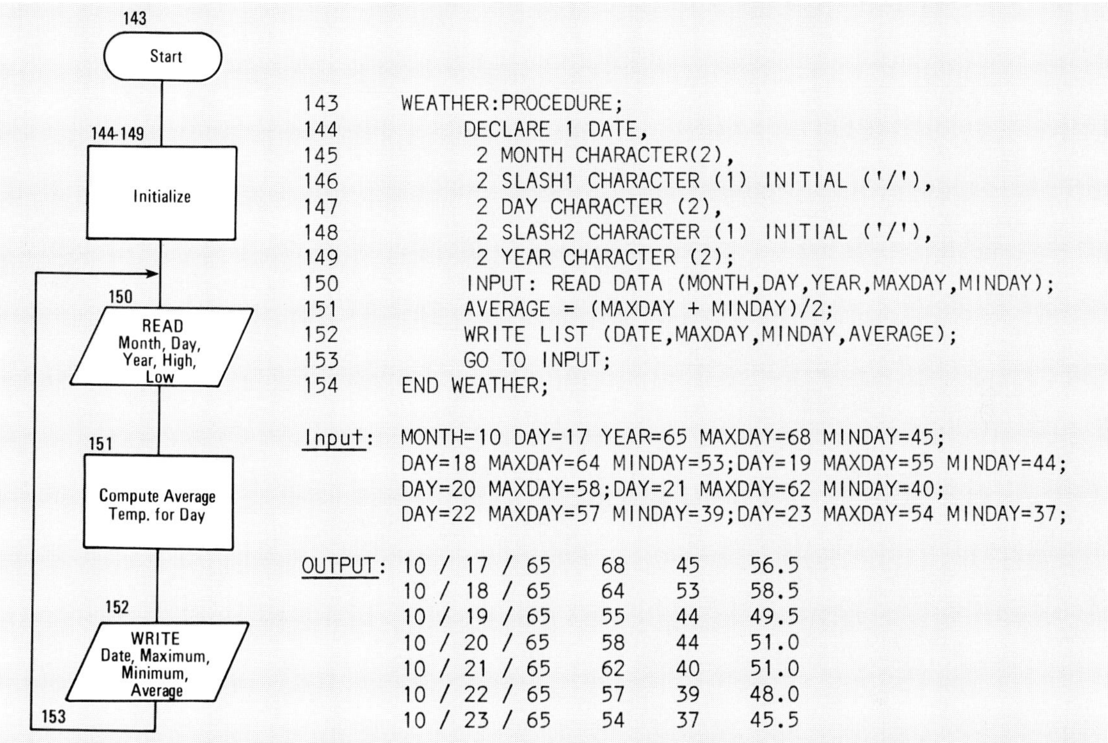

143
Start
144-149
Initialize
150
READ Month, Day, Year, High, Low
151
Compute Average Temp. for Day
152
WRITE Date, Maximum, Minimum, Average
153
143 WEATHER:PROCEDURE;
144 DECLARE 1 DATE,
145 2 MONTH CHARACTER(2),
146 2 SLASH1 CHARACTER (1) INITIAL ('/'),
147 2 DAY CHARACTER (2),
148 2 SLASH2 CHARACTER (1) INITIAL ('/'),
149 2 YEAR CHARACTER (2);
150 INPUT: READ DATA (MONTH,DAY,YEAR,MAXDAY,MINDAY);
151 AVERAGE = (MAXDAY + MINDAY)/2;
152 WRITE LIST (DATE,MAXDAY,MINDAY,AVERAGE);
153 GO TO INPUT;
154 END WEATHER;
Input: MONTH=10 DAY=17 YEAR=65 MAXDAY=68 MINDAY=45;
DAY=18 MAXDAY=64 MINDAY=53;DAY=19 MAXDAY=55 MINDAY=44;
DAY=20 MAXDAY=58;DAY=21 MAXDAY=62 MINDAY=40;
DAY=22 MAXDAY=57 MINDAY=39;DAY=23 MAXDAY=54 MINDAY=37;
OUTPUT: 10 / 17 / 65 68 45 56.5
10 / 18 / 65 64 53 58.5
10 / 19 / 65 55 44 49.5
10 / 20 / 65 58 44 51.0
10 / 21 / 65 62 40 51.0
10 / 22 / 65 57 39 48.0
10 / 23 / 65 54 37 45.5

Figure 14–9. Example—PL/1 Program to Compute Average Days Temperature.

B. *Basic elements.*

1. *Format*—no fixed length format.
2. *Coding forms*—none needed. Programs are written in free form.
3. *Character set*—sixty characters composed of alphabetic, numerical, and special characters.
4. *Words*—separated by delimiters and/or blanks.

   Identifiers—a word created by the user to identify a file or data item. It may be a *keyword* which when used in proper context has a special meaning to the compiler. Identifiers are variables that may change during the execution of the program.

   Constants—are unchanging data items. The characteristics of constants are inherent in its representation of the constant.
5. *Delimiters*

   Separators—separate elements of a list (,), terminate statements (;), follow statement labels and condition prefixes (:), separate name qualifier (.), used in expressions and for ending lists and specifying information associated with certain key words (( )).

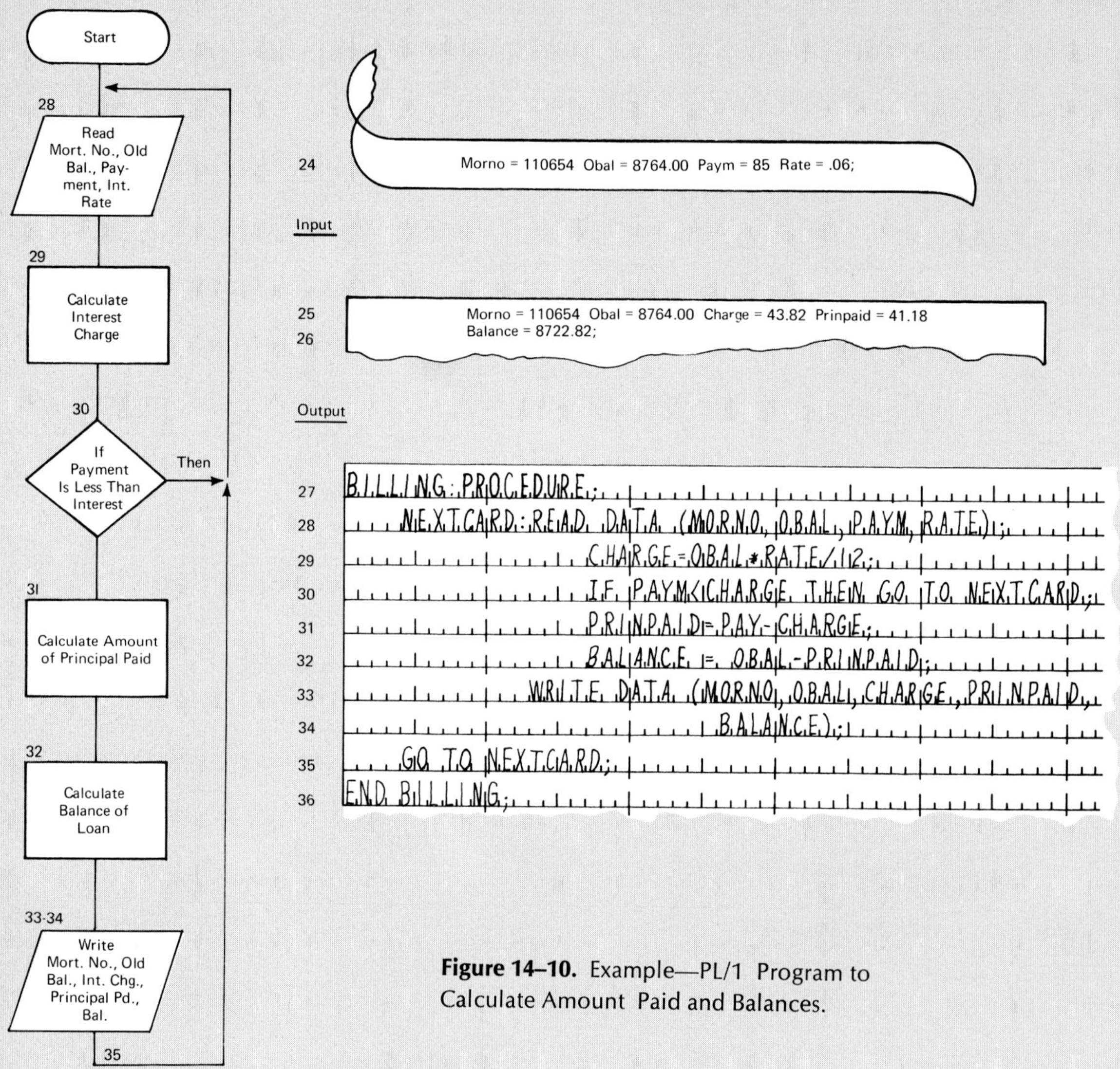

Figure 14–10. Example—PL/1 Program to Calculate Amount Paid and Balances.

Operators

Arithmetic

Denoting addition or positive quantity	+
Denoting subtraction or negative quantity	—
Denoting multiplication	*
Denoting division	/
Denoting exponentiation	**

Figure 14–11. Example—PL/1 Program for a Work Card Study.

A Work Card Study

The computer is directed to read a series of work cards showing the hours worked by employees and then to compute the daily average for each employee. Each card contains several fields, one field for each data item; a comma separates fields. The first data item on each card is a name consisting of 15 alphameric characters. The next item is five alphameric characters representing a department number. The next five items are numeric and consist of five characters each with an actual decimal point in the third character position. These are daily time items, representing the hours worked on each of five workdays.

An output file is to be created according to the conventions of list-directed output. The data items on the input cards are to be duplicated in the output file. The data for each card is to be followed by the total time and the average daily time.

In the actual processing the five daily time items are treated as an array and a subscript N is used to obtain each time value in turn.

```
Work-Card: PROCEDURE OPTIONS(Main);
DECLARE N FIXED (1), Work-File FILE,
  New-Work-File FILE, Name CHARACTER
  (15), Dept CHARACTER (5),
  Time (5) PICTURE '99.99',
  Total-Time PICTURE '99V99',
  Average-Time PICTURE'99V99';
OPEN FILE (Work-File) INPUT, FILE
  (New-Work-File) OUTPUT;
ON ENDFILE (Work-File) GO TO Close;
Read: GET FILE (Work-File) LIST (Name,
  Dept, Time);
Total-Time = 0;
DO N = 1 TO 5 BY 1;
  Total-Time = Time (N) + Total-Time;
  END;
Average-Time = Total-Time / 5;
PUT FILE (New-Work-File)
  LIST     (Name,Dept,Time,Total-Time,
    Average-Time);
GO TO Read;
Close: CLOSE FILE (Work-File), FILE
  (New-Work-File);
END Work-Card;
```

Comparison	
Denoting greater than	>
Denoting not greater than	¬>
Denoting greater than or equal to	>=
Denoting equal to	=
Denoting not equal to	¬=
Denoting less than or equal to	<=
Denoting less than	<
Denoting not less than	¬<
Logical	
Denoting not	¬
Denoting and	&
Denoting or	|
Concatenation	
Denoting linkage	||

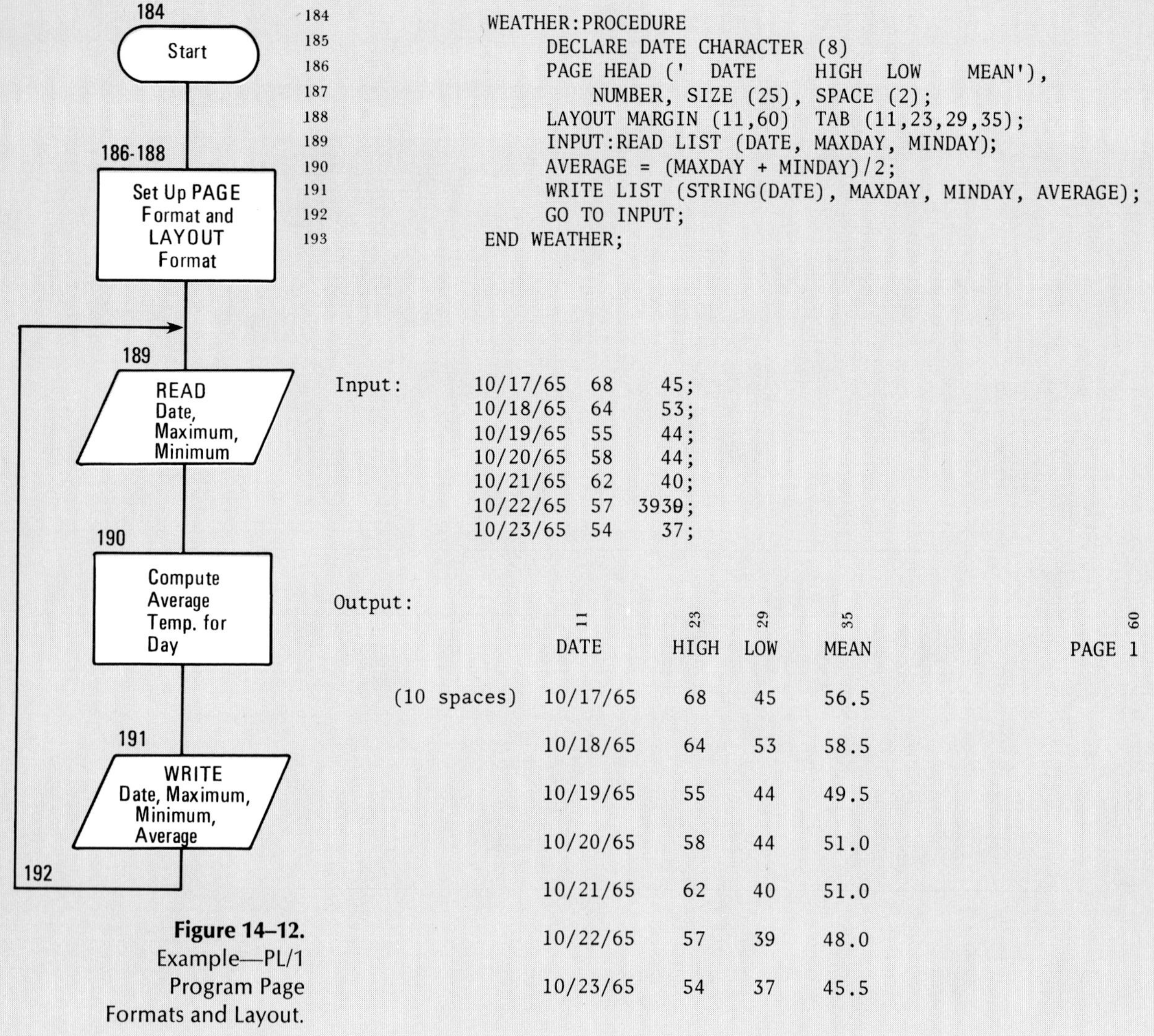
184
Start
186-188
Set Up PAGE Format and LAYOUT Format
189
READ Date, Maximum, Minimum
190
Compute Average Temp. for Day
191
WRITE Date, Maximum, Minimum, Average
192
184 WEATHER:PROCEDURE
185 DECLARE DATE CHARACTER (8)
186 PAGE HEAD (' DATE HIGH LOW MEAN'),
187 NUMBER, SIZE (25), SPACE (2);
188 LAYOUT MARGIN (11,60) TAB (11,23,29,35);
189 INPUT:READ LIST (DATE, MAXDAY, MINDAY);
190 AVERAGE = (MAXDAY + MINDAY)/2;
191 WRITE LIST (STRING(DATE), MAXDAY, MINDAY, AVERAGE);
192 GO TO INPUT;
193 END WEATHER;
Input:
10/17/65 68 45;
10/18/65 64 53;
10/19/65 55 44;
10/20/65 58 44;
10/21/65 62 40;
10/22/65 57 3939;
10/23/65 54 37;
Output:
11 23 29 35 60
DATE HIGH LOW MEAN PAGE 1
(10 spaces) 10/17/65 68 45 56.5
10/18/65 64 53 58.5
10/19/65 55 44 49.5
10/20/65 58 44 51.0
10/21/65 62 40 51.0
10/22/65 57 39 48.0
10/23/65 54 37 45.5

Figure 14–12. Example—PL/1 Program Page Formats and Layout.

6. *Expressions*—may be a single constant or a name, or it may be a combination of them, including operators or other delimiters.
7. *Comments*—used to clarify the action that occurs at a given point.

C. *Statements*—combinations of words, delimiters, expressions, blanks, and comments. The basic program element used to construct a PL/1 program.
   1. *DECLARE statement*—describes named data within storage.
   2. *GO TO statement*—transfers control to a specified statement.
   3. *IF statement*—is used to execute a statement or series of statements under certain conditions.

4. *DO statement*—is used to define and specify control for a group of statements to be used as a loop: a series of statements to be executed one or more times until a certain condition is satisfied.

D. *Input and output*—may be specified to describe the type of data transmission that is permitted for a certain file.
   1. *INPUT attribute*—is used for files that are only to be read.
   2. *OUTPUT attribute*—is used for files that are to be created.
   3. *UPDATE attribute*—is used for existing files that are to be read, or have new records added, or existing records altered or deleted.
   4. *GET statement*—is used to transmit data from external to internal storage.
   5. *PUT statement*—is used to transmit data from internal to external storage.
   6. *Stream-oriented transmission*—data set is considered to be a continuous stream of data items in character form to be assigned from stream to variables (data names) and from variables to stream.
   7. *Record-oriented transmission*—data set is considered to consist of a collection of physically separated records, each of which consists of one or more data items in any form. Each record is transmitted to and from a variable as an entity or directly to an addressable buffer.

E. *Procedures*—statements specifying the action to be processed on the data. Each PROCEDURE must be named which provides an entry through which control can be transferred to a PROCEDURE.

II. *Comparison PL/1 and COBOL.*

A. *Language notation.*
   1. *Similarities*—both languages use programmer defined words, expressions, keywords, punctuation characters to separate elements, and English-like statements.
   2. *Differences*—PL/1 allows for different meanings to keywords, requires no programming form, does not require arithmetic operators to be surrounded by blanks, allows comments to appear throughout the program, has sixty-character set compared to the fifty-one-character set of COBOL. In PL/1 statements are terminated with a semicolon, whereas in COBOL all sentences are terminated with a period.

B. *Data description.*
   1. *Similarities*—both languages use programmer-defined words to name data items, keywords specify the characteristics of the named data items, data may be collected in aggregates, constants may be specified, data names may be assigned initial values, a picture specification may be used.

The flowchart and the PL/I text illustrate an inventory control program written for a hypothetical company which has an inventory of 20,000 stock items. Four hundred of these are motors and related items built to stock; the remainder are raw materials and subassemblies.

The master file on magnetic tape will contain part number, abbreviated alphabetic description, quantity on hand, quantity on order, reorder point, reorder quantity, code character (indicating finished item, raw material, or subassembly), unit price, and year-to-date sales.

The processing required may be summarized as follows: The inventory tape is updated daily. Adjustments replace the quantity on hand in the master file record. Receipts are added to the master file quantity on hand and are subtracted from quantity on order. Issues are subtracted from the quantity on hand, and orders are added to the quantity on order. Tests and other details may be deduced from the flowchart.

Figure 14–13. Example—PL/1 Program for Inventory Control.

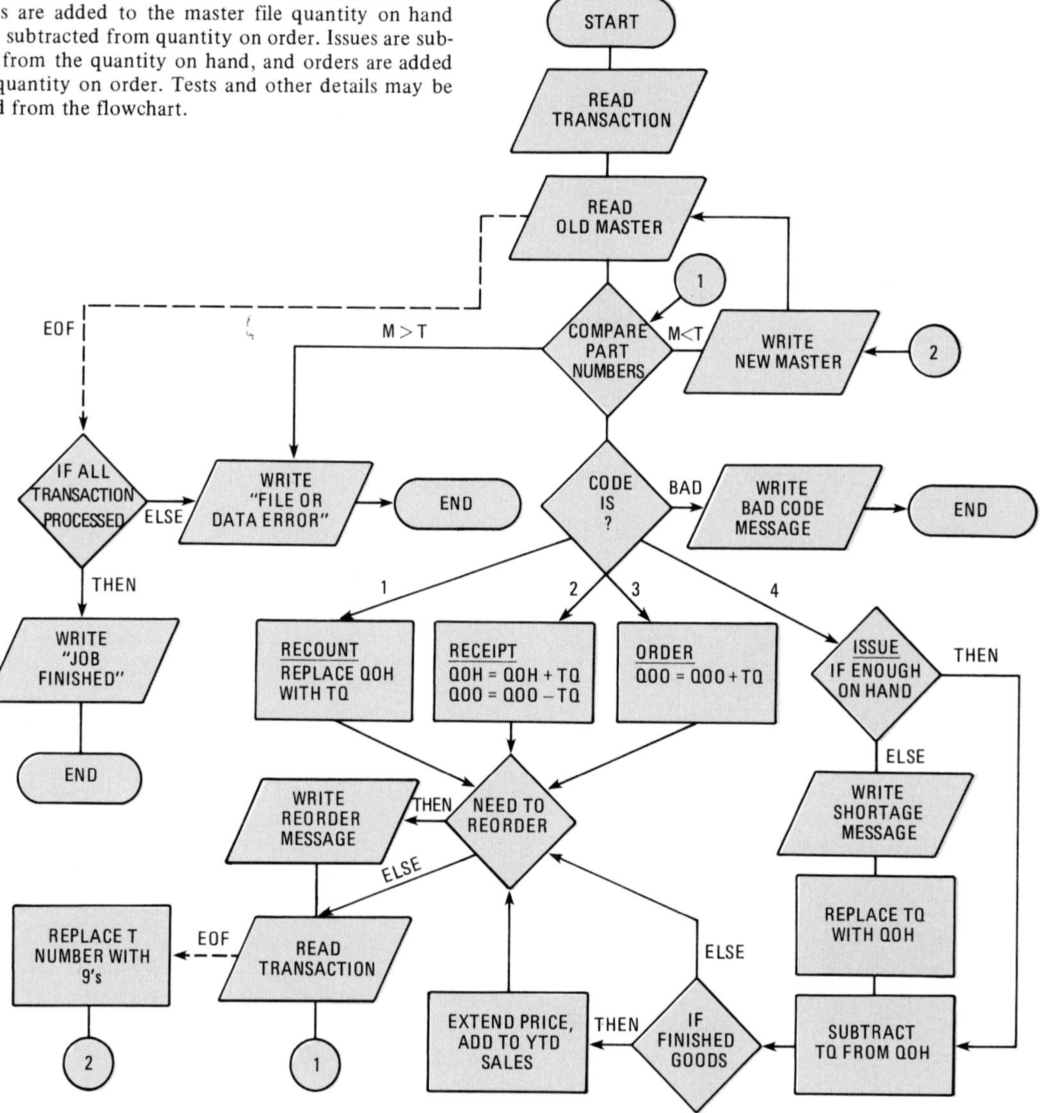

Figure 14–13. (Continued).

```
INVCTL:PROCEDURE;
    DECLARE (OLDMAST INPUT, NEWMAST OUTPUT) BLOCK (FIXED, 432,8),
        PFILE OUTPUT,
        1 WORK,
            2 PARTNO CHARACTER (7),
            2 DESCR CHAR(12),
            2 (QOH,QOO,RP,RQ)FIXED(5),
            2 UP FIXED (6),
            2 YTDSALE FIXED (8),
            2 CODE FIXED,
        1 TRANS,
            2 TNUMBER CHARACTER (7),
            2 TCODE FIXED,
            2 TQ FIXED (5),
        CODEIS (4) LABEL;
    ON ENDFILE  (STANDIN) BEGIN; TNUMBER = '9999999';GO TO WRITNM;END;
    ON ENDFILE  (OLDMAST) BEGIN; IF TNUMBER = '9999999' THEN DO;CLOSE
                                     OLDMAST DISCARD,(PFILE, NEWMAST)
                                     STORE, DISPLAY ('JOB FINISHED');
                                     END;
                                 ELSE ERROR:DISPLAY ('FILE OR DATA
                                     ERROR'); EXIT; END;
    ON SUBSCRIPTRANGE BEGIN; DISPLAY  ('BAD CLASS CODE JOB HALTED');
        EXIT; END;
    READ (TRANS) (A);

READM: READ FILE(OLDMAST), (WORK)(A);

TESTM: IF PARTNO < TNUMBER THEN WRITNM: DO; WRITE FILE (NEWMAST),
                                  (WORK)(A); GO TO READM; END;
       IF PARTNO > TNUMBER THEN GO TO ERROR;
             /*THEN PARTNO = TNUMBER*/
       GO TO CODEIS(TCODE);
CODEIS(1):QOH = TQ; GO TO JOIN;
CODEIS(2):QOH = QOH + TQ; QOO = QOO - TQ; GO TO JOIN;
CODEIS(3):QOO = QOO + TQ; GO TO JOIN;
CODEIS(4): IF QOH < TQ THEN·DO; WRITE ('ONLY', PARTNO,'AVAILABLE',
             QOH, ' REQUESTED')(3A,F(5),A); TQ=QOH; END; QOH =
             QOH-TQ; IF CODE = 1 THEN YTDSALE = YTDSALE + TQ*UP;

JOIN:  IF QOH + QOO < = RP THEN WRITE FILE(PFILE), (PARTNO, CODE,
            RQ)  (3 A);
      READ (TRANS)(A); GO TO TESTM; END INVCTL;
```

2. *Differences*—COBOL describes data in the Data Division, PL/1 uses a DECLARE statement. All programmer-supplied words used in COBOL programs must be described in the Data Division; no such restriction exists in PL/1. COBOL has figurative constants, PL/1 does not have any.

C. *Input and output.*

1. *Similarities*—both languages employ similar methods of transmitting data between internal and external areas.

2. *Differences*—COBOL provides only one form of data transmission; PL/1 has two: record-oriented and stream-oriented. PL/1 provides control format specifications for printing and spacing; COBOL does not. PL/1 has file characteristics specified in the DECLARE statement; in COBOL the file characteristics are specified in the Data Division.

IDENTIFICATION QUESTIONS

Match the following terms with the statements that follow.

A. Attributes
B. Declare
C. Default
D. Do
E. End
F. Expression
G. Get
H. Go To
I. Identifier
J. If
K. Input
L. Keyboard
M. Output
N. Put
O. Read
P. Record-Oriented Transmission
Q. Statement
R. Stream-Oriented Transmission
S. Update
T. Write

1. A statement that is used in record-oriented transmission to read the next record.
2. The statement that is used to transmit data from external to internal storage.
3. A statement that transfers control to a specified statement.
4. This statement is used to describe named data sets as it is represented within the internal storage of the computer.
5. A variable symbolic name having a value that may change during the execution of the program.
6. That attribute that is used for files that are only to be read.
7. A data set that is considered to be a continuous stream of data in character form.
8. An assumption that the compiler makes where there are alternatives and the programmer has made no choice.
9. A word that when used in the proper context has a special meaning to the compiler.
10. Those properties that characterize a data item.
11. A statement that is used to determine whether or not statement(s) are to be executed.
12. The statement that is used to transmit data from internal to external storage.
13. A statement that is used in record-oriented transmission to write the next record in the data set.
14. A single constant or name or combination of these include operators and delimiters.
15. A statement that is used to define and specify control for a group of statements to be used in a loop.

16. The attribute that is used for files that are created.
17. The basic program element used to construct a PL/1 program.
18. A data set that consists of a collection of physically separated records.
19. A statement that defines the end of a group.
20. The attribute that is used for existing files that will have records added or deleted.

QUESTIONS FOR REVIEW

1. What is the main purpose of PL/1 as a programming language?
2. Describe the PL/1 format features.
3. Explain the use of the following in PL/1 program: identifiers and constants.
4. What are the types of delimiters used in PL/1? Give examples of each.
5. Explain the use of expressions in PL/1 programs. Give examples.
6. Describe the use of statements in PL/1. Give examples.
7. Differentiate between stream-oriented data transmission and record-oriented data transmission.
8. How are the Procedures statement used in PL/1 programming?
9. Compare the features of COBOL and PL/1 programming. Show the similarities and differences in regard to Language Notation, Data Description, Input and Output.
10. What is the similarity between PL/1 and FORTRAN?
11. What is the significance of the "default" option in PL/1?

CHAPTER 15

System 360/370 Assembler Language

Not many years ago all programs were written in machine language. The most valuable tools the programmer had was an eraser. He was concerned with an enormous amount of clerical detail. He had to remember dozens of numerical codes for computer operations and try not to make mistakes when using them. He had to keep track of the storage space he used for instructions, data, and work areas, and to actually calculate any addresses he needed to refer to in his program. Revising a program (a more frequent occurrence than it is now) often meant changing every address that followed the revisions. All this detail increased possibilities for error and increased time spent on checking, calculating, keeping tables, and other clerical tasks.

The realization that the computer itself was better suited than man for doing this type of clerical work led to the development of assembler languages. In IBM system 360/370 assembler language, the programmer writes every operation code in alphabetic letters, called mnemonics, and the addresses of locations in storage can be given symbolic names such as PAY, NAME, HOURS and RATE by the programmer. The assembler program translates these symbols into machine-language instructions, assigns storage locations and performs all the other necessary operations to produce a program that will be executed by the computer.

The system 360/370 assembler language is an example of a machine-oriented language. Assembler language enables the programmer to use all system 360/370 machine functions as if he were coding in system 360/370 machine language. Of all the programming languages, it is closest to machine language in form and content. The high-level languages such as FORTRAN,

COBOL and PL/1 are procedure-oriented rather than machine-oriented. These languages are much like English or mathematical notation. Depending on what is involved, one statement in these languages may be compiled into series of two or eight or fifty machine-language instructions. The procedure-oriented languages have the advantage of letting the programmer concentrate on what he wants to accomplish and not on how it is to be done by the computer, and they may save considerable time in programming, program modification, and program testing. Choice of a programming language in any given situation usually involves weighing the cost of programming against the cost of machine time. A complex mathematical problem that can be run in a few minutes and will be run only once presents a very different situation from a program that runs for several hours and will be repeated every week.

Here we can appreciate one of the important advantages of assembler language over the high-level languages: its efficient use, in the hands of a skilled programmer, of computer storage and time. High-level languages produce generalized routines so that a wide range of data processing needs can be met with a minimum of programming effort. A routine can be written in assembler language exactly to fit some particular data processing need, thus saving storage space and execution time.

A knowledge of assembler programming has some important benefits for a programmer working in a high-level language. It can be helpful to him in analyzing and debugging programs. It also enables him to include certain language routines in his program to meet special systems or other requirements. For this and other reasons, assembler language is the principal language used in writing software programs for compilers, supervisory programs, and any other programs that will be used repeatedly.

Programming in an assembler language offers the following important advantages over programming in actual machine language.

1. Mnemonic codes are used in place of numeric codes. For example, the actual operation code for the instruction STORE is 50 in hexadecimal, while in assembler language, the mnemonic code ST is written. Many programmers never actually learn machine language codes.
2. All addressed data and instructions are written in symbolic form, thus relieving the programmer of the tedious task of effective allocation of storage to handle data. The resulting program is easier to modify. Furthermore, the use of symbolic addresses reduces the clerical aspects of programming, thereby eliminating many programming errors. The meaningful symbols are easier to read and understand than numeric addresses.
3. Assembler instructions perform many of the functions of assigning

base registers and calculating displacement factors in storage addressing.

The assembler programming language is not directly executable by the computer. The symbolic program must be written on a special coding form. Cards constituting the *source program* are later punched from this form. These cards are then combined with Job Control cards and entered into the computer. The program is processed under the control of the processor (Assembler) program supplied by the IBM Corporation.

The output from the processor run produces a listing of the source program statements and the resulting *object program* statements (Fig. 15.1, Fig. 15.2). The object program may be punched into cards or stored in mag-

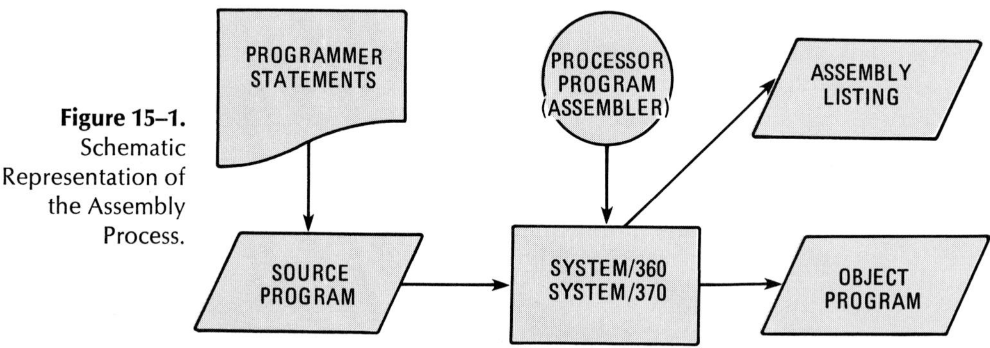

Figure 15–1. Schematic Representation of the Assembly Process.

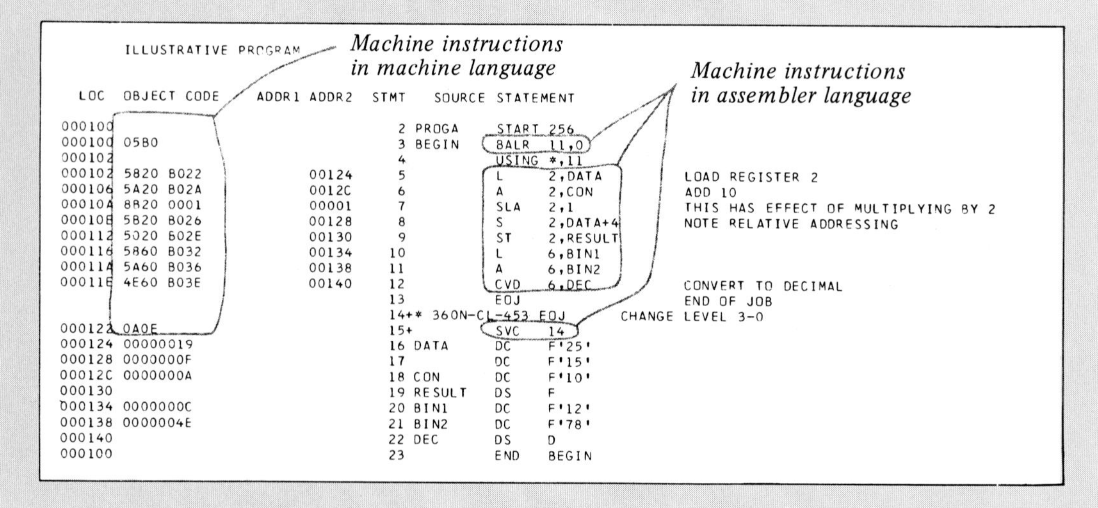


```
              ILLUSTRATIVE PROGRAM

LOC    OBJECT CODE     ADDR1 ADDR2  STMT    SOURCE STATEMENT

000100                                2 PROGA    START 256
000100 05B0                           3 BEGIN    BALR  11,0
000102                                4          USING *,11
000102 5820 B022            00124     5          L     2,DATA       LOAD REGISTER 2
000106 5A20 B02A            0012C     6          A     2,CON        ADD 10
00010A 8B20 0001            00001     7          SLA   2,1          THIS HAS EFFECT OF MULTIPLYING BY 2
00010E 5B20 B026            00128     8          S     2,DATA+4     NOTE RELATIVE ADDRESSING
000112 5020 B02E            00130     9          ST    2,RESULT
000116 5860 B032            00134    10          L     6,BIN1
00011A 5A60 B036            00138    11          A     6,BIN2
00011E 4E60 B03E            00140    12          CVD   6,DEC        CONVERT TO DECIMAL
                                     13          EOJ                END OF JOB
                                     14+* 360N-CL-453 EOJ      CHANGE LEVEL 3-0
000122 0A0E                          15+         SVC   14
000124 00000019                      16 DATA     DC    F'25'
000128 0000000F                      17          DC    F'15'
00012C 0000000A                      18 CON      DC    F'10'
000130                               19 RESULT   DS    F
000134 0000000C                      20 BIN1     DC    F'12'
000138 0000004E                      21 BIN2     DC    F'78'
000140                               22 DEC      DS    D
000100                               23          END   BEGIN
```

Figure 15–2. Translation of Machine-Oriented Language.

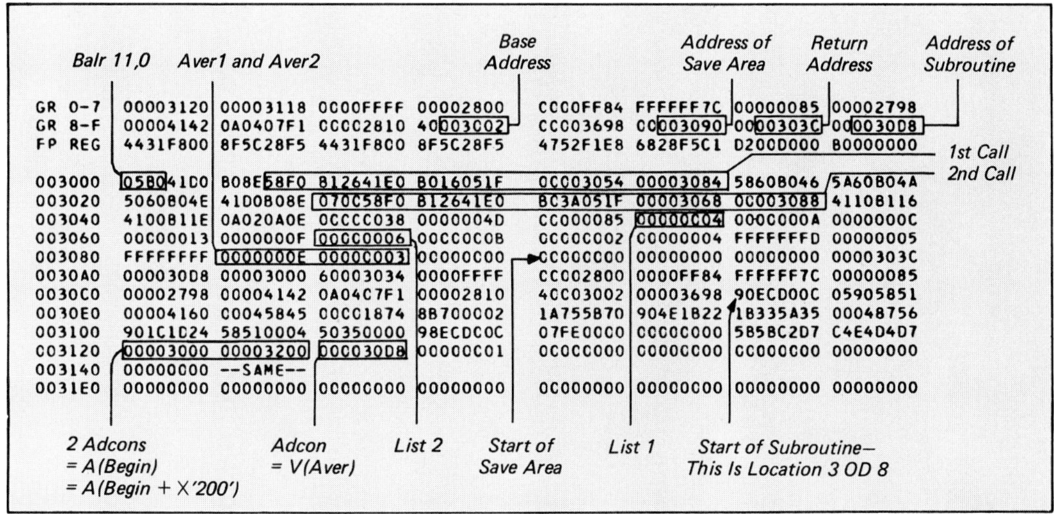

Figure 15–3. Dump of Storage.

netic core, magnetic tape, or on a magnetic disk for the subsequent processing of the program. The form and content of the listing can be partially controlled by the programmer. In addition, as the source program is being assembled, it is analyzed for actual or potential errors in the use of the assembler language. Detected errors are indicated in the program listings. The object program may be executed if no serious errors exist.

A dump (print routine) can be asked for if the program fails to execute due to serious errors in the program (Fig. 15.3). The entire contents of storage, the contents of the registers, the conditions of indicators and switches are printed in hexadecimal format which can be used by the programmer to locate the error. Selected areas of storage, instead of the entire storage area, may be dumped if so desired.

SYSTEM FEATURES—IBM SYSTEM 360/370

The system 360/370 is a general purpose computer designed to handle business as well as scientific data processing applications (Fig. 15.4). In the past, these operations were handled by separate computer families. Scientific computers were fixed word length machines using a binary form of coding in their operations. In a fixed word length machine, each storage area location is addressable by a word consisting of a fixed number of characters. Business computers, on the other hand, use a variable word length machine (character oriented) and use a binary representation of decimal information BCD (Binary Coded Decimal). See Fig. 15.5. The system 360/370 uses a binary system as well as variable word length fields. Although business data processing programmers are primary users of the decimal form of arithmetic, the ability to use binary increases the effectiveness of the programmer.

Figure 15–4. IBM System/370 Model 155.

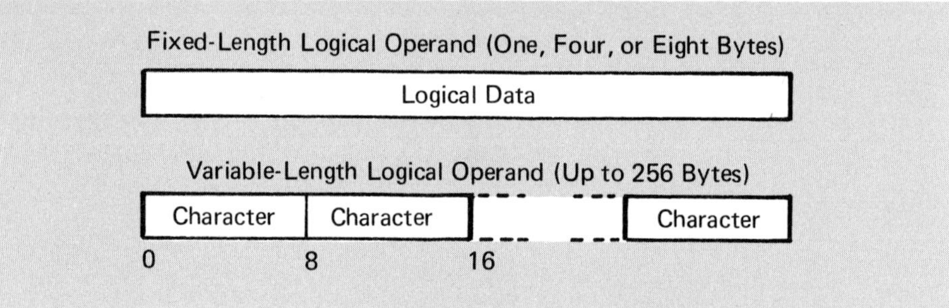

Figure 15–5. Fixed and Variable Length Logical Information.

The system 360/370 is produced in a variety of models to fit the need of the user. To allow for growth in volume, the system is so designed as to allow upward growth with a minimum of program revisions. Some of the principal features of the system 360/370 are listed below.

OVERLAPPING OF INPUT/OUTPUT OPERATIONS

The system permits the processing to continue while the relative slow operations of input and output are being performed, thus decreasing the over-all processing time.

AUTOMATIC INTERRUPTS

Through a monitoring type system, the program may be switched to another operation or to another program due to a condition encountered during the processing. This feature permits the continued processing with a minimum amount of interruptions.

COMMUNICATION APPLICATIONS

Time sharing, message switching and the whole area of teleprocessing is available to the main computer. Messages may be sent to the computer from these terminals. Inquiries for information may also be processed and relayed back to these terminals. Thus the resources can be utilized for maximum operations vital to the communications field.

MULTIPROGRAMMING

All facilities may be optimized by having the system operate upon multiple programs or routines concurrently. Depending upon the size, speed, and configuration of a system, multiprogramming permits several jobs to be processed at the same time, including the insertion of "crash" jobs with high priority ratings.

CONTROL (SUPERVISORY) PROGRAMS

There are two types of programs operating within the system 360/370 computer; a problem program and a control program. The *problem program* is written by the programmer to provide a solution to a particular problem. The *control program* is written by the computer manufacture (part of the program may be written by the user) and resides in main storage in an area not accessible to the problem programmer. The purpose of the control program is to reduce machine idle time and manual intervention, and to increase the efficiency of the data processing installation. Some of these control functions have reached a high degree of sophistication. These programs are also known as supervisory or monitor programs.

Some of the basic functions performed by a control program are:

1. The loading of the problem program into the storage area of the computer.
2. The initiation of input and output operations.
3. The supervision of the running of the problem program through an automatic interrupt system.

LOADING THE PROBLEM PROGRAM

The problem program is loaded into an assigned storage area by the control program (Fig. 15.6). After the problem program is loaded, control then passes to the first instruction of that program. When the problem program is finished (execution of the data completed), control is transferred back to the control program which then proceeds to load in the next problem program and pass control back to it. The procedure will be continued until all problem programs have been executed. The system will never stop between jobs and

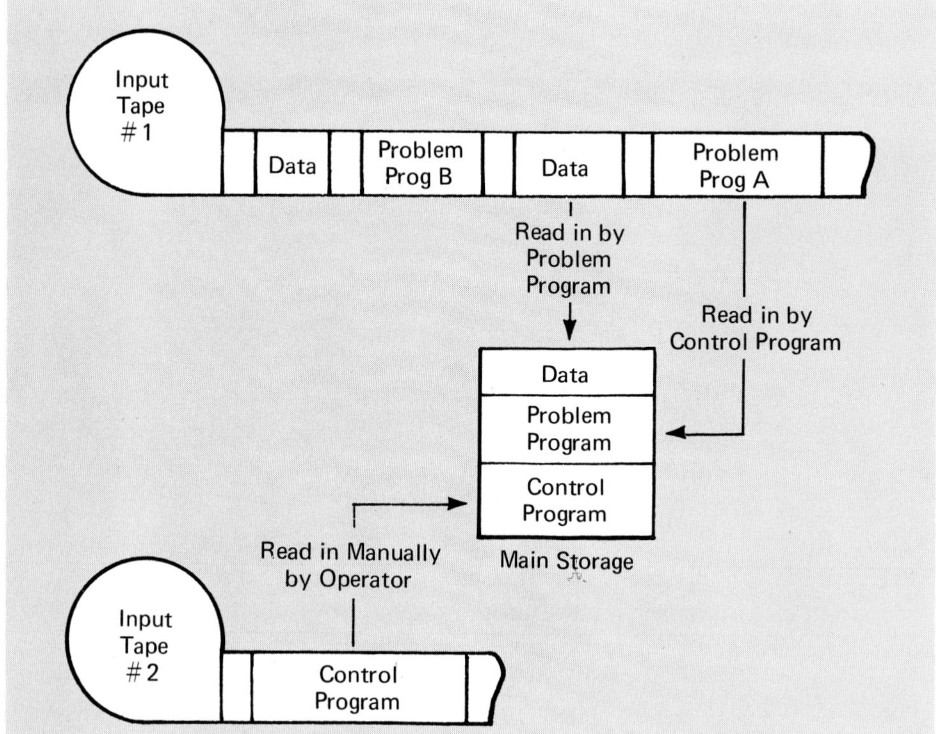

Figure 15–6. Loading the Problem Program.

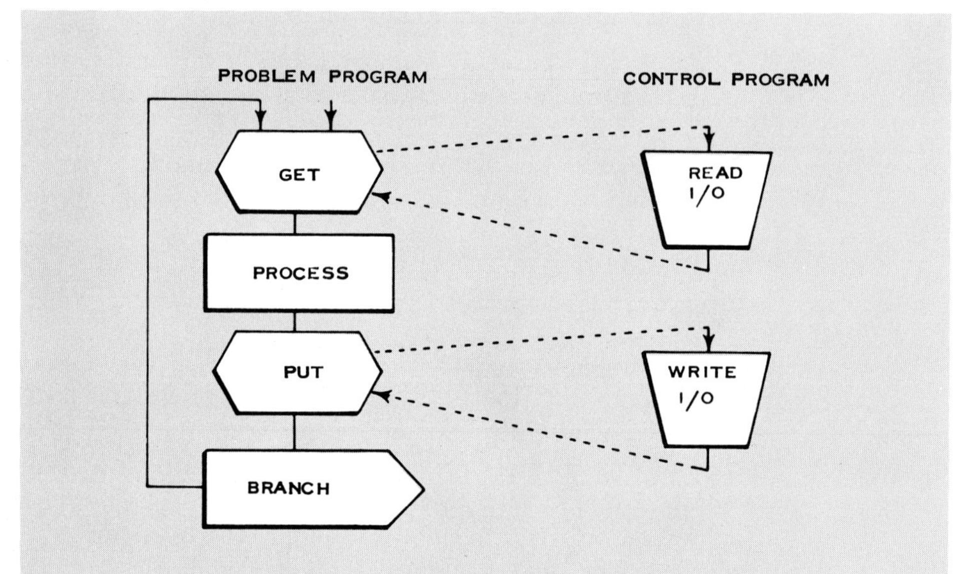

Figure 15–7. Initiation of Input/Output Operation.

the control program serves as a linkage between each of the jobs to be performed. The control program remains in storage as each problem program is executed.

INITIATION OF INPUT/OUTPUT OPERATIONS

The problem program is concerned mainly with the processing of the data (Fig. 15.7). The necessary instructions to read, write, and transfer the data between the input/output devices and main storage are handled by the control program. Each input/output operation consists of a series of instructions that informs the input/output device to start, as well as instructions for checking the validity of the data, the status of the input/ouput devices, error conditions, etc. Control will continually pass back and forth between the problem program and the control program during the execution of the program until the job is completed. The problem program transfers control to the control program whenever an input/output function is necessary.

AUTOMATIC INTERRUPTS

For a system to operate with maximum efficiency, it must be capable of redirecting its activities when prescribed or unusual conditions arise. Situations which require an interruption of the program may be the result of a condition external to the system, in the input/output unit, or possibly in the central processing unit itself. Completion of an input/output operation or an entire job, unacceptable input data, program error, machine error, corrective action, are some of the conditions that may result in an automatic interrupt (Fig. 15.8). The programmer himself can interrupt the system by asking for the supervisory program via the automatic interrupt system.

To minimize the amount of manual intervention, an automatic system was designed. The circuitry takes over the functions that were formerly the responsibility of the programmer. When an interrupt occurs, the operation of the program in progress is suspended temporarily. The control and status information needed to restart the program are automatically stored by the interrupt system itself.

An interrupt action causes an automatic branch to the control program. The current sequence of instructions are interrupted and an automatic branch occurs to a new set of instructions. The control program consists of the computer manufacturer's prepared programs as well as the user's application program plus various fix up and other corrective routines to which the machine is directed to branch after the interrupt. The interrupt will cause the "current" PSW (Program Status Word) location and the "new" PSW to replace it. The "new" PSW will now control the operations of the program. The "new" PSW

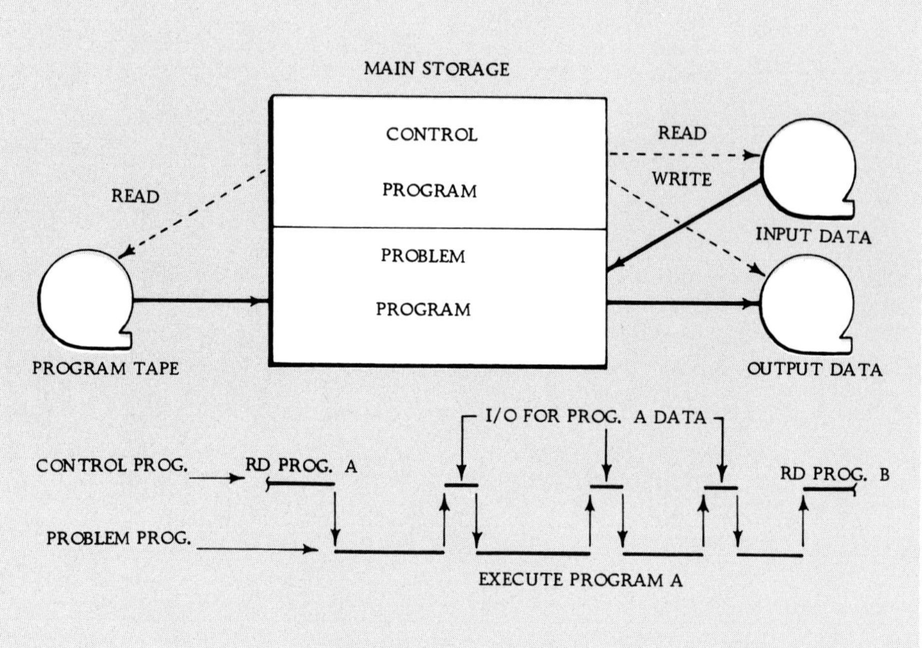

Figure 15–8. Execution of Problem Program and Automatic Interrupts.

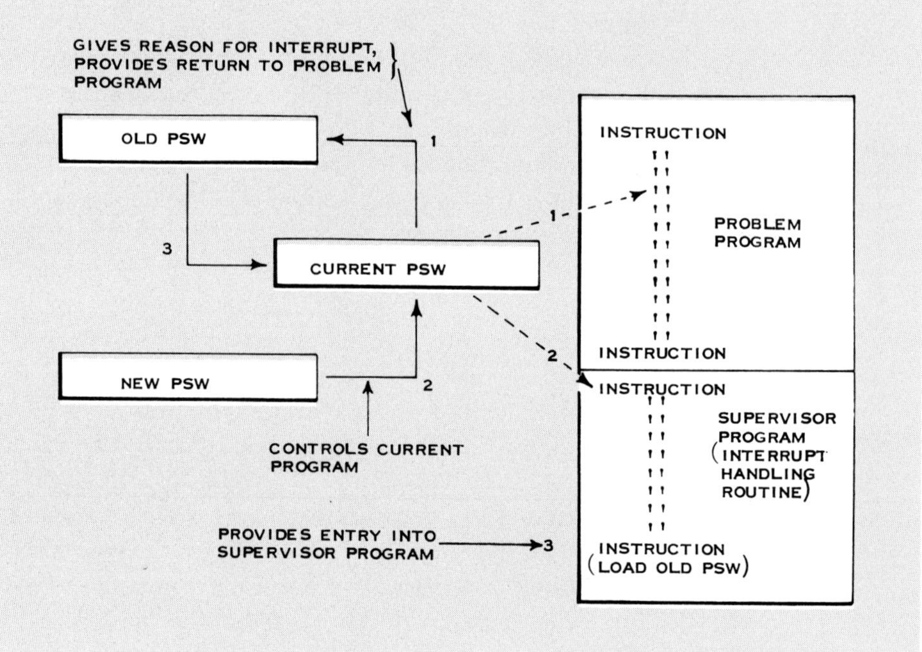

Figure 15–9. Automatic Interrupt Procedure.

will initiate a sequence of instructions designed to handle the particular interrupt action. The "new" and "old" PSW words occupy fixed storage locations. The particular PSW word that will be fetched will depend on the type of interrupt. The types of automatic interrupts are Input/Output, Program, Supervisor Call, External and Machine Check (Fig. 15.9).

INPUT/OUTPUT INTERRUPT

This interrupt can be caused by the termination of an input/output operation. This is a signal to the processing unit that the input/output channel is free and ready to accept a new operation. Special conditions in the channel or in an input/output unit cause the processing unit to take appropriate action.

PROGRAM INTERRUPT

This interrupt may be caused by various kinds of programming errors and other unusual conditions such as incorrect operands, overflow, improper divide, improper address, attempted execution of an invalid instruction, etc. There are fifteen possible conditions that may cause this interrupt.

SUPERVISOR CALL INTERRUPT

This is a special instruction available to the programmer that can cause an interrupt. The most frequent use of a Supervisor Call interrupt is to switch from the problem state to the supervisory state.

EXTERNAL INTERRUPT

Through an External Interrupt, the system can respond to a signal from the Interrupt key on the console, the built-in timer system, other processing units, terminals or special devices.

MACHINE CHECK INTERRUPT

A Machine Check interrupt is caused by various types of machine errors and hardware malfunctions as detected by the machine checking circuit. Program errors such as invalid instructions or data cannot result in a Machine Check interrupt. This interrupt initiates an automatic recording of the status of the system into a special scan-out area in main storage.

Some classes of interrupts may be ignored or held pending under program control. This postponement of the interrupt is known as "masking." Certain interrupts may be "masked" and kept pending until a later time. The

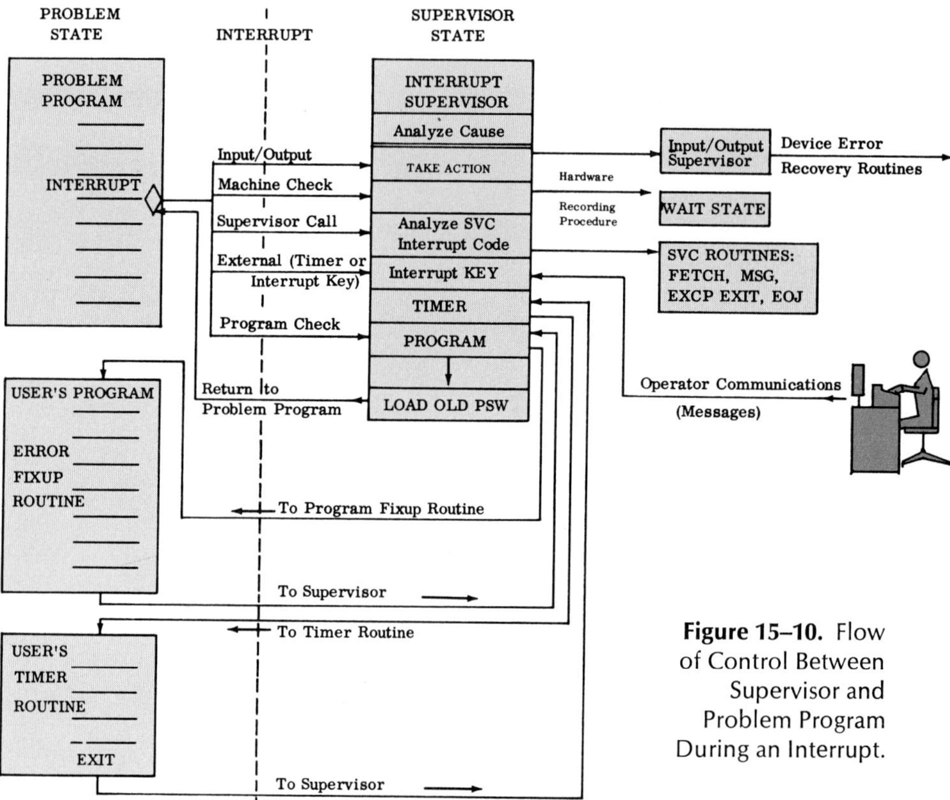

Figure 15–10. Flow of Control Between Supervisor and Problem Program During an Interrupt.

system when executing instructions of the problem program is said to be operating in the *Problem Program* state. Interrupts cause the circuitry to switch from the Problem state to the Supervisory state (Fig. 15.10).

PROGRAM STATUS WORD

The Program Status Word (PSW) contains the required information essential for proper program execution. The necessary status information includes

1. The location of the next instruction to be executed (Fig. 15.11).
2. The program status of the central processing unit (CPU)—whether interruptible or not, stopped or operating, running or waiting, in the problem state or the supervisory state (Fig. 15.12).
3. The length of the last instruction executed.
4. The outcome of arithmetic and logical operations (Fig. 15.13).

The active or controlling PSW is called the "current" PSW and is kept in some internal storage area that is not addressable by the program. The cur-

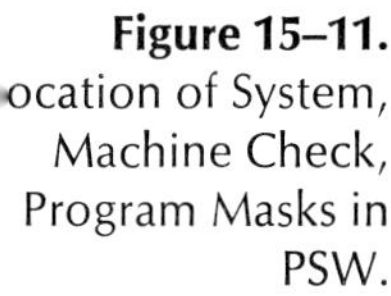

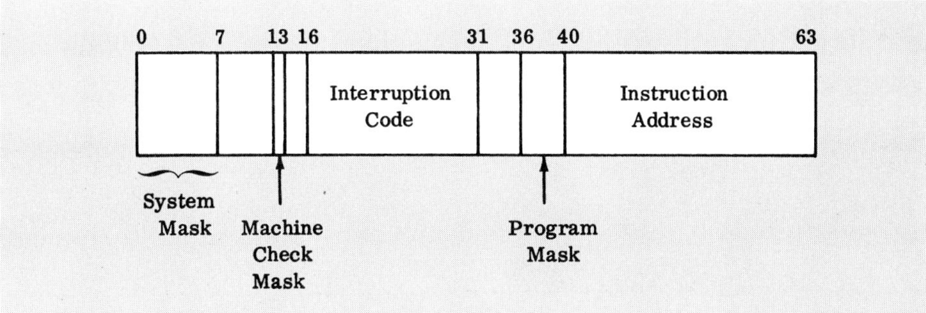

Figure 15–11. ocation of System, Machine Check, Program Masks in PSW.

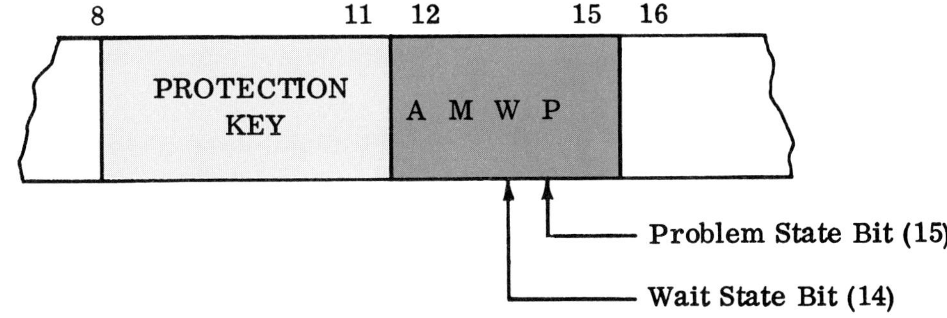

Figure 15–12. Protection Key, Problem State, Wait State, Indentification in PSW.

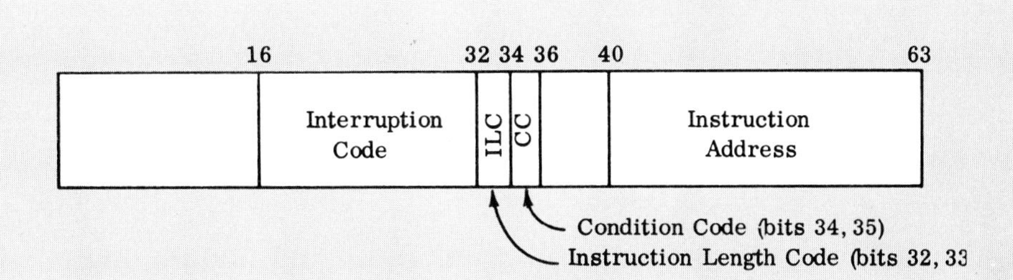

Figure 15–13. Location of Instruction Length Code and Condition Code in PSW.

rent PSW reflects the status of the program currently being executed. The current PSW is equivalent to the control register of earlier computers.

Passing control between the problem program and the supervisory program, and then returning to the correct place in the problem program to resume execution following an interrupt, is accomplished with the PSWs. Traditionally, when information was required at some later point in the program, it was the programmer's responsibility to store it. Since the problem program cannot anticipate interrupts with the system 360/370 computer, they become the responsibility of the system.

Since the relevant status information of the system is available at any time in the current PSW, all the machine need do upon an occurrence of an interrupt is to record in some way the cause of the interrupt, then file the current PSW at a fixed location in storage; it may be returned after the interrupt has been satisfied. Each major class of interrupt has its own fixed storage location for the old and new PSWs. A new PSW is fetched from the fixed location in storage for the particular type of interrupt. The new PSW replaces the current PSW in main storage. By storing the current PSW during an interruption, the status of the central processing unit (CPU) can be preserved for further inspection. By loading a new PSW, the state of the CPU can be initialized or changed. The new PSW contains the information necessary (location of the fix up routine) for handling the interrupt. After the interrupt has been serviced, a single instruction in the new PSW recalls the old PSW and the processing can continue from the point of interruption (Fig. 15.14).

Figure 15–14. Storage Addresses of Program Status Words.

ADDRESS	PROGRAM STATUS WORD
24	External OLD PSW
32	Supervisor Call OLD PSW
40	Program OLD PSW
48	Machine-check OLD PSW
56	Input Output OLD PSW
88	External NEW PSW
96	Supervisor Call NEW PSW
104	Program NEW PSW
112	Machine-check NEW PSW
120	Input/Output NEW PSW

CHANNEL CONCEPT

Input/output operations involve the transfer of information to and from main storage and an input/output device. Input/output (I/O) devices include such equipment as card readers, card punches, magnetic tape units, disk storage units, drum storage and typewriter keyboard devices, printers, teleprocessing devices, and control equipment. Since I/O devices operate at different speeds, mechanical and electronic, a control unit is provided to perform the logical and buffering operations necessary to operate the associate I/O devices.

All communication between the central processing unit and the channel takes place over a connection called the I/O interface. The I/O interface provides an information format and control sequence signals that are independent of the type of control unit. The channel provides a uniform means of attaching and controlling the various types of I/O devices (Fig. 15.15).

One of the important system features that facilitates the simultaneous operations necessary for the maximum utilization of the system's resources is the channel circuitry. The electronic circuitry of a channel may be regarded as a small computer that responds to its own set of commands. Channels provide the ability of the computer to read, write, and compete concurrently. Each channel has its own program in main storage which must be initiated by the supervisory program (Fig. 15.16).

The main function of the channel is to handle I/O requests for main storage cycles (Fig. 15.17). The channel receives the data from the I/O device. When enough data has been received, the channel will request storage cycles so as to enter the data into main storage. After the data has been placed in main storage, the channel will wait for additional information from the input device. For an output procedure, the process is reversed, with requests for main storage cycles for data. The data transfers to and from the I/O device to a channel. Since the channel is taking care of main storage cycles for I/O devices, the CPU is free to continue its processing of instructions. The simultaneous operation of an I/O device and processing instructions in main storage is known as *overlapping* (Fig. 15.18).

Figure 15–15. Channel Circuitry.

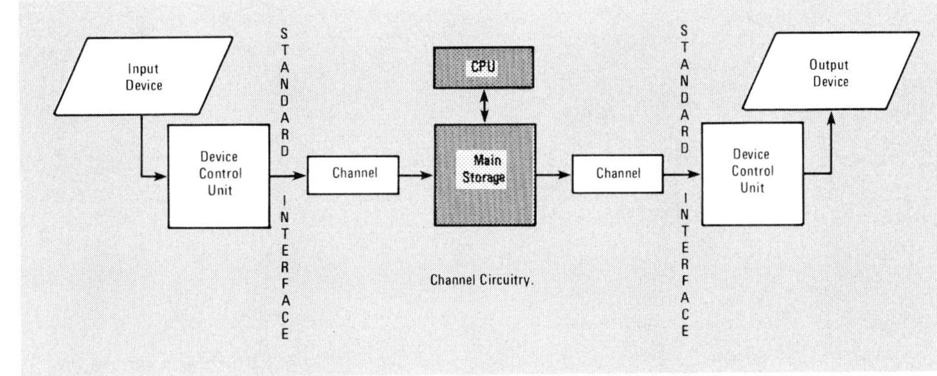

Figure 15–16. Relationship of I/O Instructions, Commands, and Orders.

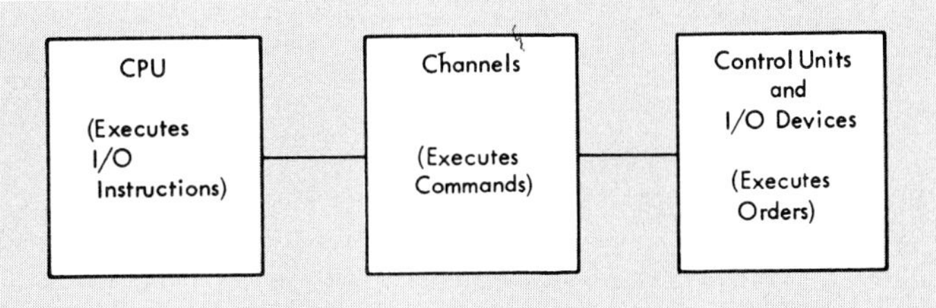

Total time to process a record

INPUT DEVICE | CPU | OUTPUT DEVICE

Read → Process → Write

X milliseconds + Y milliseconds + Z milliseconds

TOTAL TIME = X + Y + Z milliseconds

Record Process Time.

Figure 15–17. Record Process Time.

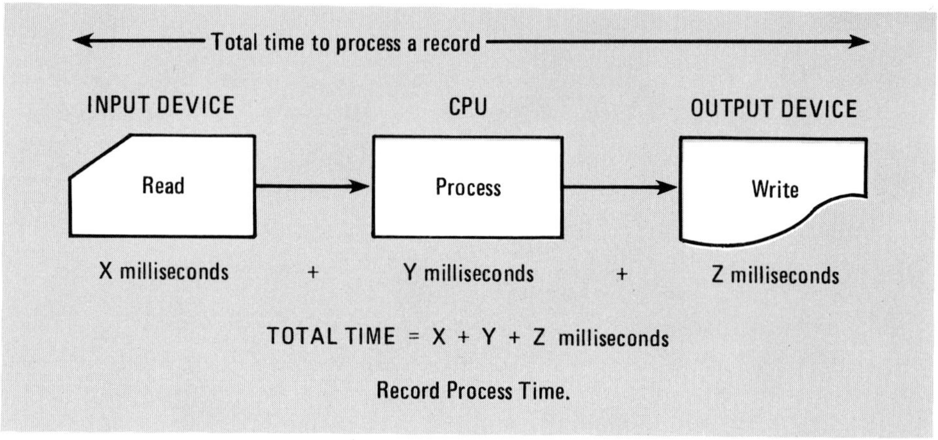

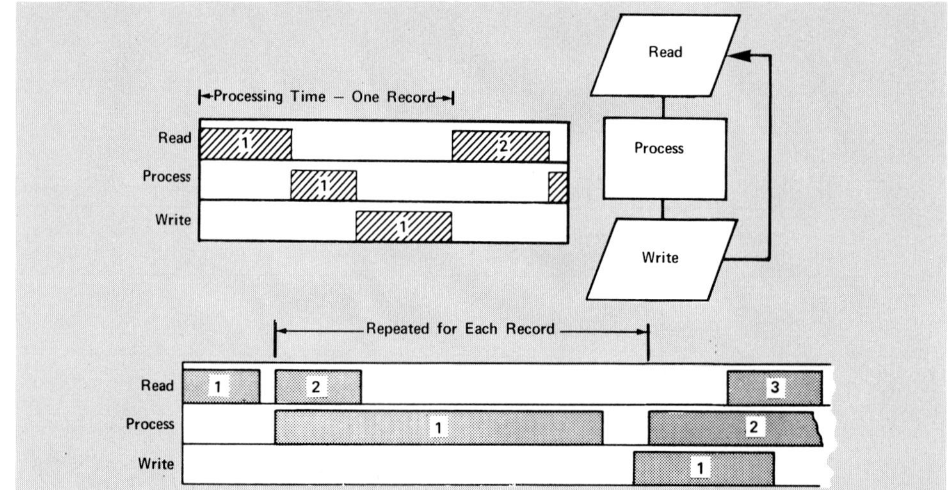

Figure 15–18. Nonoverlapped and Overlapped Processing.

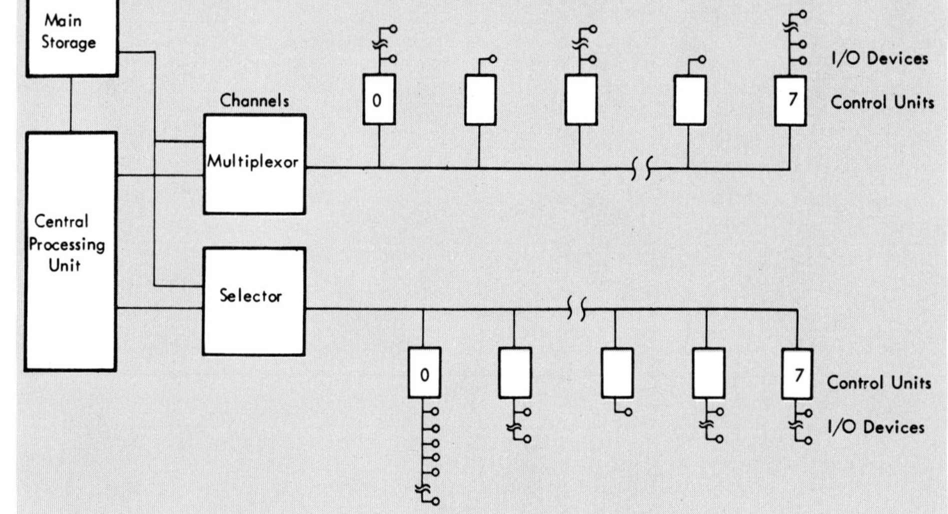

Figure 15–19. Comparison of Burst and Multiplexor Modes.

The channel relieves the CPU of the burden of communicating directly with the I/O device and thus permits the processing of data to proceed concurrently with the I/O operation.

Two types of channels are available: multiplexor and selector (Fig. 15.19). One multiplexor channel is provided with each system. Up to twelve selector channels can be provided, depending on the model number.

Multiplexor Channels are intended for use primarily with low speed I/O devices such as card readers, printers, card punches, etc. The channel is designed to operate with a number of I/O devices simultaneously. Several I/O devices can be transferring records over the multiplexor channel on a shared basis (up to 256 I/O devices can be using the channel depending on the model). The multiplexor channel stores its information from the various I/O units in a compact storage area. Each I/O device has an area of the multiplexor storage for its own individual use when operating in the multiplexor channel. Subchannels are provided for all I/O devices in this area.

Selector Channels are designed to operate with high speed devices such as magnetic tapes, disk units, drums, and buffered card devices. Only one I/O device can be selected in the channel at one time. Once selected, a complete record is transferred over the I/O interface (Burst Mode). See Fig. 15.20.

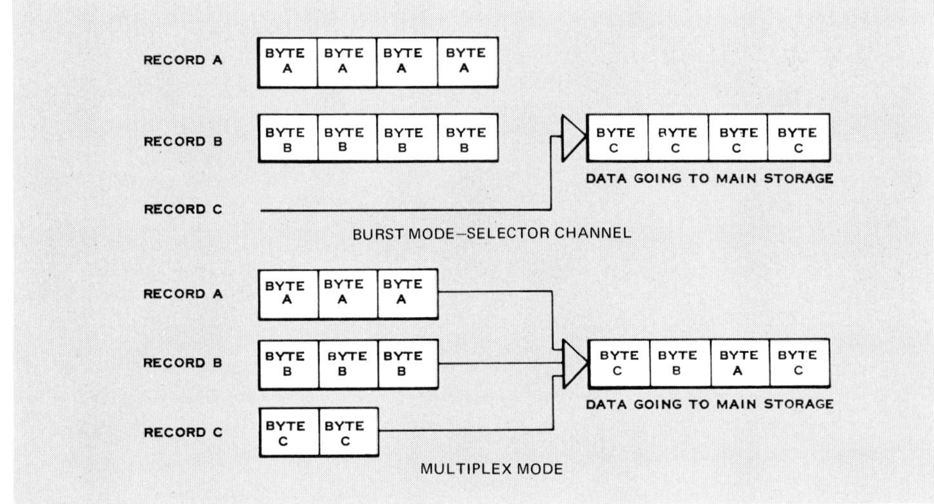

Figure 15–20. Multiplexor and Selector Channels.

REGISTERS

The CPU provides sixteen general registers for fixed point (binary) operations and four floating point registers for floating point operations (Fig. 15.21).

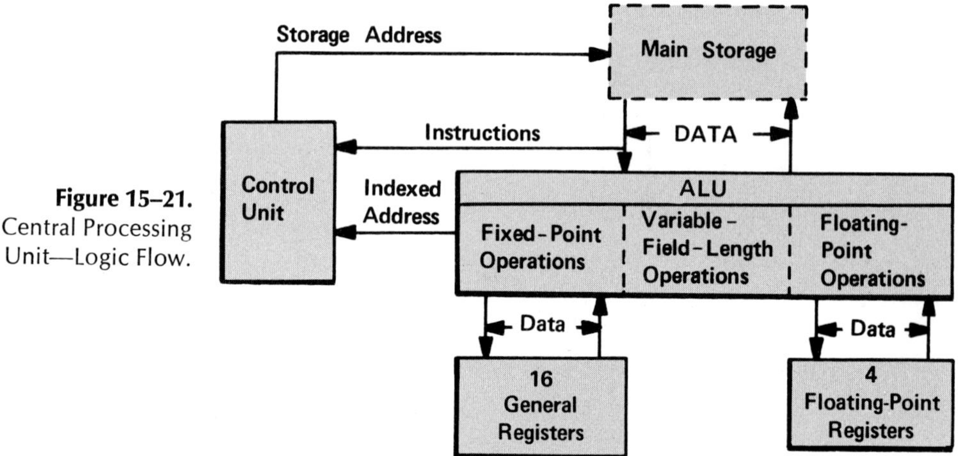

Figure 15–21. Central Processing Unit—Logic Flow.

GENERAL REGISTERS

The sixteen general purpose registers can be used as base registers, index registers, accumulators for fixed point arithmetic operations, and for logical operations. Registers decrease the overall processing time when compared to the time required for decimal (storage to storage) operations. Registers have a capacity of one word (thirty-two bits), and are identified by the numbers 0–15 in the instruction. A special field in the instruction specifies the desired register. The registers may be combined in some operations with adjacent registers to provide a capacity of two words (sixty-four bits).

FLOATING POINT REGISTERS

Four floating point registers of sixty-four bits each are available for floating point operations. These registers are principally used in mathematical and scientific operations. The instruction operation code determines which type of register is to be used. Registers improve the efficiency of arithmetic and logical operations and also provide a means of efficient address specifications and modification (Fig. 15.22).

STORAGE ADDRESSING

To permit the ready relocation of a program segment and to provide the flexible specification for input and output, and work areas, all instructions referring to main storage have been given a capacity of employing a full address.

Because the ability to address vast amounts of main storage is a desirable feature, an internal address of twenty-four binary bits permits addressing up to 16,777,216 locations in storage. An instruction involving a storage address would specify a base register, a displacement factor and possibly an index register.

BASE REGISTER (B)

A base register has a twenty-four-bit number contained in a general register specified by the programmer in the instruction. This B field is included in every address specification.

DISPLACEMENT FACTOR (D)

The displacement factor is a twelve-bit number contained in the instruction format. It provides for relative addressing up to 4095 locations beyond the base register address.

All instructions involving storage include a base register plus a displacement factor that are added together to produce an effective storage address.

INDEX REGISTER (I)

The index register is a twenty-four-bit number contained in a general register specified in the X field of the instruction. It is only permissible in certain types of instructions (RX). In these instructions, the effective address is calculated by adding together the contents of the base register, the index register, and the displacement factor (Fig. 15.23).

R Field	Reg. No.	General Registers	Floating-Point Registers
0000	0	← 32 Bits →	← 64 Bits →
0001	1		
0010	2		
0011	3		
0100	4		
0101	5		
0110	6		
0111	7		
1000	8		
1001	9		
1010	10		
1011	11		
1100	12		
1101	13		
1110	14		
1111	15		

Figure 15–22. Registers.

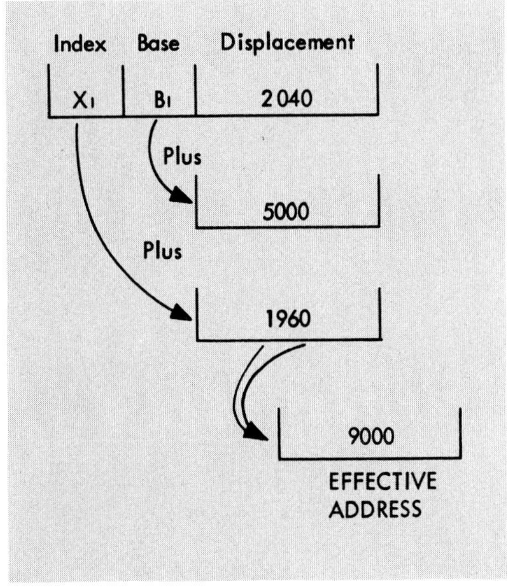

Figure 15–23. Address Generation.

INSTRUCTION FORMAT

The instruction sets were designed to process commercial and scientific applications. Four instruction sets are available to the user (Fig. 15.24).

1. A *standard* instruction set provides the basic computing functions of the system. Most of the instructions are included in this set which is supplied as a standard feature with all models.
2. A *commercial* instruction set may be added to provide decimal operations.
3. A *scientific* instruction set provides the floating point capabilities necessary for scientific operations.
4. A *universal* instruction set is a combination of all three sets, standard, commercial and scientific, and in addition provides storage protection instructions.

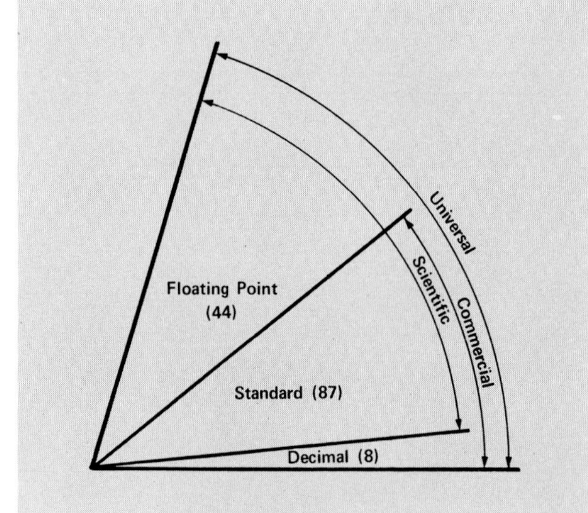

Figure 15–24. IBM System/360/370 Instruction Set.

INSTRUCTION LENGTH

Instructions specify the operations to be performed and the location of the data involved. Data may be located in main storage or in any of the sixteen general registers. To conserve storage space and save time in instruction execution, a variable instruction length is used. Instructions will be of different lengths depending on the location of the data. The length of the instruction is varied depending upon the number of addresses necessary for the operation (one, two, or three halfwords). See Fig. 15.25.

The instructions consist of the following:

1. *Op code.* The operation code supplies the following information.
   a) Specifies the operation to be performed (ADD, MOVE, BRANCH, etc.).

b) specifies the length of the instruction (1, 2, or 3 halfwords).
c) Specifies the data format, whether the data is fixed or variable in length and if fixed whether the data is in decimal or binary formats.
d) Specifies the general location of the data, and whether operands are in storage or registers; however, it does not specify the location of the data.

2. *Operands.* The programmer can specify the operands as being in registers or in main storage.

In most instruction operations, the result of the operation replaces the value at the first operand except the STORE and CONVERT TO DECIMAL instructions where the results replace the second operand value (Fig. 15.26).

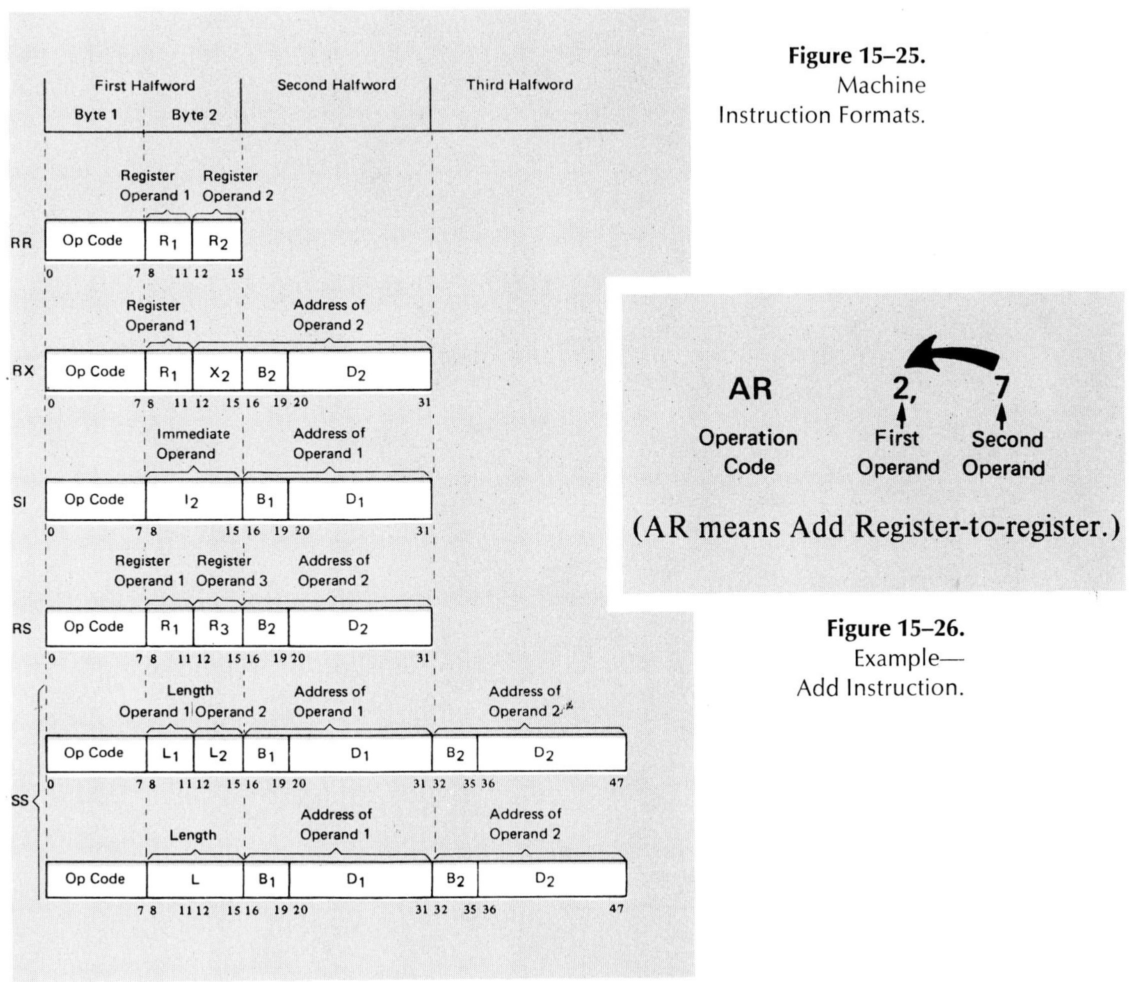

Figure 15–25. Machine Instruction Formats.

Figure 15–26. Example— Add Instruction.

DATA REPRESENTATION

The main storage of a computer contains the program to be executed as well as the data to be processed. All data must enter main storage before it can be processed by the machine. After the data has been processed and the results produced, the data must be placed back in main storage before it can be transmitted to an output device.

The most familiar data representations in commercial applications in earlier computers has been binary coded decimal (BCD) in which six bits were used to represent the sixty-four alphameric and special characters. The basic records of commercial applications consist of many fields of varying lengths. On the other hand, scientific computers generally operate in fixed word length fields of binary data.

The system 360/370 transmits information between main storage and the processing unit in units of one byte (eight bits) or in multiples of bytes at a time (Fig. 15.27). Because eight bits rather than six bits are used, up to 256 characters can be represented in Extended Binary Coded Decimal Interchange Code (EBCDIC). See Fig. 15.28. For the eight-bit configuration for EBCDIC see Fig. 15.29.

Numerals (0–9)

Zone bits are all 1111 plus numeric bits 0000—1001.

Alphabetic

Letters	Zone Bits	Numeric Bits
A – I	1100	0001 – 1001
J – R	1101	0001 – 1001
S – Z	1110	0010 – 1001

SPECIAL CHARACTERS

Zone bits 0000 up to zone 1011 are combined with various configurations of numeric bits to represent all possible special characters.

The zone bits are so arranged as to provide a collating sequence in which numbers are higher than alphabetic and special characters in alphameric fields, but zones are not used in numerals in arithmetic operations. Instead, an instruction PACK, places two decimal digits in one byte, thus eliminating the zone bits. The zone bits have to be put back into the byte if the numeric information is to be output. Special instructions are provided to accomplish this.

An eight-bit unit of information known as the *byte* is the basic building block of all formats. The byte is the smallest addressable unit in storage. All

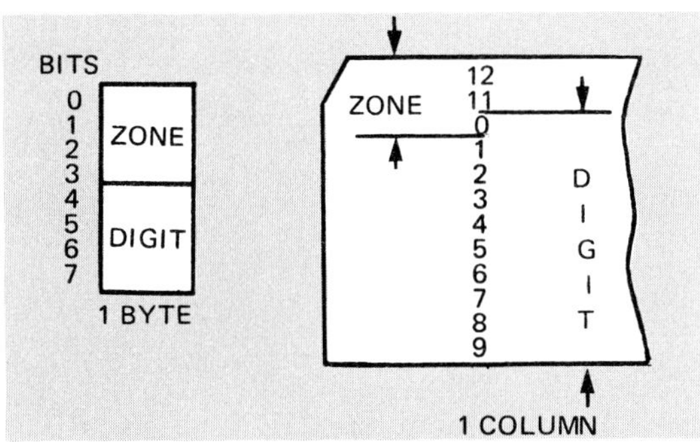

Figure 15–27.
Example—Byte.

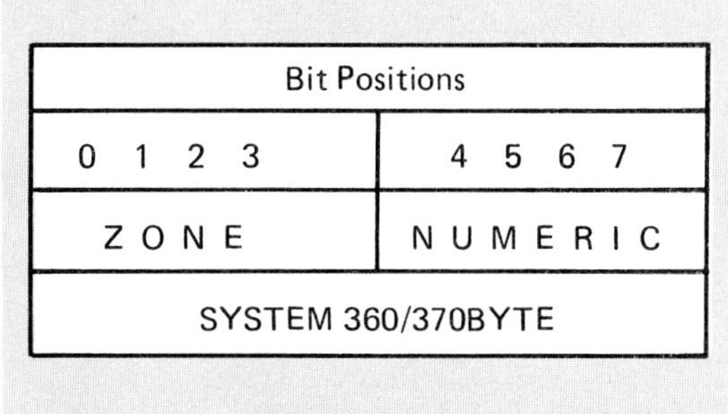

Figure 15–29.
System/360/370 Byte.

Figure 15–28.
Extended Binary Coded Decimal Interchange Code (EBCDIC) for Graphic Characters.

Graphic character	EBCDIC 8-bit code Bit Positions 0123 4567	Hex equiv-alent	Punched card code	Graphic character	EBCDIC 8-bit code Bit Positions 0123 4567	Hex equiv-alent	Punched card code
blank	0100 0000	40	no punches	u	1010 0100	A4	11-0-4
¢	0100 1010	4A	12-8-2	v	1010 0101	A5	11-0-5
.	0100 1011	4B	12-8-3	w	1010 0110	A6	11-0-6
(	0100 1101	4D	12-8-5	x	1010 0111	A7	11-0-7
+	0100 1110	4E	12-8-6	y	1010 1000	A8	11-0-8
&	0101 0000	50	12	z	1010 1001	A9	11-0-9
!	0101 1010	5A	11-8-2	A	1100 0001	C1	12-1
$	0101 1011	5B	11-8-3	B	1100 0010	C2	12-2
*	0101 1100	5C	11-8-4	C	1100 0011	C3	12-3
)	0101 1101	5D	11-8-5	D	1100 0100	C4	12-4
;	0101 1110	5E	11-8-6	E	1100 0101	C5	12-5
-	0110 0000	60	11	F	1100 0110	C6	12-6
,	0110 1011	6B	0-8-3	G	1100 0111	C7	12-7
%	0110 1100	6C	0-8-4	H	1100 1000	C8	12-8
?	0110 1111	6F	0-8-7	I	1100 1001	C9	12-9
:	0111 1010	7A	8-2	J	1101 0001	D1	11-1
#	0111 1011	7B	8-3	K	1101 0010	D2	11-2
@	0111 1100	7C	8-4	L	1101 0011	D3	11-3
'	0111 1101	7D	8-5	M	1101 0100	D4	11-4
=	0111 1110	7E	8-6	N	1101 0101	D5	11-5
"	0111 1111	7F	8-7	O	1101 0110	D6	11-6
a	1000 0001	81	12-0-1	P	1101 0111	D7	11-7
b	1000 0010	82	12-0-2	Q	1101 1000	D8	11-8
c	1000 0011	83	12-0-3	R	1101 1001	D9	11-9
d	1000 0100	84	12-0-4	S	1110 0010	E2	0-2
e	1000 0101	85	12-0-5	T	1110 0011	E3	0-3
f	1000 0110	86	12-0-6	U	1110 0100	E4	0-4
g	1000 0111	87	12-0-7	V	1110 0101	E5	0-5
h	1000 1000	88	12-0-8	W	1110 0110	E6	0-6
i	1000 1001	89	12-0-9	X	1110 0111	E7	0-7
j	1001 0001	91	12-11-1	Y	1110 1000	E8	0-8
k	1001 0010	92	12-11-2	Z	1110 1001	E9	0-9
l	1001 0011	93	12-11-3	0	1111 0000	F0	0
m	1001 0100	94	12-11-4	1	1111 0001	F1	1
n	1001 0101	95	12-11-5	2	1111 0010	F2	2
o	1001 0110	96	12-11-6	3	1111 0011	F3	3
p	1001 0111	97	12-11-7	4	1111 0100	F4	4
q	1001 1000	98	12-11-8	5	1111 0101	F5	5
r	1001 1001	99	12-11-9	6	1111 0110	F6	6
s	1010 0010	A2	11-0-2	7	1111 0111	F7	7
t	1010 0011	A3	11-0-3	8	1111 1000	F8	8
				9	1111 1001	F9	9

storage capabilities are specified in number of bytes. Bytes may be handled separately or grouped together in fields.

To be a truly general purpose computer, the machine must be designed to operate with both fixed and variable length data. Whereas variable length data has a variable number of bytes, fixed length data has a fixed number of bytes.

Variable length fields have a specified number of bytes and may start at any byte address in main storage. When the length of the field is not implied by the operation code but is stated explicitly, the information has a variable length field. Variable length fields are addressable in multiples of bytes. An initial byte may be addressed as an operand of the instruction with the number of bytes specified in the instruction.

Fixed length fields have a fixed number of bytes and must start at appropriate boundary locations. A *halfword* is a group of two consecutive bytes and is the basic building block of all instruction formats. A *word* is a group of four consecutive bytes. A *doubleword* is eight consecutive bytes in length.

The OP code of the instruction will determine whether the data is variable or fixed. In case of fixed length operands, the OP code will also determine whether the fixed length data is a halfword, word, or doubleword.

BOUNDARIES

Fixed length data such as halfwords, words, or doublewords must be located in main storage on an integral storage boundary for that unit of information. For a halfword (two bytes) the storage address must be divisible by two; for a word (four bytes) divisible by four; for a doubleword (eight bytes) divisible by eight (Fig. 15.30).

A variable length field is not limited to boundaries and may start at any byte location.

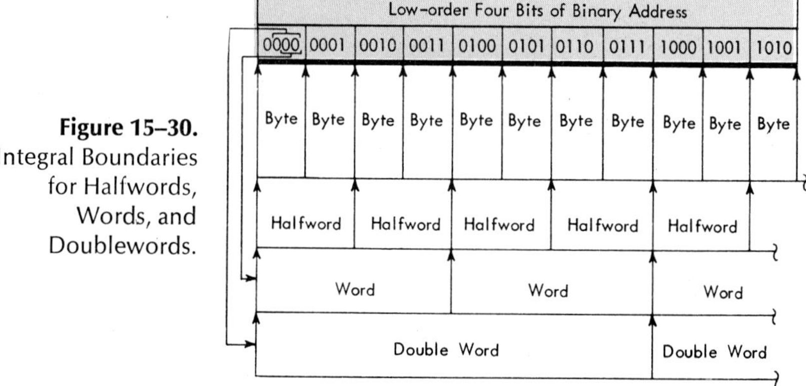

Figure 15–30. Integral Boundaries for Halfwords, Words, and Doublewords.

A group of bytes in storage is addressed by the *leftmost* byte of the group. The number of bytes in a group is either implied or explicitly defined by the operation.

ASSEMBLY PROCESS

To compile an assembly-language program, the source program is written by the programmer in the symbolic language on a special coding form. Cards are punched from these forms on a one card for one instruction basis for each line of the coding form. The source program serves as input to the assembly process, and is combined with the appropriate job control cards. The source program is translated by the processor program into the machine-language instructions of the computer (Fig. 15.31).

Two outputs result from the assembly process: an object program and an assembly listing. The *object program* consists of the actual machine-language instructions generated by the compilation of the source program written by the programmer. These machine-language instructions may be punched into cards or written on a magnetic tape or disk.

A program or *assembly listing* of the original source statements is printed side by side with the machine-language instructions (Fig. 15.32). These listings are used by the programmer to debug his program. The various programming errors are indicated by diagnostic statements in the assembly listing. If the program fails to execute, the listing will state the reason for the aborted program, together with the listing of the contents of the various registers at the point of interruption. The storage location of the next instruction to be executed will also be indicated. The programmer may also ask for a storage dump to aid him in his debugging process.

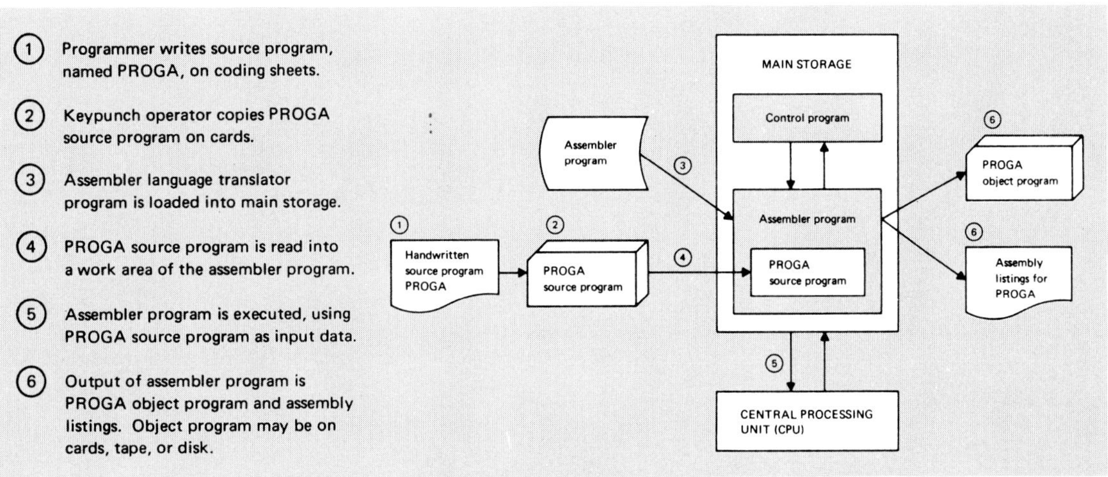
1 Programmer writes source program, named PROGA, on coding sheets.
2 Keypunch operator copies PROGA source program on cards.
3 Assembler language translator program is loaded into main storage.
4 PROGA source program is read into a work area of the assembler program.
5 Assembler program is executed, using PROGA source program as input data.
6 Output of assembler program is PROGA object program and assembly listings. Object program may be on cards, tape, or disk.
MAIN STORAGE
Control program
Assembler program
Assembler program
PROGA source program
Handwritten source program PROGA
PROGA source program
PROGA object program
Assembly listings for PROGA
CENTRAL PROCESSING UNIT (CPU)

Figure 15–31. Assembly Process.

```
                                                        A
   C        B
000100                              1         PRINT  NOGEN
000100 05B0                         2 *       TITLE  ILLUSTRATIVE PROGRAM
000102                              3         START  256
000102 5820 B022          00124     4 BEGIN   BALR   11,0
000106 5A20 B02A          0012C     5         USING  *,11
                                    6         L      2,DATA            LOAD REGISTER 2
                                    7         A      2,TEN             ADD 10
                                    8 * THE FOLLOWING SHIFT HAS THE EFFECT OF MULTIPLYING BY 2
00010A 8B20 0001          00001     9         SLA    2,1
00010E 5B20 B026          00128    10         S      2,DATA+4          NOTE RELATIVE ADDRESSING
000112 5020 B02E          00130    11         ST     2,RESULT
000116 5860 B032          00134    12         L      6,BIN1
00011A 5A60 B036          00138    13         A      6,BIN2
00011E 4E60 B03E          00140    14         CVD    6,DEC             CONVERT TO DECIMAL
                                   15         EOJ                      END OF JOB
000124 00000019                    18 DATA    DC     F'25'
000128 0000000F                    19         DC     F'15'
00012C 0000000A                    20 TEN     DC     F'10'
000130                             21 RESULT  DS     F
000134 0000000C                    22 BIN1    DC     F'12'
000138 0000004E                    23 BIN2    DC     F'78'
000140                             24 DEC     DS     D
000100                             25         END    BEGIN
```

Proceeding from right to left in the example:

- The items listed under A should be exactly the same as the handwritten entries on the coding sheet. This provides a good check on the accuracy of the keypunching.
- The items under B are a representation, in hex, of the corresponding instructions and constants.
- C shows the addresses (in hex) of the instructions, constants, and areas of storage specified by the programmer.

Figure 15–32. Assembly Listing Produced in the Assembly of the Program.

CODING FORM

The coding form is used by the programmer to code his symbolic source program (Fig. 15.33). A source program is a sequence of source statements that are punched into cards. Each line represents one symbolic statement and is punched into one card.

The body of the coding form is divided into two segments: the statement portion columns (1–71) and the identification sequence field columns (73–80). Column 72 is left blank and is used only for continuation indicators.

The statement portion is examined by the processor program and is used to produce the object program. The identification sequence field is used to identify the program and put the source cards into sequence.

STATEMENT FORMAT

Statements may consist of one to four entries separated by at least one blank and must appear in the following sequence: name, operation, operands, and comments.

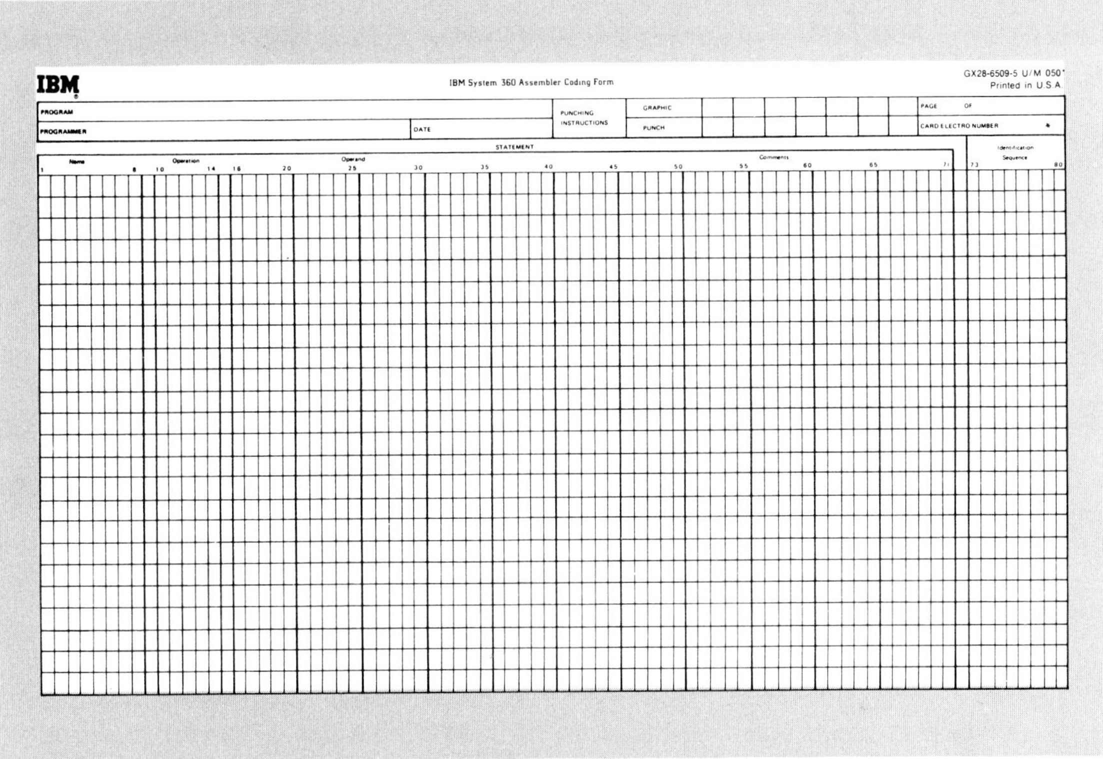
IBM

IBM System 360 Assembler Coding Form

GX28-6509-5 U/M 050
Printed in U.S.A.

PROGRAM

PROGRAMMER

DATE

PUNCHING INSTRUCTIONS

GRAPHIC

PUNCH

PAGE OF

CARD ELECTRO NUMBER

STATEMENT

Name 1 8 | Operation 10 14 | Operand 16 20 25 30 35 40 45 50 55 | Comments 60 65 71 | Identification Sequence 73 80

Figure 15–33. Coding Form.

NAME ENTRY

The name is a symbol created by the programmer to identify a statement. The entry provides a reference identification for the line if other parts of the program need refer to it. It is most commonly given to instructions to which branches are made. It is also permissible to use the name for identification without a branch operation.

1. The entry is optional, not required for each line.
2. The symbol must consist of eight characters or less, with the first character beginning in column one.
3. If column one is left blank, the assembler assumes no name is present.
4. There may be no imbedded blanks in the name.

OPERATION ENTRY

This entry specifies the operation to be performed (ADD, MOVE, BRANCH, etc.).

OPERAND ENTRY

Operand entries identify and describe the data to be acted upon by the instruction.

1. The entry indicates storage locations, masks, storage areas, lengths, and types of data.
2. One or more operands may be written, separated by commas.
3. No imbedded blanks between operands are permissable. The first blank encountered indicates the end of the operand field.
4. Operands are required for all machine instructions but many assembler instructions do not require operands.

COMMENT ENTRIES

Comments are descriptive items of information about the program that are shown in the program listing.

1. Comments may be used freely by the programmer to document the purpose and the methods of the program.
2. Comments are used as an aid in debugging and analyzing the program.
3. A comment may begin anywhere following the operand as long as there is at least one intervening blank between the operand and the comments.
4. All valid characters including space are permissible in the comments statement.
5. Comments cannot extend beyond column 71. Many programmers prefer to begin all comments on a fixed column.
6. An entire statement can be a comment if the first column contains an asterisk.

IDENTIFICATION SEQUENCE FIELD

This is an optional entry and is used to enter program identification statement or statement sequence characters. A request may be made to the assembler to check the sequence of the cards.

CONTINUATION LINES

When it is necessary to continue a statement on another line, the following rules apply.

1. Enter a continuation character (not blanks or part of the statement coding) in column 72 of the line.

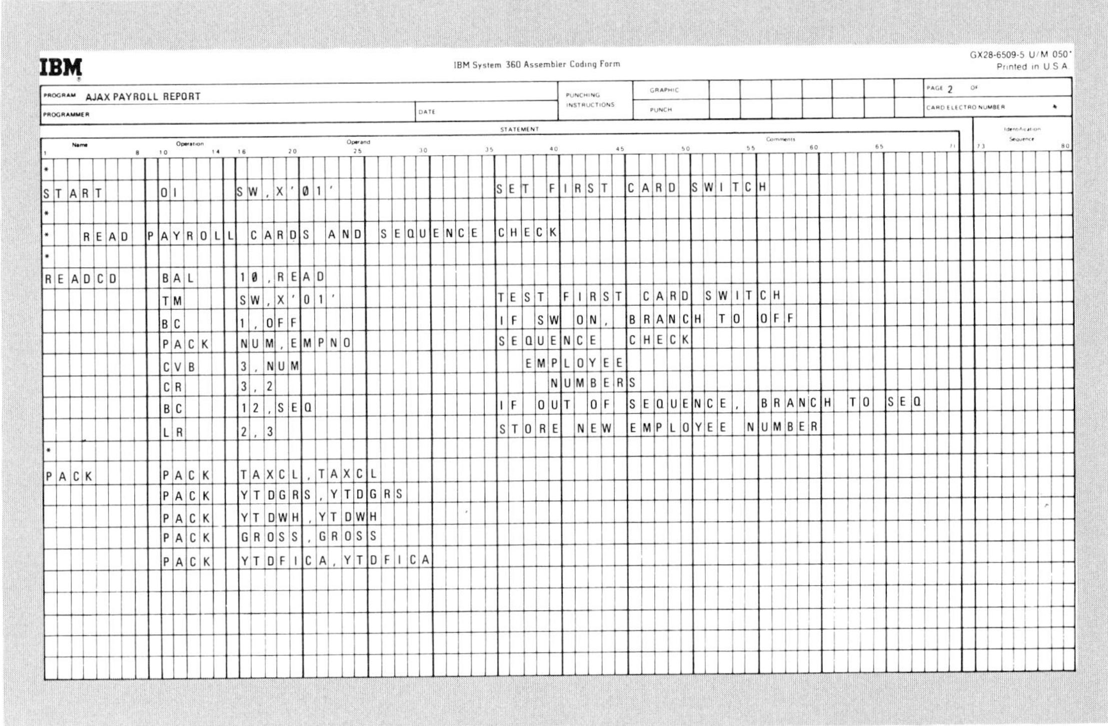

IBM — IBM System 360 Assembler Coding Form — GX28-6509-5 U/M 050* Printed in U.S.A.

PROGRAM AJAX PAYROLL REPORT — PAGE 2 OF

```
*
START    OI    SW,X'Ø1'         SET FIRST CARD SWITCH
*
*     READ PAYROLL CARDS AND SEQUENCE CHECK
*
READCD   BAL   1Ø,READ
         TM    SW,X'01'         TEST FIRST CARD SWITCH
         BC    1,OFF            IF SW ON, BRANCH TO OFF
         PACK  NUM,EMPNO        SEQUENCE CHECK
         CVB   3,NUM                EMPLOYEE
         CR    3,2                     NUMBERS
         BC    12,SEQ           IF OUT OF SEQUENCE, BRANCH TO SEQ
         LR    2,3              STORE NEW EMPLOYEE NUMBER
*
PACK     PACK  TAXCL,TAXCL
         PACK  YTDGRS,YTDGRS
         PACK  YTDWH,YTDWH
         PACK  GROSS,GROSS
         PACK  YTDFICA,YTDFICA
```

Figure 15–34. IBM System/360/370 Program Example.

2. Continue the statement in the next line starting in column 16. All columns to the left of column 16 must be left blank.
3. When more than one line is needed to complete an entry, each line to be continued must have a character (not blanks or part of the statement coding) entered in column 72.
4. Only two continuation lines may be used for all statements except macro statements which may have as many continuation lines as needed (Fig. 15.34).

ASSEMBLY PROGRAMMING ELEMENTS

CHARACTER SET

Source statements are written using the following symbols.

Letters	A through Z and $ # @
Numbers	0 through 9
Special Characters	+ — , = . * ( ) ' / % blank

In addition, any of the 256 characters may be permitted between paired apostrophes in comments and macro instruction operands.

STATEMENT STRUCTURE

A source statement may be composed of

1. A *Name Entry* (usually optional). A symbol.
2. An *Operational Entry* (required). A mnemonic operational code representing a machine, assembler, or macro instruction.
3. An *Operand Entry* (usually required). One or more expressions which in turn are composed of a term or an arithmetic combination of terms.
4. A *Comments Entry* (optional). One or more explanatory statements relating to the method and purpose of the entry.

SYMBOLS

A symbol is a character or combination of characters used to represent locations of arbitrary values. The use of symbols in operands and name fields provide the programmer with a quick and efficient method of referring to a program element. The assembler assigns a value to each symbol appearing in the name area. Values are also assigned to symbols naming storage areas, instructions, constants, etc. In addition, the assembler assigns a length attribute to the symbol.

LITERALS

A literal is a method of entering data into a program.

1. A literal represents constant data preceded by an equal (=) sign.
2. It represents data rather than an address of data.
3. It may not be combined with other items.
4. Only one literal is permitted in a machine instruction statement.
5. Literals are placed in a specified area called a literal pool by the assembler and referred to by location in the pool rather than by the literal itself.

BEGINNING A PROGRAM

The addressing scheme of the system 360/370 requires the use of a base register which contains the value of the base address, and a displacement factor which is added to the contents of the base register to arrive at the effective storage address. The programmer in his source program must specify a symbolic address and request the assembler to determine the storage address composed of the base register and the displacement factor. In order to perform this service, the assembler must know what general registers are available for assignment as base registers and what values the assembler may assume each contains. The programmer may use any number of registers for this purpose, the only requirement being that at his point of reference, a register containing an address from the control section is available and that address is less than or equal to the address of the item to which the reference is being made. Each base register setting can accommodate up to 4095 bytes of storage. To relocate a program at a definite area in storage at assembly time, all that is needed to be done is to change the initial value of the base register.

The first instruction to be written in an assembly program is concerned with the initial setting of a location counter; the placing of an initial value in the base register and informing the assembler what base address to use as the contents of the specified register. The assembler will then proceed to calculate the displacement factor and to assign addresses to the symbol as it assembles the program.

The instructions written at the beginning of an assembly program are TITLE, START, BALR, USING.

TITLE

TITLE is an optional assembler type instruction that precedes the program and produces no object program coding. It is used to specify the name of the program and other information relative to the program. This will serve to identify the listing sheet and provide for ready reference to the program. This instruction may be omitted.

START

The START statement is actually the first statement of the source program. It is used to provide a name (symbol) to the program and to provide the initial setting of the location counter. The START statement dictates the starting address of a program.

In many data processing installations, there are limitations as to the storage areas that may be used by a problem program, especially new programs to be debugged. A predefined storage area is set aside for this purpose and regardless of the value of the operand field in the START statement, the program will be assembled at this fixed location.

BALR

BALR is the mnemonic operation code for the BRANCH AND LINK REGISTER instruction which is used to place the setting of the location in a register.

USING

The USING instruction tells the assembler that one or more registers are available for use as base registers. It states the base address value that the assembler will assume will be in the registers at object time (Fig. 15.35).

DEFINING STORAGE AREAS

In order to execute a program successfully, data must be introduced into the system. Instructions are of no value unless there is data for them to act on. Basically there are three types of data used in a program.

1. The *input data* that is read directly from an input device and placed in an input/output area in storage,
2. The *constant data* that remains relatively unchanged in storage during the execution of the program, and
3. *Intermediate data* that requires work areas for the results of arithmetic and logical operations.

Input/output areas may also be used as work areas. The number, size and type of data areas needed will depend upon the complexity of the particular program. The need exists for defining storage areas that are to be used for input, output, constants, and work areas. Storage must be reserved for these needed areas and symbolic names assigned to them so that they can be referenced by the program.

IBM — IBM System 360 A

PROGRAM PROGA
PROGRAMMER J.J. JONES — DATE

```
         TITLE 'ILLUSTRATIVE PROGRAM'
PROGA    START 256
BEGIN    BALR  11,Ø
         USING *,11
         L     2,DATA          LOAD REG
         A     2,CON           ADD 1Ø
         S A   2,1             THIS HAS
         S     2,DATA+4        NOTE REL
         S     2,RESULT
         L     6,BIN1
         A     6,BIN2
         CV    6,DEC           CONVERT
         EOJ                   END OF JO
DATA     DC    F'25'
         DC    F'15'
CON      DC    F'1Ø'
RESULT   DS    F
BIN1     DC    F'12'
BIN2     DC    F'78'
DEC      DS    D
         END   BEGIN
```

Figure 15–35. IBM System 360/370 Program Example.

IBM — IBM System 360 Assembler Coding Form — GX28-6509-5 U/M 050 Printed in U.S.A.

PROGRAM AJAX PAYROLL REPORT — PAGE 7 OF

```
INPUT    DS    0CL80
ENAME    DS    CL15
EMPNO    DS    CL6
TAXCL    DS    CL2
YTDGRS   DS    CL7
YTDWH    DS    CL6
YTDFICA  DS    CL5
GROSS    DS    CL6
         DS    CL33
*
NUM      DS    D
CURWH    DC    PL6'0'
EXAMT    DC    PL5'0'
TXBLGR   DS    PL4
CURFICA  DC    PL7'0'
UNPDFICA DS    CL3
NETPAY   DS    CL4
*
SEQERR   DC    C'OUT OF SEQUENCE'
SW       DS    CL1
PATRN1   DC    X'402020206B2020202114B202020'
PATRN2   DC    X'402020202114B20200'
```

Figure 15–36. Defining Storage and Defining Constants—Examples.

There are two data statements that allow us to introduce data constants and reserve areas of storage. The statements are named so that other statements in the program can refer to them (Fig. 15.36).

DEFINING CONSTANTS (DC)

A constant is defined as a fixed data value that is entered in storage as part of the program. The value remains unchanged during the execution of the program. Constants may be used as increment counters or may be used in the actual processing of data such as withholding tax rates, social security rates, etc. (Figs. 15.37).

DEFINING STORAGE (DS)

This instruction is used to reserve areas of storage and to assign names to these areas. The use of this instruction is the preferred way of symbolically defining storage areas for input, outputs, work areas, etc. The format is similar to the DEFINE CONSTANT with the exception that no fixed data values are assembled. (Fig. 15.38)

Code	Type	Machine Format
C	Character	8-bit code for each character
X	Hexadecimal	4-bit code for each hexadecimal digit
B	Binary	Binary
F	Fixed-point	Signed, fixed-point binary; normally a fullword
H	Fixed-point	Signed, fixed-point binary; normally a halfword
E	Floating-point	Short floating-point; normally a fullword
D	Floating-point	Long floating-point; normally a doubleword
P	Decimal	Packed decimal
Z	Decimal	Zoned decimal
A	Address	Value of address; normally a fullword
Y	Address	Value of address; normally a halfword
S	Address	Base register and displacement value; a halfword
V	Address	Space reserved for external symbol addresses; each address normally a fullword

Figure 15–37. Types of Assembler Language Constants.

LOCATION CTR.	NAME	OPERATION	OPERAND
1000	RDAREA	DS	0CL80
		DS	CL20
1014	MANNO	DS	CL6
101A	HRSWKD	DS	CL4
101E	DATE	DS	0CL6
101F	DAY	DS	CL2
1020	MONTH	DS	CL2
1022	YEAR	DS	CL2
		DS	CL10
102E	GROSS	DS	CL8
1036	FEDTAX	DS	CL8
		DS	CL18

Figure 15–38. Assignment of Storage Locations to Constants.

STANDARD INSTRUCTIONS

There are four classes of operating procedures possible on the system 360/370 computer: fixed point (binary) arithmetic, floating point arithmetic, logical operations, and decimal arithmetic. Fixed point arithmetic and logical operations are part of the standard instruction set. The decimal operations are designed primarily for use in commercial applications while the floating point arithmetic is used in scientific and engineering operations.

FIXED POINT (BINARY) ARITHMETIC AND LOGICAL OPERATIONS

The decision to use binary arithmetic or decimal arithmetic in the processing of the data is made by the programmer. When extensive processing is required, the storage and circuitry of the system are more efficiently utilized when binary numbers are used. As a result, binary arithmetic is used extensively in many scientific applications where many complex mathematical operations are required. Decimal arithmetic can make the application more productive when relatively few computational steps are involved between the input and output process. However, the criterion for using a particular processing technique is the amount of processing required between the input and output stages.

The fixed point instruction set performs binary arithmetic in operands serving as addresses, index quantities, counts and fixed point data. The operands must be in the fixed point data format, that is thirty-two-bit operands (a one-bit sign followed by thirty-one-bit integer). One operand may be in main storage or in another register. The other operand must be in a register. The standard instruction set includes loading, adding, subtracting, multiplying, dividing, storing, comparing, sign control, and shifting. The condition code is set in the PSW (Program Status Word) as a result of all sign control operations, add, subtract, compare, and shift operations. The code may be tested later in the program.

Fixed point numbers occupy a fixed length of thirty-two bits (a one-bit sign followed by a thirty-one-bit integer), however, a halfword of sixteen bits (a one-bit sign followed by a fifteen-bit integer), may be used in many instructions as an operand (Fig. 15.39). As the halfword is read from storage, it is extended to a fullword by propagating the sign through the next high order sixteen positions before a fixed point operation; subsequently the halfword participates as a fullword (Figs. 15.40, 15.41).

All fixed point data must be located on an integral storage boundary: halfword (divisible by two); fullword (divisible by four); and doubleword (divisible by eight).

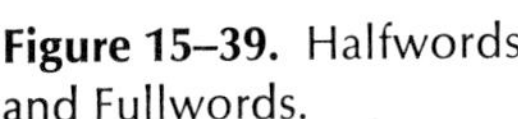

Figure 15–39. Halfwords and Fullwords.

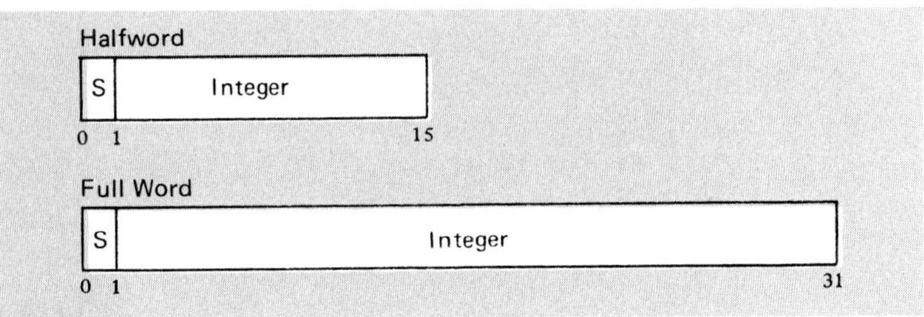

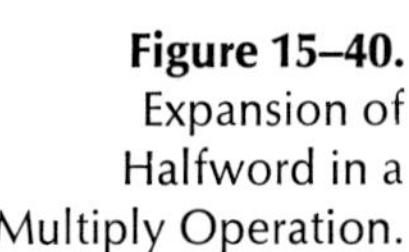

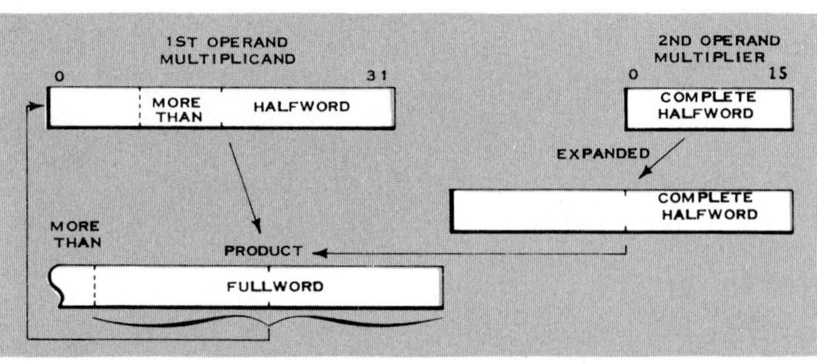

Figure 15–40. Expansion of Halfword in a Multiply Operation.

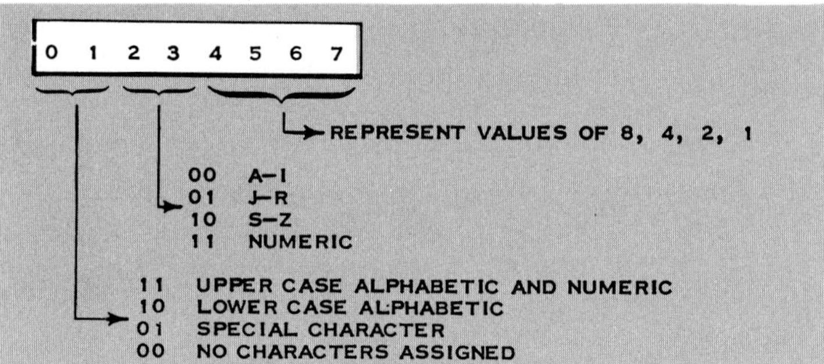

Figure 15–41. Bit Positions in EBCDIC Byte.

CONVERSION INSTRUCTIONS

PACK, CONVERT TO BINARY, CONVERT TO DECIMAL, UNPACK

To perform an operation by binary arithmetic, the input data must be converted to binary format (Fig. 15.42). The PACK instruction is used first to pack the data (Fig. 15.43). The packed format must then be converted to binary format to process the data using the fixed point arithmetic instructions (Fig. 15.44). The CONVERT TO BINARY instruction is used to convert the packed data into a binary format (Figs. 15.45, 15.46). After the processing is completed, a CONVERT TO DECIMAL and UNPACK (or editing type instruction) are used to prepare the data for output on devices such as printer or card punch. The CONVERT TO DECIMAL converts the binary data back into packed format (Figs. 15.47, 15.48) and the UNPACK instruction converts the packed data back into zoned format for subsequent outputting (Figs. 15.49, 15.50). If further processing of the data is required before output, the results can be stored in binary format in the main storage area and converted later in the program when the operation is complete and ready for output (Fig. 15.51).

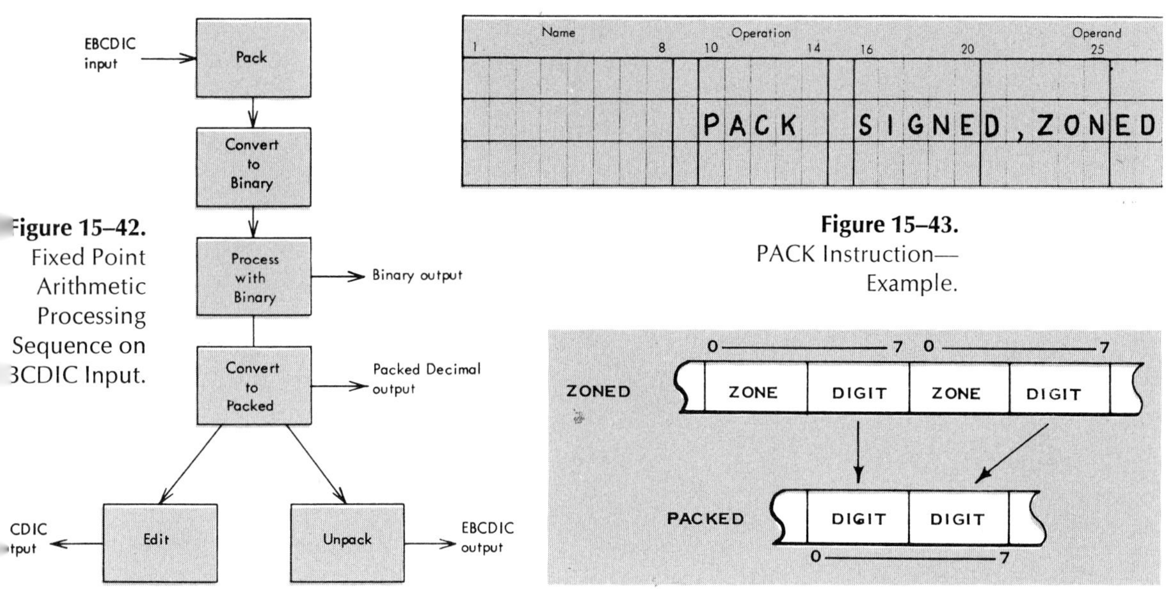

Figure 15–42. Fixed Point Arithmetic Processing Sequence on EBCDIC Input.

Figure 15–43. PACK Instruction—Example.

Figure 15–44. Zoned Format Converted to Packed Format.

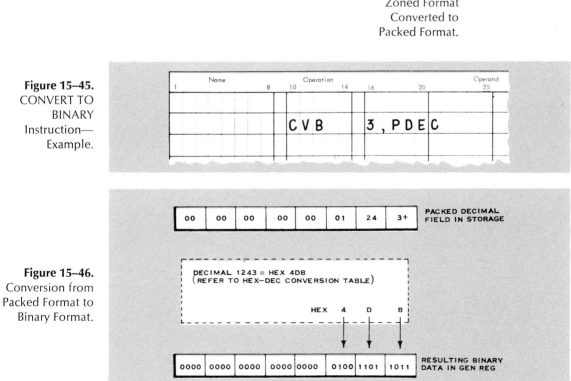

Figure 15–45. CONVERT TO BINARY Instruction—Example.

Figure 15–46. Conversion from Packed Format to Binary Format.

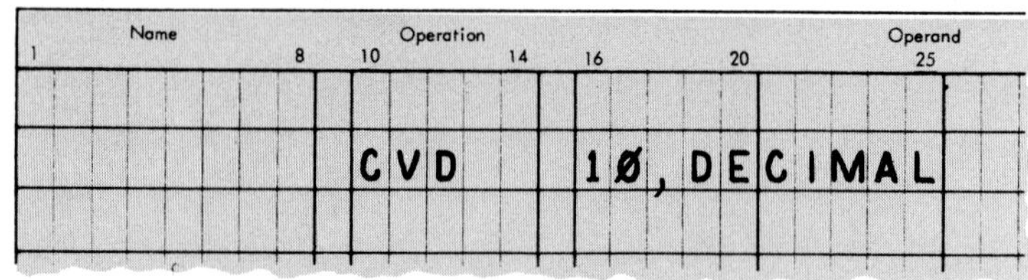

Figure 15–47. CONVERT TO DECIMAL Instruction—Example.

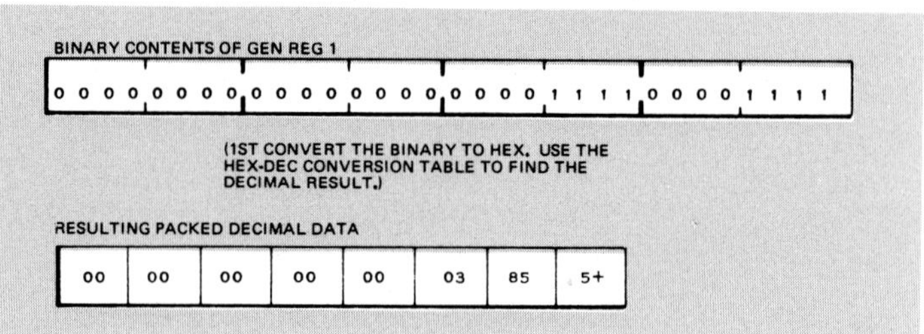

Figure 15–48. Conversion from Binary Format to Packed Decimal Format.

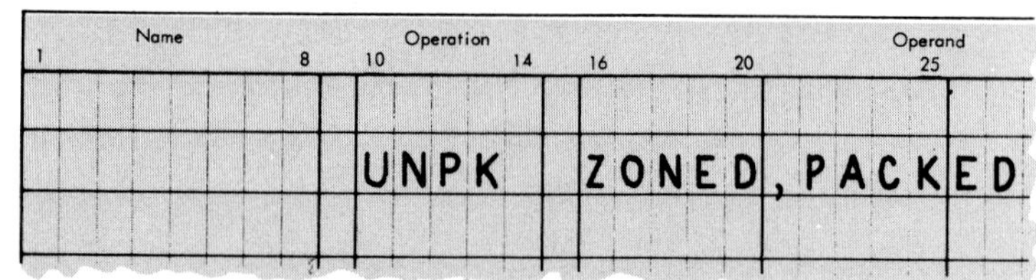

Figure 15–49. UNPACK Instruction—Example.

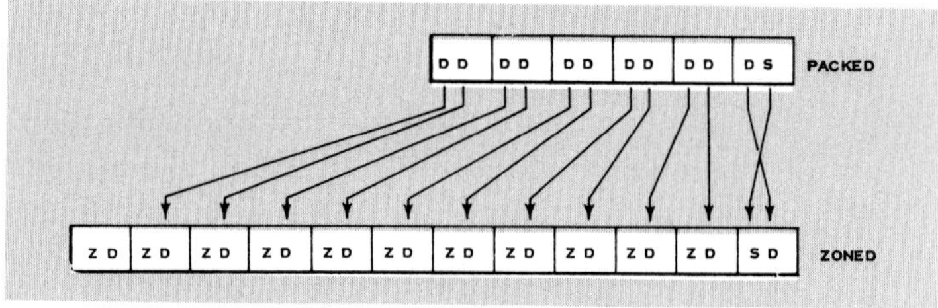

Figure 15–50. Conversion from Packed Format to Zoned Format.

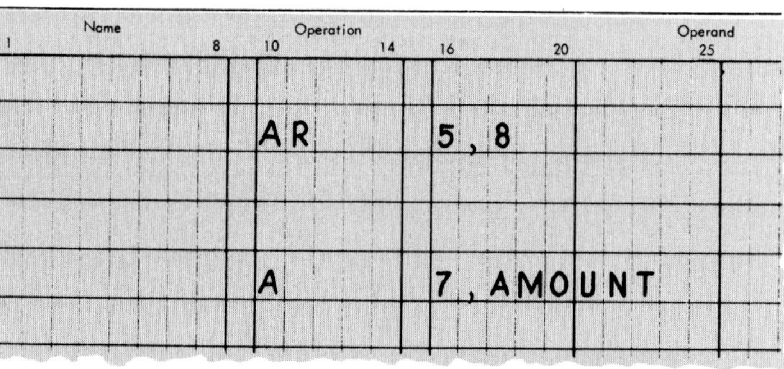

Figure 15–51. Add Instruction—Example.

FIXED POINT (BINARY) ARITHMETIC OPERATIONS

ADD, SUBTRACT, MULTIPLY, DIVIDE (Fig. 15.52)

In fixed point arithmetic, the basic arithmetic operand is a signed value recorded as a binary integer (a whole number, positive or negative) as contrasted with a fraction. The number is called *fixed point* because the machine interprets the number as a binary integer with the decimal point located to the right of the least significant digit. The programmer has the responsibility for keeping track of the decimal point (Figs. 15.53, 15.54, 15.55).

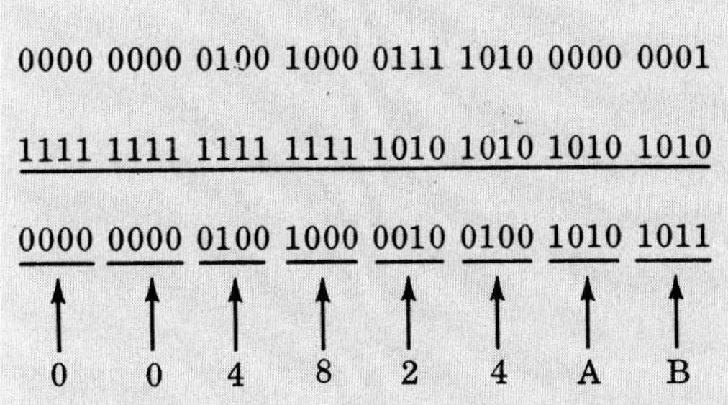

Figure 15–52. Binary Operands—Addition.

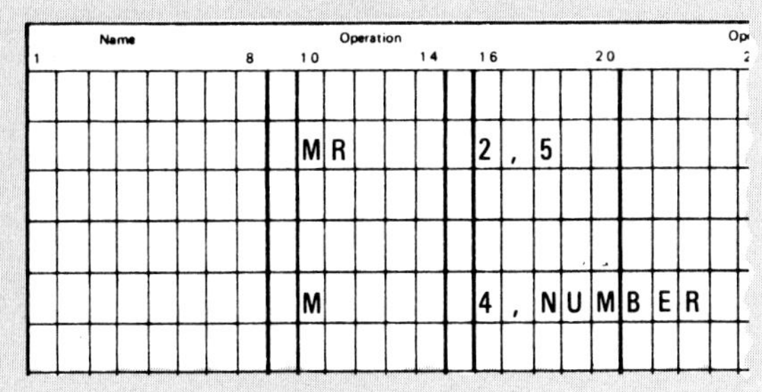

Figure 15–53. Multiply Instruction—Examples.

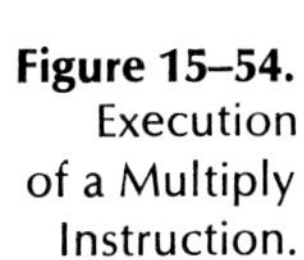

Figure 15–54. Execution of a Multiply Instruction.

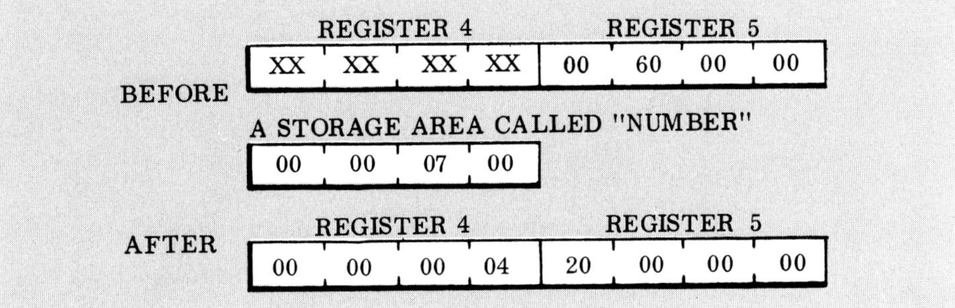

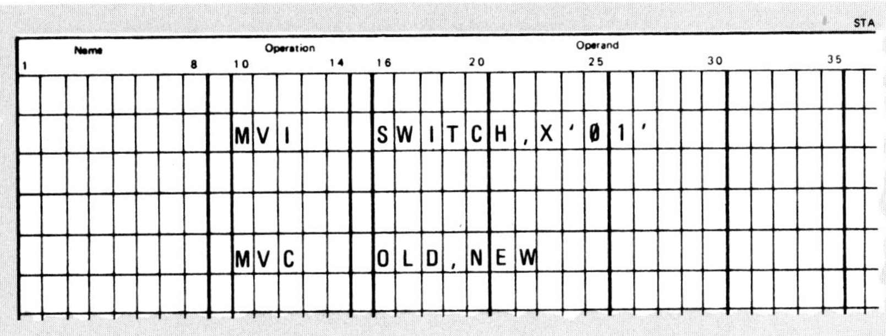

Figure 15–55. Move Instruction—Examples.

Fixed point numbers occupy a fixed length format consisting of a one-bit sign followed by a thirty-one-bit integer field. Some operations are performed in halfwords where the halfword is extended to a fullword before the operation begins. Doublewords are used in multiply and divide instructions.

DATA TRANSMISSION INSTRUCTIONS

LOAD, STORE, SHIFT, MOVE

An important function of fixed point arithmetic operation is the manipulation of data in, out of, and within registers. These functions are performed by the LOAD, STORE, and SHIFT instructions. The LOAD instructions are used to put data into a register from another register or from a storage area. The STORE instructions are used to place data from a register into a storage area. The SHIFT instructions are used to shift data within a register or a pair of registers.

The MOVE instructions are used to transfer data from one storage location to another (Figs. 15.56, 15.57).

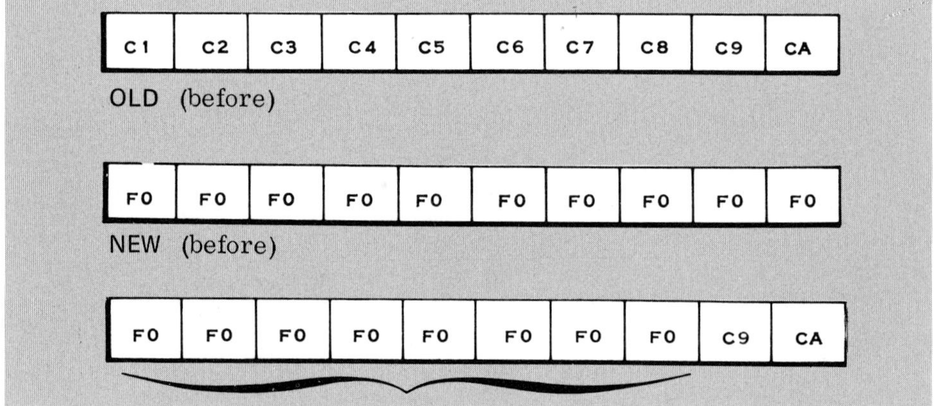

Figure 15–56. Execution of a Move Instruction.

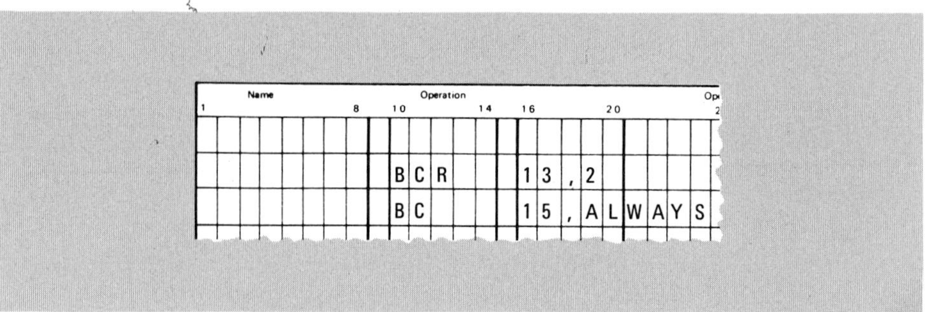

Figure 15–57. Branch Instruction—Examples.

BRANCHING OPERATION INSTRUCTIONS

BRANCH ON CONDITION, BRANCH AND LINK

Branching and decisions are important parts of data processing and the programming methods by which these operations are carried out are important aspects of the programming task. Instructions are performed by a central processing unit in the sequence in which they are written. A departure from this normal sequential procedure arises when a branch operation is performed. The branching instructions provide the facility for making a two-way choice to reference a subroutine or to repeat a segment of the program (loop).

Branching is performed by introducing a branch address as a new instruction. This new address may reside in a register or may be specified in the instruction itself. A basic operation is the setting of the condition code by any of the large number of instructions and the subsequent testing of the conditions. An unconditional branch may be indicated when a program reaches a certain point; it will branch to the address specified under all conditions for its instruction

LOGICAL OPERATION INSTRUCTIONS

COMPARE

A set of instructions is provided for the logical manipulation of data. The operands are written within storage or a register. The condition is set as a result of all logical operations which can be tested later. The COMPARE instructions of fixed point data compares on an algebraic basis treating all numbers as signed binary integers. The operands may be positive or negative.

In the COMPARE LOGICAL instructions, the operands are treated as unsigned binary numbers.

If the data consists of signed binary words or halfwords, the algebraic instructions should be used. If the data consists of unsigned binary fields, the logical instructions are used.

LOGICAL OPERATIONS—MANIPULATION OF BIT INSTRUCTIONS

AND, OR, EXCLUSIVE OR, TEST UNDER MASK, TRANSLATE, TRANSLATE AND TEST

Problems often arise in which tests of the "yes" or "no" variety are required. These instructions are used to turn switches on or off.

DECIMAL ARITHMETIC

The decimal instruction set is an optional feature of the system 360/370 but one that most users select. Decimal arithmetic lends itself to data processing applications that require few computational steps from the source input to the documented ouput. This type of processing is frequently found in commercial applications. Because of the limited number of arithmetic operations to be performed on each item of data, the conversion from decimal to binary and back to decimal is not justified. The use of registers for intermediate results yield no advantage over storage to storage processing. The *commercial* set of instructions will perform arithmetic operations in packed decimal format without first converting it to binary (Fig. 15.58).

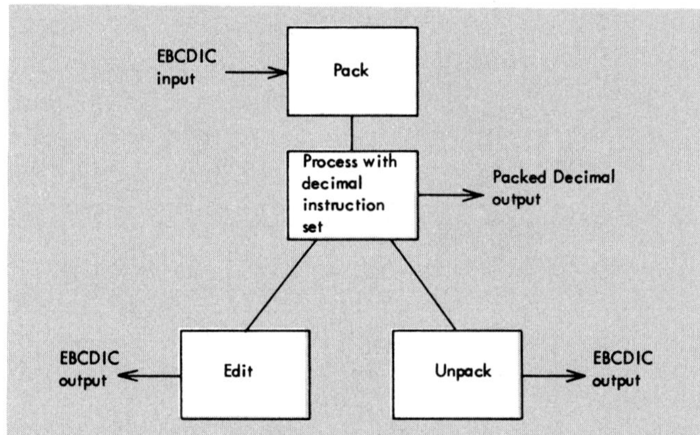

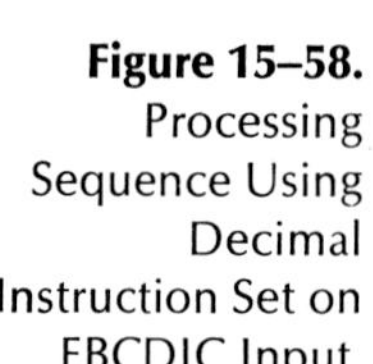
Figure 15–58. Processing Sequence Using Decimal Instruction Set on EBCDIC Input.

Data operated upon by instructions in the decimal set must be of two forms, packed or zoned. Packed format is used for arithmetic and logical operations. Zoned format is used for input/output operations. Packing digits within a byte and the use of variable field lengths within storage results in an efficient use of storage, in increased arithmetic performance, and improved rate of data transmissions between storage and files (Fig. 15.59).

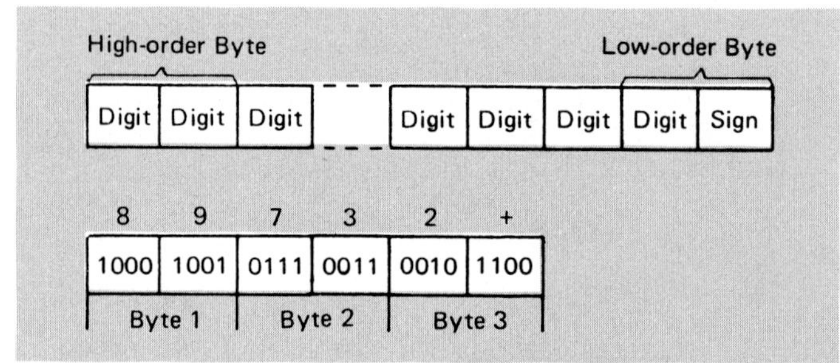

Figure 15–59. Packed Decimal Number Format.

In *packed* format, two decimal digits are placed in each byte except the rightmost byte which contains a digit and sign in the rightmost four bits. Digits and sign occupy four bits each (Fig. 15.60). Decimal digits 0–9 have binary codes 0000–1001. In the sign position, the code combinations 1010, 1100, 1110, 1111 are all taken to mean plus and 1011 and 1101 are recognized as a minus. When a sign is generated as part of an arithmetic result, a plus sign is 1100 and a minus sign is 1101.

Decimal numbers may also appear in the *zoned* format as subset of the eight bit alphameric character set (Fig. 15.61). The representation is required for character sensitive input/output devices. In the zoned format, the rightmost four bits of a byte are called the *numeric* position of a byte and contain a digit. The leftmost four bits of each byte are called the *zone* portion and contain either a zone code or in the case of the rightmost (low order) byte, the sign of the number.

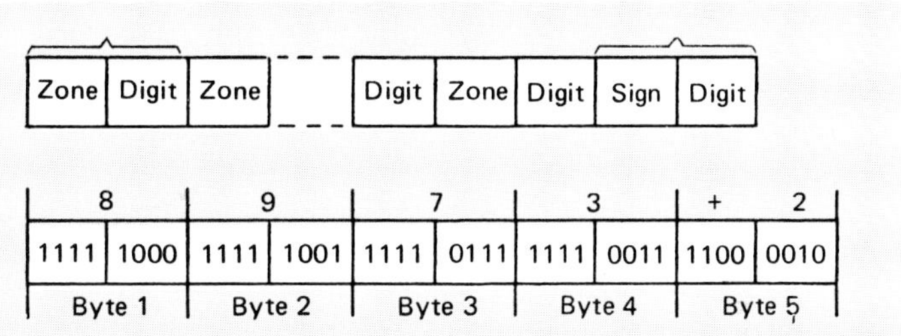

Figure 15–60. Zoned Decimal Number Format.

1. EBCDIC characters

Characters	I	B	M	3
Internal form	1100 1001	1100 0010	1101 0100	1111 0011
Hex code	C 9	C 2	D 4	F 3

2. Zoned decimal number

Decimal	8	9	7	3	+ 2
Internal form	1111 1000	1111 1001	1111 0111	1111 0011	1100 0010
Hex code	F 8	F 9	F 7	F 3	C 2

3. Packed decimal number

Decimal	8 9	7 3	2 +
Internal form	1000 1001	0111 0011	0010 1100
Hex code	8 9	7 3	2 C

4. Signed binary number

(This fixed-point fullword is equivalent to decimal +89,732)

Internal form	0000 0000	0000 0001	0101 1110	1000 0100
Hex code	0 0	0 1	5 E	8 4

Figure 15–61. EBCDIC Zoned, Packed, and Binary Format.

Decimal arithmetic has precise requirements that operands be in packed or zoned formats. The zoned format is not used in decimal arithmetic operations. Instructions are provided for packing and unpacking decimal numbers so that they may be changed from the zoned to the packed format and vice versa. The PACK and UNPACK instructions, standard instructions in the system, are available for converting from one form to another (Fig. 15.62).

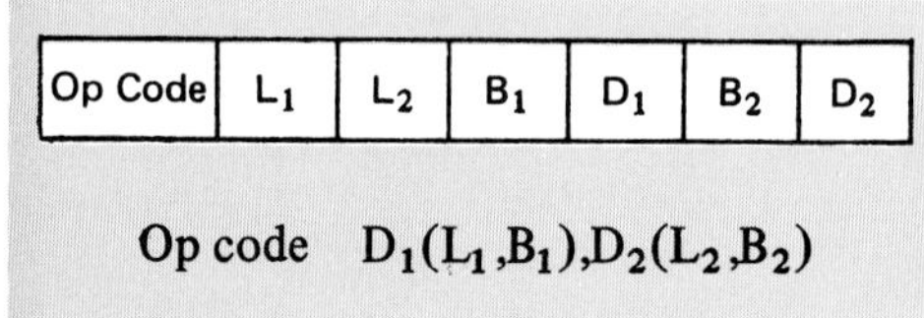

Figure 15–62. Decimal Instruction (Storage-to-Storage) Format.

The standard instruction set uses instructions of the RR (Register to Register), RX (Register to Indexed Storage) and RS (Register to Storage), which means that the data processed by the standard instruction set must be in a fixed length format occupying a thirty-two-bit word or a sixteen-bit halfword. Also, these words and halfwords must be located on an integral boundary in storage.

The decimal instruction set uses instructions that are all of the SS (Storage to Storage) format (Fig. 15.63). The data processed by these instructions may be in fields of varying lengths, starting at any address in storage (not aligned to integral storage boundaries).

Decimal instructions use the SS format as follows.

1. Two addresses are involved, both in storage. Each address is formed from the base register plus the displacement factor.

```
GO          AP    SUBTOT1,SUBTOT2

SUBTOT2     DS    PL4

SUBTOT1     DS    PL4
```

SUBTOT1 (Before): | 07 | 42 | 56 | 7C |

SUBTOT 2: | 04 | 31 | 72 | 1C |

SUBTOT1 (After): | 11 | 74 | 28 | 8C |

Figure 15–63. Decimal Addition—Example.

2. The address always refers to the leftmost byte of an operand.
3. In most instructions there is an implicit length for each operand. The length code may be up to 16 bytes (0–15).
4. The length code is actually one greater than appears in the length code of the instruction.
5. The length code will be implicit in the data definition.
6. The generation of a proper length code is the function of the assembler.
7. An explicit length may be written to "override" an implicit length code.

The decimal instruction set includes the following instructions: ADD DECIMAL, COMPARE DECIMAL, DIVIDE DECIMAL, EDIT, EDIT AND MARK, MULTIPLY DECIMAL, SUBTRACT DECIMAL, AND ZERO AND ADD DECIMAL.

DECIMAL ARITHMETIC INSTRUCTIONS

ADD, SUBTRACT, MULTIPLY, DIVIDE, ZERO AND ADD

All instructions assume SS (Storage to Storage) format and packed operands and results.

LOGICAL DECIMAL INSTRUCTIONS

COMPARE DECIMAL

The first operand is compared algebraically with the second operand and the result determines the setting of the condition code which can be tested later.

EDIT INSTRUCTIONS

EDIT, EDIT AND MARK

The EDIT instructions are some of the most powerful instructions in the repertoire of the system 360/370. They are used in the preparation of printed reports to give them a high degree of legibility and therefore greater usefulness. With proper planning, it is possible to suppress nonsignificant zeros, insert commas and decimal points, insert minus signs or credit symbols, and to specify where the suppression of zeros stops for small numbers. All these actions are performed by the machine in *one* left-to-right pass. The condition code may be used to blank all-zero fields with two simple and fast instructions.

A variation of the EDIT instruction, EDIT AND MARK makes possible the insertion of floating dollar symbols. The floating dollar sign operation permits the placing of the dollar sign immediately to the left of the first significant digit in the edited result.

The purpose of the EDIT instruction is to produce easy-to-read documents by inserting the proper punctuation into a data record. The data to be edited is called the *source field* and must be in packed format. The EDIT operation consists of moving the source field (the data to be edited) into a *pattern field.* The *pattern field* will be made up of zoned characters that will control the editing. The final edited result will replace the pattern field. The pattern is set up as a hexadecimal constant. It is given a symbolic name and is kept in storage. If the pattern field is to be used more than once, it should be moved to a storage work area before each use as it will be destroyed during the edit operation (Fig. 15.64).

INPUT/OUTPUT INSTRUCTIONS

EXCP, WAIT, OPEN, GET, PUT, CLOSE

Transferring information to and from main storage and other than to and from the central processing unit or via the direct control path is referred to as an input/output operation. Before the input data can be processed by the central processing unit, it must first reside in main storage. After the data has been processed, it must be made available to an output device for subsequent printing, punching, etc.

There are two parts to the input/output control: physical IOCS (Input Output Control System) and logical IOCS.

Physical IOCS controls the actual transfer of records between the medium and main storage. It performs the function of issuing channel commands

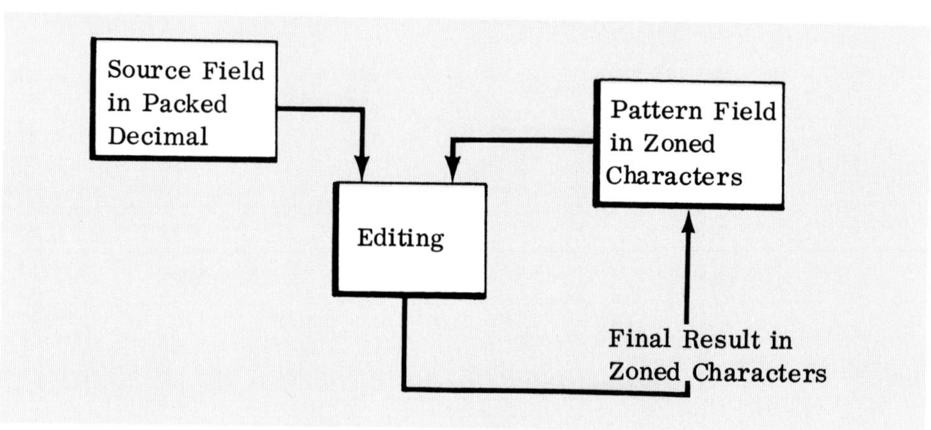

Figure 15–64. Editing—Schematic.

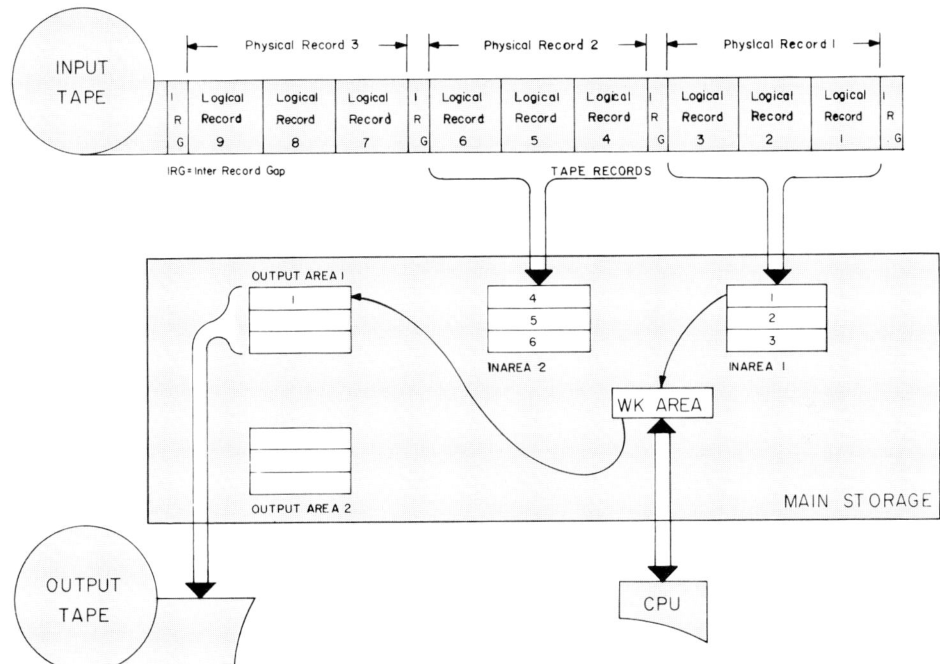

Figure 15–65. Processing Blocked Records.

and handling associated I/O interruptions. The physical IOCS routines are part of the supervisory program which is permanently located in main storage while problem programs are being executed (Fig. 15.65).

Logical IOCS controls those functions that a user would have to perform to locate a logical record for processing. A *logical record* is one unit of information in a file of like units; for example, an item of inventory, or an employee's record. One or many logical records can be included in a physical record.

Logical IOCS routines required for the execution of a problem program are assembled with that program. The particular routines required are determined on the basis of the definition of the logical files used by the program.

Logical IOCS uses physical IOCS whenever it determines that a transfer of data is required. For example, in a file of blocked records, where a block has been read into main storage, logical IOCS makes each successive record available to the user until the end of the block is reached. No physical IOCS is required during this processing. When the logical IOCS has determined that the last record in the block has been processed, it requests physical IOCS to start and I/O operation to transfer the next physical record to main storage.

Two sets of imperative macro routines are available to the programmer for handling records: a set of physical IOCS macros EXCP (Execute Channel Program) and WAIT and a set of logical IOCS macros GET and PUT (Fig. 15.66).

```
                                                                                          PAGE   1

  LOC  OBJECT CODE     ADDR1 ADDR2  STMT   SOURCE STATEMENT                               DD22APR66 11/16/66

                                       1  PRINT ON,NOGEN
000100                                 2          START 256
                                       3 CARDIN   DTFCD                                        C
                                                        DEVADDR=SYSRDR,                        C
                                                        EOFADDR=EOJ,                           C
                                                        IOAREA1=INPUT
                                      22 *
                                      23          CDMOD
                                      90 *
                                      91 ALINE    DTFPR                                        C
                                                        BLKSIZE=132,                           C
                                                        DEVADDR=SYSLST,                        C
                                                        IOAREA1=OUTPUT
                                     110 *
                                     111          PRMOD
                                     173 *
000168 0580                          174 BEGIN    BALR  11,0
00016A                               175          USING *,11
                                     176          OPEN  CARDIN,ALINE
00017E 47F0 B04A             00184   184          B     START
                                     185 *
                                     186 EOJ      CLOSE CARDIN,ALINE          END OF JOB ROUTINE
                                     194          EOJ
                                     197 *
                                     198 READ     GET   CARDIN                READ MACRO
0001A4 07FA                          203          BCR   15,10
                                     204 *
                                     205 WRITE    PUT   ALINE                 WRITE MACRO
0001B2 07FA                          210          BCR   15,10
                                     211 *
                                     212 *  ASSEMBLE AND PRINT THE HEADER LINES
                                     213 *
0001B4 D283 B147 B146 00281 00280    214 START    MVC   OUTPUT,OUTPUT-1       CLEAR OUTPUT AREA
0001BA D241 B168 B1CB 002D2 00335    215          MVC   HEADER,HDR1           MOVE FIRST HEADER TO OUTPUT AREA
0001C0 45A0 B03C             001A6   216          BAL   10,WRITE              PRINT FIRST HEADER LINE
0001C4 D241 B168 B20D 002D2 00377    217          MVC   HEADER,HDR2           MOVE SECOND HEADER TO OUTPUT AREA
0001CA 45A0 B03C             001A6   218          BAL   10,WRITE              PRINT SECOND HEADER LINE
0001CE D241 B168 B167 002D2 002D1    219          MVC   HEADER,HEADER-1       CLEAR HEADER OUTPUT AREA
                                     220 *
                                     221 *  READ THE TRANSACTION CARDS
                                     222 *
0001D4 45A0 B02E             00198   223 NEXT     BAL   10,READ               READ A CARD
0001D8 F276 B256 B0FC 003C0 00266    224          PACK  PPRIN,PRIN            REFORMAT
0001DE F273 B25E B103 003C8 0026D    225          PACK  PRATE,RATE
0001E4 F273 B266 B107 003D0 00271    226          PACK  PPAY,PAY                INPUT
0001EA 4F30 B256             003C0   227          CVB   3,PPRIN
0001EE 4F20 B25E             003C8   228          CVB   2,PRATE                   DATA
                                     229 *
                                     230 *  PERFORM THE REQUIRED CALCULATIONS
                                     231 *
0001F2 5020 B286             003F0   232          ST    2,BRATE               STORE INTEREST RATE IN BINARY FORM
```

Figure 15–66. Source Program Listing with Input/Output Macros.

The physical IOCS routines completely bypass the logical IOCS functions (for example, the blocking and deblocking of records). They permit the problem program to utilize the physical IOCS functions directly. To transfer a physical record, the program issues an EXCP instruction. This causes a request for data transfer to be placed in the channel scheduler and the program execution immediately continues with the next problem program instruction. However, the type record will not be available in main storage until some time later. Therefore when the record is needed for processing, the program must test to find out if the transfer has been completed. This is accomplished by issuing the WAIT instruction.

The logical IOCS macro routines cause all functions of both logical and physical IOCS to be performed for the program. For example, when a GET instruction for a record is executed, that record is transferred to main storage and it is available for the execution of the next program instruction (Fig. 15.67).

Additional instructions are available for combined operations of manipulation of data and bits (Figs. 15.68, 15.69, 15.70).

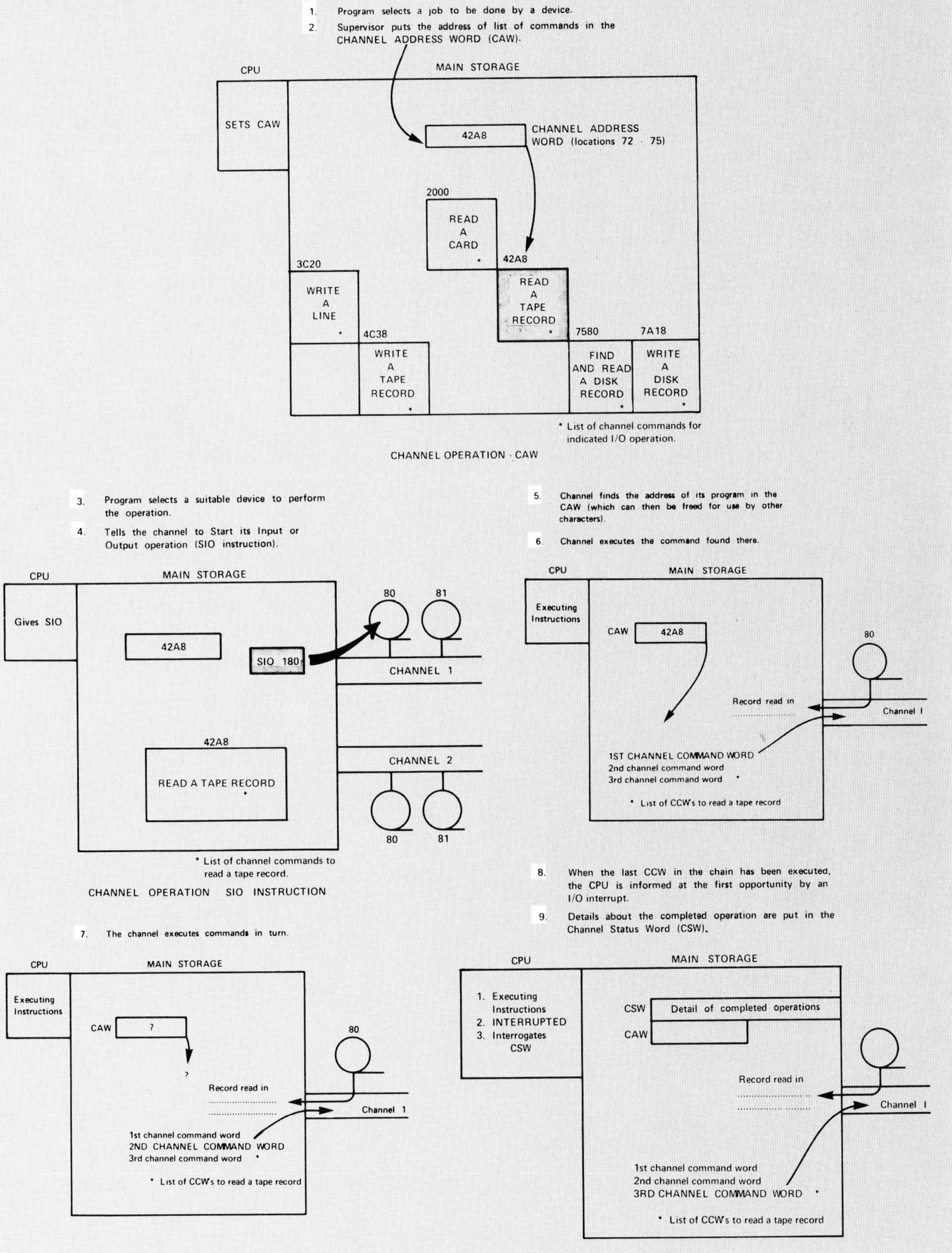

Figure 15–67. Channel Operation.

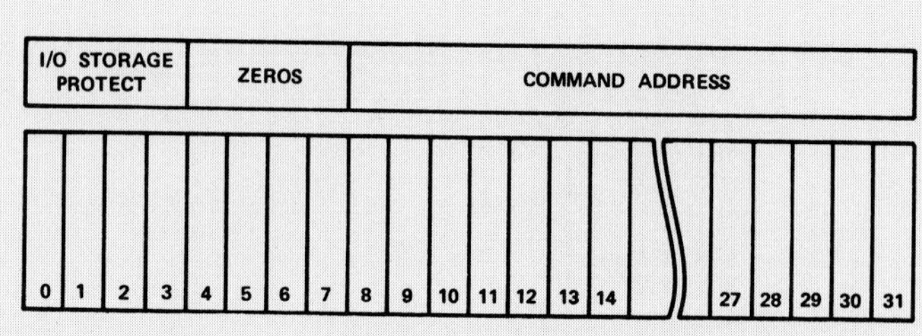

Figure 15–68. Channel Address Word.

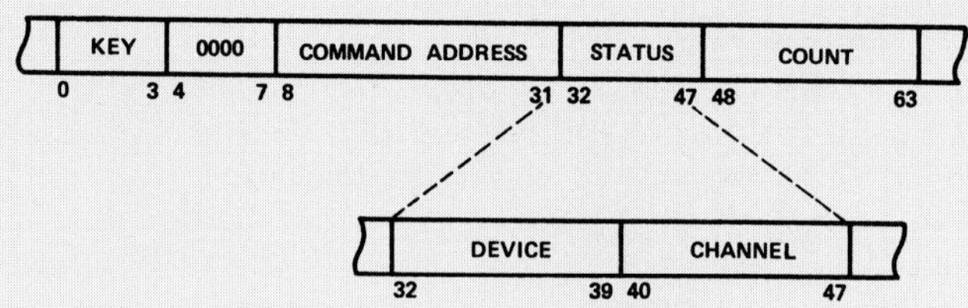

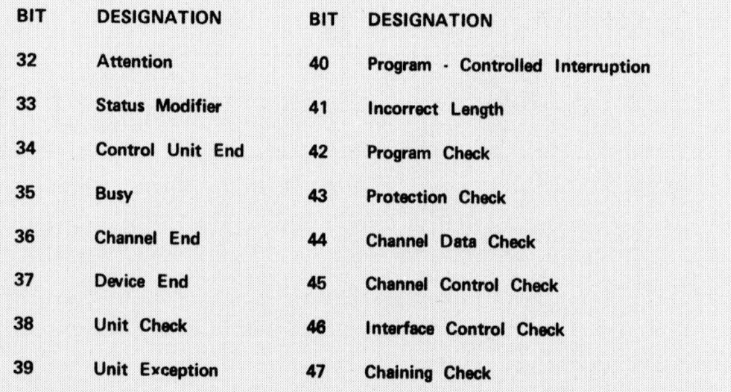

BIT	DESIGNATION	BIT	DESIGNATION
32	Attention	40	Program - Controlled Interruption
33	Status Modifier	41	Incorrect Length
34	Control Unit End	42	Program Check
35	Busy	43	Protection Check
36	Channel End	44	Channel Data Check
37	Device End	45	Channel Control Check
38	Unit Check	46	Interface Control Check
39	Unit Exception	47	Chaining Check

Figure 15–69. Channel Status Word.

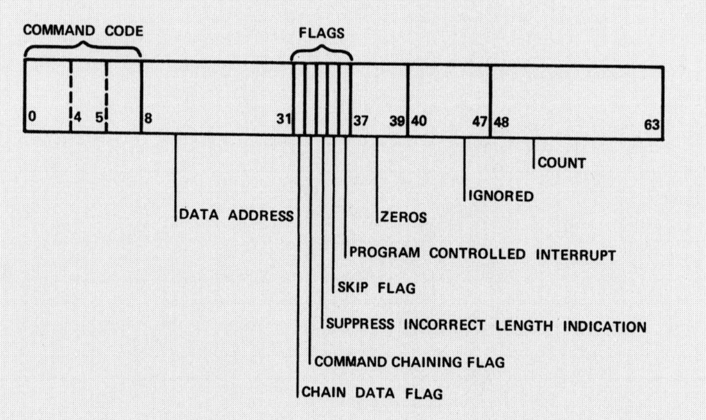

Figure 15–70. Channel Command Word.

END

Just as the START statement is the first card of the source program, the END statement will be the last card. The mnemonic END tells the assembler that the assembly is finished.

The operand of the END statement usually contains the address of the first instruction to be executed.

SUMMARY

The IBM system 360/370 Assembler language is an example of a machine-oriented programming language that is widely used for both scientific and business applications. Of all the programming languages available, it is the closest to machine language in format content. The system 360/370 Assembler language was designed to take full advantage of the capabilities and features of the IBM system /360 and system/370 computers. A routine can be written in Assembler language to fit some particular data processing need thus saving storage space and execution time. A knowledge of Assembler language has important benefits for the programmer as it enables him to include certain language routines in his program to meet special system or other requirements. For this and other reasons, Assembler language is the principal language used in writing software programs for compilers, supervisory programs, and any other programs that will be used repeatedly. It is the intent of this chapter to introduce the main features and operations of the system 360/370 Assembler language.

I. *System Features.*

   A. *Purpose*—designed to handle business and scientific applications.
   B. *Formats*—uses variable and fixed word length words.
   C. *Overlapping of input and output operations*—permits input and output operations to operate concurrently with the processing of data.
   D. *Automatic interrupts*—permit the program to switch to another operation due to a condition encountered during the processing.
   E. *Communication applications*—time sharing, teleprocessing, message switching, etc.
   F. *Multiprogramming*—operate on multiple programs or routines concurrently.
   G. *Control (supervisory) program*—controls the running of the problem program.
   H. *Program status word*—required information essential to proper program execution.
   I. *Channel concept*—the transfer of information to and from main storage and an input and output device.

J. *Registers.*
   1. *General registers*—sixteen used as base registers, index registers, accumulators for fixed point arithmetic and logical operations.
   2. *Floating point registers*—four used in floating point operations.

K. *Storage addressing*—(base register plus displacement factor plus index register).
   1. *Base register*—set at a predetermined value and included in every instruction format.
   2. *Displacement factor*—provides relative addressing beyond value in Base Register.
   3. *Index registers*—provides further relative addressing permitted in some instruction formats.

II. *Instructions.*

A. *Sets.*
   1. *Standard*—supplied as a standard feature, includes all basic computing functions of the system.
   2. *Commercial*—provides decimal operations.
   3. *Scientific*—provides floating point capabilities necessary for scientific operations.
   4. *Universal*—a combination of the instructions of standard, commercial and scientific sets.

B. *Instruction lengths*—one, two or three halfwords.

C. *Instruction format*—operation code (operation to be performed) and operation (location of data in storage).

D. *Data representation* (must be located on appropriate boundaries).
   1. *Byte* comprises four zone bits plus four numeric bits.
   2. *Halfword* comprises two bytes and must be located on a boundary divisible by two.
   3. *Fullword* comprises four bytes and must be located on boundary divisible by four.
   4. *Doubleword*—comprises eight bytes and must be located on boundary divisible by eight.

E. *Coding form.*
   1. *Name entry*—eight characters or less used for reference.
   2. *Operation code*—five characters or less defines operation to be performed.
   3. *Operand*—columns 16–71 denotes data to be acted upon.
   4. *Continuation indicator*—column 72, a nonblank character denotes a continuation of the statement from previous line.

5. *Identification sequence field*—columns 73–80 used optionally for identification of program.
6. *Comments*—may be placed freely throughout the form. An asterisk in the first column of the form will indicate the entire line as a comment.

III. *Assembler program elements.*
 A. *Character set*—fifty-one characters.
 B. *Statement structure*—Name, Operation code, Operand, Comments.
 C. *Symbols*—combinations of characters used to represent locations of data.
 D. *Literals*—represents constant data.
 E. *Beginning a program.*
  1. TITLE—optional item used to specify name of a program.
  2. START—first statement of a program—provides initial setting of location counter.
  3. BALR—instruction used to place setting of location counter in base register.
  4. USING—instruction that informs the assembler the name of the base register and its setting.
 F. *Defining storage areas.*
  1. *Defining constant*—a fixed data value that is entered into storage as part of the program.
  2. *Defining storage*—used to reserve areas of storage and assign names to these areas.
 G. *Standard instructions.*
  1. Conversion instructions.
  2. Fixed point arithmetic instructions.
  3. Data transmission instructions.
  4. Logical instructions.
 H. *Decimal instructions.*
  1. Decimal arithmetic instructions.
  2. Logical decimal instructions.
  3. Edit instructions.
 I. *Input and output instructions.*
  1. *Physical IOCS*—controls the actual transfer of records between the medium and main storage.
  2. *Logical IOCS*—controls those functions that a user would have to perform to locate a logical record for processing. *A logical record* is one unit of information in a file of like units.

IDENTIFICATION QUESTIONS

Match the following terms with the statements that follow.

A. Assembly Listing
B. Balr
C. Base Register
D. Byte
E. Channel
F. Comment
G. Commercial Instructions
H. Control Program
I. Displacement Factor
J. Doubleword
K. Edit Instructions
L. Ext. Bin. Coded Dec. Int. Code
M. Fixed Length
N. Float. Pt. Register
O. General Register
P. Halfword
Q. IBM System 360/370
R. Index Register
S. I/O Interface
T. Logical IOCS
U. Logical Record
V. Multiplexor Channel
W. Name
X. Operand
Y. Operation
Z. Packed Format
AA. Problem Program
BB. Program Status Word
CC. Physical IOCS
DD. Scientific Instructions
EE. Selector Channel
FF. Standard Instructions
GG. Start
HH. Symbol
II. Universal Instructions
JJ. Variable Length
KK. Word

1. A group of two consecutive bytes.
2. A program supplied by the computer manufacturer to reduce machine idle time and manual intervention.
3. Provides the basic computing functions for the system.
4. Specifies the operation to be performed.
5. The first statement of the source program.
6. Controls those functions that one would use to locate a logical record for processing.
7. Contains the required information necessary for successful program execution.
8. Unit used for base register, index register, and accumulator in fixed point operations.
9. Eight bits are used to represent all 256 characters.
10. A group of four consecutive bytes.
11. Identifies and decodes the data to be acted upon by the computer.
12. An instruction used to set the location register.
13. A unit of information in a file of like units.
14. Handles all the communication between the CPU and the channel.
15. Units used principally in mathematically and scientific operations.
16. Provides the functions for decimal operations.
17. Eight bits of information.
18. Descriptive items of information that appear in the program listing.
19. The original source statements are printed side by side with machine-language instruction.
20. Two decimal digits are placed in each byte position except the rightmost byte.

21. Used primarily with low speed I/O devices.
22. Specifies the beginning address in storage.
23. Provides floating point capabilities necessary for scientific operations.
24. Fields that have a specified number of bytes.
25. Instructions used in the preparation of printed output to improve readability.
26. A general purpose computer designed to handle both business and scientific applications.
27. Designed to operate with high speed I/O devices.
28. Provides for relative addressing beyond the base register.
29. Fields that have a fixed number of bytes.
30. A group of eight consecutive bytes.
31. A character or combination of characters used to represent locations or arbitrary values.
32. A symbol created by the programmer to identify a statement.
33. A program written to solve a particular problem.
34. Controls the actual transfer of records between the medium and mass storage.
35. A unit that contains its own program and is used for I/O operations.
36. Provides for effective addressing beyond the normal address.
37. A combination of all instruction sets.

QUESTIONS FOR REVIEW

1. What are the main features of a machine-oriented language?
2. What are the important advantages of using a machine-oriented language as compared to programming in actual machine language?
3. How does the system 360/370 handle both scientific and business data processing applications?
4. List the important features of the system 360/370.
5. What is the difference between a problem program and a control program?
6. Describe the steps involved in loading the program and executing a program.
7. How are input and output operations initiated?
8. How does an automatic interrupt system operate?
9. What are types of automatic interrupts and their main causes?
10. What information is stored in a Program Status Word?
11. What function does the input/output interface perform?
12. What is the main function of a channel and how does it provide overlapping of operations?
13. Explain the main difference between a multiplexor and selector channel.
14. What are the principal uses of general registers?
15. Explain the main purpose of floating point registers.
16. Describe the storage addressing scheme of the system 360/370. What are the factors involved?
17. Describe the four instruction sets available to the users of the system 360/370.

18. What is a byte of storage?
19. What is the main difference between variable length fields and fixed length fields?
20. What is a boundary and how does it apply to fixed data formats?
21. What are the steps in an assembly process?
22. What are the main purposes of the various entries on a system 360/370 assembler coding form?
23. What is the difference between a symbol and a literal?
24. What functions are provided by TITLE, START, BALR, and USING instructions?
25. Name the two instructions used for assigning storage areas. What are their main purposes?
26. What are the main characteristics of the standard instruction set?
27. What are the main functions of the commercial instruction set?
28. How do the input and output instructions operate on data?

PART VI / REAL TIME PROCESSING AND TIME SHARING

CHAPTER 16

Introduction to Real Time Processing and Time Sharing

One of the most inconvenient restrictions to the user of a computer system is having to wait for critical reports while the computer is busy and not available for other jobs at this particular time. Many users want facilities that are available for the execution of critical programs at any time. They are particularly interested in putting urgent inquiries to the information stored in the computer without being forced to abort the job on hand. In many companies, these requests for information originate at remote inquiring locations, a great distance from the central data processing system. This means that the information must be transmitted back and forth over various communication networks. In order to accommodate these needs, data has to be collected at widely dispersed points and transmitted to the central computer with ever-increasing speed. In addition, these remote inquiry stations must have access to the files stored in the central system.

REAL TIME PROCESSING

Real time processing has developed into an activity that eliminates many of the delays in processing information to and from a data processing system. *Real time is the ability of the system to provide the necessary data for a decision at such a time and in such a manner as is optimum for the needs of management.* This does not infer the instantaneous delivery of all information within a company, which would be neither economical nor required in a practical application.

The remote terminal unit can accept and transmit data to the system, thus providing *online* operation for the system. This online function allows more than one unit to share the communication line to the computer.

Real time computer systems provide instant communication between a central computer and thousands of remote points. An airline reservation clerk, for example, can press a few buttons to request a reservation on a certain flight for a certain day. In seconds, a central computer thousands of miles away can check reservations for that flight made by all the airline's ticket offices around the country, establish the availability of the space requested, and flash back an answer. The reservations clerk then keys in the information needed to make the reservation and the central computer updates the records instantly.

Real time systems are adaptable to a wide variety of business applications. Steel companies are now processing orders, inventories, and other time-critical information with real time computers. Tellers at savings banks now can give a depositor his up-to-minute balance and accrued interest without hand-searching a file, seconds after the depositor approaches the window. A manufacturer of appliances links 300 remote terminals to his real time system to speed order handling and reduce costly inventory levels. A large insurance company connects all agents and branches throughout the country to the home office. In effect, this makes the company's huge central policy file directly available to the most remote locations (Figs. 16.1, 16.2, 16.3).

With fast, flexible data communications systems like these, we are beginning to eliminate the problems of time and distance which, until now, have limited many computer applications.

DATA COMMUNICATIONS

Information is valueless unless you can get it to where it's needed. And more and more, where it's needed is far from where it originates. A production schedule in Detroit may depend on inventory data in Denver; a bookkeeping balance in New York is based on figures collected daily from dozens of widely scattered plant locations.

In order to move data around the country at speeds that bear some relation to the speed with which it can be processed, computers are learning to use the telephone. Computer information can now be transmitted over regular telephone lines almost as easily as it can be transferred from one computer to another in the same room (Fig. 16.4).

Data communications is designed to fulfill the requirements for the rapid transmission of information. Almost any transmission of data may be thought of as data communications. The term is usually limited to one particular area of technology. In this sense, a data communication system must have two characteristics: (1) the information is transferred into a special code for

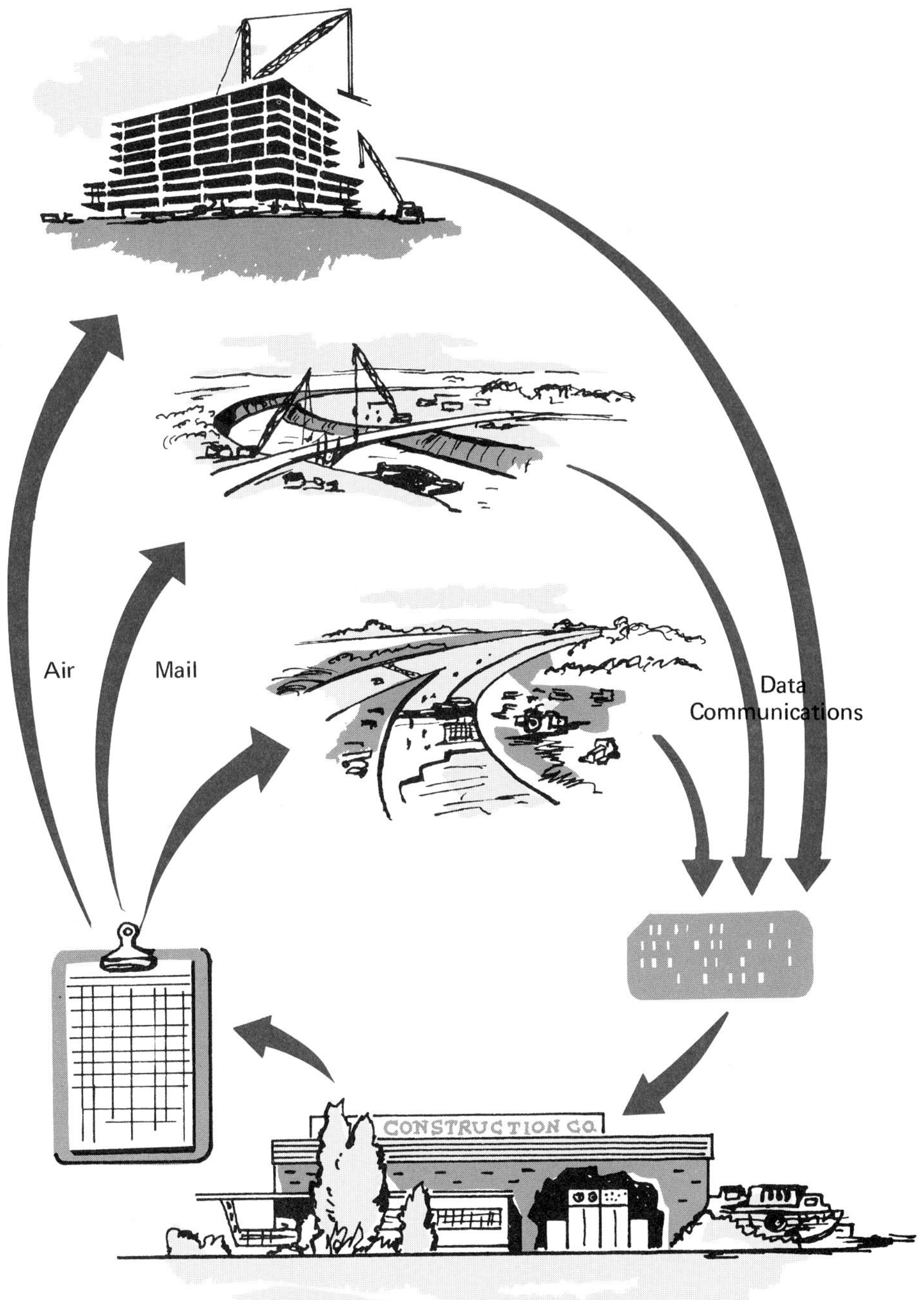

Figure 16–1. Example Real Time Processing.

Figure 16–2. Example Real Time Processing.

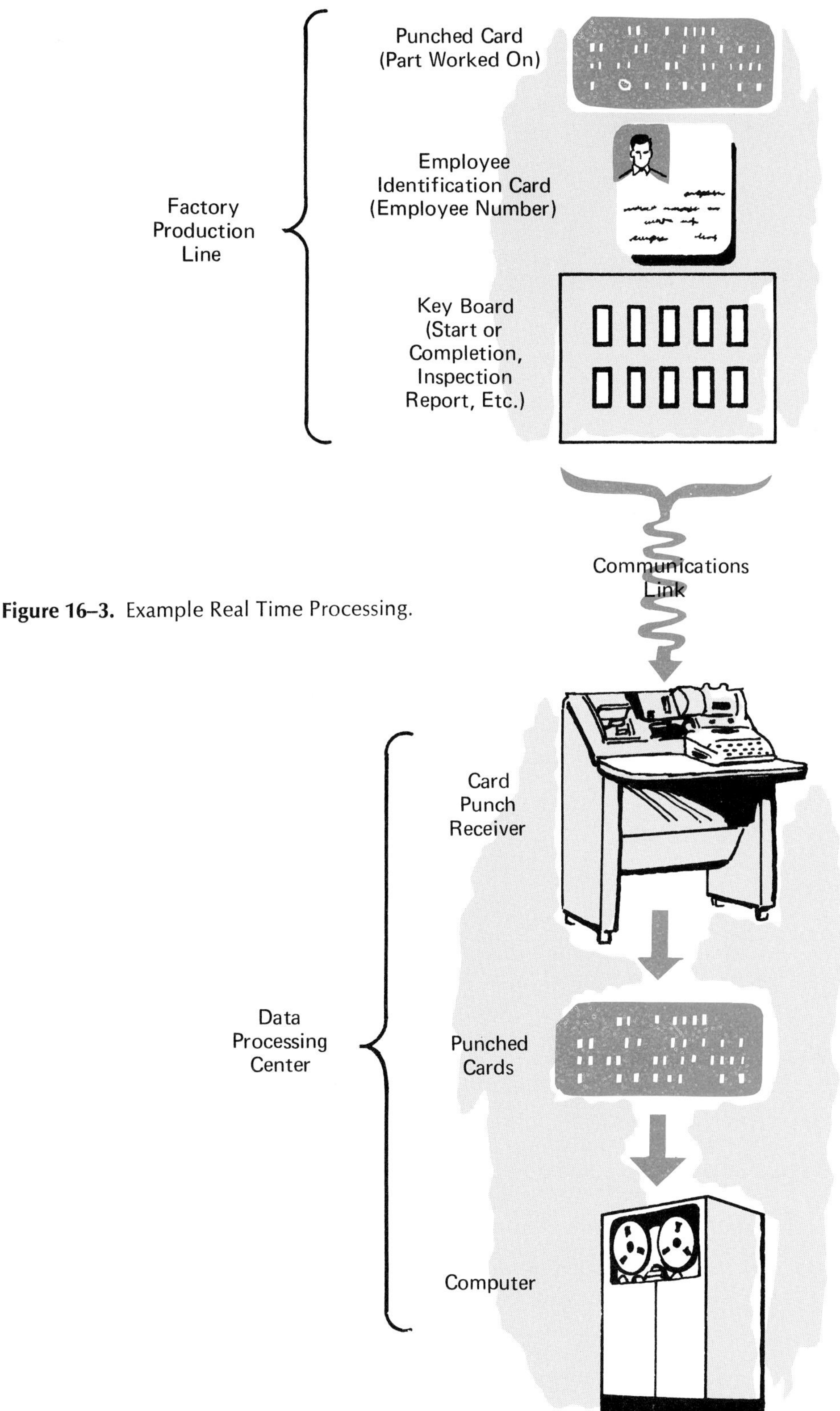

Figure 16–3. Example Real Time Processing.

Figure 16–4. Remote Terminals.

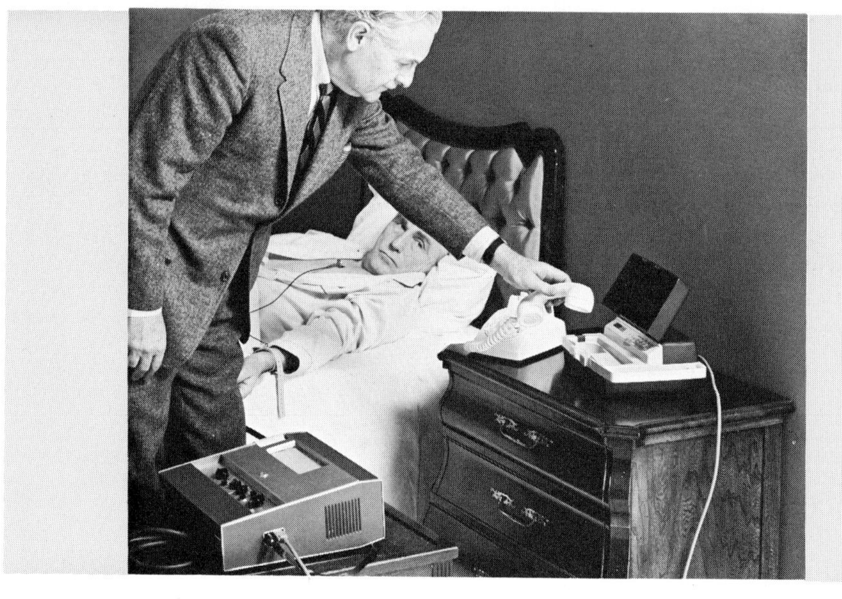

Figure 16–5. Request by a Physician for an Electrocardiogram from a Distant Hospital.

transmission and (2) the translated code is transmitted by electronic means. Thus *data communications may be defined as the movement of information by means of electronic transmission.* The transmission system includes input and output devices, the electronic and electrical transmission links, and the related circuit switching systems. A data communication system is used to transmit information almost instantaneously over considerable distances for various purposes (Fig. 16.5).

A sales manager receives a sales report of the preceding week's sales from the corporate center.

A hotel manager confirms a reservation in another city through the hotel's central office data processing system.
Payroll time card information is transmitted from a remote location to a home office computer for processing.
A physician requests an electrocardiogram from a distant hospital for a particular patient.*
A police officer requests information from the motor vehicle bureau as to the owner of an automobile.

DEFINITIONS OF TERMS USED IN MODES OF PROCESSING

Online Processing is the control by the central computer directly from the point of origin without human intervention. When human intervention becomes necessary, the system becomes *offline.* (Fig. 16.6)

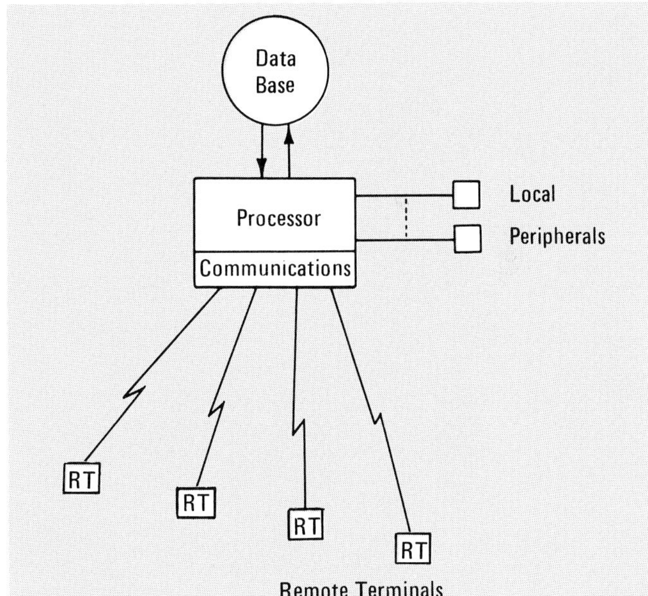

Figure 16–6. On-Line Processing.

* In June 1962, while on location for a movie on a remote mountain near Aiusha, in Kenya, Africa, veteran actor Edward G. Robinson was suddenly stricken with a heart attack. A doctor in Nairobi, responding to the distress call, flew to the camp with special emergency equipment. As he treated the 70-year-old star, those around him were unaware that an important page in medical history was being written. The electrocardiogram he took was being received over telephone lines thousands of miles away in Los Angeles by the actor's heart specialist, whose diagnosis and recommended treatment are credited with saving Mr. Robinson's life. This event marked not only the first transoceanic transmission of an electrocardiogram but the first time the new technique had ever been used for long-distance consultation. It was made possible by a newly-developed instrument that instantly converts the recorded electrocardiogram into audible sound waves of variable pitch which can be transmitted over regular telephone lines.

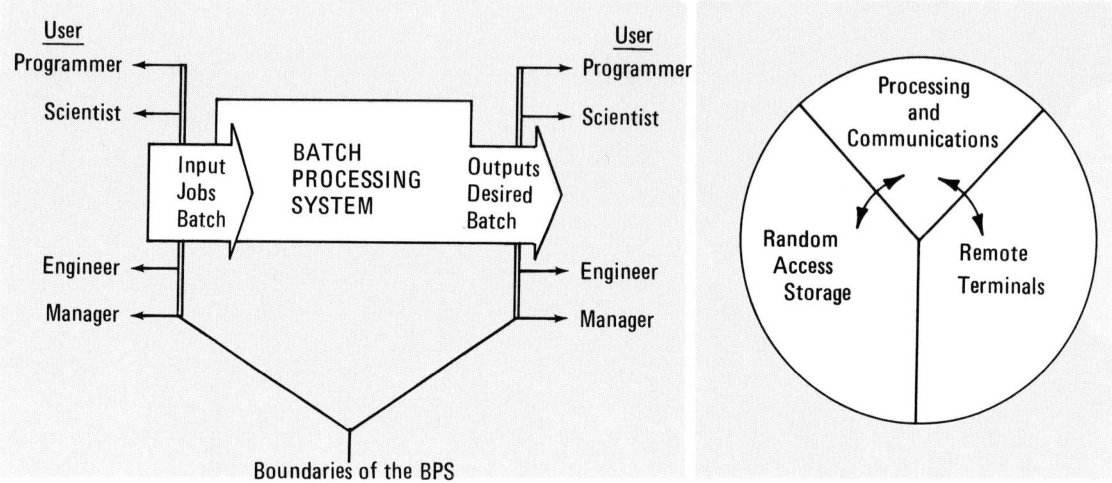

Figure 16–7. Batch Processing System.

Figure 16–8. Real Time Processing.

Batch Processing is considered a background program in an online system because it has the characteristic of not being available at all times but is run whenever a program of no higher priority takes command (Fig. 16.7).

Online Systems data is introduced into the system as soon as it occurs, is stored in the data reservoir, and is available to potential users.

Real Time is the speed at which a response is received relative to a change in the environment (Fig. 16.8).

Online Real Time Systems insure that information requirements of real time are supplied through an online terminal directly connected to a central computer with minimal direct human intervention between the source of the data or decision source and the online device.

Time Sharing aims at efficiency in processing by interspersing various problem programs for a fair share of the allocation of time on the system. Thus each user has independent control of the central computer through his terminal.

A Total System may develop from either an online or real time application. This is the ultimate goal of the entire data processing system. It may take the form of a total control system characterized by an integrated system for overall operational control through the use of a computer. Or broader still, it may develop into a total information system, which while attempting to integrate all pertinent data in an organization, focuses its attention on making data available for human decisions (Fig. 16.9).

Data base can be defined as a nonredundant collection of interrelated data items processable by one or more applications (Fig. 16.10).

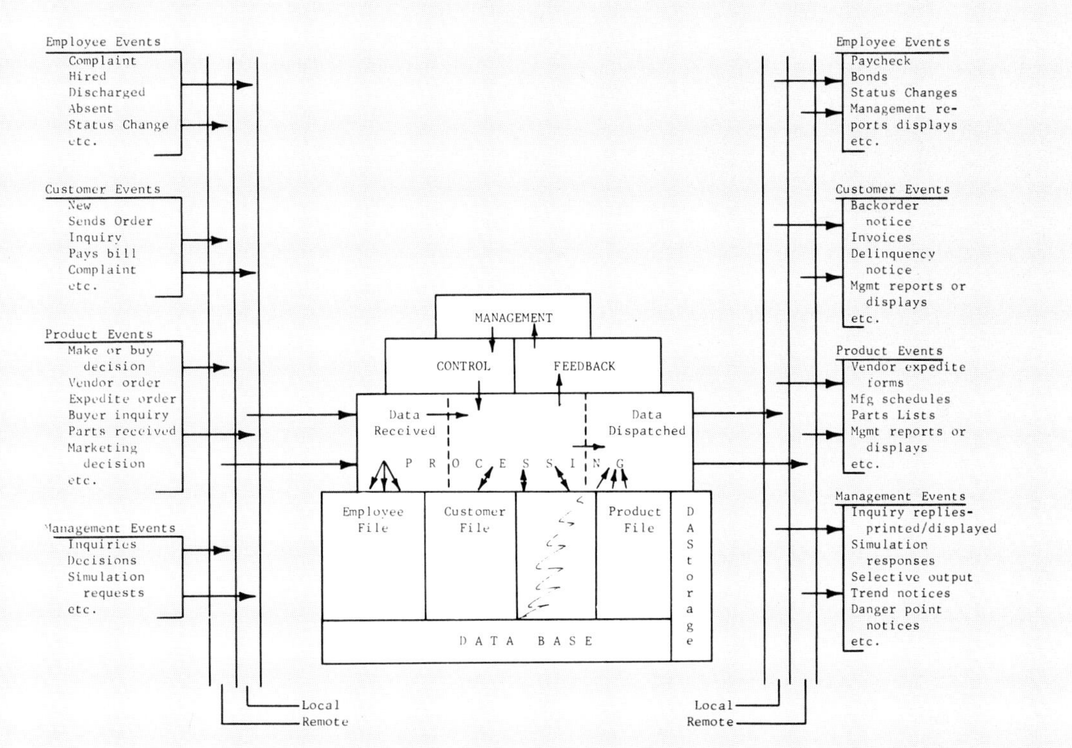

Figure 16–9. Total Integration Management Information System.

REAL TIME SYSTEMS

A real time system is considered as being composed of one or more computers and other devices which control or monitor the environment by receiving data, processing them, and outputting the results in sufficient time to affect the function of the environment at that time. A short response time from the computer is necessary for the system to be effective. The speed of the response may vary according to the type of system and the needs of the user.

Real time systems range from very small computers with relatively simple programs to the largest and most expensive multi-computer systems (Fig. 16.11). Regardless of the system involved, the major components are:

1. The *Compter*—accepts the data, applies the prescribed processes to the data, and furnishes the results in the desired format to its user.
2. The *Data Base*—the random access files containing large quantities of information that provide the necessary information for processing (Fig. 16.12).
3. The *Terminals* which are attached to the communications network and provide the necessary input and output facilities (Fig. 16.13).

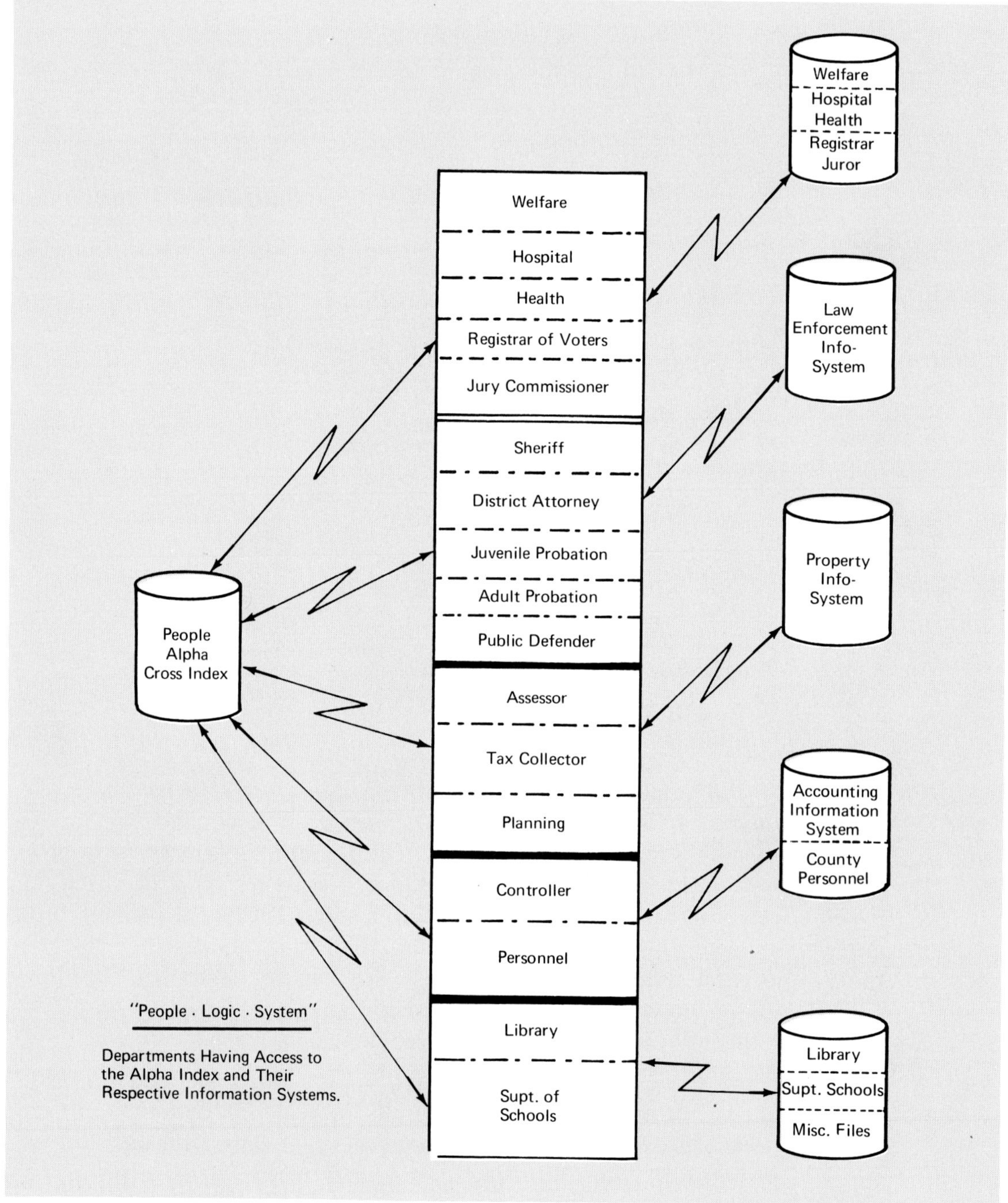

Figure 16–10. Data Bank for Cities and Counties.

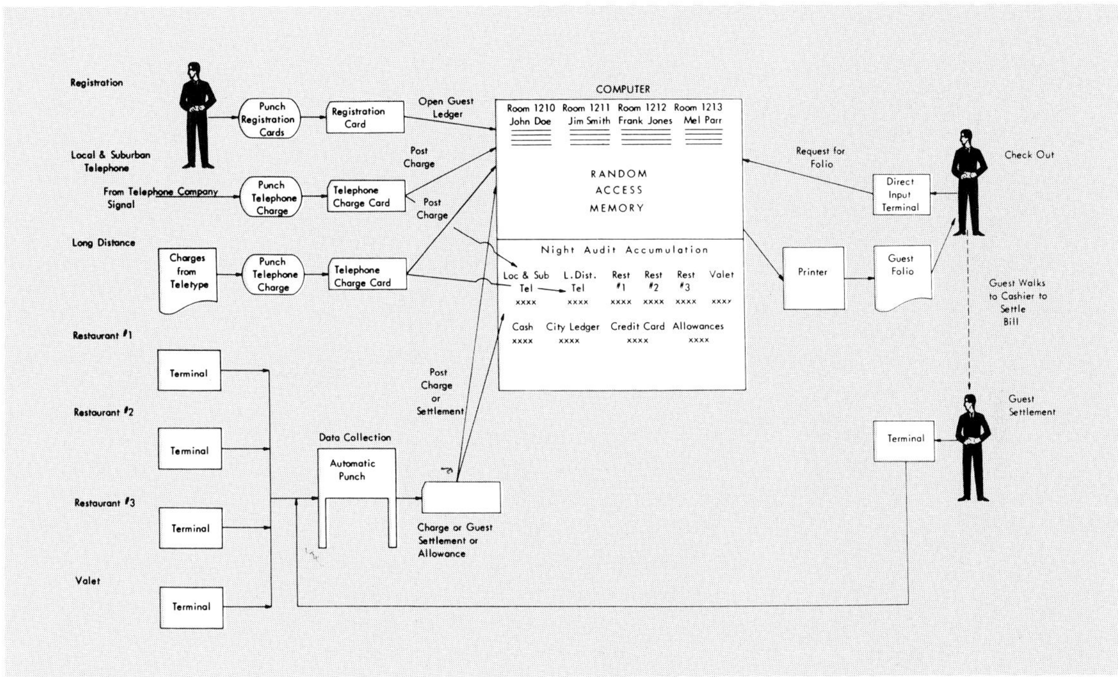

Figure 16–11. Real Time System Flowchart—Hotel.

4. The *Communication Network*—links the remote terminals with the central processing unit.
5. The *Software*—the necessary collection of the programs and routines necessary to operate the system. (Fig. 16.14).

ADVANTAGES OF REAL TIME PROCESSING SYSTEMS

SIMPLIFICATION OF INPUT PREPARATION

A real time system eliminates the need for converting the data into a machine processable format. Each piece of data is transmitted directly from the terminal to the computer.

REDUCTION IN THE NUMBER OF PROGRAMS NEEDED

Each user of a system becomes an expert in his own form of transmission of data to the system. The terminals in a real time system are designed to perform the specialized input and output functions, thus eliminating the need for transmitting data in prescribed output formats. The input itself may be the by-product of another process.

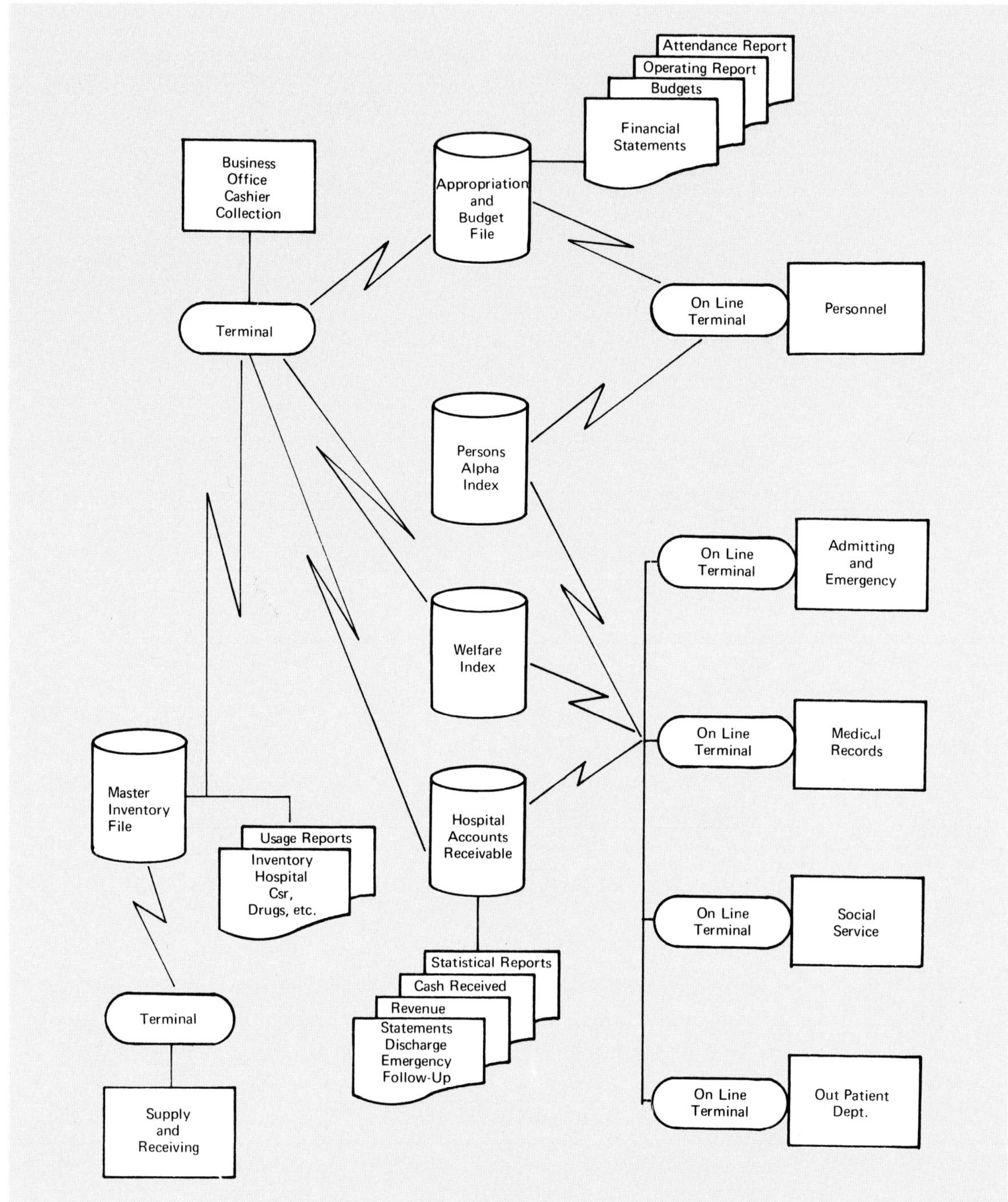

Figure 16–12. Hospital Sections Requiring Access to Information Systems.

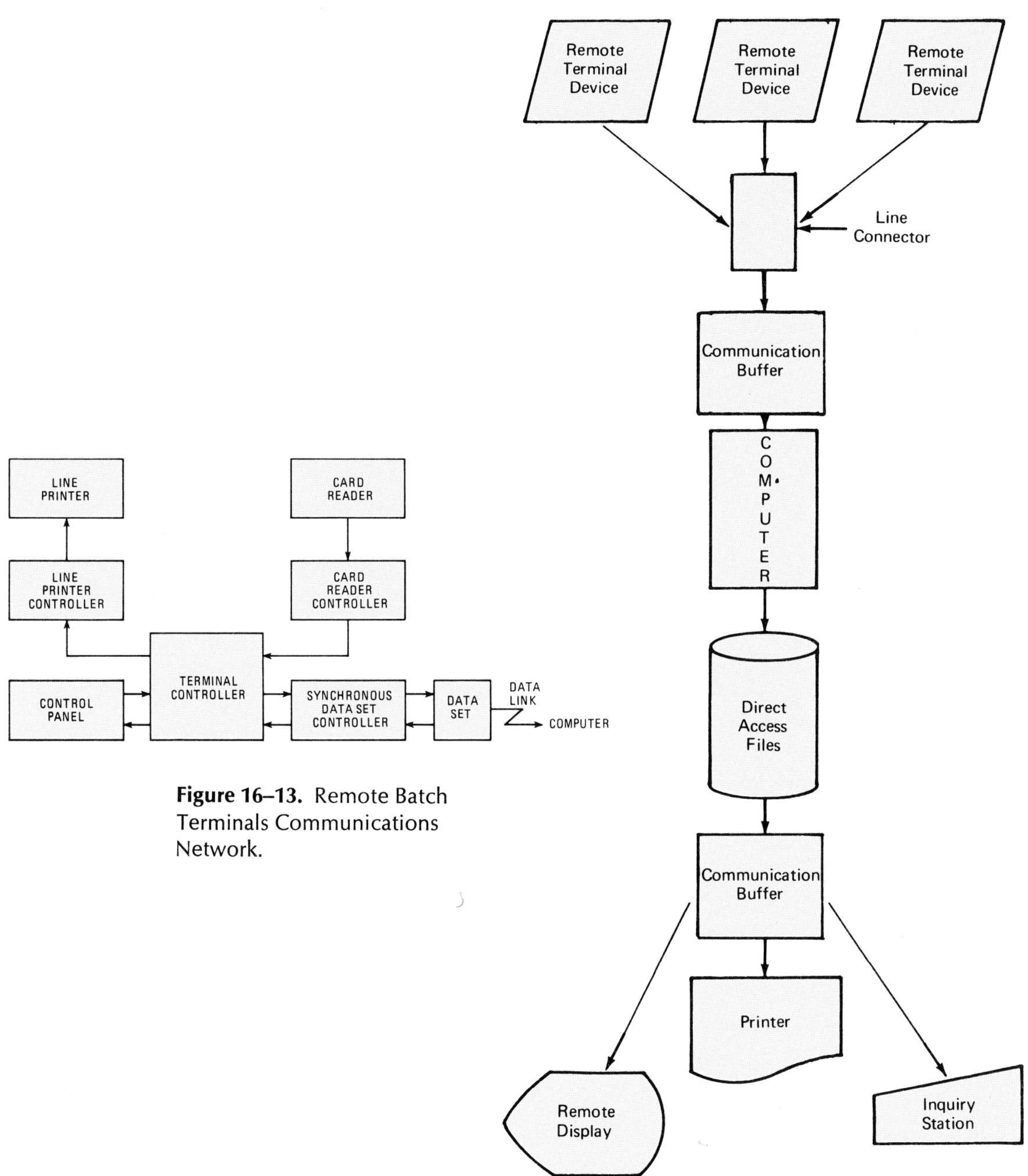

Figure 16–13. Remote Batch Terminals Communications Network.

Figure 16–14. Real Time Data Gathering and Processing.

ELIMINATION OF DUPLICATE RECORDS

Data is entered into a real time system only once, thus reducing the number of times a document is handled. This elimination of effort duplication in the clerical aspect of record keeping, by reducing the probability of clerical errors in the transcription of data, results in cost savings and greater efficiency in clerical operation.

IMPROVEMENT OF EDITING, ACCURACY AND CONTROLS

By entering the data into a real time system at the source as the transaction occurs, many errors for control are eliminated. The errors of conflicting reports, caused by varied coding or interpretation, are reduced. Moreover, each user receives faster and more economical data processing service thanks to the elimination of many of the intermediate steps.

The economy of using equipment in this manner provides a more efficient method of operation. A real time system makes the most efficient use of both hardware and software. Two or more peripheral devices can be operating while the computer is simultaneously working on a number of programs.

TIMELINESS OF THE INFORMATION PROVIDED

A real time system is a reservoir of centrally updated information which is immediately accessible to all users. Management may interrogate the computer and receive special reports vital to the successful operation of the business. All management reports can be generated automatically in a prescribed format or on a demand basis when so required by management.

DISADVANTAGES OF REAL TIME PROCESSING SYSTEMS

The expenses involved in real time processing systems constitute their main disadvantage. These costs are generally higher than those of batch processing systems.

HARDWARE COSTS

Terminals, channels, scanning mechanisms, large core storage units, vast random access processing storage memories—all necessary to a successful real time system—increase the costs of operation. The computers and files required in real time systems are usually more expensive than those used in batch processing systems.

SOFTWARE COSTS

Because of the difficulties in programming real time systems, software costs are increased. Some of the factors involved in programming for a real time system are

1. The organization and addressing of direct access devices.
2. The control of the communication network and the various remote terminals.
3. Multiprogramming—the processing of two or more transactions simutaneously.
4. Integrating a complex system with programs written by many different programmers.
5. New difficulties in program management.

As the real time systems come into more general use, programming patterns will emerge and segments of earlier programs will prove reusable in later systems. Therefore, reductions can be expected in the programming effort.

As management recognizes the practical advantages and benefits of real time systems in business applications, such systems will become more widespread. Continued improvements in computer hardware technology will provide more efficient random access devices, larger storage capacities at reduced costs, and improved communication equipment and facilities permitting reliable and economically feasible remote processing.

TIME SHARING

Computer time sharing is one of the fastest growing segments of the computer industry (Fig. 16.15). In 1969, time sharing sales rocketed to $125 million from approximately $70 million in 1968. By 1975, it is predicted that time sharing sales may approach $2 billion.

EARLY DEVELOPMENTS IN TIME SHARING

The first goal of time sharing was to eliminate the time-consuming steps of taking or sending a program to the computer, having the program sit on a shelf until other programs were run, and waiting for the results to be returned after the program was finally run. To accomplish this goal the developers decentralized access to the computer. In time sharing many users have data terminals—usually teletypewriters—through which they can gain access to the power of the computer whenever they wish. The data terminals are connected to the computer via telephone lines; they may be located anywhere there is a telephone. To allow such access to the computer, and make it practical, changes affecting the machines and the software had to be made.

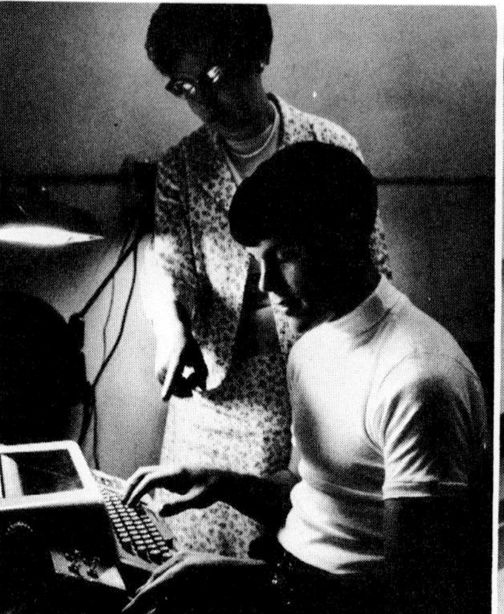

Figure 16–15. Time Sharing.

1. *Hardware Developments*—Even though such fast devices as magnetic disks had been developed to communicate with computers, users usually entered their data through a punched-card reader and received their results on printers. In time sharing, they would use even slower devices—teletypes—for communicating with the machine. To make time sharing practical designers began working on the bottleneck caused by data transfers (Fig. 16.16).

By placing a communications processor in front of the main computer (the central processor) to transfer data to and from the users' terminals, the time spent transferring data by the central processor was cut drastically. A central processor operating in a time sharing environment would always transfer data to and from a disk—one of the fastest devices for transferring data. The communications processor would store data from the terminals on the disk and inform the central processor where it was and what was to be done with it. When the central processor had a message for a teletype, it transferred it to the disk and informed the communications processor. A simple block diagram of an early time sharing system is shown below (Fig. 16.17).

As soon as the central processor had stored a message for a teletype on the disk, it would call in another user's program and begin work on it. At the same time, the communications processor would be transferring the message for the first user to his teletype. The user would receive the results of his program at his terminal in a few seconds—at about the rate a good typist can type. And the central processor was free to work on someone else's program.

2. *Software Developments*—To control operation of the time sharing machines, new programs had to be developed to coordinate the activities of the communications processor and the central processor. Because many users

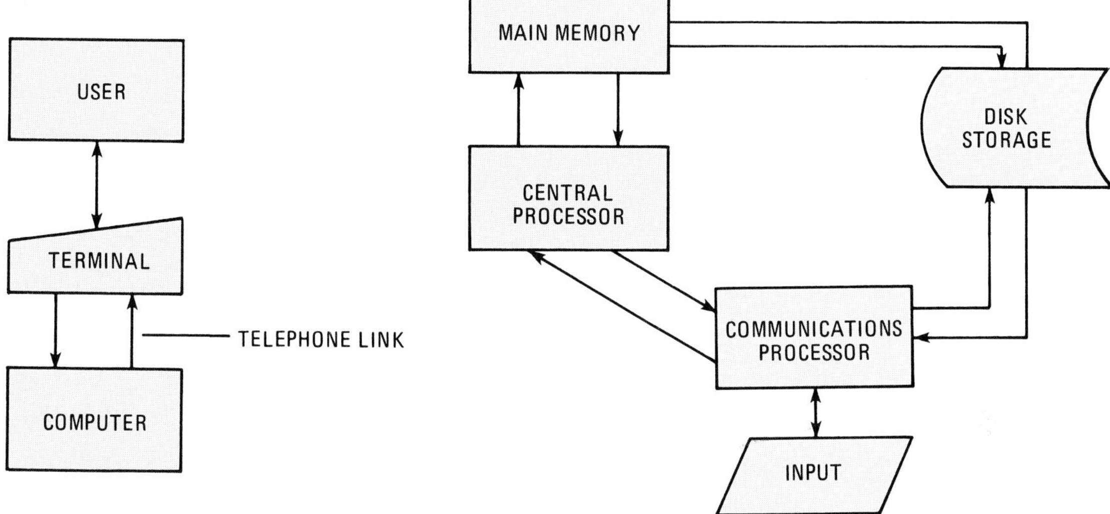

Figure 16–16. Terminal Operation.

Figure 16–17. A Teletypewriter at a Remote Location.

would have access to the machine from many different locations, programs had to be written to maintain the security of each user's information. This software, though sophisticated and necessary to the operation of the system, did not affect users as directly as did the development of new compilers.

Since time sharing makes the power of computers available to many users who never even considered using it previously, new languages were developed to make programming simple enough to be learned in a few hours. Programs were even written to teach new users to use these simplified languages. What the new languages do is simplify the use of computers so that one can express his problem in a language similar to his and thereby be able to make immediate use of the machine. It is by using the machine to solve problems that one becomes efficient in using it.

RECENT ADVANCES IN TIME SHARING

Although early time sharing systems were initially successful and popular with users, the systems could not cope efficiently with many users running large programs simultaneously. To solve this problem designers are eliminating the early time sharing systems, which were basically general purpose computers with communication processors tacked on—replacing them with integrated hardware and software and software systems built exclusively to ensure efficient time sharing.

The central processor in early time sharing systems spent as much as ten to fifteen seconds of every minute transferring data to and from the disk. In new time sharing systems an input/output processor is given direct access to the computer's main memory. In addition to handling the system's data-transferring duties, the input/output processor:

—Allocates space in main memory to as many user's programs as will fit and determines the order in which the programs will be transferred to and from the disk.
—Schedules the computing tasks to be performed by the central processor.
—Performs nearly all the system's "housekeeping" tasks, including keeping track of the usage of the system both to facilitate task scheduling and to allow correct billing to be performed.

In addition to system improvements, changes are being made to aid problem-solvers directly. New, more efficient compilers are constantly being designed to expand the capabilities and simplify the use of problem-solving languages.

Many programming languages have been modified so that they can be used in an interactive mode. COBOL, FORTRAN, PL1, APL, AND BASIC are just some of the programming languages being used in a conversational type of processing. BASIC (one of the more popular types of interactive languages) is discussed in detail in the next chapter.

The popularity of time sharing is due primarily to the fact that it allows many people at remote locations to use a central computer. Decision-making management personnel are given access to a system on a conversational basis —able to interrogate the computer from one's own office and have the system respond in the form of displays on a cathode tube or in a printed report of the various alternatives possible to management.

Although time sharing is still rather new to most users, much has already been accomplished in this field. As users become more familiar with the capabiilties of a system, they progress into more difficult problems. Time-sharing computers range from the simplest arithmetic calculations to complex mathematical formulas. Data bases, containing the records of many files, can be tapped by time-sharing terminals for information retrieval.

The development of special programs in the Question/Response mode has greatly simplified computer programming and minimized the need to learn sophisticated computer language. These programs instruct the user how to input the data and obtain the desired results.

Perhaps the single most important use of time sharing will be the development of data bases for management information systems. Until recently one of the largest obstacles to the development of management information systems has been the difficulty of gathering from many remote locals the timely data needed as a data base. A time-sharing computer system is ideally suited for this task. Information can be entered from any number of terminals into one central location. It can then be used by the remote locations as well as by the central location.

With present applications of time sharing rising steadily, data bases are required that contain huge masses of data. With the many alternatives and variables available to management, executives may predict the consequences of an action before they input it. They may construct corporate models within which to test alternative courses and select the most desirable. Capital investment analysis will become a science minimizing the number of risks involved, and enabling companies to fully exploit their markets. Budgeting will be performed quickly and precisely.

To sustain the growth of time sharing, centrally stored computer data banks or data bases that can be simultaneously accessed by remote terminals will have to be established. Computerized information retrieval will become an important industry affiliated with time sharing. There is so much documentation today that the paperwork cannot be accessed quickly and correctly. There is a vital need for a computer to store this information and to disperse it on request either in printed or visual form.

Many valuable man-hours could be saved if scientists could input a few key words of a project into a terminal and have the data bank reply with all relevant information concerning the project. Scientific information alone, it is estimated, has doubled in only 8½ years. If all the ailments of man were placed in a data bank catalogued in some manner, a physician could input his patients' symptoms through a terminal in his office. The central computer would return a diagnosis of the ailment and suggest methods for its treatment.

Data bases are being established for entire industries and are available to executives, businessmen, scientists, engineers and statisticians. When accessed by remote terminals, time-sharing computers will retrieve the data instantly from these bases, perform the necessary computations, and produce the desired output.

Computers will be kept busy around the clock offering additional associated data processing services. Data entering a computer for processing can be accessed through the remote terminal on a current basis. The retrieval of such information from these batch files can be combined with computations to yield dynamic statistics that will enhance the decision making function in all areas of management, production, sales, etc. For example, a salesman will be able to access the data base in the central computer and bid firmly and realistically on an order. The same terminals may be used to transmit data from field offices to the central computer to update files such as inventory, payroll, sales.

CONVERSATIONAL TIME SHARING PROCESSING

The two basic forms of time sharing processing are conversational, and remote batch processing. Today, most users of time sharing employ the conversational mode of computer usage. In this particular mode, a user sits at a standard terminal, dials the computer on a standard telephone, puts the receiver into an accoustical receptacle interfaced with the terminal and is on the computer in the conversational or immediate response mode (Fig. 16.18). The user may write his program in a simple language developed for this particular method of processing called BASIC. He may also call out programs that he had previously written and stored in the computer. These programs can be returned and combined with the input that the user has inserted to receive an immediate solution. Numerous "canned" programs supplied by the various vendors are stored in the computer and are available to the user instantly to solve his problem. This method of processing has several important advantages:

1. Programs may be written simply and quickly.
2. An immediate response will be available to the inquiry.
3. Easy to use terminals, most employing simple keyboards and typewriter configurations that are usually small and easy to service.

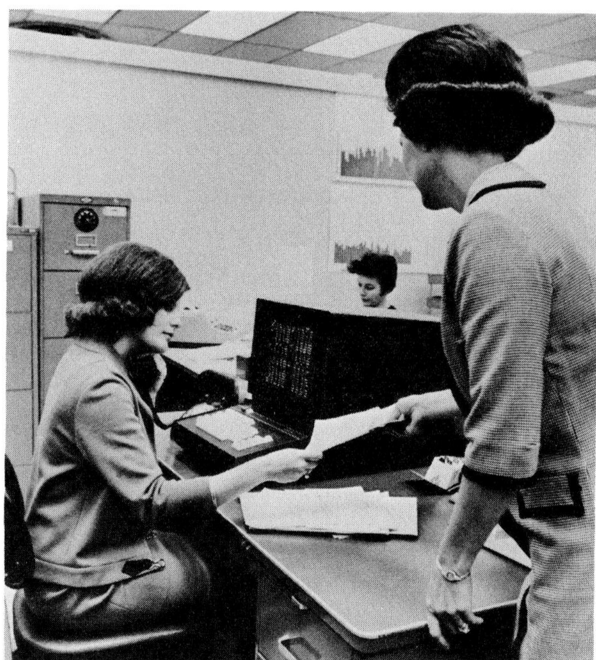

Figure 16–18. Visual Terminals Time Sharing.

4. The remote terminals may be installed anywhere where there is a telephone and electricity available.
5. Relatively low cost of operation. Most remote terminals rent for about $100 per month. The actual compute-time charges (for the actual time the terminals are connected to the central computer) range from $200 to $800 per month with the average about $500 per month.

Some typical business applications for conversational time sharing processing are:

Banking—Savings and checking deposits, cash flow projections, scheduling loan payments, pro forma balance sheets (bank clients).

Management Consulting—Cash budgets, enrollment projections for schools, lease or buy decisions, acquisition and merger analysis.

Investment—Corporate earnings projections, rate of return analysis, economic forcasting.

Manufacturing—Cost analysis, production scheduling, sales forecasting, sales analysis, inventory control.

REMOTE BATCH TIME SHARING: PROCESSING—AND LIMITATIONS

Although the smallest portion of time sharing operations, it is expected that remote batch time sharing processing will eventually become the largest segment of data processing. Remote batching is not time sharing in the conversational mode, but fits the original definition because it is a time sharing function—the shared use of a central computer by numerous remote users. There is no immediate response in remote batch processing. On the contrary, there may be a time lag factor of hours, days, or even weeks.

Remote batch processing uses terminals of entirely different types from those in the conversational time sharing. Terminals are usually small simple input and output devices, such as a small card reader and printer connected to another small computer used as the remote terminal (Fig. 16.19). This type of capability opens the potential of time sharing to the giant business field of data processing.

At the present time, and probably for the next decade, telephone lines are the only practical source of communication. In spite of the numerous advances made by the telephone company in improving the communication media, there are still some serious problems. The major problem lies in the fact that the telephone is a voice-oriented system and cannot be easily changed to a data-oriented system. The principle difference between these two systems is that voice communications need not be error-free while data

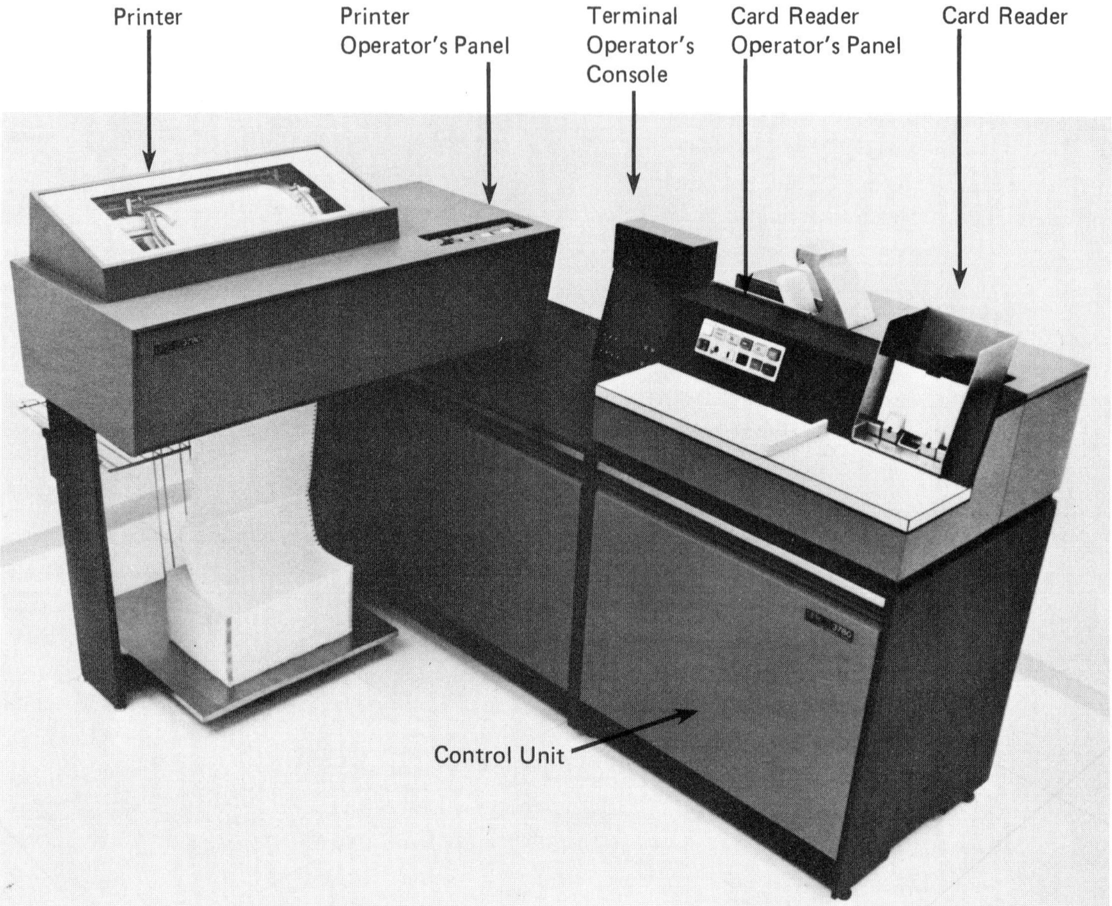

Figure 16–19. IBM 3780 Data Communications Terminal.

communications must be at least error-predictable. The telephone company has built in safeguards to prevent many of the previous errors in data transmission generated by the malfunctioning of the equipment.

Additional communication sources such as microwave transmission, satelite communicators, and laser transmission are available, but they are either too expensive or too theoretical to be considered as alternatives to the telephone lines.

TERMINALS

Limitations in terminals and peripheral equipment provide obstacles to batch time sharing. In order for time sharing to be economically feasible for batch processing, the industry must have low cost input and output equipment at the terminal end.

STORAGE

Limited disk storage is another problem hindering the development of remote batch time sharing. Magnetic disks, magnetic tapes, and magnetic core storage must be combined in a manner which utilizes the best capabilities of each. The future of data storage is the cost and performance of the input and output equipment devices at the terminal end.

SOFTWARE

The same problem of software exists in time sharing as in normal computer operation. Software has not kept pace with the rapid growth of the industry. Advanced software should provide greater capabilities in random mass storage media and terminal interface than are presently available.

MANAGEMENT

Management is still reluctant to enter the time sharing field to a large extent. They must be taught the significance and the potential of remote batch processing on a time sharing basis.

Remote batch processing has a bright future in the growth area of time sharing. Within a few years, a wide variety of terminals, printers, and small computers will be available from various manufacturers to be located on site. Data processing managers will have access through these terminals or through an installed computer to an elaborate array of sophisticated computer capabilities.

Time sharing in the remote batch mode will make massive magnetic disks storage and magnetic core storage available at greatly reduced costs. The mode of operation will be the same as if the user was completely on site, as all the input and output functions are on the terminal end. The terminal operation manager will completely control the system and programming, while using the magnetic disk and magnetic core storage in the central processing unit as an auxiliary to his operations at a fraction of the cost.

The possible applications would be identical to those presently being processed on site in the central processor, such as inventory, payroll, sales, billing.

THE GROWING THREAT TO PERSONAL PRIVACY

Day in and day out, our public personalities—actors, politicians, "beautiful people"—are hounded by intruding photographers, reporters demanding unnecessary interviews, surreptitious snooping. But you don't have to be famous to have a privacy problem. There is a less visable threat to the privacy of every citizen in the U.S.A.—existence of enormous amounts of records, both public and private, on almost every member of American society.

The Social Security number, a relatively harmless piece of paper used to identify the individual as a participant in the Social Security Administration's insurance program, is being used by government agencies, private industry, hospitals, education institutions, and other record-keepers to identify individuals, to structure files, as a condition of eligibility for benefits, and to link records.

Using one's Social Security number as a link, there can be surfaced from the unforgettable data base of the computer information pertaining to school records, earnings and tax payments, driving history, credit rating, medical treatment, and arrest records.

The twentieth century has witnessed a rapid explosion of governmental activity, coupled with new thrusts toward social action. The result has been a proliferation of programs whose cornerstone is information. We need information to determine elegibility for these programs; we must be able to identify the members of society most in need of some of the benefits. We need accounting information on payments and accounts for workers enrolled in Social Security insurance programs. We need information to evaluate these programs, to determine if they are effectively attacking the ills which our previous information had identified.

The information explosion has not been limited to government, however. The changing character of our society has created new demands for accurate records in the private sector as well, and the private sector's appetite for information is no less gluttonous than the government's. And it all adds up to the growing threat of personal privacy invasion.

Examples of the controversial threat to personal privacy are found in circumstances like these:

Banking and credit were formerly carried out on a face-to-face basis, often between persons who grew up together and lived in the same town all of their lives. That kind of familiarity and recognition is no longer possible in today's complex, mobile society, but an efficient system of credit cannot function without some process of identifying the individual who requests credit or banking services. Personal contact has been replaced by reliance on records. And where do these records come from? All over, it appears. Doctors keep detailed records on your medical history. Airlines record where you have gone; hotels and motels record where you have stayed; telephone companies record the numbers you have called, department stores' records tell how you pay your bills—and information about you is available through many other sources in the private sector. All this information is needed, either to facilitate scheduling, to allow for better delivery of products and services, or to provide prompt and efficient billing.

The issue of privacy arises, then, out of the basic facts that information is power and that we all desire some degree of control over information about ourselves. Once information has been supplied and recorded, however, we have relinquished control and laid ourselves open to certain practices that can result in an invasion of privacy.

There is a lack of controls on the accuracy of data now entered into data bases. Once recorded, there is a tendency of the part of users to assume accuracy, and then for all practical purposes, "fiction may become fact," and far-reaching decisions may be based on rumor, lies, or mistaken identity. The potential for anonymous character assassination is staggering.

Since effective regulation is virtually nonexistent at this time, our only protection seems to be that no organization is yet prepared to take real advantage of the massive quantities of fact and fiction which have already been accumulated. This lends an air of urgency to the need for effective legislative controls in the immediate future. It would probably be better to over control initially, and relax later if prudent. Establishment of strong legal damages for harm done through misuse of data bases might also serve as a deterrent to misuse.

Certain credit bureaus make it a practice to conduct broad-reaching investigations of potential customers. Investigators are detailed to find out not only about an individual's earning capacity and credit history, but also about his activities and life-style. Each of us supplies information to different institutions either to receive services (like a checking account, a credit card, or admission to a manpower training program) or as required by law (taxes, military records, etc.). We normally expect that this information will not be distributed or disclosed for other purposes. We are not aware that this information is incorporated in giant data bases and are available for all to use.

Fully aware of the need for an in depth examination of the practices and potentiality for harm that are associated with computerized data banks, the federal government appointed a citizens' advisory committee on Automated Personal Data Systems, composed of computer technologists, social scientists, representatives from state government agencies, educators, lawyers, elected public officials and members of the general public. After taking testimony from a broad spectrum of individuals involved in automated record-keeping operations—not only individuals who operate data banks, but also individuals who are file subjects to data banks—the committee reported the results of its investigation to the secretary of the Department of Health, Education, and Welfare, proposing a series of recommendations to safeguard against such unfair practices.

The principles cited in the report include:

1. That notice should be given to a record subject of this entry into a data bank. The notice should specify the kinds of data being col-

lected and the purposes for which they shall be used. Furthermore, a record subject should be advised of his right to refuse to provide data.

2. That the data should not be used unless such use is required or permitted by statute or regulation, or unless it is made with the fully informed consent of the record subject.
3. That the data should not be transferred to a third party unless specifically permitted by statue or regulation, or unless the transfer receives prior approval from the record subject. Where "the right to know" statutes compel or allow disclosure without the consent of the record subject, they should be amended to require such consent.
4. That certain classes of data should be removed from any automated data base after a specified time.
5. That record subjects should have the right to know the contents of their record and rights to contest the accuracy and timeliness of the information, in order to correct or amend that record.
6. That the record subject should have redress through court action in any instance when a record-keeping organization commits an "unfair information practice."

The plan for action of the report recommends that the secretary implement these safeguards, by departmental regulation, for all data systems used in programs operated or funded by the Department of Health, Education, and Welfare. Furthermore, the secretary is urged to generalize these safeguards for computerized data banks, in government and the private sector.

The practices that lead to the abuses of information are not new to record-keeping. The introduction of the computer to record-keeping, however, may and often does add new dimensions to the problems and magnifies the harm or potential harm from unfair information practices.

The records of criminal offenders are laboriously being converted for use in computers. Soon the computer will produce the total of those parts of a man's life he would prefer to forget. The computers will never forget.

The principal dispute centers on a Federal Bureau of Investigation program that will contain computerized records of every person in the country who has had a "significant" contact with law enforcement agencies. The information is to be supplied by local and federal law enforcement agencies.

A major objection to the FBI program is that it retains all arrest records, as well as convictions, with no provision for recording the subsequent disposition of the case. This is grossly unfair to innocent suspects who are subsequently cleared of any wrongdoing by the courts.

A governor of an Eastern state has accused the new FBI program known as the Computerized Criminal History file of posing "one of the biggest threats to our democratic system—the invasion of one's privacy." The governor and other state officials maintain that they do not oppose a computerized file of past criminal offenders but that the system now being developed by the FBI violates citizens' constitutional rights and is vulnerable to abuse.

The National Crime Information Center (NCIC) which operates the FBI computer systems was authorized to develop the computerized criminal history file in 1970 by the attorney general. The new system will represent a mammoth enlargement of the NCIC's computer program. According to an NCIC spokesman, the new file on past offenders will contain many times more entries than the present files combined.

Under the centralized version, each state virtually relinquishes control of its information when it "hooks up" to the federal system. Once in the data bank, the state's information will be available to any of the 45,000 computer terminals planned throughout the country. By 1978, three years after it becomes fully operational, plans call for the system to contain 8 million files.

The central issue is the availability of such information to persons or organizations outside the category of law enforcement. The NCIC routinely allows access to the information by federally insured banks, by private employers with defense contracts or other federal contracts, by some federal agencies outside law enforcement, by many state agencies, and by private employers with state contracts.

Although NCIC regulations governing the system discourage use by non-law enforcement agencies, control access of the information is effectively governed by whoever operates the terminal in each state. Thus, if officials in, say, South Carolina, wish information on a person who previously lived in California, they need only ask the computer. NCIC regulations are not legally binding on the states, and most states do not have local laws governing access to such computer files.

NCIC officials argue that safeguards have been built into the system guaranteeing protection of privacy. Although they concede that most states will supply arrest records to the computer whether or not a conviction is obtained, they maintain that follow-up entries indicate guilt or innocence in each case.

As for the accessibility of computer information to groups not associated with law enforcement, NCIC officials pass the responsibility along to the states, which will govern the use of terminals connected to the system. If the information on any individual is incorrect, they say, that person has the right to challenge the file and have it corrected.

SUMMARY

Time sharing with real time processing is the fastest growing segment of the computer industry. The principal reason for the popularity of time sharing is that it allows many people at remote locations to share the facilities of the computer thus eliminating many of the delays in processing information to and from a data processing system. With the increases in speed and storage capacities of computers, the input of enough data to keep the system active has become a problem. Through time sharing, both the computer time and storage facilities are divided amongst many users. The central computer can be located at a great distance from each of its users.

It is the intent of this chapter to introduce the features and operations of time-sharing real time systems. It is important that one realize the potential of time-sharing operations and what an important role it is playing today.

I. *Real Time Processing.*
   A. *Definition*—the ability of the system to provide the necessary data for a decision at such a time and in such a manner as is optimum for the needs of management.
   B. *Data communications*—designed to fulfill the requirements for the rapid transmission of data.
   C. *Definition of terms.*
      1. *Online*—direct control by the computer without human intervention.
      2. *Offline*—not controlled by central computer, requiring human intervention.
      3. *Batch processing*—a background program that is processed all at once after a certain time interval.
      4. *Online systems*—data is introduced into the system as soon as it occurs and is available to all potential users.
      5. *Real time*—the speed at which a response is received relative to a change in the environment.
      6. *Time sharing*—the interspersing of various problem programs in a system so that each user has independent control of the central computer through his terminal and receives a fair share of the allocation of time on the system.
      7. *Total system*—the ultimate goal of entire data processing system whereby all operations are integrated into a system controlled through a central computer.

II. *Real Time System.*
   A. *Definition*—is composed of one or more computers or other devices which control or monitor environment by receiving data, processing the data and outputting the results in sufficient time to affect the function of the environment of that time.
   B. *Components.*
      1. *Computer*—accepts the data, processes data and furnishes results in desired format to its user.

2. *Data base*—random access files containing large quantities of data necessary for processing.
3. *Terminals*—attached to communications network that provide the necessary input and output facilities.
4. *Communication network*—links remote terminals with central computer.
5. *Software*—necessary collection of programs and routines to operate the system.

C. *Advantages.*

1. *Simplification of input preparation*—elimination of converting data to machine processable format.
2. *Reduction in the number of programs needed*—each user designs his own program to perform his specialized input and output functions, thus eliminating the need for transmitting data in prescribed formats.
3. *Elimination of duplicate records*—data is entered into system just once.
4. *Improvement of editing, accuracy, and controls*—by entering data once, errors of conflicting records, coding, and controls are reduced.
5. *The timeliness of the information provided*—reservoir of updated information immediately available to all users.

D. *Disadvantages.*

1. *Higher costs of processing*—communications costs are high.
2. *Hardware costs are higher*—terminals, channels, scanning mechanisms, etc.
3. *Software costs are higher*—difficulties in programming real time systems.

III. *Time Sharing.*

A. *Early developments in time sharing.*

1. *Hardware developments*—communications processor, faster disk packs, etc.
2. *Software developments*—new packages to speed up operations, new time sharing programming languages.

B. *Recent advances in time sharing.*

1. Input/output processor given direct access to the computer's main memory.
2. Automatic allocation of space in main memory for user's programs.
3. Schedules the computing tasks performed by the central processor.
4. Performs nearly all of the system's "housekeeping" tasks, including

keeping track of the usage of the system both to facilitate task scheduling and to allow correct billing to be performed.

C. *Conversational time sharing.*
   1. User sits at terminal.
   2. Dials computer on standard telephone.
   3. Puts receiver into an accoustical receptacle interfaced with the terminal.
   4. Communicates with computer through some computer language in an immediate response mode.

D. *Remote batch time sharing*—no immediate response as data is entered into central computer at a convenient time.
   Limitations.
   1. Terminals range in size from small input and output devices to remote computers. Rather expensive equipment.
   2. A voice-oriented system not easily changed to data-oriented system—error prone.
   3. Limited storage capacity.
   4. Software has not kept pace with rapid growth in time sharing field.
   5. Management still reluctant to enter into time sharing field to large extent.

E. *The growing threat to personal privacy*—the information explosion resulting in the building of large data bases of personal records has raised controversial questions of the invasion of the privacy of individuals.

IDENTIFICATION QUESTIONS

Match the following terms with the statements that follow.

A. Batch Processing
B. Conversational Time Sharing
C. Data Base
D. Data Communications
E. Online Processing
F. Online Systems
G. Real Time
H. Real Time Systems
I. Software
J. Terminals
K. Time Sharing

1. A background program in an online system that is processed whenever a program with no higher priority exists.
2. The user and the computer are in the immediate response mode.
3. The ability of the system to provide the necessary data for a decision at such a time and in such a manner as is optimum for the needs of management.
4. The use of the computer facility by various independent users.
5. Attached to the communications network and provides the necessary I/O facilities.
6. Data is introduced into the system as soon as it occurs.

7. The movement of information by means of electronic transmission.
8. Random files containing large quantities of information that provide the necessary data for processing.
9. One or more computers and other devices which control or monitor the environment by receiving data, processing them, and outputting the results in sufficient time to affect the environment.
10. Direct control by the computer from the point of origin.
11. The necessary collection of programs and instructions to operate the system.

QUESTIONS FOR REVIEW

1. What is the importance of real time processing in eliminating many of the delays in transmitting data?
2. What are the characteristics of a data communications system?
3. What is meant by a real time system?
4. Describe the major components of a real time system.
5. What are the main advantages and serious disadvantages of a real time processing system?
6. What are the main reasons for the rapid growth and popularity of time sharing?
7. What were the early hardware and software developments in time sharing?
8. What are some of the important recent advances in time sharing?
9. What is meant by conversational time sharing processing?
10. List the important advantages of conversational time sharing processing.
11. What is remote batch time sharing processing?
12. Describe the serious limitations of remote batch time sharing.
13. Discuss the current problem of "The Growing Threat To Personal Privacy." What is your opinion of this controversial subject?

CHAPTER 17

Time-Sharing Programming—BASIC Programming Language

Time sharing is working directly with a computer; whether you are in the same room with the computer or hundreds of miles away, essentially you are alone with the machine. To achieve this almost instantaneous usage by several people at the same time requires that computer equipment effectively share its time among various remote input terminals permitting a continuous flow of data between the central computer and its users.

The computer can be located anywhere and access to the central computer system is through a telephone connector and a teletypewriter (Fig. 17.1). To access the central computer, the user need learn only two things: how to operate the keyboard terminal, and a language that the computer understands.

Using the system is rather simple, as the computer and its user talk back and forth via the printed page or visual display and the keyboard terminal. In the simplified form, the user calls the computer center on the telephone, identifies himself with a user number and proceeds to teletype his new problem or retrieve an old program previously stated that he wishes to use at this time. The only contact between the user and the central computer is the teletype. This "conversation" with the computer should produce the end result—the answer to a particular problem (Fig. 17.2).

The other requirement for "conversational" time sharing is a language that the computer understands. If you have used a computer before, you probably had to wait a day or more for answers to your problem. You pro-

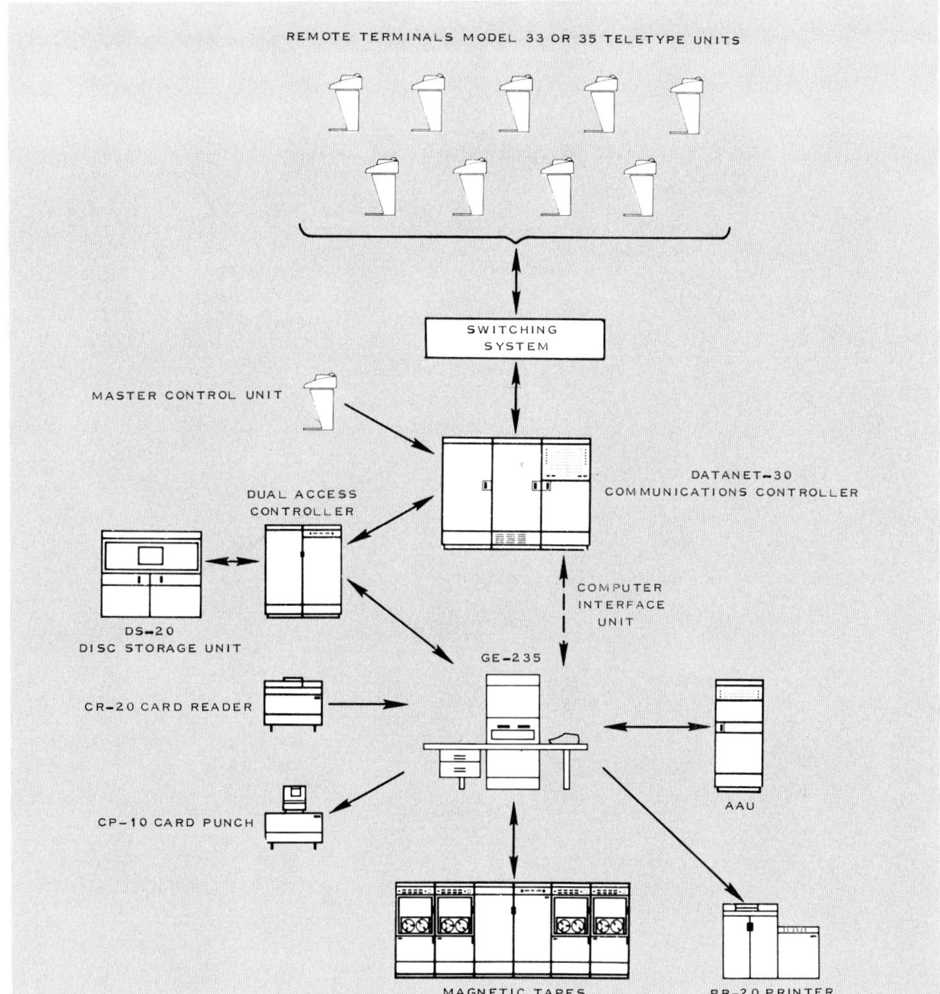

Figure 17–1. Time-Sharing System Communication.

grammed your problem (usually requiring assistance from an experienced programmer) and had it keypunched. Then you took the deck of punched cards to the computer room where your program was scheduled to run along with others. Finally, the program was processed through the computer and returned to you together with the finished results. More often than not, changes had to be made and the deck of punched cards had to be taken back to the computer room with the corrections and rerun on the computer. This entire process can take from one to three days depending upon the schedule and work load in the central computer center. Time sharing has eliminated many of these delays. Now you can check your program in a few minutes right at the machine (Fig. 17.3).

Figure 17–2. Conversation with a Computer.

USER NUMBER-X15006	The computer asks you to identify yourself. You type in your number, **X15006**.
SYSTEM-BASIC	The computer asks what computing system you want to use. You reply with **BASIC**.
NEW OR OLD-NEW	The computer asks whether the program is already stored in the system (**OLD**) or is to be introduced at this time (**NEW**). You answer **NEW**.
NEW PROBLEM NAME- SOLU	The computer requests an identifying name so the program can be saved for future use. You type in a name, **SOLU**.
READY	The computer informs you that it is ready for the input of the new program named **SOLU**, which is to be run in the **BASIC** programming system.
10 INPUT Y	In Statement **10**, the value of **Y** will be inputted at execution time when the computer requests it by typing a question mark (**?**).
20 LET X=Y↑2	Statement **20** causes the value in Statement **10** to be squared and the results to be stored in a location referred to as **X**.
30 INPUT Z	A value for **Z** is entered . . .
40 LET R=Z↑2	. . . and raised to the second power, with the results being stored in **R**.
50 LET S=X+R	This sums the values of the two squared quantities and stores this value in **S**.
60 LET T=SQR (S)	A function is requested to calculate the square root of the value of **S**, and this result is stored in **T**. A function is a series of instructions which can be called by a symbolic name to accomplish a complex task such as extracting a square root. **T** is your answer.
70 PRINT	You print a blank line for spacing.
80 PRINT "ANSWER IS" T	You print a legend **"Answer is"** with the value of **T**, the answer, following.
90 PRINT	Again, you cause a blank line to be inserted for appearance.
100 GO TO 10	Statement **100** cycles the program back to Statement **10**, so you can input another set of data and get another answer.
110 END	The **END** statement informs the computer that all the statements comprising the program have been entered.
	Now, you have the option of having your program **RUN** or **SAVED**.
RUN	Typing **RUN** causes the program to be executed.
SOLU 9:16 THURS 03-07-68	Before actual execution, the computer types out the symbolic name of the program, the time of day, the day of the week, and the date. Then it begins execution.
? 4	The computer executes the request for the first item of information by typing a question mark. This is the signal for you to input your first value, which in this case is **4**.
? 4	The computer asks for the second required item of information, and you respond with another **4**.
ANSWER IS 5.65685	The computer calculates the square of each inputted quantity, sums these squares, and extracts the square root of this sum, printing the legend and the answer.
? 6	Since this problem was programmed to do multiple combinations, a question mark indicates the computer is now ready for the first of the next set of data to be entered. In this case, you input a **6**.
? 9	The second question mark asks for the second item of data, and you input a **9**.
ANSWER IS 10.8167	The computer again makes its calculation and prints its answer.
? STOP	Another question mark awaits the next set. If you choose to stop, type in **STOP**.
RAN 6 SEC	The computer informs you that **6 seconds** of computer time were required to run your program.
STOP READY	Then it reminds you that you stopped execution and it is ready for your next desire.
SAVE	You type in **SAVE**, so the program will remain on the disc file.
LIST	If you are interested in a final copy of what has been stored, type **LIST** and the program will be typed for you by the computer.
10 INPUT Y 20 LET X=Y↑2 30 INPUT Z 40 LET R=Z↑2 50 LET S=X+R 60 LET T=SQR (S) 70 PRINT 80 PRINT "ANSWER IS" T 90 PRINT 100 GO TO 10 110 END	
BYE	You type **BYE** to tell the computer you have terminated your work at this time.
OFF AT 9:35 RAN 30 SEC	The computer tells you the time you are off the machine and the total time you consumed using it for this specific operation.

BASIC PROGRAMMING

Before a program can be successfully executed, it must fulfill two requirements: (1) The program must be presented in a language that the computer understands, and (2) the problem must be completely and precisely stated. The program should be in a programming language that resembles ordinary mathematical notation, has a simple vocabulary, and permits a complete and precise specification of your program. BASIC (*B*eginners *A*ll-Purpose *S*ymbolic *I*nstruction *C*ode) is a computer language that satisfies all these objec-

A computer program written in BASIC consists of numbered statements. The computer executes these statements in sequence unless an instruction within a statement directs otherwise. Let's examine the statements in the first program (see opposite page).

```
10  LET I = 1
```

In the first statement the variable "I" is assigned the value 1. (Note that the typewriter uses the symbol "Ø" in 1Ø to denote zero and distinguish it from the letter "O".)

```
20  IF I > 1000 THEN 50
```

If "I" were larger than 1ØØØ the computer would jump to statement 5Ø for the next instruction. Since it is not larger, the next statement is 3Ø.

```
30  LET I = I + 1
```

Here the computer is instructed to increment the value of "I" by one. I = 1 + 1 = 2.

```
40  GO TO 20
```

Here the computer is instructed to jump back to statement 2Ø, creating a program loop. The computer will cycle around and around this loop until "I" is greater than 1ØØØ at which time statement 2Ø instructs it to jump to statement 5Ø.

```
50  PRINT "PROGRAM COMPLETE"
```

The computer is instructed to print the phrase "PROGRAM COMPLETE".

Figure 17–3. BASIC Programming—Example. (Continued on p. 530).

```
60  END
```

This statement identifies the end of the program.

Instructions printed over blue tone (on the opposite page) are system commands. After the program is entered, the command "RUN" tells the computer to execute the program and the computer responds by typing:

```
PROGRAM COMPLETE
```

Suppose that at this point we wished to have the computer print the value of "I" each time around the loop. We add the statement:

```
25  PRINT I;
```

The "LIST" command causes the computer to list the new program with the new statement inserted in its proper place. The ";" in statement 25 tells the computer to space the values of "I" across the line. Without the ";" the computer would use a separate line for each value of "I" and make a vertical column.

The "RUN" command again causes the program to execute, this time printing each value. If we don't want to wait for the computer to type the full series, the command "STOP" will halt the execution.

If we now want the computer to list the value I, the square of I, the cube of I, and 2 to the power I we rewrite statement 25 as shown. The ↑ is used to indicate raising to a power since the typewriter cannot type subscripts or superscripts. Statement 5 provides column headings and statement 2Ø is rewritten to reduce the maximum value of "I" to 1Ø. The command "RUN" produces the desired results.

```
10  LET I = 1
20  IF I > 1000 THEN 50
30  LET I = I + 1
40  GO TO 20
50  PRINT "PROGRAM COMPLETE"
60  END

RUN

PROGRAM COMPLETE

READY

25  PRINT I;

LIST

10  LET I=1
20  IF I>1000 THEN 50
25  PRINT I;
30  LET I=I+1
40  GO TO 20
50  PRINT "PROGRAM COMPLETE"
60  END

READY

RUN

 1    2    3    4    5    6    7    8    9    10   11   12
 13   14   15   16   17   18   19   20   21   22   23   24
 25   26   27   28   29   30   31   32   33   34   35   36
 37   38   39   40   41   42   43   44   45   46   47   48
STOP

READY

25  PRINT I, I↑2, I↑3, 2↑I
 5  PRINT "VALUE", "SQUARE", "CUBE", "POWER"
20  IF I > 10 THEN 50

RUN

VALUE          SQUARE         CUBE           POWER
 1              1              1              2
 2              4              8              4
 3              9              27             8
 4              16             64             16
 5              25             125            32
 6              36             216            64
 7              49             343            128
 8              64             512            256
 9              81             729            512
 10             100            1000           1024
PROGRAM COMPLETE
```

Figure 17–3. (Continued).

tives. It is precise, simple, and easy to understand. BASIC is a user's language that minimizes the clerical tasks of "set-up." It can be used at a teletype in rather free-form for input and output, thus eliminating many of the problems in formulating data required by other computer languages (Fig. 17.4).

The language and logic of BASIC was developed by faculty members and undergraduates at Dartmouth College. It is not unusual for beginners to start composing their own BASIC programs within a half hour after they have been introduced to the system. Debugging, updating, or composing programs can be done right at the remote terminal keyboard. BASIC makes every man his own programmer. He need not concern himself with the fact that the computer uses binary arithmetic, rather than decimal, or that the program—as the computer sees it—is complicated by being written in binary "words."

STEP 1

Multiply 6 by $15.00 and jot down answer.	100 LET X1 = 6*15
Multiply 3 by $10.00 and jot down answer.	110 LET X2 = 2*10
Multiply 3 by $00.50 and jot down answer.	120 LET X3 = 3*0.5
Multiply 12 by minus $.02 and jot down answer.	130 LET X4 = 12*(-.02)
Add all items and jot down answer.	140 LET T = X1+X2+X3+X4
Tell me what the answer is.	150 PRINT T
That's all, thank you.	999 END

STEP 2

Say "Thank you, goodbye."	Type in BYE
Friend hangs up.	Computer advances paper to where it can be torn off, and automatically disconnects the teletypewriter.

Figure 17–4. BASIC Program. (Continued on p. 532).

HUMAN	COMPUTER
1. Pick up phone.	1. Push the ORIG button on teletypewriter.
2. Listen for dial tone.	2. Listen for dial tone on speaker.
3. Dial friend's number.	3. Dial the Time-Sharing computer's number.
4. Friend answers.	4. Computer answers (beep).
5. Say HELLO.	5. Type HELLO.
6. Friend says, "Who is this?"	6. Computer types USER NUMBER.
7. Tell him your name.	7. Type in your user number.
8. Friend says, "What language?"	8. Computer types SYSTEM.
9. Tell him: "English."	9. Type in BASIC.
10. Friend says, "Is this a new problem or the same as before?"	10. Computer types NEW OR OLD.
11. Tell him, "A new problem."	11. Type in NEW.
12. Friends says, "What kind?"	12. Computer types NEW PROBLEM NAME
13. Tell him, "Sales spree"	13. Type in SPREE.
14. Friend says, "O.K. let's go."	14. Computer types READY.

STEP 3

```
USER NUMBER--W95500
SYSTEM--BASIC
NEW ØR ØLD--NEW
NEW FILE NAME--SPREE
READY.

100 LET X1=6*15
110 LET X2=2*10
120 LET X3=3*0.5
130 LET X4=12* -0.02
140 LET T=X1+X2+X3+X4
150 PRINT T
999 END
RUN
WAIT.


SPREE       11:08        W1 WED 01/22/69

 111.26



USED                  6.17 UNITS.
BYE

*** ØFF AT 11:09        ELAPSED TERMINAL TIME =  2 MIN.
```

Figure 17–4. (Continued).

OPERATION OF BASIC PROGRAMS

BASIC is a simple and efficient problem solving language. It provides its users with efficient, rapid, flexible, and precise problem-solving activities, with which is combined ease of use and learning. Users create, execute, debug, and save BASIC programs from typewriter-like terminals, conveniently located in classrooms, offices, or laboratories, which may be far removed from the central computer (Fig. 17.5). At the terminal keyboard, the user types problem-solving statements and input data, one line at a time, transmitting them to the computer. Messages and output data are (at the user's request) printed at the terminal.

As the term "time sharing" implies, many users are sharing the same facilities of the computer. Because of the speed of computer processing, each user is unaware of any other activity at any terminal but his own. All users have immediate access to the computer, the same priority and the same share of the computer resources. The programs are executed dynamically and results are available immediately. The computer and user are in constant conversation; programs are checked as they are entered, line by line, and errors can be corrected at once (Fig. 17.6).

Figure 17–5. Keyboard and Teletype Controls.

FEATURES OF BASIC PROGRAMS

Besides the ability to *build* and *execute* BASIC programs, each user can do the following at his terminal.

1. Test and debug his programs dynamically.
2. Modify his program freely through a single or multiple line insertion, deletions or replacements.
3. Build and modify text. *Text is a collection line that is typed at the terminal.* This can be useful for preparing reports, program documentation, and for saving any kind of data. Unlike BASIC programming, text entries do not follow any programming rules.
4. Have the system save his programs and text for later use. (Each user has his own programs, text and files; the contents of a user's private library cannot be touched by any other user).
5. Every terminal user has a password (user-identifier code) that he uses to identify himself to the system every time he signs on at his terminal. This password protects the user's programs and text from use or destruction by other users (Fig. 17.7).
6. BASIC is designed to detect a wide variety of program errors and to inform the user of an error as soon as it is detected. In some cases (misspelling and other syntactical errors) an error will be found right after a BASIC statement has been typed. In other cases (missing statements and semantic errors) errors can be detected only after the user has requested that his program be executed. Whenever an error is

Explanation	Statement
Let's examine the following BASIC program which causes computer to square and cube each of the numbers 1 to 10, and provide a printout of these values.	
In the first statement, we assign the variable "I" a value of 1. (The teleprinter types a "Ø", for zero, to distinguish it from the letter O.)	1Ø LET I = 1
This statement specifies that if "I" is larger than 10, the computer will jump to statement 6Ø for the next instruction.	2Ø IF I > 1Ø THEN 6Ø
Now, since we want the computer to list the value I, the square of I, and the cube of I, we write statement 30 as shown. The ↑ is used to indicate raising to a power (the teleprinter cannot type subscripts and superscripts).	3Ø PRINT I, I↑2, I↑3
The computer is instructed to increment the value of "I" by one in this statement.	4Ø LET I = I + 1
Here the computer is instructed to jump back to statement 2Ø, creating a program loop. The computer will cycle around and around this loop until "I" is greater than 1Ø, at which time statement 2Ø instructs it to jump to statement 6Ø.	5Ø GO TO 2Ø
The computer is instructed to print the phrase "Program Complete".	6Ø PRINT "PROGRAM COMPLETE"
This statement identifies the end of the program.	7Ø END
If we want to print a heading, we add statement 5 to provide column headings. (The computer automatically places this statement in proper sequence, ahead of 1Ø.)	5 PRINT "VALUE", "SQUARE", "CUBE"

PROGRAM OUTPUT:

```
VALUE     SQUARE     CUBE
 1          1        1
 2          4        8
 3          9        27
 4          16       64
 5          25       125
 6          36       216
 7          49       343
 8          64       512
 9          81       729
 10         100      1000
 PROGRAM COMPLETE
```

Figure 17–6. BASIC Program Operation.

```
HELLO
USER NUMBER--D25727
SYSTEM--BASIC
NEW OR OLD--OLD
OLD PROBLEM NAME--INTEGR***
READY

RUN
```

Figure 17–7. Sample Identification Sequence.

```
10  READ A, B, D, E
15  LET G = A * E - B * D
20  IF G = 0 THEN 65
30  READ C, F
37  LET X = (C*E - B*F) / G
42  LET Y = (A*F - C*D) / G
55  PRINT X, Y
60  GO TO 30
65  PRINT "NO UNIQUE SOLUTION"
70  DATA 1, 2, 4
80  DATA 2, -7, 5
85  DATA 1, 3, 4, -7
90  END
```

Figure 17–8. Sample BASIC Program.

detected, a message will be printed to help the user to locate the error and correct it.

7. BASIC provides a common library into which an installation can place any programs, files, and text collections that it wants to make available to *all* users. One uses the contents of the common library in the same manner that he uses the contents of his own private library. However, he cannot in any way change the contents of the common library: only installation-authorized personnel can do that (Fig. 17.8).

TERMINAL OPERATING PROCEDURES

A BASIC program will employ many different instructions in both the English language and in mathematical notation. Before entering the program, the user must identify himself to the system. This is done in the following manner.

1. Push the ORIG button. This corresponds to lifting the telephone off the hook.
2. Listen for the dial tone (SPKR VOL controls the sound you hear from the speaker).
3. Dial the number of the time-sharing computer. If it is busy, push the CLR button, wait a while and try again.
4. When a computer answers with a beep, the typewriter will automatically type out its own identification number.
5. Type your user number and other information requested, then enter a new program or call up an old one and use it.
6. When you are through, type BYE, followed by a carriage return. The typewriter will shut itself off automatically.

IBM ITF : BASIC

To identify oneself to the system using a communications terminal (Fig. 17.9), the following procedures are performed (2741 Communications Terminal):

1. Set the terminal mode switch, located in a niche in the left side-panel of the typewriter stand, to the COM position.
2. Set the terminal power switch, located on the right-hand side of the keyboard to ON.
3. If the terminal is equipped with a dial-up mechanism, follow these instructions; otherwise, skip to step 4.
   a. Depress the TALK button on the telephone.
   b. Pick up the receiver and dial the telephone number you have been assigned.
   c. When you hear a steady, high-pitched tone on the receiver, depress the DATA button firmly for a moment and then release it; the DATA button should light and remain lit as long as the terminal is connected to ITF. When the DATA button lights, hang up the receiver.
4. When the connection has been made, the terminal keyboard will be unlocked (a faint click accompanies this unlocking). Now identify yourself to ITF.

After you have connected your terminal, you identify yourself to ITF by typing the LOGON command (Fig. 17.10). First type the word LOGON, press the space bar once, and then type the password (user-identifier code) that has been assigned to you. For example, assume that your user-identifier code is W0004, you would identify yourself to the system in this manner:

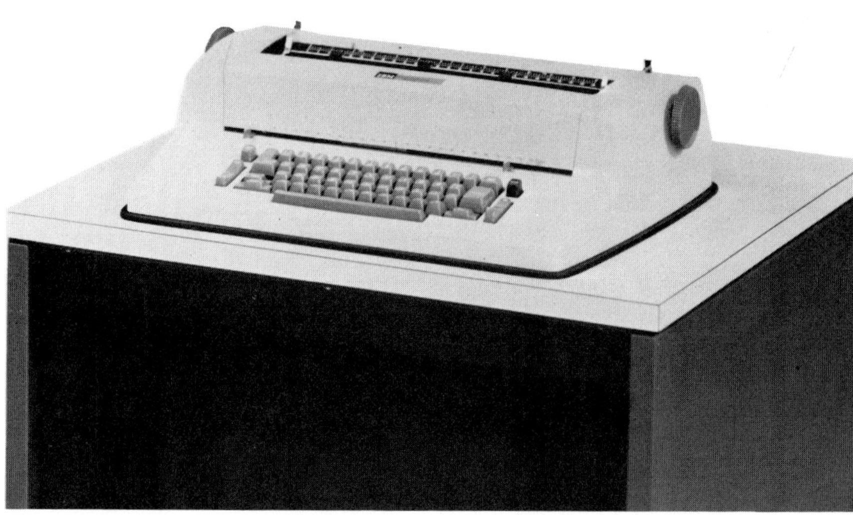

Figure 17–9. IBM 2741 Controls.

Figure 17–10. IBM 2741 BASIC Keyboard.

LOGON W0004

After typing the last character of your code, send the line to ITF by pressing the CR (carriage return) key. ITF will respond with an acknowledgment message and then skip to a new line. On this line it will type READY in the first five positions. This "system cue" indicates that ITF is in the *control mode*. You may remain in that mode or type an EDIT command to switch to the *edit mode* (Fig. 17.11).

Figure 17–11. Logging On—IBM 2741 Terminal.

```
          logon w0004
THANK YOU.                  DATE 05/17/7-        TIME 16.47.25
READY edit cbf basic
EDIT
```

The *control mode* is primarily used for log on or off and for providing access to the edit mode. You can initiate a "terminal session," perform various library functions or switch to the edit mode. In the control mode, you can list the names of all programs in your private library, delete a program from that library, or change the name of an existing program.

The *edit mode* is used to create, update, modify, test, and execute programs. In the edit mode, you build programs, changing, inserting, and deleting statements until you are satisfied with the results. You can save programs in your private library. Program testing tools for finding errors in your program are also provided in this mode so that you can readily spot errors.

In addition to these facilities, you have the ability (in the edit mode) to build collections of texts instead of building programs. This can be useful for preparing reports and for saving any kind of information. As with programs, collections of texts can be saved in your private library.

READY edit cbf basic

Note: All capitals (upper case) indicate the printing generated by the computer. You can type in upper case and/or lower case; it makes no difference to the computer since it interprets everything as upper case anyway. If you type in lower case, you can easily differentiate what you have typed from what the computer has typed.

In the above statement, we have indicated that we wished to be in the edit mode. Programs are always created in the edit mode (which we enter, from the control mode, by typing the command EDIT). Every program must have a name (in ITF: BASIC, a program name can have up to three characters). We have chosen the name *cbf* for our program, so we follow the command *edit* with the word *cbf* and the word *basic* to indicate that we wish to write a program using BASIC language.

In the edit mode, the computer will type the word EDIT in the first four positions of each line of our program; we are now ready to write our program.

When you have finished your work at the terminal, you must be in the control mode to log off. Once back in the control mode, just type LOGOFF and you will be disconnected from ITF.

The computer will indicate the time you have spent on the terminal between log on and log off (terminal session).

CONTROL MODE AND EDIT MODE COMMANDS

The following are some of the commands commonly used in ITF:BASIC programs.

Note: Collection means a text collection or program.

Control Mode

Command	Use
DELETE	Deletes a file or collection from user's library.
EDIT	Enters the Edit mode where collections are created and programs are debugged and executed.
LISTCAT	Provides a listing of the names of all collections and files in the user's private library along with its type; BASIC, TEXT, FILE.
LOGON	Identifies user to ITF and initiates terminal session.
LOGOFF	Ends the user's session on terminal.
RENAME	Assigns a new name to a collection or file, the old name is forgotten.

Edit Mode

Command	Use
DELETE	Deletes lines from the "current" collection (the collection named in the Edit command).
END	Ends Edit mode and returns it to Control mode.
LIST	Lists part or all of a current collection in line number sequence.
RENUM	Renumbers the lines of a collection from a specified point.
RUN	Executes the current program.
SAVE	Saves collection (i.e. puts it in the user's private library for future use).

STEPS IN THE OPERATION OF ITF : BASIC PROGRAM (Fig. 17.12)

1. LOGON Identify user to system.
2. READY Identify program and switch to Edit mode.
3. EDIT Write program.
4. EDIT list Type out the entire program as stored in machine. This is very useful when it is necessary to obtain up-to-date version of a program which has undergone many corrections, additions, and deletions as it is being typed.
5. EDIT run This causes the program to be executed.

```
logon w0004
THANK YOU.          DATE 05/25/7     TIME 12.40.02
READY edit avg basic
EDIT  10 rem this finds the average of any 4 values
EDIT  20 input a,b,c,d
EDIT  30 let x = a+b+c+d
EDIT  40 let y = x/4
EDIT  50 print 'the average is:',y
EDIT  60 end
EDIT  run
?     95,78,93,79
THE AVERAGE IS:   86.25
EDIT  save
EDIT  end
READY logoff
LOGGED OFF AT 12.43.12
TIME USED 00.03.10
```

Figure 17–12. Example of Creating, Executing, and Saving a Program.

6. EDIT save This causes the collection to be saved in the user's private library.
7. EDIT end The system reverts back to the Control mode.
8. READY Either a new program is initiated or the session is terminated, *logoff*.

PROGRAMMING

A program is a set of directions that is used to tell a computer how to provide an answer to some problem. It usually starts with the given data, contains a set of instructions to be performed or carried out in a certain order, and results in a set of answers.

Any program must fulfill two requirements before it can be carried out. The first is that it must be presented in a language that is understood by the computer. If the program is a set of instructions for solving a system of linear equations and the computer is an "English-speaking person," the program will be presented in some combination of mathematical notation and English.

The second requirement for all programs is that they must be completely and precisely stated. This requirement is crucial when dealing with a computer which has no ability to infer what is meant—it does what the user tells it to do, not what the user meant to tell it.

This applies to programs which provide numerical answers to numerical problems. It is easy for a programmer to present a program in the English language, but such a program poses great difficulties for the computer because English is rich in ambiguities and redundancies, those qualities which make poetry possible, but computing impossible. Instead the program must be presented to the computer in a language resembling ordinary mathematical notation which has a simple vocabulary and grammar, and which permits a complete and precise specification of the program. BASIC is precise, simple, and easy to understand.

Too often the teaching of computers and programming is unnecessarily complicated by the use of complex and hard-to-remember computer languages. The use of BASIC permits one to concentrate on the development of programming skills common to all programming rather than rules and formats peculiar to a particular language. The computer language foundation thus acquired is applicable to any future computer experience regardless of the languages then available.

With time-shared BASIC, one can get simultaneous "hands on" experience in contrast to the inherent delays and lack of interaction common to most batch processing systems.

BASIC is so simple and natural that the user need spend only a minimum amount of time mastering it, and can therefore concentrate his efforts on learning programming techniques.

INSTRUCTIONS

Each instruction must be entered on a separate line and followed by a carriage return. Each line of the program begins with a *line number* that identifies the lines, each of which is called a *statement.* Thus a program is made up of a series of statements which serve as instructions to the computer. The line number also serves to specify the sequence in which the statements are to be executed by the computer. This allows the programmer to type his program in any sequence that he desires and specify the order of execution (Fig. 17.13). Before the program is run, the computer sorts and edits the program according to its line numbers. This editing processing facilitates the correcting and changing of programs.

ELEMENTS OF BASIC INSTRUCTIONS

The following are used in BASIC instructions.

Character set.

Numerals	0 through 9.
Letters	A through Z.
Special Characters	b. : ’ < = > & +
	| ,) (; ? – ! ” / * ↑

small “b” denotes a blank character.

↑ symbol not used in IBM ITF Basic

Statement number. One to four digits may be used. 1–9999.

Label. Any group of characters enclosed in quotation marks. For example “THIS IS BASIC PROGRAM 1.” “10/24/74.”

Constant. A value, either signed or unsigned, that remains unchanged during the execution of the program. For example, 515,276.45, – 521.49645.

Variable. A variable is any letter or any letter followed by a number. It is a value that is not known by the programmer at the time the program is written. Variables are assigned values by LET, READ, or INPUT statements (Fig. 17.14). Once these values are assigned, they will not change until the next time a LET, READ, or INPUT statement is encountered with a value for that variable.

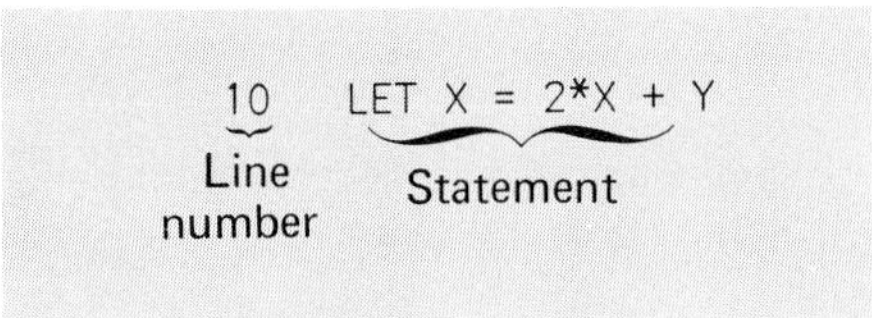

```
10      LET X = 2*X + Y
Line    Statement
number
```

Figure 17–13.
BASIC Statement Format.

```
10  let x = 40
20  let y = 172
30  let t = x + y
40  z = t + 120
```

Figure 17–14.
Assigning Values to Variables.

For example in the statement 140 LET X = T + 1, X is considered to be the variable.

Numbers. A number may be positive or negative and it may contain up to nine digits. The number must be expressed in a decimal format. For example 5, 2.641, —.0051.

Formulas. In the BASIC language, the computer performs its calculations by evaluating formulas that are supplied by the program. The formulas are similar to those used in ordinary mathematical calculations except that each BASIC formula must be completed on one line.

Arithmetic—Five operators are used to write the formulas necessary for computations.

Function	Symbol	Example	Meaning
ADDITION	+	A + B	Add B to A
SUBTRACTION	—	A — B	Subtract B from A
MULTIPLICATION	*	A*B	Multiply B by A
DIVISION	/	A/B	Divide A by B
EXPONENTIATION	↑	A↑2	Raise to the power of A^2
(IBM "ITF")	**	A**2	Raise to the power of A^2

Rules for the sequence of calculation of arithmetic expressions containing a combination of operators.

1. Parenthetical arithmetic expressions are calculated first.
2. All exponentiations are performed next.
3. Multiplication and division are calculated next from left to right.
4. Addition and subtraction are performed last from left to right.

For example, in the arithmetic expression A + B * C**D, the computer will first raise C to the power of D, then multiply the result by B, and lastly add A to the resulting product. If we wish to alter the sequence of operations, we could write the arithmetic expression as A + (B*C)**D. The execution would then be, B would be multiplied by C first, the product would then be raised to the power D and finally A would be added to the result.

Comparison Operators

Function	Symbol	Example	Meaning
IS EQUAL TO	=	A = B	A is equal to B.
IS LESS THAN	<	A < B	A is less than B.
IS LESS THAN OR EQUAL TO	<=	A <= B	A is less than or equal to B.
IS GREATER THAN	>	A > B	A is greater than B.
IS GREATER THAN OR EQUAL TO	>=	A >= B	A is greater than or equal to B.
IS NOT EQUAL TO	<>	A <> B	A is not equal to B.

Loops. It is often necessary to repeat portions of a program a number of times, perhaps with slight changes each time. In order to write a simple program where this portion is written once and the program is continually repeated, a programming device known as a loop is used. For example to repeat the same operation with fewer instructions, the following program is written

```
10 LET X = 1
20 PRINT X, SQR (X)
30 LET X = X + 1
40 IF X <= 100 THEN 20
50 END
```

1st Instruction: In the first statement, the variable "X" is assigned the value of 1.

2nd Instruction: The computer is instructed to print the values of the variable "X" by one.

3rd Instruction: Here the computer is instructed to increment the value of "X" by one.

4th Instruction: If "X" is less than or equal to 100, the computer is instructed to jump back to statement 20, creating a program loop. The computer will cycle around and around this loop until "X" is greater than 100 at which time the next statement will be executed.

5th Instruction: This statement identifies the end of the program. In the above program, five instructions were used instead of 101.

STATEMENTS

ASSIGNMENT STATEMENT

LET

The LET statement evaluates an expression and assigns it to one or more variables. It is not a statement of algebraic equality but is rather an instruction to the computer to perform certain computations and to assign the answer to the particular variable (Fig. 17.15).

Figure 17–15. LET Statement—Examples.

```
10  LET Z$ = "CAT"
20  LET X = 9
30  LET Y(X) =2
```

After execution of statement 10, the character variable z$ will contain the word CAT followed by fifteen blank characters.

After execution of statement 20, the arithmetic variable X will have the integer value 9.

After execution of statement 30, the ninth member of the one-dimensional arithmetic array Y will have the integer value 2.

The format of the LET statement is

LET variable [, variable] = formula

Note: IN IBM ITF: BASIC, the word LET is optional.

Examples

20 LET B = 6	The constant 6 is assigned to the variable B.
30 LET A,B,C = 5	The constant 5 is assigned to the variable A, then to B, and finally to C.
40 LET A1 = 62.416 * Y	The variable A1 is assigned the value of the evaluation of the expression.

INPUT AND OUTPUT STATEMENTS

READ and DATA

A READ statement is used to assign to the listed variables values determined from a DATA statement. A READ statement causes the values listed in it to be given the next available numbers in the collection of DATA statements. Before the program is run, all of the DATA statements in the order in which they are written are collected by the computer in a large created data block. Each time a READ statement is encountered anywhere in the program, the data block will supply the next available number. When the data block runs out of data, the program will be assumed to be over (Figs. 17.16, 17.17).

Since data must be read in before it can be processed, READ statements normally occur near the beginning of a program. The location of DATA statements is arbitrary as long as they occur in the correct order.

The format of the READ statements is READ [sequence of variables] and each DATA statement is DATA [sequence of numbers]. For example,

```
10 LET X = 46.215*Y
20 READ Y
30 DATA 3, 7, 23, 17
```

Whenever the computer encounters the READ statement in the program, it will read the next value of Y. The first time it will read 3, the next time 7, and so on until there is no more data left to be read. At that time, the program will terminate. If the program had been written as 10 LET X = A * B we would have to change the READ statement to READ A, B. The computer will then take two numbers from the DATA statement regarding the first number as A and the second as B, the third as A and the fourth as B and so on.

```
10  DATA 'JONES', 15.00, 'SMITH', 20.50
20  READ A$,A1,B$,B1
30  DATA 1,2,3,4,5,6
40  READ A,B,C,X(A),X(B),X(C)
```

After execution of the above statements, the character variables A$ and B$ will contain the characters strings JONES and SMITH respectively, each padded on the right with blanks to a length of eighteen. The arithmetic variables A1 and B1 will contain the decimal values 15.00 and 20.50, respectively. The arithmetic variables A, B, and C will contain the integer values 1, 2, and 3 respectively, and the first three members of the one-dimensional array named X will contain the integer values 4, 5, and 6, respectively.

Figure 17–16. READ and DATA Statement—Examples.

```
10  read a,b$,x,#$
20  data  2507,"john doe",33,"new york"
```

The values would be assigned as follows:

```
A   = 2507
B$  = JOHN DOE
X   = 33
#$  = NEW YORK
```

You can actually have more than one DATA statement in a program; the effect is cumulative. For example:

```
10  read a,b,c,d,e,f,g
20  data 10012, -73621, 4308.973, 7.2, 15.0, -3.7
30  data 10
```

The values would be assigned like this:

```
A = 10012
B = -73621
C = 4308.973
D = 7.2
E = 15.0
F = -3.7
G = 10
```

Figure 17–17. READ and DATA Statement—Examples.

PRINT *The PRINT statement is used to get information out of the computer in the form of a printed report.* PRINT causes the value of given numerical expressions, variables, and constants to be printed at the terminal. The format of a print line is to a large extent controlled by the computer; the user can control the density of a line (i.e. number of items and spacing) to a certain degree, but the format of the value is standard (Fig. 17.18). For example, if X has the value 472.15, B2 has the value "NOTHING", and Y the value 27, this PRINT statement

PRINT "X = ";X,B2,Y

will result in the following printed output

X = 472.15000   NOTHING   27

Figure 17–18.
PRINT Statement—Examples.

```
STATEMENT                  PRINTED OUTPUT
10 PRINT 'A','B'           A -14 blanks- B
20 PRINT 'A';'B'           AB
30 LET A$="B"
40 PRINT 'A' A$            AB
50 PRINT A$ 'A',A$;A$      BA -13 blanks- BB
60 PRINT A$;'A'            BA
70 LET A$ = ''
80 PRINT 'A';A$;'A'        AA
```

Note the difference in spacing. The use of semicolons and commas between expressions in the PRINT statement controls the spacing.

The PRINT statement may also be used to skip lines in the output form.

By using quotation marks, we can have the computer print out exactly what we specify for column headings, line titles, and so on. By omitting the quote marks, the computer will print out the value of an item. For example,

175 PRINT "G" will be outputted as G.
185 PRINT G will be outputted as 475.25 (the value of G).

The format of the PRINT statement is

PRINT [label or expression] [label or expression.......... label or expression]

The output form in BASIC is 75 columns wide divided into five print zones of fifteen columns each. Anything appearing in quotation marks will be printed just as it appears. When information does not appear in quotes, the comma is the signal to skip to the next print zone. As many as five printouts are possible across the page beginning at column 0, 15, 30, 45, and 60. If more than five items are listed, the sixth would be printed in the first print zone on the next line. For example,

170 PRINT X, Y, Z

The output values would be

3000 4 .09

190 PRINT U, V, W, X, Y, Z

The output values would be

```
   7         1051        6.415        3000        4
  09
```

If more than five columns are required in a report, the printout can be packed by separating the variables with a semicolon instead of a comma. The spacing between the printouts will depend upon the number of characters in each variable. When each value is printed, one space appears before the number of the sign, the sign is printed only if it is minus, and as many as four spaces appear after the number. The following table shows the field widths for the different numbers of characters.

NUMBER OF CHARACTERS	FIELD WIDTH
1	3
2, 3, 4	6
5, 6, 7	9
8, 9, 10	12
11, 12, 13	15

The rules for printing out numbers are:

1. No more than six significant digits are printed except for integers. If the number is an integer (in other words a whole number), the decimal point will not be printed and up to nine digits will be printed in full.
2. Any trailing zeros after the decimal point are not printed.
3. For numbers less than 0.1, the form X.XXXXXE-Y is used unless the significant part of the number can be printed as a six digit number. For example, .0000478 is the same as 4.78×10^{-5} and will be printed as 4.78E−5.

Some of the common uses for the PRINT statement are

1. *To print out a message in the program.* Anything included between the quote marks following the PRINT command word will be printed as is. For example, 150 PRINT "T" would cause the letter T to be printed, perhaps as a column heading.
2. *To print out the result of a computation.* For example, 150 PRINT T (without the quote marks) would cause the computer to print the value of T.
3. *To perform the combinations of A & B.* For example, 150 PRINT "THE VALUE OF T IS" T will print out the message plus the value of T.
4. *To skip a line.* For example, 190 PRINT will cause the printer to advance a line each time this statement is encountered. This is a handy technique for improving the format.

INPUT Often it is desirable to have data entered during the running of the program. This is particularly true if different people write programs. One person writes the program and the other persons doing the program are asked to supply the data. The INPUT statement is very much like the READ state-

Figure 17–19.
INPUT Statement—Example.

```
        10  INPUT  X,Y(X),Z(R+3),CI
        .
        .
        .
        90 RUN
?       25, 15.5, 4,
TOO FEW 25, 15.5,4,.35

        10  INPUT  A$,R
        .
        .
        .
        90  RUN
?       'YES, 20
MSNG QUOTE 'YES', 20
```

ment but does not draw numbers from the DATA statement. The format for the INPUT statement is INPUT [sequence of variables]. The INPUT statement allows the user to assign values dynamically during execution. When INPUT is executed, execution is interrupted and the user is asked to type values for the variables specified in the INPUT statement (Fig. 17.19). For example, if you wish the user to supply the values of L and M in a program, you would write the statement as 150 INPUT L, M before the first statement that is to use these values. When it encounters this statement, the computer types a question mark on the printout and waits for the input. The user types two numbers, separated by commas, and presses the RETURN key, and the computer goes on with the rest of the program. The two numbers will be used as the value of L and M in all subsequent computations. For example, if it is necessary to insert the values of X, Y, and Z into the program each time the program is executed, the following two instructions can be used.

```
150 PRINT "ENTER X, Y, Z"
160 INPUT X, Y, Z
```

The computer will now ask for the values of X, Y, and Z by typing; ENTER X, Y, Z? Then you can enter the values, for example 8, 15, —35, by typing them in and depressing the RETURN key. The computer will then proceed to perform the necessary calculations using the values that you have furnished and print out the result. If you have programmed a *loop* (which was explained earlier), the computer will ask you each time it encounters the INPUT statement to insert the values for the variables.

Data entered by the INPUT statement is not saved with the program as mentioned earlier. Also it may take a long time to enter a large amount of data using INPUT. INPUT statement should only be used when small amounts are to be entered, or when it is necessary to enter data during the program run.

PRINT USING

The PRINT USING statement is used in conjunction with an image statement to print values according to the format specified in the image statement. PRINT USING includes the values to be printed and the statement number of the image statement to be used; the image statement specifies the format of the print line (Fig. 17.20). Assuming that A and B have the values 5 and −372.561, respectively, consider the result of this example;

```
50 PRINT USING 120,A,B
        .
        .
        .
120 :THE ANSWER TO QUESTION # IS + ###.###
```

The colon beginning statement 120 identifies it as an image statement. This statement causes the printed line to look like this:

```
THE ANSWER TO QUESTION 5 IS − 372.561
```

The alphabetic characters in the image statement are printed as they appear in the statement; the value of A replaces the first #, and the value of B replaces the final set of symbols. Note that the decimal point in the value of B is aligned on the decimal point in the image statement. Also note that the plus sign is overriden by the minus sign, so that the negative value is accurately represented.

Another example:

```
30 PRINT USING 40, A,B
40 :RATE OF LOSS ### EQUALS ###.## POUNDS
    RATE OF LOSS 342  EQUALS   42.04 POUNDS
                  ↑                ↑
                Value            Value
                of A             of B
```

```
READY  edit int basic
EDIT   10 input p,i,n
EDIT   20 let a = p*(1+i/100)**n
EDIT   30 print using 40, n,a
EDIT   40 :in ## yrs amt = $####.##
EDIT   50 end
EDIT   run
?      1000.00, 5, 10
IN 10 YRS AMT = $1628.88
```

Statement 30 directs the computer to print the values of N and A using statement 40 as the image. The colon beginning statement 40 identifies it as the Image statement. The alphabetic characters are printed as they appear in the statement, the value of N replaces the first set of #'s, and the value of A replaces the final set of symbols. Note that the decimal point in the value of A is aligned on the decimal point in the image specification.

Figure 17–20. PRINT USING Statement—Example.

SEQUENCE CONTROL STATEMENTS

GO TO There are times when it is necessary to change the sequence of commands to be executed. *The GO TO statement causes control to be unconditionally transferred to a specific statement number (simple GO TO), see Figure 17.21, or to be transferred to one of a set of statement numbers, depending on the value of an expression (computed GO TO).*

```
READY  edit rtb basic
EDIT   10 let x = 1
EDIT   20 print x,x**2
EDIT   30 let x = x + 1
EDIT   40 go to 20
EDIT   50 end
```

In RTB we have created a loop in statements 20 through 40 so that when the program is run the PRINT statement will be executed once each time the value of X increases by 1. The statement that makes the loop possible is the GOTO statement. It alters the normal sequence of execution by actually specifying the next statement to be executed. It does this by referring to the number of that statement.

Figure 17–21. GO TO Statement—Example.

The format for the simple GO TO is

GO TO statement number

For example;

```
40 READ T,X,M
     •
     •
70 GO TO 40
```

The program will branch to line number 40 when it reaches the number 70. The computer will *loop* through the instruction 40–70.

The format for the computed GO TO is

GO TO S_1 (S_2. . . . S_n) ON arithmetic expression

This statement causes control to be transferred to the first, second. . . ., nth statement number if the truncated integer value of the expression is 1,2, ...*n*(respectively) at the time of execution. If the truncated integer value is less than 1 or greater than *n*, control passes to the next logically executable statement. For example;

```
50 GO TO 10,45,60 ON X/Y
```

Control is transferred to either the first, second, third or fouth statement number depending on whether the value of X/Y is 1,2, or 3; if it is none of these, control falls through to the next sequential statement.

IF THEN *The IF THEN instructions are used when it is desirable to skip the normal sequence of commands if a certain condition exists* (Fig. 17.22). These statements are usually based with comparison operators. The format of the statements is IF [formula] [relation] [formula] THEN [line number]. For example, 40 IF K < = L THEN 50.

If K is less than or equal to L, the program will branch to line number 50 otherwise the next line of the program will be executed.

Figure 17–22. IF THEN Statement—Example.

```
30  IF A(3)= X+2/Z THEN 85
40  IF R$ > "CAT" GO TO 70
50  IF S2  = 37.222 THEN 110
```

FOR NEXT *The FOR and NEXT statements are used in loops, one at the entrance to the loop and the other at the exit directing the computer back to the entrance.* Every FOR statement has the format:

FOR [variable] = [formula TO formula STEP formula]

The FOR and NEXT statements operate in this manner.

1. The *variable* is initialized with first formula found in the loop.
2. The *terminal value* is the second formula following TO.
3. The third formula contains the *increment* value (STEP).
4. The NEXT statement is at the bottom of the loop and must contain the same variable name as the FOR statement.

Upon encountering the FOR statement, the variable is initialized with the value of the first formula. A test is made to determine whether the variable is *greater* than the terminal value (TO formula). If the variable is *not* greater than the terminal value, the next instruction following the FOR statement is executed and each succeeding instruction until the NEXT statement is reached. The program is then transferred back to the FOR statement and the variable is incremented by the incremental value (STEP formula) and the test is made and the process is repeated. The loop is continued until the variable is greater than the terminal value. At that point, the program is transferred to the statement following NEXT. For example,

```
30 FOR X = 0 TO 3 STEP 1
        .
        .
80 NEXT X
```

In the above example, line numbers 30 to 80 will be executed *four* times. X will start with an initial value of 0 and be incremented by one (STEP) each time the loop is repeated. At the fourth loop, X will have a value of four which

The following example shows the correct technique for nesting FOR loops. The inner loop is executed 100 times for each execution of the outer loop.

```
10  FOR J= A TO B STEP C(1) **3
          .
          .
          .
(BASIC statements)
          .
          .
          .
150 FOR K = 1 TO 100
          .
          .
          .
(BASIC statements)
          .
          .
          .
280  NEXT K
          .
          .
          .
(BASIC statements)
          .
          .
          .
620  NEXT J
```

Figure 17–23. FOR NEXT Statement—Example.

Figure 17–24. FOR NEXT Statement—Example.

```
10    FOR I = 1 TO 3
20       READ P(I)
30    NEXT I
40    FOR I = 1 TO 3
50       FOR J = 1 TO 5
60          READ S(I, J)
70       NEXT J
80    NEXT I
90    FOR J = 1 TO 5
100      LET S = 0
110      FOR I = 1 TO 3
120         LET S = S + P(I) * S(I, J)
130      NEXT I
140      PRINT "TOTAL SALES FOR SALESMAN "J, "$" S
150   NEXT J
900   DATA 1.25, 4.30, 2.50
910   DATA 40, 20, 37, 29, 42
920   DATA 10, 16, 3, 21, 8
930   DATA 35, 47, 29, 16, 33
999   END

RUN

SALES1        10:50

TOTAL SALES FOR SALESMAN 1                    $180.5
TOTAL SALES FOR SALESMAN 2                    $211.3
TOTAL SALES FOR SALESMAN 3                    $131.65
TOTAL SALES FOR SALESMAN 4                    $166.55
TOTAL SALES FOR SALESMAN 5                    $169.4

TIME:   0 SECS.
```

will be greater than the terminal value (TO) and the program will branch to the next statement following NEXT (Figs. 17.23, 17.24).

FILE INPUT/OUTPUT STATEMENTS

GET *The GET statement causes values to be read from the named file and assigned to the variables included in the GET statement* (Fig. 17.25). If the file is inactive, GET activates it for input and positions it to the beginning; if the file is active, it must be an input file.

90 GET 'IN',X,Y,Z

Files are always represented as character constants in GET (and PUT) statements. Thus the GET statement reads three values from the file named IN and assigns those values to X,Y, and Z respectively.

PUT *The PUT statement has the opposite effect of GET; that is, it writes the specified values into the named file* (Fig. 17.26). If the file is inactive, PUT activates it for output and positions it to the beginning. If the file is active, it must be an output file.

Figure 17–25. Searching a File for a Single Value.

```
logon w0004
THANK YOU.            DATE 12/30/7    TIME 11.50.22
READY edit qtl basic
EDIT  10 get 'qf', m,d,y,p
EDIT  20 if y>69 then 90
EDIT  30 if p < h then 10
EDIT  40 let h = p
EDIT  50 let ml = m
EDIT  60 let dl = d
EDIT  70 let yl = y
EDIT  80 go to 10
EDIT  90 print 'high price:'
EDIT  100 print using 110, ml, dl, yl, h
EDIT  110 :##/##/##      $##.##
EDIT  120 end
EDIT  save
EDIT  run
HIGH PRICE:
1/26/69      $52.00
EDIT  end
READY logoff
LOGGED OFF AT 11.54.44
TIME USED 00.04.22
```

Figure 17–26. The Output Data File.

```
logon w0004
THANK YOU.            DATE 12/16/7     TIME 14.24.56
READY edit int basic
EDIT  10 read p
EDIT  20 data 1000.00
EDIT  30 for t = 1 to 10
EDIT  40 for r = 1 to 20
EDIT  50 let a = p*(1+r/100)**t
EDIT  60 put 'tf',t,r,a
EDIT  70 next r
EDIT  80 next t
EDIT  90 end
EDIT  save
EDIT  run
EDIT  end
READY logoff
LOGGED OFF AT 14.30.39
TIME USED 00.05.43
```

120 PUT 'OU',X,SQR(X)

This PUT statement writes the value of X and its square root in OU.

CLOSE *The CLOSE statement "deactivates" a file; such a file can subsequently be reactivated for input or output, regardless of its previous use* (Fig. 17.27). Consider this example:

```
 40 PUT 'OU',X,Y,Z
      .
      .
 90 CLOSE'OU'
100 GET 'OU',A,B,C
```

Statement 40 activates file OU for output and writes the values X,Y, and Z in that file. The CLOSE statement deactivates OU. This deactivation allows OU to be used for input in the GET statement following CLOSE. Note that the GET statement is reactivating OU for input, repositions it to the beginning and therefore assigns the *first* three values A,B, and C.

Notice what happens when an input file is closed and reactivated as an output file.

```
 .
 .
 .
40 get 'af', a, b, c, d, e
50 let b = a
60 let a = 36
70 let c = c+b
80 let d = a/b
90 let e = a**3
100 close 'af'
110 put 'af', a, b, c, d, e
 .
 .
 .
```

A previously created file, named 'AF,' is activated for input in statement 40 and five values are made available to the program. In statements 50 through 90, new values are acquired for A, B, C, D, and E. Statement 100 deactivates 'AF' as an input file; statement 110 reopens the file for output and places the new values for A through E into the file. Actually 'AF' is now a new file and any values could be placed in it, not necessarily A, B, C, D, and E.

Figure 17–27. CLOSE Statement—Example.

OTHER STATEMENTS

DIM *The DIM statement is used to create lists and tables to be used in the program.* The DIM statement informs the computer to set aside sufficient storage for the list or table (Fig. 17.28). For example,

20 DIM H(35).

This statement will allow the user to enter a list of 35 items.

```
10 dim x(5), y(12)
20 input x(1), x(2), x(3), x(4), x(5), y(4)
```

The DIM statement says that X is an array representing five arithmetic values and Y is an array representing twelve arithmetic values. The INPUT statement says that you will assign values to all five members of X and to the fourth member of Y. Execution of the INPUT statement causes the computer to print a question mark (?) at the terminal. A valid response would be:

```
? 25, 33, 17, 62, 95, 43
```

The first five values of the input line are assigned to X(1) through X(5), respectively. The last value is assigned to Y(4).

Figure 17–28. DIM Statement—Example.

END *Every program must have an END statement and it must be the statement with the highest line number.* For example,

999 END

REMARK *The REMARK statement is used to write comments for a particular program* (Fig. 17.29). The computer generates no instructions for these statements other than including them in the program listing.

10 REM this is a Remark
20 REM so is this

Figure 17–29. REM Statement—Example.

```
10  REM THIS PROGRAM DETERMINES THE COST PER UNIT
```

CORRECTIONS TO A BASIC PROGRAM

Corrections can be made to a BASIC program as it is being inputted through the teletypewriter, as follow:

1. *To correct an entire line.* Retype the line correctly using the original line number and end it with a carriage return.
2. *To delete a line.* Retype the *line number only and* follow it with a carriage return.
3. *To correct a character in a line.* Depress the backspace key. Then type the correct character. The character will not be erased from the page, but it will be deleted from the computer storage. For example, LEZ ← T Z = 4. If several incorrect characters have been typed backspace once for each incorrect character (including spaces) and then retype the correct characters.
4. If an *instruction has been omitted* several lines back, just type it in with the correct line number. The computer will automatically arrange it in the proper sequence.

If you have made numerous corrections, just type LIST followed by a carriage return and the computer will type out a list of the corrected program.

Once you are convinced that the program is correct, type RUN followed by a carriage return.

If you wish to save your program, type SAVE *before* you type the END statement, depress RETURN key and wait for the computer to answer. Unless you save your program before you logoff, the computer will "forget" it as soon as you sign off. To recall the saved program, all that is needed after the READY statement when you sign on is the name of the program that you have saved (Figs. 17.30, 17.31, 17.32).

SUMMARY

One of the major requirements for conversational time sharing is a programming language that the computer understands. BASIC is a precise, simple, easy-to-understand users' language that minimizes the clerical task of "set up." It provides the user with efficient, rapid, flexible, and precise problem-solving activities combined with ease of use and learning. Users can create, execute, debug, and save BASIC programs from typewriter-like terminals, conveniently located in classrooms, offices, or laboratories which may be far removed from the central computer. BASIC programming not only provides a sound basis for future programming efforts in the more complex pro-

```
010 PRINT "THIS PRØGRAM CØMPUTES THE DIAMETER AND AREA"
020 PRINT "ØF A CIRCLE AS A FUNCTIØN ØF THE RADIUS."
030 PRINT
040 PRINT "R", "D", "A"
050 READ R
060 LET D=2*R
070 LET A=R↑2*3.14159
080 PRINT R, D, A
090 GØ TØ 050
100 DATA 1,2,3,4,5
999 END
```

When this program is run, the following is printed:

```
CIRC-1     14:18

THIS PRØGRAM CØMPUTES THE DIAMETER AND AREA
ØF A CIRCLE AS A FUNCTIØN ØF THE RADIUS.

R               D               A
 1              2                3.14159
 2              4                12.5664
 3              6                28.2743
 4              8                50.2654
 5              10               78.5398

ØUT ØF DATA IN  50
```

Figure 17–30. Sample BASIC Program.

```
1 PRINT "DO YOU WANT INSTRUCTIONS(YES=0,NO=1)";
100 INPUT Z
110 IF Z=1 THEN 170
120 PRINT "THE INTEGRAND IS INSERTED AS STATEMENT 1000."
130 PRINT"I.E. 1000 DEF FNA(X)=2*(X↑2)"
135 PRINT"CHANGES MAY BE MADE ONLY ON THE RIGHT OF THE EQUAL SIGN."
137 PRINT "TO DO INTEGRATION RUN PROGRAM TAKING 'NO' BRANCH."
140 PRINT"THE PROGRAM WILL REQUEST THE UPPER AND LOWER LIMITS WHEN NEEDED
150 GO TO 99999
160 REM READ IN THE NUMBER OF POINTS
170 READ N
180 FOR I=1 TO N
190 READ U(I),R(I)
200 NEXT I
210 PRINT "WHAT ARE THE LOWER AND UPPER LIMITS";
220 INPUT A,B
230 LET S=0
240 FOR I=1 TO N
250 LET X = A + (B - A) * U(I)
260 LET  S = S + R(I) * FNA(X)
270 NEXT I
280 PRINT "THE ANSWER IS " S*(B-A)
300 DATA 7
310 DATA .025446,.064742,.129234,.139853
320 DATA .297077,.190915,.500000,.208980
330 DATA .702922,.190915,.870766,.139853
340 DATA .974554,.064742
1000 DEF FNA(X)=2*X
99999END
```

Figure 17–31. Sample BASIC Program.

gramming languages, but eliminates many of the problems in formulating data required by other programming languages as well.

It is the intent of this chapter to introduce the basic concepts of the programming language, BASIC.

I. *BASIC Programming.*
   A. *Operation.*
      1. User types problem-solving statements at the terminal keyboard.
      2. User programs and data are transmitted to the central computer.
      3. Messages and output data printed at terminal upon the user's request.
      4. Computer and user in constant conversation.
      5. Many users sharing the same facilities of computer with each user unaware of any activity of another but aware only of his own program.
   B. *Features.*
      1. Build and execute programs.

```
THIS PROGRAM PRINTS OUT A DEPRECIATION SCHEDULE BASED ON STRAIGHT-LINE METHOD,
DECLINING-BALANCE METHOD, AND SUM-OF-DIGITS METHOD.  YOU WILL BE ABLE TO COMPUTE
YOUR PROBLEMS BY ENTERING THE DATA YOU WISH TO COMPUTE.  THE DATA SHOULD BE ENTERED
AS LISTED COST, SCRAP VALUE, NUMBER OF YEARS AND LIMIT. . . . .USING COMMAS TO SEPARATE
EACH VALUE ONLY.  FOR EXAMPLE:
                          COST?    SCRAP?    YEARS?    LIMIT?
                          7000.00,    400.00,    6,    6,


    COST?    SCRAP?    YEARS?    LIMIT?

 ?  6000,1680,8,5



                                   DEPRECIATION SCHEDULE


    COST  6000                  SCRAP  1680                YEARS  8                     LIMIT 5
**************************************************************************************************

                   DEPRECIATION                                          BOOK VALUE


    YEAR     ST-LINE      DEC-BAL      SUM-DIGITS      ST-LINE    DEC-BAL         SUM-DIGITS

     1     $ 540.00     $1500.00        $ 960.00     $ 5460.00  $ 4500.00       $ 5040.00
     2     $ 540.00     $1125.00        $ 840.00     $ 4920.00  $ 3375.00       $ 4200.00
     3     $ 540.00     $ 843.75        $ 720.00     $ 4380.00  $ 2531.25       $ 3480.00
     4     $ 540.00     $ 632.81        $ 600.00     $ 3840.00  $ 1898.44       $ 2880.00
     5     $ 540.00     $ 474.61        $ 480.00     $ 3300.00  $ 1423.83       $ 2400.00
EDIT  end
```

Figure 17–32. Sample BASIC Program.

```
00001  PRINT'THIS PROGRAM PRINTS OUT A DEPRECIATION SCHEDULE BASED ON STRAIGHT-LINE METHOD,'
00002  PRINT'DECLINING-BALANCE METHOD, AND SUM-OF-DIGITS METHOD.  YOU WILL BE ABLE TO COMPUTE'
00003  PRINT'YOUR PROBLEMS BY ENTERING THE DATA YOU WISH TO COMPUTE.  THE DATA SHOULD BE ENTERED'
00004  PRINT'AS LISTED COST, SCRAP VALUE, NUMBER OF YEARS AND LIMIT. . . . .USING COMMAS TO SEPARATE'
00005  PRINT'EACH VALUE ONLY.  FOR EXAMPLE:'
00006  PRINT'                          COST?    SCRAP?    YEARS?    LIMIT?'
00007  PRINT'                          7000.00,    400.00,    6,    6,'
00008  PRINT
00009  PRINT
00010 PRINT'     COST?     SCRAP?     YEARS?     LIMIT?'
00011 PRINT
00012  INPUT C, S, Y, L
00013 PRINT
00014 PRINT
00015 PRINT
00016 PRINT
00017 PRINT'                                   DEPRECIATION SCHEDULE'
00018 PRINT
00019 PRINT
00022 PRINT'    COST ';C,'      SCRAP ';S,'     YEARS ';Y,'      LIMIT ';L
00023 PRINT'**************************************************************************************************'
00024 PRINT
00025 PRINT'                   DEPRECIATION                                          BOOK VALUE'
00026 PRINT
00027 PRINT
00030 PRINT'    YEAR     ST-LINE      DEC-BAL      SUM-DIGITS      ST-LINE    DEC-BAL         SUM-DIGITS'
00031 PRINT
00035 T1 = 0
00036 D1 = 0
00037 M1 = 0
00040 V = 0
00042 B =0
00044 X1 = 0
00046 I =0
00048 R =1.00 /Y
00050 IF X1 = Y THEN 60
00052 X1 =X1 +1
00054 I =I +X1
00055 GO TO 50
00060 V=V+1
00070 T= (C-S) *R
00080 D=(C-B) *2*R
00090 B=B+D
00100 M=(C-S)*(Y/I)
00101 T1 =T1+T
00102 A1 =C - T1
00103 D1 = D1 + D
00104 A2 = C - D1
00105 M1 =M1 +M
00106 A3 = C - M1
00110 PRINT USING 120, V,T,D,M,A1,A2,A3
00120 :      ##      $####.##      $####.##        $####.##      $#####.##    $#####.##       $#####.##
00130 Y=Y-1
00140 IF V=L THEN 160
00150 GO TO 60
00160 END
EDIT  save
EDIT  end
READY
```

2. Test and debug programs dynamically.
3. Build and modify texts.
4. Save programs and/or texts for future use.
5. Each user has own unique identifier code (password).
6. BASIC is designed to detect a large variety of errors.
7. A common library can be provided available to all users.

C. *Terminal Operating Procedures.*
1. Push ORIG button.
2. Listen for dial tone.
3. Dial number of computer.
4. After beep sound, type identification number.
5. Enter program (new or old).
6. When program is finished and executed, type BYE.

II. *IBM ITF:BASIC*

A. *Operation.*
1. Set the terminal code switch to the COM position.
2. Set the terminal power switch to ON position.
3. If terminal is equipped with dial-up mechanism, the following instructions are followed, otherwise skip to step 4.
   a) Depress the TALK button on the telephone.
   b) Dial number of computer.
   c) When you hear beep sound, depress DATA button which will turn the light on.
4. When connection is made, identify yourself to the computer with LOGON command and password.
5. The system cue response READY indicates that you are in the *Control* mode. The Control mode is primarily used for LOGON or LOGOFF or providing access to the *Edit* mode.
6. If you switch to the Edit mode, you will be able to create, update, modify, test, and execute programs.
7. All capitals (upper case) indicate the printing generated by the computer.
8. When you finish, you must be in the Control mode to LOGOFF.
9. LOGOFF will disconnect you from ITF.BASIC and the computer will indicate the time you spent on the terminal between LOGON and LOGOFF.

B. *Control mode and Edit mode commands.*
1. *Control mode.*
   a) DELETE—deletes a file or collection from the user's library.
   b) EDIT—enters Edit mode for programming writing.
   c) LISTCAT—provides a listing of all programs in the user's private library.

d) LOGON—identifies user to ITF:BASIC and initializes terminal session.
e) LOGOFF—ends user's terminal session.

2. *Edit mode.*
   a) DELETE—delete line from the "current" collection.
   b) END—ends Edit mode and returns to Control mode.
   c) LIST—lists part or all of a "current" collection.
   d) RENUM—renumbers the lines of a collection from a specified point.
   e) RUN—executes the current program.
   f) SAVE—saves current collection.

C. *Operation of ITF:BASIC programs.*
1. LOGON—identifies user to system.
2. READY—identifies program and switches to Edit mode.
3. EDIT—writes program.
4. EDIT list—types out entire program stored in computer.
5. EDIT run—causes program to be executed.
6. EDIT save—causes program to be saved in user's private library.
7. EDIT end—system reverts back to Control mode.
8. READY—either new program is created or session is terminated (LOGOFF).

III. *Elements of BASIC Programming.*

A. *Program Definition.* A set of instructions used to tell a computer how to provide an answer to some problem.

B. *Instructions*—each line is a *statement* beginning with a line number that specifies the order of execution of a program.

C. *Elements of BASIC instructions.*
1. *Character set*—numerals, letters, and special characters.
2. *Statement number*—one to four digits 1–9999.
3. *Label*—any group of characters enclosed in quotation marks.
4. *Constant*—unchanged value either positive or negative.
5. *Variable*—a letter which may be followed by a number whose value may change many times during the execution of a program.
6. *Numbers*—up to nine digits, either positive or negative.
7. *Formulas*—used in arithmetic calculations.
8. *Arithmetic operators*—Addition (+), subtraction (−), multiplication (*), division (/), exponentiation (↑ or ** ITF:BASIC).
9. *Comparison operators*—Equal to (=), less than (<), less than or equal to (<=), greater than (>), greater than or equal to (>=), not equal to (< >).

D. *Statements.*
   1. *Assignment.*
      a) LET—a command to the computer to perform some computation.
   2. *Input and output.*
      a) READ and DATA—used to assign to listed variable values determined from a DATA statement.
      b) PRINT—used to get data out of computer in the form of a printed report.
      c) INPUT—used to enter data during the running of the program.
      d) PRINT USING—used in conjunction with an image statement to print value according to the format specifications in the image statement.
   3. *Sequence Control.*
      a) GO TO—causes control to be transferred conditionally or unconditionally to a specified statement.
      b) IF THEN—used when it is desired to skip the normal sequence of command if a certain condition exists.
      c) FOR NEXT—used in loops, one at the entrance and other at the exit directing the computer back to the entry.
   4. *File Input/output.*
      a) GET—causes value to be read from the named file and assigned to the variables included in the GET statement.
      b) PUT—has the opposite effect of the GET statement; it writes the specified values into the named file.
      c) CLOSE—deactivates a file.
   5. *Other statements.*
      a) DIM—used to create lists and tables to be used in a program.
      b) END—must be included in every program to signal the end of the program.
      c) REMARK—used to write comment(s) for particular program.

IV. *Corrections to a BASIC Program.*
   A. *Correct an entire line* by using the original line number and retyping the entire line.
   B. *To delete a line*—type line number only.
   C. *To correct a character in a line*—depress backspace key or arrow and type corrected character.
   D. *To type in an omitted instruction*—type omitted instruction using correct line number.
   E. *To save a program*—type the word SAVE before END.

F. *If numerous corrections have been made*—type word LIST and the computer will type out a list of the corrected program.

In all of the above statements, each line typed should be followed by a carriage return.

IDENTIFICATION QUESTIONS

Match the following terms with the statements that follow.

A. Basic
B. Close
C. Control Mode
D. Dim
E. Edit Mode
F. End
G. For Next
H. Get
I. Go To
J. If Then
K. Input
L. Let
M. Line Number
N. List
O. Password
P. Print
Q. Put
R. Read
S. Remarks
T. Statement
U. Text
V. Variable

1. A mode used to create, update, modify, test, or execute programs in ITF: BASIC.
2. One letter or any letter followed by a number used to identify an item.
3. A statement that allows the user to assign values dynamically during the execution of the program.
4. This statement writes the specified values in a named file.
5. This statement must appear in every program.
6. Beginners All Purpose Language.
7. A user identifier-code.
8. A statement that evaluates an expression and assigns it one or more variables.
9. A statement that causes control to be transferred conditionally or unconditionally to another statement.
10. Statements that are used when it is desirable to skip the normal sequence of commands if a certain condition exists.
11. The statement that "deactivates" the file.
12. This statement is used to write comments in a program.
13. A collection line that is typed at the terminal.
14. Each line of the program.
15. A statement used to assign to the listed variables values determined by a DATA statement.
16. Statements that are used in loops, one at the entrance, the other at the exit, directing control back to the entrance.
17. This statement is used to create lists and tables to be used in the program.
18. This statement is used to print some or all of a "current" collection.
19. A mode primarily used for logging on or off the computer in ITF:BASIC.
20. Identifies the line.
21. A statement that is used to get information out of the computer in a printed format.

22. This statement causes values to be read from a named file and assigned to variables.

QUESTIONS FOR REVIEW

1. What two things are necessary to know before one can access a central computer from a time sharing terminal?
2. What are the two basic requirements necessary before a program can be successfully executed?
3. How does BASIC fulfill all the requirements of a time sharing programming language?
4. What steps are involved in identifying oneself to the system?
5. How does one identify themselves using ITF:BASIC?
6. What is the difference between the Control and Edit modes in ITF: BASIC? How is each used?
7. List the steps involved in a typical ITF:BASIC program.
8. How is a BASIC program written and how does it operate?
9. Name some of the basic elements of a BASIC program.
10. What are the main functions of the LET, READ, PRINT, and INPUT statements? Give examples of each.
11. What are the main uses of a PRINT statement?
12. What is the principal use of the PRINT USING statement?
13. Differentiate the uses of the GO TO, IF THEN, and FOR NEXT statements. Give examples of each.
14. What are the uses of the GET, PUT, and CLOSE statements?
15. What purpose does the DIM, END, and REMARKS statement serve?
16. What types of corrections can be made to a BASIC program before it is executed?
17. How may a BASIC program be "saved" in the computer?

PART VII / COMPUTER SYSTEMS AND MANAGEMENT

CHAPTER 18

Computer Systems—Mini, Small, and Super Computers, Virtual Storage

Computers, in their early stages, were classified on the basis of their monthly rentals: small, medium, or large. Now, with new breeds of computers for the masses being introduced almost daily, we have micro, mini, small, larger, and super computers on the market. Computer technology has swept past its accepted definitional confines so far and so fast that as yet there are no generally accepted definitions in the files for these new groups of computers. The current divisions according to an authority are:

—A microcomputer costs less than $8,000.
—A minicomputer costs less than $40,000.
—A small computer costs less than $200,000.
—An ordinary or regular computer costs less than $1 million.
—A large computer costs less than $5 million.
—A super computer costs more than $5 million.

MINI-COMPUTERS

The minicomputer industry was born with the first delivery of the PDP-8 in 1965. These early machines were dedicated to specific applications. Today, there are several dozen manufacturers making general purpose minicomputers that cover the entire spectrum of computer applications.

There is no generally accepted definition of the term "mini" but an overall definition would be, "A general purpose small computer, using a word length from 12 to 16 bits, with an average storage capacity of 16,000 bytes and costing about $25,000."

All manufacturers offer peripherals (card readers, tape units, printers, etc.) to increase the power of the computer, but these peripherals are expensive in relation to the cost of the central processing unit. A wide range of instruction sets are also offered by the manufacturers to make their systems easy to program and efficient to operate. Some of them offer microprogramming through the addition of writeable control storage.

Minicomputers in their early stages were marketed exclusively to OEM (original equipment manufacturers) who incorporated them into sophisticated systems, machine tools, or multiple-station data input devices. Today minicomputers are used as stand-alone computers capable of operating independently with software packages such as FORTRAN, COBOL, RPG, and BASIC compilers. They are often used as remote job entry terminals for a centralized computer. Vast numbers of minicomputers are being delivered for direct communications applications (Figs. 18.1, 18.2).

The minicomputer explosion is not limited merely to traditional usage in control, scientific, time sharing, and data communications applications; the mini is also turning up more and more in offbeat applications. In short, the minicomputer, normally looked upon as just another electronics black box, can be fun.

A few years ago, a computer manufacturer offered a minicomputer through a fashionable department store Christmas catalog. The so-called "kitchen computer" was programmed to provide menus and recipe references to five famous cookbooks. The computer could also be used for checkbook balancing and other household tasks.

Minicomputers were even the object of violence during the college student outbreaks of several years ago. In the absence of an accessible data processing center at one Boston area university, a group of self-appointed

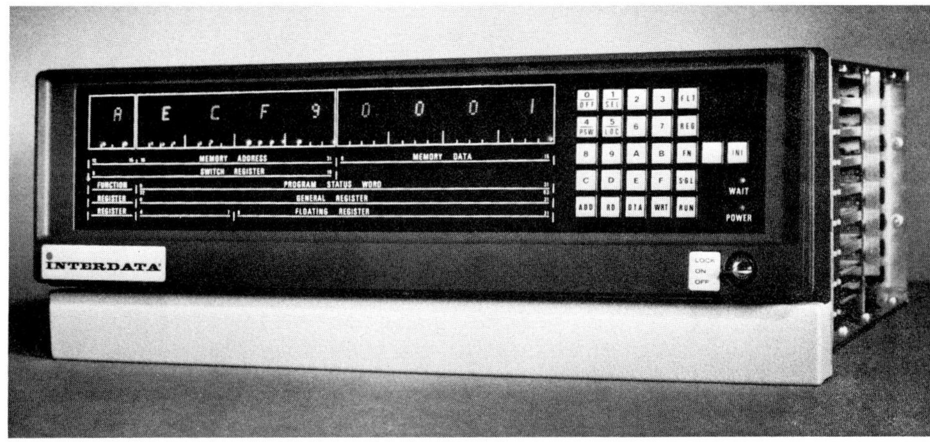

Figure 18–1. Interdata Minicomputer.

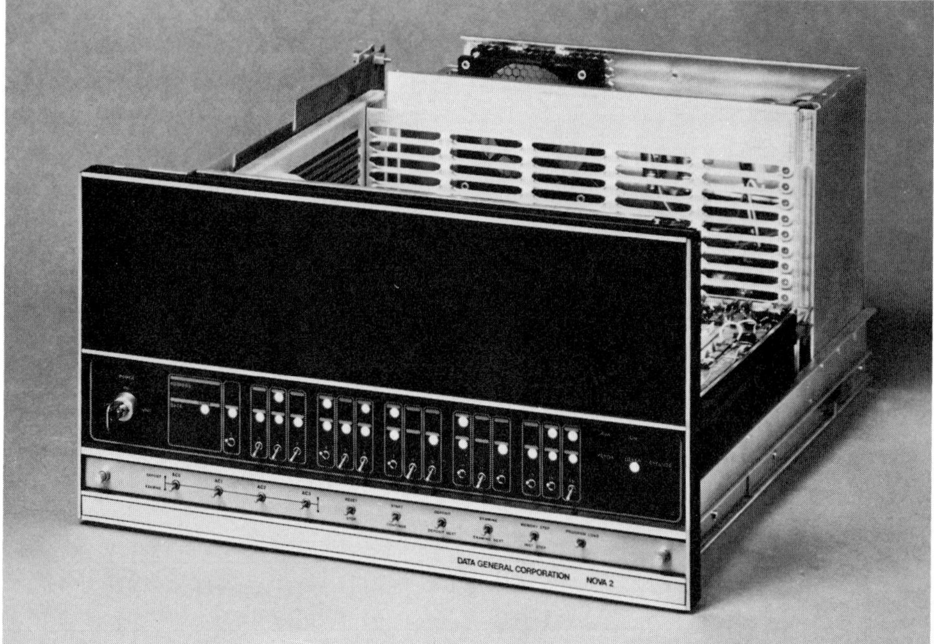

Figure 18–2. Minicomputer.

radical students set fire to the minicomputer. After the fire was extinguished, the casing was taken off the machine and soot and debris fell into the printed circuit boards. But when the minicomputer was plugged in, it still worked!

As an educational and vocational tool, the minicomputer is turning up just about everywhere. Besides the expected places like elementary and secondary schools and colleges, machines are used in prison as a vocational tool. Officers play war games on a time shared minicomputer at the Armed Forces Staff College in Norfolk, Virginia.

It is only natural that minis work their way into sports. The animated display scoreboard is used by many teams to keep a running record of the event in progress. At any given time, it can flash spot announcements, animate events, give newscasts, and lead in sing-alongs and cheers.

Many people take a mini home with them to continue working on a project they started at their regular job (inevitably, the children use the machine). Some people run stock market analyses for business or pleasure; others conduct laboratory and scientific tests.

What of the future? While many are predicting the widespread growth of minis in the home and office, there are indications that they will touch people increasingly in unusual ways. We have seen them being used in the Los Angeles Freeway System. A few years ago, minis began to play an important role in the automation of Paris' Metro system. By now that application is taken for granted. And lately, a mini has been operating an experimental driverless taxi in England. The passenger simply inserts a magnetically encoded ticket into a slot in the taxi and he is whisked to his destination. Perhaps, that application will be taken for granted in a few years.

More than anything, though, it is the sheer force of the minicomputer boom that is likely to spread the unusual applications. And in this very regard, the vast increase of machines in use will cause the unit price to decline. In five years, it is expected that minis will sell for less than $1,000.

Equally important, minicomputer peripheral prices have begun to decline at an even faster rate than central processing units, with the result that system costs are dropping rapidly. All this simply adds up to the fact that the only ultimate limits to the use of and market for minicomputers are those of the human imagination (Fig. 18.3).

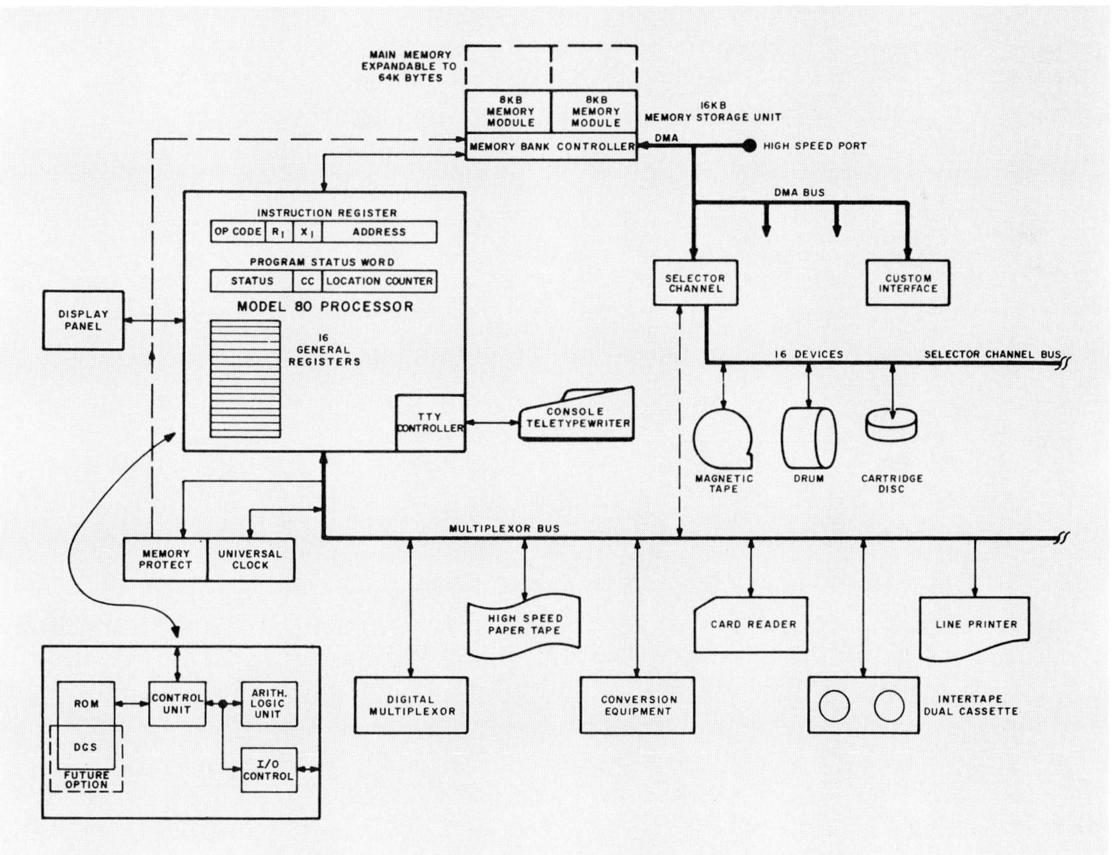

Figure 18–3. Interdata Minicomputer Model 80—Schematic.

Thus, the *function* of the minicomputer is more necessary than ever. In some situations, this function can be replaced by today's or tomorrow's electronics; in others—enough to triple the number of minis in use by the mid-1970s—minicomputers will keep doing their thing.

MICROPROGRAMMING

Higher level programs are difficult to implement on minis, because compilers and compiled programs demand large amounts of memory. But more and more users want to program in higher level languages such as COBOL and FORTRAN. As a result, mini makers have found that they must tailor their architecture to the language and its compiler, rather than the other way around. Microprograms are designed to accomplish this.

Prior to the middle or even late 1960s, this approach could not be accomplished economically, due to the cost and speed of most available memory. During the last few years, however, advances in computer technology (lowering of prices) have contributed to microprogramming's use. And as costs continue to plunge, the use of microprogramming will inevitably increase.

Microprogramming is a method of putting only the most fundamental instructions in hardware and using memory to bring these together in a combination of microprograms that are useful to the programmer.

Advantages quoted by mini manufacturers are: greater flexibility in tailoring systems to specific needs; programming at lower costs with increased efficiency; more accurate system checkout and fault detection; easier field changes and expansions at greater economies; and better emulation of other processors and the various types of peripherals that might be needed.

PROS AND CONS OF MICROPROGRAMMING

Microprogramming is a mystery to many. In the most simplistic of terms, it is a way to replace circuits with little programs; it is effective only when these programs are put in a control memory, or store, that operates many times faster than the computer's main memory.

Writable control programs have more flexibility. But the method of writing into them, via a disk, for example, has been controlled by the manufacturer so that he has the final say over what instructions the computer can execute. But with some products, the mini maker has given users the ability to modify memory. Yet there are some serious disadvantages.

For one thing, modifying a system via microprogramming requires the user to be not only versed in programming, but because of its close relationship with hardware, with computer architecture as well. This is a rare bird, and unless he is a careful one he can end up with problems as a result of microprogramming—even with a workable system—that will more than offset the sought-after improvements in system flexibility.

Additionally, there is the question of control. Who will be permitted access to the control memory to make changes? And, once the system has been changed, what about maintenance and documentation? Since the system no longer looks like the one that left the factory, it is difficult to expect the manufacturer to be able to maintain it without added costs. And what about manufacturer-supplied diagnostics, debugging, and other microroutines generally supplied free of charge with the system? Once the control memory is altered, these may be rendered virtually useless.

In summary, with alterable control memory, the user must be ready to commit the necessary time and funds to support what he creates. This may ultimately be more costly to implement and support in a microprogrammed system than dealing with the inefficiencies of a conventional mini.

REMOTE JOB ENTRY (RJE) TERMINALS

Terminal-oriented computing is a fact of data processing life. Remote locations transmit data over communication lines to their control computing facility for processing and return. It is a swift and economical way to move large volumes of data at high speeds; the terminal can read all the data for a job or a series of jobs at one time, send it out for processing and upon its return, display the results in a printed or other form of output (Figs. 18.4, 18.5, 18.6).

In the world of data processing, remote locations are remote in name only. Data communications has moved branch offices, plants, warehouses, and other remotely located sites into the data processing mainstream of the decentralized organization. Through the use of a data communication system, these locations have full use of the centralized computing facilities. Data moves from the remote location to the computer and back again and every-

Figure 18–4. Data 100 Model 78 Programmed Terminal.

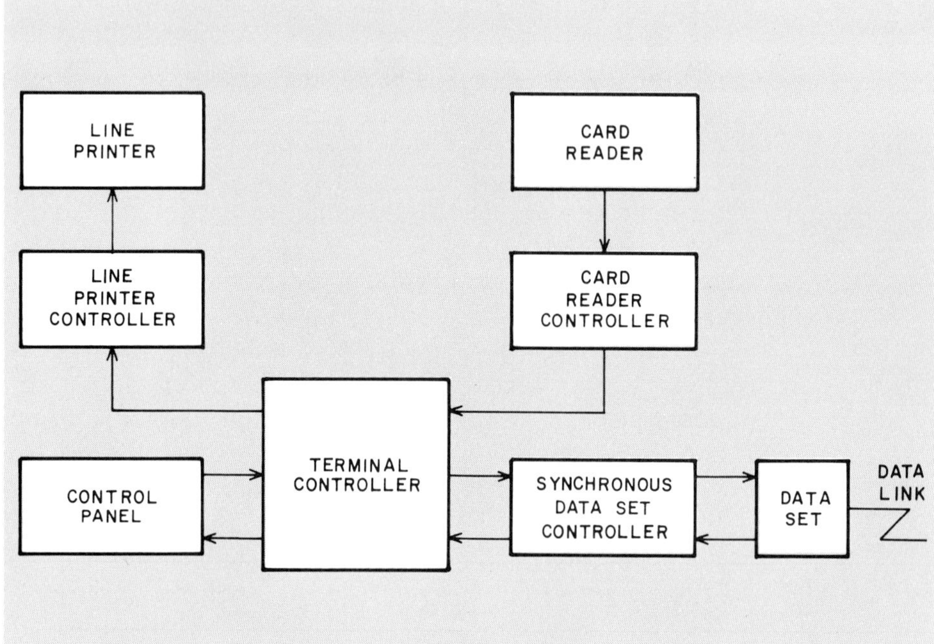

Figure 18–5. Basic Model 78–1 Configuration.

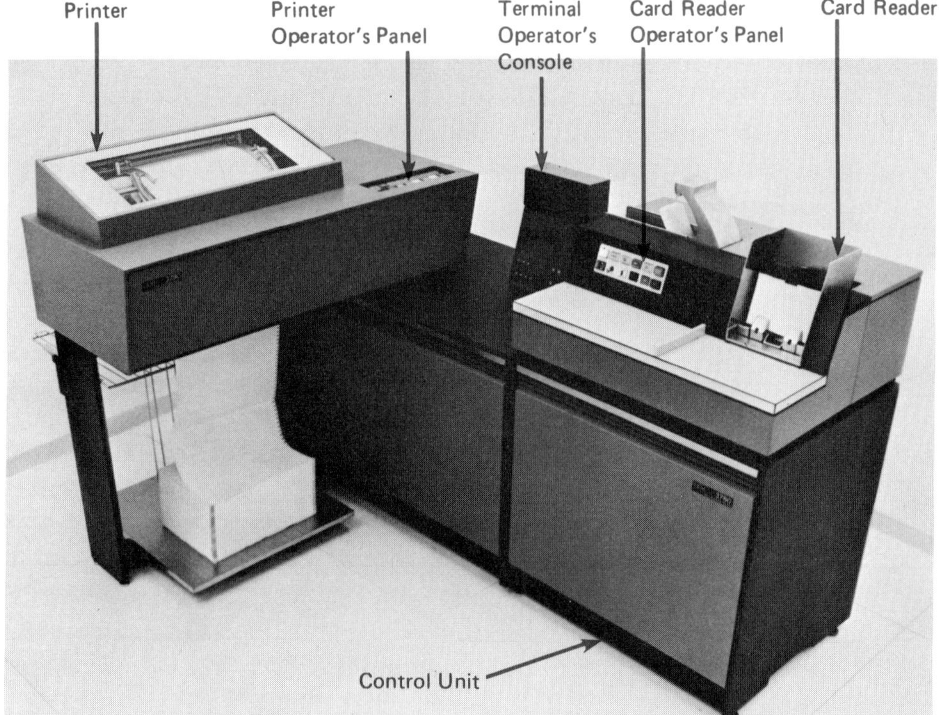

Figure 18–6. IBM 3780 Data Communications Terminal.

body benefits from this round trip. Central management receives timely operating information from all its sources for effective decision making and the specific locations have their processing work load handled without incurring attendant costs for staff or equipment.

Remote job entry is rapidly becoming one of the most active areas of minicomputer applications. Remote batch terminals users plan to increase their terminals installed over the next three years by at least 60 percent, according to a recent survey. Remote job entry techniques and applications have been firmly established for several years; however, recent advances in awareness and understanding of the capability of minicomputers is leading to an explosion in applications involving the marriage of conventional RJE processing with the flexibility of the minicomputer.

Typical examples demonstrating the versatility of RJE terminals utilization are:

—Large organizations with operations widely spread over large geographic areas utilize RJE terminals to enable the various corporate branches to access and update centralized data bases with large computer processing capability to achieve coordinated operation.

—Warehouses and production areas where RJE terminals enable inventory and production levels to be maintained in a central data file accessible to management. In many cases, the RJE terminal prints customers' invoices and shipping labels right at the remote facility under the direction of the large central computer (Fig. 18.7).

—Many universities and college campuses use RJE terminals in their instruction program, and do perform administrative jobs as well, through the use of the central computer. A single RJE terminal may be typically shared by the administrative office, engineering department, data processing, and computer science departments in order to utilize the substantial software application and processing power of the remote central processing unit (Fig. 18.8).

—In these, and many other established RJE terminal applications, the RJE terminal may be used strictly as a data communications terminal or in conjunction with the minicomputer which provides the conventional operations of RJE entry/retrieval, and in addition provides flexibility and efficiency not possible with conventional "fixed logic" or hardware RJE terminals.

COMPONENTS OF RJE TERMINALS

RJE terminals are low-cost, general purpose terminals useable in computer communications systems. The terminal was designed to move data to and from a central computer with speed and efficiency. It is a high-speed, high-volume terminal that can read batched data, transmit it swiftly, assure rapid response time, and then provide the ensuing punching or printing facil-

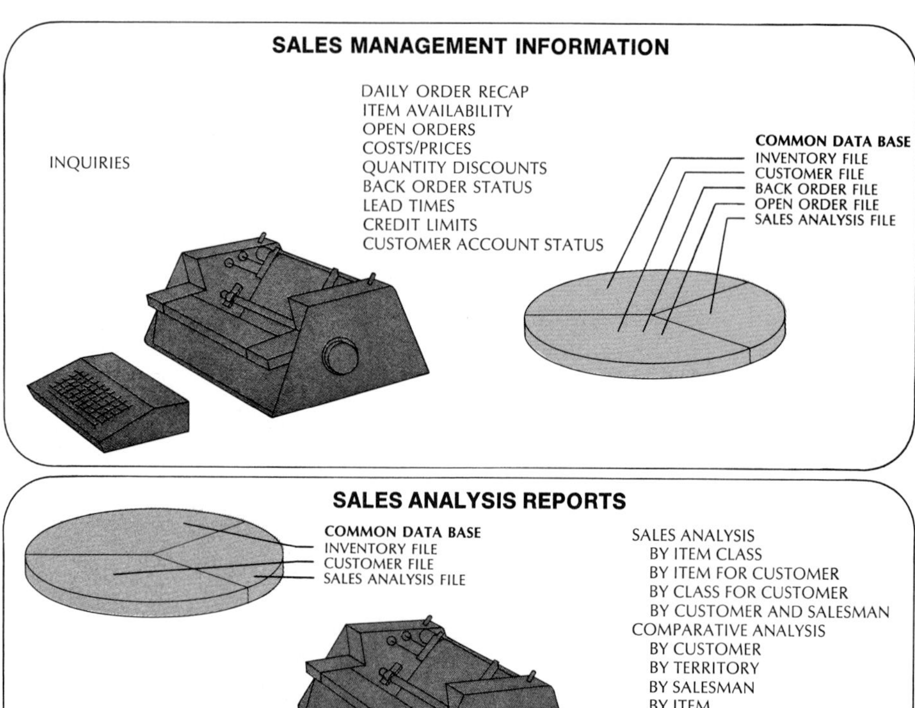

Figure 18–7. Management Reports.

ity at the remote location. As a combination control unit, card reader, card punch, and printer, the terminal concentrates on the vital areas of reading, transmitting, printing, and punching. Basic components of RJE terminals are:

Control Unit. Provides general terminal control functions and serves as an interface between the communications line and the peripheral devices. A multirecord buffer for each peripheral device improves the throughput and efficiency. These buffering techniques provide

1. Consistent transmission rate with variable input/output rates.
2. Overlapping of input/output operations with transmission.
3. Checking of data before printing, punching, or transmission.

Card Reader. A wide spectrum of card readers are available, ranging in speed from 150 to 1,200 cards per minute depending upon the needs of the user. As the cards are being read, they are checked for misrepresentation and invalid punches. The machine has dynamic load and unload capabilities.

Card Punch. The card punches available provide card output on remote terminals. Card punch speeds vary from 20 to 200 cards per minute depending

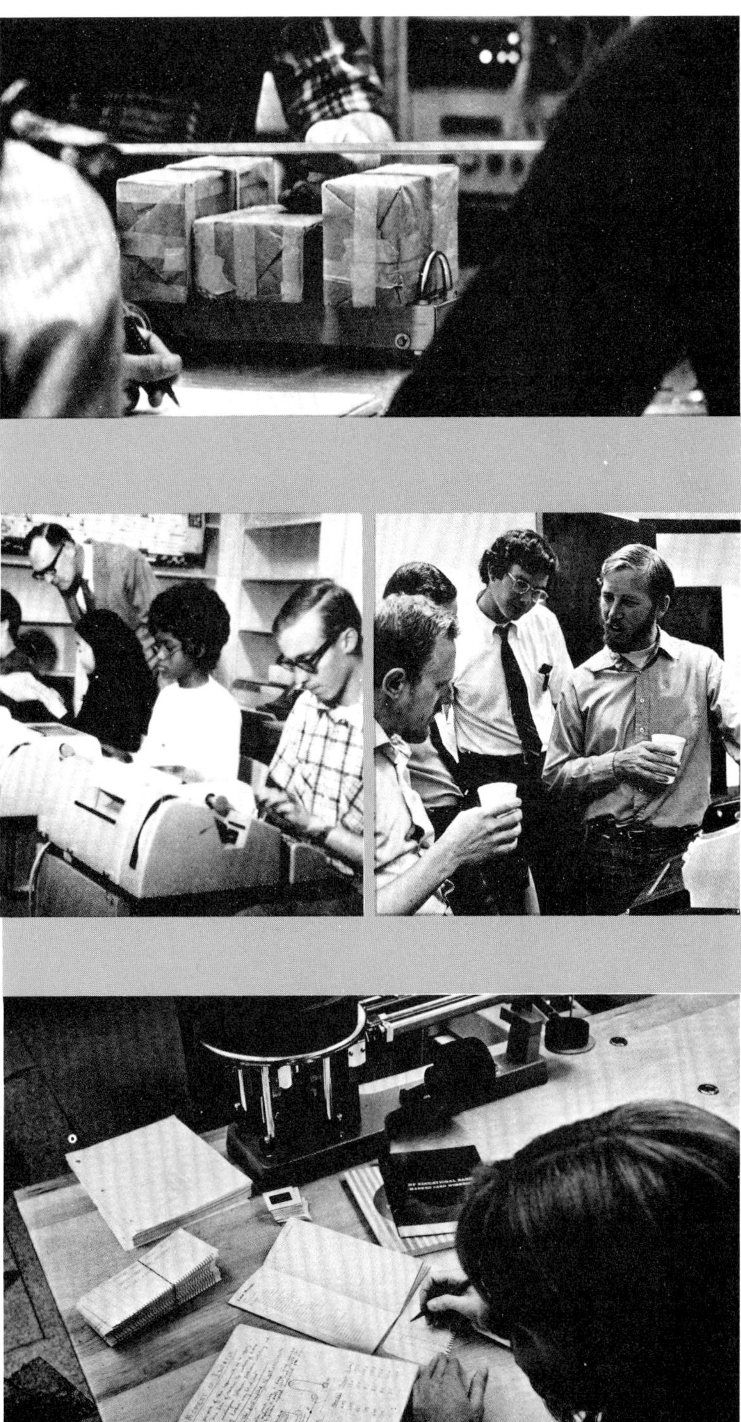

Figure 18–8. Instructional Uses.

upon the needs of the user. Card punches are automatically verified by invalid character check devices.

Printers. To complement the flexibility of the remote terminal, the user may select from a wide range of printer models to match his output requirements. The rated speed of printers is from 50 to 1,500 lines per minute. Vertical form formats, suitable at six or eight lines per inch and a choice of one or two character sets are some of the options available to users (120-column or 132-column print position options are available).

BATCH PROCESSING

The major aspects of batch processing and how the RJE relates to it, follows.

Batch processing systems support multiple jobs by queuing them to be processed into one or more "input job streams," where jobs are brought into storage by the operating system, processed to completion, and placed in an output "job stream" for delivery by the operating system to the designated output device.

Card readers typically provide job input, with printers and card punches receiving the results. Summarizing the major aspects of batch processing:

1. Jobs are "queued" or stacked in an input stream, brought into computer storage, processed to completion, and placed in an output stack or stream for printing or punching of results.
2. Job control information is provided with the input job stream itself. This setup makes it possible to proceed on job processing with a minimum of operator intervention.

REMOTE JOB ENTRY

Remote job entry addresses itself to that task of entering jobs and control information into the job stream and retrieving the processed results from a remote terminal site.

The conventional RJE terminal provides the remote user with the ability to input his job into the central computer's input job stream and retrieve the processed job results at his remote output device. Conventional remote job entry terminals utilize input and output devices typical to the equivalent functions performed at the central facility. For example, a card reader to read punched cards and transmit the data to the remote computer facility, a line printer to print the processed results.

Communications between the RJE terminal and central computer is performed via a data-link consisting of modems and point-to-point or switched phone lines.

Conventional RJE terminals offer a limited choice of data entry techniques and, through a fixed logic or hardwired implementation, provide communication capability with a single manufacturer's central facility.

Remote job entry, being a form of data collection and retrieval, consists of converting data from a "man" readable form into a format acceptable by the computer, entering the data into a format acceptable for communication transmission techniques, and retrieving the data in an intelligible manner. The conventional RJE terminal does little to accommodate the application being served.

In a typical operation, the route from card data input to job entry to the central facility, through the return of the processed job results is tailored to terminal and central computer requirements, not to the requirements or characteristics of the application. It is in the better matching of the application requirements supported by RJE terminals that the minicomputer's programmed flexibility shines.

Before looking at how a minicomputer RJE terminal would better solve the preceding application, let's identify two functional areas which constitute an RJE terminal operation. The RJE/data collection interface makes possible the entry of the "man" readable information into the computer as "machine readable" data. Once accomplished, this "machine readable" data must now be transmitted to the central facility in a format acceptable to the computer's transmission requirements. Returned processed data must now be accepted by the RJE terminal and presented to the user in the most informative way. With a minicomputer, the various RJE terminal functions are performed by programmed instructions which can be tailored to the application and the central computer facility, to optimize each requirement.

The minicomputer enables the data collection procedure to be customized for the application; not vice versa. In many cases, additional bulk storage (such as disk) can be introduced to facilitate accumulation of a local data base for immediate inventory update and order information.

The way the mini can be programmed to accommodate more than one central computer transmission convention, thus allowing a single RJE terminal to access application programs and data bases residing in diverse central facilities, is a further demonstration of the flexibility of the minicomputer for RJE terminal applications.

The minicomputer is just entering the RJE field. As the technologies of computer-communication and minicomputer application programming becomes more coordinated, the 'intelligent" mini-based RJE terminal will attain a predominant place in corporate, educational, and utility operations.

SMALL COMPUTERS

A small computer system may be defined as one which rents for less than $3,000 a month, operates under stored program control, and includes a master file capability. To qualify as a small computer system, the following criteria must be satisfied.

1. The hardware should be a general purpose, user-programmable system capable of accessing at least 1 megabyte of information from a disk or drum. Also, the system must have a high speed printer.
2. The software must include at least skeletal programs for doing engineering, payroll and accounting functions such as accounts payable, payroll, billing, accounts receivable, etc. Additionally the system must be capable of sorting files on the disk or drum.
3. The computer manufacturer must be ready to provide the system on a turnkey basis including installation and training.
4. The system should have communication capabilities to allow it to act as an efficient online terminal to a central computer.
5. Finally, the system should rent for less than $3,000 per month.

These specifications are the general description of an IBM System/3 computer system, the most common small computer system in use today. Since its introduction in 1969, more than 10,000 system/3s have been installed. (Fig. 18.9.)

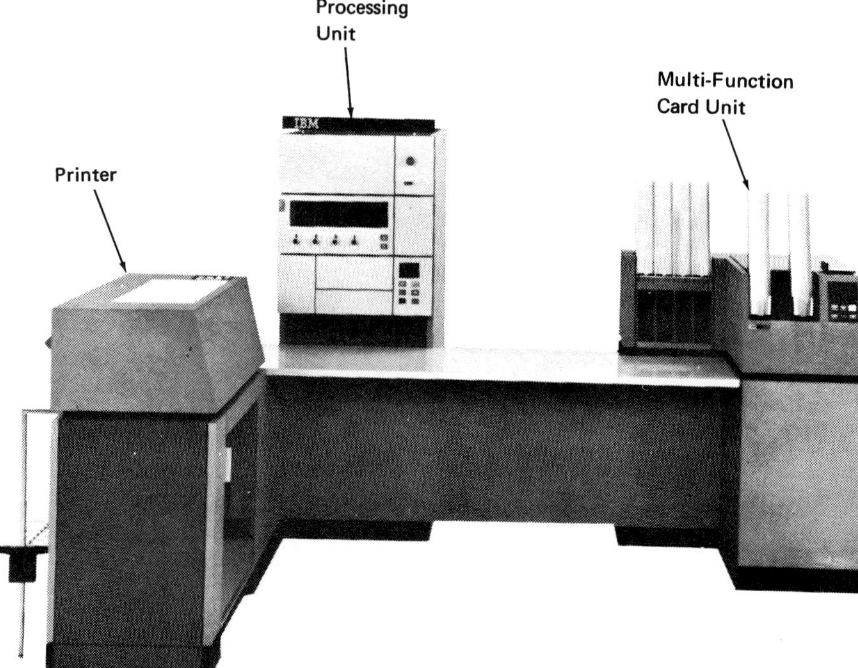

Figure 18–9. IBM System/3.

The IBM System/3 was designed to provide high speed processing capabilities to small data processing installations. Since the main input in these units is the punched card, a 96-column card was designed so that additional information covering a single transaction can be recorded. The system also can accommodate the traditional 80-column card. (More detailed information as to devices, applications and features of the IBM System/3 can be found in the Appendix.)

Another new system recently introduced that is commanding a great deal of attention is the Burroughs B1700. Much technology and design theory have been blended into a product that promises users so much performance and convenience for the price. (Fig. 18.10.)

FEATURES OF SMALL COMPUTERS

1. Storage capabilities ranging from 8,000 to 96,000 bytes allow the user to start with the storage level that efficiently meets their present requirements, and as the work load increases, to add remaining storage increments as needed.
2. Low cost disk devices reduce the cost of online random access to information. Additional data file systems available include compact magnetic tape devices and magnetic tape clusters.
3. Input and output devices for every application includes the new 96-column card equipment as well as the traditional 80-column card equipment. Line printers with speeds from 90 to 1,040 lines per minute are available.

Figure 18–10. Burroughs Model 1700.

4. A full line of terminals and terminal systems are available for such activities as data collection and input, remote site report writing, management information inquiry, and response. Online communication capabilities with other small computer systems and a larger central computer are also available.
5. Program products include software packages that allow the small computer user to operate with application programs written in high level languages such as RPGII, COBOL, FORTRAN, and BASIC. A library of well-designed application programs, such as Accounts Receivable, Billing, Sales Analysis, auxiliary routines for mathematics, and statistics calculations, etc. should significantly reduce the cost and time required to get a small system into productive operation.
6. Multiprogramming is now available so that one can program from job-at-a-time processing to multiprogramming, in which several jobs move forward at the same time. In a multiprogramming environment, the system can accept jobs in any sequence one chooses. In this manner more work is done in less time.

In addition to the two small computer systems mentioned, the IBM System/3 and the Burroughs B1700, there are over twenty-six computer manufacturers that offer products that perform approximately the same functions as those two systems. Between them, these vendors have several thousand systems installed. Every vendor has something worth considering, however, be it price, technological innovation, proximity to prospective clients, or familiarity with specific types of applications.

The potential domestic market for computers in this class is more than 200,000 units, with approximately 25 percent penetration of that market by 1975. Small computers will experience a reduction in price up to 25 percent, during the next four years, it is predicted. These reduced prices, plus increased acceptance by small business operations, will produce an annual sales growth (small computer systems) of approximately 22 percent during the next four years.

The small-scale computer provides management with the same opportunities for improved management efficiency available to users of larger systems. These computers provide a significant advance in computer design technology and should be a vital factor in the data processing field for many years to come.

SUPER COMPUTERS

These ultra high-performance data processing systems were designed for high-speed large-scale scientific and commercial applications. Their scientific applications range from nuclear physics to weather forecasting and theoretical astronomy. In commercial applications, these computers can be used as,

Figure 18–11. IBM System/370 Model 195.

for example, control center of the most complex airline reservation systems, coast-to-coast time sharing networks, or process control systems (Fig. 18.11).

The power and speed of this advanced system are primarily the result of:

1. Improved circuit technology.
2. High performance of buffer storage for main storage accesses.
3. Buffering within the processor.
4. Ultra fast execution time.
5. A high degree of concurrency in operation.
6. Highly efficient algorithms, particularly in floating-point operations.

Processing proceeds concurrently in five separate highly autonomous units; main storage; the storage control unit and buffer storage; the instruction processor; the fixed-point/variable-field-length/decimal processor; and the floating-point processor. Furthermore each unit may be performing several functions at one time. The floating-point processor, for example, can execute as many as three floating-point operations concurrently.

Contributing significantly to the speed and power of these super computers are the main storage capabilities ranging from 1 million to 4 million bytes and a high speed buffer unit, which can sharply reduce the time required for fetching currently used sections of main storage. The storage control unit is an intermediary between main storage and the other system units. As such it controls the accesses to the high-speed buffer and to main storage. As many as thirteen channels may be attached to the central processing unit.

The base rental prices for these computers range from $165,000 to $300,000 monthly, and their purchase prices range from $7 million to $12 million, depending upon the peripherals desired.

VIRTUAL STORAGE

OVERVIEW OF DATA PROCESSING OPERATIONS

Fifteen years ago, central processing units performed instructions in thousandths of a second. Today, CPUs execute instructions in billionths of a second. Main storage sizes have expanded from 16,000 to 4 million bytes. Data transfer rates for some new tape drives are up to twenty times faster than early tape drives. Storage capacity in the new disk drives is twenty-five times larger than the early disk models. Its transfer rate is eight times faster. Improvements just as dramatic have been made in card readers, card punches, and printers. This overview does not even include the new devices for applications such as teleprocessing which did not exist fifteen years ago.

A large amount of software development has accompanied this hardware evolution. Assemblers, compilers, and input/output control systems moved the programmer further from machine coding, enabling him to spend more time solving application problems.

The first operating systems enabled users to batch jobs and run them in a single stream. As CPU speeds became faster and main storage more abundant, operating systems expanded in scope. These new operating systems let users run multiple jobs concurrently—multiprogramming—by sharing the CPU, real storage, and other system resources among active jobs. They also made possible teleprocessing applications that control remote computing and data entry operations from one central location.

These technical developments have meant significant benefits for computer users and their people-system analysts, programmers, computer operators, and so forth. Users can now develop complete sophisticated systems for operational control and management information in contrast to the computer's typically confined payroll and billing applications of ten to fifteen years ago. System resources are shared among several jobs in multiprogramming systems, and among multiple users in time sharing systems. Programmers use procedure-oriented programming languages, such as COBOL, FORTRAN, and PL/1. As a result, programmers can devote more time to problem solution. Operating systems handle much of the job preparation and job-to-job transition that formerly occupied so much of the computer operators' time. Operators can now spend less time handling punched cards and tapes and more time directing system activity, keeping the system *productive*. Thus the programmer and operators who work with the computer and develop the scope of its applications, and computer users in general—all now benefit from the great amount of the past development in hardware and software.

OBJECTIVES FOR DESIGNING NEW FUNCTIONS AND FEATURES FOR A COMPUTER SYSTEM

1. Programmers should have the amount of main storage that they need for designing programs without having to use planned overlay or dynamic management techniques. Even though the size of available computer main storage has increased tremendously, users cut their storage into partitions or regions for multiprogramming efficiency. Programmers, then, are restricted to the size of the largest partition or region used in their installation. This often requires breaking a program into separate steps or using special overlay techniques to make programs "fit" into a region or partition. All of these design requirements add overhead to solving a program.

2. If the program is too large for main storage size, the operating system, not the programmer, should make the program "fit" into main storage.

3. Programs should use system resources—especially main storage—only as required during execution. For example, a program that needs 82,000 bytes of main storage when fully loaded may reference only 22,000 bytes during one part of processing. During this time, there is no need for the operating system to commit main storage to 60,000 unreferenced bytes. An example of such a situation is a teleprocessing application running at less than its maximum load.

4. The operating system should not allow main storage to become fragmented. Assume that several programs are executing, each in its own contiguous area of main storage. Three 15K-byte areas in main storage are idle (none of the executing programs occupy these areas). If the smallest program waiting to begin execution needs 30K bytes of main storage, it must wait until 30K bytes of contiguous main storage becomes available. Until then, a total of 45K bytes of main storage are idle because of storage fragmentation. They are wasted.

5. An operating system should control system resources like main storage in such a way that the user automatically gets a performance improvement by adding more storage. For example, if one has a program that must use overlays because it won't fit into main storage, adding more main storage won't help at all unless the program is redesigned and recoded. It would be nice if the operating system could somehow "automatically" overlay programs and "automatically" use added main storage.

6. A computer user should not be dependent upon the size of the main storage in which programs are executed and in which the operating system is

structured. He should be able to structure a system more according to his *needs* than to the size of main storage.

7. Main storage should be shared dynamically among the active jobs in the stream. Programs should get the main storage that they need when they need it. In other words, the system should be a captive to the demands of the systems' activities, and not the other way around.

8. Scheduling and operating a system should be easier. Operating systems, for example, still require a large amount of user participation in order to achieve good scheduling and operating results.

Most items in this list of objectives relate in some way to how an operating system manages a computer's main storage. These objectives can be fulfilled by an operating system that supports a *virtual storage*.

VIRTUAL STORAGE CONCEPT

Virtual storage is an advanced technique that can significantly speed and simplify the development of many computer applications, including remote computing networks and online inquiry systems which are considered the key applications of the seventies.

Virtual storage can be reviewed as another step in the continuing revolution of data processing systems. *Virtual storage, stated very simply, is the apparent extension of memory size beyond the available real memory (core or main storage)* (Fig. 18.12). For example, a real computing system may have 1 million positions of real storage, but an apparent memory size that is much larger, perhaps 10 million characters. It becomes the responsibility of a software and hardware combination to allow large programs to operate in a smaller real machine size. Data processing departments have been striving for a balance between the costs of computing equipment and the costs of people to implement the computer system.

Virtual storage becomes yet another step in this continuing evaluation. It has a twofold advantage for the data processing community. First the machine storage resource will be better utilized with the virtual concept, allowing a higher degree of multiprogramming. Second, virtual storage allows a system designer and programmer to become more productive by concentrating more on the needs of the end user and less on the needs of the computer.

Virtual storage provides a vehicle for extending the powers of the computer in the user's department through the implementation of advanced data bases and data communication systems. It enables applications to be designed to solve the user department need instead of the machine need. It is an aid to to the programmer in the areas of:

1. Greater accessibility of packages to ease the programming burden.

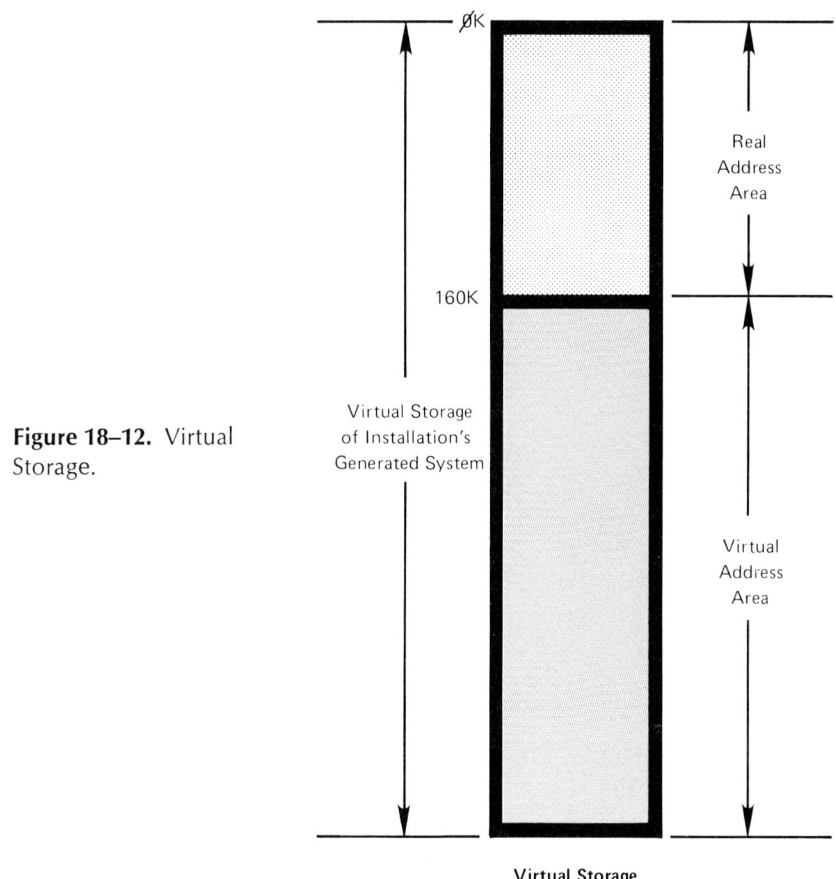

Figure 18–12. Virtual Storage.

2. More users to be capable of taking advantage of interactive computing.
3. Better turnaround time to be provided for programming testing.
4. Storage to become a much smaller consideration with the implementation of the system.

Virtual storage can increase the productivity of programmers by freeing them from time-consuming and routine work. In addition, it enables a computer to process more jobs concurrently, adding new flexibility for user operations.

To provide virtual storage for computer systems, a new system control programming and circuitry had to be developed. The most compact storage circuits ever used in computer systems were introduced.

Present computer users will be able to purchase the dynamic translation facility (DAT) which will permit their computer models to operate with virtual storage control programming.

The vast majority of existing applications programmed for present computer systems require little or no reprogramming to take advantage of virtual storage. In addition, compatibility between all computer virtual storage models makes it easier to move up to the larger and more powerful models as the processing requirements grow.

Virtual storage is a storage management technique which makes a computer system appear to the user as if it had many times the number of characters it actually has in its main storage. This makes possible concurrent processing of computer programs that, in total size, exceed main storage capacity.

The computer's virtual storage is created by circuitry and advanced control programming which links slower but less costly disk storage to main storage. During processing only the active sections of each program need occupy space in main storage; the rest are stored in the disk and are automatically moved into main storage for processing when needed.

With virtual storage, new large scale applications—such as online order entry programs—can be tested immediately, without stopping regularly scheduled processing or waiting for time on the computer.

REAL STORAGE

Computer storage has been called memory, processor storage, main storage, and real storage. In our discussion, we shall refer to it as *real storage*. Each unit of real storage can be located or addressed by the addressing structure of the computer's CPU. A computer's unit of storage contains the smallest addressable entity in real storage. In the system/370, the unit of storage is the byte.

A computer's real storage size is fixed with a variety of sizes to select from; 128K, 256K, 512K, 1024K, etc. No matter what size you select, real storage is a very valuable system resource. You select the storage size as carefully as you would select the model of the computer.

To execute a program in a computer, instructions and data in the program must eventually be loaded into specified real storage locations in the computer. This process is equivalent to allocating specific machine resources to the program. In particular, part of a computer's real storage must be allocated to hold a program's instruction, data elements, control blocks, and input/output areas. Real storage plays a central role in a computer installation because a program cannot execute until it resides in real storage. Real storage is also expensive compared with other storage media like disk and tape. Managing this valuable resource deserves special attention. Real storage management techniques affect the programmer's job. If an operating system uses storage well, the programmer's job is easier. Otherwise, a programmer spends part of his time designing the management of real storage, compensating for the operating system.

Relocation is the translation of addresses in the program to specific locations in real storage. The type of relocation depends on the time at which translation occurs. Translation may occur at two different times.

1. When a program is loaded for execution. This is called *static relocation*. The result is a program that uses fixed real storage locations when it is run. In other words, the program is bound to real storage locations at load time.

2. During the program execution, it is called *dynamic relocation* (Fig. 18.13). If a computer has a dynamic relocation capability, a program is not bound to specific real storage locations during its execution.

Static relocation occurs at program load time only while dynamic relocation occurs continually during program execution.

Each type of relocation has its effect on the use of related storage in a computer system.

VIRTUAL STORAGE OPERATIONS

Up to this point we have learned that a program is associated with its address space, which it occupies, while a computer system is associated with

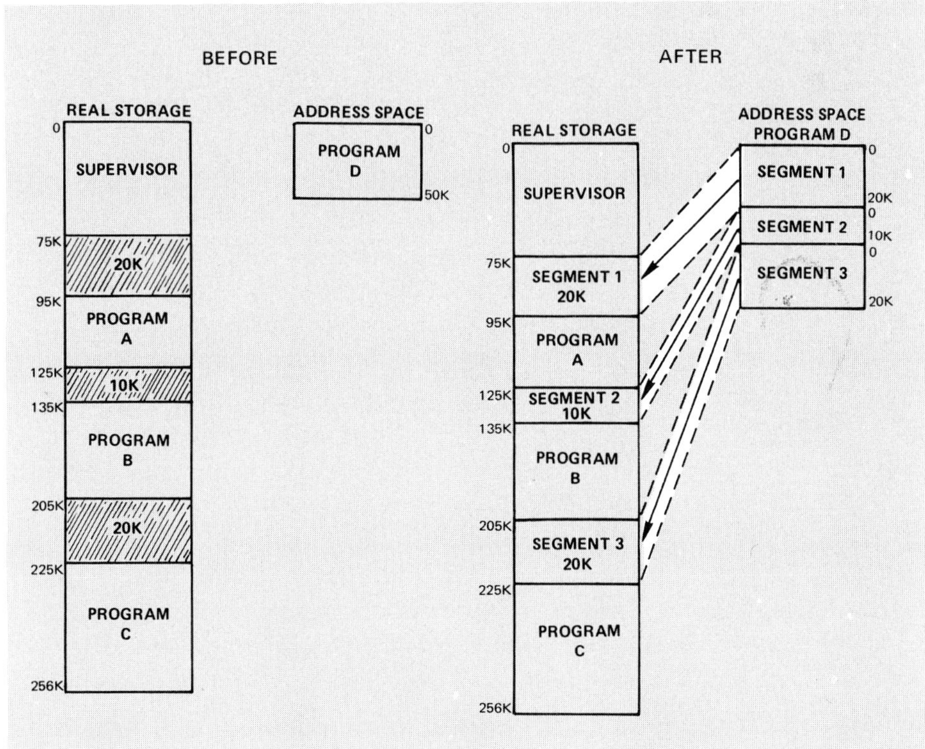

Figure 18–13. Dynamic Relocation—Example.

its real storage space. The program's address space is contiguous, or linear, and it contains the set of addresses generated for its program. The real storage space is also linear. It can be regarded as the set of physical locations addressable by the CPU. The implication is that a program address space can never be larger than real storage size, but this is not true. The maximum size of an address space is established by a computer system address structure. A computer system with a 24-bit address structure may have an address space up to 16,777,216 addressable locations (16 megabytes). This concept of an address space may be much larger than real storage and is called *virtual storage.*

A virtual storage system can be used to simulate a large real storage. Virtual storage gets its name from the fact that it extends beyond the computer's real storage. You can see real storage, but you can't see virtual storage. Virtual storage is a large address space. Where does virtual storage physically exist, if anywhere?

Because virtual storage might be much larger than real storage, it can't *all* be represented in real storage at one time. It must exist in one of the system's two levels of storage—either real or auxiliary storage. A variety of new hardware devices have been introduced for virtual storage systems. The dynamic address translation (DAT) feature translates virtual storage addresses. Some new software is required in a virtual storage system.

BENEFITS OF VIRTUAL STORAGE

The benefits and potential that result from these hardware and software requirements are numerous. In fact, they make the virtual storage concept a profitable investment in almost any application environment.

A virtual storage system's *real* storage is used only on demand, when referenced. This results in many benefits.

1. Programs only require their working set for effective execution. This may enable the system to initiate and execute more jobs.
2. Real storage fragmentation is almost eliminated.
3. It is possible to design and implement an application the size of which greatly exceeds real storage size. This would be impossible in a conventional system without the use of overlays, or a multitape job.
4. Long-run applications will use only the amount of real storage required at any point in time. Thus, a dedicated teleprocessing network will use very little real storage when idle.
5. Virtual storage systems might be unstable as backup for systems that have a larger real storage size.

From the programmer's point of view, virtual storage systems eliminate limitations that exist in static relocation systems. Because virtual storage is much larger than real storage, the programmer has much more space to design problem solutions. This greatly reduces, if not completely eliminates, the need to overlay programs. In overlayed programs, the programmer must plan for storage requirements, storage content, and branching conventions. Revising a program or application that uses overlays can be a complicated job. In virtual storage systems, the *system* manages real storage. In effect it "automatically" overlays programs too large for available real storage. The programmer develops his program for execution in a large contiguous space in virtual storage. This saves time and eliminates complicated procedures. It lets the programmer concentrate on the solution to his application. (Fig. 18.14)

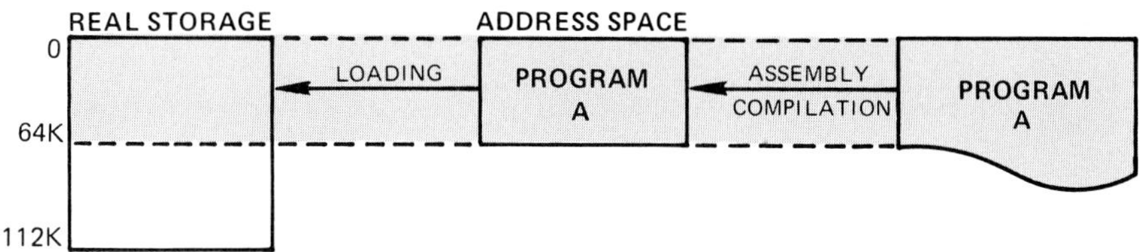

Figure 18–14. Static Relocation—Example.

SUMMARY OF VIRTUAL STORAGE

1. Virtual storage is a means of greatly expanding the computer to direct access storage devices as though they were part of the real storage itself.
2. A necessary prerequisite for accessing outside storage is that addresses in a program (virtual) need not be the same as in real storage (main). A hardware feature (DAT) accomplishes this.
3. Maximum utilization of real storage is achieved by automatically inserting "fragments" of the program into available real storage slots, even though the slots are not contiguous.
4. Through addressing, the total system storage (virtual) is able to exceed the computer's real storage by the use of secondary or auxiliary storage such as disks, as an extension of real storage.
5. The system moves programs between real storage and auxiliary storage by transferring an entire program user between real storage and auxiliary storage. Because only the most active programs are being circulated into and out of real storage, the system operates as though it has a larger real storage than is actually the case.

SUMMARY

The past decade has produced many spectacular advances in computer systems. Besides the many innovations introduced in regular general purpose computers, new concepts and uses relative to other areas of computer systems have appeared also.

There are several dozen manufacturers making general purpose minicomputers that cover the entire spectrum of computer applications. Minicomputers were used originally as parts of larger sophisticated computer systems. Today, they are used as stand-alone computers, each capable of operating independently, supported by a large number of software packages, and as a remote job entry terminal for a centralized computer. The explosion in minicomputer usage has brought about a functional explosion too—the minicomputer has expanded from its traditional applications in scientific, time sharing, and data communications areas to become an educational and vocational tool as well. The widespread use of minicomputers will continue and it is expected that the number of users will triple by the mid-1970s.

Because compilers and compiled programs demand large amounts of storage, microprogramming was designed to tailor the architecture of the machine to the language and its compiler. Microprogramming puts only the fundamental instructions in hardware and uses the memory of the computer to bring these together in a combination of microprograms that are useful to the public.

Remote job entry terminals transmit data swiftly and economically over communication lines of central computing facilities for processing and return. It has become one of the most active areas of minicomputer applications.

Small computers were designed to provide high speed capabilities to small data processing installations. They differ from minicomputers in that they provide file capabilities and other programming features normally not found in minicomputers. The price range is higher than that of the minicomputer due to the added features available.

Super computers are designed for high speed large-scale scientific and commercial applications. They offer fast processing speeds, greater storage capacities and many forms of high speed input and output devices.

Virtual storage is the apparent extension of memory size beyond the available real memory (main or core storage). It provides a vehicle for extending the power of the computer department through the implementation of advanced data base and data communications. It enables the application to be designed to solve the user department need instead of the machine need.

It is the intention of this chapter to describe the main features and operations of these new computer systems.

I. *Minicomputers.*

A. *Definition*—a general purpose small computer, using a word length from twelve to sixteen bits, with an average storage capacity of 16,000 bytes and costing approximately $25,000.

B. *Features.*
   1. A wide range of peripherals (card readers, tape units, printers, etc.).
   2. A wide range of instruction sets.
   3. Microprogramming offered.
   4. Operates independently with software packages such as FORTRAN, COBOL, RPG, BASIC compilers.
   5. Can be used as a remote job entry for a centralized computer.
   6. Used as an educational and vocational tool in schools and colleges.

C. *Microprogramming.*
   1. *Definition*—a method of putting only the most fundamental instructions in hardware and using memory to bring these together in a combination of microprograms that are useful to the programmer.
   2. *Advantages*
      a) Greater flexibility in tailoring systems to specific needs.
      b) Programming at lower costs with more efficiency.
      c) More accurate system checkout and fault detection.
      d) Easier field changes and expansions, with greater economies.
      e) Better emulation of other processors and the various types of peripherals that might be needed.
   3. *Disadvantages.*
      a) More flexibility writing control programs, but methods of writing into them is controlled by manufacturer.
      b) Modifying a system via microprogramming requires users not only versed in programming but, because of the close relationship with hardware, with computer architecture as well.
      c) There is a question of control. Who will be permitted access to the control memory to make changes? What about maintenance and documentation? Debugging, diagnostics, and other microroutines are also problems in microprogramming.
      d) With alterable control memory, the user must be ready to commit the necessary functions to support what he creates.

II. *Remote Job Entry Terminals.*

A. *Definition*—Transmits data over communication lines to the central computer facility for processing and return.

B. *Operation*—swift and economical way for moving large volumes of data at high speeds.

1. The terminal can read all the data from a job or series of jobs at one time.
2. Send it for processing.
3. Upon its return, the results can be displayed in a printed or other form of output.

C. *Components.*
1. *Control Unit*—provides general terminal control functions and serves as an interface between the communications line and peripheral devices.
2. *Card Reader*—wide spectrum of card readers are available ranging in speed from 150 to 1,200 cards per minute, depending upon the needs of the user.
3. *Card Punch*—provides card output on remote terminals.
4. *Printers*—wide range of printers to match output requirements, with rated speeds of 50 to 1,500 lines per minute.

D. *Batch processing*
1. Jobs are "queued" or stacked in an input stream, brought into computer storage, processed to completion, and placed in an output stack or stream for punching or punching of results.
2. Job control information is provided with the input job stream itself thus making it possible to proceed on the job processing with a minimum of operator intervention.

III. *Small Computers.*

A. *Definition*—A system that rents for less than $3,000 a month, operates under stored program control, includes master file capabilities.

B. *Criteria.*
1. The hardware should be a general purpose, user-programmable system capable of accessing at least one megabyte of information from a disk or drum. The system must have a high-speed printer.
2. The software must include at least skeletal programs for doing engineering, payroll, accounting functions, etc.
3. The computer manufacturer must be ready to provide the system on a turnkey basis including installation and training.
4. The system should have communication capabilities to allow it to act as an efficient online terminal to the central computer.
5. The system should lease for less than $3,000 a month.

C. *Features.*
1. Storage capabilities ranging from 8,000 to 96,000 bytes allow the user to start with the storage level that efficiently meets their present requirements and allows for future applications.

2. Low cost disk devices reduce cost of online random access processing of information.
3. A large array of input and output devices.
4. A full line of terminal and terminal system allow the small computer user to use time sharing facilities.
5. Software packages that allow the small computer user to operate with application programs written in high level languages such as FORTRAN, COBOL, RPG, BASIC, etc.
6. Multiprogramming is now available so that one can progress from job-at-a-time processing to multiprogramming, in which several jobs move forward at the same time.

IV. *Super computers.*

A. *Definition*—A large system designed for high speed, large-scale scientific and commercial applications. The base price for these systems ranges from $165,000 to $300,000 monthly. These computers are used for large scale systems, such as the control center of the most complex airline reservations systems.

B. *Features.*

1. Large main storage capacities ranging from 1 million to 4 million bytes.
2. High speed buffer unit which can sharply reduce the time required for fetching currently used sections of main storage.
3. As many as thirteen channels for input/output devices may be attached to the central processing unit.
4. High degree of concurrency in operation.
5. Very fast execution time.
6. Improved circuit technology.

V. *Virtual Storage.*

A. *Definition*—The apparent extension of memory size beyond the available real memory (core or main storage).

B. *Concept.*

1. Advanced technique that can significantly speed and simplify the development of many computer applications, including remote computing networks and online inquiry systems which are considered the key application of the seventies.
2. Frees the programmer from time-consuming and routine work, thus enabling him to increase his productivity and thereby making it possible to process more jobs concurrently on the computer.
3. New control programming and circuitry had to be developed. Compact storage circuits introduced into computer systems.

4. Present computer user will be able to purchase the dynamic translation facility (DAT) which will permit their computer models to operate with virtual storage control programming.
5. Present computer applications will require little or no reprogramming to take advantage of virtual storage.
6. A storage management technique which makes a computer system appear to the user as if it had many times the number of characters it has in its main storage. This permits concurrent processing of computer programs that, in total size, exceed main storage capacity.
7. The computer's virtual storage is created by circuitry and advanced control programming which links slower but less costly disk storage to main storage. During the processing only the active sections of each program need occupy space in main storage; the others are stored on the disk and are automatically moved into main storage for processing when needed.
8. New large scale applications can be tested immediately, without stopping regularly scheduled processing or waiting in line for the computer.

C. *Real Storage*—processor, main or core storage.

D. *Relocation*—the translation of addresses in the program to specific locations in real storage. Depends on the time when translation occurs.

1. *Static relocation*—program is loaded for execution. Program is bound to real storage locations at load time.
2. *Dynamic relocation*—occurs during the program execution. If a computer has a dynamic relocation capacity, a program is not bound to specific real storage locations during its execution.
3. Static relocation occurs at program load time only while dynamic relocation occurs continually during program execution.

E. *Benefits.*

1. Programs require only their working set for effective execution. This may make possible the initiation and execution of more jobs.
2. Real storage fragmentation is almost eliminated.
3. It is possible to design and implement an application which greatly exceeds the real storage size of the computer.
4. Long running applications will use only the amount of real storage required at any point in time. A dedicated teleprocessing system will thus use very little storage when idle.
5. Virtual storage systems might be usable as backup for systems that have a larger real storage size.

F. *Advantages to programmers.*
1. Greater accessibility of packages to ease the programming burden.
2. More users will now be capable of taking advantage of interactive computing.
3. Better turnaround time can be provided for programming and testing.
4. Storage becomes a much smaller consideration with the implementation of the system.

IDENTIFICATION QUESTIONS

Match the following terms with the statements that follow.

A. Batch Processing Systems
B. Dynamic Relocation
C. Microprogramming
D. Minicomputer
E. Real Storage
F. Relocation
G. Remote Job Entry Terminals
H. Small Computer
I. Static Relocation
J. Super Computers
K. Virtual Storage

1. A system which rents for less than $3,000 per month, operates under a stored program control, and includes a master file capability.
2. The putting of only the most fundamental instructions in hardware and using memory to bring these together in the form of programs.
3. The transmission of data to the central computing facility for processing and return.
4. Machines designed for high speed large-scale scientific and commercial applications with a base rental price ranging from $65,000 to $300,000 per month.
5. The translation of addresses in a program to specific locations in real storage.
6. The program that is bound to real storage locations at load time.
7. The apparent extension of memory size beyond the available real memory.
8. A general purpose computer with an average storage capacity of 16,000 bytes and costing about $25,000.
9. The ability to support multiple jobs by queuing them to be processed in one or more "input job streams".
10. The main storage of a computer that is fixed in a variety of sizes.
11. A program that is not bound to specific locations during its execution.

QUESTIONS FOR REVIEW

1. What is a minicomputer? Trace its phenomenal progress during the last decade.
2. What is microprogramming? What are its important advantages?
3. Discuss the pros and cons of microprogramming.
4. What is the purpose of Remote Job Entry terminals? Give some typical examples of their use.

5. List the components of Remote Job Entry terminals and their main purpose.
6. Explain batch processing and how the Remote Job Entry terminal relates to it.
7. What is a small computer? What criteria is used in defining a small computer system? Give examples.
8. What are the important features of small computers?
9. What were super computers designed for?
10. What are the objectives for designing new functions and features for a computer system?
11. Discuss the virtual storage concept and how it is used to extend the power of the computer.
12. What is real storage?
13. What is the difference between static and dynamic relocation?
14. What are the important benefits derived from virtual storage?

CHAPTER 19

Management of a Data Processing Installation

CONCEPTS OF ORGANIZATION

The organization of a data processing installation requires an unusual blending of technical and managerial skills. The data processing effort follows concepts and methods not ordinarily encountered in other functions. Data processing is a technical operation requiring highly trained, technically competent, and in many cases creative, personnel. Standards for control of data processing operations and planning are necessarily distinct from those of other managerial functions.

Although data processing performs a service function, the services it furnishes are frequently of fundamental importance to the success of the operational departments involved. Good data processing systems design aims at integrating data processing operations which cut across organizational lines, thus creating unique problems in the relationship of the data processing unit and other parts of the company (Fig. 19.1).

DATA PROCESSING OBJECTIVES

The most important influence in the structure of the data processing activity is exerted by its objectives and the ways in which these objectives relate to the large organizational units served. Defining these objectives requires a careful examination of the internal and external requirements of the organization (Fig. 19.2).

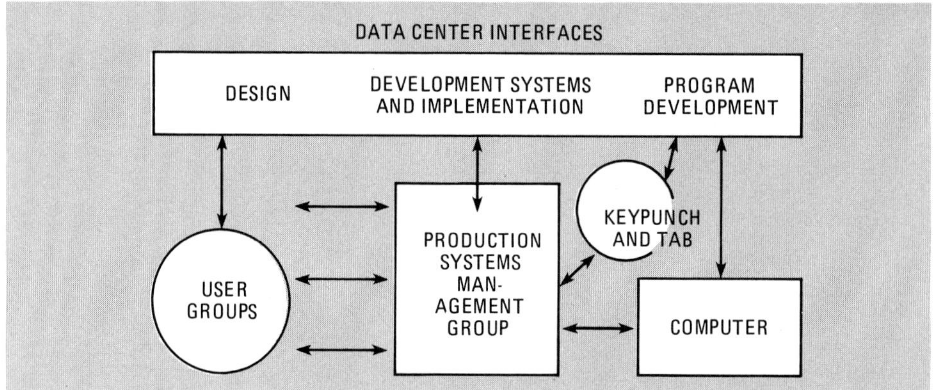

Figure 19–1. Data Center Interfaces.

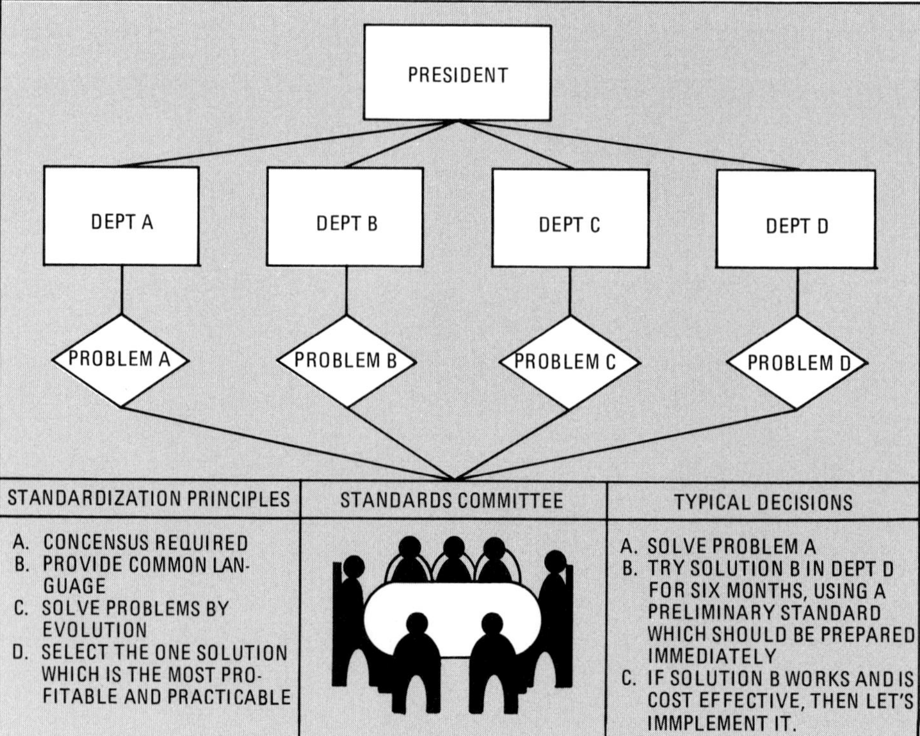

Figure 19–2. Problem Solving-Management Objectives.

MANAGEMENT PURPOSES TO BE SERVED

What important contributions can the data processing unit make to management planning and control flow? Some management functions to which the data processing may be of great importance include planning and research, control and exceptional reporting, and the maintenance of the organization's basic information files.

OPERATIONAL PURPOSES TO BE SERVED

How does the data processing participate? Data processing controls inventory orders, production, maintains personnel and payroll records, maintains customer accounts, etc.

SCOPE OF SERVICE

What are the number and different types of departments to be served? What services are to be provided? Accounting and record keeping, scientific and mathematical, real time, and data transmission services, are types of service to be furnished to users.

MEANS OF SERVICE

Will the data processing department operate an "open" or "closed" shop activity? In an open shop operation, each user has access to the equipment and provides his own personnel for programming and operations. In a closed shop the user, not permitted to program or operate the equipment, provides the data processing department with the problem. This department performs the necessary programming and operations.

Another important factor to be considered is the establishment of deadlines and turn-around schedules that must be fulfilled by the data processing activity.

FUTURE PLANS

Careful consideration should be given to the organization plans for growth, product expansion, and competitive position. Any major changes planned will have a direct bearing on the data processing procedures to be adopted.

ORGANIZATIONAL POSITION—DATA PROCESSING UNIT

The important and unusual nature of the service provided by the data processing unit makes its position within an organization of prime importance (Fig. 19.3). The unit can serve the needs of the organization either in a centralized or decentralized position. In a centralized position, the data processing unit is independent but at the same level with the departments it is servicing. In a decentralized operation, the data processing unit is within the larger organizational unit that is its major customer. There are advantages

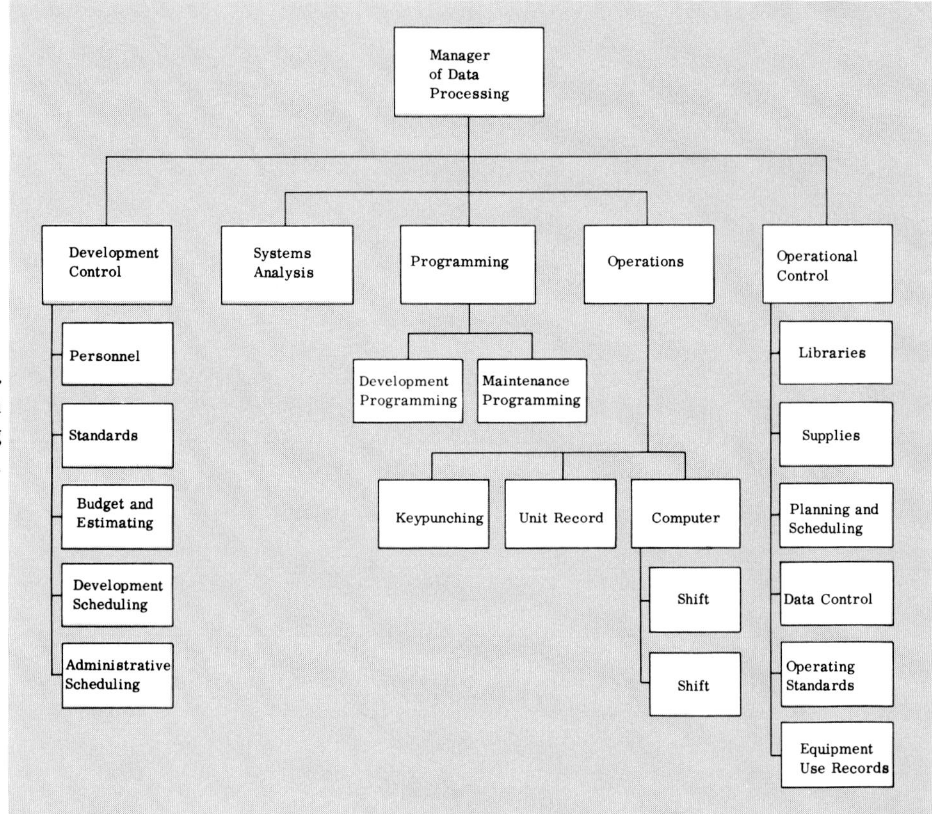

Figure 19–3. Organization of a Data Processing Unit.

and disadvantages to each position. Each has merits, which depend on the different environments and the objectives to be served within them. Recently, there has been a tendency towards the centralized use of data processing units.

CENTRALIZED DATA PROCESSING UNIT

Through the centralization of computer facilities, the following primary goals are expected to be achieved (Fig. 19.4):

1. Significant cost reduction because of improvement in the cost/efficiency ratio of the large scale systems.
2. Improved overall work load performance with better service to users.
3. Broader range of computing services offered to the user.

During the 1960s, the business fortunes of organizations had driven their computing installations through the so-familiar cycles of growth and reduction, and it was rarely true that any of them had the "right" computing capac-

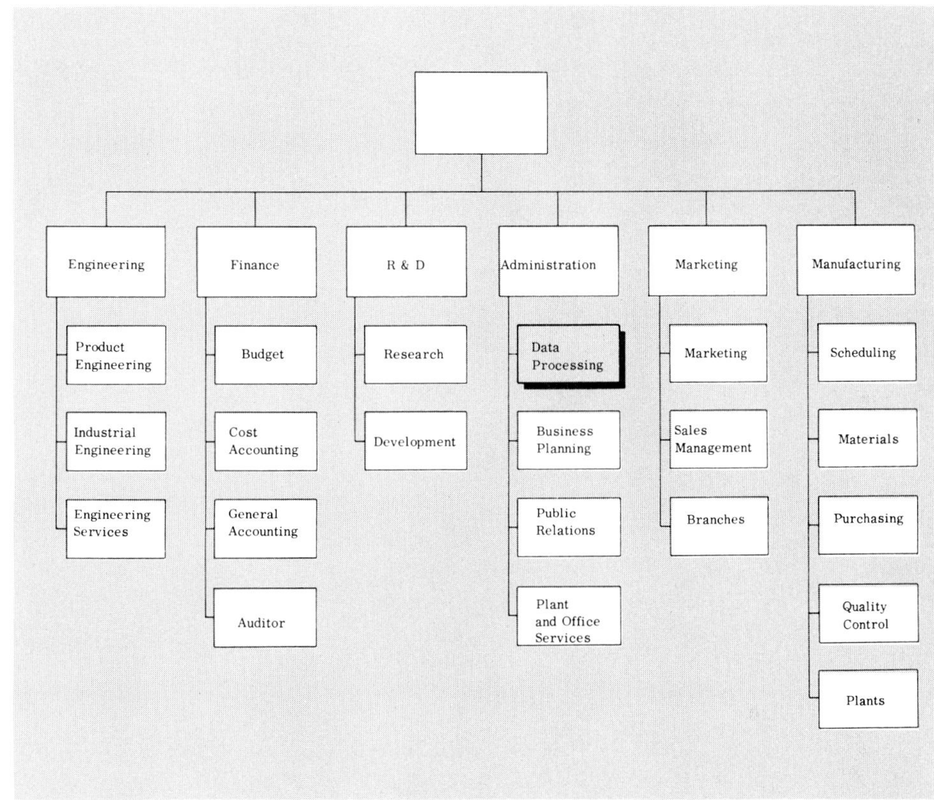

Figure 19–4. Organizational Chart—Centralized Data Processing Unit.

ity for more than a short interval of time. The advancing state of computer technology contributed to this perpetual imbalance. The situation, involving large geographically dispersed work loads, limited potency of computing hardware, and lack of data communication facilities, was badly in need of stabilizing. But no reasonable improvement appeared at hand.

Then into the breach stepped the supercomputers of the 1970s, complete with multi-operating systems and control systems, communication facilities that work and greater computer power. The speed of the central processing unit and large storage size will give the user his sought after power, and the operating system software and reliable communication capabilities will greatly improve job turn-around time.

Coincidently, the data transmission art improved during the late sixties—right on schedule with a range of capacities and techniques to make work load movements feasible.

By centralizing its data processing operations, an organization can put itself in the position to realize the full potential of very large scale computer systems.

ADVANTAGES

1. All departments receive equal consideration from the data processing unit.
2. Programming planning and systems research and development can be more efficiently integrated for the entire organization.
3. Disputes that may arise with reference to the use of data processing service can be settled by managers of comparable status.
4. The centralization of data processing personnel and equipment will reduce costs of any future expansion since additional volume can be more easily absorbed by a centralized unit.

DISADVANTAGES

1. The largest user of the data processing services may receive the same priority as the other users, thus reducing the effectiveness of the largest user's operations.
2. If each department has an equal right to use the data processing facility without a chargeback through allotment or allocation, unprofitable use of the data processing facility may result. This is due to the tendency of each department to reduce its operating budget at the expense of the data processing department.
3. The physical distance between the data processing facility and the user may create communication and deadline problems.

DECENTRALIZED DATA PROCESSING UNIT

Is the system "responsive" to the user's real needs? Many systems developed today are capable of producing more data than the user can possibly digest. The user ends up spending most of his time making corrections on several hundred sheets of output and little time for information analysis, which is why he asked for computer assistance in the first place. A new approach in the organization of information systems development is needed. User-oriented systems can be defined as those in which the user and information systems professionals together clearly delineate the thought process of the user, as opposed to the architectural approach of the technically trained systems professional.

In many large companies, the development of computer-based information systems has evolved from a central development organization dedicated to the support of users who are unfamiliar with the working concepts employed in the decentralized regional offices (Fig. 19.5). The data processing center has become a closed shop. No longer is the user knowledgeable about

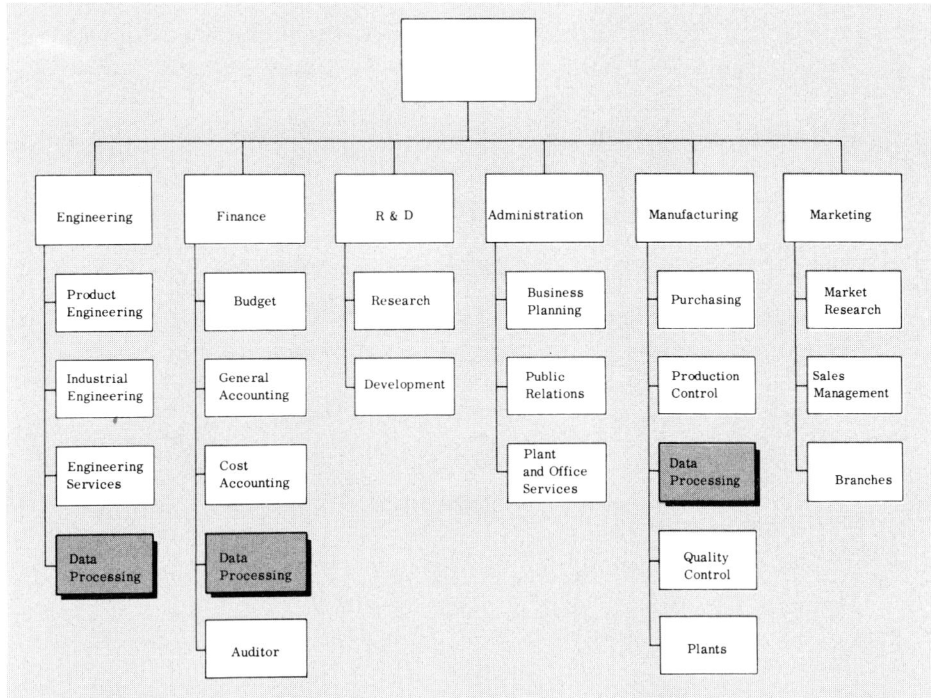

Figure 19–5. Organizational Chart—Decentralized DATA Processing Unit.

the centralized computing operations. He is not even admitted to the data center where he can see the sophisticated machinery which has aided his daily requirements.

Technically trained systems people are being drawn from the predominently nonbusiness-oriented fields, such as engineering and mathematics. While some degree of change has occurred by employing those individuals with computer science degrees, the practical business orientation is still neglected.

As information systems development enters into the fourth-generation computers, the role of the user becomes an increasingly important factor in the success of information systems, and management must take a greater role in support of these systems. This can be best accomplished by organizing the development of activities in a manner more conducive to the needs of the user.

Although many large organizations have obtained greater efficiency by centralizing their data processing operations, the question is asked whether management has become an unresponsive bureaucracy. Communication between the user and the central system has become a serious problem in recent years. One way computer systems can be made more sensitive to the needs of the user would be through decentralization of computer facilities.

ADVANTAGES

1. Within a large decentralized organization, direct control by users may be necessary for daily operations.
2. Within each unit only the minimum equipment for the purpose served need be acquired.
3. Major users may be more sensitive to the economic use of the equipment.

DISADVANTAGES

1. Establishing a formal corporate policy on the use of data processing facilities is difficult in a decentralized activity.
2. The integration of data processing functions and long-range planning will be more difficult.
3. Other departments may have difficulty in obtaining data processing services.
4. The total cost of multiple data processing units, each having its own personnel, may be much more than the cost of a centralized data processing organization.

DATA PROCESSING FUNCTIONS

An organizational structure is a logical grouping of functions and the people who perform them. Basically, data processing functions are divided into planning, operation, and management.

PLANNING FUNCTIONS

Planning is the major activity that encompasses those functions concerned with establishing a data processing installation, and with selecting, designing, and preparing programs for new data processing applications (Fig. 19.6).

INSTALLATION PLANNING

This type of planning involves organization and scheduling of human and mechanical resources into an effective plan for establishing or changing a data processing activity (Fig. 19.7). This includes the following operations:

1. Schedule development for all tasks involved in installing the organization, applications, and equipment.
2. Budget development.
3. Staffing plans including assignment of tasks, recruitment, selection, and training plans.

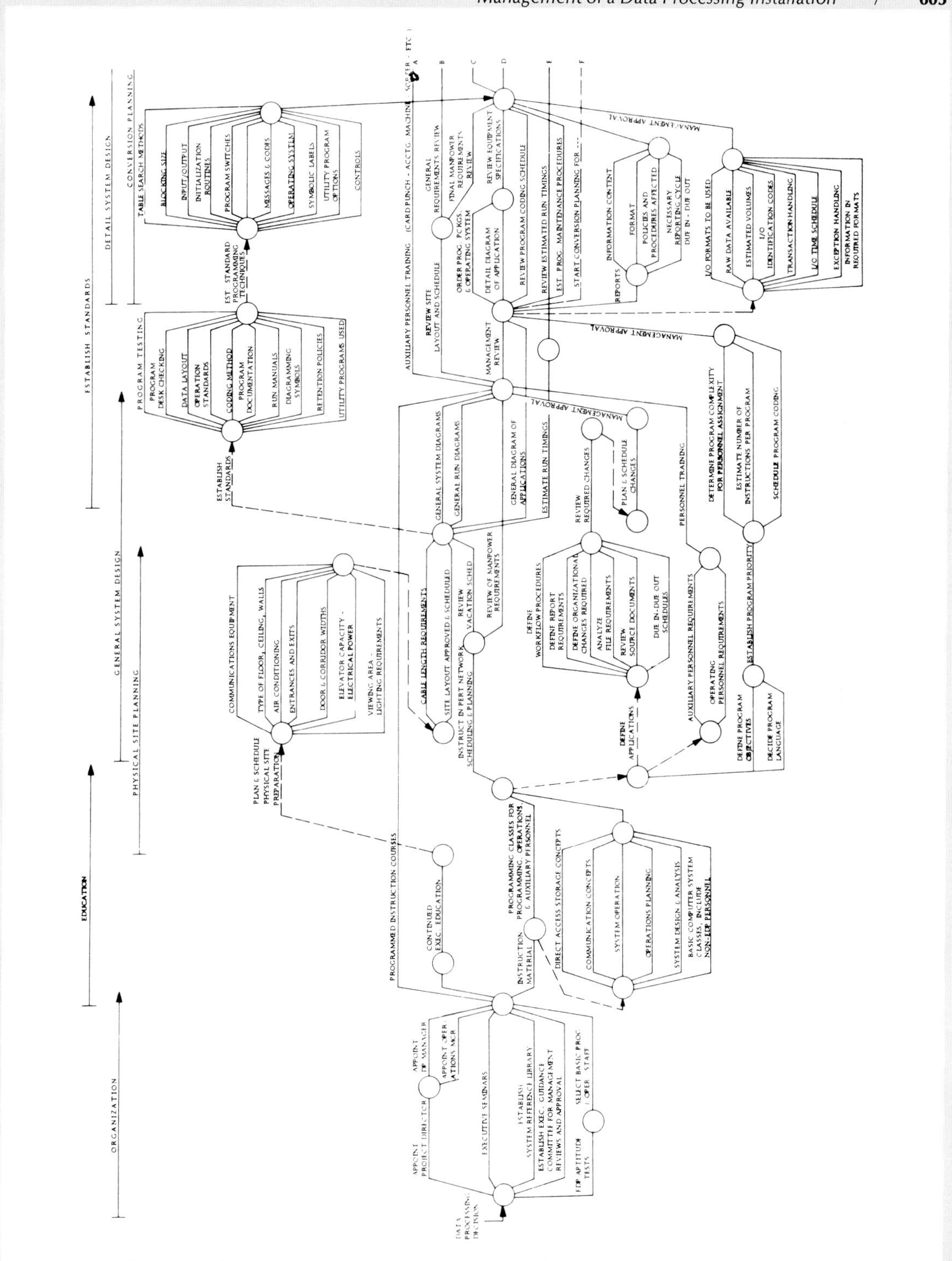

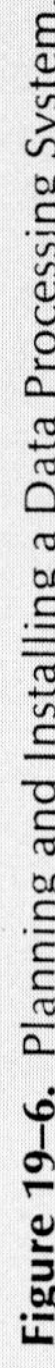

Figure 19–6. Planning and Installing a Data Processing System.

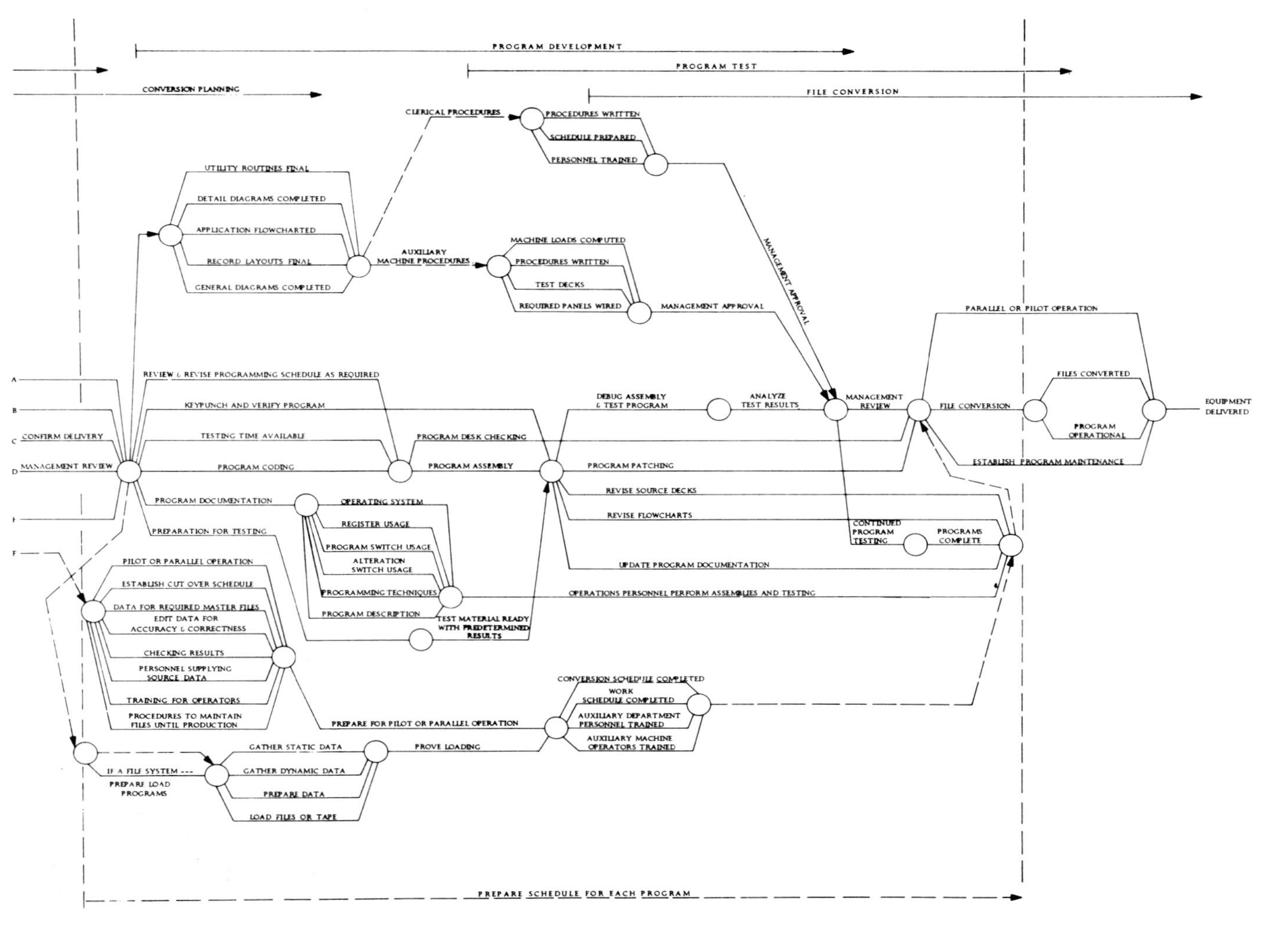

Figure 19–6. (Continued).

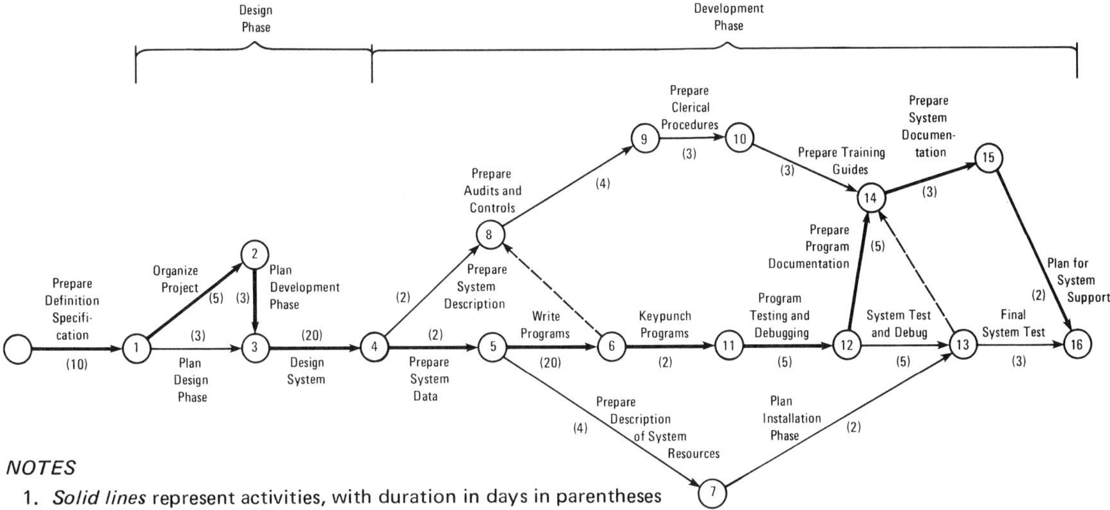

NOTES

1. *Solid lines* represent activities, with duration in days in parentheses
2. *Critical Path* is depicted by heavy lines
3. *Total Man-Days* are summary of all activity durations (77 days)
4. *Dashed lines* reflect time dependency between nodes

Figure 19–7. Specimen Critical Path Network for Design and Development Phase of a Data Processing Project.

4. Development of detailed standards for performance.
5. Site and facilities planning.

APPLICATION SELECTION

This function includes the activities relative to the selection and definition of data processing applications which fulfill the objectives of the company (Fig. 19.8), such as:

1. Review with management and other departments of information needs and their translation into stated objectives.
2. Economic analysis to determine the justification of the costs.
3. A thorough analysis of proposed applications to ascertain whether they fit into the overall plan of the data processing system.
4. Continuing liaison with other sections and management to review the need for new applications and the degree to which present applications are satisfying management goals.

SYSTEM ANALYSIS AND DESIGN

The analysis of the present methods, applications, objectives, and all pertinent data is followed by a design of improved systems using data processing equipment and techniques. The primary aim of this function is to produce.

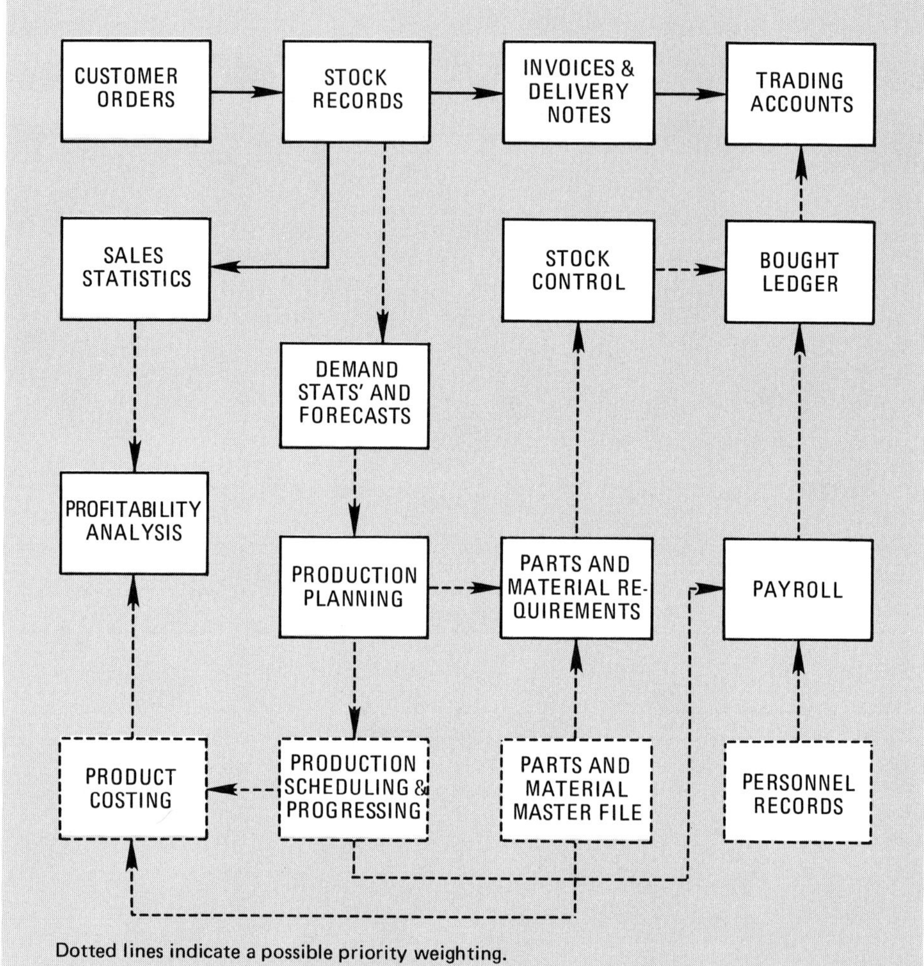

Figure 19–8. Specimen Master Plan.

the optimum solution to application needs; the most economic solution consistent with management and operating objectives, equipment capabilities and personnel resources (Fig. 19.9). The analytical tasks of the function include:

1. Gathering data about present methods.
2. Recording data in suitable form for analysis, flowcharts, tables, graphs, etc.
3. Analyzing the data to define the desired results of the application, the restraints upon systems design, time, cost, volume, the relationship of the application to other systems, and controls to be placed on the systems operations.

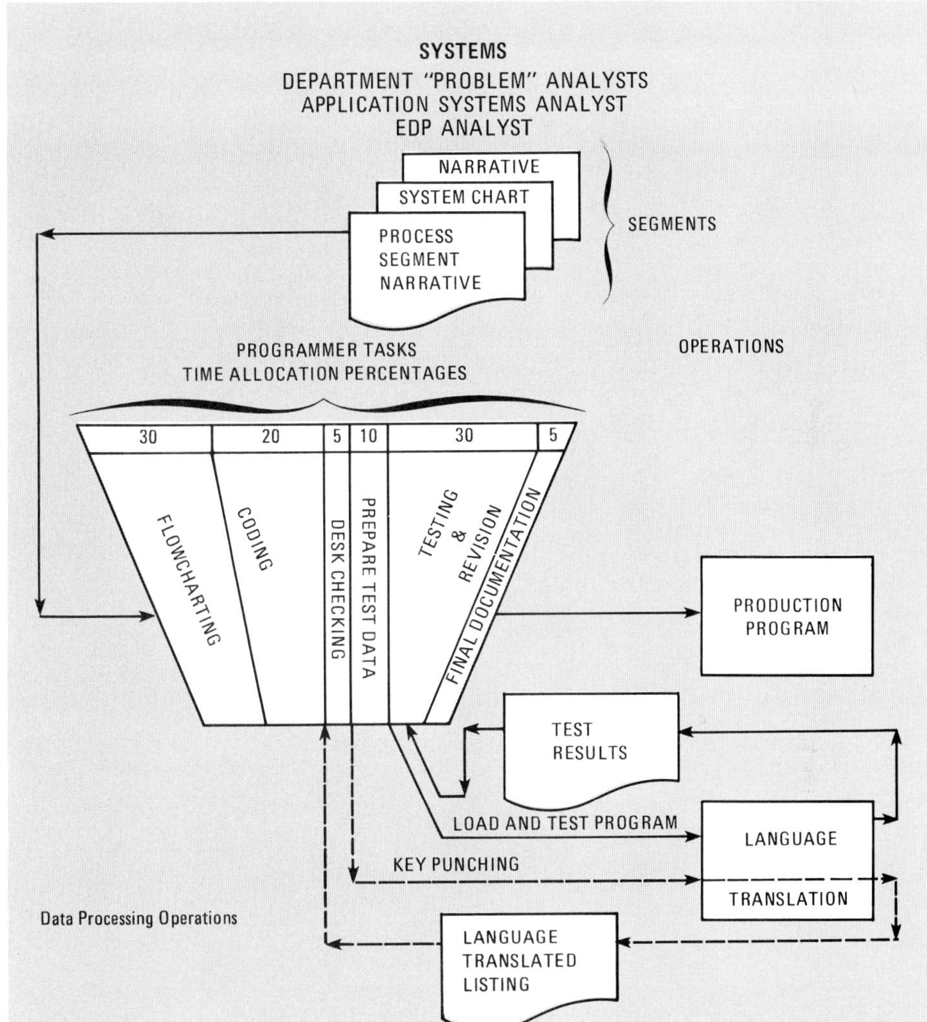

Figure 19–9. Data Processing Operations.

The tasks included in system design are

1. Matching equipment requirements to system needs.
2. Finding the best way to meet the system needs.
3. Calculating the economic and administrative effects of the new system.
4. Defining and documenting all clerical, control, and equipment procedures of the new system.
5. Getting agreement of all organizations affected by the new procedures and new systems.

RULE No.	1	2	3	4	5	6	7	8
1st Class Request	Y	Y	Y	Y				
Tourist Request					Y	Y	Y	Y
1st Class Open	Y	N	N	N		Y	N	
Tourist Open		Y	N		Y	N	N	N
Alternate Class Acceptable		Y	Y	N		Y	Y	N
Issue 1st Class Ticket	X					X		
Issue Tourist Ticket		X			X			
Subtract 1 from 1st Class Avail	X					X		
Subtract 1 from Tourist Avail		X			X			
Place on Tourist Wait List			X				X	X
Place on 1st Class Wait List			X	X			X	

Decision table, airline reservations example

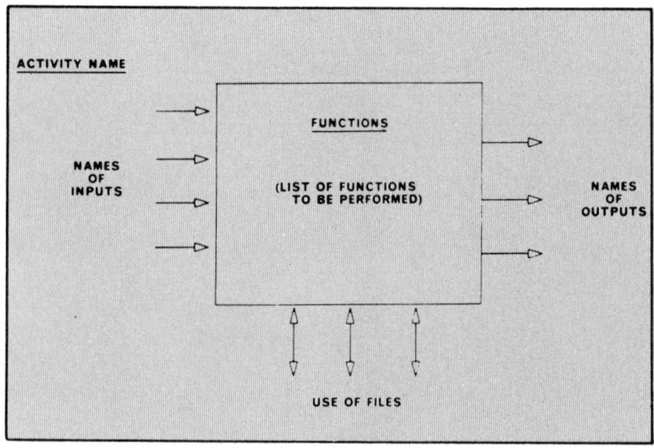

Activity requirements model

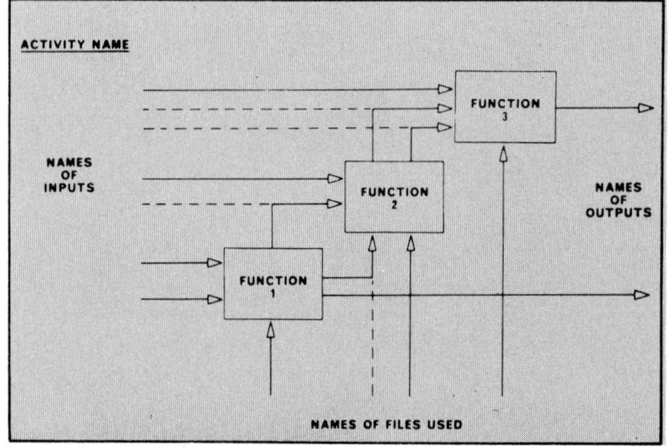

Function sequence chart

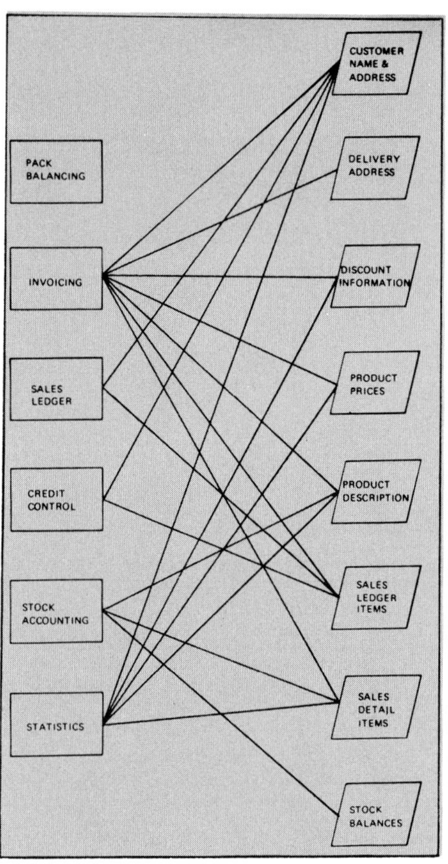

Interaction of files

Figure 19–10. Decision Table, Activity Requirements Model, Function Sequence Chart, Interaction of Files.

PROGRAMMING

Defined system requirements and procedures are translated into a logical process and a set of instructions for its operation on data processing equipment (Fig. 19.10). The major tasks in programming are:

1. Finding the best way to use the equipment efficiently to meet the needs of the system.
2. To design the logical flow of the program (Fig. 19.11).
3. The selection of standard program routines and available programming systems for incorporation into the program.
4. Preparing and coding the necessary instructions to carry out the program logic, incorporating program routines and systems as desired.

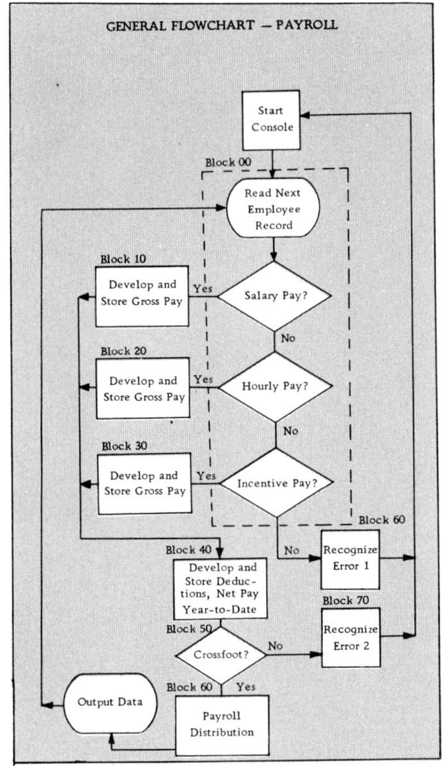

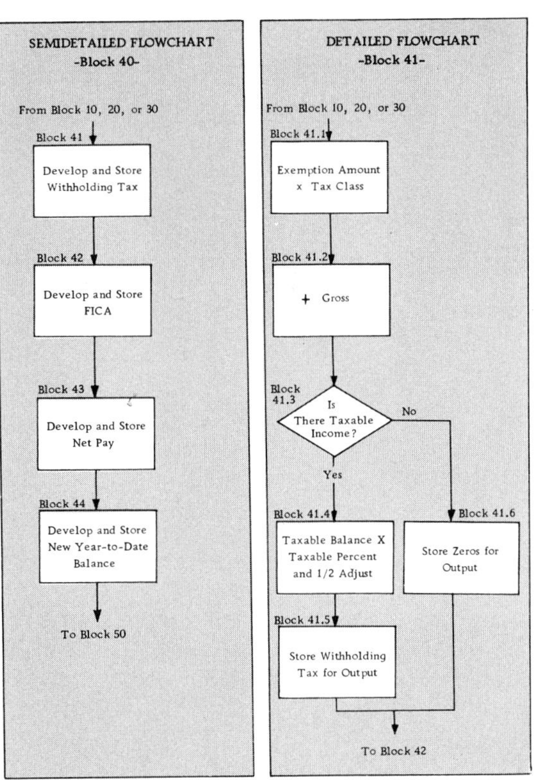

Figure 19–11. Program Flowcharts.

TESTING

Determine the success of the program in meeting the defined systems requirements and procedures of the total system in meeting the objectives of the application (Fig. 19.12). The following tasks are important to successful testing.

Figure 19–12. Machine Testing.

1. Design of testing methods that will give a thorough trial to the new system and program.
2. Selection of appropriate source data for tests.
3. Isolation and correction of programming errors with a run using test cards and computer software.
4. Testing the manner of the program as it fits into the system.
5. Final testing of the computer system including "live" actual data.

DOCUMENTATION

The documentation function requires reduction of the system and programs to a standardized written form for use in system and program modification, training, and machine operation. Documentation is usually in great detail, in rigid format, and absolutely up-to-date. Three common forms of documentation are

1. *Systems application* manuals, showing the inputs, outputs and procedures for the total system and all programs within it (Figs. 19.13, 19.14, 19.15).
2. *Program* manuals showing the detailed logic, instructions, and machine utilization for each program (Fig. 19.16).
3. *Operations* manuals providing precise instructions for running the programs and for dealing with unusual and emergency situations.

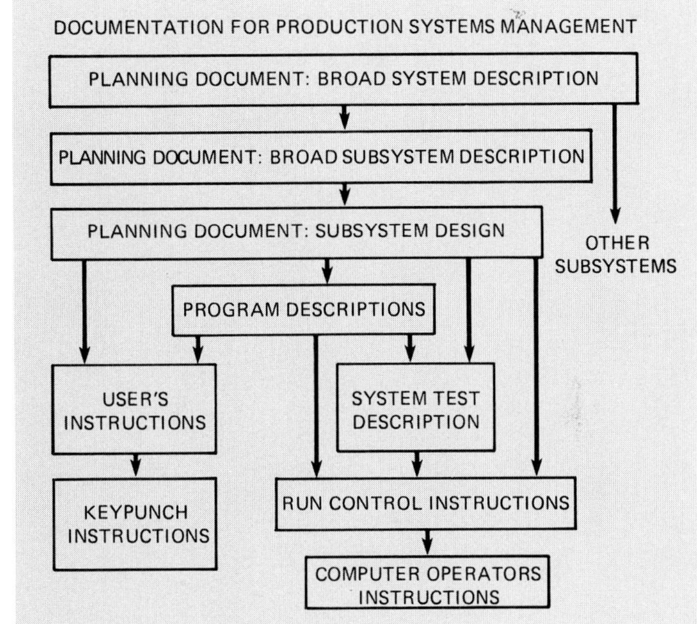

Figure 19–13. Documentation for Production Systems Management.

DOCUMENTATION CONTROL

APPLICATION ______________________________

The following documents have been completed
and are included in this binder:

DATE PLACED IN BINDER	FORM
__________	Narrative write up
__________	Overall System Flow Chart
__________	Table of Computer Runs
__________	Record of Management agreement
__________	Due in - Due out schedules
__________	Summary of Volume figures
__________	Estimate of time by job
__________	Samples of all input records
__________	Forms to be prepared
__________	Master disk layouts
__________	Card forms

Documentation of the following programs is complete
and included in this binder:

DATE PLACED IN BINDER	PROGRAM NO.	PROGRAM NAME
__________	________	________
__________	________	________
__________	________	________
__________	________	________
__________	________	________
__________	________	________
__________	________	________
__________	________	________
__________	________	________
__________	________	________
__________	________	________
__________	________	________
__________	________	________

Figure 19–14. Table of Contents—Applications Manual.

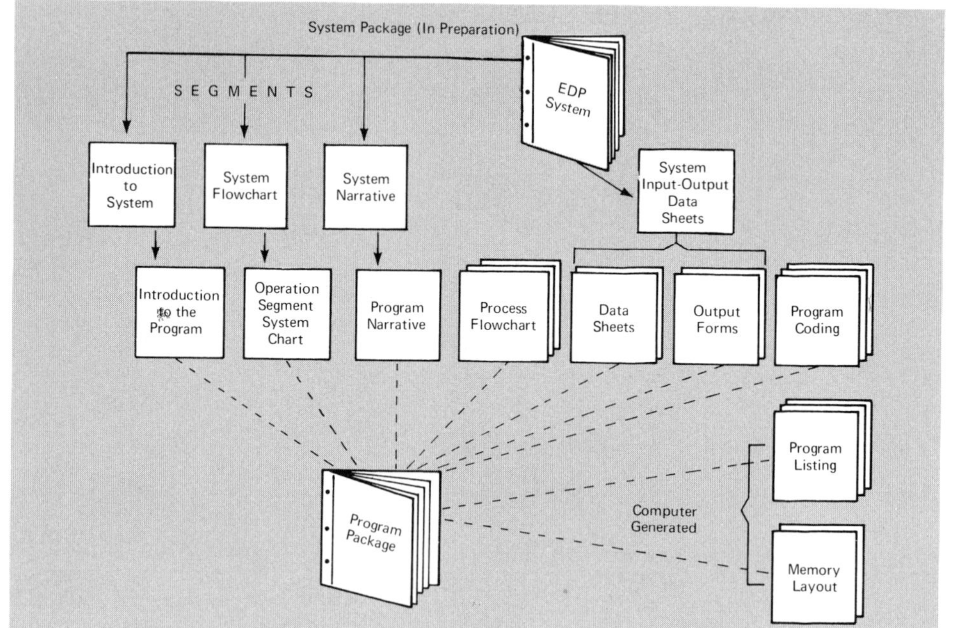

Figure 19–15. Data Processing Operations Manual.

Field Characteristics:

A = Alphabetic or Alphanumeric
AS = Alphabetic or Alphanumeric (Units Pos. is Non-Numeric)
N = Numeric (Unsigned)
NX = Numeric (Minus only is Signed, Designate Position)
NS = Numeric (Signed + and – , Designate Position)

File RECORD DESCRIPTION

Record Name	Record Number
Customer Master	CM 123

Record Source	Size	Record Medium
UD-124	150	Tape

File Sequence	Date Submitted
Account within Cycle	7/1/6-

Prepared by		Revwd. by	Date	Superceded
J.R.		J.L	7/10	N.A.

Item No.	From To	Size	No. of Dec. Pos.	Field Char.	Label	Item Name	Page of
1	1	1		N	TYPE	Type of account	
2	2-10	9		N	NUM	Customer account number	
3	11-70	60		A	NAME	Customer name and address	
4	71	1		N	LIMIT	Credit limit	
5	72	1		N	STATUS	Status code	
6	73-74	2		N	TRANS	Number of transactions this month	
7	75-80	6	2	N	CHARGE	Current month charges	
8	81-86	6	2	N	PAY	Current month payments	
9	87-92	6	2	N	CREDIT	Current month credits	
10	93-98	6	2	N	BAL	Balance	
11	99-104	6	2	N	BAL 30	Aged balance over 30 days	
12	105-110	6	2	N	BAL 60	Aged balance over 60 days	
13	111-116	6	2	N	BAL 90	Aged balance over 90 days	
14	117-120	6	2	N	BAL 120	Aged balance over 120 days	
15	123-124	2		N	OPENED	Year account opened	
16	125-126	2		N	ACTIVE	Year last active	
17	127-131	5		N	PURCHY	Total purchases this year to date	
18	132-135	4		N	RETY	Total returns this year to date	
19	136-137	2		N	ACTIVE	Number of months active	
20	138-139	2		N	90 DAY	Number of months in over-90-day category	
21	140-144	5		N	PURCAL	Total purchases last year	
22	145-147	4		N	RETLY	Total returns last year	
23	148-149	2		N	MOACT	Number of months active last year	
24	150	1		N	MO 90	Number of months in over-90-day category last year	

Figure 19–16. Illustration—Record Layout Form.

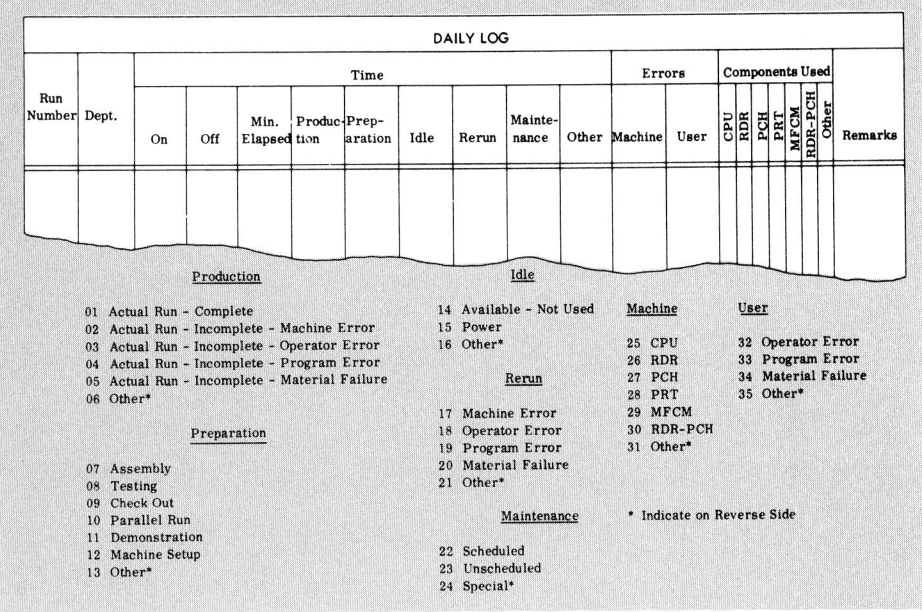

DAILY LOG

Run Number	Dept.	Time									Errors		Components Used							Remarks
		On	Off	Min. Elapsed	Production	Preparation	Idle	Rerun	Maintenance	Other	Machine	User	CPU	RDR	PCH	PRT	MFCM	RDR-PCH	Other	

Production

01 Actual Run - Complete
02 Actual Run - Incomplete - Machine Error
03 Actual Run - Incomplete - Operator Error
04 Actual Run - Incomplete - Program Error
05 Actual Run - Incomplete - Material Failure
06 Other*

Preparation

07 Assembly
08 Testing
09 Check Out
10 Parallel Run
11 Demonstration
12 Machine Setup
13 Other*

Idle

14 Available - Not Used
15 Power
16 Other*

Rerun

17 Machine Error
18 Operator Error
19 Program Error
20 Material Failure
21 Other*

Maintenance

22 Scheduled
23 Unscheduled
24 Special*

Machine

25 CPU
26 RDR
27 PCH
28 PRT
29 MFCM
30 RDR-PCH
31 Other*

User

32 Operator Error
33 Program Error
34 Material Failure
35 Other*

* Indicate on Reverse Side

Figure 19–17. System Log.

CONVERSION

A controlled transition is needed from the current system to the new one. The function requires the careful planning of the conversion steps and equally careful supervision of their execution. The conversion plan covers such items as:

1. Purging and clean up of data files.
2. Training in the use of new procedures and formats.
3. Preparation of special computer programs for the conversion of records.
4. Parallel operation of old and new systems.
5. Preparation and publication of training aids and procedure guides.

OPERATING FUNCTIONS

These functions include the activities that make up the day-to-day operation of established procedures.

MACHINE OPERATION

The actual loading, unloading, setup, and control of the equipment that a data processing installation is comprised of, is included in machine operation. Data processing equipment operations require meticulous control of schedules and the maintenance of accurate records of equipment and program performance.

INPUT PREPARATION

Input data must be translated into codes and formats suitable for data processing. The objective of this activity is to prepare accurate, properly coded input data in the manner prescribed by the system and according to the schedules.

INPUT/OUTPUT CONTROL

The control over data processing inputs and outputs requires receiving, logging, controlling, and coordinating of documents and input/output devices (Fig. 19.17).

MAINTENANCE OF RECORD LIBRARIES

The control and storage of all data files, programs, documentation, and operating records and reports is maintained in a library. Physically, the records are found in magnetic tapes, magnetic disks, data cells, punched paper

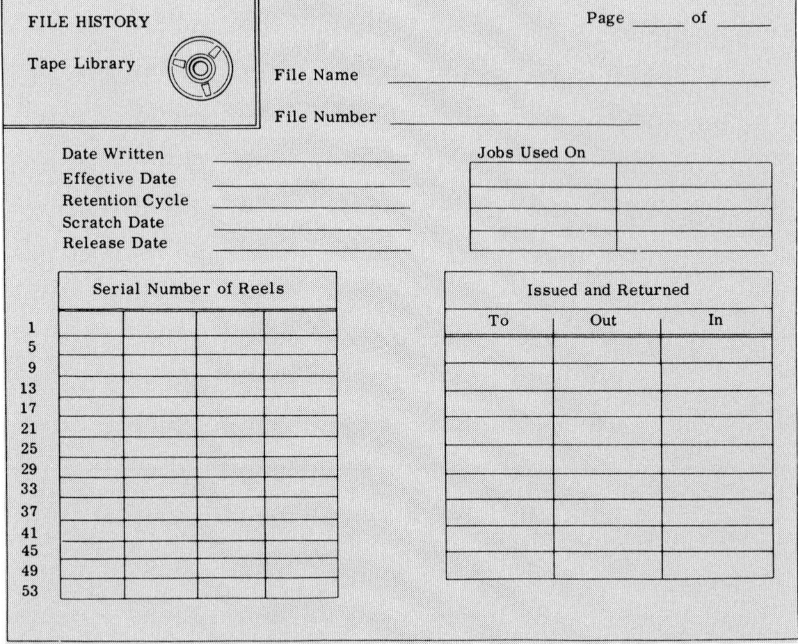

FILE HISTORY

Tape Library

Page ____ of ____

File Name ____________

File Number ____________

Date Written ____________

Effective Date ____________

Retention Cycle ____________

Scratch Date ____________

Release Date ____________

Jobs Used On

	Serial Number of Reels			
1				
5				
9				
13				
17				
21				
25				
29				
33				
37				
41				
45				
49				
53				

Issued and Returned		
To	Out	In

Figure 19–18. File History Form.

tapes, punched cards, and a variety of forms and records. These records must be controlled on an item basis, and detailed control records maintained throughout their existence (Fig. 19.18).

PROGRAM MAINTENANCE

Program maintenance includes the making of relatively minor changes in operating programs to update them, solve program-operating problems, adapt to scheduling changes, and correct errors found in programs after they have gone into an operating status. Efficient program maintenance depends to a great extent on the adequacy of the documentation prepared when the programs were developed. A significant aspect of program maintenance is a continuing liaison with system users and program operators.

MANAGEMENT FUNCTIONS

Data processing shares in common with other activities the many functions of administering and supervising an operating unit (Figs. 19.19, 19.20).

SUPERVISION AND ADMINISTRATION

Special aspects of data processing administration and supervision are as follows:

1. Good utilization of the equipment is a constant concern since meeting schedules is very important.
2. Rigid, detailed operations and creative development work must often be supervised simultaneously, as a combination.

INFORMATION CHARACTERISTICS BY DECISION CATEGORY

CHARACTERISTICS OF INFORMATION	OPERATIONAL CONTROL	MANAGEMENT CONTROL	STRATEGIC PLANNING
Source	Internal	Internal/External	External
Scope	Deterministic	Det./Prob.	Probabilistic
Level of Detail Data	Detailed	Intermediate	Aggregate
Time Horizon	Historical	Current	Future
Currency of Data Base	Current	Intermediate	Old
Units of Measurement	Quantity	Dollars & Others	Dollars
Accuracy of Data Base	High	Average	Low
Frequency of Occurrence of Information Change	High	Average	Low
Frequency of Use of Information	Very Frequent	Frequent	Infrequent
End Result	Action within Procedures	Procedures	Policies
Mental Activity	Implementation	Persuasive	Creative & Analytical
Nature of Information	Functional Departmental	Divisional Inter-Departmental	Integrated
Level of Management Involvement	Supervisors; Workers	Middle Management	Senior Management

Figure 19–19. Information Characteristics by Decision Category.

INFORMATION SYSTEMS PLANNING MATRIX

	OPERATIONAL CONTROL	MANAGEMENT CONTROL	STRATEGIC PLANNING
Deterministic	Order Entry Accts. Receivable Payroll Inventory Control Eng. Data Control Standard/Job/ Process Costs	Variance Analysis-Cost/Perf. Prod. Plan. & Sched. Sales Analysis Financial Statement Analysis PERT/CPM	Return on Investment (ROI) Simulation Linear Programming Models (Plant Location Alternatives) P & L Objectives
Probabilistic	Short Range Cash Flow Engineering Design Job Shop Scheduling	Sales Planning & Forecasting Budget Preparation Facilities Planning Capital Budgeting	New Product Selection & Planning Mergers & Acquisitions Long-Term Cash Management Risk Analysis — Alternate Investment Strategies (Simulation)

Figure 19–20. Information Systems Planning Matrix.

3. Supervision of data processing work is very difficult without a thorough knowledge of the technical details and technical skills usage capabilities of the equipment.

REPORTING

The reporting function is an important part of any manager's job. Data processing management faces two problems.

1. The translation of technical measures of progress and performance into commonly understood standards.
2. Continual reporting on planning and project performance.

LONG RANGE PLANNING AND PROJECT CONTROL

Long term plans occupy a very important part of the manager's time. Long range plans are typically subject to periodic and often major revisions. Projects may be scheduled and developed within the long range plan, available budgets, personnel availability—often in the face of conflicting pressures from the other departments served. Data processing management must keep constantly abreast of the new developments in equipment and techniques, to see how these may alter future planning.

MAINTENANCE OF STANDARDS

Keeping the standards of performance and product high is extremely important in this as in any other function. But in the relatively new and constantly growing field of data processing, the establishment of standards and the maintenance of a high quality level demands constant attention to

1. Recruitment of qualified personnel.
2. Continual training of new employees and updating the training of old employees.
3. Development of quantity and quality evaluation system based on meaningful standards.
4. Definition and publication of job description.
5. Constant review of individual and group performance.

LIAISON

The usual position of the data processing activity within an organization greatly heightens the importance of its liaison function at the management level. The data processing manager is faced with particularly difficult relationships; he often shares in making decisions that do not relate directly to his own department and acts as an intermediary with other departments. The problem of translating technical information into management terms is always with him. Finally, in day-to-day operations, he must act to assure a smooth timely flow of data.

DATA PROCESSING POSITIONS

Exact job titles and content are closely related to the size of the data processing activity, the type of installation, the kind of organization and other factors in the environment (Figs. 19.21, 19.22). The following are the five major types of data processing positions:

CLERICAL AND ADMINISTRATIVE

These positions are generally concerned with input and output control and record maintenance—operating functions in the data processing unit. Typical jobs in this category, discussed below, include:

Librarian issues and stores data files and other records of the installation.

Control clerk is responsible for the integrity of all data received, processed, and dispatched from the data processing department. The duties include such activities as batch balancing, validity checking of data, zero balancing, and other control activities specified by the application.

Scheduler and Dispatcher coordinates the input requirements of production programs, the output requirements of the user department and the processing capabilities of the data processing equipment; dispatches the outputs to the ultimate users. This is one of the few clerical positions requiring technical operations experience.

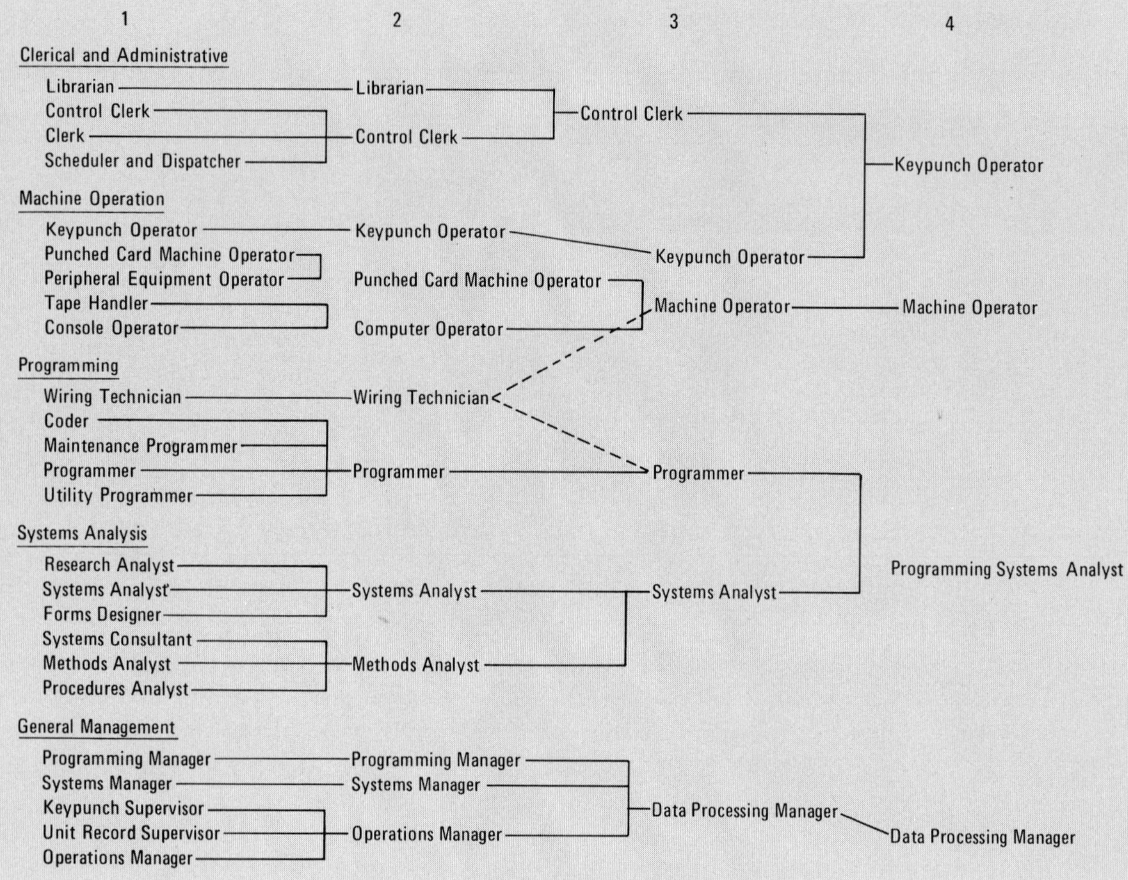

Figure 19–21. Data Processing Positions by Levels.

Clerk performs miscellaneous document and data handling tasks required for smooth work flow between machine processing steps. Also removes carbons and separates continuous form paper from the final processing of output reports.

MACHINE OPERATION

Jobs in this category are concerned with the operation of the data processing equipment. The following are typical jobs included in this category:

Keypunch Operator converts source documents into machine acceptable forms (occasionally operating a tape-to-card converter).

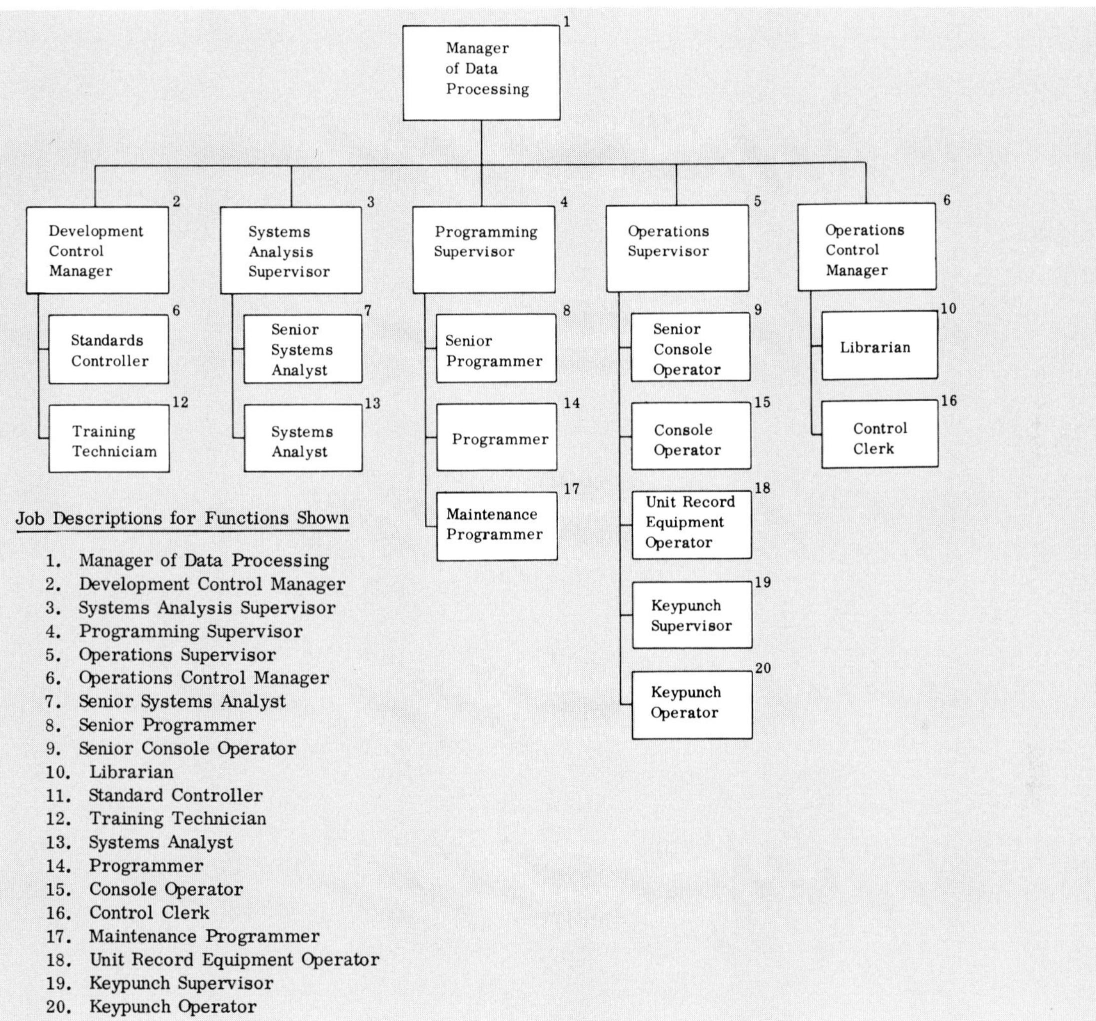

Figure 19–22. Typical Data Processing Job Titles.

Console Operator operates a computer system (including entry of variable data through the console keyboard, initialization and loading of programs), monitors the progam during the execution and records equipment utilization figures (Fig. 19.23).

Peripheral Equipment Operator operates equipment in support of the main processing configuration for such purposes as card-to-tape and tape-to-card conversion, loading and editing, and tape-to-printer report preparation.

Punched Card Equipment Operator operates punched card equipment.

File Handler obtains and returns tape reels, disk, and data cells, mounts

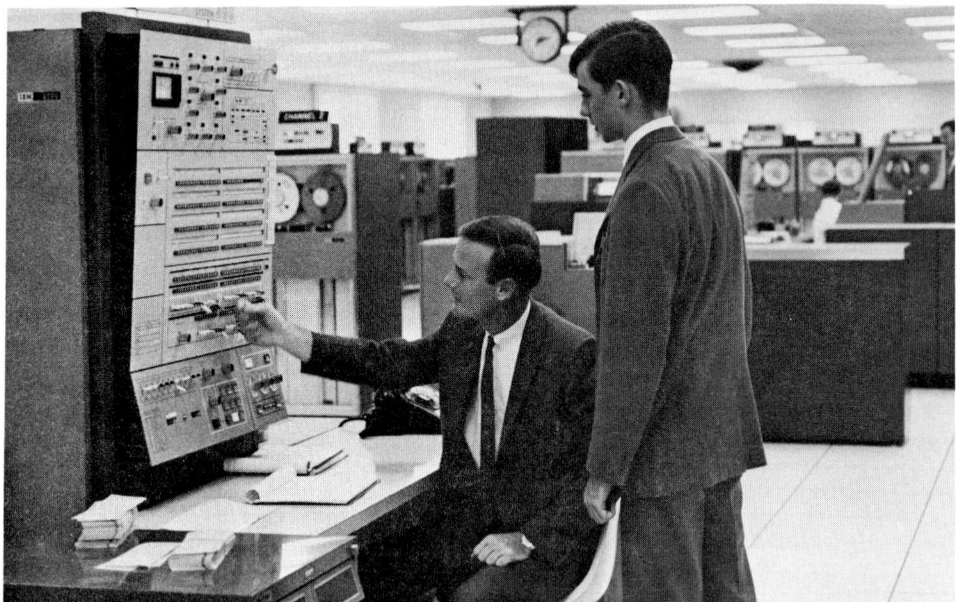

Figure 19–23. Console Operator.

and dismounts files on the proper drives assigned by program specifications and directed by the console operator, and maintains work and master files in the computer room.

PROGRAMMING

Programming positions occur both in the planning and operating functions.

Wiring Technician wires and tests control panels and defines external control switches and selectors for punched card equipment.

Coder converts detailed logical descriptions into program instructions as specified by the program specifications.

Maintenance Programmer codes and tests such revisions to production programs as are needed to maintain operations.

Programmer designs and tests program logic, selects subroutines, selects other software for use in the program.

Utility Programmer develops subroutines and special software, develops programming techniques, and trains programming staff in the use of these aids.

SYSTEMS ANALYSIS

These positions are concerned mainly with the planning of new applications. Although the general title *systems analyst* or *systems designer* is normally used in most levels, occasionally job specialization extends to these positions as follows.

Research Analyst investigates and reviews operations identified as suitable for data processing applications.

Forms Designer designs, coordinates and controls the use and circulation of all forms within an organization.

Procedures Analyst develops improved clerical and manual office procedures.

Methods Analyst designs systems, and plans for their implementation; controls and coordinates conversions to new systems.

System Consultant supplies technical assistance and direction with specific emphasis on problem identification, organization analysis, conversion planning, forms control, and analysis and report control.

MANAGEMENT

Typical job titles in the management structure are as follows:

Manager of Data Processing is responsible for the planning, development, and operation of applications and programs to meet the needs of the organization.

Manager of Systems Analysis is responsible for planning, scheduling, and supervising systems analysis and design activities.

Program Manager is responsible for the planning, scheduling, and supervising program development and maintenance work.

Manager of Operations is responsible for the operations and scheduled use of data processing equipment.

Computer Supervisor is responsible for the operation and scheduled use of the computer and peripheral devices.

Control Supervisor is responsible for input preparation, job scheduling, data control, and output control.

Punched Card Supervisor is responsible for the operation and scheduled use of punched card equipment.

Keypunch Supervisor is responsible for input preparation using keypunch and key verification equipment.

Certain management functions are sometimes delegated to staff positions such as the following:

Standards Controller develops and audits the use of standards in programming, data control, systems analysis, and operating procedures.

Training Specialist develops and conducts educational programs dealing in data processing, and guides the technical training of new and promoted employees.

Advanced Planner reviews and evaluates new developments in the data processing field and coordinates the formal planning of the data processing department with the corporate forward planning effort.

INTRODUCTION OF A SYSTEM

INSTALLATION (Fig. 19.24)

A decision to establish a new data processing system is usually reached as the result of a favorable feasibility study. Beneficial results of a good system are rarely maximized because the installation tasks were not properly met. The following are some of the important steps in a proper installation of a system:

1. All procedures must be converted to the new system and properly documented.
2. The new system must be sold to all levels of management to overcome resistance.
3. During the installation period, tight controls should be maintained over every phase of the new system. This will include the following controls.
   a) *Checkpoint Controls:* a point in the program through which every document flows.
   b) *Data Flow Controls:* the recording of input and output through log sheets, registers, documents, etc.
   c) *Accounting Controls:* dollar and unit controls on all volume quantities.
4. A calendar should be agreed upon. This includes the scheduling of personnel requirements (including training), necessary forms, and equipment for the proper installation at the appropriate time.
5. The necessary manuals and job instructions must be prepared for use during and after the installation period.
6. Necessary personnel must be educated and trained. This training may be at the computer manufacturer's school, at colleges or universities, or at the plant.
7. A method of installation must be decided upon.
   a) *All at Once* method—recommended when the system is relatively simple and does not involve too many organizational units, or the volume of data to be processed is relatively light.
   b) *Piecemeal* installation—usually recommended when there is a large volume job to be converted and it is simpler to convert a segment at a time.

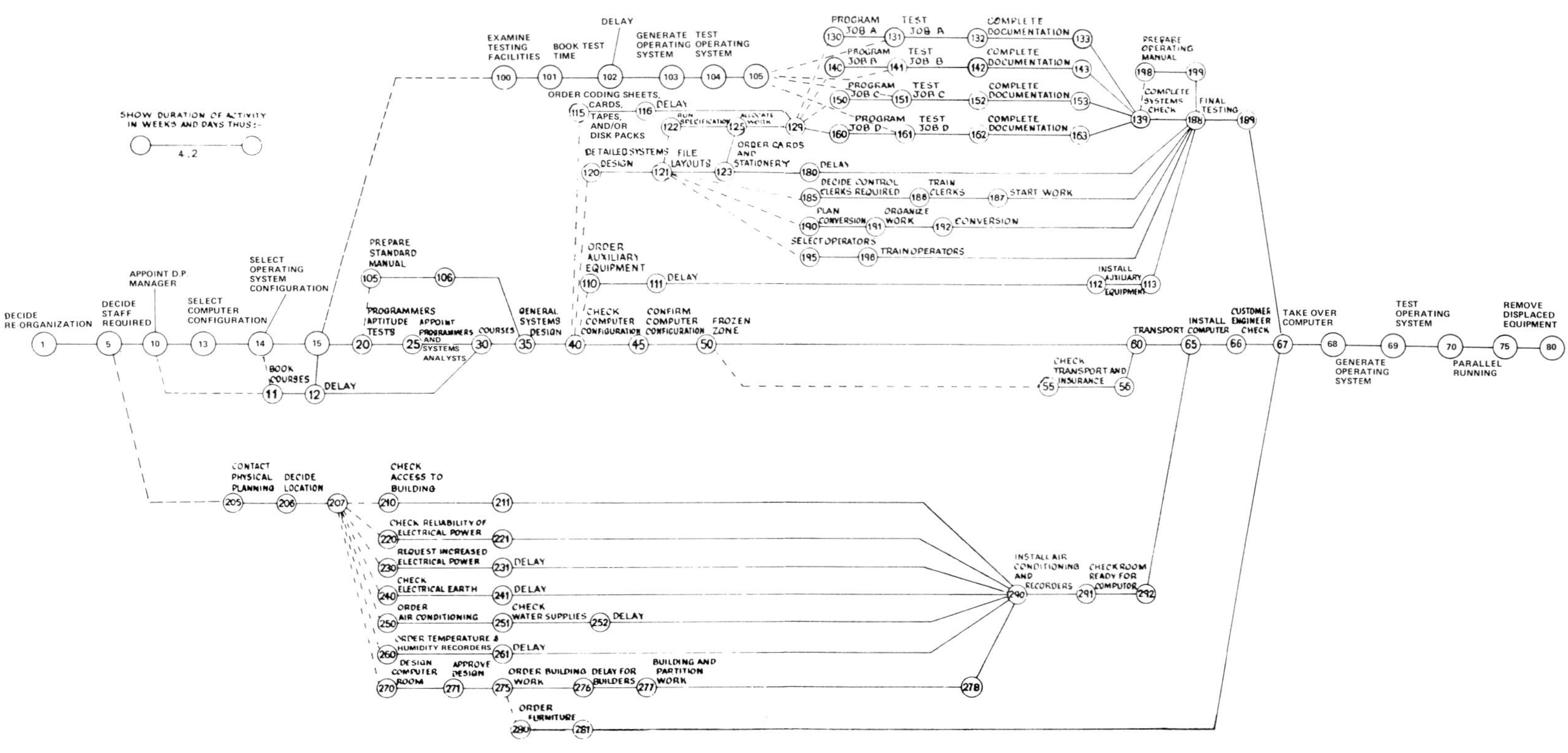

Specimen critical path for computer installation

Figure 19-24. Specimen Critical Path for Computer Installation.

c) *Parallel Operations*—usually recommended for large scale jobs involving intricate processing. A payroll application is usually converted using a parallel operation method—the old and new systems operating simultaneously. When the new system satisfies all the needs, the old system may be abandoned.

DURATION OF THE INSTALLATION PERIOD

Strict control of the system should continue until the system personnel are satisfied that the new system is functioning properly, that all problems are solved, and everyone fully trained, and that the new system will operate without the supervision of the systems personnel. At such time the system should be turned over in its entirety to the operating personnel.

REMEDIAL ACTION

The control devices will point out whether the concepts and results are deviating from established standards. When this happens, swift and accurate changes must be made to the system.

COST CONSIDERATIONS

The primary design of the system was to save money and time but during the installation period, costs may exceed those of the old system. This may be due to the following factors:

1. *Duplication of Effort.* Two systems operating at the same time.
2. *More Stringent Controls.* Excess controls during this period will require additional clerical efforts.
3. *Learning Curves.* It will take employees longer to do a new job than it took to do the old job, using the old system (after months and years of practice).
4. *One Time Costs.* Such costs as site preparation, transportation costs, additional employees, etc.
5. *Resistance to Changes.* Old employees may be hesitant about learning new systems.

PERSONNEL PROBLEMS

The new system must be properly communicated to the employees. They must be allowed the opportunity to participate in the planning of the new system and the conversion. This will satisfy their personal goals and make them more anxious to participate in the new system.

FOLLOW-UP

The prime purpose of follow-up is to consolidate all new gains made by the new system and to eliminate any losses. When to follow up depends upon the complexity of the new system. Various methods may be used.

CONTINUOUS THEORY

Every area in the system is visited and checked each time it is visited.

SPOT CHECK

Check the system at specific time intervals. First check after installation has been in operation for thirty days. The frequency thereafter will depend on the complexity of the system.

The systems analyst should assure himself that

1. The costs are in line.
2. The facilities are adequate.
3. The employee's performances are acceptable.
4. The employees are accepting the new system.
5. There is no evidence of falling back to the old system.

In addition to consolidating gains and correcting misunderstandings, there are several other reasons for follow-up.

1. A feedback on the operation of the system.
2. Possible revisions of the system.
3. To prevent and discourage backsliding to the old system by participants.
4. Discovery of new ideas and improvements during this period.
5. The preparation of justification reports to management.

SUMMARY

The problems encountered in managing a data processing installation are quite different from those found in managing other units of the enterprise. Data processing organization requires the careful blending of technical and managerial skills to achieve a well-balanced data processing unit. The data processing effort follows concepts and methods not ordinarily followed in other units of an organization. Highly trained, technically competent, and in many cases creative personnel are required in a data processing unit. Data processing has created many new positions quite different from those found in other areas of the company. Data processing performs a service function and its primary obligation is to satisfy the needs of all units of an organization.

It is the intent of this chapter to acquaint the reader with the many problems that arise in the management function of the data processing installation.

I. *Organization of a data processing unit.*
   A. *Data processing objectives.*
      1. Management purposes to be served.
      2. Operational purposes to be served.
      3. Scope of service.
      4. Means of service—open or closed shop.
      5. Future plans.
   B. *Centralized data processing unit.*
      1. *Advantages.*
         a) All departments receive equal consideration.
         b) More efficient program planning and systems research and development.
         c) Disputes between departments more easily settled.
         d) Costs of expansion reduced.
      2. *Disadvantages.*
         a) Largest users have same priority as others.
         b) May result in unprofitable use of data processing facilities.
         c) Physical distance between data processing facility and users may create problems.
   C. *Decentralized data processing unit.*
      1. *Advantages.*
         a) Direct control by users.
         b) Only minimum equipment for purpose served required for each unit.
         c) Major users more sensitive to economic use of equipment.
      2. *Disadvantages.*
         a) Formal corporate policy on use of equipment difficult.
         b) Integration of data processing functions and long range planning is difficult.
         c) Other departments may have difficulty in obtaining data processing services.
         d) Total data processing cost of multiple units usually higher.

II. *Data processing functions.*
   A. *Planning function*—the major activity that encompasses those functions concerned with the planning for a new application or establishing a data processing installation.
      1. *Installation planning*—organization and scheduling of human and mechanical resources.
      2. *Application selection*—the activities relative to the selection and definition of data processing applications which fulfill management objectives.

3. *System analysis and design*—the analysis of present methods, objectives and all pertinent data to produce the optimum solution to application needs.
4. *Programming*—defined system requirements and procedures translated into a logical process and a set of instructions for its operation on data processing equipment.
5. *Testing*—determining the success of the program in meeting defined systems requirements, and procedures of the total system in meeting the objectives of the application.
6. *Documentation*—reduction of the system and programs to a standardized written form for use in system and program modification, training, and machine operation.
7. *Conversion*—controlled transition from the current system to the new one.

B. *Operating functions.*
   1. *Machine operation*—actual loading, unloading, setup, and control of data processing equipment.
   2. *Input preparation*—preparing accurate, properly coded input data in the manner prescribed by system.
   3. *Input/output control*—control over operation of input/output devices; logging, controlling, coordination.
   4. *Maintenance of record libraries*—control and storage of all data files, programs, documentation, and operating records and reports.
   5. *Program maintenance*—making of relatively minor changes in operating programs.

C. *Management functions.*
   1. *Supervision and administration*—utilization and control of equipment.
   2. *Reporting*—translating the measure of progress and performance.
   3. *Long range planning and project control*—project scheduling and development within the long range period.
   4. *Maintenance of standards*—keeping the standards of performance and product high.
   5. *Liaison*—maintaining a good relationship with other departments that are being serviced.

III. *Data processing positions.*
   A. *Clerical and administrative*—these positions are concerned with input and output control and record maintenance. Examples: Librarian, clerks, schedulers, and dispatcher.
   B. *Machine operation*—jobs in this category are concerned with the

operation of data processing equipment. Examples: keypunch operators, equipment operators, File Handler.

C. *Programming*—these jobs are concerned with the programming both in the planning and operations functions. Example: Wiring Technician, Coder, Programmer.

D. *Systems Analyst*—these positions are concerned mainly with the planning of new applications and updating of present applications. Examples: Forms Designer, Systems Consultant, Research Analyst.

E. *Management*—typical jobs in this category are Manager of Data Processing, Program Manager, Manager of Operations, Control Supervisor, Keypunch Supervisor.

IV. *Introduction of a system.*

A. *Installation.*

1. *Checkpoint control*—a point in the program through which every document flows.
2. *Data flow controls*—the recording of input and output through log sheets, registers, documents, etc.
3. *Accounting controls*—the dollar and unit controls on all volume quantities.
4. *Scheduling*—when the new system is to be operational.
5. *Manuals and job instructions*—the preparation of necessary instruction manuals to be used during the installation period.
6. *Training of personnel*—the education and training of the necessary personnel.
7. *Method of installation.*
   a) *All at once*—entire conversion of old system to new.
   b) *Piecemeal*—conversion of one segment of the system at a time.
   c) *Parallel*—old and new systems operate simultaneously until the new system satisfies all needs.

B. *Duration of installation period*—until the system personnel are satisfied that the new system is functioning properly.

C. *Remedial action*—control devices which will point out the concepts and results which are deviating from established standards.

D. *Cost considerations.*

1. *Duplicate effort*—two systems operating at the same time.
2. *More stringent controls*—additional clerical help.
3. *Learning curves*—takes employees longer to learn new system.
4. *One time costs*—site preparation, transportation costs, etc.

E. *Personnel problems*—proper communication to employees.

F. *Follow up*—consolidate all gains and prevent backsliding to old system.

1. *Continuous theory*—every area in the system is visited and checked.
2. *Spot check*—check system at specific time intervals.

IDENTIFICATION QUESTIONS

Match the following terms with the statements that follow.

A. Accounting Controls	E. Data Flow Controls	I. Operations Manual
B. Centralized Position	F. Decentralized Position	J. Program Manuals
C. Checkpoint Controls	G. Learning Curves	K. System Application Manuals
D. Closed Shop	H. Open Shop	

1. The data processing department is independent but at the same level with the department it is servicing.
2. The inputs, outputs, and procedures for the system and all programs included therein.
3. The precise instructions for running the program and dealing with emergency and unusual conditions are included herein.
4. The recording of input and output through log sheets, registers, etc.
5. It takes employees longer to do a new job than it took to do the old job.
6. Each user has access to the equipment and provides his own personnel for programming and operations.
7. The data processing department is within a larger organizational unit that is its major customer.
8. The detail logic and machine utilization of each program are included herein.
9. A point in the program through which each document flows.
10. Dollar and unit controls of all volume quantities.
11. Each user provides the data processing department with the problem and the department provides the necessary programming and operations personnel.

QUESTIONS FOR REVIEW

1. What are some of the problems encountered in data processing installations?
2. List the important factors to be considered in establishing the managerial objectives of a data processing installation.
3. What is the important difference between a centralized and decentralized data processing unit?
4. What are the important advantages and disadvantages of a centralized data processing unit?
5. What are the important advantages and disadvantages of a decentralized data processing unit?
6. What is the necessary planning function of the data processing unit?
7. Describe the different types of planning activities involved with the planning function itself.
8. Describe the major operating functions of a data processing unit.

9. What are some of the important management functions in the operation of a data processing installation?
10. What are the five types of data processing positions? Give examples of each.
11. List the important steps in the proper installation of a system.
12. Why are costs usually higher during the installation period?
13. What is the prime purpose of follow-up?
14. What must the system analyst assure himself of before he can completely release the system to operating personnel?
15. What are the other reasons for follow-up in addition to the consolidation of gains and the correction of misunderstandings?

CHAPTER 20

Data Management

The rapid expansion of computer usage, and the vast increase in the variety of uses for computers during the past decade has created many problems for management. Today, both top management and data processing executives recognize their responsibilities to the public and to company shareholders for protecting the company's investment in computer facilities, programs and data. The survival of most companies and organizations rests on the information stored in data processing media. Hence, practical safeguards must be installed to assure the accuracy and protection of important programs, files and data.

COMPUTER SECURITY

Newspaper headlines recently have blared forth stories of embezzlement by means of the computer, and in the process have raised a dark cloud that looks far more menacing than it actually is (Fig. 20.1). The words "computer fraud" leapt into print on newspaper front pages in the wake of the celebrated insurance company scandal. The company is said to have been keeping two sets of books for several years and selling bogus life insurance policies in the "reinsurance" business. Data processing professionals were quick to scoff at the idea of a "criminal computer," but some others took the headlines literally.

A class action suit filed against the insurance company contends:

"That defendants, and each of them, so carelessly, negligently and wantonly designed, constructed and manufactured said data processing equipment that said equipment could be used for any business for the purpose of defrauding the public, of which plaintiffs are members; that there is no

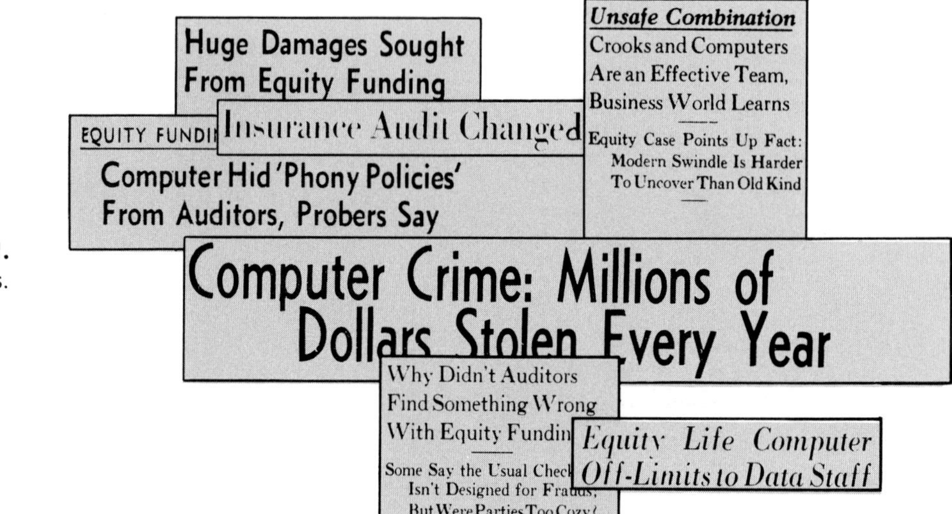

Figure 20–1. Headlines.

method available to prevent the insertion of false and fradulent material in the computer printouts and no method to discover the insertion of false and fraudulent materials in a program otherwise legitimate."

Some of the questions raised were

1. How did they get away with it?
2. What controls were missing?
3. Were improper data processing audits a factor?

How can modern business realize the full potential of the computer and still protect itself against ordinary human error, which, with no criminal intent, may scramble records and cost thousands of dollars before it is found and corrected?

Nobody can guarantee systems that are foolproof and wholly adequate in the prevention and detection of fraud. But the best line of defense against either error or fraud is a combination of properly supervised operations, systems that incorporate good management controls, and the proper kind of computer auditing (Fig. 20.2).

The computer has become faster and more versatile and has been given more and more nonaccounting functions. Today, computers are playing an important part in nearly all aspects of a business. And today's use of the computer merely sketches the shape of things to come!

The role of the internal auditor has broadened tremendously. Not long ago the auditor was pretty much restricted to verifying the accuracy of accounting department computations. Now, at least in the more progressive firms, the functions of the auditor are as broad as the total operations of the

Figure 20–2. Suggestions on How to Prevent Computer Frauds.

1. Let as few people as possible use your computer.
2. Make them give the proper password—or better yet, a series of two or three—before the computer will do anything.
3. Limit the number of miscues. For example, the computer should holler for help on the third attempt in a row to use the wrong password.
4. Change passwords often.
5. Make everyone log in and out when he uses the computer.
6. Check the log frequently. If a program takes longer to run than it should, maybe it has been tampered with.
7. Give no one blanket access to computer data. Restrict users to what they have a right to know. Then, for example, production personnel can't tamper with financial records.
8. Keep tight security over the computer center itself.
9. Use a random monitoring system to spot-check what your computer's doing.

business. The auditor's new job, which has been defined as operational or management auditing, is gradually gaining recognition.

Many companies today are trying to do today's work with yesterday's auditors. Auditors who never had even a nodding acquaintance with the older punched-card computer systems now face the huge gap between the ledgers of the past and the integrated data processing systems of today and tomorrow. Systems of the future will operate on a fast-response, online, realtime basis, and will employ input and inquiry devices unheard of previously. Unless auditors become intimately acquainted with new developments now, they will not even know what they are facing, let alone be able to cope with it.

In a very real sense, the auditor now must work through the machine, which means he must understand what the program is doing and how it does it. The auditor must be able to use the machine itself as a tool to audit its own operations. He no longer has piles of paper to paw through. The classical "paper trail" or "audit trail" is vanishing, and is being replaced by invisible arrangements of molecules in an iron oxide coating on plastic tape or drums.

AUDIT PACKAGES

A powerful new tool is now available to the computer auditor. It takes the form of computer programs known as Computer Audit Packages, which are designed to keep the auditor independent of the data processing personnel. Using this package, the accountant is able to select, summarize, and study categories of records from magnetic tape or disk, even though he has no programming background. He can select certain records for examination without the necessity of requiring programming assistance.

Computer Audit Packages are just another form of generalized computer programs designed to satisfy the particular needs of the auditor. During the past several years, many of these generalized audit programs have come on the market. All have differing features and capabilities suitable for auditing one's company computer system.

The auditor would realize that a generalized audit program is potentially a very powerful audit tool. If he uses the program only to prepare confirmation letters and test extensions and footings he will not be properly utilizing it. For with the universe of data to be audited now available in magnetic form, he has the opportunity to select data which may indicate a real or potential problem area. In short, he can perform his analysis electronically, ultimately providing his management with a more meaningful and more effective audit report.

Some of the audit functions which should be considered in evaluating a generalized audit program are as follows:

Extraction. The extraction function should enable the user to select only those records which meet predetermined criteria. These criteria should be changeable by means of control card entries which can be readily changed to fit shifting demands. These criteria should allow the selection of records on the basis of their data's inclusion or exclusion within a range of values or on a match with exact values. The possible combinations for extraction should be further expanded by AND/OR relationship tests for selection of records meeting required combinations of criteria. In addition, the ability to apply different sampling intervals to each type of extracted record is often most useful.

Mathematics. The mathematical function should allow the user to enter mathematical formulas of his own description for calculation. Possible applications are summation of payroll deductions, cross footing and balancing, checking extensions, to name but a few.

Surveying (Frequency Distribution). The surveying function allows the auditor to take item and amount totals of all records meeting a certain criterion, without extracting the individual records. On this basis file characteristics can be stratified without selecting the actual records for audit. For instance, in an accounts receivable application, the auditor may be interested in determining the number and dollar ranges: $.01 to 50.00, $50.01 to 500.00, etc.

Totaling. The subtotaling function allows for printing subtotal amounts when there is a change in the given file sequence. As many levels of subtotals should be provided as the auditor deems necessary for his applications. Final trial totals should, of course, also be provided. A possible application should be the subtotaling of a payroll file which is in order by branch, department, and section.

Aging. The aging function should make possible a comparison of the dates in the records to a given date, and the stratification of each record into selected categories such as: current, 31–60 days, 61–90 days, 91–120 days, over 120 days.

Sampling. The sampling functions can be used to select records based on a sequential interval or based on random numbers. Both are useful to the auditor and will be used in different types of audit situations.

Comparison of Two Files. The comparison should allow the user to match two files on a given sequence and compare the data in one file to that of the other. In addition, in the case of information which is split between two files, for example, one file of account numbers, transactions, etc., and the other, a corresponding name file, both files can be used simultaneously to include more meaningful data on printed reports and other reports.

Printer-File and Confirmation Outputs. The package should provide multiple output types such as report, file, and confirmations. All should be free format and under the auditor's control.

User Exits. Provide the auditor with the ability to extend the capabilities of his system in new and unique areas of his own design.

Test Auditing. In order to test the content and format of the audit results prior to processing the entire file, the auditor may wish to run a test audit on a portion of the file.

Bypass Invalid Data. In order to prevent an audit from terminating because of invalid data (fields intended to be numeric and are not) the auditor should have the ability to bypass and print out invalid data.

The concept of generalized audit programs is an excellent approach in solving a large void that exists today. The auditor should select an audit package that will suit his needs.

Although audit packages will help to prevent human errors and frauds, there are still many areas of computer processing audits that need investigation. Public accounting audit teams should include data processing professionals. Certain audit files (such as usage statistics) should be generated automatically, stored online, and be accessible only to the audit team. State insurance commissioners and other government regulatory agencies could greatly improve auditing abilities and procedures by establishing standards for master audit files, thus making it easier to maintain programs for reading them.

What has happened in the aforementioned insurance scandal will generate new interest in controls and audits. In light of this scandal, the American Institute of Certified Public Accountants has formed a special committee to investigate and to determine where there is a need for a change in auditing computer systems.

Many companies will be looking carefully into their data processing controls and a good many CPAs will be signing up for data processing courses.

DATA SECURITY

Each month brings reports of computers destroyed by bombs, fire, or other means. There are ready headlines such as: COMPUTER FACILITY BOMBED—ONE KILLED, or STUDENTS BURN COMPUTERS—DESTROY TAPES. Such occurrences can force a company out of business. Many companies have failed due to damage to their computer programs and tapes or disk files. Others have suffered losses so severe that it took years to recover.

Management has paid little attention to this problem. A catastrophe in the computer room can be just as devastating as lightning striking the plant. Without any countermeasures, there may be no company left to suffer another catastrophe. Managers can no longer ignore the risk involved in using computers. It is too vital a problem. The hazards in using computers should be analyzed and treated as any other business risk.

Various risks associated with the use of computers are; fire, explosion, natural disasters, sabotage social protests, loss of programs and/or data, mechanical or electronic breakdown, data theft, fraud, law suits, etc.

PREVENTIVE MEASURES

Few, if any data processing installations have the funds needed to take all of the following precautions which are enumerated and discussed here in order to furnish reference points for deciding which measures to employ. These possibilities are segregated into five categories; location, site construction, operating procedures, data protection, and legal protection.

Location. If choice of a building location is possible, one should consider possible catastrophes. Select or erect a strong fireproof building in a safe location. Location within the building should also be considered. One should select a location away from the regular stream of pedestrians, out of sight and not contiguous to danger.

Site Construction. Fireproof computer sites constructed in fireproof buildings provide the best protection against fire. Locked maximum-security doors provide the best protection against undesired intrusion. A plain lock, which can be opened easily from the inside is preferable.

To protect against theft, unauthorized use of the computer, and sabotage during off-hours, closed circuit television provides comparatively inexpensive protection. A continuous picture of the computer installation can be relayed to the guard's station. If the danger is great enough, an ultrasonic detector system with alarm to both the guard and to a central point will supply added protection.

Operating Procedures. There should be, if possible, only one entrance used to get into the building with a guard stationed there at all times. All windows and doors should have alarm devices. The guard should inspect all packages to insure against explosives or firearms being carried into the building.

Access to the computer facility should be limited to those whose presence is needed. The day of the computer as a showpiece is gone. Visitors should be limited in number and always accompanied by a supervisor and a log of all visitors should be kept. Any visitor permitted to take anything from the computer room or tape vault should be required to sign a receipt.

The tape room should be locked and under the control of a tape librarian. A tape log should be maintained with a complete record of tape withdrawals, returns, times, purposes, and persons involved. Access to this room should be severely limited.

Tapes are comparatively small and easily damaged. At a minimum, all tapes should have identification data, date of creation, and disposal date. Backup tapes for necessary programs and data should be maintained in a safe room, preferably in another building. As programs are changed and files updated the current program or file should be substituted for the outdated one. This is a comparatively inexpensive means of insuring safety of programs and data.

Regardless of how good a security system is, undependable employees can negate it. Computer room employees should be checked carefully before employment.

Operating procedures, no matter how carefully supervised, quickly become ineffective without good supervision. Good procedures should be established and employees should be trained to follow them. Even this is not enough. Continual inspections and audits should be carried out to ensure that these procedures are followed faithfully.

Data Protection. The degree of protection depends upon the amount of secrecy needed. Overprotection of computer records can be a very costly matter. The data processing manager normally cannot make the determination. His job is to state the risks, the possibilities of the data being stolen, his estimate of the possible consequences and the costs of protection. He should give this information, together with his recommendations, to management, which makes the final decision concerning the precautions to be taken.

Unless proper precautions are taken almost all input to or output from a computer can be read from outside the computer room without the knowledge or consent of those inside. Also data transmitted over wire or by radio can be tapped. Input/output gear should be located as close to the center of the computer room as possible. This will make reading them from outside more difficult.

Growth in the use of telecommunications, online systems, time sharing, and companies using remote terminals for access to the computer has raised an entire new crop of security problems. The ability of the computer to distinguish between different users of remote terminals and to limit their access to files accordingly is of paramount importance in today's online and time sharing systems. Most systems depend upon key words, special numbers, and person-terminal coordination for recognition. These methods require programs and the ability to make unreadable the typewritten record of the key word or special number made by an authorized person. Furthermore, these key words or numbers can be changed as often as necessary. The computer can contain a table listing of the files the user is permitted to use. This will help protect the files of other users.

No software system is 100 percent safe. Assuming that all the methods discussed have been employed, a log of all users, their queries, and the files accessed should be kept where the user cannot control what goes into the log, and can neither read nor change what is there. Regular and continual audit of this file should reveal any attempted accession of sensitive files before the accessor has accomplished his purpose.

Legal Protection. With the growth of suits by users against manufacturers, software houses and service bureaus, the data processing manager must pay attention to the matter of legal protection. In dealing with a computer manufacturer thousands, perhaps millions of dollars are at stake. A standard contract must pertain for legal obligations. Let the legal department of the company handle all matters relative to computer leases, computer purchases, software rentals and purchases, data processing supplies, etc. Particularly important are service and maintenance contracts with the computer manufacturer.

In order to protect oneself against derivative suits by stockholders, or other interested parties, files should be kept. These files should give the details and cost of possible alternatives that were considered in making decisions. Escape routes in case things go wrong should be included. With such documentation, charges would be reduced to considering the merits of the decision, instead of charges to the effect that no consideration was given to alternatives.

Additional Measures. The computers of a multicomputer company can be decentralized. Then, if anything should put a computer installation out of operation the complete data processing capability of the company would not be wiped out. Another possibility would be to have an unused but duplicate installation in a remote location. Few companies, however, could afford this expense.

Almost as much protection, but with far less cost is the use of a backup facility. The agreement with the furnisher of the backup facility should be in writing.

Although installation of fire or heat-proof safes will not prevent fire, they will lessen damage if a fire occurs.

If you are using a time sharing system, send one of your tapes to the central location. Have your files dumped on your tape, ensuring that it is clearly marked as your property. If the time sharing company goes bankrupt or suffers any catastrophe, you will be able to recover both your tape and data from the central location.

Business insurance is another preventive measure. Employees should be bonded if they are in a position to seize any assets of the company fraudulently. Fire insurance should be taken out, not only for hardware and the premises, but also for the software and the additional expenses involved in continuing operations in a backup site until the computer facility is restored. Insurance covering errors or omissions is available also. For almost any of the risks detailed previously, some form of insurance can be obtained.

What can the data processing manager do? What must he do? He must recognize the potential dangers. After recognizing these dangers he should prepare a cost/value analysis. The following, at least, should be considered; hazard, degree of damage, probability of occurrence, consequences, possible dollar damages, measures recommended, comparison of cost of probable damages with costs of measures recommended, alternative measures considered. A data processing manager completing this analysis will have qualified the major elements of hazards and countermeasures considered. He is now ready to make specific recommendations to top management.

There are many potential hazards to a computer installation. For each hazard, there is a preventive measure. It is extremely risky to fail to take appropriate preventive measures. The cost of taking all preventive measures is very high. The major problem is that of determining which measures are appropriate. The data processing manager's prime responsibility is to recognize all of the hazards that exist. Using a cost/value analysis, he should make recommendations to top management detailing those measures he believes to be appropriate for that particular installation. Top management then has the tools with which to make the best decision for the company.

TELECOMMUNICATIONS PROTECTION

The increasing use of remote terminals for file maintenance, on-line testing, data inquiry and information retrieval, and management information reporting requires new types of protection and controls.

Telecommunications permit access to information from distant locations, via terminal or telephone. Thus, online files must be protected at the source, since potential access can occur from anywhere.

CLASSIFICATION OF INFORMATION

The needs for data security must be related directly to the type of program or information that can be accessed through a terminal. Certain files probably should be restricted to only a few people, due to the proprietary value of those files to the company, or to their confidential nature. This category would include payroll information, lists of major customers and activity, unique engineering design solutions, and employee personnel files.

A second level of classification might be assigned to files, access to which is required by a large group of employees, but which, by modification, is available to a few people only. In this group are files such as demand deposit accounts, loan accounts, accounts receivable, employee personnel files (excluding payroll), and bills of material files.

A third level might permit broad access and interaction with minimal security. This might include the use of program instructions, general routines for financial or engineering problem-solving, stock market information, product catalog information, or stolen car reports.

SYSTEM DESIGN FACTORS

Systems analysts designing online systems have a continuing responsibility to build in security controls to assure that only authorized personnel can have access or modify information. Sections of a particular file can be classified with different levels of access, and individual *passwords* required to enter these sections of the file. Multiple tests can include passwords, employee numbers, and the specific terminal location entered automatically on a hardware device. If all three tests are not met, access may be refused.

Identification and passwords should be changed frequently and those of terminating or transferred employees deleted immediately.

Control Audits. Many different controls can be instituted to assure appropriate checks and balances, and to permit early detection of accidental or intentional security breaches.

Detailed logs. Records of all inquiries and access to critical data files should be maintained and computer-analyzed periodically in a search for excessive usage, unauthorized terminal locations, extra long spans of communication, and unusual times of access.

Lockword. In addition to a required password permitting access to the file, a special *lockword* may be required to permit access to portions of a file, or to accept modification. Normally, the lockword is changed frequently and limited to a very few authorized people.

Monte Carlo Validation. The internal audit group may periodically take samples from the online file and assure that no "dummy" records exist. Such techniques are frequently used to verify payroll files, banking files, and insurance files.

DATA PROCESSING RESPONSIBILITY

Data processing's foremost responsibility lies with answering management's requirements insofar as operational and statistical reports are concerned. The major areas of responsibility are: usefulness of reports, systems design, communication, accuracy, timeliness, personnel, economy, technology study, and progress reports.

USEFULNESS OF REPORTS

It should be the responsibility of all operational as well as management people connected with data processing to continually audit all output reports leaving the department, and to inform management of any cases of duplication in the material being distributed to the various user departments.

Care must be taken to consider the potential usefulness of all new requests for data. If the expected result does not warrant the time required for programming, testing, and debugging, this information should be made known to people initiating such a request.

Data processing cannot allow itself the luxury of preparing reports for the sake of additional hours on the computer meter, or for the sake of adding to the paper work within an organization.

SYSTEMS DESIGN

The major systems design generally falls with the data processing managers' realm of responsibility. It is up to the data processing manager to understand and communicate management goals before setting out in any direction in the systems effort. Large sums of money are spent in an effort to obtain a long range systems design which will enhance the competitive position of a company. However, only by bringing needed information that will, through efficient and timely operation, direct a company toward a better profit picture, can computer costs by justified.

Every effort is required to avoid the mistake of so over-emphasizing the data processing function as to include poorly-thought-out sections which should actually be done manually. Care must be taken to exclude any function from the automated system which could be accomplished more efficiently and/or more economically by a manual method.

In areas of doubtful performance, great care should be taken before the decision is made to include such tasks in the data processing function. Once a job has been erroneously included, it is very difficult to back it out.

COMMUNICATION

It is the responsibility of data processing to recognize the necessity for breaking through the so-called communication gap between data processing and the rest of the organization and to inform management, as well as all users, of situations in which it would be more expedient and feasible to not run certain data through a data processing routine.

Computers are expensive and should not become high-speed, high-priced typewriters. A large majority of computer installations are overtaxed to maintain their schedules from a timeliness standpoint; when "out-of-system" jobs are entered into the priority system, a simple request for data can create a real scheduling nightmare. Management has a right to expect that it will be kept informed of the true status of any data processing problems resulting from a conflict between scheduling and the time factor.

High sounding phrases of computerese jargon have become, in many cases, a way of life rather than a communication link for data processing specialists. Use of such phrases as "management information system" has been so overextended as to distort the original concept. *Management Information System defines an operation consisting of a series of steps designed to furnish all the data required by management, in a concise form, which will enable them to make the necessary decisions, on a timely basis, to result in a successful and profitable business operation.* It is supported by a single all-encompassing data base from which all information can be obtained.

The data processing facility owes to itself the acceptance of the fact that it, like every other facility, must justify its existence with facts and results—not with an obscure vocabulary. Management should insist that systems and reports are created and explained in language that can be understood clearly by everyone.

The responsibility for sound communication rests on the information interchanged understandably between all people in data processing, those in nondata processing management, and user departments personnel.

ACCURACY

Data processing departments are well known by many for being prone to user department criticism concerning accuracy. The first thought of the user is keypunch errors, programmer errors, or compute errors.

It is the responsibility of the data processing department to keep as tight a rein as possible on quality control of output, within the organization. By the use of check-point accounting, both internal and external crossfooting and balancing data, data processing output should be controlled to an error content of near zero.

Results can be expected to be only as good as the input. Therefore it is important that accuracy of input be made emphatic to the other departments originating the data. The work must be continuous toward the goal of a full audit trail to be absolutely certain of as near perfect accuracy as possible, in all data emanating from the department.

TIMELINESS

With the ever-changing and ever-increasing work load to schedule through today's data processing departments, a continuous effort is called for to keep schedules updated. Constant review is required to note priority changes and other happenings which may affect the timeliness of output reports.

PERSONNEL

Due to the extreme diversity of material which is processed, data processing personnel must be highly versatile. The point often missed by nondata processing personnel is that data processing people must be capable of switching their thinking through all phases of the operation. This thinking process requires a unique, alert mentality. Acceptance of one less effective person within a department causes problems with accuracy and timeliness affecting the entire department.

ECONOMY

An addiction fairly common with data processing managers appears to be the constant and everlasting desire for acquiring the latest sophisticated equipment. Study and review of all such equipment is certainly a necessity. If there is a new piece of hardware, or software, which will truly improve the operation, management should be made aware of it. The responsibility still remains with the data processing manager to be absolutely certain that the advantage is there and not just a desire to upgrade for the sake of prestige.

A great responsibility exists for the economic operation of the data processing function; it becomes more critical as uses for computer-based data increase. Under the heading of such economy falls the prolific issuance of reports and copies without a periodic review for the purpose of deleting unnecessary material. The review of such reports and copies for deletion purposes is becoming an increasingly important economy measure.

TECHNOLOGICAL STUDY

The heavy outflow of new technology inherent in the data processing profession continues unceasingly, and it is the grave responsibility of the data processing manager to keep up with the available information concerning this mass of advances and changes. It is further his responsibility to apprise management of anything which is significant and might actually apply to the particular organization. His greatest responsibility in this area lies in dissecting the mass of information and putting it into summary form for presentation to management in a manner which will keep them up-to-date and knowledgeable, but only on subjects of significance to them.

REPORTING ON PROGRESS

A formal method of reporting progress, or failure to progress, is often lacking and should be an integral part of the data processing responsibility. The tendency often exists to ignore this procedure if management is not interested enough to ask for it.

Much will be learned about his own operation if a data processing manager institutes such a form of reporting (even if he retains the result solely for his own study and consideration). All data processing managers should be eager to make a report, on a regular basis, which compares present operations and cost factors with past performance. Also of interest to top management would be the inclusion (at the very least) in each report of this kind, of a brief summary of plans for future systems and for improvements to be considered or accomplished on existing systems.

If data processing is to progress to the fulfillment of everyone's hope and dreams of a true, real-time, optimized Management Information System or similar system of management information reporting, which will lessen the chance of untimely decision making and heighten the profit expectancy of business, all of these responsibilities must be acknowledged and accepted by the people involved in the control and operation of the sophisticated data processing centers of the future.

FEASIBILITY STUDY

OVERVIEW

A feasibility study is intended to provide management with enough information about the proposed systems project so that an objective decision can be made with regard to its value.

The feasibility study must provide answers to four basic questions. Can it be done? Is it practical? Is it economical? How should it be done?

In order to answer these questions the existing system should be investigated, alternative solutions to the problem defined, alternatives compared with the existing method and an alternative chosen and supported with economic justification.

The preliminary analysis and requirements determination must be carried out in sufficient depth to allow a technical and economic evaluation of a proposed new system to be made. Attention must be paid to:

1. Possible existence of problem areas in the present system.
2. User organization's level of experience in the use of computers.
3. Type of improvements which user management will expect from a new system.
4. Future organizational changes which will be called for by the implementation of a new system.

The results of the feasibility study should be presented in a formal report. This is the master plan for the new system and will provide the basis for further systems effort. The master plan and its presentation should be regarded as the basis for a management decision. The presentation should therefore be designed to emphasize those aspects of the plan which most clearly assist the making of that decision. Fig. 20.3 shows the specific tasks to be performed during the feasibility study and the order in which they are generally performed.

THE STUDY

Before a detailed study is undertaken, a preliminary survey study should be made of the proposed data processing applications. Based on the conclu-

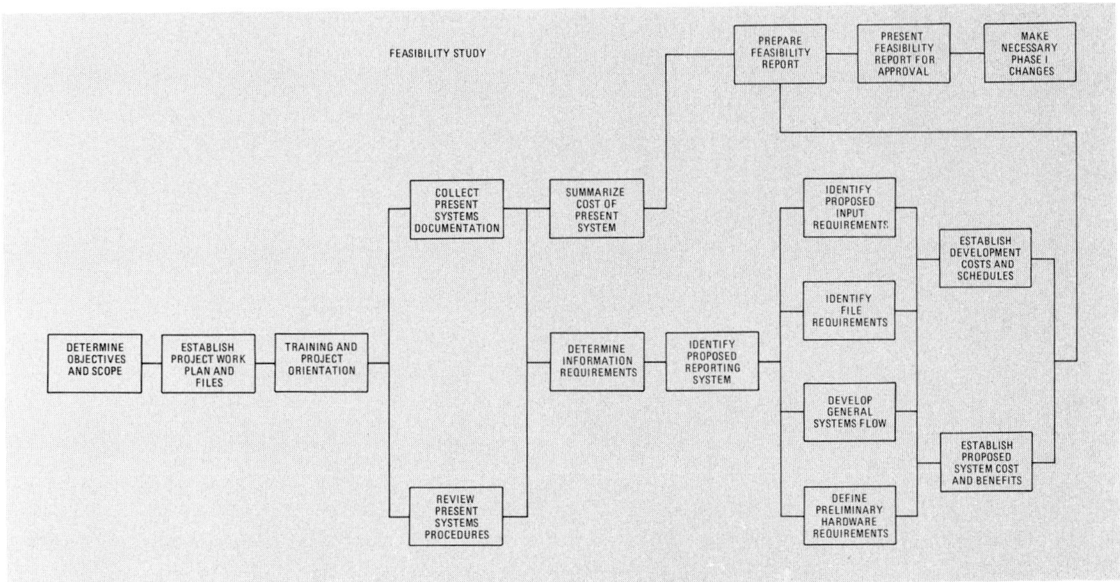

Figure 20–3. Feasibility Study.

sions and recommendations of this survey, it can be determined whether the more detailed study should be made. The primary reason for the recent interest of management in data processing feasibility studies is that the investment in an "in depth" systems study and evaluation involves a substantial expenditure regardless of whether the results support recommendation of a change of the present systems (Figs. 20.4, 20.5). Other areas of concern to management are:

1. A system study will cross established organizational lines.
2. The integration of the new system often results in the activities of some departments being altered or even eliminated.
3. Some of the basic, time honored, traditional company policies may have to be changed.
4. Methods of management control of operations may be affected.

Management will be wise to issue a statement of the objectives of the study and to outline the broad general methods by which they are to be attained.

AREAS TO BE SPECIFICALLY DELINEATED IN THE STUDY

1. Definition of the problem.
2. Scope of the study to be made.

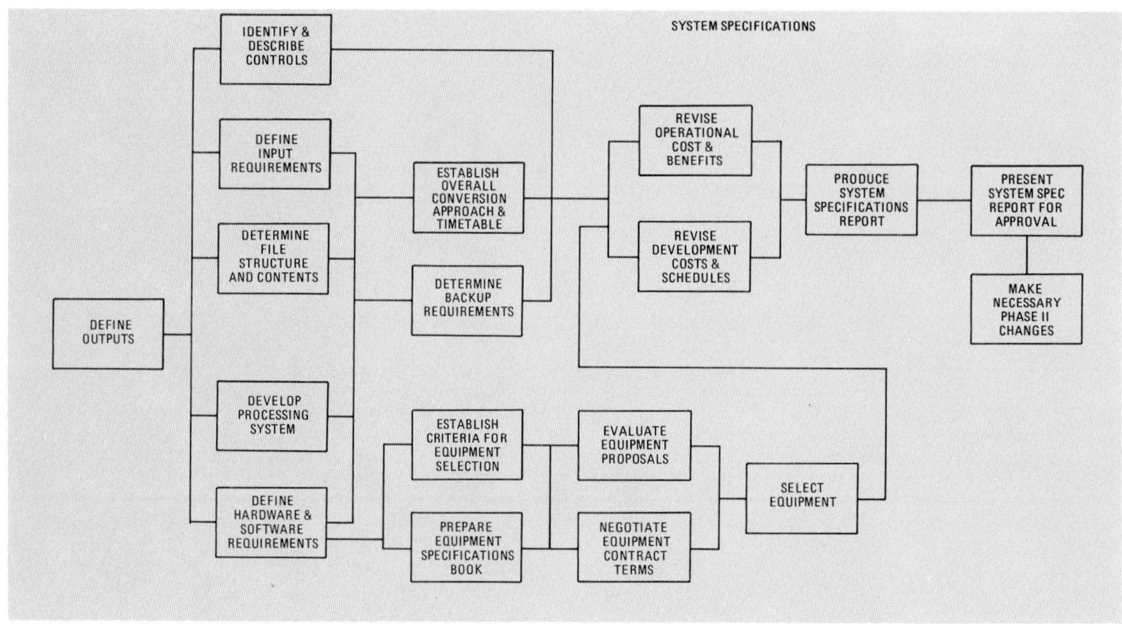

Figure 20–4. System Specification.

3. Ultimate objectives which management hopes to achieve.
4. Authority to be delegated to the team carrying out its assignment.
5. Organization, selection, and training of the study team.
6. Timetable in skeleton form to indicate to study team members and management in general time alloted to the study.

PROBLEM DEFINITION

The problem itself and the scope of the study to be made should be so stated that there is little doubt in the minds of the group as to the extent of the investigation and the areas within the firm to be covered. The problem may be as limited as one involving a delineation of the feasibility of acquiring a computer to do current record-keeping procedures. It may also be so broad in scope as to include the possibility of a complete integrated data control system involving operations research techniques and other mathematical tools of scientific management.

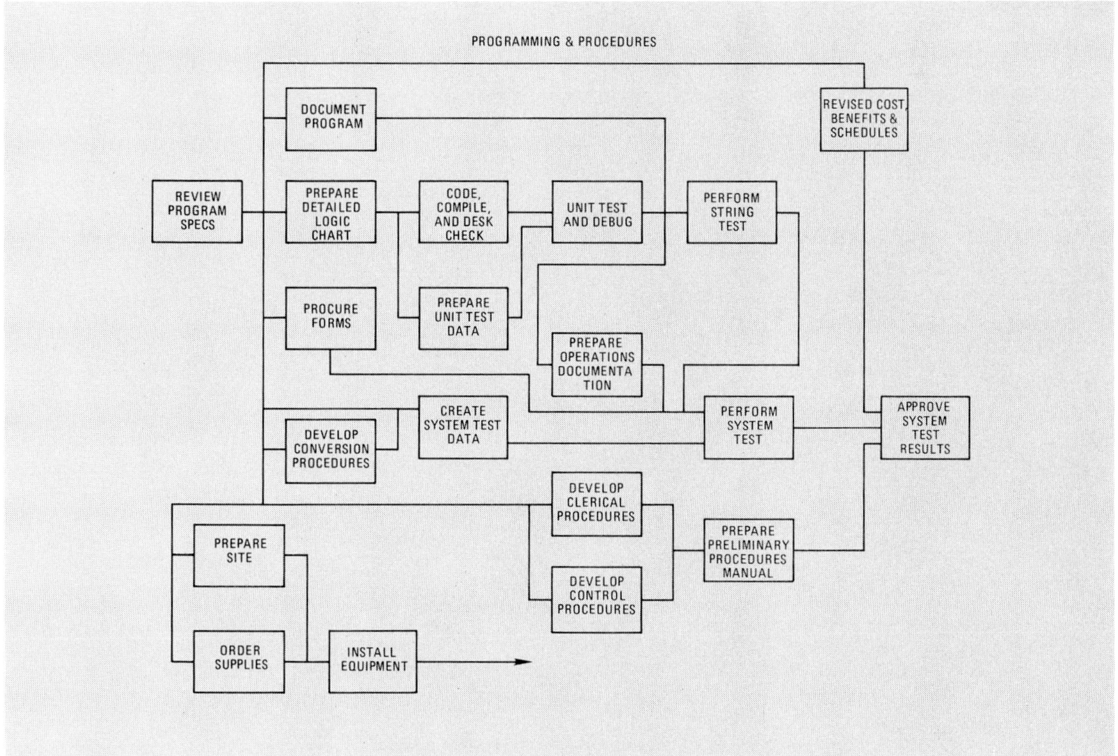

Figure 20–5. Programming and Procedures.

OBJECTIVES DESIRED

A formal set of objectives forces management to give the whole subject matter serious thought. In the process of arriving at a set of objectives, the problems involved in attaining these objectives will be clearly defined.

A framework will be developed within which the study team can operate, so it will know what is expected of it, the limitations under which it must work, and the time allowed for conclusions.

AUTHORITY DELEGATION

The authority delegated to the group should be clearly outlined. This is necessary as not only those conducting the study, but those with whom they will have contact, must fully understand the powers and responsibilities which have been assigned to the group.

COMMITTEE CONSIDERATIONS

A committee may involve only company personnel or may represent some combination of consultants and company employees. The amount of training required to qualify the members of the study team for the work expected of them will depend on the knowledgeability of the individual members in the general area of system analysis in data processing.

A tentative time schedule will have to be developed to guide the committee on the progress of the assignment.

ORGANIZATION OF THE GROUP

An individual must be selected to head the group. His duties will include review of the work of members of the study team, policy decisions within the framework management provides, seeing that the work is progressing according to schedule, and generally directing the systems study activities. The actual number of members will depend upon the size of the study.

SELECTION OF THE TEAM

If the company does not have qualified individuals, or has them but cannot spare them for the period required for the study, it may be necessary to turn over complete responsibility to professional consultants. Normally, this is not recommended because:

1. Outside consultants will rarely have any knowledge of the firm's detailed procedures and requirements.

2. Company personnel will fail to receive the training in system work, programming, and operational techniques required of them at a later date in the installation and operational stages.
3. The consultant will have little or no responsibility for the continuing operation of a computer system.
4. Most of the "know how" developed in the study will be lost to the company and belong to the consultants.

Representatives from the departments involved in the study should be included because:

1. They will bring authoritative "know how."
2. They will be more cooperative if they feel that they have a voice in the decision.
3. There will be some individuals from top management in the group who will acquire at first-hand a necessary understanding of the problems involved.

TRAINING GROUP

Since most members of the group will not possess the special knowledge required of them as the study progresses, they should undergo a period of training. This will include visists to operating data processing installations, instruction in data processing courses taken at colleges and universities, and at the computer manufacturers' schools.

TIMETABLE FOR THE STUDY

This will vary with the objectives and definition of the problem. Definite deadlines should be set for periodic progress reports.

GENERAL CONSIDERATIONS

The committee's basic obligation involves the major question as to whether data processing equipment will improve the overall company efficiency in terms of financial savings, customer relations, and operating efficiencies. To accomplish these ends, the committee will have to determine the company's requirements for data processing and place particular emphasis on the areas in which the greatest improvements can be made. These requirements should not only include those of a record-keeping system but, perhaps of even greater importance, those involving new management techniques which are so broad as to include important new areas such as inventory control, purchasing, production controls, etc.

The committee will need a broad view of the organization when charting the flow of information throughout the firm.

AREAS OF VITAL CONCERN TO MANAGEMENT IN A COMPUTER FEASIBILITY STUDY

1. *The computer feasibility study should be the work of company-oriented personnel with supplementary help from outside sources.* Many computer manufacturers offer free feasibility studies. These companies are primarily interested in selling or leasing their own equipment and it is highly unlikely that they will properly evaluate their competitor's equipment. Moreover it is probable that they will recommend equipment that will be *more* than adequate for the job.

Outside consultants, on the other hand, can definitely play an important part in the study. They can supply the necessary technical knowledge in evaluating the proposals of various equipment manufacturers. However, consultants should be used in support of the company personnel—not to supplant them. After all, the company personnel will have the ultimate responsibility of installing and operating without the benefit of the preparatory background available at the feasibility study stage.

If the management is to obtain an accurate view of the computer adoption, the entire study should be directed, conducted, and the results presented, by company personnel.

2. *The feasibility study should indicate the procedures and operations to be computerized and to demonstrate the physical feasibility of so doing.* It should take the form of a narrative summary, backed up by solid documentary evidence in the form of system flowcharts, source document formats, sample reports, etc., describing each of the operations that will be computerized and how the computer auxiliary systems will go about handling them. Sufficient factual proof of the proposed application should be presented to remove management doubts about the ability to achieve the defined goals.

3. *The physical capability of the equipment selected to do the job asked of it should be thoroughly demonstrated.* A short narrative should describe the capabilities of the proposed equipment, including speeds, capabilities, etc. Also volumes, output requirements, and data transmission facilities must all be directly linked with the timing demands of the proposed system for output report generation. In addition to this, a full analysis of other equipment considered should be presented. An explanation of the factors which caused the proposed equipment to be selected in preference to other equipment examined, should also be given.

4. *The physical facilities required to house the computer should be*

properly detailed. Many businessmen in their first dealings with the computer are under the illusion that the computer can be housed in the back of the warehouse or some other obscure location. Computers, they later learn, are delicate instruments that must be treated with extreme care. Among the other considerations, management must be made well aware of the following facts.

a) The computer must be located in an air-conditioned room properly humidified.
b) Special elevated floors are required to cover the heavy wiring required for computer operation.
c) Excess amounts of dust will disrupt the computer circuitry.
d) Proper noise abatement facilities must be provided for people working close to the computer room.

These physical facilities will increase the expense of computer operations and should be presented to management as part of the proposal.

5. *The proper cost of acquiring a computer should be presented in the proposal.* In the past, many computers have been acquired on the basis of cost saving as a justification. Many times these cost savings have not materialized, resulting in skepticism by management of the ability of the computer to achieve savings in costs. To combat this disillusionment, the following guidelines should be followed.

a) The accounting personnel should certify all cost figures presented in the feasibility proposal.
b) Equipment costs should include all costs associated with the operations: rental fees, transportation costs, programmers and analysts salaries, etc.
c) The cost of housing the equipment, mentioned earlier, should be included.
d) Itemize start-up costs before the computer operation begins to function effectively; e.g., parallel operations, dual systems in operation, etc.
e) Intangible benefits, such as better management reports and improved employee morale, often ascribed to the computer, must be discarded as they may never materialize.

6. *The personnel problems of designing, implementing, and operating a computer should be properly presented in the report.* Many computer manufacturers tend to oversimplify the operation of a computer. There is now a great awareness that to operate a computer effectively, many trained people are required: systems analysts, programmers, computer operators, key punch operators, auxiliary equipment operators, plus a data processing manager and/or a systems manager.

Many of these people are professionals—must have received considerable training. Management must be made aware that in most cases, much of the necessary professional help required to install and operate the computer must be hired from outside the company. It must also be pointed out that the hiring of outside personnel will be quite costly, possibly disruptive in terms of personnel relations within the company.

Many employees will be unhappy as there will be new routines to learn, new forms to fill in, new reports to be read and understood.

Management should also be made aware of the steps that should be taken to assign, retrain, terminate the service of, or in some other way deal with the displaced person.

7. *The proposal must demonstrate that the system and computer selected are capable of expansion and change.* The corporate structure is ever-changing and the computer selected must have at least the capability of absorbing the changes occurring in the various corporate structures without costly reprogramming and system redesign.

Evidence must be demonstrated in the feasibility study that allowance has been made for future expansion in the systems proposed, thus insuring that new, increased, or changing information requirements can be satisfied without serious reprogramming.

8. *The proposal should indicate that problems will occur during the installation and tell what these problems might be.* There must be indications that the existing information system, probably of many years standing and presently without operating difficulties, will have to be completely dismantled and rebuilt. Late reports, inaccuracies in reports, progress slower than actually planned, difficulty in getting competent help, and program "bugs" are some of the expected problem areas that should be outlined in the proposal. It must be realized that the installation of a computer is "no bed of roses."

9. *The proposal must give evidence of solid planning for the computer installation.* The solid planning is usually best expressed through a detailed critical path analysis of the steps to be completed in the implementation schedule. All activities necessary to complete the installation of the computer should be detailed and time-phased. This should be an all-inclusive schedule, including everything from the recruiting, selection, and training of the programming staff to the connecting of the air conditioning system of the computer room.

10. *The proposal must give evidence of support from other functional areas within the company.* This point is especially important if applications are projected in several areas. If the accounting department is proposing the acquisition of a computer which will do, among other things, cost distribution, payroll, billing, production scheduling, and marketing statistics, it is essential that manufacturing and marketing personnel strongly support the computer

in their areas. The most direct way to insure this is to include personnel from these departments in the investigating team.

11. *All benefits to be derived from the computer installation should be effectively presented in the report.* While it is true in most cases involving the installation of a computer that cost reduction is the most important consideration, there are often other important benefits to be derived. All benefits including cost reductions should be spelled out in the report. Some of these other benefits are better scheduling in production departments, better utilization of equipment, an ability to sell more, better cost control through budgetary reports, more accurate and quicker reports, new reports not previously possible, and advanced scientific analysis.

If a computer installation in the company is to be successful, it must have the unqualified support of management. The inclusion of this section in the feasibility report will gain the solid support of top management. Unfortunately, even if all of the eleven points (above) are covered in the feasibility study presentation, it still can fail in its main task of convincing management to go ahead with the proposal.

Finally, the reports to management, especially in the areas of computers and computer feasibility, must be written in an understandable format. Many management persons have been excessively burdened with computer feasibility reports written in "computereze." Top management does not understand the weird numeric codes that various computer manufacturers assign to their equipment or the jargon which programmers and systems personnel use when describing equipment and its applications. The final requirement is to present the case for or against the installation of a computer as simply as possible in plain everyday English. This will enable management to make a much more intelligent assessment of the advisability of installing a computer.

MANAGEMENT INFORMATION SYSTEMS

The key to good information systems planning involves a total understanding of not only the major decisions, and their causes, that are made at each management level, but also the environment (external and/or internal influence) in which these decisions are made. It is these management decisions that should govern the planning and design of all new information systems (Fig. 20.6).

The typical business-oriented data processing system user knows very little about computers. Rather than being impressed by a complex and sophisticated computer system, he may be hopelessly confused. The user must see clearly how using the computer will help him. The better he understands the information system, the more confidence he will have in the computer. The user must understand the basic plan by which his needs will be met, so that he can derive full benefit from the system.

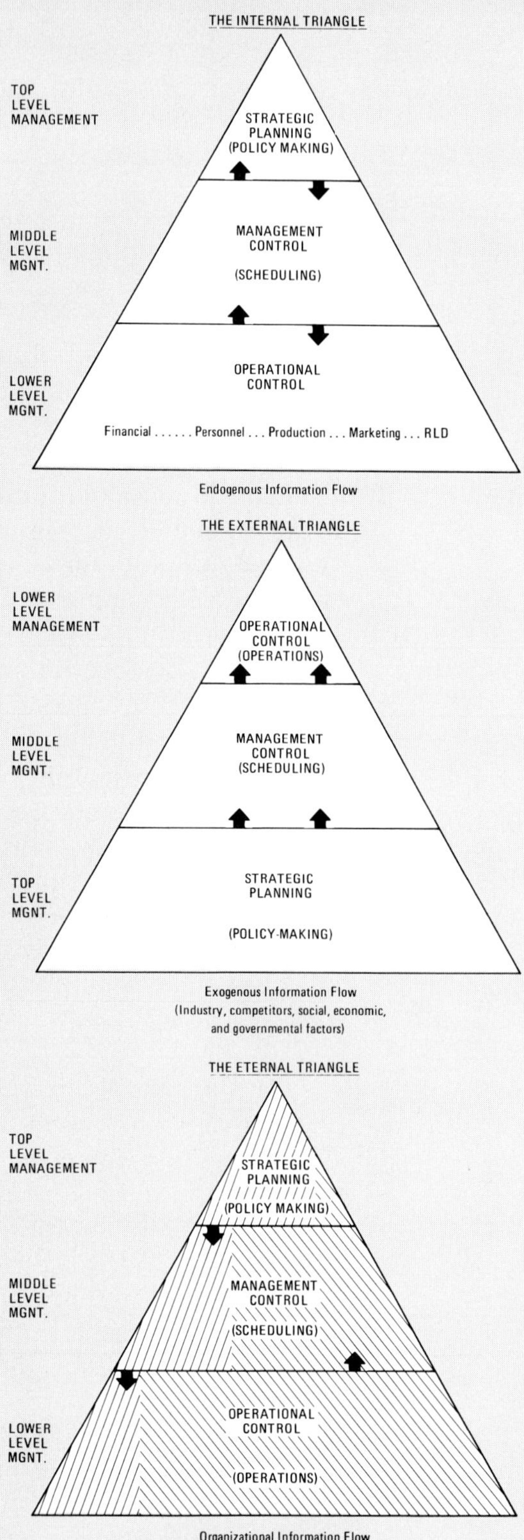

Figure 20–6. Management Information Systems— Schematic.

The user typically believes that the computer can produce results from a request instantaneously. He must be made aware that the computer does process large volumes of data very quickly, but that keypunching large volumes of data and manual intervention by the production management group are time-consuming and important for data processing accuracy and record keeping. He will surely realize that the time involved is a great deal less than that required by using an equivalent manual system.

DEFINING THE SYSTEM

When a systems analyst begins work on the information system, he studies the entire area as it is done manually, or could be done manually, and decides which portions could possibly be performed by the computer. He may interview the user at this point in an effort to discover how receptive the user is to an automated data processing system, and to make an estimate of the user's ability or potential for grasping data processing concepts. A cost analysis is performed on the parts of the system that may be automated. The analysis performed and the facts learned in the study must be documented since the outcome of the study dictates whether or not further effort will be expended in that area.

If the outcome of the feasibility study permits, a broad plan can be developed which will specify the manual portions of the system and the automated portions of the system. The plan may be further divided into subsystem definitions. The user should be involved to the extent that he agrees that he can perform the manual operations of the system and can furnish the input data needed, and that the output documents will satisfy his needs.

DESIGNING THE SYSTEM

The system designer studies the broad system plan and defines, within the plan, modules called *subsystems*. Each subsystem is then broken down into modules called runs, which are in turn broken down into modules called programs, and the programs may be divided into program modules. The modular concept of system design is desirable for many reasons, a major one being that many separate modules can be assigned to many different people who can all supply development effort simultaneously.

DATA PREPARATION FORM DESIGN

A very important and sometimes neglected part of system design is input data form design. All forms from which data will be keypunched should be approved by the production data center where keypunching will be done.

Input forms designed for the user must be logical for him to fill out and designed so that each is simple to keypunch.

USER PARTICIPATION AND SUPPORT

Output forms have to be designed with user participation. System function output reports typically must be designed within a list of requirements supplied by the user. A number of additional reports are usually generated for the purpose of data control; the user may have preferences for the content and format of these reports also. Participation in output form design can help the user become function-oriented during the design stage of the system.

PROGRAMMING TECHNIQUES

The system designer plans program interface carefully so that as much work as possible is done by a program without the program becoming too large or complicated. He makes recommendations to programmers on the use of decision tables, file processing techniques, and efficient processing methods so that each program will involve as short a run time as possible. He insures that no program reaches production if a program interrupt could occur from incorrect data; he is sure that all data is properly validated before it is used. He anticipates user misinterpretations and makes every effort to see that all programs are "fool proof."

The system designer plans all computer runs so that file changes occur conveniently; tapes and disks can be passed from program to program with very little operator intervention. He defines conditions under which a program may abort and directs the programmer to set certain condition codes for certain events so that good run control is established. Efficient program coding plus careful run planning can save a great deal of production run time.

PROGRAM MESSAGES

Program messages are of greater importance in program planning. Each message should be one of three types; user messages, computer operator messages, or production systems management messages. All user-directed messages should appear in a formatted report and should specify exactly the situation that caused the message to be generated and the action expected of the user.

Very few messages should be directed to the computer, but when they are necessary, they should appear on the console typewriter and should be meaningful facts about the computer run or actions required by the processing program.

Production systems management control messages are most critical and should include general information messages as well as program or run control error messages with action specified.

IMPLEMENTATION OF SYSTEM

System test, which takes place after development personnel have determined that all programs will run together compatibly as a system, should mark the start of an earnest effort to educate the user, the keypunch operator, the computer operator, and the production systems management groups in the proper use of the system.

Since the system test represents the initial education for all people who will be concerned with the production system, it should be well documented. It is particularly important that documentation include technical information about the computer runs and the maintenance of the data base.

PRODUCTION SYSTEMS MANAGEMENT

The production systems management group should receive maximum consideration in the design of the information system. These people have the responsibility of giving support for the lifetime of the production system and the responsibility of continually meeting the user's needs.

The outcome of system design should be a simple and easy-to-follow procedure by which an information system can fulfill the data processing needs of a user group. The procedure must be flexible so that it can fit any change that may occur in computer hardware configuration, computer software, or personnel available to support the production system. The production systems management group is responsible for updating the procedure when necessary so that the information system can be used to its fullest design intent as long as it is required.

DOCUMENTATION

System planning documentation available to the production systems management group should include the broad plan which describes the intent and purpose of the system and the design document describing the detailed manual and data processing procedure, and the system test documentation.

SUMMARY

The widespread use of computers during the last decade has created many problems for management. With tremendous investments in computer facilities, management is concerned with the accuracy of the data being processed and the protection of sensitive files and programs. Among causes of alarm to computer users is the thievery and fraudulent use of the computer which has seriously undermined the public's faith in computer processing. The success of most organizations depends on its ability to efficiently use the information stored in data processing media. Computer systems are needed to expedite procedures in our complex society and to monitor its operations. The design and installation of computer systems require extensive studies.

It is the intent of this chapter to describe some practical safeguards that can be used to assure the accuracy and protection of important programs, files, data and to present the problems inherent in the study and design of management information systems.

I. *Computer Security.*
   A. *Audit packages*—generalized computer programs designed to satisfy the particular needs of the auditor.
   B. *Extraction*—enables the user to select only those records which meet predetermined criteria for audit.
   C. *Mathematics*—allows the user to enter mathematical formulas of his own design to test the accuracy of the computations.
   D. *Surveying (Frequency Distribution)*—allows the user to select items and amount totals of all records meeting a certain criteria without extracting individual records.
   E. *Totalling*—allows for printing of subtotal amounts when there is a change in the given file sequence.
   F. *Aging*—a comparison of the data in the records to a given data and the categorization of this data.
   G. *Sampling*—selecting records based on a sequential or random numbers.
   H. *Comparison of two files*—allows the user to match two files in a given sequence, one against the other.
   I. *Printer-File and Conformation Outputs*—all reports should be under auditor control and to provide multiple outputs of significant data.
   J. *User Exits*—provides the user with the ability to extend the capabilities of the computer according to the design of the user.
   K. *Test Auditing*—testing a segment of the file prior to processing an entire file.
   L. *Bypassing Invalid Data*—to prevent an audit from termination because of invalid data.

II. *Data Security.*
   A. *Preventive Measures.*
      1. *Location*—strong fireproof building in a safe location.
      2. *Site construction*—locked maximum security doors, protection

against unauthorized entry, closed circuit TV, burglar alarm system, etc.

3. *Operating procedures*—access limited, visitors log, tape logging and identification, backup tapes and other media, etc.
4. *Data protection*—input/output gear located close to computer, keywords for telecommunications uses, logs of all users and inquiries, etc.
5. *Legal protection*—standard contract for all legal obligations for computer leases, computer purchase, software rentals and purchases, service and maintenance contracts for computer facilities, data processing supplies, etc.

B. *Additional measures.*

1. *Decentralization*—multicomputer companies may decentralize some of their computers.
2. *Backup facility*—arrangement with another user to provide computer services in case of emergency.
3. *Time sharing*—maintain tapes and records at a central location.
4. *Business insurance*—bonded employees, fire insurance, etc.

III. *Telecommunications Protection.*

A. *Classification of information.*

1. Certain files should be restricted to only a few people due to their confidential nature.
2. Access is required by many but modification of files is limited to few.
3. Permit broad access and interaction with minimal security.

B. *System Design Factors.*

1. *Passwords*—required to enter sections of a file.
2. *Detailed logs*—records of all inquiries and access to critical data files.
3. *Lockword*—in addition to password permitting access to a file or to accept modification.
4. *Monte Carlo Validation*—random sampling of online records to assure that no "dummy" records exist.

IV. *Data Processing Responsibility.*

A. *Usefulness of reports*—establish that the reports are necessary and are being used.
B. *System Design*—system effort directed toward management goals.
C. *Communication*—information exchanges between all nondata processing, data processing, and user departments.
D. *Accuracy*—tight control of the accuracy of input and output.

E. *Timeliness*—keep schedules updated and preparation of reports to meet deadlines.
F. *Personnel*—data processing personnel must be highly versatile people.
G. *Economy*—economic use and operation of equipment.
H. *Technology Study*—keeping up with the latest advances in computer technology.
I. *Reporting on Progress*—reports on a periodic basis to management on problems and progress of data processing operations.

V. *Feasibility Study.*
A. *Overview*—to provide management with enough information about the proposed systems project so that an objective decision can be made with regard to its value.
B. *Areas to be delineated in study*—problem definition, scope of study, objectives, authority of group, organization, and time table.
C. *General considerations*—improve efficiency, etc.
D. *Areas of vital concern to management in study.*
1. Work of company-oriented personnel with help from outside consultants.
2. Procedures and operations to be computerized.
3. Physical capability of equipment to do job.
4. Physical facilities to house the equipment.
5. Proper cost of acquiring the computer.
6. Personnel problems in designing, implementing, and operating a computer.
7. System and computer to be capable of expansion.
8. Indicate installation problems.
9. Indicate solid planning for computer.
10. Support from other functional units.
11. Expected benefits to be derived from computer installation.

VI. *Management Information Systems.*
A. *Defining the system*—study of the entire system to determine whether or not further effort will be expended in this area.
B. *Designing the system.*
1. *Subsystems*—modules of a system.
2. *Data Preparation Form Design*—input/output forms design.
3. *User Participation and Support*—participation of all users in design of forms and systems.
C. *Programming*—conversion of system into computer programs.
D. *Program messages*—specifies situation that caused the message to be generated and action expected of user.
E. *Implementation of System*—educate user, keypunch operator, com-

puter operator, production systems group in projected use of system.

F. *Production Systems Management*—responsibility for continually meeting the user needs.

G. *Documentation*—broad plan describing intent and purpose of system and detailed manuals of data processing procedures.

IDENTIFICATION QUESTIONS

Match the following terms with the statements that follow.

A. Aging
B. Bypassing Invalid Data
C. Computer Audit Packages
D. Extraction
E. Feasibility Study
F. Lockword
G. Management Information System
H. Monte Carlo Validation
I. Sampling
J. Surveying
K. Totalling
L. User Exits

1. A series of steps designed to find all data requested by management, in a concise form, which will enable them to make the necessary decisions in a timely basis, to result in a successful and profitable business operation.
2. This technique allows the user to take item and amount totals of all records meeting a certain criteria without extracting the individual record.
3. Generalized computer programs designed to satisfy the particular needs of the auditor.
4. This technique is used to select records based on a sequential interval or based on random numbers.
5. A report to management with enough information about the proposed system project so that a proper decision can be made relative to its value.
6. The ability to extend the capabilities of a system in a new and unique area of one's design.
7. The selection of records which meet predetermined criteria.
8. It permits access to a portion of a file or to accept modification of that file.
9. This technique allows for the printing of subtotals when there is a given change in a file sequence.
10. This technique allows the taking of samples periodically from online files to assure that there are no "dummy" records in the file.
11. The stratification of each record into selected categories.
12. This technique prevents an audit from terminating prematurely by printing out the invalid data.

QUESTIONS FOR REVIEW

1. Why is it important for the auditor to understand the operations of a computer?
2. What is the importance of audit packages? What are some of the audit functions that should be considered in evaluating an audit package?

3. Enumerate the preventative measures that may be used to assure data security.
4. Why is it important to take measures to protect telecommunications? List some of the preventive measures that may be taken.
5. List and discuss the major areas of data processing responsibility.
6. What interest does management have in a feasibility study?
7. What are the specific areas to be delineated in the study?
8. What are the areas of vital concern to management in a computer feasibility study?
9. What important contributions can outside consultants make to the feasibility study?
10. How should the feasibility study to management be written?
11. Why is it important that management have a clear understanding of computer operations?
12. What are the important phases of management information systems? List the important points in defining the system, designing the system, programming techniques, implementation of the system, and production system management.

APPENDIX

IBM System/3

The IBM System/3 was designed to provide high-speed processing capabilities to small data processing installations. Since the main input in these units is the punched card, a 96 column card was designed so that additional necessary information concerning a single item can be recorded.

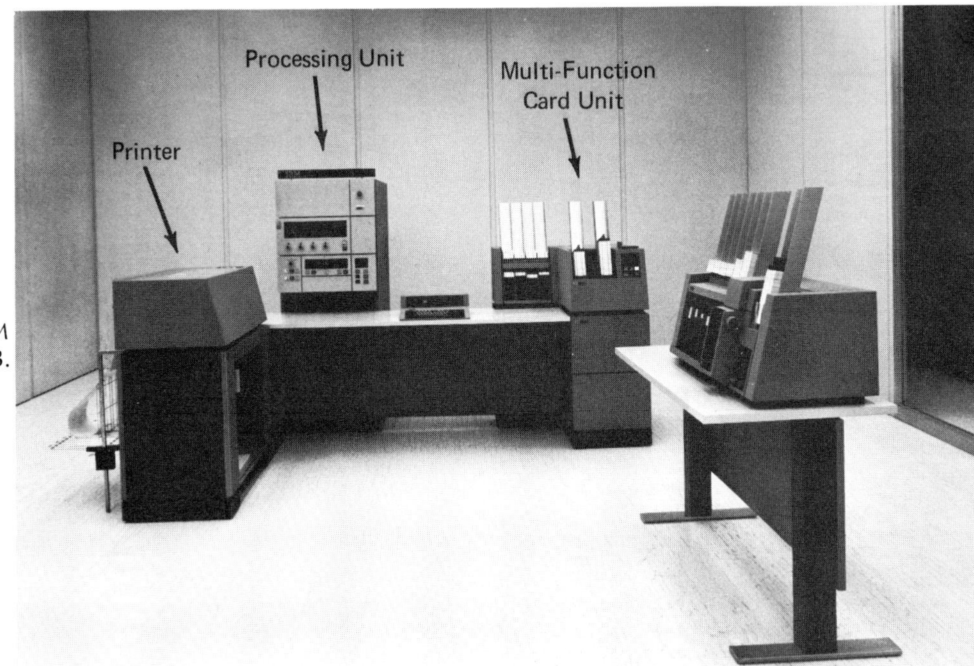

Figure A-1. IBM System/3.

SYSTEM/3 CARD

The 96 column card is divided into two sections: a print area and a punch area. The *print area* is located in the upper section of the card and represents the punched information as printed characters. The print positions correspond with the columns in the punch area. Therefore, every character punched may be read in the corresponding print area.

The *punch area* is located in the lower section of the card and is divided into three equal horizontal sections called *tiers*. There are 32 columns in each tier as follows:

Tier 1—columns 1–32
Tier 2—columns 33–64
Tier 3—columns 65–96

Each tier contains vertical groups of six punch positions. These punch positions are labelled B, A, 8, 4, 2, 1, from the top of the tier to the bottom.

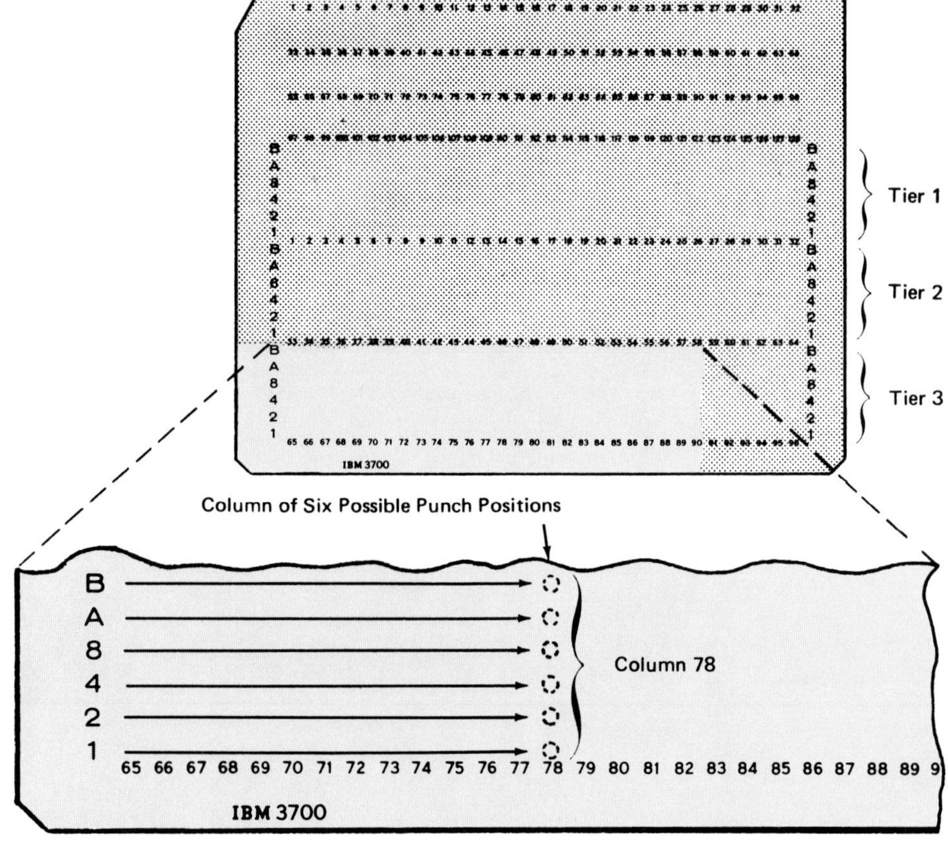

Figure A-2. Card Columns.

Each group of six positions constitutes a card column which represents a character. Up to 96 characters of information can be punched into each card.

DATA REPRESENTATION

Using the six positions, it is possible to represent 64 different characters. The 64 punch combinations include alphabetic characters (A-Z), numeric characters (0-9), and 28 special characters such as comma, dollar sign, period, and the blank.

The *zone* portion of a column includes the *B* and *A* punch positions while the 8, 4, 2, 1 positions are referred to as the *digit* positions of the card. For example, the number 1 would be represented by a hole in the 1 punch position. Since there is no 3 punch position, a 3 is represented by holes in both the 1 and 2 punch positions. The one exception is the digit 0 which is not represented by a digit punch but by a single punch in the A punch position.

Alphabetic characters are represented by a combination of punches in the zone (B, A) and the digit (8, 4, 2, 1) portions of the card. Special characters are represented by a combination of punches in the digit and/or zone portion of a card.

There is no need to memorize these codes as a depression of the appropriate key on the Data Recorder will punch the appropriate holes automatically.

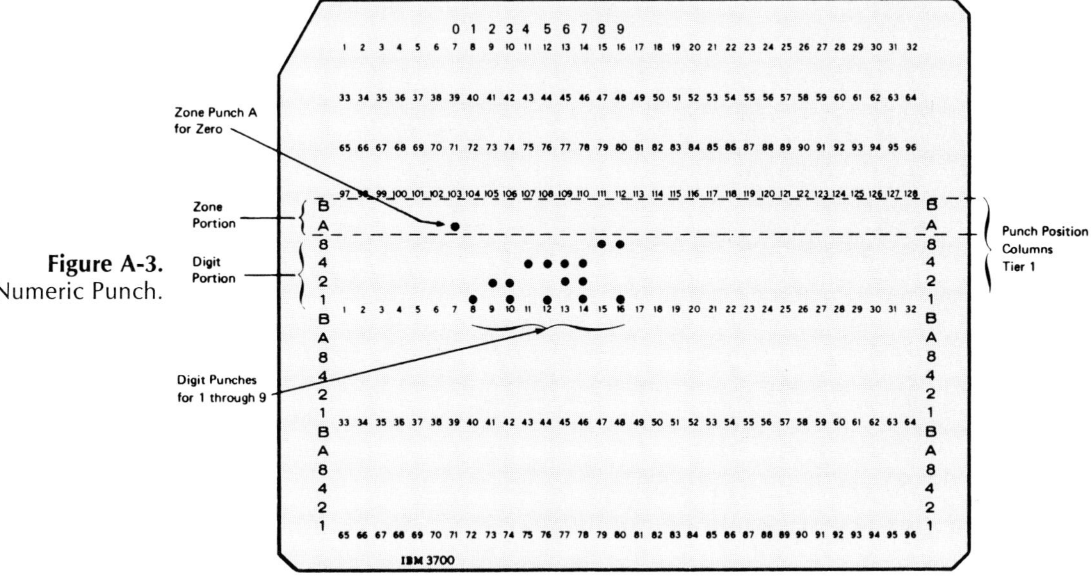

Figure A-3. Numeric Punch.

Figure A-4. Character Set and Punch Combinations.

			Numeric Characters									
			0	1	2	3	4	5	6	7	8	9
Punch Positions	Zone	B										
		A	A									
	Digit	8									8	8
		4					4	4	4	4		
		2			2	2			2	2		
		1		1		1		1		1		1

			Alphabetic Characters																									
			A	B	C	D	E	F	G	H	I	J	K	L	M	N	O	P	Q	R	S	T	U	V	W	X	Y	Z
Punch Positions	Zone	B	B	B	B	B	B	B	B	B	B	B	B	B	B	B	B	B	B	B								
		A	A	A	A	A	A	A	A	A	A										A	A	A	A	A	A	A	A
	Digit	8								8	8								8	8							8	8
		4				4	4	4	4						4	4	4	4					4	4	4	4		
		2		2	2			2	2				2	2			2	2			2	2			2	2		
		1	1		1		1		1		1	1		1		1		1		1		1		1		1		1

			Special Characters																											
			}	¢	.	<	(	+	|	!	$	*	)	;	¬	-	/	&	,	%	_	>	?	:	#	@	'	=	"	ƀ
Punch Positions	Zone	B	B	B	B	B	B	B	B	B	B	B	B	B	B	B														
		A	A	A	A	A	A	A	A								A	A	A	A	A	A	A							
	Digit	8		8	8	8	8	8	8	8	8	8	8	8	8			8	8	8	8	8	8	8	8	8	8	8	8	
		4				4	4	4	4			4	4	4	4					4	4	4	4			4	4	4	4	
		2		2	2			2	2	2	2			2	2			2	2			2	2	2	2			2	2	
		1			1		1		1		1		1		1		1		1		1		1		1		1		1	

DATA RECORDER

The IBM 5496 Data Recorder is a separate machine from the other units of the System/3. It provides the information to the system in the form of punched cards. The Data Recorder has a 64 character keyboard, a card hopper, a punch station, a read station, a print station, and a stacker. The reading, punching, and printing speeds are at the rate of 60 columns per second.

One of the outstanding features of the Data Recorder is its ability to collect the data as it is being keyed without punching it. When all the data has been keyed, the card is punched. This allows the operator to erase and rekey any data he wishes. A character, a field, or an entire card may be erased and rekeyed. The keying and punching operations are overlapped so that as one card is being keyed, the previous card is being punched. Up to four prepunched program cards may be used permitting the operator to select from one to four program formats for versatility of field controls within jobs.

A verify feature is provided in the Data Recorder. By combining these

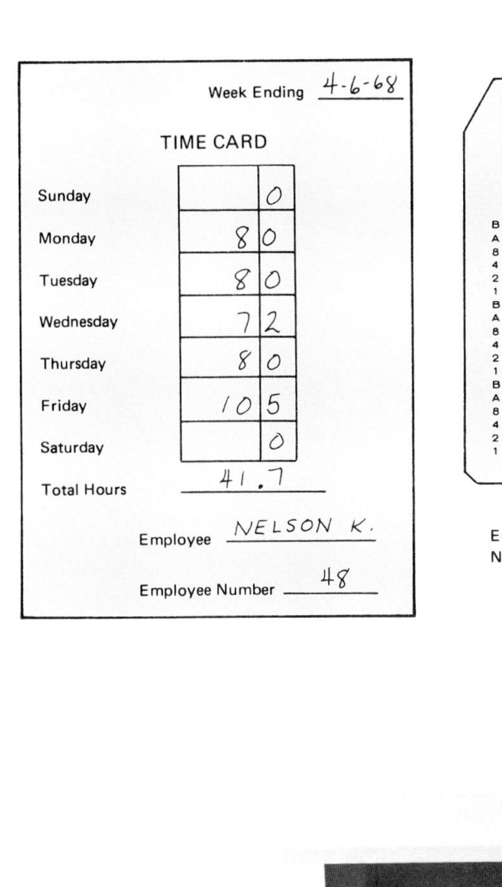

Week Ending 4-6-68

TIME CARD

Sunday	0
Monday	8 0
Tuesday	8 0
Wednesday	7 2
Thursday	8 0
Friday	10 5
Saturday	0

Total Hours 41.7

Employee NELSON K.

Employee Number 48

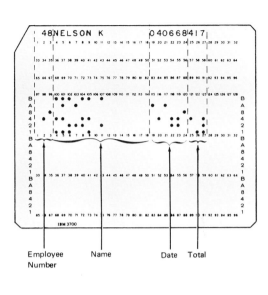

igure A-5. A Payroll Sheet and Related Card Records.

Figure A-6. IBM 5496 Data Recorder.

operations into a single unit, it is possible to correct a card immediately as it is being verified.

DEVICES

The System/3 has three basic devices to handle the input, processing, and output functions. The devices are the *Multi-Function Card Unit,* the *Processing Unit,* and the *Printer.*

MULTI-FUNCTION CARD UNIT

The IBM 5424 Multi-Function Card Unit combines the capabilities of several unit record machines into one unit. With two hoppers, a solar cell reading station, a common punching station, it offers complete card file maintenance plus the ability to print up to four lines on each card.

Cards from both hoppers can be read, punched, and printed, and sent to any of the four stackers regardless of hopper origin. The unit record functions of reproducing, gangpunching, summary punching, sorting, collating, and interpreting can be performed on the Multi-Function Card Unit under complete control of an internally stored program.

Card reading is performed at the rate of 250 to 500 cards per minute depending upon the functions to be performed. Each card is read by an array of solar cells (one for each punch position). After the card is read, it advances to the wait station. Upon receiving a command from the processing unit, the card advances to the punch station.

Card punching is performed at the rate of 60 to 120 cards per minute depending upon the particular operation. The processing unit can cause the card to be fed from either wait station. The appropriate data is transferred to the card by the program and the card is punched as it passes through the punch station. The card is automatically verified by a signal generated when each hole is punched. The signal is compared with the punched unit data. After leaving the punch station, the card then proceeds to the print station.

Card printing, up to three rows, is performed at the rate of 60 to 120 cards per minute depending upon the particular job. Four lines of printing may be printed in the upper portion of the card under the control of the stored program. Any of the 64 characters may be printed in each position. The fourth row of printing is under program control and reduces the number of cards put through each minute.

Figure A-7. IBM 5424 Multi-Function Card Unit.

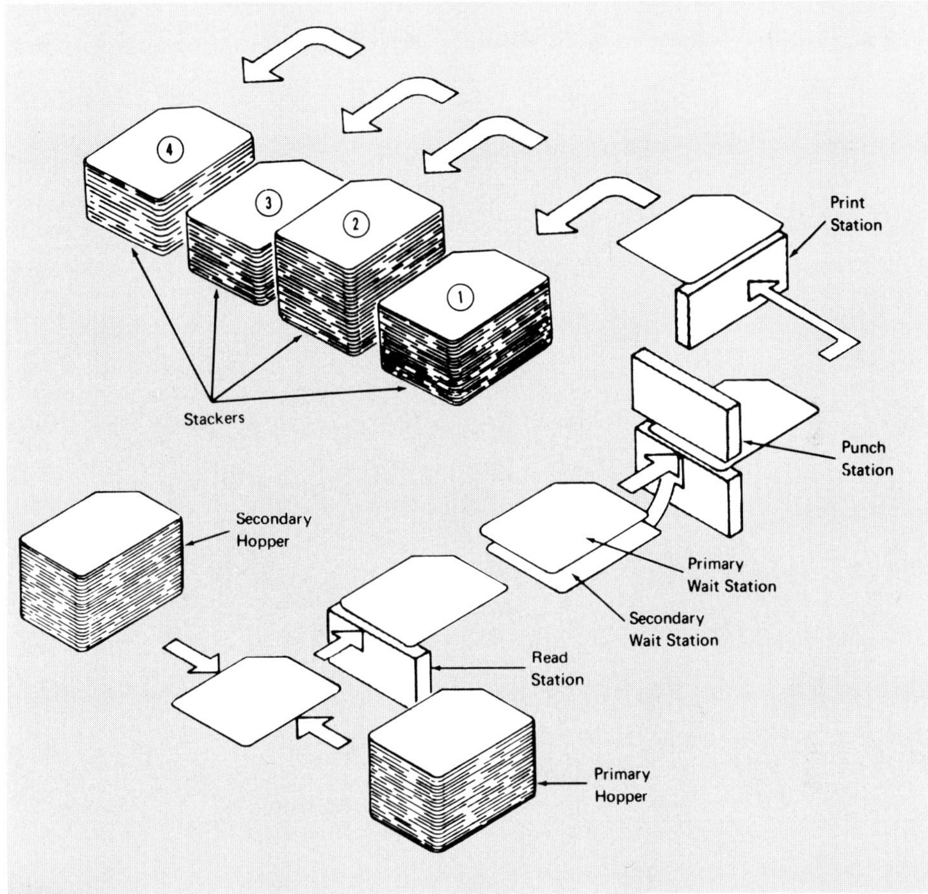

Figure A-8. Card Path Multi-Function Unit.

An *operator console* to the right of the primary hopper provides the necessary lights and switches to control start, stop, and card runouts. The console permits the operator to have complete control over the unit.

PROCESSING UNIT

The IBM 5410 Processing Unit is the control center for the entire data processing system. The processing unit stores the information in addressable locations, performs the necessary arithmetic and logical processing of the data, executes the program instructions in the desired sequence and controls the transfer of data between storage and attached input and output devices.

The system console provides the necessary switches, keys, and lights to operate and control the processing unit and the input and output unit.

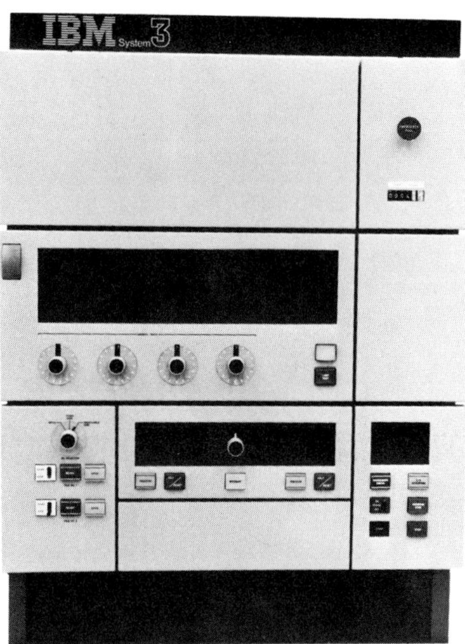

Figure A-9.
System Console.

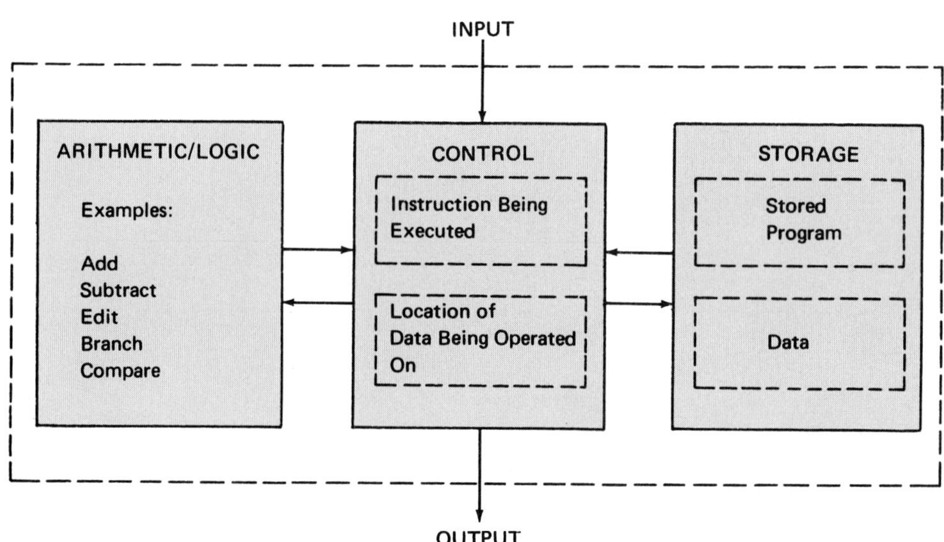

Figure A-10. Function of Processing Unit.

The 28 instructions of the processing unit permit it to manipulate data between storage locations, to manipulate data between registers and storage and to give direct orders to units of the system.

PRINTER

The IBM 5203 Printer provides the printed report output for the system. Up to 200 lines per minute can be printed when using the 48 character set. Some of the important features of the printer are:

1. An interchange chain cartridge allowing the operator to select different print formats. The Universal Character Set special feature permits the use of from 49 to 120 characters on the interchangeable chain cartridge. (The output printing rate is reduced somewhat.)
2. The standard printing capacity is 96 positions with 120 or 132 positions available as an optional feature.
3. Ten character positions are printed to an inch with vertical spacing of six or eight lines to an inch being selected manually by an operator. Normal skipping and spacing features are available.
4. A Dual-Feed Carriage, available as a special feature, allows the simultaneous printing of two forms, side by side, each form being independently controlled for line spacing and skipping.
5. As each character is being printed, checking circuits are set up to insure that the printer is operating correctly.

Figure A-11. IBM 5203 Printer.

CARD SORTER

The IBM 5486 Card Sorter is an offline operation that can be used to sequence card files before they are entered into the system. The cards can be sorted in any predetermined sequence. The sorter has a card hopper, a read station, and six stackers. Sorting speeds of 1,000 or 1,500 cards per minute are available depending upon the particular model.

Figure A-12. IBM 5486 Card Sorter.

PROGRAMS

A comprehensive package of independent programs is provided for the users of System/3 with all the required operations functions. Report Program Generator II (RPG II) is the programming language of the System/3.

RPG II

Report Program Generator II (RPG II) was designed to provide an efficient, easy-to-use technique for doing such jobs as billing, payroll, inventory, etc. RPG II language is a highly flexible problem-solving language. It permits programming solutions to a wide variety of problems. The language maintains capability with RPG (explained earlier in text) although it has been extended to provide major functional improvements.

Simply, the program is written on five different types of coding forms called *specification sheets*. Each specification sheet is self explanatory, requiring the programmer just to fill in the required blanks. Each line on the specification sheet is then punched into one card. When all the specification sheets

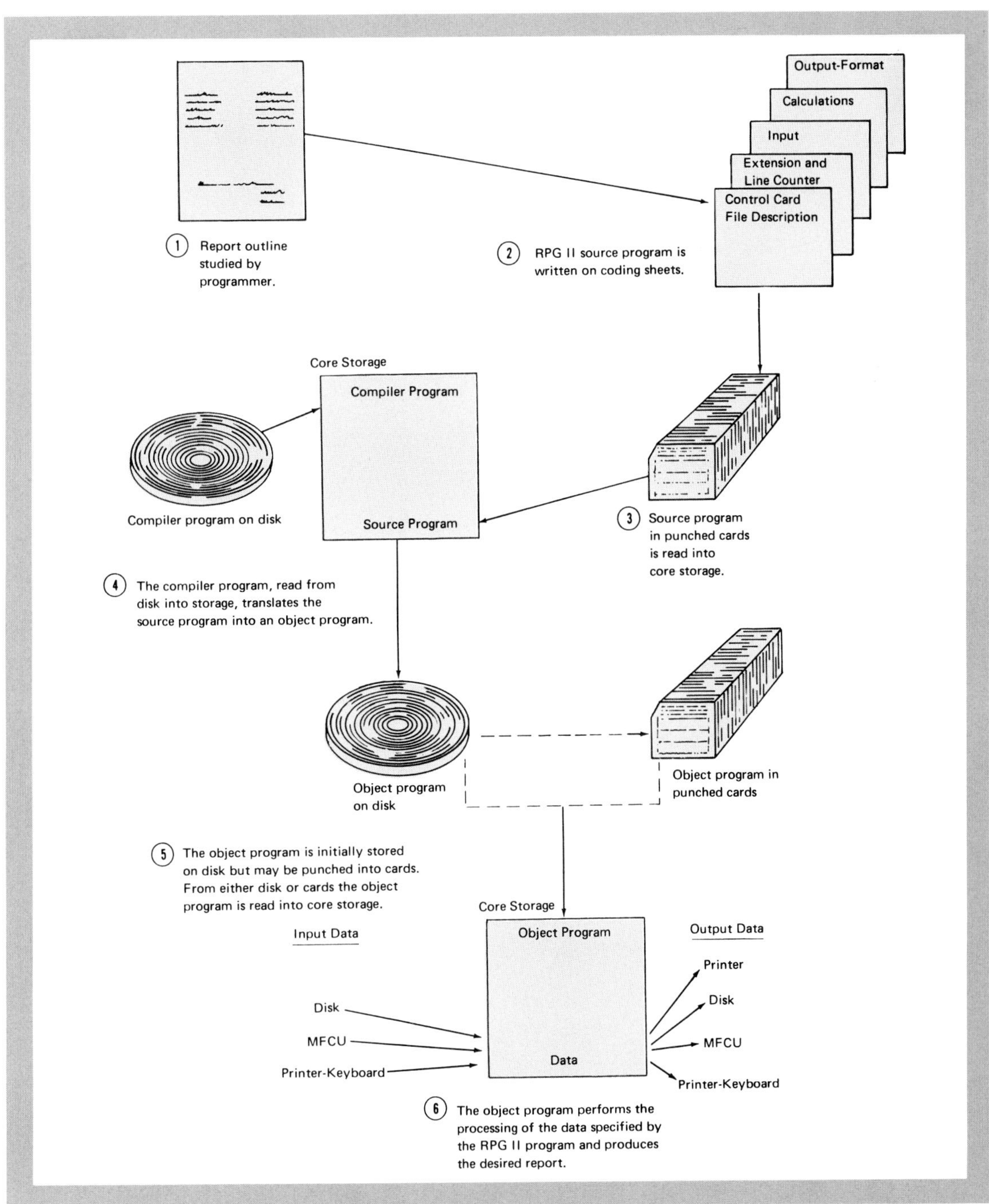

Figure A-13. Preparation of a Report Using RPG II.

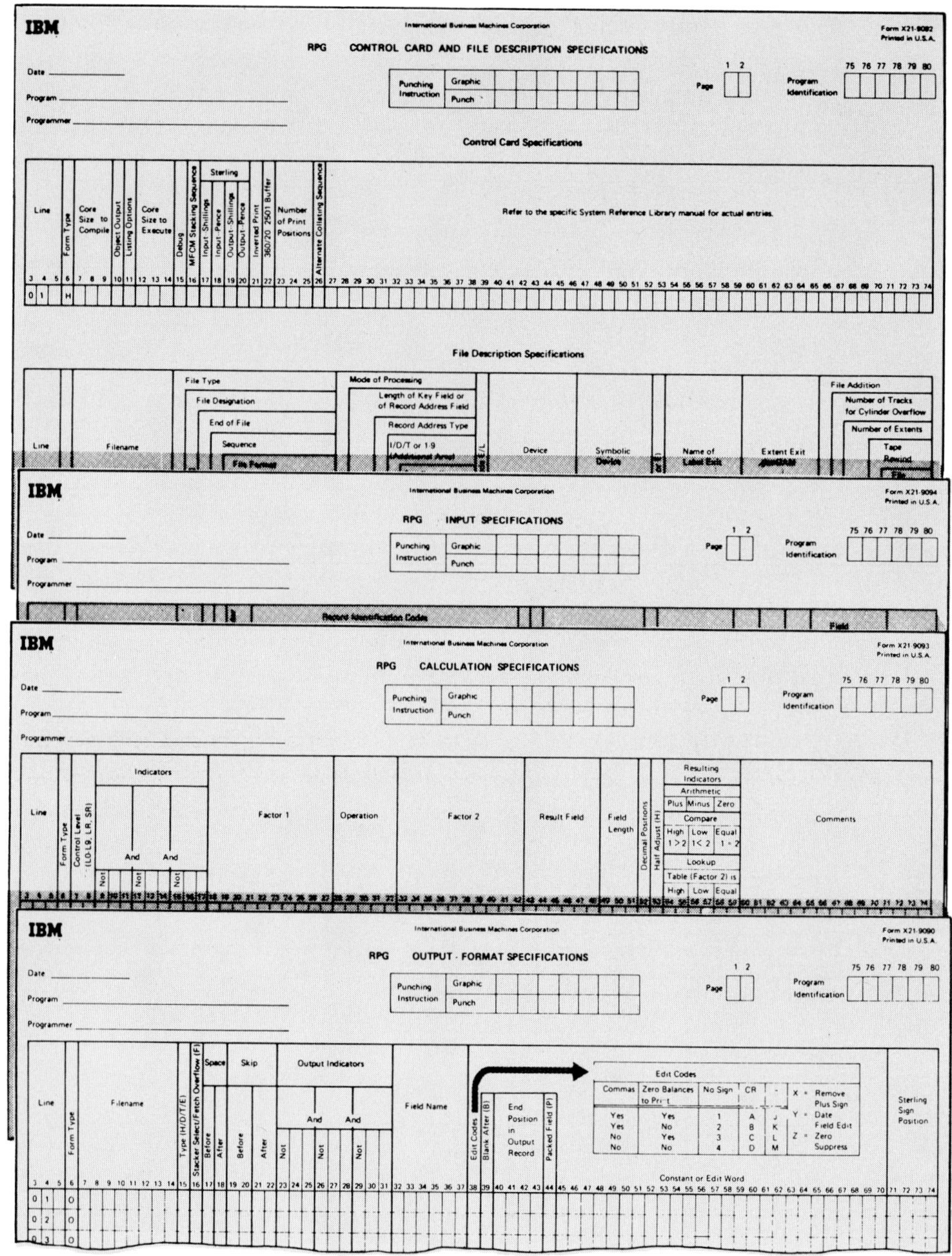

IBM International Business Machines Corporation Form X21-9092 Printed in U.S.A.

RPG CONTROL CARD AND FILE DESCRIPTION SPECIFICATIONS

Date
Program
Programmer

Punching Instruction: Graphic, Punch
Page 1 2
Program Identification 75 76 77 78 79 80

Control Card Specifications

Line; Form Type; Core Size to Compile; Object Output; Listing Options; Core Size to Execute; Debug; MFCM Stacking Sequence; Sterling: Input-Shillings, Input-Pence, Output-Shillings, Output-Pence; Inverted Print; 360/20 2501 Buffer; Number of Print Positions; Alternate Collating Sequence

Refer to the specific System Reference Library manual for actual entries.

0 1 H

File Description Specifications

Line; Filename; File Type; File Designation; End of File; Sequence; File Format; Mode of Processing; Length of Key Field or of Record Address Field; Record Address Type; I/O/T or 1-9 (Additional Area); E/L; Device; Symbolic Device; Name of Label Exit; Extent Exit (DAM/DAM); File Addition; Number of Tracks for Cylinder Overflow; Number of Extents; Tape Rewind; File

IBM International Business Machines Corporation Form X21-9094 Printed in U.S.A.

RPG INPUT SPECIFICATIONS

Date
Program
Programmer

Punching Instruction: Graphic, Punch
Page 1 2
Program Identification 75 76 77 78 79 80

Record Identification Codes; Field

IBM International Business Machines Corporation Form X21-9093 Printed in U.S.A.

RPG CALCULATION SPECIFICATIONS

Date
Program
Programmer

Punching Instruction: Graphic, Punch
Page 1 2
Program Identification 75 76 77 78 79 80

Line; Form Type; Control Level (L0-L9, LR, SR); Indicators: Not, And, Not, And, Not; Factor 1; Operation; Factor 2; Result Field; Field Length; Decimal Positions; Half Adjust (H); Resulting Indicators: Arithmetic: Plus, Minus, Zero; Compare: High 1 > 2, Low 1 < 2, Equal 1 = 2; Lookup: Table (Factor 2) is High, Low, Equal; Comments

IBM International Business Machines Corporation Form X21-9090 Printed in U.S.A.

RPG OUTPUT - FORMAT SPECIFICATIONS

Date
Program
Programmer

Punching Instruction: Graphic, Punch
Page 1 2
Program Identification 75 76 77 78 79 80

Line; Form Type; Filename; Type (H/D/T/E); Stacker Select/Fetch Overflow (F); Space: Before, After; Skip: Before, After; Output Indicators: Not, And, Not, And, Not; Field Name; Edit Codes; Blank After (B); End Position in Output Record; Packed Field (P); Sterling Sign Position

Edit Codes

Commas	Zero Balances to Print	No Sign	CR	-
Yes	Yes	1	A	J
Yes	No	2	B	K
No	Yes	3	C	L
No	No	4	D	M

X = Remove Plus Sign
Y = Date Field Edit
Z = Zero Suppress

Constant or Edit Word

0 1 O
0 2 O
0 3 O

Figure A-14. Sheets to Describe RPG II Program.

have been punched (source program); they are translated later into machine-language instructions (object program). The compiler is a program that acts as the translator.

The machine-language instructions are combined with input data files and both card groups are processed through the system to produce the desired report and output files.

The RPG II compiler may be run on a minimum configuration system as well as some of the larger computer systems. There is no restriction on the number of input, output, or combined files that may be used in a single RPG II application, other than the limitation of the number of devices. A program testing facility is also provided within RPG II to aid the programmer in "debugging" his program.

BASIC ASSEMBLER LANGUAGE

Computer programs may be written in either machine language or symbolic language. A *machine language* can be used directly by the computer but it is difficult for the programmer to use. *Symbolic languages* are more meaningful to the programmer but they must be later translated into machine language before they can be used by the computer.

The System/3 Assembler Language is a symbolic language that provides a convenient method for representing, on a one-for-one basis, machine instructions and related data necessary to write a program. Because of its one-for-one relationship to machine instructions, assembly language provides the versatility of machine language plus the facilities which greatly reduce the programming effort.

The System/3 Basic Assembler Program processes the instructions written in an assembler language, translates them into machine instructions, assigns storage locations, and performs other functions necessary to produce an executable machine-language program.

The assembler source statement is divided into five fields: name field, operation field, operand field, remarks field, and sequence field. The rules for coding assembler statements are given in the various reference manuals of the computer manufacturer.

The assembler language is composed of mnemonic symbols that represent (1) machine language operation codes (machine instruction statements) and (2) instructions to control the functions of the assembler program (assembler instruction statements). Assembler instruction statements are instructions to the assembler to perform certain operations during assembly.

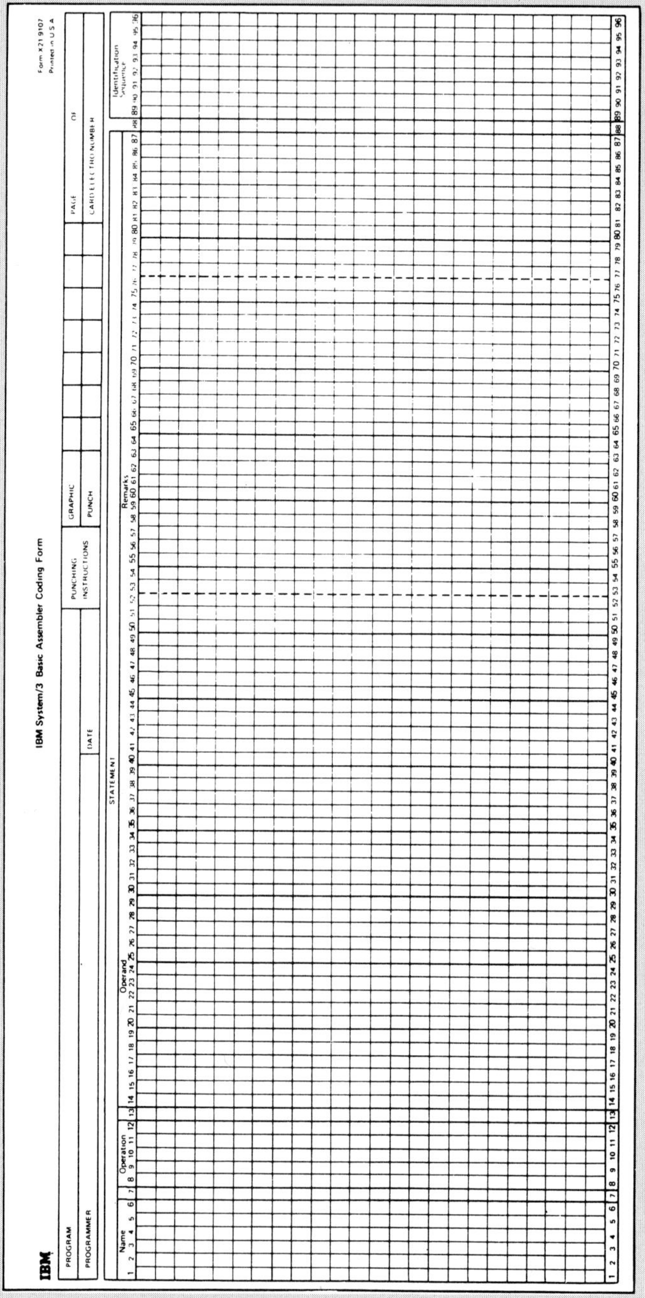

IBM

IBM System/3 Basic Assembler Coding Form

Form X21-9107
Printed in U.S.A.

PROGRAM		PUNCHING INSTRUCTIONS	GRAPHIC								PAGE	OF
PROGRAMMER	DATE		PUNCH								CARD ELECTRO NUMBER	

STATEMENT

Name | Operation | Operand | Remarks | Identification Sequence

1 2 3 4 5 6 7 8 9 10 11 12 13 14 15 16 17 18 19 20 21 22 23 24 25 26 27 28 29 30 31 32 33 34 35 36 37 38 39 40 41 42 43 44 45 46 47 48 49 50 51 52 53 54 55 56 57 58 59 60 61 62 63 64 65 66 67 68 69 70 71 72 73 74 75 76 77 78 79 80 81 82 83 84 85 86 87 88 89 90 91 92 93 94 95 96

Figure A-15. IBM System/3 Basic Assembly Coding Forms.

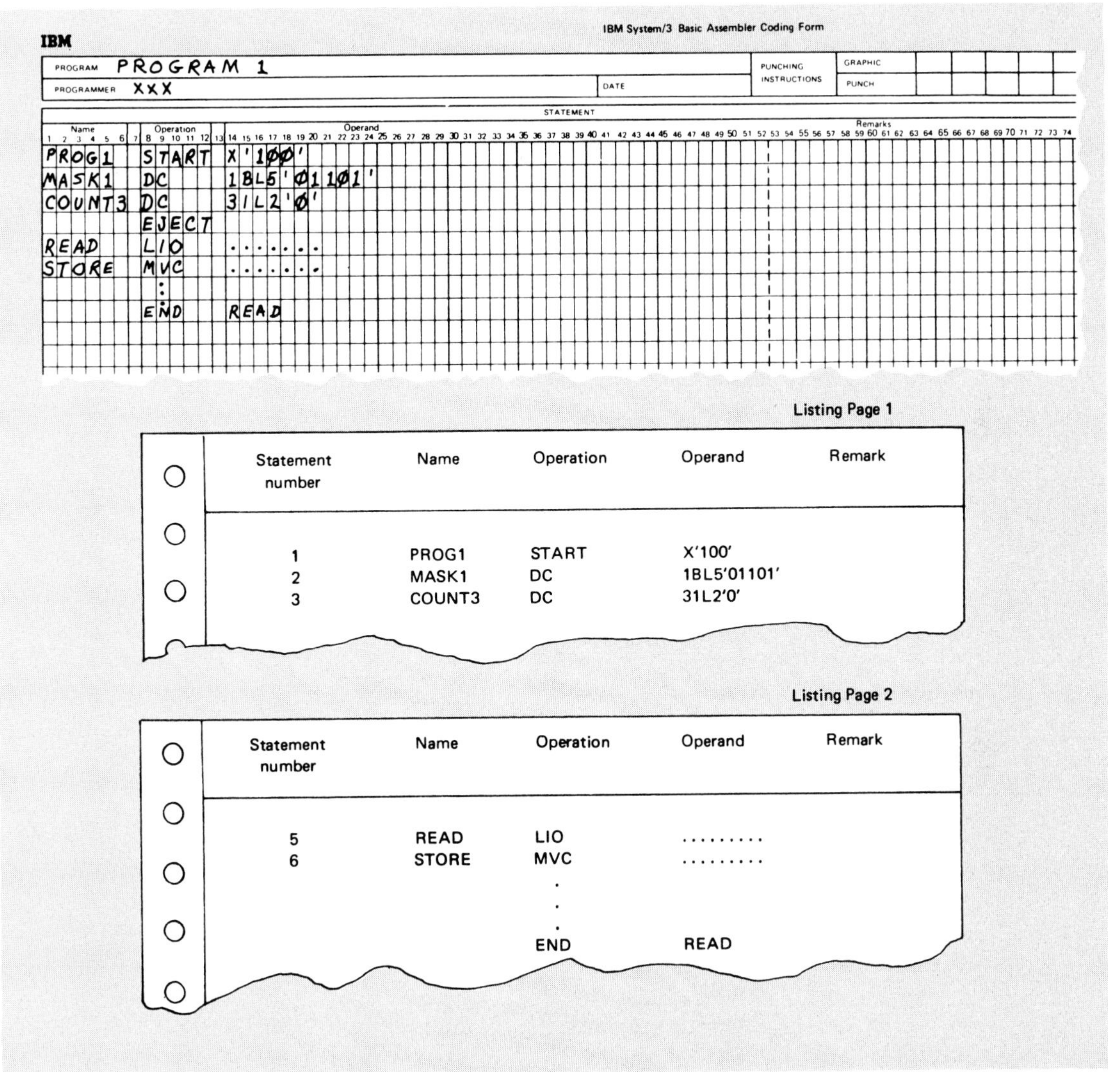

Figure A-16. Assembler Program Example.

The important features of the assembler language are

1. The variety of data representations which allows the programmer to represent his data in four possible formats; hexadecimal, decimal, binary, and character.
2. The assembler coding sheet that permits the writing of programs in rather "free form" without any column restrictions.

3. The programmer may enter from one to six character labels in the name field of an instruction which permits him to symbolically refer to an instruction in his program.
4. Mnemonics are standardized symbols representing machine and assembler operation codes which are usually abbreviated so that they are easy to remember.
5. An assembler program may be linked to a RPG II program.
6. The assembler can check the sequence of instructions and indicate any that are out of order.
7. The printing of diagnostic messages during the assembly process identifies errors in the source program.
8. The assembler listing provides
   a. A listing of the source program statements, showing the object codes generated.
   b. A cross reference of the symbols used and
   c. diagnostic messages.

SORT/COLLATE PROGRAM

The Sort/Collate program is a general purpose utility program designed to perform a variety of sorting and collating functions. The types of jobs are:

1. Sort—arrange cards in a predetermined sequence.
2. Merge—combine two card files.
3. Match—compare two card files and find cards that match.
4. Select—select cards from file.

To use the Sort/Collate program, specification sheets similar to RPG II specifications are filled in to describe the job to be performed. Cards are punched from these sheets and then are entered, compiled, and executed in the same manner as an RPG program.

PAYROLL—COMPUTATION OF GROSS EARNINGS CASE ILLUSTRATION

1. The employee master cards for hourly employees are merged with salary and current earnings file. During this processing the two files are merged and the system computes gross earnings.
2. The salaried employees are already calculated and added into the appropriate accumulated totals. Hourly employees earnings are calculated by multiplying hours worked by the hourly rate from employee master record. The resulting pay is accumulated in the same manner as salaried employees.
3. The calculated hourly earnings, salaried earnings, and employee mastercards are held for the withholding tax procedure.
4. A gross earnings control list is prepared and balanced to predetermined control totals.

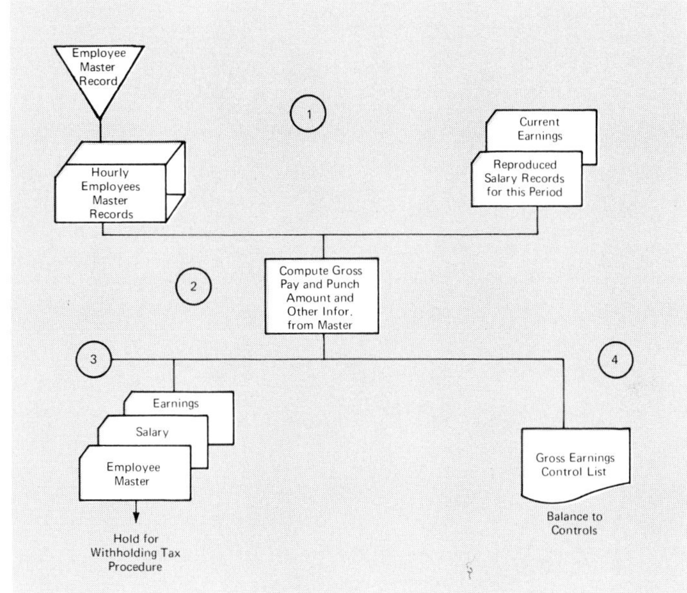

Figure A-17. Gross Earnings Calculation Data Flow.

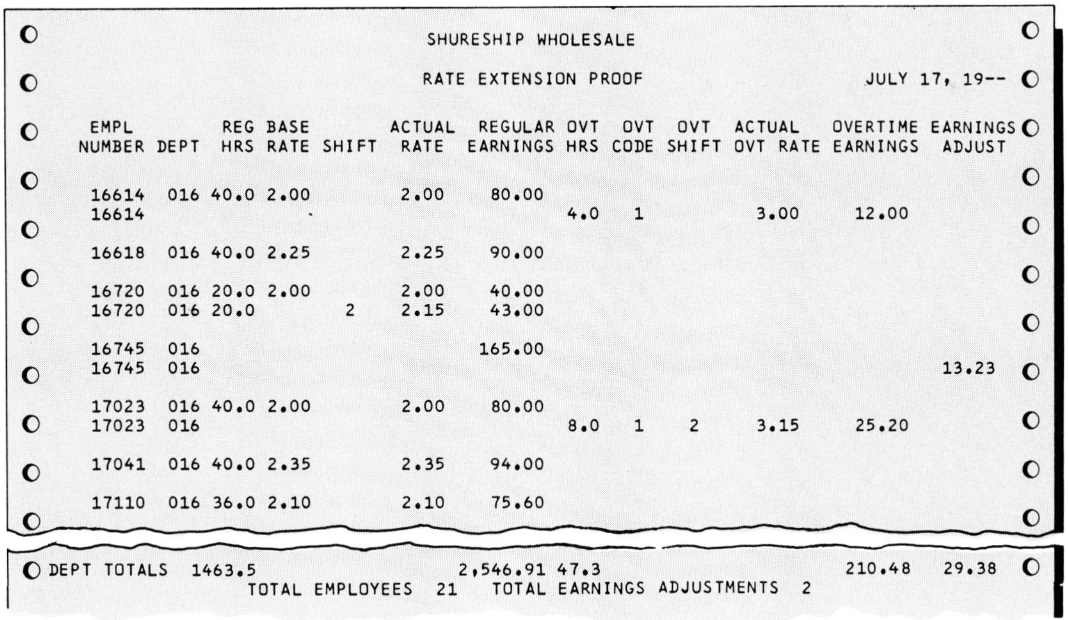

SHURESHIP WHOLESALE

RATE EXTENSION PROOF JULY 17, 19--

EMPL NUMBER	DEPT	REG HRS	BASE RATE	SHIFT	ACTUAL RATE	REGULAR EARNINGS	OVT HRS	OVT CODE	OVT SHIFT	ACTUAL OVT RATE	OVERTIME EARNINGS	EARNINGS ADJUST
16614	016	40.0	2.00		2.00	80.00						
16614							4.0	1		3.00	12.00	
16618	016	40.0	2.25		2.25	90.00						
16720	016	20.0	2.00		2.00	40.00						
16720	016	20.0		2	2.15	43.00						
16745	016					165.00						
16745	016											13.23
17023	016	40.0	2.00		2.00	80.00						
17023	016						8.0	1	2	3.15	25.20	
17041	016	40.0	2.35		2.35	94.00						
17110	016	36.0	2.10		2.10	75.60						
DEPT TOTALS		1463.5				2,546.91	47.3				210.48	29.38

TOTAL EMPLOYEES 21 TOTAL EARNINGS ADJUSTMENTS 2

Figure A-18. Gross Earnings Control List.

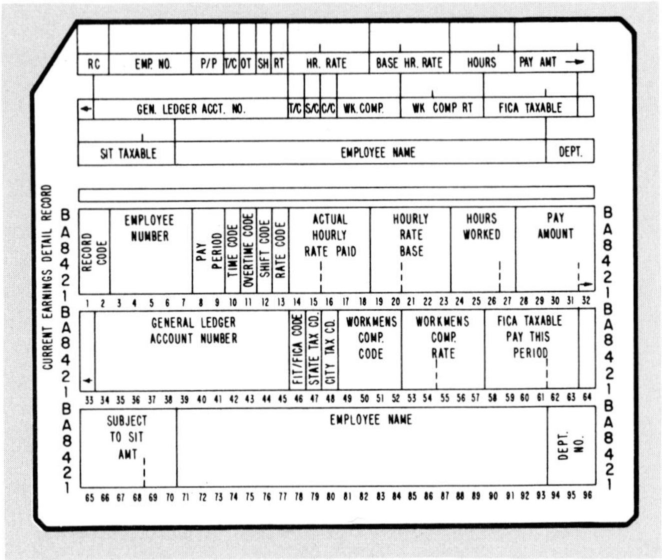

Figure A-19. Current Earnings Detail Card.

QUESTIONS FOR REVIEW

1. What is the main purpose of System/3?
2. Describe the System/3 card?
3. How are the different types of characters represented?
4. What is the main function of the Data Recorder?
5. Describe the basic devices of System/3.
6. How many lines may be printed on the face of the card?
7. What is the main function of the Card Sorter?
8. What was RPG II designed for? How are programs written in RPG II?
9. What functions does the System/3 Basic Assembler Program perform?
10. What are the important features of the Assembler Language?
11. What are the main functions of the Sort/Collate program?
12. How is a Sort/Collate job programmed?

Glossary

Absolute address* (1) An address that is permanently assigned by the machine designer to a storage location. (2) A pattern of characters that identifies a unique storage location without further modification. (3) Synonymous with "machine address" and "specific address."

Absolute coding* Coding that uses machine instructions with absolute addresses.

Abstract (Noun.) A short form or summary of a document. (Verb.) To shorten or summarize a document.

Access* (See random access, remote access, and serial access.)

Access arm* A part of a disk storage unit that is used to hold one or more reading and writing heads.

Access method Any of the data management techniques available to the user for transferring data between main storage and an input/output device.

Access mode* In COBOL, a technique that is used to obtain a specific logic record from, or to place a specific logic record into, a file assigned to a mass storage device.

Access time (1) The time interval between the instant at which data are called for from a storage device and the instant delivery is completed, that is, the read time. (2) The time interval between the instant at which data are requested to be stored and the instant at which storage is completed, that is, the write time.

Accounting machine* (1) A keyboard-actuated machine that prepares accounting records. (2) A machine that reads data from external storage media, such as cards or tapes, and automatically produces accounting records or tabulations, usually on continuous forms.

Accumulator* A register in which the result of an arithmetic or logic operation is formed.

* This material is reproduced with permission from American National Standard "Vocabulary for Information Processing" ANSI X3.12–1970 Copyright 1970 by the American National Standards Institute, copies of which may be purchased from the American National Standards Institute at 1430 Broadway, New York, New York, 10018.

ACCURACY* The degree of freedom from error, that is, the degree of conformity to truth or to a rule. Accuracy is contrasted with precision, for example, four-place numerals are less precise than six-place numerals; nevertheless, a properly computed four-place numeral might be more accurate than an improperly computed six-place numeral.

ACRONYM A word formed from the first letter or letters of the words in a name, term, or phrase, for example, COBOL from *CO*mmon *B*usiness *O*riented *L*anguage.

ACTIVITY A term to indicate that a record in a master file is used, altered, or referred to.

ACTIVITY RATIO The ratio of the number of records in a file which have activity to the total number of records in that file.

ACTUAL KEY In COBOL, a data item that may be used as a hardware address and that expresses the location of a record on a mass storage medium.

ADDER* A device whose output is a representation of the sum of the quantities represented by its inputs.

ADDRESS* (1) An identification, as represented by a name, label, or number, for a register, location in storage, or any other data source or destination such as the location of a station in a communication network. (2) Loosely, any part of an instruction that specifies the location of an operand for the instruction. (3) (See "absolute address," "base address," "content addressed storage," "direct address," "effective address," "four-plus-one address," "immediate address," "indirect address," "instruction address," "machine address," "multiaddress," "multilevel address," "n-level address," "one-level address," "one-plus-one address," "relative address," "symbolic address," "three-plus-one address," "two-plus-one address," and "zero-level address.")

ADDRESS FORMAT* (1) The arrangement of the address parts of an instruction. The expression "-plus-one" is frequently used to indicate that one of the addresses specifies the location of the next instruction to be executed, such as one-plus-one, two-plus-one, three-plus-one, four-plus-one. (2) The arrangement of the parts of a single address, such as those required for identifying channel, module, track, etc., in a disc system.

ADDRESS MODIFICATION The process of changing the address part of a machine instruction by means of coded instructions.

ADDRESS PART* A part of an instruction word that specifies the address of an operand, instruction, or result. (Contrast with instruction address.)

ADDRESS REGISTER* A register in which an address is stored.

ADD TIME The time required for one addition, not including the time required to get and return the quantities from storage.

ALGOL Algorithmic-oriented language. An international procedure-oriented language.

ALGORITHM* A prescribed set of well-defined rules or processes for the solution of a problem in a finite number of steps, for example, a full statement of an arithmetic procedure for evaluating sin x to a stated precision.

ALLOCATE To grant a resource to, or reserve it for, a job or task.

ALPHABET (1) An ordered set of all the letters and associated marks used in a language. (2) An ordered set of the letters used in a language, for example, the Morse code alphabet, the 128 characters of the USASCII alphabet.

ALPHABETIC STRING* A character string consisting solely of letters from the same alphabet.

ALPHABETIC WORD* (1) A word consisting solely of letters. (2) A word consisting of characters from the same alphabet.

ALPHAMERIC (alphanumeric) Generic term for alphabetic letters, numerical digits, and special characters which are machine-processable.

ALPHANUMERIC CHARACTER SET* A character set that contains letters, digits and, usually, other characters.

ALPHANUMERIC CODE* A code whose code set consists of letters, digits, and associated special characters.

ALTERATION SWITCH A manual switch on the computer console or a program-simulated switch which can be set on or off to control coded machine instructions.

ALU Arithmetic and logic unit.

ANALOG COMPUTER* (1) A computer in which analog representation of data is mainly used. (2) A computer that operates on analog data by performing physical processes on these data. (Contrast with digital computer.)

ANALYSIS* The methodical investigation of a problem, and the separation of the problem into smaller related units for further detailed study.

ANALYST* A person who defines problems and develops algorithms and procedures for their solution.

AND* A logic operator having the property that if P is a statement, Q is a statement, R is a statement . . . , then the AND of P, Q, R, . . . is true if all statements are true, false if any statement is false. P and Q are often represented by $P \cdot Q$, PQ, $P \wedge Q$.

ANNOTATION* An added descriptive comment or explanatory note.

ARGUMENT* An independent variable, for example, in looking up a quantity in a table the number, or any of the numbers, that identifies the location of the desired value.

ARITHMETIC OPERATION Any of the fundamental operations of arithmetic, for example, the binary operations of addition, subtraction, multiplication, and division, and the unary operations of negation and absolute value.

ARITHMETIC SHIFT* (1) A shift that does not affect the sign position. (2) A shift that is equivalent to the multiplication of a number by a positive or negative integral power of the radix.

ARITHMETIC UNIT* The unit of a computing system that contains the circuits that perform arithmetic operations.

ARM* (See access arm.)

ARRAY* An arrangement of elements in one or more dimensions.

ARTIFICIAL INTELLIGENCE* The capability of a device to perform functions that are normally associated with human intelligence, such as reasoning, learning, and self-improvement. Related to machine learning.

ARTIFICIAL LANGUAGE* A language based on a set of prescribed rules that are established prior to its usage. (Contrast with natural language.)

ASCII USA Standard Code for Information Interchange. The standard code, using a coded character set consisting of 7-bit coded characters (8 bits including parity check), used for information interchange among data processing systems, communication systems, and associated equipment. The USASCII set consists of control characters and graphic characters.

ASSEMBLE* To prepare a machine language program from a symbolic language program by substituting absolute operation codes for symbolic operation codes and absolute or relocatable addresses for symbolic addresses.

ASSEMBLER* A computer program that assembles.

ASSEMBLY ROUTINE A computer routine which assembles other routines.

ATTRIBUTE A characteristic; for example, attributes of data include record length, record format, data set name, associated device type and volume identification, use, creation date, etc.

AUTOMATIC* Pertaining to a process or device that, under specified conditions, functions without intervention by a human operator.

AUTOMATIC CARRIAGE* A control mechanism for a typewriter or other listing device that can automatically control the feeding, spacing, skipping, and ejecting of paper or preprinted forms.

AUTOMATIC COMPUTER* A computer that can perform a sequence of operations without intervention by a human operator.

AUTOMATIC DATA PROCESSING* (1) Data processing largely performed by automatic means. (2) By extension, the discipline which deals with methods and techniques related to data processing performed by automatic means. (3) Pertaining to data processing equipment such as EAM and EDP equipment.

AUTOMATIC PROGRAMMING* The process of using a computer to perform some stages of the work involved in preparing a program.

AUTOMATION* (1) The implementation of processes by automatic means. (2) The theory, art, or technique of making a process more automatic. (3) The investigation, design, development, and application of methods of rendering processes automatic, self-moving, or self-controlling. (4) The conversion of a procedure, a process, or equipment to automatic operation.

AUXILIARY EQUIPMENT Equipment not under direct control of the central processing unit.

AUXILIARY OPERATION* An operation performed by equipment not under continuous control of the central processing unit.

AUXILIARY STORAGE* A storage that supplements another storage.

AVAILABLE MACHINE TIME The elapsed time when a computer is in operating condition, whether or not it is in use.

AVAILABLE TIME Time other than maintenance time. Available time consists of idle time and operating time. Operating time consists of development time, production time, and makeup time.

BACKGROUND PROCESSING* The automatic execution of lower-priority programs when higher-priority programs are not using the system resources. (Contrast with foreground processing.)

BACKSPACE* To move back the reading or display position according to a prescribed format.

BAND* A group of circular recording tracks on a storage device such as a drum or disc.

BASE* (1) A reference value. (2) A number that is multiplied by itself as many times as indicated by an exponent. (3) (See radix.)

BASE ADDRESS* A given address from which an absolute address is derived by combination with a relative address.

BATCH PROCESSING (1) Pertaining to the technique of executing a set of programs such that each is completed before the next program of the set is started. (2) Loosely, the execution of programs serially.

BAUD* A unit of signaling speed equal to the number of discrete conditions or signal events per second. For example, one baud equals one-half dot cycle per second in Morse code, one bit per second in a train of binary signals, and one 3-bit value per second in a train of signals each of which can assume one of eight different states.

BCD* (See binary–coded decimal notation.)

BEGINNING OF TAPE MARKER* A marker on a magnetic tape used to indicate the beginning of the permissible recording area, for example, a photo-reflective strip, a transparent section of tape.

BENCHMARK A point of reference from which measurements can be made.

BENCHMARK PROBLEM A problem used to evaluate the performance of computers relative to each other.

BINARY (1) Pertaining to a characteristic or property involving a selection, choice, or condition in which there are two possibilities. (2) Pertaining to the numeration system with a radix of two.

BINARY CARD* A card containing data in column binary or row binary form.

BINARY CELL* A storage cell of one binary digit capacity, for example, a single bit register.

BINARY CODE* A code that makes use of exactly two distinct characters, usually 0 and 1.

BINARY-CODED DECIMAL NOTATION* A positional notation in which the individual decimal digits expressing a number in decimal notation are each represented by a binary numeral, for example, the number twenty-three is represented by 0010 0011 in the 8-4-2-1 type of binary-coded decimal notation and by 10111 in binary notation. (Synonymous with BCD.)

BINARY DIGIT (1) In binary notation, either of the characters 0 or 1. (2) (Same as bit.)

BINARY NOTATION* A fixed radix notation where the radix is two. For example, in binary notation the numeral 110.01 represents the number 1 x 2 squared plus 1 x 2 to the first power plus 1 x 2 to the minus 2 power, that is, six and a quarter.

BINARY TO DECIMAL CONVERSION Conversion of a binary number to the equivalent decimal number, that is, a base two number to a base ten number.

BINARY UNIT (1) A binary digit. (2) A unit of information content, equal to one binary decision, or the designation of one of two possible and equally likely values or states of anything used to store or convey information. (3) (See check bit and parity bit.) (4) (Same as bit.)

BIT Contraction of "binary digit," the smallest unit of information in a binary system. A bit may be either a one or a zero.

BIT STREAM A binary signal without regard to grouping by character.

BIT STRING A string of binary digits in which each bit position is considered as an independent unit.

BLANK* A part of a medium in which no characters are recorded.

BLOCK (1) A set of things, such as words, characters, or digits, handled as a unit. (2) A collection of contiguous records recorded as a unit. Blocks are separated by block gaps, and each block may contain one or more records. (3) In data communication, a group of contiguous characters formed for transmission purposes. The groups are separated by interblock characters.

BLOCK DIAGRAM A diagram of a system, instrument, or computer in which the principal parts are represented by suitably associated geometrical figures to show both the basic functions and functional relationship between the parts.

BLOCKING Combining two or more records into one block.

BLOCK LENGTH The total number of records, words, or characters contained in one block.

BLOCK LOADING The form of fetch that brings the control sections of a load module into contiguous positions of main storage.

BLOCK RECORDS (Verb.) To group records for the purpose of conserving storage space or increasing the efficiency of access or processing. (Noun.) A physical record so constituted, or a portion of a telecommunications message defined to be a unit of data transmission.

BLOCK SORT Sorting by separation of the entire file on the highest-order portion of the key, usually implying separate ordering of these segments, and then adjoining the entire file.

BLOCK TRANSFER* The process of transmitting one or more blocks of data where the data are organized in such blocks.

BOOLEAN* (1) Pertaining to the processes used in the algebra formulated by George Boole. (2) Pertaining to the operations of formal logic.

BOOLEAN OPERATOR* A logic operator each of whose operands and whose result have one of two values.

BOOTSTRAP* A technique or device designed to bring itself into a desired state by means of its own action, for example, a machine routine whose first few instructions are sufficient to bring the rest of itself into the computer from an input device.

BORROW* An arithmetically negative carry.

BPS Bits per second. In serial transmission, the instantaneous bit speed within one character, as transmitted by a machine or a channel.

BRANCH* (1) A set of instructions that are executed between two successive decision instructions. (2) To select a branch as in (1). (3) A direct path joining two nodes of a network or graph. (4) Loosely, a conditional jump.

BRANCHPOINT* A place in a routine where a branch is selected.

BUFFER (1) A routine or device used to compensate for a difference in rate of flow of data, or time of occurrence of events, when transmitting data from one device to another. (2) An isolating circuit used to prevent a driven circuit from influencing the driving circuit.

BUG* A mistake or malfunction.

BUSINESS DATA PROCESSING* (1) Use of automatic data processing in accounting or management. (2) Data processing for business purposes, for example, recording and summarizing the financial transactions of a business.

BYTE A sequence of adjacent binary digits operated upon as a unit and usually shorter than a word.

CALCULATOR A data processor especially suitable for performing arithmetic operations which require frequent intervention by a human operator. (2) A device capable of performing arithmetic. (3) A calculator, as in (2), that requires frequent manual intervention. (4) Generally and historically, a device for carrying out logic and arithmetic digital operations of any kind.

CALL* (1) To transfer control to a specified closed subroutine. (2) In communications, the action performed by the calling party, or the operations necessary in making a call, or the effective use made of a connection between two stations.

CALLING SEQUENCE* A specified arrangement of instructions and data necessary to set up and call a given subroutine.

CARD* (See binary card, header card, laced card, magnetic card, punched card, and tape-to-card.)

CARD CODE The combinations of punched holes which represent characters (letters, digits, etc.) in a punched card.

CARD COLUMN One of the vertical lines of punching positions on a punched card.

CARD DECK* (See deck.)

CARD FEED A mechanism which moves cards into a machine one at a time.

CARD FIELD A fixed number of consecutive card columns assigned to data of a specific nature. For example, card columns 15-20 can be assigned to identification.

CARD HOPPER A device that holds cards and makes them availbale to a card feed mechanism. (Contrast with card stacker.)

CARD PUNCH A device to record information in cards by punching holes in the cards to represent letters, digits, and special characters.

CARD READER A device which senses and translates into internal form the holes in punched cards.

CARD STACKER An output device that accumulates punched cards in a deck. (Contrast with card hopper.)

CARD-TO-TAPE Pertaining to equipment which transfers information directly from punched cards to punched or magnetic tape.

CARRIAGE* (See automatic carriage.)

CARRIAGE CONTROL TAPE* A tape that contains line feed control data for a printing device.

CARRIAGE RETURN* The operation that prepares for the next character to be printed or displayed at the specified first position on the same line.

CARRY (1) One or more characters, produced in connection with an arithmetic operation on one digit place of two or more numerals in positional notation, that are forwarded to another digit place for processing here. (2) The number represented by the character or characters in (1). (3) Most commonly, a character as defined in (1), that arises when the sum of two or more digits equals or exceeds the radix of the number representation system. (4) Less commonly, a borrow. (5) To forward a carry. (6) The command directing that a carry be forwarded.

CATALOG* An ordered compilation of item descriptions and sufficient information to afford access to the items.

CATHODE RAY STORAGE* An electrostatic storage device that utilizes a cathode ray beam for access to the data.

CATHODE RAY TUBE DISPLAY (1) A device that presents data in visual form by means of controlled electron beams. (Abbreviated "CRT display.") (2) The data display produced by the device as in (1).

CENTRAL PROCESSING UNIT A unit of a computer that includes circuits controlling the interpretation and execution of instructions. (Synonymous with "main frame.")

CHAINING A system of storing records in which each record belongs to a list or group of records and has a linking field for tracing the chain.

CHAINING SEARCH A technique for retrieving data from a file by using addresses in the records that link each record to the next in the chain.

CHAIN PRINTER* A printer in which the type slugs are carried by the links of a revolving chain.

CHANNEL* (1) A path along which signals can be sent, for example, data channel, output channel. (2) The portion of a storage medium that is accessible to a given reading or writing station, for example, track, band. (3) In communication, a means of one-way transmission. Several channels may share common equipment. For example, in frequency multiplexing carrier systems, each channel uses a particular frequency band that is reserved for it. (Contrast with circuit.)

CHARACTER* A letter, digit, or other symbol that is used as part of the organization, control, or representation of data. A character is often in the form of a spatial arrangement of adjacent or connected strokes.

CHARACTER PRINTER* A device that prints a single character at a time. (Contrast with line printer.)

CHARACTER RECOGNITION* The identification of graphic, phonic, or other characters by automatic means. (See also, magnetic ink character recognition and optical character recognition.)

CHARACTER SET An ordered set of unique representation called characters, for example, the 26 letters of the English alphabet, 0 and 1 of the Boolean alphabet, the set of signals in the Morse code alphabet, the 128 characters of the USASCII alphabet.

CHARACTER STRING* A string consisting solely of characters.

CHART* (See flowchart.)

CHECK BIT* A binary check digit, for example, a parity bit.

CHECK CHARACTER* A character used for the purpose of performing a check.

CHECK DIGIT* A digit used for the purpose of performing a check.

CHECKPOINT* A place in a routine where a check, or a recording of data for restart purposes, is performed.

CHIP In microcircuitry, a single device, either a transistor or a diode, that has been cut from a larger wafer of silicon.

CIRCUIT* In communications, a means of two-way communication between two points, comprising associated "go" and "return" channels. (Contrast with channel.)

CLASSIFY To arrange into classes of information according to a system or method.

CLEAR (1) To place a storage device into a prescribed state, usually that denoting zero or blank. (2) To place a binary cell into the zero state.

CLEAR AREA* In character recognition, a specified area that is to be kept free of printing or any other markings not related to machine reading.

CLOSED LOOP A group of instructions which are repeated indefinitely.

CLOSED SHOP Pertaining to the operation of a computer facility in which most productive problem programming is performed by a group of programming specialists rather than by the problem originators. The use of the computer itself may also be described as closed shop if full-time trained operators, rather than user/programmers, serve as the operators. (Contrast with open shop.)

CLOSED SUBROUTINE A subroutine that can be stored at one place and can be connected to a routine by linkages at one or more locations. (Contrast with open subroutine.)

COBOL Common business-oriented language. A business data processing language.

CODE (1) A set of unambiguous rules specifying the way in which data may be represented, for example, the set of correspondences in the standard code for information interchange. (Synonymous with coding scheme.) (2) In telecommunications, a system of rules and conventions according to which the signals representing data can be formed. (3) In data processing, to represent data or a program in a symbolic form that can be accepted by a data processor. (4) To write a routine.

COLLATE To compare and merge two or more similarly ordered sets of items into one ordered set.

COLLATING SEQUENCE* An ordering assigned to a set of items, such that any two sets in that assigned order can be collated.

COLLATOR A device to collate sets of punched cards or other documents into a sequence.

COLUMN* (1) A vertical arrangement of characters or other expressions. (2) Loosely, a digit place.

COLUMN BINARY Pertaining to the binary representation of data on punched cards in which adjacent positions in a column correspond to adjacent bits of data.

COLUMN SPLIT* Pertaining to the sensing or punching of punched card data in a manner that permits certain punch positions within a single column to be ignored or treated separately from the other punch positions of the same column.

COMMAND* (1) A control signal. (2) Loosely, an instruction in machine language. (3) Loosely, a mathematical or logic operator.

COMMON LANGUAGE A language in machine-sensible form which is common to a group of computers and associated equipment.

COMMUNICATION LINK The physical means of connecting one location to another for the purpose of transmitting and receiving information.

COMPARISON The examination of the relationship between two similar items of data. Usually followed by a decision.

COMPILE To prepare a machine language program from a computer program written in another programming language by making use of overall logic structure of the program, or generating more than one machine instruction for each symbolic statement, or both, as well as performing the function of an assembler.

COMPILER* A program that compiles.

COMPLEMENT A number that can be derived from a specified number by subtracting it from a specified number. For example, in radix notation, the specified number may be a given power of the radix or one less than a given power of the radix. The negative of a number is often represented by its complement.

COMPONENT A basic part. An element.

COMPUTER (1) A data processor that can perform substantial computation, including numerous arithmetic or logic operations, without intervention by a human operator during the run. (2) A device capable of solving problems by accepting data, performing described operations on the data, and supplying the results of these operations. Various types of computers are calculators, digital computers, and analog computers.

COMPUTER CODE* A machine code for a specific computer.

COMPUTER INSTRUCTION* A machine instruction for a specific computer.

COMPUTER NETWORK A complex consisting of two or more interconnected computing units.

COMPUTER PROGRAM* A series of instructions or statements in a form acceptable to a computer prepared in order to achieve a certain result.

COMPUTER WORD* A sequence of bits or characters treated as a unit and capable of being stored in one computer location.

CONCATENATED DATA SET A collection of logically connected data sets.

CONCURRENT* Pertaining to the occurrence of two or more events or activities within the same specified interval of time. (Contrast with simultaneous, sequential, and consecutive.)

CONDITIONAL JUMP* A jump that occurs if specified criteria are met.

CONFIGURATION The group of machines, devices, etc., which make up a data processing system.

CONNECTOR On a flowchart, the means of representing the convergence of more than one flowline into one, or the divergence of one flowline into more than one. It may also represent a break in a single flowline for continuation in another area.

CONSECUTIVE* Pertaining to the occurrence of two sequential events without the intervention of any other such event. (Contrast with concurrent, sequential, and simultaneous.)

CONSOLE* That part of a computer used for communication between the operator or maintenance engineer and the computer.

CONSTANT A fixed or invariable value or data item.

CONTROL CARD A punched card containing input data or parameters for initializing or modifying a program.

CONTROL CHARACTER A character whose occurrence in a particular context initiates, modifies, or stops a control action—for example, a character that controls carriage return, or a character that controls transmission of data over communication networks. A control character may be recorded for use in a subsequent action. It may have a graphic representation in some circumstances.

CONTROL MODE The state that all terminals on a line must be in to allow line discipline, line control, or terminal selection to occur. When all terminals on a line are in the control mode, characters on the line are viewed as control characters performing line discipline, that is, polling or addressing.

CONTROL PANEL* (1) A part of a computer console that contains manual controls. (2) (See plugboard.)

CONTROL PROGRAM A group of programs that provides such functions as the handling of input/output operations, error detection and recovery, program loading, and communication between the program and the operator. IPL, Supervisor, and Job Control make up the control program in the Disk and Tape Operating Systems.

CONTROL SECTION The smallest separately relocatable unit of a program. That portion of text specified by the programmer to be an entity, all elements of which are to be loaded into contiguous main storage locations.

CONTROL TOTAL A sum resulting from the addition of a specified field from each record in a group of records, used for checking machine, program, and data reliability.

CONTROL UNIT In a digital computer, those parts that effect the retrieval of instructions in proper sequence, the interpretation of each instruction, and the application of the proper signals to the arithmetic unit and other parts in accordance with this interpretation.

CONVERSATIONAL MODE Communication between a terminal and the computer in which each entry from the terminal elicits a response from the computer and vice versa.

CONVERSION (1) The process of changing from one method of data processing to another or from one data processing system to another. (2) The process of changing from one form of representation to another.

CONVERT* To change the representation of data from one form to another, for example, to change numerical data from binary to decimal or from cards to tape.

COPY* To reproduce data in a new location or other destination, leaving the source data unchanged, although the physical form of the result may differ from that of the source. For example, to copy a deck of cards onto a magnetic tape. (Contrast with duplicate.)

CORE* (See magnetic core.)

CORE STORAGE A form of high-speed storage using magnetic cores.

CORNER CUT A corner removed from a card for orientation purposes.

COUNTER* A device such as a register or storage location used to represent the number of occurrences of an event.

CPS "Character per second" or "cycles per second," depending on context.

CPU* Central processing unit, q.v.

CR The carriage return character, q.v.

CRT DISPLAY (See cathode ray tube display.)

CYCLE* (1) An interval of space or time in which one set of events or phenomena is completed. (2) Any set of operations that is repeated regularly in the same sequence. The operations may be subject to variations on each repetition.

DATA* (1) A representation of facts, concepts, or instructions in a formalized manner suitable for communication, interpretation, or processing by humans or automatic means. (2) Any representations such as characters or analog quantities to which meaning is, or might be, assigned.

DATA BANK* A comprehensive collection of libraries of data. For example, one line of an invoice may form an item, a complete invoice may form a record, a complete set of such records may form a file, the collection of inventory control files may form a library, and the libraries used by an organization are known as its data bank. (Synonymous with data base.)

DATA BASE (See data bank.)

DATA CODE A structured set of characters used to represent the data items of a data element. For example, the data codes 1, 2, . . . 7 may be used to represent the data items Sunday, Monday, . . . Saturday.

DATA COLLECTION The act of bringing data from one or more points to a central point.

DATA COMMUNICATION The transmission of data from one point to another.

DATA CONTROL BLOCK A control block through which the information required by access routines to store and retrieve data is communicated to them.

DATA CONVERSION The process of changing data from one form of representation to another.

DATA, DIGITAL Information represented by a code consisting of a sequence of discrete elements.

DATA ELEMENTS The name for a class or category of data based on natural or assigned relationship that can be used to denote a set of data items. For example, the data item "Tuesday" is a member of the set denoted by the data element "weekday." (Contrast with data item.)

DATA FLOWCHART* A flowchart representing the path of data through a problem solution. It defines the major phases of the processing as well as the various data media used. (Synonymous with data flow diagram.)

DATA FLOW DIAGRAM* (See data flowchart.)

DATA HIERARCHY* A data structure consisting of sets and subsets such that every subset of a set is of lower rank than the data of the set.

DATA ITEM The name for an individual member of a set of data denoted by a data element. For example, the data item "Tuesday" is a member of the set denoted by the data element "weekday." (Contrast with data element.)

DATA MANAGEMENT A general term that collectively describes those functions of the control program that provide access to data sets, enforce data storage conventions, and regulate the use of input/output devices.

DATA NAME An identifier that names unambiguously an item of data.

DATA ORGANIZATION A term that refers to any one of the data management conventions for the arrangement of a data set.

DATA ORIGINATION The translation of information from its original form into a machine-readable form or directly into electrical signals.

DATA PROCESSING* The execution of a systematic sequence of operations performed upon data. (Synonymous with information processing.)

DATA PROCESSING SYSTEM A network of machine components capable of accepting information, processing it according to a plan, and producing the desired results.

DATA PROCESSOR A device capable of performing data processing—for example, a desk calculator, punched card machine, or computer.

DATA TRANSMISSION The sending of data from one part of a system to another part.

DEBUG* To detect, locate, and remove mistakes from a routine or malfunctions from a computer.

DECIMAL (1) Pertaining to a characteristic or property involving a selection, choice, or condition in which there are ten possibilities. (2) Pertaining to the numeration system with a radix of ten. (3) (See binary–coded decimal.)

DECIMAL DIGIT* In decimal notation, one of the characters 0 thru 9.

DECIMAL NOTATION A fixed radix notation, where the radix is ten. For example, in decimal notation, the numeral 576.2 represents the number 5 x 10 squared plus 7 x 10 to the first power plus 6 times 10 to the zero power plus 2 x 10 to the minus 1 power.

DECIMAL NUMERAL* A decimal representation of a number.

DECIMAL POINT* The radix point in decimal representation.

DECISION* A determination of future action.

DECISION INSTRUCTION An instruction that effects the selection of a branch of program, for example, a conditional jump instruction.

DECISION TABLE* A table of all contingencies that are to be considered in the description of a problem, together with the actions to be taken. Decision tables are sometimes used in place of flowcharts for problem description and documentation.

DECK* A collection of punched cards. (Synonymous with card deck.)

DECODER* (1) A device that decodes. (2) A matrix of logic elements that selects one or more output channels according to the combination of input signals present.

DECOLLATE* To separate the plies of a multipart form or paper stock.

DELIMITER* A flag that separates and organizes items of data.

DESTRUCTIVE READ A read process that also erases the data in the source.

DEVICE A mechanical, electrical, and/or electronic contrivance with a specific purpose.

DEVICE INDEPENDENCE The ability to request input/output operations without regard to the characteristics of the input/output devices.

DIAGNOSTIC* Pertaining to the detection and isolation of a malfunction or mistake.

DIAGNOSTIC ROUTINE A program that facilitates computer maintenance by detection and isolation of malfunctions or mistakes.

DIGIT* A symbol that represents one of the nonnegative integers smaller than the radix. For example, in decimal notation, a digit is one of the characters from 0 to 9. (Synonymous with numeric character.)

DIGITAL COMPUTER* (1) A computer in which discrete representation of data is mainly used. (2) A computer that operates on discrete data by performing arithmetic and logic processes on these data. (Contrast with analog computer.)

DIGIT PUNCH A punch in rows 0-9 in a punched card. The 0-punch may also function as a zone punch in alphabetic representation.

DIODE An electronic device used to permit current flow in one direction and to inhibit current flow in the other.

DIRECT ACCESS* (See random access.)

DIRECT ACCESS DEVICE* (See random access device.)

DIRECT ADDRESS* An address that specifies the location of an operand.

DISK A physical element of disk storage.

DISK STORAGE A storage device which uses magnetic recording on flat rotating disks.

DISPLAY* A visual presentation of data.

DISPLAY TUBE* A tube, usually a cathode ray tube, used to display data.

DISPLAY UNIT A device which provides a visual representation of data. (Compare hard copy.)

DOCUMENT* (1) A medium and the data recorded on it for human use, for example, a report sheet, a book. (2) By extension, any record that has permanence and that can be read by man or machine.

DOCUMENTATION* (1) The creating, collecting, organizing, storing, citing, and disseminating of documents, or the information recorded in documents. (2) A collection of documents or information on a given subject.

DOS Disk Operating System.

DOUBLE PRECISION* Pertaining to the use of two computer words to represent a number.

DOUBLE PUNCH More than one numeric punch in any one column of a card.

DOWNTIME* The time interval during which a device is malfunctioning.

DRUM STORAGE A storage device which uses magnetic recording on a rotating cylinder. A type of addressable storage associated with some computers.

DUMP* (1) To copy the contents of all or part of a storage, usually from an internal storage into an external storage. (2) A process as in (1). (3) The data resulting from the process as in (1).

DUPLICATE* To copy so that the result remains in the same physical form as the source. For example, to make a new punched card with the same pattern of holes as an original punched card. (Contrast with copy.)

DYADIC OPERATION* An operation on two operands.

DYNAMIC STORAGE ALLOCATION A storage allocation technique in which the location of programs and data is determined by criteria applied at the moment of need.

EAM Electrical Accounting Machine. Pertaining to data processing equipment that is predominantly electromechanical, such as a keypunch, mechanical sorter, collator, and tabulator.

EDIT* To modify the form or format of data, for example, to insert or delete characters such as page numbers or decimal points.

EDP* Electronic Data Processing.

EFFECTIVE ADDRESS* The address that is derived by applying any specified indexing or indirect addressing rules to the specified address and that is actually used to identify the current operand.

ELECTRICAL ACCOUNTING MACHINE (See EAM.)

ELECTRONIC DATA PROCESSING* (1) Data processing largely performed by electronic devices. (2) Pertaining to data processing equipment that is predominantly electronic, such as electronic digital computer.

EMULATE* To imitate one system with another such that the imitating system accepts the same data, executes the same programs, and achieves the same results as the imitated system.

END-AROUND CARRY* A carry from the most significant digit place to the least significant digit place.

END-OF-FILE MARK A code which signals that the last record of a file has been read.

END OF TAPE MARKER* A marker on a magnetic tape used to indicate the end of the permissible recording area, for example, a photo-reflective strip, a transparent section of tape, or a particular bit pattern.

ENTRY POINT In a routine, any place to which control can be passed.

ERASE* To obliterate information from a storage medium, for example, to clear, to overwrite.

ERROR* Any discrepancy between a computed, observed, or measured quantity and the true, specified, or theoretically correct value or condition.

ERROR MESSAGE* An indication that an error has been detected.

EXECUTE To carry out an instruction or perform a routine.

EXECUTE STATEMENT (EXEC) A job control statement that designates a job step by identifying the load module to be fetched and executed.

EXECUTIVE ROUTINE* A routine that controls the execution of other routines.

EXPONENT* In a floating-point representation, the numeral of a pair of numerals representing a number, that indicates the power to which the base is raised.

EXPRESSION A source-language combination of one or more operations.

EXTERNAL STORAGE A storage device outside the computer which can store information in a form acceptable to the computer, for example, cards and tapes.

EXTRACT (1) To separate specific parts of a word from the whole word. (2) To remove specific items from a file.

FACILITY Anything used or available for use in furnishing communication service. Commonly, a general term for communications paths.

FEEDBACK The return of part of the output of a machine, process, or system to the computer as input for another phase, especially for self-correcting or control purposes.

FEED HOLES Holes punched in a paper tape to enable it to be driven by a sprocket wheel.

FETCH* To locate and load a quantity of data from storage.

F. FORMAT A data set record format in which the logical records are the same length.

FIELD* In a record, a specified area used for a particular category of data, for example, a group of card columns used to represent a wage rate or a set of bit locations in a computer word used to express the address of the operand.

FIGURATIVE CONSTANT* A preassigned, fixed, character string with a preassigned, fixed, data name in a particular programming language.

FILE* A collection of related records treated as a unit. For example, one line of an invoice may form an item, a complete invoice may form a record, a complete set of such records may form a file, the collection of inventory control files may form a library, and the libraries used by an organization are known as its data bank.

FILE GAP* An area on a data medium intended to be used to indicate the end of a file and possibly, the start of another. A file gap is frequently used for other purposes, in particular, as a mark to indicate the end or beginning of some other group of data.

FILE LAYOUT* The arrangement and structure of data in a file, including the sequence and size of its components. By extension, a file layout might be the description thereof.

FILE MAINTENANCE* The activity of keeping a file up-to-date by adding, changing, or deleting data.

FILTER* (1) A device or program that separates data, signals, or material in accordance with specified criteria. (2) A mask.

FIRST GENERATION COMPUTER A computer utilizing vacuum tube components.

FIXED-LENGTH RECORD Pertaining to a file in which all records are constrained to be of equal, predetermined length. (Contrast with variable-length record.)

FIXED-POINT Pertaining to a numeration system in which the position of the point is fixed with respect to one end of the numerals, according to some convention.

FIXED WORD LENGTH COMPUTER A computer in which data is treated in units of a fixed number of characters or bits (as contrasted with variable word length).

FLAG* (1) Any of various types of indicators used for identification, for example, a wordmark. (2) A character that signals the occurrence of some condition, such as the end of a word.

FLIP-FLOP* A circuit or device containing active elements, capable of assuming either one of two stable states at a given time. (Synonymous with toggle -1.)

FLOATING-POINT Pertaining to a numeration system in which the position of the point does not remain fixed with respect to one end of the numerals.

FLOATING-POINT REPRESENTATION (1) A numeration system in which the position of the radix point does not remain fixed with respect to one end of the numerals.

(2) A numeration system in which each number equals one of the numerals times a power of an understood fixed positive integer base, where the power is equal to the understood base raised to the exponent represented by the other numeral, e.g., 123-03.

FLOWCHART (1) A graphical representation of the definition, analysis, or solution of a problem, in which symbols are used to represent operations, data, flow, equipment, etc. (2) (See data flowchart.)

FLOWCHART SYMBOL* A symbol used to represent operations, data, flow, or equipment on a flowchart.

FLOW DIRECTION* In flowcharting, the antecedent-to-successor relation, indicated by arrows or other conventions, between operations on a flowchart.

FLOWLINE* On a flowchart, a line representing a connecting path between flowchart symbols, for example, a line to indicate a transfer of data or control.

FOREGROUND PROCESSING The automatic execution of the programs that have been designed to preempt the use of the computing facilities. Usually a real time program. (Contrast with background processing.)

FORMAT (1) A specific arrangement of data. (2) (See address format.)

FORTRAN FORmula TRANslating system. Any of several specific procedure-oriented languages.

FOUR-PLUS-ONE ADDRESS* Pertaining to an instruction containing four operand addresses and one control address.

GANG-PUNCH To punch all or part of the information from one punched card into succeeding cards.

GENERAL PURPOSE COMPUTER A computer that is designed to handle a wide variety of problems.

GENERATE* To produce a program by selection of subsets from a set of skeletal coding under the control of parameters.

GET To obtain a record from an input file.

GROUPED RECORDS Records combined into a unit to conserve storage space or reduce access time.

GROUP INDICATE The printing of indicative information from only the first record of a group.

HALF-ADJUST To round by one-half of the maximum value of the number base of the counter.

HALF-WORD* A contiguous sequence of bits or characters which comprises half a computer word and is capable of being addressed as a unit.

HARD COPY A printed copy of machine output in a visually readable form, for example, printed reports, listings, documents, summaries, etc. (Compare display unit.)

HARDWARE Physical equipment, as opposed to the program or method of use, for example, mechanical, magnetic, electrical, or electronic devices. (Contrast with software -2.)

HASH TOTAL A summation for checking purposes of one or more corresponding fields of a file which would ordinarily not be summed.

HEAD* A device that reads, records, or erases data on a storage medium, for example, a small electromagnet used to read, write, or erase data on a magnetic drum or tape, or the set of perforating, reading, or marking devices used for punching, reading, or printing on paper tape.

HEADER (message heading). The initial character of a message designating addressee, routing, time of origination, etc.

HEADER CARD* A card that contains information about the data in cards that follow.

HEXADECIMAL* (See sexadecimal.)

HIGH-SPEED CARRY* Any technique in parallel addition for speeding up carry propagation, for example, standing-on-nines carry.

HIT* A successful comparison of two items of data.

HOLLERITH A particular type of code or punched card utilizing 12 rows per column and usually 80 columns per card.

HOPPER* (See card hopper.)

HOUSEKEEPING Operations or routines which do not contribute directly to the solution of the problem but do contribute directly to the operation of the computer.

I/O Input/output. Input or output, or both.

IDENTIFIER* A symbol whose purpose is to identify, indicate, or name a body of data.

IDLE TIME* That part of available time during which the hardware is not being used. (Contrast with operating time.)

IDP* Integrated data processing, q.v.

INDEX (1) An ordered reference list of the contents of a file or document, together with keys or reference notations for identification or location of those contents. (2) To prepare a list as in (1). (3) A symbol or number used to identify a particular quantity in an array of similar quantities. For example, the terms of an array represented by $X_1, X_2, \ldots X_{100}$ have the indexes 1, 2, . . . , 100, respectively. (4) Pertaining to an index register. (5) To move a machine part to a predetermined position, or by a predetermined amount, on a quantized scale.

INDICATOR A device which registers a condition in the computer.

INDIRECT ADDRESS* An address that specifies a storage location that contains either a direct address or another indirect address. (Synonymous with multilevel address.)

INFORMATION The meaning that a human assigns to data by means of the known conventions used in its representation.

INFORMATION PROCESSING* (See data processing.)

INFORMATION RETRIEVAL* The methods and procedures for recovering specific information from stored data.

INITIALIZE* To set counters, switches, and addresses to zero or other starting values at the beginning of, or at prescribed point in, a computer routine.

INITIATOR/TERMINATOR The job scheduler function that selects jobs and job steps to be executed, allocates input/output devices for them, places them under task control, and at completion of the job, supplies control information for writing job output on a system output unit.

INLINE PROCESSING The processing of data in random order, not subject to preliminary editing or sorting.

INPUT* (1) (See input data.) (2) One or a sequence of input states. (3) (See input device.) (4) (See input channel.) (5) (See input process.) (6) Pertaining to a device, process, or channel involved in the insertion of data or states, or to the data or states involved. (7) (See manual input.)

INPUT AREA* An area of storage reserved for input.

INPUT DATA* Data to be processed.

INPUT DEVICE* The device or collective set of devices used for conveying data into another device.

INPUT JOB STREAM A sequence of job control statements entering the system, which may also include input data.

INPUT/OUTPUT (1) Commonly called I/O. A general term for the equipment used to communicate with a computer. (2) The data involved in such communication. (3) The media carrying the data for input/output.

INPUT PROCESS* (1) The process of receiving data by a device. (2) The process of transmitting data from peripheral equipment, or external storage, to internal storage.

INQUIRY A request for information from storage, for example, a request for the number of available airline seats or a machine statement to initiate a search of library documents.

INQUIRY STATION* Data terminal equipment used for inquiry into a data processing system.

INSTALLATION TIME Time spent in installing, testing, and accepting equipment.

INSTRUCTION A statement that specifies an operation and the values or locations of its operands. In this context, the term instruction is preferable to the terms command or order which are sometimes used synonymously. Command should be reserved for electronic signals, and order should be reserved for sequence, interpolation, and related usage.

INSTRUCTION ADDRESS The address of the location where an instruction word is stored. (Contrast with address part.)

INSTRUCTION COUNTER* A counter that indicates the location of the next computer instruction to be interpreted.

INSTRUCTION FORMAT The allocation of bits or characters of a machine instruction to specific functions.

INTEGRATED DATA PROCESSING* Data processing in which the coordination of data acquisition and all other stages of data processing is achieved in a coherent system, for example, a business data processing system, in which data for orders, and buying are combined to accomplish the functions of scheduling, invoicing, and accounting.

INTERFACE A shared boundary. An interface might be a hardware component to link two devices or it might be a portion of storage or registers accessed by two or more programs.

INTERLEAVE* To arrange parts of one sequence of things or events so that they alternate with parts of one or more other sequences of things or events and so that each sequence retains its identity, for example, to organize storage into banks with independent busses so that sequential data references may be overlapped in a given period of time.

INTERLEAVING (1) The act of accessing two or more bytes or streams of data from distinct memory banks simultaneously. (2) The alternating of two or more operations or functions through the overlapped use of a computer facility.

INTERLOCK To prevent a machine or device from initiating further operations until the operation in process is completed.

INTERMEDIATE TOTAL The result when a summation is terminated by a change of group which is neither the most nor the least significant.

INTERNAL STORAGE* Addressable storage directly controlled by the central processing unit of a digital computer.

INTERPRETER (1) A program that translates and executes each source language expression before translating and executing the next one. (2) A device that prints on a punched card the data already punched in the card. (3) A program element which handles job control language statements.

INTERPRETING Printing on paper tape or cards the meaning of the holes punched on the same tape or cards.

INTER-RECORD GAP* (See record gap.)

INTERRUPT* To stop a process in such a way that it can be resumed.

IOCS Input/Output Control System. (See also WATS.)

ITEM (1) In general, one member of a group. For example, a record may contain a number of items, such as fields or groups of fields. A file may consist of a number of items, such as records. A table may consist of a number of items, such as entries. (2) A collection of related characters treated as a unit. (3) (See data item.)

ITERATE To repeatedly execute a loop or series of steps, for example, a loop in a routine.

JACK A connecting device to which a wire or wires of a circuit may be attached and which is arranged for the insertion of a plug.

JOB A specified group of tasks prescribed as a unit of work for a computer. By extension, a job usually includes all necessary programs, linkages, files, and instructions to the Operating System.

JOB CONTROL STATEMENT A statement in a job that is used in identifying the job or describing its requirements to the Operating System.

JOB LIBRARY A concatenation of user-identified, partitioned data sets used as the primary sources of load modules for a given job.

JOB MANAGEMENT A general term that collectively describes the functions of the job scheduler and master scheduler.

JOB-ORIENTED TERMINAL A terminal designed for a particular application.

JOB SCHEDULER The control program function that controls input job streams and system output, obtains input/output resources for jobs and job steps, attaches tasks corresponding to job steps, and otherwise regulates the use of the computing system by jobs.

JOB STATEMENT The control statement in the input job stream that identifies the beginning of a series of job control statements for a single job.

JOB STEP The execution of a computer program explicitly identified by a job control statement. A job may specify that several job steps be executed.

JUSTIFICATION The act of adjusting, arranging, or shifting digits to the left or right, to fit a prescribed pattern.

JUSTIFY To align data about a specified reference.

KEY* One or more characters within an item of data that are used to identify it or control its use.

KEYBOARD A device for the encoding of data by key depression, which causes the generation of the selected code element.

KEYPUNCH* A keyboard-actuated device that punches holes in a card to represent data.

KEYWORD One of the significant and informative words in a title or document which describe the content of that document.

LABEL One or more characters used to identify an item of data.

LACED CARD* A punched card that has a lace-like appearance, usually without information content.

LANGUAGE* A set of representations, conventions, and rules used to convey information.

LANGUAGE TRANSLATOR A general term for any assembler, compiler, or other routine that accepts statements in one language and produces equivalent statements in another language.

LAYOUT* (See file layout and record layout.)

LETTER A graphic, which, when used alone or combined with others, represents in a written language one or more sound elements of the spoken language. Diacritical marks used alone and punctuation marks are not letters.

LIBRARY (1) A collection of organized information used for study and reference. (2) A collection of related files. For example, one line of an invoice may form an item, a complete invoice may form a record, a complete set of such records may form a file, the collection of inventory control files may form a library, and the libraries used by an organization are known as its data bank.

LIBRARY ROUTINE* A proven routine that is maintained in a program library.

LINEAR PROGRAMMING In operations research, a procedure for locating the maximum or minimum of a linear function of variables which are subject to linear constraints.

LINE PRINTER A device that prints all characters of a line as a unit. (Contrast with character printer.)

LINE PRINTING* The printing of an entire line of characters as a unit.

LINKAGE* In programming, coding that connects two separately coded routines.

LINKAGE EDITOR A program that produces a load module by transforming object modules into a format that is acceptable to fetch, combining separately produced object modules and previously processed load modules into a single load module, resolving symbolic cross-references among them, replacing, deleting, and adding control sections automatically on request, and providing overlay facilities for modules requesting them.

LIST An ordered set of items.

LIST To print every relevant item of input data.

LITERAL A symbol or a quantity in a source program that is itself data, rather than a reference to data.

LOAD* In programming, to enter data into storage or working registers.

LOAD-AND-GO* An operating technique in which there are no stops between the loading and execution phases of a program, and which may include assembling or compiling.

LOCATION Loosely, anyplace in which data may be stored.

LOGICAL FILE* A collection of one or more logical records.

LOGICAL RECORD* A collection of items independent of their physical environment. Portions of the same logical record may be located in different physical records.

LOGIC INSTRUCTION* An instruction that executes an operation that is defined in symbolic logic, such as AND, OR, NOR.

LOGIC SYMBOL (1) A symbol used to represent a logic element graphically. (2) A symbol used to represent a logic connective.

LOOP A sequence of instructions that is executed repeatedly until a terminal condition prevails.

MACHINE CODE* An operation code that a machine is designed to recognize.

MACHINE-INDEPENDENT Pertaining to procedures or programs created without regard for the actual devices which will be used to process them.

MACHINE INSTRUCTION* An instruction that a machine can recognize and execute.

MACHINE LANGUAGE* A language that is used directly by a machine.

MACHINE-READABLE MEDIUM A medium that can convey data to a given sensing device.

MACHINE-SENSIBLE INFORMATION Information in a form which can be read by a specific machine.

MACRO INSTRUCTION* An instruction in a source language that is equivalent to a specified sequence of machine instructions.

MACROPROGRAMMING* Programming with macro instructions.

MAGNETIC CARD* A card with a magnetic surface on which data can be stored by selective magnetization of portions of the flat surface.

MAGNETIC CORE* A configuration of magnetic material that is, or is intended to be, placed in a spatial relationship to current-carrying conductors and whose magnetic properties are essential to its use. It may be used to concentrate an induced magnetic field as in a transformer, induction coil, or armature, to retain a magnetic polarization for the purpose of storing data, or for its nonlinear properties as in a logic element. It may be made of such material as iron, iron oxide, or ferrite and in such shapes as wires, tapes, toroids, or thin film.

MAGNETIC DISC* A flat circular plate with a magnetic surface on which data can be stored by selective magnetization of portions of the flat surface.

MAGNETIC DRUM* A right circular cylinder with a magnetic surface on which data can be stored by selective magnetization of portions of the curved surface.

MAGNETIC INK* An ink that contains particles of a magnetic substance whose presence can be detected by magnetic sensors.

MAGNETIC INK CHARACTER RECOGNITION* (See MICR.)

MAGNETIC STORAGE* A storage device that utilizes the magnetic properties of materials to store data, for example, magnetic cores, tapes, and films.

MAGNETIC TAPE* (1) A tape with a magnetic surface on which data can be stored by selective polarization of portions of the surface. (2) A tape of magnetic material used as the constituent in some forms of magnetic cores.

MAGNETIC THIN FILM* A layer of magnetic material, usually less than one micron thick, often used for logic or storage elements.

MAIN FRAME* (Same as central processing unit.)

MAIN STORAGE The fastest general purpose storage of a computer.

MAINTENANCE (1) Any activity intended to eliminate faults or to keep hardware or programs in satisfactory working condition, including tests, measurements, replacements, adjustments, and repairs. (2) (See file maintenance.)

MAINTENANCE TIME Time used for hardware maintenance. It includes preventive maintenance time and corrective maintenance time. (Contrast with available time.)

MALFUNCTION The effect of a fault.

MANAGEMENT INFORMATION SYSTEMS Management performed with the aid of automatic data processing.

MANUAL INPUT (1) The entry of data by hand into a device at the time of processing. (2) The data entered as in (1).

MAP To establish a correspondence between the elements of one set and the elements of another set.

MARK-SENSE To mark a position on a punched card with an electrically conductive pencil, for later conversion to machine punching.

MARK SENSING* The electrical sensing of manually recorded conductive marks on a nonconductive surface.

MASK* (1) A pattern of characters that is used to control the retention or elimination of portions of another pattern of characters. (2) A filter.

MASS STORAGE (online) The storage of a large amount of data which is also readily accessible to the central processing unit of a computer.

MASS STORAGE DEVICE* A device having a large storage capacity, for example, magnetic disc, magnetic drum.

MASTER FILE A file that is either relatively permanent, or that contains relatively permanent data, or that is treated as an authority in a particular job.

MATCH To check for identity between two or more items of data.

MATRIX* (1) In mathematics, a two-dimensional rectangular array of quantities. Matrices are manipulated in accordance with the rules of matrix algebra. (2) In computers, a logic network in the form of an array of input leads and output leads with logic elements connected at some of their intersections. (3) By extension, an array of any number of dimensions.

MEDIUM The material, or configuration thereof, on which data is recorded, for example, paper tape, cards, magnetic tape.

MEMORY (See storage.)

MERGE To combine two or more sets of items into one, usually in a specified sequence.

MESSAGE An arbitrary amount of information whose beginning and end are defined or implied.

MICR Magnetic ink character recognition. The machine recognition of characters printed with magnetic ink. (Contrast with OCR.)

MICRO INSTRUCTION A basic or elementary machine instruction.

MICROPROGRAMMING Programming with micro instructions.

MICROSECOND One-millionth of a second.

MICROWAVE Any electromagnetic wave in the radio frequency spectrum above 890 megacycles per second.

MILLISECOND One-thousandth of a second.

MINOR TOTAL The result when a summation is terminated by the least significant change of group.

MISTAKE A human action that produces an unintended result.

MNEMONIC* (See mnemonic symbol.)

MNEMONIC SYMBOL A symbol chose to assist the human memory, for example, an abbreviation such as MPY for "multiply."

MODE (See access mode.)

MODEM Contraction of modulator-demodulator. A device which modulates and demodulates signals transmitted over communications facilities.

MODIFY To alter a part of an instruction or routine.

MODULE (1) A program unit that is discrete and identifiable with respect to compiling, combining with other units, and loading, for example, the input to, or output from, an assembler, compiler, linkage editor, or executive routine. (2) A packaged functional hardware unit designed for use with other components.

MONITOR* Software or hardware that observes, supervises, controls, or verifies the operations of a system.

MONTE CARLO METHOD A method of obtaining an approximate solution to a numerical problem by the use of random numbers, for example, the random walk method, q.v.

MOVE (See transmit.)

MULTIPLEX* To interleave or simultaneously transmit two or more messages on a single channel.

MULTIPROCESSING (1) Pertaining to the simultaneous execution of two or more programs or sequences of instructions by a computer or computer network. (2) Loosely, parallel processing.

MULTIPROCESSOR A computer that can execute one or more computer programs employing two or more processing units under integrated control of programs or devices.

MULTIPROGRAMMING Pertaining to the concurrent execution of two or more programs by a single computer.

MYLAR* A DuPont trademark for polyester film, often used as a base for magnetically coated or perforated information media.

NANOSECOND One-thousand-millionth of a second.

NATURAL LANGUAGE A language whose rules reflect and describe current usage rather than prescribed usage. (Contrast with artificial language.)

NEEDLE* A probe that may be passed through holes or notches to assist in sorting or selecting cards.

NEGATE To perform the logic operator "NOT."

NEST* To imbed subroutines or data in other subroutines or data at a different hierarchial level such that the different levels of routines or data can be executed or accessed recursively.

NETWORK (1) A series of points interconnected by communications channels. (A private line network is a network confined to the use of one customer, while a switched telephone network is a network of telephone lines normally used for dialed telephone calls.) (2) The interconnection of electrical components.

NONDESTRUCTIVE READ A read process that does not erase the data in the source.

No OP* An instruction that specifically instructs the computer to do nothing, except to proceed to the next instruction in sequence.

NOT A logic operator having the property that if P is a statement, then the NOT of P is true if P is false, false if P is true. The NOT of P is often represented by P, P, ~P, |P'.

NOTATION A representational system which utilizes characters and symbols in positional relationships to express information.

NUCLEUS That portion of the control program that must always be present in main storage. Also, the main storage area used by the nucleus and other transient control program routines.

NULL CHARACTER A control character that serves to accomplish media fill or time fill, for example, in USASCII, the "all zeros" character (not numeric zero). Null characters may be inserted into or removed from, a sequence of characters without affecting the meaning of the sequence, but control of equipment or the format may be affected. Abbreviated NUL.

NUMBER (1) A mathematical entity that may indicate quantity or amount of units. (2) Loosely, a numeral.

NUMERIC Pertaining to numerals or to representation by means of numerals.

NUMERIC CHARACTER (See digit.)

OBJECT CODE Output from a compiler or assembler which is itself executable machine code or is suitable for processing to produce executable machine code.

OBJECT LANGUAGE The language in which the output from a compiler or assembler is expressed.

OBJECT MODULE* A module that is the output of an assembler or compiler and is input to a linkage editor.

OBJECT PROGRAM A fully compiled or assembled program that is ready to be loaded into the computer.

OCR Optical character recognition. Machine identification of printed characters through use of light-sensitive devices. (Contrast with MICR.)

OCTAL (1) Pertaining to a characteristic or property involving a selection, choice, or condition in which there are eight possibilities. (2) Pertaining to the numeration system with a radix of eight.

OFFLINE Pertaining to equipment or devices not under direct control of the central processing unit.

ONE-FOR-ONE A phrase often associated with an assembly routine where one source language instruction is converted to one machine language instruction.

ONLINE* (1) Pertaining to equipment or devices under direct control of the central processing unit. (2) Pertaining to a user's ability to interact with a computer.

ONLINE SYSTEM (1) In teleprocessing, a system in which the input data enters the computer directly from the point of origin and/or in which output data is transmitted directly to where it is used. (2) In the telegraph sense, a system of transmitting directly into the system.

OPENENDED* Pertaining to a process or system that can be augmented.

OPEN SHOP Pertaining to the operation of a computer facility in which most productive problem programming is performed by the problem originator rather than by a group of programming specialists. The use of the computer itself may also be described as open shop if the user/programmer also serves as the operator, rather than a full-time trained operator. (Contrast with closed shop.)

OPEN SUBROUTINE A subroutine that must be relocated and inserted into a routine at each place it is used. (Contrast with closed subroutine.)

OPERAND* That which is operated upon. An operand is usually identified by an address part of an instruction.

OPERATING SYSTEM Software which controls the execution of computer programs and which may provide scheduling, debugging, input/output control, accounting, compilation, storage assignment, data management, and related services.

OPERATING TIME That part of available time during which the hardware is operating and assumed to be yielding correct results. It includes development time, production time, and makeup time. (Contrast with idle time.)

OPERATION (1) A defined action, namely, the act of obtaining a result from one or more operands in accordance with a rule that completely specifies the result for any permissible combination of operands. (2) The set of such acts specified by such a rule, or the rule itself. (3) The act specified by a single computer instruction. (4) A program step undertaken or executed by a computer, for example, addition, multiplication, extraction, comparison, shift, transfer. The operation is usually specified by the operator part of an instruction. (5) The event or specific action performed by a logic element.

OPERAION CODE A code that represents specific operations.

OPERATION RESEARCH The use of the scientific method to provide criteria for decisions concerning the operations of people, machines, and other resources in a system involving repeatable operations.

OPERATOR (1) In the description of a process, that which indicates the action to be performed on operands. (2) A person who operates a machine.

OPTICAL CHARACTER RECOGNITION (See OCR.)

OPTICAL SCANNER* (1) A device that scans optically and usually generates an analog or digital signal. (2) A device that optically scans printed or written data and generates their digital representations.

OPTIMIZE To arrange the instructions or data in storage so that a minimum amount of machine time is spent for access when instructions or data are called out.

OR (1) A logic operator having the property that if P is a statement, Q is a statement, R is a statement, . . . , then the OR of P, Q, R, . . . is true if at least one statement is true, false if all statements are false, P or Q is often represented by P+Q, PVQ. (Synonymous with inclusive OR, Boolean add; contrast with exclusive OR.) (2) Operations research.

OS Operating System, q.v.

OUTPUT (1) Data that has been processed. (2) The state or sequence of states occurring on a specified output channel. (3) The device or collective set of devices used for taking data out of a device. (4) A channel for expressing a state of a device or logic element. (5) The process of transferring data from an internal storage to an external storage.

OVERFLOW (1) That portion of the result of an operation that exceeds the capacity of the intended unit of storage. (2) Pertaining to the generation of overflow as in (1).

OVERFLOW INDICATOR A bi-stable trigger which changes state when overflow occurs in the register with which it is associated. It may be interrogated and/or restored to the original state.

OVERLAP To do something at the same time that something else is being done; for example, to perform input/output operations while instructions are being executed by the central processing unit.

OVERLAY The technique of repeatedly using the same blocks of internal storage during different stages of a problem. When one routine is no longer needed in storage, another routine can replace all or part of it.

PACK To compress several items of data in a storage medium in such a way that the individual items can later be recovered.

PANEL (See control panel.)

PAPER TAPE READER A device that senses and translates the holes in perforated tape into electrical signals.

PARALLEL OPERATION Pertaining to the concurrent or simultaneous execution of two or more operations in devices such as multiple arithmetic or logic units. (Contrast with serial operation.)

PARALLEL PROCESSING Pertaining to the concurrent or simultaneous execution of two or more processes in multiple devices such as channels or processing units. (Contrast with serial processing.)

PARAMETER* A variable that is given a constant value for a specific purpose or process.

PARITY BIT A binary digit appended to an array of bits to make the sum of all the bits always odd or always even.

PARITY CHECK A check that tests whether the number of ones or zeros in an array of binary digits is odd or even.

PATCH* (1) To modify a routine in a rough or expedient way. (2) A temporary electrical connection.

PERIPHERAL EQUIPMENT* In a data processing system, any unit of equipment, distinct from the central processing unit, which may provide the system with outside communication.

PHYSICAL RECORD A record from the standpoint of the manner or form in which it is stored, retrieved, and moved—that is, one that is defined in terms of physical qualities.

PL/I Programing Language/I, a high level programming language.

PLATEN A backing, commonly cylindrical, against which printing mechanisms strike to produce an impression.

PLOT To map or diagram. To connect the point-by-point coordinate values.

PLUGBOARD A perforated board that accepts manually-inserted plugs to control the operation of equipment. (Synonymous with control panel -2.)

POSITION In a string, each location that may be occupied by a character or binary digit, and may be identified by a serial number.

POSITIONAL NOTATION A numeration system with which a number is represented by means of an ordered set of digits such that the value contributed by each digit depends on its position as well as upon its value. (Synonymous with positional representation.)

POSITIONAL REPRESENTATION (See positional notation.)

POST To enter a unit of information on a record.

PRECISION The degree of discrimination with which a quantity is stated; for example, a three-digit numeral discriminates among 1000 possibilities.

PREDEFINED PROCESS* A process that is identified only by name and that is defined elsewhere.

PREFIX NOTATION A method of forming mathematical expressions in which each operator precedes its operands. In prefix notation, the expression "A plus B multiplied by C" would be represented by "ABxC."

PREVENTIVE MAINTENANCE Maintenance specifically intended to prevent faults from occurring during subsequent operation. (Contrast with corrective maintenance.) Corrective maintenance and preventive maintenance are both performed during maintenance time.

PRIMARY STORAGE The main internal storage.

PRINTER A device which expresses coded characters as hard copy.

PRINTING (See line printing.)

PROBLEM DESCRIPTION In information processing, a statement of a problem. The statement may also include a description of the method of solution, the procedures and algorithms, etc.

PROBLEM-ORIENTED LANGUAGE* A programming language designed for the convenient expression of a given class of problems.

PROBLEM PROGRAM* Any program that is not part of the operating system.

PROCEDURE The course of action taken for the solution of a problem.

PROCEDURE-ORIENTED LANGUAGE* A programming language designed for the convenient expression of procedures used in the solution of a wide class of problems.

PROCESS A systematic sequence of operations to produce a specified result.

PROCESSING PROGRAM A general term for any program that is not a control program; a problem program.

PROCESSOR (1) In hardware, a data processor. (2) In software, a computer program that includes the compiling, assembling, translating, and related functions for a specific programming language, for example, COBOL processor, FORTRAN processor.

PROGRAM (1) A series of actions proposed in order to achieve a certain result. (2) Loosely, a routine. (3) To design, write, and test a program as in (1). (4) Loosely, to write a routine.

PROGRAM LIBRARY* A collection of available computer programs and routines.

PROGRAMMED CHECK A check procedure designed by the programmer and implemented specifically as a part of his program.

PROGRAMMER A person mainly involved in designing, writing, and testing programs.

PROGRAMMING The design, the writing, and testing of a program.

PROGRAMMING LANGUAGE* A language used to prepare computer programs.

PUNCH A perforation, as in a punched card or paper tape.

PUNCHED CARD* (1) A card punched with a pattern of holes to represent data. (2) A card as in (1) before being punched.

PUNCHED TAPE* A tape on which a pattern of holes or cuts is used to represent data.

PUNCH POSITION A site on a punched tape or card where holes are to be punched.

PUT To place a single data record into an output file.

QUEUE (Noun.) A waiting line formed by items in a system waiting for service—for example, customers at a bank teller window or messages to be transmitted in a message switching system. (Verb.) To arrange in, or form, a queue.

RADIX In positional representation, the integral ratio of the significances of any two specified adjacent digit positions. For example, if the radix is five, then 142.3 means 1 times 5 to the second power, plus 4 times 5 to the first power, plus 3 times 5 to the zero power, plus 2 times 5 to the minus one power. (Synonymous with base.)

RADIX COMPLEMENT A complement obtained by subtracting each digit from one less than the radix, then adding to the least significant digit, executing all carries required. For example, tens complement in decimal notation, twos complement in binary notation. (Synonymous with true complement.)

RANDOM ACCESS (1) Pertaining to the process of obtaining data from, or placing data into, storage where the time required for such access is independent of the location of the data most recently obtained or placed in storage. (2) Pertaining to a storage device in which the access time is effectively independent of the location of the data. (3) (Synonymous with direct access.)

RANDOM ACCESS DEVICE* A device in which the access time is effectively independent of the location of the data. (Synonymous with direct access device.)

RANDOM NUMBERS (1) A series of numbers obtained by chance. (2) A series of numbers considered appropriate for satisfying certain statistical tests. (3) A series of numbers believed to be free from conditions which might bias the result of a calculation.

RANDOM PROCESSING The treatment of data without respect to its location in external storage, and in an arbitrary sequence governed by the input against which it is to be processed.

RANGE (1) The set of values that a quantity or function may assume. (2) The difference between the highest and lowest value that a quantity or function may assume.

RANK To arrange in an ascending or descending series according to importance.

RAW DATA* Data which has not been processed or reduced.

READ (1) To acquire or interpret data from a storage device, a data medium, or in any other source. (2) (See destructive read and nondestructive read.)

READER A device converts information in one form of storage to information in another form of storage.

READY CONDITION The condition of a task such that it is contention for the central processing unit, all other requirements for its activation having been satisfied.

REAL TIME (1) Pertaining to the actual time during which a physical process transpires. (2) Pertaining to the performance of a computation during the actual time that the related physical process transpires in order that results of the computation can be used in guiding the physical process.

REAL-TIME INPUT* Input data inserted into a system at the time of generation by another system.

REAL-TIME OUTPUT* Output data removed from a system at time of need by another system.

RECORD (1) A collection of related items of data, treated as a unit. For example, one line of an invoice may form a record. A complete set of such records may form a file. (2) (See fixed-length record and variable-length record.)

RECORD GAP An area on a data medium used to indicate the end of a block or record. (Synonymous with inter-record gap.)

RECORDING DENSITY* The number of bits in a single linear track measured per unit of length of the recording medium.

RECORD LAYOUT* The arrangement and structure of data in a record, including the sequence and size of its components. By extension, a record layout might be the description thereof.

RECORD LENGTH* A measure of the size of a record, usually specified in units such as words or characters.

REDUNDANCY In the transmission of information, that fraction of the gross information content of a message which can be eliminated without loss of essential information.

REEL A mounting for a roll of tape.

REGISTER A device capable of storing a specified amount of data, such as one word.

REGISTRATION* The accurate positioning relative to a reference.

RELATIVE ADDRESS* The number that specifies the difference between the absolute address and the base address.

RELIABILITY The probability that a device will function without failure over a specified time period or amount of usage.

RELOCATE In programming, to move a routine from one portion of storage to another and to adjust the necessary address references so that the routine, in its new location, can be executed.

REMOTE ACCESS* Pertaining to communication with a data processing facility by one or more stations that are distant from that facility.

REMOTE STATION* Data terminal equipment for communicating with a data processing system from a location that is time, space, or electrically distant.

REPORT GENERATION A technique for producing complete machine reports from information which describes the input file and the format and content of the output report.

REPRODUCE To prepare a duplicate of stored information, especially for punched cards, punched paper tape, or magnetic tape.

REPRODUCER A device which will duplicate, in one card, all or part of the information contained in another card.

RERUN* A repeat of a machine run, usually because of a correction, an interrupt, or a false start.

RERUN POINT That location in the sequence of instructions in a computer program at which all information pertinent to the rerunning of the program is available.

RESET* (1) To restore a storage device to a prescribed initial state, not necessarily that denoting zero. (2) To place a binary cell into the state denoting zero.

RESOURCE Any facility of the computing system or operating system required by a job or task, and including main storage, input/output devices, the central processing unit, data sets, and control processing programs.

RESPONSE TIME The elapsed time between the generation of a message at a terminal and the receipt of a reply in case of an inquiry or receipt of message by addressee.

RESTART* To reestablish the execution of a routine, using the data recorded at a checkpoint.

RETRIEVAL (See information retrieval.)

RETURN (See carriage return.)

REWIND To return a magnetic or paper tape to its beginning.

ROUND To adjust the least significant digits retained in truncation to partially reflect the dropped portion. For example, when rounded to three digits, the decimal number 2.7561 becomes 2.76.

ROUNDING ERROR An error due to round off. (Contrast with truncation error.)

ROUND OFF To delete the least significant digit or digits of a numeral and to adjust the part retained in accordance with some rule.

ROUTINE An ordered set of instructions that may have some general or frequent use.

RUN A single, continuous performance of a computer routine.

SAMPLING (1) Obtaining the values of a function for discrete, regularly or irregularly spaced values of the independent variable. (2) In statistics, obtaining a sample from a population.

SCALE To change a quantity by a factor in order to bring its range within prescribed limits.

SCAN* To examine sequentially part by part.

SEARCH To examine a set of items for those that have a desired property.

SECOND GENERATION COMPUTER A computer utilizing solid state components.

SEEK To position the access mechanism of a direct access device at a specified location.

SEGMENT* (1) To divide a computer program into parts such that the program can be executed without the entire program being in internal storage at any one time. (2) A part of a computer program as in (1).

SEQUENTIAL CONTROL* A mode of computer operation in which instructions are executed in an implicitly defined sequence until a different sequence is explicitly initiated by a jump instruction.

SERIAL (1) Pertaining to the sequential or consecutive occurrence of two or more related activities in a single device or channel. (2) Pertaining to the time-sequencing of two or more processes. (3) Pertaining to the time-sequential processing of the individual parts of a whole, such as the bits of a character or the characters of a word, using the same facilities for successive parts.

SERIAL ACCESS (1) Pertaining to the sequential or consecutive transmission of data to or from storage. (2) Pertaining to the process of obtaining data from, or placing data into, storage where the time required for such access is dependent upon the location of the data most recently obtained or placed in storage. (Contrast with random access.)

SERIAL COMPUTER (1) A computer having a single arithmetic and logic unit. (2) A computer, some specified characteristic of which is serial, for example, a computer that manipulates all bits of a word serially.

SET (1) A collection. (2) To place a storage device into a specified state, usually other than that denoting zero or blank. (3) To place a binary cell into the state denoting one.

SETUP (1) An arrangement of data or devices to solve a particular problem. (2) In a computer which consists of an assembly of individual computing units, the arrangement of interconnections between the units, and the adjustments needed for the computer to solve a particular problem.

SEXADECIMAL (1) Pertaining to a characteristic or property involving a selection, choice, or condition in which there are sixteen possibilities. (2) Pertaining to the numeration system with a radix of sixteen. (3) (Synonymous with hexadecimal.)

SHARED FILE A direct access device which may be used by two systems at the same time; a shared file may link two systems.

SHIFT A movement of data to the right or left.

SIGHT CHECK* A check performed by sighting through the holes of two or more aligned punched cards toward a source of light to verify the punching, for example, to determine if a hole has been punched in a corresponding punching position on all cards in the deck.

SIGNAL (1) The event or phenomenon that conveys data from one point to another. (2) A time dependent value attached to a physical phenomenon and conveying data.

SIGN BIT* A binary digit occupying the sign position.

SIGN DIGIT* A digit occupying the sign position.

SIGNED FIELD* A field which has a character in it to designate its algebraic sign.

SIGNIFICANCE In positional representation, the factor, dependent on the digit position, by which a digit is multiplied to obtain its additive contribution in the representation of a number.

SIGNIFICANT DIGIT* A digit that is needed for a certain purpose, particularly one that must be kept to preserve a specific accuracy or precision.

SIGN POSITION A position, normally located at one end of a numeral, that contains an indication of the algebraic sign of the number represented by the numeral.

SIMULATE To represent certain features of the behavior of a physical or abstract system by the behavior of another system.

SIMULATION The representation of certain features of the behavior of a physical or abstract system by the behavior of another system; for example, the representation of physical phenomena by means of operations performed by a computer or the representation of operations of a computer by those of another computer.

SIMULATOR A device, system, or computer program that represents certain features of the behavior of a physical or abstract system.

SIMULTANEOUS Pertaining to the occurrence of two or more events at the same instant of time. (Contrast with concurrent, sequential, and consecutive.)

SKIP* To ignore one or more instructions in a sequence of instructions.

SOFTWARE (1) A set of programs, procedures, rules, and possibly associated documentation concerned with the operation of a data processing system. For example, compilers, library routines, manuals, circuit diagrams. (2) (Contrast with hardware.)

SOLID STATE COMPONENT* A component whose operation depends on the control of electric or magnetic phenomena in solids, for example, a transistor, crystal diode, ferrite core.

SORT To arrange data or items in an ordered sequence by applying specific rules.

SORTER* A person, device, or computer routine that sorts.

SOURCE LANGUAGE A language that is an input to a given translation process.

SOURCE MODULE A series of statements in the symbolic language of an assembler or compiler, which constitutes the entire input to a single execution of the assembler or compiler.

SOURCE PROGRAM A program written in a source language.

SPACE (1) A site intended for the storage of data, for example, a site on a printed page of a location in a storage medium. (2) A basic unit of area, usually the size of a single character. (3) One or more blank characters. (4) To advance the reading or display position according to a prescribed format, for example, to advance the printing or display position horizontally to the right or vertically down. (Contrast with backspace.)

STACKER (See card stacker.)

STANDARD (1) An accepted criterion or an established measure for performance, practice, design, terminology, size, etc. (2) A rule of test by which something is judged.

STANDBY (1) Condition of equipment which will permit complete resumption of stable operation within a short span of time. (2) A duplicate set of equipment to be used if the primary unit becomes unusable because of malfunction.

STATEMENT In computer programming, a meaningful expression or generalized instruction in a source language.

STATION One of the input or output points of a communications system; for example, the telephone set in the telephone system or the point where the business machine interfaces the channel on a leased private line.

STEP (1) One operation in a computer routine. (2) To cause a computer to execute one operation. (3) (See single step.)

STORAGE (1) Pertaining to a device into which data can be entered, in which it can be held, and from which it can be retrieved at a later time. (2) Loosely, any device that can store data. (3) (Synonymous with memory.)

STORAGE ALLOCATION (1) The assignment of blocks of data to specified blocks of storage. (2) (See dynamic storage allocation.)

STORAGE CAPACITY* The amount of data that can be contained in a storage device.

STORAGE DEVICE A device into which data can be inserted, in which it can be retained, and from which it can be retrieved.

STORAGE KEY An indicator associated with a storage block or blocks, which requires that tasks have a matching protection key to use the blocks.

STORAGE PROTECTION An arrangement for preventing access to storage for either reading or writing, or both.

STORE (1) To enter data into a storage device. (2) To retain data in a storage device. (3) A storage device.

STRING A linear sequence of entities, such as characters or physical elements.

SUBROUTINE (1) A routine that can be part of another routine. (2) (See closed subroutine and open subroutine.)

SUBSET (1) A set contained within a set. (2) In communications, a subscriber set, such as a telephone. (3) A modulation and demodulation device.

SUMMARY PUNCH (Noun.) A card-punching machine which can be connected to an accounting machine to punch totals or balance cards. (Verb.) To punch summary information in cards.

SUPERVISOR A routine or routines executed in response to a requirement for altering or interrupting the flow of operations through the central processing unit, or for performance of input/output operations, and, therefore, the medium through which the use of resources is coordinated and the flow of operations through the central processing unit is maintained. Hence, a control routine that is executed in supervisor state.

SUPPRESSION (See zero suppression.)

SWITCH* A device or programming technique for making a selection, for example, a toggle, a conditional jump.

SYMBOL (1) A reprensentation of something by reason of relationship, association, or convention. (2) (See flowchart symbol, logic symbol, and mnemonic symbol.)

SYMBOLIC ADDRESS An address expressed in symbols convenient to the programmer.

SYMBOLIC CODING* Coding that uses machine instructions with symbolic addresses.

SYMBOLIC LOGIC The discipline that treats formal logic by means of a formalized artificial language or symbolic calculus whose purpose is to avoid the ambiguities and logical inadequacies of natural languages.

SYNCHRONIZE To lock one element of a system into step with another. The term usually refers to locking a receiver to a transmitter, but it can refer to locking the data terminal equipment bit rate to the data set frequency.

SYNCHRONOUS Occurring concurrently, and with a regular or predictable time relationship.

SYNTAX* (1) The structure of expressions in a language. (2) The rules governing the structure of a language.

SYNTHESIS The combination of parts to form a whole.

SYSTEM (1) An assembly of methods, procedures, or techniques united by regulated interaction to form an organized whole. (2) An organized collection of men, machines, and methods required to accomplish a set of specific functions.

SYSTEM INPUT UNIT A device specified as a source of an input job stream.

SYSTEM LIBRARY The collection of all cataloged data sets at an installation.

SYSTEM OUTPUT UNIT An output device shared by all jobs, onto which specified output data is transcribed.

SYSTEMS ANALYSIS The analysis of an activity to determine precisely what must be accomplished and how to accomplish it.

TABLE A collection of data in which each item is uniquely identified by a label, by its position relative to the other items, or by some other means.

TABLE LOOK-UP* A procedure for obtaining the function value corresponding to an argument from a table of function values.

TABULATE* (1) To form data into a table. (2) To print totals.

TAG One or more characters attached to an item or record for the purpose of identification.

TAPE (See magnetic tape and punched tape.)

TAPE-CONTROLLED CARRIAGE An automatic paper-feeding carriage controlled by a punched paper tape.

TAPE DECK (See tape unit.)

TAPE DRIVE A device that moves tape past a head.

TAPE-TO-CARD* Pertaining to equipment or methods that transmit data from either magnetic tape or punched tape to punched cards.

TAPE UNIT A device containing a tape drive, together with reading and writing heads and associated controls.

TASK A unit of work for the central processing unit from the standpoint of the control program; therefore, the basic multiprogramming unit under the control program.

TELECOMMUNICATIONS* Pertaining to the transmission of signals over long distances, such as by telegraph, radio, or television.

TELEPROCESSING A form of information handling in which a data processing system utilizes communication facilities.

TEMPORARY STORAGE In programming, storage locations reserved for intermediate results. (Synonymous with working storage.)

TENS COMPLEMENT* The radix complement in decimal notation.

TERMINAL* A point in a system or communication network at which data can either enter or leave.

TERMINAL, JOB-ORIENTED A terminal specially designed to receive source data in an environment associated with the job to be performed, and capable of transmission to and from the system of which it is a part.

TEXT The control sections of an object or load module, collectively.

THIRD GENERATION COMPUTER A computer utilizing SLT components.

THROUGHPUT A measure of system efficiency; the rate at which work can be handled by a system.

TIME-SHARE* To use a device for two or more interleaved purposes.

TIME SHARING* Pertaining to the interleaved use of the time of a device.

TIME SHARING Participation in available computer time by multiple users, via terminals. Characteristically, the response time is such that the computer seems dedicated to each user.

TOGGLE (1) (See flip-flop.) (2) Pertaining to any device having two stable states.

TRACING ROUTINE A routine that provides a historical record of specified events in the execution of a program.

TRACK The portion of a moving storage medium, such as a drum, tape, or disc, that is accessible to a given reading head position.

TRANSACTION FILE A file containing relatively transient data to be processed in combination with a master file. For example, in a payroll application, a transaction file indicating hours worked might be processed with a master file containing employee name and rate of pay.

TRANSCRIBE To copy from one external storage medium to another.

TRANSFORM* To change the form of data according to specific rules.

TRANSISTOR A small solid-state, semiconducting device, ordinarily using germanium, that performs nearly all the functions of an electronic tube, especially amplification.

TRANSLATE To convert from one language to another language.

TRANSLATOR (1) A device that converts information from one system of representation into equivalent information in another system of representation. In telephone equipment, it is the device that converts dialed digits into call-routing information. (2) A routine for changing information from one representation or language to another.

TRANSMISSION The electrical transfer of a signal, message, or other form of intelligence from one location to another.

TRANSMIT To send data from one location and to receive the data at another location.

TRUE COMPLEMENT (See radix complement.)

TRUNCATE* To terminate a computational process in accordance with some rule, for example, to end the evaluation of a power series at a specified term.

TRUNCATION ERROR An error due to truncation. (Contrast with rounding error.)

TURNAROUND TIME (1) The elapsed time between submission of a job to a computing center and the return of results. (2) The actual time required to reverse the direction of transmission from send to receive or vice versa when using a half-duplex circuit. For most communication facilities, there will be time required by line propagation and line effects, modem timing, and machine reaction. A typical time is 200 milliseconds on a half-duplex telephone connection.

TWELVE PUNCH A punch in the top row of a card.

TYPEBAR A linear type of element containing all printable symbols.

U FORMAT A data set format in which blocks are of unspecified or otherwise unknown length.

UNIT (1) A device having a special function. (2) A basic element.

UNIT RECORD Historically, a card containing one complete record. Currently, the punched card.

UNPACK To separate various sections of packed data.

UPDATE To modify a master file with current information according to a specified procedure.

USASCII* Same as ASCII.

USER Anyone utilizing the services of a computing system.

VALIDITY CHECK A check that a code group is actually a character of the particular code in use.

VARIABLE A quantity that can assure any of a given set of values.

VARIABLE-LENGTH RECORD Pertaining to a file in which the record length is not constrained. (Contrast with fixed-length record.)

VERIFIER A device similar to a card punch used to check the inscribing of data by rekeying.

VERIFY* (1) To determine whether a transcription of data or other operation has been accomplished accurately. (2) To check the results of keypunching.

V FORMAT A data set format in which logical records are of varying length and include a length indicator, and in which V format logical records may be blocked, with each block containing a block length indicator.

VOLATILE STORAGE* A storage device in which stored data are lost when the applied power is removed, for example, an accoustic delay line.

VOLUME That portion of a single unit of storage media which is accessible to a single read/write mechanism.

WATS Wide Area Telephone Service. A service provided by telephone companies which permits a customer, by use of an access line, to make calls to telephones in a specific zone on a dial basis for a flat monthly charge. Monthly charges are based on the size of the area in which the calls are placed, not on the number or length of calls. Under the WATS arrangement, the U.S. is divided into six zones to be called on a full-time or measured-time basis.

WORD A character string or a bit string considered as an entity.

WORD LENGTH* A measure of the size of a word, usually specified in units such as characters or binary digits.

WORD TIME* In a storage device that provides serial access to storage locations, the time interval between the appearance of corresponding parts of successive words.

WORKING STORAGE (See temporary storage.)
WRITE* To record data in a storage device or a data medium. The recording need not be permanent, such as on a cathode ray tube display device.
X-PUNCH A punch in the top row, two rows above the zero row, on a Hollerith punched card.
ZERO SUPPRESSION* The elimination of nonsignificant zeroes in a numeral.
ZONE PUNCH A punch in the O, X, or Y row of a Hollerith punched card.

Index